The CRB Commodity Yearbook 2012

Commodity Research Bureau

www.crbyearbook.com

Published by Commodity Research Bureau, Chicago, Illinois

For general information on our other products and services or for technical support, please contact our Customer Support Department within the United States at (800) 621-5271, outside the United States at (312) 554-8456 or fax (312) 939-4135.

ISBN 978-0-910418-90-4

Printed in the United States of America

10 9 8 7 6 5 4 3 2 1

Commodity Research Bureau
330 South Wells Street, Sixth Floor
Chicago, Illinois 60606-7110 USA
800.621.5271 or +1.312.554.8456
Fax: +1.312.939.4135
Website: www.crbyearbook.com
Email: info@crbyearbook.com

Contents

barchart
market data solutions

Put Barchart on your desk.

Quotes. Charts. News. Trading.

Premier desktop solutions.

Barchart.com, Inc. provides a variety of high-performance Desktop Solutions for monitoring real-time quotes, accessing charts, news and electronic trading. Our Desktop Solutions provide access to Barchart's premier data and superior reliability. We offer several levels of services for traders, brokers, analysts and other market participants. Our Desktop Solutions provide access to a broad range of markets including: **Futures, Stocks, Indices and Foreign Exchange.**

QuotePlus	**AgPlus**	**WebStation**	**Professional**
Basic solution for streaming real-time quotes.	Agricultural quotes, charts, news and weather.	Full-featured solution delivered in your web browser.	Professional PC application for high-end trading tools.

Barchart Desktop Solutions provide many features, including: customizable quote boards, advanced charts, time and sales, option analysis, market depth, fundamental data, technical data, news, weather, alerts, mobile add-ons and other market data tools. Detailed information including all features and exchange coverage is available at www.barchart.com/solutions.

For more information:
www.barchart.com/solutions

Barchart Sales
312-566-9235
sales@barchart.com

The Commodity Price Trend

The Continuous Commodity Index (CCI) in early 2011 extended the post-crisis recovery rally that started in 2009 and reached a new record high of 691.09 in April 2011. That brought the 2001-11 bull market to a total gain of 278%, making it the largest commodity rally in post-war history. After reaching its peak in April 2011, however, the CCI index then moved lower through the end of 2011. The CCI index moved lower in the latter part of 2011 due to the softer U.S. economy, a slowdown in the Chinese economy during 2011, the end of the Fed's second quantitative easing program in June 2011, and a moderate recovery rally in the dollar in 2011. Yet the global economy continued to grow in 2011 and there was generally strong demand for commodities during the year.

Only two of the six CCI futures sub-sectors closed higher in 2011 and the rest closed lower: Meats +8.9%, Energy +0.2%, Metals -6.9%, Grains -9.7%, Softs -16.4%, and Industrials -29.7%. The sub-sector changes noted above are calculated by taking the average of the percentage changes of the constituents in each sub-sector.

Energy

The CCI Energy sub-sector, which is composed of Crude Oil, Heating Oil, and Natural Gas, accounts for 18% of the overall CCI Index. The constituents in the Energy sub-sector on average in 2011 closed up 0.2%, adding to the 8.4% gain seen in 2010 and the sharp 57.8% gain seen in 2009. On a nearest-futures basis, crude oil in 2011 closed up 8.2%, gasoline closed up +9.5%, heating oil closed up +15.4%, and natural gas closed down −32.1%. Crude oil prices extended the 2009/2010 rally in early 2011, but then faded as OPEC raised production. Still, crude oil, gasoline and heating oil prices closed higher in 2011 due to firm global demand, the temporary shut-down of Libyan oil production in early 2011 due to the Libyan revolution, and tensions with Iran over its nuclear program. Natural gas prices plunged by -32.1% in 2011, adding to the -20.9% plunge seen in 2010, due to high U.S. production and a supply glut.

Grains

The CCI Grains and Oilseeds sub-sector, which is composed of Corn, Soybeans, and Wheat, accounts for 18% of the overall CCI Index. The constituents in the Grains and Oilseeds sub-sector on average closed down -9.7% in 2011, giving back part of the extraordinary gain of 44.2% seen in 2010. On a nearest-futures basis, corn in 2011 rose +2.8%, soybeans fell -14.0%, and wheat closed -17.8%. Corn was the leader in 2011 with a small gain on strong demand and tight U.S. and global supplies for the second straight year. Soybeans fell -14.0% on the year due to long liquidation pressure and adequate global supplies with a global stocks-to-use ratio of 23.4%. Wheat fell -17.8% during 2011 due to above-average U.S. inventories with the U.S. stocks-to-use ratio at a high 39.5%.

Industrials

The CCI Industrials sub-sector, which is composed of Copper and Cotton, accounts for 12% of the overall Index. The constituents in the Industrials sub-sector on average showed a sharp -29.7% decline during 2011, giving back some of the extraordinary increases of +62.6% seen in 2010 and +96.4% in 2009. Copper closed -22.7% in 2011 on softer demand and a technical correction after sharp increases in the previous two years. Cotton prices fell by -36.6% in 2011 on an increase in global cotton production, an increase in inventories, flat Chinese demand, and a technical correction after the sharp rallies seen in the previous two years.

Livestock

The CCI Livestock sub-sector, which is composed of Live Cattle and Lean Hogs, accounts for 12% of the CCI Index. The constituents in the Livestock sub-sector on average closed up +8.9% in 2011, adding to the 23.7% rally in 2010. On a nearest-futures basis, cattle closed +12.1% while lean hogs closed +5.7%. Livestock prices in 2011 were supported by strong demand and limited supply as continued high feed costs caused livestock producers to minimize their herd sizes.

Precious Metals

The CCI Precious Metals sub-sector, which is composed of Gold, Platinum, and Silver, accounts for 17% of the overall Index. The constituents in the Precious Metals sub-sector on average closed down -6.9% in 2011, falling back after extraordinary gains of +45.0% in 2010 and +43.1% in 2009. Precious metals prices in 2011 continued to see support from safe-haven demand tied to the European debt crisis and potentially inflationary central bank policies. Precious metals prices nevertheless fell back on technical long liquidation pressure and the stronger dollar seen in the latter part of 2011.

Softs

The CCI Softs sub-sector, which is composed of Cocoa, Coffee, Orange Juice, and Sugar #11, accounts for 23% of the CCI Index. The constituents in the Softs sub-sector on average in 2011 closed down -16.4%, falling back after the sharp gains of +31.8% seen in 2010 and +63.5% in 2009. All four soft commodities fell in 2011 with declines of -1.9% for Orange Juice, -5.7% for coffee, -27.5% for sugar and -30.5% for cocoa. The softs complex saw weakness during 2011 mainly because of dollar strength in the latter part of 2011 and technical long liquidation pressure after two years of sharp gains.

Continuous Commodity Index (CCI) (weekly close) as of December 30, 2011

Continuous Commodity Index (CCI)   (High, Low and Close 1967 = 100)

Year		Jan.	Feb.	Mar.	Apr.	May	June	July	Aug.	Sept.	Oct.	Nov.	Dec.	Range
2002	High	195.97	193.53	205.45	208.39	205.33	209.33	215.10	219.24	229.62	231.67	231.83	238.39	238.39
	Low	186.38	187.19	192.26	195.21	197.42	199.56	207.24	208.46	217.60	223.82	223.29	230.17	186.38
	Settle	187.29	192.33	204.92	201.16	204.20	209.29	210.97	219.20	226.53	228.91	230.64	234.52	----
2003	High	248.92	251.59	247.23	236.62	242.16	238.25	237.20	243.74	246.07	250.67	257.54	263.60	263.60
	Low	234.58	245.39	228.10	228.77	231.26	231.39	230.36	233.96	236.79	241.68	244.79	249.60	228.10
	Settle	248.45	247.25	232.15	232.53	235.55	233.78	234.21	243.70	243.66	247.58	248.44	255.29	----
2004	High	271.08	275.02	285.28	284.42	277.94	282.03	275.38	278.10	285.37	289.29	292.49	291.02	292.49
	Low	257.49	258.94	270.52	268.53	266.80	264.34	265.50	265.20	269.12	280.53	280.20	276.15	257.49
	Settle	262.57	274.73	283.77	272.54	277.25	265.94	267.78	276.50	284.98	283.70	290.94	283.90	----
2005	High	288.38	305.00	323.33	313.23	304.25	315.79	316.46	321.60	333.58	338.19	332.58	349.20	349.20
	Low	277.07	280.19	304.22	297.47	292.06	300.76	302.71	309.21	317.05	326.36	326.09	332.62	277.07
	Settle	284.75	305.00	313.57	303.74	300.83	306.91	315.24	318.99	333.33	326.68	332.49	347.89	----
2006	High	363.70	364.28	365.66	382.46	399.66	387.52	396.16	399.90	393.51	389.24	408.91	409.65	409.65
	Low	348.57	345.49	346.56	360.85	376.35	363.63	375.73	380.15	359.07	361.19	385.23	391.77	345.49
	Settle	363.30	353.27	361.91	379.53	379.80	385.63	391.49	390.95	370.10	383.92	408.79	394.89	----
2007	High	396.93	414.62	411.26	411.97	408.05	418.59	426.79	424.78	450.36	454.40	461.06	477.48	477.48
	Low	377.59	390.76	395.75	401.53	401.16	402.80	409.78	395.03	412.70	436.88	446.46	450.94	377.59
	Settle	394.37	410.64	407.45	403.54	407.58	410.36	424.52	413.49	447.56	454.29	451.26	476.08	----
2008	High	503.45	567.84	577.64	556.09	556.84	599.36	615.04	553.81	517.81	457.69	388.82	364.82	615.04
	Low	475.91	501.42	509.00	507.82	523.37	539.42	538.86	498.36	449.70	350.53	341.55	322.53	322.53
	Settle	503.27	565.65	516.38	536.23	541.30	595.98	548.86	516.47	452.42	369.56	361.74	363.06	----
2009	High	382.99	372.28	378.55	379.59	418.80	430.20	413.47	430.19	436.06	473.86	479.70	489.61	489.61
	Low	348.96	342.97	341.44	363.16	372.57	391.97	381.65	403.08	408.80	420.83	454.64	466.83	341.44
	Settle	364.50	352.45	368.83	371.55	417.04	398.76	413.41	415.49	430.67	452.69	479.22	484.42	----
2010	High	504.76	480.49	482.57	483.24	483.27	480.22	499.05	510.69	540.01	566.54	604.30	630.45	630.45
	Low	464.91	451.79	459.65	466.90	447.39	447.89	464.97	486.39	497.50	523.93	553.65	565.80	447.39
	Settle	465.29	478.32	467.25	481.11	458.70	471.37	499.05	496.73	536.12	566.28	565.96	629.53	----
2011	High	650.99	678.07	689.50	691.09	685.98	662.37	656.33	662.01	661.31	613.73	608.55	587.61	691.09
	Low	613.49	649.96	635.07	668.01	625.18	619.27	623.44	615.27	570.59	563.19	570.81	546.36	546.36
	Settle	650.80	676.96	672.81	687.66	656.42	632.23	645.77	661.93	571.38	604.28	584.22	563.00	----

Source: Thomson-Reuters

Continuous Commodity Index (CCI)
(monthly close) through December 2011

Continuous Commodity Index (CCI), CRB Spot Index, and CPI
(monthly close) through December 2011

Continuous Commodity Index (CCI) vs. 30-year T-Bond Yield - 12-month (RoC)
(monthly close) through December 2011

Continuous Commodity Index (CCI) vs. CPI - 12-month Rate of Change
(monthly close) through December 2011

CRB Fats & Oils Sub-Index (1967=100) (monthly close) through December 2011

CRB Fats & Oils Sub-Index (1967=100) (weekly close) as of December 31, 2010

CRB Livestock Sub-Index (1967=100) (monthly close) through December 2011

CRB Livestock Sub-Index (1967=100) (weekly close) as of December 30, 2011

CRB INDICIES

CRB Spot Index (monthly close) through December 2011

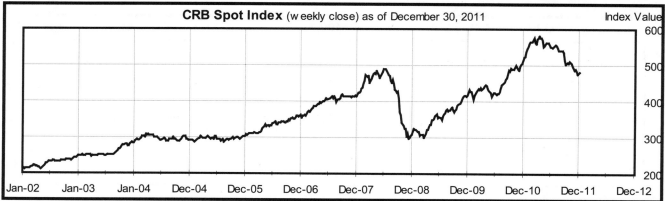

CRB Spot Index (weekly close) as of December 30, 2011

Reuters-CRB Index (CCI) and Goldman Sachs Commodity Index (GSCI^{TM/SM}) (weekly close) as of December 30, 2011

Reuters-CRB Index (CCI) and CRB Spot Index (weekly close) as of December 30, 2011

Continuous Commodity Index (CCI) (1967=100)

Year	Jan.	Feb.	Mar.	Apr.	May	June	July	Aug.	Sept.	Oct.	Nov.	Dec.	Average
2002	191.44	190.91	201.86	200.74	201.69	203.92	211.42	214.01	226.00	227.52	228.54	234.62	211.06
2003	242.04	247.89	237.81	231.73	237.38	235.11	234.05	238.13	241.44	246.15	250.66	258.44	241.74
2004	266.65	264.93	278.19	276.48	272.78	270.78	270.41	271.18	276.47	285.36	286.02	283.28	275.21
2005	282.96	289.01	312.70	305.26	298.11	308.07	311.47	315.00	324.05	333.46	330.39	343.83	312.86
2006	354.56	354.30	353.74	371.33	385.81	374.50	386.50	389.11	372.98	376.70	395.21	397.28	376.00
2007	386.38	400.96	403.41	405.99	404.24	410.22	418.88	411.65	432.37	446.95	453.23	467.28	420.13
2008	490.38	531.00	547.16	538.62	544.56	572.19	573.12	517.71	475.59	392.21	360.19	346.15	490.74
2009	364.14	356.43	358.81	372.81	399.62	410.96	400.35	417.38	421.88	450.93	466.10	479.51	408.24
2010	488.95	470.99	472.21	476.18	464.23	465.76	478.19	495.62	523.97	549.42	572.44	604.78	505.23
2011	631.79	660.83	666.50	680.23	644.45	644.55	645.72	640.13	623.06	590.36	591.50	564.53	631.97

Average.   *Source: Thomson-Reuters*

Reuters/Jefferies-CRB Futures Index[1] (1967=100)

Year	Jan.	Feb.	Mar.	Apr.	May	June	July	Aug.	Sept.	Oct.	Nov.	Dec.	Average
2002	191.44	190.91	201.86	200.74	201.69	203.92	211.42	214.01	226.00	227.52	228.54	234.62	211.06
2003	242.04	247.89	237.81	231.73	237.38	235.11	234.05	238.13	241.44	246.15	250.66	258.44	241.74
2004	266.65	264.93	278.19	276.48	272.78	270.78	270.41	271.18	276.47	285.36	286.02	283.28	275.21
2005	282.96	289.01	312.70	305.26	298.11	306.97	308.04	318.76	326.19	326.44	315.27	327.58	309.77
2006	340.95	331.30	325.98	345.84	351.22	339.21	346.86	340.18	310.28	304.36	310.84	311.60	329.89
2007	292.18	305.63	309.03	314.35	310.77	314.32	320.89	308.89	323.89	336.20	349.82	349.36	319.61
2008	363.88	386.31	403.95	409.23	422.29	445.14	438.75	394.23	360.98	288.86	249.29	221.26	365.35
2009	224.69	212.16	215.45	222.70	241.36	255.94	244.10	260.66	253.92	269.88	274.27	276.58	245.98
2010	281.42	270.35	273.37	276.86	259.57	258.08	262.43	269.78	278.38	295.45	305.25	321.54	279.37
2011	331.13	341.89	354.86	363.97	344.60	340.75	344.57	331.26	323.58	311.24	315.49	305.14	334.04

Average.   [1] New Calculation begins June 20, 2005.   *Source: Thomson-Reuters*

Reuters/Jefferies-CRB Total Return Index[1] (01/02/1982=100)

Year	Jan.	Feb.	Mar.	Apr.	May	June	July	Aug.	Sept.	Oct.	Nov.	Dec.	Average
2002	123.82	124.53	135.70	138.03	138.93	138.66	143.23	145.91	153.53	153.91	151.63	161.51	142.45
2003	171.83	182.79	178.17	171.17	175.28	178.21	178.96	184.60	182.27	191.06	194.53	204.73	182.80
2004	213.15	215.30	226.72	227.21	234.19	230.03	232.57	236.76	238.75	254.24	248.91	241.10	233.24
2005	244.84	250.48	273.57	267.03	254.14	267.60	271.16	281.23	288.68	289.74	280.70	292.65	271.82
2006	305.70	298.05	294.39	313.52	319.76	310.00	318.32	313.52	287.18	282.84	290.08	291.98	302.11
2007	275.02	288.82	293.24	299.54	297.32	301.96	309.52	299.14	314.90	327.82	342.08	342.69	307.67
2008	357.92	380.80	398.78	404.43	417.85	441.16	435.51	391.90	359.36	287.82	248.68	220.56	362.06
2009	224.05	211.60	214.92	222.20	240.85	255.44	243.66	260.22	253.80	269.50	273.89	276.21	245.53
2010	281.07	270.02	273.08	276.59	259.36	257.89	262.29	269.66	278.28	295.38	305.20	321.54	279.20
2011	331.68	341.98	354.99	364.13	344.76	340.92	344.76	331.46	323.78	311.43	315.69	305.34	334.24

Average.   [1] Theoretical data prior to June 20, 2005.   *Source: Thomson-Reuters*

CRB INDICIES

CRB Spot Metals Sub-Index (1967=100)

Year	Jan.	Feb.	Mar.	Apr.	May	June	July	Aug.	Sept.	Oct.	Nov.	Dec.	Average
2002	174.76	176.41	181.22	186.31	189.12	189.38	192.66	184.51	184.03	185.61	183.21	186.27	184.46
2003	199.71	204.17	206.72	202.78	205.57	207.77	212.24	214.09	220.24	240.20	248.49	266.70	219.06
2004	287.40	306.07	320.96	321.90	314.73	308.28	312.29	318.21	333.97	350.45	359.77	361.92	324.66
2005	355.95	364.50	371.99	371.31	365.83	369.32	361.39	363.75	364.70	369.68	370.47	425.84	371.23
2006	458.64	485.21	504.91	571.37	623.28	616.35	621.31	617.86	623.05	660.11	681.87	693.51	596.46
2007	668.94	691.71	761.81	798.96	798.65	803.29	834.00	840.13	835.06	868.19	828.50	812.12	795.11
2008	843.66	883.22	947.21	1,011.63	1,006.52	914.50	901.61	837.56	728.05	545.95	404.38	400.04	785.36
2009	409.17	416.80	421.44	455.21	410.21	552.61	591.59	651.17	688.67	704.55	716.43	767.81	565.47
2010	830.98	773.24	833.04	850.73	765.47	717.04	728.15	804.22	853.40	896.08	905.01	971.85	827.43
2011	1,029.49	1,085.28	1,066.15	1,096.80	1,033.85	1,023.86	1,063.60	994.80	942.14	874.77	868.19	849.37	994.03

Average.   *Source: Commodity Research Bureau*

CRB Spot Textiles Sub-Index (1967=100)

Year	Jan.	Feb.	Mar.	Apr.	May	June	July	Aug.	Sept.	Oct.	Nov.	Dec.	Average
2002	218.08	216.84	218.40	214.72	211.21	220.16	222.95	221.74	219.02	220.10	225.85	227.76	219.74
2003	231.25	235.31	235.04	234.64	231.66	235.24	240.88	237.50	244.30	256.99	257.59	254.25	241.22
2004	257.58	253.15	252.37	247.97	249.74	242.65	233.48	233.58	237.31	235.03	235.88	236.39	242.93
2005	239.93	240.36	247.12	247.73	246.60	244.69	247.21	243.08	246.64	251.24	248.96	250.83	246.20
2006	255.02	255.52	251.74	248.26	244.26	244.16	242.03	243.89	245.78	244.89	246.37	251.15	247.76
2007	252.50	251.35	251.91	248.99	245.40	250.72	260.09	256.51	261.58	264.79	265.79	265.28	256.24
2008	267.18	269.60	271.76	267.02	264.71	262.29	263.92	261.98	255.47	241.15	231.28	235.84	257.68
2009	241.13	237.01	229.83	240.05	252.00	253.03	258.94	253.52	257.42	265.67	280.85	293.96	255.28
2010	290.62	287.34	291.16	294.69	292.22	290.03	284.28	295.19	310.18	329.04	341.31	344.99	304.25
2011	347.26	365.82	372.19	365.44	352.18	344.70	319.66	310.92	310.19	303.37	299.19	289.50	331.70

Average.   *Source: Commodity Research Bureau*

CRB Spot Raw Industrials Sub-Index (1967=100)

Year	Jan.	Feb.	Mar.	Apr.	May	June	July	Aug.	Sept.	Oct.	Nov.	Dec.	Average
2002	219.05	222.33	231.03	230.38	231.81	243.72	245.38	240.53	240.77	240.68	243.04	248.21	236.41
2003	255.85	258.59	260.97	258.79	257.65	260.47	263.77	263.99	273.24	291.18	295.88	302.30	270.22
2004	312.24	309.54	316.77	318.52	312.98	308.40	308.84	307.54	315.25	315.13	320.52	322.65	314.03
2005	320.94	324.57	333.31	336.68	331.99	331.88	325.29	324.52	329.36	332.79	332.83	349.53	331.14
2006	363.05	371.00	372.08	385.69	400.62	399.97	403.50	403.90	403.19	415.76	426.67	434.25	398.31
2007	430.87	434.54	452.81	465.37	468.44	475.75	485.36	478.47	483.09	492.43	486.68	475.95	469.15
2008	487.92	502.29	522.98	534.29	532.30	517.02	517.29	495.17	460.96	392.49	329.86	317.83	467.53
2009	335.09	331.50	321.35	343.49	370.17	391.18	403.99	431.59	439.72	435.97	455.27	480.02	394.95
2010	492.93	476.13	499.63	510.22	489.56	476.07	474.97	498.86	518.04	539.43	555.01	574.70	508.80
2011	595.51	619.22	621.89	628.72	606.29	602.99	596.81	573.01	559.74	536.77	528.95	519.49	582.45

Average.   *Source: Commodity Research Bureau*

CRB Spot Foodstuffs Sub-Index (1967=100)

Year	Jan.	Feb.	Mar.	Apr.	May	June	July	Aug.	Sept.	Oct.	Nov.	Dec.	Average
2002	203.33	202.39	204.04	197.88	195.85	207.11	218.25	222.32	226.98	230.63	230.76	237.99	214.79
2003	238.60	237.01	234.16	234.55	239.15	239.53	232.81	234.30	244.69	251.04	255.36	257.99	241.60
2004	263.90	275.85	287.49	287.41	285.33	278.05	273.83	270.42	272.10	257.76	268.47	261.77	273.53
2005	252.84	246.44	253.58	252.19	254.21	255.43	251.31	247.65	249.22	253.37	252.74	242.54	250.96
2006	243.31	241.95	239.60	243.17	250.70	253.86	261.17	267.04	269.14	267.52	271.19	273.16	256.82
2007	275.31	286.30	297.37	299.85	311.98	320.79	322.44	319.95	325.01	322.19	325.40	337.97	312.05
2008	346.56	383.11	390.10	391.07	405.44	421.87	427.47	405.89	385.15	334.27	303.48	284.65	373.26
2009	299.83	286.21	284.71	302.35	316.81	318.81	301.83	304.44	305.01	314.86	338.56	339.54	309.41
2010	349.28	344.48	352.89	357.94	359.11	352.01	361.74	385.62	415.09	424.20	411.58	423.33	378.11
2011	464.45	489.47	494.49	506.33	497.04	497.00	495.67	503.38	484.57	466.21	451.87	429.91	481.70

Average.   *Source: Commodity Research Bureau*

CRB Spot Fats and Oils Sub-Index   (1967=100)

Year	Jan.	Feb.	Mar.	Apr.	May	June	July	Aug.	Sept.	Oct.	Nov.	Dec.	Average
2002	169.64	165.91	177.34	167.61	164.38	193.38	193.29	192.85	193.20	193.90	211.97	230.05	187.79
2003	222.39	209.89	215.72	216.91	219.56	229.01	225.83	223.36	251.40	285.47	288.08	292.22	239.99
2004	305.30	300.47	318.53	330.54	302.31	295.32	304.60	290.52	302.51	267.12	279.42	271.36	297.33
2005	248.45	238.13	252.70	263.98	262.93	266.01	245.81	243.51	259.50	268.43	269.77	231.17	254.20
2006	231.10	221.46	217.14	214.75	222.03	221.97	247.09	271.97	267.18	257.29	264.75	270.94	242.31
2007	274.74	274.35	300.01	313.08	339.65	366.31	376.09	357.79	365.74	365.51	381.69	364.06	339.92
2008	381.95	418.92	459.52	457.65	467.23	498.89	526.26	467.08	443.38	366.91	283.76	238.42	417.50
2009	283.42	254.79	243.41	285.09	321.74	335.76	308.54	340.28	324.64	298.33	343.85	344.85	307.06
2010	337.27	329.26	366.69	378.35	381.68	374.59	379.27	399.57	444.83	471.40	463.11	458.65	398.72
2011	536.41	542.91	553.67	561.25	569.84	588.10	587.94	578.55	567.28	536.83	502.49	499.60	552.07

Average.   *Source: Commodity Research Bureau*

CRB Spot Livestock Sub-Index   (1967=100)

Year	Jan.	Feb.	Mar.	Apr.	May	June	July	Aug.	Sept.	Oct.	Nov.	Dec.	Average
2002	251.61	260.32	274.95	257.32	256.33	289.40	288.22	279.03	274.13	276.94	288.86	313.14	275.85
2003	316.67	308.65	310.49	311.25	320.03	333.29	324.58	327.63	361.30	386.60	385.63	372.48	338.22
2004	372.16	353.19	362.41	369.65	369.31	374.28	395.48	392.33	395.40	365.68	373.69	370.63	374.52
2005	359.25	341.74	353.05	373.63	377.41	361.10	330.39	331.75	349.24	358.04	369.98	337.97	353.63
2006	331.93	328.72	320.09	314.72	327.28	340.29	359.18	388.13	384.78	366.35	364.05	372.08	349.80
2007	379.93	388.03	407.19	425.25	449.92	462.39	459.18	445.81	444.91	434.88	425.72	412.45	427.97
2008	417.36	451.42	468.41	483.09	510.01	522.82	556.10	526.98	492.24	426.75	342.41	288.42	457.17
2009	333.60	310.58	288.18	321.58	347.01	368.85	362.91	393.37	389.53	350.90	386.75	403.06	354.69
2010	411.55	408.71	450.01	478.92	488.46	470.53	465.13	475.55	498.82	495.89	485.02	505.23	469.49
2011	561.16	577.76	601.55	629.36	618.46	635.68	646.41	644.21	626.64	618.26	580.65	580.02	610.01

Average.   *Source: Commodity Research Bureau*

CRB Spot Sub-Index   (1967=100)

Year	Jan.	Feb.	Mar.	Apr.	May	June	July	Aug.	Sept.	Oct.	Nov.	Dec.	Average
2002	212.55	214.02	219.65	216.54	216.43	228.09	233.96	232.98	235.10	236.59	238.01	244.06	227.33
2003	248.72	249.60	249.73	248.66	250.00	251.77	250.71	251.49	261.25	274.11	278.66	283.38	258.17
2004	291.55	295.38	304.54	305.49	301.44	295.70	294.10	291.86	296.90	290.35	298.19	296.26	296.81
2005	291.19	290.08	298.13	299.24	297.73	298.26	292.80	290.63	293.94	297.75	297.48	301.05	295.69
2006	308.31	311.58	310.86	319.47	330.81	332.19	337.82	341.11	341.85	347.18	354.58	359.35	332.93
2007	358.84	366.47	381.36	388.90	396.79	405.08	410.71	405.97	410.96	414.11	412.79	413.88	397.16
2008	424.32	449.73	464.01	470.41	476.34	475.87	478.60	456.61	428.42	367.61	318.88	303.90	426.23
2009	320.03	312.26	305.91	326.11	347.44	359.84	358.67	374.28	378.72	381.73	403.44	416.74	357.10
2010	428.27	417.21	433.51	441.48	431.40	420.89	425.03	449.12	473.29	489.05	491.25	507.30	450.65
2011	538.09	562.60	566.40	575.61	559.14	557.32	553.30	543.59	527.83	506.85	496.08	480.93	538.98

Average.   *Source: Commodity Research Bureau*

S&P Goldman Sachs Commodity Index (GSCI)   (12/31/1969=100)

Year	Jan.	Feb.	Mar.	Apr.	May	June	July	Aug.	Sept.	Oct.	Nov.	Dec.	Average
2002	168.97	172.75	193.58	199.87	200.65	197.07	203.12	208.76	223.69	222.70	212.18	230.03	202.78
2003	241.74	264.19	246.70	221.68	228.18	235.01	233.18	241.35	228.54	242.22	246.24	261.23	240.86
2004	269.18	266.23	280.10	284.06	303.19	292.63	298.97	308.01	315.29	356.70	341.12	314.25	302.48
2005	324.47	332.80	374.05	371.68	350.65	382.96	396.64	431.85	455.28	444.90	418.56	435.45	393.27
2006	442.12	422.49	427.47	469.73	477.93	471.65	490.32	485.65	434.56	431.13	442.05	444.62	453.31
2007	406.98	435.26	446.69	469.60	470.72	485.26	504.65	490.16	528.83	559.36	600.37	593.12	499.25
2008	606.71	638.88	689.26	717.94	778.15	832.31	818.90	716.84	644.00	496.05	405.96	338.27	640.27
2009	346.03	327.48	350.86	367.12	410.82	458.22	429.21	466.68	453.77	492.51	509.71	505.07	426.46
2010	520.05	503.83	523.07	543.90	499.87	497.00	503.57	517.41	526.98	561.66	579.86	614.79	532.67
2011	634.64	661.44	707.87	744.48	695.62	679.91	689.47	651.63	638.94	625.65	653.51	642.72	668.82

Average.   *Source: Goldman Sachs*

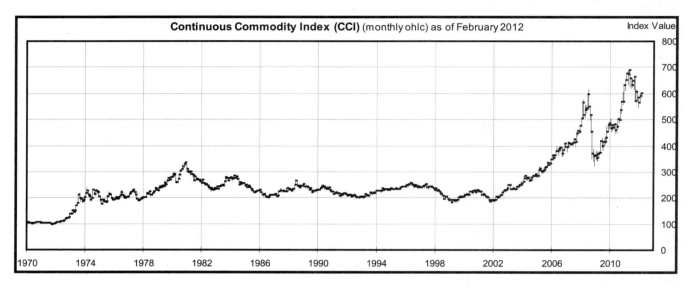

The Continuous Commodity Index (CCI) in early 2011 extended the recovery rally seen after the 2008/09 financial crisis and posted a new record high of 691.09 in April 2011. That brought the bull market seen since 2001 to a total of 278%. That decade-long rally is by far the largest bull market in post-war history, exceeding even the rallies seen in the 1970s. The 1971-74 and 1977-80 commodity bull markets were separated by two years of consolidation in 1975-76. Even if those two rallies are counted as one large bull market, that bull market of 250% is less than the current 2001-2011 bull market of 278%.

The 2001-11 commodity bull market has been driven mainly by strong commodity demand from the fast-growing emerging markets such as China, India, Brazil, and others. The fact that the rally has been driven by demand, as opposed to a temporary supply disruption, accounts for its size and longevity. The commodity rallies in the 1970s, by contrast, were driven mainly by supply disruptions and inflation, not by demand. A rally caused by demand is a much more durable rally, unlike a rally driven by inflation, a weak dollar, or supply disruptions, which are usually reversed after a period of time.

Along with strong demand, the weak dollar was an important driver of the commodity bull market from 2001 through 2008. During that time frame, the dollar plunged and provided a powerful bullish factor for commodity prices. As the value of the dollar falls, the price of hard assets tends to rise to account for the lower value of the currency in which the hard assets are priced. Since 2008, however, the dollar has had less impact on commodity prices because the dollar has been in a sideways consolidation mode.

The 2001-11 commodity bull market occurred during a period of low inflation, which means that inflation was not a big factor behind the commodity rally. Inflation during the 2001-11 rally averaged only 2.4% annually, which was just modestly above the Fed's inflation target of 2%. Nevertheless, commodity prices have seen some support more recently from fears that inflation may rise substantially in coming years in response to the Federal Reserve's extraordinarily easy monetary policy seen since the financial crisis began in 2008. Commodities are thus seeing demand from their status as an inflation hedge.

Investment demand for commodities has in fact been an important component in the commodity bull market. The total amount of commodity assets under management reached a massive $412 billion in October 2011, according to a report by Barclays Capital, which was just $39 billion below the record high of $451 billion posted in April 2011. The academic literature has concluded that the commodity sector is a separate asset class relative to equities, bonds, or other asset classes. Many institutional and individual investors now devote at least a small percentage of their portfolio to commodities. Smaller investors now have an easy way to invest in commodities through the multitude of commodity-based exchange-traded products.

Commodity Bull Markets Ranked by Percentage Gain of Continuous Commodity Index (CCI) (1960-2012[1])							
	-------- Low --------		-------- High --------		Percent Rally	Rally Duration Months	Avg CPI (yr-yr%)
2001-11	Oct-01	182.83	Apr-11	691.09	278.0%	114	2.4%
1971-74	Oct-71	96.40	Feb-74	237.80	146.7%	28	4.9%
1977-80	Aug-77	184.70	Nov-80	337.60	82.8%	39	10.2%
1986-88	Jul-86	196.16	Jun-88	272.19	38.8%	23	3.2%
1992-96	Aug-92	198.17	Apr-96	263.79	33.1%	44	2.8%

[1] Data as of February 16, 2012.   *Source: Commodity Research Bureau*

The long-term outlook for commodity prices continues to look bullish based on the likelihood that global demand for basic commodities will remain strong in coming years and that commodity suppliers will continue to lag in investing in new production capacity. The commodity demand story is mainly tied to the developing world. The need is enormous for food, shelter and infrastructure, which are all sectors that utilize raw commodities. According to the World Bank's Development Indicators, 80% of the world's population lives on less than $10 per day. As these people are slowly integrated into the global economy, their food, shelter and transportation needs expand and they use more commodities. Commodity demand will also continue to be driven by population growth. The United Nations forecasts that there will be a net 2.2 billion more people on earth by 2050, bringing the world's population to 9 billion from its current level near 6.8 billion. These people will need more food, shelter and infrastructure.

While the long-term outlook remains bullish for commodity prices, commodity prices in the latter part of 2011 entered into a downward correction. The commodity rally started to run out of steam in May 2011 when it became obvious that the Fed was not going to extend its second quantitative easing program (QE2) beyond its scheduled end in June 2011. The Fed's QE2 program injected $600 billion into the financial system and was a major bullish factor for commodity prices in late 2010 and early 2011.

Commodity prices also traded lower in the latter part of 2011 due to the dip in the U.S. economy during spring and summer 2011. Commodity prices bottomed out in December 2011 and recovered a bit in early 2012 due to the improvement in the U.S. economy and some short-covering after the 2011 sell-off.

Commodity prices have the potential to trade mildly higher during 2012. The U.S. economy should show steady, if unimpressive, growth during 2012, thus providing steady commodity demand. In addition, commodity demand should remain relatively strong from China where the market consensus is for a soft landing. On the other hand, commodity prices are not likely to get much support from the dollar, which does not appear to be headed for any big sell-off. Commodity prices are also unlikely to get any more

help from the Fed in terms of additional easing. With the stronger U.S. economy seen in late 2011 and early 2012, the Federal Reserve dialed down market expectations for a third quantitative easing program (QE3), which would have represented a major bullish factor for commodity prices.

The main risks to the forecast for mildly higher commodity prices in 2011 are the European debt crisis, the possibility of an oil spike on Iranian tensions, and the possibility of a hard landing in China. If the European debt crisis should suddenly blow up and cause a global recession, then commodity prices would be forced sharply lower. If there is an upward oil spike on a military showdown with Iran, then higher oil prices would obviously have an upward impact on the overall commodity indexes. However, an oil price spike would also likely cause a global recession that would push other commodity prices lower, resulting in a mixed effect on the overall commodity indexes. A hard landing in China would obviously have a very negative effect on commodity demand and would produce a sharp drop in commodity prices. These risks indicate there are still events that could extend the 2011 commodity sell-off. However, this weakness would likely be only a downward correction in a long-term bull market.

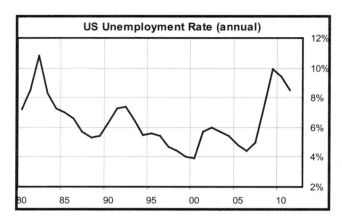

The U.S. economy has technically been in an expansion mode for more than two years but the economy is still hamstrung and has yet to fully normalize. The U.S. experienced its worst recession since the Great Depression in the 1930's from December 2007 through June 2009, according to the National Bureau of Economic Research (NBER), the official arbiter of recession dating. U.S. GDP growth in 2007/09 fell by a total of -5.0% from peak to trough, making it much worse than the 1957-58 recession of -3.7% and the 1973-75 recession of -3.2%.

The U.S. economy showed relatively strong growth in 2010 with an annual GDP rate of +3.0%. However, the U.S. economy then hit the skids in the first half of 2011 with GDP growth of only +0.4% in Q1-2011 and +1.3% in Q2-2012. GDP for all of 2011 was weak at +1.7%. The U.S. economy in early 2011 was hit by a confluence of negative events. First, gasoline prices in early 2011 soared above $4 per gallon due to overall commodity price strength caused by the Fed's quantitative easing program. High gasoline prices undercut consumer confidence and spending. Second, the Japanese Tohohu earthquake disaster occurred in March 2011 and caused significant disruptions to the U.S. economy. Third, the U.S. political battle over raising the debt ceiling in July 2011 caused a near default on U.S. Treasury securities, resulting in the loss of America's AAA credit rating from Standard & Poors. The debt ceiling debacle hurt confidence among

U.S. businesses and consumers and foreign investors. Fourth, the European debt crisis worsened in early 2011

and the European banking system was in a systemic crisis until the European Central Bank finally took relief action starting in November 2011.

After the economic slowdown in the first half of 2011, the U.S. economy finally started to show signs of life again in late 2011 and early 2012. U.S. GDP improved to +1.8% in Q3-2011 and then to +3.0% in Q4-2011. Confidence in the manufacturing sector improved in late 2011 and the ISM manufacturing index showed three straight monthly increases starting in November 2011 and posted a 5-month high of 54.1 in January 2012. The ISM non-manufacturing index rose to 56.8 in January 2012 from the trough of 52.6 seen in Sep-Nov 2011.

Most importantly, the U.S. labor market started to substantially improve in late 2011 and early 2012. That lifted some of the gloom on consumer confidence and provided consumers with more disposable income. U.S. non-farm payrolls rose by 203,000 in December 2011 and by 243,000 in January 2012. The U.S. civilian unemployment rate showed a sharp and unexpected drop to a 3-year low of 8.3% by January 2012.

Yet despite the improvement in the U.S. economy, the market consensus in early 2012 was that U.S. economy would continue to show sub-par growth during 2012 and 2013. The market consensus is for GDP growth of only about +2.4% in 2012 and 2013, which is well below the post-war average of +3.3% and is far below the typical GDP surge following a recession.

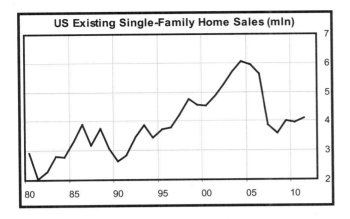

US Existing Single-Family Home Sales (mln)

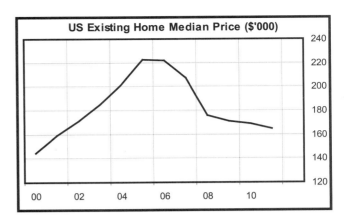

US Existing Home Median Price ($'000)

There continue to be headwinds that are likely to hold back the U.S. economy in 2012. First, the European debt crisis has yet to be fully contained, which keeps alive the risks for the global equity markets, for the U.S. banking system, and for U.S. exports to Europe.

Second, the U.S. housing market continues to struggle, keeping downward pressure on consumer confidence and household wealth. U.S. home prices have yet to bottom out. The U.S. home price index from the Federal Housing Financing Agency hit an 8-year low in March 2011 and then moved mildly higher through 2011. However, the U.S. home price index from Case-Shiller, which measures home prices in the top 20 metropolitan areas, fell to a new 8-3/4 year low in December 2011. Still, there were some rays of light for the housing market in late 2011 and early 2012 with existing home sales showing a 4.3% increase in January 2012 and with the supply of existing homes available for sale falling to a 5-3/4 year low of 6.1 months. Moreover, the 30-year mortgage rate was at a record low of 3.87% in early 2012, which provided a boost for home affordability.

Short-term U.S. interest rates have remained extraordinarily low since the financial crisis emerged in September 2008. The 3-month dollar Libor rate is currently at 0.47%. The Federal Reserve at its meeting in January 2012 said that it expect rates to remain "exceptionally low" until at least late 2014. The market is therefore not expecting an increase in the federal funds rate from its current target range of zero to 0.25% until late 2014. The

low federal funds rate will keep the 3-month Libor rate and T-bill rates low.

Yields on the longer end of the yield curve also remain exceptionally low. The 10-year T-note yield in late 2011 and early 2012 traded near 2.00% after posting a record low of 1.67% in September 2011. The Federal Reserve is pursuing an explicit policy of trying to keep long-term Treasury yields as low as possible as a means to hold down mortgage rates, corporate bond yields, and all other private interest rates that are priced off Treasury yields. The Federal Reserve in its second quantitative easing program (QE2) from November 2010 through June 2011 purchased $600 billion of longer-term Treasury securities in an explicit attempt to push Treasury yields lower. The Fed in September 2011 then began its $400 billion Operation Twist program which involved swapping short-term for long-term Treasury securities, thus keeping long-term Treasury yields low.

The S&P 500 index took a sharp hit in the first half of 2011 on the confluence of negative events mentioned earlier. However, the S&P 500 index then came roaring back in late 2011 and edged to a new 3-3/4 year high in February 2012. The stock market recovered on the improved U.S. economic data, continued strong U.S. earnings growth, and hopes that the European debt crisis was close to being contained. The main risks to the stock market as of late February 2012 included any flare-up in the European debt crisis and a possible oil price spike on Iranian tensions.

S&P 500

10-year T-Note Yield

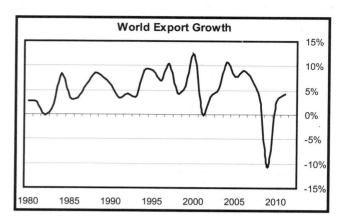

The global economy in 2011 extended its recovery that began in the second half of 2009. The World Bank reported that the global economy in 2011 grew by +4.0%. That was lower than the +5.1% growth rate seen in 2010 but was the second straight annual gain after the -0.7% decline seen in 2009. The GDP decline of -0.7% in 2009 was the first decline in the overall global economy in post-war history. The World Bank expects global economic growth to be steady near +4.0% in 2012 and then to improve to +4.5% in 2013.

The global economy remains on a two-speed path with the emerging world continuing to far outpace the developed world. The developed world remains mired in a host of problems including high debt, poor consumer confidence, and ongoing housing market problems. The World Bank is forecasting 2012 real GDP growth of only +1.4% for the developed countries but stronger growth of +5.4% for the emerging world.

Even GDP in the emerging world, however, is showing weaker growth due to reduced exports and efforts to curb inflation. China's real GDP growth rate eased to +9.2% in 2011 from +10.4% in 2010, and the consensus is for a continue decline to +8.5% in 2012 and +8.4% in 2013. India's real GDP peaked at +9.4% in Q1-2010 but then steadily slid to a 2-year low of +6.9% in Q3-2011. The consensus is that India's economic growth will stabilize near +8% in 2012. Brazil's GDP peaked at +9.3% in Q1-2010 and then steadily slid to +2.1% by Q3-2011. The market consensus

is that Brazil's GDP growth will stabilize at +3.4% in 2012 and then improve to +4.1% in 2013.

There are two main risks for the global economy in 2012. First, the European debt crisis has yet to be fully contained and there is a risk that the Eurozone may show a worse-than-expected recession. Second, there is the threat of an oil price spike in 2012. The U.S. and Europe are tightening sanctions against Iran due to its nuclear program and a European oil embargo on Iranian oil is scheduled to begin on July 1, 2012. There is also the threat of a military strike by Israel and/or the U.S. later in 2012, which would likely cause a big oil price spike. With the global economy already in vulnerable shape, a big oil price spike could easily cause a global recession.

Inflation also continues to be a significant problem in the emerging world and has caused the need for higher interest rates. Inflation is at +4.5% in China, +6.2% in Brazil, and +6.5% in India, for example. The recent rally in oil prices will put additional upward pressure on inflation and reduce the flexibility of the world's central banks to cut interest rates.

Yet even with all the obstacles, the global economy is expected to show +4.0% growth in 2012. In fact, if the European debt crisis can be contained and if the Iranian nuclear situation can be resolved without an oil spike, then the global economic outlook will start to look increasingly positive.

West Texas Intermediate Crude Oil Prices (monthly close, US$/barrel)

The petroleum market has been extremely volatile in recent years. Nymex West Texas Intermediate (WTI) crude oil futures prices from 2002 through 2008 more than quadrupled due to a combination of strong emerging country demand, lagging capacity and production, the weak dollar, and speculative fervor. That rally culminated in mid-2008 at a record high of $147 per barrel.

Oil prices then plunged in the latter half of 2008 to a 7-year low of $32.40 per barrel in December 2008 in response to the global financial crisis and heavy long liquidation pressure by speculators and hedge funds. The global recession caused world oil demand to fall by -4.7% from the peak of 86.9 million bpd in November 2007 to the 4-year low of 82.8 million bpd posted in May 2009.

Oil prices in 2009 were then able to recover after OPEC (ex-Iraq) slashed production by 16.5% to 25.320 million bpd in March 2009 from the peak of 30.315 million bpd in July 2008. Crude oil prices in the latter half of 2009 and through most of 2010 then traded sideways in the relatively narrow range of about $60-85 per barrel. During that time, oil prices traded near OPEC's target as OPEC maintained its subdued level of production and as demand remained on the weak side.

Oil prices in late 2010, however, started to rally as

Real WTI Crude Oil Prices (current US$)

the global economy picked up steam and demand started to increase. OPEC kept its production unchanged but was pleased with the rally in oil prices above its former target range since OPEC members were looking to increase their revenues, which had been depressed by the weak dollar and by the low production levels in 2008-2010. OPEC's general strategy was to keep production low during the recession and early recovery period until excess global inventories slowly declined in response to an improvement in the global economy and higher fuel demand.

World Crude Oil Demand (mln bpd)

China Crude Oil Imports (Prev. 12-mo, mln tons)

OPEC Oil Production (mln barrels/day)

Non-OPEC Crude Oil Production (mln bpd)

The situation in the oil market then changed dramatically in early 2011 when the Arab world erupted in protest. The initial revolutions in Tunisia and Egypt did not have much impact on the oil market. However, oil prices then rose sharply above $100 per barrel after an armed rebellion emerged in Libya that was ultimately successful in ousting the Qaddafi regime. Libya's oil production plunged from normal levels of 1.58 million barrels per day in January 2011 to only 390,000 bpd in March 2011 and to virtually zero by August 2011. After the revolution was over, Libyan production rose in late 2011 but still only reached 925,000 bpd in January 2012, about 60% of its normal level.

Saudi Arabia and its Persian Gulf partners sharply boosted their production in early 2011 in order to offset the loss of Libyan production. In fact, OPEC production after the initial dip on the Libya revolution rose sharply through the remainder of 2011 and reached a 3-year high of 30.9 million bpd by January 2012. This increase in production was successful in preventing a major upward spike in oil prices due to the Libyan revolution.

After peaking in May 2011, oil prices then fell through October 2011 due to (1) increased production by Saudi Arabia and its Persian Gulf partners to offset the loss of Libyan crude oil production, (2) the European debt crisis and the mild European recession that started in Q4-2011, (3) reduced demand from China as its economy slowed during 2011, and (4) weak petroleum demand from the U.S. due to a weaker economy, record ethanol production,

and energy conservation efforts.

Crude oil prices then rallied sharply in late 2011 and early 2012 as the U.S. economy strengthened and as tensions increased with Iran over its nuclear program. In early 2012, Europe agreed to put an embargo on Iranian oil imports as of July 1, 2012. In addition, the U.S. and Europe tightened financial restrictions on the Iranian banking system, which crimped Iran's ability to receive payment for its oil exports. The U.S. also lobbied Iran's big oil customers such as China, Japan and India to reduce their imports from Iran. Meanwhile, the U.S. received commitments from Saudi Arabia to boost production to offset the slow loss of Iranian oil exports. However, it remains to be seen whether Saudi Arabia and its Gulf partners have sufficient excess capacity to fully offset the loss of Iranian exports.

As of March 2012, Iran was being as intransigent as ever and refused to engage in serious negotiations or allow any inspections of its sensitive nuclear facilities. Iran was also threatening to close the Straight of Hormuz, through which about 20% of the world's oil passes. Meanwhile, Israel was explicitly threatening military action. The U.S. continued to try to resolve the situation through tougher sanctions, but at the same time was making plans for a possible military conflict with Iran.

Even aside from the current geopolitical problems, oil prices are likely to see upward pressure over the long term The reality is that most of the cheap oil has already been found in the earth's crust. Major new sources of oil can usually be found only in very remote places or under miles of ocean, or have to be extracted from oil shale or tar sands, which is an expensive process. The marginal cost of developing new oil supplies is in the neighborhood of $7580 per barrel and is rising. Oil producers will only invest the huge sums of capital that are necessary to find new oil supplies if oil prices stay consistently above the cost of extracting new reserves plus a reasonable profit margin. Lagging production and reserves will be an increasingly important factor in coming years as the global economic expansion continues and as fuel demand grows. This is likely to keep upward pressure on oil prices over the long term.

Crude Oil Inventories (mln bbls) vs 5-yr avg

26T

The U.S. dollar index hit a record low in early 2008 and has since traded in a wide consolidation range just moderately above that record low. The dollar index took a huge -41% hit during 2002-07 bear market when the dollar plunged on the Fed's easy monetary policy and on the sharp widening of America's trade deficit. However, the dollar index during the last four years has been trading in a choppy, sideways range.

The biggest factor affecting the dollar since the financial crisis began in September 2008 has been safe-haven demand. The dollar is the world's reserve currency and has the greatest depth of investment opportunities. The dollar is therefore perceived to be a necessary place to park assets during times of stress.

The dollar during 2008-10 saw two major rallies, but both were based on safe-haven demand and therefore reversed once the initial panic wore off. The first rally in late 2008 and early 2009 was due to the global financial crisis that erupted in September 2008 with the Lehman bankruptcy. That crisis caused a rush to dollar liquidity by global financial institutions. The second dollar rally occurred in early 2010 with the start of the European debt crisis. That crisis caused flight to quality in the dollar and caused a sharp sell-off in the euro due to doubts about the ability of the Eurozone to hold together.

Aside from safe-haven demand, the dollar has had few supportive factors during the past several years. The dollar has been undercut mainly by the Fed's extraordinarily easy

monetary policy. The Fed during the financial crisis cut its federal funds target to nearly zero with a target range of zero to 0.25%. The Fed also engaged in the aggressive purchase of Treasury and mortgage securities in its so-called "quantitative easing" moves that flooded the banking system with liquidity. By 2011, the Fed's balance sheet assets had soared to $2.9 trillion, which represented about $2 trillion of excess liquidity in the banking system beyond normal levels. The Fed also conducted dollar swap loans with global central banks, supplying foreign banks with the dollar liquidity they needed to ride out the financial crisis and its aftermath. This excess liquidity continues to be a major bearish factor for the dollar.

The European Central Bank (ECB), by contrast, did not cut interest rates as far as the Fed during the financial crisis. The ECB cut its key refinancing rate only as far as 1.00% in the wake of the financial crisis, which meant that the euro had about a 75 basis point interest rate advantage over the dollar. That interest rate advantage was bullish for the euro because global investors can earn more interest on their cash if they park it in the European money markets rather than in the U.S. money markets.

The dollar index in the past several years has also continued to be undercut by the wide U.S. trade deficit. The U.S. trade deficit temporarily narrowed sharply during the 2008/09 financial crisis due to the fact that imports fell much more sharply than exports. However, the U.S. trade deficit widened again once the initial crisis was over. The U.S. trade deficit during 2010-11 moved in the

US Export & Import Growth (yoy%)

3-mo Eurodollar vs Euribor Futures Curve

range of $40-50 billion. Excluding petroleum imports, the U.S. trade deficit was in much better shape in the range of about $15-25 billion.

The U.S. current account deficit, the broadest measure of U.S. trade, was most recently reported at -$110 billion in Q3-2011. That means that a net $1.2 billion worth of dollars are flowing out of the U.S. each calendar day to pay for goods and services. That dollar outflow puts downward pressure on the dollar since the recipients of those dollars sell them into the foreign exchange market if they do not want to hold them and invest them in dollar-denominated investments.

In terms of GDP, the U.S. trade position has improved substantially in the past several years. The U.S. current account deficit peaked at 6.4% of GDP in Q4-2005 and has since narrowed sharply to 2.9% of GDP. That means the U.S. trade deficit is now much less of a bearish factor for the dollar than it was during the 2000-07 period.

A potentially bearish long-term factor for the dollar is that Asian central banks would like to reduce their dollar risks by reducing the percentage of their reserves that are held in dollars. Asian central banks in China, Japan and South Korea, for example, hold most of reserves in dollars, making them vulnerable to any sell-off in the dollar. Confidence in the U.S. dollar has been hurt by the global financial crisis that started with the melt-down of the U.S. housing market. Confidence in the U.S. has also been hurt by the fact that the U.S. is on a path towards fiscal disaster

if major course corrections are not made soon. Asian central banks do not have much alterative to the dollar, however, because the euro's structural flaws have been exposed and the other currencies in the world do not have anything approaching the size and depth of the U.S. markets. The U.S. dollar will remain the primary global reserve currency in coming decades and will likely suffer only a slow decline in its share of currency reserves.

The dollar/yen (USDJPY) during 2011 was mainly affected by the massive earthquake disaster that hit Japan in March 2011. The earthquake required Japanese insurance companies to repatriate investments from overseas to pay for earthquake damages, thus providing strong support for the yen. The Bank of Japan tried to intervene to halt the yen's rise but the intervention had little net impact. The yen repatriation, plus Japan's trade surplus, provided strong support for the yen through 2011 and offset the bearish factors for the yen such as (1) the Bank of Japan's near-zero interest rates and quantitative easing program, and (2) Japan's dangerous fiscal condition. While Fed policy and the U.S. trade deficit continue to present major bearish factors for the dollar, the dollar is already trading at a relatively low level that reflects those bearish factors. In addition, there are offsetting bullish factors for the dollar such as the fact that the U.S. economy is in much better shape than the European or Japanese economies and that the dollar is still seeing safe-haven demand. With these largely offsetting factors, the dollar may therefore continue to range-trade over the near-term.

US - Europe 3-mo Rate Diff. vs. Dollar Index

US - Japan 3-mo Rate Diff. vs. Dollar Index

Five years have passed since the U.S. housing bubble started deflating in 2006 and more than two years have passed since the U.S. 2007/09 recession officially ended in June 2009, according to the National Bureau of Economic Research (NBER). Yet the U.S. Federal Reserve still has a record amount of liquidity in the banking system and recently announced its goal of keeping interest rates "exceptionally low" until late 2014. The Fed is trying to encourage the U.S. economy to enter a sustained and normalized expansion, overcoming obstacles such as the European debt crisis, the continued depression in the U.S. housing market, and hamstrung U.S. consumers and small businesses.

The Fed responded aggressively to the financial crisis in 2008 with a wide range of measures. The Fed started cutting its federal funds rate target in October 2007 from 5.25% when the housing crisis started causing strains. By February 2008 the Fed had cut the funds rate to 3.00% and by early 2009 the Fed had cut the funds rate to the current range of zero to 0.25%.

After the financial crisis erupted into global proportions in September 2008 with the bankruptcy of Lehman Brothers, the Fed began a broad range of liquidity programs to lend money not only to banks, but also to securities firms and directly into the commercial paper and mortgage markets. The Fed, in its first quantitative easing move (QE1), purchased $300 billion in Treasury securities from March through September 2009, directly monetizing U.S. government debt and permanently injecting reserves into the banking system. The Fed from January 2009 through March 2010 also conducted a program of buying $1.25 trillion in agency mortgage-backed securities and about $175 billion of agency debt securities. That program kept mortgage rates down and helped to revive the mortgage securitization market.

When the economy continued to struggle in the first half of 2010, the Fed on November 3, 2010 officially announced its second quantitative easing program (QE2) to buy $600 billion worth of Treasury securities from November 2010 through June 2011. The QE2 program, plus the Fed's policy of using proceeds from maturing securities to purchase new securities, resulted in the increase of the Fed's balance

sheet asset level to about $2.9 trillion by June 2011. That represented a massive $2 trillion in excess liquidity above the $900 billion level seen before the financial crisis began.

The purpose of the Fed's QE2 program was two-fold: (1) to keep banks fully supplied with excess reserves to reduce the chance of any liquidity squeeze and to provide plenty of reserves as a base for expanded lending, and (2) to keep long-term Treasury yields relatively low in order to hold down private rates such as corporate bond yields and mortgage rates. The Fed also intended for the QE2 program to change market psychology to one of expecting some inflation versus fears of deflation. The Fed's measures were intended to prevent the U.S. economy from slipping into a deflationary trap such as the one seen in Japan for most of the last two decades.

QE2 turned out to be very effective in helping to improve consumer, business, and market confidence and gave the stock market a big boost, thus expanding household wealth. The U.S. economy by late 2010 and early 2011 showed a pickup in growth. The labor market by February 2011 was even showing some signs of life with a decline in the unemployment rate to a 2-year low of 8.9%. The threat of deflation receded by enough to convince the Fed not to extend its QE2 program when it ended in June 2011.

The U.S. economy in the first half of 2011, however, started to falter again due to a confluence of negative events that included high gasoline prices, the Japanese earthquake in March 2011, and the U.S. debt ceiling debacle in early summer 2011. In addition, the European debt crisis flared up in 2011 and the European banking system was near an all-out systemic crisis during 2011.

The Fed responded to the European debt crisis and the soft U.S. economy in the first half of 2011 with additional stimulus measures. The Fed did not go so far as to launch a new quantitative easing program, but it did announce that it would keep its balance sheet asset level unchanged by buying new Treasury and mortgage securities with cash from maturing securities, thus preventing a back-door tightening through a falling balance sheet asset level.

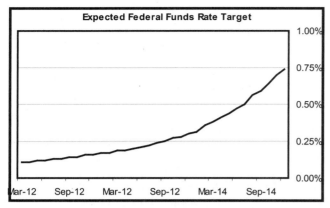

Expected Federal Funds Rate Target

U.S. 10-year Inflation Expectations

10-yr T-note minus TIPS

The Fed in September 2011 also began a new program dubbed "Operation Twist," in which the Fed sold shorter-term Treasury securities from its portfolio and used the cash to buy longer-term securities. The clear purpose of this program was to keep long-term Treasury yields low. Low Treasury yields in turn minimize other key rates including mortgage rates and corporate bond yields. The Fed successfully pushed the 30-year mortgage rates down to record low levels below 4.0%. The Fed's Operation Twist program did not result in an increase in the Fed's balance sheet asset level, which meant that the Fed could not be accused of permanently printing more money. The Fed's plan is to wrap up its $400 billion Operation Twist program by June 2012.

The European debt crisis continued to negatively affect the U.S. and global economy through late 2011. The Fed in November 2011 announced an expanded program to provide dollar loans to European and other foreign banks through dollar swap agreements with foreign central banks. This program was helpful in offsetting tight dollar liquidity in Europe that was exacerbating the European debt crisis.

The Fed in January 2012 then announced that it expects its federal funds target rate to remain "exceptionally low" until late-2014, which was later than its previous forecast of mid-2013. The Fed also announced a new program of transparency whereby individual FOMC members will provide forecasts for the federal funds rate. The members forecast, on balance, that the Fed will not begin raising interest rates until at least 2014.

The Fed's current policy is therefore to keep the federal funds rate near zero for all of 2012 and 2013 and likely well into 2014. The Fed also plans to keep its balance sheet asset level unchanged near $2.9 trillion, which will keep $2 trillion worth of excess liquidity in the banking system until at least 2014. The Fed has also said that it will consider a new quantitative easing program (QE3), likely involving the purchase of mortgage securities, should the U.S. economy start to stumble again or if there is a global shock (e.g., from Europe or China, or an oil price spike). The Fed's aggressive policy reflects its pessimism about the U.S. and global economy and the high level of risks that the global economy and banking system still face.

Despite the Fed's extraordinarily easy monetary policy, U.S. inflation expectations remain stable. The 10-year breakeven inflation expectations rate, which measures the difference between nominal and inflation-protected Treasury securities, fell from a peak of 2.66% in April 2011 and remained below 2.5% for the remainder of 2011 and into early 2012. Due to the slack in the U.S. economy and the continued overhang from the housing market and the European debt crisis, the markets are not currently worried about an inflation outbreak. However, as the economy likely picks up in 2012 and 2013, the question is whether the Fed will act fast enough to prevent a burst in inflation expectations. If not, there is the risk of an upward spike in bond yields if the markets start to worry that the Fed is falling behind the inflation curve.

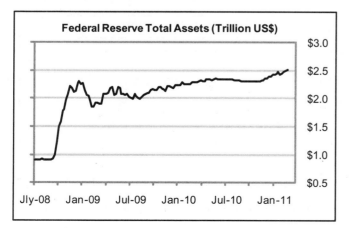

Federal Reserve Total Assets (Trillion US$)

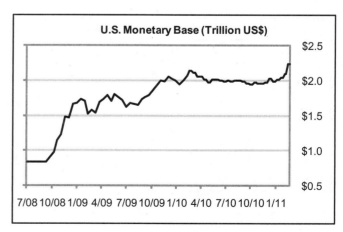

U.S. Monetary Base (Trillion US$)

TWO-YEAR EUROPEAN DEBT CRISIS IS CLOSE TO CONTAINMENT

After two years of falling behind the debt crisis with half measures, Eurozone officials in late 2011 and early 2012 finally started to hit on the right combination of tools to contain the crisis. The biggest step forward came from the European Central Bank (ECB), which made a complete U-turn when Mario Draghi took over as the new ECB President on November 1, 2011. Mr. Draghi at each of his first two meetings in November and December 2011 cut the ECB's refinancing rate by 25 basis points. That reversed former ECB President Jean-Claude Trichet's 50 bp rate hike earlier in 2011 and put the refinancing rate back at the 1.00% level that prevailed in the aftermath of the 2008/09 financial crisis. More importantly, the ECB at its December 2011 meeting announced that it would conduct two unlimited 36-month lending operations to European banks. More than 800 European banks borrowed more than 1 trillion euros worth of 36-month funds at the ECB's two loan operations in December and February.

The ECB's two 36-month lending operations went a long way toward containing the European debt crisis by easing bank funding stress and by bringing down Eurozone bond yields. Some banks used their 1.00% loans from the ECB to buy Eurozone government bonds, thus capturing a wide yield spread. The ECB's 36-month loans essentially removed the threat of a major European bank failure because banks then had access to unlimited 36-month funding, providing alternative funding for the many European banks that had effectively been shut out of both the interbank lending market and the bond market during 2011 because of concerns about counter-party risk.

The Eurozone debt crisis started as a crisis of confidence in the sovereign debt of the GIIPS countries (Greece, Ireland, Italy, Portugal, Spain) due to excessively high budget deficits and total debt loads. However, the sovereign debt crisis quickly morphed into a systemic European banking crisis because European banks held so much bad sovereign debt that their own solvency came into question. The banking system problems in turn spilled over into the real economy because of a crisis of business and consumer confidence and because of the possibility of a severe credit crunch. Banks in Europe are the primary conduit for loans to the corporate and consumer sector. If banks are in trouble and reduce their lending, then businesses and consumers cannot borrow and they in turn cut their spending, causing weaker economic growth.

Greece kicked off the Eurozone debt crisis at the beginning of 2010 when the 2008/09 financial crisis laid bare the country's massive underlying fiscal problems. Greece received its first bailout in May 2010. Portugal and Ireland quickly ran into problems as well and required bailouts. Ireland received an IMF/Eurozone bailout in November 2010 and Portugal received a bailout in April 2011.

While Italy and Portugal have largely been stabilized, Greece continues to present a major problem because there is no way that Greece can possibly pay back all its debt, which has ballooned to nearly 200% of GDP. However, Greek and Eurozone officials in March 2012 were putting the final touches on a second 130 billion euro bailout package and a voluntary bond swap by Greek bond holders that would help cut Greece's debt load to 120% of GDP by 2020.

Eurozone leaders in early 2012 also agreed to a new fiscal treaty to fix defects in the Eurozone's fiscal integration. The fiscal treaty requires members to enshrine debt limits in national constitutions and imposes automatic sanctions on fiscal violators. German Chancellor Angela Merkel required the fiscal treaty in return for boosting bailout amounts. The Eurozone accelerated its bailout resources by planning to get the permanent 500 billion euro European Stability Mechanism (ESM) running by July 2012, a year earlier than previously planned. Eurozone officials may also decide to add the remaining 250 billion euros of unused resources in the temporary European Financial Stability Facility to the permanent ESM facility, thus bringing the total to 750 billion euros.

The European crisis is certainly not over since the question is whether the region can produce enough economic growth and tax revenue growth to outweigh the harsh austerity measures. Moreover, the Eurozone does not have sufficiently large bailout facilities to save both Italy and Spain if that becomes necessary. However, the ECB's liquidity measures and Eurozone bailout facilities now have at least a chance of stabilizing the European debt crisis for long enough for the region to outgrow its debt problems and eventually regain the trust of investors.

Volume - U.S.

U.S. Futures Volume Highlights
2011 in Comparison with 2010

2011 Rank	Top 50 Contracts Traded in 2009	2011 Contracts	%	2010 Contracts	%	2010 Rank
1	E-Mini S&P 500 Index, CME	620,368,790	22.44%	555,328,670	20.09%	1
2	Eurodollars (3-month), CME	564,086,746	20.40%	510,955,113	18.48%	2
3	T-Notes (10-year), CBT	317,402,598	11.48%	293,718,907	10.62%	3
4	Crude Oil, NYMEX	175,036,216	6.33%	168,652,141	6.10%	4
5	T-Notes (5-year), CBT	170,563,052	6.17%	132,149,948	4.78%	5
6	T-Bonds (30-year), CBT	92,338,638	3.34%	83,509,754	3.02%	7
7	Euro FX, CME	84,236,825	3.05%	86,232,358	3.12%	6
8	Corn, CBT	79,004,801	2.86%	69,841,420	2.53%	9
9	Natural Gas, NYMEX	76,864,334	2.78%	64,323,068	2.33%	11
10	E-Mini NASDAQ 100, CME	75,165,277	2.72%	79,637,745	2.88%	8
11	T-Notes (2-year), CBT	72,178,803	2.61%	66,977,168	2.42%	10
12	COMEX Gold (100 oz.), NYMEX	49,175,593	1.78%	44,730,345	1.62%	12
13	Soybeans, CBT	45,143,755	1.63%	36,933,960	1.34%	14
14	E-Mini Russell 2000 Index, ICE	43,594,169	1.58%	39,747,503	1.44%	13
15	Mini ($5) Dow Jones Industrial Index, CBT	32,496,922	1.18%	34,059,544	1.23%	15
16	Heating Oil #2, NYMEX	31,838,626	1.15%	26,970,106	0.98%	20
17	Gasoline, RBOB, NYMEX	31,129,256	1.13%	27,898,698	1.01%	19
18	Australian Dollar, CME	30,751,538	1.11%	25,903,355	0.94%	21
19	British Pound, CME	29,028,755	1.05%	30,220,239	1.09%	17
20	Japanese Yen, CME	28,369,147	1.03%	31,862,793	1.15%	16
21	Sugar #11, ICE	24,629,369	0.89%	29,052,539	1.05%	18
22	Wheat, CBT	24,283,331	0.88%	23,090,255	0.84%	22
23	Soybean Oil, CBT	24,156,509	0.87%	20,791,164	0.75%	24
24	Canadian Dollar, CME	22,416,680	0.81%	22,083,807	0.80%	23
25	Henry Hub Swap, NYMEX	20,825,660	0.75%	20,417,178	0.74%	25
26	COMEX Silver (5,000 oz.), NYMEX	19,608,557	0.71%	12,826,666	0.46%	27
27	Soybean Meal, CBT	16,920,194	0.61%	14,052,845	0.51%	26
28	Ultra T-Bond, CBT	15,461,984	0.56%	7,713,395	0.28%	34
29	Live Cattle, CME	13,532,554	0.49%	11,332,739	0.41%	30
30	High Grade Copper, NYMEX	12,491,517	0.45%	10,305,670	0.37%	31
31	Federal Funds (30-day), CBT	12,306,131	0.45%	12,753,228	0.46%	28
32	CBOE Volatility Index, CFE	12,031,528	0.44%	4,392,796	0.16%	44
33	Eurodollars, NYSE	11,752,482	0.43%			
34	Swiss Franc, CME	10,238,684	0.37%	12,011,173	0.43%	29
35	Lean Hogs, CME	9,969,961	0.36%	8,076,535	0.29%	33
36	Mexican Peso, CME	9,203,730	0.33%	6,763,808	0.24%	37
37	US Dollar Index, ICE	7,751,270	0.28%	6,369,517	0.23%	38
38	E-mini S&P MidCap 400 Index, CME	7,689,306	0.28%	7,657,372	0.28%	36
39	Nikkei 225 Index (JPY), CME	7,670,282	0.28%	5,108,015	0.18%	42
40	Natural Gas Penultimate Swap, NYMEX	7,384,147	0.27%	8,995,324	0.33%	32
41	S&P 500 Index, CME	7,220,582	0.26%	7,689,961	0.28%	35
42	Wheat, KCBT	6,342,782	0.23%	5,549,842	0.20%	40
43	Cotton #2, ICE	5,288,454	0.19%	5,732,906	0.21%	39
44	Coffee "C", ICE	5,174,538	0.19%	5,488,196	0.20%	41
45	Cocoa, ICE	4,948,052	0.18%	3,797,679	0.14%	45
46	Eurodollar, ELX	3,888,256	0.14%	1,287,250		
47	30-Year Treasury Bond, ELX	3,785,858	0.14%	1,243,519		
48	5-Year Treasury Note, ELX	3,599,102	0.13%	3,565,576		
49	Crude Oil, miNY, NYMEX	3,000,140	0.11%	3,157,814	0.11%	49
50	10-Year Treasury Note, ELX	2,970,234	0.11%	3,600,261	0.13%	46
	Top 50 Contracts	2,985,315,715	97.67%	2,694,560,061	97.46%	
	Contracts Below the Top 50	71,226,042	2.33%	70,224,375	2.54%	
	TOTAL	3,056,541,757	100.00%	2,764,784,436	100.00%	

* For 2010 Top 50 contracts totaled 2,703,318,609 including 4 contracts that are not among 2011's Top 50.

U.S. Futures Volume Highlights
2011 in Comparison with 2010

2011 Rank	EXCHANGE	2011 Contracts	%	2010 Contracts	%	2010 Rank
1	Chicago Mercantile Exchange (CME Group)	1,535,793,841	55.55%	1,418,240,658	60.92%	1
2	Chicago Board of Trade (CME Group)	906,707,754	32.79%	799,926,808	34.36%	2
3	New York Mercantile Exchange (CME Group)	458,412,470	16.58%	419,914,148	18.04%	3
4	ICE Futures U.S.	94,106,767	3.40%	92,520,026	3.97%	4
5	NYSE Liffe U.S.	20,896,432	0.76%	4,064,780	0.17%	9
6	ELX Futures	16,757,952	0.61%	13,142,541	0.56%	5
7	CBOE Futures Exchange	12,040,074	0.44%	4,402,616	0.19%	8
8	Kansas City Board of Trade	6,342,782	0.23%	5,549,842	0.24%	6
9	OneChicago	3,679,484	0.13%	4,971,160	0.21%	7
10	Minneapolis Grain Exchange	1,732,331	0.06%	1,690,207	0.07%	10
11	Chicago Climate Exchange	71,870	0.00%	361,650	0.02%	11
	Total Futures	3,056,541,757	100.00%	2,764,784,436	100.00%	

Chicago Climate Futures Exchange (CCFE)

FUTURE	2011	2010	2009	2008	2007
CA Climate Action Registry-Climate Res Tons (CCAR)	25	193	684		
Carbon Financial Instrument (CFI-US)	356	522	891		
Event Linked (IFEX)	1,464	2,148	4,499	10,373	2,321
Event Linked (IFEX) FLW	1,100	1,000	1,860	2	
Nitrogen Financial Instrument - Annual (NFI-A)	33,321	100,491	209,223	21,730	205
Nitrogen Financial Instrument (NFI-OS)	490	1,220	808	1,348	3,465
Renewable Energy Certificate Funds-Connecticut	7,818	2,172	261		
Renewable Energy Certificate Funds-Massachusetts	7,455	4,805			
Renewable Energy Certificate Funds-New Jersey	3,052	7,401	2,262		
Regional Greenhouse Gas Initiatives (RGGI)	8,980	52,494	693,863	17,043	
Sulfur Financial Instrument (SFI)	7,809	184,637	317,749	289,398	181,030
Total Futures	71,870	361,650	1,246,123	370,505	191,899

CBOE Futures Exchange (CFE)

FUTURE	2011	2010	2009	2008	2007
CBOE Volatility Index (VIX)	12,031,528	4,392,796	1,144,858	1,088,105	1,046,475
CBOE Mini-Volatility Index (VM)	8,388	9,429	9,268		
CBOE Gold ETF-Volatility Index (GVZ)	129				
S&P 500 3-Month Variance (VTI)	29	388	123	2,078	9,302
Total Futures	12,040,074	4,402,616	1,155,969	1,161,397	1,136,295

Chicago Board of Trade (CBT)

FUTURE	2011	2010	2009	2008	2007
Wheat	24,283,331	23,090,255	17,677,547	19,011,928	19,582,706
Mini Wheat	149,102	91,560	61,355	70,971	79,282
Corn	79,004,801	69,841,420	50,948,804	59,957,118	54,520,152
Mini Corn	363,832	237,394	203,474	219,562	156,210
Oats	349,316	344,587	314,305	441,588	432,741
Soybeans	45,143,755	36,933,960	35,758,855	36,373,096	31,726,316
Mini Soybeans	394,119	412,732	466,367	475,231	540,940
Soybean Oil	24,156,509	20,791,164	17,132,082	16,928,361	13,170,914
Soybean Meal	16,920,194	14,052,845	12,880,767	13,354,174	12,213,315
Grain Bais Swap	235,642	57,423	7,918		
Rough Rice	555,854	448,724	277,065	362,565	358,905
Fertilizer Products	360				
T-Bonds (30-year)	92,338,638	83,509,754	62,232,671	89,464,546	107,630,211
Ultra T-Bond	15,461,984	7,713,395			
T-Notes (10-year)	317,402,598	293,718,907	189,852,019	256,770,689	349,229,371
T-Notes (5-year)	170,563,052	132,149,948	98,391,120	168,127,469	166,207,391
T-Notes (2-year)	72,178,803	66,977,168	48,158,948	79,311,002	68,610,392
Interest Rate Swap (30-year)	13,966	31,564	55,228	80,169	12,555
Interest Rate Swap (10-year)	316,847	444,751	871,074	1,004,309	848,372
Interest Rate Swap (7-year)	12,347	33,036	21,957	320	
Interest Rate Swap (5-year)	658,376	1,039,064	1,331,017	1,147,170	551,505
OTR 2-Year T-Note	22,583	14,853			
OTR 5-Year T-Note	36,286	27,570			
OTR 10-Year T-Note	43,843	70,067			
30-Day Federal Funds	12,306,131	12,753,228	10,349,071	19,434,295	16,597,188
Ethanol	238,946	162,725	67,168	29,451	12,516
OTC Ethanol Forward Swap	632,211	636,444	270,596	249,147	60,729
Dow Jones Industrial Index ($25)	224	1,907	3,867	12,392	14,301
Dow Jones Industrial Index ($10)	286,697	188,109	395,584	1,147,657	1,483,817
Mini Dow Jones Industrial Index ($5)	32,496,922	34,059,544	39,889,836	55,348,312	40,098,882
DJ US Real Estate	6				
Dow-UBS Commodity Index	140,479	84,314	97,223	73,445	51,651
Total Futures	799,926,808	587,984,965	825,257,796	895,521,149	678,262,052

Chicago Mercantile Exchange (CME Group)

FUTURE	2011	2010	2009	2008	2007
Live Cattle	13,532,554	11,332,739	8,797,033	9,801,360	8,587,973
Feeder Cattle	1,580,387	1,330,421	1,059,109	1,250,324	1,099,863
Lean Hogs	9,969,961	8,076,535	6,819,061	8,505,138	7,264,832
Pork Bellies, Frozen	2	4,722	27,852	56,705	68,409
Class III Milk	368,614	277,860	280,636	304,754	311,459
Class IV Milk	10,744	968	332	624	314
Nonfat Dry Milk	6,372	5,696	1,480	2,239	1,072
Cash Butter	16,939	14,197	16,983	17,495	20,067
Cash Settled Cheese	15,990	3,189			
Dry Whey	10,601	7,490	5,246	4,141	6,378
USD Crude Palm Oil	1,016	572			
Wood Pulp	686	1,263	3,364	8,740	1,038
Random Lumber	319,333	311,902	317,227	437,613	334,689
One Month LIBOR	187,511	385,821	452,340	571,710	1,194,200
Eurodollar (3-month)	564,086,746	510,955,113	437,585,193	596,974,081	621,470,328
Euroyen	10,388	22,833	40,879	122,917	561,220

Chicago Mercantile Exchange (CME Group) (continued)

FUTURE	2011	2010	2009	2008	2007
Sovereign Yield	367				
Euro Bonds	4,568				
Australian Dollar	30,751,538	25,903,355	16,732,682	11,212,985	10,785,897
British Pound	29,028,755	30,220,239	24,853,787	20,497,378	20,799,827
Brazilian Real	260,730	50,020	30,398	67,168	127,879
Canadian Dollar	22,416,680	22,083,807	15,481,166	11,378,024	12,224,845
Czech Koruna	219	727	224	787	496
DJ CME FX$ Index	322	1,694			
Euro FX	84,236,825	86,232,358	54,393,644	53,652,590	43,063,060
E-Mini Euro FX	1,426,462	1,245,374	664,350	774,078	491,401
Hungarian Forint	2,117	2,080	975	901	148
Israeli Shekel	5,599	6,329	7,495	3,014	3,070
Japanese Yen	28,369,147	31,862,793	22,749,569	32,844,404	30,820,442
E-Mini Japanese Yen	129,518	67,354	28,906	24,657	19,116
Korean Won	3,939	5,271	1,411	268	2,312
Mexican Peso	9,203,730	6,763,808	4,298,939	5,302,297	5,154,636
New Zealand Dollar	2,077,277	2,235,390	1,220,227	808,296	928,816
Norwegian Krone	13,082	11,241	11,652	7,327	10,289
Polish Zloty	38,951	20,318	19,848	20,554	25,977
Russian Ruble	687,845	238,490	162,314	213,341	173,613
South African Rand	143,544	138,144	77,848	99,413	84,376
Swedish Krona	3,217	6,972	5,396	2,436	12,374
Swiss Franc	10,238,684	12,011,173	10,618,630	14,814,153	14,478,658
Turkish Lira	13,729	26,521	12,011		
Australian Dollar / Canadian Dollar	1,694	4,079	3,582	2,762	1,749
Australian Dollar / Japanese Yen	26,857	26,094	3,493	1,088	44
Australian Dollar / New Zealand Dollar	438	167	281	1,346	903
British Pound / Japanese Yen	36,105	28,977	6,395	3,430	332
British Pound / Swiss Franc	10,610	8,762	2,610	702	3,031
Canadian Dollar / Japanese Yen	624	838	301	14	236
Chinese Renimibi / US Dollar	7,563	4,937	7,024	16,790	8,179
Swiss Franc / Japanese Yen	8,337	3,323	302	1,968	2,754
Euro / Australian Dollar	4,816	9,290	531	246	210
Euro / British Pound	341,899	275,335	125,657	73,554	80,232
Euro / Canadian Dollar	4,049	1,213	277	85	180
Euro / Japanese Yen	369,522	295,766	219,109	320,060	365,895
Euro / Norwegian Krone	1,386	104	356	3,760	6,605
Euro / Polish Zloty	31,006	46,514	35,455	14,693	18,349
Euro / Swedish Krona	1,110	174	110	50	48
Euro / Swiss Franc	351,429	152,038	85,059	50,923	97,478
Euro / Turkish Lira	10,825	39,549	22,280		
Euro/US Dollar Realized Vol	844				
Micro JPY/USD	68,499	29			
Micro CHF/USD	59,900	78			
Micro CAD/USD	24,582	13			
E-micro EUR/USD	1,532,755	1,063,133	424,726		
E-micro GBP/USD	206,527	240,081	170,411		
E-micro USD/CAD	12,898	48,573	39,809		
E-micro USD/CHF	19,911	27,384	15,182		
E-micro USD/JPY	29,465	34,453	94,508		
E-micro AUD/USD	240,406	89,358	65,031		
S&P 500 Index	7,220,582	7,689,961	10,435,912	16,763,071	15,837,593
E-mini S&P 500 Index	620,368,790	555,328,670	556,314,143	633,889,466	415,348,228
E-mini S&P SmallCap 600 Index	13,422	32,168	66,471	107,039	28,894
E-mini S&P MidCap 400 Index	7,689,306	7,657,372	9,133,223	8,580,467	7,352,427
S&P MidCap 400 Index	42,724	38,467	59,360	97,224	118,140
E-micro S&P CNX Nifty Index	44,757	143,753			
E-mini S&P CNX Nifty Index	1,495	5,888			
S&P Citigroup Growth	554	1,463	1,351	8,163	25,132
S&P Citigroup Value	697	4,971	5,437	6,450	6,418
E-Mini NASDAQ 100 Index	75,165,277	79,637,745	77,972,143	108,734,456	95,309,053
NASDAQ 100 Index	472,587	507,824	756,919	1,407,413	1,683,378
Nikkei 225 Index (USD)	2,766,559	2,951,246	2,935,616	4,399,966	3,421,085
Nikkei 225 Index (JPY)	7,670,282	5,108,015	4,167,340	4,769,567	3,290,909
S&P 500 Financial Sector	60	555	5,866	9,032	4,202
E-mini S&P Financial Sector	10,000				
E-mini S&P Consumer Discretionary Sector	5,570				
E-mini S&P Consumer Staples Sector	7,766				
E-mini S&P Energy Sector	17,788				
E-mini S&P Health Sector	6,810				
E-mini S&P Industrial Sector	15,953				
E-mini S&P Materials Sector	16,133				
E-mini S&P Technology Sector	6,581				
E-mini S&P Utilities Sector	8,197				
E-Mini MSCI EAFE	380,551	1,068,082	602,104	450,138	172,371

Chicago Mercantile Exchange (CME Group) (continued)

FUTURE	2011	2010	2009	2008	2007
E-mini MSCI Emerging Markets Index	509,064	715,849	324,722	171,064	26,793
TRAKRS BXY	1,100				
TRAKRS PIMCO	221,332	306,642	792,148	3,668,906	8,712,135
TRAKRS PIMCO SPTR	48,485	104,344	134,141	451,858	2,324,128
Bespoke Custom Indexes	30				
HDD Weather	28,491	64,388	70,619	119,533	135,702
HDD Seasonal Weather Strips	3,975	6,257	3,550	6,600	12,350
CDD Weather	22,856	57,993	53,398	117,729	114,044
CDD Seasonal Weather Strips	3,150	250	2,900	3,610	7,300
Euro HDD Weather	4,664	8,275	16,950	4,625	3,625
Euro CAT Weather	1,650	1,025	775	350	750
Euro HDD Seasonal Strip Weather	1,028	5,435	300	2,850	1,750
Weekly Average Temperature	50		1,850	100	5
CSI Housing Index	195	88	295	1,178	2,995
Goldman Sachs Commodity Index	328,281	521,886	520,462	526,036	644,761
GSCI Excess Return Index	92,046	16,085	55,178	27,206	15,136
OTC SP GSCI ER 3-Month Swap	11,422	14,967			
OTC SP GSCI ER Swap	4,708	12,216			
S&P 500 ETF	101	977	1,809	1,109	1,165
Russell 2000 ETF	16	145	71	550	470
Nasdaq 100 ETF	10	292	328	833	1,470
Total Futures	1,535,793,841	1,418,240,658	1,276,264,462	1,612,884,857	1,415,423,615

ELX Futures Exchange (ELX)

FUTURE	2011	2010	2009	2008	2007
2-Year Treasury Note (ZTE)	2,443,559	3,424,750	1,075,171		
5-Year Treasury Note (ZFE)	3,599,102	3,565,576	2,012,132		
10-Year Treasury Note (ZNE)	2,970,234	3,600,261	1,322,429		
Ultra Long-Term US T-Bond (ZUE)	70,943	20,989			
30-Year Treasury Bond (ZBE)	3,785,858	1,243,715	594,251		
Eurodollar (GEE)	3,888,256	1,287,250			
Total Futures	16,757,952	13,142,541	5,003,983		

ICE Futures U.S. (ICE)

FUTURE	2011	2010	2009	2008	2007
Coffee 'C'	5,174,538	5,488,196	4,235,349	5,446,516	5,128,623
Sugar #11	24,629,369	29,052,539	27,300,259	27,019,704	21,263,799
Sugar #16	74,876	99,049	66,719	250	
Cocoa	4,948,052	3,797,679	3,086,966	3,592,268	3,335,283
Cotton #2	5,288,454	5,732,906	3,574,995	6,162,963	6,334,979
Orange Juice, Frozen Concentrate	627,610	691,583	656,995	710,512	845,792
US Dollar / Swedish Krona (Half Size)	70,409	35,785	42,749	50,858	
US Dollar / Norwegian Krone (Half Size)	80,993	58,091	30,359	48,976	
US Dollar / Czech Koruna (Half Size)	32,584	17,901	31,581	12,711	
US Dollar / Hungarian Forint (Half Size)	39,723	18,500	21,426	29,945	
US Dollar / South African Rand	102,942	123,105	149,046	81,401	88,260
Australian Dollar / US Dollar (AU)	4,671	2,520	2,858	4,920	17,666
Australian Dollar / US Dollar (KAU)	4,219				
Australian Dollar / Canadian Dollar	18,411	18,378	6,671	26,637	25,922
Australian Dolar / New Zealand Dollar	17,688	18,768	9,326	12,307	32,262
Australian Dollar / Japanese Yen	19,346	16,593	17,871	39,382	53,049
Canadian Dollar / Japanese Yen	17,562	16,147	6,719	13,078	20,463
Canadian Dollar / US Dollar (KSV)	178				
Japanese Yen / US Dollar (KSN)	371				
New Zealand Dollar / Japanese Yen	12,900	19,141	2,461	558	1,502
New Zealand Dollar / US Dollar (ZX)	2,262	4,870	8,156	45,134	61,657
New Zealand Dollar / US Dollar (KZX)	191				
Norwegian Krone / Japanese Yen	176	83	1,333		
Norwegian Krone / Swedish Koruna	17,044	22,460	29,257	38,021	20,866
Swiss Franc / Japanese Yen (KY)	8,079	17,356	15,721	76,734	74,148
Swiss Franc / Japanese Yen (KZY)	1,820				
Swiss Franc / US Dollar (KMF)	137				
Euro / US Dollar (EO)	5,691	10,251	61,953	112,675	24,382
Euro / US Dollar (KEO)	79,547				
Euro / Australian Dollar (RA)	49,763	99,371	43,084	62,986	73,821
Euro / Australian Dollar (KRA)	28,941				
Euro / British Pound (GB)	67,870	80,847	105,056	169,921	241,409
Euro / British Pound (KGB)	30,679				
Euro / Canadian Dollar (EP)	16,058	23,478	12,746	21,972	43,266
Euro / Canadian Dollar (KEP)	5,609				
Euro / Czech Koruna	34,069	39,172	25,233	16,204	49,442
Euro / Hungarian Forint	42,289	49,112	40,094	18,525	31,105
Euro / Japanese Yen (EJ)	111,413	149,485	182,157	346,417	418,725
Euro / Japanese Yen (KEJ)	31,351				
Euro / Swedish Krona (RK)	46,683	51,498	37,438	55,039	64,617

ICE Futures U.S. (ICE) (continued)

FUTURE	2011	2010	2009	2008	2007
Euro / Swedish Krona (KRK)	11,268				
Euro / Norwegian (OL)	72,240	42,275	18,857	52,084	58,664
Euro / Norwegian (KOL)	17,743				
Euro / South African Rand	183	113	117	244	318
Euro / Swiss Franc (RZ)	25,418	41,269	65,200	159,849	215,173
Euro / Swiss Franc (KRZ)	3,934				
Million Australian Dollar / US Dollar	924		259	3	
Million British Pound / US Dollar	408	54	250	327	
Million Euro / British Pound	60				
Million Euro / US Dollar	3,752	1,198	3,062	4,804	
Million US Dollar / Swiss Franc	20		102	49	
Million US Dollar / Japanese Yen	36		4,780	1,783	
Million US Dollar / Canadian Dollar	8	46			
British Pound / Australian Dollar	19,111	18,216	6,271	8,104	5,994
British Pound / Canadian Dollar	14,099	12,598	1,033	3,204	5,195
British Pound / New Zealand Dollar	7,019	6,535	2,245	16	
British Pound / Norwegian Krone	17,952	10,717	383		
British Pound / Swiss franc	15,076	13,911	16,317	43,558	66,586
British Pound / Japanese Yen	82,549	48,674	25,686	46,231	111,274
Small British Pound / US Dollar	20,833	12,402	31,175	55,127	14,279
Small US Dollar / Canadian Dollar	6,539	7,621	3,587	6,572	14,672
Small US Dollar / Japanese Yen	25,945	25,061	8,842	26,973	28,251
Small US Dollar / Swiss Franc	4,840	4,414	5,853	9,462	17,866
US Dollar Index	7,751,270	6,369,517	2,523,927	1,825,326	1,099,800
Revised NYSE Composite Index	157	252	209	698	4,605
Russell 1000 Mini Index	414,079	326,645	445,752	177,768	81,432
Russell 1000 Growth Index Mini	120,758	35,031			
Russell 1000 Value Index Mini	129,021	31,506			
Russell 2000 Mini Index	43,594,169	39,747,503	38,686,673	16,526,331	57,540
Reuters-CRB Futures Index (CCI)	2,787	9,500	15,973	19,185	19,973
RJ/CRB Futures Index	1	55	354	44	3
Total Futures	94,106,767	92,520,026	81,715,275	63,433,647	40,658,718

Kansas City Board of Trade (KCBT)

FUTURE	2011	2010	2009	2008	2007
Wheat	6,342,782	5,549,842	3,660,343	3,778,266	4,318,007
Total Futures	6,342,782	5,549,842	3,660,343	3,778,266	4,318,007

Minneapolis Grain Exchange (MGE)

FUTURE	2011	2010	2009	2008	2007
Spring Wheat	1,732,331	1,687,228	1,198,013	1,361,042	1,792,310
Total Futures	1,732,331	1,687,228	1,198,013	1,361,042	1,792,310

New York Mercantile Exchange (NYMEX)

FUTURE	2011	2010	2009	2008	2007
Gold	49,175,593	44,730,345	35,139,541	38,377,367	25,060,440
Platinum	1,993,263	1,486,507	802,884	675,543	501,545
Palladium	1,139,529	901,584	400,821	483,828	400,993
Silver	19,608,557	12,826,666	7,990,528	8,917,183	6,817,137
Gold, E-mini	963	11,008	13,341		
Gold, miNY	192,575	105,236	59,900	20,034	10,988
E-micro Gold	474,444	23,534			
Volatility Gold (GVF)	8				
Silver, E-mini	15	1,975	660		
Silver, miNY	106,576	24,722	13,367	8,115	5,120
Copper	12,491,517	10,305,670	6,398,967	4,618,068	3,753,168
Copper, miNY	23,655	10,566	5,987	4,890	4,927
Hot-Rolled Steel	31,738	21,613	13,494	23	
Australian Coke Coal	102				
Uranium	22,598	26,097	6,149	13,291	1,268
Crude Oil, Physical	175,036,216	168,652,141	137,428,494	134,674,264	121,525,967
Crude Oil	313,463	453,557	1,139,308	1,360,899	625,839
Crude Oil, miNY	3,000,140	3,157,814	3,368,983	5,641,145	5,185,214
Brent Crude Oil, Last Day	787,768	144,625	31,708	465,056	506,075
No. 2 Heating Oil, NY	31,838,626	26,970,106	21,426,015	19,583,052	18,078,976
Heating Oil Financial	44,784	50,834	91,152	70,561	46,828
Heating Oil, miNY	289	411	415	637	21,296
NY Harbor RBOB Gasoline	31,129,256	27,898,698	21,159,516	20,522,571	19,791,439
RBOB Gasoline, miNY	49	205	84	307	563
Natural Gas (HP)	27,786				
LTD Natural Gas	63,980	1,540			
Natural Gas, miNY	547,462	670,266	1,030,118	1,058,665	1,403,525
Singapore 380 Fuel Oil	280	50	300	650	150
NY Harbor ULSD Diesel (LH)	4				
PJM Financially Settled Monthly - Peak	215,741	115,132	126,778	77,287	84,154

New York Mercantile Exchange (NYMEX) (continued)

FUTURE	2011	2010	2009	2008	2007
Natural Gas	76,864,334	64,323,068	47,951,353	38,730,519	29,786,318
RBOB Gas	45,008	48,088	9,800		
3.5% Fuel Oil (Platts) CIF MED Swap	29	34	278		
AER-Dayton Hub Monthly - Peak	20,332	5,718	4,000	12,258	4,262
AER Dayton Hub Monthly - Off-Peak	17,979	5,892	11,716	35,148	14,604
Alberta Electricity (AOM)	4,418				
Algonquin City - Gates Natural Gas Index Swap	5,839	3,454			
Algonquin City - Gates Natural Gas Basis Swap	9,891	3,243	1,924	214	
Algonquin City - Gates Natural Gas Swing Swap (C8)	636				
ANR - LA Natural Gas Index Swap	788	1,518			
ANR - Louisiana Basis Swap	5,140	15,887	46,530	34,499	13,127
ANR - Oklahoma Basis	20,157	28,380	70,712	124,501	99,106
Central Appalachian Coal	95,330	162,020	139,732	108,887	127,529
Argus Biodiesel RME FOB Rdam Swap	5,168	15,765	8,457		
Argus LLS vs WTI (Arg) T	35,595	7,187	843		
Argus Propane Far East Index Swap	5,952	4,583	2,220		
Argus Propane (Saudi Aramco) Swap	8,313	2,792	433	20	
Brent (ICE) Crude Oil BALMO Swap	2,363	3,145	4,619		
Brent (ICE) Calendar Swap	221,197	157,237	313,572	335,640	71,534
Brent CFD (Platts) vs Front Month Swap	3,685	7,639	12,357		
Brent (CFD) Swap	7,753	25,585	61,632		
Brent Bullet Swap	241,343	176,357	276,532	114,701	42,053
Brent 25-Day (Platts) (NBZ)	30				
Centerpoint Basis Swap	19,409	79,471	188,819	319,716	159,048
Centerpoint East Index	1,524	10,476	9,617	4,644	1,671
Chicago Basis Swap	480	428	73,011	575,663	486,313
Chicago Ethanol Swap	227,267	55,779	15,169	15,617	4,590
Chicago ULSD PL vs HO SPR	971	110			
Chicago Unleaded Gasoline vs RBOB Spread Swap	61		300		
CIG Basis Swap	21,569	28,833	42,065	117,473	100,525
CIG Rockies Natural Gas Index Swap	877	3,664	5,364	1,041	
CIG Rockies Natural Gas Swing Swap	448	236	726	62	
Cinergy Hub Off-Peak LMP Swap	5,840	12,348	32,146	27,524	10,202
Cinergy Hub Daily Peak Swap	460	1,040		200	1,358
Cinergy Hub LMP Swap-Peak	12,722	23,962	43,856	17,280	10,586
Cinergy Hub 5mw Day Ahead Off-Peak	571,672	680,344	604,840		
Cinergy Hub 5mw Day Ahead Peak	44,471	42,043	46,939		
Cinergy Hub 5mw Real-Time Off-Peak	171,600	185,328	236,576		
Cinergy Hub 5mw Real-Time Peak	25,243	19,088	15,321		
China Coal Swap (CMC)	55				
Columbia Gulf Mainline Basis Swap	21,690	71,361	99,036		
Columbia Gulf Mainline Natural Gas	11,066	20,880	556		
Columbia Gulf Onshore Basis	1,476	34,980	105,653	211,645	80,422
Conway Natural Gas (OPIS) Swap	3,890	1,575	220		
Conway Normal Butane (OPIS) Swap	2,523	490	362		
Conway Propane 5 decimals Swap	13,514	18,067	4,129		
Crude Oil Last Day Financial Futures	531	347	130		
Crude Oil Outrights	3,001	1,883			
Dated to Frontline Brent BALMO Swap (FE)	2,792				
Canadian Heavy Crude Oil (Net Energy) Index	18,615	2,040			
Micro Crude Oil (MCL)	1,320,004				
Argus Sour Crude Index vs WTI Diff Spread Calendar	800				
Brent CFD (Platts) vs Brent Front Month (Platts)	263				
Brent CFD (Platts) vs Brent Second Month (Platts)	250				
RME Biodiesel (Argus) FOB Rdam vs ICE Gasoil	15,858	4,850			
Fame 0 Biodiesel FOB Rdam vs ICE Gasoil Spread	27,945	5,170			
Dated Brent (Platts) Daily Swap	11,816	35,626	1,802		
Dated-to-Frontline Brent Swap	44,615	48,303	141,760	183,262	90,783
Demarc Natural Gas Index Swap	2,696	7,906	3,461	13,913	3,460
Demarc Natural Gas Swing Swap	374	662	1,356	3,169	1,423
Diesel 10ppm Barge FOB Rdam vs ICE Gasoil BALMO	389	335	254		
Diesel 10ppm Barge FOB Rdam BALMO Swap (U7)	1				
Diesel 10ppm NEW Le Harve CIF Swap	32	198	5		
Dominion Natural Gas Index Swap (IH)	25,127	2,816	46,703	34,100	18,657
Dominion Basis Swap (PG)	28,072	46,950	102,937	229,043	458,950
Dubai Crude Oil BALMO Swap (BI)	1,975	6,847	3,774	2,276	
Dubai Crude Oil Calendar Swap (DC)	207,050	413,157	923,539	325,802	107,329
Eastern Rail CSX Coal Swap	66,795	40,325	29,060	30,488	4,815
East-West Fuel Oil Spread Swap	20,056	13,850	18,589	11,622	2,532
EIA Flat Tax On-Highway Diesel Swap (A5)	3,929	4,986	6,974		
Electric Ercot Daily Peak (I9)	1,260				
Electric Financially Settled	7,072	9,495			
PJM PENELEC Zone Peak Cal Mth Day Ahead LMP	2,550	7,172			
PJM DOM Zone Peak Cal mth Day Ahead LMP Swap	220	210			
Electric MISO Peak	6,968	8,225	800		

New York Mercantile Exchange (NYMEX) (continued)

FUTURE	2011	2010	2009	2008	2007
Electric NYISO Off-Peak	122,528	117,598	15,520		
PJM Meted Zone Off-Peak Cal Mth Day Ahead LMP	118,041	173,870			
PJM PECO Zone Off-Peak Cal Mth Day Ahead LMP	52,992	598,550			
PJM PENELEC Zone Off-Peak Cal Mth Day Ahead	47,040	131,411			
El Paso/Permian Index Swap	1,484	6,919	42,447	46,469	34,194
ERCOT Houston ZMCPE 5mw Peak	1,713	105	1,275		
ERCOT North ZMCPE 5mw Peak	4,233	745	4,285		
Ethanol T1 FOB Rdam Ex Duty Swap	210	3,831	2,427		
Ethanol T2 FOB Rdam Incl Duty Swap	6,149	2,338	300		
European 1% Fuel Oil BALMO Swap	258	532	1,886	815	15
European 3.5% Fuel Oil Rdam BALMO Swap	1,790	2,295	5,121	2,300	20
European 3.5% Fuel Oil Spread Swap	1,295	1,540	740	282	53
European Gasoil 10ppm Rdam Barges Swap	508	379	42	116	
European Gasoil 10ppm Rdam Barges vs Gasoil	4,848	6,228	4,789	2,850	436
Europe 1% Fuel Oil Calendar Swap	12,576	18,943	24,162	24,565	8,048
Europe 1% Fuel Oil Rdam Calendar Swap	2,092	4,517	9,115	18,743	2,872
European 6.5% Fuel Oil MED Calendar Swap	175	541	533	244	15
Europe 3.5% Fuel Oil Rotterdam Calendar Swap	89,321	76,245	126,496	77,769	20,075
European Gasoil (ICE)	17,317	5,871	1,644		
European Naptha BALMO Swap	1,423	1,804	936	139	9
European Naptha Crack Spread	99,444	126,917	110,560	34,053	13,268
European Dated Brent Crude Oil Calendar Swap	45,517	94,187	91,481	34,610	7,815
European Jet Kero NWE Calendar Swap	430	969	782	250	71
European Jet Kero Rotterdam Calendar Swap (UR)	5				
European Naptha Calendar Swap	27,807	30,006	25,031	5,430	1,143
European Propane CIF ARA Swap	12,819	6,016	3,555	389	
FAME 0 Biodiesel FOB Rdam Swap	3,027	21,840	7,198		
Florida Gas, Zone 3 Natural Gas Index Swap	10,532	1,150	668		
Florida Gas Transmission Zone 3 Basis Swap	4,929	12,779	38,300	87,760	28,098
Freight Routet TC5 (Platts) Forward	20	20			
Freight Routet TC6 (Platts) Forward	30				
Freight Routet TD3 (Baltic) Forward	30	65			
Freight Routet TD5 (Baltic) Forward	40	40			
3.5% Fuel Oil Rdam Crack Swap	130,348	80,788	78,398	39,551	921
1% Fuel Oil NWE Crack Spread Swap	15,426	3,469	9,042	5,322	1,385
Fuel Oil (Platts) CAR CM	875	116	785		
1% Fuel Oil (Platts) Cargoes CIF NEW Swap	579	856	210		
High-Low Sulfur Fuel Oil Spread Swap	20,067	7,328	21,931	14,528	2,860
Gas EuroBob OXY NWE Barges	73,570	70,147	12,549		
Gas EuroBob OXY NWE Barges Crack	140,943	78,732	15,321		
Gasoil 0.1 Barges FOB Rdam vs ICE Gasoil BALMO	60	134	137		
Gasoil 0.1 Cargoes CIF NEW Swap	79	195	104		
Gasoil 0.1 CIF MED	58	243	110		
Gasoil 0.1 CIF MED vs ICE Gasoil Swap	1,043	1,589	3,233	124	
Gasoil 0.1 Cargoes CIF NWE vs ICE Gasoil Swap	93	609	1,294	773	
Gasoil 0.1 CIF MED vs ICE Gasoil BALMO Swap	89	197	230		
Gasoil 0.1 Cargoes NWE vs ICE Gasoil BALMO Swap	14	75	59		
Gasoil 0.1 Barges FOB Rdam vs ICE Gasoil Swap	10,455	4,111	14,180	10,104	
Gasoil 0.1 Barges FOB Rdam Swap	517	3,790	1,833	965	
Gasoil 10ppm Cargoes CIF NEW vs ICE Gasoil	347	491	495		
Gasoil 10ppm Cargoes CIF NWE Swap	805	599	351	42	
Gasoil 10ppm Cargoes CIF NWE vs ICE Gasoil Swap	7,439	6,895	9,233	1,968	
Gasoil (ICE) Bullet Swap	417	4,081	3,488	4,311	676
Gasoil (ICE) Calendar Swap	10,202	17,272	14,669	6,791	220
Gasoil Crack Spread Swap	97,917	76,952	257,528	190,522	14,287
Gasoil (ICE) Mini Calendar Swap	14,106	22,064			
Gasoline Up-Down (Argus) Swap	3,227	3,946	2,992	125	
Gasoline Up-Down BALMO Swap	4,234	3,547	697		
Group Three (Platts) vs Heating Oil Spread Swap	3,671	217			
Group Three Unlead Gas (Platts) vs RBOB Gas Spread	1,695	124			
Gulf Coast 3.0% Fuel Oil BALMO Swap	32,679	22,229	16,852	3,170	
Gulf Coast Gasoline Calendar Swap	1,042	8,130	3,473	7,283	6,142
Gulf Coast Jet Fuel Calendar Swap	870	522	410	960	1,725
Gulf Coast Jet vs NY Harbor No 2 HO Spread Swap	114,056	113,926	97,772	27,511	6,470
Gulf Coast No 6 Fuel Oil 3.0% Sulfur Swap	854,111	644,907	683,433	180,907	53,150
Gulf Coast No 6 Fuel Oil Crack Swap	66,893	139,544	75,852	30,872	1,400
Gulf Coast ULSD Calendar Swap	9,143	8,729	7,538	3,506	305
Gulf Coast ULSD Crack Spread Swap	17,900	4,155	106	825	325
Heating Oil BALMO Calendar Swap	62	139			
Heating Oil Last Day Financial Futures	78				
Heating Oil vs ICE Gasoil	28,587	33,564	72,340	16,561	
Henry Hub Basis Swap	66,870	98,290	309,092	287,216	264,818
Henry Hub Index Swap	48,277	65,144	187,879	187,463	207,234
Henry Hub Swap	20,825,660	20,417,178	25,670,240	31,401,575	16,207,044
Henry Hub Swing	4,074	8,055	19,156	66,875	73,750

New York Mercantile Exchange (NYMEX) (continued)

FUTURE	2011	2010	2009	2008	2007
Houston Ship Channel Basis Swap	33,836	184,062	595,698	787,312	1,088,654
Houston Ship Channel Index Swap	2,139	23,394	69,071	101,690	132,368
ICE Brent-Dubai Swap	51,835	72,518	207,977	60,009	19,400
ICE Gasoil BALMO Swap	138	101	40	114	
Midwest ISO IL Hub Peak Calendar Month LMP	40				
Midwest ISO IL Hub Off-Peak Calendar Month LMP	80				
In Delivery Month CER	852	15,245	4,927		
MISO Indiana Hub 5MW Off-Peak Calendar Month	4,704				
MISO Indiana Hub 5MW Off-Peak Calendar Month	575,856				
MISO Indiana Hub 5MW Peak Calendar Month Day-	1,530				
MISO Indiana Hub 5MW Peak Calendar Month Real	27,443				
Indonesian Coal (MCC)	195				
ISO New England Off-Peak	16,802	18,038	27,468	20,279	11,258
ISO New England LMP Swap Peak	24,342	19,322	38,225	24,971	21,110
Japan C&F Naptha Swap	24,965	40,120	32,132	5,114	195
Japan Naptha BALMO Swap	312	500	201		
Jet AV Fuel (P) Car FM ICE Gas Swap	42	39	290		
European Jet Rotterdam Barges vs Gasoil Swap	145	392	384	672	
European Jet CIF NWE vs Gasoil Swap	6,428	9,156	17,561	11,358	2,832
Jet Fuel Barges FOB Rdam vs ICE Gasoil BALMO	12	4	5		
Jet Fuel Cargoes CIF NEW vs ICE Gasoil BALMO	504	397	941		
Jet Fuel Up-Down BALMO CL	2,908	1,703	75		
Jet Up-Down (Argus)	20,630	14,980	9,125		
Los Angeles CARB Diesel (OPIS) Outright Swap	291	550	259	25	25
Los Angeles CARB Diesel (OPIS) Spread Swap	22,688	19,997	13,142	5,189	25
Los Angeles CARBOB (OPIS) Spread Swap	20,325	21,024	4,075	1,592	
Los Angeles Jet Fuel vs NYH #2 Heating Oil Spread	1,260	1,100	162	39	300
Los Angeles Jet (OPIS) Spread Swap	21,548	28,818	33,572	6,425	775
LL Jet (OPIS) Swap	75	550			
LLS (Argus) Calendar Swap (XA)	100				
LLS (Argus) vs WTI Spread Calendar Swap	36,158	13,250	2,135	5,049	
Los Angeles CARB Gasoline Swap (OPIS)	176	25	36		
Mars (Argus) vs WTI Spread Calendar Swap	2,202	3,180	1,500		
Mars (Argus) vs WTI Spread Trade Month Swap	3,699	2,035	3,720	180	
Coal (API2) cis ARA (Argus/McCloskey) Swap	2,592	24			
Coal (API4) fob Richards Bay (Argus/McCloskey) Swap	1,140	24			
MichCon Natural Gas Index Swap	2,322	5,994	5,413	1,414	
MichCon Natural Gas Swing Swap	120	267	62		
MichCon Basis Swap	11,495	73,658	173,256	283,962	289,738
Michigan Hub Off-Peak LMP Swap	48				
Michigan Hub LMP Swap-Peak	48	20	246	28	620
MISO 5mw Off-Peak	246,704	460,896	120,520		
MISO 5mw Peak	16,069	25,768	7,732		
Mini European Jet Kero (Platts) Cargoes CIF NEW vs	672				
Mini European Naptha CIF NEW Swap	2,369	78			
Mont Belvieu Ethane 5 Decimals (OPIS) Swap	46,216	97,340	38,404		
Mont Belvieu Ethane (OPIS) BALMO	920	2,938	126		
Mont Belvieu LDH Propane 5 Decimal (OPIS) Swap	114,417	210,632	66,945		
Mont Belvieu LDH Propane (OPIS) BALMO Swap	5,009	6,389	1,059		
Mont Belvieu Natural Gas 5 Decimal (OPIS) Swap	58,523	54,771	15,257		
Mont Belvieu Natural Gas (OPIS) BALMO Swap	1,677	939	355		
Mont Belvieu Normal Butane 5 Decimal (OPIS) Swap	46,202	56,408	28,214		
Mont Belvieu Normal Butane (OPIS) BALMO Swap	2,477	3,002	148		
Natural Gas Penultimate Swap	7,384,147	8,995,324	11,038,692	12,352,928	10,117,889
NEPOOL CNCTCT Day Ahead Off-Peak	159,019	461,528	1,194,942		
NEPOOL CONECTIC 5mw Day Ahead Peak	12,271	27,569	66,666		
NEPOOL INTR HUB 5mw Day Ahead Off-Peak	851,583	1,021,109	2,433,442		
NEPOOL INTR HUB 5mw Day Ahead Peak	42,914	67,190	140,169		
NE Maine HUB 5mw Day Ahead Off-Peak	89,376	46,848	75,404		
NE Maine HUB 5mw Day Ahead Peak	7,520	5,928	4,415		
NEPOOL NE Mass 5mw Day Ahead Off-Peak	107,570	306,500	204,984		
NEPOOL NE Mass 5mw Day Ahead Peak	8,104	16,226	14,849		
NEPOOL New Hamp 5MW Day Ahead Peak	3,058	7,073			
NEPOOL New Hamp 5MW Day Ahead Off-Peak	56,460	129,365			
NEPOOL Rhode Island 5MW Day Ahead Peak	15,934	255			
NEPOOL Rhode Island 5MW Day Ahead Off-Peak	294,247				
NEPOOL SE Mass 5mw Day Ahead Peak	510	2,849	12,432		
NEPOOL W CNTR Mass 5mw Day Ahead Off-Peak	74,173	82,358	277,045		
NEPOOL W CNTR Mass 5mw Day Ahead Peak	5,290	4,961	17,055		
New England Hub Daily Peak Swap	282	996	276	1,060	464
New York 0.3% Fuel Oil HiPr (Platts) Swap	2,897	7,973	3,850	775	
New York Ethanol Swap	11,158	16,371	8,215	3,814	1,739
New York Hub Zone G Peak Swap	840	100	320		
NGPL Mid-Continent Basis Swap	21,895	116,520	275,602	355,491	392,899
NGPL Mid-Continent Natural Gas Index Swap	542	3,965	14,420	12,004	8,698

New York Mercantile Exchange (NYMEX) (continued)

FUTURE	2011	2010	2009	2008	2007
NGPL STX Natural Gas Basis Swap	4,290	17,256	61,843	11,686	
NGPL STX Natural Gas Index Swap	2,969	5,596	1,592		
NGPL TEX/OK Basis Swap	43,928	184,279	430,388	524,326	675,365
NGPL TEX/OK Natural Gas Index Swap	1,838	1,763	33,584	43,322	14,304
Northern Illinois Hub Monthly Peak	16,542	12,508	38,455	23,978	19,359
No 2 Heating Oil Up-Down Spread Calendar Swap	14,564	29,118	20,285	8,762	3,735
Northern Natural Gas Demarcation Basis Swap	7,084	59,065	177,130	334,235	278,478
Northern Natural Gas Ventura Basis Swap	36,903	71,867	259,500	361,503	353,186
Northern Illinois Hub Monthly Off-Peak	18,323	5,383	29,433	113,666	63,896
Northwest Rockies Basis Swap	23,587	88,194	293,089	792,219	1,040,846
New York 0.7% Fuel Oil (Platts)	267	888	300		
New York 1% Fuel Oil vs Gulf Coast 3% Fuel Oil Swap	70,946	103,093	42,976	8,468	
New York 2.2% Fuel Oil (Platts) Swap (Y3)	1,927	1,580	5,770		
New York 3.0% Fuel Oil Swap (H1)	4,653	3,904	2,293		
New York 0.3% Fuel Oil Swap (VQ)	200				
NY Harbor Fuel Oil 1.0% Sulfur BALMO Swap	7,927	8,425	5,375	1,161	
NY Harbor Heating Oil Calendar Swap	93,313	157,545	141,753	115,500	49,074
NY Harbor Residual Fuel 1.0% Sulfur Swap	141,667	209,696	189,772	93,845	67,130
NY Harbor Residual Fuel Oil Crack Swap	1,070	14,622	6,672	5,255	11,464
NY Harbor No 2 Crack Spread Calendar Swap	63,503	102,877	148,936	53,929	42,335
New York Heating Oil (Platts) vs NYMEX Heating Oil	2,962	1,981	1,895	50	
NYISO Zone A LBMP Swap Peak	9,728	8,401	12,687	24,128	13,950
NYISO Zone A LBMP Swap Off-Peak	4,982	4,164	5,600	16,232	17,784
NYISO NYC In-City Capacity Calendar Month Swap	125				
NYISO Rest of the State Capacity Calendar Month	56				
NYISO Zone G LBMP Swap Peak	7,814	8,224	10,459	15,500	16,990
NYISO Zone G LBMP Swap Off-Peak	3,608	3,780	10,050	22,442	26,608
NYISO Zone J LBMP Swap Peak	5,680	7,361	8,221	5,265	9,767
NYISO Zone J LBMP Swap Off-Peak	2,264	2,834	2,660	4,218	4,510
NYISO Zone A 5mw Day Ahead Off-Peak	267,274	129,788	284,962		
NYISO Zone A 5mw Day Ahead Peak	12,809	12,994	18,320		
NYISO Zone C 5mw Day Ahead Off-Peak	118,395	82,560	108,840		
NYISO Zone C 5mw Day Ahead Peak	6,454	4,780	8,555		
NYISO Zone G 5mw Day Ahead Off-Peak	213,204	57,833	154,380		
NYISO Zone G 5mw Day Ahead Peak	26,581	21,407	11,162		
NYISO Zone J 5mw Day Ahead Off-Peak	73,623	93,738	37,768		
NYISO Zone J 5mw Day Ahead Peak	10,947	8,287	7,512		
NY Jet Fuel (Argus) vs Heating Oil Swap	350	50	50		
NY Jet Fuel (Platts) vs Heating Oil Swap	4,850	350	1,150		
NYMEX Iron Ore	1,854	80			
DME Oman Crude Oil BALMO Swap (DOB)	100	930			
DME Oman Crude Oil Swap (DOO)	1,237	1,250			
NYMEX ULSD vs NYMEX Heating Oil Spread Swap	782	517	558	510	100
NY ULSD (Argus) vs Heating Oil Spread Swap	4,653	6,068	530		
OneOk, OK Natural Gas Index Swap	434	724	1,020		
OneOk, OK Basis Swap	6,739	11,179	21,659		
Ontario Off-Peak Calendar Day Swap (OFD)	2,480				
Ontario Off-Peak Calendar Month Swap (OFM)	122,410				
Ontario Peak Calendar Day Swap (OPD)	965				
Ontario Peak Calendar Month Swap (OPM)	4,103				
OPIS Physical Ethane	20	3,010	475		
OPIS Physical LDH Propane	760	2,866	1,245		
OPIS Physical Natural Gas	655	4,637	4,535		
OPIS Physical Non-LDH Propane	240	1,405	1,405		
OPIS Physical Normal Nutane	960	8,823	5,676		
Panhandle Basis Swap	121,303	417,511	1,277,176	2,017,371	1,497,748
Panhandle Index Swap	2,899	11,966	24,002	37,250	31,609
Panhandle Swing Swap	354	1,797	6,264	21,182	8,493
El Paso Natural Gas Permian Basin Basis Swap	31,758	68,883	152,858	432,177	521,914
Argus Propane Far East Index BALMO Swap	637	262			
European Propane CIF ARA (Argus) BALMO Swap	1,063	299			
Mont Belvieu LDH Propane (OPIS) vs European CIF	42				
Mont Belvieu Mini LDH Propane	1,905	380			
Mont Belvieu Iso-Butane	3,761	2,735	90		
Argus Propane Far East Index vs European Propane	325				
Conway Physical Propane In-Well	20	55			
HDPE High Density Polyethylene In-Well	546	8			
LLDPE (PCW) Calendar Swap (LPE)	1,038				
Mont Belvieu Spot Ethylene In-Well	7,020	880			
Mont Belvieu Normal Butane LDH (OPIS) Swap (MNB)	10,871	10			
Singapore Fuel Oil 180 cst (Platts) 6.35 Dubai Crack	750				
Gulf Coast CBOB Gasoline A1 (Platts) vs RBOB Spread	500				
Gulf Coast CBOB Gasoline A2 (Platts) vs RBOB	187				
RBOB Gasoline vs Eurobob Oxy (Argus) NEW Barges	1,051				
NY 3% Fuel Oil vs GC #6 Fuel Oil 3% (Platts) Swap	637				

New York Mercantile Exchange (NYMEX) (continued)

FUTURE	2011	2010	2009	2008	2007
Gulf Coast #6 Fuel Oil 3% (Platts) vs Brent Crack	5,006				
Gulf Coast #6 Fuel Oil 3% vs European 3.5% Fuel Oil	159,564				
Gulf Coast #6 Fuel Oil (Platts) Crack Spread BALMO	695				
Heating Oil vs Brent Crack Spread Swap (HOB)	1,345				
NY 1% Fuel Oil (Platts) Crack Spread BALMO Swap	100				
NY 1% Fuel Oil (Platts) vs Gulf Coast 3% Fuel Oil	1,917				
NY 1% Fuel Oil vs European 1% Fuel Oil Cargoes FOB	21,103				
RBOB Gasoline vs Brent Crack Spread Swap (RBB)	68,379				
Gulf Coast Unleaded 87 Gasoline M2 (Argus) vs RBOB	75				
Gulf Coast Unleaded 87 Gasoline MD (Platts) vs	4,490				
Singapore Mogas 92 Unleaded (Platts) Brent Crack	260				
Petro European Naptha Crack Spread BALMO Swap	3,739	4,688			
3.5% Fuel Oil (Platts) Barges FOB Crack Spread Swap	452	53			
Argus Gasoline Eurobob Oxy Barges NWE Crack	30	15			
European Propane CIF ARA (Argus) vs Naptha CIF	1,659				
Gulf Coast #5 Fuel Oil 3% vs Euro 3.5% Fuel Oil	1,162				
Gasoil (ICE) Crack Spread Swap (GOC)	820	23			
Gasoil 50 ppm (Platts) Barges FOB Rdam vs ICE	40				
Gasoil 50 ppm (Platts) Barges FOB Rdam vs ICE	320				
Naptha Cargoes CIF NEW vs Gasoil Swap (NOB)	136	101			
NY Fuel Oil 1% vs Euro 1% Fuel Oil Cargoes FOB	131				
Singapore Fuel Oil 180 Crack Spread Swap (SFC)	214	240			
Mini Japan C&F Naptha (Platts) Swap (MJN)	226				
Mini European 1% Fuel Oil (Platts) Cargoes FOB	60				
Mini European 3.5% Fuel Oil Barges FOB Rdam Swap	28,573	4,940			
Mini Singapore Fuel Oil 180 cst (Platts) SWAP (0F)	811				
Jet Aviation Fuel (Platts) Cargoes FOB MED Swap	15				
1% Fuel Oil Rdam vs 1% Fuel Oil NWE (Platts) Swap	2,212	144			
3.5% Fuel Oil Rdam vs 3.5% FOB MED Spread Balmo	742	133			
European 1% Fuel Oil (Platts) Barges FOB Rdam	8				
Gasoil EuroBob Oxy NWE Barges Crack Spread	1,996	2,115			
EuroBob Gasoline 10ppm (Platts) Barges FOB Rdam	19	39			
Gasoil EuroBob Oxy NWE Barges BALMO Swap (7R)	3,615	4,976	3		
EuroBob Gasoline 10ppm Barges FOB Rdam BALMO	11	5			
Conway Normal Butane (OPIS) BALMO Swap (CBB)	75				
Conway Natural Gas (OPIS) BALMO Swap (CGB)	210				
Gulf Coast CBOB Gasoline A1 (Platts) Crack Spread	229	265			
European 1% Fuel Oil Cargoes FOB MED Swap (EFM)	173	20			
Euro 1% Fuel Oil Cargoes FOB MED vs Euro 1% Fuel	100	20			
Mont Belvieu Ethylene (PCW) Financial Swap (MBN)	942	1,023			
Mini European 1% Fuel Oil Barges FOB Rdam Swap	804	28			
Singapore Mogas 95 Unleaded Swap (V0)	750	275			
Singapore Mogas 95 Unleaded (Platts) BALMO Swap	15				
Singapore Mogas 95 Unleaded (Platts) Swap (X0)	516				
Gulf Coast Jet (Argus) Up-Down BALMO Swap (GBA)	55				
Biodiesel SME Houston B-100 (Argus) Swap (GSI)	1				
Gulf Coast ULSD (Argus) Up-Down BALMO Swap	50				
New York 0.3% Fuel Oil HiPr (Platts) BALMO Swap	75				
New York 2.2% Fuel Oil (Platts) BALMO Swap (NYE)	107				
New York 3% Fuel Oil (Platts) BALMO Swap (NYE)	558				
PG&E Citygate Basis Swap (PC)	1,488	48	31,019	387,422	328,283
PJM AD Hub 5mw Real-Time Off-Peak (V3)	853,031	430,142	72,498		
PJM AD Hub 5mw Real-Time Peak (Z9)	51,695	14,608	9,962		
PJM APS Zone Day Ahead Off-Peak (W4)	60,680	33,886			
PJM APS Zone Day Ahead Peak	3,805	1,876			
PJM BGE Day Ahead Off-Peak	246,229	305,027	823,697	3,800	
PJM BGE Day Ahead Peak	10,928	21,080	49,163		
PJM ComEd 5mw Day Ahead Off-Peak	155,803	4,648	149,456		
PJM ComEd 5mw Day Ahead Peak	8,559	515	10,144		
PJM Financially Settled Daily Peak	860	3,220	350	1,626	26,610
PJM Dayton Day Ahead Off-Peak	640,076	287,026	269,270	32,648	
PJM Dayton Day Ahead Peak	45,571	17,026	38,051	9,514	
PJM DPL Day Ahead Off-Peak	14,832	67,864	99,290	4,688	
PJM DPL Day Ahead Peak	1,037	2,957	5,635	512	
PJM DUQUE SNE 5MW Day Ahead Peak	2,194	7,324			
PJM DUQUE SNE 5MW Day Ahead Off-Peak	40,257	132,176			
PJM Eastern Day Ahead Off-Peak	36,030	230,010	421,819	19,864	
PJM Eastern Day Ahead Peak	3,325	15,876	58,876	5,416	
PJM JCPL Zone Hub Off-Peak Cal-Mth Day Ahead	141,238	329,176	653,460	4,664	
PJM JCPL Zone Hub Peak Cal-Mth Day Ahead LMP	9,896	23,322	44,379	1,516	
PJM Northern IL Hub 5mw Real-Time Off-Peak	65,570	26,815	32,478		
PJM Northern IL Hub 5mw Real-Time Peak	1,619,448	440,021	465,914		
PJM Northern IL Hub Day Ahead Off-Peak	1,057,271	402,357	1,683,800	86,888	
PJM Northern IL Hub Day Ahead Peak	58,068	27,594	91,606	10,702	
PJM Off-Peak LMP Swap	41,402	32,744	61,397	68,172	50,940

New York Mercantile Exchange (NYMEX) (continued)

FUTURE	2011	2010	2009	2008	2007
PJM PECO Zone 5mw Peak Calendar Month Day	3,827	36,696	3,840		
PJM PEPCO Day Ahead Off-Peak	222,125	338,949	1,254,275	147,640	
PJM PEPCO Day Ahead Peak	9,685	25,532	97,197	7,690	
PJM PPL Day Ahead Off-Peak	203,108	608,959	332,772		
PJM PPL Day Ahead Peak	10,729	41,097	37,398		
PJM PSEG Day Ahead Off-Peak	789,728	1,249,809	2,801,488	18,240	
PJM PSEG Day Ahead Peak	48,385	82,035	203,264	5,690	
PJM WES Hub 50MW Peak Cal Mth Real Time LMP	256	82			
PJM Western Hub Day Ahead Off-Peak	1,671,911	4,913,517	6,810,613	231,232	
PJM Western Hub Day Ahead Peak	115,898	317,505	531,995	23,435	
PJM Western Hub Real-Time Off-Peak	2,248,985	1,565,616	1,727,213	202,312	
PJM Western Hub Real-Time Peak	83,776	78,894	98,311	11,905	
PGP Polymer Grade Propylene (PCW) Calendar Swap	1,722				
Polypropylene (PCW) Calendar Swap (PPP)	227	336			
High Density Polyethylene (P6)	815	806			
Premium Unld Gasoline 10ppm FOB MED (3G)	2,987	1,736	1,234		
Premium Unld Gasoline 10ppm CARGOE (4G)	98	17	37		
Premium Unleaded Gasoline 10ppm (Platts) Cargoes	5				
Premium Unld Gasoline 10ppm FOB (8G)	527	442	280		
Premium Unld Gasoline 10ppm Rdam FOB BALMO	52	94	60		
Premium Unld Gasoline 10ppm FOB Swap (7L)	467	121	234		
Propane Non-LDH Mt Belvieu (OPIS) BALMO Swap	399	28	315		
Propane Non-LDH Mt Belvieu (OPIS) Swap (1R)	4,905	1,986	3,390		
RBOB Calendar Swap (RL)	151,780	156,852	112,652	81,874	30,235
RBOB Crack Spread Swap (RM)	37,893	144,319	151,414	83,269	57,793
RBOB Gasoline BALMO Swap (1D)	4,891	6,262	3,274		
NY RBOB (Platts) Calendar Swap (RY)	1,600				
RBOB Up-Down Calendar Swap (RV)	114,851	97,772	93,703	53,431	22,724
RBOB vs Heating Oil Swap (RH)	13,450	14,707	2,860	2,638	8,455
Rockies Natural Gas Index Swap	67	5,804	29,993	26,500	19,440
San Juan Basis Swap	13,109	28,434	93,864	169,655	246,858
San Juan Natural Gas Index Swap	62	20,785	12,700	2,766	3,425
Singapore Fuel Oil 180cst BALMO Swap	2,718	3,478	5,762	2,085	90
Singapore Fuel Oil 380cst BALMO Swap	901	1,169	929	514	15
Singapore Fuel Oil 380cst Calendar Swap	17,417	16,529	5,982	3,662	2,142
Singapore Fuel Oil 180cst Calendar Swap	105,335	121,756	133,362	79,252	48,516
Singapore Fuel Oil Spread Swap (SD)	10,611	11,980	11,276	4,823	1,532
Mini Singapore Fuel Oil 380 cst (Platts) BALMO Swap	55				
Mini Singapore Fuel Oil 380 cst (Platts) Swap (MTS)	401				
Singapore Gasoil 10ppm Swap (STF)	75				
Singapore Gasoil 10ppm BALMO Swap (STL)	75				
Singapore Gasoil 10ppm vs 0.5% Sulfur Spread	8,730				
Singapore Gasoil 0.05% Sulfur (Platts) Swap (SZF)	10				
Singapore Gasoil 0.05% Sulfur (Platts) BALMO Swap	25				
Singapore Gasoil 0.05% vs 0.5% Sulfur Spread (Platts)	105				
Singapore Gasoil BALMO Swap (VU)	19,196	23,926	28,166	15,214	425
Singapore Gasoil Calendar Swap (SG)	192,079	260,561	321,662	128,359	52,955
Singapore Gasoil vs Rdam Gasoil Swap (GA)	35,079	33,009	69,019	37,975	18,564
Singapore Jet Kerosene BALMO Swap (BX)	1,921	3,567	7,740	4,754	150
Singapore Jet Kerosene vs Gasoil Spread Swap (RK)	31,603	35,730	64,490	32,980	18,740
Singapore Jet Kerosene Swap	48,422	66,582	81,705	36,688	20,045
Singapore Jet Kero vs Gasoil BALMO	1,775	2,690	255		
Singapore Mogas 92 Unleaded BALMO	3,438	1,236	425		
Singapore Mogas 92 Unleaded Swap	105,150	31,649	11,224		
Singapore Naptha BALMO Swap	49	139	550	375	
Singapore Naptha Swap	3,504	9,286	13,887	25,374	9,955
SoCal Basis Swap	6,880	15,349	113,568	1,082,052	1,784,378
SoCal Pipe Swap (XN)	15,768				
SONAT Basis Swap	11,144	27,493	72,505	130,742	36,106
Southern Star LA Natural Gas Index Swap	3,916	10,580	4,354		
Southern Star TX,OK,KS Natural Gas Basis Swap	12,698	19,049	4,304		
Sumas Basis Swap	7,049	6,102	6,652	63,684	83,641
TC2 Rotterdam to USAC 37K	435	2,135	395	449	205
TC4 Singapore to Japan 30	55	629	305	445	10
TC5 Ras Tanura to Yokohama Freight	2,566	3,275	5,256	560	50
TCO Basis Swap (TC)	11,872	34,315	110,615	236,679	394,285
TCO Natural Gas Index Swap (Q1)	240	6,180	25,207	2,648	
TCO Natural Gas Swing Swap	81		208		
TD3 Middle Eastern Gulf to Japan 250K MT	1,292	2,505	651	460	
TD5 West Africa to USAC 1	235	1,320	105		
Tennessee 800 Leg Natural Gas Index Swap (L4)	35,017				
Tennessee 500 Leg Basis Swap	17,781	32,620	126,840	79,271	29,621
Tennessee 500 Leg Natural Gas Index Swap	10,360	8,576	11,895	62	
Tennessee 800 Basis Swap	47,179	4,560	6,426		
Tennessee Zone 0 Basis Swap	5,448	11,083	12,040	23,876	53,705

New York Mercantile Exchange (NYMEX) (continued)

FUTURE	2011	2010	2009	2008	2007
Tennesse Zone 0 Natural Gas Index Swap	6,392	17,216	7,777	2,804	
TETCO East Louisiana Basis Swap (TE)	2,268	6,229	44,184	43,217	5,382
TETCO M-3 Natural Gas Index Swap (IX)	3,252	5,777	120,561	121,290	54,619
TETCO South Texas Basis Swap (TX)	4,528	5,334	12,289	37,702	51,664
TETCO South Texas Natural Gas Index Swap (Q2)	1,570	3,816	7,388	2,195	
Texas Eastern Zone M-3 Basis Swap (NX)	28,924	94,942	232,939	412,686	765,236
TETCO M-3 Natural Gas Swing Swap (SX)	108				
Texas Eastern West Louisiana Natural Gas Index Swap	76,411	9,344	6,878		
Texas Eastern West Louisiana Basis Swap	78,027	25,066	19,300		
Texas Gas Zone 1 Basis Swap	492	6,391	11,113		
Texas Gas Zone SL Basis Swap	3,476	18,023	81,101	71,598	46,454
Texas Gas Zone SL Natural Gas	216	92	232		
Texas Gas Zone 1 Basis Swap (Platts IFERC)	304	2,462	124		
Transco Zone 3 Basis Swap	2,619	24,328	73,501	157,593	126,442
Transco Zone 3 Natural Gas Index Swap	560	5,370	12,980	9,215	
Transco Zone 4 Basis Swap	4,761	34,684	70,159	107,097	11,004
Transco Zone 4 Natural Gas Index	5,000	14,467	1,611		
Transco Zone 6 Basis Swap	8,324	32,080	94,997	165,105	545,492
Transco Zone 6 Natural Gas Swing Swap (ST)	1,240				
Trunkline, LA Basis Swap	428	950	10,210	31,481	17,364
ULSD 10ppm Cargoes CIF MED BALMO Swap (X7)	13				
ULSD 10ppm CIF MED Swap (Z6)	325	238	146		
ULSD 10ppm CIF MED vs ICE Gasoil Swap (Z7)	4,018	4,725	3,057	125	
ULSD 10ppm CIF NW BALMO Swap (B1)	12		4		
ULSD 10ppm CIF MED vs ICE Gasoil BALMO Swap	507	193	334		
ULSD Up-Down (Argus) Swap	35,305	16,155	6,620		
ULSD Up-Down BALMO Swap	20,681	9,483	1,206		
Up Down GC ULSD vs NYMEX Heating Oil Spread	556,663	525,152	228,195	105,423	19,834
US Gulf Coast Unleaded 87 Crack Spread Calendar	7,500	7,805	8,045	10,724	8,517
Ventura Natural Gas Index Swap (VI)	5,184	14,731	6,267	17,671	12,748
WAHA Basis Swap (NW)	41,601	149,767	425,807	624,817	727,707
WAHA Index Swap (IY)	1,754	11,996	101,880	71,755	72,219
Western Rail Powder River Basin Coal Swap (QP)	19,145	17,580	24,085	28,340	10,680
WTI Brent (ICE) Bullet Swap (BY)	4,200				
WTI-Brent (ICE) Calendar Swap (BK)	99,413	70,919	107,192	240,916	60,008
WTI Crude Oil Calendar Swap (CS)	879,489	1,216,576	1,057,843	847,658	489,274
WTS (Argus) vs WTI Spread Calendar Swap (FF)	576		3,600		
WTS (Argus) vs WTI Spread Trade Month Swap (FH)	7,414	2,646	1,460	3,082	
NYMEX Columbian Peso (V2)	11,437	17,308	10,405		
In Delivery Month EUA (6T)	14,167	47,267	9,029		
Daily EUA (EUL)	1,450	2,200			
NYMEX Cocoa	1,608	1,338	1,318	2,222	1,769
NYMEX Coffee	1,077	1,847	1,335	9,780	5,784
NYMEX Cotton	2,949	4,964	1,764	8,495	7,407
NYMEX Sugar #11	3,516	9,244	7,197	26,107	10,470
Total Futures	419,908,616	362,428,100	338,490,891	277,408,465	216,252,995

NYSE LIFFE U.S.

FUTURE	2011	2010	2009	2008	2007
100 oz Gold	103,864	471,446	1,467,450	847,778	
Mini New York Gold	1,955,899	2,090,555	2,122,569	675,114	
5,000 oz Silver	45,694	108,114	107,941	72,722	
Mini New York Silver	1,550,088	1,060,631	647,314	236,327	
Eurodollar	11,752,482				
2-Year Treasury Note	477,387				
5-Year Treasury Note	1,094,298				
10-Year Treasury Note	1,484,004				
US Bond	343,038				
Ultra Bond	24,215				
MSCI EAFE	860,513	194,080	75,697		
MSCI EM	1,148,430	139,613	49,373		
MSCI EAFE NTR	234	6			
MSCI EM NTR	4,989				
MSCI Pan Euro	51,297				
Total Futures	20,896,432	4,064,780	4,474,734	1,831,941	

ONECHICAGO

FUTURE	2011	2010	2009	2008	2007
Single Stock Futures	3,599,917	4,758,640	2,624,496	3,404,201	7,835,289
Exchange Traded Funds	42,157	44,842	101,660	299,547	51,034
Narrow-Based Equity Index	37,410	167,678	256,992	308,533	219,640
Total Futures	3,679,484	4,971,160	2,983,148	4,012,281	8,105,963

VOLUME - U.S.

Total Futures Volume

	2011	2010	2009	2008	2007
Total Futures	3,056,541,757	2,764,784,436	2,328,123,926	2,904,518,236	2,680,196,142
Precent Change	10.55%	18.76%	-19.84%	8.37%	29.57%

Options Traded on U.S. Futures Exchanges Volume Highlights
2011 in Comparison with 2010

2011 Rank	EXCHANGE	2011 Contracts	%	2010 Contracts	%	2010 Rank
1	Chicago Mercantile Exchange (CME Group)	268,518,626	71.71%	238,175,073	45.90%	1
2	Chicago Board of Trade (CME Group)	131,039,321	34.99%	123,666,496	23.83%	2
3	New York Mercantile Exchange (CME Group)	86,514,666	23.10%	80,574,639	15.53%	3
4	ICE Futures U.S.	13,180,700	3.52%	14,654,805	2.82%	4
5	Kansas City Board of Trade	239,891	0.06%	148,032	0.03%	6
6	Minneapolis Grain Exchange	43,315	0.01%	32,290	0.01%	7
7	Chicago Climate Futures Exchange	12,710	0.00%	79,951	0.02%	5
8	NYSE Liffe U.S.	1,742	0.00%	5,736	0.00%	8
	Total Options	**499,550,971**	**100.00%**	**457,337,022**	**100.00%**	

Chicago Climate Futures Exchange (CCFE)

OPTION	2011	2010	2009	2008	2007
CA Climate Action Registry-Climate Res Tons (CCAR)	160		415		
Carbon Financial Instrument (CFI-US)	50	848	1,212		
Nitrogen Financial Instrument - Annual (NFI-A)	12,350	26,800	13,800	6,500	
Regional Greenhouse Gas Initiatives (RGGI)	150	8,453	74,363	10,373	
Total Options	12,710	79,951	126,456	113,817	91,859

Chicago Board of Trade (CBT)

OPTION	2011	2010	2009	2008	2007
Wheat	4,680,418	4,495,955	3,635,792	4,060,865	3,893,354
Corn	28,650,380	20,810,260	14,435,687	20,992,582	14,691,277
Oats	19,727	18,312	20,830	23,843	16,381
Soybeans	13,236,367	10,046,345	9,555,840	9,806,935	8,215,582
Soybean Crush	1,016	3,044	3,254	2,452	3,267
Soybean Oil	2,360,836	1,843,307	1,255,304	1,458,568	1,277,884
Soybean Meal	946,723	1,021,831	891,551	884,721	713,821
Rough Rice	37,222	38,317	15,674	26,681	23,374
Corn Nearby + 2 Calendar Spread	41,790	5,946	186		
Soybean Nearby + 2 Calendar Spread	18,973	5,106	603		
Wheat Nearby + 2 Calendar Spread	43,257	2,618	510		
Soy Meal Nearby + 2 Calendar Spread	70	300			
Wheat - Corn ICSO	1,109	90			
Soybean - Corn Ratio	291				
Soy Oil Nearby + 2 Calendar Spread	4,380	2,470			
Dec-July Wheat Calendar Spread	4,686	255	150		
Jan-May Soybean Calendar Spread	20				
July-Nov Soybean Calendar Spread	104,727	78,669	20,799		
Aug-Nov Soybean Calendar Spread	530				
Nov-Nov Soybean Calendar Spread	16,105				
Nov-July Soybean Calendar Spread	9,607	1			
July-Dec Soy Meal Calendar Spread	50	1,040			
July-Dec Soy Oil Calendar Spread	585	625			
July-Dec Corn Calendar Spread	64,105	21,673	50		
Dec-July Corn Calendar Spread	400	80			
Dec-Dec Corn Calendar Spread	1,926	7,340			
July-July Wheat Calendar Spread	5,934	5,254	451		
July-Dec Wheat Calendar Spread	1,375	669	320		
Ethanol Forward Month Swap	13,468	23,639	8,933	42,477	6,048
Treasury Bonds (30-year)	12,849,585	14,447,974	11,142,149	18,209,855	17,391,744
Treasury Notes (10-year)	50,797,081	55,280,257	40,206,023	56,753,688	61,528,219
Treasury Notes (5-year)	10,849,707	6,064,380	4,803,364	12,752,318	15,392,035
Treasury Notes (2-year)	2,686,449	2,400,459	2,397,210	2,333,092	1,056,738
Federal Funds (30-Day)	3,272,313	6,666,619	4,217,906	7,478,025	8,020,547
Federal Funds Midcurve	2,950				
Ultra T-Bond	185,581	51,022			
Flexible US T-Bonds	14,960	188,620	117,292	287,136	252,780
Flexible Treasury Notes (10-year)	5,050	45,404	7,550	12,575	910,609
Flexible Treasury Notes (2-year)	231		500		2,046
Dow Jones Industrial Index	1,948	3,188	22,718	75,840	105,860
Mini ($5) Dow Jones Industrial Index	107,389	85,425	85,934	281,062	300,307
Total Options	131,039,321	123,666,496	92,848,854	135,519,960	134,047,704

Chicago Mercantile Exchange (CME Group)

OPTION	2011	2010	2009	2008	2007
Live Cattle	3,012,718	2,089,701	1,355,251	1,226,704	726,003
Live Cattle Calendar ISO	135	94			
Feeder Cattle	153,216	119,382	74,777	99,911	106,587
Lean Hogs	1,070,098	653,785	651,731	512,159	321,258
Lean Hogs CSO	20				
Class III Milk	304,232	172,384	153,513	167,779	94,640
Class IV Milk	4,667	48			
Nonfat Dry Milk	177	2	59	60	
Mini BFP Milk	2,365	1,057	562	367	967
Cash Settled Cheese	1,368	25			
Dry Whey	974	468	862	670	
Cash Butter	2,310	758	223	322	17
Random Lumber	7,226	8,840	13,883	17,485	18,127
Eurodollar (3-month)	100,855,181	106,893,369	117,553,569	187,341,383	313,032,284
Eurodollar Mid-Curve	92,429,741	76,490,147	43,369,605	40,883,014	
Treasury Matched Eurodollar Mid-Curve	60,121	196,301	107,128	287,662	
Eurodollar Calendar Spreads	2,500	2,000	1,400	11,752	
Australian Dollar	946,663	551,060	273,516	206,649	74,874
British Pound	735,630	1,208,577	465,413	565,050	352,736
Canadian Dollar	782,225	889,708	465,264	380,894	530,023
Euro FX	5,684,036	6,651,318	2,207,616	2,696,811	1,801,681
Japanese Yen	1,292,246	1,366,149	758,564	850,340	929,733
Russian Ruble	15,600	750			
Swiss Franc	306,134	174,320	112,861	198,694	78,675
Euro FX European	69,717	107,476	94,244	375,621	230,615
Euro FX / Swiss Franc	1,000	1,440	400		
Australian Dollar European	1,966	1,682	3,800		
British Pound European	6,845	23,463	61,434	89,910	98,323
Canadian Dollar European	14,484	21,403	26,775	54,138	50,899
Japanese Yen European	6,654	14,468	40,178	136,921	155,394
Swiss Franc European	3,479	10,226	20,423	37,868	30,079
S&P 500 Index	11,718,229	10,719,451	10,350,127	16,378,218	19,458,815
E-Mini S&P 500 Index	36,130,942	22,778,255	18,142,915	22,167,648	16,213,737
EOM S&P 500 Index	1,521,319	1,859,912	1,470,660	2,512,846	816,354
EOM E-Mini S&P 500 Index	3,793,860	1,872,924	845,519	1,028,368	950,829
EOW1 S&P 500 Index	212,794	287,033	153,184		
EOW1 E-mini S&P 500 Index	1,885,408	769,266	88,404		
EOW2 S&P 500 Index	382,127	287,542	114,594		
EOW2 E-mini S&P 500 Index	1,961,040	708,912	82,869		
EOW4 E-mini S&P 500 Index	1,973,286	404,518			
E-Mini S&P MidCap 400 Index	581	3,534	5,272	5,507	235
NASDAQ 100 Index	13,005	607	1,535	13,096	79,900
E-Mini NASDAQ 100 Index	923,266	514,551	440,634	542,497	742,395
CDD Weather	7,875	61,325	27,050	25,100	19,400
HDD Weather	27,220	40,215	40,250	50,850	63,835
HDD Seasonal Weather Strip	83,086	99,150	115,300	139,800	295,450
CDD Seasonal Weather Strip	67,600	84,000	98,950	245,850	258,350
HDD Weather European	20,000	4,500	3,500		
CAT Weather European	500				
Euro HDD Seasonal Strip Weather	9,000	21,300	3,000	4,200	
Euro CAT Seasonal Strip Weather	500		7,500	14,000	3,500
Seasonal Maximum Hurricane	300			26,000	
Binary Seasonal Hurricane	2,950	3,000			
Binary Seasonal Hurricane Event 2	1,000	1,000	1,000		
Snowfall	190	287			
Seasonal Snowfall	320	160			
Pacific Rim Dat SS Weather	8,500	1,000	4,400		
Total Options	238,172,901	199,818,941	280,517,713	360,005,823	301,551,501

ICE Futures U.S. (ICE)

OPTION	2011	2010	2009	2008	2007
Coffee 'C'	2,624,667	2,292,800	1,427,032	2,826,331	2,999,648
Coffee Calendar Spread	5,463	3,428			
Sugar #11	6,667,573	8,448,556	7,280,380	9,179,779	5,548,668
Sugar #11 Options on Futures Spreads	82,813	204,668	109,849	145,368	204,100
Cocoa	652,080	322,121	318,805	376,444	370,429
Cotton #2	2,794,411	2,911,509	1,709,004	4,468,327	3,451,217
Cotton #2 Options on Futures Spreads	425				
Orange Juice Frozen Concentrate	153,176	237,790	243,741	238,616	385,219
US Dollar Index	41,793	22,248	55,822	72,768	50,562
Russell 1000 Index Mini	2,336	4,836	7,798	877	
Russell 2000 Index Mini	155,824	206,624	157,126	73,634	
Reuters-CRB Futures Index (CCI)	139	175	192	892	435
Total Options	13,180,700	14,654,805	11,309,749	17,521,134	13,124,201

VOLUME - U.S.

Kansas City Board of Trade (KCBT)

OPTION	2011	2010	2009	2008	2007
Wheat	239,891	148,032	108,317	187,658	352,948
Total Options	239,891	148,032	108,317	187,658	352,948

New York Mercantile Exchange (NYMEX)

OPTION	2011	2010	2009	2008	2007
COMEX Copper	6,897	17,509	18,568	22,559	24,467
COMEX Gold	10,080,754	7,730,488	4,755,427	4,392,737	3,554,858
COMEX Silver	2,124,108	1,640,232	1,066,721	1,700,882	1,257,505
NYMEX Platinum	84,927	10,643	20		300
Palladium	37,389	12,214			
Short Term Gold (L01-L30)	10,937				
Iron Ore China (ICT)	6,633				
AEP-Dayton HUB Monthly (OT)	1,000				
Appalachian Coal	1,815	1,200			
Brent Crude Oil Average Price	566,278	139,273	137,549	92,549	
Brent Crude Oil 1 M CSO	4,525	11,350			
Brent Crude Oil European Style Look-Alike	516,740	79,143	18,562	31,181	
Brent Crude Oil American Style	139,652	29,880	2,410	8,904	
Central Appalachian Coal	160	585	255		
Cinergy Hub Peak Month	27,080	94,552	142,190	14,240	8,930
Crude Oil 1-month CSO	2,886,427	2,049,582	719,802	1,016,327	1,851,827
Crude Oil APO	2,488,882	4,621,556	3,203,460	2,227,738	1,445,930
Dubai Crude Oil Average Price (AH)	3,104	100			
Dated Brent (Platts) Average Price (DBP)	4,200				
Crude Oil Physical (CD)	113,280	130,902	86,932	132,590	134,537
Crude Oil European Style (LC)	860,949	1,195,827	1,507,042	3,580,861	1,879,999
Crude Oil (LO)	36,716,805	32,785,267	28,551,730	35,255,326	28,398,793
Brent Option on Calendar Futures Strip (BPC)	30				
Daily Crude Oil (DNM)	3,350				
PJM Peak Calendar Day LMP Swap (J01-J31)	1,603				
ISO NE Internal Hub Peak LMP Swap (NEL)	316				
PJM 50MW Calendar Month LMP Swap (PML)	34,087				
Ethanol Swap (CVR)	2,135				
European Jet Kerosene NEW APO (30)	312	344	10		
Gasoil Crack Spread APO (3U)	2,550				
Heating Oil-Crude Oil Spread	1,080	24,529	6,238	824	5,783
Heating Oil Crack Spread Average Price	252	3,000			
Heating Oil Physical - European	3,201	6,261	11,479	112,488	32,438
Heating Oil	889,524	884,849	686,270	781,003	620,761
Henry Hub Financial Last Day	27,294	28,775	16,892		
Heating Oil 1-month CSO (FA)	25,785	10,350	16,345	275	
Heating Oil 6-month CSO (FM)	150				
In Delivery Month EUA (6U)	2,000	16,000	1,250		
ISO New England Calendar-Month LMP Swap	49,790	7,186	17,410	43,082	45,240
Henry Hub Natural Gas 12-Month CSO Financial (G7)	1,000				
Natural Gas 1-month CSO Financial (G4)	303,810	258,719	15,874		
Natural Gas 1-month CSO Financial (IA)	7,400	37,875	43,290	174,940	120,608
Natural Gas 2-month CSO Financial (G2)	7,800	1,650			
Natural Gas 3-month CSO Financial (G3)	567,772	338,267	52,855		
Natural Gas 6-month CSO Financial (G6)	109,575				250
Texas Eastern Zone M-3 Basis Swap (5N)	1,216				
Natural Gas Calendar Strip (6J)	98,055	11,801	3,240		
Natural Gas Physical (KD)	466,319	369,439	213,170	112,303	13,320
Natural Gas Physical - European (LN)	23,773,183	23,957,725	25,309,214	31,158,326	29,921,068
Natural Gas Physical (ON)	2,064,055	1,360,225	1,135,135	2,336,287	5,051,879
Natural Gas Summer Strip (4D)	3,300	400	1,000		
Natural Gas Winter Strip (6I)	1,600	5,800			
Natural Gas 3-month CSO (IC)	1,133	1,301	10,877	26,605	14,233
Northern Rockies Pipe (ZR)	20,506	51,800	87,840	11,460	1,960
NW Pipeline Rockies Basis (5I)	2,620	12,680	9,508		
NY Harbor Heating Oil Swap (AT)	423,583	858,571	661,036	240,362	60,471
NYISO Zone G 5mw Peak (9U)	26,640	26,120	63,960		
NYMEX European Gasoil APO (F7)	12,826	32,369	9,957	96	
NYMEX European Style Gasoil (F8)	144	590	317		
Panhandle Basis (5K)	3,548	7,184	4,528		
Panhandle Pipe Swap (PU)	5,508	65,996	105,368	47,092	
Petrochemicals (4H)	7,318	9,035	645		
Mont Belvieu Natural Gas 5 Decimals (OPIS) APO (4I)	1,380				
Petrochemicals - Mt Bel Ethane (OPIS) APO (4J)	6,540	4,735			
Petrochemicals - Mt Bel Normal Butane (OPIS) APO	267	735			
Conway Propane (OPIS) APO (CPR)	300				
Singapore Fuel Oil 380 cst (Platts) APO (8H)	18				
Gulf Coast No 6 Fuel Oil 3.0% APO (FG)	148	1,071			
PGE Citygate Pipe Swap (CW)	12,000			3,600	

New York Mercantile Exchange (NYMEX) (continued)

OPTION	2011	2010	2009	2008	2007
PJM Calendar Strip (6O)	82,040	13,484			
PJM Monthly Financially Settled Electricity (JO)	107,834	707,300	528,316	365,316	370,108
RBOB 1-Month CSO (ZA)	18,830	30,517	32,381		
RBOB 3-Month CSO (ZC)	700				
RBOB Calendar Swap (RA)	28,167	90,392	57,384	27,402	6,219
RBOB Crack Spread (RX)	754	7,214	225	13,072	6,362
RBOB Gasoline (OB)	470,606	546,878	680,635	884,839	1,016,963
RBOB Gasoline European style (RF)	165	10,016	21,007	84,382	44,382
Rotterdam 3.5% Fuel Oil CL (Q6)	12,047	6,857	1,881		
San Juan Pipe (PJ)	6,216	5,652	22,118	3,240	
Short Term Natural Gas (U11-U25)	1,325				
Light Sweet Crude Oil (C01-C23)	117				
Short Term Natural Gas (U01-U31)	2,075				
Singapore Fuel Oil 180 CST (C5)	3,305	1,157	318		
Singapore Gasoil APO (M2)	1,200	150			
Singapore Jet Fuel Calendar (N2)	6,060	2,395	3,023		
SoCal Basis (5M)	1,104	3,240			
SoCal Pipe Swap (ZN)	53,688	46,172	119,320	26,445	
WTI Crude Oil 12-month CSO (WZ)	15,575	42,570	20,675	70,137	83,126
WTI Crude Oil 6-month CSO (WM)	1,000	6,100		5,450	2,300
WTI-Brent Bullet Swap (BV)	24,943	1,000			
WTI Crude Oil 1-month CSO Financial (7A)	21,350	33,450	5,370		
Total Options	86,514,666	80,574,639	70,210,423	85,014,980	75,976,972

NYSE LIFFE U.S.

OPTION	2011	2010	2009	2008	2007
100 oz Gold	1,725	5,631	8,702	4,972	
5,000 oz Silver	17	105	505	630	
Total Options	1,742	5,736	9,207	5,602	

Minneapolis Grain Exchange (MGE)

OPTION	2011	2010	2009	2008	2007
American Spring Wheat	43,315	27,354	24,937	47,935	34,354
Total Options	43,315	32,290	25,137	47,935	34,354

Total Volume

	2011	2010	2009	2008	2007
Total Options	499,550,971	457,337,022	374,457,084	518,928,799	583,633,862
Percent Change	9.23%	22.13%	-27.84%	-11.09%	16.37%

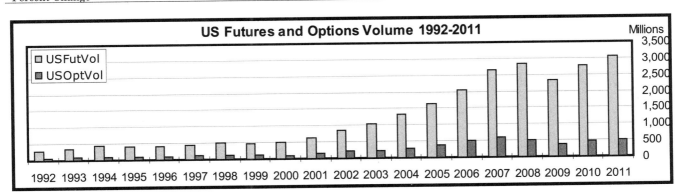

US Futures and Options Volume 1992-2011

Options Traded on U.S. Securities Exchanges Volume Highlights
2011 in Comparison with 2010

2011 Rank	EXCHANGE	2011 Contracts	%	2010 Contracts	%	2010 Rank
1	Chicago Board of Options Exchange	1,152,063,469	29.55%	1,115,491,922	30.88%	1
2	Nasdaq OMX PHLX	983,485,204	25.22%	846,895,365	23.44%	2
3	International Securities Exchange	778,086,425	19.96%	745,176,328	20.63%	3
4	NYSE-ARCA	495,343,827	12.70%	488,093,760	13.51%	4
5	NYSE-AMEX	618,733,066	15.87%	440,021,234	12.18%	5
6	Nasdaq Options Market	194,199,918	4.98%	142,922,225	3.96%	6
7	Boston Options Exchange	139,679,281	3.58%	91,754,121	2.54%	7
8	BATS Exchange	148,338,460	3.80%	25,103,245	0.69%	8
9	C2 Exchange	52,818,616	1.35%	3,610,470	0.10%	9
	Total Options	4,562,748,266	100.00%	3,899,068,670	100.00%	

Volume - Worldwide

Athens Derivatives Exchange S.A. (ADEX), Greece

	2011	2010	2009	2008	2007
FTSE/Athex 20	2,482,713	2,987,458	2,371,733	2,808,788	2,588,908
FTSE/Athex-CSE Banking Index	2,100	4,964			
All Futures on Individual Equities	7,553,643	4,767,973	5,037,065	3,713,266	3,101,602
Total Futures	**10,038,456**	**7,760,395**	**7,408,798**	**6,545,423**	**5,843,937**
FTSE/Athex 20	328,391	615,122	383,555	440,650	591,476
All Options on Individual Equities	64,238	105,764	67,590	182,757	106,913
Total Options	**392,629**	**720,886**	**451,154**	**626,697**	**737,607**

Australian Stock Exchange (ASX), Australia

	2011	2010	2009	2008	2007
S&P/ASX Index	270,236	370,800	396,723	309,499	238,823
All Futures on Individual Equities	3,460,934	543,676	777,732	971,261	706,656
Total Futures	**3,731,170**	**914,476**	**1,174,455**	**1,280,760**	**945,479**
S&P / ASX Index	10,321,625	5,274,603	3,486,914	2,819,582	1,797,754
All Options on Individual Equities	108,860,114	15,455,208	14,465,066	16,070,022	22,226,578
Total Futures	**119,181,739**	**20,729,811**	**17,951,980**	**18,889,604**	**24,024,332**

Bolsa de Mercadorias & Futuros (BM&F), Brazil

	2011	2010	2009	2008	2007
Arabica Coffee	450,802	640,754	596,435	760,761	724,319
Arabica Coffee Rollover	8,002	33,252	48,764	22,476	
Live Cattle	975,362	1,153,778	834,304	1,633,113	934,422
Ethanol	81,725	20,925	1	16,608	17,234
Corn Cash Settled	464,387	364,045	259,610	7,767	
Soybean	30,734	95,598	168,168	284,382	188,279
Soybean Cash Settled	37,465				
Gold Forward	14,147	1,195	176	520	283
Gold Spot	23,579	9,567	12,403	12,579	9,118
Pound Sterling	42,771	46,600			
Australian Dollar	138,216	49,090			
Canadian Dollar	74,623	7,725			
New Zealand Dollar	260				
Mexican Peso	58,419	31,650			
South African Rand	600				
Swiss Franc	6,468				
Turkish Lira	2,032				
Japanese Yen	30,303	7,140			
Bovespa Stock Index Futures	21,650,138	18,039,345	16,350,493	20,226,662	26,550,491
Bovespa Rollover	3,075,094	1,943,040	1,382,060	118,680	
Bovespa Mini Index	26,234,515	16,705,118	12,374,969	9,928,406	10,692,141
Interest Rate	320,821,062	293,065,417	151,958,184	166,983,583	221,627,417
Interest Rate Swap	161,230	144,440	71,545	547,146	91,503
Interest Rate x Stock Basket Swap	879	1,022			
Interest Rate x Exchange Rate Swap	193,759	449,476	368,853	449,784	483,342
Interest Rate x Reference Rate Swap	12,800	3,600	14,000	22,234	20,200
Interest Rate x Price Index Swap (formerly Inflation)	1,646,628	1,303,131	655,582	1,054,533	1,486,734
Exchange Rate Swap	32,571	138,165	27,883	43,007	54,887
Forward Exchange Rate	2,205	79			
Price Index	6,200	1,728			
Interest Rate x IBrX-50	1,440	1,610	3,901	9,254	10,467
ID x US Dollar Spread Futures	1,685,441	1,045,712	738,389	1,150,157	396,326
FRA on ID x US Dollar Spread	33,933,356	21,075,685	17,487,272	21,217,283	20,907,906
ID x US Dollar Spread Swap	28,639	21,650	256,434	336,560	44,049
ID x IPCA Spread	4,425	39,485	6,240	69,350	111,025
Global 2020	2,460				
Global 2040	1,020	2,070	3,409	48,533	94,845
US T-Note	30,065	13,563	26,291	107,576	73,123
US Dollar	86,167,955	82,453,621	66,776,180	87,442,346	84,774,568
US Dollar Rollover	20,145,632	19,223,570	15,280,530	7,179,600	
Mini US Dollar	2,259,014	1,969,427	573,839	147,424	3,460,153
US Dollar forward points	3,303,276	4,337,700	3,157,515	3,488,158	2,850,000
Euro	552,481	390,295	75,265	37,550	2,725
Total Futures	**524,392,180**	**464,830,782**	**289,549,270**	**323,770,173**	**375,885,135**
Gold on Actuals	710,184	361,960	369,564	363,867	193,380
US $ Denominated Arabica Coffee	4,009	17,453	8,459	48,166	80,523
Corn Cash Settled	88,833	114,619	17,364	51	
Soybeans	1,718	47,163	6,611	6,616	7,184
Soybean Cash Settled	33,174				
Live Cattle	172,660	166,319	46,001	75,622	5,108
Hydrous Ethanol	9,556	1,305			
Bovespa Stock	5,586,998	1,995,760	1,714,845	1,229,734	727,015
Interest Rate	9,361,846	12,477,540	4,545,435	7,317,364	1,886,247
Interest Rate (volatility)	3,637,180	3,148,715	1,455,990	3,724,645	2,436,765

Bolsa de Mercadorias & Futuros (BM&F), Brazil (continued)

	2011	2010	2009	2008	2007
Interest Rate (IDI)	95,790,772	88,014,027	40,174,869	13,915,878	12,316,359
IDI Index (volatility)	7,156,160	12,415,185	5,894,010	1,823,370	3,068,460
Flexible Spot Interest Rate Index	53,402	35,192	159,582		
Flexible Bovespa Stock Index	191,537	358,446	622,374	469,747	323,459
Flexible FIND11 Index	37,898				
US Dollar on Actuals	11,136,468	24,170,975	21,631,255	30,588,575	24,682,702
US Dollar Volatility	597,785	1,395,970	1,485,170	2,887,345	2,241,390
Flexible Currency	514,642	732,042	357,381	495,007	339,827
Total Options	**135,084,822**	**153,803,010**	**83,836,882**	**67,844,442**	**50,478,357**

BOVESPA, Brazil

	2011	2010	2009	2008	2007
Ibovespa Index	623,103	281,815	199,147	210,868	384,837
Exchange Traded Funds	2,018,403	959,093	242,863	17,063	
All Options on Individual Equities	838,325,495	802,229,293	546,547,550	350,046,567	367,305,446
Total Options	**840,967,001**	**803,470,201**	**546,989,560**	**350,274,498**	**367,690,283**

Budapest Stock Exchange (BSE), Hungary

	2011	2010	2009	2008	2007
Feed Corn	3,352	3,476	5,068	6,879	7,452
Feed Corn Index	2				
Feed Wheat	53	220	801	1,213	528
Mill Wheat	298	7			
Euro Wheat	203	1,021	874	2,819	3,447
Feed Wheat II	26	9			
Feed Barley	135	290	391	621	260
Sunflower Seed	872	1,070	1,874	1,942	564
Rapeseed	377	750	1,785	1,426	428
Budapest Stock Index (BUX)	1,881,620	3,635,407	2,881,483	3,082,870	3,950,947
Government Bond	1				
CAD/HUF	500				
CHF/HUF	1,322,258	254,925	101,249	159,947	91,977
EUR/HUF	1,894,259	2,764,599	3,426,699	2,481,943	2,669,580
GBP/HUF	16,350	24,080	14,700	22,050	42,750
JPY/HUF	17,900	29,300	17,780	14,350	62,877
NOK/HUF	400				
PLN/HUF	120	4,320	7,040	40	880
TRY/HUF	37,775	3,300	20,400	138,400	131,950
USD/HUF	1,086,439	1,046,731	700,606	1,446,993	1,152,754
AUD/CAD	850	200			
AUD/CHF	1,200	400			
AUD/JPY	2,600	1,800	5,550	3,300	2,700
AUD/USD	14,180	27,700	29,400	150,650	32,940
CAD/CHF	200				
CAD/JPY	200	500	1,000	1,500	12,700
CHF/JPY	100	800	3,750	2,750	5,050
CHF/PLN	600	200			
GBP/AUD	1,400	4,200			
GBP/CAD	2,600	600			
GBP/CHF	4,250	11,300	35,200	188,850	102,456
GBP/JPY	8,300	17,800	116,050	328,270	1,353,100
GBP/PLN	100				
GBP/SEK	800	6,200	15,500	32,300	83,050
GBP/USD	12,300	56,900	103,010	146,068	354,640
EURO/AUD	1,000				
EURO/CAD	100				
EURO/CHF	196,790	124,600	44,300	18,700	86,650
EURO/CZK	1,200	600	1,900	10,400	3,200
EURO/GBP	5,650	29,300	17,650	210,150	100,700
EURO/JPY	69,400	199,170	241,440	227,340	306,673
EURO/NOK	3,700	3,300	23,600	29,100	34,200
EURO/PLN	26,000	23,050	51,400	17,600	14,450
EURO/RON	4,675	17,300	35,750	20,300	3,500
EURO/RUB	200		400	8,350	7,700
EURO/TRY	126,835	26,625	99,385	352,440	315,540
EURO/USD	365,652	582,380	416,160	999,736	1,555,406
USD/CAD	5,600	12,840	34,120	78,332	251,316
USD/CHF	33,000	23,300	20,400	73,900	183,200
USD/JPY	99,300	106,500	64,900	176,150	759,300
USD/PLN	2,000	21,400	7,800	4,600	52,600
USD/TRY	12,750	7,400	21,625	86,100	48,550
EUR (1 week)	43,700	367,650	493,066	360,950	594,650
GBP (1 week)	3,500	23,900	56,830	7,200	27,300
USD (1 week)	49,500	91,800	140,290	111,920	71,500

Budapest Stock Exchange (BSE), Hungary (continued)

	2011	2010	2009	2008	2007
AUD/CAD (1 week)	3,500	800			
AUD/CHF (1 week)	2,600	600			
AUD/JPY (1 week)	200				
AUD/USD (1 week)	27,200	27,200	12,800	800	87,000
CAD/CHF (1 week)	100				
CHF/PLN (1 week)	1,600	600			
EURO/CAD (1 week)	400				
EUR/CHF (1 week)	16,600	2,100			
EUR/GBP (1 week)	200	3,800	31,100	4,900	17,000
EUR/JPY (1 week)	15,000	158,000	110,550	85,650	522,900
EUR/USD (1 week)	424,150	561,303	429,700	189,250	330,900
GBP/AUD (1 week)	7,700	1,200			
GBP/CAD (1 week)	9,800	2,300			
GBP/CHF (1 week)	7,200	23,600	33,773	27,300	8,100
GBP/JPY (1 week)	2,200	42,550	189,750	231,400	432,000
GBP/PLN (1 week)	800				
GBP/USD (1 week)	25,500	90,100	106,100	57,200	232,400
USD/CAD (1 week)	16,900	36,900	40,850	84,700	362,040
USD/CHF (1 week)	7,600	40,800	51,600	26,200	22,400
USD/JPY (1 week)	4,400	59,150	45,000	23,400	29,500
USD/PLN (1 week)	7,200	8,600			
All Futures on Individual Equities	806,061	1,033,190	1,204,849	1,163,252	1,529,194
Total Futures	**8,750,083**	**11,780,544**	**11,570,661**	**12,958,135**	**18,221,627**
US Dollar	2,000	500	4,750	31,450	21,240
CHF	8,150	500	52,830	13,350	10,300
EUR	12,775	20,750	155,350	130,559	126,766
EUR/CHF	1,300				
EURO/PLN	3,750				
EURO/RON	100				
EURO/TRY	1,700				
EUR/USD	1,000	8,000	6,600	26,958	23,100
USD/CHF	1,250				
USD/JPY	750				
USD/TRY	3,900		225	102	200
Total Options	**36,675**	**29,750**	**224,345**	**411,290**	**606,601**

Central Japan Commodity Exchange (CJCE), Japan

	2011	2010	2009	2008	2007
Gasoline	364,282	984,956	1,745,785	3,635,329	4,953,168
Kerosene	282,728	716,338	1,430,843	2,685,345	4,027,192
Hen Egg	11	486	6,362	7,077	12,275
Rubber (RSS3)	160	996	19,638	90,983	314,914
Rubber Index	57	4,198	30,822	78,198	180,654
Gold	72,038	65,393			
Total Futures	**719,276**	**1,773,603**	**3,272,665**	**6,549,417**	**9,635,688**

China Financial Futures Exchange (CFFE)

	2011	2010	2009	2008	2007
CSI 300 Index	50,411,860	45,873,295			
Total Futures	**50,411,860**	**45,873,295**			

Dalian Commodity Exchange (DCE), China

	2011	2010	2009	2008	2007
Corn	26,849,738	35,999,573	16,744,088	59,918,460	59,436,742
No 1 Soybeans	25,239,532	37,393,600	42,507,076	113,681,550	47,432,721
No 2 Soybeans	10,662	14,709	32,048	42,791	21,107
Palm Oil	22,593,961	41,799,813	44,426,498	6,302,478	339,175
Soybean Oil	58,012,550	91,406,238	94,836,881	43,695,993	13,283,866
Soybean Meal	50,170,334	125,581,888	155,404,029	81,265,439	64,719,466
Linear Low Density Polyethylene (LLDPE)	95,219,058	62,488,306	44,752,979	13,252,982	381,836
Coke	1,512,734				
Polyvinyl Cloride (PVC)	9,438,431	8,483,624	18,078,662		
Total Futures	**289,047,000**	**403,167,751**	**416,782,261**	**318,159,693**	**185,614,913**

Dubai Mercantile Exchange (DME)

	2011	2010	2009	2008	2007
Oman Crude Oil	883,359	744,727	553,888	322,294	200,892
Total Futures	**883,359**	**744,727**	**553,888**	**322,294**	**200,892**

EUREX, Frankfurt, Germany

	2011	2010	2009	2008	2007
DAX	44,990,070	40,994,689	40,101,438	49,237,082	50,413,122
DJ Global Titans 50	1,700	130	160	646	10,358
DivDAX	3,948	3,409	1,803	22,679	
Euro Stoxx 50	408,860,002	372,229,766	333,407,299	432,298,342	327,034,149
Euro Stoxx Select Dividend 30 Index	92,084	73,762	132,793	103,422	21,118
Euro Stoxx	2,663	190			
Euro Stoxx Large	2,735	186			
Euro Stoxx Mid	9,699	3,737			
Euro Stoxx Small	22,009	5,921			
MDAX	422,382	404,815	297,724	595,273	824,809
MSCI Japan Index	1,112	892	426		
MSCI Russia Index	41,514				
MSCI Russia Index Futures	31,638	30,861	46,704	94,697	
OMX-Helsinki 25	255,060	250,475	148,333	186,127	100,795
SENSEX	246				
Swiss Leader index (SLI)	21,384	9,007	43,871	122,721	36,577
Swiss Market Index Mid-Cap (SMIM)	181,654	100,531	80,081	99,254	152,977
Swiss Market Index (SMI)	13,482,706	11,626,179	12,135,437	17,658,178	14,391,903
Stoxx Europe 50 Index	1,330,841	1,417,882	1,300,945	1,607,048	1,387,401
Stoxx Europe 600	1,247,960	93,633			
Stoxx Europe Large 200	75,207	7,657			
Stoxx Europe Mid 200	490,301	57,847			
Stoxx Europe Small 200	428,524	38,155			
TecDAX	203,962	232,025	245,270	435,556	585,377
Euro Stoxx Automobiles	58,072	54,507	84,664	212,427	142,146
Euro Stoxx Banks	5,229,347	1,156,447	437,131	651,855	640,667
Euro Stoxx Basic Resources	32,098	44,913	30,634	39,168	22,501
Euro Stoxx Chemicals	29,076	65,913	36,940	39,868	18,750
Euro Stoxx Construction & Materials	39,676	38,599	44,989	34,171	36,663
Euro Stoxx Financial Services	8,502	10,227	22,295	34,470	27,007
Euro Stoxx Food and Beverage	24,402	25,563	22,160	36,888	11,226
Euro Stoxx Healthcare	49,145	42,894	36,312	50,893	40,201
Euro Stoxx Industrial Goods & Services	24,727	46,383	35,546	26,200	29,283
Euro Stoxx Insurance	220,847	204,346	192,823	234,726	153,642
Euro Stoxx Media	25,575	42,233	34,959	39,198	39,462
Euro Stoxx Oil & Gas	67,219	148,169	85,545	182,422	107,664
Euro Stoxx Personal & Household Goods	15,058	18,442	21,120	21,440	15,420
Euro Stoxx Real Estate	4,706	3,508	2,413	2,742	
Euro Stoxx Retail	41,504	17,663	28,668	27,085	18,399
Euro Stoxx Technology	44,757	51,565	89,955	171,420	153,129
Euro Stoxx Telecom	125,229	127,420	143,714	257,493	274,843
Euro Stoxx Travel & Leisure	19,914	19,712	32,092	36,451	24,433
Euro Stoxx Utilities	89,787	131,250	109,173	117,898	74,923
Euro Stoxx 600 Automobiles & Parts	303,586	151,258	145,939	377,947	184,908
Euro Stoxx 600 Banks	2,456,184	1,727,129	1,178,604	1,634,005	541,557
Euro Stoxx 600 Basic Resources	707,868	490,447	491,332	441,871	214,640
Euro Stoxx 600 Chemicals	114,697	74,946	75,880	89,156	72,184
Euro Stoxx 600 Construction & Materials	130,865	67,965	69,729	144,268	85,996
Euro Stoxx 600 Financial Services	38,373	22,647	28,542	69,389	96,472
Euro Stoxx 600 Food & Beverage	268,565	189,505	212,780	175,795	85,753
Euro Stoxx 600 Healthcare	411,857	372,362	366,782	379,849	305,236
Euro Stoxx 600 Industrial Goods & Services	577,074	452,187	306,558	285,522	174,806
Euro Stoxx 600 Insurance	757,845	412,506	333,646	433,779	349,726
Euro Stoxx 600 Media	254,493	271,169	201,928	273,233	74,664
Euro Stoxx 600 Oil & Gas	645,483	425,478	490,611	534,071	387,825
Euro Stoxx 600 Personal & Household Goods	116,613	104,779	101,473	60,153	15,092
Euro Stoxx 600 Real Estate	24,520	32,431	34,407	17,321	
Euro Stoxx 600 Retail	148,710	114,683	164,015	221,545	105,297
Euro Stoxx 600 Technology	172,508	177,025	124,442	168,702	199,401
Euro Stoxx 600 Telecom	346,960	414,900	396,821	386,335	268,292
Euro Stoxx 600 Travel & Leisure	138,866	207,146	158,307	113,510	86,329
Euro Stoxx 600 Utilities	361,392	290,852	229,079	266,804	153,117
KOPSI 200 Index	17,442,744	166,170			
DAX - Kursindex Index Dividend	80	275	120		
DivDAX Index Dividend	4	1,530	8,030		
Euro Stoxx 50 Index Dividend	4,232,260	3,585,955	2,534,348	183,058	
SMI Index Dividend	14,375	13,691	2,576		
Mini-Futures auf VStoxx	1,889,492	431,669	14,576		
Swiss Government Bond (CONF)	181,740	205,109	279,720	407,583	360,355
Euro-BTP	2,386,768	1,396,953	327,914		
Euro-BOBL	142,309,151	133,851,275	105,820,542	155,090,861	170,909,055
Euro-BUND	236,188,831	231,484,529	180,755,004	257,827,619	338,319,416
Euro-BUXL	1,806,195	1,360,503	925,627	1,155,127	1,582,859
Euro-SCHATZ	165,798,952	140,923,898	125,607,110	174,226,719	181,101,310
Short-term Euro-BTP	575,349	131,195			

EUREX, Frankfurt, Germany (continued)

	2011	2010	2009	2008	2007
Mid-term Euro-BTP	10,156				
3-Month Euribor	125,557	267,985	403,243	703,273	792,635
CER MidDec	252	175	23		
EUA MidDec	44,172	125,875	876		
European Carbon	36,624	735			
Butter	510	10			
European Processing Potatoes	52,918	49,336	15,575		
Hogs	2,009	2,215	1,367		
Piglets	258	579	289		
Skimmed Milk Powder	7	16			
DJ UBS Agriculture Sub-Index	6,481	10,298	5,552		
DJ UBS Commodity Index	54,974	57,255	14,177	12,982	9,694
DJ UBS Energy Sub-Index	2,898	5,148	2,238	17,537	11,220
DJ UBS Ex-Energy Sub-Index	4,792	2,236		192,065	169,198
DJ UBS Grains Sub-Index	2,214	214		30,860	26,035
DJ UBS Industrial Metals Sub-Index	4,771	3,528	308	101,586	118,601
DJ UBS Livestock Sub-Index	937			8,326	5,910
DJ UBS Petroleum Sub-Index	2,337	1,263			
DJ UBS Precious Metals Sub-Index	8,649	3,241		2,441	9,568
DJ UBS Softs Sub-Index	2,125	843			
IPD UK Annual All Industrial Index	35			210,081	218,982
IPD UK Annual All Office Index	15			246,288	177,863
IPD UK Annual All Retail Index	89				
IPD UK Annual All Property Index	3,337	1,652	547		
Gold	2,105	777	4,154		
Xetra-Gold	668	135			
Silver	948	474	81		
Exchange Traded Funds	5		30	89	1,188
Single Stock Dividend	938,950	779,542			
All Futures on Individual Equities	174,271,102	202,195,229	116,771,129	130,210,348	52,460,383
Total Futures	**1,234,731,337**	**1,153,336,562**	**928,766,700**	**1,231,646,824**	**1,146,081,579**
DAX	67,616,997	75,123,356	95,926,938	104,939,881	91,850,835
DAX 1st Friday Weekly	603,610	529,697	180,486	136,941	192,587
DAX 2nd Friday Weekly	542,074	500,470	117,787	99,993	149,972
DAX 4th Friday Weekly	654,937	539,207	193,299	118,099	209,868
DAX 5th Friday Weekly	144,953	251,562	68,591	41,279	74,790
Euro STOXX 50 Index	369,241,952	284,707,318	300,208,574	400,931,635	251,438,870
Euro STOXX 50 Index - 1st Friday	792,380	227,729	72,606	36,992	149,414
Euro STOXX 50 Index - 2nd Friday	527,710	223,769	78,701	16,865	167,282
Euro STOXX 50 Index - 4th Friday	855,663	248,929	73,304	23,379	200,733
Euro STOXX 50 Index - 5th Friday	299,572	95,331	38,518	19,418	50,709
MDAX	44,866	78,895	60,560	187,159	91,140
HEX 25	911	1,333	755	20	1,307
Swiss Leader Index (SLI)	53,573	53,685	48,110	49,519	19,599
Swiss Market Index Mid-Cap (SMIM)	33,981	74,286	54,287	49,610	44,920
Swiss Market Index (SMI)	5,679,053	4,236,899	4,094,103	5,588,591	5,773,269
Stoxx Europe 50 Index	41,866	15,701	52,816	103,080	140,197
Euro Stoxx Mid	8,770				
Stoxx Europe 600 Index	5,367	529	16,113	37,529	30,593
Stoxx Europe Mid 200	105,985	520			
Stoxx Europe Mid 200 Index	826	23,669	11,251	112,858	172,017
TecDAX	16,566	23,590	53,753	52,968	37,848
Euro Stoxx Automobiles & Parts	14,662	4,790			
Euro Stoxx Banks	1,888,904	389,123	32,571	103,585	644,500
Euro Stoxx Basic Resources	694	120	21	50	415
Euro Stoxx Chemicals	3,620	6,950	12,317	5,899	12,790
Euro Stoxx Construction & Materials	132	80			
Euro Stoxx Financial Services	191		1,511	1,575	5,381
Euro Stoxx Food and Beverage	2,581	8	1,200	104	3,486
Euro Stoxx Healthcare	281	157	74	502	
Euro Stoxx Industrial Goods & Services	24				8,765
Euro Stoxx Insurance	21,056	34,497	5,430	47,709	19,955
Euro Stoxx Media	103	1,276	2,000	5,408	16,559
Euro Stoxx Oil & Gas	2,406	1,109	1,652	14,544	17,870
Euro Stoxx Personal & Household Goods	868	5,200	10	165	
Euro Stoxx Retail	341				337
Euro Stoxx Technology	80	3,907	7,600	24,702	10,000
Euro Stoxx Telecom	12,189	5,043	9,741	51,047	40,018
Euro Stoxx Travel & Leisure	577		75	90	150
Euro Stoxx Utilities	2,383	7,362	15,989	13,781	62,494
Euro Stoxx 600 Automobiles & Parts	33,677	21,211	8,580	95,635	85,135
Euro Stoxx 600 Banks	916,728	642,558	245,012	535,531	377,343
Euro Stoxx 600 Basic Resources	313,369	180,572	95,564	179,574	95,047
Euro Stoxx 600 Chemicals	15,389	6,395	2,221	31,488	9,684
Euro Stoxx 600 Construction & Materials	9,535	4,550	1,018	60,216	50,582

EUREX, Frankfurt, Germany (continued)

	2011	2010	2009	2008	2007
Euro Stoxx 600 Financial Services	259	741	1,246	6,947	6,115
Euro Stoxx 600 Food & Beverage	8,070	1,462	1,384	29,802	623
Euro Stoxx 600 Healthcare	23,403	19,709	28,654	46,305	65,188
Euro Stoxx 600 Industrial Goods & Services	104,553	68,363	57,026	111,988	142,189
Euro Stoxx 600 Insurance	72,791	121,461	147,459	525,853	195,790
Euro Stoxx 600 Media	3,196	15,260	5,990	15,632	10,744
Euro Stoxx 600 Oil & Gas	163,125	69,994	39,455	173,140	89,956
Euro Stoxx 600 Personal & Household Goods	11,365	1,714	706	4,587	7,063
Euro Stoxx 600 Retail	12,747	11,685	19,958	19,431	
Euro Stoxx 600 Technology	323	382	1,550	11,612	11,539
Euro Stoxx 600 Telecom	15,088	6,941	76,903	46,994	43,478
Euro Stoxx 600 Travel & Leisure	559	40,610	9,208	922	9,653
Euro Stoxx 600 Utilities	14,372	11,804	38,748	84,162	106,487
Euro Stoxx 50 Index Dividend	804,612	144,620			
Stoxx	553,463	562,745			
Euro-Bobl	16,188,346	7,803,983	6,955,457	15,083,076	15,135,182
Euro-Bund	38,154,098	39,301,301	28,392,790	33,317,879	44,441,961
Euro-Schatz	26,531,383	17,712,470	16,215,924	20,438,378	19,085,515
3-Month Euribor	100,003	371,000			
Gold	14,543	10,799	13,181		
Xetra-Gold	1,488	142			
Silver	747	426	106		
All Options on Exchange Traded Funds	62,623	141,718	5,515	330,944	31,730
All Options on Austrian Equities	559,998	308,428	188,289	113,901	19,025
All Options on Belgian Equities	309,027	244,081	104,865	31,017	
All Options on Dutch Equities	6,552,069	5,646,218	6,813,332	7,243,976	11,811,227
All Options on Scandinavian Equities	24,569,269	28,816,601	19,342,143	18,414,654	17,291,936
All Options on French Equities	17,081,302	13,138,701	10,539,983	9,429,765	7,795,177
All Options on German Equities	156,521,894	178,639,023	186,930,541	234,948,892	214,969,289
All Options on Great Britain Equities	121,109	85,034			
All Options on Italian Equities	2,439,964	1,457,602	1,394,120	1,784,585	1,146,488
All Options on Russian Equities	44,789	18,119	59,885	179,672	22,398
All Options on Spanish Equities	2,160,580	1,794,803	1,202,642	1,319,054	860,700
All Options on Swedish Equities	1,500	121,600			
All Options on Individual Swiss Equities	64,969,435	78,588,478	77,977,503	75,864,298	68,122,792
Total Options	**808,683,495**	**743,579,836**	**758,392,598**	**933,396,359**	**753,780,347**

Hong Kong Futures Exchange (HKFE), Hong Kong

	2011	2010	2009	2008	2007
Hang Seng Index	23,085,833	21,031,085	20,728,034	21,716,508	17,160,964
Mini Hang Seng Index	10,294,537	8,300,654	9,279,877	7,961,028	4,325,977
H-Shares Index	15,003,870	12,429,800	12,394,116	14,440,965	10,846,277
Mini H-Shares Index	1,845,116	992,224	799,894	318,395	
HSI Dividend Point Index	11,196	2,123			
HSCEI Dividend Point Index	53,054	4,667			
1-Month HIBOR	245	14	204	881	574
3-Month HIBOR	414	1,055	2,573	23,818	31,678
Gold	3,716	5,642	6,773	3,075	
All Futures on Individual Equities	444,014	239,259	271,766	257,015	351,514
Total Futures	**50,741,995**	**43,006,523**	**43,483,237**	**44,721,743**	**32,723,598**
Hang Seng Index	10,667,426	8,515,049	5,367,403	3,820,797	7,480,183
Mini Hang Seng Index	954,414	482,691	286,591	156,957	69,512
Flexible Hang Seng Index	9,260	11,222			
H-Shares Index	3,771,799	2,910,713	1,961,131	1,613,988	1,727,847
Flexible H-Shares Index	23,510	2,532			
All Options on Individual Equities	74,325,068	61,125,647	47,439,896	54,692,865	45,982,968
Total Options	**89,751,477**	**73,047,854**	**55,055,021**	**60,284,993**	**55,262,088**

ICE Futures Canada (ICE), Canada

	2011	2010	2009	2008	2007
Canola (Rapeseed)	4,653,153	4,118,428	3,351,793	3,132,188	3,169,182
Western Barley	429	2,632	54,839	167,381	214,672
Total Futures	**4,653,582**	**4,121,060**	**3,406,632**	**3,299,999**	**3,430,324**
Canola	68,375	87,818	85,115	21,206	17,067
Total Options	**68,375**	**87,818**	**85,115**	**21,211**	**21,841**

ICE Futures Europe (ICE), United Kingdom

	2011	2010	2009	2008	2007
Brent Crude Oil (Monthly)	132,045,563	100,022,169	74,137,750	68,368,145	59,728,941
Brent Crude Oil (Quarters)	1,947				
Brent Crude Oil (Calendars)	8,940				
Brent NX Crude Oil (Monthly)	150				
Gas Oil (Monthly)	65,774,151	52,296,582	36,038,870	28,805,192	24,509,884
Gas Oil (Quarters)	1,503				

VOLUME - WORLDWIDE

ICE Futures Europe (ICE), United Kingdom (continued)

	2011	2010	2009	2008	2007
LS Gas Oil (Monthly)	1,149				
UK Natural Gas Monthly (NBP)	2,788,240	2,105,730	1,629,980	879,420	1,058,290
UK Natural Gas (Quarters)	651,180	423,585	255,435	103,440	37,905
UK Natural Gas (Seasons)	2,604,150	1,638,720	907,470	279,930	136,740
ECX EUA (Monthly)	5,444,050	4,263,655	3,775,621	1,991,276	980,780
ECX EUA (Daily)	5,855	194,981	38,214		
WTI Crude (Monthly)	51,097,818	52,586,415	46,393,671	51,091,712	51,388,362
WTI Crude (Quarters)	1,206				
WTI Crude (Calendars)	6,540				
NYH (RBOB) Gasoline (Monthly)	664,784	2,257	4,965	26,356	14,805
Heating Oil (Monthly)	876,937	118,863	135,265	116,911	205,072
ECX CER (Monthly)	1,272,128	864,089	766,349	507,779	
ECX CER (Daily)	546	16,494	3,780		
Rotterdam Coal (Monthly)	40,976	39,901	28,735	5,895	465
Rotterdam Coal (Quarters)	266,238	216,516	135,240	24,720	3,870
Rotterdam Coal (Seasons)	5,238	5,790	2,190	630	
Rotterdam Coal (Calendar)	529,464	357,336	255,420	70,860	4,500
Richards Bay Coal (Monthly)	30,281	33,601	14,225	1,900	240
Richards Bay Coal (Quarters)	88,221	102,915	44,265	8,880	525
Richards Bay Coal (Calendar)	91,200	159,564	91,680	34,020	480
Richards Bay Coal (Seasons)	258	780	210	30	
gCNewcastle Coal (Monthly)	10,634	8,295	4,625		
gCNewcastle Coal (Quarters)	66,669	52,050	18,210		
gCNewcastle Coal (Calendars)	33,996	62,880	39,240		
Dutch TTF Gas (Monthly)	21,040	10,860			
Dutch TTF Gas (Seasons)	9,600	25,860			
Dutch TTF Gas (Quarter)	14,040	4,800			
Dutch TTF Gas (Calendars)	21,360	41,040			
GASPOOL Natural Gas (Monthly)	360				
GASPOOL Natural Gas (Seasons)	2,760	732			
GASPOOL Natural Gas (Quarter)	6,870	270			
GASPOOL Natural Gas (Calendars)	11,280	240			
NCG Natural Gas (Monthly)	30				
ECX ERU (Monthly)	61,119	3,045			
UK Peak Electricity (Monthly)	60				
UK Peak Electricity (Seasons)	90				
UK Base Electricity (Monthly)	3,315	1,020	895	370	990
UK Base Electricity (Quarters)	1,395	255	1,140	975	330
UK Base Electricity (Seasons)	16,470	18,180	16,830	2,790	1,920
Central Appalachian Coal (Monthly)	132				
Central Appalachian Coal (Quarters)	630				
Total Futures	**264,580,563**	**215,679,470**	**164,741,409**	**152,322,268**	**138,169,680**
Brent Crude Oil	2,191,733	165,286	212,341	121,024	74,056
ECX EUA	700,929	740,889	416,567	242,966	57,541
ECX CER	81,784	77,134	91,130	69,565	
ECX ERU	3,750	250			
Richards Bay Coal	1,470				
Rotterdam Coal	1,560				
UK Natural Gas	204,195				
WTI Crude Oil	829,972	198,245	18,200	11,131	10,416
Gasoil	407,827	259,499	213,884	183,179	159,263
Total Options	**4,423,220**	**1,441,303**	**952,122**	**627,865**	**301,276**

JSE Securities Exchange of South Africa, Africa

	2011	2010	2009	2008	2007
White Maize (WMAZ)	863,992	773,177	687,472	859,920	956,026
Yellow Maize (YMAZ)	376,723	313,899	311,589	337,429	268,780
Corn	132,886	63,997	15,016		
Wheat	449,532	441,738	379,365	469,471	378,289
Sunflower Seeds	156,785	89,194	127,807	165,088	64,402
Soybeans	218,111	136,802	116,530	73,111	44,062
Sorghum	218	274			
CBOT Soybeans	795	190			
CBOT Soybean Meal	28	173			
CBOT Soybean Oil	2	1			
CBOT Wheat	3,784				
Copper	480	317			
Gold	21,285	3,838	1,725		
Silver	3,743	395			
Platinum	7,240	1,745	1,596		
Crude Oil	25,313	3,002	742		
FTSE/JSE Top 40 Index	13,214,316	11,782,186	12,145,844	15,924,693	16,150,010
FTSE/JSE Top 40 Index - Mini	146,690	29,253	10,876	450	
FTSE/JSE African Banks Index	1,386	754	56		
Top 100 FTSE/JSE All Share Index	910	100			

JSE Securities Exchange of South Africa, Africa (continued)

	2011	2010	2009	2008	2007
FTSE/JSE 25 Index	20,741	1,379	3,058	25,723	22,845
FTSE/JSE General Retailers Index	84	200			
FTSE/JSE Gold Mining Index	1,243	1,219	2,352	1,651	7,893
FTSE/JSE FINI 15 Index	2,520	4,471	17,826	43,660	16,309
FTSE/JSE FNDI 30 Index	105,506	131,351	183,311	217,863	125,960
FTSE/JSE Capped Top 40 Index	4,600	7,585	11,420	47,687	19,977
FTSE/JSE Shareholder Weighted Top 40 Index (DTOP)	4,742,391	4,603,466	4,361,957	3,037,960	2,359,997
FTSE/JSE RESI 20 Index	994	360	780	14,528	5,390
Can-Do	1,347,604	9,304,664	10,619,562	1,128,772	736,044
Kruger Rand	1,017	55	12	519	9,922
Dollar / Rand	9,052,270	5,243,573	5,604,875		
Euro / Rand	675,946	321,554	370,297		
British Pound / Rand	630,975	434,603	328,838		
ZAAD / Rand	283,494	178,492	873,552		
Japanese Yen / Rand	86,378	18,093			
Canadian Dollar / Rand	11,425	9,525			
Swiss Franc / Rand	15,893	1,897			
Maxi Dollar / Rand	916,400	210			
Any-Day Expiry Dollar/Rand	1,163,137				
Currency Can-Do	398,349				
Dividend Futures	20,305,731	15,266,618	16,364,671	20,097,204	11,891,790
IDX Futures	22,287,098	15,475,728	4,321,081	28,362	
IDX Dividend Futures	19,365,740	6,764,568	172,914	1,364,561	
All Futures on Individual Equities	50,769,051	78,620,861	88,791,925	431,212,627	265,493,735
Total Futures	**147,812,806**	**150,037,770**	**145,845,620**	**475,051,729**	**298,567,616**
White Maize (WMAZ)	234,436	191,223	182,400	455,403	471,727
Yellow Maize (YMAZ)	46,162	39,934	41,635	69,339	55,695
Corn	10,421	26,304	61		
Wheat (WEAT)	57,962	47,078	28,620	176,079	140,545
Sunflower Seeds (SUNS)	6,860	12,343	7,108	21,073	5,983
Soybeans (SOYA)	26,061	10,922	6,914	5,978	1,986
Grade 2 White Maize (WOPT)	26,061				
Sorghum (SORG)	19	14			
Crude Oil	302				
FTSE/JSE Top 40 Index (ALSI)	3,291,168	3,483,237	5,691,546	9,834,294	9,008,828
FTSE/JSE Top 40 Index - Mini (ALMI)	21				
FTSE/JSE 25 Index (INDI)	296	20			
FTSE/JSE Shareholder Weighted Top 40 Index (DTOP)	1,318,751	1,808,511	4,975,451	4,722,544	4,026,943
Can-Do	567,128	645,553	1,247,761	3,604,877	2,978,981
Dollar / Rand	993,499	1,136,585	578,442		
Euro / Rand	193,736	112,417	68,919		
British Pound / Rand	76,726	7,824	87,924		
Maxi Dollar/Rand	20,600				
Any-Day Expiry Dollar/Rand	186,694				
All Options on Individual Equities	11,327,943	12,313,211	15,670,869	19,591,351	14,312,446
Total Options	**18,384,846**	**19,860,839**	**28,659,600**	**38,532,275**	**31,074,787**

Kansai Commodities Exchange (KCE), Japan

	2011	2010	2009	2008	2007
Red Beans	9,458	10,212	4,750	4,362	4,362
US Soybeans	6,408	8,766	11,816	16,238	19,712
Corn	51,846	14,930	24,336	133,592	101,401
Raw Sugar	4,664	4,912	5,340	4,559	4,380
Rice	97,901				
Frozen Shrimp	4,655	5,832	5,789	5,853	6,248
Corn 75 Index	6,398	8,754	8,682	8,754	8,910
Coffee Index	5,873	8,754	8,683	8,903	11,248
Total Futures	**187,203**	**63,092**	**69,900**	**183,999**	**164,743**

Korea Futures Exchange (KFE), Korea

	2011	2010	2009	2008	2007
3-Year Treasury Bond	34,140,210	26,922,414	20,050,788	15,958,864	13,555,136
10-Year Treasury Bond	3,503,677	33,054		9,686	
KOPSI 200*	87,274,461	86,214,025	83,117,030	64,835,148	47,758,294
STAR Index	39	59	490	13,325	21,919
Lean Hogs	5,981	13,943	13,703	16,258	
Mini Gold	182,278				
US Dollar	70,212,467	64,256,678	41,161,819	6,672,438	5,752,134
Japanese Yen	803,734	411,117	272,531	104,012	271,043
Euro	205,395	388,294	310,540	103,762	212,790
All Futures on Individual Equities	59,966,166	44,711,133	36,971,510	11,293,134	
Total Futures	**256,294,408**	**222,950,753**	**181,900,142**	**99,007,894**	**67,571,815**
*KOPSI 200 Index	3,671,662,258	3,525,898,562	2,920,990,655	2,766,474,404	2,709,844,077
Total Options	**3,671,662,258**	**3,525,910,648**	**2,920,991,635**	**2,766,474,425**	**2,709,844,283**

VOLUME - WORLDWIDE

London Metal Exchange (LME), United Kingdom

	2011	2010	2009	2008	2007
High Grade Primary Aluminium	59,558,330	46,537,180	46,988,069	48,307,389	40,229,693
Aluminium Alloy	610,935	466,206	427,452	582,398	492,868
North American Special Aluminium Alloy	699,863	588,269	920,336	1,519,811	1,236,484
Copper - Grade A	34,537,310	29,949,765	24,922,949	26,507,242	21,420,450
Standard Lead	10,921,882	7,744,747	5,983,323	6,188,753	4,697,862
Primary Nickel	8,056,421	7,325,219	6,717,299	5,202,609	3,792,788
Special High Grade Zinc	21,984,302	18,065,641	15,901,774	16,120,770	12,556,285
Mediterranean Steel (MS)	219,163	191,179	30,764	13,206	
Tin	1,891,633	1,554,269	4,567,910	1,410,450	1,293,722
LMEmini Copper Grade A	399	736	10	45	1,099
LMEmini Special High Grade Zinc	11	5		7	195
Cobalt	6,578	6,812			
Molybdenum	513	510			
PE Europe	2	20	8	22	29
PN North America	134	1,235	2,713	2,449	401
LN North America	182	1,869	710	1,705	282
Total Futures	**138,487,658**	**112,439,117**	**106,463,839**	**105,861,588**	**85,736,480**
High Grade Primary Aluminium	3,218,299	3,479,888	2,505,499	3,702,232	3,115,989
Aluminium Alloy	270	270	216,735	267,722	316,496
North American Special Aluminium Alloy	4,178	17,428	4,333	24,052	10,052
Copper - Grade A	3,371,191	3,111,996	1,624,350	1,987,291	2,027,181
Standard Lead	189,831	199,884	145,354	346,672	298,965
Primary Nickel	233,837	172,075	142,168	152,744	167,428
Special High Grade Zinc	913,771	732,279	712,526	715,970	1,111,080
Tin	26,114	26,009	33,562	67,716	18,407
Primary Aluminium TAPOS	44,196	38,299	55,149	37,748	43,621
Copper Grade A TAPOS	24,309	21,532	15,212	16,146	16,667
Lead TAPOS	6,806	1,622	3,065	9,411	3,210
Nickel TAPOS	2,091	2,547	3,541	11,347	35,220
Tin TAPOS	20	25	12	810	48
NASAA TAPOS	36	140	100	2,290	42
Special High Grade Zinc TAPOS	74,938	9,648	5,335	8,538	10,314
Total Options	**8,109,887**	**7,819,002**	**5,466,989**	**7,353,711**	**7,178,248**

Malaysia Derivatives Exchange, Malaysia

	2011	2010	2009	2008	2007
Crude Palm Oil (FCPO)	5,871,587	4,064,361	4,008,882	3,003,529	2,793,560
3-Month KLIBOR (FKB3)	101,979	95,477	126,690	195,203	239,314
KLSE Composite Index (FKLI)	2,489,204	1,994,907	1,997,955	2,920,728	3,157,341
Total Futures	**8,462,770**	**6,154,745**	**6,137,827**	**6,120,032**	**6,202,686**
KLSE Composite Index (OKLI)	16				
Total Options	**16**				

MEFF Renta Fija (RF), Spain

	2011	2010	2009	2008	2007
10-Year Notional Bond	16	14	18	4	13
Total Futures	**16**	**14**	**18**	**4**	**13**

MEFF Renta Variable (RV), Spain

	2011	2010	2009	2008	2007
IBEX 35 Plus Index	5,281,218	6,280,999	5,436,989	7,275,299	8,435,258
Mini IBEX 35 Index	3,099,647	3,579,263	3,148,292	3,300,418	2,865,739
Ibex Dividends	3,154				
All Futures on Individual Equities	27,578,789	19,684,108	44,586,779	46,237,568	21,294,315
Total Futures	**35,962,808**	**29,544,370**	**53,172,060**	**56,813,285**	**32,595,312**
IBEX 35 Plus Index	2,198,967	3,072,418	4,357,260	8,286,224	5,670,773
All Options on Individual Equities	29,410,340	37,607,374	35,527,914	18,317,249	13,593,493
Total Options	**31,609,307**	**40,679,792**	**39,885,174**	**26,603,473**	**19,264,266**

Mercado a Termino de Buenos Aires (MATBA), Argentina

	2011	2010	2009	2008	2007
Wheat	22,810	24,496	25,921	37,243	41,781
Corn	17,114	12,549	15,144	22,269	32,012
Sunflower	32	30	99	101	135
Sorghum	293	99			
Soybeans	116,719	117,440	101,654	82,164	80,016
Total Futures	**156,968**	**154,614**	**142,818**	**141,873**	**154,069**
Wheat	539	2,328	2,584	1,449	5,243
Corn	2,415	1,773	356	1,538	4,068
Sunflower	2			64	1,221
Soybeans	45,431	40,954	35,126	10,831	12,963
Total Options	**48,387**	**45,055**	**38,066**	**13,882**	**23,495**

Mexican Derivatives Exchange (MEXDER), Mexico

	2011	2010	2009	2008	2007
US Dollar	7,189,846	5,662,462	1,587,858	3,186,832	3,223,044
Euro FX	24,397	36,168	64,327	44,172	2,105
IPC Stock Index	1,231,048	1,321,686	1,130,528	1,085,663	951,955
CETE 91	4,990,595	3,802,874	4,877,430	4,087,066	2,812,500
TIIE 28	26,906,390	26,208,542	37,545,841	57,881,101	220,608,024
M3 Bond	197,623	1,051,818	216,150	43,000	36,500
M5 Bond	50,575				
M10 Bond	2,917,800	2,281,187	2,613,021	3,005,307	1,182,069
M20 Bond	2,241,045	1,377,266	269,904		
M30 Bond	396,078				
10-Year Interest Rate Swap	10,794	43,742	67,144	170,949	25,332
10-Year Interest Rate Swap (Centrally Cleared)	6,434	5,226			
2-Year Interest Rate Swap (Centrally Cleared)	19,580	14,571			
Exchange Traded Funds	511	10			
All Futures on Individual Equities	63,711	12,044		2,000	2
Total Futures	**46,246,427**	**41,827,321**	**48,394,113**	**69,506,090**	**228,841,531**
MXN / USD	422	963	145	7	10
IPC Stock Index	65,631	147,411	40,723	52,556	130,410
Exchange Traded Funds	2	10		7,585	
All Options on Individual Equities	446,547	619,870	345,718	577,452	78
Total Options	**512,602**	**768,254**	**386,586**	**637,600**	**130,498**

Montreal Exchange (ME), Canada

	2011	2010	2009	2008	2007
3-Month Bankers Acceptance (BAX)	20,865,769	13,698,870	7,668,781	9,958,833	15,237,958
S&P/TSX Composite Index Mini (SCF)	232	261	1,151		
2-Year Canadian Gov't Bond (CGZ)	59,650	611			6,363
5 Year Canadian Gov't Bond (CGF)	105,580		12,055		
10-Year Canadian Gov't Bond (CGB)	7,788,218	6,405,525	5,310,537	7,363,569	9,337,754
S&P Canada 60 Index (SXF)	4,228,938	4,070,604	4,157,917	4,575,352	3,885,872
S&P/TSX 60 Index Mini (SXM)	100,554				
Total Futures	**33,148,941**	**24,176,031**	**17,150,708**	**22,043,015**	**28,493,454**
3-Month Bankers Acceptance (OBX)	635,046	349,675	234,861	282,190	748,991
10-Year Canadian Gov't Bond (OGB)	8,775	9,742	12,531	23,553	13,782
US Dollar (USX)	16,947	17,705	29,902	23,795	34,889
S&P Canada 60 Index (SXO) (incl LEAPS)	93,151	77,820	34,056	38,666	26,484
i60 Index (XIU)	2,473,873	2,333,095	1,956,588	661,286	364,924
Claymore Global Agriculture (COW)	2,101	1,562	1,460	64	
Horizons BetaPro S&P/TSX Global Gold Bear Plus Fund	10,524	2,740	2,728		
Horizons BetaPro S&P/TSX Global Gold Bull Plus Fund	16,216	7,658	4,789		
Horizons BetaPro S&P/TSX 60 Bear Plus ETF (HXD)	14,859	8,476	13,137	3,896	
Horizons BetaPro S&P/TSX 60 Bull Plus ETF (HXU)	6,538	2,898	10,109	7,651	
iShares DJ Canada Select Div Index Fund (XDV)	5,526	4,567	3,159		
iShares CDN S&P/TSX Capped Com Index Fund (XIC)	16,143	4,532	3,022		
iShares CDN S&P/TSX Capped REIT Index Fund (XRE)	3,347	2,117	1,978		
Horizons BetaPro NYMEX Crude Oil Bear Plus Fund	36,818	12,054	9,491		
Horizons BetaPro NYMEX Crude Oil Bull Plus Fund	99,245	68,123	75,439		
Horizons BetaPro S&P/TSX Capped Fin Bear Plus ETF	12,448	2,107	2,662		
Horizons BetaPro S&P/TSX Capped Fin Bull Plus ETF	2,843	1,169	2,553		
iShares CDN MSCI EAFE 100% Hedged to CAD $ Index	8,736	7,768	1,624		
iShares CDN S&P 500 Hedged to CAD $ Index Fund (XSP)	7,343	5,938	1,268		
Horizons BetaPro S&P/TSX Cap Energy Bear ETF (HED)	1,247	403	634		
Horizons BetaPro S&P/TSX Cap Energy Bull ETF (HEU)	1,288	733	378		
Claymore Natural Gas Commodity ETF (GAS)	12,113	75,100	79,444		
iShares CDN DEX Corporate Bond Index Fund (XCB)	3,226	4,418	1,280		
iShares CDN DEX Short-term Bond Index Fund (XSB)	1,405	1,685	763		
Horizons BetaPro NYMEX Natural Gas Bear Plus Fund	20,174	12,806	451		
Horizons BetaPro NYMEX Natural Gas Bull Plus Fund	105,827	101,575	2,038		
Claymore Gold Bullion ETF (CGL)	2,426	3,015			
BMO DJ Canada Titans 60 Index (ZCN)	210	1,906			
Horizon Beta Pro S&P/TSX 60 Inverse ETF (HIX)	168	170			
Horizon Beta Pro S&P/TSX 60 Index ETF (HXT)	463				
BMO S&P/TSX Equal Weight Banks Index ETF (ZEB)	7,617				
CDN S&P/TSX Capped Gold Index Fund (XGD)	184,669	127,824	114,884	58,438	89,435
CDN S&P/TSX Capped Financials Index Fund (XFN)	317,119	248,487	356,040	195,820	101,499
CDN S&P/TSX Capped IT Index Fund (XIT)	602	1,339	2,110	3,248	14,989
CDN S&P/TSX Capped Materials Index Fund (XMA)	17,447	5,711	14,669	5,811	59,371
CDN S&P/TSX Capped Energy Index Fund (ZEG)	474,128	262,674	121,064	80,838	158,178
All Options on Individual Equities	24,211,857	16,353,284	14,507,261	14,633,599	12,634,060
Total Options	**28,832,465**	**20,120,876**	**17,602,373**	**16,021,887**	**14,248,756**

National Stock Exchange of India

	2011	2010	2009	2008	2007
US Dollar/Indian Rupee	697,825,411	699,042,420	226,362,368		
EUR/Indian Rupee	18,065,186	17,326,787			
GBP/Indian Rupee	5,569,204	1,488,555			
JPY/Indian Rupee	5,411,351	1,491,520			
Bank Nifty Index	17,131,900	13,732,237			
CNX INFRA	1,072				
CNX IT Index	71,672	67,577			
CNX PSE	984				
DJIA Index	230,828				
Mini S&P CNX Nifty Index	14,994,257	14,154,716			
Nifty Midcap 50 Index	2,935	4,117			
S&P CNX Nifty Index	123,144,880	128,392,858	195,759,414	202,390,223	138,794,235
S&P 500 Index	135,323				
All Futures on Individual Equities	160,878,260	175,674,069	161,053,345	225,777,205	179,324,970
Total Futures	**1,043,463,263**	**1,051,374,856**	**583,175,127**	**428,167,428**	**318,119,205**
US Dollar/Indian Rupee	252,807,126	6,277,165			
Bank Nifty Index	1,867,147	777,136			
CNX INFRA	3,779				
CNX IT Index	873	640			
CNX PSE	3,044				
Mini S&P CNX Nifty Index	309,211	147,415			
Nifty Midcap 50 Index	23,639	18,445			
S&P CNX Nifty Index	868,684,582	528,831,609	321,265,217	150,916,778	52,707,150
S&P 500 Index	31,023				
All Options on Individual Equities	33,172,963	28,363,426	14,066,778	11,067,082	9,048,495
Total Options	**1,156,903,387**	**564,415,836**	**335,331,995**	**161,983,860**	**61,755,645**

NYSE-LIFFE European Derivatives Market

	2011	2010	2009	2008	2007
3-Month Eonia	15,110	85,181	135,594	31,322	
3-Month Euribor	241,950,875	248,504,960	192,859,090	228,487,462	221,411,485
3-Month Eurodollar	16,035	9,103	6,343	26,692	15,926
3-Month Euroswiss	8,233,176	7,179,251	4,768,825	8,572,662	12,219,848
3-Month Short Sterling	115,586,702	112,944,490	104,073,092	104,572,875	119,675,947
Long Gilt	34,362,932	28,525,983	23,977,779	24,717,249	27,367,489
Medium Gilt	36,307	166,521	11,455		
Short Gilt	432,744	365,824	30,680		
Japanese Government Bond	40,614	49,610	50,953	105,584	173,810
10-Year Swapnote EUR	77,825	78,536	76,200	104,460	273,961
5-Year Swapnote EUR	220,966	254,717	251,078	212,746	407,029
2-Year Swapnote EUR	357,849	392,976	452,362	703,608	512,872
US Dollar/Euro	331	1,404	829	1,394	918
Euro/US Dollar	2,949	5,206	6,588	5,124	5,087
AEX Stock Index	12,602,311	11,958,934	10,524,741	12,477,916	12,850,137
AEX Dividend Index	550	880			
Bel 20 Index	106,922	158,047	296,543	615,088	596,144
CAC 40 Stock Index 10 Euro	43,403,809	44,559,669	41,940,487	49,242,000	44,668,975
CAC 40 Dividend Index	20,643	82,139	322		
FTSE 100 Index	39,283,942	37,627,230	38,515,933	42,314,080	33,535,934
FTSE 100 Dividend Index	447,151	910,456	667,052		
FTSE Mid 250 Index	81,345	101,194	91,362	163,652	181,735
FTSE EPRA Eurozone	9,859	13,592	28,659	12,265	3,742
FTSE EPRA Europe	79,618	78,147	87,274	53,533	4,278
FTSE Eurotop 100 Index	233	737	9,882	13,907	27,352
FTSEurofirst 100	239	407	122	501	21,281
FTSEurofirst 80	52,345	107,837	186,634	473,365	397,110
MSCI Pan-Euro Index	23,077	203,263	358,168	641,354	835,603
PSI-20 Index	77,939	126,127	61,225	75,904	110,485
TOPIX	985	363			
Index F Other Bclear	1,032,135	550,503	95,287		
All Futures on Individual Equities	250,441,783	289,334,111	199,044,957		
Cocoa #7	4,079,975	3,519,409	3,218,726	3,577,010	3,319,396
Corn	402,397	240,028	149,008	112,408	94,606
Malted Barley	25,009	6,200			
Rapeseed	1,908,310	1,202,153	812,779	680,765	438,849
Robusta Coffee - 10 Tonne	3,502,508	2,789,953	2,514,457	207,443	
Skimmed Milk Powder	9	7			
Wheat	162,683	147,684	114,133	131,358	128,073
Wheat #2	5,687,888	4,374,323	1,925,916	1,464,484	980,742
White Sugar	1,497,216	1,854,156	1,852,702	1,654,446	2,091,654
Total Futures	**766,265,296**	**798,511,326**	**629,257,336**	**610,023,995**	**562,443,027**
3-Month Euribor	126,535,338	121,077,679	121,612,383	106,730,522	74,276,297
3-Month Euribor 2-Year Mid-curve	131,056	134,920	30,402		
3-Month Euribor Mid Curve	16,617,712	20,425,277	18,498,853	7,955,894	6,188,559
3-Month Short Sterling	21,575,685	26,157,563	37,876,416	59,079,440	50,747,710

NYSE-LIFFE European Derivatives Market (continued)

	2011	2010	2009	2008	2007
3-Month Sterling 2-Year Mid-curve	94,370	45,000	10,550		
3-Month Sterling Mid-curve	11,784,839	20,766,671	12,109,210	12,994,233	4,330,981
Long Gilt	2,050	184,618	384,145		
US Dollar / Euro	9,181	30,178	45,603	55,414	52,499
Euro / US Dollar (EDX)	170,392	266,086	388,488	394,315	439,811
AEX Stock Index (AEX)	25,079,752	26,158,523	24,660,898	27,534,800	26,292,719
Bel 20 (E10) Index	149	20			
Bel 20 (E2) Index	4,846	9,691	10,192	15,404	133,467
CAC 40 Index, 10 EUR	5,281,378	6,329,140	6,126,542	8,628,618	9,793,350
FTSE 100 Index (ESX)	20,341,926	23,440,064	30,155,112	29,261,814	23,700,667
Other Bclear	578,002	1,246,316	2,400,296	1,434,196	1,021,680
All Options on Individual Equities	150,562,241	175,228,607	170,870,365		
Cocoa	79,238	730,027	556,860	251,614	177,788
Corn	43,794	20,245	5,720	3,738	4,656
Malted Barley	3,100	390			
Rapeseed	408,554	271,993	79,385	134,370	50,962
Robusta Coffee - 10 Tonne	898,109	482,483	192,398	48,987	
Wheat	1,363	873	656	523	5,284
Wheat	1,298,748	1,016,600	655,099	325,464	129,365
White Sugar	17,624	22,482	50,195	224,977	254,307
Total Options	**381,519,447**	**424,045,446**	**426,754,760**	**439,705,657**	**386,582,425**

New Zealand Futures Exchange (NZFOE), New Zealand

	2011	2010	2009	2008	2007
10-Year Government Stock	260	1,742	4,329	691	664
NZ 30-Day OCR Interbank	1,780	400	20		
90-Day Bank Bill	2,018,667	1,426,513	1,484,030	1,453,947	1,638,294
NZ Electricity (Otahuhu)	537	195	6		
NZ Electricity (Benmore)	816	272	52		
Total Futures	**2,022,060**	**1,430,222**	**1,490,947**	**1,454,638**	**1,638,988**
90-Day Bank Bill	600	1,200	3,100	1,850	4,450
Total Options	**600**	**1,200**	**3,100**	**4,450**	**12,050**

NASDAQ OMX Oslo, Norway

	2011	2010	2009	2008	2007
CER Spot	38	40			
CER Forward	1,528	4,870	5,113	52,107	
EUA	41,567	40			
EUA Spot	1,122	9,818			
EUA Forward	7,307	16,732	40,850	69,624	
German Power Base (Year)	2,161	1,826	2,710	4,225	
German Power Base (Quarter)	303	554	1,002	1,212	
German Power Base (Month)	287	706	449	2,387	
German Power Base (Week)	125	235	100	895	
German Power Peak (Quarter)	10		28		
German Power Peak (Month)	220		40	31	
German Power Peak (Week)	300	20			
Nordic Power Base (Year)	79,667	82,382	118,404	128,352	
Nordic Power Base (Quarter)	287,396	408,218	307,694	422,468	
Nordic Power Base (Month)	163,672	192,260	136,195	167,644	
Nordic Power Base (Week + Day)	133,201	140,954	214,819	185,966	
Nordic Power Base (Day)	57,766	52,380			
Nordic Power Base (CfD Year)	11,428	11,561	50,148	46,458	
Nordic Power Base (CfD Month)	22,930	27,198			
Nordic Power Base (CfD Quarter)	20,864	22,729			
Nordic Power Peak (Month)	1	20		40	
Total Futures	**831,893**	**972,685**	**877,992**	**1,081,668**	
Nordic Power Base (Year)	7,642	10,531	28,104	33,182	
Nordic Power Base (Quarter)	9,210	20,978			
Total Options	**16,852**	**31,509**	**28,104**	**33,182**	

OMX Exchanges, Swedish, Finnish, Danish & Icelandic Exchanges

	2011	2010	2009	2008	2007
3-Month STIBOR	19,872,815	15,640,119	12,923,736	16,929,736	14,892,134
NIBOR-FRA	638,600				
CIBOR	15,016				
Mortgage Bond (MBF)	25,747	28,899			
Mortgage Bond Short (MBFS)	29,250				
5% Danish Mortgage Bond (5MBF)	1,925				
Policy Rate (RIBA)	4,680,389	2,114,300	1,040,006		
NASDAQ OMX Interest Rate Swap (NOIS)	124,800	3,648	1,250		
2-Year Swedish Gov't Bond Forward (R2)	2,303,865	2,950,624	2,096,471	4,049,661	3,568,792
5-Year Swedish Gov't Bond Forward (R5)	1,445,999	1,511,946	1,179,563	1,366,872	1,930,006
10-Year Swedish Gov't Bond Forward (R10)	1,339,726	1,063,189	885,565	892,169	798,640
2-Year Nordea Hypotek Bond Forward (NBHYP2)	175,208	340,514	345,156	389,973	168,119

OMX Exchanges, Swedish, Finnish, Danish & Icelandic Exchanges (continued)

	2011	2010	2009	2008	2007
5-Year Nordea Hypotek Bond Forward (NBHYP5)	216,357	290,635	202,314	186,936	118,052
2-Year Spintab Bond Forward (SPA2)	252,565	310	176,791	215,937	154,457
5-Year Spintab Bond Forward (SPA5)	250,373	477,440	240,372	226,499	178,072
2-Year Stadshypotek Bond Forward (ST2)	275,194	385,412	257,681	674,731	386,189
5-Year Stadshypotek Bond Forward (ST5)	298,374	352,728	331,842	294,279	328,507
OMX Index	37,462,177	32,427,696	33,700,054	39,307,915	31,609,782
All Futures on Individual Equities	4,012,218	2,468,839	6,718,987	15,841,312	9,013,489
Total Futures	**73,420,598**	**60,056,299**	**60,099,788**	**80,376,020**	**63,376,025**
Interest Rate	2,043,400	1,170,505	629,000	685,010	
Interest Rate	1,312,800	2,043,400	1,170,505	629,000	685,010
NIBOR-FRA	32,500				
2-Year Sewdish Government Bond Forward (R2)	14,700				
5-Year Sewdish Government Bond Forward (R5)	4,250				
10-Year Sewdish Government Bond Forward (R10)	50				
OMX Index	12,485,788	13,761,881	14,225,611	19,654,145	19,715,476
All Options on Individual Equities	**43,686,686**	**48,559,140**	**44,171,207**	**63,050,552**	**80,061,305**

Osaka Securities Exchange (OSE), Japan

	2011	2010	2009	2008	2007
Nikkei 225 Index	19,294,064	22,483,722	25,368,919	35,546,016	30,084,781
Nikkei 225 Mini	117,905,210	125,113,769	104,738,309	95,446,729	49,107,059
Nikkei 300 Index	16	148	405	35,509	81,907
US Dollar/Japanese Yen	2,906,939	1,813,592	243,611		
Euro/Japanese Yen	2,438,817	929,577	108,118		
British Pound/Japanese Yen	1,056,471	390,457	51,086		
Australian Dollar/Japanese Yen	2,652,305	1,002,638	52,858		
Swiss Franc/Japanese Yen	229,941	27,224	4,953		
Canadian Dollar/Japanese Yen	111,099	46,340	13,069		
New Zealand/Japanese Yen	312,812	118,211	7,567		
South African Rand/Japanese Yen	76,872				
Euro/US Dollar	582,463	218,219	71,516		
British Pound/US Dollar	85,917	24,566	30,241		
Australian Dollar/US Dollar	98,760				
Total Futures	**147,751,686**	**152,168,463**	**130,690,652**	**131,028,334**	**79,291,064**
Nikkei 225 Index	45,192,519	43,791,011	34,986,005	32,126,060	29,181,438
All Options on Individual Equities	1,231,796	390,805	408,752	534,954	444,149
Total Options	**46,424,315**	**44,181,816**	**35,394,757**	**32,661,014**	**29,625,747**

Oslo Stock Exchange (OSE), Norway

	2011	2010	2009	2008	2007
Forwards	2,279,603	1,460,982	1,173,476	1,637,407	2,630,772
OBX	6,468,392	8,001,664	9,041,941	9,195,919	4,755,934
Total Futures	**8,747,995**	**9,462,646**	**10,215,417**	**10,833,326**	**7,386,706**
OBX	711,566	734,458	746,589	1,460,422	1,797,651
All Options on Individual Equities	4,131,235	3,363,236	2,549,240	3,754,682	4,783,490
Total Options	**4,842,801**	**4,097,694**	**3,295,829**	**5,215,104**	**6,581,141**

Rosario Futures Exchange (ROFEX), Argentina

	2011	2010	2009	2008	2007
Wheat	3,074	1,654	267	106	405
Corn	4,635	2,622	88	208	294
Soybeans	68,583	72,183	26,047	17,421	40,000
Chicago Soybeans	4,698				
Rosafe Soybean Index (ISR)	227,596	154,872	133,712	77,766	143,824
Gold	139,207	20,869			
WTI Crude Oil	9,928				
US Dollar (EMT)	4,559				
US Dollar (DLR)	54,373,381	61,729,396	51,107,696	41,796,793	25,042,919
Euro (EC)	132,020	30,023	11,974	151,620	20
Total Futures	**54,967,681**	**62,011,935**	**51,286,802**	**42,092,168**	**25,249,072**
Soybeans	113	7,114			
Rosafe Soybean Index (ISR)	25,755	23,273	53,114	24,986	36,972
Gold	2,444				
US Dollar (DLR)	4,048	4,353	128,362	95,960	129,601
Total Options	**32,360**	**34,885**	**196,627**	**124,493**	**174,878**

Russian Trading Systems Stock Exchange (RTS), Russia

	2011	2010	2009	2008	2007
Ruble 3 Monthly Credit Interbank Mkt Moscow	141,858	123,375	17,861	6,940	591
Moscow Money Market MosPrime Overnight	6,993	9,673	8,884	10,278	
2-Year Federal Bond issued by Russian Federation	2,530,693				
4-Year Federal Bond issued by Russian Federation	4,645,995				
6-Year Federal Bond issued by Russian Federation	159,000				
AUD/USD	1,228,766	73,446			
EUR/USD	45,657,240	39,476,420	13,658,237		

Russian Trading Systems Stock Exchange (RTS), Russia (continued)

	2011	2010	2009	2008	2007
EUR/RUB	1,736,514	1,298,081	479,084		
GBP/USD	1,361,481	124,956			
USD/RUB	206,820,695	81,122,195	8,468,200		
RTS Consumer & Retail Index	8,380	1,265	1,246	9,157	100,103
RTS Index	377,845,640	224,696,733	150,019,917	87,469,405	34,228,973
RTS Oil & Gas Index	48,882	7,289	29,798	316,255	345,439
RTS Standard Index	1,197,521	2,327,517			
MICEX Index	663,411				
Russian Volatility Index	47,244				
Gas Oil	16,969			1,292	5,107
Brent Oil	18,707,384	11,127,254	7,471,665	153,438	
Diesel Fuel (Summer grades)	152,922	101,628			
Center Base Load Annual (C1)	128				
Center Base Load Quarterly (C3)	10				
Center Base Load Power (CB)	238,354	73,270			
Center Peak Load Power (CP)	113,797	39,604			
East Siberia Base Load Power	132,839	81,017			
West Siberia Base Load Power	131,773	8,962			
URAL Base Load Annual (C2)	80				
URAL Base Load Quarterly (C4)	4,020				
URAL Base Load Power (UB)	107,325	74,391			
URAL Peak Load Power (UP)	102,959	21,511			
Urals Oil	284	785	28,070	701,975	357,145
Copper	118,593	18,912			
Gold	13,018,359	5,562,423	2,903,120	5,199,919	1,632,410
Palladium	10,871	1,982	391		
Platinum	379,285	275,555	34,570		
Refined Silver	3,923,342	714,645	104,531	169,276	17,731
Sugar (Cash settled - SA)	605,513	80,809			
Sugar (Deliverable - SU)	184	2,071	12,602	6,684	1,222
Cash Settled Corn	14,041				
Cash Settled Cotton	11,282				
Cash Settled Soybean	4,710				
Cash Settled Wheat	357,917				
All Futures on Individual Equities	355,374,012	226,711,751	249,278,962	83,652,425	75,393,694
Total Futures	**1,037,627,266**	**600,216,411**	**454,465,573**	**191,981,604**	**119,622,650**
RTS Index	35,389,828	13,179,587	5,062,653	11,446,411	7,150,531
MICEX Index	6,195				
US Dollar	853,367	1,280,316	1,863,930	311,990	154,196
EUR/USD	24,332	17,522			
Gold	139,284	98,002	84,164	675,707	117,580
Platinum	20,453	13,420			
Refined Silver	40,481	21,784	1,336	8,435	
Brent Crude Oil	45,911	12,251			
All Options on Individual Equities	8,411,748	9,153,070	12,962,387	33,796,561	16,933,254
Total Options	**44,931,599**	**23,775,952**	**19,974,470**	**46,239,104**	**24,355,561**

Shanghai Metal Exchange, China

	2011	2010	2009	2008	2007
Copper	48,961,130	50,788,568	81,217,436	20,773,258	16,328,011
Aluminum	9,953,918	17,261,995	20,530,548	14,788,920	4,823,552
Lead	293,280				
Zinc	53,663,483	146,589,373	32,253,386	23,538,897	10,215,449
Steel Rebar	81,884,789	225,612,417	161,574,521		
Wire Rod	3,242	151,702	1,092,016		
Gold	7,221,758	3,397,044	3,406,233	3,890,467	
Rubber	104,286,399	167,414,912	89,035,959	46,461,103	42,191,727
Fuel Oil	1,971,141	10,682,204	45,753,969	30,810,540	12,005,094
Total Futures	**308,239,140**	**621,898,215**	**434,864,068**	**140,263,185**	**85,563,833**

Singapore Exchange (SGX), Singapore

	2011	2010	2009	2008	2007
RSS3	22,454	35,712	20,027		
TSR20 (FOB)	205,439	191,160	48,544		
Robusta Coffee	108	2,843			
Euroyen TIBOR	59,250	85,840	161,492	562,063	1,916,702
10-Year Japanese Gov't Bond	4				5
Mini Japanese Gov't Bond	759,703	741,764	694,655	831,196	1,457,309
Nikkei 225 Index	29,022,284	28,785,870	25,353,225	26,149,701	21,937,499
Nikkei 225 Index (USD)	2,695	3,010	666	3,154	10,913
Mini Nikkei 225 Index	68,298	134,449	1,857	31,640	29,378
Nikkei Stock Average Dividend Point Index	62,653	21,216			
Straits Times Index	229	436	2,916	2,734	22
Euro Stoxx 50 Index	5,139	200			
FTSE/China A50 Index	3,071,428	531,865	1	34,232	12,349

VOLUME - WORLDWIDE

Singapore Exchange (SGX), Singapore (continued)

	2011	2010	2009	2008	2007
S&P CNX Nifty Index	14,678,520	10,479,168	7,115,255	12,435,118	750,361
MSCI Hong Kong Index	100				
MSCI Singapore Index	4,358,862	3,718,450	3,947,690	4,635,517	4,012,860
MSCI Taiwan Index	17,624,091	15,576,877	15,718,096	16,913,325	13,611,314
Fuel Oil 380	1,746	6,490			
LME-SGX Copper	35,115				
LME-SGX Aluminum	16,751				
LME-SGX Zinc	33,155				
Gold	550	645,354			
Total Futures	**70,028,574**	**60,961,099**	**53,065,083**	**61,605,338**	**43,741,573**
MSCI Taiwan Index	10,695	5,400	9,901	385	16,010
MSCI Singapore Index	9,397	16,953	2,628		
Nikkei 225 Index	2,070,984	610,630	102,142	233,545	397,704
Total Options	**2,091,076**	**632,983**	**114,671**	**235,930**	**465,253**

Sydney Futures Exchange (SFE), Australia

	2011	2010	2009	2008	2007
SPI 200	12,130,237	10,061,779	9,538,554	10,174,823	8,407,052
30-Day Interbank Cash Rate	6,296,489	5,214,205	2,315,374	2,785,693	3,585,675
90-Day Bank Bills	22,391,055	17,910,061	14,435,474	20,192,284	22,682,851
3-Year Treasury Bonds	41,662,349	34,482,136	24,197,537	26,116,381	33,585,015
3-Year Interest Rate Swaps	1,980				
10-Year Treasury Bonds	15,954,349	13,454,773	10,072,494	13,188,549	19,169,641
10-Year Interest Rate Swaps	2,650	4,799	6,001		
d-cypha NSW Base Load Electricity	64,143	52,543	42,330	30,173	39,076
d-cypha QLD Base Load Electricity	49,345	38,211	28,811	30,469	36,357
d-cypha SA Base Load Electricity	4,530	2,733	1,751	2,191	4,372
d-cypha VIC Base Load Electricity	42,174	49,574	34,867	23,870	34,788
d-cypha NSW Peak Period Electricity	7,668	2,883	1,501	1,236	1,491
d-cypha QLD Peak Period Electricity	1,819	2,130	1,436	1,274	1,804
d-cypha SA Peak Period Electricity	319	28	105	251	338
d-cypha VIC Peak Period Electricity	5,476	2,831	1,774	2,538	4,089
d-cypha NSW Base $300 CAP	12,051	12,378	1,728	1,887	1,397
d-cypha QLD Base $300 CAP	5,729	4,537	2,734	1,625	902
d-cypha SA Base $300 CAP	1,185	768	232	101	260
d-cypha VIC Base $300 CAP	9,837	12,401	3,085	3,621	2,422
Fine Wool	314	128	375	698	1,828
Greasy Wool	6,996	6,377	9,971	21,612	19,629
WA Wheat	12,283				
NSW Wheat	93,940				
Eastern Australian Feed Barley	8,558				
Australian Sorghum	1,690				
Renewable Energy Certificate	15				
Total Futures	**98,767,181**	**81,315,280**	**60,696,359**	**72,580,096**	**87,595,681**
SPI 200	423,390	382,378	319,735	436,869	564,156
90-Day Bank Bills	53,602	40,840	33,146	287,103	774,472
3-Year Treasury Bond	509,638	205,816	446,182	326,323	466,507
Overnight 3-Year Treasury Bond	1,433,184	1,740,511	1,136,306	680,333	1,121,860
3-Year Bonds Intra-Day	1,249,257	1,049,240	430,590	288,288	472,047
10-Year Treasury Bonds	2,052	5,475	9,335	5,034	38,217
Overnight 10-Year Treasury Bond	2,250	2,150	2,250	1,200	19,115
NSW Wheat	160				
Total Options	**3,673,533**	**3,426,510**	**2,377,784**	**2,025,460**	**3,525,481**

Tokyo Commodity Exchange (TOCOM), Japan

	2011	2010	2009	2008	2007
Gold	16,075,145	12,198,340	11,913,502	15,163,975	18,203,194
Gold Mini	3,312,107	2,477,688	5,010,476	5,736,883	455,212
Silver	373,445	236,296	111,775	301,216	536,583
Platinum	3,455,529	4,390,452	3,617,988	6,940,348	9,169,890
Platinum Mini	287,322	308,711	413,310	119,606	
Palladium	110,163	156,946	107,829	684,682	207,867
Gasoline	2,462,261	2,509,734	2,732,376	4,054,761	7,529,706
Kerosene	900,700	1,196,729	1,026,529	1,319,014	2,350,819
Chukyo Gasoline	65,225	7,800			
Chukyo Kerosene	52,213	3,856			
Gas Oil	11,314	4,366			
Crude Oil	1,297,512	943,450	624,307	755,520	1,489,018
Rubber	3,259,984	3,130,073	3,320,088	5,914,747	7,062,252
Nikkei-TOCOM Commodity Index	7,075	71,646			
Nikkei-TOCOM Sub-Commodity Index	36				
Total Futures	**31,670,031**	**27,636,367**	**28,881,948**	**41,026,955**	**47,070,048**

Taiwan Futures Exchange, Taiwan

	2011	2010	2009	2008	2007
TAIEX (TX)	30,611,932	25,332,827	24,625,062	19,819,775	11,813,150
Mini TAIEX (MTX)	19,128,802	13,893,559	13,926,904	9,058,436	2,964,042
Taiwan 50 Index	2,503	618	888	602	506
Taiwan Stock Exchange Electronic Sector Index	1,552,291	1,092,763	1,166,622	1,356,290	1,004,603
Taiwan Stock Exchange Bank & Insurance Sector Index	2,287,601	1,257,861	1,482,264	1,285,074	909,383
MSCI Taiwan Index (MSF)	172	1,020	466	1,425	1,132
GreTai Securities Weighted Stock Index (GTF)	30,478	43,335	66,610	94,144	21,231
Taiwan Stock Exch NonFin/NonElec SubIndex (XIF)	181,233	106,768	157,613	168,534	37,197
30-Day Commercial Paper Interest Rate	27	2	13,149	114,558	36,243
Gold (GDF)	383	677	205	40,174	48,925
NT Dollar Gold (TGF)	105,458	75,218	3,342,838	5,314,069	
All Futures on Individual Equities	2,471,605	724,375			
Total Futures	**56,372,485**	**42,529,023**	**44,886,570**	**37,724,589**	**16,987,659**
TAIEX	125,767,624	95,666,916	72,082,548	92,757,254	92,585,637
TSE Electronic Sector Index	187,576	382,747	786,132	1,068,755	1,066,141
TSE Financial Sector Index	352,241	797,910	761,886	927,888	1,203,084
GreTai Securities Weighted Stock Index (GTO)	36,595	123,537	688,481	835,892	187,967
Taiwan Stock Exch NonFin/NonElec SubIndex (XIO)	46,334	118,565	741,908	891,575	186,161
MSCI Taiwan Index (MSO)	50	27,048	1,116,142	1,640,944	1,634,117
DTB-demoninated Gold (TGO)	101,708	76,873	5,821,638		
All Options on Individual Equities	130,558	70,272	8,240,390	872,880	1,299,858
Total Options	**126,622,686**	**97,263,868**	**90,239,125**	**98,995,188**	**98,162,965**

Thailand Futures Exchange, Thailand

	2011	2010	2009	2008	2007
SET 50	4,316,437	2,362,845	2,522,465	2,099,098	1,228,238
Gold, 50 Baht	1,817,483	792,960	311,591		
Gold, 10 Baht	2,171,795	178,463			
Silver	31,567				
Brent Crude Oil	3,320				
5-Year Government Bond	253	40			
3-Month BIBOR	78	1			
6-Month THBFIX	98				
All Futures on Individual Equities	1,578,092	804,156	142,837	3,838	
Total Futures	**9,919,123**	**4,138,465**	**2,976,893**	**2,102,936**	**1,228,238**
SET 50	107,993	107,317	95,504	45,684	2,428
Total Options	**107,993**	**107,317**	**95,504**	**45,684**	**2,428**

Tel-Aviv Stock Exchange (TASE), Israel

	2011	2010	2009	2008	2007
TA-25 Index	35,429	24,484	43,025	29,694	19,802
TA-Banks Index	19,496	21,524	8,435		
Shekel-Dollar Rate	105,304	336,208	51,198	80	
Shekel-Euro Rate	28,505	25,290	4,008		
Total Futures	**188,734**	**407,506**	**106,666**	**29,774**	**20,445**
TA-25 Index	87,133,824	70,573,392	62,271,157	81,483,701	94,520,236
TA-Banks Index	22,489	75,248	73,937	72,486	87,445
Shekel-Dollar Rate	10,400,167	7,927,235	8,067,320	10,596,199	9,508,185
Shekel-Euro Rate	392,139	484,415	73,937	391,882	235,452
IL GOV 5.0 01/20	262				
IL GOV 5.5 02/17	187				
All Options on Individual Equities	827,357	973,129	321,228		
Total Options	**98,776,425**	**80,033,419**	**70,807,579**	**92,544,268**	**104,351,318**

Tokyo International Financial Futures Exchange (TIFFE), Japan

	2011	2010	2009	2008	2007
3-Month Euroyen TIBOR	7,201,901	11,274,925	13,066,020	22,372,133	38,952,553
Nikkei 225 Margin	812,346	62,000			
DAX Margin	100,509	3,616			
FTSE 100 Margin	80,189	1,857			
FTSE China 25 Margin	13,112	218			
US Dollar / Japanese Yen	31,441,164	27,551,634	20,198,781	13,177,698	7,629,879
Euro / Japanese Yen	26,769,174	19,921,565	9,961,673	5,883,330	4,070,296
British pound / Japanese Yen	11,782,185	17,108,444	16,266,521	7,634,056	6,041,411
Australian Dollar / Japanese Yen	41,589,199	34,272,436	17,793,787	9,246,469	6,835,958
Swiss Franc / Japanese Yen	1,631,739	368,567	183,224	768,754	669,032
Canadian Dollar / Japanese Yen	1,156,599	927,926	467,812	1,334,653	2,005,416
New Zealand Dollar / Japanese Yen	5,781,332	2,196,138	2,097,853	4,966,753	6,330,039
South African Rand / Japanese Yen	2,138,750	1,185,379	860,162	48,086	
Norway Krone / Japanese Yen	80,369	36,144	27,956	1,948	
Hong Kong Dollar / Japanese Yen	42,391	53,830	21,825	2,014	
Sweden Krona / Japanese Yen	56,304	21,591	15,926	592	
Paland Zloty / Japanese Yen	259,632	152,485	217,530	22,335	
Chinese Yuan / Japanese Yen	31,992				
Korean Won / Japanese Yen	90,877				

VOLUME - WORLDWIDE

Tokyo International Financial Futures Exchange (TIFFE), Japan (continued)

	2011	2010	2009	2008	2007
Indian Rupee / Japanese Yen	90,019				
Euro / US Dollar	8,246,516	3,674,987	1,116,564	141,449	
British Pound / US Dollar	772,999	555,891	426,937	19,796	
British Pound / Swiss Franc	186,041	79,909	27,895	2,329	
US Dollar / Swiss Franc	497,869	145,093	75,115	11,313	
US Dollar / Canadian Dollar	178,483	111,927	45,869	3,939	
Australian Dollar / US Dollar	2,369,321	1,003,682	542,598	15,763	
Euro / Swiss Franc	522,352	82,892	20,485	1,100	
Euro / British Pound	157,660	100,441	88,194	10,453	
New Zealand Dollar / US Dollar	195,778	94,114	38,640	5,000	
Euro / Australian Dollar	355,969	208,708	24,891	2,351	
British Pound / Australian Dollar	233,642	81,296	59,698	1,087	
Total Futures	**144,866,413**	**121,277,695**	**83,645,956**	**65,675,700**	**72,535,144**
3-Month Euroyen	35,547	400	32,088	1,251,367	3,660,673
Total Options	**35,547**	**400**	**32,088**	**1,251,367**	**3,660,673**

Tokyo Grain Exchange (TGE), Japan

	2011	2010	2009	2008	2007
American Soybeans	1,199,496	1,147,425	2,320,782	910,992	1,247,786
Non-GMO Soybeans	5,431	35,749	189,020	2,899,301	12,280,932
Arabic Coffee	22,938	50,526	46,281	282,446	595,871
Azuki (Red Beans)	114,724	180,591	243,415	346,356	388,643
Corn	1,131,856	1,084,049	1,867,864	3,645,293	4,645,239
Rice	52,304				
Robusta Coffee	51	2,981	1,860	11,197	72,971
Raw Sugar	133,953	365,267	157,102	331,976	433,329
Total Futures	**2,660,753**	**2,866,588**	**4,829,183**	**8,433,346**	**19,674,560**

Tokyo Stock Exchange (TSE), Japan

	2011	2010	2009	2008	2007
10-Year Government Yen Bond	6,802,032	7,914,448	6,765,074	10,639,934	13,545,239
Mini 10-Year Government Yen Bond	7,734		46		
REIT Index	51,457	46,696	52,799	89,922	
TOPIX Stock Index	14,608,165	14,541,751	15,190,781	18,375,802	16,578,731
Mini TOPIX Stock Index	621,569	1,044,343	681,248	599,692	
TOPIX Core 30 Index	91,715	242,105	362,882	202,189	
Nikkei 225 Dividend Index	61,050	19,553			
Total Futures	**22,243,722**	**23,814,704**	**23,052,830**	**29,907,539**	**30,123,970**
TOPIX	21,342	120,040	52,523	62,045	19,555
10-Year Government Yen Bond	1,853,672	1,999,282	2,433,217	2,442,598	2,804,811
All Options on Individual Equities	601,156	834,941	662,813	88,256	145,449
Total Options	**2,476,170**	**2,954,263**	**3,148,553**	**2,592,899**	**2,969,815**

Turkish Derivatives Exchange (TurkDEX), Turkey

	2011	2010	2009	2008	2007
Cotton	8	2		11	29
Wheat	4	2	4	5,503	
Psysically Delivered Live Cattle	2				
Gold	165,729	144,965	118,347	21,641	81
US Dollar/Ounce Gold	595,495	2,523			
Base Load Electricity	32				
ISE-100 Index	9,788	8,066	6,654	2,961	1,561
ISE-30 Index	54,612,000	56,508,907	65,393,094	40,332,007	17,015,352
ISE 30 - 100 Index Spread	5,576	2,331			
US Dollar	16,028,342	7,095,340	13,687,292	13,979,082	7,832,542
Euro	1,416,367	171,375	225,314	131,210	17,067
Euro/US Dollar Cross Currency	1,453,964	12,906			
Physically Delivered US Dollar	10	146	54		
T-Benchmark	313	5,584	564	420	401
Total Futures	**74,287,630**	**63,952,177**	**79,431,343**	**54,472,835**	**24,867,033**

Warsaw Stock Exchange, Poland

	2011	2010	2009	2008	2007
WIG 20 Index	13,642,282	13,481,633	12,766,415	11,743,240	8,792,219
WIG 40 Index	29,439	32,998	30,182	25,349	15,819
CHFPLN	73,155	7,673	9,418	5,669	
EURPLN	21,885	22,625	59,438	28,600	532
USDPLN	104,450	88,777	93,382	98,219	5,517
All Futures on Individual Equities	737,742	375,496	465,757	331,646	111,457
Total Futures	**14,608,953**	**14,009,202**	**13,424,593**	**12,233,935**	**8,936,225**
WIG20 Index	897,801	675,112	396,208	326,583	405,657
Total Options	**897,801**	**675,112**	**396,208**	**326,583**	**405,733**

Wiener Borse - Derivatives Market of Vienna, Austria

	2011	2010	2009	2008	2007
ATF Index	42,764	42,254	34,664	32,408	35,043
ATX Index	284,229	266,786	219,038	156,376	108,020
AXD	60				
CeCe (5 Eastern European Indices)	15,109	22,167	13,362	59,692	89,335
All Futures on Individual Equities	4,430	4,575	6,053	6,981	11,199
Total Futures	**346,592**	**335,782**	**273,117**	**255,462**	**243,602**
ATF Index	4,994	7,588	3,993	3,236	8,117
ATX Index	23,338	26,005	14,821	22,894	28,067
All Options on Individual Equities	499,139	469,216	474,697	848,021	1,036,975
Total Options	**527,471**	**503,129**	**493,511**	**874,157**	**1,073,293**

Zhengzhou Commodity Exchange (ZCE), China

	2011	2010	2009	2008	2007
Cotton #1	139,044,152	86,955,310	8,534,688	5,400,835	2,955,235
Early Rice	5,925,454	26,854,086	1,950,083		
Methanol	316,107				
Rapeseed Oil	4,320,115	9,527,915	10,956,863	6,429,404	659,612
White Sugar	128,193,356	305,303,131	146,063,344	165,485,978	45,468,481
Strong Gluten Wheat	7,909,755	5,804,642	13,735,956	27,509,312	38,982,788
Hard White Winter Wheat	152,901	35,095	20,170	164,309	25,719
PTA	120,528,824	61,424,805	45,851,417	17,567,296	4,960,879
Total Futures	**406,390,664**	**495,904,984**	**227,112,521**	**222,557,134**	**93,052,714**

Total Worldwide Volume

	2011	2010	2009	2008	2007
Total Futures	9,110,583,338	8,539,315,985	5,859,892,391	5,444,906,611	4,573,165,703
Percent Change	6.69%	45.72%	7.62%	19.06%	41.31%
Total Options	7,742,264,165	6,772,535,597	5,569,496,199	5,259,609,949	4,862,456,753
Percent Change	14.32%	21.60%	5.89%	8.17%	20.06%
Total Futures and Options	16,852,847,503	15,311,851,582	11,429,388,590	10,704,516,560	9,435,622,456
Percent Change	10.06%	33.97%	6.77%	13.45%	29.50%

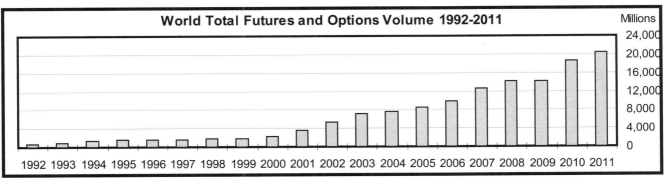

Conversion Factors

Commonly Used Agricultural Weights and Measurements

Bushel Weights:
Corn, Sorghum and Rye = 56 lbs.
Wheat and Soybeans = 60 lbs.
Canola = 50 lbs.
Barley Grain = 48 lbs.
Barley Malt = 34 lbs.
Oats = 32 lbs.

Bushels to tonnes:
Corn, Sorghum and Rye = bushels x 0.0254
Wheat and Soybeans = bushels x 0.027216
Barley Grain = bushels x 0.021772
Oats = bushels x 0.014515

1 tonne (metric ton) equals:
2204.622 lbs.
1,000 kilograms
22.046 hundredweight
10 quintals

Ethanol
1 bushel Corn = 2.75 gallons Ethanol = 18 lbs Dried Distillers Grain
1 tonne Corn = 101.0 gallons Ethanol = 661 lbs Dried Distillers Grain
1 tonne Sugar = 149.3 gallons Ethanol

1 tonne (metric ton) equals:
39.3679 bushels of Corn, Sorghum or Rye
36.7437 bushels of Wheat or Soybeans
22.046 hundredweight
45.9296 bushels of Barley Grain
68.8944 bushels of Oats
4.5929 Cotton bales (the statistical bale used by the USDA and ICAC contains a net weight of 480 pounds of lint)

Area Measurements:
1 acre = 43,560 square feet = 0.040694 hectare
1 hectare = 2.4710 acres = 10,000 square meters
640 acres = 1 square mile = 259 hectares

Yields:
Rye, Corn: bushels per acre x 0.6277 = quintals per hectare
Wheat: bushels per acre x 0.6725 = quintals per hectare
Barley Grain: bushels per acre x 0.538 = quintals per hectare
Oats: bushels per acre x 0.3587 = quintals per hectare

Commonly Used Weights

The troy, avoirdupois and apothecaries' grains are identical in U.S. and British weight systems, equal to 0.0648 gram in the metric system. One avoirdupois ounce equals 437.5 grains. The troy and apothecaries' ounces equal 480 grains, and their pounds contain 12 ounces.

Troy weights and conversions:
24 grains = 1 pennyweigh
20 pennyweights = 1 ounce
12 ounces = 1 pound
1 troy ounce = 31.103 grams
1 troy ounce = 0.0311033 kilogram
1 troy pound = 0.37224 kilogram
1 kilogram = 32.1507 troy ounces
1 tonne = 32,151 troy ounces

Avoirdupois weights and conversions:
27 11/32 grains = 1 dram
16 drams = 1 ounce
16 ounces = 1 lb.
1 lb. = 7,000 grains
14 lbs. = 1 stone (British)
100 lbs. = 1 hundredweight (U.S.)
112 lbs. = 8 stone = 1 hundredweight (British)
2,000 lbs. = 1 short ton (U.S. ton)
2,240 lbs. = 1 long ton (British ton)
160 stone = 1 long ton
20 hundredweight = 1 ton
1 lb. = 0.4536 kilogram
1 hundredweight (cwt.) = 45.359 kilograms
1 short ton = 907.18 kilograms
1 long ton = 1,016.05 kilograms

Metric weights and conversions:
1,000 grams = 1 kilogram
100 kilograms = 1 quintal
1 tonne = 1,000 kilograms = 10 quintals
1 kilogram = 2.204622 lbs.
1 quintal = 220.462 lbs.
1 tonne = 2204.6 lbs.
1 tonne = 1.102 short tons
1 tonne = 0.9842 long ton

U.S. dry volumes and conversions:
1 pint = 33.6 cubic inches = 0.5506 liter
2 pints = 1 quart = 1.1012 liters
8 quarts = 1 peck = 8.8098 liters
4 pecks = 1 bushel = 35.2391 liters
1 cubic foot = 28.3169 liters

U.S. liquid volumes and conversions:
1 ounce = 1.8047 cubic inches = 29.6 milliliters
1 cup = 8 ounces = 0.24 liter = 237 milliliters
1 pint = 16 ounces = 0.48 liter = 473 milliliters
1 quart = 2 pints = 0.946 liter = 946 milliliters
1 gallon = 4 quarts = 231 cubic inches = 3.785 liters
1 milliliter = 0.033815 fluid ounce
1 liter = 1.0567 quarts = 1,000 milliliters
1 liter = 33.815 fluid ounces
1 imperial gallon = 277.42 cubic inches = 1.2 U.S. gallons = 4.546 liters

Energy Conversion Factors

U.S. Crude OIl (average gravity)
1 U.S. barrel = 42 U.S. gallons
1 short ton = 6.65 barrels
1 tonne = 7.33 barrels

Barrels per tonne for various origins

Abu Dhabi	7.624
Algeria	7.661
Angola	7.206
Australia	7.775
Bahrain	7.335
Brunei	7.334
Canada	7.428
Dubai	7.295
Ecuador	7.580
Gabon	7.245
Indonesia	7.348
Iran	7.370
Iraq	7.453
Kuwait	7.261
Libya	7.615
Mexico	7.104
Neutral Zone	6.825
Nigeria	7.410
Norway	7.444
Oman	7.390
Qatar	7.573
Romania	7.453
Saudi Arabia	7.338
Trinidad	6.989
Tunisia	7.709
United Arab Emirates	7.522
United Kingdom	7.279
United States	7.418
Former Soviet Union	7.350
Venezuela	7.005
Zaire	7.206

Barrels per tonne of refined products:

aviation gasoline	8.90
motor gasoline	8.50
kerosene	7.75
jet fuel	8.00
distillate, including diesel	7.46

(continued above)

residual fuel oil	6.45
lubricating oil	7.00
grease	6.30
white spirits	8.50
paraffin oil	7.14
paraffin wax	7.87
petrolatum	7.87
asphalt and road oil	6.06
petroleum coke	5.50
bitumen	6.06
LPG	11.6

Approximate heat content of refined products:

(Million Btu per barrel, 1 British thermal unit is the amount of heat required to raise the temperature of 1 pound of water 1 degree F.)

Petroleum Product	Heat Content
asphalt	6.636
aviation gasoline	5.048
butane	4.326
distillate fuel oil	5.825
ethane	3.082
isobutane	3.974
jet fuel, kerosene	5.670
jet fuel, naptha	5.355
kerosene	5.670
lubricants	6.065
motor gasoline	5.253
natural gasoline	4.620
pentanes plus	4.620

Petrochemical feedstocks:

naptha less than 401*F	5.248
other oils equal to or greater than 401*F	5.825
still gas	6.000
petroleum coke	6.024
plant condensate	5.418
propane	3.836
residual fuel oil	6.287
special napthas	5.248
unfinished oils	5.825
unfractionated steam	5.418
waxes	5.537

Source: U.S. Department of Energy

Natural Gas Conversions

Although there are approximately 1,031 Btu in a cubic foot of gas, for most applications, the following conversions are sufficient:

Cubic Feet			MMBtu		
1,000	(one thousand cubic feet)	=	1 Mcf	=	1
1,000,000	(one million cubic feet)	=	1 MMcf	=	1,000
10,000,000	(ten million cubic feet)	=	10 MMcf	=	10,000
1,000,000,000	(one billion cubic feet)	=	1 Bcf	=	1,000,000
1,000,000,000,000	(one trillion cubic feet)	=	1 Tcf	=	1,000,000,000

Acknowledgments

The editors wish to thank the following for source material:

Agricultural Marketing Service (AMS)

Agricultural Research Service (ARS)

American Bureau of Metal Statistics, Inc. (ABMS)

American Forest & Paper Association (AFPA)

The American Gas Association (AGA)

American Iron and Steel Institute (AISI)

American Metal Market (AMM)

Bureau of the Census

Bureau of Economic Analysis (BEA)

Bureau of Labor Statistics (BLS)

Chicago Board of Trade (CBT)

Chicago Mercantile Exchange (CME / IMM / IOM)

Commodity Credit Corporation (CCC)

Commodity Futures Trading Commision (CFTC)

The Conference Board

Economic Research Service (ERS)

Edison Electric Institute (EEI)

Farm Service Agency (FSA)

Federal Reserve Bank of St. Louis

Fiber Economics Bureau, Inc.

Florida Department of Citrus

Food and Agriculture Organization of the United Nations (FAO)

Foreign Agricultural Service (FAS)

Futures Industry Association (FIA)

ICE Futures U.S, Canada, Europe (ICE)

International Cotton Advisory Committee (ICAC)

International Cocoa Organization (ICCO)

International Rubber Study Group (IRSG)

Johnson Matthey

Kansas City Board of Trade (KCBT)

Leather Industries of America

Minneapolis Grain Exchange (MGEX)

National Agricultural Statistics Service (NASS)

New York Mercantile Exchange (NYMEX)

Oil World

The Organisation for Economic Co-Operation and Development (OECD)

Random Lengths

The Silver Institute

The Society of the Plastics Industry, Inc. (SPI)

United Nations (UN)

United States Department of Agriculture (USDA)

Wall Street Journal (WSJ)

Aluminum

Aluminum (symbol Al) is a silvery, lightweight metal that is the most abundant metallic element in the earth's crust. Aluminum was first isolated in 1825 by a Danish chemist, Hans Christian Oersted, using a chemical process involving a potassium amalgam. A German chemist, Friedrich Woehler, improved Oersted's process by using metallic potassium in 1827. He was the first to show aluminum's lightness. In France, Henri Sainte-Claire Deville isolated the metal by reducing aluminum chloride with sodium and established a large-scale experimental plant in 1854. He displayed pure aluminum at the Paris Exposition of 1855. In 1886, Charles Martin Hall in the U.S. and Paul L.T. Heroult in France simultaneously discovered the first practical method for producing aluminum through electrolytic reduction, which is still the primary method of aluminum production today.

By volume, aluminum weighs less than a third as much as steel. This high strength-to-weight ratio makes aluminum a good choice for construction of aircraft, railroad cars, and automobiles. Aluminum is used in cooking utensils and the pistons of internal-combustion engines because of its high heat conductivity. Aluminum foil, siding, and storm windows make excellent insulators. Because it absorbs relatively few neutrons, aluminum is used in low-temperature nuclear reactors. Aluminum is also useful in boat hulls and various marine devices due to its resistance to corrosion in salt water.

Futures and options on Primary Aluminum and Aluminum Alloy are traded on the London Metal Exchange. Aluminum futures are traded on the Tokyo Commodity Exchange (TOCOM), the Osaka Mercantile Exchange (OME), and the Shanghai Futures Exchange (SHFE). The London Metals Exchange aluminum futures contracts are priced in terms of dollars were metric tons.

Prices – The London Metals Exchange spot aluminum contract opened 2011 at about $2,460 per metric ton and then moved steadily higher to $2,759 on 4/22/11. From there the price moved sharply lower to about $1,994 on 11/30/11. The contract then turned higher and ended the year at about $2,200. The 2011 close was below the average of about $2,700 seen from 2006 through mid-2008 but still at a relatively high level, well above the average of about $1500 seen during the 1990-2003 period.

Supply – World production of aluminum in 2011 rose by +8.1% to a new record high of 44.100 million metric tons. The world's largest producers of aluminum are China with 41% of world production in 2011, Russia (9%), Canada (7%), U.S. (5%), and Australia (4%). U.S. production of primary aluminum in 2011 rose +15.3% yr/yr to 1.998 million metric tons. U.S. production of aluminum from secondary sources in 2011 rose +7.9% yr/yr to 3.020 million metric tons.

Demand – World consumption of aluminum in 2001, the latest reporting year for the series, fell -4.8% yr/yr to 23.613 million metric tons, which was moderately below the record high of 24.811 million metric tons consumed in 2000. U.S. consumption of aluminum in 2011 rose +12.7% yr/yr to 3.900 million metric tons, up from the three decade low of 3.320 million metric tons in 2009.

Trade – U.S. exports in 2011 rose +10.2% yr/yr to 3.350 million metric tons, which was a new record high. U.S. imports of aluminum in 2011 rose +1.7% yr/yr to 3.670 million metric tons, down from the 2005 record high of 4.850 million metric tons. The U.S. was a net importer in 2011 and relied on imports for 13% of its consumption.

World Production of Primary Aluminum   In Thousands of Metric Tons

Year	Australia	Brazil	Canada	China	France	Germany	Norway	Russia	Spain	United Kingdom	United States	Vene-zuela	World Total
2002	1,836	1,318	2,709	4,300	463	653	1,096	3,347	380	344	2,707	605	26,100
2003	1,857	1,381	2,792	5,450	443	661	1,192	3,478	389	343	2,703	601	28,000
2004	1,890	1,460	2,590	6,670	451	668	1,320	3,590	398	360	2,516	624	29,900
2005	1,903	1,499	2,894	7,800	442	648	1,372	3,647	394	369	2,481	615	31,900
2006	1,932	1,605	3,051	9,360	442	516	1,331	3,718	349	360	2,284	610	33,900
2007	1,957	1,655	3,083	12,600	428	551	1,357	3,955	408	365	2,554	610	38,000
2008	1,974	1,661	3,120	13,200	389	606	1,358	4,190	408	326	2,658	610	39,600
2009	1,943	1,536	3,030	12,900	345	292	1,130	3,815	360	253	1,727	410	36,900
2010[1]	1,928	1,536	2,963	16,200	356	394	800	3,947	340	186	1,726	335	40,800
2011[2]	1,930	1,410	2,970	18,000		450	800	4,000			1,990	380	44,100

[1] Preliminary.   [2] Estimate.   NA = Not available.   *Source: U.S. Geological Survey (USGS)*

Production of Primary Aluminum (Domestic and Foreign Ores) in the U.S.   In Thousands of Metric Tons

Year	Jan.	Feb.	Mar.	Apr.	May	June	July	Aug.	Sept.	Oct.	Nov.	Dec.	Total
2002	210	197	220	216	228	225	238	237	227	235	232	241	2,707
2003	242	220	238	225	228	221	226	225	217	224	215	221	2,702
2004	216	202	217	209	217	204	209	210	203	211	207	211	2,516
2005	209	191	214	211	214	206	210	208	199	207	204	208	2,481
2006	197	179	198	190	197	189	192	185	183	190	188	197	2,285
2007	202	185	217	209	210	209	219	220	216	224	220	225	2,556
2008	233	219	234	228	236	224	225	222	214	217	202	204	2,658
2009	193	149	154	145	147	132	135	133	129	137	133	140	1,727
2010	142	130	146	142	148	141	146	146	143	148	144	148	1,724
2011[1]	152	140	162	162	170	167	171	172	169	175	171	177	1,988

[1] Preliminary.   *Source: U.S. Geological Survey (USGS)*

ALUMINUM

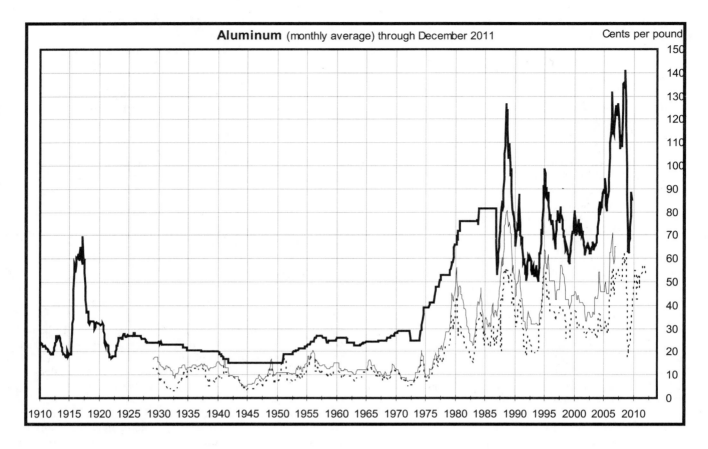

Aluminum (monthly average) through December 2011 — Cents per pound

Salient Statistics of Aluminum in the United States In Thousands of Metric Tons

Year	Net Import Reliance as a % of Apparent Consumption	Production Primary	Secondary	Primary Shipments	Recovery from Scrap Old	New	Apparent Consumption	Plate, Sheet, Foil	Rolled Structural Shapes[3]	Extruded Shapes[4]	All	Permanent Mold	Die	Sand	Total All Net Shipments	Total All Net Shipments
2001	35	2,637	2,970	9,310	1,210	1,760	6,230	4,370	512	1,550	6,580	484	873	251	1,760	8,340
2002	39	2,707	2,930	9,640	1,170	1,750	6,320	4,450	559	1,550	6,710	693	1,280	279	2,450	9,160
2003	38	2,703	2,820	9,760	1,070	1,750	7,120	4,370	531	1,670	6,580	719	1,210	285	2,400	8,970
2004	39	2,516	3,030	10,400	1,160	1,870	6,570	4,750	579	1,810	7,140	735	1,250	221	2,370	9,510
2005	41	2,481	3,030	10,461	1,080	1,950	6,530	5,330	1,080	2,090	8,500	785	1,110	289	2,290	10,790
2006	31	2,284	3,540	10,500	1,580	2,800	5,700	4,690	608	192	5,490	754	1,170	335	2,310	7,800
2007	18	2,554	3,790	9,730	1,660	2,450	5,170	5,000	888	1,580	7,468	615	1,260	315	2,230	9,698
2008	E	2,658	3,330	8,570	1,500	2,130	3,940	4,770	789	1,380	6,939	570	1,030	255	1,900	8,839
2009	10	1,727	2,710	6,810	1,260	1,570	3,320	4,050	632	1,070	5,752	371	691	160	1,230	6,982
2010[1]	14	1,726	2,800	8,300	1,250	1,550	3,460	4,700	760	1,400	6,860	570	1,000	250	1,860	8,720

[1] Preliminary. [2] To domestic industry. [3] Also rod, bar & wire. [4] Also rod, bar, tube, blooms & tubing. [5] Consists of total shipments less shipments to other mills for further fabrication. *Source: U.S. Geological Survey (USGS)*

Supply and Distribution of Aluminum in the United States In Thousands of Metric Tons

Year	Apparent Consumption	Production Primary	From Old Scrap	Imports	Exports	Inventories December 31 - Private	Government[2]	Year	Apparent Consumption	Production Primary	From Old Scrap	Imports	Exports	Inventories December 31 - Private	Government[2]
2000	7,530	3,668	1,370	3,910	1,760	1,550	----	2006	5,700	2,284	1,580	4,660	2,820	1,410	----
2001	6,230	2,637	1,210	3,740	1,590	1,300	----	2007	5,170	2,554	1,660	4,020	2,840	1,400	----
2002	6,320	2,707	1,170	4,060	1,590	1,320	----	2008	3,940	2,658	1,500	3,710	3,280	1,220	----
2003	7,120	2,703	1,070	4,130	1,540	1,400	----	2009	3,320	1,727	1,260	3,680	2,710	937	----
2004	6,570	2,516	1,160	4,720	1,820	1,470	----	2010[1]	3,460	1,726	1,250	3,610	3,040	1,010	----
2005	6,530	2,481	1,080	4,850	2,370	1,430	----	2011[2]	3,900	1,986	1,400	3,670	3,350	900	

[1] Preliminary. [2] Estimate. [3] National Defense Stockpile. [4] Less than 1/2 unit. *Source: U.S. Geological Survey (USGS)*

Aluminum Products Distribution of End-Use Shipments in the United States   In Thousands of Metric Tons

Year	Building & Construction	Consumer Durables	Containers and Packaging	Electrical	Exports	Machinery and Equipment	Trans-portation	Other	Total
2001	1,500	681	2,250	686	902	641	3,190	367	10,200
2002	1,560	722	2,260	677	1,070	616	3,410	390	10,700
2003	1,560	689	2,240	653	905	659	3,540	415	10,700
2004	1,680	713	2,310	720	930	730	3,860	416	11,400
2005	1,671	708	2,320	746	1,125	741	3,939	336	11,586
2006	1,650	746	2,320	774	1,270	762	3,930	330	11,800
2007	1,410	664	2,230	762	1,450	736	3,580	359	11,200
2008	1,180	607	2,240	700	1,490	688	2,830	334	10,100
2009	964	458	2,150	593	1,280	475	1,910	254	8,090
2010[1]	1,000	600	2,200	700	1,500	700	2,800	300	9,800

[1] Preliminary.   Source: U.S. Geological Survey (USGS)

World Consumption of Primary Aluminum   In Thousands of Metric Tons

Year	Brazil	Canada	China	France	Germany	India	Italy	Japan	Rep. of Korea	Russia	United Kingdom	United States	World Total
1992	377.1	420.4	1,253.8	730.5	1,457.1	414.3	660.0	2,271.6	397.0	1,242.0	550.0	4,616.9	18,529.5
1993	378.9	492.5	1,339.9	667.2	1,150.7	475.3	554.0	2,138.3	524.8	657.0	540.0	4,877.1	18,122.6
1994	414.1	559.0	1,500.1	736.3	1,370.3	475.0	660.0	2,344.8	603.9	470.0	570.0	5,407.1	19,670.8
1995	500.6	611.9	1,941.6	743.8	1,491.3	581.0	665.4	2,335.6	675.4	476.0	620.0	5,054.8	20,480.9
1996	497.0	619.9	2,135.3	671.7	1,355.4	584.8	585.1	2,392.6	674.3	443.8	571.0	5,348.0	20,596.4
1997	478.6	628.2	2,260.3	724.2	1,558.4	553.4	671.0	2,434.3	666.3	469.2	583.0	5,390.0	21,721.8
1998	521.4	720.6	2,425.4	733.8	1,519.0	566.5	675.4	2,082.0	505.7	489.2	579.0	5,813.6	21,797.2
1999	463.1	777.2	2,925.9	774.2	1,438.6	569.5	735.3	2,112.3	814.0	562.8	496.8	6,203.3	23,323.0
2000	513.8	798.7	3,499.1	780.4	1,490.3	602.4	780.3	2,224.9	822.6	748.4	575.5	6,079.5	24,811.4
2001[1]	550.8	759.6	3,545.4	772.9	1,590.9	558.0	770.4	2,014.0	849.6	786.2	433.3	5,117.0	23,612.8

[1] Preliminary.   Source: American Metal Market (AMM)

Salient Statistics of Recycling Aluminum in the United States

Year	Percent Recycled	New Scrap[1]	Old Scrap[2]	Recycled Metal[3]	Apparent Supply	New Scrap[1]	Old Scrap[2]	Recycled Metal[3]	Apparent Supply
		In Thousands of Metric Tons				Value in Millions of Dollars			
2000	36	2,080	1,370	3,450	9,610	3,420	2,260	5,670	15,800
2001	37	1,760	1,210	2,970	7,990	2,670	1,830	4,500	12,100
2002	36	1,750	1,170	2,930	8,070	2,510	1,680	4,190	11,500
2003	32	1,750	1,070	2,820	8,870	2,620	1,610	4,230	13,300
2004	33	1,870	1,160	3,030	9,080	3,460	2,140	5,600	16,800
2005	33	1,950	1,080	3,030	9,220	3,910	2,160	6,070	18,500
2006	39	2,290	1,260	3,540	8,190	6,160	3,380	9,540	22,000
2007	47	2,250	1,540	3,790	7,990	6,110	4,170	10,300	21,700
2008	48	1,960	1,370	3,330	6,900	5,240	3,650	8,890	18,500
2009	46	1,520	1,190	2,710	5,840	2,650	2,080	4,740	10,200

[1] Scrap that results from the manufacturing process.   [2] Scrap that results from consumer products.   [3] Metal recovered from new plus old scrap.
Source: U.S. Geological Survey (USGS)

Producer Prices for Aluminum Used Beverage Can Scrap   In Cents Per Pound

Year	Jan.	Feb.	Mar.	Apr.	May	June	July	Aug.	Sept.	Oct.	Nov.	Dec.	Average
2002	44.50	44.66	47.21	49.41	48.68	48.50	46.89	45.06	46.36	47.07	49.76	50.29	47.37
2003	50.50	52.30	52.45	49.43	50.17	49.75	49.22	49.83	47.43	50.17	52.00	53.73	50.58
2004	57.44	61.64	61.65	63.00	57.85	60.00	62.23	60.57	59.48	62.07	61.45	63.81	60.93
2005	64.80	65.79	71.91	71.40	64.75	62.23	60.05	62.96	60.40	61.76	65.25	72.90	65.35
2006	81.03	85.76	85.13	91.08	99.41	83.50	83.40	82.74	80.70	79.66	83.90	85.00	85.11
2007	89.05	89.58	90.18	93.14	93.16	87.86	85.90	80.39	76.37	79.57	82.98	79.68	85.66
2008	82.81	90.35	100.19	100.09	97.52	98.88	98.75	88.83	79.38	63.43	55.67	46.33	83.52
2009	43.70	41.42	41.91	44.00	46.80	50.64	54.27	61.62	58.00	61.43	64.42	71.16	53.28
2010	73.95	68.05	75.48	78.77	69.10	65.77	67.43	72.45	74.76	82.57	79.38	82.26	74.16
2011	86.78	89.11	90.98	96.08	94.72	940.50	90.95	86.54	83.69	78.07	75.25	73.18	157.15

Source: American Metal Market (AMM)

ALUMINUM

Average Price of Cast Aluminum Scrap (Crank Cases) in Chicago[1]   In Cents Per Pound

Year	Jan.	Feb.	Mar.	Apr.	May	June	July	Aug.	Sept.	Oct.	Nov.	Dec.	Average
2002	26.00	27.47	28.95	30.00	30.00	30.00	30.00	29.64	28.00	28.00	28.00	28.00	28.67
2003	28.10	30.00	30.00	29.00	29.00	27.90	26.68	26.00	26.00	26.00	26.00	26.00	27.56
2004	30.00	31.26	36.00	36.00	33.00	29.00	29.00	29.00	29.00	29.00	29.00	29.00	30.77
2005	29.00	29.00	31.61	33.00	31.33	28.00	28.00	28.00	28.00	28.00	28.00	39.71	30.14
2006	42.50	42.50	43.80	47.50	47.50	55.91	46.48	45.46	44.50	46.45	51.15	51.10	47.07
2007	52.50	52.50	54.00	55.50	55.50	53.07	52.50	52.50	51.34	50.50	50.50	50.50	52.58
2008	50.50	52.00	58.50	62.09	60.12	57.50	60.00	60.60	53.69	35.76	26.94	18.45	49.68
2009	17.50	17.50	22.27	22.50	22.50	22.50	24.55	27.50	37.50	37.50	37.50	42.24	27.63
2010	45.39	47.50	48.80	55.23	51.50	43.41	42.50	47.27	47.50	51.31	52.50	47.50	48.37
2011	48.75	52.50	52.50	52.50	52.50	52.50	56.00	57.50	56.93	54.50	54.70	52.45	53.61

[1] Dealer buying prices.   Source: American Metal Market (AMM)

Aluminum Exports of Crude Metal and Alloys from the United States   In Thousands of Metric Tons

Year	Jan.	Feb.	Mar.	Apr.	May	June	July	Aug.	Sept.	Oct.	Nov.	Dec.	Total
2002	17.1	15.2	15.6	16.4	19.4	18.3	15.0	15.5	17.5	19.8	19.4	16.4	205.6
2003	14.3	14.8	14.5	16.9	17.0	17.8	16.5	20.4	18.7	22.9	20.4	19.7	213.9
2004	18.2	20.8	24.3	25.2	25.1	27.6	23.7	23.0	28.3	26.9	28.0	27.4	298.5
2005	26.5	23.4	24.3	27.0	28.9	29.6	25.9	33.1	27.2	29.5	29.6	23.9	328.9
2006	40.0	26.0	30.5	29.4	38.8	25.3	23.7	32.0	26.1	25.8	27.0	22.0	346.6
2007	32.1	27.1	27.0	28.6	33.8	31.1	26.4	30.3	28.5	29.9	29.6	24.5	348.9
2008	30.8	26.8	26.4	30.4	28.4	27.6	25.9	26.4	27.4	25.3	17.3	15.6	308.3
2009	15.9	15.9	12.7	14.8	24.7	24.9	24.6	24.7	24.4	28.0	26.4	25.1	262.1
2010	20.2	22.0	22.4	16.8	20.5	25.6	22.8	24.5	35.2	24.4	26.0	23.5	283.9
2011[1]	25.5	24.2	30.2	34.6	26.1	23.1	25.7	23.2	23.2	24.3	29.5		315.9

[1] Preliminary.   Source: U.S. Geological Survey (USGS)

Aluminum General Imports of Crude Metal and Alloys into the United States   In Thousands of Metric Tons

Year	Jan.	Feb.	Mar.	Apr.	May	June	July	Aug.	Sept.	Oct.	Nov.	Dec.	Total
2002	272.0	205.0	223.0	221.0	221.0	263.0	228.0	279.0	235.0	196.0	264.0	186.0	2,793.0
2003	215.0	246.0	350.0	202.0	265.0	261.0	233.0	194.0	215.0	210.0	233.0	243.0	2,867.0
2004	211.0	288.0	248.0	254.0	282.0	309.0	297.0	225.0	279.0	286.0	272.0	294.0	3,245.0
2005	334.0	289.0	262.0	372.0	372.0	324.0	324.0	264.0	282.0	298.0	240.0	299.0	3,660.0
2006	348.0	247.0	289.0	353.0	315.0	298.0	249.0	315.0	289.0	259.0	233.0	241.0	3,436.0
2007	251.0	258.0	238.0	259.0	220.0	254.0	236.0	266.0	268.0	244.0	238.0	215.0	2,947.0
2008	240.0	208.0	247.0	238.0	237.0	263.0	227.0	204.0	229.0	249.0	219.0	233.0	2,794.0
2009	270.0	204.0	333.0	233.0	292.0	200.0	299.0	216.0	212.0	207.0	211.0	217.0	2,894.0
2010	238.0	209.0	230.0	257.0	233.0	232.0	223.0	207.0	224.0	203.0	209.0	179.0	2,644.0
2011[1]	211.0	212.0	232.0	220.0	285.0	263.0	220.0	241.0	263.0	243.0	192.0		2,816.7

[1] Preliminary.   Source: U.S. Geological Survey (USGS)

Average Open Interest of Aluminum Futures in New York   In Contracts

Year	Jan.	Feb.	Mar.	Apr.	May	June	July	Aug.	Sept.	Oct.	Nov.	Dec.
2002	3,277	2,744	2,738	2,250	2,397	2,902	3,903	4,618	4,643	5,139	8,057	10,479
2003	9,573	9,163	6,960	7,190	7,686	8,529	8,402	8,445	7,655	7,283	8,434	9,427
2004	8,815	7,384	9,666	10,575	10,363	10,370	9,626	10,287	10,292	10,035	9,706	8,879
2005	8,183	8,487	7,464	6,612	5,654	5,061	4,359	3,223	3,225	2,676	2,232	1,670
2006	1,066	708	482	1,110	948	816	1,068	1,125	1,116	865	994	950
2007	608	614	491	450	415	368	329	276	237	194	156	132
2008	0	0	0	0	0	0	0	0	0	0	0	0

Source: CME Group; New York Mercantile Exchange (NYMEX)

Volume of Trading of Aluminum Futures in New York   In Contracts

Year	Jan.	Feb.	Mar.	Apr.	May	June	July	Aug.	Sept.	Oct.	Nov.	Dec.	Total
2002	2,774	4,635	4,924	2,593	5,388	5,389	8,953	4,194	2,571	7,328	16,185	9,066	74,000
2003	12,565	9,625	8,163	5,440	10,567	8,463	11,797	9,451	5,119	6,222	8,536	11,542	107,490
2004	9,425	9,621	9,548	9,770	5,438	5,453	5,280	2,063	5,533	4,822	2,525	2,691	72,169
2005	5,294	2,829	3,244	2,627	2,613	1,832	1,247	902	1,625	623	3,135	2,520	28,491
2006	633	245	1,343	1,558	210	471	1,046	1,546	662	323	842	270	9,149
2007	94	332	82	28	2	56	84	19	25	0	1	0	723
2008	0	0	0	0	0	0	0	0	0	0	0	0	

Source: CME Group; New York Mercantile Exchange (NYMEX)

Antimony

Antimony (symbol Sb) is a lustrous, extremely brittle and hard crystalline semi-metal that is silvery white in its most common allotropic form. Antimony is a poor conductor of heat and electricity. In nature, antimony has a strong affinity for sulfur and for such metals as lead, silver, and copper. Antimony is primarily a byproduct of the mining, smelting and refining of lead, silver, and copper ores. There is no longer any mine production of antimony in the U.S.

The most common use of antimony is in antimony trioxide, a chemical that is used as a flame retardant in textiles, plastics, adhesives and building materials. Antimony trioxide is also used in battery components, ceramics, bearings, chemicals, glass, and ammunition.

Prices – Antimony prices in 2011 rose by 63.5% to a new record high of 671.10 cents per pound. Antimony prices in 2011 were more than ten times the 35-year low price of 66.05 cents per pound posted as recently as 1999. Bullish factors included stronger U.S. and global economic growth in 2011, the weak dollar, and tight supplies.

Supply – World mine production of antimony in 2011 was almost the same as in 2010 at 169,000 metric tons, but still down from the 2008 record high of 182,000 metric tons. China accounted for 89% of world antimony production in 2011. After China, the only significant producers were Bolivia (3.0% of world production) and South Africa (2.0%). U.S. secondary production of antimony in 2011 fell by -2.0% yr/yr to 3,450 metric tons.

Demand – U.S. industrial consumption of antimony in 2010 (latest data available) rose +31.68% to 8,910 metric tons. Of the consumption in the U.S. in 2008, 40% was used for non-metal products, 36% was used for flame-retardants, and 25% was used for metal products.

Trade – The total U.S. gross weight of imports of antimony ore in 2010 (latest data available) rose +14.9% to 308 metric tons. The antimony content of that ore rose by +8.4% to 181 metric tons. The gross weight of U.S. imports of antimony oxide in 2010 rose by +36.1% to 24,900 metric tons. U.S. exports of antimony oxide in 2011 fell by -7.8% to 2,350 metric tons.

World Mine Production of Antimony (Content of Ore)   In Metric Tons

Year	Australia	Bolivia	Canada	China[2]	Guat-emala	Kyrgy-zstan	Mexico[3]	Peru[4]	Russia	South Africa	Thailand	Turkey	World Total
2008	1,500	3,905	132	166,000	----	10	----	531	3,500	3,370	----	1,300	182,000
2009	1,000	2,990	66	140,000	----	10	----	530	3,500	2,800	----	1,200	154,000
2010[1]	1,000	4,980	1,000	150,000	----	10	----	530	3,000	3,000	----	1,500	167,000
2011[2]		5,000		150,000					3,000	3,000			169,000

[1] Preliminary.   [2] Estimate.   [3] Includes antimony content of miscellaneous smelter products.   [4] Recoverable.
Source: U.S. Geological Survey (USGS)

Salient Statistics of Antimony in the United States   In Metric Tons

Year	Avg. Price Cents/lb. C.i.f. U.S. Ports	Production[3] Primary[2] Mine	Production[3] Primary[2] Smelter	Secondary (Alloys)[2]	Imports for Consumption Ore Gross Weight	Imports for Consumption Ore Antimony Content	Oxide (Gross Weight)	Exports (Oxide)	Industry Stocks, December 31[3] Metallic	Industry Stocks, December 31[3] Oxide	Industry Stocks, December 31[3] Sulfide	Industry Stocks, December 31[3] Other	Industry Stocks, December 31[3] Total
2007	257.3	W	W	3,480	313	226	26,100	1,980	470	1,410	W	18	1,900
2008	279.5	----	W	3,180	286	164	26,200	2,200	217	916	W	357	1,490
2009[1]	235.6	----	W	3,020	268	167	18,300	2,060	155	900	W	363	1,420
2010[2]	401.2	----	W	3,520	308	181	24,900	2,550	129	1,060	W	372	1,560

[1] Preliminary.   [2] Estimate.   [3] Antimony content.   [4] Including primary antimony residues & slag.   W = Withheld proprietary data.
Source: U.S. Geological Survey (USGS)

Industrial Consumption of Primary Antimony in the United States   In Metric Tons (Antimony Content)

Year	Metal Products Ammu-nition	Metal Products Anti-monial Lead[3]	Metal Products Sheet & Pipe[4]	Metal Products Bearing Metal & Bearings	Metal Products Solder	Metal Products Products	Flame Retardants Plastics	Flame Retardants Total	Non-Metal Products Ceramics & Glass	Non-Metal Products Pigments	Non-Metal Products Plastics	Non-Metal Products Total	Grand Total
2007	W	W	W	21	71	2,520	2,710	3,580	231	329	W	3,500	9,590
2008	W	W	W	18	54	1,690	2,290	3,190	259	448	W	2,680	8,140
2009	W	W	W	14	44	2,000	1,820	2,330	W	403	W	2,430	6,770
2010[1]	W	W	W	26	34	2,190	2,610	3,180	W	399	W	3,540	8,910

[1] Preliminary.   [2] Estimated coverage based on 77% of the industry.   W = Withheld proprietary data.   *Source: U.S. Geological Survey (USGS)*

Average Price of Antimony[1] in the United States   In Cents Per Pound

Year	Jan.	Feb.	Mar.	Apr.	May	June	July	Aug.	Sept.	Oct.	Nov.	Dec.	Average
2008	257.27	275.29	281.23	281.23	287.42	292.57	294.84	294.84	294.84	294.84	294.84	294.84	287.00
2009	294.84	294.84	202.98	198.35	200.77	212.06	235.57	265.46	276.69	278.14	292.57	277.04	252.44
2010	286.41	299.37	303.07	378.70	417.80	392.26	406.90	440.56	470.86	476.28	505.76	547.72	410.47
2011	609.29	651.09	712.14	765.95	718.79	696.68	635.94	635.04	683.64	700.48	652.50	591.71	671.10

[1] Prices are for antimony metal (99.65%) merchants, minimum 18-ton containers, c.i.f. U.S. Ports.   *Source: American Metal Market (AMM)*

Apples

The apple tree is the common name of trees from the rose family, Rosaceae, and the fruit that comes from them. The apple tree is a deciduous plant and grows mainly in the temperate areas of the world. The apple tree is believed to have originated in the Caspian and Black Sea area. Apples were the favorite fruit of the ancient Greeks and Romans. The early settlers brought apple seeds with them and introduced them to America. John Champman, also known as Johnny Appleseed, was responsible for extensive planting of apple trees in the Midwestern United States.

Prices – The average monthly price of apples received by growers in the U.S.in 2011 rose by +8.2% yr/yr to 33.8 cents per pound.

Supply – World apple production in the 2011-12 marketing year rose +4.5% yr/yr to 65.228 million metric tons. The world's largest apple producers in 2011-12 were China (with 53.7% of world production), the European Union (18.1%), the U.S. (6.5%), and Turkey (4.1%). U.S. apple production in 2011-12 rose 1.1% to 4.227, down from the 7-year high of 4.686 million metric tons in 2004-05 and far above the 2-decade low of 3.798 million metric tons posted in 2002-03.

Demand – The utilization breakdown of the 2010 apple crop showed that 68.3% of apples were for fresh consumption, 14.5% for juice and cider, 11.3% for canning, 2.0% for frozen apples, and 1.8% for dried apples. U.S. per capita apple consumption in 2009 was 16.4 pounds.

World Production of Apples[3], Fresh (Dessert & Cooking) In Thousands of Metric Tons

Year	Argentina	Canada	Chile	China	European Union	Japan	Mexico	New Zealand	Russia	South Africa	Turkey	United States	World Total
2006-07	1,047	403	1,250	26,059	11,134	832	510	425	1,250	710	2,000	4,414	54,418
2007-08	980	446	1,350	24,800	10,295	840	505	436	1,300	749	2,458	4,103	53,080
2008-09	933	427	1,280	29,800	12,655	911	512	457	1,115	747	2,600	4,327	60,550
2009-10	830	413	1,370	31,681	12,021	892	561	439	1,230	781	2,750	4,288	62,342
2010-11[1]	1,040	347	1,506	33,263	10,889	810	585	480	910	790	2,500	4,184	62,407
2011-12[2]	850	360	1,500	35,000	11,834	850	605	475	955	800	2,700	4,227	65,228

[1] Preliminary.   [2] Estimate.   NA = Not available.   *Source: Foreign Agricultural Service, U.S. Department of Agriculture (FAS-USDA)*

Salient Statistics of Apples[2] in the United States

	-- Production --		- Growers Prices -		----------- Utilization of Quantities Sold -------------						Avg. Farm		------ Foreign Trade[4] ------			Fresh Per Capita
							---------------- Processed[5] ----------------						---- Domestic ----			
			Fresh Cents/ lb.	Processing $/ton					Juice &		Price Cents/	Farm Value	Exports Fresh	Imports Fresh		Consumption
Year	Total	Utilized			Fresh	Canned	Dried	Frozen	Cider	Other[3]	lb.	Million $		Dried[5] & Dried[5]	Fresh	Lbs.
			---------------------------- Millions of Pounds ----------------------------									----- Metric Tons -----			
2005	9,667	9,567	24.2	106.0	6,097	1,164	191	259	1,695	64	17.3	1,675.1	654.1	27.4	198.5	16.7
2006	9,823	9,730	31.6	129.0	6,309	1,167	253	272	1,550	61	22.7	2,213.2	652.8	32.9	255.3	17.7
2007	9,089	9,045	38.3	190.0	6,077	1,091	204	258	1,257	60	28.8	2,608.2	681.1	31.7	238.4	16.4
2008	9,633	9,540	30.1	198.0	6,274	1,253	213	211	1,349	112	23.2	2,599.5	780.9		164.9	15.9
2009	9,705	9,453	31.4	132.0	6,314	1,158	161	236	1,389	55	23.1	2,187.0	808.3		155.8	16.4
2010[1]	9,302	9,223	31.0	183.0	6,297	1,043	166	181	1,336	69	24.1	2,220.8	780.3		153.9	

[1] Preliminary.   [2] Commercial crop.   [3] Mostly crushed for vinegar, jam, etc.   [4] Year beginning July.   [5] Fresh weight basis.
NA = Not available.   Source: Economic Research Service, U.S. Department of Agriculture (ERS-USDA)

Price of Apples Received by Growers (for Fresh Use) in the United States In Cents Per Pound

Year	Jan.	Feb.	Mar.	Apr.	May	June	July	Aug.	Sept.	Oct.	Nov.	Dec.	Average
2006	21.7	20.6	19.8	19.3	18.9	22.9	42.3	35.9	42.0	36.2	36.1	31.0	28.9
2007	29.9	29.7	29.2	28.1	26.9	29.6	30.6	34.4	40.2	37.9	40.3	35.0	32.7
2008	35.5	34.8	34.4	33.8	36.2	41.2	44.6	53.7	50.6	42.5	36.0	29.3	39.4
2009	27.2	23.7	21.5	20.4	18.7	18.1	17.2	23.8	35.7	31.2	33.3	27.5	24.9
2010	29.0	28.9	29.5	29.7	30.9	30.8	29.9	29.1	36.5	35.7	35.3	29.3	31.2
2011[1]	30.0	28.5	29.2	26.6	25.9	26.3	28.9	43.4	48.0	43.4	38.3	36.7	33.8

[1] Preliminary.   *Source: Economic Research Service, U.S. Department of Agriculture (ERS-USDA)*

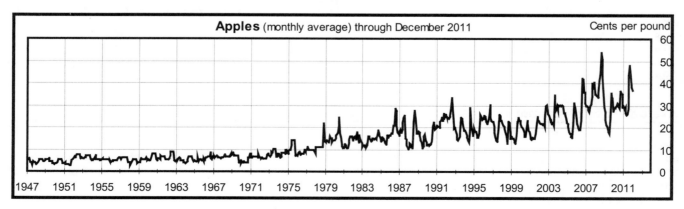

Apples (monthly average) through December 2011   Cents per pound

Arsenic

Arsenic (symbol As) is a silver-gray, extremely poisonous, semi-metallic element. Arsenic, which is odorless and flavorless, has been known since ancient times, but it wasn't until the Middle Ages that its poisonous characteristics first became known. Metallic arsenic was first produced in the 17th century by heating arsenic with potash and soap. Arsenic is rarely found in nature in its elemental form and is generally recovered as a by-product of ore processing. Recently, small doses of arsenic have been found to put some forms of cancer into remission. It can also help thin blood. Homoeopathists have successfully used undetectable amounts of arsenic to cure stomach cramps.

The U.S. does not produce any arsenic and instead imports all its consumption needs for arsenic metals and compounds. More than 95 percent of the arsenic consumed in the U.S. is in compound form, mostly as arsenic trioxide, which in turn is converted into arsenic acid. Production of chromated copper arsenate, a wood preservative, accounts for about 90% of the domestic consumption of arsenic trioxide. Three companies in the U.S. manufacture chromate copper arsenate. Another company used arsenic acid to produce an arsenical herbicide. Arsenic metal is used to produce nonferrous alloys, primarily for lead-acid batteries.

One area where there is increased consumption of arsenic is in the semiconductor industry. Very high-purity arsenic is used in the production of gallium arsenide. High speed and high frequency integrated circuits that use gallium arsenide have better signal reception and lower power consumption. An estimated 30 metric tons per year of high-purity arsenic is used in the production of semiconductor materials.

In the early 2000's, as much as 88% of U.S. arsenic production was used for wood preservative treatments, so the demand for arsenic was closely tied to new home construction, home renovation, and deck construction. However, the total demand for arsenic in 2004 dropped by 69% from 2003, and due to arsenic's toxicity and tighter environmental regulation; only 65% of that much smaller amount was used for wood preservative treatments. Since then the specific percentage used for wood preservative treatments is no longer available.

Supply – World production of white arsenic (arsenic trioxide) in 2011 fell by -1.5% to 52,000 metric tons. The world's largest producer is China with about 48% of world production, followed by Chile with 22% of world production, Peru with 9%, Russia with 3%, and Belgium with 2%. China's production of arsenic use to be fairly constant at about 40,000 metric tons per year but that has dropped to about 25,000 to 30,000 in the last eight years. The U.S. supply of arsenic in 2011 fell by -25.3% to a nine decade low of 3,960 metric tons.

Demand – U.S. demand for arsenic in 2011 fell by -31.7% to a ten decade low of 3,290 metric tons. The use for arsenic is no longer available but in 2004 (latest data) about 65% was for wood preservatives, 10% was for non-ferrous alloys and electric usage, 10% was for glass, and 3% was for other uses.

Trade – U.S. imports of trioxide arsenic in 2010 (latest data available) fell by -3.4% to a record low of 5,920 metric tons. U.S. exports of trioxide arsenic in 2010 rose by +35.8% to 481 metric tons, but still far below the record high of 3,270 metric tons in 2005.

World Production of White Arsenic (Arsenic Trioxide)   In Metric Tons

Year	Belgium	Bolivia	Canada[4]	Chile	China	France	Germany	Mexico	Namibia[3]	Peru	Philip-pines	Russia	World Total
2004	1,000	168	250	11,500	30,000	----	----	1,829	----	3,037	----	1,500	57,800
2005	1,000	120	250	11,700	30,000	----	----	1,664	----	3,150	----	1,500	60,000
2006	1,000	120	----	11,700	30,000	----	----	1,595	----	4,399	----	1,500	60,900
2007	1,000	----	----	11,400	25,000	----	----	1,600	----	4,321	----	1,500	55,400
2008	1,000	74	----	10,000	25,000	----	----	513	----	4,822	----	1,500	53,400
2009	1,000	115	----	11,000	25,000	----	----	500	----	4,850	----	1,500	54,100
2010[1]	1,000	155	----	11,000	25,000	----	----	----	----	4,500	----	1,500	52,800
2011[2]	1,000			11,500	25,000					4,500		1,500	52,000

[1] Preliminary.   [2] Estimate.   [3] Output of Tsumeb Corp. Ltd. only.   [4] Includes low-grade dusts that were exported to the U.S. for further refining.
Source: U.S. Geological Survey (USGS)

Salient Statistics of Arsenic in the United States   (In Metric Tons -- Arsenic Content)

	---- Imports ----		Industry Stocks Jan. 1	Total	Apparent Demand	Industry Stocks Dec. 31	Agricul-tural Chem-icals	Glass	Wood Preserv-atives	Non-Ferrous Alloys & lectric	Other	Total	Trioxide Mexican	Metal Chinese	Imports Trioxide[3]	Exports
Year	Metal	pounds Com-											-- Cents/Pound --			
2004	872	6,150	----	7,022	6,800	----	----	650	4,450	650	200	6,800	32	88	8,090	220
2005	812	8,330	----	9,142	5,870	----	----	NA	NA	NA	NA	5,870	67	95	11,000	3,270
2006	1,070	9,430	----	10,500	7,450	----	----	----	----	----	----	7,450	NA	62	12,400	3,060
2007	759	7,010	----	7,769	5,280	----	----	----	----	----	----	5,280	----	122	9,220	2,490
2008	376	4,810	----	5,186	4,130	----	----	----	----	----	----	4,130	----	125	6,320	1,050
2009	438	4,660	----	5,098	4,740	----	----	----	----	----	----	4,740	----	121	6,130	354
2010[1]	769	4,530	----	5,299	4,820	----	----	----	----	----	----	4,820	----	72	5,920	481
2011[2]	410	3,550	----	3,960	3,290							3,290		70		

[1] Preliminary.   [2] Estimate.   [3] For Consumption.   *Source: U.S. Geological Survey (USGS)*

Barley

Barley is the common name for the genus of cereal grass and is native to Asia and Ethiopia. Barley is an ancient crop and was grown by the Egyptians, Greek, Romans and Chinese. Barley is now the world's fourth largest grain crop, after wheat, rice, and corn. Barley is planted in the spring in most of Europe, Canada and the United States. The U.S. barley crop year begins June 1. It is planted in the autumn in parts of California, Arizona and along the Mediterranean Sea. Barley is hardy and drought resistant and can be grown on marginal cropland. Salt-resistant strains are being developed for use in coastal regions. Barley grain, along with hay, straw, and several by-products are used for animal feed. Barley is used for malt beverages and in cooking. Barley, like other cereals, contains a large proportion of carbohydrate (67%) and protein (12.8%). Barley futures are traded on the ICE Futures Canada (ICE) exchange, the NYSE-LIFFE exchange in Paris, the Budapest Stock Exchange (BSE), the Multi Commodity Exchange of India (MCX), and the National Commodity & Derivatives Exchange of India.

Prices – The monthly average price for all barley received by U.S. farmers in the 2011-12 marketing year (through January 2012) rose by +35.4% yr/yr to $5.27 per bushel.

Supply – World barley production in the 2011-12 marketing year rose +8.8% yr/yr to 134.042 million metric tons. The world's largest barley crop of 179.038 million metric tons occurred in 1990-91. The world's largest barley producers are the European Union with 39.0% of world production in 2011-12, Russia (12.6%), Ukraine (6.7%), Australia (6.3%), Canada (5.8%), Turkey (4.9%), and the U.S. (2.5%).

U.S. barley production in the 2011-12 marketing year fell by -13.6% yr/yr to 155.780 million bushels and that is less than 40% of the record U.S. barley crop of 608.532 million bushels seen in 1986-87. U.S. farmers harvested -9.2% yr/yr fewer acres in 2011-12 at 2.239 million acres, not much less than the 2006-07 level of 2.951 million acres which was the lowest acreage since 1885. Barley yield in 2011-12 fell -4.8% yr/yr to 69.6 bushels per acre, down from last year's record high yield of 73.1 bushels per acre. Ending stocks for the 2011-12 marketing year fell -49.5% to 45.13 million bushels, a new record low.

Demand – U.S. total barley disappearance in 2011-12 fell -2.7% yr/yr to 210.0 million bushels. About 77.0% of barley is used for food and alcoholic beverages, 20.0% for animal feed, and 3.0% for seed.

Trade – World exports of barley in 2011-12 rose +11.7% yr/yr to 17.015 million metric tons. The largest world exporters of barley in 2011-12 were Australia with 21.2% of world exports, the European Union with 16.5%, Canada with 5.9%, and the U.S. with only 1.2%. The single largest importer of barley is Saudi Arabia with 7.500 million metric tons of imports in 2011-12, which is about 45.7% of total world imports.

World Barley Supply and Demand   In Thousands of Metric Tons

	------------------------- Exports -------------------------					-------- Imports --------			-------- Utilization --------		------ Ending Stocks ------		
Year	Aus- tralia	Can- ada	European Union	Total Non-US	United States	Total	Saudi Arabia	Unac- counte	Total	Russia	United States	Total	Can- ada	United States	Total
2002-03	2,159	304	6,102	15,754	552	16,306	7,650	225	16,496	15,500	5,179	136,881	1,475	1,510	27,499
2003-04	6,104	1,937	986	14,452	384	14,836	5,700	444	14,720	18,600	4,990	145,345	2,102	2,619	23,413
2004-05	4,481	1,476	4,240	16,199	771	16,970	6,500	530	16,581	16,500	5,672	143,675	3,435	2,796	33,010
2005-06	5,231	1,876	2,587	17,171	357	17,528	7,100	660	16,993	15,500	4,570	140,424	3,289	2,350	28,087
2006-07	1,927	1,337	4,366	14,113	528	14,641	6,200	350	14,665	16,400	4,596	143,441	1,491	1,500	21,444
2007-08	3,377	2,947	3,888	17,693	901	18,594	8,000	455	18,182	15,050	4,324	134,519	1,568	1,485	20,418
2008-09	3,278	1,618	2,374	18,045	158	18,203	7,700		17,876	17,100	5,127	143,639	2,843	1,932	31,375
2009-10	3,846	1,203	2,389	17,125	152	17,277	7,200		16,770	16,650	4,604	144,590	2,583	2,515	37,451
2010-11[1]	4,088	1,052	4,594	15,053	181	15,234	6,200		15,265	9,500	4,537	134,372	1,441	1,945	24,664
2011-12[2]	3,600	1,000	2,800	16,815	200	17,015	7,500		16,415	14,300	4,354	136,007	951	983	21,949

[1] Preliminary.   [2] Estimate.   *Source: Foreign Agricutural Service, U.S. Department of Agriculture (FAS-USDA)*

World Production of Barley   In Thousands of Metric Tons

Year	Australia	Belarus	Canada	China	European Union	India	Iran	Kazak- hstan	Russia	Turkey	Ukraine	United States	World Total
2002-03	3,865	1,681	7,489	3,322	58,168	1,420	3,085	2,209	18,738	7,200	10,364	4,940	134,325
2003-04	10,387	1,800	12,164	2,717	55,818	1,410	2,908	2,154	18,003	6,900	6,833	6,059	142,246
2004-05	7,740	2,000	12,557	3,222	64,085	1,300	2,940	1,388	17,180	7,400	11,084	6,091	152,250
2005-06	9,483	1,864	11,678	3,400	54,752	1,200	2,857	1,528	15,791	7,600	8,975	4,613	136,241
2006-07	4,257	1,831	9,573	3,115	56,220	1,220	2,956	1,953	18,155	7,500	11,341	3,923	137,118
2007-08	7,160	1,911	10,984	2,785	57,545	1,330	3,104	2,441	15,663	6,000	5,981	4,575	133,250
2008-09	7,997	2,212	11,781	2,823	65,509	1,200	1,547	2,059	23,148	5,700	12,612	5,230	155,232
2009-10	7,865	2,123	9,517	2,318	62,149	1,690	3,446	2,519	17,881	6,500	11,833	4,949	150,917
2010-11[1]	8,145	1,966	7,605	2,500	53,028	1,350	3,500	1,313	8,350	5,900	8,484	3,925	123,247
2011-12[2]	8,500	1,800	7,760	2,600	52,254	1,570	3,000	2,593	16,935	6,500	9,000	3,392	134,042

[1] Preliminary.   [2] Estimate.   *Source: Foreign Agricutural Service, U.S. Department of Agriculture (FAS-USDA)*

Barley Acreage and Prices in the United States

Crop Year Beginning June 1	Acreage 1,000 Acres Planted	Acreage 1,000 Acres Harvested for Grain	Yield Per Harvested Acre -- Bushels --	Received by Farmers[3] All	Received by Farmers[3] Feed[4]	Received by Farmers[3] Malting[4]	Portland No. 2 Western	National Average Loan Rate	Target Price	Put Under Support (mil. Bu.)	Percent of Production
2004-05	4,527	4,021	69.6	2.46	1.76	2.79	2.39	1.85	2.24	8.3	3.0
2005-06	3,875	3,269	64.8	2.54	1.89	2.80	2.44	1.85	2.24	12.0	5.7
2006-07	3,452	2,951	61.0	2.90	2.72	2.98	4.08	1.85	2.24	9.3	5.1
2007-08	4,018	3,502	60.0	4.14	4.42	4.00	5.71	1.85	2.24	4.4	2.1
2008-09	4,246	3,779	63.6	5.23	3.61	5.56	5.29	1.85	2.24	6.8	2.9
2009-10	3,567	3,113	73.0	4.58	2.62	4.95	NQ	1.85	2.24	----	----
2010-11[1]	2,872	2,465	73.1	3.90	3.35	4.07	NQ				
2011-12[2]	2,559	2,239	69.6	5.27	4.81	5.36	NQ				

[1] Preliminary. [2] Estimate. [3] Excludes support payments. *Source: Economic Research Service, U.S. Department of Agriculture (ERS-USDA)*

Salient Statistics of Barley in the United States   In Millions of Bushels

Crop Year Beginning June 1	Supply Beginning Stocks	Supply Pro- duction	Supply Imports	Supply Total Supply	Domestic Use Food & Alcohol Beverage	Domestic Use Seed	Domestic Use Feed & Residual	Domestic Use Total	Exports	Total Disap- pearance	Ending Stocks Gov't Owned	Ending Stocks Privately Owned	Ending Stocks Total Stocks
2004-05	120.3	279.7	12.1	412.2	151.3	6.4	103.3	260.5	23.3	283.8	0	128.4	128.4
2005-06	128.4	211.9	5.4	345.7	152.2	5.7	52.0	209.9	27.8	237.8	0	107.9	107.9
2006-07	107.9	180.2	12.1	300.2	155.3	6.6	49.2	211.1	20.3	231.3	0	68.9	68.9
2007-08	68.9	210.1	29.2	308.2	161.6	7.0	30.0	198.6	41.4	240.0	0	68.2	68.2
2008-09	68.2	240.2	29.0	337.4	163.0	5.9	66.6	235.5	13.2	248.7	0	88.7	88.7
2009-10	88.7	227.3	16.6	332.7	158.7	5.0	47.8	211.5	5.7	217.2	0	115.5	115.5
2010-11[1]	115.5	180.3	9.5	305.3	153.7	4.8	49.8	208.3	7.6	215.9	0	89.4	89.4
2011-12[2]	89.4	155.8	10.0	255.1	153.7	6.3	40.0	200.0	10.0	210.0	0	45.1	45.1

[1] Preliminary. [2] Estimate. [3] Uncommitted inventory. [4] Includes quantity under loan & farmer-owned reserve. [5] Included in Food & Alcohol.
Source: Economic Research Service, U.S. Department of Agriculture (ERS-USDA)

Barley (monthly average) through December 2011 — Cents per pound

BARLEY

Average Price Received by Farmers for All Barley in the United States — In Dollars Per Bushel

Year	June	July	Aug.	Sept.	Oct.	Nov.	Dec.	Jan.	Feb.	Mar.	Apr.	May	Average
2004-05	2.63	2.54	2.77	2.43	2.29	2.45	2.49	2.41	2.31	2.49	2.26	2.46	2.46
2005-06	2.54	2.37	2.50	2.36	2.41	2.58	2.48	2.42	2.55	2.70	2.65	2.97	2.54
2006-07	2.77	2.71	2.70	2.53	2.76	2.92	2.93	3.03	3.09	3.11	3.07	3.12	2.90
2007-08	3.30	3.46	3.55	4.05	4.53	4.31	4.44	4.35	4.38	4.18	4.56	4.52	4.14
2008-09	4.78	5.12	5.46	5.97	5.73	5.44	5.49	5.34	4.99	5.03	4.84	4.59	5.23
2009-10	4.70	5.09	5.17	4.78	4.41	4.46	4.54	4.68	4.53	4.22	4.08	4.25	4.58
2010-11	3.64	3.79	3.69	3.61	3.73	3.86	3.86	3.86	3.95	4.31	4.27	4.15	3.89
2011-12[1]	4.66	5.07	5.20	5.46	5.52	5.39	5.44	5.40	5.05				5.24

[1] Preliminary. *Source: National Agricultural Statistical Service, U.S. Department of Agriculture (NASS-USDA)*

Average Price Received by Farmers for Feed Barley in the United States — In Dollars Per Bushel

Year	June	July	Aug.	Sept.	Oct.	Nov.	Dec.	Jan.	Feb.	Mar.	Apr.	May	Average
2004-05	2.20	2.21	1.83	1.64	1.58	1.78	1.66	1.65	1.60	1.67	1.56	1.71	1.76
2005-06	1.91	1.88	1.77	1.84	1.81	1.91	1.76	1.94	1.83	1.80	1.81	2.45	1.89
2006-07	2.08	2.04	2.06	2.31	2.68	2.84	2.79	3.11	3.15	3.19	3.20	3.20	2.72
2007-08	3.50	3.27	3.60	4.47	4.89	5.05	4.79	4.89	4.67	4.29	4.67	4.99	4.42
2008-09	5.49	4.72	4.54	4.46	3.82	3.43	3.00	2.90	2.63	2.73	2.65	2.99	3.61
2009-10	3.16	2.94	2.49	2.14	2.29	2.50	2.63	2.63	3.11	2.66	2.40	2.49	2.62
2010-11	2.24	2.40	2.39	2.89	3.38	3.34	3.40	3.46	3.56	4.27	4.32	4.61	3.36
2011-12[1]	4.75	5.04	4.85	5.04	4.76	4.87	4.89	4.84	4.28				4.81

[1] Preliminary. *Source: National Agricultural Statistical Service, U.S. Department of Agriculture (NASS-USDA)*

Average Open Interest of Western Feed Barley Futures in Winnipeg — In Contracts

Year	Jan.	Feb.	Mar.	Apr.	May	June	July	Aug.	Sept.	Oct.	Nov.	Dec.
2004	6,731	6,881	6,262	9,779	10,497	9,930	9,992	9,743	11,140	11,956	12,786	10,916
2005	9,321	8,164	9,144	9,476	9,475	9,140	6,481	6,880	6,046	5,839	6,538	7,281
2006	8,179	10,505	10,719	12,131	12,543	12,762	12,948	13,680	14,938	16,026	13,803	14,620
2007	16,178	16,769	16,969	15,901	16,351	16,951	13,808	13,941	14,270	15,480	14,337	13,830
2008	14,224	15,626	15,758	14,304	14,394	13,462	12,975	12,052	10,528	9,502	8,462	8,486
2009	7,616	5,100	4,380	3,819	3,216	2,522	3,058	3,398	2,484	1,825	1,478	1,286
2010	973	439	35	21	15	36	22	28	119	74	57	2
2011	2	7	11	55	55	48	30	60	117	44	32	25

Contract size = 20 tonnes. *Source: ICE Futures Canada (ICE)*

Volume of Trading of Western Feed Barley Futures in Winnipeg — In Contracts

Year	Jan.	Feb.	Mar.	Apr.	May	June	July	Aug.	Sept.	Oct.	Nov.	Dec.	Total
2004	11,405	16,265	12,784	23,806	13,179	27,081	15,326	14,933	23,072	15,790	22,516	8,478	204,635
2005	15,452	12,171	19,849	9,325	16,469	14,741	4,100	11,815	7,573	12,665	8,452	3,952	136,564
2006	16,241	9,238	23,987	9,361	26,466	8,083	4,294	25,858	14,903	37,489	12,620	6,484	195,024
2007	24,784	10,380	21,229	12,525	21,161	23,044	11,151	20,457	27,030	27,072	11,926	3,913	214,672
2008	20,322	15,642	20,495	13,025	19,547	14,392	5,719	15,473	13,251	14,171	11,529	3,815	167,381
2009	11,518	6,580	5,388	6,579	3,955	3,876	1,887	4,910	3,222	4,064	950	1,910	54,839
2010	1,075	991	104	16	9	62	42	55	141	19	86	32	2,632
2011	0	12	30	20	0	25	0	166	155	11	10	----	644

Contract size = 20 tonnes. *Source: ICE Futures Canada (ICE)*

Western Barley Futures - ICE Futures Canada
(weekly close) as of December 30, 2011
CAD per metric ton

Bauxite

Bauxite is a naturally occurring, heterogeneous material comprised of one or more aluminum hydroxide minerals plus various mixtures of silica, iron oxide, titanium, alumina-silicates, and other impurities in trace amounts. Bauxite is an important ore of aluminum and forms by the rapid weathering of granite rocks in warm, humid climates. It is easily purified and can be converted directly into either alum or metallic aluminum. It is a soft mineral with hardness varying from 1 to 3, and specific gravity from 2 to 2.55. Bauxite is dull in appearance and may vary in color from white to brown. It usually occurs in aggregates in pea-sized lumps.

Bauxite is the only raw material used in the production of alumina on a commercial scale in the United States. Bauxite is classified according to the intended commercial application, such as abrasive, cement, chemical, metallurgical, and refractory. Of all the bauxite mined, about 95 percent is converted to alumina for the production of aluminum metal with some smaller amounts going to nonmetal uses as various forms of specialty alumina. Small amounts are used in non-metallurgical bauxite applications. Bauxite is also used to produce aluminum chemicals and is used in the steel industry.

Supply – World production of bauxite in 2011 rose +5.3% yr/yr to a record high of 220.000 million metric tons.

The world's largest producer of bauxite is Australia with 31% of the world's production in 2011, followed by China (21%), Brazil (14%), India (9%), Guinea (8%), and Jamaica (5%). Chinese production of bauxite has almost quadrupled in the past 10 years. India's bauxite production has also risen rapidly and is about triple the amount seen 15 years ago.

Demand – U.S. consumption of bauxite in 2010 (latest data) rose by +68.3% yr/yr to 9.240 million metric tons but still well below the record high of 15.962 million metric tons seen in 1980. The alumina industry took almost 99% of bauxite production in 2010, or 9,910 million metric tons. According to 2004 data (the latest data available) the refractory industry usually takes about 1.4% of the U.S. bauxite supply, the abrasive industry takes about 0.2%, and the chemical industry takes the rest.

Trade – The U.S. relies on imports for almost 100% of its consumption needs. Domestic ore, which provides less than 1 percent of the U.S. requirement for bauxite, is mined by one company from surface mines in the states of Alabama and Georgia. U.S. imports of bauxite rose +16.5% yr/yr to 8.210 million metric tons in 2010, which was still well below the record of 14.976 million metric tons seen in 1974. U.S. exports of bauxite in 2010 were negligible at 21,000 metric tons but still up +133% yr/yr.

World Production of Bauxite   In Thousands of Metric Tons

Year	Australia	Brazil	China	Greece	Guinea	Guyana[3]	Hungary	India	Jamaica[3]	Russia[3]	Sierra Leone	Suriname	Total
2002	54,135	13,260	12,000	2,492	15,300	1,690	720	9,647	13,120	4,500	----	4,002	144,000
2003	55,602	17,363	13,000	2,418	15,000	1,846	666	10,414	13,444	5,500	----	4,215	153,000
2004	56,593	20,950	17,000	2,444	15,254	1,506	647	11,285	13,296	6,000	----	4,052	164,000
2005	59,959	22,034	22,000	2,495	16,817	1,694	535	12,385	14,116	5,000	----	4,757	178,000
2006	61,780	23,236	27,000	2,163	18,784	1,479	538	13,940	14,865	6,300	1,071	4,924	193,000
2007	62,398	25,461	30,000	2,126	18,519	2,243	546	20,343	14,568	5,775	1,169	5,054	204,000
2008	61,389	28,098	35,000	2,176	18,400	2,092	511	21,210	14,363	5,675	954	5,200	211,000
2009	65,231	25,628	40,000	2,100	15,600	1,760	317	16,000	7,817	5,475	757	4,000	196,000
2010[1]	68,414	28,100	44,000	2,100	17,400	1,760	350	18,000	8,540	5,475	1,089	4,000	209,000
2011[2]	67,000	31,000	46,000	2,100	18,000	2,000		20,000	10,200	5,800	1,700	5,000	220,000

[1] Preliminary.   [2] Estimate.   [3] Dry Bauxite equivalent of ore processed.   *Source: U.S. Geological Survey (USGS)*

Salient Statistics of Bauxite in the United States   In Thousands of Metric Tons

Year	Net Import Reliance as a % of Apparent Consumption	Average Price F.O.B. Mine $ per Ton	Consumption by Industry — Total	Alumina	Abrasive	Chemical	Refractoty	Dry Equivalent — Imports[4]	Exports[3]	Consumption	Stocks, December 31 — Producers & Consumers	Gov't Owned	Total
2001	100	23	9,770	9,010	61	W	175	8,300	67	9,770	1,740	2,070	3,810
2002	100	20	9,980	9,290	52	W	115	7,340	27	9,980	1,280	1,770	3,050
2003	100	19	11,300	10,600	53	W	150	8,390	55	11,300	3,830	66	3,830
2004	100	22	13,600	12,500	53	W	260	9,640	42	13,600	3,120	----	3,120
2005	100	26	12,400	11,900	W	W	W	11,800	34	12,400	W	----	W
2006	100	28	12,300	11,800	W	W	W	11,600	20	12,300	W	----	W
2007	100	31	10,200	9,830	W	W	W	9,840	15	10,200	W	----	W
2008	100	26	9,550	9,310	W	W	W	10,500	14	9,550	W	----	W
2009[1]	100	30	5,490	5,330	W	W	W	6,970	9	5,490	W	----	W
2010[2]	100	29	9,240	9,110	W	W	W	8,120	21	9,240	W	----	W

[1] Preliminary.   [2] Estimate.   [3] Including concentrates.   [4] For consumption.   W = Withheld.   *Source: U.S. Geological Survey (USGS)*

Bismuth

Bismuth (symbol Bi) is a rare metallic element with a pinkish tinge. Bismuth has been known since ancient times, but it was confused with lead, tin, and zinc until the middle of the 18th century. Among the elements in the earth's crust, bBismuth (symbol Bi) is a rare metallic element with a pinkish tinge. Bismuth has been known since ancient times, but it was confused with lead, tin, and zinc until the middle of the 18th century. Among the elements in the earth's crust, bismuth is ranked about 73rd in natural abundance. This makes bismuth about as rare as silver. Most industrial bismuth is obtained as a by-product of ore extraction.

Bismuth is useful for castings because of the unusual way that it expands after solidifying. Some of bismuth's alloys have unusually low melting points. Bismuth is one of the most difficult of all substances to magnetize. It tends to turn at right angles to a magnetic field. Because of this property, it is used in instruments for measuring the strength of magnetic fields.

Bismuth finds a wide variety of uses such as pharmaceutical compounds, ceramic glazes, crystal ware, and chemicals and pigments. Bismuth is found in household pharmaceuticals and is used to treat stomach ulcers. Bismuth is opaque to X-rays and can be used in fluoroscopy. Bismuth has also found new use as a nontoxic substitute for lead in various applications such as brass plumbing fixtures, crystal ware, lubricating greases, pigments, and solders. There has been environmental interest in the use of bismuth as a replacement for lead used in shot for waterfowl hunting and in fishing sinkers. Another use has been for galvanizing to improve drainage characteristics of galvanizing alloys. Zinc-bismuth alloys have the same drainage properties as zinc-lead without being as hazardous.

Prices – The average price of bismuth (99.99% pure) in the U.S. in 2011 rose by +29.9% to $11.20 per pound, but still below the 2007 record high of $13.32 per pound. Up until 2007 the prices were in the $3.00 to $5.00 per pound range.

Supply – World mine production of bismuth in 2011 rose +11.8% to a new record high of 8,500 metric tons. The world's largest producer in 2011 was China with 71% of world production, followed by Peru with 13%, Mexico with 12%, and Canada far behind with 1%. Regarding production of the refined metal in 2010 (latest data), China had 81% of production, Mexico had 5%, Belgium had 5%, and Peru had 4%. The U.S. does not have any significant domestic refinery production of bismuth.

Demand – U.S. consumption of bismuth in 2011 rose by +13.1% to 1,000 metric tons, but still below the record high of 2,420 metric tons in 2004. In 2010 (latest data) the consumed uses of bismuth were 67% for chemicals, 26% for metallurgical additives, 7% for fusible alloys, and 0.5% for other alloy uses.

Trade – U.S. imports of bismuth in 2011 fell -25.9% to 1,200 metric tons, down from the 2007 record high of 3,070 metric tons. Of U.S. imports in 2010, 42% came from Belgium and unusually almost none came from Mexico. U.S. exports of bismuth and alloys in 2011 fell 29.0.8% yr/yr to 500 metric tons, down from the 2010 record high of 704 metric tons.

World Production of Bismuth   In Metric Tons (Mine Output=Metal Content)

| | | ---------- Mine Output, Metal Content ---------- | | | | | ---------- Refined Metal ---------- | | | | | |
Year	Canada	China	Japan	Mexico	Peru	Total	Belgium	China	Kazak-hastan[3]	Japan	Mexico	Peru	Total
2005	185	3,000	23	970	952	5,400	800	10,600	120	463	970	600	14,000
2006	177	3,000	21	1,186	950	5,800	800	11,800	115	425	1,186	600	15,000
2007	137	3,500	20	1,200	950	6,200	800	12,100	120	408	1,200	600	16,000
2008	71	5,000	20	1,170	960	7,600	800	13,100	125	480	1,170	600	17,000
2009	86	6,000	21	854	1,000	8,200	800	12,300	125	423	854	600	15,000
2010[1]	91	6,500	20	850	1,100	7,600	800	13,000	125	420	850	600	16,000
2011[2]	100	6,000		1,000	1,100	8,500							

[1] Preliminary.   [2] Estimate.   *Source U.S. Geological Survey (USGS)*

Salient Statistics of Bismuth in the United States   In Metric Tons

| | | | | ---------- Bismuth Consumed, By Uses ---------- | | | | Imports from | | | | Dealer Price |
| | Metal-lurgical | Other Alloys | Fusible | Chem- | Total Con- | Consumer Stocks | Exports of Metal | ---------- Metallic Bismuth from ---------- | | | | $ Per |
Year	Additives	& Uses	Alloys	icals[3]	sumption	Dec. 31	& Alloys	Belgium	Mexico	Preu	Total	Pound
2005	1,150	14	685	498	2,340	175	142	1,050.0	480.0	----	2,530	3.91
2006	1,050	12	260	660	1,990	120	311	876.0	552.0	17.6	2,300	5.04
2007	1,130	45	709	744	2,630	139	421	1,020.0	420.0	3.7	3,070	14.07
2008	375	38	75	597	1,090	228	375	509.0	40.0	55.7	1,930	12.73
2009	232	2	58	528	820	134	397	450.0	59.4	29.4	1,250	7.84
2010[1]	231	4	62	589	884	134	704	674.0	0.4	0.5	1,620	8.76
2011[2]					1,000	170	500				1,200	11.60

[1] Preliminary.   [2] Estimate.   [3] Includes pharmaceuticals.   *Source: U.S. Geological Survey (USGS)*

Average Price of Bismuth (99.99%) in the United States   In Dollars Per Pound

Year	Jan.	Feb.	Mar.	Apr.	May	June	July	Aug.	Sept.	Oct.	Nov.	Dec.	Average
2008	13.00	12.35	12.00	12.00	14.94	13.70	12.75	12.21	10.50	10.50	10.50	10.50	12.08
2009	10.50	10.50	8.00	7.68	7.44	7.08	6.86	6.85	8.50	8.99	8.56	8.03	8.25
2010	7.72	7.84	8.10	9.36	9.32	8.58	7.94	8.11	8.91	9.38	9.24	9.00	8.63
2011	9.18	9.46	10.21	11.06	11.41	11.45	11.45	11.45	12.83	12.88	12.31	10.75	11.20

Source: American Metal Market (AMM)

Broilers

Broiler chickens are raised for meat rather than for eggs. The broiler industry was started in the late 1950's when chickens were selectively bred for meat production. Broiler chickens are housed in massive flocks mainly between 20,000 and 50,000 birds, with some flocks reaching over 100,000 birds. Broiler chicken farmers usually rear five or six batches of chickens per year.

After just six or seven weeks, broiler chickens are slaughtered (a chicken's natural lifespan is around seven years). Chickens marketed as pouissons, or spring chickens, are slaughtered after four weeks. A few are kept longer than seven weeks to be sold as the larger roasting chickens.

Prices – The average monthly price received by farmers for broilers (live weight) fell in 2011 by -4.9% yr/yr to 46.7 cents per pound. The average monthly price for wholesale broilers (ready-to-cook) in 2011 rose +1.3% to 86.37 cents per pound, setting a new record high.

Supply – Total production of broilers in 2011 rose +1.1% yr/yr to 37.318 billion pounds. The number of broilers raised for commercial production in 2010 was down -2.3% yr/yr to 8.356 billion birds, down from the 2008 record high of 9.009 billion birds. The average live-weight per bird rose +2.3% to 5.71 pounds, which was a new record high and was about 50% heavier than the average bird weight of 3.62 pounds seen in 1970, attesting to the increased efficiency of the industry.

Demand – U.S. per capita consumption of broilers in 2011 rose by +1.1% to 83.2 pounds (ready-to-cook) per person per year, down very slightly from the 2006 record high of 86.5. U.S. consumption of chicken has nearly doubled in the past two decades, up from 47.0 pounds in 1980, as consumers have increased their consumption of chicken because of the focus on low-carb diets and because chicken is a leaner and healthier meat than either beef or pork.

Broiler Supply and Prices in the United States

Years and Quarters	Number (Million)	Federally Inspected Slaughter Average Weight (Pounds)	Liveweight Pounds (Mil. Lbs.)	Certified RTC[3] Weight (Mil. Lbs.)	Total Production RTC[3] (Mil. Lbs.)	Per Capita Consumption RTC[3] Basis (Mil. Lbs.)	Prices Farm Cents per Pound	Georgia Dock[4]
2006	8,838	5.47	48,333	35,750	35,500	86.5	38.92	68.25
2007	8,889	5.51	48,983	35,964	36,126	85.4	44.92	77.46
2008	8,915	5.51	49,753	35,863	36,906	83.5	46.58	83.11
2009	8,519	5.59	47,604	35,505	35,511	79.6	45.17	84.97
2010[1]	8,649	5.70	49,313	36,909	36,911	82.3	49.08	85.25
2011[2]	8,532	5.80	49,520	37,176	37,318	83.2	46.67	86.37
I	2,137	5.79	12,374	9,291	9,291	21.5	46.00	84.72
II	2,182	5.79	12,643	9,501	9,501	21.4	49.33	85.86
III	2,186	5.80	12,690	9,526	9,526	20.8	46.33	86.57
IV	2,027	5.83	11,814	8,858	9,000	19.5	45.00	88.31

[1] Preliminary. [2] Estimate. [3] Total production equals federal inspected slaughter plus other slaughter minus cut-up & further processing condemnation. [4] Ready-to-cook basis. *Source: Economic Research Service, U.S. Department of Agriculture (ERS-USDA)*

Salient Statistics of Broilers in the United States

Year	Commercial Production Number (Mil. Lbs.)	Commercial Production Liveweight (Mil. Lbs.)	Average Liveweight Per Bird (Mil. Lbs.)	Average Price (cents Lb.)	Value of Production (Mil. $)	Total Chickens[3] Supply and Distribution — Production Federally Inspected	Other Chickens	Total	Storage Stocks January 1	Exports	Broiler Feed Ratio (pounds)	Consumption Total (Mil. Lbs.)	Per Capita[4] (Pounds)
2004	8,741	45,796	5.24	44.6	20,446	33,699	504	34,203	611	4,783	5.9	34,063	84.30
2005	8,872	47,856	5.39	43.6	20,878	35,365	516	35,881	716	5,203	7.0	35,293	85.90
2006	8,868	48,830	5.51	36.3	17,739	35,500	505	36,005	926	5,205	6.2	36,325	86.60
2007	8,907	49,331	5.54	43.6	21,514	36,159	498	36,657	750	5,904	5.1	29,827	85.20
2008	9,009	50,442	5.60	45.8	23,203	36,906	559	37,465	719	6,961	3.7	30,800	83.40
2009[1]	8,550	47,752	5.58		21,823	35,510	500	36,011	745	6,835	4.1		79.60
2010[2]	8,356	47,747	5.71		23,696	36,904	504	37,407			4.5		

[1] Preliminary. [2] Estimate. [3] Ready-to-cook. [4] Retail weight basis. Source: Economic Research Service, U.S. Department of Agriculture (ERS-USDA)

Average Wholesale Broiler[1] Prices RTC (Ready-to-Cook)   In Cents Per Pound

Year	Jan.	Feb.	Mar.	Apr.	May	June	July	Aug.	Sept.	Oct.	Nov.	Dec.	Average
2005	71.40	71.43	72.81	73.21	72.54	72.19	72.47	71.45	72.51	69.02	66.95	63.98	70.83
2006	63.13	63.19	61.77	58.91	59.57	64.44	67.10	68.26	68.18	65.16	65.93	66.48	64.34
2006	63.13	63.19	61.77	58.91	59.57	64.44	67.10	68.26	68.18	65.16	65.93	66.48	76.42
2007	70.43	75.89	78.66	78.63	81.00	81.34	80.68	78.82	78.19	70.60	71.74	71.06	79.68
2008	75.91	78.79	79.51	77.84	81.58	82.48	84.60	79.34	77.98	77.65	78.51	82.01	77.60
2009	81.90	80.17	77.01	76.39	82.96	86.22	82.95	74.50	72.81	71.00	71.76	73.56	82.92
2010	81.57	81.07	84.00	82.12	86.35	86.63	86.12	83.25	84.04	80.42	81.12	78.38	79.03
2011[2]	76.28	75.43	81.97	82.12	83.38	82.44	79.97	80.89	75.42	73.71	76.46	80.28	

[1] 12-city composite wholesale price. [2] Preliminary. *Source: Economic Research Service, U.S. Department of Agriculture (ERS-USDA)*

Butter

Butter is a dairy product produced by churning the fat from milk, usually cow's milk, until it solidifies. In some parts of the world, butter is also made from the milk of goats, sheep, and even horses. Butter has been in use since at least 2,000 BC. Today butter is used principally as a food item, but in ancient times it was used more as an ointment, medicine, or illuminating oil. Butter was first churned in skin pouches thrown back and forth over the backs of trotting horses.

It takes about 10 quarts of milk to produce 1 pound of butter. The manufacture of butter is the third largest use of milk in the U.S. California is generally the largest producing state, followed closely by Wisconsin, with Washington as a distant third. Commercially finished butter is comprised of milk fat (80% to 85%), water (12% to 16%), and salt (about 2%). Although the price of butter is highly correlated with the price of milk, it also has its own supply and demand dynamics.

The consumption of butter has dropped in recent decades because pure butter has a high level of animal fat and cholesterol that have been linked to obesity and heart disease. The primary substitute for butter is margarine, which is produced from vegetable oil rather than milk fat. U.S. per capita consumption of margarine has risen from 2.6 pounds in 1930 to recent levels near 8.3 pounds, much higher than U.S. butter consumption.

Futures on butter are traded at the Chicago Mercantile Exchange (CME). The CME's butter futures contract calls for the delivery of 40,000 pounds of Grade AA butter and is priced in cents per pound.

Prices – The average monthly price of butter at the Chicago Mercantile Exchange in 2011 rose +13.5% yr/yr to 196.18 cents/pound, a new record high.

Supply – World production of butter in 2012 is expected to rise +2.2% yr/yr to 8.724 million metric tons, a new record high. The world's largest producers of butter will be India with 51.6% of the world production in 2012, the European Union with 23.4%, the United States with 9.3%, New Zealand with 5.6%, and Russia with 2.4%. Production of creamery butter by U.S. factories in 2011 rose +15.6% yr/yr to 1.805 billion pounds. The record high was 1.872 billion pounds in 1941.

Demand – Total commercial use of creamery butter in the U.S rose by +12.3% yr/yr to 1.829 million pounds in 2011, a new record high. That is about one-third higher that the commercial use of butter back in the 1950's. Cold storage stocks of creamery butter in the U.S. on December 1, 2011 rose +33.7% yr/yr to 93.523 million pounds.

Trade – World imports of butter in 2011 rose +6.1% yr/yr to 311,000 metric tons. U.S. imports of butter in 2011 fell -10.0% yr/yr to 9,000 metric tons. World exports of butter in 2011 rose +5.7% yr/yr to 783,000 metric tons. U.S exports in 2011 rose +13.6% yr/yr to 67,000 metric tons, down from the 1993 record high of 145,000 metric tons.

Supply and Distribution of Butter in the United States — In Millions of Pounds

	---------------- Supply ----------------				----------------------- Distribution -----------------------							------- 93 Score --------
		Cold Storage				-- Domestic Disappearance --			-- Department of Agriculture --				AA Wholesale Price
Year	Pro-duction	Stocks[3] Jan. 1	Imports	Total Supply	Total	Per Capita (Pounds)	Exports	Stocks[4] Jan. 1	Stocks[4] Dec 31	Removed by USDA Programs	Total Use	$ per Pound
2003	1,242	158	32.200	1,432	1,307	4.5	9	1	6	29.1	1,332	1.1450
2004	1,250	100	50.600	1,400	1,326	4.5	26	6	0	-6.6	1,356	1.8166
2005	1,347	45	31.418	1,424	1,335	4.6	20	0			1,370	1.5484
2006	1,448	59	39.683	1,548	1,415	4.7	24				1,548	1.2360
2007	1,533	109	37.478	1,678	1,435	5.0	88				1,678	1.3680
2008	1,645	154	37.478	1,836	1,521	5.0	196				1,836	
2009	1,572	119	37.478	1,728	1,530		66				1,728	
2010[1]	1,563	132	22.046	1,717	1,506		130				1,717	
2011[2]	1,764	82	19.841	1,865	1,601		148				1,865	

[1] Preliminary. [2] Estimates. [3] Includes butter-equivalent. [4] Includes butteroil. [5] Includes stocks held by USDA.
Source: Economic Research Service, U.S. Department of Agriculture (ERS-USDA)

Quarterly Commercial Disappearance of Creamery Butter in the United States — In Millions of Pounds

Year	First Quarter	Second Quarter	Third Quarter	Fourth Quarter	Total	Year	First Quarter	Second Quarter	Third Quarter	Fourth Quarter	Total
2000	300.8	286.9	332.3	380.6	1,300.6	2006	320.2	308.5	333.2	471.6	1,433.5
2001	290.9	278.4	316.1	397.0	1,282.4	2007	344.6	299.2	376.8	498.3	1,518.9
2002	313.5	263.5	317.4	393.4	1,287.8	2008	399.3	381.4	424.9	512.2	1,717.8
2003	304.2	275.4	317.2	411.8	1,308.6	2009	372.9	374.0	352.8	464.4	1,564.1
2004	286.3	303.2	340.8	421.1	1,351.4	2010	382.5	382.7	398.9	464.8	1,628.9
2005	287.1	304.9	349.6	423.1	1,364.7	2011[1]	420.9	411.4	447.4	549.5	1,829.2

[1] Preliminary.   *Source: Economic Research Service, U.S. Department of Agriculture (ERS-USDA)*

World Production of Butter[3]   In Thousands of Metric Tons

Year	Australia	Brazil	Canada	Egypt	European Union	India	Japan	Mexico	New Zealand	Russia	Ukraine	United States	World Total
2005	131	77	84	12	2,155	2,749	84	93	381	275	118	611	6,828
2006	129	79	75	10	2,035	3,050	80	109	415	290	105	657	7,096
2007	117	82	79	10	2,053	3,360	75	214	413	300	100	695	7,565
2008	111	84	85	----	2,040	3,690	72	180	413	305	85	746	7,872
2009	118	76	86	----	2,030	3,910	81	171	482	246	75	713	8,039
2010	108	78	80	----	1,980	4,162	74	182	441	205	79	709	8,155
2011[1]	105	79	84	----	2,025	4,320	67	187	492	212	80	820	8,535
2012[2]	107	81	85	----	2,040	4,500	70	185	490	210	80	810	8,724

[1] Preliminary.   [2] Forecast.   [3] Factory (including creameries and dairies) & farm.   NA = Not available.
Source: Foreign Agricultural Service, U.S. Department of Agriculture (FAS-USDA)

Production of Creamery Butter in Factories in the United States   In Millions of Pounds

Year	Jan.	Feb.	Mar.	Apr.	May	June	July	Aug.	Sept.	Oct.	Nov.	Dec.	Total
2004	129.3	108.6	100.4	100.3	110.1	99.2	92.6	90.3	94.2	104.4	101.4	118.8	1,249.7
2005	128.0	116.9	122.4	117.1	120.7	106.6	95.9	93.2	100.6	108.9	110.9	126.0	1,347.2
2006	149.8	136.8	141.7	127.7	128.6	101.1	94.7	88.9	104.3	119.1	118.1	137.6	1,448.5
2007	150.6	134.0	138.4	133.0	124.0	110.0	116.5	110.9	112.9	130.4	130.8	141.5	1,532.9
2008	168.8	146.8	151.9	150.1	142.6	119.8	114.2	115.7	121.0	130.0	133.7	156.3	1,651.1
2009	174.7	145.7	147.2	142.5	139.4	125.5	114.3	100.9	94.6	112.9	120.5	150.8	1,568.9
2010	162.1	141.1	138.8	133.2	130.5	117.3	111.0	101.7	113.8	121.6	133.3	158.1	1,562.2
2011[1]	166.4	149.3	164.9	158.8	155.5	140.7	135.1	133.0	137.3	146.1	152.3	165.9	1,805.5

[1] Preliminary.   *Source: Economic Research Service, U.S. Department of Agriculture (ERS-USDA)*

Cold Storage Holdings of Creamery Butter in the United States, on First of Month   In Millions of Pounds

Year	Jan.	Feb.	Mar.	Apr.	May	June	July	Aug.	Sept.	Oct.	Nov.	Dec.
2004	99.6	152.4	159.1	158.1	155.7	178.7	189.2	193.5	161.0	133.0	107.2	57.2
2005	45.0	77.2	110.9	132.4	164.5	178.0	179.6	176.7	148.9	124.1	98.1	60.4
2006	58.6	125.3	169.1	195.3	227.7	261.5	263.0	259.8	215.2	190.6	157.6	108.1
2007	108.6	148.7	185.4	193.1	245.9	270.2	273.0	271.5	260.9	240.3	196.6	143.2
2008	155.2	188.1	210.4	224.8	251.5	269.5	258.4	246.1	213.7	186.9	149.4	119.9
2009	119.0	176.5	204.9	212.5	240.0	253.3	262.9	262.8	259.6	227.9	190.6	142.7
2010	133.0	168.1	202.9	195.9	206.3	212.5	197.6	193.5	155.3	130.0	108.8	69.9
2011[1]	81.7	118.8	138.7	144.2	141.7	170.1	190.3	187.8	165.7	151.0	130.7	93.5

[1] Preliminary.   *Source: Agricultural Statistics Board, U.S. Department of Agriculture (ASB-USDA)*

Average Price of Butter at Chicago Mercantile Exchange   In Cents Per Pound

Year	Jan.	Feb.	Mar.	Apr.	May	June	July	Aug.	Sept.	Oct.	Nov.	Dec.	Average
2004	143.2	171.3	213.5	222.0	203.6	193.0	174.6	154.1	176.6	164.8	192.4	170.8	181.7
2005	157.8	161.5	155.3	149.3	140.4	153.1	162.1	168.6	169.9	162.0	142.6	135.5	154.8
2006	133.7	119.3	116.6	116.3	117.6	116.4	116.5	130.4	131.7	132.1	129.2	124.1	123.6
2007	122.5	121.9	132.2	137.3	148.3	150.2	149.1	144.6	137.8	130.2	135.9	131.9	136.8
2008	122.5	120.9	134.5	139.1	147.5	150.0	153.9	162.8	169.7	173.2	161.7	120.1	146.3
2009	111.0	111.0	117.7	120.4	125.3	122.4	123.5	120.1	122.0	128.3	150.1	139.7	124.3
2010	139.5	135.6	146.4	154.6	159.0	163.8	177.9	199.0	222.6	219.0	193.0	163.3	172.8
2011	203.5	206.2	208.6	199.7	207.2	210.8	204.4	208.8	187.2	183.0	173.6	161.2	196.2

Source: Economic Research Service, U.S. Department of Agriculture (ERS-USDA)

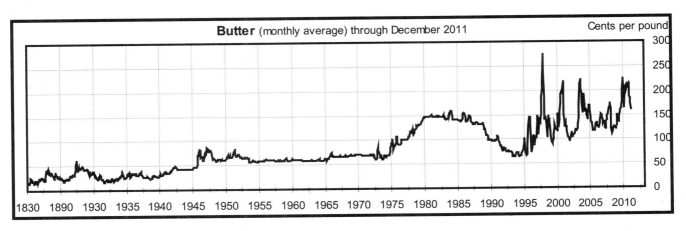

Butter (monthly average) through December 2011

Cadmium

Cadmium (symbol Cd) is a soft, bluish-white, metallic element that can easily be shaped and cut with a knife. Cadmium melts at 321 degrees Celsius and boils at 765 degrees Celsius. Cadmium burns brightly in air when heated, forming the oxide CdO. In 1871, the German chemist Friedrich Stromeyer discovered cadmium in incrustations in zinc furnaces.

Rare greenockite is the only mineral bearing cadmium. Cadmium occurs most often in small quantities associated with zinc ores, such as sphalerite. Electrolysis or fractional distillation is used to separate the cadmium and zinc. About 80% of world cadmium output is a by-product from zinc refining. The remaining 20% comes from secondary sources and recycling of cadmium products. Cadmium recycling is practical only from nickel-cadmium batteries and from some alloys and dust from electric-arc furnaces.

Cadmium is used primarily for metal plating and coating operations in transportation equipment, machinery, baking enamels, photography, and television phosphors. It is also used in pigments and lasers, and in nickel-cadmium and solar batteries.

Prices – Cadmium prices for the 8 years up to 2005 were at severely depressed levels, reflecting the decreased demand for the substance. In 2005, however, cadmium prices rose very sharply by +172.7% to $1.50 cents per pound. In 2007 the price rose further to a 21-year high of $3.45 per pound. In 2011 the price fell by -29.5% yr/yr to

$1.25 per pound. The record high of $7.89 per pound was posted in 1988.

Supply – World cadmium production in 2011 fell by -2.3% yr/yr to 21,500 metric tons, down from the 2010 record high of 22,000 metric tons but still above the 30-year low of 17,800 metric tons seen in 2002. The largest producer was China with 35% of total world production followed by Japan with 9% and Kazakhstan with 8%. The U.S produced only 3% of world. The U.S. production in 2011 fell by -7.7% to 600 metric tons, which is the lowest level since 1932.

Demand – Consumption of cadmium has been declining over the last few years due to environmental concerns. However, U.S. cadmium consumption in 2011 rose by +2.7% yr/yr to 490 metric tons. Of the total apparent consumption, generally about 75% is used for batteries, 12% for pigments, 8% for coatings and plating, 4% for nonferrous alloys, and 1% for other uses.

Trade – The U.S. in 2004 relied on imports for 20% of its cadmium usage, down from 38% in 1998 but since 2004 the U.S. has been a net exporter. U.S. imports of cadmium had decreased sharply over the past 17 years but recovered to post a 12-year high in 2007 at 315 metric tons. That, however, was still far below the 1,110 metric tons seen as recently as 1994. In 2011 the U.S. imported 150 metric tons which was down -30.6% from 2010. U.S. exports of cadmium in 2011 fell -5.2% yr/yr to 290 metric tons.

World Refinery Production of Cadmium   In Metric Tons

Year	Australia	Canada	China	Germany	India	Japan	Kazakh-stan	Rep of Korea	Mexico	Nether-lands	Russia	United States[3]	World Total
2004	347	1,880	2,800	640	489	2,233	1,900	2,362	1,615	493	532	1,480	18,600
2005	358	1,727	4,080	640	409	2,297	2,000	2,582	1,653	494	621	1,470	20,100
2006	329	2,090	3,790	640	457	2,287	2,000	3,320	1,401	524	690	723	19,900
2007	351	1,388	4,210	400	583	1,933	2,100	2,846	1,617	495	810	735	19,400
2008	350	1,409	6,960	420	599	2,116	2,100	3,090	1,550	530	800	777	20,100
2009	370	1,299	7,000	278	610	1,824	1,800	2,500	1,210	490	700	633	18,800
2010[1]	350	1,300	7,200	400	620	2,053	1,800	2,500	1,483	580	NA	650	22,000
2011[2]	380	1,300	7,500	400	660	2,000	1,800	2,500	1,500	580	NA	600	21,500

[1] Preliminary.   [2] Estimate.   [3] Primary and secondary metal.   *Source: U.S. Geological Survey (USGS)*

Salient Statistics of Cadmium in the United States   In Metric Tons of Contained Cadmium

Year	Net import Reliance As a % of Apparent Consumption	Production (Metal)	Producer Shipments	Cadmium Sulfide Production	Production Other Compounds	Imports of Cadmium Metal[3]	Exports[4]	Apparent Consumption	Industry Stocks Dec. 31[5]	New York Dealer Price $ Per Lb.
2004	20	1,480	1,410	----	----	263	154	1,840	1,170	.55
2005	E	1,470	1,680	----	----	288	686	2,060	1,540	1.50
2006	E	723	833	----	----	179	483	530	1,400	1.35
2007	E	735	692	----	----	315	424	594	1,440	3.45
2008	E	777	774	----	----	153	421	528	1,460	2.69
2009	E	633	737	----	----	117	661	199	1,450	1.30
2010[1]	E	637	563	----	----	216	306	477		1.77
2011[2]	E	600				150	290	490		1.25

[1] Preliminary.   [2] Estimate.   [3] For consumption.   [4] Cadmium metal, alloys, dross, flue dust.   [5] Metallic, Compounds, Distributors.   [6] Sticks & Balls in 1 to 5 short ton lots of metal (99.95%).   E = Net exporter.   *Source: U.S. Geological Survey (USGS)*

Average Price of Cadmium (99.95%) in the United States   In Dollars Per Pound

Year	Jan.	Feb.	Mar.	Apr.	May	June	July	Aug.	Sept.	Oct.	Nov.	Dec.	Average
2009	280.00	280.00	157.27	141.43	121.38	142.05	141.25	166.67	180.00	189.05	190.00	167.63	179.73
2010	173.42	193.16	238.91	225.34	212.88	203.41	197.50	187.27	185.00	185.00	185.00	180.00	197.24
2011	161.38	144.61	140.00	140.00	140.00	140.00	140.00	140.00	125.71	125.00	121.63	116.18	136.21

Source: American Metal Market (AMM)

Canola (Rapeseed)

Canola is a genetic variation of rapeseed that was developed by Canadian plant breeders specifically for its nutritional qualities and its low level of saturated fat. The term *Canola* is a contraction of "Canadian oil." The history of canola oil begins with the rapeseed plant, a member of the mustard family. The rape plant is grown both as feed for livestock and birdfeed. For 4,000 years, the oil from the rapeseed was used in China and India for cooking and as lamp oil. During World War II, rapeseed oil was used as a marine and industrial lubricant. After the war, the market for rapeseed oil plummeted. Rapeseed growers needed other uses for their crop, and that stimulated the research that led to the development of canola. In 1974, Canadian plant breeders from the University of Manitoba produced canola by genetically altering rapeseed. Each canola plant produces yellow flowers, which then produce pods. The tiny round seeds within each pod are crushed to produce canola oil. Each canola seed contains approximately 40% oil. Canola oil is the world's third largest source of vegetable oil accounting for 13% of world vegetable oils, following soybean oil at 32%, and palm oil at 28%. The rest of the seed is processed into canola meal, which is used as high protein livestock feed.

The climate in Canada is especially suitable for canola plant growth. Today, over 13 million acres of Canadian soil are dedicated to canola production. Canola oil is Canada's leading vegetable oil. Due to strong demand from the U.S. for canola oil, approximately 70% of Canada's canola oil is exported to the U.S. Canola oil is used as a salad oil, cooking oil, and for margarine as well as in the manufacture of inks, biodegradable greases, pharmaceuticals, fuel, soap, and cosmetics.

Canola futures and options are traded at the ICE Futures Canada (ICE) exchange. The futures contract calls for the delivery of 20 metric tons of canola and 5 contracts are together called a "1 board lot." The futures contract is priced in Canadian dollars per metric ton.

Prices – Canola prices on the ICE nearest-futures chart traded sideways in the first half of 2011 and then drifted lower later in the year to close 2011 down -10% at CD$525.80 per metric ton.

The average monthly wholesale price of canola oil in the Midwest in 2011 rose +29.3% yr/yr to 59.10 cents per pound. The average monthly wholesale price of canola meal (delivery Pacific Northwest) in the 2011-12 crop year (through November 2011) fell by -8.0% to $263.63 per short ton.

Supply – World canola production in the 2011-12 marketing year rose by +0.7% yr/yr to 60.832 million metric tons, just below 2009-10 record high of 60.964 million metric tons. The world's largest canola producers were the European Union with 31.4% of world production in 2011-12, Canada (23.3%), China (21.4%), and India (11.5%). U.S. production of canola and canola oil in 2011-12 fell -37.2% yr/yr to 699,000 metric tons. Regarding canola products, world production of canola oil in 2011-12 rose +0.1% to 23.326 million metric tons, which was a new record high. U.S. production of canola oil in 2011-12 rose +2.2% to 552,000 metric tons, which is a new record high. World production of canola meal in 2011-11 rose +0.4% to a record high of 34.975 million metric tons.

Demand – World crush demand for canola in 2011-12 rose +0.4% yr/yr to 59.111 million metric tons, which was a new record high. World consumption of canola oil in 2011-12 fell -0.4% yr/yr to 23.198 million metric tons, just below last year's record high of 23.301 million metric tons. World consumption of canola meal in 2011-12 rose by +0.4% to 34.975, a new record high.

Trade – World canola exports in 2011-12 rose +6.5% to 11.536 million metric tons, world canola oil exports rose +3.4% to a record high of 3.576 million metric tons, and world canola meal exports rose +3.7% yr/yr to a record high of 5.429 million metric tons. World canola imports in 2011-12 rose +12.7% to 11.300 million metric tons, world canola oil imports rose +3.9% to 3.413 million metric tons, and world canola meal imports rose +2.7% to a record high of 5.099 million metric tons. Regarding U.S. canola trade, U.S. canola imports in 2011-12 rose +78.8% to 699,000 metric tons and U.S. exports fell -37.5% to 180,000 metric tons.

World Production of Canola (Rapeseed)   In Thousands of Metric Tons

Year	Australia	Bangla-desh	Belarus	Canada	China	European Union	India	Pakistan	Romania	Russia	Ukraine	United States	World Total
2002-03	871	233	60	4,521	10,552	11,752	4,050	235	----	115	61	697	33,262
2003-04	1,703	218	55	6,771	11,420	11,185	6,800	238	----	192	51	686	39,436
2004-05	1,542	211	143	7,674	13,182	15,432	6,500	215	----	276	149	613	46,112
2005-06	1,419	191	150	9,483	13,052	15,523	7,000	181	----	303	285	718	48,542
2006-07	573	235	115	9,000	10,966	16,092	5,800	318	----	523	606	633	45,127
2007-08	1,214	210	240	9,601	10,573	18,358	5,450	190	----	630	1,047	650	48,500
2008-09	1,844	220	514	12,643	12,100	19,000	6,700	225	----	752	2,873	656	57,805
2009-10[1]	1,920	225	611	12,889	13,657	21,551	6,400	230	----	667	1,873	669	60,964
2010-11[2]	2,382	225	374	12,773	13,100	20,706	7,000	230	----	670	1,470	1,113	60,399
2011-12[3]	2,940	230	400	14,165	13,000	19,100	7,000	280	----	1,050	1,500	699	60,832

[1] Preliminary.   [2] Estimate.   [3] Forecast.   *Source: Economic Research Service, U.S. Department of Agriculture (ERS-USDA); The Oil World*

CANOLA

Canola Futures - ICE Futures Canada
(weekly close) as of December 30, 2011

CAD per metric ton

Volume of Trading of Canola Futures in Winnipeg   In 20 Metric Ton Units

Year	Jan.	Feb.	Mar.	Apr.	May	June	July	Aug.	Sept.	Oct.	Nov.	Dec.	Total
2002	164,945	179,753	166,889	159,981	133,202	139,256	132,524	174,527	131,034	170,873	105,661	169,477	1,828,122
2003	129,903	152,738	108,991	153,528	120,178	152,979	90,909	66,768	109,760	217,310	90,950	153,269	1,547,283
2004	145,339	204,567	178,516	192,429	120,218	128,843	73,417	97,483	113,368	175,776	110,922	196,094	1,736,972
2005	116,678	207,198	141,717	124,636	102,424	178,001	87,724	121,749	138,701	200,004	145,231	258,922	1,822,985
2006	195,189	240,070	237,537	229,470	211,688	238,967	129,433	145,133	212,164	284,033	191,676	291,994	2,607,354
2007	204,893	309,278	198,589	273,755	281,240	321,022	160,846	181,145	212,288	396,852	268,743	360,531	3,169,182
2008	368,963	388,180	307,536	318,641	209,631	290,152	172,089	170,596	220,479	293,978	126,273	265,670	3,132,188
2009	265,415	345,108	267,276	358,030	286,069	326,924	161,569	188,651	268,629	340,368	211,160	332,594	3,351,793
2010	239,347	349,512	283,156	415,932	232,711	534,781	200,250	277,736	351,663	500,943	284,703	447,694	4,118,428
2011	345,505	483,744	342,887	417,453	326,805	436,050	268,144	331,289	490,065	443,909	361,250	406,052	4,653,153

Contract size = 20 tonnes.   *Source: ICE Futures Canada (ICE)*

Average Open Interest of Canola Futures in Winnipeg   In 20 Metric Ton Units

Year	Jan.	Feb.	Mar.	Apr.	May	June	July	Aug.	Sept.	Oct.	Nov.	Dec.
2002	57,821	56,443	53,321	56,830	50,924	38,901	48,329	54,286	53,630	50,379	56,896	57,983
2003	52,818	54,749	55,369	53,480	50,549	49,930	47,479	45,314	44,510	49,008	45,423	48,655
2004	54,524	57,944	71,624	77,357	69,783	59,012	50,669	51,009	49,659	53,855	65,215	68,719
2005	64,147	75,090	65,205	63,514	54,341	53,390	57,706	56,305	65,700	68,186	66,117	87,246
2006	82,651	88,576	84,828	88,970	84,710	81,561	81,243	77,356	81,597	80,800	90,694	102,651
2007	103,317	103,250	94,001	102,050	114,244	124,321	117,967	111,470	121,589	122,965	146,879	156,698
2008	164,326	172,229	165,282	135,226	111,687	102,353	91,891	82,272	90,075	90,062	91,459	88,373
2009	88,487	100,072	97,016	104,423	111,922	109,921	94,574	104,426	95,168	99,968	93,108	99,736
2010	112,406	125,895	122,112	133,172	134,768	159,949	154,881	150,209	155,712	181,660	199,487	193,948
2011	204,715	207,186	188,138	176,678	166,554	166,105	150,624	166,066	188,592	166,852	160,276	140,345

Contract size = 20 tonnes.   *Source: ICE Futures Canada (ICE)*

World Supply and Distribution of Canola and Products   In Thousands of Metric Tons

| | ----- Canola ----- | | | | ----- Canola Meal ----- | | | | | ----- Canola oil ----- | | | | |
Year	Pro-duction	Exports	Imports	Crush	Ending Stocks	Pro-duction	Exports	Imports	Con-sumption	Ending Stocks	Pro-duction	Exports	Imports	Con-sumption	Ending Stocks
2004-05	46,112	4,902	5,000	40,606	4,765	24,235	2,239	2,298	24,398	345	15,756	1,293	1,202	15,582	480
2005-06	48,542	6,976	6,657	44,646	5,514	26,559	2,509	2,553	26,358	590	17,369	1,645	1,465	17,020	649
2006-07	45,127	6,616	6,987	43,636	4,642	25,918	2,962	3,050	26,347	249	17,148	1,990	2,198	17,540	465
2007-08	48,500	8,152	7,548	46,639	3,550	27,591	3,692	3,556	27,430	274	18,442	1,899	2,020	18,254	774
2008-09	57,805	12,045	12,126	52,088	6,575	30,810	3,607	3,581	30,814	244	20,509	2,426	2,430	20,150	1,137
2009-10[1]	60,964	10,788	10,742	56,545	7,977	33,517	3,612	3,625	33,435	339	22,316	2,741	2,929	22,416	1,225
2010-11[2]	60,399	10,828	10,028	58,857	6,261	34,835	5,236	4,967	34,546	359	23,319	3,459	3,285	23,301	1,069
2011-12[3]	60,832	11,536	11,300	59,111	5,136	34,975	5,429	5,099	34,689	315	23,326	3,576	3,413	23,198	1,034

[1] Preliminary.   [2] Estimate.   [3] Forecast.   *Source: Economic Research Service, U.S. Department of Agriculture (ERS-USDA); The Oil World*

Salient Statistics of Canola and Canola Oil in the United States   In Thousands of Metric Tons

| | ----- Canola ----- | | | | | | | ----- Canola Oil ----- | | | | | | |
| | --- Supply --- | | | | --- Disappearance --- | | | --- Supply --- | | | | --- Disappearance --- | | |
Year	Stocks June 1	Pro-duction	Imports	Total Supply	Crush	Exports	Total[3]	Stocks Oct. 1	Pro-duction	Imports	Total Supply	Domestic	Exports	Total
2004-05	40	613	467	1,120	901	140	1,120	42	378	514	934	754	122	934
2005-06	60	718	518	1,296	1,030	157	1,296	58	421	726	1,205	871	214	1,205
2006-07	87	633	647	1,367	963	246	1,367	120	423	712	1,255	901	286	1,255
2007-08	135	650	874	1,659	1,050	423	1,659	68	460	1,016	1,544	1,326	158	1,544
2008-09	158	656	825	1,639	1,218	191	1,639	60	501	1,050	1,611	1,284	249	1,611
2009-10	203	669	568	1,440	1,116	176	1,440	78	491	1,067	1,636	1,297	251	1,636
2010-11[1]	122	1,113	482	1,717	1,310	288	1,717	88	540	1,421	2,049	1,681	232	2,049
2011-12[2]	91	699	862	1,652	1,310	180	1,652	136	552	1,497	2,185	1,837	249	2,185

[1] Preliminary.   [2] Forecast.   [3] Includes planting seed and residual.   *Source: Economic Research Service, U.S. Department of Agriculture (ERS-USDA)*

Wholesale Price of Canola Oil in Midwest   In Cents Per Pound

Year	Jan.	Feb.	Mar.	Apr.	May	June	July	Aug.	Sept.	Oct.	Nov.	Dec.	Average
2004	33.44	37.19	38.19	36.81	35.60	32.88	31.63	29.50	31.38	28.35	31.75	31.75	33.21
2005	29.80	28.88	31.38	31.00	31.25	33.00	31.95	29.75	30.50	31.50	30.88	28.81	30.73
2006	38.63	29.06	30.19	29.70	31.56	31.69	33.95	33.06	32.94	34.50	37.63	37.42	33.36
2007	38.56	40.06	38.95	38.44	40.44	42.56	45.00	44.25	48.00	50.38	57.30	61.50	45.45
2008	64.94	71.80	70.56	71.38	73.05	76.69	74.13	61.05	54.88	42.85	39.81	37.19	61.53
2009	38.80	35.66	35.38	39.75	41.50	42.38	39.80	42.00	39.31	41.55	44.38	42.90	40.28
2010	40.56	41.88	42.50	42.20	40.00	40.00	44.00	47.19	47.38	51.45	53.63	58.25	45.75
2011[1]	59.50	60.13	60.25	62.05	60.19	59.56	60.70	60.00	58.45	56.81	56.13	55.40	59.10

[1] Preliminary.   *Source: Economic Research Service, U.S. Department of Agriculture (ERS-USDA)*

Average Price of Canola in Vancouver   In Canadian Dollars Per Metric Ton

Year	Jan.	Feb.	Mar.	Apr.	May	June	July	Aug.	Sept.	Oct.	Nov.	Dec.	Average
2004	345.51	370.53	402.02	395.92	384.09	378.62	360.93	349.57	341.29	288.64	275.37	265.15	346.47
2005	261.56	250.02	270.29	273.13	275.58	286.78	279.45	259.58	240.30	235.00	233.21	226.39	257.61
2006	230.48	231.43	241.57	248.63	267.11	263.66	277.90	265.70	265.20	295.90	335.39	348.60	272.63
2007	354.09	357.65	350.26	348.36	357.87	368.11	372.55	380.70	401.35	402.61	417.23	453.82	380.38
2008	519.88	608.92	618.85	594.74	578.47	616.27	601.79	517.00	457.86	391.62	399.41	371.48	523.02
2009	413.77	416.13	409.67	428.95	459.08	461.29	422.69	429.38	394.03	377.19	377.74	389.42	414.95
2010	376.26	373.42	374.40	377.22	372.83	400.29	439.34	443.06	453.22	481.16	514.84	542.25	429.02
2011	567.16	577.71	558.19	569.44	555.48	574.44	563.30	547.52	528.64	509.52	513.06	502.88	547.28

Source: ICE Futures Canada (ICE)

Average Wholesale Price of Canola Meal, 36% Pacific Northwest   In Dollars Per Short Ton

Year	Oct.	Nov.	Dec.	Jan.	Feb.	Mar.	Apr.	May	June	July	Aug.	Sept.	Average
2004-05	133.39	138.81	135.13	129.21	139.55	146.08	140.85	139.25	153.98	150.48	138.12	132.10	139.75
2005-06	130.13	139.55	158.06	150.05	143.94	134.74	136.04	136.59	139.63	137.83	143.28	136.38	140.52
2006-07	149.77	166.80	163.17	173.30	198.37	195.37	169.01	168.19	189.11	171.14	159.33	176.98	173.38
2007-08	167.24	192.25	226.30	276.78	285.83	276.85	268.14	258.75	293.20	310.19	239.88	220.42	251.32
2008-09	192.55	217.99	228.62	279.23	243.30	217.02	230.06	287.99	325.48	261.55	277.30	224.74	248.82
2009-10	220.90	177.69	NA	248.63	218.18	214.11	226.95	222.28	224.56	245.18	244.44	231.20	224.92
2010-11	251.03	257.73	265.54	275.80	261.20	260.32	254.68	267.82	263.45	277.55	271.04	257.34	263.63
2011-12[1]	238.70	235.20	NA	253.98									242.63

[1] Preliminary.   *Source: Economic Research Service, U.S. Department of Agriculture (ERS-USDA)*

Cassava

Cassava is a perennial woody shrub with an edible root. Cassava, which is also called manioc, mandioca, or yucca, grows in tropical and subtropical areas of the world. Cassava has been known since the 1500s and originates in Latin America. The cassava's starchy roots are a major source of dietary energy for more than 500 million people. Cassava is the highest producer of carbohydrates among staple crops, and it ranks fourth in food crops in developing countries. The leaves of the cassava plant are also edible and are relatively rich in protein and vitamins A and B.

Cassava is drought-tolerant and needs less soil preparation and weeding than other crops. Because cassava can be stored in the ground for up to 3 years, it also serves as a reserve food when other crops fail. The cassava is propagated by cuttings of the woody stem, thereby resulting in a low multiplication rate compared to crops propagated by true seeds.

One problem with cassava is the poisonous cyanides, which need to be destroyed before consumption. The cyanide content differs with each variety of cassava, but higher cyanide is usually correlated to high yields. The cyanide content can be destroyed through heat and various processing methods such as grating, sun drying, and fermenting.

Cassava is the primary source of tapioca. Cassava is also eaten raw or boiled, and is processed into livestock feed, starch and glucose, flour, and pharmaceuticals. One species of cassava has been successfully grown for its rubber.

Supply – World production of cassava in 2010 fell by -2.6% to 228.549, below the 2009 record high of 234.550 million metric tons. The world's largest producers of cassava in 2010 were Nigeria (with 16.4% of world production), Brazil (10.7%), Indonesia (10.5%), and Thailand (9.6%).

Trade – World exports of tapioca in 2010 fell -19.3% to 5.610 million metric tons, below the 2009 record high of 6.950 million metric tons. Thailand accounted for 76.2% of world exports in 2010, followed by Vietnam with 18.6%, and Indonesia with 2.6%. The world's main importers of tapioca in 2010 were China with 92.5% of world imports, the Republic of Korea with 4.7%, and the European Union with 0.4%.

World Cassava Production   In Thousands of Metric Tons

Year	Brazil	China	Congo[2]	Ghana	India	Indonesia	Mozam-bique	Nigeria	Paraguay	Tanzania	Thailand	Uganda	World Total
2003	21,961	4,015	878	10,239	5,426	18,524	6,150	36,304	4,669	3,962	19,718	5,450	191,125
2004	23,927	3,816	932	9,739	5,950	19,425	6,413	38,845	5,500	4,441	21,441	5,500	201,388
2005	25,872	4,016	935	9,567	7,463	19,321	6,500	41,565	4,785	5,539	16,938	5,576	207,609
2006	26,639	4,313	1,000	9,638	7,855	19,987	6,659	45,721	4,800	6,158	22,584	4,926	223,853
2007	26,541	4,362	950	10,218	8,232	19,988	5,039	43,410	4,800	5,199	26,916	4,973	226,301
2008	26,703	4,409	1,113	11,351	9,056	21,593	5,410	44,582	2,219	5,392	25,156	5,072	233,498
2009	24,404	4,506	1,149	12,231	9,623	22,039	5,672	36,804	2,610	5,916	30,088	5,179	234,550
2010[1]	24,354	4,684	1,149	13,504	8,060	23,909	5,700	37,504	2,624	4,392	22,006	5,282	228,549

[1] Estimate.   [2] Formerly Zaire.   *Source: Food and Agriculture Organization of the United Nations (FAO-UN)*

World Trade in Tapioca   In Thousands of Metric Tons

| | ---------- Exports ---------- | | | | ---------- Imports ---------- | | | | | | |
Year	Costa Rica	Indonesia	Thailand	Vietnam	World Total	China	European Union	Japan	Korea	Philippines	Singapore	World Total
2003	14	42	3,994	681	4,785	2,368	1,869	21	247	6	19	4,624
2004	17	234	4,579	730	5,626	3,442	2,075	30	460	12	19	6,134
2005	18	230	3,028	545	3,889	3,335	362	23	265	----	21	4,062
2006	22	132	4,361	1,106	5,690	4,950	263	20	268	3	22	5,570
2007	25	210	4,798	1,256	6,360	4,625	1,325	27	302	----	19	6,500
2008	76	130	2,984	846	4,085	1,976	619	37	900	----	2	3,752
2009	82	168	4,357	2,291	6,950	6,107	42	32	552	----	2	6,862
2010[1]	92	145	4,273	1,041	5,610	5,763	26	21	293	31	2	6,230

[1] Estimate.   [2] Intra-EU trade is excluded.   *Source: The Oil World*

Prices of Tapioca, Hard Pellets, F.O.B. Rotterdam   U.S. Dollars Per Tonne

Year	Jan.	Feb.	Mar.	Apr.	May	June	July	Aug.	Sept.	Oct.	Nov.	Dec.	Average
2001	83	80	77	78	80	82	84	84	87	83	84	84	82
2002	86	82	82	84	87	91	96	97	95	93	93	89	90
2003	91	92	95	96	101	101	103	108	114	134	138	143	110
2004	138	132	121	118	117	118	120	122	128	134	139	148	128
2005	147	149	153	145	142	130	----	----	----	----	----	----	144
2006	----	----	----	----	----	----	----	----	----	----	----	----	----
2007	165	169	164	171	185	203	229	273	317	299	265	247	224
2008	255	261	264	257	249	241	247	226	214	212	172	171	214

Source: The Oil World

Castor beans

Castor bean plants are native to the Ethiopian region of tropical east Africa. The seeds of the castor bean are used to produce castor oil. The average castor bean seed contains 35% to 55% oil. The oil is removed from the bean seeds by either pressing or solvent extraction. Castor oil is used in many products. In the U.S., the paint and varnish industry is the single largest market for castor oil. Castor oil is also used for coating fabrics, insulation, cosmetics, skin emollients, hair oils, inks, nylon plastics, greases, and hydraulic fluids.

Ricin is found in all parts of the castor bean plant, but the most concentrated amounts are found in the cake by-product after oil extraction. Ricin is one of the most deadly, naturally occurring poisons known. Ricin received attention when it was used in a subway attack in Japan in 1995 and again when it was sent to a Congressional office in an envelope in February 2004. One non-deadly use for ricin is for medical research where it is being studied for use as a potential treatment for cancer.

Supply – World production of castor-seed beans in the 2010-11 marketing year rose by +15.1% to 1.542 million metric tons. The world's largest producer of castor-seed beans by far is India with 74.6% of world production in 2010-11 at 1.150 million metric tons. The second and third largest producers are China with 11.7% of world production (180,000 metric tons) and Brazil with 6.6% of world production (101,000 metric tons).

Demand – U.S. consumption of castor oil in 2009-10 fell by -35.5% to 39.311 million pounds, down from the 2007-08 record high of 97.769 million pounds. The 2009-10 consumption is estimated to be only about 58 million pounds based on the first three months of the year.

World Production of Castorseed Beans — In Thousands of Metric Tons

Year	Brazil	China	Ecuador	India	Mexico	Paraguay	Pakistan	Philip-pines	Sudan	Tanzania	Thailand	Former U.S.S.R.	Total
2003-04	78	258	4	720	1	10	10	4	1	3	10	2	1,154
2004-05	129	250	2	870	1	11	7	4	1	3	10	2	1,350
2005-06	162	220	2	930	1	12	8	4	1	3	11	2	1,418
2006-07	92	190	3	820	1	9	8	4	1	3	11	2	1,210
2007-08	94	170	3	1,000	1	10	8	4	1	3	11	2	1,376
2008-09	123	190	3	980	1	5	8	4	1	4	11	2	1,402
2009-10[1]	93	170	3	970	1	5	8	4	1	3	11	2	1,340
2010-11[2]	101	180	3	1,150	1	5	8	4	1	3	12	2	1,542

[1] Preliminary. [2] Estimate. [3] Forecast. *Sources: Foreign Agricultural Service, U.S.Department of Agriculture (FAS-USDA); The Oil World*

Castor Oil Consumption[2] in the United States — In Thousands of Pounds

Year	Oct.	Nov.	Dec.	Jan.	Feb.	Mar.	Apr.	May	June	July	Aug.	Sept.	Total
2004-05	2,155	1,391	1,581	1,365	1,915	1,992	2,175	2,211	1,827	1,689	2,021	1,162	21,484
2005-06	1,389	1,761	1,654	1,602	1,610	1,426	1,457	1,766	1,899	1,516	1,768	1,379	19,227
2006-07	1,583	2,026	1,642	2,021	4,011	6,577	5,105	4,107	5,360	5,123	2,161	3,813	43,529
2007-08	2,616	4,583	W	7,664	7,890	7,942	9,327	9,190	9,101	10,361	11,406	9,542	89,622
2008-09	10,137	7,123	7,775	7,231	5,447	2,994	4,758	4,322	4,718	W	2,109	4,363	60,977
2009-10	4,294	5,658	4,529	4,850	4,590	4,243	W	1,763	3,583	3,696	1,097	1,008	39,311
2010-11[1]	W	W	W										

[1] Preliminary. [2] In inedible products (Resins, Plastics, etc.). W = Withheld. *Source: Bureau of the Census, U.S. Department of Commerce*

Castor Oil Stocks in the United States, on First of Month — In Thousands of Pounds

Year	Oct.	Nov.	Dec.	Jan.	Feb.	Mar.	Apr.	May	June	July	Aug.	Sept.
2004-05	34,525	31,608	24,287	19,476	32,641	25,318	27,876	19,098	31,493	22,919	15,963	35,604
2005-06	38,357	45,720	37,111	29,428	21,047	25,076	15,756	25,543	25,070	22,165	21,329	14,389
2006-07	39,635	24,055	18,780	43,896	30,734	46,850	58,989	50,455	49,276	46,715	37,668	26,019
2007-08	16,945	34,444	23,661	36,046	30,034	20,303	22,240	14,167	39,649	27,285	14,907	W
2008-09	W	W	47,243	38,349	56,845	50,612	38,987	32,208	42,361	34,222	25,908	25,111
2009-10	28,817	21,217	20,504	22,054	19,057	21,675	W	W	W	W	W	W
2010-11[1]	W	W	W									

[1] Preliminary. W = Withheld proprietary data. *Source: Bureau of the Census, U.S. Department of Commerce*

Average Wholesale Price of Castor Oil No. 1, Brazilian Tanks in New York — In Cents Per Pound

2003	47.00	47.00	47.00	47.00	47.00	47.00	47.00	47.00	47.00	47.00	47.00	47.00	47.00
2004	47.00	47.00	47.00	47.00	47.00	47.00	47.00	47.00	47.00	47.00	47.00	48.00	47.08
2005	50.00	50.00	50.00	50.00	50.00	50.00	50.00	49.00	49.00	47.00	45.50	45.00	48.79
2006	45.00	45.00	44.00	43.00	43.00	43.00	43.00	43.00	44.00	44.00	44.00	43.50	43.71
2007	46.60	49.75	52.00	54.60	58.00	57.50	56.00	NA	60.00	60.00	60.00	60.29	55.89
2008	63.57	66.11	70.20	72.00	72.00	74.29	78.00	82.00	82.00	80.18	79.21	77.67	74.77
2009	76.00	72.58	70.00	69.00	67.00	64.45	64.09	65.00	65.00	67.00	67.00	70.64	68.15
2010	71.00	71.00	72.04	74.95	80.45	82.00	83.05	84.09	NA	NA	NA	NA	77.32

Source: Foreign Agricultural Service, U.S.Department of Agriculture (FAS-USDA)

Cattle and Calves

The beef cycle begins with the cow-calf operation, which breeds the new calves. Most ranchers breed their herds of cows in summer, thus producing the new crop of calves in spring (the gestation period is about nine months). This allows the calves to be born during the milder weather of spring and provides the calves with ample forage through the summer and early autumn. The calves are weaned from the mother after 6-8 months and most are then moved into the "stocker" operation. The calves usually spend 6-10 months in the stocker operation, growing to near full-sized by foraging for summer grass or winter wheat. When the cattle reach 600-800 pounds, they are typically sent to a feedlot and become "feeder cattle." In the feedlot, the cattle are fed a special food mix to encourage rapid weight gain. The mix includes grain (corn, milo, or wheat), a protein supplement (soybean, cottonseed, or linseed meal), and roughage (alfalfa, silage, prairie hay, or an agricultural by-product such as sugar beet pulp). The animal is considered "finished" when it reaches full weight and is ready for slaughter, typically at around 1,200 pounds, which produces a dressed carcass of around 745 pounds. After reaching full weight, the cattle are sold for slaughter to a meat packing plant. Futures and options on live cattle and feeder cattle are traded at the Chicago Mercantile Exchange. Both the live and feeder cattle futures contracts trade in terms of cents per pound.

Prices – Live cattle futures prices began 2011 on a firm note and trended higher into April 2011 when they posted a then record high of $1.22875 a pound. Tight supplies pushed prices higher as the USDA's Jan 2011 bi-annual cattle report showed the US cattle herd as of Jan 1, 2011 at 92.582 million head, the smallest since 1958. Another major bullish factor was the catastrophic earthquake in Japan in March 2011 that damaged the Fukushima nuclear plant and caused Japan to boost its imports of U.S. meats due to radiation contamination of its food supply. Live cattle prices tumbled into mid-year and in May 2011 posted a 1-1/4 year low of $1.00750 a pound as a persistent drought in the Great Plains scorched pastures and prompted ranchers to move cattle out of pastures and to slaughter. The Aug 2011 Cattle on Feed report showed feedlots purchased 2.153 million head of cattle in July 2011, the most for a July since USDA data began in 1996. This temporary boost in supplies was easily absorbed by continued strong foreign demand as 2011 US beef exports rose +21% y/y. Live cattle prices strengthened into year-end and posted an all-time high of $1.25575 a pound in December 2011, the highest since cattle futures trading began in 1964, and finished the year at $1.2290, up +13.9%.

Supply – The world's number of cattle as of January 1, 2012 rose +0.6% to 1.017 million head, which is below the decade high of 1.029 million. As of January 1, 2012 the number of cattle and calves on farms in the U.S. fell -2.1% to 90.768 million, which was the lowest level since the 1952 figure of 88.072. World production of beef and veal in 2011 fell -0.3% to 56.848 million metric tons (carcass weight equivalent). The USDA is forecasting that world production will be virtually unchanged at 56.798 million metric tons in 2012. U.S. commercial production of beef in 2011 fell -0.1% to 26.277 billion pounds.

Demand – World consumption of beef and veal in 2011 fell -0.7% to 55.834 million metric tons. The USDA is forecasting a further drop of -0.3% in 2012 to 55.649 million metric tons. U.S. consumption of beef and veal in 2011 fell -2.4% to 11.750 million metric tons. The USDA is forecasting a further drop of 5.0% in 2012 to 11.158 million metric tons.

Trade – U.S. imports of live cattle in 2011 fell -7.7% to 2.107 million head, but remained well above the low levels seen when mad cow disease caused the U.S. to close the Canadian border to live cattle in 2003. U.S. exports of live cattle in 2011 rose +109.2% yr/yr to 190.538 head, an eight year record high. By weight, U.S. imports of beef in 2011 rose +11.7% to 2.029 billion pounds. U.S. exports of beef in 2011 rose +20.3% to 2.765 billion pounds, a new record high.

World Cattle and Buffalo Numbers as of January 1   In Thousands of Head

Year	Argentina	Australia	Brazil	Canada	China	European Union	India	Mexico	Russia	South Africa	Ukraine	United States	World Total (Mil. Head)
2003	53,069	27,870	161,463	13,466	115,678	91,597	284,329	26,011	26,846	13,635	9,108	96,100	1,020.6
2004	53,968	26,640	165,492	14,555	114,344	90,375	283,103	25,199	25,091	13,540	7,712	94,403	1,015.3
2005	53,767	27,270	169,567	14,925	112,354	89,319	286,200	24,309	23,154	13,510	6,992	95,018	1,017.6
2006	54,266	27,782	172,111	14,655	109,908	89,672	291,700	23,669	21,625	13,790	6,514	96,342	1,023.5
2007	55,664	28,400	173,830	14,155	104,651	88,463	297,700	23,316	21,562	13,934	6,175	96,573	1,025.9
2008	55,662	28,040	175,437	13,870	105,948	89,043	304,418	22,850	21,546	14,082	5,491	96,035	1,029.1
2009	54,260	27,321	179,540	13,195	105,722	88,837	309,900	22,666	21,040	14,195	5,079	94,521	1,023.8
2010	49,057	27,907	185,159	12,905	105,430	88,300	316,400	22,192	20,677		4,827	93,881	1,010.2
2011[1]	48,156	26,733	190,925	12,457	104,814	86,993	320,800	21,456	20,000		4,494	92,582	1,012.1
2012[2]	48,856	27,500	197,280	12,615	103,944	85,750	324,300	20,075	19,600		4,320	91,450	1,017.7

[1] Preliminary.   [2] Forecast.   *Source: Foreign Agricultural Service, U.S. Department of Agriculture (FAS-USDA)*

Cattle Supply and Distribution in the United States   In Thousands of Head

Year	Cattle & Calves on Farms Jan. 1	Imports	Calves Born	Total Supply	Federally Inspected	Other[3]	All Commercial	Farm	Total Slaughter	Deaths on Farms	Exports	Total Disappearance
2002	96,704	2,503	38,224	137,431	36,139	641	36,780	190	36,970	4,076	244	41,290
2003	96,100	1,752	37,903	135,755	35,883	611	36,494	192	36,686	4,030	99	40,815
2004	94,888	1,371	37,505	133,764	32,979	592	33,571	189	33,760	4,003	16	37,779
2005	95,438	1,816	37,575	134,829	32,549	573	33,122	189	33,311	4,052	22	37,385
2006	96,342	2,289	37,016	135,646	33,844	566	34,410	187	34,597	4,167	50	38,813
2007	96,573	2,495	36,759	135,827	34,465	557	35,022	187	35,209	4,251	66	39,526
2008	96,035	2,284	36,153	134,471	34,747	574	35,322	186	35,507	4,074	107	39,688
2009	94,521	2,002	35,939	132,462	33,696	587	34,283	185	34,468	4,064	58	38,590
2010[1]	93,881	2,284	35,695	131,860	34,566	561	35,128	203	35,331		91	35,422
2011[2]	92,682	2,107	35,313	130,103	34,394						191	

[1] Preliminary.   [2] Estimate.   [3] Wholesale and retail.   *Source: Economic Research Service, U.S. Department of Agriculture (ERS-USDA)*

Beef Supply and Utilization in the United States

Years and Quarters	Beginning Stocks	Production Commercial	Total	Imports	Total Supply	Exports	Ending Stocks	Total Disappearance	Per Capita Disappearance - Carcass Weight	Retail Weight Total
2008	630	26,561	27,191	2,537	29,728	1,888	642	27,303	89.6	62.8
I	630	6,372	7,002	637	7,639	360	553	6,764	22.3	15.6
II	553	6,899	7,452	661	8,113	471	559	7,097	23.3	16.3
III	559	6,908	7,467	584	8,051	609	590	6,865	22.5	15.8
IV	590	6,382	6,972	655	7,627	448	642	6,576	21.5	15.1
2009	642	25,963	26,605	2,628	29,233	1,869	565	26,836	87.3	61.2
I	642	6,248	6,890	704	7,594	384	556	6,651	21.7	15.3
II	556	6,602	7,158	751	7,909	471	570	6,855	22.3	15.7
III	570	6,689	7,259	623	7,882	496	560	6,841	22.2	15.6
IV	560	6,524	7,084	550	7,634	518	565	6,489	21.0	14.7
2010	----	26,304	26,304	2,297	28,601	2,299	----	----	----	59.6
I	565	6,248	6,813	573	7,386	478	502	6,445	20.9	14.6
II	502	6,547	7,049	690	7,739	585	487	6,684	21.6	15.1
III	487	6,768	7,255	598	7,853	590	514	6,767	21.8	15.3
IV	----	6,741	6,741	436	7,177	646	----	----	----	14.6
2011[1]	----	26,187	26,187	2,052	28,239	2,779	----	----	----	57.4
I	----	6,411	6,411	461	6,872	633	----	----	----	14.1
II	----	6,559	6,559	593	7,152	702	----	----	----	14.5
III	----	6,737	6,737	548	7,285	769	----	----	----	14.6
IV	----	6,480	6,480	450	6,930	675	----	----	----	14.1
2011[2]	----	24,965	24,965	2,090	27,055	2,775	----	----	----	54.1
I	----	6,195	6,195	500	6,695	695				13.4
II	----	6,330	6,330	565	6,895	735				13.7
III	----	6,420	6,420	535	6,955	700				13.8
IV	----	6,020	6,020	490	6,510	645				13.2

[1] Preliminary.   [2] Forecast.   *Source: Economic Research Service, U.S. Department of Agriculture (ERS-USDA)*

United States Cattle on Feed in 13 States   In Thousands of Head

Year	Number on Feed[3]	Placed on Feed	Marketings	Other Disappearance	Year	Number on Feed[3]	Placed on Feed	Marketings	Other Disappearance
2008	12,092	22,299	22,404	753	2010[1]	10,983	23,389	22,078	781
I	12,092	5,246	5,471	183	I	10,983	5,352	5,395	198
II	11,684	4,954	6,128	215	II	10,742	5,292	5,719	244
III	10,295	5,998	5,733	145	III	10,071	6,492	5,626	149
IV	10,415	6,101	5,072	210	IV	10,788	6,253	5,338	190
2009	11,234	22,187	21,692	746	2011[2]	11,513	23,835	22,590	899
I	11,234	5,344	5,243	173	I	11,513	5,470	5,555	169
II	11,162	4,629	5,812	227	II	11,271	5,300	5,911	212
III	9,752	6,370	5,502	146	III	10,448	6,861	5,770	227
IV	10,474	5,844	5,135	200	IV	11,312	6,204	5,354	291

[1] Preliminary.   [2] Estimate.   [3] Beginning of period.   *Source: Economic Research Service, U.S. Department of Agriculture (ERS-USDA)*

Live Cattle (monthly average) through December 2011 — Cents per pound

United States Cattle on Feed, 1000+ Capacity Feedlots, on First of Month   In Thousands of Head

Year	Jan.	Feb.	Mar.	Apr.	May	June	July	Aug.	Sept.	Oct.	Nov.	Dec.
2002	11,565	11,572	11,518	11,587	10,971	10,990	10,507	10,109	10,159	10,452	10,785	10,946
2003	10,658	10,700	10,546	10,713	10,535	10,539	9,923	9,590	9,839	10,218	11,043	11,335
2004	11,253	11,138	10,987	10,763	10,375	10,640	10,132	9,868	9,988	10,502	11,334	11,334
2005	11,299	11,342	11,154	10,873	10,641	10,771	10,394	10,093	10,000	10,482	11,473	11,726
2006	11,804	12,110	12,023	11,812	11,559	11,187	10,872	10,822	10,986	11,385	11,969	11,973
2007	11,974	11,726	11,599	11,644	11,297	11,272	10,737	10,299	10,302	10,967	11,769	12,099
2008	12,092	11,966	11,853	11,684	11,135	10,815	10,295	9,869	9,997	10,415	10,972	11,346
2009	11,234	11,288	11,228	11,162	10,822	10,407	9,752	9,637	9,900	10,474	11,134	11,277
2010	10,983	10,959	10,849	10,742	10,428	10,495	10,071	9,880	10,181	10,788	11,497	11,620
2011[1]	11,513	11,571	11,399	11,271	11,200	10,928	10,448	10,589	10,730	11,312	11,914	12,055

[1] Preliminary.   *Source: Economic Research Service, U.S. Department of Agriculture (ERS-USDA)*

United States Cattle Placed on Feed, 1000+ Capacity Feedlots   In Thousands of Head

Year	Jan.	Feb.	Mar.	Apr.	May	June	July	Aug.	Sept.	Oct.	Nov.	Dec.	Total
2002	2,179	1,810	1,963	1,463	2,267	1,644	1,840	2,228	2,194	2,396	1,982	1,610	23,576
2003	2,089	1,650	2,032	1,870	2,307	1,672	1,997	2,384	2,474	2,781	1,926	1,748	24,930
2004	1,754	1,612	1,810	1,600	2,370	1,647	1,719	2,102	2,375	2,701	1,743	1,834	23,267
2005	1,888	1,523	1,750	1,660	2,223	1,769	1,678	1,993	2,355	2,788	2,045	1,884	23,556
2006	2,199	1,588	1,837	1,619	1,903	1,946	1,958	2,290	2,227	2,430	1,884	1,714	23,595
2007	1,690	1,659	1,960	1,568	2,159	1,657	1,622	2,119	2,415	2,725	2,125	1,701	23,400
2008	1,787	1,723	1,736	1,536	1,900	1,518	1,656	2,061	2,281	2,438	2,016	1,647	22,299
2009	1,858	1,678	1,808	1,600	1,638	1,391	1,863	2,119	2,388	2,474	1,844	1,526	22,187
2010	1,822	1,674	1,856	1,634	2,030	1,628	1,758	2,271	2,463	2,505	1,959	1,789	23,389
2011[1]	1,889	1,667	1,914	1,795	1,810	1,695	2,133	2,259	2,469	2,496	2,035	1,673	23,835

[1] Preliminary.   *Source: Economic Research Service, U.S. Department of Agriculture (ERS-USDA)*

Live Cattle Futures - CME Group
(weekly close) as of December 30, 2011

United States Cattle Marketings, 1000+ Capacity Feedlots[2]   In Thousands of Head

Year	Jan.	Feb.	Mar.	Apr.	May	June	July	Aug.	Sept.	Oct.	Nov.	Dec.	Total
2002	2,083	1,801	1,825	1,996	2,171	2,076	2,193	2,135	1,848	1,979	1,731	1,799	23,637
2003	1,972	1,733	1,803	1,985	2,238	2,227	2,270	2,075	2,032	1,855	1,537	1,740	23,467
2004	1,775	1,694	1,967	1,891	2,026	2,085	1,925	1,926	1,800	1,803	1,635	1,777	22,304
2005	1,772	1,634	1,963	1,801	1,997	2,083	1,918	2,033	1,816	1,739	1,701	1,715	22,172
2006	1,810	1,602	1,958	1,785	2,160	2,198	1,950	2,067	1,760	1,765	1,797	1,625	22,477
2007	1,841	1,711	1,843	1,816	2,085	2,140	1,999	2,066	1,696	1,876	1,738	1,650	22,461
2008	1,853	1,776	1,842	2,010	2,140	1,978	2,037	1,884	1,812	1,814	1,575	1,683	22,404
2009	1,737	1,682	1,824	1,871	1,952	1,989	1,935	1,800	1,767	1,755	1,635	1,745	21,692
2010	1,776	1,716	1,903	1,857	1,865	1,997	1,901	1,923	1,802	1,734	1,774	1,830	22,078
2011[1]	1,774	1,791	1,990	1,807	2,002	2,102	1,911	2,046	1,813	1,796	1,782	1,776	22,590

[1] Preliminary.   Source: Economic Research Service, U.S. Department of Agriculture (ERS-USDA)

Quarterly Trade of Live Cattle in the United States   In Head

| | ---------- Imports ---------- | | | | | ---------- Exports ---------- | | | | |
Year	First Quarter	Second Quarter	Third Quarter	Fourth Quarter	Total	First Quarter	Second Quarter	Third Quarter	Fourth Quarter	Total
2002	785,559	398,072	474,185	845,157	2,502,973	73,060	62,140	50,859	58,335	244,394
2003	630,381	409,239	142,296	569,980	1,751,896	36,692	34,152	11,114	16,860	98,818
2004	306,555	315,996	280,824	467,236	1,370,611	176	7,208	2,629	5,708	15,721
2005	336,216	348,368	342,661	788,293	1,815,538	5,580	6,446	5,977	3,604	21,607
2006	708,680	470,176	418,117	691,870	2,288,843	8,721	12,473	10,249	18,235	49,678
2007	629,157	518,173	462,359	885,276	2,494,965	13,723	15,112	10,441	27,107	66,383
2008	682,174	562,566	405,199	634,054	2,283,993	38,319	30,581	15,175	23,417	107,492
2009	612,188	423,742	342,988	622,956	2,001,874	6,903	18,153	16,354	16,613	58,023
2010	598,853	596,339	406,926	681,767	2,283,885	15,526	20,853	17,552	37,150	91,081
2011[1]	580,696	488,313	376,517	661,777	2,107,303	33,640	39,994	45,260	71,644	190,538

[1] Preliminary.   Source: Economic Research Service, U.S. Department of Agriculture (ERS-USDA)

Feeder Cattle (monthly average) through December 2011 — Cents per pound

Average Slaughter Steer Price, Choice 2-4, Nebraska Direct (1100-1300 Lb.)   In Dollars Per 100 Pounds

Year	Jan.	Feb.	Mar.	Apr.	May	June	July	Aug.	Sept.	Oct.	Nov.	Dec.	Average
2005	87.77	87.73	91.78	91.98	88.83	83.06	79.37	80.80	85.19	87.40	90.32	93.08	87.28
2006	92.90	89.09	85.73	81.30	79.02	80.85	81.14	85.87	89.18	87.43	86.56	85.83	85.41
2007	86.75	88.68	96.39	98.04	95.50	86.81	89.09	91.49	93.49	91.69	93.37	90.50	91.82
2008	88.63	90.85	89.28	89.04	93.86	95.55	98.83	99.14	97.37	90.61	90.40	83.66	92.27
2009	81.60	79.68	81.66	87.02	85.27	81.31	82.72	82.48	83.13	83.53	83.43	80.34	82.68
2010	83.46	87.41	92.93	99.58	97.93	92.25	93.12	96.42	97.22	97.85	99.89	102.30	95.03
2011	105.12	109.50	116.81	119.80	111.42	109.00	110.87	114.17	117.17	121.25	124.76	122.80	115.22

Source: Economic Research Service, U.S. Department of Agriculture (ERS-USDA)

Average Price of Feeder Steers in Oklahoma City   In Dollars Per 100 Pounds

Year	Jan.	Feb.	Mar.	Apr.	May	June	July	Aug.	Sept.	Oct.	Nov.	Dec.	Average
2005	112.40	116.87	120.48	126.77	127.13	126.91	122.73	119.96	119.61	120.29	122.84	122.75	121.56
2006	125.49	123.56	121.41	122.29	119.35	122.29	124.55	120.35	123.90	114.85	100.78	99.80	118.22
2007	96.54	97.50	103.38	107.97	107.74	107.65	112.29	116.30	117.20	112.79	108.80	105.13	107.77
2008	98.62	102.81	100.17	100.45	107.08	108.90	111.07	112.53	109.69	98.84	95.76	90.76	103.06
2009	95.57	93.19	92.47	98.05	99.58	97.74	100.65	100.39	97.75	93.56	93.33	93.29	96.30
2010	96.25	100.06	103.82	112.43	111.44	109.75	112.68	113.53	111.92	109.65	112.58	119.32	109.45
2011	125.33	127.22	130.02	133.94	128.32	126.90	136.72	134.25	132.02	137.54	142.47	144.22	133.25

Source: Economic Research Service, U.S. Department of Agriculture (ERS-USDA)

Federally Inspected Slaughter of Cattle in the United States   In Thousands of Head

Year	Jan.	Feb.	Mar.	Apr.	May	June	July	Aug.	Sept.	Oct.	Nov.	Dec.	Total
2005	2,477	2,297	2,675	2,517	2,751	2,894	2,677	2,948	2,729	2,625	2,623	2,619	31,831
2006	2,591	2,302	2,806	2,566	2,993	3,116	2,795	3,089	2,721	2,803	2,797	2,566	33,145
2007	2,748	2,518	2,747	2,660	3,008	3,035	2,860	3,088	2,621	3,046	2,787	2,603	33,721
2008	2,847	2,598	2,684	2,914	3,095	2,912	3,017	2,866	2,842	2,933	2,475	2,623	33,805
2009	2,668	2,479	2,681	2,724	2,806	2,936	2,878	2,738	2,766	2,829	2,556	2,704	32,765
2010	2,657	2,503	2,864	2,802	2,743	3,004	2,860	2,912	2,851	2,809	2,830	2,868	33,702
2011[1]	2,687	2,580	2,913	2,678	2,777	3,058	2,728	3,053	2,830	2,804	2,739	2,706	33,555

[1] Preliminary.   *Source: National Agricultural Statistics Service, U.S. Department of Agriculture (NASS-USDA)*

Feeder Cattle Futures - CME Group
(weekly close) as of December 30, 2011

Cents per Pound

Average Open Interest of Live Cattle Futures in Chicago   In Contracts

Year	Jan.	Feb.	Mar.	Apr.	May	June	July	Aug.	Sept.	Oct.	Nov.	Dec.
2002	93,589	91,566	98,176	98,343	98,846	91,129	93,541	92,966	109,651	111,338	121,671	116,588
2003	111,874	105,882	98,943	96,875	107,193	111,397	113,324	115,417	130,836	124,525	113,224	106,522
2004	98,752	99,491	112,449	124,930	128,727	126,481	114,656	109,588	104,928	109,832	112,709	123,483
2005	142,333	140,869	146,062	141,610	145,235	133,768	135,971	134,329	148,094	167,175	174,496	197,090
2006	225,313	220,947	220,042	240,567	261,496	235,783	231,914	213,918	214,583	205,776	211,814	224,501
2007	257,373	273,121	296,235	281,239	261,866	240,526	235,110	212,154	234,754	234,584	240,710	241,614
2008	252,555	273,397	276,043	285,956	298,370	298,937	300,862	278,808	265,436	227,860	215,054	211,836
2009	207,768	203,912	207,221	206,462	204,424	211,978	222,562	233,578	251,083	260,285	266,293	262,738
2010	276,265	294,225	343,951	362,939	362,895	327,910	323,477	339,349	344,298	317,349	321,039	332,858
2011	344,671	358,852	366,250	380,138	346,614	326,592	322,313	309,147	324,714	336,225	325,195	315,700

Contract size = 40,000 lbs.   *Source: CME Group; Chicago Mercantile Exchange (CME)*

Volume of Trading of Live Cattle Futures Chicago   In Thousands of Contracts

Year	Jan.	Feb.	Mar.	Apr.	May	June	July	Aug.	Sept.	Oct.	Nov.	Dec.	Total
2002	331.0	275.7	387.1	448.5	304.9	247.9	286.2	288.5	314.9	352.5	315.7	298.7	3,851.7
2003	378.9	343.9	334.0	306.7	391.5	311.2	450.0	319.7	473.2	469.4	324.7	332.9	4,436.1
2004	362.3	265.4	442.6	353.9	419.9	345.6	381.2	341.0	382.5	344.5	511.5	359.7	4,510.1
2005	519.8	395.8	598.2	377.5	503.8	405.7	506.3	406.0	569.0	438.6	627.6	485.3	5,833.6
2006	783.0	498.8	849.5	570.0	817.5	709.7	718.8	670.4	698.3	631.9	757.8	504.0	8,209.7
2007	907.2	663.1	1,046.7	575.8	814.4	513.7	849.1	634.5	724.5	638.9	761.9	458.3	8,588.0
2008	982.6	596.4	954.2	724.4	936.2	731.3	1,006.4	738.2	998.2	801.1	773.9	558.4	9,801.4
2009	819.5	616.8	789.3	641.3	721.5	617.8	855.4	657.9	854.6	739.7	844.3	638.9	8,797.0
2010	901.0	782.9	1,167.2	863.2	1,204.5	785.8	923.8	868.3	1,158.8	827.1	1,066.3	783.9	11,332.7
2011	1,181.8	910.9	1,531.6	928.4	1,293.3	1,097.4	1,148.8	1,034.4	1,325.4	1,067.2	1,136.1	877.4	13,532.6

Contract size = 40,000 lbs.   *Source: CME Group; Chicago Mercantile Exchange (CME)*

CATTLE AND CALVES

Beef Steer-Corn Price Ratio[1] in the United States

Year	Jan.	Feb.	Mar.	Apr.	May	June	July	Aug.	Sept.	Oct.	Nov.	Dec.	Average
2004	35.7	31.5	32.0	30.8	32.3	33.6	36.4	38.9	40.7	42.6	44.0	45.0	37.0
2005	44.5	47.7	47.1	49.1	48.5	45.3	41.8	45.0	48.5	52.8	54.9	51.9	48.1
2006	51.0	48.3	45.0	42.3	39.8	41.2	42.1	43.8	43.3	36.7	31.3	29.6	41.2
2007	29.4	26.6	28.5	29.4	28.1	26.4	28.0	29.4	30.0	29.4	27.9	25.3	28.2
2008	23.5	20.8	19.8	17.9	18.2	17.6	19.0	19.0	19.8	21.3	21.3	20.9	19.9
2009	19.7	21.7	21.8	22.9	22.1	21.2	23.7	25.6	26.3	23.4	23.4	23.3	22.9
2010	23.9	25.5	27.0	29.6	28.6	27.8	27.5	26.9	24.4	22.9	22.2	21.6	25.7
2011[1]	22.3	19.6	21.3	19.2	18.3	17.2	18.2	16.6	18.4	21.4	21.6	21.5	19.6

[1] Bushels of corn equal in value to 100 pounds of steers and heifers.   [2] Preliminary.   *Source: Economic Research Service, U.S. Department of Agriculture*

Farm Value, Income and Wholesale Prices of Cattle and Calves in the United States

Year	January 1 Per Head Dollars	January 1 Total Million $	Gross Income From C & C[2] Million $	At Omaha Steers Choice	At Omaha Steers Select	At Omaha Heifers[4] Select	At Omaha Heifers[4] Choice	Feeder Heifers at Oklahoma City[5]	Cows, Boning Utility Sioux Falls[6]	Cows, Commercial Sioux Falls	Wholesale Prices, Central U.S. Choice 700-850 lb.	Wholesale Prices, Central U.S. Select 700-850 lb.	Cow[6], Canner, Cutter
								Dollars per 100 Pounds					
2005	916	87,024	49,668	86.54	----	----	87.35	106.87	55.52	54.36	145.78	136.36	54.36
2006	1,009	97,230	49,423	85.55	----	----	86.58	102.00	50.50	47.56	146.82	132.56	47.56
2007	922	89,063	50,284	91.87	----	----	91.86	102.06	54.77	52.12	149.80	140.09	52.12
2008	990	95,113	48,934	93.24	----	----	93.06	96.85	57.75	54.92	153.17	147.68	54.92
2009	872	82,436	44,261	82.70	----	----	82.71	90.49	50.87	47.94	140.77	135.70	46.00
2010[1]	829	77,677	51,975					104.22	NA	NA	156.91	150.99	56.10
2011[1]								125.56	NA	NA	181.29	173.31	67.91

[1] Preliminary.   [2] Excludes interfarm sales & Gov't. payments. Cash receipts from farm marketings + value of farm home consumption.
[3] 1,000 to 1,100 lb.   [4] 1,000 to 1,200 lb.   [5] 700 to 750 lb.   [6] All weights.
Source: Economic Research Service, U.S. Department of Agriculture (NASS-USDA)

Average Price Received by Farmers for Beef Cattle in the United States   In Dollars Per 100 Pounds

Year	Jan.	Feb.	Mar.	Apr.	May	June	July	Aug.	Sept.	Oct.	Nov.	Dec.	Average
2004	80.90	78.50	83.70	85.00	88.50	89.80	88.10	87.70	85.90	86.50	85.40	86.80	85.57
2005	89.40	88.80	91.00	93.70	92.10	88.00	85.00	84.40	88.00	90.40	90.80	93.30	89.58
2006	95.10	92.40	87.90	84.80	82.20	84.00	85.80	87.20	90.00	88.20	84.40	83.10	87.09
2007	84.30	86.10	91.60	93.70	92.80	88.80	89.00	91.40	93.10	90.90	89.90	89.20	90.07
2008	87.30	89.00	87.80	86.80	91.30	91.90	95.00	95.80	94.20	87.40	84.30	79.70	89.21
2009	80.10	78.90	79.10	83.80	83.20	80.10	80.90	80.40	80.50	79.20	79.60	78.50	80.36
2010	82.10	85.70	90.40	95.60	94.70	90.40	91.70	93.50	94.10	93.10	94.00	98.10	91.95
2011[1]	107.00	108.00	115.00	119.00	112.00	107.00	111.00	111.00	112.00	117.00	120.00	120.00	113.25

[1] Preliminary.   *Source: National Agricultural Statistics Service, U.S. Department of Agriculture (NASS-USDA)*

Average Price Received by Farmers for Calves in the United States   In Dollars Per 100 Pounds

Year	Jan.	Feb.	Mar.	Apr.	May	June	July	Aug.	Sept.	Oct.	Nov.	Dec.	Average
2004	110.00	111.00	115.00	117.00	121.00	125.00	130.00	131.00	128.00	126.00	123.00	122.00	121.58
2005	125.00	129.00	136.00	141.00	143.00	140.00	133.00	133.00	135.00	135.00	137.00	137.00	135.33
2006	141.00	143.00	139.00	137.00	134.00	135.00	137.00	136.00	136.00	128.00	119.00	116.00	133.42
2007	115.00	114.00	122.00	125.00	124.00	124.00	126.00	127.00	126.00	123.00	122.00	120.00	122.33
2008	117.00	120.00	118.00	116.00	120.00	118.00	114.00	117.00	113.00	106.00	105.00	98.90	113.58
2009	106.00	104.00	106.00	109.00	111.00	109.00	108.00	108.00	105.00	103.00	104.00	105.00	106.50
2010	109.00	113.00	117.00	124.00	124.00	122.00	122.00	123.00	118.00	121.00	125.00	130.00	120.67
2011[1]	136.00	139.00	148.00	147.00	137.00	133.00	138.00	134.00	132.00	145.00	153.00	157.00	141.58

[1] Preliminary.   *Source: National Agricultural Statistics Board, U.S. Department of Agriculture (NASS-USDA)*

Federally Inspected Slaughter of Calves and Vealers in the United States   In Thousands of Head

Year	Jan.	Feb.	Mar.	Apr.	May	June	July	Aug.	Sept.	Oct.	Nov.	Dec.	Total
2004	77	70	75	69	63	65	67	71	66	61	66	73	823
2005	66	61	67	60	57	58	57	64	57	54	55	59	718
2006	54	52	58	47	56	58	57	65	55	62	66	67	699
2007	73	66	70	56	58	60	62	65	55	64	58	60	745
2008	70	68	70	72	70	74	87	78	80	94	80	93	942
2009	84	73	79	67	64	76	79	76	80	70	72	77	930
2010	82	73	79	67	59	72	72	72	70	70	72	77	864
2011[1]	71	68	72	58	60	72	72	79	73	72	72	72	839

[1] Preliminary.   *Source: Crop Reporting Board, U.S. Department of Agriculture (CRB-USDA)*

Cement

Cement is made in a wide variety of compositions and is used in many different ways. The best-known cement is *Portland cement*, which is bound with sand and gravel to create concrete. Concrete is used to unite the surfaces of various materials and to coat surfaces to protect them from various chemicals. Portland cement is almost universally used for structural concrete. It is manufactured from lime-bearing materials, usually limestone, together with clays, blast-furnace slag containing alumina and silica or shale. The combination is usually approximately 60 percent lime, 19 percent silica, 8 percent alumina, 5 percent iron, 5 percent magnesia, and 3 percent sulfur trioxide. To slow the hardening process, gypsum is often added. In 1924, the name "Portland cement" was coined by Joseph Aspdin, a British cement maker, because of the resemblance between concrete made from his cement and Portland stone. The United States did not start producing Portland cement in any great quantity until the 20th century. Hydraulic cements are those that set and harden in water. Clinker cement is an intermediate product in cement manufacture. The production and consumption of cement is directly related to the level of activity in the construction industry.

Prices – The average value (F.O.B. mill) of Portland cement in 2011 fell -1.1% yr/yr to $91 per ton, down from the 2007 record high $104.00 per ton.

Supply – World production of hydraulic cement in 2011 rose +3.0% yr/yr to 3.400 billion tons, a new record high. The world's largest hydraulic cement producers were China with 58.8% of world production in 2011, India (6.2%), U.S. (2.0%), and Turkey (1.9%).

U.S. production of Portland cement in 2009 fell -25.6% yr/yr to 61.961, further down from the 2005 record high of 93.904 million tons. U.S. shipments of finished Portland cement from mills in the U.S. in 2011 rose +5.4% to 67.812 million metric tons, falling farther below the 2005 record high of 95.588 million metric tons.

Demand – U.S. consumption of cement in 2011 rose +1.5% to 72.300 million metric tons, well below the 2005 record high of 128.260 million metric tons.

Trade – The U.S. relied on imports for 6% of its cement consumption in 2011. The two main suppliers of cement to the U.S. were Canada and Mexico. U.S. exports of cement in 2011 rose +44.3% yr/yr to 1.700 million metric tons.

World Production of Hydraulic Cement   In Thousands of Short Tons

Year	Brazil	China	France	Germany	India	Italy	Japan	Rep. of Korea	Russia	Spain	Turkey	United States	World Total
2004	34,413	970,000	20,962	31,854	130,000	45,343	67,376	56,955	45,700	45,593	38,796	99,015	2,190,000
2005	38,705	1,068,850	21,277	31,009	145,000	40,284	69,629	51,391	48,500	50,347	42,787	100,903	2,350,000
2006	41,895	1,236,770	22,540	33,630	160,000	47,814	69,942	53,971	54,700	54,033	47,499	99,712	2,610,000
2007	46,551	1,361,170	22,300	33,382	170,000	47,542	67,685	52,182	59,900	54,720	49,553	96,850	2,810,000
2008	51,970	1,400,000	21,700	33,581	185,000	43,030	62,810	51,653	53,600	42,088	54,027	87,610	2,850,000
2009	51,748	1,629,000	18,300	30,441	205,000	36,317	54,800	50,127	44,300	29,505	53,973	64,864	3,040,000
2010[1]	59,000	1,800,000		31,000	220,000	35,000	56,000	46,000	49,000	50,000	60,000	63,500	3,300,000
2011[2]	62,600	2,000,000		33,000	210,000	35,000	47,000	46,000	52,000	20,700	64,000	68,400	3,400,000

[1] Preliminary.   [2] Estimate.   *Source: U.S. Geological Survey (USGS)*

Salient Statistics of Cement in the United States

Year	Net Import Reliance as a % of Apparent Consumption	Production Portland	Production Other[3]	Production Total	Capacity Used at Portland Mills %	Shipments From Mills Total (Mil. MT)	Shipments From Mills Value[4] (Mil. $)	Average Value (F.O.B. Mill) $ per MT	Stocks at Mills Dec. 31	Exports	Apparent Consumption	Imports for Consumption[5] by Country Canada	Imports for Consumption[5] by Country Japan	Imports for Consumption[5] by Country Mexico	Imports for Consumption[5] by Country Spain	Total
		1,000 Metric tons										1,000 Metric Tons				
2004	21	92,434	5,000	97,434	81.6	120,000	9,520	79.50	6,740	749	121,950	5,753	2	1,429	408	27,026
2005	23	93,904	5,415	99,319	82.3	128,000	11,700	91.00	7,450	766	128,260	5,404	4	2,173	236	33,261
2006	27	92,768	5,399	98,167	80.6	127,000	12,900	101.50	9,380	723	127,660	5,059	3	2,264	69	35,566
2007	19	91,144	4,320	95,464	78.2	115,426	11,900	104.00	8,890	886	116,600	5,326	5	1,684	29	22,468
2008	11	83,283	3,027	86,310	70.9	97,322	9,990	103.50	8,360	823	96,800	4,104	6	1,071	1	11,365
2009	8	61,961	1,968	63,929	49.9	71,489	7,020	99.00	6,080	884	71,500	3,426	1	366	----	6,767
2010[1]	8			66,452		71,194		92.00	6,166	1,178	71,200					6,626
2011[2]	6			67,700		72,300		91.00	5,500	1,700	72,300					6,100

[1] Preliminary.   [2] Estimate.   [3] Masonry, natural & pozzolan (slag-line).   [4] Value received F.O.B. mill, excluding cost of containers.   [5] Hydraulic & clinker cement for consumption.   [6] Less than 1/2 unit.   *Source: U.S. Geological Survey (USGS)*

Shipments of Finished Portland Cement from Mills in the United States   In Thousands of Metric Tons

Year	Jan.	Feb.	Mar.	Apr.	May	June	July	Aug.	Sept.	Oct.	Nov.	Dec.	Total
2005	5,337	5,732	7,498	8,316	9,102	9,595	8,305	9,604	8,847	8,870	8,065	6,317	95,588
2006	6,542	6,088	7,704	7,763	8,871	9,230	7,917	9,144	8,011	8,539	7,549	6,097	93,456
2007	5,574	5,207	7,241	7,697	9,082	8,869	8,693	9,426	8,218	9,182	7,890	5,189	92,268
2008	5,503	5,323	6,347	7,768	8,064	8,182	8,640	7,974	7,822	8,291	6,021	4,555	84,490
2009	4,022	4,242	4,908	5,539	5,727	6,508	6,615	6,306	6,167	5,624	5,215	3,545	64,418
2010	3,167	3,133	5,012	6,051	5,776	6,459	6,144	6,673	6,226	6,461	5,411	3,853	64,366
2011[1]	3,395	3,391	4,999	5,272	5,964	6,688	6,262	7,297	6,472	6,745	5,676		67,812

[1] Preliminary.   *Source: U.S. Geological Survey (USGS)*

Cheese

Since prehistoric times, humans have been making and eating cheese. Dating back as far as 6,000 BC, archaeologists have discovered that cheese had been made from cow and goat milk and stored in tall jars. The Romans turned cheese making into a culinary art, mixing sheep and goat milk and adding herbs and spices for flavoring. By 300 AD, cheese was being exported regularly to countries along the Mediterranean coast.

Cheese is made from the milk of cows and other mammals such as sheep, goats, buffalo, reindeer, camels, yaks, and mares. More than 400 varieties of cheese exist. There are three basic steps common to all cheese making. First, proteins in milk are transformed into curds, or solid lumps. Second, the curds are separated from the milky liquid (or whey) and shaped or pressed into molds. Finally, the shaped curds are ripened according to a variety of aging and curing techniques. Cheeses are usually grouped according to their moisture content into fresh, soft, semi-soft, hard, and very hard. Many classifications overlap due to texture changes with aging.

Cheese is a multi-billion-dollar a year industry in the U.S. Cheddar cheese is the most common natural cheese produced in the U.S., accounting for 35% of U.S. production. Cheeses originating in America include Colby, cream cheese, and Monterey Jack. Varieties other than American cheeses, mostly Italian, now have had a combined level of production that easily exceeds American cheeses.

Prices – Average monthly cheese prices at the Chicago Mercantile Exchange in 2011 rose by +20.7% yr/yr to 180.64 cents per pound, below the 2008 record high of 185.58 cents per pound.

Supply – World production of cheese in 2012 is expected to rise +1.9% yr/yr to 15.222 million metric tons, well below the 2007 record high of 21.440 million metric tons. The European Union is the world's largest producer of cheese with 46.8% of the total world production in 2011. The U.S. production was the next largest with 32.4% of the total. U.S. production of cheese in 2011 rose +2.6% to 10.609 billion pounds, which was a new record high.

World Production of Cheese   In Thousands of Metric Tons

Year	Argentina	Australia	Brazil	Canada	Egypt	European Union	Japan	Mexico	New Zealand	Russia	Ukraine	United States	World Total
2003	325	368	460	342	450	6,205	35	126	301	335	169	3,882	13,119
2004	370	389	470	345	455	6,481	35	134	295	350	224	4,025	13,638
2005	400	375	495	352	480	6,625	39	143	307	375	274	4,150	14,112
2006	480	362	528	291	408	6,801	40	145	292	405	210	4,320	14,385
2007	520	360	580	308	420	6,760	43	184	331	435	244	4,435	14,721
2008	525	344	607	285	----	6,800	47	188	288	430	249	4,496	14,299
2009	530	321	614	291	----	6,810	45	242	308	400	228	4,570	14,397
2010	540	319	648	297	----	6,970	48	264	268	435	212	4,734	14,777
2011[1]	555	325	675	305	----	7,070	48	267	257	425	185	4,800	14,946
2012[2]	575	332	700	311	----	7,120	49	270	280	420	200	4,925	15,222

[1] Preliminary.   [2] Forecast.   NA = Not available.   *Source: Foreign Agricultural Service, U.S. Department of Agriculture (FAS-USDA)*

Supply and Distribution of All Cheese in the United States   In Millions of Pounds

	Supply					Cheese 40-lb. Blocks Wisconsin Assembly Points (Cents/Lb.)	Distribution				Domestic Disappearance		
Year	Production Whole Milk[2]	All Cheese[3]	Commercial Stocks Jan. 1	Imports[4]	Total Supply		Exports & Shipments[5]	Gov't - Stocks Dec. 31	American Cheese Removed by USDA Programs	Total Disappearance	American Cheese Donated	Total	Per Capita
2001	3,544	8,261	706	445	9,412	144.92	115	4.0	3.9	8,741	----	8,586	30.00
2002	3,691	8,547	659	475	9,681	118.22	119	2.7	15.8	8,933	----	8,819	30.60
2003	3,622	8,557	730	476	9,763	131.24	115	27.4	41.3	9,007			
2004	3,739	8,873	715	472	10,060	164.92	134	9.0	5.9	9,342			
2005	3,808	9,149	701	460	10,310	145.53	128			9,519			
2006	3,913	9,525	758			123.85				9,869			
2007	3,877	9,777	817			175.78				10,112			
2008	4,109	9,913	798			185.58							
2009	4,203	10,074	852			129.61							
2010[1]	4,275	10,436				149.64							

[1] Preliminary.   [2] Whole milk American cheddar.   [3] All types of cheese except cottage, pot and baker's cheese.   [4] Imports for consumption.
[5] Commercial.   *Source: Economic Research Service, U.S. Department of Agriculture (ERS-USDA)*

Production of Cheese in the United States   In Millions of Pounds

Year	American Whole Milk	American Part Skim	American Total	Swiss, Including Block	Munster	Brick	Lim- burger	Crean & Neufchatel Cheese	Italian Varieties	Blue Mond	All Other Varieties	Total of All Cheese[2]	Cottage Cheese Lowfat	Cottage Cheese Curd[3]	Cottage Cheese Creamed[4]
2001	3,544	----	3,544	245.5	82.2	8.7	.7	645.1	3,425.9	5	199.6	8,261	370.2	453.2	371.6
2002	3,691	----	3,691	254.1	81.1	10.0	.7	686.2	3,470.0	5	229.8	8,547	374.3	436.6	374.2
2003	3,622	----	3,622	264.7	79.4	9.8	.7	676.7	3,524.0	5	246.7	8,557	384.4	448.0	385.2
2004	3,739	----	3,739	281.3	72.8	8.1	.9	699.1	3,661.6	5	268.1	8,873	396.4	464.0	382.4
2005	3,808	----	3,808	300.1	77.9	8.9	.8	714.8	3,803.0	5	268.3	9,149	407.9	468.6	376.7
2006	3,913	----	3,913	314.5	95.5	8.6	.8	756.2	3,972.9	5	281.5	9,525	409.2	459.0	368.8
2007	3,877	----	3,877	313.7	103.6	7.4	.7	772.8	4,198.8	5	311.9	9,777	425.4	458.5	348.6
2008	4,109	----	4,109	294.0	117.2	6.9	.6	763.6	4,120.8	5	307.5	9,913	389.2	428.1	325.0
2009	4,203	----	4,203	322.3	115.5	9.4	5	766.9	4,180.6	5	270.0	10,074	389.0	432.3	342.4
2010[1]	4,275	----	4,275	336.5	117.6	6.7	5	744.9	4,423.8	5	315.9	10,436	389.0	428.9	331.2

[1] Preliminary.   [2] Excludes full-skim cheddar and cottage cheese.   [3] Includes cottage, pot, and baker's cheese with a butterfat content of less than 4%.
[4] Includes cheese with a butterfat content of 4 to 19 %.   [5] Included in All Other Varieties.   NA = Not available.
Source: Economic Research Service, U.S. Department of Agriculture ERS-USDA)

Average Price of Cheese, 40-lb. Blocks, Chicago Mercantile Exchange[2]   In Cents Per Pound

Year	Jan.	Feb.	Mar.	Apr.	May	June	July	Aug.	Sept.	Oct.	Nov.	Dec.	Average
2002	132.4	120.8	121.3	124.5	120.1	113.0	108.9	115.8	120.4	119.5	108.9	113.1	118.2
2003	109.3	109.2	108.2	112.3	114.2	118.6	151.2	160.0	160.0	158.8	139.3	133.8	131.2
2004	130.6	139.6	182.0	216.9	199.3	171.1	144.9	157.3	157.0	151.7	169.6	159.2	164.9
2005	162.7	149.3	153.2	154.1	147.7	150.7	105.4	142.5	156.4	144.7	137.6	142.2	145.5
2006	133.4	119.9	116.4	116.5	118.6	119.2	116.3	123.5	129.3	123.5	137.5	132.2	123.8
2007	131.8	134.1	138.2	146.3	172.1	201.0	191.4	195.5	199.3	189.6	209.3	200.8	175.8
2008	182.6	200.2	182.3	188.3	209.8	203.5	196.7	174.0	187.6	179.6	171.0	151.3	185.6
2009	108.3	121.7	124.6	120.5	113.9	113.5	115.2	134.7	132.9	147.1	157.9	165.0	129.6
2010	145.4	145.3	129.8	141.8	144.2	139.6	155.5	163.7	173.7	172.5	146.2	138.1	149.6
2011[1]	151.4	190.6	181.3	160.4	168.6	210.0	211.5	197.3	175.6	172.3	187.2	161.7	180.6

[1] Preliminary.   [2] Data through December 2001 are for Wholesale Price of Cheese, 40-lb. Blocks, Wisconsin Assembly Points.
Source: Economic Research Service, U.S. Department of Agriculture (ERS-USDA)

Production[2] of Cheese in the United States   In Millions of Pounds

Year	Jan.	Feb.	Mar.	Apr.	May	June	July	Aug.	Sept.	Oct.	Nov.	Dec.	Total
2002	717.5	667.9	742.8	719.2	748.3	708.3	692.2	714.3	683.9	732.2	725.4	747.2	8,599
2003	714.8	648.6	730.3	718.8	737.0	712.3	718.3	700.1	708.7	740.0	710.0	758.9	8,598
2004	738.0	705.5	785.6	761.0	752.1	715.3	708.7	719.5	714.4	748.0	754.3	773.9	8,876
2005	754.0	704.6	797.5	754.8	783.9	764.5	739.5	757.4	745.5	760.4	766.1	798.9	9,127
2006	782.7	720.5	820.8	793.6	820.0	796.1	775.4	795.1	788.6	812.3	798.1	831.1	9,534
2007	822.9	754.1	840.5	803.8	824.6	792.6	799.5	797.0	777.2	825.8	815.2	847.3	9,700
2008	812.7	784.6	834.7	810.2	831.8	809.4	813.2	820.7	796.5	843.5	824.0	859.0	9,840
2009	826.9	768.0	870.5	847.6	856.1	838.1	842.8	850.7	842.5	862.8	839.5	863.9	10,109
2010	841.6	775.3	891.6	862.0	879.3	880.9	881.6	875.2	878.6	891.9	883.0	907.8	10,449
2011[1]	886.9	807.5	911.5	881.8	915.5	894.9	855.4	868.9	867.8	897.7	891.8	929.5	10,609

[1] Preliminary.   [2] Excludes cottage cheese.   *Source: National Agricultural Statistics Service, U.S. Department of Agriculture (NASS-USDA)*

Cold Storage Holdings of All Varieties of Cheese in the United States, on First of Month   In Millions of Pounds

Year	Jan.	Feb.	Mar.	Apr.	May	June	July	Aug.	Sept.	Oct.	Nov.	Dec.
2002	660.0	693.6	720.3	731.7	765.6	789.0	797.6	833.6	801.5	753.9	720.4	697.1
2003	730.1	761.2	770.0	771.3	781.1	791.0	800.1	809.0	794.2	762.2	722.4	695.5
2004	724.4	756.9	766.1	759.5	767.6	804.5	842.0	870.0	811.5	790.7	756.1	704.3
2005	705.8	713.8	723.7	749.2	780.8	815.6	823.4	837.2	812.9	769.0	755.9	720.8
2006	758.2	765.0	782.8	810.7	832.8	863.3	876.0	898.9	862.3	843.1	810.2	784.8
2007	817.4	850.0	875.7	892.9	894.3	898.9	891.2	886.0	846.2	820.4	810.6	805.9
2008	798.3	781.4	801.0	824.3	855.9	881.3	902.5	902.8	880.3	834.2	829.0	818.6
2009	852.0	882.4	892.5	915.2	938.9	970.3	987.4	1,000.2	997.6	983.9	969.2	961.7
2010	966.8	981.6	995.9	1,004.8	1,018.6	1,026.8	1,037.8	1,070.1	1,059.0	1,060.6	1,057.8	1,026.1
2011[1]	1,047.9	1,052.4	1,034.6	1,028.9	1,039.4	1,048.3	1,049.9	1,083.2	1,061.0	1,041.4	1,013.4	969.0

Quantities are given in "net weight."   [1] Preliminary.   *Source: National Agricultural Statistics Service, U.S. Department of Agriculture (NASS-USDA)*

Chromium

Chromium (symbol Cr) is a steel-gray, hard, and brittle, metallic element that can take on a high polish. Chromium and its compounds are toxic. Discovered in 1797 by Louis Vauquelin, chromium is named after the Greek word for color, *khroma*. Vauquelin also discovered that an emerald's green color is due to the presence of chromium. Many precious stones owe their color to the presence of chromium compounds.

Chromium is primarily found in chromite ore. The primary use of chromium is to form alloys with iron, nickel, or cobalt. Chromium improves hardness and resistance to corrosion and oxidation in iron, steel, and nonferrous alloys. It is a critical alloying ingredient in the production of stainless steel, making up 10% or more of the final composition. More than half of the chromium consumed is used in metallic products, and about one-third is used in refractories. Chromium is also used as a lustrous decorative plating agent, in pigments, leather processing, plating of metals, and catalysts.

Supply – World production of chromium in 2011 rose +1.3% yr/yr to 24.000 million metric tons, only slightly below the 2008 record high of 24.100 million metric tons. The world's largest producers of chromium in 2011 were South Africa with 46% of world production, India with 16%,

and Kazakhstan with 16%. India has emerged as a major producer of chromium in the past two decades. India's 2011 production level of 3.800 million metric tons was more than ten times the level of 360,000 metric tons seen 20 years earlier. South Africa's production in 2011 was up +29.4% yr/yr at a record high of 11.0 million metric tons and that is more than double the levels seen as recently as the early 1990s. Kazakhstan's production in 2011 was up +14.7% yr/yr at a record high of 3.900 million metric tons. Zimbabwe's chromium production in 2009 (latest available data) was 279,360 metric tons. U.S. Government stocks of chromium as of Dec 31, 2006 (latest available data) fell 98.4% yr/yr to a record low of 1.160 metric tons.

Demand – Based on the most recently available data from 1994, the metallurgical and chemical industry accounts for about 94% of chromium usage in the U.S., with the remaining 6% used by the refractory industry.

Trade – The U.S. relied on imports for a record low of 56% of its chromium consumption in 2010 (latest available data). That is well below the record high of 91% posted back in the 1970s. U.S. chromium imports in 2009 (latest available data) fell -55.0% yr/yr to 181,170 metric tons. U.S. exports of chromium in 2009 (latest available data) fell -55.1% yr/yr to 16,243 metric tons.

World Mine Production of Chromite   In Thousands of Metric Tons (Gross Weight)

Year	Albania	Brazil	Cuba	Finland	India	Iran	Kazakhstan	Madagascar	philippines	South Africa	Turkey	Zimbabwe	Total[1]
2002	73	284	20	566	2,699	513	2,369	11	22	6,436	314	749	14,600
2003	98	377	33	549	2,210	97	2,928	45	34	7,405	229	637	15,500
2004	160	593	40	580	2,949	139	3,287	77	42	7,677	506	621	17,900
2005	183	617	34	571	3,255	224	3,581	141	38	7,552	688	820	19,200
2006	213	563	28	549	3,600	245	3,366	132	47	7,418	1,060	713	19,700
2007	200	628	25	556	3,320	186	3,687	122	32	9,647	1,679	664	22,900
2008	207	706	25	614	3,900	188	3,629	84	15	9,683	1,886	484	24,100
2009[1]	256	700	25	247	3,760	255	3,333	60	14	6,866	1,770	279	19,300
2010[2]					3,800		3,400			8,500			23,700
2011[2]					3,800		3,900			11,000			24,000

[1] Preliminary.   [2] Estimate.   *Source: U.S. Geological Survey (USGS)*

Salient Statistics of Chromite in the United States   In Thousands of Metric Tons (Gross Weight)

Year	Net Import Reliance as a % of Appearent Consumption	Production of Ferro-chromium	Exports	Imports for Consumption	Reexports	Consumption by -- Primary Consumer Group --- Total	Metal-lurgical & Chemical	Refractory	Government[5] Stocks, Dec. 31 - Metal-lurgical & Chemical	Refractory	Total Stocks	South Africa[3]	Turkish[4]
2000	77	W	86	453	----	W	W	W	396	241	637	60-65	140-150
2001	63	W	43	239	----	W	W	W	396	241	637	NA	NA
2002	69	W	29	263	----	W	W	W	78	126	204	NA	NA
2003	57	W	46	317	----	W	W	W	78	156	234	NA	NA
2004	64	W	35	326	----	W	W	W	46	88	135	NA	NA
2005	68	W	57	353	----	W	W	W	4	70	73	NA	NA
2006	70	W	56	342	----	W	W	W	----	1	1	NA	NA
2007	67	W	60	328	----	W	W	W	----	----	----	NA	NA
2008[1]	66	W	36	402	----	W	W	W	----	----	----	NA	NA
2009[2]	12	W	16	181	----	W	W	W	----	----	----	NA	NA

[1] Preliminary.   [2] Estimate.   [3] Cr_2O_3, 44% (Transvaal).   [4] 48% Cr_2O_3.   [5] Data through 1999 are for Consumer.   W = Withheld.
Source: U.S. Geological Survey (USGS)

Coal

Coal is a sedimentary rock composed primarily of carbon, hydrogen, and oxygen. Coal is a fossil fuel formed from ancient plants buried deep in the Earth's crust over 300 million years ago. Historians believe coal was first used commercially in China for smelting copper and for casting coins around 1,000 BC. Almost 92% of all coal consumed in the U.S. is burned by electric power plants, and coal accounts for about 55% of total electricity output. Coal is also used in the manufacture of steel. The steel industry first converts coal into coke, then combines the coke with iron ore and limestone, and finally heats the mixture to produce iron. Other industries use coal to make fertilizers, solvents, medicine, pesticides, and synthetic fuels.

There are four types of mined coal: anthracite (used in high-grade steel production), bituminous (used for electricity generation and for making coke), sub-bituminous, and lignite (both used primarily for electricity generation).

Coal futures trade at the New York Mercantile Exchange (NYMEX). The contract trades in units of 1,550 tons and is priced in terms of dollars and cents per short ton.

Supply – U.S. production of bituminous coal in 2011 (annualized through November) fell -0.9% yr/yr to 1.073 billion tons, down from the 2008 record high of 1.169 billion tons.

Demand – U.S. consumption of coal in 2010 rose +5.1% to 1.048 billion tons, below the 2007 record high of 1.128 billion tons.

Trade – U.S. exports of coal in 2010 rose +38.3% yr/yr to 81.715, a new record high. U.S. imports fell -14.5% yr/yr to 19.353 million tons, down from the 2007 record high of 36.347 million tons. The major exporting destinations for the U.S. are Canada and Europe.

World Production[3] of Coal (Monthly Average)   In Thousands of Metric Tons

Year	Australia	Canada	China	Czech-Republic	Germany	India	Indonesia	Kazak-hstan	Poland	Russia	Ukraine	United Kingdom	United States
2002	23,123	2,468	92,339	1,206	2,197	27,938	8,588	6,493	8,642	15,198	5,163	2,499	66,565
2003	30,000	2,215	109,602	1,137	2,396	29,036	9,551	6,734	8,573	16,329	5,354	2,353	81,023
2004	31,250	2,438	130,434	1,109	2,429	31,438	11,021	6,922	8,436	17,495	4,947	2,089	92,953
2005	32,917	2,382	150,891	1,104	2,335	33,129	11,755	6,899	8,159	18,472	5,033	1,667	94,439
2006	33,583	2,492	171,288	1,115	1,980	35,088	12,571	7,631	7,935	19,468	5,135	1,544	96,782
2007	35,167	2,734	192,229	1,074	1,794	37,134	14,569	8,199	7,316	20,178	4,897	1,417	95,550
2008	35,917	2,737	215,472	1,054	1,431	40,289	15,131	8,773	7,020	20,464	4,939	1,504	97,624
2009	35,583	2,330	248,666	917	1,141	43,448	17,445	8,015	6,493	19,193	4,568	1,489	89,577
2010[1]	37,417	2,809	249,629	953	1,068	42,614	18,723		6,383	20,661	4,537	1,506	90,440
2011[2]	28,000	2,813		964	1,011	52,864			6,279	20,971	5,069	1,565	89,896

[1] Preliminary.   [2] Estimate.   [3] All grades of anthracite and bituminous coal, but excludes recovered slurries, lignite and brown coal.
Source: United Nations

Production of Bituminous & Lignite Coal in the United States   In Thousands of Short Tons

Year	Alabama	Colorado	Illinois	Indiana	Kentucky	Montana	Ohio	Pennsyl-vania	Texas	West Virginia	Virgina	Wyoming	Total
2002	19,062	35,103	33,358	35,513	124,388	37,386	21,157	67,104	45,247	30,126	150,222	373,161	1,092,916
2003	20,207	35,831	31,760	35,512	113,126	36,994	22,009	63,792	47,517	31,771	139,755	376,270	1,071,753
2004	22,329	39,870	31,912	35,206	114,743	39,989	23,222	66,023	45,863	31,647	148,017	396,493	1,110,393
2005	21,453	38,510	32,014	34,457	120,029	40,354	24,718	65,852	45,939	27,964	153,655	404,319	1,129,794
2006	18,830	36,322	32,729	35,119	120,848	41,823	22,722	64,500	45,548	29,740	152,374	446,742	1,162,750
2007	19,522	36,384	32,857	35,003	115,530	43,390	22,575	63,621	41,948	25,462	153,522	453,568	1,145,067
2008	21,157	32,028	33,074	36,040	120,778	44,786	26,251	63,742	39,017	24,748	157,805	467,644	1,170,096
2009	19,171	28,267	34,021	35,850	107,802	39,486	27,651	57,222	35,093	21,019	137,194	431,107	1,073,002
2010[1]	20,396	25,163	33,465	35,317	105,267	44,732	26,728	57,188	40,982	22,385	135,307	442,522	1,082,592
2011[2]	19,969	27,776	36,471	36,758	108,586	41,591	27,455	58,003	44,546	22,322	136,592	436,092	1,087,010

[1] Preliminary.   [2] Estimate.   *Source: Energy Information Administration, U.S. Department of Energy (EIA-DOE)*

Production[2] of Bituminous Coal in the United States   In Thousands of Short Tons

Year	Jan.	Feb.	Mar.	Apr.	May	June	July	Aug.	Sept.	Oct.	Nov.	Dec.	Total
2002	101,939	90,208	90,108	90,039	91,673	85,555	86,190	92,054	92,212	94,033	87,836	91,058	1,092,905
2003	92,649	82,130	88,976	89,202	90,435	88,348	88,301	89,355	90,344	93,928	84,155	94,154	1,071,977
2004	93,182	86,306	94,876	91,739	87,210	94,835	92,260	95,209	93,525	92,618	92,268	95,478	1,109,506
2005	92,804	89,039	102,178	93,296	90,168	95,374	91,930	97,907	95,493	93,532	94,842	92,774	1,129,337
2006	98,385	88,826	101,339	95,288	99,706	97,023	94,861	100,504	94,029	98,674	96,400	95,939	1,160,974
2007	99,221	88,084	97,490	92,923	96,867	95,432	92,884	100,493	92,288	98,691	96,769	93,010	1,144,152
2008	98,488	93,428	96,805	96,991	96,425	90,096	99,014	100,312	99,203	104,222	95,264	99,604	1,169,852
2009	96,418	89,126	95,457	88,797	84,989	88,435	90,435	89,902	87,775	87,898	85,396	86,053	1,070,681
2010	85,458	82,838	96,601	90,848	85,313	88,510	90,860	93,419	93,430	91,700	91,418	92,648	1,083,043
2011[1]	90,529	84,800	95,482	86,457	84,576	86,652	83,419	93,190	91,823	92,638	92,082	92,116	1,073,764

[1] Preliminary.   [2] Includes small amount of lignite.   *Source: Energy Information Administration, U.S. Department of Energy (EIA-DOE)*

COAL

Production[2] of Pennsylvania Anthracite Coal   In Thousands of Short Tons

Year	Jan.	Feb.	Mar.	Apr.	May	June	July	Aug.	Sept.	Oct.	Nov.	Dec.	Total
2002	131	117	116	121	122	240	116	126	119	130	120	126	1,584
2003	108	98	98	115	114	107	97	95	101	130	111	116	1,290
2004	197	183	147	111	101	214	141	145	150	145	151	127	1,812
2005	133	129	149	137	135	157	125	140	135	156	179	127	1,704
2006	138	121	147	117	128	125	124	140	115	134	126	123	1,538
2007	141	125	139	125	133	134	120	135	116	134	141	128	1,568
2008	131	126	127	160	162	103	147	146	148	168	140	154	1,712
2009	150	141	153	153	139	154	172	168	171	176	168	177	1,921
2010	129	128	156	158	140	151	161	169	168	131	140	143	1,776
2011[1]	191	183	206	171	174	180	185	218	205	155	162	162	2,190

[1] Preliminary.   [2] Represents production in Pennsylvania only.   *Source: Energy Information Administration, U.S. Department of Energy (EIA-DOE)*

Salient Statistics of Coal in the United States   In Thousands of Short Tons

Year	Production	Imports	Consumption	Exports Brazil	Canada	Europe	Asia	Total	Total Ending Stocks[2]	Losses & Unaccounted For[3]
2001	1,127,689	19,787	1,060,146	4,574	17,633	20,821	3,246	48,666	181,912	7,120
2002	1,094,283	16,875	1,066,355	3,538	16,686	15,574	1,735	39,601	192,127	4,039
2003	1,071,753	25,044	1,094,861	3,514	20,760	15,148	266	43,014	165,468	-4,403
2004	1,112,099	27,280	1,107,255	4,361	17,760	15,211	7,475	47,998	154,006	6,887
2005	1,131,498	30,460	1,125,978	4,199	19,466	18,825	5,082	49,942	144,304	9,092
2006	1,162,750	36,246	1,112,292	4,534	19,889	20,805	2,008	49,647	186,946	8,824
2007	1,146,635	36,347	1,127,998	6,512	18,389	27,119	1,202	59,163	192,758	4,085
2008	1,171,809	34,208	1,120,548	6,380	22,979	40,306	5,269	81,519	205,112	5,740
2009	1,074,923	22,639	997,478	7,416	10,599	30,073	6,483	59,097	244,780	14,985
2010[1]	1,085,281	19,353	1,048,295	7,925	11,400	38,208	17,896	81,716	224,315	8,950

[1] Preliminary.   [2] Producer & distributor and consumer stocks, excludes stocks held by retail dealers for consumption by the residential and commercial sector.   [3] Equals production plus imports minus the change in producer & distributor and consumer stocks minus consumption minus exports.
Source: Energy Information Administraion, U.S. Department of Energy (EIA-DOE)

Consumption and Stocks of Coal in the United States   In Thousands of Short Tons

Year	Electric Utilities Anthracite	Bituminous	Lignite	Total	Industrial Coke Plants	Other Industrial[2]	Residential and Commercial	Total	Stocks, Dec. 31 Consumer Electric Utilities	Coke Plants	Other Industrials	Producers and Distributors
2001	NA	NA	NA	964,433	26,075	65,268	4,369	1,060,146	138,496	1,510	6,006	35,900
2002	NA	NA	NA	977,507	23,656	60,747	4,445	1,066,355	141,714	1,364	5,792	43,257
2003	NA	NA	NA	1,005,116	24,248	61,261	4,236	1,094,861	121,567	905	4,718	38,277
2004	NA	NA	NA	1,016,268	23,670	62,195	5,122	1,107,255	106,669	1,344	4,842	41,151
2005	NA	NA	NA	1,037,485	23,434	60,340	4,720	1,125,978	101,237	2,615	5,582	34,971
2006	NA	NA	NA	1,026,636	22,957	59,472	3,226	1,112,292	140,964	2,928	6,506	36,548
2007	NA	NA	NA	1,045,141	22,715	56,615	3,526	1,127,998	151,221	1,936	5,624	33,977
2008	NA	NA	NA	1,040,580	22,070	54,393	3,506	1,120,548	161,589	2,331	6,007	34,688
2009	NA	NA	NA	933,627	15,326	45,314	3,210	997,478	189,467	1,957	5,109	47,718
2010[1]	NA	NA	NA	975,052	21,092	52,082	3,081	1,051,307	174,917	1,925	6,350	49,820

[1] Preliminary.   [2] Including transportation.   [3] Excludes stocks held at retail dealers for consumption by the residential and commercial sector.
Source: Energy Information Administration, U.S. Department of Energy (EIA-DOE)

Average Prices of Coal in the United States   In Dollars Per Short Ton

Year	End-Use Sector Electric Utilities	Coke Plants	Other Industrial[2]	Imports[3]	Exports Steam	Metal-lurgical	Total Average[3]	Year	End-Use Sector Electric Utilities	Coke Plants	Other Industrial[2]	Imports[3]	Exports Steam	Metal-lurgical	Total Average[3]
2001	24.68	46.42	32.26	34.00	31.88	41.63	36.97	2006	34.26	92.87	51.67	49.10	46.25	90.81	70.93
2002	24.74	50.67	35.49	35.51	34.51	45.41	40.44	2007	NA	94.97	54.42	47.64	47.90	88.99	70.25
2003	25.29	50.63	34.70	31.45	26.94	44.55	35.98	2008	NA	118.09	63.44	59.83	57.35	134.62	97.68
2004	27.30	61.50	39.30	37.52	42.03	63.63	54.11	2009	NA	143.01	64.87	63.91	73.63	117.73	101.44
2005	31.22	83.79	47.63	46.71	47.64	81.56	67.10	2010[1]	NA	153.59	64.24	71.77	65.54	145.44	120.41

[1] Preliminary.   [2] Manufacturing plants only.   [3] Based on the free alongside ship (F.A.S.) value.
Source: Energy Information Administration, U.S. Department of Energy (EIA-DOE)

Trends in Bituminous Coal, Lignite and Pennsylvania Anthracite in the United States   In Thousands of Short Tons

| | ------ Bituminous Coal and Lignite ------ | | | | | | | ---- Pennsylvania Anthracite ---- | | | | | All Mines |
| | ------ Production ------ | | | | ---- Labor Productivity ---- | | | | | | | Labor Productivity | Labor Productivity |
Year	Under-Ground	Surface	Total	Miners[1] Employed	Under-Ground Short Tons	Surface Per Miner	Average Per Hour	Under-Ground	Surface	Total	Miners[1] Employed	Short Tons Miner/Hr.	Short Tons Miner/Hr.
2001	380,627	745,308	1,127,689	77,088	4.02	10.60	6.82	341	1,143	1,484	955	.81	6.82
2002	357,385	735,910	1,094,283	75,466	3.98	10.38	6.80	305	998	1,303	872	.78	6.80
2003	352,785	717,870	1,071,753	71,023	4.04	10.76	6.95	282	961	1,243	814	.82	6.95
2004	367,557	743,552	1,112,099	73,912	3.96	10.57	6.80	271	1,408	1,679	890	.97	6.80
2005	368,612	762,190	1,131,498	79,283	3.62	10.04	6.36	264	1,296	1,560	891	.95	6.36
2006	359,022	802,976	1,161,998	82,959	3.37	10.19	6.26	239	1,132	1,371	869	.95	6.26
2007	351,790	793,690	1,145,480	81,278	3.34	10.25	6.27	224	1,199	1,423	910	.89	6.27
2008	357,079	813,322	1,170,401	86,859	3.15	9.82	5.96	227	2,455	2,682	929	.91	5.96
2009	332,062	740,174	1,072,236	87,592	2.99	9.22	5.61	176	1,555	1,731	941	.95	5.61
2010	337,155	745,357	1,082,512	86,057	2.89	9.47	5.55	139	1,566	1,705	928	.98	5.55

[1] Excludes miners employed at mines producing less than 10,000 tons.
Source: Energy Information Administration, U.S. Department of Energy (EIA-DOE)

Average Mine Prices of Coal in the United States   In Dollars Per Short Ton

| | ---- Average Mine Prices by Method ---- | | | ---- Average Mine Prices by Rank ---- | | | | Bituminous & Lignite FOB Mines[2] | Anthracite FOB Mines[2] | All Coal CIF[3] Electric Utility Plants |
Year	Under-ground	Surface	Total	Lignite	Sub-bituminous	Bituminous	Anthracite[1]			
2001	25.37	13.18	17.38	11.52	6.67	25.36	47.67	25.36	47.67	24.68
2002	26.68	13.65	17.98	11.07	7.34	26.57	47.78	26.57	47.78	24.74
2003	26.71	13.42	17.85	11.20	7.73	26.73	49.55	26.73	49.55	25.29
2004	30.36	14.75	19.93	12.27	8.12	30.56	39.77	30.56	39.77	27.30
2005	36.42	17.37	23.59	13.49	8.68	36.80	41.00	36.80	41.00	31.22
2006	38.28	18.88	25.16	14.00	9.95	39.32	43.61	39.32	43.61	34.26
2007	40.29	19.41	26.20	14.89	10.69	40.80	52.24	40.80	52.24	36.06
2008	51.35	22.35	31.25	16.50	12.31	51.40	60.76	51.40	60.76	
2009	55.77	23.24	33.24	17.26	13.35	55.44	57.10	55.44	57.10	
2010	60.73	24.13	35.61	18.76	14.11	60.88	59.61	60.88	59.61	

[1] Produced in Pennsylvania.   [2] FOB = free on board.   [3] CIF = cost, insurance and freight.   W = Withheld data.
Source: Energy Information Adminstration, U.S. Department of Energy (EIA-DOE)

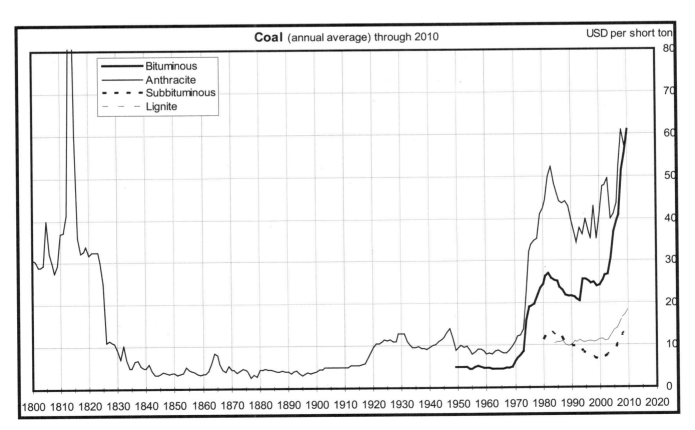

Coal (annual average) through 2010 — USD per short ton

Cobalt

Cobalt (symbol Co) is a lustrous, silvery-white, magnetic, metallic element used chiefly for making alloys. Cobalt was known in ancient times and used by the Persians in 2250 BC to color glass. The name *cobalt* comes from the German word *kobalt* or *kobold*, meaning evil spirit. Miners gave cobalt its name because it was poisonous and troublesome since it polluted and degraded other mined elements, like nickel. In the 1730s, George Brandt first isolated metallic cobalt and was able to show that cobalt was the source of the blue color in glasses. In 1780, it was recognized as an element. Cobalt is generally not found in nature as a free metal and is instead found in ores. Cobalt is generally produced as a by-product of nickel and copper mining.

Cobalt is used in a variety of applications: high temperature steel alloys; fasteners in gas turbine engines; magnets and magnetic recording media; drying agents for paints and pigments; and steel-belted radial tires. Cobalt-60, an important radioactive tracer and cancer-treatment agent, is an artificially produced radioactive isotope of cobalt.

Prices – The price of cobalt in 2010 (latest data available) rose by 17.6% to $21.00 per pound, well below the 2008 record high of $39.01 per pound, but triple the 20-year low of $6.91 per pound in 2002, just eight years ago.

Supply – World production of cobalt in 2010 (latest data) rose by 21.7% to a record high of 88,000 metric tons. The world's largest cobalt mine producers in 2010 were the Congo with 51% of world production, Zambia (13%), Russia (7%), Australia (5%), and Canada (3%).

The U.S. does not specifically mine or refine cobalt although some cobalt is produced as a by-product of other mining operations. Imports, stock releases, and secondary materials comprise the U.S. cobalt supply. Secondary production includes extraction from super-alloy scrap, cemented carbide scrap, and spent catalysts. In the U.S. there are two domestic producers of extra-fine cobalt powder. One company produces the powder from imported primary metal and the other from recycled materials. There are only about seven companies that produce cobalt compounds. U.S. secondary production of cobalt in 2010 (latest data) rose +11.7% yr/yr to 2,000 metric tons but remains well below the record high of 3,080 metric tons seen in 1998.

Demand – U.S. consumption of cobalt in 2010 (latest data) rose by +33.0% yr/yr to 10,000 metric tons, but still below the 2005 record high of 11,800 metric tons. The largest use of cobalt by far was for super-alloys 43% of consumption in 2008 consumption. Other smaller-scaled applications for cobalt include cutting and wear-resistant materials (8.0%), magnetic alloys (3.6%), and welding materials (2.2%). Demand for some other uses is not available as proprietary information.

Trade – U.S. imports of cobalt in 2010 (latest data) rose +43.2% to 11,000 metric tons, but still below the 2006 record high of 11,600 metric tons. In 2009 the U.S. relied on imports for 81% of its cobalt consumption, which is down from the 99% level seen in the early 1970s.

World Mine Production of Cobalt   In Metric Tons (Cobalt Content)

Year	Australia	Botswana	Canada	Cuba	Finland (Refinery)	France (Refinery)	Japan (Refinery)	New Caledonia	Norway (Refinery)	Russia	Congo[3]	Zambia	World Total
2001	6,300	325	1,003	5,326	150	12,000	3,425	----	1,242	1,400	4,600	8,000	44,800
2002	6,800	269	1,099	5,148	1,000	14,600	3,442	----	1,453	2,780	4,600	10,000	52,200
2003	6,000	294	1,300	4,327	700	14,800	3,274	----	1,391	2,602	6,100	11,300	52,900
2004	5,600	223	1,400	5,060	1,260	20,200	3,554	1,700	1,600	2,726	6,000	10,000	60,300
2005	4,590	326	1,400	5,767	2,100	24,500	4,798	1,600	1,600	1,769	6,300	9,300	65,200
2006	5,130	303	1,100	7,115	1,840	27,100	5,602	1,600	1,500	1,629	6,300	8,000	69,800
2007	4,730	242	1,311	8,692	6,100	25,300	4,540	1,600	1,600	1,620	6,300	7,500	72,600
2008	4,780	337	1,215	8,953	6,630	31,000	3,175	1,300	1,700	1,600	6,200	6,900	75,900
2009[1]	4,630	335	1,200	4,072	6,000	35,500	3,500	1,200	1,600	1,000	6,100	5,000	72,300
2010[2]	4,600		1,500	2,500	6,200	45,000	3,500			1,500	1,700	6,100	11,000	88,000

[1] Preliminary.   [2] Estimate.   [3] Formerly Zaire.   *Source: U.S. Geological Survey (USGS)*

Salient Statistics of Cobalt in the United States   In Metric Tons (Cobalt Content)

Year	Net Import Reliance As a % of Apparent Consumption	Cobalt Secondary Production	Processor and Consumer Stocks Dec. 31	Imports for Consumption	Ground Coat Frit	Stainless & Heat Resisting	Catalysts	Super-alloys	Tool Steel	Magnetic Alloys	Pigments	Drier in Paints, etc.	Cutting & Wear-Resistant Material	Welding Materials	Total Apparent Uses	Price $ Per Pound[4]
2001	76	2,780	852	9,410	W	W	W	4,850	W	472	W	W	720	661	11,800	10.55
2002	72	2,800	917	8,450	W	W	W	3,700	W	416	W	W	618	634	9,830	6.91
2003	79	2,130	649	8,080	W	W	W	3,400	W	282	W	W	662	632	10,000	10.60
2004	77	2,300	719	8,720	W	W	W	3,650	W	396	W	W	765	627	9,950	23.93
2005	83	2,030	705	11,100	W	W	W	4,140	W	343	W	W	762	227	11,800	15.96
2006	82	2,010	1,180	11,600	W	W	W	4,170	W	386	W	W	808	224	11,000	17.22
2007	80	1,930	1,310	10,300	W	W	W	4,410	W	385	W	W	726	225	9,630	30.55
2008	81	1,930	1,160	10,700	W	W	W	4,320	W	368	W	W	827	226	10,100	39.01
2009[1]	76	1,790	840	7,680	W	W	W	3,680	W	295	W	W	503	221	7,520	17.86
2010[2]	81	2,000	880	11,000											10,000	21.00

[1] Preliminary.   [2] Estimate.   [3] Or related usage.   [4] Annual spot for cathodes.   W = Withheld.   *Source: U.S. Geological Survey (USGS)*

Cocoa

Cocoa is the common name for a powder derived from the fruit seeds of the cacao tree. The Spanish called cocoa "the food of the gods" when they found it in South America 500 years ago. Today, it remains a valued commodity. Dating back to the time of the Aztecs, cocoa was mainly used as a beverage. The processing of the cacao seeds, also known as cocoa beans, begins when the harvested fruit is fermented or cured into a pulpy state for three to nine days. The cocoa beans are then dried in the sun and cleaned in special machines before they are roasted to bring out the chocolate flavor. After roasting, they are put into a crushing machine and ground into cocoa powder. Cocoa has a high food value because it contains as much as 20 percent protein, 40 percent carbohydrate, and 40 percent fat. It is also mildly stimulating because of the presence of theobromine, an alkaloid that is closely related to caffeine. Roughly two-thirds of cocoa bean production is used to make chocolate and one-third to make cocoa powder.

Four major West African cocoa producers, the Ivory Coast, Ghana, Nigeria and Cameroon, together account for about two-thirds of world cocoa production. Outside of West Africa, the major producers of cocoa are Indonesia, Brazil, Malaysia, Ecuador, and the Dominican Republic. Cocoa producers like Ghana and Indonesia have been making efforts to increase cocoa production while producers like Malaysia have been switching to other crops. Ghana has had an ongoing problem with black pod disease and with smuggling of the crop into neighboring Ivory Coast. Brazil was once one of the largest producers of cocoa but has had problems with witches' broom disease. In West Africa, the main crop harvest starts in the September-October period and can be extended into the January-March period. Cocoa trees reach maturity in 5-6 years but can live to be 50 years old or more. During the course of a growing season, the cocoa tree will produce thousands of flowers but only a few will develop into cocoa pods.

Cocoa futures and options are traded at the ICE Futures U.S. (ICE) exchange and on NYSE-LIFFE exchange in London. The futures contracts call for the delivery of 10 metric tons of cocoa and the contract is priced in US dollars per metric ton.

Prices – Cocoa prices rallied sharply in early 2011 as the presidential election in the Ivory Coast in November 2010 was disputed and disrupted cocoa exports from the Ivory Coast, the world's biggest producer. Cocoa prices rallied to a 33-year nearest-future high of $3,826 per metric ton in March 2011 as the Ivory Coast's President-elect banned exports starting in January and extended the export ban into March of 2011as the presidential dispute continued. The market was also concerned that stockpiled Ivory Coast cocoa beans from the export ban would quickly go bad in hot and humid Ivory Coast warehouses. After the Ivory Coast President-elect regained power in April 2011 and Ivory Coast cocoa exports resumed, prices plunged the rest of the year and posted a 3-1/4 year low in December 2011 at $1898 a metric ton and finished the year down -30.5% at $2109 per metric ton. Another bearish factor for cocoa was increased cocoa production in Ghana, the world's second-biggest producer, which posted a record 2010/11 harvest of 1.025 MMT. This increase in supply prompted the ICO to hike its 2010/11 global cocoa ending stocks estimate +18.5% y/y to a record high of 1.93 MMT.

Supply – The world production of cocoa beans in the 2010-11 (latest data) crop year rose +2.2% to 4.231 million metric tons. The world's largest cocoa producer by far is the Ivory Coast with 29.4% of total world production in 2010-11(latest data). The Ivory Coast's production in 2010-11, rose +1.6% yr/yr. After the Ivory Coast the major producers are Indonesia with 19.2% of total world production in 2010-11, Ghana with 15.0%, Nigeria with 10.1%, Cameroon with 6.2% and Brazil with 5.5%. Closing stocks of cocoa in the 2010-11 (latest data) crop year rose +22.8% yr/yr to 1.834 metric tons.

Demand – World seasonal grindings of cocoa in 2010-11 rose +4.1% yr/yr to 3.867 million metric tons, a new record high. Europe is by far the largest global consumer of cocoa, consuming about 36.3% of the global crop.

Trade – U.S. imports of cocoa and cocoa products in 2011(annualized through November) rose +7.4% yr/yr to 1.313 million metric tons, a new record high.

World Supply and Demand Cocoa   In Thousands of Metric Tons

Crop Year Beginning Oct. 1	Stocks Oct. 1	Net World Production[4]	Total Availability	Seasona Grindings	Closing Stocks	Stock Change	Stock/Consumption Ratio %
2001-02	1,344	2,857	4,201	2,886	1,315	-29	45.6
2002-03	1,315	3,157	4,472	3,077	1,395	80	45.3
2003-04	1,395	3,526	4,921	3,237	1,682	287	52.0
2004-05	1,682	3,347	5,029	3,372	1,654	-28	49.1
2005-06	1,654	3,773	5,427	3,522	1,902	248	54.0
2006-07	1,902	3,399	5,301	3,670	1,628	-274	44.4
2007-08	1,628	3,713	5,341	3,759	1,569	-59	41.7
2008-09[1]	1,569	3,566	5,135	3,512	1,614	45	46.0
2009-10[2]	1,614	3,611	5,225	3,716	1,493	-121	40.2
2010-11[3]	1,493	3,899	5,392	3,867	1,834	341	47.4

[1] Preliminary.   [2] Estimate.   [3] Forecast.   [4] Obtained by adjusting the gross world crop for a one percent loss in weight.
Source: International Cocoa Organization (ICO

COCOA

World Production of Cocoa Beans   In Thousands of Metric Tons

Crop Year Beginning Oct. 1	Brazil	Came-roon	Colom-bia	Côte d'Ivoire	Dominican Republic	Ecuador	Ghana	Indo-nesia	Malaysia	Mexico	Nigeria	Papau New Guinea	World Total
2001-02	186	122	36	1,212	45	76	390	428	58	47	340	39	3,109
2002-03	175	125	34	1,265	45	88	341	571	48	46	362	42	3,271
2003-04	170	155	42	1,352	47	88	497	573	36	50	385	43	3,580
2004-05	196	167	39	1,407	48	90	737	642	33	44	412	39	4,020
2005-06	209	140	37	1,360	31	94	740	643	28	36	441	48	4,016
2006-07	212	165	35	1,372	47	88	734	769	32	38	485	51	4,273
2007-08	202	213	40	1,384	43	86	615	740	35	30	361	49	4,037
2008-09[1]	202	229	45	1,382	46	94	681	793	28	28	367	52	4,228
2009-10[2]	218	236	49	1,223	50	121	711	800	18	23	364	51	4,142
2010-11[3]	233	264	40	1,242	53	132	632	810	18	27	428	57	4,231

[1] Preliminary.   [2] Estimate.   [3] Forecast.   Source: Food and Agricultural Organization of the United Nations (FAO)

World Consumption of Cocoa[4]   In Thousands of Metric Tons

Crop Year Beginning Oct. 1	Canada	Côte d'Ivoire	Brazil	European Union	Ghana	Indonesia	Japan	Malaysia	Singa-pore	Turkey	United States	Russia	World Total
2001-02	56	265	173	1,159	80	108	50	93	62	39	393	69	2,886
2002-03	57	290	196	1,190	69	115	64	129	71	50	400	60	3,077
2003-04	72	321	207	1,256	78	122	57	200	59	71	401	63	3,237
2004-05	65	320	209	1,328	76	111	53	228	57	58	409	68	3,372
2005-06	76	336	223	1,328	85	130	60	265	70	56	432	70	3,522
2006-07	66	360	226	1,390	121	140	50	301	87	64	418	65	3,670
2007-08	59	374	232	1,409	123	160	42	331	89	60	391	65	3,759
2008-09[1]	55	419	216	1,320	133	120	41	278	80	52	361	54	3,512
2009-10[2]	59	400	161	1,373	212	120	42	298	80	65	382	54	3,716
2010-11[3]		350	190	1,403	275	130	40	315	80	70	390	55	3,867

[1] Preliminary.   [2] Estimate.   [3] Forecast.   [4] Figures represent the "grindings" of cocoa beans in each country.   NA = Not available.
Source: International Cocoa Organization (ICO)

Imports of Cocoa Butter in Selected Countries   In Metric Tons

Year	Australia	Austria	Belgium	Canada	France	Germany	Italy	Japan	Nether-lands	Sweden	Switzer-land	United Kingdom	United States
2002	20,800	3,777	48,992	24,397	63,814	82,313	12,099	20,212	47,562	6,401	21,545	46,912	84,788
2003	22,310	3,823	54,621	26,309	58,759	77,880	13,337	22,579	55,523	6,564	21,555	39,092	78,035
2004	23,514	4,536	56,328	27,646	70,386	79,155	13,891	22,166	63,657	6,668	22,960	50,593	94,890
2005	21,527	4,281	61,200	28,382	72,561	82,050	16,114	24,633	70,255	6,276	24,264	70,777	96,876
2006	19,172	4,729	68,173	23,803	75,572	82,726	16,285	25,603	82,864	5,774	25,725	48,447	96,455
2007	15,845	4,367	75,283	31,301	78,858	85,113	20,973	24,417	70,598	3,441	27,265	48,911	86,258
2008	14,970	4,847	64,782	23,516	69,153	85,605	21,706	23,368	72,786	3,993	27,193	42,879	102,868
2009	13,113	4,110	69,909	20,758	64,516	84,942	21,086	22,037	70,262	3,698	24,790	43,244	84,499
2010	15,024	4,779	65,642	20,889	57,614	88,718	22,438	19,363	69,397	6,414	26,460	50,632	102,585
2011[1]	16,252	5,252	75,316	22,632	52,436	79,604	22,212	22,620	96,828	6,152	27,916	46,340	94,612

[1] Preliminary.   Sources: Food and Agricultural Organization of the United Nations (FAO)

Imports of Cocoa Liquor and Cocoa Powder in Selected Countries   In Metric Tons

Year	Cocoa Liquor						Cocoa Powder						
	France	Germany	Japan	Nether-lands	United Kingdom	United States	Denmark	France	Germany	Italy	Japan	Nether-lands	United States
2002	64,820	28,100	1,193	46,369	14,038	22,215	2,895	35,128	39,871	19,642	10,859	54,422	126,443
2003	71,337	31,391	1,764	35,089	20,154	20,018	3,142	43,915	37,065	18,757	12,895	38,713	136,813
2004	72,057	42,975	2,773	40,847	17,753	20,758	3,447	44,213	35,460	19,538	14,973	38,692	147,392
2005	80,194	42,537	3,327	46,409	6,574	33,540	3,996	43,626	33,202	23,085	13,705	45,859	141,044
2006	86,767	43,918	14,684	43,885	6,541	24,359	3,053	39,833	41,050	22,485	15,831	34,770	145,820
2007	58,344	39,985	7,659	48,960	6,725	20,357	3,106	41,030	47,480	28,241	16,218	35,979	158,132
2008	58,469	60,364	8,438	44,435	6,603	20,135	3,046	45,652	47,232	28,576	18,050	24,364	156,028
2009	58,994	64,205	7,513	44,521	6,798	19,369	2,617	42,069	49,685	24,692	15,611	34,518	163,827
2010	60,808	77,908	5,950	57,146	10,030	36,686	2,402	51,364	52,764	26,756	17,728	43,524	157,778
2011[1]	74,212	74,556	9,640	75,284	10,968	13,668	1,696	56,560	50,216	29,456	16,848	48,852	151,804

[1] Preliminary.   NA = Not available.   Source: Food and Agricultural Organization of the United Nations (FAO)

Imports of Cocoa and Products in the United States   In Thousands of Metric Tons

Year	Jan.	Feb.	Mar.	Apr.	May	June	July	Aug.	Sept.	Oct.	Nov.	Dec.	Total
2002	84	74	73	60	76	70	85	96	60	65	88	71	902
2003	114	73	91	70	68	73	93	81	78	95	85	116	1,038
2004	110	79	130	100	101	103	94	94	100	90	81	88	1,169
2005	129	109	156	108	104	93	91	104	84	87	113	129	1,307
2006	114	104	109	94	92	86	108	140	103	91	90	124	1,255
2007	111	121	110	102	82	76	83	83	84	95	76	106	1,130
2008	108	115	109	87	80	65	88	82	79	90	84	128	1,114
2009	114	98	88	95	82	99	80	88	103	103	94	126	1,170
2010	154	100	134	85	94	78	80	84	110	89	100	115	1,222
2011[1]	132	144	88	90	92	138	125	122	94	98	90	101	1,313

[1] Preliminary.   *Source: Foreign Agricultural Service, U.S. Department of Agriculture (FAS-USDA)*

Visible Stocks of Cocoa in Port of Hampton Road Warehouses[1], at End of Month   In Thousands of Bags

Year	Jan.	Feb.	Mar.	Apr.	May	June	July	Aug.	Sept.	Oct.	Nov.	Dec.
2002	509.7	462.8	436.7	415.4	383.8	353.4	322.9	273.3	255.1	194.8	181.5	169.9
2003	149.9	121.7	102.6	100.7	80.5	71.8	69.2	67.7	56.9	53.0	48.4	49.3
2004	48.6	47.8	47.5	47.5	45.8	43.9	41.2	40.4	40.1	38.0	38.0	36.8
2005	31.1	30.9	28.6	28.0	28.0	27.4	27.4	27.4	27.4	27.4	27.4	27.4
2006	18.3	17.9	17.3	17.3	17.3	17.3	17.3	17.3	17.1	17.1	17.1	17.1
2007	16.8	16.8	16.8	16.8	16.8	16.8	16.8	15.6	15.6	15.6	15.6	15.6
2008	15.6	15.6	15.6	15.6	15.8	15.8	15.8	15.8	15.8	15.6	15.6	15.6
2009	14.9	14.9	14.9	14.9	14.9	14.9	13.7	13.7	13.7	13.7	13.7	13.7
2010	13.3	12.3	12.3	12.3	12.3	12.3	12.3	12.3	12.3	12.3	12.3	12.3
2011	10.4	12.3	12.3	12.3	12.3	12.3	12.3	12.3	11.6	11.6	11.6	11.6

[1] Licensed warehouses approved by ICE.   *Source: ICE Futures U.S. (ICE)*

Visible Stocks of Cocoa in Philadelphia (Del. River) Warehouses[1], at End of Month   In Thousands of Bags

Year	Jan.	Feb.	Mar.	Apr.	May	June	July	Aug.	Sept.	Oct.	Nov.	Dec.
2002	1,705.4	1,876.7	1,849.3	1,702.0	1,746.4	1,689.5	1,899.2	1,832.7	1,736.2	1,334.5	1,162.7	1,250.6
2003	1,347.2	1,422.0	1,327.9	1,311.7	1,217.2	1,178.5	1,170.9	1,123.7	868.7	798.9	765.0	806.0
2004	1,294.9	1,061.5	1,067.1	1,187.1	1,232.7	1,366.8	1,432.6	1,529.3	1,379.5	1,569.4	1,378.2	1,335.7
2005	1,588.9	1,809.8	2,066.3	2,264.5	2,434.3	2,258.3	2,465.0	2,481.0	2,470.5	2,385.2	2,382.8	2,566.4
2006	2,888.5	2,828.9	3,013.5	3,246.1	3,111.0	2,913.8	2,754.7	3,404.0	3,382.1	3,307.2	3,085.7	3,293.0
2007	3,488.8	4,113.3	4,326.8	4,324.0	4,226.5	3,860.3	3,437.9	3,106.8	2,883.0	2,660.0	2,327.4	2,334.5
2008	2,431.0	2,679.8	2,920.4	2,787.6	2,733.9	2,486.3	2,223.6	2,110.8	1,717.5	1,571.2	1,390.4	1,533.4
2009	2,062.7	2,339.1	2,292.6	2,530.2	2,456.1	2,405.8	2,137.2	2,059.1	1,938.5	1,931.4	2,105.8	2,196.4
2010	2,699.9	3,217.3	3,442.6	3,400.3	3,317.0	3,128.8	2,935.7	2,602.8	2,491.2	2,159.6	1,985.2	2,197.6
2011	2,551.7	2,900.4	2,856.1	2,633.1	2,546.0	2,971.6	3,388.2	3,089.4	3,055.1	2,758.3	2,559.1	2,856.1

[1] Licensed warehouses approved by ICE.   *Source: ICE Futures U.S. (ICE)*

Visible Stocks of Cocoa in New York Warehouses[1], at End of Month   In Thousands of Bags

Year	Jan.	Feb.	Mar.	Apr.	May	June	July	Aug.	Sept.	Oct.	Nov.	Dec.
2002	1,104.1	870.8	892.0	806.6	739.1	736.0	628.7	553.6	669.2	525.7	473.1	554.8
2003	614.6	625.4	593.5	604.4	515.1	470.3	446.8	388.2	451.7	301.9	260.7	342.9
2004	229.9	415.2	615.4	579.9	711.3	680.1	676.3	596.1	485.9	334.5	210.2	209.6
2005	201.2	446.3	495.9	677.7	813.6	916.5	805.2	625.2	457.2	430.3	388.3	599.2
2006	758.4	971.5	869.7	820.6	758.3	691.8	634.1	685.8	654.2	649.1	532.3	502.8
2007	532.2	460.2	632.6	667.1	611.9	605.4	577.7	530.5	496.8	442.2	394.8	343.2
2008	408.9	411.1	574.4	618.7	614.0	554.4	527.9	434.6	396.1	375.6	323.1	242.5
2009	291.7	413.2	423.9	472.0	501.5	557.3	672.2	664.2	653.9	726.0	714.6	722.3
2010	831.4	1,005.7	1,099.3	1,042.0	954.2	825.2	730.7	662.7	618.4	572.3	524.9	487.3
2011	499.4	604.9	701.2	711.1	639.3	661.5	719.8	734.1	807.6	884.8	875.5	857.6

[1] Licensed warehouses approved by ICE.   *Source: ICE Futures U.S. (ICE)*

COCOA

Cocoa (monthly average) through December 2011 — USD per metric ton

Average Cash Price of Cocoa, Ivory Coast in New York In Dollars Per Metric Ton

Year	Jan.	Feb.	Mar.	Apr.	May	June	July	Aug.	Sept.	Oct.	Nov.	Dec.	Average
2002	1,586	1,674	1,794	1,800	1,814	1,836	2,081	2,191	2,391	2,471	2,123	2,322	2,007
2003	2,483	2,506	2,258	2,232	1,996	1,818	1,803	1,843	1,877	1,713	1,737	1,832	2,008
2004	1,840	1,763	1,695	1,610	1,588	1,571	1,733	1,889	1,698	1,654	1,867	1,848	1,730
2005	1,740	1,827	1,950	1,744	1,656	1,687	1,625	1,626	1,640	1,598	1,585	1,670	1,696
2006	1,752	1,729	1,739	1,749	1,806	1,794	1,862	1,795	1,764	1,725	1,773	1,897	1,782
2007	1,883	1,996	2,120	2,169	2,214	2,225	2,361	2,185	2,242	2,198	2,251	2,396	2,187
2008	2,486	2,806	2,922	2,867	2,971	3,307	3,248	3,078	2,972	2,533	2,371	2,837	2,867
2009	2,985	2,977	2,781	2,830	2,699	2,892	3,047	3,186	3,427	3,634	3,596	3,782	3,153
2010	3,851	3,611	3,452	3,580	3,535	3,539	3,602	3,455	3,269	3,314	3,279	3,354	3,487
2011	3,507	3,937	3,992	3,697	3,565	3,360	3,422	3,312	3,199	2,949	2,831	2,396	3,347

Source: Economic Research Service, U.S. Department of Agriculture (ERS-USDA)

Total Visible Stocks of Cocoa in Warehouses[1], at End of Month In Thousands of Bags

Year	Jan.	Feb.	Mar.	Apr.	May	June	July	Aug.	Sept.	Oct.	Nov.	Dec.
2002	3,319.2	3,210.2	3,177.9	2,924.0	2,869.4	2,778.9	2,850.8	2,659.6	2,660.4	2,055.0	1,817.3	1,975.3
2003	2,111.7	2,169.1	2,024.1	2,016.8	1,812.7	1,720.6	1,686.9	1,579.6	1,377.3	1,153.8	1,074.1	1,198.1
2004	1,573.5	1,524.4	1,730.0	1,814.5	1,989.8	2,090.9	2,150.1	2,165.8	1,905.5	1,941.9	1,626.4	1,582.0
2005	1,821.1	2,287.0	2,590.8	2,970.3	3,276.0	3,202.2	3,297.5	3,133.6	2,955.1	2,842.9	2,798.5	3,192.9
2006	3,665.1	3,818.4	3,900.5	4,249.5	4,021.8	3,737.7	3,512.1	4,375.5	4,271.5	4,166.7	3,811.4	4,194.0
2007	4,366.4	4,882.4	5,239.0	5,347.3	5,148.4	4,821.1	4,322.9	3,897.1	3,604.0	3,297.4	2,867.8	2,832.9
2008	3,211.7	3,453.9	3,916.2	3,757.7	3,648.4	3,322.8	3,003.3	2,771.8	2,322.7	2,114.2	1,875.9	1,950.5
2009	2,557.4	2,996.2	2,956.0	3,266.2	3,177.1	3,166.2	3,000.9	2,909.0	2,751.1	2,783.3	2,932.8	3,027.8
2010	3,639.8	4,330.1	4,727.3	4,636.9	4,477.2	4,170.8	3,901.1	3,492.1	3,318.1	2,884.6	2,645.7	2,801.8
2011	3,158.1	3,611.9	3,757.3	3,520.8	3,324.1	3,729.7	4,185.3	3,892.5	3,928.4	3,704.4	3,491.6	3,767.1

[1] Licensed warehouses approved by ICE. *Source: ICE Futures U.S. (ICE)*

Cocoa Futures - ICE Futures U.S.
(weekly close) as of December 30, 2011

USD per metric ton

Average Open Interest of Cocoa Futures in New York   In Contracts

Year	Jan.	Feb.	Mar.	Apr.	May	June	July	Aug.	Sept.	Oct.	Nov.	Dec.
2002	97,563	98,169	96,336	98,851	103,746	100,701	107,080	102,441	107,294	107,880	82,236	82,844
2003	96,375	91,944	83,625	83,230	95,307	96,813	89,846	78,197	76,468	86,392	99,038	94,010
2004	88,879	84,078	99,918	100,429	108,150	99,476	103,350	111,318	101,998	119,033	117,876	118,769
2005	117,091	115,007	144,055	124,417	124,925	128,203	126,388	129,562	118,468	132,629	131,733	123,302
2006	131,527	127,471	129,426	129,814	131,035	138,004	154,163	134,942	139,544	153,485	136,329	140,099
2007	145,503	152,358	172,846	157,373	154,649	148,608	167,565	134,823	123,171	133,362	137,208	165,522
2008	188,039	182,389	166,939	136,591	146,759	160,366	151,896	134,715	127,674	122,381	113,422	113,240
2009	119,496	118,145	114,051	111,859	117,027	114,792	112,079	112,935	121,226	133,635	129,171	129,296
2010	137,675	127,994	129,562	128,298	130,258	119,074	124,335	119,070	127,315	138,385	136,708	137,345
2011	148,426	158,965	163,700	159,411	157,851	162,945	172,670	166,766	176,524	191,211	168,734	167,339

Source: ICE Futures U.S. (ICE)

Volume of Trading of Cocoa Futures in New York   In Contracts

Year	Jan.	Feb.	Mar.	Apr.	May	June	July	Aug.	Sept.	Oct.	Nov.	Dec.	Total
2002	155,699	187,550	129,833	217,590	160,364	220,289	176,450	209,249	138,394	207,310	162,982	114,270	2,079,980
2003	172,845	215,240	136,564	179,956	176,969	207,255	143,888	206,428	146,113	197,316	209,775	135,857	2,128,206
2004	174,684	180,693	181,667	244,946	174,452	238,201	219,018	260,025	146,090	150,443	290,227	128,604	2,389,050
2005	185,624	239,511	231,917	249,209	134,330	288,809	151,339	252,868	222,122	182,337	283,663	161,198	2,582,927
2006	235,410	264,557	201,604	295,814	244,032	333,275	331,108	313,591	174,246	264,490	308,782	202,293	3,169,202
2007	239,568	338,998	273,605	333,551	212,318	328,646	242,710	378,897	213,143	265,018	273,419	235,410	3,335,283
2008	322,864	434,965	316,509	328,981	293,874	353,593	280,275	345,973	197,765	313,220	228,699	175,550	3,592,268
2009	265,308	282,200	242,110	279,621	214,640	303,030	216,046	292,552	188,138	289,133	338,296	175,892	3,086,966
2010	255,025	361,068	282,222	372,997	290,545	366,645	253,289	425,322	247,749	284,483	404,682	253,652	3,797,679
2011	395,349	401,740	390,590	423,879	357,282	454,217	328,156	571,410	335,481	388,486	554,320	347,142	4,948,052

Source: ICE Futures U.S. (ICE)

Coconut Oil and Copra

Coconut oil and copra come from the fruit of the coconut palm tree, which originated in Southeast Asia. Coconut oil has been used for thousands of years as cooking oil, and is still a staple in the diets of many people living in tropical areas. Until shortages of imported oil developed during WWII, Americans also used coconut oil for cooking.

Copra is the meaty inner lining of the coconut. It is an oil-rich pulp with a light, slightly sweet, nutty flavor. Copra is used mainly as a source of coconut oil and is also used shredded for baking. High-quality copra contains about 65% to 72% oil, and oil made from the copra is called crude coconut oil. Crude coconut oil is processed from copra by expeller press and solvent extraction. It is not considered fit for human consumption until it has been refined, which consists of neutralizing, bleaching and deodorizing it at high heat with a vacuum. The remaining oil cake obtained as a by-product is used for livestock feed.

Premium grade coconut oil, also called virgin coconut oil, is oil made from the first pressing without the addition of any chemicals. Premium grade coconut oil is more expensive than refined or crude oil because the producers use only selected raw materials and there is a lower production yield due to only one pressing.

Coconut oil accounts for approximately 20% of all vegetable oils used worldwide. Coconut oil is used in margarines, vegetable shortening, salad oils, confections, and in sports drinks to boost energy and enhance athletic performance. It is also used in the manufacture of soaps, detergents, shampoos, cosmetics, candles, glycerin and synthetic rubber. Coconut oil is very healthy, unless it is hydrogenated, and is easily digested.

Prices – The average monthly price of coconut oil (crude) in 2010 rose +46.3% yr/yr to 50.69 cents per pound. The record high of 60.21 cents per pound was posted in 1984.

Supply – World production of copra in 2011 fell by -10.5% yr/yr to 5.230 million metric tons, remaining below the record high of 5.662 million metric tons posted in 2001. The world's largest producers of copra are the Philippines with 38.2% of world production, Indonesia with 28.7%, India with 13.0%, and Mexico with 4.2%. World production of coconut oil in the 2010-11 marketing year fell by -10.3% yr/yr to 3.274 million metric tons.

Demand – Virtually all of world production of copra goes for crushing into coconut meal and oil (over 99%). World consumption of coconut oil in 2010-11 fell by -6.6% yr/yr to 3.353 million metric tons, below the 2009-10 record high of 3.588 million metric tons.

Trade – Copra is generally crushed in the country of origin, meaning that less than 4% of copra itself is exported; the rest is exported in the form of coconut oil. World exports of coconut oil in 2010-11 fell by -12.6% yr/yr to 2.075 million metric tons, below the 2009-10 record high of 2.374 million metric tons.

World Production of Copra   In Thousands of Metric Tons

Year	India	Indonesia	Ivory Coast	Malaysia	Mexico	Mozambique	Papua New Guinea	Philippines	Sri Lanka	Thailand	Vanuatu	Vietnam	World Total
2002	713	1,290	45	50	203	50	71	2,010	59	61	25	46	4,920
2003	690	1,260	45	51	185	55	85	2,406	50	68	25	49	5,267
2004	700	1,300	45	51	182	50	90	1,980	60	71	35	49	4,915
2005	690	1,460	45	48	209	50	112	2,100	67	72	30	50	5,252
2006	680	1,370	45	51	187	48	94	2,100	65	65	30	51	5,110
2007	670	1,570	45	49	217	46	97	1,880	69	68	30	54	5,121
2008	680	1,435	46	52	226	48	123	1,910	73	68	32	55	5,076
2009[1]	680	1,520	46	54	228	48	100	2,040	89	69	31	55	5,284
2010[2]	690	1,440	46	53	211	48	100	2,680	85	70	32	57	5,841
2011[3]	680	1,500	46	55	220	48	105	2,000	87	70	32	57	5,230

[1] Preliminary.   [2] Estimate.   [3] Forecast.   *Source: The Oil World*

World Supply and Distribution of Coconut Oil   In Thousands of Metric Tons

Year	India	Indonesia	Malaysia	Philippines	Total	Exports	Imports	European Union	India	Indonesia	Philippines	United States	Total	Philippines	United States	Total
	-------- Production --------							**-------- Consumption --------**						**---- Ending Stocks ----**		
2001-02	421	773	45	1,403	3,183	1,846	1,872	712	448	278	332	506	3,274	62	103	507
2002-03	418	758	41	1,425	3,180	1,958	1,991	786	454	273	352	384	3,301	53	98	418
2003-04	419	731	41	1,379	3,104	1,860	1,833	713	428	246	311	399	3,125	58	60	370
2004-05	416	881	42	1,263	3,164	2,116	2,067	814	434	175	253	361	3,083	73	110	402
2005-06	409	789	45	1,450	3,240	2,189	2,176	768	437	180	253	494	3,223	66	101	405
2006-07	402	960	47	1,220	3,185	1,924	1,903	704	417	187	351	435	3,170	105	58	399
2007-08	405	887	44	1,346	3,248	2,001	2,025	685	420	179	428	506	3,274	85	82	398
2008-09[1]	407	851	44	1,239	3,117	1,763	1,792	632	425	181	441	419	3,107	145	83	438
2009-10[2]	411	890	45	1,732	3,649	2,374	2,328	783	417	183	440	587	3,589	60	84	451
2010-11[3]	408	888	44	1,360	3,275	2,076	2,063	757	420	178	330	492	3,354	70	64	359

[1] Preliminary.   [2] Estimate.   [3] Forecast.   *Source: The Oil World*

Supply and Distribution of Coconut Oil in the United States   In Millions of Pounds

Year	Rotterdam Copra Tonne $ U.S.	Rotterdam Coconut Oil, CIF $ U.S.	Imports For Consumption	Stocks Oct. 1	Total Supply	Exports	Disapearance Total Domestic	Edible Products	Inedible Products	Production Total	Oct.-Dec.	Jan.-Mar.	April-June	July-Sept.
2001-02	245	388	1,150	260	1,410	11	1,100	294	302	501.8	139.5	126.1	115.4	120.8
2002-03	286	450	866	226	1,092	28	1,205	305	310	546.7	128.8	137.0	155.6	125.2
2003-04	424	630	812	216	1,028	17	1,312	330	274	594.9	160.7	132.8	162.8	138.6
2004-05	431	636	936	131	1,067	29	1,374	341	280	623.3	153.7	157.5	160.8	151.3
2005-06	387	583	1,127	242	1,369	58	1,323	366	270	599.9	141.9	156.2	160.5	141.4
2006-07	537	812	892	222	1,114	26	1,443	339	309	654.6	162.6	152.2	165.4	174.4
2007-08	867	1,306	1,196	128	1,325	28	1,383	373	447	627.4	139.9	165.9	161.1	160.5
2008-09	487	735	961	181	1,143	37	1,293	364	394	586.6	147.6	131.1	122.8	185.2
2009-10[1]	613	921	1,338	183	1,521	41	1,836	441	W	833.0	190.1	214.9	211.2	216.8
2010-11[2]	1,239	1,850	1,102	186	1,288	62	1,783	467	W	808.8	202.2			

[1] Preliminary.   [2] Forecast.   *Source: Bureau of Census, U.S. Department of Commerce*

Consumption of Coconut Oil in End Products (Edible and Inedible) in the United States   In Millions of Pounds

Year	Jan.	Feb.	Mar.	Apr.	May	June	July	Aug.	Sept.	Oct.	Nov.	Dec.	Total
2002	55.4	41.3	50.8	59.3	53.9	46.4	50.7	51.8	45.9	54.3	56.1	49.4	615.4
2003	51.2	49.3	56.8	50.6	52.3	46.7	48.9	49.6	50.3	47.8	41.8	38.5	583.7
2004	50.0	51.7	58.5	54.6	48.5	55.6	52.9	55.1	48.9	48.2	64.3	51.7	640.0
2005	46.7	52.0	47.9	48.8	51.4	55.5	47.2	58.1	49.2	52.8	53.4	58.1	621.1
2006	70.4	62.7	50.4	47.5	50.7	51.6	43.1	51.6	43.8	49.6	44.4	40.8	606.4
2007	49.8	48.5	47.0	51.2	53.7	60.3	60.3	74.2	67.5	71.8	71.3	62.7	718.3
2008	63.6	72.1	64.8	74.4	69.7	70.4	65.8	67.6	65.8	63.0	63.6	53.6	794.5
2009	67.9	62.8	60.2	66.9	66.9	27.6	36.5	28.1	29.4	32.8	32.1	30.6	541.8
2010	41.0	36.6	45.3	34.9	39.8	38.6	37.2	40.4	32.1	41.4	39.9	70.8	498.0
2011[1]	34.6	37.0	40.6	38.0	39.0	37.0	26.7						433.5

[1] Preliminary.   *Source: Bureau of Census, U.S. Department of Commerce*

Stocks of Coconut Oil (Crude and Refined) in the United States, on First of Month   In Millions of Pounds

Year	Jan.	Feb.	Mar.	Apr.	May	June	July	Aug.	Sept.	Oct.	Nov.	Dec.
2002	245.9	238.8	249.6	251.3	233.5	231.6	303.3	301.6	245.8	226.5	273.8	264.1
2003	195.2	194.0	214.3	224.9	223.7	187.8	162.2	202.9	195.6	218.9	184.6	186.1
2004	167.2	160.3	192.6	181.7	131.4	108.7	90.6	132.8	149.2	131.3	147.7	182.5
2005	225.9	163.7	188.4	191.0	170.6	187.7	263.5	250.4	253.7	242.1	252.3	273.3
2006	268.3	236.9	224.5	227.3	260.2	229.1	213.8	214.4	204.7	224.5	179.2	180.2
2007	214.4	228.5	261.5	223.1	191.8	157.9	171.2	154.4	127.7	128.4	142.5	212.6
2008	205.6	192.9	180.9	191.9	223.9	203.9	187.8	181.5	180.4	182.2	163.3	174.6
2009	164.1	183.7	215.6	167.2	143.9	138.0	134.8	133.2	102.3	182.3	159.0	154.7
2010	220.2	204.5	172.1	144.6	119.3	120.3	172.2	179.3	197.1	185.8	166.7	167.2
2011[1]	181.5	150.2	162.7	154.6	150.0	157.6	158.4	190.9				

[1] Preliminary.   *Source: Bureau of Census, U.S. Department of Commerce*

Average Price of Coconut Oil (Crude) Tank Cars in New York   In Cents Per Pound

Year	Jan.	Feb.	Mar.	Apr.	May	June	July	Aug.	Sept.	Oct.	Nov.	Dec.	Average
2001	26.00	24.00	22.75	22.50	21.00	21.00	24.00	26.50	26.50	26.50	24.50	24.50	24.15
2002	16.38	17.38	17.25	18.75	20.05	21.13	21.06	21.35	28.50	28.25	27.13	26.00	21.94
2003	26.00	26.00	24.60	24.50	24.50	25.00	25.00	25.00	25.00	25.00	28.75	31.00	25.86
2004	32.00	33.38	34.56	39.20	45.00	46.00	46.00	46.00	39.25	32.65	31.25	31.25	38.05
2005	31.05	31.00	32.67	35.00	34.67	34.00	33.00	33.00	33.00	35.00	29.13	27.75	32.44
2006	27.75	27.75	27.75	37.50	40.13	45.75	48.00	NA	42.50	45.16	45.38	46.32	41.68
2007	35.75	36.00	36.00	37.50	40.13	45.75	48.00	NA	42.50	45.16	45.38	46.32	41.68
2008	58.02	62.33	70.98	67.38	67.38	71.73	70.33	59.62	55.82	47.73	37.46	35.51	58.69
2009	35.25	33.14	30.07	31.58	37.84	37.34	32.78	35.00	35.75	35.75	35.75	35.53	34.65
2010[1]	36.20	35.75	37.88	41.99	43.60	44.00	46.49	54.31	55.94	63.65	69.00	79.50	50.69

[1] Preliminary.   *Source: Economic Research Service, U.S. Department of Agriculture (ERS-USDA)*

Coffee

Coffee is one of the world's most important cash commodities. Coffee is the common name for any type of tree in the genus madder family. It is actually a tropical evergreen shrub that has the potential to grow 100 feet tall. The coffee tree grows in tropical regions between the Tropics of Cancer and Capricorn in areas with abundant rainfall, year-round warm temperatures averaging about 70 degrees Fahrenheit, and no frost. In the U.S., the only areas that produce any significant amount of coffee are Puerto Rico and Hawaii. The coffee plant will produce its first full crop of beans at about 5 years old and then be productive for about 15 years. The average coffee tree produces enough beans to make about 1 to 1 ½ pounds of roasted coffee per year. It takes approximately 4,000 handpicked green coffee beans to make a pound of coffee. Wine was actually the first drink made from the coffee tree using the coffee cherries, honey, and water. In the 17th century, the first coffee house, also known as a "penny university" because of the price per cup, opened in London. The London Stock Exchange grew from one of these first coffee houses.

Coffee is generally classified into two types of beans: arabica and robusta. The most widely produced coffee is arabica, which makes up about 70 percent of total production. It grows mostly at high altitudes of 600 to 2,000 meters, with Brazil and Colombia being the largest producers. Arabic coffee is traded on the ICE Futures U.S. (ICE) exchange. The stronger of the two types is robusta. It is grown at lower altitudes with the largest producers being Indonesia, West Africa, Brazil, and Vietnam. Robusta coffee is traded on NYSE-LIFFE exchange in London.

Ninety percent of the world coffee trade is in green (unroasted) coffee beans. Seasonal factors have a significant influence on the price of coffee. There is no extreme peak in world production at any one time of the year, although coffee consumption declines by 12 percent or more below the year's average in the warm summer months. Therefore, coffee imports and roasts both tend to decline in spring and summer and pick up again in fall and winter.

The very low prices for coffee in 2000-03 created serious problems for coffee producers. When prices fall below the costs of production, there is little or no economic incentive to produce coffee. The result is that coffee trees are neglected or completely abandoned. When prices are low, producers cannot afford to hire the labor needed to maintain the trees and pick the crop at harvest. The result is that trees yield less due to reduced use of fertilizer and fewer employed coffee workers. One effect is a decline in the quality of the coffee that is produced. Higher quality Arabica coffee is often produced at higher altitudes, which entails higher costs. It is this coffee that is often abandoned. Although the pressure on producers can be severe, the market eventually comes back into balance as supply declines in response to low prices.

Coffee prices are subject to upward spikes in June, July and August due to possible freeze scares in Brazil during the winter months in the Southern Hemisphere. The Brazilian coffee crop is harvested starting in May and extending for several weeks into what are the winter months in Brazil. A major freeze in Brazil occurs roughly every five years on average.

Coffee futures are traded on the Bolsa de Mercadorias & Futuros (BM&F), the Tokyo Grain Exchange (TGE), the NYSE-LIFFE exchange in London, and the ICE Futures U.S. (ICE) exchange. Options are traded on the BM&F, the LIFFE and the ICE.

Prices – ICE Arabica coffee futures prices in early 2011 extended the rally that began in mid-2010 and posted a 14-year high of 306.25 cents per pound in May 2011. Coffee prices then consolidated modestly below that 14-year high into October and fell to a 1-year low of 210.95 cents per pound in December 2011, finishing the year down -5.7% at 226.85 cents per pound. Bullish factors in 2011 included (1) tight coffee supplies after flooding in Columbia, the second-largest supplier of Arabica beans, decimated its 2011 coffee crop to only 7.81 million bags, a 35-year low, (2) USDA's cut in its 2011 global coffee ending stocks estimate to an 11-year low of 24 million bags, and (3) ICO's cut in its 2011/12 global coffee production estimate to 127.4 million bags from a Jan 2011 estimate of 132.4 million. Negative factors that prompted a slide in coffee prices from their 14-year high included (1) ICO data that showed 2011 global coffee exports climbed 7.4% y/y to a record 104 million bags, and (2) Brazil's forecast for a 2011/12 crop of 43.15 million bags, the largest off-cycle crop in 11 years.

Supply – World coffee production in the 2011-12 marketing year (July-June) fell -1.9% yr/yr to 133.801 million bags (1 bag equals 60 kilograms or 132.3 pounds), down from last year's record high of 136.377 million bags. The decrease in production caused the 2011-12 ending stocks to fall -8.3% to 23.979 million bags.

Brazil is the world's largest coffee producer by far with 49.2 million bags of production in 2011-12, which was 36.8% of total world production. Other key producers include Vietnam with 15.4% of the world's production and with Columbia and Indonesia each with 6.2%. Brazil's coffee production in 2011-12 fell -9.7% yr/yr to 49.2 million bags. Vietnam has become a major coffee producer in recent years, boosting its production to 20.600 million bags in 2011-12, up from less than a million bags in 1990.

Demand – U.S. coffee consumption in 2011 rose 7.5% to 24.907 million bags, not far below the record high of 25.377 million bags seen in 1968.

Trade – World coffee exports in 2011-12 fell -5.7% yr/yr to 103.655 million bags, down from last year's record high of 109.871 million bags. The world's largest exporters of coffee in 2011-12 were Brazil with 28.0% of world exports, Vietnam with 18.7%, and Columbia with 8.2%. U.S. coffee imports in 2011 rose +7.5% yr/yr from the previous year to 24.908 million bags. The all-time high of 24.549 million bags was posted in 1962. The key countries from which the U.S. imported coffee in 2011 were Brazil (which accounted for 28.0% of U.S. imports), Columbia (14.3%), Mexico (6.6%), and Guatemala (6.3%).

World Supply and Distribution of Coffee for Producing Countries   In Thousands of 60 Kilogram Bags

Year	Beginning Stocks	Production	Imports	Total Supply	Total Exports	Bean Exports	Rst/Grn Exports	Soluble Exports	Domestic Use	Ending Stocks
2002-03	39,422	127,102	90,663	150,977	94,108	87,255	293	6,560	115,720	47,359
2003-04	47,359	110,750	90,698	182,140	90,071	82,760	231	7,080	119,391	39,345
2004-05	39,345	121,262	93,011	247,139	93,195	84,272	130	8,793	120,149	40,274
2005-06	40,274	116,721	92,195	242,277	92,829	84,128	170	8,531	125,107	31,254
2006-07	31,254	131,819	97,470	260,501	102,859	93,814	134	8,911	124,107	33,577
2007-08	33,577	122,153	96,809	252,539	96,551	86,158	226	10,167	126,971	29,017
2008-09	29,017	134,103	96,821	259,941	99,451	89,311	167	9,973	123,592	36,898
2009-10[1]	36,898	126,705	99,416	263,019	101,746	90,157	207	11,382	135,249	26,024
2010-11[2]	26,024	136,377	104,788	267,189	109,871	96,523	162	13,186	131,159	26,159
2011-12[3]	26,159	133,801	101,529	261,489	103,655	91,246	172	12,237	133,855	23,979

[1] Preliminary.   [2] Estimate.   [3] Forecast.   132.276 Lbs. Per Bag   *Source: Foreign Agricultural Service, U.S. Department of Agriculture (FAS-USDA)*

World Production of Green Coffee   In Thousands of 60 Kilogram Bags

Crop Year	Brazil	Colombia	Costa Rica	Cote d'Ivoire	El Salvador	Ethiopia	Guate-mala	India	Indo-nesia	Mexico	Uganda	Vietnam	World Total
2002-03	53,600	11,712	2,207	3,145	1,351	3,693	3,802	4,588	6,140	4,350	2,890	11,167	127,102
2003-04	33,200	11,053	2,106	2,689	1,343	3,875	3,671	4,508	6,000	4,428	2,599	15,000	110,750
2004-05	43,600	11,532	1,907	2,301	1,329	4,575	3,817	4,672	8,450	3,900	2,593	14,500	121,262
2005-06	36,100	11,953	1,751	1,962	1,387	4,000	3,605	4,617	9,450	4,000	2,159	16,335	116,721
2006-07	46,700	12,164	1,782	2,447	1,400	4,036	4,050	4,665	7,500	4,500	2,300	19,500	131,819
2007-08	39,100	12,515	1,867	2,098	1,650	3,906	4,110	4,660	8,000	4,350	2,500	18,000	122,153
2008-09	53,300	8,664	1,580	1,853	1,550	3,650	3,980	4,375	10,000	4,550	3,200	16,980	134,103
2009-10[1]	44,800	8,100	1,475	2,350	1,300	4,000	4,010	4,825	10,500	4,150	2,700	18,500	126,705
2010-11[2]	54,500	8,525	1,575	1,600	1,750	4,400	3,810	5,040	9,325	4,000	2,300	18,735	136,377
2011-12[3]	49,200	8,500	1,640	2,000	1,600	4,700	3,810	5,200	8,300	4,300	2,400	20,600	133,801

[1] Preliminary.   [2] Estimate.   [3] Forecast.   132.276 Lbs. Per Bag   *Source: Foreign Agricultural Service, U.S. Department of Agriculture (FAS-USDA)*

World Exportable[4] Production of Green Coffee   In Thousands of 60 Kilogram Bags

Crop Year	Brazil	Colombia	Cote d'Ivoire	Ethiopia	Guate-mala	Honduras	India	Indo-nesia	Mexico	Peru	Uganda	Vietnam	World Total
2002-03	29,396	10,478	3,278	2,277	3,500	2,438	3,567	5,446	3,520	2,575	2,810	11,176	94,108
2003-04	24,920	10,049	2,622	2,200	3,314	2,794	3,826	5,658	2,470	2,685	2,175	14,075	90,071
2004-05	27,920	11,405	1,390	2,250	3,451	2,450	3,207	6,700	1,950	3,306	2,050	14,400	93,195
2005-06	24,543	10,678	2,010	2,250	3,325	2,850	4,120	8,040	2,485	2,270	1,410	15,748	92,829
2006-07	29,260	11,155	2,095	2,225	3,980	3,370	3,609	6,400	2,865	4,200	2,160	15,735	102,859
2007-08	27,290	11,525	1,890	2,110	3,890	3,440	3,820	6,110	2,610	2,660	2,770	15,565	96,551
2008-09	31,475	8,935	1,555	1,850	3,783	3,050	3,120	7,700	2,735	3,150	2,290	18,670	99,451
2009-10[1]	29,780	7,435	2,045	2,325	3,860	3,200	4,110	8,750	2,480	3,880	1,885	17,867	101,746
2010-11[2]	35,010	8,395	985	2,660	3,850	3,900	5,300	9,680	2,435	3,700	2,000	17,867	109,871
2011-12[3]	29,000	8,450	2,000	2,800	3,700	3,925	4,700	7,250	2,600	3,700	2,000	19,350	103,655

[1] Preliminary.   [2] Estimate.   [3] Forecast.   [4] Marketing year begins in October in some countries and April or July in others. Exportable production represents total harvested production minus estimated domestic consumption.   132.276 Lbs. Per Bag
Source: Foreign Agricultural Service, U.S. Department of Agriculture (FAS-USDA)

Coffee[2] Imports in the United States   In Thousands of 60 Kilogram Bags

Year	Brazil	Colombia	Costa Rica	Republic	Ecuador	El Salvador	Ethiopia	Guate-mala	Indo-nesia	Mexico	Peru	Vene-zuela	World Total
2002	5,060	3,597	987	51	145	470	74	1,626	759	2,034	842	170	20,632
2003	5,321	3,884	914	80	133	569	101	2,023	966	1,510	807	180	21,695
2004	4,475	3,714	957	2	157	524	121	1,624	1,636	1,477	788	103	22,049
2005	4,464	4,090	920	2	74	406	177	1,752	1,599	1,285	587	0	21,791
2006	4,795	3,904	751	60	147	435	250	1,654	1,677	1,528	850	2	22,659
2007	4,968	4,064	823	35	123	565	234	1,815	1,122	1,495	919	25	23,216
2008	4,970	4,245	953	35	40	657	348	1,901	1,351	1,427	963	93	23,217
2009	5,642	3,425	750	56	65	463	202	1,739	1,318	1,642	854	7	22,465
2010	6,302	3,017	715	6	56	366	306	1,311	1,352	1,371	882	7	23,165
2011[1]	6,971	3,549	707	26	73	657	283	1,579	990	1,635	1,051	0	24,908

[1] Preliminary.   132.276 Lbs. Per Bag   *Source: Bureau of Census, U.S. Department of Commerce*

COFFEE

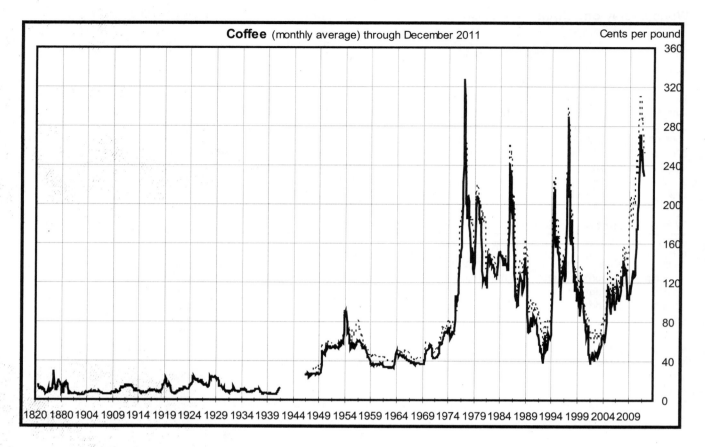

Coffee (monthly average) through December 2011 — Cents per pound

Monthly Coffee Imports in the United States In Thousands of 60 Kilogram Bags (132.276 Lbs. Per Bag)

Year	Jan.	Feb.	Mar.	Apr.	May	June	July	Aug.	Sept.	Oct.	Nov.	Dec.	Total
2002	1,652	1,364	1,613	1,697	1,672	1,547	1,802	1,794	1,850	1,877	1,807	1,958	20,631
2003	1,994	1,755	2,007	1,916	1,715	1,710	2,015	1,732	1,712	1,750	1,525	1,863	21,694
2004	1,813	1,635	1,967	1,862	2,049	2,034	1,784	1,766	1,708	1,684	1,798	1,947	22,047
2005	1,939	1,942	2,072	1,965	1,893	1,891	1,781	1,606	1,481	1,718	1,699	1,803	21,791
2006	1,853	1,647	2,043	1,672	2,007	1,916	1,780	2,091	2,089	1,894	1,834	1,833	22,659
2007	2,167	1,760	1,992	2,016	1,888	1,743	2,005	2,249	2,037	2,038	1,712	1,608	23,216
2008	1,985	1,867	2,119	2,073	2,034	1,913	1,980	1,856	1,973	1,863	1,542	2,012	23,217
2009	1,872	1,680	1,998	1,978	2,042	2,197	2,357	1,895	1,661	1,605	1,389	1,793	22,465
2010	1,705	1,696	1,989	1,989	2,036	1,988	1,870	2,095	1,863	1,826	2,054	2,053	23,165
2011[1]	2,058	1,914	2,391	2,188	2,105	2,091	2,048	1,831	1,871	2,012	2,139	2,259	24,908

[1] Preliminary.   *Source: Bureau of the Census, U.S. Department of Commerce*

Average Price of Brazilian[1] Coffee in New York   In Cents Per Pound

Year	Jan.	Feb.	Mar.	Apr.	May	June	July	Aug.	Sept.	Oct.	Nov.	Dec.	Average
2002	42.56	42.79	48.79	49.90	45.19	42.96	43.58	40.55	44.46	45.28	48.37	46.70	45.09
2003	49.14	48.54	43.77	48.71	51.06	47.11	49.64	52.88	55.19	53.51	54.15	56.92	50.89
2004	64.32	66.08	65.79	62.89	64.31	67.62	59.39	60.25	69.46	68.63	80.20	89.17	68.18
2005	94.00	108.05	117.03	112.82	111.89	105.08	94.66	95.66	87.02	94.54	99.35	96.23	101.36
2006	115.89	109.51	103.52	105.89	99.00	91.26	91.01	98.90	97.36	97.39	109.34	115.60	102.89
2007	111.99	109.78	102.34	100.84	99.66	105.89	105.25	112.47	116.43	120.95	118.99	124.06	110.72
2008	126.26	142.25	130.45	123.15	125.18	130.52	131.10	131.85	126.82	104.57	102.74	95.22	122.51
2009	101.43	100.45	97.48	101.46	113.13	109.81	104.55	114.01	114.12	122.84	126.21	131.23	111.39
2010	128.11	121.61	125.28	124.94	121.66	136.18	146.74	152.91	162.02	163.86	179.16	186.05	145.71
2011	209.26	237.43	257.24	271.39	266.02	247.19	242.66	251.78	251.70	230.62	233.13	225.59	243.67

[1] And other Arabicas.   *Source: Foreign Agricultural Service, U.S. Department of Agriculture (FAS-USDA)*

Average Monthly Retail[1] Price of Coffee in the United States   In Cents Per Pound

Year	Jan.	Feb.	Mar.	Apr.	May	June	July	Aug.	Sept.	Oct.	Nov.	Dec.	Average
2004	289.2	285.6	293.2	290.8	283.1	275.0	287.8	287.8	287.4	284.0	277.8	277.6	284.9
2005	304.9	294.0	300.9	324.0	332.9	341.6	333.4	342.8	337.6	344.7	329.3	323.5	325.8
2006	323.2	317.4	330.1	329.2	334.9	315.8	315.4	319.6	317.3	313.8	315.8	311.3	320.3
2007	328.8	345.6	347.5	343.7	330.8	340.7	352.9	349.7	NA	NA	360.7	368.5	346.9
2008	NA	NA	NA	NA	NA	NA	NA	NA	NA	NA	NA	NA	NA
2009	NA	NA	NA	NA	NA	NA	NA	NA	NA	NA	NA	366.9	366.9
2010	381.1	373.6	356.5	364.1	366.4	369.7	385.7	393.5	417.4	417.5	446.7	414.6	390.6
2011	441.7	421.8	464.2	510.1	512.9	523.4	554.7	576.6	565.1	551.1	563.6	543.7	519.1

[1] Roasted in 13.1 to 20 ounce cans.   *Source: Foreign Agricultural Service, U.S. Department of Agriculture (FAS-USDA)*

Average Price of Colombian Mild Arabicas[1] in the United States   In Cents Per Pound

Year	Jan.	Feb.	Mar.	Apr.	May	June	July	Aug.	Sept.	Oct.	Nov.	Dec.	Average
2004	76.61	79.34	80.12	77.08	80.61	85.62	78.27	78.85	85.71	85.52	95.63	106.48	84.15
2005	110.03	124.34	137.10	129.80	128.36	122.47	112.48	111.21	101.31	108.77	111.66	106.54	117.01
2006	129.64	123.17	117.00	119.87	113.03	106.84	109.45	116.22	112.26	113.73	126.23	132.85	118.36
2007	127.54	125.54	119.92	117.51	116.14	122.35	122.32	126.68	131.51	137.71	133.81	139.87	126.74
2008	143.37	161.30	151.48	142.41	143.51	150.60	151.56	154.23	150.20	133.37	133.40	134.72	145.85
2009	148.88	149.58	162.00	190.94	225.58	195.27	192.11	181.61	169.90	175.16	180.08	199.38	180.87
2010	214.55	208.36	206.37	195.18	197.76	229.06	230.88	241.77	239.26	225.83	239.59	256.52	223.76
2011	280.05	289.49	300.93	314.26	301.48	290.19	286.46	288.43	283.51	256.86	259.74	254.41	283.82

[1] ICO monthly and composite indicator prices on the New York Market, 1979 ICA Agreement basis.   *Source: Foreign Agricultural Service, U.S. Department of Agriculture (FAS-USDA)*

Average Price of Other Mild Arabicas[1] in the United States   In Cents Per Pound

Year	Jan.	Feb.	Mar.	Apr.	May	June	July	Aug.	Sept.	Oct.	Nov.	Dec.	Average
2004	74.25	77.51	77.29	74.24	76.40	82.24	73.64	72.99	81.22	79.90	89.88	102.19	80.15
2005	107.07	122.20	134.81	128.80	126.21	119.87	108.45	108.43	98.17	106.09	108.81	102.68	114.30
2006	124.26	118.46	112.20	114.65	107.96	101.21	102.77	112.13	109.36	110.91	123.57	129.93	113.95
2007	124.40	122.34	116.44	114.59	112.35	118.76	116.80	123.53	128.04	134.43	130.28	136.47	123.20
2008	139.10	158.03	148.07	138.06	139.32	144.90	145.13	146.03	141.50	122.04	120.76	116.87	138.32
2009	128.03	128.63	127.76	134.44	147.34	145.17	137.87	146.87	145.67	151.95	150.23	155.86	141.65
2010	154.40	155.92	162.13	171.32	174.21	193.52	205.25	212.80	222.10	215.84	227.96	237.33	194.40
2011	262.94	288.08	294.48	303.59	293.06	277.78	269.18	273.54	274.38	248.49	249.50	243.40	273.20

[1] ICO monthly and composite indicator prices on the New York Market, 1979 ICA Agreement basis.   *Source: Foreign Agricultural Service, U.S. Department of Agriculture (FAS-USDA)*

Average Price of Robustas 1976[1] in the United States   In Cents Per Pound

Year	Jan.	Feb.	Mar.	Apr.	May	June	July	Aug.	Sept.	Oct.	Nov.	Dec.	Average
2004	41.32	39.10	38.61	38.02	38.04	41.09	36.44	34.81	35.10	31.77	34.07	38.98	37.28
2005	39.63	44.61	50.70	53.32	58.66	62.96	60.57	55.60	50.07	50.84	54.72	58.79	53.37
2006	66.46	65.50	62.92	64.45	63.97	64.14	68.66	75.73	77.88	76.26	79.67	77.71	70.28
2007	80.55	80.97	78.95	81.64	86.06	94.76	93.47	88.51	93.61	97.34	92.28	91.37	88.29
2008	100.68	117.10	122.44	112.06	109.58	112.16	115.09	113.48	106.67	89.69	92.81	83.99	106.31
2009	85.77	81.66	77.48	76.50	77.00	75.88	74.83	75.04	77.31	76.68	73.08	74.68	77.16
2010	75.09	73.49	72.53	76.26	76.21	82.51	89.95	89.06	87.11	90.57	97.94	98.32	84.09
2011	106.03	114.62	122.46	121.55	126.30	122.15	116.58	119.00	113.47	107.34	108.18	114.23	115.99

[1] ICO monthly and composite indicator prices on the New York Market, 1979 ICA Agreement basis.   *Source: Foreign Agricultural Service, U.S. Department of Agriculture (FAS-USDA)*

Average Price of Composite 1979[1] in the United States   In Cents Per Pound

Year	Jan.	Feb.	Mar.	Apr.	May	June	July	Aug.	Sept.	Oct.	Nov.	Dec.	Average
2004	58.69	59.87	60.80	58.80	59.91	64.28	58.46	56.98	61.47	61.10	67.74	77.72	62.15
2005	79.35	89.40	101.44	98.20	99.78	96.29	88.48	85.31	78.79	82.55	85.93	86.85	89.36
2006	101.20	97.39	92.76	94.20	90.00	86.04	101.20	95.78	95.98	95.53	103.48	108.01	96.80
2007	105.81	104.18	100.09	99.30	100.09	107.03	106.20	107.98	113.20	115.71	114.43	118.16	107.68
2008	122.33	138.82	136.17	126.55	126.76	130.51	132.78	131.14	126.69	108.31	107.88	103.07	124.25
2009	108.39	107.60	105.87	111.61	123.05	119.05	112.90	117.45	116.40	121.09	119.67	124.96	115.67
2010	126.85	123.37	125.30	126.89	128.10	142.20	153.41	157.46	163.61	161.56	173.90	184.26	147.24
2011	197.35	216.03	224.33	231.24	227.97	215.58	210.36	212.19	213.04	193.90	193.66	189.02	210.39

[1] ICO monthly and composite indicator prices on the New York Market, 1979 ICA Agreement basis.   *Source: Foreign Agricultural Service, U.S. Department of Agriculture (FAS-USDA)*

COFFEE

Coffee 'C' Futures - ICE Futures U.S.
(weekly close) as of December 30, 2011

Cents per pound

Average Open Interest of Coffee "C" Futures in New York   In Contracts

Year	Jan.	Feb.	Mar.	Apr.	May	June	July	Aug.	Sept.	Oct.	Nov.	Dec.
2002	57,897	66,825	66,798	66,207	66,289	68,994	69,197	69,635	70,079	73,753	73,431	69,343
2003	69,508	71,682	76,934	77,954	72,716	72,155	72,110	68,259	73,809	79,038	81,253	76,670
2004	92,388	103,966	102,281	98,430	96,738	102,276	89,446	88,021	83,001	78,047	83,360	107,832
2005	102,163	107,715	117,419	105,245	96,063	94,139	93,303	89,662	85,518	86,489	81,525	81,234
2006	102,195	102,614	99,982	102,882	104,230	120,907	120,007	107,928	105,175	111,392	117,469	123,259
2007	128,158	132,849	141,033	146,723	159,011	157,086	168,019	163,288	162,445	173,426	158,146	160,331
2008	176,128	193,555	179,957	160,544	150,017	146,166	147,056	133,178	126,573	132,112	116,643	118,223
2009	129,577	130,101	135,143	134,290	134,827	127,263	107,711	100,880	97,935	114,065	118,016	123,699
2010	129,749	126,850	124,238	133,961	136,711	151,959	169,669	156,086	143,454	139,801	138,738	134,477
2011	139,619	133,869	123,270	120,639	113,874	109,539	108,411	108,089	114,318	119,559	107,527	102,687

Source: ICE Futures U.S. (ICE)

Volume of Trading of Coffee "C" Futures in New York   In Contracts

Year	Jan.	Feb.	Mar.	Apr.	May	June	July	Aug.	Sept.	Oct.	Nov.	Dec.	Total
2002	201,327	279,966	229,764	295,701	159,670	225,177	174,567	254,563	232,255	250,483	236,307	178,728	2,718,508
2003	205,420	283,317	169,611	334,188	255,935	270,424	237,210	278,746	332,473	309,930	314,182	219,595	3,211,031
2004	389,864	397,656	301,270	395,552	324,849	467,887	247,439	366,171	305,196	280,733	424,146	292,540	4,193,303
2005	280,912	469,605	356,855	459,018	240,989	428,227	224,531	404,307	259,177	266,697	376,844	220,616	3,987,778
2006	357,994	416,964	326,256	429,249	322,932	476,542	289,027	481,870	238,953	313,459	492,904	261,362	4,407,512
2007	334,593	468,712	383,506	474,542	373,291	600,122	361,467	596,622	373,925	484,038	468,987	208,818	5,128,623
2008	419,096	729,397	515,528	556,002	354,887	642,074	317,917	512,002	381,241	384,451	383,346	250,575	5,446,516
2009	309,386	406,786	328,940	404,635	305,326	435,239	244,504	388,567	244,371	332,043	535,063	300,489	4,235,349
2010	336,188	544,197	388,468	586,602	372,641	791,873	384,464	601,583	336,930	370,233	519,808	255,209	5,488,196
2011	390,345	471,890	408,416	516,121	388,052	555,238	332,701	577,095	391,134	420,084	483,740	239,722	5,174,538

Source: ICE Futures U.S. (ICE)

Coke

Coke is the hard and porous residue left after certain types of bituminous coals are heated to high temperatures (up to 2,000 degrees Fahrenheit) for about 17 hours. It is blackish-gray and has a metallic luster. The residue is mostly carbon. Coke is used as a reducing agent in the smelting of pig iron and the production of steel. Petroleum coke is made from the heavy tar-like residue of the petroleum refining process. It is used primarily to generate electricity.

Supply – Production of petroleum coke in the U.S.

in 2011 (annualized through April) rose +2.9% yr/yr to 304.904 million barrels. That was below the 2006 three-decade high of 309.980 and far below the U.S. production record of 369.305 million barrels posted back in 1957. U.S. stocks of coke at coke plants (Dec 31) in 2010 fell by -7.1% yr/yr to 721,000 short tons.

Trade – U.S. coke exports in 2010 rose +11.9% to 1.426 million tons, and over a third of those exports were to Canada. U.S. coke imports in 2010 rose to 1.213 million short tons. About 20% of the imports were from Japan.

Salient Statistics of Coke in the United States — In Thousands of Short Tons

| | Coke and Breeze Production at Coke Plants | | | | | | | Producer and Distributor | Exports | | Imports | |
| | By Census Division | | | | | | | Stocks | | | | |
Year	Middle Atlantic	East North Central	East South Central	Other	Total	Coke Total	Breeze Total	Con-sumption[2]	Dec. 31	Canada	Total	Japan	Total
2005	W	8,448	W	9,456	17,904	16,719	1,184	18,239	614	764	1,747	699	3,529
2006	W	8,439	W	9,112	17,551	16,404	1,147	18,784	685	840	1,616	838	4,068
2007	W	8,009	W	9,409	17,418	16,201	1,217	17,270	632	589	1,444	791	2,460
2008	W	7,578	W	9,153	16,731	15,646	1,085	17,006	916	758	1,959	604	3,603
2009	W	5,972	W	5,796	11,768	11,143	625	10,323	776	419	1,307	46	347
2010[1]	W	8,385	W	7,803	16,188	15,022	1,166	14,847	702	400	1,463	245	1,214

[1] Preliminary. [2] Equal to production plus imports minus the change in producer and distributor stocks minus exports.
W = Withheld. *Source: Energy Information Administration, U.S. Department of Energy (EIA-DOE)*

Production of Petroleum Coke in the United States — In Thousands of Barrels

Year	Jan.	Feb.	Mar.	Apr.	May	June	July	Aug.	Sept.	Oct.	Nov.	Dec.	Total
2005	25,093	23,806	26,896	25,648	27,209	26,950	26,612	26,410	22,209	22,039	24,372	26,575	303,819
2006	26,180	23,706	25,722	24,987	26,690	26,128	26,372	26,395	26,300	25,957	25,048	26,495	309,980
2007	25,883	22,117	25,369	24,592	26,071	24,904	26,345	26,316	24,613	24,143	24,220	26,050	300,623
2008	25,862	22,994	24,616	24,100	25,432	25,801	26,691	25,993	21,350	24,796	25,196	25,875	298,706
2009	25,902	21,991	25,071	24,741	24,402	25,339	25,205	24,862	24,364	23,823	22,490	23,857	292,047
2010	23,127	20,913	24,490	23,911	25,878	25,618	26,761	26,089	23,986	NA	24,394	26,437	296,295
2011[1]	25,976	20,975	24,952	23,904	25,635	25,745	27,115	27,363	25,962	26,460			304,904

[1] Preliminary. *Source: Energy Information Administration, U.S. Department of Energy (EIA-DOE)*

Coal Receipts and Average Prices at Coke Plants in the United States

| | Coal Receipts at Coke Plants | | | | | Average Price of Coal Receipts at Coke Plants | | | | |
| | By Census Division, in Thousands of Short Tons | | | | | By Census Division, In Dollars per Short Ton | | | | |
Year	Middle Atlantic	East North Central	East South Central	Other	Total	Middle Atlantic	East North Central	East South Central	Other	Total
2005	W	11,523	W	12,778	24,301	W	89.97	W	W	83.79
2006	W	11,488	W	11,865	23,353	W	99.48	W	W	92.87
2007	W	9,907	W	11,725	21,632	W	99.20	W	W	94.97
2008	W	10,362	W	12,067	22,429	W	122.18	W	W	118.09
2009	W	7,772	W	7,333	15,105	W	150.93	W	W	143.01
2010[1]	W	11,081	W	10,000	21,081	W	164.08	W	W	153.59

[1] Preliminary. W = Withheld. *Source: Energy Information Administration, U.S. Department of Energy (EIA-DOE)*

Coal Carbonized and Coke and Breeze Stocks at Coke Plants in the United States — In Thousands of Short Tons

| | Coal Carbonized at Coke Plants | | | | | Stocks at Coke Plants, Dec. 31 | | | | | | |
| | By Census Division | | | | | By Census Division | | | | | | |
Year	Middle Atlantic	East North Central	East South Central	Other	Total	Middle Atlantic	East North Central	East South Central	Other	Total	Coke Total	Breeze Total
2005	W	11,064	W	12,370	23,434	W	363	W	383	746	614	132
2006	W	11,100	W	11,857	22,957	W	487	W	284	771	685	87
2007	W	10,486	W	12,229	22,715	W	414	W	296	710	632	78
2008	W	10,228	W	11,842	22,070	W	658	W	335	993	916	77
2009	W	7,849	W	7,477	15,326	W	538	W	320	858	776	82
2010[1]	W	10,952	W	10,140	21,092	W	644	W	189	833	721	112

[1] Preliminary. W = Withheld. *Source: Energy Information Administration, U.S. Department of Energy (EIA-DOE)*

Copper

The word *copper* comes from name of the Mediterranean island Cyprus that was a primary source of the metal. Dating back more than 10,000 years, copper is the oldest metal used by humans. From the Pyramid of Cheops in Egypt, archeologists recovered a portion of a water plumbing system whose copper tubing was found in serviceable condition after more than 5,000 years.

Copper is one of the most widely used industrial metals because it is an excellent conductor of electricity, has strong corrosion-resistance properties, and is very ductile. It is also used to produce the alloys of brass (a copper-zinc alloy) and bronze (a copper-tin alloy), both of which are far harder and stronger than pure copper. Electrical uses of copper account for about 75% of total copper usage, and building construction is the single largest market (the average U.S. home contains 400 pounds of copper). Copper is biostatic, meaning that bacteria will not grow on its surface, and it is therefore used in air-conditioning systems, food processing surfaces, and doorknobs to prevent the spread of disease.

Copper futures and options are traded on the London Metal Exchange (LME) and the New York Mercantile Exchange (NYMEX). Copper futures are traded on the Shanghai Futures Exchange. The NYMEX copper futures contract calls for the delivery of 25,000 pounds of Grade 1 electrolyte copper and is priced in terms of cents per pound.

Prices – Nymex copper futures prices in February 2011 posted a record high of $4.6495 per pound. Prices consolidated moderately below that high through mid-year but then plummeted to a 1-1/2 year low of $2.9940 a pound in October 2011. Copper prices then bounced into the year-end and finished 2011 down -22.7% at $3.4315 a pound. The main bearish factors were concern that the European sovereign-debt crisis would intensify and drag the global economy into a recession along with a slowdown in China, the world's biggest copper consumer. Supporting copper prices in 2011 was decreased mine production that prompted the ICSG to call for a 201,000 MT global copper deficit in 2011 and a wider deficit of 256,000 MT in 2012.

Supply – World production of copper in 2011 rose by +1.3% yr/yr to 16.100 million metric tons, which was a new record high. The largest producer of copper was Chile with 33.7% of the world's production, followed by the Peru with 7.6%, China with 7.4%, the US with 7.0%, and Australia with 5.8%. U.S. production of refined copper in 2011 rose +0.9% yr/yr to 1.120 million short tons, which was far below the record U.S. production level of 2.490 million short tons seen in 1998.

Demand – U.S. consumption of copper in 2010 (latest data) rose +6.7% yr/yr to 1.760 million metric tons. The primary users of copper in the U.S. in 2010 (latest data) by class of consumer were wire rod mills with 71.0% of usage, brass mills with 26.1% of usage, and nominal use of 1.2% or less by each of foundries, ingot makers, and chemical plants.

Trade – U.S. exports of refined copper in 2011 fell by -53.3% to 36,480 metric tons, a new nine year low. U.S. imports of copper in 2011 rose +14.0% yr/yr to 690,000 metric tons, below the record high of 1.1 million metric tons in 2006.

World Mine Production of Copper (Content of Ore)   In Thousands of Metric Tons

Year	Australia	Canada[3]	Chile	China	Indonesia	Mexico	Peru	Poland	Russia	South Africa	United States[3]	Zambia	World Total[2]
2002	867.8	603.5	4,581.0	593	1,171.7	329.9	844.6	502.8	695	129.6	1,140	330.0	13,600
2003	839.6	557.1	4,904.2	620	1,005.8	355.7	862.6	505.0	675	89.5	1,120	378.0	13,800
2004	854.1	562.8	5,412.5	752	840.3	405.5	1,035.6	531.0	675	87.0	1,160	402.9	14,700
2005	916.3	595.4	5,320.5	777	1,064.2	429.1	1,009.9	512.0	700	88.6	1,140	432.0	15,000
2006	858.8	603.3	5,360.8	889	818.0	327.5	1,048.5	497.0	725	89.5	1,200	474.0	15,100
2007	870.0	596.2	5,557.0	946	796.9	337.5	1,190.3	452.0	740	97.0	1,170	509.0	15,500
2008	886.0	607.0	5,327.6	960	632.6	246.6	1,267.9	429.0	750	97.2	1,310	546.0	15,400
2009	854.0	490.6	5,389.6	995	996.0	227.7	1,274.7	444.0	725	92.9	1,180	697.0	15,900
2010[1]	870.0	525.0	5,420.0	1190	872.0	260.0	1,250.0	425.0	703		1,110	690.0	15,900
2011[2]	940.0	550.0	5,420.0	1190	625.0	365.0	1,220.0	425.0	710		1,120	715.0	16,100

[1] Preliminary.   [2] Estimate.   [3] Recoverable.   *Source: U.S. Geological Survey (USGS)*

Commodity Exchange Inc. Warehouse Stocks of Copper, on First of Month   In Thousands of Short Tons

Year	Jan.	Feb.	Mar.	Apr.	May	June	July	Aug.	Sept.	Oct.	Nov.	Dec.
2002	269.2	284.8	304.0	314.1	326.0	337.4	355.7	374.6	375.9	380.3	381.6	382.8
2003	399.3	395.2	373.7	362.7	351.2	336.7	320.5	310.6	303.9	299.0	294.4	288.1
2004	280.9	262.7	241.9	213.3	171.7	130.7	95.1	79.0	62.3	49.2	45.5	42.4
2005	48.2	45.8	46.8	43.3	30.1	22.0	15.3	11.0	9.3	7.2	3.7	3.7
2006	6.8	11.7	30.4	20.7	16.7	9.5	7.9	6.8	12.4	22.3	23.2	31.3
2007	34.0	36.2	37.0	36.4	33.7	27.2	22.1	21.8	20.7	20.1	19.0	18.0
2008	14.1	14.0	13.1	11.9	10.8	11.1	11.0	5.4	5.4	9.9	9.9	24.5
2009	NA	40.2	45.3	46.5	54.1	56.8	59.8	54.1	53.5	55.0	55.0	70.7
2010	94.5	94.5	94.5	102.0	101.2	101.9	101.9	100.4	95.3	84.9	74.3	70.8
2011	65.0	73.2	82.9	84.7	82.5	80.7	80.7	82.8	85.8	88.5	89.9	87.7

Source: CME Group; New York Mercantile Exchange (NYMEX)

Salient Statistics of Copper in the United States   In Thousands of Metric Tons

| | New Copper Produced | | | | | | Imports[5] | | Exports | | | | Blister & | Apparent Consumption | |
| | From Domestic Ores | | From | | Secon- | | | Ore, | | | Primary | Material | Refined | Primary |
Year	Mines	Smelters	Refin-eries	Foreign Ores	Total New	dary Re-covery	Unmanu-factured	Refined	Concen-trate[6]	Refined[7]	COMEX	Producers (Refined)	in Solution	Copper (Reported)	& Old Copper[8]
2002	1,140	683	725	116	1,440	190	1,230	927	23	27	362	1,030	44	2,370	2,610
2003	1,120	539	532	130	1,250	207	1,140	882	10	93	255	656	57	2,290	2,430
2004	1,160	542	531	140	1,260	191	1,060	807	24	118	44	134	51	2,410	2,550
2005	1,140	523	524	130	1,210	183	1,230	1,000	137	40	6	64	44	2,270	2,420
2006	1,200	501	531	144	1,210	151	1,320	1,070	108	106	31	194	19	2,110	2,200
2007	1,170	617	702	62	1,270	158	1,100	832	134	51	14	130	26	2,140	2,270
2008	1,310	574	603	109	1,220	156	934	721	301	37	31	199	24	2,020	1,990
2009	1,180	597	588	48	1,110	138	788	645	151	81	90	434	16	1,650	1,580
2010[1]	1,110				1,060	131	760	583	137	78		440		1,760	1,740
2011[2]	1,120				1,000	130		650	220	35				1,780	1,750

[1] Preliminary.   [2] Estimate.   [3] Also from matte, etc., refinery reports.   [4] From old scrap only.   [5] For consumption.   [6] Blister (copper content).
[7] Ingots, bars, etc.   [8] Old scrap only.   W = Withheld.   *Source: U.S. Geological Survey (USGS)*

Consumption of Refined Copper[3] in the United States   In Thousands of Metric Tons

| | | | By-Products | | | | | | By Class of Consumer | | | | Total |
Year	Cathodes	Wire Bars	Ingots and Ingot Bars	Cakes & Slabs	Billets	Other[4]	Wire Rod Mills	Brass Mills	Chemical Plants	Ingot Makers	Foundries	Miscel-laneous[5]	Con-sumption
2000	2,730.0	W	23.8	101.0	W	175.0	2,240.0	723.0	1.2	4.6	24.3	32.5	3,030.0
2001	2,360.0	W	24.0	95.9	W	140.0	1,940.0	623.0	1.2	4.6	21.6	28.6	2,620.0
2002	2,140.0	W	22.8	72.6	W	126.0	1,710.0	593.0	1.0	4.6	19.8	35.7	2,370.0
2003	2,070.0	W	22.3	41.8	W	153.0	1,640.0	587.0	1.0	4.6	21.9	36.7	2,290.0
2004	2,160.0	W	21.4	57.0	W	173.0	1,780.0	573.0	1.2	4.6	21.0	35.2	2,410.0
2005	2,040.0	W	28.8	35.3	W	167.0	1,680.0	528.0	1.2	4.5	20.2	39.3	2,270.0
2006	1,910.0	W	30.8	37.1	W	135.0	1,570.0	490.0	1.0	4.5	21.4	24.1	2,110.0
2007	1,930.0	W	28.8	42.7	W	135.0	1,610.0	476.0	1.0	4.5	19.4	25.7	2,140.0
2008[1]	1,820.0	W	28.6	45.0	W	130.0	1,490.0	479.0	0.3	4.5	20.4	24.7	2,020.0
2009[2]	1,450.0	W	27.4	43.6	W	125.0	1,140.0	454.0	0.4	4.5	19.1	30.1	1,650.0

[1] Preliminary.   [2] Estimate.   [3] Primary & secondary.   [4] Includes Wirebars and Billets.   [5] Includes iron and steel plants, primary smelters producing alloys other than copper, consumers of copper powder and copper shot, and other manufacturers.   W = Withheld.
Source: U.S. Geological Survey (USGS)

London Metals Exchange Warehouse Stocks of Copper, at End of Month   In Thousands of Metric Tons

Year	Jan.	Feb.	Mar.	Apr.	May	June	July	Aug.	Sept.	Oct.	Nov.	Dec.
2002	855.5	910.9	950.9	973.8	958.3	892.1	893.6	896.6	870.6	863.2	862.8	855.9
2003	833.8	825.9	813.2	768.2	740.8	665.8	612.6	620.3	580.4	516.5	467.0	430.7
2004	358.2	281.6	187.5	151.3	132.3	101.5	87.7	111.3	91.8	77.9	59.8	48.9
2005	46.4	52.5	45.3	61.0	44.4	28.9	31.6	68.0	79.9	65.1	72.6	92.3
2006	96.0	115.3	120.7	117.6	111.2	93.6	100.6	125.4	116.9	135.2	156.8	190.7
2007	216.2	205.4	181.1	156.6	127.5	122.4	144.6	173.8	199.1	238.0	291.3	240.7
2008	177.9	141.4	111.3	110.1	124.0	122.4	144.6	173.8	346.2	372.2	441.1	502.5
2009	491.3	536.8	501.9	398.8	312.1	265.8	282.2	300.0	346.2	372.2	441.1	502.5
2010	543.6	551.4	512.6	497.1	475.7	449.5	413.2	398.4	373.9	367.7	355.0	377.8
2011[1]	394.0	420.4	438.9	463.9	471.0	463.6	466.2	464.8	475.0	424.9	386.8	

[1] Preliminary.   *Source: American Bureau of Metal Statistics (ABMS)*

Copper Refined from Scrap in the United States   In Thousands of Metric Tons

Year	Jan.	Feb.	Mar.	Apr.	May	June	July	Aug.	Sept.	Oct.	Nov.	Dec.	Total
2002	7.1	6.2	7.2	7.6	8.2	7.8	7.0	7.6	7.1	6.3	5.1	3.9	81.1
2003	5.8	3.9	5.7	3.9	4.1	4.9	4.9	3.9	4.2	4.5	4.1	4.1	53.8
2004	4.2	3.9	4.3	4.4	4.2	4.5	4.1	3.9	4.7	4.5	4.2	4.0	50.8
2005	4.4	4.4	4.2	4.2	3.8	3.6	3.9	3.6	3.6	3.8	3.8	3.9	47.1
2006	3.8	3.7	3.8	3.7	3.7	3.7	3.7	3.7	3.8	3.7	3.7	3.8	44.8
2007	3.9	3.9	3.4	3.5	3.4	3.4	3.4	3.4	3.5	3.4	3.6	3.5	42.1
2008	4.1	4.2	4.1	4.3	4.6	5.0	4.3	4.5	4.3	4.6	4.6	4.6	53.2
2009	5.4	4.8	4.4	4.4	4.0	4.2	4.1	2.9	3.0	3.0	3.0	3.2	46.4
2010	2.9	3.2	2.8	3.3	3.0	3.3	3.2	3.5	3.3	3.2	3.2	2.9	37.7
2011[1]	3.8	3.0	3.2	3.0	3.2	3.1	3.0	3.2	3.0				38.1

[1] Preliminary.   *Source: U.S. Geological Survey (USGS)*

COPPER

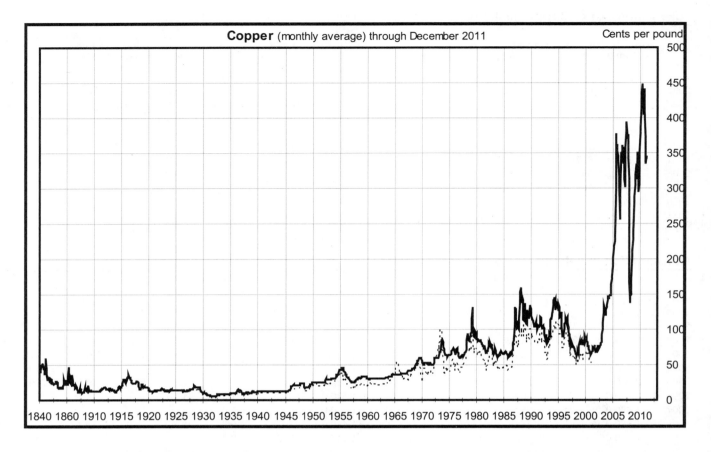

Copper (monthly average) through December 2011 — Cents per pound

Average Open Interest of Copper Futures in New York   In Contracts

Year	Jan.	Feb.	Mar.	Apr.	May	June	July	Aug.	Sept.	Oct.	Nov.	Dec.
2002	72,823	79,806	79,156	75,229	74,350	80,981	82,661	102,056	99,225	99,470	89,213	79,218
2003	81,820	81,499	72,484	85,485	77,704	81,509	82,868	94,517	92,768	106,924	103,218	90,208
2004	91,726	88,136	77,158	71,705	65,531	64,879	65,310	71,096	81,162	85,421	81,928	88,822
2005	85,363	96,537	116,004	120,138	98,240	106,218	109,156	109,481	102,652	106,829	110,972	104,062
2006	102,227	93,813	93,069	97,283	83,758	75,841	74,471	72,158	69,004	72,023	72,517	68,402
2007	69,972	70,373	69,324	78,919	80,834	79,257	88,691	78,113	72,469	86,909	78,385	71,626
2008	81,778	94,021	101,503	105,050	98,787	103,055	109,591	96,254	76,523	80,961	76,869	71,809
2009	82,402	85,831	90,636	103,517	106,511	111,555	111,849	118,935	117,782	127,204	146,612	149,621
2010	147,311	126,659	131,619	151,712	132,069	134,323	132,119	140,543	142,628	160,288	156,869	162,683
2011	162,325	157,918	138,261	134,959	122,036	128,861	148,876	130,312	120,015	126,973	124,770	115,634

Source: CME Group; New York Mercantile Exchange (NYMEX)

Volume of Trading of Copper Futures in New York   In Thousands of Contracts

Year	Jan.	Feb.	Mar.	Apr.	May	June	July	Aug.	Sept.	Oct.	Nov.	Dec.	Total
2002	217.6	233.7	164.7	254.3	218.1	267.2	263.4	303.6	195.6	232.7	276.5	179.8	2,807.3
2003	232.9	269.8	249.3	274.1	221.4	301.7	252.7	324.2	196.5	230.4	363.9	172.4	3,089.3
2004	213.5	385.8	265.3	340.2	203.9	280.9	208.4	310.3	212.1	245.0	317.2	207.9	3,190.6
2005	199.9	391.9	298.2	469.8	288.4	475.8	227.9	435.8	252.7	265.2	458.3	186.8	3,950.8
2006	234.3	401.4	284.5	407.0	260.4	321.6	182.2	310.0	189.4	216.4	320.8	153.4	3,281.3
2007	241.3	334.0	264.5	402.8	292.4	367.2	272.4	451.6	225.6	289.3	412.9	199.1	3,753.2
2008	345.5	459.5	298.5	466.5	344.5	462.0	382.1	463.2	349.5	403.8	414.4	228.4	4,618.1
2009	343.5	446.0	361.0	592.9	373.6	661.9	499.5	746.2	511.2	599.7	809.3	454.0	6,399.0
2010	645.5	996.3	772.6	1,049.0	894.7	1,051.1	724.9	980.5	604.4	822.3	1,132.3	631.8	10,305.7
2011	777.6	1,079.7	931.9	1,079.4	915.2	1,170.7	765.9	1,312.5	1,142.5	1,268.8	1,234.6	812.7	12,491.5

Source: CME Group; New York Mercantile Exchange (NYMEX)

Copper Futures - CME Group (NYMEX)
(weekly close) as of December 30, 2011

Cents per pound

Producers' Price of Electrolytic (Wirebar) Copper, Delivered to U.S. Destinations   In Cents Per Pound

Year	Jan.	Feb.	Mar.	Apr.	May	June	July	Aug.	Sept.	Oct.	Nov.	Dec.	Average
2002	81.79	84.23	86.60	85.11	85.22	88.23	84.44	79.82	79.71	80.16	84.57	75.56	82.62
2003	78.62	80.21	78.87	75.60	78.56	80.44	81.55	83.51	85.34	91.50	96.47	103.72	84.53
2004	113.93	129.91	139.96	135.82	129.44	129.11	134.34	135.50	138.74	142.01	147.99	151.88	135.72
2005	151.25	152.89	154.68	155.42	154.19	168.31	169.62	178.39	182.00	197.61	208.60	224.25	174.77
2006	225.07	230.74	238.31	302.74	382.65	346.65	368.49	359.91	353.01	345.83	322.45	307.00	315.24
2007	263.89	265.67	298.65	356.76	355.24	346.59	370.42	343.65	351.87	364.48	318.93	306.74	328.57
2008	325.53	364.78	385.98	399.96	383.39	375.08	382.31	349.89	320.54	224.32	174.59	145.09	319.29
2009	153.55	155.38	176.45	209.36	215.36	233.23	243.36	285.81	285.91	292.24	307.45	320.57	239.89
2010	337.71	315.88	343.54	356.46	315.33	299.00	312.18	337.50	357.31	382.81	390.16	419.69	347.30
2011	439.85	454.13	436.70	435.63	410.49	415.91	445.11	412.86	378.78	339.15	349.89	348.73	405.60

Source: American Metal Market (AMM)

Dealers' Buying Price of No. 2 Heavy Copper Scrap in Chicago   In Cents Per Pound

Year	Jan.	Feb.	Mar.	Apr.	May	June	July	Aug.	Sept.	Oct.	Nov.	Dec.	Average
2002	41.00	41.00	41.00	41.00	41.00	41.00	41.00	41.00	41.00	41.00	41.00	41.00	41.00
2003	41.00	41.00	41.00	41.00	41.00	41.00	41.00	41.00	41.00	48.17	56.00	56.00	43.99
2004	56.65	69.00	69.00	69.32	76.00	76.00	76.64	90.00	90.00	90.00	90.00	90.00	78.55
2005	90.00	90.00	90.00	90.00	90.00	94.09	100.00	100.00	100.00	100.00	100.00	129.52	97.80
2006	137.50	137.50	139.46	145.00	145.00	171.36	203.60	216.83	213.97	224.72	210.20	191.87	196.92
2007	155.83	153.92	164.32	197.83	210.09	203.60	216.83	219.89	226.07	141.85	97.50	87.02	200.92
2008	198.21	210.00	238.21	246.82	247.02	237.50	240.00	233.93	192.50	194.40	203.55	224.61	154.49
2009	80.00	92.24	104.32	124.40	134.00	155.23	166.59	182.02	192.50	194.40	203.55	224.61	154.49
2010	245.13	220.92	258.37	275.68	244.50	214.32	214.64	255.68	260.36	273.93	277.50	268.29	250.78
2011	285.00	292.50	299.13	295.00	290.72	295.23	315.00	311.41	293.69	241.55	261.50	256.97	286.48

Source: American Metal Market (AMM)

COPPER

Imports of Refined Copper into the United States   In Thousands of Metric Tons

Year	Jan.	Feb.	Mar.	Apr.	May	June	July	Aug.	Sept.	Oct.	Nov.	Dec.	Total
2002	82.5	87.8	53.0	92.6	59.9	76.2	80.3	90.5	69.9	79.0	82.0	73.0	927.0
2003	60.7	87.8	69.9	78.5	72.7	62.3	74.0	78.1	81.7	82.0	73.2	61.1	882.0
2004	55.4	48.8	70.7	59.3	70.8	51.3	83.9	78.7	91.7	68.4	77.0	51.1	807.1
2005	85.2	66.5	75.8	63.7	107.0	64.7	75.8	79.4	79.4	99.4	101.0	106.0	1,003.9
2006	138.0	108.0	80.1	69.1	100.0	94.1	91.4	101.0	106.0	96.4	58.3	56.5	1,098.9
2007	87.3	76.4	68.4	65.8	80.1	58.9	66.6	77.7	68.5	66.9	54.5	NA	841.2
2008	58.6	57.8	53.6	59.8	63.6	48.9	77.5	86.9	54.5	49.7	51.0	61.7	723.6
2009	76.4	67.7	80.0	53.9	52.6	35.7	54.2	36.4	56.0	39.9	55.2	55.5	663.5
2010	60.3	61.3	46.2	46.7	46.7	61.6	66.0	37.7	35.3	45.6	34.4	63.3	605.1
2011[1]	57.4	50.5	66.2	73.1	65.5	45.5	69.5	32.3					690.0

[1] Preliminary.   Source: U.S. Geological Survey (USGS)

Exports of Refined Copper from the United States   In Thousands of Metric Tons

Year	Jan.	Feb.	Mar.	Apr.	May	June	July	Aug.	Sept.	Oct.	Nov.	Dec.	Total
2002	.4	.7	3.2	.7	.8	6.8	7.7	2.6	1.3	.6	.5	1.5	26.6
2003	2.5	.8	1.5	.6	15.9	23.0	5.1	4.1	4.3	4.6	8.5	22.3	93.2
2004	11.0	18.5	23.9	28.4	3.7	2.7	5.5	9.4	.6	3.9	2.5	8.4	118.4
2005	4.5	3.2	2.8	1.9	7.2	4.3	3.0	2.7	1.8	3.3	3.3	3.0	40.9
2006	5.6	7.3	6.8	9.6	6.3	13.1	6.0	9.6	9.3	13.7	6.2	12.6	106.1
2007	3.1	2.7	5.1	3.6	3.9	6.6	3.6	3.4	5.4	7.1	3.0	NA	51.8
2008	6.0	5.7	6.3	3.2	1.9	1.4	2.0	2.0	1.5	3.2	1.7	1.6	36.5
2009	.9	1.7	3.8	6.5	21.4	19.2	8.9	6.3	4.0	2.1	3.0	3.2	80.9
2010	6.2	13.9	13.6	10.4	4.7	4.5	4.2	5.3	7.0	1.5	1.2	5.7	78.2
2011[1]	1.6	5.0	3.1	2.1	3.5	1.9	1.9	5.1					36.5

[1] Preliminary.   Source: U.S. Geological Survey (USGS)

Stocks of Refined Copper in the United States, on First of Month   In Thousands of Short Tons

Year	Jan.	Feb.	Mar.	Apr.	May	June	July	Aug.	Sept.	Oct.	Nov.	Dec.
2002	1,045.1	1,096.2	1,132.4	1,155.3	1,175.0	1,158.8	1,126.7	1,132.2	1,123.0	1,123.7	1,110.5	1,109.0
2003	1,119.8	109.7	1,038.8	1,042.1	998.3	959.8	891.8	848.9	855.6	825.5	761.2	768.0
2004	733.8	646.3	566.7	463.9	367.0	311.8	247.8	218.3	194.5	169.2	158.9	147.4
2005	145.8	151.0	143.4	134.4	129.3	116.2	105.3	98.5	83.0	68.2	56.8	59.4
2006	66.8	76.9	103.3	109.0	88.2	84.5	68.3	76.4	80.1	88.4	103.4	152.3
2007	194.9	222.1	216.8	197.7	165.8	130.7	114.3	118.8	114.0	110.3	115.0	123.8
2008	147.2	122.5	106.3	105.9	74.4	81.3	72.8	83.8	106.3	123.6	134.6	165.7
2009	231.1	290.3	321.7	376.8	380.1	355.9	320.8	331.1	336.3	362.9	384.3	431.7
2010	480.2	523.4	544.8	525.4	509.6	486.9	479.9	471.9	454.5	425.6	408.5	400.2
2011[1]	429.5	427.3	427.2	418.5	409.0	410.0	400.6	412.0	412.5	420.6	427.7	

Recoverable Copper Content.   [1] Preliminary.   Source: American Bureau of Metal Statistics (ABMS)

Stocks of Refined Copper Outside the United States, on First of Month   In Thousands of Short Tons

Year	Jan.	Feb.	Mar.	Apr.	May	June	July	Aug.	Sept.	Oct.	Nov.	Dec.
2002	1,241.3	1,273.5	1,291.5	1,370.4	1,391.1	1,399.4	1,289.0	1,342.6	1,369.1	1,321.1	1,219.7	1,224.5
2003	1,238.8	2,147.6	1,188.0	1,216.3	1,147.4	1,109.8	1,129.2	1,139.9	1,150.9	1,140.2	1,170.8	1,157.1
2004	1,191.5	1,149.9	1,139.5	995.5	968.4	826.0	807.1	812.4	830.2	825.2	778.0	816.8
2005	833.8	802.2	929.8	848.0	758.2	771.3	822.6	786.4	846.9	774.3	803.4	805.0
2006	871.2	956.8	923.2	797.7	816.4	819.2	789.1	812.9	872.4	830.1	877.6	905.9
2007	1,016.2	969.5	966.6	994.3	973.0	873.8	893.9	845.9	880.9	894.4	884.8	860.7
2008	947.7	920.0	833.9	1,257.0	1,253.4	1,311.1	1,309.1	1,315.5	1,318.0	1,487.6	366.8	957.6
2009	931.3	1,155.7	1,125.6	1,024.3	853.1	788.4	817.5	752.9	864.3	943.4	958.9	1,032.0
2010	1,083.3	1,105.2	1,131.6	1,084.3	1,122.5	1,088.1	1,030.7	933.6	985.4	910.9	970.0	966.7
2011[1]	980.1	1,064.6	1,119.6	1,220.9	1,063.8	1,038.2	1,058.7	1,062.2	1,040.0	1,057.8	964.9	

Recoverable Copper Content.   [1] Preliminary.   Source: American Bureau of Metal Statistics (ABMS)

Production of Refined Copper in the United States   In Thousands of Short Tons

Year	Jan.	Feb.	Mar.	Apr.	May	June	July	Aug.	Sept.	Oct.	Nov.	Dec.	Total
2002	134.0	117.0	124.0	129.0	134.0	128.0	130.0	124.0	120.0	129.0	120.0	119.0	1,508
2003	124.0	110.0	118.0	98.7	98.8	106.0	110.0	110.0	112.0	108.0	101.0	111.0	1,308
2004	104.0	98.9	105.0	111.0	109.0	113.0	104.0	107.0	112.0	111.0	109.0	123.0	1,307
2005	102.0	102.0	104.0	105.0	109.0	101.0	100.0	102.0	103.0	104.0	108.0	115.0	1,255
2006	99.9	101.0	117.0	109.0	113.0	114.0	100.0	101.0	102.0	89.8	94.4	108.0	1,249
2007	101.0	97.1	116.0	113.0	116.0	112.0	116.0	117.0	108.0	120.0	91.5	103.0	1,311
2008	109.0	107.0	108.0	102.0	107.0	102.0	98.7	107.0	108.0	110.0	107.0	113.0	1,279
2009	105.0	96.7	95.9	93.7	91.8	90.3	94.4	97.6	94.3	101.0	98.0	101.0	1,160
2010	96.2	91.3	95.2	89.5	85.4	89.3	95.6	94.4	94.2	90.1	84.1	89.2	1,095
2011[1]	86.8	76.3	84.9	79.7	82.9	86.4	79.2	79.7	93.6				999

Recoverable Copper Content.   [1] Preliminary.   *Source: U.S. Geological Survey (USGS)*

Production of Refined Copper Outside North America   In Thousands of Short Tons

Year	Jan.	Feb.	Mar.	Apr.	May	June	July	Aug.	Sept.	Oct.	Nov.	Dec.	Total
2002	1,197.9	1,091.1	1,196.4	1,159.7	1,183.4	1,161.3	1,174.1	1,195.8	1,159.6	1,200.9	1,172.9	1,187.2	14,080
2003	1,182.0	1,103.7	1,191.7	1,158.4	1,202.9	1,175.1	1,212.2	1,192.0	1,179.5	1,218.7	1,205.0	1,241.5	14,263
2004	1,183.7	1,143.0	1,233.5	1,195.3	1,185.3	1,208.2	1,262.3	1,268.9	1,276.5	1,287.6	1,300.0	1,301.2	14,846
2005	1,312.6	1,166.7	1,285.0	1,251.8	1,290.3	1,292.7	1,309.0	1,302.7	1,317.0	1,331.1	1,342.1	1,393.0	15,594
2006	1,335.6	1,260.3	1,371.2	1,340.5	1,373.2	1,377.9	1,388.8	1,366.9	1,362.2	1,423.7	1,397.8	1,469.4	16,468
2007	1,467.9	1,351.6	1,445.2	1,407.0	1,420.3	1,397.2	1,411.5	1,411.9	1,442.0	1,454.4	1,460.7	1,506.1	17,176
2008	1,463.3	1,387.4	1,513.4	1,487.8	1,481.1	1,518.3	1,555.6	1,549.1	1,520.6	1,535.6	1,512.0	1,517.7	18,042
2009	1,458.4	1,398.3	1,483.0	1,464.8	1,528.2	1,488.8	1,525.5	1,556.0	1,562.9	1,584.9	1,581.6	1,616.6	18,249
2010	1,557.1	1,462.9	1,585.7	1,581.5	1,612.8	1,645.2	1,637.3	1,631.5	1,572.8	1,591.1	1,627.1	1,683.3	19,188
2011[1]	1,614.9	1,460.1	1,664.2	1,608.0	1,683.4	1,664.7	1,661.8	1,655.7	1,644.9	1,707.1	1,777.1		19,631

Recoverable Copper Content.   [1] Preliminary.   *Source: American Bureau of Metal Statistics (ABMS)*

Deliveries of Refined Copper to Fabricators in the United States   In Thousands of Short Tons

Year	Jan.	Feb.	Mar.	Apr.	May	June	July	Aug.	Sept.	Oct.	Nov.	Dec.	Total
2002	152.1	126.0	140.7	149.3	148.6	136.2	147.9	141.1	129.5	141.6	124.5	129.7	1,667
2003	136.4	123.4	124.6	106.6	107.7	117.0	127.1	120.6	125.8	127.9	114.4	133.8	1,465
2004	126.4	131.1	137.6	137.7	130.9	143.5	133.3	132.9	136.8	129.3	128.8	137.5	1,606
2005	120.1	120.0	131.2	125.4	125.7	119.2	106.9	112.8	108.0	110.9	112.6	115.9	1,409
2006	124.8	110.3	131.5	121.9	121.8	132.7	117.5	119.9	112.7	95.5	95.6	100.5	1,385
2007	115.9	118.9	131.9	127.4	128.1	126.2	131.3	132.3	112.2	134.9	113.3	100.9	1,473
2008	134.1	118.8	123.2	114.7	111.6	120.8	105.4	118.3	121.4	129.7	109.4	110.6	1,418
2009	117.6	105.0	104.3	99.4	97.6	105.7	115.3	110.1	100.7	101.6	104.9	117.3	1,280
2010	100.9	102.0	111.1	101.7	102.4	96.7	107.9	105.1	100.7	100.3	92.3	92.7	1,214
2011[1]	95.1	86.3	98.6	95.2	96.9	95.6	87.2	96.6	92.3	96.5	102.2		1,137

Recoverable Copper Content.   [1] Preliminary.   *Source: American Bureau of Metal Statistics (ABMS)*

Deliveries of Refined Copper to Fabricators Outside the United States   In Thousands of Short Tons

Year	Jan.	Feb.	Mar.	Apr.	May	June	July	Aug.	Sept.	Oct.	Nov.	Dec.	Total
1990	419.9	466.3	436.7	392.9	408.3	466.7	303.7	373.5	370.8	448.9	469.1	420.7	4,972
1991	405.0	404.4	391.5	361.2	406.3	433.5	368.5	323.4	420.7	499.1	391.4	483.4	4,807
1992	453.7	408.9	441.8	416.4	413.4	432.4	410.4	364.7	432.6	403.5	406.1	461.3	5,045
1993	427.9	392.9	452.3	361.7	422.2	442.6	384.4	347.9	387.5	414.8	463.4	458.5	4,956
1994	399.8	429.5	481.2	466.5	468.9	428.1	387.9	369.2	423.5	448.9	457.1	436.0	5,197
1995[2]	758.5	810.1	892.8	882.2	853.0	867.3	863.7	814.1	803.4	835.1	796.6	726.2	9,903
1996	875.2	859.4	934.3	907.2	816.7	950.7	908.3	817.4	911.5	1,056.0	922.7	918.3	10,878
1997	862.2	889.7	977.9	1,007.1	991.1	982.7	897.8	873.9	886.2	1,009.0	980.4	966.6	11,349
1998	1,091.7	973.8	1,062.0	1,055.5	995.7	1,014.8	986.8	924.8	913.3	987.9	982.1	1,023.0	12,011
1999[1]	314.5	745.5	NA	NA	NA	NA	NA	NA	NA	NA	NA	NA	6,360

Recoverable Copper Content.   [1] Preliminary.   [2] New reporting method beginning January 1995, includes crude copper deliveries.
Source: American Bureau of Metal Statistics (ABMS)

Corn

Corn is a member of the grass family of plants and is a native grain of the American continents. Fossils of corn pollen that are over 80,000 years old have been found in lake sediment under Mexico City. Archaeological discoveries show that cultivated corn existed in the southwestern U.S. for at least 3,000 years, indicating that the indigenous people of the region cultivated corn as a food crop long before the Europeans reached the New World. Corn is a hardy plant that grows in many different areas of the world. It can grow at altitudes as low as sea level and as high as 12,000 feet in the South American Andes Mountains. Corn can also grow in tropical climates that receive up to 400 inches of rainfall per year, or in areas that receive only 12 inches of rainfall per year. Corn is used primarily as livestock feed in the United States and the rest of the world. Other uses for corn are alcohol additives for gasoline, adhesives, corn oil for cooking and margarine, sweeteners, and as food for humans. Corn is the largest crop in the U.S., both in terms of the value of the crop and of the acres planted.

The largest futures market for corn is at the Chicago Board of Trade. Corn futures also trade at the Bolsa de Mercadorias & Futuros (BM&F) in Brazil, the Budapest Commodity Exchange, the Marche a Terme International de France (MATIF), the Mercado a Termino de Buenos Aires in Argentina, the Kanmon Commodity Exchange (KCE) in Korea, and the Tokyo Grain Exchange (TGE). The CBOT futures contract calls for the delivery of 5,000 bushels of No. 2 yellow corn at par contract price, No. 1 yellow at 1-1/2 cents per bushel over the contract price, or No. 3 yellow at 1-1/2 cents per bushel below the contract price.

Prices – Corn futures prices in 2011 rallied through the first half of the year and posted an all-time high of $7.9975 a bushel in June 2011. Price rallied as the wet spring prompted the USDA to cut its 2011 U.S. corn production estimate to 13.2 billion bushels from 13.5 billion bushels since flooded fields reduced U.S. planted acres to 90.7 million from 92.2 million acres. U.S. corn supplies also tightened as the USDA in the same month cut its 2011/12 U.S. ending stocks estimate to a 15-year low of 695 million bushels. In addition, the International Grains Council predicted global corn inventories would fall to 111 MMT in 2011/12 or about 13% of consumption, the smallest stocks-to-use ratio since 1974. U.S. corn demand for ethanol continued to expand as U.S. ethanol production rose to a record of 963,000 barrels a day in December 2011. Corn prices remained firm through the summer of 2011 but then sold off to a 1-year low of $5.70 a bushel in December 2011, finishing the year up +2.8% at $6.4650 a bushel. The surge in prices in the first half of the year reduced corn demand from livestock producers who switched to wheat as a cheaper feed alternative to corn. Record high corn prices also dented foreign demand as the USDA in October reduced its 2011 U.S. corn export estimate to a 13-year low of 1.60 billion bushels. Other bearish factors for corn prices during the second half of 2011 included the +9.2%

y/y increase in the 2011 China corn harvest to a record 192 MMT, along with the increase in corn plantings for Argentina, the world's second-largest corn exporter, by +7.2% to 12 million acres. Going into 2012, corn supplies remain tight after the USDA cut its 2012 global ending stocks estimate to a 5-year low of 125.35 MMT and with the U.S. stocks/use ratio at a 16-year low of 6.3%. However, the USDA projects 2012 US corn plantings on 94 million acres, the most acres planted since 1944.

Supply – World production of corn in the 2011-12 marketing year rose +4.4% to a new record high of 864.107 million metric tons. The world's largest corn producers are the U.S. with 36.3% of world production, China (22.2%), and Brazil (7.1%). Corn production in both China and Brazil has nearly tripled since 1980. Production in the U.S. over that same time frame has risen by about 50%. The world area harvested with corn in 2011-12 rose +1.6% yr/yr to 314.4 million hectares, just under the 13-year high of 318.7 million hectares in 2007-08. World ending stocks of corn and coarse grains in 2011-12 fell –4.6% to 158.5 million metric tons.

U.S. corn production estimates for the 2011-12 marketing year (Aug-Nov) fell by -0.8% yr/yr to 12.358 billion bushels. U.S. farmers harvested 83.981 million acres of corn for grain usage in 2011-12, which was up +3.1% yr/yr. U.S. corn yield in 2011-12 fell -3.7% to 147.2 bushels per acre. U.S. carry-over stocks on June 1, 2011 fell by -14.9% to 3.669 billion bushels. The largest corn producing states in the U.S. in 2011 were Iowa with 19.1% of U.S. production, Illinois (15.6%), Nebraska (12.4%), Minnesota (9.7%), and Indiana (6.8%). The value of the U.S. corn crop in 2011-12 was $76.464 billion.

Demand – World consumption of corn and rough grains in 2011-12 rose by +2.1% yr/yr to 1,149.9 million metric tons, which was a new record high. The U.S. distribution tables for corn show that in 2011-12 the largest category of usage, aside from animal feed, is for ethanol production (alcohol fuel) with 4.950 billion bushels. That was up +8.36% yr/yr and is 78.0% of total non-feed usage. Corn usage for ethanol is more than seven times the usage in 2000 and that usage category is likely to grow if there is a return of the high prices of crude oil and gasoline. After ethanol, the largest non-feed usage categories are for high fructose corn syrup (HFCS) with 8.4% of U.S. usage, glucose and dextrose sugars (4.1%), corn starch (4.0%), cereal and other corn products (3.1%), and alcoholic beverages (2.1%).

Trade – U.S. exports of corn in 2010-11 (latest data available) fell -9.0% yr/yr to 45.200 million metric tons, which is farther below the record high of 61.417 million metric tons posted in 1979-80. The largest destination countries for U.S. corn exports are Japan, which accounted for 30.7% of U.S. corn exports in 2010-11, South Korea (16.6%), Mexico (13.4%), Egypt (6.5%), Taiwan (6.2%), and Canada (2.1%).

World Production of Corn or Maize   In Thousands of Metric Tons

Crop Year Beginning Oct. 1	Argentina	Brazil	Canada	China	European Union	Egypt	India	Mexico	Romania	South Africa	Ukraine	United States	World Total
2002-03	15,500	44,500	8,999	121,300	57,660	6,000	11,150	19,280	7,300	9,675	4,180	227,767	603,179
2003-04	14,951	42,000	9,587	115,830	47,905	5,740	14,980	21,800	7,020	9,700	6,875	256,229	627,516
2004-05	20,483	35,000	8,837	130,290	66,471	5,840	14,180	22,050	12,000	11,716	8,867	299,876	715,809
2005-06	15,800	41,700	9,332	139,365	60,668	5,932	14,710	19,500	10,300	6,935	7,167	282,263	699,723
2006-07	22,500	51,000	8,990	151,600	53,829	6,149	15,100	22,350	8,500	7,300	6,426	267,503	714,031
2007-08	22,017	58,600	11,649	152,300	47,555	6,174	18,960	23,600	----	13,164	7,421	331,177	794,698
2008-09	15,500	51,000	10,592	165,914	62,321	6,645	19,730	24,226	----	12,567	11,447	307,142	799,151
2009-10[1]	23,300	56,100	9,561	163,974	56,947	6,280	16,720	20,374	----	13,420	10,486	332,549	819,234
2010-11[2]	22,500	57,500	11,714	177,245	55,795	6,500	21,280	21,130	----	10,924	11,919	316,165	827,537
2011-12[3]	22,000	61,000	10,700	191,750	64,524	3,800	21,000	20,500	----	12,500	22,500	313,918	864,107

[1] Preliminary.   [2] Estimate.   [3] Forecast.   *Source: Foreign Agricultural Service, U.S. Department of Agriculture (FAS-USDA)*

World Supply and Demand of Coarse Grains   In Millions of Metric Tons/Hectares

Crop Year Beginning Oct. 1	Area Harvested	Yield	Production	World Trade	Total Consumption	Ending Stocks	Stocks as % of Consumption[3]
2002-03	291.6	3.00	873.6	102.8	901.1	172.0	19.1
2003-04	306.0	3.00	916.1	102.6	944.8	143.3	15.2
2004-05	300.5	3.40	1,015.6	101.3	978.8	180.2	18.4
2005-06	301.1	3.30	980.4	108.6	994.4	166.2	16.7
2006-07	305.5	3.20	988.9	114.7	1,013.8	141.3	13.9
2007-08	318.7	3.40	1,080.8	128.9	1,057.9	164.2	15.5
2008-09	313.5	3.50	1,111.2	110.7	1,081.0	194.4	18.0
2009-10	310.5	3.60	1,115.6	119.0	1,114.5	195.4	17.5
2010-11[1]	309.5	3.50	1,097.6	116.0	1,126.8	166.2	14.7
2011-12[2]	314.4	3.60	1,142.2	120.1	1,149.9	158.5	13.8

[1] Preliminary.   [2] Estimate.   [3] Represents the ratio of marketing year ending stocks to total consumption.   *Source: Foreign Agricultural Service, U.S. Department of Agriculture (FAS-USDA)*

Acreage and Supply of Corn in the United States   In Millions of Bushels

Crop Year Beginning Sept. 1	Planted	Harvested For Grain	Harvested For Silage	Yield Per Harvested Acre Bushels	Carry-over, Sept. 1 On Farms	Carry-over, Sept. 1 Off Farms	Beginning Stocks	Supply Production	Supply Imports	Total Supply
	In Thousands of Acres									
2002-03	78,894	69,330	7,122	129.3	586.8	1,009.6	1,596	8,967	14	10,578
2003-04	78,603	70,944	6,583	142.2	484.9	601.8	1,087	10,089	14	11,188
2004-05	80,930	73,632	6,103	160.4	438.0	520.1	958	11,807	11	12,775
2005-06	81,759	75,107	5,920	147.9	820.5	1,293.5	2,114	11,112	9	13,235
2006-07	78,327	70,648	6,477	149.1	749.5	1,217.7	1,967	10,531	12	12,510
2007-08	93,527	86,520	6,060	150.7	460.1	843.5	1,304	13,038	20	14,362
2008-09	85,982	78,570	5,965	153.9	500.0	1,124.2	1,624	12,092	14	13,729
2009-10	86,382	79,490	5,605	164.7	607.5	1,065.8	1,673	13,110	8	14,774
2010-11[1]	88,192	81,446	5,567	152.8	485.1	1,222.7	1,708	12,447	25	14,180
2011-12[2]	91,921	83,981	5,928	147.2	315.0	812.7	730	12,358	20	14,255

[1] Preliminary.   [2] Estimate.   *Source: Economic Research Service, U.S. Department of Agriculture (ERS-USDA)*

Production of Corn (For Grain) in the United States, by State   In Million of Bushels

Year	Illinois	Indiana	Iowa	Kansas	Michigan	Minnesota	Missouri	Nebraska	Ohio	South Dakota	Texas	Wisconsin	Total
2002	1,471.5	631.6	1,931.6	301.6	234.0	1,051.9	283.5	940.8	264.3	308.8	202.3	391.5	8,966.8
2003	1,812.2	786.9	1,868.3	300.0	259.8	970.9	302.4	1,124.2	478.9	427.4	194.7	367.7	10,089.2
2004	2,088.0	929.0	2,244.4	432.0	257.3	1,121.0	466.6	1,319.7	491.4	539.5	233.5	353.6	11,807.2
2005	1,708.9	888.6	2,162.5	465.8	288.9	1,191.9	329.7	1,270.5	464.8	470.1	210.9	429.2	11,112.1
2006	1,817.5	844.7	2,050.1	345.0	286.7	1,102.9	362.9	1,178.0	470.6	312.3	175.5	400.4	10,531.1
2007	2,283.8	981.0	2,376.9	507.8	287.8	1,146.1	457.8	1,472.0	541.5	542.1	291.6	442.8	13,037.9
2008	2,130.1	873.6	2,188.8	486.4	295.3	1,180.8	381.6	1,393.7	421.2	585.2	253.8	394.6	12,091.6
2009	2,053.2	933.7	2,420.6	598.3	309.3	1,244.1	446.8	1,575.3	546.4	706.7	254.8	448.3	13,110.1
2010	1,946.8	898.0	2,153.3	581.3	315.0	1,292.1	369.0	1,469.1	533.0	569.7	301.6	502.2	12,446.9
2011[1]	1,946.8	839.5	2,356.4	449.4	335.1	1,201.2	350.0	1,536.0	508.8	653.4	136.7	517.9	12,358.4

[1] Preliminary.   *Source: National Agricultural Statistics Service, U.S. Department of Agriculture (NASS-USDA)*

CORN

Quarterly Supply and Disappearance of Corn in the United States   In Millions of Bushels

Crop Year Beginning Sept. 1	Beginning Stocks	Pro- duction	Imports[3]	Total Supply	Food & Alcohol	Seed	Feed & Residual	Total	Exports[3]	Total Disap- pearance	Gov't Owned[4]	Privately Owned[5]	Total Stocks
								Disappearance				**Ending Stocks**	
2007-08	1,304	13,038	20.0	14,362	4,420	21.8	5,858	10,300	2,437	12,737			1,624
Sept.-Nov.	1,304	13,038	2.2	14,344	986	0	2,387	3,372	693	4,066			10,278
Dec.-Feb.	10,278	----	2.8	10,281	1,046	0	1,734	2,780	642	3,422			6,859
Mar.-May	6,859	----	9.7	6,868	1,167	20.7	1,069	2,257	583	2,840			4,028
June-Aug.	4,028	----	5.3	4,033	1,221	1.1	668	1,890	519	2,409			1,624
2008-09	1,624	12,092	13.5	13,729	5,003	21.9	5,182	10,207	1,849	12,056			1,673
Sept.-Nov.	1,624	12,092	2.8	13,719	1,219	0	1,978	3,198	449	3,647			10,072
Dec.-Feb.	10,072	----	4.1	10,076	1,178	0	1,573	2,751	371	3,122			6,954
Mar.-May	6,954	----	5.1	6,959	1,238	20.4	947	2,205	493	2,698			4,261
June-Aug.	4,261	----	1.5	4,263	1,368	1.5	684	2,053	536	2,590			1,673
2009-10	1,673	13,092	8.3	14,774	5,939	22.3	5,125	11,086	1,980	13,066			1,708
Sept.-Nov.	1,673	13,092	1.0	14,766	1,382	0	2,015	3,397	467	3,864			10,902
Dec.-Feb.	10,902	----	1.3	10,904	1,447	0	1,341	2,788	422	3,210			7,694
Mar.-May	7,694	----	3.1	7,697	1,543	21.7	1,273	2,838	549	3,387			4,310
June-Aug.	4,310	----	2.9	4,313	1,566	.7	495	2,062	543	2,605			1,708
2010-11[1]	1,708	12,447	27.7	14,182	6,405	23.0	4,793	11,220	1,835	13,055			1,128
Sept.-Nov.	1,708	12,447	5.3	14,160	1,580	0	2,069	3,649	454	4,103			10,057
Dec.-Feb.	10,057	----	8.5	10,065	1,579	0	1,559	3,138	404	3,542			6,523
Mar.-May	6,523	----	10.4	6,534	1,619	20.2	716	2,356	508	2,864			3,670
June-Aug.	3,670	----	3.5	3,673	1,626	2.8	448	2,077	469	2,546			1,128
2011-12[2]	1,128	12,358	20.0	13,506	6,382	23.5	4,600	11,005	1,700	12,705			801
Sept.-Nov.	1,128	12,358	4.1	13,490	1,616	0	1,825	3,441	407	3,848			9,642

[1] Preliminary.   [2] Estimate.   [3] Uncommitted inventory.   [4] Includes quantity under loan and farmer-owned reserve.   *Source: Economic Research Service, U.S. Department of Agriculture (ERS-USDA)*

Corn Production Estimates and Cash Price in the United States

Year	Aug. 1	Sept. 1	Oct. 1	Nov. 1	Final	St. Louis No. 2 Yellow	Omaha No. 2 Yellow	Gulf Ports No. 2 Yellow	Kansas City No. 2 White	Chicago No. 2 Yellow	Average Farm Price[2]	Value of Pro- duction (Mil. $)
		Corn for Grain Production Estimates										
	In Thousands of Bushels					**Dollars Per Bushel**						
2002-03	8,886,009	8,848,529	8,969,836	9,003,364	8,966,787	2.49	2.29	2.71	2.94	2.46	2.32	20,882
2003-04	10,064,452	9,944,418	10,207,141	10,277,932	10,089,222	2.49	2.29	2.94	2.66	2.66	2.50	24,477
2004-05	10,923,099	10,960,710	11,613,226	11,740,920	11,807,217	2.73	2.50	2.48	2.01	2.08	2.05	24,381
2005-06	10,349,841	10,638,661	10,857,440	11,032,105	11,112,072	2.13	1.82	2.69	2.11	2.10	2.01	22,198
2006-07	10,975,740	11,113,766	10,905,194	10,744,806	10,531,123	2.19	1.88	3.95	4.18	3.46	3.13	32,083
2007-08	13,053,617	13,307,999	13,318,102	13,167,741	13,037,875	3.60	3.33	5.54	5.19	4.98	4.45	54,667
2008-09	12,287,875	12,072,365	12,199,908	12,019,894	12,091,648	5.05	4.84	4.39	4.13	3.89	4.05	49,313
2009-10	12,760,986	12,954,500	13,018,058	12,920,928	13,110,062	3.88	3.80	4.14	3.71	3.64	3.53	46,734
2010-11	13,365,225	13,159,700	12,663,949	12,539,646	12,446,865	3.69	3.49	7.04	6.55	6.38	5.51	64,643
2011-12[1]	12,914,085	12,497,070	12,432,910	12,309,936	12,358,412	6.50	6.29	6.99	7.07	6.41	6.00	76,464

[1] Preliminary.   [2] Season-average price based on monthly prices weigthed by monthly marketings.
Source: Economic Research Service, U.S. Department of Agriculture (ERS-USDA)

Distribution of Corn in the United States   In Millions of Bushels

Crop Year Beginning Sept. 1	HFCS	Glucose & Dextrose	Starch	Fuel	Bev- rage[3]	Seed	Cereal & Other Products	Total	Livestock Feed[4]	Exports (Including Grain Equiv. of Products)	Domestic Disap- pearance	Total Utilization
			Food, Seed and Industrial Use									
			Alcohol									
2002-03	532	219	256	996	131	20.0	187	2,340	5,563	1,587.9	7,903	9,491
2003-04	530	228	271	1,168	132	20.6	187	2,537	5,793	1,899.8	8,330	10,230
2004-05	521	222	277	1,323	133	20.8	189	2,666	6,155	1,818.1	8,842	10,661
2005-06	529	229	275	1,603	135	19.9	190	2,961	6,152	2,133.8	9,134	11,268
2006-07	510	239	272	2,117	136	23.8	190	3,464	5,591	2,437.4	9,081	11,207
2007-08	490	236	262	3,049	135	21.8	192	4,387	5,858	1,848.9	10,300	12,737
2008-09	489	245	234	3,709	134	22.0	192	5,025	5,182	1,980.0	10,207	12,056
2009-10	512	257	250	4,591	134	22.3	194	5,961	5,125	1,834.5	11,086	13,066
2010-11[1]	521	272	258	5,021	135	23.0	197	6,428	4,793	1,834.5	11,220	13,055
2011-12[2]	520	265	260	5,000	135	23.5	202	6,405	4,600	1,700.0	11,005	12,705

[1] Preliminary.   [2] Estimate.   [3] Also includes nonfuel industrial alcohol.   [4] Feed and waste (residual, mostly feed).
Source: Economic Research Service, U.S. Department of Agriculture (ERS-USDA)

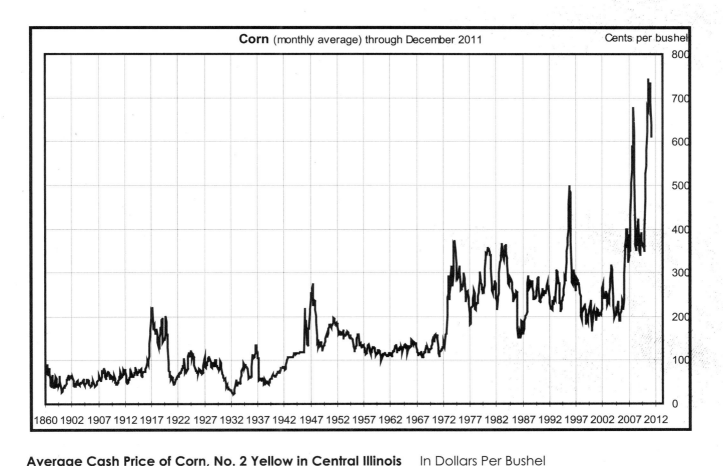

Corn (monthly average) through December 2011 — Cents per bushel

Average Cash Price of Corn, No. 2 Yellow in Central Illinois   In Dollars Per Bushel

Year	Sept.	Oct.	Nov.	Dec.	Jan.	Feb.	Mar.	Apr.	May	June	July	Aug.	Average
2002-03	2.57	2.41	2.36	2.32	2.29	2.33	2.31	2.36	2.40	2.37	2.13	2.26	2.34
2003-04	2.25	2.11	2.26	2.38	2.52	2.73	2.89	3.03	2.90	2.76	2.26	2.17	2.52
2004-05	1.98	1.77	1.79	1.87	1.86	1.86	1.97	1.94	1.93	2.02	2.20	1.98	1.93
2005-06	1.75	1.67	1.75	1.89	1.98	2.07	2.04	2.18	2.22	2.15	2.22	2.07	2.00
2006-07	2.21	2.82	3.43	3.53	3.66	3.90	3.76	3.36	3.52	3.68	3.03	3.08	3.33
2007-08	3.15	3.28	3.66	4.03	4.55	4.91	5.15	5.59	5.58	6.55	5.97	5.04	4.79
2008-09	5.00	3.69	3.42	3.33	3.61	3.46	3.60	3.69	3.98	3.97	3.22	3.21	3.68
2009-10	3.10	3.52	3.62	3.59	3.52	3.39	3.40	3.36	3.43	3.24	3.49	3.77	3.45
2010-11	4.51	5.19	5.33	5.65	6.10	6.69	6.59	7.33	7.08	7.17	6.96	7.30	6.33
2011-12[1]	6.77	6.23	6.26	5.88									6.29

[1] Preliminary.   Source: Economic Research Service, U.S. Department of Agriculture (ERS-USDA)

Average Cash Price of Corn, No. 2 Yellow at Gulf Ports[2]   In Dollars Per Bushel

Year	Sept.	Oct.	Nov.	Dec.	Jan.	Feb.	Mar.	Apr.	May	June	July	Aug.	Average
2002-03	2.89	2.79	2.77	2.71	2.69	2.69	2.67	2.68	2.74	2.72	2.48	2.56	2.70
2003-04	2.63	2.65	2.75	2.85	2.95	3.12	3.27	3.39	3.29	3.13	2.66	2.64	2.94
2004-05	2.49	2.37	2.39	2.43	2.44	2.40	2.54	2.45	2.42	2.49	2.69	2.59	2.48
2005-06	2.47	2.58	2.44	2.61	2.61	2.72	2.67	2.74	2.81	2.78	2.90	2.92	2.69
2006-07	3.05	3.82	4.17	4.08	4.19	4.50	3.81	3.88	4.07	4.20	3.73	3.84	3.95
2007-08	4.05	4.17	4.35	4.58	5.25	5.59	5.99	6.26	6.18	7.29	6.74	5.97	5.54
2008-09	5.94	4.65	4.18	4.02	4.39	4.15	4.18	4.29	4.58	4.56	3.86	3.87	4.39
2009-10	3.82	4.25	4.36	4.18	4.25	4.11	4.04	3.99	4.15	3.88	4.15	4.46	4.14
2010-11	5.23	5.99	6.05	6.36	6.73	7.44	7.38	8.11	7.82	7.89	7.64	7.88	7.04
2011-12[1]	7.50	6.98	6.97	6.51									6.99

[1] Preliminary.   [2] Barge delivered to Louisiana Gulf.   Source: Economic Research Service, U.S. Department of Agriculture (ERS-USDA)

CORN

Weekly Outstanding Export Sales and Cumulative Exports of U.S. Corn   In Thousands of Metric Tons

Marketing Year 2009/2010 Week Ending	Out- standing Sales	Cumu- lative Exports	Marketing Year 2010/2011 Week Ending	Out- standing Sales	Cumu- lative Exports	Marketing Year 2011/2012 Week Ending	Out- standing Sales	Cumu- lative Exports
Sep 03, 2009	12,131.4	537.0	Sep 02, 2010	15,102.5	285.8	Sep 01, 2011	13,170.5	136.0
Sep 10, 2009	11,934.6	1,699.4	Sep 09, 2010	14,587.5	1,385.0	Sep 08, 2011	13,812.9	620.9
Sep 17, 2009	11,569.5	2,737.7	Sep 16, 2010	14,157.5	2,376.8	Sep 15, 2011	13,783.6	1,248.3
Sep 24, 2009	11,827.8	3,702.9	Sep 23, 2010	14,141.6	3,318.6	Sep 22, 2011	13,748.4	2,071.4
Oct 01, 2009	11,205.5	4,847.1	Sep 30, 2010	13,770.2	4,297.1	Sep 29, 2011	14,282.1	2,728.1
Oct 08, 2009	11,167.2	5,516.8	Oct 07, 2010	13,868.4	5,104.9	Oct 06, 2011	14,630.0	3,738.1
Oct 15, 2009	10,584.1	6,334.8	Oct 14, 2010	13,247.4	5,938.4	Oct 13, 2011	15,829.2	4,301.6
Oct 22, 2009	10,284.3	7,001.7	Oct 21, 2010	13,216.5	6,501.5	Oct 20, 2011	15,488.3	4,978.7
Oct 29, 2009	10,140.1	7,709.9	Oct 28, 2010	12,797.8	7,381.8	Oct 27, 2011	15,364.0	5,725.6
Nov 05, 2009	9,870.5	8,468.0	Nov 04, 2010	12,620.4	8,132.8	Nov 03, 2011	14,991.4	6,350.0
Nov 12, 2009	9,540.2	9,151.2	Nov 11, 2010	12,375.4	8,911.6	Nov 10, 2011	14,305.3	7,245.1
Nov 19, 2009	10,135.9	9,779.1	Nov 18, 2010	12,415.5	9,694.5	Nov 17, 2011	13,643.3	8,219.1
Nov 26, 2009	9,915.4	10,658.6	Nov 25, 2010	12,389.1	10,479.0	Nov 24, 2011	13,113.6	9,029.4
Dec 03, 2009	10,056.6	11,365.1	Dec 02, 2010	12,365.0	11,174.2	Dec 01, 2011	12,772.5	10,061.0
Dec 10, 2009	10,507.3	12,141.5	Dec 09, 2010	12,365.3	11,984.7	Dec 08, 2011	12,390.3	10,947.9
Dec 17, 2009	11,684.4	12,556.2	Dec 16, 2010	12,442.6	12,813.5	Dec 15, 2011	11,804.4	12,248.7
Dec 24, 2009	11,593.4	13,419.8	Dec 23, 2010	12,058.9	13,896.3	Dec 22, 2011	11,176.9	13,195.0
Dec 31, 2009	11,160.1	14,217.8	Dec 30, 2010	11,814.2	14,510.1	Dec 29, 2011	10,900.2	13,771.2
Jan 07, 2010	10,829.3	14,875.9	Jan 06, 2011	11,737.7	15,025.8	Jan 05, 2012	10,473.5	14,519.4
Jan 14, 2010	11,603.8	15,711.8	Jan 13, 2011	12,055.4	15,612.9	Jan 12, 2012	10,479.6	15,273.1
Jan 21, 2010	11,974.3	16,243.6	Jan 20, 2011	11,700.0	16,383.0	Jan 19, 2012	10,497.1	16,213.8
Jan 28, 2010	11,774.5	17,366.6	Jan 27, 2011	12,004.9	17,244.8	Jan 26, 2012	10,739.4	16,883.4
Feb 04, 2010	11,913.9	17,970.5	Feb 03, 2011	12,443.1	17,913.9	Feb 02, 2012	10,344.6	17,972.4
Feb 11, 2010	12,236.3	18,598.2	Feb 10, 2011	12,797.6	18,589.8	Feb 09, 2012	10,664.4	18,658.4
Feb 18, 2010	11,397.0	19,838.7	Feb 17, 2011	13,238.3	19,650.4	Feb 16, 2012	10,728.9	19,434.7
Feb 25, 2010	11,103.1	20,894.1	Feb 24, 2011	13,518.7	20,450.5	Feb 23, 2012	10,600.7	20,252.8
Mar 04, 2010	10,476.8	21,858.9	Mar 03, 2011	12,791.0	21,655.4	Mar 01, 2012	10,277.2	21,022.0
Mar 11, 2010	10,269.2	22,814.2	Mar 10, 2011	12,946.7	22,536.0	Mar 08, 2012	10,078.0	22,057.6
Mar 18, 2010	9,715.2	23,975.0	Mar 17, 2011	12,961.9	23,415.8	Mar 15, 2012		
Mar 25, 2010	9,326.7	25,189.6	Mar 24, 2011	13,856.8	24,435.8	Mar 22, 2012		
Apr 01, 2010	9,809.1	26,065.0	Mar 31, 2011	13,460.9	25,451.3	Mar 29, 2012		
Apr 08, 2010	9,702.2	27,178.2	Apr 07, 2011	13,210.8	26,549.4	Apr 05, 2012		
Apr 15, 2010	10,027.6	28,333.8	Apr 14, 2011	12,888.9	27,484.7	Apr 12, 2012		
Apr 22, 2010	10,342.5	29,228.2	Apr 21, 2011	12,330.0	28,392.5	Apr 19, 2012		
Apr 29, 2010	11,337.9	30,083.6	Apr 28, 2011	11,815.7	29,191.1	Apr 26, 2012		
May 06, 2010	11,123.7	31,116.8	May 05, 2011	11,389.2	30,051.4	May 03, 2012		
May 13, 2010	11,498.9	32,095.8	May 12, 2011	11,270.8	31,013.0	May 10, 2012		
May 20, 2010	11,289.9	33,335.6	May 19, 2011	11,043.7	31,966.8	May 17, 2012		
May 27, 2010	10,262.1	34,562.1	May 26, 2011	10,614.8	32,867.3	May 24, 2012		
Jun 03, 2010	10,369.0	35,474.1	Jun 02, 2011	9,931.1	33,871.3	May 31, 2012		
Jun 10, 2010	10,386.4	36,547.1	Jun 09, 2011	9,406.6	34,691.6	Jun 07, 2012		
Jun 17, 2010	10,691.7	37,365.2	Jun 16, 2011	8,649.6	35,859.4	Jun 14, 2012		
Jun 24, 2010	10,388.9	38,317.6	Jun 23, 2011	8,686.1	36,514.6	Jun 21, 2012		
Jul 01, 2010	9,859.6	39,348.1	Jun 30, 2011	8,267.1	37,555.4	Jun 28, 2012		
Jul 08, 2010	9,495.0	40,390.9	Jul 07, 2011	7,888.0	38,415.9	Jul 05, 2012		
Jul 15, 2010	9,160.7	41,339.3	Jul 14, 2011	7,390.9	39,341.7	Jul 12, 2012		
Jul 22, 2010	8,393.7	42,538.5	Jul 21, 2011	6,716.5	40,347.6	Jul 19, 2012		
Jul 29, 2010	8,032.6	43,371.2	Jul 28, 2011	6,235.5	41,126.0	Jul 26, 2012		
Aug 05, 2010	7,464.1	44,379.4	Aug 04, 2011	5,728.2	42,074.7	Aug 02, 2012		
Aug 12, 2010	7,052.9	45,385.5	Aug 11, 2011	5,069.2	42,977.2	Aug 09, 2012		
Aug 19, 2010	5,923.3	46,557.4	Aug 18, 2011	4,626.7	43,803.4	Aug 16, 2012		
Aug 26, 2010	4,752.6	47,699.6	Aug 25, 2011	3,540.0	44,569.2	Aug 23, 2012		
						Aug 30, 2012		

Source: Foreign Agricultural Service, U.S. Department of Agriculture (FAS-USDA)

Average Price Received by Farmers for Corn in the United States   In Dollars Per Bushel

Year	Sept.	Oct.	Nov.	Dec.	Jan.	Feb.	Mar.	Apr.	May	June	July	Aug.	Average
2002-03	2.47	2.34	2.28	2.32	2.33	2.34	2.33	2.34	2.38	2.34	2.17	2.15	2.32
2003-04	2.20	2.12	2.20	2.31	2.39	2.61	2.75	2.89	2.87	2.79	2.51	2.34	2.50
2004-05	2.20	2.14	2.05	2.04	2.12	1.95	2.02	2.00	1.98	2.03	2.11	1.95	2.05
2005-06	1.90	1.82	1.77	1.92	2.00	2.02	2.06	2.11	2.17	2.14	2.14	2.09	2.01
2006-07	2.20	2.55	2.88	3.01	3.05	3.44	3.43	3.39	3.49	3.53	3.32	3.26	3.13
2007-08	3.28	3.29	3.44	3.77	3.98	4.54	4.70	5.14	5.27	5.47	5.25	5.26	4.45
2008-09	5.01	4.37	4.26	4.11	4.36	3.87	3.85	3.85	3.96	4.01	3.60	3.33	4.05
2009-10	3.25	3.61	3.65	3.60	3.66	3.55	3.55	3.41	3.48	3.41	3.49	3.65	3.53
2010-11	4.08	4.32	4.55	4.82	4.94	5.65	5.53	6.35	6.30	6.38	6.32	6.88	5.51
2011-12[1]	6.37	5.71	5.84	5.86	6.07	6.16							6.00

[1] Preliminary.   Source: Economic Research Service, U.S. Department of Agriculture (ERS-USDA)

Corn Price Support Data in the United States

Crop Year Beginning Sept. 1	National Average Loan Rate[3] --- Dollars Per Bushel -----	Target Price	Placed Under Loan	% of Pro-duction	Acquired by CCC	Owned by CCC Aug. 31	CCC Inventory ----- As of Dec. 31 ----- CCC Owned	Under CCC Loan	Quantity Pledged (Thousands of Bushels)	Face Amount (Thousands of Dollars)
				----------------------------- Millions of Bushels -----						
2001-02	1.89	NA	1,395	14.7	0	6	24	----	1,394,561	2,557,874
2002-03	1.98	2.60	1,367	15.2	0	4	18	----	1,366,513	2,622,823
2003-04	1.98	2.60	1,327	13.2	1	0	16	----	1,326,884	2,555,183
2004-05	1.95	2.63	1,366	11.6	25	0	12	----	40,814	87,053
2005-06	1.95	2.63	1,064	9.6	2	2	12	----	47,595	99,406
2006-07	1.95	2.63	1,108	10.5	0	0	1	----	31,873	65,968
2007-08	1.95	2.63	1,217	9.3	0	0	1	----	56,674	117,648
2008-09	1.95	2.63	1,074	8.9	0	0	30	----	46,573	91,966
2009-10[1]	1.95	2.63	890	6.8	0	0	9	----	80,876	147,579
2010-11[2]	1.95	2.63								

[1] Preliminary.   [2] Estimate.   [3] Findley or announced loan rate.   NA = Not available.
Source: National Agricultural Statistics Service, U.S. Department of Agriculture (NASS-USDA)

U.S. Exports[1] of Corn (Including Seed), By Country of Destination   In Thousands of Metric Tons

Crop Year Beginning Oct. 1	Algeria	Canada	Egypt	Israel	Japan	Mexico	Rep. of Korea	Russia	Saudi Arabia	Spain	Taiwan	Vene-zuela	Total
2001-02	1,343	3,979	4,283	847	14,817	1,085	4,025	86	670	5	4,599	502	47,058
2002-03	1,009	3,811	2,904	313	14,384	272	5,220		222		4,139	651	40,780
2003-04	1,158	2,014	3,120	1,154	14,968	3,942	5,730	70	402	5	4,757	669	48,724
2004-05	1,036	2,210	3,738	393	15,036	2,210	5,935	13	126	14	4,446	90	45,262
2005-06	1,255	1,901	4,156	725	16,361	5,866	6,755	15	619	8	4,519	133	56,038
2006-07	940	2,142	3,522	844	14,840	3,873	8,886	9	540	3	4,213	514	54,159
2007-08	898	3,051	2,971	1,207	15,043	8,380	9,526	7	985	10	3,792	1,085	60,593
2008-09	95	1,810	2,445	138	15,491	5,735	7,710		440	3	3,713	1,145	47,658
2009-10	64	1,935	2,961	330	14,616	6,795	8,243		706	3	3,011	1,121	49,668
2010-11[2]		952	2,939	679	13,863	6,065	7,482		574	296	2,780	852	45,200

[1] Excludes exports of corn by-products.   [2] Preliminary.   *Source: Foreign Agricultural Service, U.S. Department of Agriculture (FAS-USDA)*

Stocks of Corn (Shelled and Ear) in the United States   In Millions of Bushels

Year	On Farms Mar. 1	June 1	Sept. 1	Dec. 1	Off Farms Mar. 1	June 1	Sept. 1	Dec. 1	Total Stocks Mar. 1	June 1	Sept. 1	Dec. 1
2002	3,355.0	2,020.6	586.8	4,800.0	2,440.3	1,576.3	1,009.6	2,838.0	5,795.3	3,596.9	1,596.4	7,638.0
2003	2,940.0	1,620.2	484.9	5,286.0	2,191.9	1,364.7	601.8	2,667.8	5,131.9	2,984.9	1,086.7	7,953.8
2004	3,030.0	1,540.0	438.0	6,144.0	2,241.5	1,430.1	520.1	3,308.5	5,271.5	2,970.1	958.1	9,452.5
2005	4,137.0	2,462.3	820.5	6,325.0	2,619.3	1,858.5	1,293.5	3,490.0	6,756.3	4,320.8	2,114.0	9,815.0
2006	4,055.0	2,350.5	749.5	5,627.0	2,932.3	2,011.2	1,217.7	3,305.7	6,987.3	4,361.7	1,967.2	8,932.7
2007	3,330.0	1,826.6	460.1	6,530.0	2,738.3	1,706.8	843.5	3,748.1	6,068.3	3,533.4	1,303.6	10,278.1
2008	3,780.0	1,970.9	500.0	6,482.0	3,078.7	2,057.1	1,124.2	3,590.1	6,858.7	4,028.0	1,624.2	10,072.1
2009	4,085.0	2,205.4	607.5	7,405.0	2,869.1	2,056.0	1,065.8	3,497.5	6,954.1	4,261.4	1,673.3	10,902.5
2010	4,548.0	2,131.4	485.1	6,302.0	3,145.8	2,178.7	1,222.7	3,754.8	7,693.8	4,310.1	1,707.8	10,056.8
2011[1]	3,384.0	1,681.5	315.0	6,175.0	3,139.2	1,988.3	812.7	3,466.9	6,523.2	3,669.8	1,127.6	9,641.9

[1] Preliminary.   *Source: National Agricultural Statistics Service, U.S. Department of Agriculture (NASS-USDA)*

CORN

Corn Futures - CME Group (CBT)
(weekly close) as of December 30, 2011

Cents per bushel

Volume of Trading of Corn Futures in Chicago   In Thousands of Contracts

Year	Jan.	Feb.	Mar.	Apr.	May	June	July	Aug.	Sept.	Oct.	Nov.	Dec.	Total
2002	996.3	1,449.6	944.7	1,498.0	1,434.5	1,851.5	1,958.4	2,158.7	1,635.4	1,523.3	1,801.4	880.5	18,132.4
2003	1,204.0	1,559.1	1,156.9	1,633.1	1,657.0	1,951.2	1,499.3	1,830.6	1,389.7	2,057.7	1,815.9	1,364.3	19,118.7
2004	2,025.7	2,367.0	2,190.9	2,870.9	1,855.3	2,538.6	1,740.5	1,883.0	1,446.9	1,476.4	2,473.3	1,169.6	24,038.2
2005	1,467.8	2,680.8	2,278.1	2,519.1	2,188.3	3,446.1	2,626.0	2,993.6	1,618.5	1,504.2	2,892.2	1,750.3	27,965.1
2006	2,494.6	3,599.1	3,041.0	3,507.5	3,773.1	4,693.4	3,743.6	4,226.9	3,760.5	5,300.2	6,279.4	2,820.6	47,239.9
2007	5,166.5	5,111.6	4,959.0	6,095.4	4,519.9	6,090.9	4,035.7	4,344.1	3,128.9	3,306.5	4,615.6	3,145.9	54,520.2
2008	4,213.2	5,808.2	4,350.8	6,501.1	4,876.9	7,593.8	5,402.2	4,989.1	3,934.7	4,572.5	4,448.6	3,266.2	59,957.1
2009	3,041.3	4,487.1	3,684.9	4,567.6	4,151.8	5,636.8	4,765.8	4,441.8	3,153.8	4,374.0	5,509.1	3,134.9	50,948.6
2010	4,025.9	5,217.5	3,935.4	6,466.0	4,240.6	6,207.8	4,863.8	6,899.6	7,033.7	7,501.1	9,169.7	4,280.4	69,841.4
2011	5,981.0	7,473.1	7,552.4	8,715.1	5,676.9	8,639.5	5,119.3	6,834.9	5,385.7	5,568.2	8,003.4	4,055.2	79,004.8

Contract size = 5,000 bu.   *Source: CME Group; Chicago Board of Trade (CBT)*

Average Open Interest of Corn Futures in Chicago   In Thousands of Contracts

Year	Jan.	Feb.	Mar.	Apr.	May	June	July	Aug.	Sept.	Oct.	Nov.	Dec.
2002	459.3	464.4	431.9	430.7	411.3	430.9	458.1	509.1	501.5	485.9	497.0	450.0
2003	456.0	469.6	445.3	412.0	407.0	385.8	384.6	383.6	356.2	420.7	470.2	447.5
2004	544.0	641.4	678.0	704.9	637.4	621.9	566.5	562.2	548.8	606.3	639.5	588.9
2005	629.3	654.1	659.7	673.8	677.3	702.4	713.1	733.6	714.2	794.4	852.5	774.2
2006	875.3	1,048.8	1,066.0	1,176.0	1,288.2	1,327.8	1,360.2	1,347.2	1,302.1	1,312.6	1,405.7	1,381.5
2007	1,448.2	1,498.8	1,427.3	1,345.9	1,257.6	1,244.1	1,213.4	1,132.8	1,108.5	1,161.7	1,202.6	1,211.5
2008	1,383.2	1,463.1	1,421.8	1,445.3	1,409.2	1,396.1	1,279.9	1,170.4	1,050.9	995.5	967.6	820.5
2009	806.7	801.1	767.8	823.3	860.6	971.7	894.1	862.6	850.1	923.9	1,002.9	969.2
2010	1,105.4	1,149.6	1,124.2	1,169.6	1,196.2	1,204.5	1,161.3	1,324.5	1,405.8	1,509.8	1,629.6	1,511.5
2011	1,595.6	1,697.7	1,598.8	1,617.6	1,439.8	1,406.3	1,196.7	1,244.3	1,214.8	1,220.0	1,268.5	1,156.4

Contract size = 5,000 bu.   *Source: CME Group; Chicago Board of Trade (CBT)*

Corn Oil

Corn oil is a bland, odorless oil produced by refining the crude corn oil that is mechanically extracted from the germ of the plant seed. High-oil corn, the most common type of corn used to make corn oil, typically has an oil content of 7% or higher compared to about 4% for normal corn. Corn oil is widely used as cooking oil, for making margarine and mayonnaise, and for making inedible products such as soap, paints, inks, varnishes, and cosmetics. For humans, studies have shown that no vegetable oil is more effective than corn oil in lowering blood cholesterol levels.

Prices –The average monthly price of corn oil (wet mill price in Chicago) in the 2011-12 marketing year (Oct-Sep) fell -11.3% yr/yr to 53.90 cents per pound, down from 2007-08 record high of 69.37 cents per pound. Seasonally, prices tend to be highest around March/April and lowest late in the calendar year.

Supply – U.S. corn oil production in the 2010-11 marketing year rose +1.2% yr/yr to 2.515 billion pounds, below the 2006-07 high of 2.560 billion pounds. Seasonally, production tends to peak around December and March and reaches a low in July. U.S. stocks in the 2010-11 marketing year (Oct 1) fell -52,6% yr/yr to 136.0 million pounds.

Demand – U.S. usage (domestic disappearance) in 2010-11 fell -1.5% to 1.871 billion pounds.

Exports – U.S. corn oil exports in 2010-11 fell -12.2% to 680 million pounds. U.S. corn oil imports in 2010-11 fell by -5.7% to 35.000 million pounds.

Supply and Disappearance of Corn Oil in the United States   In Millions of Pounds

	Supply			Baking and Frying Fats	Salad and Cooking Oil	Margarine	Total Edible Products	Domestic Disappearance	Exports	Total Disappearance
Year	Stocks Oct. 1	Production	Imports	Total Supply							
2004-05	153	2,396	49.1	2,598	W	1,466	W	1,690	1,653	789	2,442
2005-06	156	2,483	45.0	2,683	W	1,407	W	1,607	1,685	799	2,483
2006-07	200	2,560	43.1	2,803	W	1,335	W	1,735	1,832	793	2,625
2007-08	179	2,507	45.2	2,731	W	1,722	W	1,606	1,756	769	2,525
2008-09	205	2,418	43.5	2,667	W	1,722	W	1,591	1,568	814	2,382
2009-10[1]	286	2,485	37.1	2,808	W	1,930	W	1,589	1,898	774	2,672
2010-11[2]	136	2,515	35.0	2,686	W	2,387	W	1,691	1,871	680	2,551

[1] Preliminary.   [2] Estimate.   W = Withheld.   *Source: Economic Research Service, U.S. Department of Agriculture (ERS-USDA)*

Production[2] of Crude Corn Oil in the United States   In Millions of Pounds

Year	Oct.	Nov.	Dec.	Jan.	Feb.	Mar.	Apr.	May	June	July	Aug.	Sept.	Total
2004-05	208.8	187.1	191.0	205.2	182.5	206.6	217.2	188.2	211.5	206.7	198.5	189.0	2,392
2005-06	207.5	199.9	200.3	209.2	184.8	217.6	191.7	218.7	206.7	215.3	222.0	209.0	2,483
2006-07	228.7	216.0	226.1	224.7	187.9	222.5	190.7	220.9	193.7	214.9	217.3	207.3	2,560
2007-08	213.5	213.0	214.0	205.4	193.7	218.8	189.4	202.5	189.0	186.0	201.4	215.8	2,507
2008-09	206.3	210.6	198.7	200.3	199.8	212.4	214.7	205.4	214.7	216.8	201.4	200.1	2,419
2009-10	212.9	205.2	203.2	197.9	188.1	199.4	220.9	198.9	211.2	216.8	213.6	200.1	2,485
2010-11[1]	205.7	216.3	215.0	203.1	218.1	199.4	220.9	198.9	211.2	205.1			2,512

[1] Preliminary.   [2] Not seasonally adjusted.   *Source: Bureau of the Census, U.S. Department of Commerce*

Consumption Corn Oil, in Refining, in the United States   In Millions of Pounds

Year	Oct.	Nov.	Dec.	Jan.	Feb.	Mar.	Apr.	May	June	July	Aug.	Sept.	Total
2004-05	W	165.4	131.6	140.3	W	147.3	132.2	124.8	149.0	142.9	142.4	132.1	1,690
2005-06	148.4	140.4	140.3	148.4	123.4	128.0	110.8	145.2	138.9	121.6	131.6	130.0	1,607
2006-07	143.6	146.7	153.3	155.3	131.1	137.2	W	W	147.7	142.2	146.0	143.0	1,735
2007-08	155.2	W	133.8	119.5	119.2	143.8	124.2	142.9	109.7	131.8	150.3	141.8	1,606
2008-09	137.8	132.1	130.8	131.4	113.7	134.3	102.7	129.4	121.6	158.2	144.2	154.6	1,591
2009-10	146.8	126.4	133.9	119.1	W	138.2	W	W	W	127.7	130.7	136.5	1,589
2010-11[1]	128.0	135.6	122.7	147.0	127.6	159.3	144.4	W	155.3	148.3			1,691

[1] Preliminary.   W = Withheld proprietary data.   *Source: Bureau of Census, U.S. Department of Commerce*

Average Corn Oil Price, Wet Mill in Chicago   In Cents Per Pound

Year	Oct.	Nov.	Dec.	Jan.	Feb.	Mar.	Apr.	May	June	July	Aug.	Sept.	Average
2005-06	27.50	27.08	26.08	25.22	23.65	22.61	23.19	25.25	25.70	25.75	25.42	24.71	25.18
2006-07	24.70	26.47	28.05	28.05	28.66	29.08	29.93	31.56	34.71	37.25	39.61	43.61	31.81
2007-08	52.50	56.32	59.47	63.67	74.89	83.55	87.09	87.29	82.33	76.64	60.00	48.71	69.37
2008-09	34.76	31.06	26.88	25.19	29.05	29.64	31.31	37.23	39.57	36.30	35.23	36.83	32.75
2009-10	37.59	38.12	40.02	40.34	37.54	38.37	38.50	38.50	38.93	39.29	41.48	42.85	39.29
2010-11	47.50	51.96	54.71	57.91	63.39	67.72	68.89	68.33	66.70	62.00	62.00	57.95	60.76
2011-12[1]	54.24	53.98	53.36	54.00									53.90

[1] Preliminary.   *Source: Economic Research Service, U.S. Department of Agriculture (ERS-USDA)*

Cotton

Cotton is a natural vegetable fiber that comes from small trees and shrubs of a genus belonging to the mallow family, one of which is the common American Upland cotton plant. Cotton has been used in India for at least the last 5,000 years and probably much longer, and was also used by the ancient Chinese, Egyptians, and North and South Americans. Cotton was one of the earliest crops grown by European settlers in the U.S.

Cotton requires a long growing season, plenty of sunshine and water during the growing season, and then dry weather for harvesting. In the United States, the Cotton Belt stretches from northern Florida to North Carolina and westward to California. In the U.S., planting time varies from the beginning of February in Southern Texas to the beginning of June in the northern sections of the Cotton Belt. The flower bud of the plant blossoms and develops into an oval boll that splits open at maturity. At maturity, cotton is most vulnerable to damage from wind and rain. Approximately 95% of the cotton in the U.S. is now harvested mechanically with spindle-type pickers or strippers and then sent off to cotton gins for processing. There it is dried, cleaned, separated, and packed into bales.

Cotton is used in a wide range of products from clothing to home furnishings to medical products. The value of cotton is determined according to the staple, grade, and character of each bale. Staple refers to short, medium, long, or extra-long fiber length, with medium staple accounting for about 70% of all U.S. cotton. Grade refers to the color, brightness, and amount of foreign matter and is established by the U.S. Department of Agriculture. Character refers to the fiber's diameter, strength, body, maturity (ratio of mature to immature fibers), uniformity, and smoothness. Cotton is the fifth leading cash crop in the U.S. and is one of the nation's principal agricultural exports. The weight of cotton is typically measured in terms of a "bale," which is deemed to equal 480 pounds.

Cotton futures and options are traded on the ICE Futures U.S. (ICE) exchange. Cotton futures are also traded on the Bolsa de Mercadorias & Futuros (BM&F). Cotton yarn futures are traded on the Central Japan Commodity Exchange (CCOM) and the Osaka Mercantile Exchange (OME). The ICE's futures contract calls for the delivery of 50,000 pounds net weight (approximately 100 bales) of No. 2 cotton with a quality rating of Strict Low Middling and a staple length of 1-and-2/32 inch. Delivery points include Texas (Galveston and Houston), New Orleans, Memphis, and Greenville/Spartanburg in South Carolina.

Prices – Cotton prices in 2011 continued their parabolic rally into March 2011 and posted an all-time high of 227.00 cents a pound, the highest price since cotton began recorded-trading 140 years ago. Cotton prices then collapsed the remainder of the year and posted a 1-1/2 year low in December 2011 at 84.35 cents a pound, finishing the year down 36.6% at 91.80 cents a pound. Cotton prices plummeted as global production expanded and Chinese demand waned. The USDA in October raised its 2011 global production estimate to a record 124.19 million bales and hiked its global ending stocks estimate to a 3-year high of 54.83 million bales as Chinese cotton demand

sank. Chinese cotton imports fell for seven consecutive months through August 2011 on a year-over-year basis, while Chinese cotton yarn exports fell for eleven of twelve months in 2011. The insatiable Chinese cotton demand in 2010 couldn't be repeated in 2011 as the global economy slowed, although overall 2011 Chinese cotton demand remained respectable with imports up 18.6% y/y to 3.36 MMT. Despite the worst drought in Texas in 100 years that reduced 2011 U.S. cotton production by -13.4% y/y to 15.67 million bales, increased output in India and Pakistan took up the slack and pushed the 2011/12 global stocks/use ratio to a 3-year high of 53.1%.

Supply – World cotton production in 2011-12 rose +5.9% yr/yr to 123.342 million bales (480 pounds per bale), a new record high. The world's largest cotton producers were China with 27.2% of world production in 2011-12, India with 21.9%, the U.S. with 12.7%, and Pakistan with 8.4%. World beginning stocks in 2011-12 rose +3.8% yr/yr below the record high of 62.480 million bales in 2007-08.

The U.S. cotton crop in 2011-12 fell by -13.4% yr/yr to 15.673 million bales, down from the 2005-06 record high of 23.890 million bales. U.S. farmers harvested 9.747 million acres of cotton in 2011-12, down -8.9% yr/yr. The U.S. cotton yield in 2011-12 fell -5.0% to 772 pounds per acre, not far behind the 2007-08 record high of 879 pounds per acre. The leading U.S. producing states of Upland cotton are Texas with 22.6% of U.S. production in 2011, Georgia (16.3%), California (8.4%), Arkansas (8.2%), Mississippi (7.8%), Tennessee (5.3%), Arizona (5.2%). U.S. production of cotton cloth has fallen sharply by almost half in the past decade due to the movement of the textile industry out of the U.S. to low-wage foreign countries. Specifically, U.S. production of cotton cloth in 2010 fell –0.3% yr/yr to a record low of 1.316 billion square yards, less than one-fourth of the production level seen in 1950.

Demand – World consumption of cotton in 2011-12 fell by -4.5% yr/yr to 109.565 million bales, but still below the 2006-07 record high of 121.986. Consumption of cotton continues to move toward countries with low wages, where the raw cotton is utilized to produce textiles and other cotton products. The largest consumers of cotton in 2011-12 were China (40.2% of world total), India (17.8%), and Pakistan (9.4%). U.S. consumption of cotton by mills in 2011-12 fell –2.6% yr/yr to 3.800 million bales, and accounted for 25% of U.S. production. The remaining 75% of U.S. cotton production went for exports.

Trade – World exports of cotton in 2011-12 rose by +4.7% yr/yr to 37.415 million bales, but still below the 2005-06 record high of 44.854 million bales. The U.S. is the world's largest cotton exporter by far and accounts for 29.4% of world cotton exports. Key world cotton importers include Turkey with 6.7% of total world imports in 2011-12, Indonesia with 5.2%, Mexico with 2.7%, and Russia with 1.5%. U.S. cotton exports in 2010-11 (latest data) rose by +18.1% yr/yr to 14.783 million bales. The main destinations for U.S. exports in 2010-11 (latest data) were China (33.0%), Mexico (8.4%), Indonesia (6.1%), Thailand (4.8%), and Taiwan (2.4%).

Supply and Distribution of All Cotton in the United States   In Thousands of 480-Pound Bales

Crop Year Beginning Aug. 1	Planted --- 1,000 Acres ---	Harvested	Yield Lbs./Acre	Beginning Stocks[3]	Pro- duction[4]	Imports	Total	Mill Use	Exports	Total	Unac- counted	Ending Stocks	Farm Price[5]	"A" Index Price[6]	Value of Pro- duction Million USD
2002-03	13,958	12,417	665	7,448	17,209	67	24,724	7,273	11,900	19,173	-166	5,385	45.7	55.81	3,777.1
2003-04	13,480	12,003	730	5,385	18,255	45	23,685	6,266	13,758	20,024	-211	3,450	63.0	68.22	5,516.8
2004-05	13,659	13,057	855	3,450	23,251	29	26,730	6,691	14,436	21,127	-108	5,495	44.7	52.22	4,993.6
2005-06	14,245	13,803	831	5,495	23,890	28	29,413	5,871	17,673	23,544	200	6,069	49.7	56.19	5,695.2
2006-07	15,274	12,732	814	6,069	21,588	19	27,676	4,935	12,959	17,894	-303	9,479	48.4	59.22	5,013.2
2007-08	10,827	10,489	879	9,479	19,207	12	28,698	4,584	13,634	18,218	-429	10,051	61.3	73.02	5,652.9
2008-09	9,471	7,569	813	10,051	12,815	0	22,866	3,541	13,261	16,802	273	6,337	49.1	61.10	3,021.5
2009-10	9,150	7,529	777	6,337	12,188	0	18,525	3,550	12,037	15,587	9	2,947	62.8	78.13	3,788.0
2010-11[1]	10,974	10,699	812	2,947	18,104	9	21,060	3,900	14,376	18,376	-184	2,600	84.2	164.29	7,348.1
2011-12[2]	14,732	9,748	772	2,600	15,674	10	18,910	3,800	11,300	15,100	10	3,800	87-100		7,262.9

[1] Preliminary.   [2] Estimate.   [3] Excludes preseason ginnings (adjusted to 480-lb. bale net weight basis).   [4] Includes preseason ginnings.   [5] Marketing year average price.   [6] Average of 5 cheapest types of SLM 1 3/32" staple length cotton offered on the European market.
Source: Economic Research Service, U.S. Department of Agriculture (ERS-USDA)

World Production of All Cotton   In Thousands of 480-Pound Bales

Crop Year Beginning Aug. 1	Argentina	Australia	Brazil	Burkina	China	Egypt	Greece	India	Pakistan	Turkey	United States	Uzbek- istan	Total
2002-03	290	1,680	3,890	750	25,200	1,331	1,715	10,600	7,972	4,179	17,209	4,600	90,987
2003-04	515	1,700	6,015	965	23,800	920	1,530	14,000	7,845	4,100	18,255	4,100	96,791
2004-05	675	3,000	5,900	1,180	30,300	1,356	1,800	19,000	11,138	4,150	23,251	5,200	121,500
2005-06	625	2,800	4,700	1,367	28,400	938	1,975	19,050	9,850	3,550	23,890	5,550	116,412
2006-07	800	1,350	7,000	1,300	35,500	975	1,550	21,800	9,600	3,800	21,588	5,350	122,245
2007-08	703	640	7,360	675	37,000	970	1,550	24,000	8,600	3,100	19,207	5,350	119,697
2008-09	600	1,500	5,480	850	36,700	483	1,150	22,600	8,700	1,930	12,815	4,600	107,474
2009-10	1,000	1,775	5,450	700	32,000	432	940	23,800	9,600	1,750	12,188	3,900	102,591
2010-11[1]	1,275	4,200	9,000	650	30,500	600	900	26,400	8,800	2,100	18,104	4,100	116,458
2011-12[2]	1,200	5,000	9,000	700	33,500	800	1,350	27,000	10,400	3,100	15,674	4,200	123,342

[1] Preliminary.   [2] Estimate.   *Source: Foreign Agricultural Service, U.S. Department of Agriculture (FAS-USDA)*

World Stocks and Trade of Cotton   In Thousands of 480-Pound Bales

Crop Year Beginning Aug. 1	Beginning Stocks United States	Uzbek- istan	China	World Total	Imports Indo- nesia	Mexico	Russia	Turkey	World Total	Exports United States	Uzbek- istan	China	World Total
2002-03	7,448	918	18,848	54,545	2,228	2,330	1,650	2,265	30,187	11,900	3,400	751	30,457
2003-04	5,385	1,018	17,474	47,651	2,150	1,858	1,475	2,370	34,112	13,758	3,100	173	33,213
2004-05	3,450	923	18,983	48,152	2,200	1,810	1,450	3,414	33,840	14,436	3,950	30	35,010
2005-06	5,495	1,298	18,388	60,573	2,200	1,744	1,375	3,501	44,671	17,673	4,800	36	44,854
2006-07	6,069	1,248	22,536	61,759	2,200	1,353	1,325	4,029	38,145	12,959	4,500	88	37,566
2007-08	9,479	1,198	20,536	62,480	2,600	1,530	1,075	3,267	39,321	13,634	4,200	62	39,052
2008-09	10,051	1,348	20,504	60,974	2,300	1,315	900	2,919	30,476	13,261	3,000	84	30,402
2009-10	6,337	1,948	22,366	60,808	2,200	1,393	845	4,394	36,349	12,037	3,800	23	35,593
2010-11[1]	2,947	948	15,246	45,287	2,100	1,196	510	3,350	35,685	14,376	2,650	122	35,747
2011-12[2]	2,600	1,148	11,603	46,990	1,950	1,000	550	2,500	37,420	11,000	2,700	50	37,415

[1] Preliminary.   [2] Estimate.   *Source: Foreign Agricultural Service, U.S. Department of Agriculture (FAS-USDA)*

World Consumption of All Cottons in Specified Countries   In Thousands of 480-Pound Bales

Crop Year Beginning Aug. 1	Bangla- desh	Brazil	China	Egypt	India	Indonesia	Mexico	Pakistan	Russia	Thailand	Turkey	United States	Total
2002-03	1,552	3,585	28,950	913	13,300	2,300	2,125	9,425	1,650	1,975	6,300	7,439	97,611
2003-04	1,802	3,865	30,950	913	13,500	2,200	2,025	9,625	1,500	1,875	6,000	6,477	97,189
2004-05	2,205	4,160	37,250	963	14,800	2,200	2,125	10,525	1,425	2,125	7,100	6,799	107,909
2005-06	2,505	4,302	43,500	1,013	16,700	2,225	2,125	11,525	1,375	2,075	6,900	5,671	115,043
2006-07	3,210	4,423	48,000	1,013	18,100	2,225	2,125	12,025	1,325	1,975	7,204	5,238	122,103
2007-08	3,510	4,450	48,500	963	18,600	2,550	2,025	12,025	1,100	1,975	6,090	5,013	121,472
2008-09	3,810	4,050	41,750	938	17,750	2,300	1,875	11,275	925	1,625	5,013	3,268	107,714
2009-10	3,910	4,250	50,000	863	19,750	2,200	1,925	10,825	875	1,800	5,720	3,541	118,868
2010-11[1]	3,710	4,150	46,000	763	21,050	2,100	1,675	10,025	550	1,725	5,520	4,084	114,693
2011-12[2]	3,410	4,150	44,000	763	19,500	2,000	1,675	10,325	550	1,375	5,220	3,484	109,565

[1] Preliminary.   [2] Estimate.   *Source: Foreign Agricultural Service, U.S. Department of Agriculture (FAS-USDA)*

COTTON

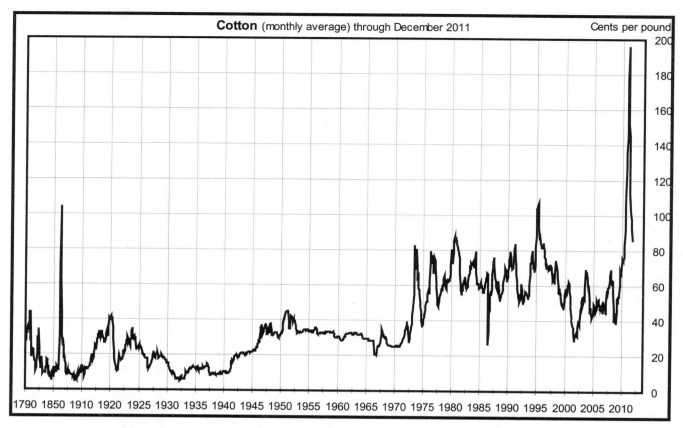

Cotton (monthly average) through December 2011 — Cents per pound

Average Spot Cotton Prices[2], C.I.F. Northern Europe   In U.S. Cents Per Pound

Crop Year Beginning Aug. 1	Argentina "C"[3] 1 1/16" M 1 3/32"	Australia M 1 3/32"	Cotlook Index A	Cotlook Index B	Egypt Giza[4] 81 M 1 3/32"	Greece M 1 3/32"	Mexico[5] M 1 3/32"	Pakistan Sind/ Punjab[6]	Tanzania AR[7] Type 3	Turkey Izmir[8] 1 3/32"	U.S. Calif. ACALA SJV[9]	U.S. Memphis Terr.[10] M 1 3/32"	U.S. Orleans/ Texas[11] M 1 1/32"
1990-1	77.06	85.58	82.90	77.80	177.43	84.24	84.46	77.19	89.62	81.32	92.84	88.13	80.35
1991-2	55.08	65.97	63.05	58.50	128.10	65.90	68.19	58.14	68.90	74.66	74.47	66.35	63.41
1992-3	64.31	64.01	57.70	53.70	99.24	56.92	----	52.66	62.24	----	68.37	63.08	58.89
1993-4	80.20	72.81	70.60	67.30	88.35	58.81	----	54.42	69.83	59.80	77.55	72.80	69.78
1994-5	101.88	81.05	92.75	92.40	93.70	88.64	82.65	73.75	----	----	106.40	98.67	95.70
1995-6	82.98	93.75	85.61	81.06	----	84.95	94.94	81.86	96.20	90.38	103.49	94.71	90.37
1996-7	79.71	83.24	78.59	74.80	----	75.85	79.60	73.37	79.22	----	89.55	82.81	79.77
1997-8	69.96	77.49	72.19	70.69	----	72.03	81.70	72.93	84.04	----	85.11	78.12	74.74
1998-9	57.19	66.48	58.94	54.26	----	58.66	65.78	----	72.70	----	78.57	74.20	70.95
1999-00[1]	----	61.97	52.85	49.55	----	51.71	56.43	----	55.67	----	68.76	66.29	55.67

[1] Preliminary.   [2] Generally for prompt shipment.   [3] 1-1/32" prior to January 20, 1984; 1-1/16" since.   [4] Dendera until 1969/70; Giza 67 1969/70 until December 1983; Giza 69/75/81 until November 1990; Giza 81 since.   [5] S. Brazil Type 5, 1-1/32" prior to 1968-69; 1-1/16" until 1987/88; Brazilian Type 5/6, 1-1/16" since.   [6] Punjab until 1979/80; Sind SG until June 1984; Sind/Punjab SG until January 1985; Afzal 1" until January 1986; Afzal 1-1/32" since.   [7] No. 1 until 1978/79; No. 1/2 until February 1986; AR' Mwanza No. 3 until January 1992; AR' Type 3 since.   [8] Izmir ST 1 White 1-1/16" RG prior to 1981/82; 1-3/32" from 1981/82 until January 1987; Izmir/Antalya ST 1 White 1-3/32" RG since.   [9] SM 1-3/32" prior to 1975/76; SM 1-1/8" since.   [10] SM 1-1/16" prior to 1981/82; Middling 1-3/32" since.   [11] Middling 1" prior to 1988/89; Middling 1-1/32" since.
Source: International Cotton Advisory Committee (ICAC)

Average Producer Price Index of Gray Cotton Broadwovens   Index 1982 = 100

Year	Jan.	Feb.	Mar.	Apr.	May	June	July	Aug.	Sept.	Oct.	Nov.	Dec.	Average
2002	110.7	109.9	110.1	108.1	107.3	108.0	106.9	107.0	106.9	105.9	105.7	106.2	107.7
2003	105.7	105.2	105.0	105.9	106.0	106.7	107.2	109.1	110.1	111.0	110.6	108.9	107.6
2004	109.9	111.2	110.6	111.5	112.3	112.6	113.7	113.2	113.5	113.6	113.3	112.5	112.3
2005	112.6	112.0	111.9	111.8	111.2	111.2	111.1	111.2	111.2	111.3	110.9	111.1	111.5
2006	111.1	110.5	109.9	109.9	110.1	110.1	110.1	110.1	110.1	110.0	110.0	109.9	110.2
2007	110.0	109.9	109.9	110.1	109.8	109.9	109.9	109.9	109.9	110.0	109.9	109.9	109.9
2008	110.1	110.1	110.1	110.1	110.0	109.9	110.2	111.7	111.7	111.7	111.6	111.4	110.7
2009	111.0	111.0	111.0	107.2	107.2	107.2	107.2	107.5	107.5	107.5	108.9	108.9	108.5
2010	109.8	113.7	113.7	113.7	114.9	116.6	119.0	118.8	118.8	118.8	119.1	119.1	116.3
2011[1]	144.8	145.4	147.0	153.5	154.3	154.3	162.1	162.0	161.3	159.0	157.8	157.8	154.9

[1] Preliminary.   *Source: Bureau of Labor Statistics (0337-01), U.S. Department of Commerce*

Average Price of SLM 1-1/16", Cotton/5 at Designated U.S. Markets   In Cents Per Pound (Net Weight)

Year	Aug.	Sept.	Oct.	Nov.	Dec.	Jan.	Feb.	Mar.	Apr.	May	June	July	Average
2002-03	39.20	37.91	39.62	44.98	46.38	48.60	51.35	53.82	53.38	48.94	50.92	54.45	47.46
2003-04	51.94	58.02	69.38	68.88	65.09	68.21	63.35	61.78	57.50	60.22	52.35	45.05	60.15
2004-05	44.92	47.48	44.55	42.62	41.68	43.21	42.90	48.19	49.58	48.57	45.92	47.78	45.62
2005-06	45.38	47.43	51.02	48.80	49.53	51.91	52.39	50.04	49.00	47.00	47.90	47.15	48.96
2006-07	48.65	46.80	45.15	46.32	49.85	49.90	48.77	49.21	46.97	44.62	50.35	57.50	48.67
2007-08	53.46	57.08	59.06	59.59	59.44	63.34	65.92	69.27	63.91	60.67	63.34	62.85	61.49
2008-09	60.93	56.72	46.90	39.83	42.07	44.87	41.81	38.53	45.11	52.92	50.80	53.98	47.87
2009-10	53.77	55.78	60.44	64.90	68.11	65.93	68.08	74.54	75.46	74.70	75.19	76.16	67.76
2010-11	81.16	91.53	108.26	126.62	135.46	144.79	177.65	195.79	181.98	151.93	144.77	113.03	137.75
2011-12[1]	102.89	102.06	97.63	93.59	85.99	89.83							95.33

[1] Preliminary.   [2] Grade 41, leaf 4, staple 34, mike 35-36 and 43-49 , strength 23.5-26.4.   *Source: Agricultural Marketing Service, U.S. Department of Agriculture (AMS-USDA)*

Average Spot Cotton, 1-3/32", Price (SLM) at Designated U.S. Markets[2]   In Cents Per Pound (Net Weight)

Year	Aug.	Sept.	Oct.	Nov.	Dec.	Jan.	Feb.	Mar.	Apr.	May	June	July	Average
2002-03	42.31	41.07	43.08	48.78	50.70	52.87	55.34	57.88	57.54	52.96	55.09	58.46	51.34
2003-04	55.87	61.76	73.27	72.63	68.90	71.96	67.34	66.42	63.11	65.97	57.99	51.11	64.69
2004-05	50.45	52.55	49.45	47.23	46.41	48.16	48.17	53.37	54.67	53.76	51.26	52.97	50.70
2005-06	50.59	52.81	56.01	53.78	54.47	56.69	57.16	55.03	54.07	52.02	52.97	52.35	54.00
2006-07	53.80	51.95	50.20	51.13	54.71	54.75	53.66	54.05	51.59	49.12	54.71	61.59	53.44
2007-08	57.53	61.15	63.08	63.71	63.50	67.22	69.73	72.68	67.25	63.99	66.67	66.17	65.22
2008-09	64.25	60.01	50.52	43.76	45.95	48.76	45.67	42.40	49.02	56.81	54.70	57.94	51.65
2009-10	57.77	59.82	64.58	69.23	72.59	70.45	72.47	79.02	79.81	78.99	79.37	80.30	72.03
2010-11	87.38	95.48	112.06	130.62	139.68	148.24	181.61	199.76	185.94	155.89	148.73	117.00	141.87
2011-12[1]	106.41	105.50	100.97	97.13	89.53								99.91

[1] Preliminary.   *Source: Agricultural Marketing Service, U.S. Department of Agriculture (AMS-USDA)*

Average Spot Prices of U.S. Cotton,[2] Base Quality (SLM) at Designated Markets   In Cents Per Pound

Crop Year Beginning Aug. 1	Dallas (EastTex.-Okl.)	Fresno (San Joaquin Valley)	Greenville (South-east)	Greenwood (South Delta)	Lubbock (West Texas)	Memphis (North Delta)	Phoenix Desert (South-west)	Average
2002-03	46.76	47.52	48.28	48.46	46.51	48.47	46.27	47.46
2003-04	59.95	59.71	60.80	60.85	59.71	60.78	59.23	60.15
2004-05	44.22	47.38	45.91	46.02	44.08	46.02	45.66	45.61
2005-06	47.69	50.06	49.65	49.63	47.78	49.67	48.26	48.96
2006-07	48.17	48.58	49.90	49.46	48.06	49.46	47.08	48.67
2007-08	60.89	60.57	63.95	62.67	60.64	62.67	59.07	61.50
2008-09	47.08	49.10	48.97	47.99	46.93	47.99	47.03	47.87
2009-10	66.57	67.20	70.13	69.30	66.38	69.30	65.40	67.76
2010-11	135.51	138.91	139.70	139.10	135.11	139.02	137.91	137.88
2011-12[1]	87.92	92.64	92.24	91.59	87.92	91.55	91.50	90.76

[1] Preliminary   [2] Prices are for mixed lots, net weight, uncompressed in warehouse.
Source: Agricultural Marketing Service, U.S. Department of Agriculture (AMS-USDA)

Average Price[1] Received by Farmers for Upland Cotton in the United States   In Cents Per Pound

Year	Aug.	Sept.	Oct.	Nov.	Dec.	Jan.	Feb.	Mar.	Apr.	May	June	July	Average
2002-03	33.0	35.2	39.4	43.0	44.3	45.5	46.5	48.6	45.4	45.9	45.5	46.3	43.2
2003-04	46.3	55.7	67.8	63.0	63.3	62.2	61.9	61.6	60.3	59.7	59.9	53.8	59.6
2004-05	53.7	49.3	50.6	43.2	39.3	38.5	38.3	40.3	41.4	39.6	41.9	41.1	43.1
2005-06	42.1	44.3	48.5	48.5	48.0	48.6	48.9	50.0	48.5	46.4	47.4	46.8	47.3
2006-07	45.8	47.3	45.9	47.4	49.0	49.4	47.4	46.4	46.3	44.0	45.4	45.2	46.6
2007-08	44.9	52.0	55.5	57.4	59.6	61.5	63.0	63.0	65.5	64.6	64.0	66.2	59.8
2008-09	58.5	61.1	58.8	54.8	53.3	46.0	41.2	40.4	44.7	44.9	45.0	43.6	49.4
2009-10	47.7	55.0	58.5	59.5	63.4	60.8	65.0	65.0	66.7	66.6	68.5	68.5	62.1
2010-11	77.2	74.7	77.3	81.5	81.2	82.1	92.9	82.3	87.3	81.3	81.4	80.1	81.6
2011-12[2]	94.0	93.5	92.3	92.5	88.5	90.3	92.3						91.9

[1] Weighted average by sales.   [2] Preliminary.   *Source: Agricultural Marketing Service, U.S. Department of Agriculture (AMS-USDA)*

COTTON

Purchases Reported by Exchanges in Designated U.S. Spot Markets[1]   In Running Bales

Crop Year Beginning Aug. 1	Aug.	Sept.	Oct.	Nov.	Dec.	Jan.	Feb.	Mar.	Apr.	May	June	July	Market Total
2002-03	43,047	49,671	194,020	204,564	369,838	481,730	432,055	169,064	170,951	213,679	149,780	86,830	2,565,229
2003-04	125,240	245,295	273,028	167,285	321,083	417,090	267,237	167,357	62,031	70,979	79,061	58,400	2,254,086
2004-05	135,568	46,749	91,390	263,999	369,597	402,504	445,448	424,472	210,285	93,471	95,154	20,398	2,599,035
2005-06	67,318	63,884	138,910	220,961	363,287	434,818	183,744	183,273	62,703	73,726	117,934	60,708	1,971,266
2006-07	87,527	58,849	111,619	112,634	214,384	174,852	140,273	125,562	207,478	310,748	168,730	137,204	1,849,860
2007-08	85,183	133,709	126,008	149,748	197,651	359,180	303,523	95,053	104,513	64,281	119,022	46,555	1,784,426
2008-09	79,487	75,191	89,246	92,960	113,117	149,362	106,701	175,099	265,718	92,969	66,390	77,746	1,383,986
2009-10	34,279	54,457	57,362	179,007	199,006	75,580	175,053	69,900	34,523	9,790	13,412	1,732	904,101
2010-11	1,431	5,498	69,122	126,009	153,780	130,932	59,520	27,102	10,609	27,288	33,804	7,581	652,676
2011-12	9,762	31,213	95,360	122,388	131,642	227,089	115,427						1,256,367

[1] Seven markets.   *Source: Agricultural Marketing Service, U.S. Department of Agriculture (AMS-USDA)*

Production of Cotton (Upland and American-Pima) in the United States   In Thousands of 480-Pound Bales

	-- Upland --												Total American-Pima
Year	Alabama	Arizona	Arkansas	California	Georgia	Louisiana	sippi	Missouri	Carolina	Carolina	nessee	Texas	
2002	570	613	1,669	1,460	1,578	739	1,935	610	806	131	818	5,040	678.3
2003	820	550	1,804	1,495	2,110	1,027	2,120	700	1,037	326	890	4,330	432.3
2004	814	723	2,089	1,790	1,797	885	2,346	830	1,360	390	984	7,740	745.6
2005	848	615	2,202	1,065	2,140	1,098	2,147	864	1,437	410	1,122	8,440	630.5
2006	675	556	2,525	779	2,334	1,241	2,107	985	1,285	433	1,368	5,800	765.4
2007	416	514	1,896	650	1,660	699	1,318	764	783	160	600	8,250	851.8
2008	469	405	1,296	367	1,600	281	683	698	755	246	530	4,450	430.8
2009	345	443	852	240	1,860	349	415	502	763	207	492	4,620	399.9
2010[1]	480	610	1,176	380	2,250	437	848	685	951	376	681	7,840	504.1
2011[2]	710	800	1,290	540	2,550	515	1,220	735	1,050	485	830	3,500	845.7

[1] Preliminary.   [2] Forecast.   *Source: Agricultural Statistics Board, U.S. Department of Agriculture (ASB-USDA)*

Cotton Production and Yield Estimates in the United States

	--------- Forecasts of Production (1,000 Bales of 480 Lbs.[1]) ---------						Actual Crop	---- Forecasts of Yield (Lbs. Per Harvested Acre) ----						Actual Yield
Year	Aug.1	Sept.1	Oct. 1	Nov. 1	Dec. 1	Jan. 1		Aug.1	Sept.1	Oct. 1	Nov. 1	Dec. 1	Jan. 1	
2002	18,439	18,134	18,070	17,815	17,375	----	17,209	675	675	674	665	648	----	665
2003	17,104	16,939	17,559	18,215	18,215	----	18,255	667	667	696	722	722	----	730
2004	20,183	20,895	21,545	22,545	22,815	----	23,251	727	758	782	818	828	----	855
2005	21,291	22,282	22,717	23,161	23,703	----	23,890	748	782	797	813	832	----	831
2006	20,431	20,345	20,659	21,299	21,297	----	21,588	765	762	774	798	798	----	814
2007	17,346	17,812	18,154	18,862	18,987	----	19,207	783	811	826	859	864	----	879
2008	13,767	13,846	13,711	13,528	13,613	----	12,815	842	849	849	837	843	----	813
2009	13,207	13,438	12,998	12,496	12,592	----	12,188	816	816	807	776	782	----	777
2010	18,534	18,841	18,873	18,418	18,268	----	18,104	837	839	841	821	814	----	812
2011	16,554	16,556	16,608	16,300	15,827	----	15,674	822	807	809	794	771	----	772

[1] Net weight bales.   *Source: Agricultural Statistics Board, U.S. Department of Agriculture (ASB-USDA)*

Supply and Distribution of Upland Cotton in the United States   In Thousands of 480-Pound Bales

Crop Year Beginning Aug. 1	-------------- Area --------------			-------------------- Supply --------------------				-------------- Disappearance --------------				Farm Price[5] Cents/ Lb.
	Planted	Harvested	Yield	Beginning Stocks[3]	Pro- duction	Imports	Total Supply	Mill Use	Exports	Total	Ending Stocks	
	----- 1,000 Acres -----		Lbs./Acre									
2002-03	13,714	12,174	652	7,120	16,530	10	23,661	7,170	11,266	18,436	5,140	43.2
2003-04	13,301	11,826	723	5,140	17,823	4	22,967	6,204	13,239	19,443	3,384	59.6
2004-05	13,409	12,809	843	3,384	22,505	8	25,897	6,629	13,683	20,312	5,482	43.1
2005-06	13,975	13,534	825	5,482	23,260	9	28,751	5,820	17,115	22,935	5,991	47.3
2006-07	14,948	12,408	806	5,991	20,822	10	26,824	4,896	12,324	17,220	9,291	46.6
2007-08	10,535	10,201	864	9,291	18,355	6	27,652	4,548	12,801	17,349	9,895	59.8
2008-09	9,297	7,400	803	9,895	12,385	0	22,279	3,512	13,029	16,541	6,032	49.4
2009-10	9,008	7,391	766	6,032	11,788	0	17,820	3,529	11,343	14,872	2,929	62.1
2010-11[1]	10,770	10,497	805	2,929	17,600	2	20,531	3,874	13,881	17,755	2,572	81.6
2011-12[2]	14,426	9,444	754	2,572	14,828	5	18,140	3,775	10,625	14,400	3,730	91.9

[1] Preliminary.   [2] Estimate.   [3] Excludes preseason ginnings (adjusted to 480-lb. bale net weight basis).   [4] Includes preseason ginnings.
[5] Marketing year average price.   *Source: Economic Research Service, U.S. Department of Agriculture (ERS-USDA)*

Cotton Futures - ICE Futures U.S.
(weekly close) as of December 30, 2011

Cents per pound

Average Open Interest of Cotton #2 Futures in New York   In Contracts

Year	Jan.	Feb.	Mar.	Apr.	May	June	July	Aug.	Sept.	Oct.	Nov.	Dec.
2002	64,096	64,572	63,451	63,827	67,601	65,848	74,892	72,612	69,554	71,526	82,802	74,685
2003	83,775	89,852	91,336	78,658	73,146	69,137	62,565	62,781	80,348	108,981	97,809	79,627
2004	93,191	81,871	84,600	89,082	81,988	79,310	77,029	75,449	69,514	76,556	86,280	84,409
2005	92,651	94,047	118,183	120,416	103,446	93,818	92,284	99,959	105,874	117,889	103,466	100,660
2006	118,234	129,108	129,728	141,156	165,386	170,190	161,719	166,806	178,539	184,002	170,275	164,797
2007	177,495	199,342	214,628	225,473	223,839	212,296	214,893	206,042	215,820	239,217	229,629	219,185
2008	264,235	279,240	286,505	259,800	258,309	239,935	219,979	216,387	211,933	177,277	146,431	127,380
2009	130,049	120,331	128,054	128,973	134,079	120,861	122,153	127,019	136,585	165,683	180,594	182,489
2010	178,305	166,475	185,608	190,458	184,193	171,459	160,118	201,962	231,513	235,834	217,587	201,510
2011	204,871	198,798	176,675	180,626	150,430	148,695	138,168	144,300	150,834	155,592	149,292	146,219

Contract size = 50,000 lbs.   *Source: ICE Futures U.S. (ICE)*

Volume of Trading of Cotton #2 Futures in New York   In Contracts

Year	Jan.	Feb.	Mar.	Apr.	May	June	July	Aug.	Sept.	Oct.	Nov.	Dec.	Total
2002	156,834	248,299	162,781	237,861	188,340	234,442	170,893	128,185	145,946	199,779	296,859	157,741	2,327,960
2003	202,615	267,234	217,791	325,627	249,314	271,822	164,027	127,080	283,988	422,132	356,052	148,310	3,035,992
2004	272,948	359,105	300,820	376,669	184,869	357,548	159,924	195,886	196,739	224,431	341,709	185,370	3,156,018
2005	356,817	407,277	317,486	465,210	306,971	456,584	171,139	189,584	271,268	290,650	408,580	207,424	3,848,990
2006	311,926	495,729	375,624	515,709	330,785	601,971	184,482	259,259	268,847	308,584	587,710	249,781	4,490,407
2007	366,579	713,894	375,964	765,244	439,838	745,901	428,059	445,099	435,529	520,221	759,829	338,822	6,334,979
2008	684,489	971,319	730,160	651,281	427,731	690,183	281,522	306,004	418,279	401,064	426,785	174,146	6,162,963
2009	276,977	326,853	272,091	373,379	274,983	372,124	187,347	177,989	228,815	347,989	509,375	227,073	3,574,995
2010	321,331	570,117	344,389	567,774	365,998	550,206	327,296	331,579	440,411	600,977	887,594	425,234	5,732,906
2011	457,454	719,075	590,294	602,903	325,606	536,555	293,608	290,265	307,617	350,452	598,711	215,914	5,288,454

Contract size = 50,000 lbs.   *Source: ICE Futures U.S. (ICE)*

COTTON

Daily Rate of Upland Cotton Mill Consumption[2] on Cotton-System Spinning Spindles in the United States
In Thousands of Running Bales

Crop Year Beginning Aug. 1	Aug.	Sept.	Oct.	Nov.	Dec.	Jan.	Feb.	Mar.	Apr.	May	June	July	Average
2001-02	28.8	28.1	27.5	26.3	27.1	27.1	27.5	27.9	27.4	28.4	29.3	30.6	28.0
2002-03	28.0	28.3	27.9	27.4	27.2	26.5	26.8	26.4	26.0	25.0	24.3	24.7	26.5
2003-04	23.0	22.7	22.6	23.0	22.7	22.4	23.1	23.1	22.8	23.1	23.2	24.2	23.0
2004-05	25.1	25.1	24.9	24.4	25.2	24.8	23.7	23.7	24.0	23.6	25.2	24.4	24.5
2005-06	23.2	22.0	22.6	21.2	20.5	22.9	23.1	22.4	20.7	20.2	19.9	19.5	21.5
2006-07	18.9	18.8	18.5	W	W	W	W	W	W	W	W	W	18.7
2007-08	W	W	W	W	W	16.7	17.0	16.0	17.2	16.6	16.9	16.4	16.7
2008-09	17.4	15.9	16.7	14.3	9.4	13.0	11.2	11.5	11.7	12.2	11.8	12.8	13.1
2009-10	12.8	10.6	13.0	12.9	10.3	13.2	12.8	12.4	12.9	13.6	13.2	13.1	12.6
2010-11[1]	13.8	13.7	14.6	13.4	11.7	14.4	14.0	13.5	13.3	13.5	13.4	12.2	13.5

[1] Preliminary. [2] Not seasonally adjusted. W = Withheld. *Source: Bureau of the Census: U.S. Department of Commerce*

Consumption of American and Foreign Cotton in the United States   In Thousands of Running Bales

Year	Aug.	Sept.	Oct.	Nov.	Dec.	Jan.	Feb.	Mar.	Apr.	May	June	July	Total
2001-02	616	751	600	521	563	541	580	759	575	594	754	571	7,425
2002-03	574	733	585	545	598	671	556	708	541	523	616	456	7,106
2003-04	476	599	482	468	504	478	475	609	461	473	582	446	6,053
2004-05	484	604	483	460	500	470	472	601	469	463	581	449	6,035
2005-06	454	574	472	415	438	452	476	593	430	422	531	381	5,637
2006-07	385	492	389	357	370	361	363	461	371	371	476	348	4,744
2007-08	358	467	366	343	362	423	341	402	346	333	430	329	4,499
2008-09	349	399	333	285	234	261	230	302	230	251	311	254	3,439
2009-10	263	280	261	266	267	266	259	313	261	275	338	270	3,318
2010-11[1]	286	351	303	274	301	287	280	337	266	270	334	244	3,533

[1] Preliminary. *Source: Bureau of the Census, U.S. Department of Commerce*

Exports of All Cotton[2] from the United States   In Thousands of Running Bales

Year	Aug.	Sept.	Oct.	Nov.	Dec.	Jan.	Feb.	Mar.	Apr.	May	June	July	Total
2002-03	472	653	373	626	935	1,206	873	1,597	1,174	1,150	1,273	1,231	11,561
2003-04	810	555	446	758	1,116	1,194	1,238	1,869	1,453	1,117	1,576	1,021	13,154
2004-05	760	374	422	632	1,087	1,179	1,214	1,839	1,461	1,094	1,411	1,828	13,301
2005-06	1,407	742	533	763	1,236	946	1,541	2,195	1,758	1,725	1,906	1,903	16,655
2006-07	688	412	487	599	812	683	824	1,266	1,269	1,385	2,174	1,745	12,342
2007-08	1,116	1,337	883	977	781	981	945	955	1,096	1,360	1,292	1,427	13,150
2008-09	994	983	1,159	923	747	733	813	1,128	1,442	1,475	1,266	1,106	13,179
2009-10	885	809	664	570	778	942	1,174	1,447	1,174	1,354	1,344	1,373	12,513
2010-11	1,023	467	449	1,146	1,696	2,067	1,864	2,087	1,568	1,171	708	536	14,783
2011-12[1]	302	303	422	776	934								6,568

[1] Preliminary. *Source: Foreign Agricultural Service, U.S. Department of Agriculture (FAS-USDA)*

U.S. Exports of American Cotton to Countries of Destination   In Thousands of 480-Pound Bales

Crop Year Beginning Aug. 1	Canada	China	Hong Kong	Indonesia	Italy	Japan	Rep. of Korea	Mexico	Philippines	Taiwan	Thailand	United Kingdom	Total
2001-02	235	306	407	947	58	385	577	1,516	126	693	693	0	10,397
2002-03	303	1,840	364	869	81	380	480	1,777	104	592	556	4	11,607
2003-04	303	4,919	169	889	63	284	469	1,620	100	527	396	20	13,758
2004-05	305	4,085	274	1,138	75	301	643	1,589	110	846	711	60	14,436
2005-06	178	9,095	280	933	33	265	431	1,511	46	660	530	23	18,039
2006-07	101	3,641	238	928	36	265	307	1,200	39	429	456	0	12,219
2007-08	40	4,491	177	1,261	62	376	361	1,432	26	390	838	0	13,972
2008-09	19	3,770	184	1,057	23	158	302	1,320	52	436	615		13,179
2009-10[1]	9	3,885	69	660	21	150	353	1,490	51	424	605		12,513
2010-11[2]	10	4,881	47	899	53	186	514	1,246	37	357	712	1	14,783

[1] Preliminary. [2] Estimate. *Source: Foreign Agricultural Service, U.S. Department of Agriculture (FAS-USDA)*

Cotton[1] Government Loan Program in the United States

Crop Year Beginning Aug. 1	Support Price	Target Price	Put Under Support	% of Pro-duction	Acquired	Owned July 31	Crop Year Beginning Aug. 1	Support Price	Target Price	Put Under Support	% of Pro-duction	Acquired	Owned July 31
	--- Cents Per Lb. ---		Ths Bales		----- Ths. Bales -----			--- Cents Per Lb. ---		Ths Bales		----- Ths. Bales -----	
2001-02	51.92	NA	13,655	67.3	31	2	2006-07	52.00	72.4	17,839	82.6	79	29
2002-03	52.00	72.4	12,740	74.0	0	106	2007-08	52.00	72.4	14,636	76.2	169	14
2003-04	52.00	72.4	10,466	57.3	16	0	2008-09	52.00	71.3	10,005	78.1	4	13
2004-05	52.00	72.4	17,092	73.5	8	0	2009-10	52.00	71.3	8,233	67.6	0	6
2005-06	52.00	72.4	17,783	74.4	181	11	2010-11[2]	52.00	71.3				

[1] Upland. [2] Preliminary. NA = Not applicable. *Source: Economic Research Service, U.S. Department of Agriculture (ERS-USDA)*

Production of Cotton Cloth[1] in the United States   In Millions of Square Yards

Year	First Quarter	Second Quarter	Third Quarter	Fourth Quarter	Total	Year	First Quarter	Second Quarter	Third Quarter	Fourth Quarter	Total
2002	893	912	894	825	3,524	2007	521	507	488	453	1,969
2003	836	780	662	620	2,898	2008	447	460	451	393	1,751
2004	648	644	640	614	2,547	2009	336	357	320	307	1,320
2005	672	640	653	664	2,629	2010	327	321	340	328	1,315
2006	583	609	551	487	2,230	2011[2]	347	331	X	X	1,356

[1] Cotton broadwoven goods over 12 inches in width. [2] Preliminary. *Source: Bureau of Census, U.S. Department of Commerce*

Cotton Ginnings[1] in the United States To: In Thousands of Running Bales

Crop Year	Aug. 1	Sept. 1	Sept. 15	Oct. 1	Oct. 15	Nov. 1	Nov. 15	Dec. 1	Dec. 15	Jan. 1	Jan. 15	Feb. 1	Total Crop
2002-03	56	538	898	1,656	3,520	6,697	9,265	12,368	14,392	15,654	16,285	16,576	16,710
2003-04	29	567	958	2,001	3,819	7,393	10,507	13,466	15,678	16,883	17,409	17,601	17,709
2004-05	48	563	1,157	2,227	4,788	8,758	12,019	14,754	17,072	18,925	20,155	21,249	22,556
2005-06	69	592	976	2,314	4,556	8,691	12,569	15,991	18,401	20,108	21,282	22,255	23,253
2006-07	23	406	996	2,572	5,039	8,604	11,833	15,139	17,657	19,212	20,062	20,559	20,998
2007-08	W	182	375	1,566	3,793	7,072	10,099	12,593	14,341	15,700	16,690	17,585	18,713
2008-09	13	335	476	797	2,027	4,358	6,800	8,928	10,463	11,572	12,094	12,370	12,462
2009-10	5	110	175	234	552	2,189	4,957	7,873	9,728	10,812	11,383	11,706	11,832
2010-11	W	287	747	2,284	4,716	7,947	10,576	13,170	15,126	16,442	17,138	17,518	17,643
2011-12[2]	203	825	1,095	1,764	3,504	6,492	9,220	11,703	13,098	13,952	14,468	14,809	

[1] Excluding linters. [2] Preliminary. W = Withheld. *Source: National Agricultural Statistics Service, U.S. Department of Agriculture (NASS-USDA)*

Fiber Prices in the United States   In Cents Per Pound

Year	Cotton[1] Actual	Cotton[1] Raw[5] Equivalent	Rayon[2] Actual	Rayon[2] Raw[5] Equivalent	Polyester[3] Actual	Polyester[3] Raw[5] Equivalent	Price Ratios[4] In Percent Cotton/ Rayon	Price Ratios[4] In Percent Cotton/ Polyester
2000	64.06	71.17	97.58	101.65	57.08	59.46	70.0	119.1
2001	47.08	52.32	98.50	102.61	60.42	62.93	52.0	83.0
2002	45.56	50.63	97.83	101.91	61.17	63.72	50.0	79.0
2003	62.54	69.49	90.25	94.01	60.67	63.20	74.1	111.0
2004	60.42	67.13	99.08	103.21	62.67	65.28	66.5	103.5
2005	54.75	60.00	114.58	119.36	67.75	70.57	51.0	86.2
2006	56.70	63.00	113.00	117.71	69.00	71.86	53.5	88.0
2007	61.97	68.86	113.00	117.71	74.00	77.08	58.5	89.3
2008[6]	73.79	82.01	113.00	117.71	74.00	77.08	69.7	121.1
Jan.	73.32	81.47	113.00	117.71	74.00	77.08	69.2	120.3
Feb.	74.25	82.54	113.00	117.71	74.00	77.08	70.1	121.8
Mar.	NA	NA	NA	NA	NA	NA	NA	NA
Apr.	NA	NA	NA	NA	NA	NA	NA	NA
May	NA	NA	NA	NA	NA	NA	NA	NA
June	NA	NA	NA	NA	NA	NA	NA	NA
July	NA	NA	NA	NA	NA	NA	NA	NA
Aug.	NA	NA	NA	NA	NA	NA	NA	NA
Sept.	NA	NA	NA	NA	NA	NA	NA	NA
Oct.	NA	NA	NA	NA	NA	NA	NA	NA
Nov.	NA	NA	NA	NA	NA	NA	NA	NA
Dec.								

[1] SLM-1 1/16" at group B Mill points, net weight. [2] 1.5 and 3.0 denier, regular rayon staples. [3] Reported average market price for 1.5 denier polyester staple for cotton blending. [4] Raw fiber equivalent. [5] Actual prices converted to estimated raw fiber equivalent as follows: cotton, divided by 0.90, rayon and polyester, divided by 0.96. [6] Preliminary.
Source: Economic Research Service, U.S. Department of Agriculture (ERS-USDA)

Cottonseed and Products

Cottonseed is crushed to produce both oil and meal. Cottonseed oil is typically used for cooking oil and cottonseed meal is fed to livestock. Before the cottonseed is crushed for oil and meal, it is de-linted of its linters. Linters are used for padding in furniture, absorbent cotton swabs, and for the manufacture of many cellulose products. The sediment left by cottonseed oil refining, called foots, provides fatty acids for industrial products. The value of cottonseeds represents a substantial 18% of a cotton producer's income.

Prices – The average monthly price of cottonseed oil in 2011 rose by +27.2% yr/yr to 54.60 cents per pound, below the 2008 record high of 68.09 cents per pound. The average monthly price of cottonseed meal in 2011 rose by +29.1% yr/yr to $275.16 per short ton, a new record high.

Supply – World production of cottonseed in the 2010-11 marketing year rose +13.0% yr/yr to 43.910 million metric tons, below the record high of 45.136 million metric tons posted in 2004-05. The world's largest cottonseed

producers are China with 26.2% of world production, India with 24.2%, the U.S. with 12.6%, and Pakistan with 8.7%. U.S. production of cottonseed in the 2011-12 marketing year fell by -13.6% yr/yr to 5.2676 million tons. U.S. production of cottonseed oil in 2011-12 fell by -9.6% yr/yr to 755 million pounds, below the 12-year high of 957 million pounds posted in 2004-05. U.S. annualized production of cottonseed cake and meal for the first five months of the 2010-11 marketing year (Aug-Jul) rose by +30.0% yr/yr to 1.082 million short tons.

Demand – U.S. cottonseed crushed (consumed) in the U.S. annualized for the first five months of the 2010-11 marketing year rose by +27.4% to 2.420 million tons. That was far below the levels of over 4 million tons seen in the 1970s.

Trade – U.S. exports of cottonseed in 2011-12 fell -41.8% to 160,000 short tons, while imports were 100,000 short tons, up from last year's imports of zero.

World Production of Cottonseed   In Thousands of Metric Ton

Crop Year Beginning Oct. 1	Argentina	Australia	Brazil	China	Egypt	Greece	India	Mexico	Pakistan	Turkey	United States	Former USSR	World Total
2002-03	90	470	1,451	8,750	475	718	4,624	68	3,472	1,457	5,610	2,584	33,641
2003-04	159	494	2,390	8,651	338	611	6,018	115	3,416	1,337	6,046	2,442	36,131
2004-05	247	912	2,309	11,257	487	645	8,250	212	4,853	1,402	7,437	2,938	45,226
2005-06	230	770	1,816	10,171	399	677	8,200	221	4,428	1,291	7,414	3,165	42,953
2006-07	300	330	2,498	13,409	372	520	9,300	249	4,065	1,477	6,666	3,100	45,866
2007-08	271	180	2,422	13,571	389	500	10,400	209	3,695	1,321	5,977	3,158	45,248
2008-09	214	466	1,785	13,330	185	420	9,800	201	3,760	1,077	3,901	3,070	41,132
2009-10[1]	374	550	1,786	11,390	160	370	10,100	151	4,010	1,021	3,764	2,629	38,845
2010-11[2]	485	1,170	2,923	11,500	220	310	10,600	230	3,800	1,270	5,532	2,908	43,910

[1] Preliminary.   [2] Estimate.   *Source: The Oil World*

Salient Statistics of Cottonseed in the United States   In Thousands of Short Tons

Crop Year Beginning Aug. 1	Supply			Disappearance				Farm Price USD/Ton	Value of Production Mil. USD	Products Produced	
	Stocks	Production	Total Supply	Crush	Exports	Other	Total				Total
2003-04	347	6,665	7,013	2,643	354	3,595	6,592	117	779.0	874	1,244
2004-05	421	8,242	8,664	2,923	379	4,770	8,072	107	872.8	957	1,362
2005-06	592	8,172	8,764	3,010	523	4,630	8,163	96	779.5	951	1,372
2006-07	602	7,348	7,950	2,680	616	4,165	7,461	111	814.2	849	1,241
2007-08	489	6,589	7,080	2,706	599	3,132	6,437	162	1,069.8	856	1,262
2008-09	643	4,300	4,943	2,240	190	1,999	4,429	230	962.7	669	938
2009-10	514	4,149	4,687	1,901	296	2,149	4,345	200-260	670.0	617	883
2010-11[1]	342	6,098	6,440	2,563	275	2,984	5,822		988.7	835	1,150
2011-12[2]	618	5,267	5,985	2,400	160	2,995	5,555		1,387.9	755	1,090

[1] Preliminary.   [2] Estimate.   *Source: Economic Research Service, U.S. Department of Agriculture (ERS-USDA)*

Average Wholesale Price of Cottonseed Meal (41% Solvent)[2] in Memphis   In Dollars Per Short Ton

Year	Jan.	Feb.	Mar.	Apr.	May	June	July	Aug.	Sept.	Oct.	Nov.	Dec.	Average
2003	157.38	143.60	142.40	142.40	131.75	131.50	143.00	151.70	153.20	163.50	182.50	185.00	152.33
2004	188.00	193.00	205.10	219.67	203.00	185.40	177.50	156.20	142.75	126.75	119.00	117.00	169.45
2005	112.50	111.25	110.80	108.00	110.40	138.75	151.00	143.00	140.00	133.13	132.50	175.00	130.53
2006	172.50	152.50	148.75	144.38	131.50	135.00	132.50	134.50	139.00	132.40	131.88	152.50	142.28
2007	161.00	174.75	185.50	148.25	137.00	131.25	137.50	144.75	167.50	183.40	176.25	196.67	161.99
2008	273.60	292.00	245.00	230.00	240.50	293.25	333.00	290.00	292.00	238.75	225.00	229.50	265.22
2009	237.50	236.25	213.00	212.50	236.25	306.00	305.00	315.00	308.00	250.00	260.00	283.75	263.60
2010	286.25	253.75	213.00	175.00	171.25	176.00	183.75	198.00	200.00	225.31	235.00	240.63	213.16
2011	245.63	258.75	256.50	240.00	275.50	307.50	313.13	342.50	345.63	255.63	240.50	220.63	275.16

[1] Preliminary.   *Source: Economic Research Service, U.S. Department of Agriculture (ERS-USDA)*

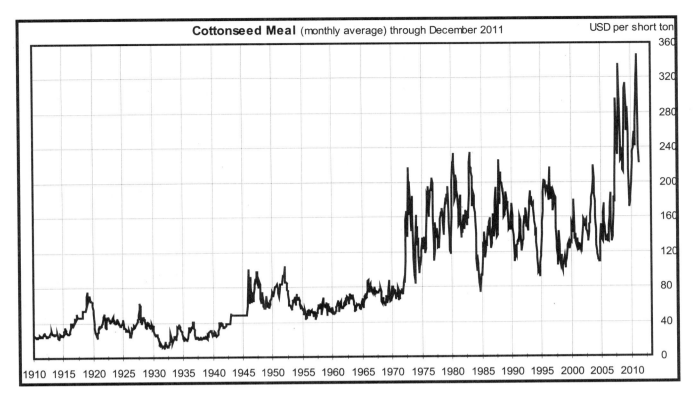

Cottonseed Meal (monthly average) through December 2011 — USD per short ton

Supply and Distribution of Cottonseed Oil in the United States — In Millions of Pounds

Crop Year Beginning Oct. 1	Supply				Disappearance			Per Capita Consumption of Salad & Cooking Oils --- In Lbs. ---	Utilization Food Uses			Prices	
	Stocks	Pro- duction	Imports	Total Supply	Domestic	Exports	Total		Short- ening	Salad & Cooking Oils	Total	U.S.[3] (Crude) --- $/Metric Ton ---	Rott[4] (Cif)
2005-06	76	951	1.0	1,028	860	67	927	43	213	389	602	649	669
2006-07	101	849	1.0	951	714	138	852	45	162	547	709	787	804
2007-08	99	856	0	956	623	186	809	50	166	567	733	1,622	1,648
2008-09	147	669	0	815	502	192	694	54	W	638	638	820	829
2009-10	121	617	0	738	551	94	646	48	W	509	509	888	895
2010-11[1]	93	835	0	928	599	164	763						1,250
2011-12[2]	165	755	0	920	695	125	820						

[1] Preliminary. [2] Estimate. [3] Valley Points FOB; Tank Cars. [4] Rotterdam; US, PBSY, fob gulf. W = Withheld.
Source: Economic Research Service, U.S. Department of Agriculture (ERS-USDA)

Consumption of Crude Cottonseed Oil, in Refining[2], in the United States — In Millions of Pound

Year	Oct.	Nov.	Dec.	Jan.	Feb.	Mar.	Apr.	May	June	July	Aug.	Sept.	Total
2004-05	60.0	66.4	67.0	73.7	69.2	66.8	72.6	52.9	64.7	57.0	71.8	55.2	777.1
2005-06	72.7	79.0	75.1	70.9	64.0	71.1	58.2	71.6	61.2	52.6	61.4	52.4	790.2
2006-07	65.7	55.7	61.4	63.9	55.3	63.7	60.1	63.6	54.1	56.3	56.5	55.6	711.9
2007-08	59.6	60.9	61.7	74.0	70.2	68.0	70.9	62.2	52.3	55.3	57.1	52.8	744.8
2008-09	47.2	56.4	63.5	58.3	58.4	57.5	44.0	48.1	50.6	36.9	39.3	37.5	597.6
2009-10	32.6	46.2	51.6	45.0	41.4	43.9	38.5	42.7	39.5	W	45.6	47.4	517.6
2010-11[1]	38.7	60.1	59.0	56.6	51.6	60.2	56.4	56.8	56.0	45.6			649.4

[1] Preliminary. *Source: U.S. Bureau of Census, U.S. Department of Commerce*

Exports of Cottonseed Oil (Crude and Refined) from the United States — In Thousands of Pounds

Year	Jan.	Feb.	Mar.	Apr.	May	June	July	Aug.	Sept.	Oct.	Nov.	Dec.	Total
2005	3,490	3,161	5,191	3,461	5,873	3,029	3,147	3,763	4,823	3,847	2,926	4,676	47,387
2006	5,084	5,724	5,410	7,738	5,519	6,640	7,539	6,608	5,755	8,827	9,377	14,365	88,586
2007	7,461	17,932	9,732	14,573	10,676	10,647	11,768	10,404	12,055	12,697	17,137	11,420	146,503
2008	11,089	21,546	25,577	11,565	12,436	17,019	17,441	11,300	17,263	22,083	20,819	18,611	206,747
2009	14,423	20,981	15,258	19,313	12,296	14,087	12,070	10,915	11,370	8,506	14,923	8,455	162,597
2010	6,880	9,414	7,075	6,728	6,450	4,234	3,539	5,523	12,740	20,331	16,878	7,038	106,827
2011	8,142	11,103	19,377	17,105	15,053	9,531	11,479	14,273	13,515	25,841	31,753	18,691	195,864

[1] Preliminary. *Source: Economic Research Service, U.S. Department of Agriculture (ERS-USDA)*

COTTONSEED AND PRODUCTS

Cottonseed Crushed (Consumption) in the United States   In Thousands of Short Tons

Year	Aug.	Sept.	Oct.	Nov.	Dec.	Jan.	Feb.	Mar.	Apr.	May	June	July	Total
2002-03	195.1	131.4	207.8	242.5	236.6	274.5	224.5	230.4	241.5	203.6	179.4	127.4	2,495
2003-04	138.7	98.9	251.6	254.8	252.0	265.2	242.3	278.0	217.1	240.2	217.7	182.4	2,639
2004-05	193.8	141.0	247.9	260.3	263.5	283.1	266.3	270.2	287.7	221.0	266.6	221.6	2,923
2005-06	240.7	170.3	272.2	289.4	296.9	291.3	245.0	276.7	235.0	280.3	227.2	203.4	3,028
2006-07	204.8	158.2	252.4	223.3	236.7	251.2	222.5	249.1	230.8	243.2	204.6	203.3	2,680
2007-08	173.4	163.8	242.5	241.2	252.1	267.5	264.1	236.3	245.2	233.4	190.3	193.1	2,703
2008-09	202.3	147.4	175.2	206.5	230.0	234.3	217.6	206.5	170.7	168.1	158.1	133.2	2,250
2009-10	107.1	92.8	131.2	169.2	189.7	202.4	184.6	187.0	180.0	191.3	141.2	124.0	1,900
2010-11[1]	151.0	143.9	172.8	245.7	251.3	249.0	229.4	258.8	235.6	235.6	211.1	178.3	2,563

[1] Preliminary.   *Source: Economic Research Service, U.S. Department of Agriculture (ERS-USDA)*

Production of Cottonseed Cake and Meal in the United States   In Thousands of Short Tons

Year	Aug.	Sept.	Oct.	Nov.	Dec.	Jan.	Feb.	Mar.	Apr.	May	June	July	Total
2002-03	92.4	79.3	95.5	112.6	108.0	123.0	100.3	96.7	108.9	89.8	81.4	63.0	1,151
2003-04	74.9	59.5	112.3	111.0	112.5	113.9	105.1	123.4	94.2	104.7	97.7	91.0	1,200
2004-05	95.3	82.5	105.4	110.4	118.7	125.7	119.3	120.4	124.4	103.6	121.0	106.2	1,333
2005-06	116.4	91.1	109.6	134.6	129.3	128.8	108.2	119.4	104.5	129.3	107.2	99.0	1,377
2006-07	102.0	83.0	118.8	101.8	102.4	115.3	101.8	114.6	105.9	112.6	97.4	102.3	1,258
2007-08	81.3	87.3	112.5	111.0	111.9	125.6	119.9	116.3	110.4	103.2	86.8	90.7	1,257
2008-09	96.5	76.9	74.8	89.7	103.5	102.7	99.2	90.8	76.6	73.0	75.6	60.7	1,020
2009-10	46.9	40.8	60.9	73.4	82.1	92.2	81.0	78.6	76.8	87.2	59.9	53.0	833
2010-11[1]	63.2	74.9	82.2	103.8	112.0	107.7	104.0	113.5	106.8	110.1	98.0	82.7	1,159

[1] Preliminary.   *Source: Bureau of Census, U.S. Department of Commerce*

Production of Crude Cottonseed Oil[2] in the United States   In Millions of Pounds

Year	Aug.	Sept.	Oct.	Nov.	Dec.	Jan.	Feb.	Mar.	Apr.	May	June	July	Total
2002-03	60.2	53.7	62.8	72.1	67.9	80.8	65.6	66.7	71.0	59.9	52.8	39.9	753
2003-04	45.0	40.7	77.5	78.2	79.0	82.4	75.7	87.2	67.0	73.8	66.7	59.7	833
2004-05	68.6	58.1	77.1	82.2	81.4	88.7	83.4	84.3	90.7	71.3	81.6	69.5	937
2005-06	84.3	62.0	86.9	95.7	90.9	92.8	77.2	87.8	70.9	90.4	70.4	68.1	977
2006-07	68.4	59.2	77.1	71.7	73.9	78.6	67.1	78.1	72.5	77.2	65.2	66.7	856
2007-08	58.2	62.5	77.5	73.8	76.8	83.5	82.1	77.1	77.1	70.3	58.5	60.3	858
2008-09	64.4	55.0	49.4	64.4	71.2	70.4	68.4	65.9	53.5	57.2	58.7	39.6	718
2009-10	34.5	35.5	38.3	54.1	59.1	59.8	55.9	60.0	51.5	59.8	41.1	36.6	586
2010-11[1]	48.0	52.9	54.3	79.1	79.8	79.3	71.4	84.6	77.3	80.0	70.6	59.4	837

[1] Preliminary.   [2] Not seasonally adjusted.   *Source: Bureau of Census, U.S. Department of Commerce*

Production of Refined Cottonseed Oil in the United States   In Millions of Pounds

Year	Aug.	Sept.	Oct.	Nov.	Dec.	Jan.	Feb.	Mar.	Apr.	May	June	July	Total
2002-03	52.7	47.1	48.3	59.2	55.7	66.5	55.6	56.8	58.9	49.4	42.4	31.7	624
2003-04	38.5	34.6	59.8	63.5	61.4	64.3	58.4	68.3	55.1	55.1	52.4	43.8	655
2004-05	53.4	52.0	59.7	66.1	66.9	73.4	68.8	66.6	72.3	52.7	64.6	56.6	753
2005-06	71.2	54.7	72.8	78.5	74.7	70.3	63.8	70.8	57.8	71.2	60.8	52.3	799
2006-07	61.0	52.0	65.2	55.3	61.1	63.5	55.3	62.9	58.9	63.5	54.0	56.1	709
2007-08	56.4	55.5	59.6	60.9	61.6	73.8	70.0	67.8	70.5	62.1	52.3	55.2	746
2008-09	56.9	52.6	46.9	56.3	63.2	57.9	58.1	57.2	43.7	47.9	50.3	36.7	628
2009-10	39.2	37.5	32.6	46.2	51.6	44.9	41.4	43.9	38.5	42.7	39.5	W	500
2010-11[1]	45.6	47.3	38.7	60.1	59.0	56.6	51.6	60.2	56.4	56.7	56.0	45.6	634

[1] Preliminary.   *Source: Bureau of the Census, U.S. Department of Commerce*

Stocks of Cottonseed Oil (Crude and Refined) in the U.S., at End of Month   In Millions of Pounds

Year	Aug.	Sept.	Oct.	Nov.	Dec.	Jan.	Feb.	Mar.	Apr.	May	June	July
2002-03	46.1	39.7	32.8	40.2	38.0	46.1	58.8	72.2	83.3	84.2	91.4	64.0
2003-04	50.5	36.0	51.9	56.1	68.7	85.9	100.6	117.6	116.8	125.7	121.0	123.0
2004-05	123.3	109.0	106.6	110.6	111.3	116.6	122.0	112.9	121.2	111.5	90.0	86.2
2005-06	90.6	76.4	69.0	76.1	74.0	84.0	99.0	108.5	103.3	110.8	105.8	95.6
2006-07	98.9	101.1	93.2	92.3	106.8	119.2	117.0	112.2	124.5	126.1	119.5	160.2
2007-08	132.9	105.8	92.8	91.6	94.9	114.3	138.4	143.5	156.1	161.4	158.7	143.1
2008-09	153.8	146.6	139.7	124.7	120.0	126.7	134.1	149.4	151.4	160.9	144.7	150.3
2009-10	141.0	120.6	98.1	85.4	114.2	112.2	122.7	130.4	126.6	128.8	121.2	97.5
2010-11[1]	78.6	84.9	72.1	78.0	109.7	139.6	152.1	163.5	163.2	180.1	189.1	180.7

[1] Preliminary.   *Source: Bureau of the Census, U.S. Department of Commerce*

Cottonseed Oil (monthly average) through December 2011 — Cents per pound

Average Price of Crude Cottonseed Oil, PBSY, Greenwood, MS.[1] in Tank Cars — In Cents Per Pound

Year	Jan.	Feb.	Mar.	Apr.	May	June	July	Aug.	Sept.	Oct.	Nov.	Dec.	Average
2002	16.38	15.89	16.77	16.98	17.95	19.48	21.30	22.32	22.32	26.84	36.90	46.89	23.34
2003	49.82	49.90	47.52	44.57	42.33	28.69	24.38	25.51	29.64	32.93	32.24	33.26	36.73
2004	32.76	34.21	34.91	34.47	32.57	30.72	27.83	25.29	23.29	22.74	23.88	23.81	28.87
2005	23.70	24.38	28.19	29.80	30.63	33.13	34.15	30.44	31.25	34.44	34.09	30.50	30.39
2006	29.63	29.50	29.75	27.05	28.06	27.25	29.20	26.69	27.13	27.44	30.25	30.75	28.56
2007	31.00	32.69	33.00	34.38	37.75	40.00	42.44	42.15	46.56	52.20	63.60	66.63	43.53
2008	71.69	78.60	78.94	79.75	82.75	87.56	86.06	72.55	62.44	46.45	37.38	32.88	68.09
2009	35.70	33.19	32.63	37.38	39.90	38.75	36.55	39.13	36.44	37.90	40.69	41.40	37.47
2010	39.00	39.13	39.88	38.75	37.38	40.00	42.45	43.69	43.00	47.20	50.75	54.00	42.94
2011	55.92	56.75	55.50	57.70	56.06	55.25	54.75	54.75	55.35	51.56	50.50	51.10	54.60

Source: Economic Research Service, U.S. Department of Agriculture (ERS-USDA)

Exports of Cottonseed Oil to Important Countries from the United States — In Thousands of Metric Tons

Year	Canada	Dominican Republic	Egypt	Guate-mala	Japan	Mexico	Nether-lands	El Salvador	Rep. of Korea	Turkey	Venez-uela	Total
2002	36.4	0	3.0	0	5.4	6.9	0	1.8	4.7	.3	0	63.2
2003	33.6	0	0	0	3.5	7.2	0	.0	.7	0	0	46.2
2004	26.5	0	0	0	11.6	8.6	0	0	.0	0	0	47.9
2005	12.7	0	0	0	1.0	6.5	0	0	.1	0	0	21.5
2006	10.0	.0	0	.0	1.3	11.2	0	0	14.1	0	.1	40.2
2007	24.0	.1	0	0	7.1	11.6	0	0	17.3	0	.0	66.5
2008	40.8	.1	0	0	9.0	22.3	0	0	14.5	0	0	93.8
2009	37.0	0	0	0	2.6	18.1	.1	.2	8.7	0	0	73.8
2010	17.6	0	0	0	1.4	26.0	0	0	.9	0	0	48.5
2011[1]	40.0	.0	0	0		45.8	0	0	.9	.0	0	88.8

[1] Preliminary.   *Source: Foreign Agricultural Service, U.S. Department of Agriculture (FAS-USDA)*

Continuous Commodity Index (CCI)

The Continuous Commodity Index (CCI) was first calculated by Commodity Research Bureau, Inc. in 1957 and made its inaugural appearance in the 1958 CRB Commodity Year Book.

The Index originally consisted of two cash markets and 26 futures markets which were traded on exchanges in the U.S. and Canada. It included barley and flaxseed from the Winnipeg exchange; cocoa, coffee "B", copper, cotton, cottonseed oil, grease wool, hides, lead, potatoes, rubber, sugar #4, sugar #6, wool tops and zinc from New York exchanges; and corn, oats, wheat, rye, soybeans, soybean oil, soybean meal, lard, onions, and eggs from Chicago exchanges. In addition to those 26, the Index also included the spot New Orleans cotton and Minneapolis wheat markets.

Like the Bureau of Labor Statistics spot index, the CCI is calculated to produce an unweighted geometric mean of the individual commodity price relatives. In other words, a ratio of the current price to the base year average price. Currently, 1967 is the base year the Index is calculated against (1967=100).

The formula considers all future delivery contracts that expire on or before the end of the sixth calendar month from the current date, using up to a maximum of five contracts per commodity. However, a minimum of two contracts must be used to calculate the current price, even if the second contract is outside the six-month window. Contracts are excluded when in their delivery period.

The 2011 closing value of 563.00 was -10.57 percent lower than the 2010 close of 629.53. 11 of the 17 component commodities finished lower for the year.

Futures and options on the CCI are traded on the ICE Futures U.S. (ICE) exchange.

Continuous Commodity Index (CCI) Component Commodities by Group

Group:	Components
Energy:	Crude Oil, Heating Oil, Natural gas
Grains and Oilseeds:	Corn, Soybeans, Wheat
Industrials:	Copper, Cotton
Livestock:	Live Cattle, Lean Hogs
Precious Metals:	Gold, Platinum, Silver
Softs:	Cocoa, Coffee, Orange Juice, Sugar #11

The Continuous Commodity Index (CCI) is computed using a three-step process:

1) Each of the Index's 17 component commodities is arithmetically averaged using the prices for all of the designated contract months which expire on or before the end of the sixth calendar month from the current date, except that: a) no contract shall be included in the calculation while in delivery; b) there shall be a minimum of two contract months for each component commodity (adding contracts beyond the six month window if necessary); c) there shall be a maximum of five contract months for each commodity (dropping the most deferred contracts to remain at five, if necessary). The result is that the Index extends six to seven months into the future depending on where one is in the current month. For example, live cattle's average price on October 30, 1995 would be computed as follows:

$$\text{Cattle Average} = \frac{\text{Dec. '96} + \text{Feb. '97}}{2}$$

2) These 17 component averages are then geometrically averaged by multiplying all of the numbers together and taking the 17th root.

$$\text{Geometric Average} = \sqrt[17]{\text{Crude Avg. * Heating Oil Avg. * Sugar Avg....}}$$

3) The resulting average is divided by 30.7766, the 1967 base-year average for these 17 commodities. That result is then multiplied by an adjustment factor of .8486. This adjustment factor is necessitated by the nine revisions to the Index since its inception in 1957. Finally, that result is multiplied by 100 in order to convert the Index into percentage terms:

$$\text{CCI} = \frac{\text{Current Geometric Average}}{\text{1967 Geometric Avg. (30.7766) * .8486 * 100}}$$

Continuous Commodity Index (CCI) - ICE Futures U.S.
(weekly close) as of December 30, 2011

Average Open Interest of Continuous Commodity Index (CCI) in New York   In Contracts

Year	Jan.	Feb.	Mar.	Apr.	May	June	July	Aug.	Sept.	Oct.	Nov.	Dec.
2002	422	514	458	384	400	412	489	399	583	646	684	710
2003	748	877	835	849	939	905	858	917	1,078	1,029	1,013	760
2004	838	870	942	704	357	305	413	412	539	600	581	604
2005	540	561	710	663	644	683	861	1,023	1,016	1,024	1,016	1,035
2006	1,045	1,025	998	1,061	1,045	964	939	919	935	948	955	959
2007	927	914	995	1,251	1,526	1,500	1,409	1,560	1,416	1,603	1,864	1,484
2008	1,349	1,355	1,241	1,159	1,168	1,226	1,329	1,302	1,435	1,677	1,541	1,392
2009	1,540	1,449	1,551	1,634	1,411	1,288	1,247	1,283	1,251	1,422	1,319	1,324
2010	1,306	1,422	1,553	1,550	1,528	1,528	1,465	1,185	1,197	1,204	1,211	867
2011	643	621	598	539	515	492	500	450	283	272	269	270

Contract size = $500.   *Source: ICE Futures U.S. (ICE)*

Volume of Trading of Continuous Commodity Index (CCI) in New York   In Contracts

Year	Jan.	Feb.	Mar.	Apr.	May	June	July	Aug.	Sept.	Oct.	Nov.	Dec.	Total
2002	1,251	1,231	896	1,472	785	1,191	1,217	915	1,100	1,654	1,430	1,141	14,283
2003	2,289	2,154	1,826	1,634	1,514	2,106	1,632	1,350	1,712	2,123	2,502	2,314	23,156
2004	2,477	1,695	3,169	2,672	1,209	1,618	792	1,341	759	813	1,630	979	19,154
2005	1,154	861	2,023	1,891	1,027	2,105	1,623	1,931	605	707	1,258	882	16,067
2006	2,231	1,114	1,017	1,836	1,563	1,323	927	1,020	892	461	1,220	708	14,312
2007	1,156	249	1,698	1,648	885	3,164	1,716	927	802	1,837	5,615	276	19,973
2008	1,888	1,454	2,139	2,186	745	1,758	2,162	1,311	1,408	499	2,692	943	19,185
2009	2,525	124	724	3,213	1,047	2,560	697	938	74	2,856	778	437	15,973
2010	453	1,778	958	143	860	49	1,409	252	68	62	1,277	2,191	9,500
2011	427	88	190	86	57	1,053	167	459	128	19	74	39	2,787

Contract size = $500.   *Source: ICE Futures U.S. (ICE)*

Currencies

A currency rate involves the price of the base currency (e.g., the dollar) quoted in terms of another currency (e.g., the yen), or in terms of a basket of currencies (e.g., the dollar index). The world's major currencies have traded in a floating-rate exchange rate regime ever since the Bretton-Woods international payments system broke down in 1971 when President Nixon broke the dollar's peg to gold. The two key factors affecting a currency's value are central bank monetary policy and the trade balance. An easy monetary policy (low interest rates) is bearish for a currency because the central bank is aggressively pumping new currency reserves into the marketplace and because foreign investors are not attracted to the low interest rate returns available in the country. By contrast, a tight monetary policy (high interest rates) is bullish for a currency because of the tight supply of new currency reserves and attractive interest rate returns for foreign investors.

The other key factor driving currency values is the nation's current account balance. A current account *surplus* is bullish for a currency due to the net inflow of the currency, while a current account *deficit* is bearish for a currency due to the net outflow of the currency. Currency values are also affected by economic growth and investment opportunities in the country. A country with a strong economy and lucrative investment opportunities will typically have a strong currency because global companies and investors want to buy into that country's investment opportunities. Futures on major currencies and on cross-currency rates are traded primarily at the Chicago Mercantile Exchange.

Dollar – The dollar index in early 2011 extended the sell-off that started in 2010 and posted a new 3-year low of 72.70 in May 2011. That sell-off was caused by (1) reduced safe-haven support for the dollar as the global economy improved after the 2008/09 financial crisis, and (2) poor U.S. interest rate differentials as the U.S. Federal Reserve kept its federal funds rate target locked near zero and engaged in a second quantitative easing program from November 2010 through June 2011. The Fed cut its federal funds rate target to the range of zero to 0.25% in the aftermath of the 2008/09 financial crisis, but the European Central Bank (ECB) never cut its policy rate below 1.00%. In fact in the first half of 2011, the ECB raised its refinancing rate by 25 basis points twice to bring its policy rate to 1.50%, far higher than the U.S. rate. The dollar was also undercut in the first half of 2011 by the soft U.S. economy and by shaken global investor confidence when the U.S. lost its AAA rating from Standard & Poors due to the battle over raising the U.S. debt ceiling.

The dollar index was able to recover modestly in the second half of 2011 due to the improvement in the U.S. economy and due to revived safe-haven demand tied to the worsening European debt crisis. The European debt crisis nearly caused an all-out European systemic banking crisis during 2001, which boosted demand for dollars. The dollar was also boosted in the latter part of 2011 when the ECB in November and December cut its policy rate by a total of 50 basis points to 1.00%, thus causing U.S. interest rate differentials to improve.

Euro – The euro saw some strength in early 2011 due to some temporary optimism about the European debt crisis and strong European interest rate differentials. In fact, the European Central Bank was optimistic enough about the Eurozone economy in the first half of 2011 that it raised its refinancing rate by 25 basis points in April 2011 to 1.25% and then by another 25 basis points to 1.50% in July 2011. The higher refinancing rate drew more global money market cash into Europe to take advantage of comparatively high short-term interest rates, thus boosting the euro. However, the European debt crisis worsened during the year along with the Eurozone economy. When Mario Draghi took over as the new ECB President in November 2011, he quickly took action by cutting the refinancing rate by 25 basis points in November and again in December to 1.00%. The ECB also announced that it would conduct two unlimited 36-month loan operations in December 2011 and February 2012. Those operations flooded the European banking system with liquidity and substantially eased the European debt crisis problems. However, the ECB's interest rate cuts and the flood of 36-month liquidity was bearish for the euro, which sank in the latter part of 2011 and hit a 1-1/4 year low in January 2012.

Yen – The yen continued to strengthen during 2011 with USDJPY falling to a record low of 75.35 yen in October 2011. The yen continued its 5-year strengthening trend in 2011 mainly because of the Japanese trade surplus, which is bullish for a currency. The yen was also boosted in 2011 by the massive Japanese Tohoku earthquake in March 2011, which created the need for Japanese insurance companies to sell foreign assets and repatriate capital to pay insurance claims, thus boosting the yen. The yen maintained its strength during 2011 despite bearish factors such as near-zero interest rates and a massive fiscal debt load.

British Pound Futures - International Monetary Market
(weekly close) as of December 30, 2011

USD per GBP

U.S. Dollars per British Pound

Year	Jan.	Feb.	Mar.	Apr.	May	June	July	Aug.	Sept.	Oct.	Nov.	Dec.	Average
2002	1.4314	1.4233	1.4233	1.4434	1.4601	1.4849	1.5566	1.5375	1.5562	1.5576	1.5718	1.5882	1.5029
2003	1.6184	1.6077	1.5832	1.5751	1.6230	1.6606	1.6242	1.5942	1.6141	1.6778	1.6899	1.7536	1.6352
2004	1.8223	1.8675	1.8273	1.8050	1.7888	1.8292	1.8433	1.8195	1.7932	1.8069	1.8608	1.9298	1.8328
2005	1.8783	1.8883	1.9034	1.8961	1.8538	1.8179	1.7518	1.7947	1.8078	1.7649	1.7355	1.7454	1.8198
2006	1.7665	1.7478	1.7446	1.7690	1.8693	1.8435	1.8451	1.8934	1.8858	1.8766	1.9124	1.9634	1.8431
2007	1.9585	1.9586	1.9479	1.9874	1.9834	1.9870	2.0344	2.0112	2.0202	2.0453	2.0709	2.0168	2.0018
2008	1.9692	1.9640	2.0012	1.9815	1.9662	1.9675	1.9897	1.8870	1.7997	1.6899	1.5290	1.4869	1.8526
2009	1.4484	1.4417	1.4197	1.4727	1.5460	1.6379	1.6387	1.6532	1.6312	1.6196	1.6610	1.6230	1.5661
2010	1.6160	1.5621	1.5059	1.5337	1.4658	1.4758	1.5302	1.5652	1.5575	1.5858	1.5953	1.5599	1.5461
2011	1.5789	1.6137	1.6158	1.6385	1.6338	1.6219	1.6150	1.6359	1.5776	1.5773	1.5799	1.5587	1.6039

Average.   *Source: FOREX*

Volume of Trading of British Pound Futures in Chicago   In Thousands of Contracts

Year	Jan.	Feb.	Mar.	Apr.	May	June	July	Aug.	Sept.	Oct.	Nov.	Dec.	Total
2002	182.0	168.2	230.4	168.2	174.1	239.8	133.3	138.3	185.3	177.5	160.9	198.0	2,155.9
2003	158.3	161.8	217.4	158.1	164.7	288.6	214.9	163.5	284.5	212.6	206.2	364.5	2,595.2
2004	310.3	291.6	470.3	293.1	282.5	427.8	373.4	367.1	471.4	405.4	348.4	635.2	4,676.5
2005	376.7	410.5	628.7	453.3	555.5	763.5	640.2	735.3	1,034.5	887.8	1,080.6	1,203.1	8,769.8
2006	1,013.7	1,012.0	1,479.2	1,207.6	1,465.1	1,262.1	963.1	1,262.2	1,486.2	1,387.1	1,563.9	1,997.4	16,099.5
2007	1,639.3	1,485.2	2,151.4	1,330.1	1,705.8	2,066.0	1,946.6	1,964.1	1,668.3	1,729.8	1,793.9	1,319.3	20,799.8
2008	1,541.0	1,442.5	1,886.1	1,979.0	1,633.7	2,058.8	1,896.4	1,805.7	2,151.8	1,584.1	1,240.3	1,278.1	20,497.4
2009	1,446.3	1,457.1	1,721.8	1,509.2	1,736.4	2,609.0	2,127.0	2,126.5	2,644.3	2,864.8	2,389.1	2,222.4	24,853.8
2010	2,258.4	2,538.3	3,253.0	2,367.8	3,139.4	2,906.1	2,170.7	2,349.4	2,541.7	2,305.1	2,299.2	2,091.1	30,220.2
2011	2,520.0	2,519.3	2,933.2	2,170.3	2,578.2	2,683.0	2,159.4	2,348.8	2,732.7	2,313.8	2,015.5	2,054.4	29,028.8

Contract size = 62,500 GBP.   *Source: CME Group; Chicago Mercantile Exchange (CME)*

Average Open Interest of British Pound Futures in Chicago   In Contracts

Year	Jan.	Feb.	Mar.	Apr.	May	June	July	Aug.	Sept.	Oct.	Nov.	Dec.
2002	26,450	31,023	30,474	39,952	46,178	47,355	38,138	31,320	31,513	29,599	40,901	36,671
2003	36,892	33,066	27,042	25,274	36,171	50,118	41,702	46,979	40,183	55,884	66,660	70,197
2004	61,694	68,173	51,968	43,830	45,843	53,615	68,262	71,503	60,274	66,565	87,487	86,572
2005	67,140	70,872	81,799	80,850	88,397	79,278	75,387	73,199	81,479	79,854	84,884	91,497
2006	83,051	97,226	83,641	83,275	106,555	98,417	91,563	129,334	120,737	106,288	145,026	157,837
2007	147,183	152,892	135,618	130,611	130,861	145,405	157,336	124,948	110,905	118,737	128,761	96,974
2008	87,465	94,154	98,154	109,464	158,836	126,688	100,775	105,857	112,717	110,761	113,147	93,313
2009	81,141	84,191	88,354	82,933	91,683	92,365	90,994	98,358	88,658	104,344	96,882	83,847
2010	86,016	116,480	136,357	122,843	145,514	136,099	126,486	138,872	97,056	89,011	95,465	80,042
2011	92,434	118,770	118,434	114,166	111,901	103,047	106,501	100,953	142,668	174,087	162,814	206,391

Contract size = 62,500 GBP.   *Source: CME Group; Chicago Mercantile Exchange (CME)*

CURRENCIES

Canadian Dollar Futures - International Monetary Market
(weekly close) as of December 30, 2011

USD per CAD

Canadian Dollars per U.S. Dollar

Year	Jan.	Feb.	Mar.	Apr.	May	June	July	Aug.	Sept.	Oct.	Nov.	Dec.	Average
2002	1.5996	1.5961	1.5872	1.5814	1.5491	1.5312	1.5447	1.5685	1.5747	1.5783	1.5715	1.5588	1.5701
2003	1.5395	1.5119	1.4752	1.4567	1.3819	1.3520	1.3801	1.3948	1.3638	1.3226	1.3128	1.3121	1.4003
2004	1.2967	1.3292	1.3282	1.3410	1.3774	1.3582	1.3225	1.3127	1.2880	1.2476	1.1958	1.2177	1.3013
2005	1.2248	1.2386	1.2157	1.2368	1.2553	1.2402	1.2239	1.2048	1.1781	1.1777	1.1813	1.1619	1.2116
2006	1.1573	1.1488	1.1571	1.1440	1.1094	1.1139	1.1287	1.1191	1.1161	1.1281	1.1365	1.1531	1.1343
2007	1.1757	1.1708	1.1687	1.1351	1.0948	1.0655	1.0512	1.0585	1.0260	0.9752	0.9680	1.0021	1.0743
2008	1.0114	1.0001	1.0031	1.0130	0.9999	1.0170	1.0133	1.0539	1.0582	1.1797	1.2204	1.2337	1.0670
2009	1.2244	1.2449	1.2638	1.2244	1.1502	1.1274	1.1225	1.0878	1.0812	1.0547	1.0587	1.0558	1.1413
2010	1.0435	1.0561	1.0233	1.0052	1.0415	1.0397	1.0433	1.0408	1.0335	1.0180	1.0128	1.0081	1.0305
2011	0.9939	0.9875	0.9767	0.9574	0.9682	0.9771	0.9558	0.9814	1.0023	1.0201	1.0253	1.0238	0.9891

Average.   *Source: FOREX*

Volume of Trading of Canadian Dollar Futures in Chicago   In Thousands of Contracts

Year	Jan.	Feb.	Mar.	Apr.	May	June	July	Aug.	Sept.	Oct.	Nov.	Dec.	Total
2002	222.9	191.5	338.3	249.6	222.2	358.7	278.8	204.2	279.1	245.3	207.4	324.4	3,122.3
2003	270.8	256.7	475.5	289.2	353.1	494.2	331.3	266.2	393.3	285.7	294.4	509.3	4,219.6
2004	380.7	328.0	516.3	380.3	337.1	504.0	366.5	419.4	640.8	512.0	499.5	726.8	5,611.3
2005	548.6	483.0	678.0	592.9	555.2	761.5	562.2	566.3	914.2	671.3	736.0	861.0	7,930.2
2006	695.1	648.6	1,040.9	654.9	816.6	1,043.4	658.3	811.0	1,073.7	805.8	960.8	1,070.4	10,279.6
2007	795.9	724.5	1,089.4	749.9	949.9	1,348.4	1,101.2	1,015.5	1,226.6	1,054.0	1,238.3	931.2	12,224.8
2008	960.2	957.8	1,202.2	948.1	958.2	1,151.9	932.0	966.4	1,240.9	812.9	601.8	645.8	11,378.0
2009	625.5	685.7	1,040.2	964.4	1,222.0	1,691.7	1,318.6	1,319.2	1,644.8	1,626.3	1,569.5	1,773.2	15,481.2
2010	1,391.4	1,623.9	1,989.7	1,742.0	2,329.7	2,120.7	1,774.7	1,839.7	1,905.7	1,841.7	1,889.4	1,635.3	22,083.8
2011	1,477.5	1,505.0	2,143.4	1,403.3	1,943.9	2,213.2	1,557.3	2,545.8	2,479.4	2,000.8	1,624.9	1,522.3	22,416.7

Contract size = 100,000 CAD.   *Source: CME Group; Chicago Mercantile Exchange (CME)*

Average Open Interest of Canadian Dollar Futures in Chicago   In Contracts

Year	Jan.	Feb.	Mar.	Apr.	May	June	July	Aug.	Sept.	Oct.	Nov.	Dec.
2002	68,927	72,132	70,484	68,120	81,574	86,250	74,347	63,116	63,605	57,031	60,648	71,852
2003	82,870	105,051	107,507	97,515	96,689	85,665	68,741	63,518	70,261	79,754	82,366	74,271
2004	74,577	64,032	61,981	72,750	84,356	68,458	73,164	83,483	97,486	112,648	110,035	81,976
2005	74,703	84,753	93,986	77,680	95,229	79,464	86,451	101,128	120,542	108,095	106,773	122,584
2006	103,427	118,978	103,066	92,541	114,587	107,605	89,443	91,591	112,788	99,209	121,729	146,474
2007	151,511	144,025	140,775	119,430	163,570	180,961	147,966	132,910	136,952	145,923	120,912	99,261
2008	86,448	99,650	109,567	103,486	115,665	103,145	95,618	120,175	116,163	103,135	94,297	66,313
2009	59,962	70,940	70,863	63,119	83,214	88,873	87,203	98,521	91,989	97,587	89,022	94,758
2010	106,475	92,349	143,969	148,414	125,802	102,117	87,121	100,655	101,319	113,964	116,126	110,800
2011	123,984	139,328	141,949	141,548	124,951	108,081	118,209	111,898	102,180	118,239	127,296	143,821

Contract size = 100,000 CAD.   *Source: CME Group; Chicago Mercantile Exchange (CME)*

Euro¹ per U.S. Dollar

Year	Jan.	Feb.	Mar.	Apr.	May	June	July	Aug.	Sept.	Oct.	Nov.	Dec.	Average
2002	.8828	.8706	.8767	.8866	.9179	.9567	.9924	.9781	.9810	.9818	1.0020	1.0210	.9456
2003	1.0636	1.0778	1.0795	1.0875	1.1580	1.1670	1.1374	1.1154	1.1260	1.1701	1.1714	1.2314	1.1321
2004	1.2604	1.2633	1.2263	1.1999	1.2013	1.2147	1.2265	1.2192	1.2226	1.2504	1.3001	1.3415	1.2439
2005	1.3110	1.3020	1.3178	1.2940	1.2685	1.2156	1.2049	1.2299	1.2246	1.2030	1.1796	1.1861	1.2448
2006	1.2121	1.1940	1.2033	1.2282	1.2773	1.2665	1.2693	1.2811	1.2734	1.2623	1.2893	1.3200	1.2564
2007	1.2989	1.3087	1.3249	1.3512	1.3511	1.3422	1.3720	1.3620	1.3918	1.4234	1.4681	1.4561	1.3709
2008	1.4722	1.4759	1.5527	1.5760	1.5560	1.5569	1.5765	1.4954	1.4367	1.3286	1.2723	1.3518	1.4709
2009	1.3253	1.2805	1.3074	1.3207	1.3675	1.4014	1.4087	1.4267	1.4565	1.4817	1.4926	1.4577	1.3939
2010	1.4270	1.3681	1.3574	1.3427	1.2536	1.2212	1.2803	1.2899	1.3092	1.3899	1.3640	1.3227	1.3272
2011	1.3374	1.3661	1.4018	1.4472	1.4324	1.4400	1.4289	1.4339	1.3754	1.3727	1.3551	1.3148	1.3921

Average.   Source: FOREX

Volume of Trading of Euro FX Futures in Chicago   In Thousands of Contracts

Year	Jan.	Feb.	Mar.	Apr.	May	June	July	Aug.	Sept.	Oct.	Nov.	Dec.	Total
2002	567.8	582.3	783.3	650.2	611.4	917.7	821.6	525.5	675.3	525.2	426.7	625.4	7,712.3
2003	610.6	749.2	977.9	785.5	902.7	1,103.8	866.2	824.5	1,112.4	1,069.6	958.9	1,232.6	11,193.9
2004	1,487.3	1,469.2	1,837.7	1,326.7	1,328.9	1,682.2	1,491.2	1,518.5	1,798.7	1,786.0	2,138.5	2,591.9	20,456.7
2005	2,646.0	2,266.4	2,772.9	2,992.0	2,771.6	3,656.1	2,732.6	2,765.1	3,206.6	2,613.6	3,164.2	2,943.6	34,530.7
2006	2,956.0	2,563.9	3,411.2	2,984.4	4,496.3	3,765.7	2,789.0	3,229.5	3,364.0	3,123.5	3,790.4	4,316.6	40,790.4
2007	3,701.9	3,032.1	4,427.3	2,979.1	3,337.4	3,877.6	3,560.5	4,074.2	3,286.6	3,831.5	3,793.1	3,161.6	43,063.1
2008	3,669.9	3,327.5	4,709.2	4,596.3	4,537.8	5,312.0	4,661.3	5,009.7	6,216.8	4,556.3	3,607.9	3,447.8	53,652.6
2009	3,574.5	3,903.4	4,564.5	3,155.7	3,758.9	5,261.4	4,675.6	4,220.4	5,123.9	5,429.9	5,419.9	5,305.7	54,393.6
2010	5,407.6	6,439.6	7,562.4	7,157.1	9,578.8	7,913.1	6,006.4	6,418.2	7,294.2	7,476.0	8,241.8	6,737.2	86,232.4
2011	7,402.8	6,451.9	7,437.7	5,453.1	7,657.0	7,504.8	6,906.8	8,061.0	8,376.7	7,008.3	6,638.4	5,338.4	84,236.8

Contract size = 125,000 EUR.   *Source: CME Group; Chicago Mercantile Exchange (CME)*

Average Open Interest of Euro FX Futures in Chicago   In Contracts

Year	Jan.	Feb.	Mar.	Apr.	May	June	July	Aug.	Sept.	Oct.	Nov.	Dec.
2002	100,258	108,955	113,075	112,413	136,660	135,364	112,462	101,992	99,365	85,462	103,156	108,602
2003	105,762	106,905	100,759	85,604	108,619	111,651	96,338	98,671	95,553	102,568	113,601	131,560
2004	125,879	133,690	115,712	112,361	138,193	120,281	140,430	160,315	121,180	136,959	202,074	175,374
2005	135,748	152,110	140,879	130,131	154,751	163,584	142,826	148,309	149,184	142,879	171,035	160,065
2006	133,092	150,085	152,674	166,920	196,057	177,700	155,865	173,151	155,567	152,410	182,079	214,241
2007	173,989	196,963	205,366	217,899	222,019	204,945	218,401	221,095	221,268	207,644	221,736	204,536
2008	179,767	206,661	200,084	178,993	211,068	193,878	170,675	153,423	163,948	180,955	169,315	144,926
2009	127,134	156,321	141,863	110,261	124,438	130,793	129,062	133,469	156,493	168,629	169,331	155,488
2010	169,083	199,832	211,780	216,500	285,206	251,763	226,656	242,448	198,817	203,635	198,138	172,703
2011	190,755	202,950	225,190	244,014	257,695	222,331	184,688	178,500	231,100	228,018	251,778	297,070

Contract size = 125,000 EUR.   *Source: CME Group; Chicago Mercantile Exchange (CME)*

CURRENCIES

Japanese Yen Futures - International Monetary Market
(weekly close) as of December 30, 2011

USD per JPY

Japanese Yen per U.S. Dollar

Year	Jan.	Feb.	Mar.	Apr.	May	June	July	Aug.	Sept.	Oct.	Nov.	Dec.	Average
2002	132.77	133.50	131.11	130.75	126.29	123.25	118.02	119.04	120.88	123.92	121.50	121.83	125.24
2003	118.76	119.39	118.76	119.81	117.37	118.31	118.64	118.61	114.94	109.51	109.17	107.70	115.91
2004	106.38	106.70	108.51	107.61	112.05	109.44	109.46	110.24	110.10	108.81	104.71	103.79	108.15
2005	103.29	104.98	105.35	107.19	106.71	108.75	111.92	110.62	111.19	114.84	118.42	118.39	110.14
2006	115.53	117.92	117.31	116.97	111.77	114.65	115.69	115.95	117.14	118.61	117.28	117.43	116.35
2007	120.45	120.40	117.33	118.96	120.82	122.65	121.47	116.78	115.08	115.92	110.92	112.37	117.76
2008	107.71	107.11	100.80	102.69	104.33	106.88	106.87	109.41	106.62	100.15	96.80	91.13	103.37
2009	90.33	92.86	97.74	98.94	96.49	96.67	94.46	94.90	91.40	90.32	89.12	89.99	93.60
2010	91.13	90.17	90.71	93.49	91.88	90.81	87.56	85.38	84.38	81.79	82.58	83.23	87.76
2011	82.61	82.57	81.65	83.18	81.14	80.47	79.29	77.05	76.88	76.68	77.54	77.83	79.74

Average. *Source: FOREX*

Volume of Trading of Japanese Yen Futures in Chicago   In Thousands of Contracts

Year	Jan.	Feb.	Mar.	Apr.	May	June	July	Aug.	Sept.	Oct.	Nov.	Dec.	Total
2002	415.7	417.5	630.8	391.7	318.5	461.7	301.2	234.2	499.2	349.5	255.4	535.8	4,811.1
2003	423.9	388.3	634.4	453.4	495.6	621.0	518.8	427.0	731.0	396.6	353.4	641.8	6,085.2
2004	410.1	484.9	741.8	516.4	415.5	685.8	487.5	490.7	807.6	629.6	650.5	1,074.9	7,395.3
2005	789.9	718.8	1,045.2	915.4	876.2	1,263.0	946.9	1,012.4	1,285.4	963.7	1,001.0	1,653.9	12,471.7
2006	1,221.1	1,128.7	1,950.5	1,385.9	1,890.9	1,905.3	1,317.9	1,395.9	1,965.8	1,525.1	1,852.8	2,137.5	19,677.4
2007	1,602.2	2,006.6	3,286.7	1,771.1	1,802.4	2,777.8	3,083.8	3,954.2	2,860.7	2,493.1	3,125.2	2,056.6	30,820.4
2008	3,013.2	2,558.7	3,384.5	2,632.6	2,502.9	3,193.9	2,898.0	2,428.9	3,446.2	3,117.8	1,937.5	1,730.2	32,844.4
2009	1,644.2	1,802.9	1,796.0	1,469.3	1,600.9	1,932.6	2,061.8	1,924.0	2,260.9	2,157.6	1,916.7	2,182.7	22,749.6
2010	2,321.3	2,382.1	2,664.8	2,397.2	3,481.7	3,094.9	2,712.4	2,591.6	3,065.3	2,171.1	2,484.6	2,495.8	31,862.8
2011	2,542.6	2,572.2	3,764.0	2,438.4	2,297.9	2,563.3	2,023.5	2,701.8	2,393.6	2,135.9	1,425.0	1,510.9	28,369.1

Contract size = 12,500,000 JPY.   *Source: CME Group; Chicago Mercantile Exchange (CME)*

Average Open Interest of Japanese Yen Futures in Chicago   In Contracts

Year	Jan.	Feb.	Mar.	Apr.	May	June	July	Aug.	Sept.	Oct.	Nov.	Dec.
2002	129,917	123,735	95,535	72,358	88,905	88,324	77,168	71,683	79,980	80,104	74,584	99,643
2003	116,574	107,929	101,809	81,168	107,090	102,507	107,450	125,884	149,978	152,368	138,799	147,255
2004	156,929	156,416	120,848	117,483	108,078	105,505	106,280	110,234	93,780	127,644	181,093	172,526
2005	164,708	155,593	132,268	134,802	172,574	164,580	161,763	170,290	159,227	186,631	202,939	191,591
2006	168,309	198,855	203,450	201,459	210,578	197,160	191,480	218,893	239,426	258,509	242,216	265,490
2007	312,252	338,933	246,715	234,352	303,537	347,031	302,278	272,937	227,242	225,047	202,361	195,324
2008	197,886	233,558	224,932	176,577	171,298	171,516	185,657	207,309	168,119	142,938	128,891	130,118
2009	112,194	108,893	90,828	79,142	86,624	81,378	95,456	80,087	119,014	118,478	123,821	110,809
2010	116,578	121,216	117,096	131,315	143,384	111,812	129,460	135,623	130,539	142,646	133,612	111,840
2011	112,265	119,793	118,104	123,251	102,290	101,702	121,491	128,615	135,195	151,744	147,224	168,945

Contract size = 12,500,000 JPY.   *Source: CME Group; Chicago Mercantile Exchange (CME)*

Swiss Franc Futures - International Monetary Market
(weekly close) as of December 30, 2011

USD per CHF

Swiss Francs per U.S. Dollar

Year	Jan.	Feb.	Mar.	Apr.	May	June	July	Aug.	Sept.	Oct.	Nov.	Dec.	Average
2002	1.6710	1.6972	1.6741	1.6527	1.5868	1.5389	1.4731	1.4968	1.4929	1.4922	1.4647	1.4360	1.5564
2003	1.3748	1.3609	1.3617	1.3770	1.3091	1.3196	1.3597	1.3813	1.3741	1.3234	1.3314	1.2627	1.3446
2004	1.2425	1.2458	1.2773	1.2954	1.2818	1.2501	1.2458	1.2625	1.2624	1.2338	1.1702	1.1455	1.2428
2005	1.1802	1.1906	1.1763	1.1955	1.2183	1.2663	1.2935	1.2626	1.2657	1.2872	1.3100	1.3056	1.2460
2006	1.2781	1.3056	1.3044	1.2822	1.2185	1.2319	1.2362	1.2319	1.2440	1.2597	1.2351	1.2102	1.2532
2007	1.2438	1.2385	1.2179	1.2128	1.2217	1.2329	1.2076	1.2034	1.1847	1.1743	1.1229	1.1397	1.2000
2008	1.1001	1.0894	1.0116	1.0141	1.0443	1.0363	1.0278	1.0843	1.1091	1.1429	1.1923	1.1393	1.0826
2009	1.1280	1.1635	1.1540	1.1472	1.1057	1.0810	1.0784	1.0677	1.0399	1.0218	1.0117	1.0304	1.0858
2010	1.0341	1.0719	1.0660	1.0682	1.1325	1.1263	1.0531	1.0392	1.0012	.9688	.9852	.9671	1.0428
2011	.9567	.9495	.9187	.8964	.8733	.8404	.8221	.7810	.8734	.8963	.9086	.9335	.8875

Average. *Source: FOREX*

Volume of Trading of Swiss Franc Futures in Chicago   In Thousands of Contracts

Year	Jan.	Feb.	Mar.	Apr.	May	June	July	Aug.	Sept.	Oct.	Nov.	Dec.	Total
2002	195.3	183.2	281.3	211.5	208.1	297.0	187.2	218.5	323.1	237.6	207.8	271.6	2,822.1
2003	236.1	289.9	412.7	256.9	277.8	384.9	315.0	252.1	349.9	237.2	283.8	300.5	3,596.7
2004	216.1	230.1	359.6	260.0	255.7	370.9	331.4	313.7	404.5	428.3	329.0	568.4	4,067.8
2005	444.3	389.1	575.5	605.0	521.4	753.4	546.4	596.4	888.8	765.9	797.1	901.2	7,784.5
2006	803.5	745.9	1,129.0	837.5	1,011.3	993.3	771.2	1,014.8	1,046.8	919.6	1,078.1	1,118.9	11,470.0
2007	994.4	998.5	1,418.5	959.4	1,100.0	1,507.0	1,660.0	1,588.2	1,113.7	1,129.8	1,067.3	941.8	14,478.7
2008	1,090.5	1,082.4	1,311.8	1,350.7	1,362.8	1,789.1	1,650.0	1,330.3	1,578.9	1,042.4	574.0	651.3	14,814.2
2009	677.7	624.5	813.9	641.5	731.2	1,094.1	844.8	727.0	1,015.2	1,098.5	1,206.6	1,143.5	10,618.6
2010	1,046.8	954.5	1,218.2	1,105.8	1,299.4	1,066.8	813.5	806.1	997.7	847.7	940.4	914.3	12,011.2
2011	848.8	1,025.6	1,266.4	827.0	928.5	1,074.6	936.2	1,098.0	643.1	539.6	489.5	561.4	10,238.7

Contract size = 125,000 CHF.   *Source: CME Group; Chicago Mercantile Exchange (CME)*

Average Open Interest of Swiss Franc Futures in Chicago   In Contracts

Year	Jan.	Feb.	Mar.	Apr.	May	June	July	Aug.	Sept.	Oct.	Nov.	Dec.
2002	35,116	44,388	45,434	38,248	55,039	54,573	42,060	38,102	37,675	35,796	48,951	50,107
2003	56,268	57,099	50,008	37,451	53,642	49,688	41,489	50,677	52,641	54,259	62,584	60,475
2004	45,259	42,950	41,250	38,563	38,024	48,654	51,116	40,256	33,539	47,200	74,988	70,330
2005	51,858	56,240	50,827	41,322	55,995	78,794	72,596	67,489	66,009	75,088	91,072	98,443
2006	80,904	107,509	101,445	82,280	98,416	89,254	67,127	69,406	83,545	73,433	81,366	74,522
2007	83,176	103,073	70,627	66,246	89,737	121,557	108,394	118,597	100,948	73,433	81,366	73,025
2008	67,993	67,786	71,972	60,528	65,029	58,511	56,337	61,521	53,448	39,448	42,315	31,420
2009	26,083	32,701	33,518	28,613	34,585	40,027	35,918	39,324	49,537	51,736	52,912	41,890
2010	36,523	41,531	36,834	38,093	49,842	48,989	52,203	55,870	58,484	53,703	45,087	44,460
2011	42,658	46,656	62,300	65,373	70,315	61,349	50,716	20,516	33,972	25,587	29,848	44,100

Contract size = 125,000 CHF.   *Source: CME Group; Chicago Mercantile Exchange (CME)*

CURRENCIES

United States Merchandise Trade Balance[1]   In Millions of Dollars

Year	Jan.	Feb.	Mar.	Apr.	May	June	July	Aug.	Sept.	Oct.	Nov.	Dec.	Total
2002	-33,731	-36,175	-36,071	-38,623	-39,158	-39,583	-38,650	-41,047	-41,094	-39,426	-43,722	-47,212	-474,492
2003	-44,579	-43,367	-47,001	-45,579	-45,030	-43,808	-44,859	-43,526	-45,511	-45,234	-43,873	-48,040	-540,407
2004	-48,758	-48,921	-51,439	-52,043	-52,435	-58,815	-55,995	-56,858	-55,825	-59,476	-63,398	-59,543	-663,506
2005	-61,048	-63,303	-58,797	-62,464	-61,534	-63,391	-63,163	-63,748	-70,335	-72,974	-69,634	-70,340	-780,731
2006	-72,784	-67,368	-67,870	-68,551	-71,120	-69,534	-72,573	-74,130	-71,165	-65,810	-65,670	-69,113	-835,688
2007	-65,644	-66,263	-70,371	-68,432	-67,763	-68,470	-68,971	-66,883	-67,579	-68,099	-71,565	-68,846	-818,886
2008	-71,456	-73,922	-70,706	-74,158	-73,696	-72,092	-77,388	-71,326	-70,225	-69,967	-53,436	-51,736	-830,108
2009	-46,762	-36,862	-38,691	-39,272	-35,776	-36,868	-42,973	-41,091	-45,461	-44,117	-47,918	-50,118	-505,909
2010	-48,932	-51,466	-52,434	-52,686	-54,323	-58,950	-53,675	-57,669	-56,477	-52,347	-52,499	-54,399	-645,857
2011[1]	-61,290	-59,363	-60,715	-57,805	-65,104	-66,801	-60,941	-60,667	-59,260	-58,471	-62,836	-65,039	-738,292

[1] Not seasonally adjusted.   [2] Preliminary.   *Source: Bureau of Economic Analysis, U.S. Department of Commerce (BEA)*

Index of Real Trade-Weighted Dollar Exchange Rates for Total Agriculture[3]   (2000 = 100)

Year		Jan.	Feb.	Mar.	Apr.	May	June	July	Aug.	Sept.	Oct.	Nov.	Dec.
2004	U.S. Markets	101.5	102.2	103.0	103.6	106.0	105.0	103.9	103.7	103.3	102.0	99.5	98.2
	U.S. Competitors	100.4	100.6	102.8	103.9	105.4	104.9	103.5	103.7	103.2	101.4	98.4	95.9
2005	U.S. Markets	98.5	98.7	98.4	99.8	99.7	100.2	100.7	100.0	100.6	101.6	101.3	100.1
	U.S. Competitors	97.0	97.2	96.7	98.2	98.8	101.1	102.0	100.6	101.3	102.4	102.6	101.7
2006	U.S. Markets	99.2	99.4	99.9	100.0	98.6	100.2	100.1	99.2	98.9	98.6	97.7	97.0
	U.S. Competitors	100.7	101.1	101.1	100.1	97.8	99.3	99.1	98.0	97.9	97.6	95.8	93.9
2007	U.S. Markets	98.2	98.2	98.2	97.6	97.0	96.9	95.7	95.6	94.2	92.3	91.4	91.7
	U.S. Competitors	95.0	94.7	94.3	92.8	92.4	92.7	90.9	91.7	90.2	87.7	86.1	86.3
2008	U.S. Markets	91.3	90.3	89.0	88.9	89.4	89.9	89.4	90.5	92.1	97.1	97.5	95.8
	U.S. Competitors	85.9	85.1	82.6	81.9	82.5	82.8	82.1	84.8	88.3	94.8	97.4	93.8
2009	U.S. Markets	97.1	100.0	101.5	98.5	95.7	95.5	94.9	93.7	93.0	91.5	91.0	90.8
	U.S. Competitors	95.9	98.9	98.4	96.1	92.9	91.2	90.7	89.3	88.0	86.3	85.6	86.5
2010[1]	U.S. Markets	90.8	91.4	90.5	89.9	92.0	92.4	91.0	90.0	89.2	86.7	86.6	87.1
	U.S. Competitors	87.5	89.8	89.6	89.5	93.8	95.4	92.3	91.3	90.0	86.1	86.8	88.2
2011[2]	U.S. Markets	86.6	86.1	85.9	85.1	85.1	85.1	84.2	84.8	87.2	86.2	86.5	86.9
	U.S. Competitors	87.7	86.4	85.4	83.3	83.9	83.6	83.7	84.0	87.3	87.6	88.4	89.2

[1] Not seasonally adjusted.   [2] Preliminary.   *Source: Bureau of Economic Analysis, U.S. Department of Commerce (BEA)*

United States Balance on Current Account[1]   In Millions of Dollars

Year	First Quarter	Second Quarter	Third Quarter	Fourth Quarter	Annual
2002	-90,578	-115,483	-127,439	-123,747	-457,247
2003	-121,771	-130,453	-140,772	-126,094	-519,090
2004	-122,939	-156,708	-170,077	-178,795	-628,519
2005	-157,499	-180,858	-198,197	-209,220	-745,774
2006	-179,410	-203,977	-229,364	-187,870	-800,621
2007	-178,113	-187,484	-181,362	-163,345	-710,304
2008	-153,313	-177,568	-193,833	-152,421	-677,135
2009	-78,632	-83,888	-110,832	-103,200	-376,552
2010	-97,320	-122,085	-139,537	-111,956	-470,898
2011[1]	-94,881	-128,115	-128,517	-121,927	-473,440

[1] Not seasonally adjusted.   [2] Estimate.   *Source: Bureau of Economic Analysis, U.S. Department of Commerce (BEA)*

Merchandise Trade and Current Account Balances[1]   In Billions of Dollars

Year	Merchanise Trade Balance					Current Account Balance				
	Canada	Germany	Japan	Switzerland	United Kingdom	Canada	Germany	Japan	Switzerland	United Kingdom
2003	32.5	96.3	69.3	21.4	-43.1	10.6	47.6	136.4	43.4	-30.0
2004	42.7	135.2	89.0	25.0	-59.8	22.9	125.0	172.3	48.6	-45.5
2005	42.5	143.6	63.3	25.0	-77.6	21.6	138.5	166.8	52.4	-59.1
2006	32.0	164.6	54.5	32.4	-75.0	18.0	181.4	171.2	58.6	-79.6
2007	27.1	235.8	73.3	44.6	-85.4	11.8	250.8	210.2	39.1	-69.4
2008	24.3	226.6	6.1	57.2	-73.7	6.4	228.9	158.8	9.5	-35.8
2009	-22.8	165.6	15.7	54.6	-39.9	-40.3	189.5	142.6	56.8	-31.4
2010	-29.6	176.7	62.4	59.9	-61.5	-49.3	184.1	196.1	82.7	-56.9
2011[2]	-25.2	159.9	-49.6	75.9	-40.3	-49.0	177.2	130.0	85.5	-14.1
2012[3]	-28.9	149.6	-54.8	66.9	-29.8	-50.7	173.5	136.4	79.5	2.2

[1] Not seasonally adjusted.   [2] Estimate.   [3] Projection.   *Source: Organization for Economic Cooperation and Development (OECD)*

Euro / Swiss Franc (weekly close) as of December 30, 2011   EUR per CHF

Euro / British Pound (weekly close) as of December 30, 2011   EUR per GBP

Japanese Yen / British Pound (weekly close) as of December 30, 2011   JPY per GBP

Euro / Japanese Yen (weekly close) as of December 30, 2011   JPY per EUR

Diamonds

The diamond, which is the mineral form of carbon, is the hardest, strongest natural material known on earth. The name *diamond* is derived from adamas, the ancient Greek term meaning "invincible." Diamonds form deep within the Earth's crust and are typically billions of years old. Diamonds have also have been found in and near meteorites and their craters. Diamonds are considered precious gemstones but lower grade diamonds are used for industrial applications such as drilling, cutting, grinding and polishing.

Supply – World production of natural gem diamonds in 2009 rose by +4.5% yr/yr to 90.900 million carats, but still down from the 2006 record high of 93.800 million

carats (one carat equals 1/5 gram or 200 milligrams). The world's largest producers of natural gem diamonds are Botswana with 35% of world production in 2009, Russia with 24%, Australia with 8%, Angola with 9%, South Africa with 6%, and the Congo with 6%. World production of natural industrial diamonds in 2009 was down -18.9% yr/yr to 54.600 million carats. World production of synthetic diamonds in 2009 was down -0.9% yr/yr to 4.380 million carats. The main producer of synthetic diamonds was China with 91.3% of world production.

Trade – The U.S. in 2010 relied on net imports for 85% of its consumption of natural diamonds.

World Production of Natural Gem Diamonds   In Thousands of Carats

Year	Angola	Australia	Botswana	Brazil	Central African Republic	China	Dem Rep. of Congo	Ghana	Namibia	Russia	Suerra Leone	South Africa	World Total
2004	5,490	6,058	23,300	300	263	100	5,900	725	2,004	23,700	318	5,800	88,400
2005	6,371	8,577	23,900	208	300	100	7,000	810	1,902	23,000	401	6,400	92,800
2006	8,258	7,305	24,000	181	340	100	5,800	780	2,400	23,400	362	6,100	93,700
2007	8,732	231	25,000	182	370	100	5,700	720	2,200	23,300	362	6,100	91,500
2008[1]	8,016	273	25,000	182	302	100	4,200	520	1,500	21,925	223	5,200	87,000
2009[2]	8,100	60	24,000	182	300	100	3,600	500	2,000	17,791	200	2,400	90,900

[1] Preliminary.   [2] Estimate.   *Source: U.S. Geological Survey (USGS)*

World Production of Natural Industrial Diamonds[4]   In Thousands of Carats

Year	Angola	Australia	Botswana	Brazil	Central African Republic	China	Ghana	Russia	Leone	South Africa	Venezuela	Dem. Rep of Congo[3]	World Total
2004	610	18,172	7,800	600	88	960	23,600	180	15,200	374	8,500	60	76,700
2005	708	25,730	8,000	600	80	960	28,200	200	15,000	267	9,400	69	90,400
2006	918	21,915	8,000	600	85	965	23,100	190	15,000	241	9,100	70	81,400
2007	970	18,960	8,000	600	93	970	22,600	180	15,000	241	9,100	70	77,800
2008[1]	900	15,397	8,000	600	75	1,000	16,700	130	15,000	149	7,700	70	67,300
2009[2]	900	10,700	7,000	600	60	1,000	14,400	120	15,000	100	3,100	70	54,600

[1] Preliminary.   [2] Estimate.   [3] Formerly Zaire.   *Source: U.S. Geological Survey (USGS)*

World Production of Synthetic Diamonds   In Thousands of Carats

Year	Belarus	China	Czech Republic	France	Greece	Ireland	Japan	Russia	South Africa	Sweden	Ukraine	United States	World Total
2004	25,000	3,800,000	5	3,000	----	60,000	34,000	80,000	60,000	20,000	8,000	252,000	4,340,000
2005	25,000	3,800,000	5	3,000	----	60,000	34,000	80,000	60,000	20,000	8,000	126,000	4,220,000
2006	25,000	3,900,000	5	3,000	----	60,000	34,000	80,000	60,000	20,000	8,000	128,000	4,320,000
2007	25,000	4,000,000	5	3,000	----	60,000	34,000	80,000	60,000	20,000	8,000	130,000	4,420,000
2008[1]	25,000	4,000,000	5	3,000	----	60,000	34,000	80,000	60,000	20,000	8,000	131,000	4,420,000
2009[2]	25,000	4,000,000	5	3,000		60,000	34,000	80,000	60,000	20,000	8,000	91,000	4,380,000

[1] Preliminary.   [2] Estimate.   *Source: U.S. Geological Survey (USGS)*

Salient Statistics of Industrial Diamonds in the United States   In Millions of Carats

	Bort, Grit & Powder & Dust Natural and Synthetic								Stones (Natural)					Net
	Production													Import
Year	Manufactured Diamond	Secondary	Imports for Consumption	Exports & Reexports	In Manufactured Products	Gov't Sales	Apparent Consumption	Price Value of Imports $/Carat	Secondary Production	Imports for Consumption	Exports & Reexports	Gov't Sales	Apparent Consumption	Price Value of Imports $/Carat	Reliance % of Consumption
2005	256.0	4.6	284.0	92.0	----	----	453.0	.27	[3]	2.1	[3]	----	2.2	13.91	77
2006	258.0	34.2	371.0	90.0	----	----	362.0	.22	[3]	2.2	[3]	[3]	2.8	12.61	78
2007	260.0	34.4	411.0	107.0	----	----	386.0	.19	[3]	3.1	----	[3]	3.5	11.54	79
2008	261.0	33.9	492.0	116.0	----	----	458.0	.15	----	3.2	[3]	.5	4.1	12.89	82
2009[1]	260.0	33.5	246.0	67.0	----	----	271.0	.17	----	1.4	----	----	3.0	13.31	71
2010[2]		33.0	520.0	100.0	----	----	490.0	.15	----	1.7	----	----	3.0	18.09	85

[1] Preliminary.   [2] Estimate.   [3] Less than 1/2 unit.   *Source: U.S. Geological Survey (USGS)*

Eggs

Eggs are a low-priced protein source and are consumed worldwide. Each commercial chicken lays between 265-280 eggs per year. In the United States, the grade and size of eggs are regulated under the federal Egg Products Inspection Act (1970). The grades of eggs are AA, A, and B, and must have sound, whole shells and must be clean. The difference among the grades of eggs is internal and mostly reflects the freshness of the egg. Table eggs vary in color and can be determined by the color of the chicken's earlobe--white earlobes lay white eggs, reddish--brown earlobes lay brown eggs, etc. In the U.S., egg size is determined by the weight of a dozen eggs, not individual eggs, and range from Peewee to Jumbo. Store-bought eggs in the shell stay fresh for 3 to 5 weeks in a home refrigerator, according to the USDA.

Eggs are primarily used as a source of food, although eggs are also widely used for medical purposes. Fertile eggs, as a source of purified proteins, are used to produce many vaccines. Flu vaccines are produced by growing single strains of the flu virus in eggs, which are then extracted to make the vaccine. Eggs are also used in biotechnology to create new drugs. The hen's genetic make-up can be altered so the whites of the eggs are rich in tailored proteins that form the basis of medicines to fight cancer and other diseases. The U.S. biotech company Viragen and the Roslin Institute in Edinburgh have produced eggs with 100 mg or more of the easily-extracted proteins used in new drugs to treat various illnesses including ovarian and breast cancers.

Prices – The average monthly price of all eggs received by farmers in the U.S. in 2011 rose by +12.7% yr/yr to 97.5 cents per dozen, below the 2008 record high of 106.5 cents per dozen.

Supply – World egg production in 2010 was 1.193 billion eggs. The world's largest egg producers at that time were China with 39.9% of world production, the U.S. with 7.7%, Mexico with 4.0%, Japan with 3.5%, Russia with 3.4%, and Brazil with 3.3%. U.S. egg production in 2011 rose +0.5% to 91.877 billion eggs, a new record high. The average number of hens and pullets on U.S. farms in 2011 fell by -0.6% yr/yr to 338.3428 million, down further from the 2006 record high of 347.880 million.

Demand – U.S. consumption of eggs in 2011 fell -0.3% yr/yr to 6.400 billion dozen eggs. That was down from the 2006 record high of 6.468 billion dozen, but still up about 20% from ten years earlier, reflecting sharply higher egg consumption due to the popularity of a low-carbohydrate diet since eggs are high in protein. U.S. per capita egg consumption in 2011 rose +0.3% yr/yr to 248.0 eggs per year per person. Per capita egg consumption was at a high of 277.2 eggs in 1970, then fell sharply in the 1990s to a low of 174.9 in 1995, and then began rebounding in 1997 to current levels of about 250 eggs per year.

Trade – U.S. imports of eggs in 2011 fell -3.2% yr/yr to 12.0 million dozen eggs. U.S. exports of eggs in 2011 fell -3.0% yr/yr to 237.0 million dozen eggs, below the record export level of 253.1 million dozen eggs in 1996.

World Production of Eggs   In Millions of Eggs

Year	Brazil	China	France	Germany	Italy	Japan	Mexico	Russia	Spain	Ukraine	United Kingdom	United States	World Total
2002	30,951	393,179	16,480	14,262	12,855	42,157	38,012	36,106	13,113	11,159	10,272	87,216	1,008,368
2003	31,423	403,660	16,598	12,588	12,838	42,173	37,451	36,296	13,722	11,380	10,116	87,473	1,021,075
2004	32,319	410,015	15,757	12,353	13,054	41,346	40,033	35,562	15,213	11,883	10,704	89,091	1,044,306
2005	33,499	420,951	15,502	12,028	12,896	41,377	40,494	36,691	13,122	12,955	10,608	90,027	1,066,577
2006	35,207	418,718	15,138	12,137	12,123	41,611	45,801	37,651	13,122	14,122	10,166	91,800	1,090,433
2007	35,584	436,664	14,640	11,974	12,929	43,050	45,817	37,889	13,095	13,978	9,920	91,044	1,122,242
2008	36,893	465,486	13,355	12,103	13,393	42,567	46,744	37,804	12,896	14,809	10,277	90,012	1,160,022
2009[1]	38,438	472,673	13,174	10,577	14,509	41,750	46,700	39,188	13,166	15,303	10,300	90,408	1,177,577
2010[2]	38,961	476,498	13,522	10,220	14,509	41,900	47,623	40,368	13,330	16,865	10,300	91,557	1,193,558

[1] Preliminary.   [2] Forecast.   [3] Selected countries.   *Source: Food and Agricultural Organization of the United Nations (FAO)*

Salient Statistics of Eggs in the United States

	--- Hens & Pullets ---		Rate of Lay Per Layer	----- Eggs -----						----- Consumption -----		
	On Farm Dec. 1[3]	Average Number During Year	During Year[4]	Total Produced	Price in cents Per Dozen	Value of Production[5] Million USD	Total Egg Production	Imports[6]	Exports[6]	Used for Hatching	Total	Per Capita Eggs[6]
Year	----- Thousands -----		(Number)	----- Millions -----			-------------------- Million Dozen --------------------					Number
2003	340,979	338,393	259	87,473	73.2	5,333	7,299	13.3	146.0	959.4	6,204	255.7
2004	344,278	341,956	261	89,091	71.4	5,299	7,450	12.7	167.6	988.1	6,306	257.3
2005	347,917	343,792	262	90,027	54.0	4,049	7,538	8.5	203.3	996.7	6,345	255.8
2006	348,719	347,880	263	91,328	58.2	4,432	7,650	8.6	202.1	992.2	6,468	257.8
2007	344,492	346,498	263	91,101	88.5	6,719	7,587	13.6	250.3	1,016.3	6,335	250.1
2008	339,643	339,131	266	90,040	109.0	8,216	7,501	14.6	206.3	996.3	6,307	248.9
2009	339,526	337,848	268	90,484	81.7	6,166	7,534	11.0	242.2	955.1	6,347	247.7
2010[1]	341,551	340,335	269	91,482		6,518	7,638	12.4	244.3	985.4	6,421	247.3
2011[2]	338,449	338,428	271	91,855			7,635	12.0	237.0	1,010.0	6,400	247.3

[1] Preliminary.   [2] Forecast.   [3] All layers of laying age.   [4] Number of eggs produced during the year divided by the average number of all layers of laying age on hand during the year.   [5] Value of sales plus value of eggs consumed in households of producers. 6/ Shell-egg equivalent of eggs and egg products.   *Source: National Agricultural Statistics Service, U.S. Department of Agriculture (NASS-USDA)*

EGGS

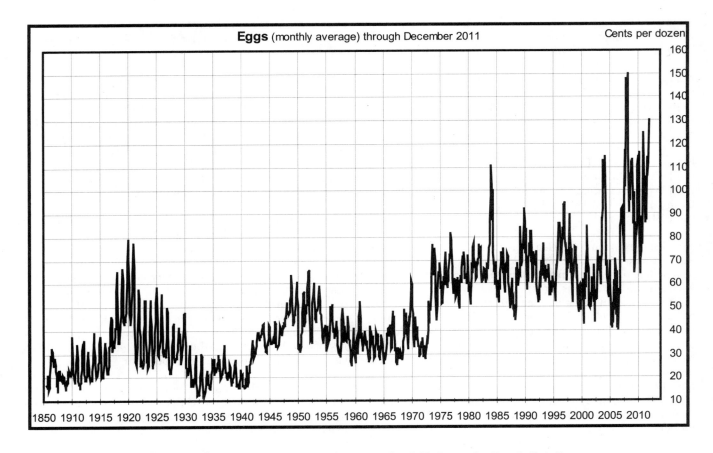

Eggs (monthly average) through December 2011   Cents per dozen

Average Price Received by Farmers for All Eggs in the United States   In Cents Per Dozen

Year	Jan.	Feb.	Mar.	Apr.	May	June	July	Aug.	Sept.	Oct.	Nov.	Dec.	Average
2002	62.3	55.9	68.5	52.2	50.5	62.1	60.8	66.4	57.1	56.0	70.7	62.8	60.4
2003	63.6	59.3	68.7	68.6	58.7	67.2	68.7	80.8	77.6	83.8	102.0	86.8	73.8
2004	92.6	87.5	110.0	76.7	62.6	77.3	64.0	52.6	53.8	49.4	60.4	65.4	71.0
2005	55.8	55.1	52.6	47.4	45.6	45.2	52.7	47.1	63.6	51.1	65.0	71.9	54.4
2006	61.0	49.5	67.0	51.2	42.7	54.7	43.5	55.0	53.4	54.1	81.2	80.7	57.8
2007	91.5	78.1	82.8	72.9	78.0	73.4	94.5	86.6	107.0	93.5	126.0	136.0	93.4
2008	129.0	131.0	138.0	103.0	86.8	106.0	84.1	96.3	99.6	102.0	102.0	99.9	106.5
2009	103.0	80.9	81.6	92.0	61.7	59.4	70.8	75.8	74.4	80.0	101.0	105.0	82.1
2010	103.0	91.7	116.0	79.4	63.3	61.9	70.9	78.9	68.4	83.6	113.0	108.0	86.5
2011[1]	85.0	95.4	80.7	105.0	82.3	88.3	88.0	117.0	102.0	102.0	102.0	122.0	97.5

[1] Preliminary.   *Source: Economic Research Service, U.S. Department of Agriculture (ERS-USDA)*

Average Wholesale Price of Shell Eggs (Large) Delivered, Chicago   In Cents Per Dozen

Year	Jan.	Feb.	Mar.	Apr.	May	June	July	Aug.	Sept.	Oct.	Nov.	Dec.	Average
2002	60.43	52.00	68.00	47.23	43.73	56.40	53.02	57.16	53.20	54.43	74.00	66.38	57.17
2003	69.57	65.39	71.05	68.83	59.10	68.76	72.39	88.26	86.21	92.07	113.16	101.09	79.66
2004	105.10	103.89	115.00	86.88	67.28	70.00	63.12	59.45	55.81	53.79	60.36	69.83	75.88
2005	54.78	60.26	48.32	42.00	41.57	40.72	51.38	42.78	61.19	48.38	62.41	70.21	52.00
2006	65.40	46.08	65.11	57.11	41.32	56.14	40.30	57.46	54.97	55.64	84.38	87.65	59.30
2007	91.75	92.71	89.23	80.00	83.55	69.60	99.95	97.37	117.50	101.89	128.93	147.70	100.02
2008	144.55	142.70	150.15	115.23	90.64	107.33	95.43	100.07	108.98	103.85	110.50	109.50	114.91
2009	113.40	92.29	85.64	99.26	64.55	72.41	73.55	85.69	80.17	86.14	110.75	114.41	89.86
2010	111.50	107.55	116.80	84.81	64.15	69.68	73.74	88.73	83.17	76.88	124.79	124.73	93.88
2011[1]	100.20	99.08	86.37	106.05	87.31	86.95	92.70	114.07	105.93	111.79	112.50	130.07	102.75

[1] Preliminary.   *Source: National Agricultural Statistics Service, U.S. Department of Agriculture (NASS-USDA)*

Total Egg Production in the United States   In Millions of Eggs

Year	Jan.	Feb.	Mar.	Apr.	May	June	July	Aug.	Sept.	Oct.	Nov.	Dec.	Total
2002	7,264	6,581	7,417	7,105	7,297	7,126	7,347	7,356	7,147	7,412	7,226	7,451	86,729
2003	7,390	6,665	7,424	7,187	7,327	7,105	7,403	7,367	7,112	7,439	7,326	7,554	87,299
2004	7,386	6,901	7,547	7,358	7,513	7,289	7,557	7,538	7,344	7,659	7,482	7,721	89,295
2005	7,626	6,928	7,738	7,407	7,572	7,346	7,563	7,528	7,348	7,665	7,514	7,793	90,028
2006	7,727	6,980	7,843	7,543	7,637	7,401	7,645	7,647	7,430	7,678	7,549	7,815	90,895
2007	7,675	6,951	7,806	7,472	7,622	7,380	7,599	7,594	7,393	7,726	7,542	7,808	90,568
2008	7,646	7,114	7,675	7,373	7,564	7,367	7,599	7,551	7,339	7,625	7,490	7,778	90,121
2009	7,678	6,903	7,737	7,472	7,607	7,360	7,590	7,593	7,376	7,696	7,569	7,853	90,434
2010	7,724	6,935	7,839	7,578	7,716	7,484	7,719	7,765	7,514	7,698	7,573	7,920	91,465
2011[1]	7,821	7,006	7,836	7,617	7,777	7,505	7,740	7,734	7,510	7,790	7,612	7,929	91,877

[1] Preliminary.   Source: National Agricultural Statistics Service, U.S. Department of Agriculture (NASS-USDA)

Per Capita Disappearance of Eggs[4] in the United States   In Number of Eggs

Year	First Quarter	Second Quarter	Third Quarter	Fourth Quarter	Total	Total Con-sumption (Million Dozen)	Year	First Quarter	Second Quarter	Third Quarter	Fourth Quarter	Total	Total Con-sumption (Million Dozen)
2001	64.5	64.2	64.7	66.6	252.7	6,043	2007	62.2	61.7	62.4	63.8	250.1	6,335
2002	62.4	62.6	64.0	64.6	256.0	6,150	2008	61.8	61.3	62.0	63.8	248.9	6,307
2003	62.6	63.0	63.8	65.3	255.7	6,204	2009	62.0	61.5	61.4	62.9	247.7	6,347
2004	63.7	63.9	64.1	65.5	257.3	6,306	2010[1]	61.4	61.3	62.0	62.7	247.3	6,421
2005	63.4	63.0	63.5	65.0	255.8	6,345	2011[2]	60.9	61.2	62.1	63.0	247.3	6,400
2006	64.1	63.7	63.9	64.7	257.8	6,468	2012[3]	61.9	61.8	61.8	62.6	248.0	

[1] Preliminary.   [2] Estimate.   [3] Forecast.   Source: Economic Research Service, U.S. Department of Agriculture (ERS-USDA)

Egg-Feed Ratio[1] in the United States

Year	Jan.	Feb.	Mar.	Apr.	May	June	July	Aug.	Sept.	Oct.	Nov.	Dec.	Average
2002	10.2	8.4	11.6	7.4	6.7	9.5	7.5	7.9	7.1	6.6	10.5	8.9	8.5
2003	9.0	8.0	9.5	9.3	6.9	8.8	9.8	12.7	11.6	12.6	15.7	12.2	10.5
2004	12.9	10.7	13.2	7.8	6.0	6.6	5.9	5.6	6.5	5.8	8.8	9.8	8.3
2005	7.2	7.4	6.3	5.2	4.6	4.4	5.9	5.1	9.3	6.6	10.3	11.3	7.0
2006	8.5	5.9	9.8	6.3	4.2	7.1	4.6	7.5	6.9	6.4	10.6	10.1	7.3
2007	11.7	8.4	9.1	7.6	8.1	6.4	10.7	9.5	12.3	10.2	13.9	13.9	10.2
2008	12.7	11.1	11.8	7.4	5.8	7.3	5.4	6.6	7.7	8.9	9.4	9.2	8.6
2009	9.0	7.0	7.2	8.4	4.3	3.8	5.6	6.5	6.8	7.3	10.0	10.3	7.2
2010	10.1	8.9	12.2	7.0	5.1	5.0	6.0	6.9	4.6	6.5	9.5	8.1	7.5
2011[1]	5.8	6.0	5.1	6.4	4.5	4.9	4.9	6.7	5.6	6.8	6.8	8.7	6.0

[1] Pounds of laying feed equivalent in value to one dozen eggs.   [2] Preliminary.   Source: Economic Research Service, U.S. Department of Agriculture (ERS-USDA)

Hens and Pullets of Laying Age (Layers) in the United States, on First of Month   In Thousands

Year	Jan.	Feb.	Mar.	Apr.	May	June	July	Aug.	Sept.	Oct.	Nov.	Dec.
2002	339,423	338,465	337,478	337,376	336,131	335,547	335,236	335,717	336,561	337,923	338,350	339,827
2003	340,752	341,019	340,080	339,645	336,678	335,611	333,925	334,381	334,248	334,103	336,528	339,989
2004	338,272	338,774	340,479	342,879	342,305	343,233	342,392	342,522	343,405	344,794	345,267	344,278
2005	347,273	348,412	349,117	344,759	342,346	341,247	338,424	338,674	339,984	341,803	343,789	347,917
2006	349,763	349,930	350,452	350,453	346,809	343,596	341,733	340,728	342,309	343,946	345,090	348,719
2007	349,192	348,563	349,081	347,280	343,835	341,057	339,373	340,648	340,604	341,322	343,909	344,492
2008	345,535	343,891	342,666	341,320	340,318	339,867	337,416	335,094	335,396	333,534	336,301	339,643
2009	341,373	341,388	340,716	341,067	339,239	334,953	333,064	332,371	332,808	334,917	336,671	339,526
2010	341,411	339,747	341,191	342,969	339,635	339,018	340,442	339,384	340,749	336,691	337,300	341,551
2011[1]	343,745	339,626	339,021	341,872	339,471	336,327	336,574	335,657	336,353	335,067	337,307	338,449

[1] Preliminary.   Source: National Agricultural Statistics Service, U.S. Department of Agriculture (NASS-USDA)

EGGS

Eggs Laid Per Hundred Layers in the United States   In Number of Eggs

Year	Jan.	Feb.	Mar.	Apr.	May	June	July	Aug.	Sept.	Oct.	Nov.	Dec.	Average
2002	2,143	1,947	2,198	2,110	2,173	2,125	2,190	2,188	2,119	2,192	2,139	2,189	2,143
2003	2,168	1,957	2,184	2,125	2,180	2,122	2,215	2,203	2,128	2,218	2,166	2,223	2,157
2004	2,182	2,032	2,209	2,148	2,192	2,126	2,207	2,198	2,134	2,220	2,170	2,234	2,171
2005	2,192	1,986	2,230	2,156	2,215	2,162	2,234	2,218	2,155	2,236	2,172	2,234	2,183
2006	2,210	1,994	2,238	2,164	2,212	2,160	2,240	2,239	2,165	2,228	2,176	2,234	2,188
2007	2,200	1,993	2,242	2,162	2,226	2,169	2,235	2,229	2,168	2,255	2,191	2,255	2,194
2008	2,218	2,072	2,244	2,163	2,224	2,175	2,260	2,252	2,194	2,277	2,216	2,283	2,215
2009	2,249	2,024	2,269	2,197	2,256	2,203	2,281	2,283	2,209	2,292	2,239	2,303	2,234
2010	2,268	2,037	2,291	2,220	2,274	2,203	2,271	2,283	2,218	2,286	2,231	2,311	2,241
2011[1]	2,289	2,065	2,302	2,236	2,301	2,231	2,303	2,302	2,237	2,317	2,253	2,344	2,265

[1] Preliminary.   Source: National Agricultural Statistics Service, U.S. Department of Agriculture (NASS-USDA)

Egg-Type Chicks Hatched by Commercial Hatcheries in the United States   In Thousands

Year	Jan.	Feb.	Mar.	Apr.	May	June	July	Aug.	Sept.	Oct.	Nov.	Dec.	Total
2002	35,655	34,473	36,985	38,096	38,760	35,144	35,581	35,689	35,742	32,157	31,154	32,113	421,549
2003	33,521	30,474	36,775	37,820	37,630	36,602	35,578	33,199	35,763	34,812	30,241	33,588	416,003
2004	35,155	31,923	37,545	37,466	38,347	37,508	34,919	36,854	36,631	34,866	38,758	37,332	437,304
2005	38,339	34,365	41,883	37,646	38,999	35,078	34,721	38,548	33,812	35,450	32,300	35,925	437,066
2006	35,230	33,473	38,910	35,549	39,827	37,475	32,860	35,779	37,048	36,345	31,623	33,254	427,373
2007	36,176	37,071	38,672	39,634	37,744	40,421	35,927	36,969	35,386	36,310	36,219	36,033	446,562
2008	40,156	38,429	42,189	42,329	41,829	40,704	37,234	35,594	37,179	40,288	34,247	37,585	467,763
2009	37,826	36,809	41,752	42,808	40,772	41,980	36,227	38,078	40,310	37,392	34,525	39,502	467,981
2010	38,819	39,218	44,914	47,558	43,231	42,331	38,089	37,014	40,130	41,300	38,849	37,759	489,212
2011[1]	41,366	37,336	43,974	43,429	43,305	39,313	37,405	41,564	40,298	37,845	37,508	38,879	482,222

[1] Preliminary.   Source: National Agricultural Statistics Service, U.S. Department of Agriculture (NASS-USDA)

Cold Storage Holdings of Frozen Eggs in the United States, on First of Month   In Millions of Pounds[2]

Year	Jan.	Feb.	Mar.	Apr.	May	June	July	Aug.	Sept.	Oct.	Nov.	Dec.
2002	13.7	13.1	13.9	11.7	10.2	11.1	12.7	12.9	13.2	13.2	13.1	11.2
2003	13.5	15.3	17.1	17.0	15.7	17.7	18.0	18.6	18.0	16.6	16.9	14.9
2004	18.0	21.3	21.1	19.2	20.9	20.6	18.3	16.7	17.3	18.7	17.9	17.3
2005	19.1	18.6	17.9	18.5	18.9	17.7	19.7	19.6	19.9	18.8	17.6	17.6
2006	21.0	22.5	24.5	20.8	23.3	21.0	22.1	23.6	21.6	19.0	16.3	17.1
2007	16.5	17.2	15.7	14.6	14.3	15.2	17.4	17.5	18.5	17.7	17.6	15.2
2008	14.7	12.0	16.7	16.3	16.0	12.4	16.1	21.1	20.8	21.9	22.4	21.3
2009	22.6	22.6	22.1	20.3	18.2	21.7	21.7	22.6	22.6	21.6	22.9	21.2
2010	23.6	24.3	24.1	21.6	22.4	22.4	25.0	24.7	24.7	26.1	25.6	22.9
2011[1]	25.4	26.8	28.1	27.3	27.7	29.0	33.8	33.9	31.0	31.9	33.9	33.0

[1] Preliminary.   [2] Converted on basis 39.5 pounds frozen eggs equals 1 case.   Source: National Agricultural Statistics Service, U.S. Department of Agriculture (NASS-USDA)

Electric Power

The modern electric utility industry began in the 1800s. In 1807, Humphry Davy constructed a practical battery and demonstrated both incandescent and arc light. In 1831, Michael Faraday built the first electric generator proving that rotary mechanical power could be converted into electric power. In 1879, Thomas Edison perfected a practical incandescent light bulb. The electric utility industry evolved from gas and electric carbon-arc commercial and street lighting systems. In 1882, in New York City, Thomas Edison's Pearl Street electricity generating station established the industry by displaying the four key elements of a modern electric utility system: reliable central generation, efficient distribution, successful end use, and a competitive price.

Electricity is measured in units called watts and watt-hours. Electricity must be used when it is generated and cannot be stored to any significant degree. That means the power utilities must match the level of electricity generation to the level of demand in order to avoid wasteful over-production. The power industry has been deregulated to some degree in the past decade and now major utility companies sell power back and forth across major national grids in order to meet supply and demand needs. The rapid changes in the supply-demand situation mean that the cost of electricity can be very volatile.

Electricity futures trade at the New York Mercantile Exchange (NYMEX). The futures contract is a financially settled contract, which is priced based on electricity prices in the PJM western hub at 111 delivery points, mainly on the utility transmission systems of Pennsylvania Electric Co. and the Potomac Electric Co. The contract is priced in dollars and cents per megawatt hours.

Supply – U.S. electricity production in 2010 (annualized through September) rose +3.7% yr/yr to 2.460 trillion kilowatt-hours. That was well below the record high of 3.212 trillion kilowatt-hours in 1998 and indicated that recent electricity production has been reduced by more efficient production and distribution systems, and to some extent by conservation of electricity by both business and residential consumers.

U.S. electricity generation in 2009 required the use of 2.911 trillion cubic feet of natural gas (+6.6% yr/yr), 695 million tons of coal (8.5% yr/yr), and 45 million barrels of fuel oil (-9.6% yr/yr).

In terms of kilowatt-hours, coal is the most widely used source of electricity production in the U.S. accounting for 46.6% of electricity production in 2010 (latest data), followed by natural gas (24.7%), nuclear (20.3%), hydro (6.5%), and fuel oil (0.9%). Alternative sources of fuel for electricity generation that are gaining favor include geothermal, biomass, solar, wind, etc. but so far account for only 4.7% of total electricity production in the U.S.

Demand – Residential use of electricity accounts for the largest single category of electricity demand with usage of 1.362 trillion kilowatt hours in 2009 accounting for 38.1% of overall usage. Business users in total use more electricity than residential users, but business users are broken into the categories of commercial with 37.0% of usage and industrial with 24.7% of usage.

World Electricity Production (Monthly Average) In Millions of Kilowatt Hours

Year	Australia	Canada	China	Germany	India	Italy	Japan	Rep. of Korea	Russia	South Africa	Ukraine	United Kingdom	United States
2002	15,646	57,873	133,513	47,211	44,141	23,638	77,139	25,500	74,078	18,142	14,477	29,220	321,538
2003	15,564	56,294	153,229	49,060	52,773	24,386	76,661	26,856	76,158	19,267	15,030	35,006	307,250
2004	16,095	56,844	176,169	44,439	48,968	24,975	71,574	28,472	77,562	20,648	15,180	34,924	316,000
2005	16,870	49,559	199,780	48,840	51,125	25,754	72,667	30,363	79,355	20,673	15,505	33,377	336,499
2006	19,077	48,758	229,119	45,030	54,309	26,037	74,906	31,773	82,619	21,150	16,115	33,272	338,725
2007	18,958	50,265	265,047	43,565	57,933	26,070	82,731	33,594	84,656	21,957	16,272	30,117	346,395
2008	19,793	50,141	282,692	43,565	59,874	26,393	82,573	35,313	86,429	21,524	15,982	29,607	343,282
2009	19,287	47,910	301,774	39,528	63,035	24,160	76,494	36,109	82,681	20,796	14,412	28,456	329,426
2010[1]	19,392	47,229	343,943	41,190	66,179	24,851	77,414	39,679	86,413	21,632	15,640	28,967	343,336
2011[2]		49,216	381,680	38,467	70,968	25,054	74,519	41,024	85,184	21,367	15,653	25,693	351,564

[1] Preliminary. [2] Estimate. NA = Not avaliable. *Source: United Nations*

Installed Capacity, Capability & Peak Load of the U.S. Electric Utility Industry In Thousands of Megawatts (Nameplate)

| | Total Electric Utility | ------- Type of Prime Mover ------- | | | | | -------------- Type of Ownership -------------- | | | | | Capability at Winter Peak | Non-Coincident Winter Peak | Capacity Margin Non-Coincident Peak | Total Electric Utility Industry Generation | Annual Peak Load Factor |
Year	Industry	Hydro & Steam	Gas Turbine & Steam	Nuclear Power	Internal Combustion	Investor	Cooper-ative	Sub-total Gov't.	Munic-ipal Utilities	Federal	Power Districts, State Projects	Load	Load	Load (%)	(Mil. kWh)	(%)
1990	735.1	87.2	531.1	108.0	8.7	568.8	26.3	139.9	40.1	65.4	34.4	696.8	484.8	20.4	2,901.3	60.4
1991	740.0	88.7	534.1	108.4	8.8	573.0	26.5	140.5	40.4	65.6	34.5	703.2	486.4	20.2	2,935.6	60.9
1992	741.7	89.7	534.5	107.9	9.6	572.9	26.0	142.7	41.6	66.1	35.0	707.8	493.6	21.1	2,934.4	61.1
1993	744.7	90.2	536.9	107.8	9.8	575.2	26.1	143.4	41.8	66.1	35.5	712.0	522.4	17.1	3,043.9	61.0
1994	764.0	90.3	537.9	107.9	9.9	574.8	26.4	144.7	42.0	66.3	36.4	715.1	518.9	16.7	3,088.7	61.2
1995	769.0	91.1	541.6	107.9	9.9	578.7	27.1	144.8	42.2	65.9	36.6	727.7	545.4	13.2	3,194.2	59.8
1996	463.0	91.0	546.6	109.0	9.9	582.2	27.2	147.1	43.0	67.2	36.9	740.5	554.1	27.7	3,284.1	61.0
1997	775.9	92.5	549.7	107.6	10.0	582.5	28.0	149.4	43.8	68.9	36.7	743.8	529.9	26.0	3,329.4	61.3
1998	778.6	91.2	522.1	104.8	10.2	531.3	32.5	164.5	50.5	68.7	45.3	835.3	567.6	25.7	3,457.4	62.0
1999[1]	775.9	89.8	476.3	102.3	9.6	483.7	34.6	159.6	50.2	68.7	40.7	848.9	570.9	26.7	3,530.0	61.2

[1] Preliminary. *Source: Edison Electric Institute (EEI)*

ELECTRIC POWER

Available Electricity and Energy Sales in the United States In Billions of Kilowatt Hours

	Net Generation — Electric Utility Industry							Sales to Ultimate Customer								
Year	Total[2]	Hydro	Natural Gas	Coal	Fuel Oil	Nu-clear	Other Sources[3]	Total	Total Million $	Total	Resi-den-tial	Inter-depart-mental	Com-mercial	Indus-trial	Street & highway Lighting	Other Public Auth.	Rail-ways & Rail-roads
2001	3,580	217.0	639.1	1,904	124.9	768.8	82.9	3,737	247,343	3,394	1,202	[4]	1,083.1	997	[4]	113.2	[4]
2002	3,698	264.3	691.0	1,933	94.6	780.1	95.4	3,858	249,411	3,465	1,265	[4]	1,104.5	990	[4]	105.6	[4]
2003	3,721	275.8	649.9	1,974	119.4	763.7	100.6	3,883	259,767	3,494	1,276	[4]	1,198.7	1,012	[4]	NA	[4]
2004	3,808	268.4	710.1	1,978	121.1	788.5	104.1	3,971	270,119	3,547	1,292	[4]	1,230.4	1,018	[4]	NA	[4]
2005	3,902	270.3	761.0	2,013	122.2	782.0	107.1	4,055	298,003	3,661	1,359	[4]	1,275.1	1,019	[4]	NA	[4]
2006	3,908	289.2	816.4	1,991	64.2	787.2	117.1	4,065	326,506	3,670	1,352	[4]	1,299.7	1,011	[4]	NA	[4]
2007	4,005	247.5	896.6	2,016	65.7	806.4	124.0	4,157	343,703	3,765	1,392	[4]	1,336.3	1,028	[4]	NA	[4]
2008	3,974	254.8	883.0	1,986	46.2	806.2	143.3	4,119	363,650	3,733	1,380	[4]	1,336.0	1,009	[4]	NA	[4]
2009	3,810	273.4	921.0	1,756	38.9	798.9	162.2	3,950	353,280	3,597	1,364	[4]	1,307.2	917	[4]	NA	[4]
2010[1]	3,971	257.1	981.8	1,851	36.9	807.0	186.5	4,120	368,906	3,754	1,446	[4]	1,330.2	971	[4]	NA	[4]

[1] Preliminary. [2] Includes internal combustion. [3] Includes electricity produced from geothermal, wood, waste, wind, solar, etc. [4] Included in Other.
NA = Not available. *Source: Edison Electric Institute (EEI)*

Electric Power Production by Electric Utilities in the United States In Millions of Kilowatt Hours

Year	Jan.	Feb.	Mar.	Apr.	May	June	July	Aug.	Sept.	Oct.	Nov.	Dec.	Total
2002	215,684	187,929	200,833	194,038	208,436	227,940	248,962	241,449	215,408	201,705	194,205	212,868	2,549,457
2003	217,338	189,944	193,305	181,914	200,634	212,297	234,888	234,675	201,966	192,198	189,362	213,758	2,462,281
2004	221,782	198,675	193,763	182,744	207,224	219,767	235,266	227,785	209,507	197,320	191,813	219,585	2,505,231
2005	212,654	185,283	196,136	178,408	197,082	221,116	239,381	238,790	211,139	193,687	188,255	212,914	2,474,845
2006	204,976	192,304	197,249	184,803	204,107	223,950	243,526	242,624	200,655	193,321	189,435	206,705	2,483,655
2007	218,288	197,329	197,229	184,017	202,783	218,554	234,728	246,147	209,641	197,285	189,498	208,631	2,504,130
2008	220,229	197,368	194,959	185,415	201,811	225,775	239,383	230,563	201,631	186,930	184,192	207,111	2,475,367
2009	216,218	179,859	184,963	174,130	189,695	213,482	221,545	222,452	193,720	184,019	179,276	213,417	2,372,776
2010	222,362	195,895	188,491	172,441	199,835	228,551	243,756	240,185	203,521	178,917	179,858	217,820	2,471,632
2011[1]	220,793	188,371	194,814	183,282	197,103	225,296	253,150	242,139	198,767	181,030			2,501,694

[1] Preliminary. *Source: Energy Information Administration, U.S. Department of Energy (EIA-DOE)*

Use of Fuels for Electric Generation in the United States

Year	Coal (Thousand ShortTons)	Fuel Oil (Thousand Barrels)	Gas (Million Cubic Feet)	Total Fuel in Coal Equiva-lent[3]	Net Generation by Fuels[4] (Million Kilowatt Hour)	Pounds of Coal Per Kilowatt Hour (Pounds)	Cost of Fossil-Fuel at Elec. Utilities (Cents/MMBTU)	Average Cost of Fuel Per Kilowatt Hour (In Cents)	Heat Rate BTU Per Kilowatt Hour	Cost Per Million BTU Consumed (In Cents)
2000	859,335	125,788	3,043,094				173.8			174.0
2001	806,269	133,456	2,686,287				173.0			173.0
2002	767,803	99,219	2,259,684				151.5			186.0
2003	757,384	118,087	1,763,764							228.0
2004	772,224	124,541	1,809,443							248.0
2005	761,349	118,874	2,134,859							325.0
2006	753,390	71,624	2,478,396							302.0
2007	764,765	70,950	2,736,418							323.0
2008	760,326	50,475	2,730,134							411.0
2009[1]	695,615	45,651	2,911,279							304.0

[1] Preliminary. [2] 42-gallon barrels. [3] Coal equivalents are calculated on the basis of Btu instead of generation data. [4] Excludes wood & waste fuels.
Source: Edison Electric Institute (EEI)

Ethanol

World Production of Ethanol   In Millions of Gallons

Year	Brazil	China	France	Germany	India	Russia	Saudi Arabia	South Africa	Spain	Thailand	United Kingdom	United States	World Total
2004	3,989	964	219	71	462	198	79	110	79	74	106	3,404	10,770
2005	4,227	1,004	240	114	449	198	32	103	93	79	92	3,904	12,150
2006	4,491	1,017	251	202	502	171	52	102	122	93	74	4,885	13,489
2007	5,019	486			53						79	6,519	13,102
2008	6,472	502			66						90	9,307	17,335
2009[1]	6,578	542			92						435	10,939	19,535
2010[2]	6,922	542										13,229	

[1] Preliminary.   [2] Estimate.   *Source: Renewable Fuels Association*

Salient Statistics of Ethanol in the United States

Year	Ethanol Plants	Ethanol Production Capacity (mgy)	Plants Under Con-struction	Capacity Under Construction (mgy)	Farmer Owned Plants	Farmer Owned Capacity (mgy)	Percent of Total Capacity Farmer	Farmer Owned UC Plants	Farmers Owned UC Capacity	Percent of Total UC Capacity	States with Ethanol Plants
2004	72	3,100.8	15	598.0	33	1,041.1	34	12	447	75	19
2005	81	3,643.7	16	754.0	40	1,388.6	38	10	450	60	18
2006	95	4,336.4	31	1,778.0	46	1,677.1	39	4	187	11	20
2007	110	5,493.4	76	5,635.5	46	1,677.1	39	4	187	11	21
2008	139	7,888.4	61	5,536.0	49	1,948.6	28	13	771	12	21
2009	170	12,475.4	24	2,066.0	NA	NA	NA	NA	NA	NA	26
2010[1]	189	13,028.4	15	1,432.0	NA	NA	NA	NA	NA	NA	26
2011[2]	204	13,507.9	10	522.0	NA	NA	NA	NA	NA	NA	29

[1] Preliminary.   [2] Estimate.   *Source: Renewable Fuels Association*

Production of Fuel Ethanol in the United States   In Thousands of Barrels Per Day

Year	Jan.	Feb.	Mar.	Apr.	May	June	July	Aug.	Sept.	Oct.	Nov.	Dec.	Average
2004	211	212	214	218	221	222	218	225	226	226	232	233	222
2005	241	245	243	238	237	249	258	260	261	269	275	280	255
2006	288	302	301	289	293	318	316	330	336	339	348	362	319
2007	375	386	384	391	406	418	422	438	447	459	486	492	425
2008	518	535	565	572	605	588	614	647	645	647	671	656	605
2009	631	652	649	646	678	704	738	746	741	757	804	811	713
2010	827	850	854	846	847	854	858	870	874	886	925	918	867
2011[1]	920	907	909	886	895	902	891	907	888	906	945	960	910

[1] Preliminary.   *Source: Energy Information Administration, U.S. Department of Energy (EIA-DOE)*

Production of Fuel Ethanol in the United States   In Thousands of Barrels

Year	Jan.	Feb.	Mar.	Apr.	May	June	July	Aug.	Sept.	Oct.	Nov.	Dec.	Total
2004	6,551	6,155	6,648	6,525	6,857	6,648	6,749	6,977	6,766	7,007	6,946	7,229	81,058
2005	7,461	6,847	7,530	7,135	7,357	7,463	8,007	8,050	7,841	8,335	8,259	8,676	92,961
2006	8,935	8,463	9,333	8,663	9,086	9,531	9,791	10,235	10,088	10,512	10,442	11,215	116,294
2007	11,621	10,795	11,892	11,716	12,573	12,553	13,083	13,581	13,402	14,221	14,568	15,258	155,263
2008	16,058	15,527	17,527	17,152	18,756	17,651	19,040	20,059	19,338	20,048	20,139	20,342	221,637
2009	19,561	18,255	20,121	19,374	21,024	21,125	22,887	23,136	22,218	23,467	24,122	25,134	260,424
2010	25,625	23,802	26,486	25,384	26,244	25,632	26,584	26,964	26,221	27,471	27,747	28,457	316,617
2011[1]	28,524	25,400	28,194	26,591	27,756	27,064	27,624	28,110	26,645	28,092			328,800

[1] Preliminary.   *Source: Energy Information Administration, U.S. Department of Energy (EIA-DOE)*

Stocks of Fuel Ethanol in the United States   In Thousands of Barrels

Year	Jan.	Feb.	Mar.	Apr.	May	June	July	Aug.	Sept.	Oct.	Nov.	Dec.
2004	5,830	5,469	5,578	5,433	5,796	5,345	5,971	6,367	6,641	6,664	6,414	6,002
2005	6,142	6,261	6,605	6,861	6,810	6,064	5,926	5,398	5,317	5,591	5,723	5,563
2006	6,099	7,268	8,626	8,990	7,767	6,675	7,706	9,133	9,725	9,723	9,232	8,760
2007	8,656	8,765	8,539	8,807	8,966	9,171	9,866	11,011	11,555	11,449	11,218	10,535
2008	11,383	11,173	12,288	12,572	13,297	13,323	13,448	14,771	16,110	15,214	15,286	14,226
2009	14,514	15,834	16,411	15,322	14,173	13,974	14,223	14,671	15,283	14,933	15,578	16,594
2010	18,251	19,297	20,222	20,042	19,851	18,565	17,809	17,380	17,437	17,278	18,150	17,941
2011[1]	20,672	20,809	21,440	20,807	20,387	18,833	18,700	17,900	18,437	18,072		

[1] Preliminary.   *Source: Energy Information Administration, U.S. Department of Energy (EIA-DOE)*

ETHANOL

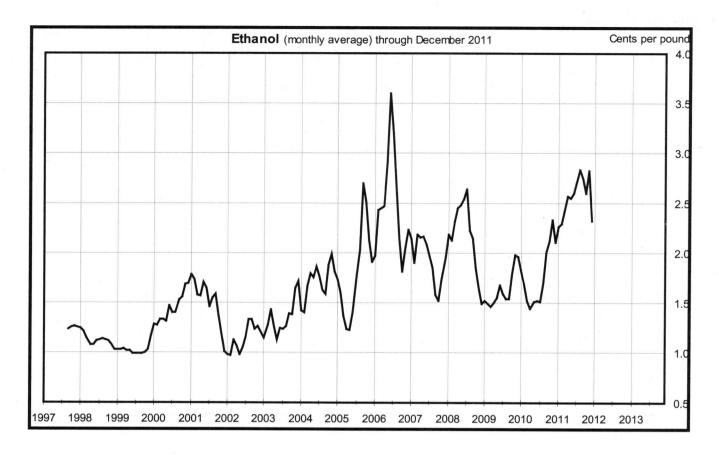

Ethanol (monthly average) through December 2011   Cents per pound

Average Price of Ethanol in the United States[1]   In Dollars Per Gallon

Year	Jan.	Feb.	Mar.	Apr.	May	June	July	Aug.	Sept.	Oct.	Nov.	Dec.	Average
2004	1.423	1.398	1.666	1.791	1.753	1.862	1.762	1.624	1.585	1.878	1.995	1.812	1.712
2005	1.733	1.597	1.365	1.237	1.221	1.405	1.786	2.031	2.695	2.511	2.130	1.916	1.802
2006	1.967	2.428	2.450	2.475	2.903	3.597	3.208	2.668	2.148	1.815	2.045	2.234	2.495
2007	2.144	1.899	2.185	2.159	2.169	2.089	1.970	1.849	1.581	1.523	1.739	1.950	1.938
2008	2.188	2.129	2.316	2.455	2.485	2.535	2.642	2.224	2.150	1.846	1.648	1.493	2.176
2009	1.518	1.488	1.461	1.497	1.553	1.673	1.585	1.535	1.540	1.798	1.984	1.962	1.633
2010	1.817	1.689	1.515	1.439	1.508	1.523	1.507	1.692	2.012	2.120	2.331	2.108	1.772
2011	2.268	2.292	2.435	2.564	2.546	2.600	2.718	2.830	2.745	2.596	2.825	2.324	2.562

[1] Northeast and Northwest Iowa.   *Source: Agricultural Marketing Service, U.S. Department of Agriculture (AMS-USDA)*

Volume of Trading of Ethanol Futures in Chicago   In Contracts

Year	Jan.	Feb.	Mar.	Apr.	May	June	July	Aug.	Sept.	Oct.	Nov.	Dec.	Total
2006	443	508	329	421	330	686	1,141	365	779	348	97	117	5,564
2007	191	526	945	1,153	784	1,163	792	969	704	966	1,436	2,887	12,516
2008	1,889	1,045	1,634	2,594	1,956	2,843	2,156	3,556	2,969	2,857	2,327	3,625	29,451
2009	2,969	2,116	7,158	4,673	4,031	5,535	4,707	4,843	7,439	6,530	6,521	10,646	67,168
2010	9,629	9,887	19,404	12,659	12,794	17,809	15,406	15,073	13,694	13,176	11,952	11,242	162,725
2011	12,857	1,589	18,387	16,665	21,406	25,489	22,550	22,026	22,766	21,370	19,710	20,131	224,946

Contract size = 29,000 US gallons.   *Source: CME Group; Chicago Board of Trade (CBT)*

Month-End Open Interest of Ethanol Futures in Chicago   In Contracts

Year	Jan.	Feb.	Mar.	Apr.	May	June	July	Aug.	Sept.	Oct.	Nov.	Dec.
2006	774	856	860	900	745	735	829	599	474	442	396	322
2007	402	478	593	623	842	1,227	1,100	1,378	1,326	1,642	1,853	2,141
2008	2,328	2,245	2,257	1,862	2,053	2,659	2,763	2,447	2,641	3,055	3,114	2,935
2009	3,146	3,228	4,644	4,145	4,381	4,174	3,877	4,631	4,940	5,575	5,932	6,904
2010	7,186	8,478	7,827	8,603	10,531	11,833	11,720	10,118	10,013	8,267	7,437	7,209
2011	8,259	8,200	7,507	7,748	8,275	9,240	9,619	10,325	9,462	10,658	10,355	9,985

Contract size = 29,000 US gallons.   *Source: CME Group; Chicago Board of Trade (CBT)*

Fertilizer

Fertilizer is a natural or synthetic chemical substance, or mixture, that enriches soil to promote plant growth. The three primary nutrients that fertilizers provide are nitrogen, potassium, and phosphorus. In ancient times, and still today, many commonly used fertilizers contain one or more of the three primary ingredients: manure (containing nitrogen), bones (containing small amounts of nitrogen and large quantities of phosphorus), and wood ash (containing potassium).

At least fourteen different nutrients have been found essential for crops. These include three organic nutrients (carbon, hydrogen, and oxygen, which are taken directly from air and water), three primary chemical nutrients (nitrogen, phosphorus, and potassium), and three secondary chemical nutrients (magnesium, calcium, and sulfur). The others are micronutrients or trace elements and include iron, manganese, copper, zinc, boron, and molybdenum.

Prices – The average price of ammonia, a key source of ingredients for fertilizers, rose by +31.3% yr/yr in 2011 to $520 per metric ton, below the 2008 record high of $590 per metric ton. The average price of potash in the U.S. in 2011 rose by +15.7% yr/yr to a record high of $700.00 per metric ton.

Supply – World production of nitrogen (as contained in ammonia) in 2011 rose +3.8% 136.000 million metric tons, a new record high. The world's largest producers of nitrogen in 2011 were China with 30.2% of world production, India (8.8%), Russia (8.1%), and the U.S. (6.0%). U.S. nitrogen production in 2011 fell -2.3% to 8.100 million metric tons.

World production of phosphate rock, basic slag and guano in 2011 rose +5.5% yr/yr to 191.000 million metric tons. The world's largest producers of phosphate rock in 2011 were China (with 37.7% of world production), U.S. (14.9%), Morocco (14.2%), and Russia (5.8%). U.S. production in 2011 rose +10.1% y/y to 28.400 million metric tons.

World production of marketable potash in 2011 rose +9.8% yr/yr to 37.000 million metric tons, a new record high. The world's largest producers of potash in 2011 were Canada with 30.3% of world production, Russia (20.0%), Belarus (14.9%), and Germany (8.9%). U.S. production of potash in 2011 rose +18.3% yr/yr to 1.100 million metric tons.

Demand – U.S. consumption of nitrogen in 2010 rose +1.9% yr/yr to 10.700 million metric tons, below the 2007decade high of 12.000 million metric tons. U.S. consumption of phosphate rock in 2011 rose +4.3% yr/yr to 31.800 million metric tons. U.S. consumption of potash in 2011 rose +20.4% yr/yr to 6.500 million metric tons, below 2008's decade high of 6.700 million metric tons.

Trade – U.S. imports of nitrogen in 2011 rose +4.9% yr/yr to 5.810 million metric tons and the U.S. relied on imports for 41% of consumption. U.S. imports of phosphate rock in 2011 rose +37.5% yr/yr to 3.300 million metric tons. U.S. imports of potash in 2011 rose +17.7% to 5.600 million metric tons up from the 2009 4-decade low of 2.400 million metric tons. Imports accounted for 83% of U.S. consumption.

World Production of Ammonia   In Thousands of Metric Tons of Contained Nitrogen

Year	Canada	China	France	Germany	India	Indonesia	Japan	Mexico	Nether-lands	Poland	Russia	United States	Total
2003	3,662	31,500	1,153	2,803	10,048	4,250	1,061	439	1,750	1,906	9,100	8,450	110,000
2004	4,107	34,770	1,120	2,741	10,718	4,120	1,101	560	1,970	1,984	9,800	8,990	117,000
2005	4,100	37,850	1,206	2,789	10,800	4,400	1,083	423	1,700	2,080	10,000	8,338	122,000
2006	4,100	40,660	616	2,718	10,900	4,300	1,091	487	1,800	2,007	10,500	8,190	125,000
2007	4,498	42,480	800	2,746	11,000	4,400	1,114	714	1,800	1,995	10,500	8,540	131,000
2008	4,781	41,140	800	2,819	11,100	4,500	1,244	826	1,800	1,995	10,425	7,870	130,000
2009	4,000	42,290	800	2,363	11,200	4,600	1,021	895	1,800	1,990	10,441	7,700	127,000
2010[1]	4,000	40,870	800	2,677	11,500	4,800	1,000	826	1,800	1,900	10,400	8,290	131,000
2011[2]	4,100	41,000		2,700	12,000	4,800	1,000		1,800		11,000	8,100	136,000

[1] Preliminary.   [2] Estimate.   *Source: U.S. Geological Survey (USGS)*

Salient Statistics of Nitrogen[3] (Ammonia) in the United States   In Thousands of Metric Tons

Year	Net Import Reliance As a % of Apparent Consumption	Production[3] (Fixed) Fertilizer	Production[3] (Fixed) Non-fertilizer	Total	Imprts[4] (Fixed)	Exports	Nitrogen[5] Compounds Produced	Nitrogen[5] Compounds Consumption	Stocks, Dec. 31 Ammonia	Stocks, Dec. 31 Fixed Nitrogen Compounds	Ammonia Consumption (Apparent)	Urea FOB Gulf[6] Coast	Urea FOB Corn Belt	Ammonium Nitrate: FOB Corn Belt	Ammonia FOB Gulf Coast
2003	39	7,490	961	8,450	5,720	400	9,122	11,000	195	476	13,900	192-195	215-225	190-195	245
2004	38	8,470	524	8,990	5,900	381	9,258	11,900	298	590	14,400	225-230	255-270	195-210	274
2005	42	7,450	884	8,340	6,520	525	9,099	11,300	254	605	14,400	260-267	300-325	265-270	304
2006	41	7,270	921	8,190	5,920	194	9,083	11,000	201	485	14,000	265-280	295-305	250-260	302
2007	43	7,610	930	8,540	6,530	145	9,485	12,000	157	407	15,000	435-445	465-490	590-620	307
2008	42	6,730	1,140	7,870	6,020	192	8,605	11,500	302	794	13,600	190-210	270-330	450-650	590
2009	38	6,470	1,240	7,700	4,530	16	8,071	10,500	167	364	12,300	307-315	350-360	340-390	251
2010[1]	40	7,130	1,160	8,290	5,540	35	8,597	10,700	165	328	13,800	370-380	415-440	640-685	396
2011[2]	41			8,100	5,810	22			207		13,800				520

[1] Preliminary.   [2] Estimate.   [3] Anhydrous ammonia, synthetic.   [4] For consumption.   [5] Major downstream nitrogen compounds.   [6] Granular.
Source: U.S. Geological Survey (USGS)

FERTILIZER

World Production of Phosphate Rock, Basic Slag & Guano   In Thousands of Metric Tons (Gross Weight)

Year	Brazil	China	Egypt	Israel	Jordan	Morocco	Russia	Senegal	Syria	Togo	Tunisia	United States	World Total
2002	5,084	23,000	1,550	4,091	7,179	23,028	10,700	1,551	2,483	1,271	7,461	36,100	136,000
2003	5,584	25,200	2,183	3,708	6,650	23,338	11,000	1,765	2,414	1,471	7,890	35,000	138,000
2004	5,690	25,500	2,219	3,290	6,188	26,675	11,000	1,580	2,883	1,115	8,051	35,800	143,000
2005	5,450	30,400	2,144	3,236	6,375	28,788	11,000	1,455	3,500	1,350	8,220	36,100	150,000
2006	5,932	38,600	2,177	2,949	5,805	27,400	11,000	584	3,664	1,650	7,801	30,100	151,000
2007	6,185	45,400	3,890	3,069	5,552	27,800	11,400	600	3,678	750	8,005	29,700	160,000
2008	6,343	50,700	5,523	3,088	6,265	24,500	10,400	700	3,221	842	7,623	30,200	165,000
2009	6,000	60,200	6,627	2,697	5,281	18,400	9,500	650	2,466	726	7,398	26,400	161,000
2010[1]	5,700	68,000	6,000	3,135	6,000	25,800	11,000	650	3,000	850	7,600	25,800	181,000
2011[2]	6,200	72,000	6,000	3,200	6,200	27,000	11,000	950	3,100	800	5,000	28,400	191,000

[1] Preliminary.   [2] Estimate.   *Source: U.S. Geological Survey (USGS)*

Salient Statistics of Phosphate Rock in the United States   In Thousands of Metric Tons

Year	Mine Production	Marketable Production	Value Million Dollars	Imports for Consumption	Exports	Apparent Consumption	Producer Stocks, Dec. 31	Avg. Price FOB Mine $/Metric Ton	Avg. Price of Florida & N. Carolina - $/Met. Ton - FOB Mine (-60% to +74%) - Domestic	Export	Average
2002	154,000	36,100	$993	2,700	62	37,400	8,860	$27.47	$27.69	W	$27.69
2003	153,000	35,000	$946	2,400	64	38,800	7,540	$27.01	$26.95	W	$26.95
2004	146,000	35,800	$995	2,500	----	39,000	7,220	$27.79	$27.76	NA	$27.76
2005	151,000	36,100	$1,070	2,630	----	37,800	6,970	$29.61	$29.67	NA	$29.60
2006	111,000	30,100	$919	2,420	----	32,600	7,070	$30.49	W	NA	$30.52
2007	126,000	29,700	$1,520	2,670	----	33,800	4,970	$51.10	W	NA	$51.36
2008	124,000	30,200	$2,320	2,750	----	31,600	6,340	$76.76	W	NA	$76.64
2009	107,000	26,400	$3,360	2,000	----	27,500	8,120	$127.19	W	NA	
2010[1]	106,000	25,800	$1,980	2,400	----	30,500	5,620	$78.50	W	NA	
2011[2]		28,400		3,300	----	31,800	4,800	$94.00	W	NA	

[1] Preliminary.   [2] Estimate.   *Source: U.S. Geological Survey (USGS)*

World Production of Marketable Potash   In Thousands of Metric Tons (K₂O Equivalent)

Year	Belarus	Brazil	Canada	Chile	China	Germany	Israel	Jordan	Russia	Spain	United Kingdom	United States	World Total
2002	3,800	337	8,515	575	450	3,472	1,950	1,191	4,400	481	540	1,200	27,100
2003	4,230	416	9,104	563	650	3,564	1,960	1,194	5,465	594	1,040	1,100	29,900
2004	4,600	403	10,100	559	770	3,627	2,138	1,180	6,405	590	547	1,200	32,200
2005	4,844	405	10,140	547	1,500	3,664	2,224	1,115	7,131	575	439	1,200	33,800
2006	4,605	403	8,518	496	1,800	3,625	2,187	1,036	3,720	435	420	1,100	30,400
2007	4,972	424	11,085	515	2,600	3,637	2,182	1,096	7,275	435	427	1,100	35,700
2008	4,968	383	10,455	559	2,750	3,280	2,170	1,223	6,730	435	427	1,100	34,500
2009	2,485	385	4,318	692	3,000	1,800	2,100	683	3,727	435	427	700	20,800
2010[1]	5,250	453	9,788	800	3,200	3,000	1,960	1,200	6,280	415	427	930	33,700
2011[2]	5,500	400	11,200	800	3,200	3,300	2,000	1,400	7,400	430	430	1,100	37,000

[1] Preliminary.   [2] Estimate.   *Source: U.S. Geological Survey (USGS)*

Salient Statistics of Potash in the United States   In Thousands of Metric Tons (K₂O Equivalent)

Year	Net Import Reliance As a % of Apparent Consumption	Production	Sales by Producers	Value Million Dollars	Imports for Consumption	Exports	Apparent Consumption	Producer Stocks Dec. 31	Dollars per Ton Avg Value of Product	Avg Value of K₂O Equiv	Avg. Price[3] (Metric Ton)
2002	80	1,200	1,200	$280.0	4,620	371	5,400	----	$110.00	$230.00	$155.00
2003	80	1,100	1,200	$280.0	4,720	329	5,600	----	$110.00	$230.00	$170.00
2004	80	1,200	1,300	$340.0	4,920	233	6,000	----	$125.00	$270.00	$200.00
2005	80	1,200	1,200	$410.0	4,920	200	5,900	----	$165.00	$350.00	$280.00
2006	79	1,100	1,100	$410.0	4,470	332	5,200	----	$170.00	$375.00	$290.00
2007	81	1,100	1,200	$480.0	4,970	199	5,900	----	$185.00	$400.00	$400.00
2008	84	1,100	1,100	$740.0	5,800	222	6,700	----	$300.00	$675.00	$700.00
2009	73	720	630	$500.0	2,220	303	2,600	----	$330.00	$800.00	$800.00
2010[1]	83	930	1,000		4,760	297	5,400	----		$600.00	$605.00
2011[2]	83	1,100	1,000		5,600	215	6,500				$700.00

[1] Preliminary.   [2] Estimate.   [3] Unit of K₂O, standard 60% muriate F.O.B. mine.   *Source: U.S. Geological Survey (USGS)*

Fish

Fish are the primary source of protein for a large portion of the world's population. The worldwide yearly harvest of all sea fish (including aquaculture) is between 85 and 130 million metric tons. There are approximately 20,000 species of fish, of which 9,000 are regularly caught. Only 22 fish species are harvested in large amounts. Ground-fish, which are fish that live near or on the ocean floor, account for about 10% of the world's fishery harvest, and include cod, haddock, pollock, flounder, halibut and sole. Large pelagic fish such as tuna, swordfish, marlin, and mahi-mahi, account for about 5% of world harvest. The fish eaten most often in the United States is canned tuna.

Rising global demand for fish has increased the pressure to harvest more fish to the point where all 17 of the world's major fishing areas have either reached or exceeded their limits. Atlantic stocks of cod, haddock and blue-fin tuna are all seriously depleted, while in the Pacific, anchovies, salmon and halibut are all over-fished. Aquaculture, or fish farming, reduces pressure on wild stocks and now accounts for nearly 20% of world harvest.

Supply – The U.S. grand total of fishery products in 2010 rose +4.5% to 19.747 billion pounds, down from a record high of 20.959 billion pounds in 2006. The U.S. total domestic catch in 2010 rose by +2.5% to 8.230 billion pounds, and that comprised 42% of total U.S. supply. Of the U.S. total domestic catch in 2010, 45.3% of the catch was finfish for human consumption, 14.8% of the catch was a variety of fish for industrial use, and 11.4% was shellfish for human consumption. The principal species of U.S. fishery landings in 2008 were Pollock (with 1.958 billion pounds landed), Menhaden (1.471 billion pounds), Pacific Salmon (787 million pounds), Flounder (624 million pounds), and Sea Herring (253 million pounds).

About 30% of the fish harvested in the world are processed directly into fishmeal and fish oil. Fishmeal is used primarily in animal feed. Fish oil is used in both animal feed and human food products. World fishmeal production in the 2010-11 marketing year rose by +4.3% to 4.775 million metric tons. World production of fish oil in 2010-11 rose +7.4% to 1.017 million metric tons. Peru and Chile are by far the world's largest producers of fishmeal and fish oil.

Trade – U.S. imports of fishery products in 2010 rose +6.0% yr/yr to 11.517, a new record high, comprising 58% of total U.S. supply.

| | | | | | -------------- Domestic Catch ----------------- | | | | | ----------------------- Imports ---------------------- | | | | |
Year	Grand Total	**For Human Food** Finfish	Shellfish[3]	For Industrial Use[4]	Total	Percent of Grand Total	**For Human Food** Finfish	Shellfish[3]	Industrial Use[4]	Total	Percent of Grand Total	**For Human Food** Finfish	Shellfish[3]	For Industrial Use[4]
2004	20,413	12,959	4,689	2,765	9,683	47.4	6,641	1,153	1,889	10,730	52.6	6,318	3,536	876
2005	20,612	13,567	4,588	2,457	9,707	47.1	6,914	1,084	1,710	10,905	52.9	6,653	3,505	747
2006	20,960	13,484	5,110	2,366	9,483	45.2	6,671	1,171	1,641	11,477	54.8	6,813	3,939	725
2007	20,561	13,339	4,914	2,308	9,309	45.3	6,415	1,075	1,819	11,252	54.7	6,925	3,838	489
2008	19,200	12,295	4,742	2,163	8,326	43.4	5,590	1,043	1,692	10,874	56.6	6,705	3,699	471
2009	18,899	11,700	4,936	2,262	8,031	42.5	4,930	1,268	1,833	10,868	57.5	6,771	3,668	430
2010[1]	19,748	12,505	5,055	2,188	8,231	41.7	5,216	1,310	1,705	11,517	58.3	7,288	3,746	483

[1] Preliminary.   [2] Live weight, except percent.   [3] For univalue and bivalues mollusks (conchs, clams, oysters, scallops, etc.) the weight of meats, excluding the shell is reported.   [4] Fish meal and sea herring.   *Source: Fisheries Statistics Division, U.S. Department of Commerce*

Fisheries -- Landings of Principal Species in the United States   In Millions of Pounds

| | | | | | | | | | | | --------------------------- Shellfish --------------------------- | | | | |
| | -- Fish ----------------------------- | | | | | | | | | Clams | | Lobsters | Oysters | Scallops | |
Year	Cod, Atlantic	Flounder	Halibut	Herring, Sea	Man-haden	Pollock	Salmon, Pacific	Tuna	Whiting	(Meats)	Crabs	American	----- (Meats) -----		Shrimp
2004	16	360	80	265	1,498	3,365	739	57	19	119	316	88	88	39	65	309
2005	14	419	76	303	1,244	3,426	899	44	17	106	299	93	34	34	59	261
2006	13	446	71	290	1,307	3,414	664	50	12	111	340	81	34	38	59	320
2007	17	483	70	233	1,484	3,085	885	51	14	116	294	82	30	30	54	281
2008	19	663	67	259	1,341	2,298	658	48	14	108	325	97	36	36	58	257
2009	20	575	60	313	1,568	1,883	705	49	17	101	326	115	28	36	58	301
2010[1]	18	624	56	253	1,472	1,959	788	48	18	89	350	115	28	28	58	259

[1] Preliminary.   *Source: National Marine Fisheries Service, U.S. Department of Commerce*

U.S. Fisheries: Quantity & Value of Domestic Catch & Consumption & World Fish Oil Production

| | ------------------------- Disposition ------------------------- | | | | | For Human Food | For Industrial Products | Ex-vessel Value[3] | Average Price | Fish Per Capita Consumption | World[2] Fish Oil Production |
| Year | Fresh & Frozen | Canned | Cured | For Meal, Oil, etc. | Total | | | | | | |
	---------------------------- Millions of Pounds ----------------------------							- Million $ -	- Cents /Lb. -	- Pounds -	1,000 Tons -
2004	7,488	552	137	1,506	9,683	7,794	1,889	3,756	38.8	16.6	1,128
2005	7,776	563	160	1,208	9,707	7,997	1,710	3,942	40.6	16.2	976
2006	7,627	573	117	1,166	9,483	7,842	1,641	4,024	42.4	16.5	983
2007	7,450	514	121	1,224	9,309	7,490	1,819	4,192	45.0	16.3	1,061
2008	6,538	336	138	1,313	8,325	6,633	1,692	4,383	52.6	16.0	1,056
2009	6,204	392	103	1,332	8,031	6,035	1,833	3,891		15.8	1,031
2010[1]	6,515	373	102	1,241	8,231	6,526	1,705	4,520			889

[1] Preliminary.   [2] Crop years on a marketing year basis.   [3] At the Dock Prices.   *Source: Fisheries Statistics Division, U.S. Department of Commerce*

FISH

Imports of Seafood Products into the United States   In Thousands of Pounds

| | Fresh | | | Fresh & Frozen | Frozen | | | Canned & Prepared | Fresh & Prepared | | | | |
Year	Atlantic Salmon	Pacific Salmon[2]	Shrimp	Trout	Atlantic Salmon	Pacific Salmon[2]	Shrimp	Salmon[3]	Shrimp[4]	Oysters[5]	Mussels[6]	Clams[7]	Tilapia[8]
2004	8,580	121,724	22,396	7,917	40,860	871,856	264,586	24,632	271,199	249,167	23,120	50,817	31,111
2005	7,171	142,244	22,514	5,052	42,270	870,595	275,501	25,672	301,534	297,639	22,912	51,662	32,912
2006	10,215	171,848	20,905	5,137	52,161	920,922	257,970	27,456	385,701	348,707	24,599	50,796	34,454
2007	11,717	178,778	17,577	6,619	52,643	912,953	265,078	30,470	317,735	383,153	24,041	53,091	30,618
2008	9,137	182,929	12,843	6,219	52,407	943,989	250,282	28,468	304,907	395,559	20,544	54,261	33,143
2009	12,021	198,260	12,278	7,844	61,750	896,045	220,550	32,444	321,372	404,132	20,503	57,062	37,657
2010	16,326	203,913	18,956	6,058	80,859	914,925	178,868	27,222	321,800	474,967	23,802	56,921	40,145
2011[1]	11,053	192,222	19,653	5,694	85,348	948,094	201,606	25,108	323,610	425,271	26,785	63,813	44,789

[1] Preliminary.   [2] Also contains salmon with no specific species noted.   [3] Includes smoked and cured salmon.   [4] Shrimp, canned, breaded, or prepared.
[5] Oysters fresh or prepared.   [6] Mussels fresh or prepared.   [7] Clams, fresh or prepared.   [8] Tilapia, frozen whole fish plus fresh and frozen fillets.
Source: Bureau of the Census, U.S. Department of Commerce

Exports of Seafood Products From the United States   In Thousands of Pounds

| | Fresh | | | Fresh & Frozen | Frozen | | | Canned & Prepared | Fresh & Prepared | | | |
Year	Atlantic Salmon	Pacific Salmon[2]	Shrimp	Trout	Atlantic Salmon	Pacific Salmon[2]	Shrimp	Salmon[3]	Shrimp[4]	Oysters[5]	Mussels[6]	Clams[7]
2004	1,180	13,995	34,249	197	187,954	12,730	138,455	14,620	7,688	924	12,506	16,909
2005	972	11,760	18,965	379	261,124	9,105	146,064	13,026	7,852	1,026	10,523	25,591
2006	875	8,759	19,869	106	219,019	7,544	137,538	12,944	6,241	2,525	12,257	29,110
2007	817	7,303	15,778	257	300,386	8,723	139,103	14,153	6,231	1,896	12,470	23,908
2008	1,107	17,705	16,198	247	277,331	7,902	138,048	17,684	7,241	1,855	14,366	24,694
2009	978	14,039	11,661	173	263,564	7,841	115,974	12,842	6,396	1,498	12,907	26,183
2010	667	20,958	18,344	205	316,240	6,037	112,905	11,287	7,664	1,069	12,773	24,577
2011[1]	491	7,550	20,511	667	337,295	9,890	137,819	16,430	10,369	1,141	13,104	32,124

[1] Preliminary.   [2] Also contains salmon with no specific species noted.   [3] Includes smoked and cured salmon.   [4] Shrimp, canned, breaded, or prepared.
[5] Oysters fresh or prepared.   [6] Mussels fresh or prepared.   [7] Clams, fresh or prepared.   *Source: Bureau of the Census, U.S. Department of Commerce*

World Production of Fish Meal   In Thousands of Metric Tons

Year	Chile	Denmark	European Union	Iceland	Japan	Norway	Peru	Russia	South Africa	Spain	Thailand	United States	World Total
2003-04	929.7	255.9	520.4	214.6	319.0	234.2	1,842.2	61.3	136.6	83.4	404.3	305.0	6,245.9
2004-05	886.1	231.2	472.8	202.1	318.0	155.6	1,949.2	59.6	121.3	53.2	407.9	269.4	6,129.8
2005-06	857.2	213.7	434.4	137.7	250.0	162.4	1,503.3	64.0	72.7	43.4	430.0	260.7	5,419.3
2006-07	798.5	164.8	386.3	151.6	204.0	173.1	1,400.1	67.3	88.6	40.9	429.0	258.1	5,187.0
2007-08	740.8	161.9	375.6	144.0	202.0	141.3	1,426.9	70.3	80.7	35.0	409.0	223.9	5,020.4
2008-09[1]	685.9	178.8	390.8	122.3	198.9	130.2	1,442.6	75.3	69.8	33.0	400.0	224.4	4,916.8
2009-10[2]	450.0	180.5	391.6	97.0	195.0	147.0	1,189.6	85.3	84.8	31.2	455.0	193.8	4,578.4
2010-11[3]	542.0	163.0	382.0	88.0	190.0	150.0	1,220.0	90.3	92.5	30.4	465.0	242.0	4,775.0

[1] Preliminary.   [2] Estimate.   [3] Forecast.   *Source: The Oil World*

World Production of Fish Oil   In Thousands of Metric Tons

Year	Canada	Chile	China	Denmark	Iceland	Japan	Norway	Peru	Africa	Russia	United States	World Total	Fish Oil CIF[4] $ Per Tonne
2003-04	4.8	176.5	14.0	107.4	74.2	68.1	40.5	263.5	7.1	3.6	81.9	1,036.0	648
2004-05	5.2	182.3	12.0	74.7	59.3	65.8	29.7	342.2	7.1	3.7	77.6	1,042.9	716
2005-06	5.0	179.0	12.1	75.0	49.5	68.5	36.1	277.4	7.5	3.8	62.7	989.0	792
2006-07	5.2	179.7	13.0	52.6	55.4	66.9	41.5	307.9	4.5	3.9	71.4	1,014.0	885
2007-08	5.4	166.6	12.5	63.5	74.2	64.3	42.9	298.6	4.0	4.0	81.7	1,064.2	1,612
2008-09[1]	5.5	164.3	14.0	67.5	74.0	59.6	38.8	302.1	4.2	4.0	80.5	1,048.0	855
2009-10[2]	5.6	93.0	15.4	67.4	57.0	61.0	46.0	238.4	6.4	4.1	54.6	947.5	994
2010-11[3]	5.8	130.0	16.0	59.4	56.0	60.0	46.0	243.0	7.3	4.2	90.0	1,017.4	1,514

[1] Preliminary.   [2] Estimate.   [3] Forecast.   [4] Any origin, N.W. Europe.   *Source: The Oil World*

Monthly Production of Catfish--Round Weight Processed--in the United States   In Thousands of Pounds (Live Weight)

Year	Jan.	Feb.	Mar.	Apr.	May	June	July	Aug.	Sept.	Oct.	Nov.	Dec.	Total
2004	53,849	54,173	60,272	53,896	52,324	50,155	51,055	53,295	51,329	52,396	49,536	48,170	630,450
2005	53,856	51,720	57,117	50,306	51,552	49,626	47,241	50,686	47,151	49,034	46,674	45,707	600,670
2006	50,703	49,145	56,315	43,126	42,865	41,214	45,528	51,736	47,296	50,788	45,680	41,735	566,131
2007	46,079	44,083	45,477	37,954	38,867	37,275	39,168	42,626	39,519	45,890	40,307	39,001	496,246
2008	45,992	47,634	47,908	45,018	44,326	43,265	42,583	40,985	39,057	43,344	36,869	32,616	509,597
2009	36,406	37,702	44,912	40,768	39,925	39,370	40,966	39,490	36,408	40,191	36,211	33,751	466,100
2010	40,042	40,977	46,650	37,111	38,244	38,656	39,302	39,231	39,494	40,455	36,683	34,838	471,683
2011[1]	35,076	27,782	30,372	23,605	24,749	24,337	26,595	30,680	30,271	32,446	25,814	22,598	334,325

[1] Preliminary.   *Source: Economic Research Service, U.S. Department of Agriculture ERS-USDA)*

Average Price Paid to Producers for Farm-Raised Catfish in the United States   In Cents Per Pound (Live Weight)

Year	Jan.	Feb.	Mar.	Apr.	May	June	July	Aug.	Sept.	Oct.	Nov.	Dec.	Average
2004	66.8	70.3	72.3	72.8	72.0	68.9	68.2	68.3	68.3	69.5	68.9	69.0	69.6
2005	72.5	73.1	73.3	72.5	72.2	72.1	72.3	72.4	72.4	72.4	72.4	72.6	72.5
2006	72.7	72.9	74.5	78.5	79.6	80.7	81.2	81.1	83.2	83.6	83.7	83.8	79.6
2007	83.7	83.8	83.8	84.1	84.0	81.7	76.2	73.1	69.7	68.2	66.6	65.0	76.7
2008	65.8	68.8	74.3	75.7	77.6	79.4	81.8	82.7	82.7	82.5	82.3	82.1	78.0
2009	81.0	77.0	77.3	76.3	76.2	76.3	77.1	76.9	77.2	76.8	76.5	76.3	77.1
2010	76.4	76.5	78.5	80.4	79.6	78.6	78.8	79.0	81.6	83.2	84.1	86.1	80.2
2011[1]	93.1	100.3	107.5	114.1	116.9	123.1	125.2	127.7	127.5	126.5	125.7	125.1	117.7

[1] Preliminary.   Source: Economic Research Service, U.S. Department of Agriculture (ERS-USDA)

Sales of Fresh Catfish in the United States   In Thousands of Pounds

Year	Jan.	Feb.	Mar.	Apr.	May	June	July	Aug.	Sept.	Oct.	Nov.	Dec.	Total
Whole
2006	3,195	3,331	4,024	2,940	2,795	2,464	2,715	2,679	2,594	2,696	2,426	2,543	34,402
2007	2,756	2,824	3,247	2,631	2,715	2,679	2,489	2,737	2,730	2,944	2,541	2,432	32,725
2008	3,338	3,585	3,194	2,908	2,868	2,612	2,552	2,605	2,227	2,830	2,302	2,517	33,538
2009	2,537	2,752	3,137	2,733	2,551	2,546	2,582	2,332	2,321	2,830	2,352	2,461	31,134
2010	2,811	3,156	3,743	3,046	2,844	2,730	2,277	2,582	2,518	2,863	2,297	2,434	33,301
2011[1]	2,488	2,046	2,614	2,259	2,061	2,025	1,484	1,701	1,635	2,024	2,021	1,878	24,236
Fillets[2]
2006	5,160	5,109	6,090	5,077	4,653	4,446	4,276	4,411	4,075	4,334	3,549	3,579	54,759
2007	4,282	4,405	4,685	4,001	4,280	3,708	4,005	4,045	3,959	4,468	3,473	3,417	48,728
2008	4,489	4,922	4,823	4,145	4,000	4,761	3,943	3,803	3,503	3,723	3,083	3,075	48,270
2009	3,795	3,732	4,196	3,894	3,864	3,621	3,649	3,554	3,444	3,495	2,989	3,038	43,271
2010	3,607	4,221	3,905	3,495	3,720	3,475	3,411	3,606	3,456	3,343	2,791	3,045	42,075
2011[1]	3,220	2,650	2,880	2,351	2,199	2,105	2,227	2,199	2,047	2,173	1,892	1,877	27,820
Other[3]
2006	1,126	1,024	1,214	987	915	807	862	868	811	866	768	816	11,064
2007	812	814	884	809	850	723	753	766	759	816	669	633	9,288
2008	913	819	755	786	736	704	653	665	642	713	717	568	8,671
2009	709	810	797	684	751	783	646	709	644	685	616	611	8,445
2010	695	735	807	668	713	641	631	650	647	621	516	564	7,888
2011[1]	615	535	556	551	485	461	456	462	444	476	423	420	5,884

[1] Preliminary.   [2] Includes regular, shank and strip fillets; excludes breaded products.   [3] Includes steaks, nuggets and all other products not reported.
Source: Economic Research Service, U.S. Department of Agriculture (ERS-USDA)

Prices of Fresh Catfish in the United States   In Dollars Per Pound

Year	Jan.	Feb.	Mar.	Apr.	May	June	July	Aug.	Sept.	Oct.	Nov.	Dec.	Average
Whole
2006	1.53	1.49	1.54	1.65	1.70	1.74	1.72	1.74	1.78	1.81	1.76	1.80	1.69
2007	1.79	1.77	1.71	1.75	1.71	1.71	1.73	1.70	1.65	1.59	1.56	1.56	1.69
2008	1.49	1.50	1.56	1.59	1.60	1.68	1.68	1.76	1.73	1.71	1.72	1.66	1.64
2009	1.72	1.67	1.65	1.68	1.70	1.64	1.66	1.69	1.66	1.59	1.57	1.57	1.65
2010	1.55	1.49	1.50	1.55	1.55	1.58	1.67	1.58	1.63	1.57	1.61	1.71	1.58
2011[1]	1.90	2.06	2.17	2.28	2.40	2.49	2.64	2.61	2.65	2.54	2.42	2.45	2.38
Fillets[2]
2006	2.86	2.87	2.89	2.98	3.08	3.14	3.18	3.17	3.22	3.23	3.24	3.25	3.09
2007	3.28	3.24	3.27	3.27	3.27	3.26	3.18	3.08	3.03	2.96	2.93	2.91	3.14
2008	2.90	2.88	2.96	3.03	3.10	3.08	3.25	3.33	3.33	3.31	3.30	3.31	3.15
2009	3.30	3.24	3.24	3.23	3.23	3.22	3.21	3.21	3.20	3.19	3.18	3.19	3.22
2010	3.16	3.10	3.18	3.22	3.25	3.26	3.25	3.22	3.24	3.29	3.32	3.32	3.23
2011[1]	3.47	3.75	4.18	4.43	4.55	4.60	4.84	4.77	4.88	4.86	4.84	4.78	4.50
Other[3]
2006	1.64	1.63	1.65	1.75	1.73	1.86	1.86	1.83	1.86	1.75	1.74	1.79	1.76
2007	1.71	1.79	1.78	1.80	1.76	1.76	1.72	1.63	1.56	1.53	1.54	1.52	1.68
2008	1.46	1.51	1.57	1.61	1.65	1.80	1.81	1.77	1.76	1.73	1.68	1.62	1.66
2009	1.64	1.52	1.61	1.75	1.60	1.68	1.64	1.64	1.67	1.64	1.66	1.67	1.64
2010	1.66	1.60	1.65	1.81	1.76	1.71	1.72	1.72	1.69	1.68	1.74	1.75	1.71
2011[1]	1.77	1.95	2.07	2.14	2.24	2.29	2.17	2.26	2.29	2.25	2.23	2.20	2.16

[1] Preliminary.   [2] Includes regular, shank and strip fillets; excludes breaded products.   [3] Includes steaks, nuggets and all other products not reported.
Source: Economic Research Service, U.S. Department of Agriculture (ERS-USDA)

Flaxseed and Linseed Oil

Flaxseed, also called linseed, is an ancient crop that was cultivated by the Babylonians around 3,000 BC. Flaxseed is used for fiber in textiles and to produce oil. Flaxseeds contain approximately 35% oil, of which 60% is omega-3 fatty acid. Flaxseed or linseed oil is obtained through either the expeller extraction or solvent extraction method. Manufacturers filter the processed oil to remove some impurities and then sell it as unrefined. Unrefined oil retains its full flavor, aroma, color, and naturally occurring nutrients. Flaxseed oil is used for cooking and as a dietary supplement as well as for animal feed. Industrial linseed oil is not for internal consumption due to possible poisonous additives and is used for making putty, sealants, linoleum, wood preservation, varnishes, and oil paints.

Prices – The average monthly price received by U.S. farmers for flaxseed in the 2011-12 marketing year (through January 2012) rose by +7.6% yr/yr to $14.04 per bushel, a new record high.

Supply – World production of flaxseed in the 2010-11 marketing year fell by -13.3% yr/yr to 1.984 million metric tons, below the 9-year high of 2.864 million metric tons in 2005-06. The world's largest producer of flaxseed is China with 23.7% of world production in 2010-11, followed by the Canada (21.3%), the former USSR (14.4%), the US (11.6%), and India (8.0%). U.S. production of flaxseed in 2011-12 fell -69.2% to 2.791 million bushels, a new record low. North Dakota is by far the largest producing state of flaxseed and accounted for 86.9% of flaxseed production in 2011, followed by Montana with 7.5% of production and South Dakota with 4.0% of production.

World production of linseed oil in 2010-11 fell by -2.0% yr/yr to 620.100 million metric tons. The world's largest producers of linseed oil are China (with 26.2% of world production in 2010-11), the U.S. (18.4%), Belgium (17.3%), and India (8.4%). U.S. production of linseed oil in 2010-11 fell by −6.8% yr/yr to 218.000 million pounds.

Demand – U.S. distribution of flaxseed in 2010-11 fell by −5.0% yr/yr to 13.973 million bushels. The breakdown was 80% for crushing into meal and oil, 13% for exports, 5% for residual, and 3% for seed.

Trade – U.S. exports of flaxseed in 2010-11 rose by +12.7% yr/yr to 1.768 million bushels. U.S. imports of flaxseed in 2010-11 fell by -18.7% yr/yr to 5.110 million bushels.

World Production of Flaxseed   In Thousands of Metric Tons

Crop Year	Argen-tina	Australia	Bang-ladesh	Canada	China	Egypt	France	Hungary	India	Romania	United States	Former USSR	World Total
2001-02	16	9	50	770	273	26	23	1	240	2	291	82	1,980
2002-03	11	9	50	750	409	15	17	1	200	2	301	60	1,974
2003-04	29	9	3	835	450	22	11	1	230	2	265	85	2,169
2004-05	36	10	3	592	460	31	13	2	200	3	263	98	2,008
2005-06	54	10	3	1,150	475	28	25	3	210	----	480	105	2,870
2006-07	38	7	9	1,040	480	27	43	2	200	----	280	157	2,551
2007-08	13	8	8	660	480	12	34	2	190	----	150	135	1,942
2008-09[1]	19	8	8	861	475	12	15	1	150	----	145	145	2,098
2009-10[2]	52	8	7	930	435	8	21	1	160	1	189	204	2,288
2010-11[3]	31	7	8	423	470	12	35	1	160	1	230	286	1,984

[1] Preliminary.   [2] Estimate.   [3] Forecast.   *Source: The Oil World*

Supply and Distribution of Flaxseed in the United States   In Thousands of Bushels

Crop Year Beginning June 1	Planted	Harvested	Yield Per Acre (Bushels)	Beginning Stocks	Pro-duction	Imports	Total Supply	Seed	Crush	Exports	Residual	Total
	---- 1,000 Acres ----											
2002-03	784	703	16.9	893	11,863	2,901	15,657	482	10,500	3,181	416	14,579
2003-04	595	588	17.9	1,078	10,516	4,580	16,174	424	11,260	2,516	686	14,886
2004-05	523	516	20.3	1,288	10,471	5,413	17,069	796	13,600	1,510	301	16,206
2005-06	983	955	20.6	863	19,695	4,256	24,814	659	16,400	3,780	440	21,279
2006-07	813	767	14.4	3,535	11,019	5,464	20,018	287	14,900	1,788	599	17,574
2007-08	354	349	16.9	2,444	5,896	8,019	16,359	287	11,700	2,221	640	14,847
2008-09	354	340	16.8	1,512	5,716	4,794	12,022	257	8,150	432	631	9,470
2009-10[1]	317	314	23.6	2,552	7,423	6,283	16,258	341	12,000	1,751	609	14,701
2010-11[2]	421	418	21.7	1,557	9,056	6,040	16,653	185	11,635	2,130	532	14,483
2011-12[3]	178	173	16.1	2,170	2,791	7,881	12,842	284	8,700	1,786	522	11,292

[1] Preliminary.   [2] Estimate.   [3] Forecast.   NA = not avaliable.   *Source: Economic Research Service, U.S. Department of Agriculture (ERS-USDA)*

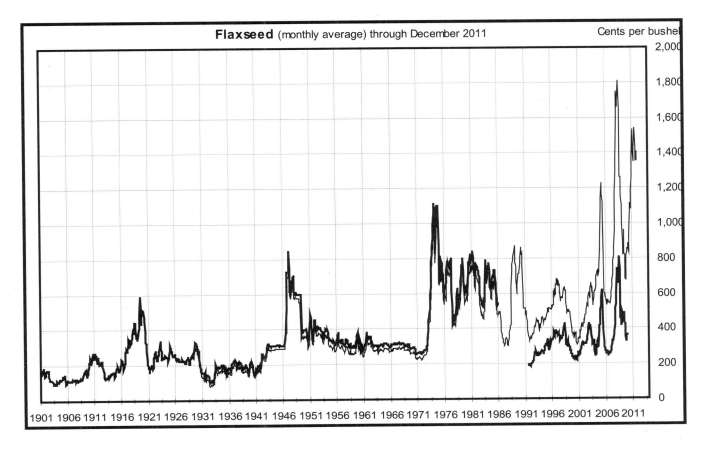

Flaxseed (monthly average) through December 2011 — Cents per bushel

Production of Flaxseed in the United States, by States — In Thousands of Bushels

Year	Minnesota	North Dakota	South Dakota	Montana[2]	Total	Year	Minnesota	North Dakota	South Dakota	Montana[2]	Total
2002	64	11,560	44	195	11,863	2007	72	5,548	96	180	5,896
2003	161	9,990	144	221	10,516	2008	69	5,491	84	72	5,716
2004	51	9,840	135	342	10,471	2009	63	7,032	168	160	7,423
2005	132	18,165	480	918	19,695	2010	56	8,536	209	255	9,056
2006	126	10,368	228	297	11,019	2011[1]	45	2,426	112	208	2,791

[1] Preliminary.   [2] Data through 1999 are "Other".   Source: National Agricultural Statistics Service, U.S. Department of Agriculture (NASS-USDA)

Factory Shipments of Paints, Varnish and Lacquer in the United States — In Millions of Dollars

Year	First Quarter	Second Quarter	Third Quarter	Fourth Quarter	Total	Year	First Quarter	Second Quarter	Third Quarter	Fourth Quarter	Total
2002	3,729.9	4,440.7	4,251.4	3,600.7	16,023	2007	4,311.4	5,483.2	5,245.9	4,277.0	19,318
2003	3,981.5	4,671.8	4,374.7	3,905.8	16,934	2008	4,211.2	5,160.9	5,197.9	3,885.7	18,456
2004	4,306.1	5,000.1	4,843.2	4,104.7	18,254	2009	3,713.7	4,582.9	4,510.2	3,413.3	16,220
2005	4,061.1	5,268.4	4,953.6	4,254.9	18,538	2010	3,943.5	5,060.6	4,898.1	3,820.9	17,723
2006	4,626.5	5,408.8	5,050.5	4,305.7	19,392	2011[1]	4,289.6	5,290.4	X	X	19,160

[1] Preliminary.   Source: Bureau of the Census, U.S. Department of Commerce

Consumption of Linseed Oil (Inedible Products) in the United States — In Millions of Pounds

Year	July	Aug.	Sept.	Oct.	Nov.	Dec.	Jan.	Feb.	Mar.	Apr.	May	June	Average
2003-04	7.9	6.9	6.0	6.8	3.5	5.0	5.6	7.3	6.0	7.7	8.1	8.2	79.1
2004-05	7.3	7.3	6.7	5.6	4.8	5.1	3.7	4.8	4.9	4.0	5.7	4.7	64.6
2005-06	4.8	4.5	4.2	3.7	2.7	2.7	3.9	3.8	4.9	3.3	5.9	6.0	50.5
2006-07	4.4	5.8	5.7	3.5	3.7	2.8	3.6	4.3	4.2	5.0	6.8	7.2	56.8
2007-08	8.6	W	W	W	W	W	5.8	W	W	W	W	W	86.4
2008-09	W	W	W	W	W	W	W	9.7	18.0	10.2	10.3	10.2	139.9
2009-10	10.0	W	10.1	10.1	9.8	W	W	W	W	W	W	W	120.4
2010-11[1]	W	W	W	W	W	W	W	W	W	W	W	W	W

[1] Preliminary.   W = Withheld.   Source: Bureau of the Census, U.S. Department of Commerce

FLAXSEED AND LINSEED OIL

Supply and Distribution of Linseed Oil in the United States   In Millions of Pounds

Crop Year Beginning June 1	Stocks June 1	Supply Production	Total	Disappearance Exports	Domestic	Total	Average Price at Minneapolis Cents/Lb.
2001-02	45	195	250	50	169	219	38.1
2002-03	31	205	249	70	145	215	39.9
2003-04	34	220	268	76	172	248	42.0
2004-05	20	265	301	107	149	256	59.5
2005-06	45	320	375	98	248	346	54.0
2006-07	29	291	328	76	202	278	44.4
2007-08	51	228	291	74	191	265	70.3
2008-09	26	159	191	66	52	118	86.5
2009-10[1]	73	234	312	103	177	280	67.5
2010-11[2]	32	218	260	80	145	225	66.0-70.0

[1] Preliminary.   [2] Forecast.   *Source: Economic Research Service, U.S. Department of Agriculture (ERS-USDA)*

World Production and Price of Linseed Oil   In Thousands of Metric Tons

Year	Argentina	Bangladesh	Belgium	China	Egypt	Germany	India	Japan	United Kingdom	United States	Former USSR	World Total	Rotterdam Ex-Tank USD $/Tonne
2001-02	3.8	13.5	95.0	75.3	15.6	57.3	72.4	18.9	9.9	95.7	20.7	584.1	454
2002-03	2.1	7.5	92.1	111.4	15.1	64.4	63.3	8.6	5.9	105.5	15.1	582.4	679
2003-04	2.3	0.6	119.6	124.0	11.3	66.6	67.7	7.5	6.7	103.8	17.1	624.1	757
2004-05	6.9	0.6	97.9	127.0	12.0	37.9	62.7	6.8	3.5	135.5	16.3	625.7	1,191
2005-06	13.1	2.6	97.9	137.6	14.8	65.2	63.7	5.7	3.5	147.7	16.2	695.0	686
2006-07	5.0	4.3	118.9	146.6	16.5	59.3	61.7	6.2	5.3	140.3	15.8	705.1	809
2007-08	2.8	2.8	114.6	148.1	8.6	53.6	58.4	4.6	2.8	98.1	21.0	635.1	1,635
2008-09	2.1	2.3	77.0	157.4	6.4	37.7	46.9	2.6	3.2	84.8	16.6	561.7	975
2009-10[1]	1.7	2.1	96.5	192.3	5.2	34.5	47.7	2.0	2.6	116.1	20.8	632.7	1,114
2010-11[2]	3.1	2.3	107.0	162.5	4.4	29.1	52.0	1.7	3.5	114.3	21.8	620.1	1,448

[1] Preliminary.   [2] Forecast.   *Source: The Oil World*

Average Price Received by Farmers for Flaxseed in the United States   In Dollars Per Bushel

Year	July	Aug.	Sept.	Oct.	Nov.	Dec.	Jan.	Feb.	Mar.	Apr.	May	June	Average
2002-03	5.38	5.27	5.55	5.76	6.04	5.92	5.71	6.25	6.47	6.57	6.05	6.02	5.92
2003-04	6.38	5.30	5.43	5.77	6.02	6.15	6.08	6.39	6.53	7.01	7.10	7.23	6.28
2004-05	7.33	6.90	7.19	7.36	8.62	8.42	8.89	10.90	11.40	12.30	11.60	11.20	9.34
2005-06	10.40	6.28	6.10	6.05	5.94	5.81	5.64	5.59	5.31	5.56	5.59	5.40	6.14
2006-07	5.47	5.50	5.46	5.41	5.38	5.73	6.03	6.39	6.79	6.72	7.08	7.81	6.15
2007-08	8.14	8.64	9.55	11.60	12.90	13.10	13.50	16.00	17.50	16.60	16.90	18.00	13.54
2008-09	18.10	16.50	15.60	12.60	12.60	11.50	11.00	9.98	8.84	8.13	8.96	9.59	11.95
2009-10	8.28	8.14	6.79	6.78	8.12	8.40	8.53	8.57	8.82	8.53	8.34	9.26	8.21
2010-11	10.70	11.10	10.80	11.90	12.60	13.10	13.80	15.30	14.20	13.50	14.20	15.40	13.05
2011-12[1]	15.40	14.30	13.50	13.90	14.00	13.60	13.60	13.20					13.94

[1] Preliminary.   *Source: National Agricultural Statistics Service, U.S. Department of Agriculture (NASS-USDA)*

Stocks of Linseed Oil (Crude and Refined) at Factories and Warehouses in the U.S.   In Millions of Pounds

Year	July 1	Aug. 1	Sept. 1	Oct. 1	Nov. 1	Dec. 1	Jan. 1	Feb. 1	Mar. 1	Apr. 1	May 1	June 1
2002-03	27.8	17.7	12.8	21.8	30.5	29.0	31.9	35.9	34.6	36.2	33.7	33.7
2003-04	30.2	27.2	22.3	78.5	42.0	35.0	40.0	43.4	37.6	32.9	24.5	19.9
2004-05	15.1	15.8	8.0	13.0	17.1	26.9	31.3	35.4	35.4	41.0	43.9	47.2
2005-06	38.1	24.8	14.1	33.9	31.1	21.0	29.4	38.4	42.2	32.2	25.5	29.8
2006-07	22.2	27.9	21.6	23.6	28.4	33.5	38.5	41.5	44.9	44.3	49.6	51.6
2007-08	41.5	44.4	49.5	39.4	50.3	49.9	34.3	22.8	37.1	28.0	35.6	26.5
2008-09	22.4	26.1	31.8	28.5	30.3	37.7	37.6	47.5	43.1	39.7	58.3	60.5
2009-10	48.7	49.4	70.3	28.3	41.7	34.9	41.7	33.1	46.2	34.8	36.0	32.1
2010-11	34.4	35.6	39.9	32.7	59.0	50.2	58.8	53.5	47.1	50.8	41.1	38.2
2011-12[1]	40.3	29.3	W	W	W	W						

[1] Preliminary.   *Source: Bureau of the Census, U.S. Department of Commerce*

Wholesale Price of Raw Linseed Oil at Minneapolis in Tank Cars   In Cents Per Pound

Year	Jan.	Feb.	Mar.	Apr.	May	June	July	Aug.	Sept.	Oct.	Nov.	Dec.	Average
2002-03	40.00	38.00	41.00	31.75	41.00	41.00	41.00	41.00	41.00	41.00	41.19	41.75	39.97
2003-04	41.75	41.75	42.00	42.75	43.13	43.25	42.60	40.00	40.00	40.00	45.00	45.50	42.31
2004-05	48.50	50.00	55.00	57.20	60.00	58.17	60.80	64.00	66.00	73.75	75.00	75.00	61.95
2005-06	75.00	75.00	75.00	48.75	42.75	43.50	42.40	42.00	42.38	42.94	43.10	42.35	51.26
2006-07	43.30	43.25	43.44	43.83	44.00	44.38	44.60	44.67	46.00	46.10	46.50	47.75	44.82
2007-08	49.00	NA	65.67	70.00	72.64	75.00	77.43	77.16	85.55	86.00	86.10	89.14	75.79
2008-09	93.18	95.71	90.00	87.86	87.21	85.82	86.35	83.42	82.59	80.00	77.00	75.36	85.38
2009-10	73.27	70.29	70.00	70.00	70.00	70.00	65.11	62.95	62.00	60.95	60.00	61.82	66.37
2010-11	70.00	70.00	NA	NA	NA	NA	NA	NA	NA	NA	NA	NA	70.00
2011-12[1]	NA	NA	NA	NA	NA	NA							NA

[1] Preliminary.   Source: Economic Research Service, U.S. Department of Agriculture (ERS-USDA)

Average Price of Linseed Meal (34% protein) at Minneapolis   In Dollars Per Ton

Year	Jan.	Feb.	Mar.	Apr.	May	June	July	Aug.	Sept.	Oct.	Nov.	Dec.	Average
2002-03	127.50	143.80	127.10	114.00	113.10	112.50	118.40	120.10	133.00	126.70	125.00	127.30	124.04
2003-04	129.10	130.60	125.20	139.90	178.80	162.30	166.30	174.40	193.60	197.80	181.80	151.80	160.97
2004-05	139.80	112.40	112.40	99.50	114.60	109.10	111.60	109.90	109.80	104.00	96.00	116.00	111.26
2005-06	159.40	157.80	99.00	100.40	113.60	118.00	127.30	130.20	129.00	126.60	119.10	116.90	124.78
2006-07	111.50	101.10	92.80	100.80	118.10	123.30	134.20	156.40	156.30	149.00	135.10	132.00	125.88
2007-08	135.80	123.90	131.40	170.20	184.60	186.80	242.70	250.00	247.10	253.70	240.30	265.40	202.66
2008-09	273.70	231.30	200.00	160.80	164.00	189.60	248.80	270.00	231.90	233.50	263.10	250.00	226.39
2009-10	226.90	217.00	195.20	185.00	220.00	256.50	228.75	222.50	201.50	200.83	202.75	189.50	212.20
2010-11	199.38	204.00	200.00	208.75	237.50	234.38	255.00	256.25	236.50	225.63	231.88	254.38	228.64
2011-12[1]	260.63	247.50	239.38	243.75	239.00	221.25							241.92

[1] Preliminary.   Source: Economic Research Service, U.S. Department of Agriculture (ERS-USDA)

Flaxseed Futures - Winnipeg Commodity Exchange
(weekly close) as of October 31, 2005
CAD per metric ton

Fruits

A fruit is any seed-bearing structure produced from a flowering plant. A widely used classification system divides fruit into fleshy or dry types. Fleshy fruits are juicy and include peaches, mangos, apples, and blueberries. Dry fruits include tree nuts such as almonds, walnuts, and pecans. Some foods that are commonly called vegetables, such as tomatoes, squash, peppers and eggplant, are technically fruits because they develop from the ovary of a flower.

Worldwide, over 430 million tons of fruit are produced each year and are grown everywhere except the Arctic and the Antarctic. The tropics, because of their abundant moisture and warm temperatures, produce the most diverse and abundant fruits. Mexico and Chile produce more than half of all the fresh and frozen fruit imported into the U.S. In the U.S., the top three fruits produced are oranges, grapes, and apples. Virtually all U.S. production of almonds, pistachios, and walnuts occurs in California, which leads the U.S. in tree nut production.

Prices – Overall fruit prices were fairly strong in 2010 with the fresh fruit Consumer Price Index (CPI) falling -0.7% to 322.3 and the processed fruit CPI index falling -1.3% to 141.0. Individual fruit prices, however, were mixed in 2010: Red Delicious Apples (+3.3% to $1.220 per pound), bananas (-5.2% to 58.0 cents per pound), Anjou pears (-1.4% to $1.287 per pound), Thompson seedless grapes (+3.4% to $2.181 per pound), lemons (+7.5% to $1.634 per pound), grapefruit (+2.8% to 92.7 cents per pound), navel oranges (+1.1% to $1.062 cents per pound), and Valencia oranges (+6.4% to $1.017 per pound).

Supply – U.S. commercial production of selected fruits in 2010 fell -4.9% to 28.307 million short tons. By weight, oranges accounted for 29.1% of that U.S. fruit production figure, followed by grapes at 26.2%, and apples at 16.4%. The value of U.S. fruit production in 2010 rose +11.2% yr/yr to $20.858 billion.

Demand – U.S. per capita fresh fruit consumption in 2010 rose +3.9% to 102.01 pounds per year, but remained just below the 2004 record high of 102.49. The highest per capita consumption categories for non-citrus fruits in 2010 were bananas (25.59 pounds) and apples (15.41 pounds).

Per capital consumption of citrus fruits were oranges (9.69 pounds), tangerines & tangelos (3.78 pounds), lemons (2.79 pounds), and grapefruit (2.76 pounds). The utilization breakdown for 2010 shows that total U.S. non-citrus fruit was used for fresh fruit (41.9%), wine (24.0%), dried fruit (12.6%), canned fruit (7.7%), juice (6.4%), and frozen fruit (4.0%). The value of utilized non-citrus fruit production in 2010 rose +1.8% yr/yr to $12.053 billion.

Commercial Production for Selected Fruits in the United States   In Thousands of Short Tons

Year	Apples	Cherries[2]	Cran-berries	Grapes	Grape-fruit	Lemons	Nect-arines	Oranges	Peaches	Pears	Pine-apple[3]	Prunes & Plums	Straw-berries	Tang-elos	Tang-erines	Total All Fruits
2004	5,206	390	309	6,240	2,165	798	269	12,872	1,307	878	220	325	1,107	45	417	33,012
2005	4,834	386	312	7,814	1,018	870	251	9,251	1,185	823	212	476	1,161	70	335	29,549
2006	4,912	425	345	6,378	1,232	980	232	9,020	1,010	842	185	813	1,202	63	417	28,390
2007	4,545	437	328	7,057	1,627	798	283	7,625	1,127	873	W	405	1,223	56	361	27,145
2008	4,817	355	393	7,319	1,548	619	303	10,076	1,135	870	W	544	1,266	68	527	30,150
2009	4,853	623	346	7,307	1,304	912	220	9,128	1,104	957	W	627	1,401	52	443	29,761
2010[1]	4,651	408	341	7,414	1,238	882	233	8,243	1,150	814	W	532	1,425	41	596	28,308

[1] Preliminary.   [2] Sweet and tart.   [3] Utilized production.   *Source: Economic Research Service, U.S. Department of Agriculture (ERS-USDA)*

Utilized Production for Selected Fruits in the United States   In Thousands of Short Tons

Year	Utilized Production Citrus[2]	Utilized Production Noncitrus	Utilized Production Tree nuts[3]	Utilized Production Total	Value of Production Citrus[2]	Value of Production Noncitrus	Value of Production Tree nuts[3]	Value of Production Total
	In Thousands of Short Tons				In Thousands of Dollars			
2004	16,360	16,823	1,524	34,706	2,485,052	8,553,060	3,527,904	14,566,016
2005	11,573	18,272	1,467	31,312	2,303,425	9,805,757	4,175,893	16,285,075
2006	11,744	16,816	1,598	30,158	2,738,361	10,510,417	3,680,383	16,929,161
2007	10,467	17,048	2,000	29,515	3,147,755	11,436,449	4,273,279	18,857,483
2008	12,838	17,603	2,144	32,585	3,240,271	11,270,860	3,828,207	18,339,338
2009	11,839	18,069	2,014	31,923	2,742,010	11,839,538	4,172,838	18,754,386
2010[1]	11,000	17,775	2,373	31,148	2,973,629	12,053,940	5,830,978	20,858,547

[1] Preliminary.   [2] Year harvest was completed.   [3] Tree nuts on an in-shell equivalent.
Source: Economic Research Service, U.S. Department of Agriculture (ERS-USDA)

Annual Average Retail Prices for Selected Fruits in the United States   In Dollars Per Pound

Year	Red Delicious Apples	Bananas	Anjou Pears	Thompson Seedless Grapes	Lemons	Grapefruit	Oranges Navel	Oranges Valencias
2004	1.043	.495	NA	2.059	1.235	.819	.859	.691
2005	.949	.492	1.114	2.078	1.411	.998	.996	.897
2006	1.067	.500	1.133	2.246	1.529	1.114	1.087	1.001
2007	1.115	.510	1.273	2.092	1.857	.964	1.284	1.074
2008	1.319	.609	1.331	2.212	2.004	.965	1.155	1.016
2009	1.182	.611	1.305	2.109	1.520	.903	1.050	.956
2010[1]	1.220	.580	1.287	2.181	1.634	.927	1.062	1.017

[1] Estimate.   *Source: Economic Research Service, U.S. Department of Agriculture (ERS-USDA)*

Utilization of Noncitrus Fruit Production, and Value in the United States   1,000 Short Tons (Fresh Equivalent)

Year	Utilized Production	Fresh	Canned	Dried	Processed Juice	Frozen	Wine	Other Processed	Value of Utilized Production $1,000
2001	16,740	6,488	1,859	2,290	1,462	665	3,568	169	7,918,636
2002	17,122	6,549	1,727	2,582	1,251	591	3,999	138	8,137,640
2003	16,848	6,672	1,762	2,293	1,295	716	3,582	219	8,434,610
2004	16,823	7,168	1,710	1,425	1,418	685	3,819	290	8,553,060
2005	18,272	7,188	1,575	2,101	1,555	712	4,551	277	9,805,757
2006	16,816	6,930	1,400	2,219	1,256	710	3,726	235	10,510,417
2007	17,048	7,013	1,453	2,030	1,277	748	3,921	278	11,436,449
2008	17,603	7,248	1,406	2,413	1,228	682	3,944	290	11,270,860
2009	18,069	7,562	1,394	2,148	1,235	742	4,373	269	11,839,538
2010[1]	17,775	7,453	1,364	2,244	1,134	693	4,274	273	12,053,940

[1] Preliminary.   *Source: Economic Research Service, U.S. Department of Agriculture (ERS-USDA)*

Average Price Indexes for Fruits in the United States

Year	Index of all Fruit & Nut Prices Received by Growers (1990-92=100)	Producer Price Index — Fresh Fruit 1982=100	Dried Fruit	Canned Fruits and Juices	Frozen Fruits and Juices	Consumer Price Index — Fresh Fruit 1982-84=100	Processed Fruit
2001	109	97.7	120.3	143.3	111.9	265.1	109.0
2002	105	91.5	120.7	141.7	112.5	270.2	111.6
2003	106	84.1	122.1	142.3	115.7	279.1	113.7
2004	124	104.9	NA	143.1	113.3	286.8	114.0
2005	128	102.8	NA	148.1	112.4	297.4	118.4
2006	154	111.0	NA	153.0	119.7	315.2	121.5
2007	158	123.4	NA	156.9	138.5	329.5	125.2
2008	149	122.9	NA	167.5	146.7	345.4	135.6
2009	134	110.4	NA	181.5	150.5	324.4	142.8
2010[1]	146	123.8	NA	175.6	148.7	322.3	141.0

[1] Estimate.   NA = Not availavle.   *Source: Economic Research Service, U.S. Department of Agriculture (ERS-USDA)*

Fresh Fruit: Per Capita Consumption[1] in the United States   In Pounds

Year	Oranges	Citrus Fruit — Tangerines & Tangelos	Lemons	Grapefruit	Total	Noncitrus Fruit — Apples	Apricots	Avocados	Bananas	Cherries	Cranberries
2001	11.88	2.73	2.96	4.85	23.92	15.61	.08	2.50	26.64	.77	.13
2002	11.74	2.57	3.34	4.63	23.37	16.00	.09	2.34	26.78	.70	.11
2003	11.90	2.73	3.33	4.10	23.83	16.91	.13	2.74	26.18	.92	.10
2004	10.80	2.78	3.12	4.14	22.69	18.79	.12	3.06	25.79	.99	.11
2005	11.42	2.51	2.95	2.65	21.62	16.66	.13	3.48	25.20	.87	.09
2006	10.25	2.69	4.15	2.31	21.64	17.73	.08	3.59	25.13	1.07	.09
2007	7.46	2.57	2.81	2.84	17.94	16.39	.16	3.50	25.98	1.22	.10
2008	9.93	3.08	1.97	3.16	20.61	15.90	.13	3.81	25.06	1.00	.10
2009	9.06	3.17	3.12	2.80	20.69	16.25	.14	4.24	22.03	1.56	.09
2010[2]	9.69	3.78	2.79	2.76	21.59	15.41	.12	3.45	25.59	1.33	.06

[1] All data on calendar-year basis except for citrus fruits; apples, August; grapes and pears, July; grapefruit, September; lemons, August of prior year; all other citrus, November.   [2] Preliminary.   *Source: Economic Research Service, U.S. Department of Agriculture (ERS-USDA)*

Fresh Fruit: Per Capita Consumption[1] in the United States   In Pounds

Year	Noncitrus Fruit Continued — Grapes	Kiwifruit	Mangos	& Peaches	Pears	Pineapples	Papaya	Prunes	Strawberries	Total Noncitrus	Total Fruit
2001	7.38	.44	1.79	5.16	3.25	3.16	.78	1.33	4.21	73.58	97.50
2002	8.42	.38	1.97	5.23	3.06	3.82	.79	1.26	4.65	75.98	99.35
2003	7.66	.38	2.06	5.17	3.08	4.40	.87	1.24	5.29	77.52	101.35
2004	7.80	.41	2.02	5.15	2.96	4.43	1.03	1.12	5.48	79.79	102.49
2005	8.60	.45	1.88	4.83	2.91	4.91	.94	1.11	5.83	78.32	99.93
2006	7.59	.47	2.10	4.58	3.19	5.21	1.04	1.02	6.14	79.59	101.23
2007	8.01	.44	2.11	4.47	3.09	5.02	1.08	1.01	6.27	79.42	97.36
2008	8.52	.46	2.11	5.09	3.11	5.08	.98	.92	6.45	79.54	100.15
2009	7.92	.50	2.02	4.41	3.19	5.09	1.20	.73	7.17	77.50	98.20
2010[2]	8.16	.49	2.23	4.73	2.89	5.69	1.16	.78	7.21	80.42	102.01

[1] All data on calendar-year basis except for citrus fruits; apples, August; grapes and pears, July; grapefruit, September; lemons, August of prior year; all other citrus, November.   [2] Preliminary.   *Source: Economic Research Service, U.S. Department of Agriculture (ERS-USDA)*

FRUITS

Average Price Received by Growers for Grapefruit in the United States   In Dollars Per Box

Year	Jan.	Feb.	Mar.	Apr.	May	June	July	Aug.	Sept.	Oct.	Nov.	Dec.	Average
2006	11.06	9.92	8.18	8.12	11.41	10.98	11.16	9.42	11.38	11.17	8.34	7.98	9.93
2007	5.66	4.02	2.91	2.10	4.49	9.89	8.95	7.53	8.55	10.06	9.93	5.97	6.67
2008	4.67	3.30	2.70	2.89	4.94	6.61	5.59	4.58	5.50	10.64	5.49	4.52	5.12
2009	4.19	3.74	3.61	2.99	6.21	8.23	7.15	6.15	6.55	16.41	10.78	8.82	7.07
2010	8.86	7.10	5.93	4.19	4.05	5.40	1.30	0.50	4.70	7.62	12.06	8.06	5.81
2011[1]	6.94	6.31	6.48	6.26	6.77	9.50	8.20	7.10	9.50	9.62	6.29	6.21	7.43

On-tree equivalent.   [1]Preliminary.   *Source: National Agricultural Statistics Service, U.S. Department of Agriculture (NASS-USDA)*

Average Price Received by Growers for Lemons in the United States   In Dollars Per Box

Year	Jan.	Feb.	Mar.	Apr.	May	June	July	Aug.	Sept.	Oct.	Nov.	Dec.	Average
2006	3.78	9.42	9.44	13.50	15.09	16.98	18.88	21.19	27.80	28.83	20.71	12.98	16.55
2007	11.50	27.69	8.68	9.18	8.14	13.04	13.64	31.67	33.08	37.98	29.80	23.89	20.69
2008	23.90	29.41	23.67	22.13	20.54	27.04	24.17	24.64	21.33	11.08	10.40	7.86	20.51
2009	5.90	2.62	1.80	4.26	5.68	11.34	12.21	20.79	17.60	15.59	14.60	11.81	10.35
2010	9.88	8.48	8.68	10.06	9.13	11.24	12.59	16.60	19.72	19.92	18.51	9.51	12.86
2011[1]	8.84	3.91	5.84	8.36	10.41	12.79	15.26	21.99	15.34	12.93	14.40	14.02	12.01

On-tree equivalent.   [1]Preliminary.   *Source: National Agricultural Statistics Service, U.S. Department of Agriculture (NASS-USDA)*

Average Price Received by Growers for Grapes in the United States   In Dollars Per Box

Year	Jan.	Feb.	Mar.	Apr.	May	June	July	Aug.	Sept.	Oct.	Nov.	Dec.	Average
2006	NQ	NQ	NQ	NQ	NQ	2,400	1,030	880	910	830	930	1,320	1,186
2007	NQ	NQ	NQ	NQ	NQ	710	660	680	790	940	1,200	1,710	956
2008	NQ	NQ	NQ	NQ	420	590	660	530	480	370	360	300	464
2009	NQ	NQ	NQ	NQ	1,720	1,400	610	310	470	630	630	1,220	874
2010	NQ	NQ	NQ	NQ	NQ	630	460	430	420	430	500	750	517
2011[1]	NQ	NQ	NQ	NQ	NQ	1,270	NA	960	810	790	980	1,080	982

Fresh.   [1]Preliminary.   NQ = No quote.   *Source: National Agricultural Statistics Service, U.S. Department of Agriculture (NASS-USDA)*

Average Price Received by Growers for Peaches in the United States   In Dollars Per Box

Year	Jan.	Feb.	Mar.	Apr.	May	June	July	Aug.	Sept.	Oct.	Nov.	Dec.	Average
2006	NQ	NQ	NQ	NQ	NQ	809	721	746	589	NQ	NQ	NQ	716
2007	NQ	NQ	NQ	NQ	820	522	579	593	563	NQ	NQ	NQ	615
2008	NQ	NQ	NQ	NQ	960	442	485	510	468	NQ	NQ	NQ	573
2009	NQ	NQ	NQ	NQ	846	822	644	676	655	NQ	NQ	NQ	729
2010	NQ	NQ	NQ	NQ	1,080	604	573	540	497	NQ	NQ	NQ	659
2011[1]	NQ	NQ	NQ	NQ	1,290	646	632	622	606	NQ	NQ	NQ	759

Fresh.   [1]Preliminary.   NQ = No quote.   *Source: National Agricultural Statistics Service, U.S. Department of Agriculture (NASS-USDA)*

Average Price Received by Growers for Pears in the United States   In Dollars Per Box

Year	Jan.	Feb.	Mar.	Apr.	May	June	July	Aug.	Sept.	Oct.	Nov.	Dec.	Average
2006	404	392	339	356	419	596	759	286	283	568	570	563	461
2007	541	517	544	597	651	714	584	374	380	526	514	557	542
2008	560	552	537	527	525	654	638	546	543	628	581	574	572
2009	543	473	452	462	518	642	537	424	383	481	449	398	480
2010	381	368	350	426	533	640	598	496	486	622	549	587	503
2011[1]	639	636	653	618	588	675	521	620	585	562	542	521	597

Fresh.   [1]Preliminary.   *Source: National Agricultural Statistics Service, U.S. Department of Agriculture (NASS-USDA)*

Average Price Received by Growers for Strawberries in the United States   In Dollars Per Box

Year	Jan.	Feb.	Mar.	Apr.	May	June	July	Aug.	Sept.	Oct.	Nov.	Dec.	Average
2006	142.00	99.90	68.80	61.10	61.80	51.40	64.00	63.70	77.60	72.90	96.10	189.00	87.36
2007	131.00	147.00	88.90	64.90	68.60	66.10	53.00	79.30	57.40	80.00	116.00	171.00	93.60
2008	194.00	131.00	95.30	65.50	83.30	61.90	65.90	91.00	70.10	72.00	87.60	208.00	102.13
2009	116.00	128.00	91.10	78.90	76.10	62.80	74.80	73.50	75.00	108.00	87.60	210.00	98.48
2010	218.00	179.00	116.00	75.70	78.90	67.70	62.00	81.70	73.30	87.60	139.00	285.00	121.99
2011[1]	217.00	126.00	98.00	96.20	80.80	72.70	89.20	92.80	87.60	66.90	84.40	153.00	105.38

Fresh.   [1]Preliminary.   *Source: National Agricultural Statistics Service, U.S. Department of Agriculture (NASS-USDA)*

Cold Storage Stocks of Frozen Blueberries in the United States, on First of Month   In Thousands of Pounds

Year	Jan.	Feb.	Mar.	Apr.	May	June	July	Aug.	Sept.	Oct.	Nov.	Dec.
2006	77,360	68,466	58,454	47,039	36,613	28,909	26,785	62,220	123,072	114,351	110,139	99,826
2007	98,719	83,196	75,709	65,398	56,362	45,921	37,700	84,342	154,880	147,570	134,715	125,577
2008	114,114	100,696	94,652	78,106	66,604	58,282	51,960	69,783	172,145	182,478	174,334	164,703
2009	153,445	141,089	130,964	115,615	100,820	87,790	81,404	106,327	189,893	189,628	173,849	154,647
2010	141,883	123,579	109,095	93,342	75,482	61,331	57,332	100,100	163,387	155,105	140,707	129,877
2011[1]	116,485	104,091	93,103	80,016	65,583	50,865	57,467	76,551	167,015	174,805	160,156	149,989

[1] Preliminary.   *Source: Economic Research Service, U.S. Department of Agriculture (ERS-USDA)*

Cold Storage Stocks of Frozen Cherries[2] in the United States, on First of Month   In Thousands of Pounds

Year	Jan.	Feb.	Mar.	Apr.	May	June	July	Aug.	Sept.	Oct.	Nov.	Dec.
2006	110,359	102,319	92,935	78,660	71,560	61,316	47,806	137,736	143,082	133,717	123,486	112,606
2007	110,361	97,425	88,896	76,170	66,958	58,337	48,989	168,436	158,643	153,812	142,039	132,845
2008	126,646	117,609	109,423	100,479	87,495	75,690	63,055	118,790	137,994	120,386	113,867	108,046
2009	101,892	96,533	90,052	79,608	69,139	59,714	53,206	128,571	193,312	185,263	179,608	167,716
2010	156,136	145,923	136,313	124,138	113,941	103,008	96,431	161,826	150,298	136,233	128,236	118,223
2011[1]	110,166	97,223	87,153	71,167	62,380	50,776	40,803	96,444	124,645	108,842	98,395	91,497

[1] Preliminary.   [2] Tart (ripe tart pitted).   *Source: Economic Research Service, U.S. Department of Agriculture (ERS-USDA)*

Cold Storage Stocks of Frozen Raspberries[2] in the United States, on First of Month   In Thousands of Pounds

Year	Jan.	Feb.	Mar.	Apr.	May	June	July	Aug.	Sept.	Oct.	Nov.	Dec.
2006	55,801	50,804	46,381	39,472	34,752	30,989	36,572	85,911	78,993	64,459	60,612	56,486
2007	52,208	45,239	39,593	34,686	33,569	30,317	27,572	72,044	60,685	52,212	44,626	39,369
2008	33,681	27,326	25,349	19,566	15,043	12,548	10,744	49,092	55,382	49,094	45,873	41,861
2009	34,083	29,155	25,817	24,155	20,797	18,742	15,963	75,263	65,422	59,133	52,459	48,339
2010	41,572	38,012	30,972	28,317	25,137	20,192	19,296	67,816	63,950	59,331	53,098	46,875
2011[1]	42,151	37,949	33,062	28,466	27,424	23,199	21,531	66,893	73,113	71,489	65,330	62,173

[1] Preliminary .   [2] Red: Includes IQF, Pails and Tubs, Barrels (400 lbs net), and Concentrate.   *Source: Economic Research Service, U.S. Department of Agriculture (ERS-USDA)*

Cold Storage Stocks of Frozen Strawberries[2] in the United States, on First of Month   In Thousands of Pounds

Year	Jan.	Feb.	Mar.	Apr.	May	June	July	Aug.	Sept.	Oct.	Nov.	Dec.
2006	421,491	399,423	353,776	301,890	274,713	249,472	224,001	212,044	160,851	172,959	424,987	495,447
2007	458,222	396,189	371,397	319,167	276,074	254,816	232,344	215,691	196,806	209,121	451,052	498,790
2008	464,609	425,313	402,895	350,167	312,823	269,330	251,309	234,242	206,201	219,247	537,319	527,876
2009	509,807	467,363	414,907	360,587	343,101	311,835	286,675	246,058	215,985	198,200	551,910	530,591
2010	486,760	449,112	399,408	355,773	318,497	289,097	246,690	209,745	174,476	225,587	502,560	473,224
2011[1]	439,996	404,540	367,245	345,891	294,806	254,167	217,588	189,747	150,499	160,415	452,305	452,560

[1] Preliminary.   [2] Includes IQF and Poly, Pails and Tubs, Barrels and Drums, and Juice Stock.   *Source: Economic Research Service, U.S. Department of Agriculture (ERS-USDA)*

Cold Storage Stocks of Other Frozen Fruit in the United States, on First of Month   In Thousands of Pounds

Year	Jan.	Feb.	Mar.	Apr.	May	June	July	Aug.	Sept.	Oct.	Nov.	Dec.
2006	421,491	399,423	353,776	301,890	274,713	249,472	224,001	212,044	160,851	172,959	424,987	495,447
2007	458,222	396,189	371,397	319,167	276,074	254,816	232,344	215,691	196,806	209,121	537,319	498,790
2008	464,609	425,313	402,895	350,167	312,823	269,330	251,309	234,242	206,201	219,247	537,319	527,876
2009	509,807	467,363	414,907	360,587	343,101	311,835	286,675	246,058	215,985	198,200	551,910	530,591
2010	486,760	449,112	399,408	355,773	318,497	289,097	246,690	209,745	174,476	225,587	502,560	473,224
2011[1]	439,996	404,540	367,245	345,891	294,806	254,167	217,588	189,747	150,499	160,415	452,305	452,560

[1] Preliminary.   *Source: Economic Research Service, U.S. Department of Agriculture (ERS-USDA)*

Cold Storage Stocks of Total Frozen Fruit in the United States, on First of Month   In Millions of Pounds

Year	Jan.	Feb.	Mar.	Apr.	May	June	July	Aug.	Sept.	Oct.	Nov.	Dec.
2006	1,067.1	972.0	863.5	747.0	710.9	740.3	849.1	1,057.4	1,027.2	963.3	1,179.7	1,192.4
2007	1,136.5	1,019.9	950.7	853.6	882.8	866.8	949.6	1,218.4	1,226.8	1,200.0	1,352.4	1,319.9
2008	1,239.5	1,140.3	1,068.7	920.5	866.2	839.8	864.1	1,043.1	1,125.7	1,130.7	1,393.6	1,337.5
2009	1,245.6	1,134.2	1,038.1	911.0	916.8	910.6	973.2	1,154.3	1,257.8	1,200.7	1,501.1	1,428.2
2010	1,328.6	1,226.0	1,125.9	1,014.5	971.8	902.7	921.1	1,124.3	1,118.5	1,113.1	1,335.7	1,259.8
2011[1]	1,165.1	1,060.7	950.9	847.7	770.1	750.6	785.5	953.4	1,058.5	1,063.6	1,316.9	1,282.6

[1] Preliminary.   *Source: Economic Research Service, U.S. Department of Agriculture (ERS-USDA)*

Gas

Natural gas is a fossil fuel that is colorless, shapeless, and odorless in its pure form. It is a mixture of hydrocarbon gases formed primarily of methane, but it can also include ethane, propane, butane, and pentane. Natural gas is combustible, clean burning, and gives off a great deal of energy. Around 500 BC, the Chinese discovered that the energy in natural gas could be harnessed. They passed it through crude bamboo-shoot pipes and then burned it to boil sea water to create potable fresh water. Around 1785, Britain became the first country to commercially use natural gas produced from coal for streetlights and indoor lights. In 1821, William Hart dug the first well specifically intended to obtain natural gas and he is generally regarded as the "father of natural gas" in America. There is a vast amount of natural gas estimated to still be in the ground in the U.S. Natural gas as a source of energy is significantly less expensive than electricity per Btu.

Natural gas futures and options are traded on the New York Mercantile Exchange (NYMEX). The NYMEX natural gas futures contract calls for the delivery of natural gas representing 10,000 million British thermal units (mmBtu) at the Henry Hub in Louisiana, which is the nexus of 16 intra-state and inter-state pipelines. The contract is priced in terms of dollars per mmBtu. NYMEX also has basic swap futures contracts available for 30 different natural gas pricing locations versus the benchmark Henry Hub location. Natural gas futures are also listed in London on the International Petroleum Exchange (IPE).

Prices – NYMEX natural gas futures on the nearest-futures chart during 2011 traded sideways in the first half of the year and then steadily sold off during the remainder of the year to close 2011 down 32% at $2.989 per mmBtu.

Supply – U.S. recovery of natural gas in 2010 rose +3.2% to a record high of 26.851 billion cubic feet. The top U.S. producing states for natural gas were Texas with 30.0% of U.S. production in 2010, Wyoming with 10.3%, Louisiana with 9.9%, Oklahoma with 8.2%, and Colorado with 7.1%. In 2010 the world's largest natural gas producers were the U.S. with 2,054,478 terajoules and Russia with 1,839,759 terajoules of production.

Demand – U.S.- delivered consumption of natural gas in 2010 rose +5.7% yr/yr to 24.134 billion cubic feet, of which about 30.6% was delivered to electrical utility plants, 27.4% to industrial establishments, 20.5% to residences, and 13.3% to commercial establishments.

Trade – U.S. imports of natural gas (consumed) in 2010 fell -0.3% yr/yr to 3.740 billion cubic feet, down from the 2007 record high of 4,607 billion cubic feet. U.S. exports of natural gas in 2010 rose +4.7% yr/yr to 1,122 billion cubic feet, which is a new record high.

World Production of Natural Gas (Monthly Average Marketed Production[3])   In Terajoule[4]

Year	Australia	Canada	China	Germany	India	Indonesia	Italy	Mexico	Nether-lands	Romania	Russia	United Kingdom	United States
2002	96,841	553,183	106,720	61,147	92,568	280,939	46,190	168,675	186,206	38,004	1,934,011	361,414	1,792,367
2003	99,771	534,434	111,352	61,441	89,570	289,371	42,812	174,733	178,853	38,831	2,016,895	358,798	1,726,221
2004	104,731	537,643	132,281	55,108	83,996	282,364	39,760	177,650	232,485	41,725	2,055,061	333,492	1,564,674
2005	108,249	547,204	163,802	55,089	92,451	267,057	38,167	187,151	218,699	40,959	2,065,477	307,775	1,636,149
2006	115,535	551,543	193,124	55,557	101,144	279,573	34,670	208,018	191,741	33,977	2,134,095	278,935	1,682,950
2007	115,541	540,070	223,107	49,895	101,150	292,656	30,839	230,885	189,494	34,001	2,116,869	251,428	1,745,050
2008	113,672	507,412	261,162	51,475	102,793	266,428	28,893	264,454	210,393	32,374	1,862,664	242,895	1,861,285
2009	125,739	473,792	277,124	49,268	130,868	278,445	25,778	269,628	195,122	31,328	1,638,043	208,190	1,896,952
2010[1]	133,676	463,813	303,564	42,939	167,753	299,422	26,346	269,073	219,495	30,990	1,829,291	199,306	1,953,277
2011[2]	131,257	467,606	322,095	41,198	154,856		26,331	254,549		30,815	1,839,759	154,366	2,054,478

[1] Preliminary.   [2] Estimate.   [3] Compares all gas collected & utilized as fuel or as a chemical industry raw material, including gas used in oilfields and/or gasfields as a fuel by producers.   [4] Terajoule = 10 to the 12th power Joule = approximately 10 to the 9th power BTU.   *Source: United Nations*

Marketed Production of Natural Gas in the United States, by States   In Million Cubic Feet

Year	Alaska	Arkansas	California	Colorado	Kansas	Louisiana[2]	New Mexico	Oklahoma	Pennsyl-vania	Texas[2]	Wyoming	Total
2001	471,440	166,804	377,824	817,206	480,145	1,502,086	1,689,125	1,615,384	130,853	5,282,723	1,363,879	20,570,295
2002	463,301	161,871	360,205	937,245	454,901	1,361,751	1,632,080	1,581,606	157,800	5,141,075	1,453,957	19,884,780
2003	489,757	169,599	337,216	1,011,285	418,893	1,350,399	1,604,015	1,558,155	159,827	5,243,567	1,539,318	19,974,360
2004	471,899	187,069	319,919	1,079,235	397,121	1,353,249	1,632,539	1,655,769	197,217	5,067,315	1,592,203	19,517,491
2005	487,282	190,533	317,637	1,133,086	377,229	1,296,048	1,645,166	1,639,310	168,501	5,276,401	1,639,317	18,927,095
2006	444,724	270,293	315,209	1,202,821	371,044	1,361,119	1,609,223	1,688,985	175,950	5,548,022	1,816,201	19,409,674
2007	433,485	269,886	307,160	1,242,571	365,877	1,365,333	1,517,922	1,783,682	182,277	6,123,180	2,047,882	20,196,346
2008	398,442	446,457	296,469	1,389,399	374,310	1,377,969	1,446,204	1,886,710	198,295	6,960,693	2,274,850	21,112,053
2009	397,077	679,952	276,575	1,499,070	354,440	1,548,607	1,383,004	1,901,556	273,869	6,818,973	2,335,328	21,647,936
2010[1]	374,226	926,638	286,841	1,578,379	324,720	2,210,099	1,292,185	1,827,328	572,902	6,715,294	2,305,525	22,402,141

[1] Preliminary.   *Source: Energy Information Administration, U.S. Department of Energy (EIA-DOE)*

World Production of Natural Gas Plant Liquids   Thousand Barrels per Day

Year	Algeria	Canada	Mexico	Saudi Arabia	Russia	United States	Persian Gulf[2]	OAPEC[3]	OPEC-12[4]	OPEC-11[4]	World
2002	270	698	408	1,095	246	1,880	1,797	2,137	2,326	2,403	6,872
2003	280	724	418	1,220	390	1,719	1,972	2,312	2,473	2,548	7,134
2004	292	658	442	1,310	456	1,809	2,100	2,437	2,634	2,702	7,382
2005	295	645	426	1,460	457	1,717	2,282	2,667	2,874	2,930	7,658
2006	310	685	427	1,427	417	1,739	2,289	2,804	2,955	2,999	7,893
2007	342	726	396	1,440	426	1,783	2,313	2,862	3,031	3,083	8,015
2008	357	677	365	1,434	422	1,784	2,339	2,891	3,088	-----	7,976
2009	345	640	370	1,422	423	1,910	2,365	2,896	3,097	-----	8,103
2010[1]	350	651	378	1,521	436	1,989	2,528	3,039	3,272	-----	8,360

Average. [1] Preliminary. [2] Bahrain, Iran, Iraq, Kuwait, Qatar, Saudi Arabia, and the United Arab Emirates. [3] Organization of Arab Petroleum Exporting Countriess: Algeria, Iraq, Kuwait, Libya, Qatar, Saudi Arabia, and the United Arab Emirates. [4] OPEC-12: Organization of the Petroleum Exporting Countries: Algeria, Angola, Indonesia, Iran, Iraq, Kuwait, Libya, Nigeria, Qatar, Saudi Arabia, the United Arab Emirates, and Venezuela. OPEC-11 does not include Angola. *Source: Energy Information Administration, U.S. Department of Energy (EIA-DOE)*

Recoverable Reserves and Deliveries of Natural Gas in the United States   In Billions of Cubic Feet

Year	Gross With-drawals	Recoverable Reserves of Natural Gas Dec. 31[2]	Residential	Commercial	Electric Utility Plants[3]	Industrial	Total	Lease & Plant Fuel	Used as Pipline Fuel	Heating Value BTU per Cubic Foot
2002	23,941	186,946	4,889	3,144	5,672	7,507	23,007	1,113	667	1,027
2003	24,119	189,044	5,079	3,179	5,135	7,150	22,277	1,122	591	1,031
2004	23,970	192,513	4,869	3,129	5,464	7,243	22,389	1,098	566	1,026
2005	23,457	204,385	4,827	2,999	5,869	6,597	22,011	1,112	584	1,028
2006	23,535	211,085	4,368	2,832	6,222	6,512	21,685	1,142	584	1,028
2007	24,664	237,726	4,722	3,013	6,841	6,648	23,097	1,226	621	1,029
2008	25,636	244,656	4,892	3,153	6,668	6,661	23,268	1,220	648	1,027
2009	26,013	272,509	4,778	3,119	6,872	6,167	22,839	1,275	598	1,025
2010[1]	26,852		4,952	3,206	7,379	6,600	24,134	1,332	632	

[1] Preliminary. [2] Estimated proved recoverable reserves of dry natural gas. [3] Figures include gas other than natural (impossible to segregate); therefore, shown separately from other consumption. *Source: Energy Information Administration, U.S. Department of Energy (EIA-DOE)*

Gas Utility Sales in the United States by Types and Class of Service   In Trillions of BTUs

Year	Total Utility Sales	Number of Customers (Millions)	Resi-dental	Commer-cial	Industrial	Electric Generation	Other	Total	Resi-dental	Commer-cial	Industrial	Electric Generation	Other
			Class of Service						Revenue - Million $ From Sales to Customers				
2000	9,232	61.3	4,741	2,077	1,698	709	6	59,243	35,828	13,338	7,432	2,612	33
2001	8,667	61.4	4,525	2,053	1,461	620	8	69,150	42,454	16,848	7,513	2,286	49
2002	8,864	62.0	4,589	2,055	1,748	459	13	57,112	35,062	13,512	6,840	1,639	59
2003	8,927	62.6	4,722	2,125	1,672	397	11	72,606	43,664	17,349	9,478	2,048	68
2004	8,766	63.3	4,566	2,075	1,763	351	12	79,929	47,275	18,689	11,230	2,653	83
2005	8,848	64.4	4,516	2,056	1,654	610	12	96,909	55,680	22,653	13,751	4,718	107
2006	8,222	65.0	4,117	1,861	1,576	606	62	91,928	53,961	21,557	12,006	3,921	484
2007[1]	8,565	65.4	4,418	1,943	1,522	626	57	92,131	55,027	21,248	11,323	4,076	457
2008[2]	8,594	65.5	4,541	2,009	1,410	614	21	102,641	60,195	23,592	13,205	5,406	243

[1] Preliminary. [2] Estimate. *Source: American Gas Association (AGA)*

Salient Statistics of Natural Gas in the United States

Year	Mar-keted Pro-duction	Extrac-tion Loss	Dry Pro-duction	Storage With-drawals	Imports (Con-sumed)	Total Supply	Con-sump-tion	Exports	Added to Storage	Total Dis-position	Well-head Price	Imports	Exports	Resi-dential	Com-mercial	Indus-trial	Electric Utilities
				In Billions of Cubic Feet								Dollars Per Thousand Cubic Feet					
2002	19,885	957	18,928	3,138	4,015	26,767	23,007	516	2,670	26,767	2.95	3.14	3.41	7.89	6.63	4.02	3.68
2003	19,974	876	19,099	3,099	3,944	26,963	22,277	680	3,292	26,963	4.88	5.17	5.54	9.63	8.40	5.89	5.57
2004	19,517	927	18,591	3,037	4,259	26,985	22,389	854	3,150	26,985	5.46	5.81	6.09	10.75	9.43	6.53	6.11
2005	18,927	876	18,051	3,057	4,341	26,325	22,011	729	3,002	25,741	7.33	8.12	7.59	12.70	11.34	8.56	8.47
2006	19,410	906	18,504	2,493	4,186	26,089	21,685	724	2,924	25,333	6.39	6.88	6.83	13.73	12.00	7.87	7.11
2007	20,196	930	19,266	3,325	4,608	28,129	23,097	822	3,133	27,053	6.25	6.87	6.92	13.08	11.34	7.68	7.31
2008	21,112	953	20,159	3,374	3,984	28,470	23,268	963	3,340	27,572	7.97	8.70	8.58	13.89	12.23	9.65	9.26
2009[1]	21,604	1,024	20,580	2,966	3,751	28,322	22,839	1,072	3,315	27,227	3.67	4.19	4.47	12.14	10.06	5.33	4.93
2010[2]	22,563	992	21,571	3,303	3,741	29,606	24,134	1,122	3,291	28,547	4.48	4.52	5.02	11.39	9.47	5.49	5.27

[1] Preliminary. [2] Estimate. *Source: Energy Information Administration, U.S. Department of Energy (EIA-DOE)*

Natural Gas (monthly average) through December 2011   USD per MMBtu

Average Price of Natural Gas at Henry Hub   In Dollars Per MMBtu

Year	Jan.	Feb.	Mar.	Apr.	May	June	July	Aug.	Sept.	Oct.	Nov.	Dec.	Average
2002	2.25	2.31	3.03	3.42	3.49	3.22	2.98	3.09	3.55	4.12	4.04	4.75	3.35
2003	5.49	7.41	6.08	5.27	5.81	5.83	5.03	4.97	4.61	4.66	4.47	6.13	5.48
2004	6.17	5.39	5.38	5.71	6.30	6.29	5.93	5.44	5.11	6.39	6.15	6.64	5.91
2005	6.13	6.13	6.91	7.22	6.48	7.15	7.63	9.46	11.87	13.42	10.28	13.05	8.81
2006	8.65	7.54	6.90	7.16	6.23	6.19	6.22	7.14	4.90	5.84	7.36	6.73	6.74
2007	6.60	7.92	7.10	7.59	7.63	7.35	6.21	6.23	6.08	6.78	7.15	7.13	6.98
2008	7.98	8.54	9.44	10.13	11.28	12.68	11.06	8.25	7.67	6.73	6.67	5.81	8.85
2009	5.23	4.52	3.95	3.50	3.83	3.81	3.39	3.15	3.01	4.02	3.70	5.33	3.95
2010	5.77	5.33	4.29	4.03	4.15	4.81	4.62	4.31	3.91	3.43	3.73	4.24	4.38
2011	4.49	4.09	3.97	4.24	4.30	4.55	4.42	4.05	3.89	3.57	3.25	3.17	4.00

Source: Energy Information Administration, U.S. Department of Energy (EIA-DOE)

Volume of Trading of Natural Gas Futures in New York   In Thousands of Contracts

Year	Jan.	Feb.	Mar.	Apr.	May	June	July	Aug.	Sept.	Oct.	Nov.	Dec.	Total
2002	1,942.5	1,668.6	2,381.1	2,421.7	2,281.4	1,911.7	2,266.1	2,115.6	1,990.0	2,103.4	1,569.2	1,706.4	24,357.8
2003	2,134.4	1,909.1	1,362.4	1,321.3	1,521.7	1,584.8	1,543.7	1,315.3	1,503.7	1,948.9	1,376.6	1,515.2	19,037.1
2004	1,162.1	1,125.1	1,420.3	1,443.1	1,587.5	1,588.5	1,508.8	1,724.1	1,885.6	1,458.3	1,320.0	1,218.6	17,441.9
2005	1,442.2	1,490.4	1,653.3	1,586.0	1,504.1	1,931.9	1,528.4	2,044.4	1,587.6	1,433.1	1,449.5	1,491.7	19,142.5
2006	1,609.9	1,833.9	1,682.2	1,911.6	2,272.5	1,920.6	1,786.2	2,428.7	2,017.7	1,935.1	1,799.6	1,832.0	23,030.0
2007	2,597.6	2,417.5	1,922.6	2,163.2	2,266.2	2,683.7	2,346.7	3,049.9	2,468.5	3,044.3	2,452.0	2,374.2	29,786.3
2008	2,921.9	3,330.7	2,983.6	3,382.9	3,168.0	3,379.1	4,274.0	3,756.1	3,458.5	3,151.7	2,539.9	2,384.3	38,730.5
2009	2,343.7	2,780.6	2,989.9	2,493.1	3,479.0	4,486.6	3,979.4	4,445.9	5,597.7	5,594.7	4,413.7	5,347.2	47,951.4
2010	4,501.7	4,557.7	4,690.9	5,740.4	4,729.9	5,911.9	5,267.7	5,791.0	5,428.1	5,920.0	5,780.8	6,002.9	64,323.1
2011	6,468.6	6,123.2	7,284.0	6,432.0	6,015.2	6,759.5	5,317.9	6,904.9	6,363.8	7,199.9	6,117.1	5,878.3	76,864.3

Contract size = 10,000 MMBtu.   *Source: CME Group; New York Mercantile Exchange (NYMEX)*

Average Open Interest of Natural Gas Futures in New York   In Contracts

Year	Jan.	Feb.	Mar.	Apr.	May	June	July	Aug.	Sept.	Oct.	Nov.	Dec.
2002	458,924	491,215	527,765	559,413	556,277	526,016	494,133	437,285	419,532	413,312	393,953	391,424
2003	415,642	420,329	367,673	354,154	365,838	366,610	357,299	343,622	354,568	352,685	356,622	340,756
2004	322,762	312,475	322,366	338,786	382,160	366,135	373,853	378,787	393,477	392,626	383,712	387,605
2005	401,829	405,692	458,013	479,880	480,318	472,631	498,440	524,235	544,165	551,121	545,270	551,444
2006	545,165	582,231	634,072	700,588	795,375	851,655	883,492	938,024	940,339	931,949	903,355	889,759
2007	905,449	839,142	761,701	747,721	752,596	787,099	823,127	776,747	778,512	749,480	789,360	843,361
2008	881,812	942,089	906,497	875,484	885,165	946,673	963,953	922,474	915,638	859,278	744,821	702,918
2009	693,269	708,968	652,412	649,925	678,413	709,236	737,506	731,555	713,822	709,965	713,612	719,561
2010	761,998	786,388	839,164	855,385	860,760	817,712	783,921	819,168	812,356	800,760	783,715	774,390
2011	820,828	916,971	922,068	948,064	956,531	980,350	977,018	990,293	952,145	969,639	977,228	981,241

Contract size = 10,000 MMBtu.   *Source: CME Group; New York Mercantile Exchange (NYMEX)*

Gasoline

Gasoline is a complex mixture of hundreds of lighter liquid hydrocarbons and is used chiefly as a fuel for internal-combustion engines. Petroleum crude, or crude oil, is still the most economical source of gasoline with refineries turning more than half of every barrel of crude oil into gasoline. The three basic steps to all refining operations are the separation process (separating crude oil into various chemical components), conversion process (breaking the chemicals down into molecules called hydrocarbons), and treatment process (transforming and combining hydrocarbon molecules and other additives). Another process, called hydro treating, removes a significant amount of sulfur from finished gasoline as is currently required by the state of California.

Octane is a measure of a gasoline's ability to resist pinging or knocking noise from an engine. Most gasoline stations offer three octane grades of unleaded fuel—regular at 87 (R+M)/2, mid-grade at 89 (R+M)/2, and premium at 93 (R+M)/2. Additional refining steps are needed to increase the octane, which increases the retail price. This does not make the gasoline any cleaner or better, but yields a different blend of hydrocarbons that burn more slowly.

In an attempt to improve air quality and reduce harmful emissions from internal combustion engines, Congress in 1990 amended the Clean Air Act to mandate the addition of ethanol to gasoline. Some 2 billion gallons of ethanol are now added to gasoline each year in the U.S. The most common blend is E10, which contains 10% ethanol and 90% gasoline. Auto manufacturers have approved that mixture for use in all U.S. vehicles. Ethanol is an alcohol-based fuel produced by fermenting and distilling crops such as corn, barley, wheat and sugar.

Unleaded gasoline futures and options trade at the New York Mercantile Exchange (NYMEX). The NYMEX gasoline futures contract calls for the delivery of 1,000 barrels (42,000 gallons) of unleaded gasoline in the New York harbor and is priced in terms of dollars and cents per gallon.

Prices – NYMEX gasoline futures prices in early 2011 extended the rally that began in 2010 and posted a new 3-year high of $3.48 per gallon in April 2011. Gasoline prices fell during the remainder of the year but still closed 2011 up 10.5% at $2.6863 per gallon.

The average monthly retail price of regular unleaded gasoline in 2011 (through November) rose +26.5% yr/yr to $3.52 per gallon. The average monthly retail price of unleaded premium motor gasoline in the U.S. in 2011 (through November) rose +24.5% to $3.79 per gallon. The average monthly refiner price of finished aviation gasoline to end users in 2011 (through September) rose +25.9% yr/yr to $3.81 per gallon.

Supply – U.S. production of gasoline in 2011 (through November, annualized) fell -0.3% yr/yr to 9.025 million barrels per day. Gasoline stocks in October of 2011 were 59.290 million barrels, down from 63.257 million barrels in December of 2010.

Demand – U.S. consumption of finished motor gasoline in 2011 (through November, annualized) fell -2.7% yr/yr to 8.750 million barrels per day, below 2007's record high of 9.284 million barrels per day.

Production of Finished Motor Gasoline in the United States   In Thousand Barrels per Day

Year	Jan.	Feb.	Mar.	Apr.	May	June	July	Aug.	Sept.	Oct.	Nov.	Dec.	Average
2002	8,160	8,117	8,072	8,626	8,729	8,661	8,665	8,666	8,320	8,190	8,738	8,734	8,475
2003	7,870	7,800	7,724	8,161	8,311	8,293	8,320	8,355	8,228	8,253	8,450	8,540	8,194
2004	7,956	7,979	8,102	8,233	8,447	8,336	8,370	8,357	7,993	8,384	8,346	8,659	8,264
2005	8,157	8,194	8,119	8,549	8,475	8,589	8,352	8,326	8,129	7,953	8,468	8,503	8,318
2006	8,189	7,969	7,765	8,032	8,613	8,957	8,624	8,610	8,465	8,210	8,335	8,567	8,361
2007	8,348	8,012	8,101	8,122	8,491	8,686	8,504	8,547	8,320	8,276	8,353	8,501	8,355
2008	8,516	8,495	8,373	8,560	8,700	8,564	8,523	8,513	7,855	8,889	8,722	8,850	8,547
2009	8,445	8,408	8,646	8,724	8,793	9,068	8,952	8,856	8,829	8,770	8,905	9,006	8,784
2010	8,348	8,510	8,913	9,062	9,113	9,211	9,500	9,426	9,143	9,049	9,134	9,252	9,055
2011[1]	8,671	8,793	8,824	8,931	9,142	9,286	9,165	9,265	9,132	8,953	9,038	9,104	9,025

[1] Preliminary.   Source: Energy Information Administration, U.S. Department of Energy (EIA-DOE)

Disposition of Finished Motor Gasoline, Total Product Supplied in the United States   In Thousand Barrels per Day

Year	Jan.	Feb.	Mar.	Apr.	May	June	July	Aug.	Sept.	Oct.	Nov.	Dec.	Average
2002	8,227	8,607	8,655	8,766	9,078	9,140	9,143	9,313	8,687	8,814	8,829	8,893	8,848
2003	8,414	8,525	8,602	8,838	9,042	9,170	9,192	9,411	8,926	9,108	8,946	9,011	8,935
2004	8,705	8,838	9,024	9,126	9,179	9,322	9,357	9,327	9,015	9,097	9,055	9,206	9,104
2005	8,813	8,861	8,994	9,128	9,278	9,373	9,534	9,537	8,915	9,036	9,115	9,296	9,157
2006	8,839	8,911	9,054	9,154	9,308	9,478	9,607	9,564	9,236	9,267	9,244	9,338	9,250
2007	8,886	9,006	9,178	9,215	9,434	9,491	9,640	9,582	9,254	9,236	9,229	9,251	9,284
2008	8,810	8,866	9,066	9,112	9,251	9,110	9,150	9,134	8,497	9,024	8,904	8,927	8,988
2009	8,623	8,836	8,903	9,029	9,084	9,180	9,260	9,295	8,911	8,986	8,906	8,931	8,995
2010	8,520	8,579	8,793	9,108	9,162	9,311	9,301	9,255	9,112	9,016	8,816	8,911	8,990
2011[1]	8,412	8,648	8,750	8,762	8,784	9,046	8,960	8,907	8,753	8,623	8,645	8,713	8,750

[1] Preliminary.   Source: Energy Information Administration, U.S. Department of Energy (EIA-DOE)

GASOLINE

RBOB Gasoline Futures - CME Group (NYMEX)
(weekly close) as of December 30, 2011

USD per gallon

Average Spot Price of Unleaded Gasoline in New York   In Cents Per Gallon

Year	Jan.	Feb.	Mar.	Apr.	May	June	July	Aug.	Sept.	Oct.	Nov.	Dec.	Average
2002	54.30	55.41	69.64	74.66	70.32	71.65	76.62	76.75	78.36	82.34	76.08	80.56	72.22
2003	87.56	99.62	95.51	80.08	76.16	80.65	87.17	100.42	90.41	87.12	87.33	88.37	88.37
2004	99.66	104.63	109.12	112.02	133.98	115.70	122.65	120.89	126.17	137.75	126.96	106.90	118.04
2005	123.85	122.42	143.90	147.06	137.06	151.02	158.89	191.13	214.78	170.87	147.73	159.88	155.72
2006	173.39	149.98	175.87	214.62	204.68	206.50	223.99	203.23	158.42	152.00	158.71	166.70	182.34
2007	141.63	164.55	193.58	210.05	224.09	218.30	213.51	199.83	209.72	216.93	242.33	232.69	205.60
2008	233.09	238.37	249.09	277.45	309.23	329.79	315.86	290.20	280.69	190.84	129.29	97.18	245.09
2009	115.11	121.66	128.84	137.77	169.79	190.79	174.74	193.01	178.43	192.30	198.63	192.00	166.09
2010	204.28	199.38	214.86	222.10	201.35	201.13	200.38	195.01	197.47	216.07	224.31	238.74	209.59
2011	244.61	252.95	283.48	316.55	302.77	283.41	302.40	282.05	281.44	276.53	263.11	263.19	279.37

Source: Energy Information Administration, U.S. Department of Energy (EIA-DOE)

Volume of Trading of Gasoline, RBOB[1] Futures in New York   In Contracts

Year	Jan.	Feb.	Mar.	Apr.	May	June	July	Aug.	Sept.	Oct.	Nov.	Dec.	Total
2002	795.0	744.7	942.7	1,019.3	985.2	834.5	967.8	893.6	867.6	1,105.0	865.9	958.4	10,979.7
2003	1,054.1	968.7	1,010.9	909.0	933.7	944.0	987.5	1,021.5	943.0	877.1	760.8	761.6	11,172.1
2004	956.1	998.7	1,169.2	1,169.0	1,203.8	1,194.5	1,027.0	1,177.7	1,052.9	983.7	849.0	995.9	12,777.5
2005	974.6	1,000.9	1,193.5	1,252.5	1,060.2	1,104.7	1,103.2	1,341.3	1,221.3	999.2	928.1	989.0	13,168.4
2006	1,149.6	1,233.0	1,259.1	1,079.6	1,122.7	1,039.8	939.8	1,145.5	891.4	839.6	838.1	966.0	12,504.2
2007	1,172.9	1,272.2	1,722.5	1,826.7	2,134.5	1,811.8	1,770.2	1,872.8	1,627.3	1,706.1	1,531.3	1,343.2	19,791.4
2008	1,660.6	1,887.5	2,111.9	1,986.3	1,917.6	1,854.4	1,621.6	1,667.7	1,862.1	1,452.9	1,193.4	1,306.4	20,522.6
2009	1,597.7	1,592.3	1,594.4	1,612.9	1,841.8	2,060.8	1,748.6	1,773.9	1,600.3	2,082.5	1,908.8	1,746.5	21,160.5
2010	1,979.2	1,978.8	2,318.0	2,829.9	2,537.8	2,186.6	1,946.1	2,402.3	2,325.4	2,614.0	2,529.1	2,251.3	27,898.7
2011	2,315.2	2,274.1	2,342.8	2,592.4	3,390.6	2,720.4	2,078.4	2,874.5	2,745.1	2,791.8	2,780.3	2,223.6	31,129.3

[1] Data thru September 2005 are Unleaded, October 2005 thru December 2006 are Unleaded and RBOB.
Contract size = 42,000 US gallons.   *Source: CME Group; New York Mercantile Exchange (NYMEX)*

Average Open Interest of Gasoline, RBOB[1] Futures in New York   In Contracts

Year	Jan.	Feb.	Mar.	Apr.	May	June	July	Aug.	Sept.	Oct.	Nov.	Dec.
2002	136,795	139,191	133,649	129,274	120,224	114,663	106,463	94,648	95,754	100,427	105,175	109,737
2003	117,558	124,288	113,380	98,627	96,405	93,285	95,433	99,394	85,457	90,007	95,002	105,919
2004	125,207	141,837	150,573	146,375	148,782	138,248	140,691	146,532	147,088	150,643	138,280	153,907
2005	162,432	161,603	172,012	166,620	145,587	148,482	156,730	156,282	140,270	134,833	138,659	144,396
2006	157,562	173,978	168,067	165,233	150,913	138,578	146,173	135,367	131,771	124,963	128,906	135,085
2007	161,557	161,335	166,936	170,675	172,870	183,443	189,084	184,342	188,954	196,730	206,392	208,238
2008	230,032	253,303	241,781	250,852	264,988	256,220	238,170	219,229	198,263	162,480	172,267	194,234
2009	192,691	187,748	199,423	204,956	220,450	215,256	200,537	217,625	205,517	219,883	256,151	238,789
2010	262,247	258,312	304,437	320,529	275,659	245,923	239,242	246,901	241,014	270,830	282,949	273,638
2011	280,084	274,277	275,857	293,452	280,369	251,349	245,309	250,244	268,974	273,495	280,706	275,994

[1] Data thru September 2005 are Unleaded, October 2005 thru December 2006 are Unleaded and RBOB.
Contract size = 42,000 US gallons.   *Source: CME Group; New York Mercantile Exchange (NYMEX)*

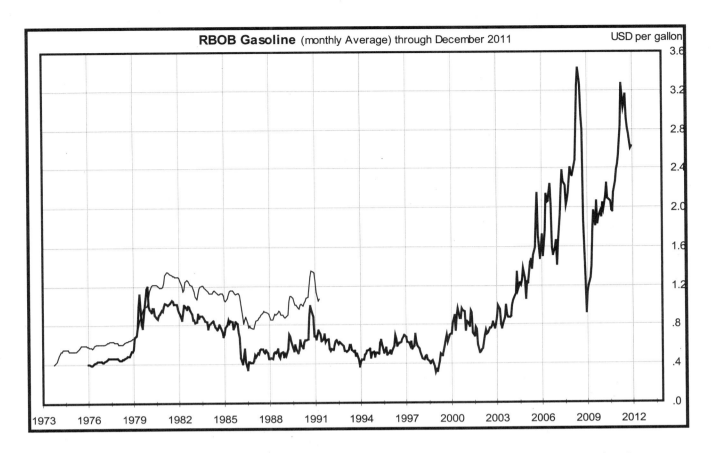

RBOB Gasoline (monthly Average) through December 2011 — USD per gallon

Stocks of Finished Gasoline[2] on Hand in the United States, at End of Month — In Millions of Barrels

Year	Jan.	Feb.	Mar.	Apr.	May	June	July	Aug.	Sept.	Oct.	Nov.	Dec.
2002	169.7	165.5	159.8	167.0	168.3	167.6	164.8	157.3	157.4	148.2	158.0	161.9
2003	157.2	151.1	144.7	151.4	155.2	153.0	150.1	145.2	146.1	140.4	146.3	146.9
2004	138.7	133.5	132.1	133.1	137.2	140.2	140.5	137.9	135.7	138.4	141.5	143.2
2005	145.6	146.4	136.4	141.1	140.7	140.9	133.6	122.5	127.3	131.3	135.4	135.8
2006	142.2	137.9	124.2	115.4	121.5	119.1	117.9	116.6	120.5	112.8	113.8	116.1
2007	124.3	116.0	109.2	108.5	114.5	116.6	114.2	110.6	113.2	108.8	110.5	111.4
2008	117.4	119.9	110.6	106.2	106.0	107.3	102.3	97.8	92.6	95.9	96.9	98.3
2009	95.3	86.9	85.9	86.0	83.5	88.6	86.1	86.7	84.7	79.4	83.0	84.9
2010	87.2	83.6	81.9	78.1	75.2	71.8	71.9	72.4	70.2	65.1	65.5	63.3
2011[1]	69.4	67.8	60.8	54.8	56.8	56.4	54.3	55.5	57.1	56.3	58.4	61.4

[1] Preliminary. [2] Includes oxygenated and other finished. *Source: Energy Information Administration, U.S. Department of Energy (EIA-DOE)*

Average Refiner Price of Finished Motor Gasoline to End Users[1] in the United States — In Cents Per Gallon

Year	Jan.	Feb.	Mar.	Apr.	May	June	July	Aug.	Sept.	Oct.	Nov.	Dec.	Average
2002	70.6	71.8	87.2	100.4	99.9	99.1	100.3	100.1	100.1	104.0	101.2	98.1	94.7
2003	106.0	122.1	130.0	120.1	110.0	109.3	110.6	123.1	126.5	115.0	109.5	106.5	115.7
2004	117.3	125.6	133.8	139.6	156.9	154.4	148.3	145.1	145.0	158.6	155.1	141.3	143.4
2005	139.5	146.8	163.7	180.3	171.4	172.1	185.0	208.0	241.7	226.2	182.4	173.9	182.6
2006	187.2	183.3	198.3	233.1	245.8	243.6	252.8	248.6	207.6	178.9	178.8	186.8	212.1
2007	179.1	184.2	213.8	240.5	266.9	256.9	248.8	232.0	233.7	235.0	261.4	255.2	234.0
2008	257.1	256.6	278.3	298.4	331.6	358.0	356.8	327.9	320.7	253.7	161.7	121.9	276.9
2009	135.8	146.8	150.3	160.1	185.6	218.7	206.7	215.7	208.6	210.4	217.3	214.4	189.2
2010	224.0	217.3	230.1	237.0	235.3	225.1	224.7	225.0	221.9	231.9	237.8	251.4	230.1
2011[2]	261.5	271.2	307.2	334.0	341.9	318.4	317.2	313.4	309.0	294.8			306.9

[1] Excludes aviation and taxes. [2] Preliminary. *Source: Energy Information Administration, U.S. Department of Energy (EIA-DOE)*

GASOLINE

Average Retail Price of Unleaded Premium Motor Gasoline[2] in the United States   In Cents per Gallon

Year	Jan.	Feb.	Mar.	Apr.	May	June	July	Aug.	Sept.	Oct.	Nov.	Dec.	Average
2002	132.3	133.0	145.0	162.2	162.5	160.8	160.7	162.0	161.9	164.3	164.3	158.9	157.8
2003	166.6	182.8	192.4	184.6	172.9	170.0	171.0	180.8	191.1	178.9	172.4	168.6	177.7
2004	177.9	185.8	194.9	201.2	218.6	222.5	213.0	209.1	208.2	221.5	220.3	208.0	206.8
2005	201.7	210.5	225.1	246.8	240.3	236.5	250.2	270.1	313.0	300.1	256.0	239.3	249.1
2006	252.1	251.9	260.3	296.7	316.9	313.9	321.9	320.7	281.9	249.3	245.9	255.0	280.5
2007	250.1	250.9	281.8	309.3	334.8	328.1	320.0	301.8	302.1	303.7	330.7	326.4	303.3
2008	329.1	327.2	350.2	369.0	400.3	431.9	435.0	404.5	394.0	343.2	243.3	195.1	351.9
2009	203.6	218.2	219.7	230.9	251.1	288.3	280.6	288.7	284.5	282.6	291.7	288.2	260.7
2010	298.7	292.2	303.5	311.3	312.4	300.0	299.7	301.5	296.8	305.5	310.9	323.4	304.7
2011[1]	334.5	342.4	380.7	407.4	419.2	397.2	391.5	389.3	388.7	374.5	370.0	355.3	379.2

[1] Preliminary.   [2] Including taxes.   *Source: Energy Information Administration, U.S. Department of Energy (EIA-DOE)*

Average Retail Price of Unleaded Regular Motor Gasoline[2] in the United States   In Cents per Gallon

Year	Jan.	Feb.	Mar.	Apr.	May	June	July	Aug.	Sept.	Oct.	Nov.	Dec.	Average
2002	113.9	113.0	124.1	140.7	142.1	140.4	141.2	142.3	142.2	144.9	144.8	139.4	135.8
2003	147.3	164.1	174.8	165.9	154.2	151.4	152.4	162.8	172.8	160.3	153.5	149.4	159.1
2004	159.2	167.2	176.6	183.3	200.9	204.1	193.9	189.8	189.1	202.9	201.0	188.2	188.0
2005	182.3	191.8	206.5	228.3	221.6	217.6	231.6	250.3	292.7	278.5	234.3	218.6	229.5
2006	231.5	231.0	240.1	275.7	294.7	291.7	299.9	298.5	258.9	227.2	224.1	233.4	258.9
2007	227.4	228.5	259.2	286.0	313.0	305.2	296.1	278.2	278.9	279.3	306.9	302.0	280.1
2008	304.7	303.3	325.8	344.1	376.4	406.5	409.0	378.6	369.8	317.3	215.1	168.9	326.6
2009	178.7	192.8	194.9	205.6	226.5	263.1	254.3	262.7	257.4	256.1	266.0	262.1	235.0
2010	273.1	265.9	278.0	285.8	286.9	273.6	273.6	274.5	270.4	279.5	285.2	298.5	278.8
2011[1]	309.1	316.7	354.6	381.6	393.3	370.2	365.4	363.0	361.2	346.8	342.3	327.8	352.7

[1] Preliminary.   [2] Including taxes.   *Source: Energy Information Administration, U.S. Department of Energy (EIA-DOE)*

Average Retail Price of All-Types[2] Motor Gasoline[3] in the United States   In Cents per Gallon

Year	Jan.	Feb.	Mar.	Apr.	May	June	July	Aug.	Sept.	Oct.	Nov.	Dec.	Average
2002	120.9	121.0	132.4	149.3	150.8	148.9	149.6	150.8	150.7	153.5	153.4	147.7	144.1
2003	155.7	168.6	179.1	170.4	158.7	155.8	156.7	167.1	177.1	164.6	157.8	153.8	163.8
2004	163.5	171.5	180.9	187.5	205.0	208.3	198.2	194.1	193.4	207.2	205.3	192.6	192.3
2005	186.6	196.0	210.7	232.5	225.7	221.8	235.7	254.8	296.9	283.0	238.7	223.0	233.8
2006	235.9	235.4	244.4	280.1	299.3	296.3	304.6	303.3	263.7	231.9	228.7	238.0	263.5
2007	232.1	233.3	263.9	290.9	317.6	310.0	301.3	283.3	283.9	284.3	311.8	306.9	284.9
2008	309.6	308.3	330.7	349.1	381.3	411.5	414.2	383.8	374.9	322.5	220.8	174.2	331.7
2009	183.8	197.9	200.0	210.7	231.4	268.1	259.4	267.7	262.6	261.3	270.9	267.1	240.1
2010	277.9	270.9	282.9	290.6	291.5	278.3	278.3	279.5	275.4	284.3	289.9	303.1	283.6
2011[1]	313.9	321.5	359.4	386.3	398.2	375.3	370.3	368.0	366.4	352.1	347.5	332.9	357.7

[1] Preliminary.   [2] Also includes types of motor oil not shown separately.   [3] Including taxes.   *Source: Energy Information Administration, U.S. Department of Energy (EIA-DOE)*

Average Refiner Price of Finished Aviation Gasoline to End Users[2] in the United States   In Cents per Gallon

Year	Jan.	Feb.	Mar.	Apr.	May	June	July	Aug.	Sept.	Oct.	Nov.	Dec.	Average
2002	111.8	110.6	122.6	129.8	128.9	127.3	139.2	136.9	139.1	143.0	141.8	139.8	128.8
2003	139.7	W	W	W	139.8	145.1	151.9	162.2	158.9	150.8	W	146.6	149.4
2004	W	W	W	177.4	194.4	192.3	185.4	184.9	187.8	195.5	187.0	176.7	186.8
2005	173.8	186.7	201.5	221.7	212.1	211.6	223.0	238.6	280.8	270.8	218.6	219.3	221.5
2006	239.1	232.4	247.3	286.9	301.3	305.7	310.3	305.8	253.2	238.5	235.3	234.9	265.9
2007	217.9	228.5	262.7	296.9	309.6	297.8	305.3	282.3	290.0	285.5	306.7	297.5	281.7
2008	298.7	295.4	329.6	335.8	361.5	396.5	392.9	379.2	383.7	297.5	223.0	181.4	322.9
2009	185.7	197.4	197.7	215.0	242.3	270.7	260.7	276.4	268.4	269.3	284.5	279.9	245.7
2010	291.4	285.5	310.3	320.1	312.9	298.1	302.8	296.7	289.3	300.0	309.5	321.8	303.2
2011[1]	332.3	337.4	376.7	413.2	409.1	391.3	402.7	392.0	391.5	369.7			381.6

[1] Preliminary.   [2] Excluding taxes.   NA = Not available.   W = Withheld proprietary data.   *Source: Energy Information Administration, U.S. Department Energy (EIA-DOE)*

Gold

Gold is a dense, bright yellow metallic element with a high luster. Gold is an inactive substance and is unaffected by air, heat, moisture, and most solvents. Gold has been coveted for centuries for its unique blend of rarity, beauty, and near indestructibility. The Egyptians mined gold before 2,000 BC. The first known, pure gold coin was made on the orders of King Croesus of Lydia in the sixth century BC.

Gold is found in nature in quartz veins and secondary alluvial deposits as a free metal. Gold is produced from mines on every continent with the exception of Antarctica, where mining is forbidden. Because it is virtually indestructible, much of the gold that has ever been mined still exists above ground in one form or another. The largest producer of gold in the U.S. by far is the state of Nevada, with Alaska and California running a distant second and third.

Gold is a vital industrial commodity. Pure gold is one of the most malleable and ductile of all the metals. It is a good conductor of heat and electricity. The prime industrial use of gold is in electronics. Another important sector is dental gold where it has been used for almost 3,000 years. Other applications for gold include decorative gold leaf, reflective glass, and jewelry.

In 1792, the United States first assigned a formal monetary role for gold when Congress put the nation's currency on a bimetallic standard, backing it with gold and silver. Under the gold standard, the U.S. government was willing to exchange its paper currency for a set amount of gold, meaning the paper currency was backed by a physical asset with real value. However, President Nixon in 1971 severed the convertibility between the U.S. dollar and gold, which led to the breakdown of the Bretton Woods international payments system. Since then, the prices of gold and of paper currencies have floated freely. U.S. and other central banks now hold physical gold reserves primarily as a store of wealth.

Gold futures and options are traded at the New York Mercantile Exchange (NYMEX). Gold futures are traded on the Bolsa de Mercadorias and Futuros (BM&F) and on the Tokyo Commodity Exchange (TOCOM), the NYSE-LIFFE exchange, the Central Japan Commodity Exchange (CJCE), the Hong Kong Futures Exchange (HKFE) and the Korea Futures Exchange (KOFEX). The NYMEX gold futures contract calls for the delivery of 100 troy ounces of gold (0.995 fineness), and the contract trades in terms of dollars and cents per troy ounce.

Prices – Nymex gold futures prices on a nearest-futures basis continued to strengthen in the first half of 2011 and exploded to an all-time high of $1,921 an ounce in September 2011 as the credit rating downgrades of the U.S., Italy and Japan fueled demand for gold as an alternative asset. European sovereign-debt contagion fears, however, prompted a rally in the dollar index to a 1-year high that fueled massive long liquidation in gold prices. Investors held a record 2,360.8 tons of in exchange-traded products as of December 2011. Gold prices then slumped to a 6-month low in December and finished the year up +10% at $1,567 an ounce. Gold prices remain in a secular bull market and retain strong long-term support from the Federal Reserve's pledge to extend its record low interest rates until at least late 2014, the ongoing European debt crisis, and extraordinary easy G7 monetary policies.

Supply – World mine production of gold rose +5.5% yr/yr to 2.700 million kilograms in 2011, a new record high (1 kilogram = 32.1507 troy ounces). The world's largest producers of gold in 2011 were China with 13.2% of world production, followed by Australia (10.0%), the U.S (8.8%), Russia (7.4%), and South Africa (7.0%).

Gold mine production has been moving lower in most major gold-producing countries such as South Africa, Australia, and the U.S. For example, South Africa's production of 192,000 kilograms in 2010 was down -4.0% yr/yr and that was about one-third the production levels of more than 600,000 kilograms seen in the 1980s and early 1990s. On the other hand, China's gold production in 2011 rose +7.8% to a record 355,000 kilograms. U.S. gold mine production in 2011 rose +2.6% yr/yr to 237,000 kilograms, just above 2009 production level which was the lowest production since 1988. U.S. refinery production of gold from domestic and foreign ore sources in 2011 rose +8.6% yr/yr to 190,000 kilograms. U.S. refinery production of gold from secondary scrap sources in 2011 rose +13.6% yr/yr to 225,000 kilograms.

Demand – U.S. consumption of gold in 2011 rose +11.1% yr/yr kilograms. The most recent data available from the early 1990s showed that 71% of that gold demand came from jewelry and the arts, 22% from industrial uses, and 7% from dental uses.

Trade – U.S. exports of gold (excluding coinage) in 2011 rose +22.7% yr/yr to 470,000 kilograms, down from the 16-year high of 568,000 kilograms seen in 2008. U.S. imports of gold for consumption in 2011 rose +11.0% yr/yr to 670,000 kilograms, a new record high.

World Mine Production of Gold   In Kilograms (1 Kilogram = 32.1507 Troy Ounces)

Year	Australia	Brazil	Canada	Chile	China	Ghana	Indonesia	Papua New Guinea	Russia	South Africa	United States	Uzebistan	World Total
2003	282,000	40,416	140,861	38,954	205,000	70,749	141,019	67,832	170,068	373,300	277,000	90,000	2,540,000
2004	259,000	47,596	129,478	39,986	215,000	63,139	91,710	73,670	163,148	337,223	258,000	93,000	2,420,000
2005	262,000	38,293	119,549	40,447	225,000	66,852	130,620	68,483	164,186	294,671	256,000	90,000	2,470,000
2006	247,000	43,082	103,513	42,100	245,000	69,817	93,176	58,349	159,340	272,128	252,000	85,000	2,370,000
2007	247,000	50,000	102,211	41,527	275,000	83,558	117,851	65,000	156,975	252,598	238,000	85,000	2,360,000
2008	215,000	54,000	95,004	39,162	285,000	80,503	64,390	68,000	172,031	212,744	233,000	85,000	2,290,000
2009	222,000	60,000	97,367	40,834	320,000	86,000	130,000	66,000	109,693	197,698	223,000	90,000	2,450,000
2010[1]	261,000	58,000	91,000	38,000	345,000	82,000	120,000	68,000	192,000	189,000	231,000	90,000	2,560,000
2011[2]	270,000	55,000	110,000	45,000	355,000	100,000	100,000	70,000	200,000	190,000	237,000	90,000	2,700,000

[1] Preliminary.   [2] Estimate.   *Source: U.S. Geological Survey (USGS)*

GOLD

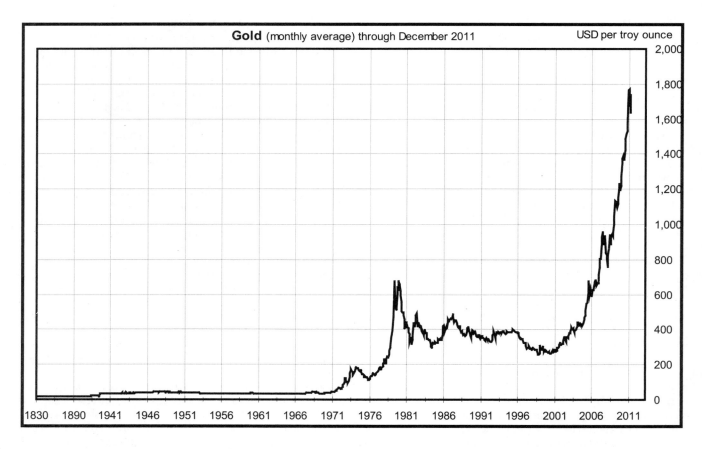

Gold (monthly average) through December 2011 — USD per troy ounce

Salient Statistics of Gold in the United States   In Kilograms (1 Kilogram = 32.1507 Troy Ounces)

	Mine Pro-	Value	Domestic & Foreign	Secondary	Exports, Excluding	Imports for Con-	Treasury Depart-	Futures		Official World		Indus-	Jewelry	
Year	duction	Million $	Ores	(Old Scrap)	Coinage	sumption	ment[3]	Exchange	Industry	Reserves[4]	Dental	trial[5]	& Arts	Total
2002	298,000	2,980.0	196,000	78,100	257,000	217,000	8,140,000	63,900	3,490	32,200	----	----	----	163,000
2003	277,000	3,250.0	194,000	89,100	352,000	249,000	8,140,000	97,100	3,590	31,800	----	----	----	183,000
2004	258,000	3,400.0	222,000	91,700	257,000	283,000	8,140,000	180,000	1,080	31,400	----	----	----	185,000
2005	256,000	3,670.0	195,000	81,300	324,000	341,000	8,140,000	211,000	2,040	30,800	----	----	----	183,000
2006	252,000	4,910.0	181,000	89,100	389,000	263,000	8,140,000	234,000	2,000	30,400	----	----	----	185,000
2007	238,000	5,350.0	176,000	135,000	519,000	170,000	8,140,000	229,000	1,140	29,900	----	----	----	180,000
2008	233,000	6,550.0	168,000	181,000	567,000	231,000	8,140,000	265,000	W	28,700	----	----	----	176,000
2009	223,000	7,000.0	170,000	189,000	381,000	320,000	8,140,000	305,000	9,200	30,700	----	----	----	150,000
2010[1]	231,000		175,000	198,000	383,000	604,000	8,140,000				----	----	----	180,000
2011[2]	237,000		190,000	225,000	470,000	670,000	8,140,000				----	----	----	200,000

[1] Preliminary.   [2] Estimate.   [3] Includes gold in Exchange Stabilization Fund.   [4] Held by market economy country central banks and governments and international monetary orgainzations.   [5] Including space and defense.   NA = Not available.   *Source: U.S. Geological Survey (USGS)*

Monthly Average Gold Price (Handy & Harman) in New York   Dollars Per Troy Ounce

Year	Jan.	Feb.	Mar.	Apr.	May	June	July	Aug.	Sept.	Oct.	Nov.	Dec.	Average
2002	281.47	295.40	294.06	302.68	314.08	321.81	313.51	310.18	319.49	316.56	319.14	333.21	310.13
2003	356.91	359.60	340.55	328.25	355.03	356.35	351.01	359.91	379.07	378.92	389.13	407.44	363.51
2004	414.09	404.52	405.99	403.96	383.94	392.73	398.08	400.86	405.45	420.46	438.21	442.20	409.21
2005	424.39	423.15	433.91	429.23	422.53	430.66	424.33	438.03	456.52	469.90	474.87	510.01	444.79
2006	549.27	555.02	557.09	610.41	673.97	596.15	634.89	632.10	596.76	585.78	627.12	629.38	604.00
2007	630.97	664.43	655.30	679.20	667.86	655.40	665.83	665.21	714.79	749.73	806.68	803.20	696.55
2008	890.47	923.25	966.30	909.70	886.29	889.49	940.16	838.30	830.30	806.62	754.95	816.09	870.99
2009	859.98	943.20	924.27	890.50	927.34	945.67	934.31	949.34	996.76	1043.16	1122.03	1212.50	979.09
2010	1116.74	1095.26	1114.36	1147.70	1204.50	1232.92	1192.25	1217.11	1272.02	1342.02	1370.46	1389.70	1224.59
2011	1359.39	1371.13	1424.01	1478.55	1511.63	1528.66	1576.70	1757.21	1765.99	1665.36	1743.83	1645.50	1569.00

[1] Preliminary.   *Source: U.S. Geological Survey (USGS)*

Gold Futures - CME Group (NYMEX)
(weekly close) as of December 30, 2011

USD per troy ounce

Volume of Trading of Gold Futures in New York (COMEX)   In Thousands of Contracts

Year	Jan.	Feb.	Mar.	Apr.	May	June	July	Aug.	Sept.	Oct.	Nov.	Dec.	Total
2002	733.6	613.2	717.7	559.8	1,089.6	775.5	998.9	585.8	621.8	669.0	844.8	808.5	9,018.2
2003	1,260.1	1,007.5	987.6	667.8	1,160.3	824.3	1,191.7	837.5	1,034.0	1,091.3	1,397.3	776.3	12,235.5
2004	1,581.3	962.6	1,649.5	1,202.9	1,344.8	960.6	1,405.0	953.0	944.9	1,067.2	1,864.7	1,053.2	14,989.6
2005	1,502.3	944.4	1,599.0	858.1	1,451.7	1,240.0	1,432.4	1,234.4	1,380.2	1,174.0	1,852.7	1,221.5	15,890.6
2006	2,018.8	1,162.7	2,052.7	1,302.9	2,071.0	1,148.6	1,487.2	804.5	884.7	857.1	1,284.7	842.7	15,917.6
2007	1,929.8	1,455.9	2,195.9	1,405.2	2,336.6	1,610.8	2,292.2	1,710.7	2,024.6	2,584.4	3,837.1	1,677.2	25,060.4
2008	4,041.7	2,617.6	3,901.8	2,765.5	3,328.0	2,624.0	4,269.9	3,066.1	4,109.4	3,045.1	2,687.1	1,921.1	38,377.4
2009	3,073.0	2,444.2	3,385.0	1,808.4	2,766.7	2,305.0	2,846.2	1,815.6	2,831.4	3,216.7	4,564.3	4,083.1	35,139.5
2010	4,574.3	3,616.1	4,385.6	2,932.3	4,824.1	3,024.7	4,097.3	2,184.9	2,732.1	3,858.8	5,530.4	2,969.7	44,730.3
2011	4,724.6	2,740.4	4,512.3	3,145.2	4,955.3	3,078.9	4,278.2	6,406.6	5,300.5	3,026.4	4,105.3	2,901.9	49,175.6

Contract size = 100 oz.   *Source: CME Group; New York Mercantile Exchange (NYMEX)*

Average Open Interest of Gold in New York (COMEX)   In Contracts

Year	Jan.	Feb.	Mar.	Apr.	May	June	July	Aug.	Sept.	Oct.	Nov.	Dec.
2002	124,222	142,763	142,638	159,892	190,845	174,123	166,042	146,596	167,620	162,456	164,581	191,594
2003	221,495	210,247	186,656	176,033	191,459	198,808	199,741	224,694	284,906	258,238	275,346	277,183
2004	283,813	238,816	256,873	274,898	250,963	225,001	239,579	237,940	259,181	306,522	344,665	329,669
2005	277,112	263,191	301,758	283,546	277,469	275,508	268,068	304,000	339,269	356,526	334,562	331,527
2006	348,949	338,851	331,223	350,380	336,735	288,309	316,969	309,186	320,850	330,152	346,141	335,204
2007	350,958	387,321	372,781	377,094	405,645	401,337	379,066	339,923	394,400	479,735	530,775	500,409
2008	556,302	487,373	471,320	418,693	435,847	401,914	460,178	382,302	378,216	321,545	290,706	280,402
2009	331,891	359,420	376,201	341,491	366,468	382,960	380,301	383,826	454,286	493,909	522,556	504,102
2010	512,723	469,214	489,600	521,976	574,107	579,416	561,781	541,408	595,118	619,536	626,630	589,823
2011	556,448	479,014	507,118	522,520	513,744	504,841	522,091	517,064	494,932	438,488	453,477	424,014

Contract size = 100 oz.   *Source: CME Group; New York Mercantile Exchange (NYMEX)*

GOLD

Commodity Exchange, Inc. (COMEX) Depository Warehouse Stocks of Gold   In Thousands of Troy Ounces

Year	Jan. 1	Feb. 1	Mar. 1	Apr. 1	May 1	June 1	July 1	Aug. 1	Sept. 1	Oct. 1	Nov. 1	Dec. 1
2002	1,220.3	1,186.7	1,285.7	1,322.3	1,372.3	1,764.1	1,850.7	1,835.6	1,915.0	1,892.4	1,994.9	2,046.5
2003	2,056.5	2,159.8	2,262.4	2,383.9	2,460.7	2,474.9	2,675.1	2,743.8	2,729.4	2,822.6	2,912.1	3,058.9
2004	3,122.2	3,324.0	3,476.9	3,677.1	4,142.0	4,391.8	4,399.6	4,657.0	4,880.1	5,122.4	5,334.7	5,374.3
2005	5,795.6	5,962.6	5,913.9	5,960.7	6,156.7	6,036.6	5,751.0	5,713.8	6,008.5	6,737.1	6,351.5	6,614.3
2006	6,657.7	7,320.9	7,518.9	7,426.6	7,334.4	7,796.0	8,031.2	8,199.0	7,980.8	7,695.2	7,565.8	7,491.1
2007	7,534.5	7,459.2	7,487.2	7,302.5	7,624.8	7,633.1	7,276.1	7,130.5	7,077.1	7,211.9	7,346.7	7,366.1
2008	7,492.5	7,588.0	7,371.3	7,623.1	7,760.4	7,588.9	7,611.6	8,266.0	8,442.8	8,594.9	8,171.8	8,540.3
2009	NA	8,556.8	8,635.9	8,508.6	8,322.6	8,725.8	8,893.4	9,144.6	9,173.0	9,316.2	9,316.2	9,508.9
2010	9,679.4	9,679.4	9,679.4	10,022.9	10,184.3	10,736.8	10,923.5	11,112.1	10,816.9	10,896.7	11,311.9	11,488.4
2011	11,694.3	11,401.9	11,075.3	11,033.0	11,140.8	11,310.3	11,439.7	11,431.5	11,559.8	11,246.8	11,236.9	11,301.8

Source: CME Group; New York Mercantile Exchange (NYMEX)

Central Gold Bank Reserves   In Millions of Troy Ounces

Year	Belgium	Canada	France	Germany	Italy	Japan	Netherlands	Switzerland	United Kingdom	United States	Industrial Total	Developing Oil	Developing Non-Oil	IMF[2]	Bank for Int'l Settlements	World Total
2001	8.3	1.1	97.2	111.1	78.8	24.6	28.4	70.7	11.4	262.0	791.3	42.3	111.3	103.4	6.5	1,054.7
2002	8.3	0.6	97.2	110.8	78.8	24.6	27.4	61.6	10.1	262.0	----	----	----	----	----	1,042.1
2003	8.3	0.1	97.2	110.6	78.8	24.6	25.0	52.5	10.1	261.5	----	----	----	----	----	1,024.3
2004	8.3	0.1	96.0	110.4	78.8	24.6	25.0	43.5	10.0	261.6	----	----	----	----	----	1,007.7
2005	7.3	0.1	90.9	110.2	78.8	24.6	22.3	41.5	10.0	261.6	----	----	----	----	----	988.4
2006	7.3	0.1	87.4	110.0	78.8	24.6	20.6	41.5	10.0	261.5	----	----	----	----	----	976.6
2007	7.3	0.1	83.7	109.9	78.8	24.6	20.0	36.8	10.0	261.5	----	----	----	----	----	960.3
2008	7.3	0.1	80.1	109.7	78.8	24.6	19.7	33.4	10.0	261.5	----	----	----	----	----	960.2
2009	7.3	0.1	78.3	109.5	78.8	24.6	19.7	33.4	10.0	261.5	----	----	----	----	----	977.0
2010[1]	7.3	0.1	78.3	109.3	78.8	24.6	19.7	33.4	10.0	261.5	----	----	----	----	----	981.6

[1] Preliminary.   [2] International Monetary Fund.   *Source: American Metal Market (AMM)*

Mine Production of Recoverable Gold in the United States   In Kilograms

Year	Arizona	California	Idaho	Montana	Nevada	Alaska	Colorado	South Dakota	New Mexico	Utah	Other States	Total
2002	W	9,180	W	W	240,000	W	W	W	W	W	48,820	298,000
2003	W	4,270	W	W	227,000	W	W	W	W	W	45,730	277,000
2004	W	3,260	W	W	216,000	W	W	W	W	W	38,740	258,000
2005	W	W	W	W	212,000	W	W	W	W	W	44,200	256,000
2006	W	W	W	W	206,000	W	W	W	W	W	45,800	252,000
2007	W	W	W	W	186,000	W	W	W	W	W	52,400	238,000
2008	W	W	W	W	178,000	W	W	W	W	W	55,400	233,000
2009	W	W	W	W	161,000	W	W	W	W	W	62,500	223,000
2010	W	W	W	W	166,000	28,100	W	W	W	W	36,900	231,000
2011[1]	W	W	W	W	174,000	26,600	W	W	W	W	35,800	237,000

[1] Preliminary.   W = Withheld proprietary data, included in "Other States."   *Source: U.S. Geological Survey (USGS)*

U.S. Exports of Gold   In Kilograms

Year	Australia	Canada	Hong Kong	India	Mexico	Peru	Singapore	Africa	Switzerland	Thailand	United Arab Emirates	United Kingdom	Total
2000	10,900	8,900	2,200	18	31,700	6,180	1,090	1	368,000	----	3,290	107,000	547,000
2001	----	7,390	1,540	----	16,300	5,530	32	----	363,000	1,450	10,800	77,900	489,000
2002	3	971	45	9	9,700	3,210	24	39	165,000	1	2,760	65,600	257,000
2003	----	2,160	98	11	11,600	1,440	----	8	237,000	[1]	1,050	94,500	352,000
2004	5,250	18,100	30	10	12,500	8	1,970	14	174,000	23	7,910	29,300	257,000
2005	1,980	738	6,270	2,500	5,980	265	3,510	----	197,000	5,980	22,200	64,900	324,000
2006	6,010	1,530	2,320	67	7,430	194	5	----	213,000	505	10,200	145,000	389,000
2007	2,470	9,210	1,170	17,000	5,890	----	24	----	266,000	1,330	20,000	191,000	519,000
2008	12,300	11,800	4,280	18,800	4,660	128	911	5,270	296,000	8,510	20,700	181,000	568,000
2009	26,700	3,110	844	21,000	3,120	95	79	----	103,000	----	147	220,000	381,000

[1] Less than 1/2 unit.   *Source: U.S. Geological Survey (USGS)*

Gold in British Pound (weekly close) as of December 30, 2011   GBP per troy ounce

Gold in Euro (weekly close) as of December 30, 2011   EUR per troy ounce

Gold in Japanese Yen (weekly close) as of December 30, 2011   JPY per troy ounce

Gold in Swiss Franc (weekly close) as of December 30, 2011   CHF per troy ounce

Grain Sorghum

Grain sorghums include milo, kafir, durra, feterita, and kaoliang. Grain sorghums are tolerant of drought by going into dormancy during dry and hot conditions and then resuming growth as conditions improve. Grain sorghums are a staple food in China, India, and Africa but in the U.S. they are mainly used as livestock feed. The two key U.S. producing states are Texas and Kansas, each with about one-third of total U.S. production. U.S. sorghum production has become more popular with the breeding of dwarf grain sorghum hybrids which are only about 3 feet tall (versus up to 10 feet tall for wild sorghum) and are easier to harvest with a combine. The U.S. sorghum crop year begins September 1.

Prices – The monthly average price for sorghum grain received by U.S. farmers in the 2011-12 marketing year (Sep-Aug) rose by +7.2% yr/yr to $10.56 per hundred pounds (annualized through January 2012). The value of U.S. grain sorghum production in the 2011-12 marketing year fell 20.6% to $1.284 billion.

Supply – World production of sorghum in the 2011-12 marketing year fell -7.4% to 60.946 million metric tons, well below the 13-year high of 65.909 million metric tons posted in 2007-08. U.S. grain sorghum production in 2011-

12 fell -38.0% yr/yr to 214.443 million bushels. Sorghum acreage harvested in 2011-12 is forecasted to fall 18.4% to 3,929 million acres, only slightly below the 2006-07 figure of 4.937 acres which was the smallest sorghum acreage since the late 1930s. Yield in 2011-12 was 54.6 bushels per acre, but that was still below the record high of 73.2 bushels per acre in 2007-08.

Demand – World utilization (consumption) of grain sorghum in the 2011-12 marketing year fell -4.2% to 61.752 million metric tons. The biggest consumers are Mexico utilizing 14.7% of the world supply and the U.S. utilizing 6.4% of the world supply.

Trade – World exports of sorghum in the 2011-12 marketing year fell -20.6% to 5.541 million metric tons, well below the 21-year high of 9.730 million metric tons seen in 2007-08. U.S. exports in 2011-12 fell -40.1% yr/yr to 2.286 million metric tons, accounting for 41.3% of total world exports. Argentina is the world's other major exporter with 2.200 million metric tons of exports in 2011-12, accounting for 40.0% of total world exports. World imports of sorghum in 2011-12 fell -13.9% yr/yr to 5.770 million metric tons. Major world importers are Mexico and Japan.

World Supply and Demand of Grain Sorghum   In Thousands of Metric Tons

	Exports				Imports				Total	Pro-	Utilization				Ending Stocks		
Crop Year	Argen- tina	Non- U.S.	U.S.	Total	Japan	Mexico	Unac- counted	Total	duction	China	Mexico	U.S.	Total	Non- U.S.	U.S.	Total
2006-07	1,083	1,587	3,876	5,463	1,276	1,954	406	4,839	57,650	2,050	8,100	4,012	57,789	3,847	814	4,661
2007-08	1,223	2,700	7,030	9,730	1,084	1,156	525	9,679	65,909	2,000	7,200	5,081	64,472	4,707	1,340	6,047
2008-09	1,113	2,352	3,632	5,984	1,629	2,496		6,177	64,846	2,000	8,600	8,319	64,555	5,141	1,390	6,531
2009-10[1]	1,771	2,404	4,211	6,615	1,649	2,528		6,258	59,278	1,900	9,700	5,859	61,265	3,139	1,048	4,187
2010-11[2]	1,900	3,158	3,819	6,977	1,419	2,400		6,700	65,797	1,800	9,400	5,306	64,467	4,543	697	5,240
2011-12[3]	2,200	3,255	2,286	5,541	1,600	2,100		5,770	60,946	1,900	9,100	3,937	61,752	3,943	720	4,663

[1] Preliminary.   [2] Estimate.   [3] Forecast.   *Source: Foreign Agricultural Service, U.S. Department of Agriculture (FAS-USDA)*

Salient Statistics of Grain Sorghum in the United States

	Acreage Planted[4]		For Grain				For Silage			Sorghum Grain Stocks				
Crop Year Beginning Sept. 1	for All Purposes	Acreage Harvested	Pro- duction (1,000 Bushels)	Yield Per Harvested Acre (Bushels)	Price in Cents Per Bushel	Value of Pro- duction (Million $)	Acreage Harvested (1,000 Acres)	Pro- duction (1,000 Tons)	Yield Per Harvested Acre (Tons)	Dec. 1		June 1		
	-- 1,000 Acres --									On Farms	Off Farms	On Farms	Off Farms	
										1,000 Bushels				
2006-07	6,522	4,937	277,538	56.2	329	883.2	347	4,642	13.4	38,100	174,094	5,380	69,490	
2007-08	7,712	6,792	497,445	73.2	408	1,925.3	392	5,246	13.4	51,400	239,850	7,000	94,019	
2008-09	8,284	7,271	472,342	65.0	320	1,631.1	408	5,646	13.8	54,400	243,290	12,000	90,215	
2009-10[1]	6,633	5,520	382,983	69.4	322	1,207.1	254	3,680	14.5	48,000	202,759	10,700	77,162	
2010-11[2]	5,404	4,813	345,625	71.8	520-560	1,617.9	268	3,370	12.6	30,500	207,168	3,140	76,894	
2011-12[3]	5,481	3,929	214,443	54.6		1,284.2	224	2,298	10.3	27,850	121,983			

[1] Preliminary.   [2] Estimate.   [3] Forecast.   *Source: Foreign Agricultural Service, U.S. Department of Agriculture (FAS-USDA)*

Production of All Sorghum for Grain in the United States, by States   In Thousands of Bushels

Year	Arkansas	Colo- rado	Illinois	Kansas	Louis- iana	Miss- issippi	Missouri	Nebraska	New Mexico	Okla- homa	South Dakota	Texas	Total
2006	5,100	3,380	6,408	145,000	8,352	1,040	8,075	18,720	2,100	6,800	2,880	62,400	277,538
2007	20,640	5,550	6,237	209,350	23,275	9,775	9,600	22,560	3,000	12,320	7,800	159,250	497,445
2008	10,120	4,500	7,828	214,500	9,570	5,822	7,760	19,110	3,440	13,950	7,360	158,600	472,342
2009	2,923	6,750	2,952	224,400	5,330	770	3,698	13,020	2,300	12,320	7,320	98,400	382,983
2010	2,695	7,520	3,168	171,000	7,410	650	2,574	6,750	4,488	13,000	5,270	119,000	345,625
2011[1]	6,480	4,900	1,820	110,000	10,788	3,700	2,376	6,580	1,344	1,680	6,600	56,350	214,443

[1] Preliminary.   *Source: National Agricultural Statistics Service, U.S. Department of Agriculture (NASS-USDA)*

Quarterly Supply and Disappearance of Grain Sorghum in the United States — In Millions of Bushels

Crop Year Beginning Sept. 1	Beginning Stocks	Pro-duction	Imports[3]	Total Supply	Food & Alcohol	Seed	Feed & Residual	Total	Exports[3]	Total Disap-pearance	Gov't Owned[4]	Privately Owned[5]	Total Stocks
2008-09	52.8	472.3	.1	525.2	94.1	.8	232.6	327.5	143.0	470.5			54.7
Sept.-Nov.	52.8	472.3	.1	525.2	27.3	0	156.0	183.4	44.2	227.5			297.7
Dec.-Feb.	297.7	----	.0	297.7	27.3	0	32.4	59.7	32.2	91.9			205.9
Mar.-May	205.9	----	0	205.9	27.8	.5	40.1	68.4	35.2	103.6			102.2
June-Aug.	102.2	----	0	102.2	11.7	.3	4.1	16.1	31.4	47.5			54.7
2009-10	54.7	383.0	.0	437.7	89.3	.7	140.7	230.7	165.8	396.5			41.2
Sept.-Nov.	54.7	383.0	0	437.7	25.0	0	115.7	140.7	46.2	186.9			250.8
Dec.-Feb.	250.8	----	.0	250.8	25.0	0	7.0	32.0	43.2	75.2			175.6
Mar.-May	175.6	----	0	175.6	25.2	.4	15.2	40.8	46.9	87.7			87.9
June-Aug.	87.9	----	0	87.9	14.0	.4	2.8	17.2	29.5	46.6			41.2
2010-11[1]	41.2	345.6	.0	386.9	84.4	.7	124.1	209.1	150.4	359.4			27.5
Sept.-Nov.	41.2	345.6	.0	386.9	23.6	0	89.7	113.3	35.9	149.2			237.7
Dec.-Feb.	237.7	----	.0	237.7	24.9	0	16.2	41.1	25.6	66.6			171.0
Mar.-May	171.0	----	.0	171.0	26.5	.3	14.3	41.0	50.0	91.0			80.0
June-Aug.	80.0	----	0	80.0	9.4	.3	3.9	13.7	38.9	52.6			27.5
2011-12[2]	27.5	214.4	.0	241.9	89.3	.7	65.0	155.0	60.0	215.0			26.9
Sept.-Nov.	27.5	214.4	.0	241.9	24.5		45.5	70.0	22.1	92.1			149.8

[1] Preliminary.   [2] Estimate.   [3] Uncommitted inventory.   [4] Includes quantity under loan and farmer-owned reserve.   *Source: Economic Research Service, U.S. Department of Agriculture (ERS-USDA)*

Average Price of Sorghum Grain, No. 2, Yellow in Kansas City — In Dollars Per Hundred Pounds (Cwt.)

Year	Sept.	Oct.	Nov.	Dec.	Jan.	Feb.	Mar.	Apr.	May	June	July	Aug.	Average
2004-05	3.45	3.21	3.17	3.21	3.13	3.23	3.44	3.30	3.36	3.56	3.90	3.53	3.37
2005-06	3.22	3.08	2.93	3.30	3.46	3.58	3.65	3.79	4.03	3.90	4.15	3.79	3.57
2006-07	3.82	5.07	5.97	6.03	6.36	6.72	6.38	5.69	5.97	6.09	5.33	5.50	5.75
2007-08	5.68	5.60	6.13	7.34	8.36	8.86	9.13	9.70	9.65	11.63	10.10	8.37	8.38
2008-09	8.43	5.92	5.49	5.19	5.67	5.48	5.51	5.76	6.37	6.29	4.66	4.75	5.79
2009-10	4.81	5.49	5.72	6.44	5.81	5.58	5.69	5.64	5.77	5.50	6.03	6.59	5.75
2010-11	8.23	9.10	9.40	9.91	10.62	11.62	11.37	12.64	12.08	12.21	12.27	12.97	11.04
2011-12[1]	11.79	10.90	11.30	10.91	11.27								11.26

[1] Preliminary.   *Source: Economic Research Service, U.S. Department of Agriculture (ERS-USDA)*

Exports of Grain Sorghum, by Country of Destination from the United States — In Metric Tons

Year	Canada	Ecuador	Ethiopia	Israel	Japan	Jordan	Mexico	South Africa	Spain	Sudan	Turkey	World Total
2004-05	5,270	0	53,540	26,654	1,088,171	0	2,883,335	2,000	167,896	116,577	0	4,474,017
2005-06	4,227	0	31,500	16,177	1,193,039	0	3,004,518	30,398	131,995	211,021	0	4,929,700
2006-07	3,999	0	4,100	54,533	674,824	0	1,914,111	0	1,018,325	299,650	0	4,333,212
2007-08	5,775	0	27,600	137,284	505,919	125	1,150,231	45,498	1,929,955	303,818	0	6,653,444
2008-09	4,987	0	28,170	0	313,179	0	2,476,004	41,000	0	268,160	0	3,585,632
2009-10[1]	3,928	0	0	20,681	818,807	0	2,517,214	21,000	0	344,283	0	4,058,108
2010-11[2]	3,704	0	0	101,990	327,689	0	2,366,523	23,039	447,974	191,658	0	3,774,424

[1] Preliminary.   [2] Estimate.   *Source: Economic Research Service, U.S. Department of Agriculture (ERS-USDA)*

Grain Sorghum Price Support Program and Market Prices in the United States

	Price Support Operations								No. 2 Yellow ($ Per Cwt.)			
	Price Support		Aquired by CCC	Owned by CCC at Year End	Basic Loan Rate	Target Price	Findley Loan Rate	Effective Base[3] (Million Acres)	Partici-pation Rate[4] % of Base	Kansas City	Texas High Plains	Los Angeles	Gulf Ports
Year	Quantity	% of Pro-duction											
	Million Cwt.				Dollars Per Bushel								
2003-04	3.5	1.6	0	0	3.54	4.54	1.98	12.1	----	4.57	5.01	----	5.45
2004-05	5.5	2.2	.2	0	3.48	4.59	1.95	12.0	----	3.37	3.95	----	4.42
2005-06	5.4	2.4	0	0	3.48	4.59	1.95	11.9	----	3.57	3.84	----	5.04
2006-07	1.9	1.2	0	0	3.48	4.59	1.95	11.8	----	5.75	6.09	----	7.39
2007-08	1.8	.7	0	0	3.48	4.59	1.95	11.7	----	8.38	8.49	----	9.81
2008-09[1]	4.5	1.7	0	0	3.48	4.59	1.95	11.6	----	5.79	5.44	----	7.18
2009-10[2]	1.7				3.48	4.59	1.95		----	5.75	5.73	----	7.74

[1] Preliminary.   [2] Estimate.   [3] National effective crop acreage base as determined by ASCS.   [4] Percentage of effective base acres enrolled in acreage reduction programs.   5/ Beginning with the 1996-7 marketing year, target prices are no longer applicable.   *Source: Economic Research Service, U.S. Department of Agriculture (ERS-USDA)*

Hay

Hay is a catchall term for forage plants, typically grasses such as timothy and Sudan-grass, and legumes such as alfalfa and clover. Alfalfa and alfalfa mixtures account for nearly half of all hay production. Hay is generally used to make cured feed for livestock. Curing, which is the proper drying of hay, is necessary to prevent spoilage. Hay, when properly cured, contains about 20% moisture. If hay is dried excessively, however, there is a loss of protein, which makes it less effective as livestock feed. Hay is harvested in virtually all of the lower 48 states.

Prices – The average monthly price of hay received by U.S. farmers in the first nine months of the 2011-12 marketing year (May/April) as of January 2012 rose by +5.4% yr/yr to $115.75 per ton, below the 2008-09 record high of $148.42 per ton. The farm production value of hay produced in 2011-12 was $17.746 million.

Supply – U.S. hay production in 2011-12 fell -9.9% yr/yr to 131,144 million tons. U.S. farmers harvested 55.633 million acres of hay in 2011-11, down -7.1% yr/yr. The yield in 2011-12 was 2.36 tons per acre, below the 2004-05 record high of 2.55. U.S. carryover (May 1) in 2011-12 rose +6.1% to 22.217 million tons.

The largest hay producing states in the U.S. for 2011 were South Dakota, (with 6.6% of U.S. hay production), California (6.0%), Missouri (4.8%), Nebraska (4.3%), Minnesota (4.2%), North Dakota (4.0%), Idaho (3.9%), and Texas (3.4%).

Salient Statistics of All Hay in the United States

Crop Year Beginning May 1	Acres Harvested (1,000 Acres)	Yield Per Acre (Tons)	Pro-duction	Carry-over May 1	Disap-pearance	Supply	Disap-pearance Per Animal Unit	Animal Units Fed[3] (Millions)	Farm Price ($ Per Ton)	Farm Pro-duction Value Million $	Alfalfa (Certified)	Timothy	Red Clover	Sudan-grass
			------- Millions of Tons -------				------ In Tons ------				----------- Dollars Per Cwt. -----------			
2006-07	60,632	2.32	140.8	21.3	147.1	2.26	2.05	71.8	111.1	13,634	286.00	106.00	177.00	50.20
2007-08	61,006	2.41	146.9	15.0	140.3	2.26	1.96	71.5	130.8	16,842	292.00	112.00	202.00	56.70
2008-09	60,152	2.43	146.3	21.6	145.8	2.37	2.06	70.9	148.4	18,639	342.00	133.00	241.00	62.10
2009-10	59,775	2.47	147.7	22.1	148.6	2.41	2.11	69.7	109.8	14,716	379.00	149.00	289.00	72.50
2010-11[1]	59,872	2.43	145.6	20.9		2.40	2.08		115.8	14,656				
2011-12[2]	55,633	2.36	131.1	22.2		2.27				17,746				

Retail Price Paid by Farmers for Seed, April 15

[1] Preliminary. [2] Estimate. [3] Roughage-consuming animal units fed annually. NA = Not available.
Source: Economic Research Service, U.S. Department of Agriculture (ERS-USDA)

Production of All Hay in the United States, by States   In Thousands of Tons

Year	California	Idaho	Iowa	Minne-sota	Missouri	New York	North Dakota	Ohio	Okla-homa	South Dakota	Texas	Wisconsin	Total
2006	9,568	5,505	5,189	5,679	6,944	5,588	3,137	3,421	3,556	4,180	8,675	5,264	140,783
2007	9,042	5,345	4,944	4,240	7,528	6,185	5,063	2,804	6,858	7,275	14,740	4,392	146,901
2008	9,414	5,588	5,330	5,265	8,820	6,232	4,118	2,802	5,536	7,840	9,211	4,810	146,270
2009	8,890	5,528	4,002	5,250	8,040	6,235	5,240	2,876	5,278	7,830	8,250	4,430	147,700
2010	8,304	5,460	3,760	5,400	7,512	6,349	5,321	2,871	5,953	7,335	10,800	4,526	145,624
2011[1]	7,908	5,070	3,460	5,530	6,250	5,624	5,224	2,772	2,330	8,625	4,440	4,075	131,144

[1] Preliminary.   *Source: Agricultural Statistics Board, U.S. Department of Agriculture (ASB-USDA)*

Hay Production and Farm Stocks in the United States   In Thousands of Short Tons

Year	Alfalfa & Mixtures	All Others	All Hay	Corn for Silage[1]	Sorghum Silage[1]	Farm Stocks May 1	Farm Stocks Dec. 1
2006	70,548	70,235	140,783	105,294	4,612	21,345	96,400
2007	69,880	77,021	146,901	106,229	5,246	14,990	104,089
2008	70,180	76,090	146,270	111,619	5,646	21,585	103,658
2009	71,072	76,628	147,700	108,209	3,680	22,065	107,222
2010	67,971	77,653	145,624	107,314	3,370	20,931	102,134
2011[2]	65,332	65,812	131,144	108,926	2,298	22,217	90,726

[1] Not included in all tame hay.   [2] Preliminary.   *Source: Agricultural Statistics Board, U.S. Department of Agriculture (ASB-USDA)*

Mid-Month Price Received by Farmers for All Hay (Baled) in the United States   In Dollars Per Ton

Year	May	June	July	Aug.	Sept.	Oct.	Nov.	Dec.	Jan.	Feb.	Mar.	Apr.	Average
2006-07	113.0	109.0	107.0	106.0	108.0	109.0	106.0	110.0	109.0	113.0	119.0	124.0	111.1
2007-08	138.0	131.0	131.0	124.0	127.0	128.0	129.0	127.0	126.0	129.0	133.0	147.0	130.8
2008-09	168.0	161.0	164.0	163.0	161.0	156.0	149.0	138.0	135.0	131.0	129.0	126.0	148.4
2009-10	130.0	123.0	116.0	104.0	105.0	105.0	105.0	105.0	106.0	104.0	107.0	108.0	109.8
2010-11	116.0	114.0	112.0	110.0	112.0	111.0	110.0	111.0	112.0	116.0	124.0	141.0	115.8
2011-12[1]	169.0	163.0	170.0	172.0	176.0	181.0	176.0	177.0	172.0	176.0			

[1] Preliminary.   [2] Marketing year average.   *Source: Economic Research Service, U.S. Department of Agriculture (ERS-USDA)*

Heating Oil

Heating oil is a heavy fuel oil that is derived from crude oil. Heating oil is also known as No. 2 fuel oil and accounts for about 25% of the yield from a barrel of crude oil. That is the second largest "cut" after gasoline. The price to consumers of home heating oil is generally comprised of 42% for crude oil, 12% for refining costs, and 46% for marketing and distribution costs (Source: EIA's Petroleum Marketing Monthly, 2001). Generally, a $1 increase in the price of crude oil translates into a 2.5-cent per gallon rise in heating oil. Because of this, heating oil prices are highly correlated with crude oil prices, although heating oil prices are also subject to swift supply and demand shifts due to weather changes or refinery shutdowns.

The primary use for heating oil is for residential heating. In the U.S., approximately 8.1 million households use heating oil as their main heating fuel. Most of the demand for heating oil occurs from October through March. The Northeast region, which includes the New England and the Central Atlantic States, is most reliant on heating oil. This region consumes approximately 70% of U.S. heating oil. However, demand for heating oil has been dropping as households switch to a more convenient heating source like natural gas. In fact, demand for heating oil is down by about 10 billion gallons/year from its peak use in 1976 (Source: American Petroleum Institute).

Refineries produce approximately 85% of U.S. heating oil as part of the "distillate fuel oil" product family, which includes heating oil and diesel fuel. The remainder of U.S. heating oil is imported from Canada, the Virgin Islands, and Venezuela.

Recently, a team of Purdue University researchers developed a way to make home heating oil from a mixture of soybean oil and conventional fuel oil. The oil blend is made by replacing 20% of the fuel oil with soybean oil, potentially saving 1.3 billion gallons of fuel oil per year. This soybean heating oil can be used in conventional furnaces without altering existing equipment. The soybean heating oil is relatively easy to produce and creates no sulfur emissions.

The "crack-spread" is the processing margin earned when refiners buy crude oil and refine it into heating oil and gasoline. The crack-spread ratio commonly used in the industry is the 3-2-1, which involves buying 1 heating oil contract and 2 gasoline futures contracts, and then selling 3 crude oil contracts. As long as the crack spread is positive, it is profitable for refiners to buy crude oil and refine it into products. The NYMEX has a crack-spread calculator on their web site at www.NYMEX.com.

Heating oil futures and options trade at the New York Mercantile Exchange (NYMEX). The heating oil futures contract calls for the delivery of 1,000 barrels of fungible No. 2 heating oil in the New York harbor. In London, gas/oil futures and options are traded on the ICE Futures Europe (ICE) exchange.

Prices – NYMEX heating oil futures prices on the nearest-futures chart rallied in early 2011 to extend the rally that began in 2010 and posted a 3-year high of $3.33 per gallon in April 2011. Heating oil futures then traded sideways during the remainder of the year and closed 2011 up 15% at $2.935 per gallon.

Supply – U.S. production of distillate fuel oil in 2011 (through November, annualized) rose by +6.0% yr/yr to 4.474 million barrels per day, a new record high. Stocks of distillate fuel oil in November 2011 were 144.013 million barrels. U.S. production of residual fuel in 2011 (through November, annualized) fell by -8.5% yr/yr to an average of 536,000 barrels per day, which was less than half the production level of over 1 million barrels per day produced in the 1970s. U.S. stocks of residual fuel oil as of January 1, 2011 fell -3.2% to 38.991 million barrels, down from the 2007 record of 42.329 million barrels.

Demand – U.S. usage of distillate fuel oil in 2011 (through November, annualized) rose +1.2% yr/yr to 3.846 million barrels per day, further down from 2007's record high of 4.198 million barrels per day.

Trade – U.S. imports of distillate fuel oil in 2011 (through November, annualized) fell -23.4% to an average of 175,000 barrels per day, down from the 2006 record high of 365,000 barrels per day. U.S. exports of distillate fuel oil in 2007 rose by +2.7% yr/yr to a 13-year high average of 221 barrels per day. U.S. imports of residual fuel oil in 2011 fell -1.9% yr/yr to 359,000 barrels per day, which was less than a third of the levels of over 1 million barrels per day seen back in the 1970s.

Average Price of Heating Oil #2 In Cents Per Gallon

Year	Jan.	Feb.	Mar.	Apr.	May	June	July	Aug.	Sept.	Oct.	Nov.	Dec.	Average
2002	53.52	54.03	63.52	66.60	66.54	64.50	67.79	69.81	77.25	76.55	72.14	81.70	67.83
2003	90.09	112.84	99.70	79.75	74.31	75.95	79.03	81.61	73.54	81.97	83.35	89.04	85.10
2004	97.91	91.19	90.88	91.87	101.65	99.41	109.42	116.86	125.73	148.55	138.16	127.32	111.58
2005	132.01	134.26	155.44	152.35	140.89	161.20	163.71	180.75	196.50	188.75	168.67	170.32	162.07
2006	174.99	163.68	177.70	198.27	197.17	191.76	192.30	198.25	169.17	154.53	165.00	167.85	179.22
2007	151.99	169.48	174.05	186.30	188.47	200.31	206.99	198.36	218.06	228.32	258.79	257.54	203.22
2008	255.64	264.17	306.80	322.96	361.64	379.99	375.67	317.16	290.76	222.44	185.15	138.93	285.11
2009	146.43	127.78	128.30	135.95	147.87	174.72	163.18	186.59	173.05	193.34	198.48	197.22	164.41
2010	205.23	197.52	208.47	221.26	203.78	203.44	197.75	202.24	209.48	224.23	231.74	246.43	212.63
2011	260.35	276.38	303.39	319.56	295.14	296.51	306.92	294.27	291.99	295.00	305.24	288.75	294.46

Source: Energy Information Administration, U.S. Department of Energy (EIA-DOE)

Heating Oil Futures - CME Group (NYMEX)
(weekly close) as of December 30, 2011

USD per gallon

Average Open Interest of Heating Oil #2 Futures in New York   In Contracts

Year	Jan.	Feb.	Mar.	Apr.	May	June	July	Aug.	Sept.	Oct.	Nov.	Dec.
2002	166,824	173,110	160,205	144,936	139,979	136,201	131,742	141,084	147,692	153,739	161,137	156,268
2003	178,932	174,224	134,616	111,706	118,822	124,675	127,273	146,821	150,893	156,142	145,857	145,555
2004	153,794	145,924	161,945	174,618	176,784	167,331	193,291	206,099	197,783	188,843	176,298	163,629
2005	155,528	152,479	174,437	179,923	176,770	185,831	182,710	185,185	174,229	172,772	178,199	178,008
2006	170,094	165,627	168,415	170,955	171,732	169,123	179,773	185,648	208,848	221,942	228,152	216,033
2007	219,690	219,715	209,805	208,829	210,128	224,289	239,109	218,913	235,403	232,165	224,475	209,578
2008	202,976	220,716	230,646	227,140	224,480	218,004	223,645	221,733	212,561	212,981	224,465	224,359
2009	237,894	252,753	261,552	259,008	260,646	283,068	294,270	308,022	311,296	312,653	322,505	309,113
2010	317,506	306,607	319,389	310,085	311,994	313,624	304,866	305,549	325,342	327,588	319,732	308,661
2011	306,262	312,145	305,872	310,288	310,053	316,026	306,360	307,607	323,485	303,460	291,931	274,679

Contract size = 42,000 US gallons.   *Source: CME Group; New York Mercantile Exchange (NYMEX)*

Volume of Trading of Heating Oil #2 Futures in New York   In Thousands of Contracts

Year	Jan.	Feb.	Mar.	Apr.	May	June	July	Aug.	Sept.	Oct.	Nov.	Dec.	Total
2002	998.5	810.8	885.5	844.1	789.8	720.1	798.8	866.0	794.4	1,017.9	1,039.5	1,129.9	10,695.2
2003	1,340.1	1,158.9	965.9	757.7	811.6	802.9	849.9	891.3	1,118.5	1,095.5	817.3	971.8	11,581.7
2004	1,153.8	1,059.7	1,139.9	1,007.8	910.0	1,100.5	920.7	1,105.7	1,060.8	1,148.6	1,112.7	1,164.4	12,884.5
2005	1,090.6	1,046.1	1,204.2	1,062.5	999.7	1,193.5	1,058.5	1,150.4	1,165.1	1,019.5	1,009.5	1,136.0	13,135.6
2006	1,157.5	1,131.2	1,121.7	974.8	1,185.1	1,114.0	1,027.1	1,166.1	1,235.9	1,291.1	1,228.6	1,357.5	13,990.6
2007	1,655.6	1,507.5	1,370.3	1,326.0	1,462.2	1,605.8	1,478.9	1,579.8	1,394.7	1,687.2	1,544.1	1,467.0	18,079.0
2008	1,611.7	1,726.3	1,763.3	1,639.2	1,825.3	1,651.9	1,571.3	1,641.9	1,578.0	1,646.4	1,297.3	1,630.4	19,583.1
2009	1,789.0	1,512.9	1,670.1	1,633.3	1,644.5	1,809.7	2,004.2	1,652.6	1,777.3	1,975.9	1,921.9	2,035.1	21,426.5
2010	2,096.3	1,872.5	2,230.6	2,459.2	2,493.3	2,305.2	1,963.7	2,409.5	2,548.9	2,230.9	2,165.8	2,194.1	26,970.1
2011	2,545.9	2,600.7	2,805.0	2,206.5	2,645.6	2,624.9	2,022.6	2,843.7	2,889.1	2,964.2	3,071.0	2,619.4	31,838.6

Contract size = 42,000 US gallons.   *Source: CME Group; New York Mercantile Exchange (NYMEX)*

Heating Oil (monthly average) through December 2011 — USD per gallon

Stocks of Distillate and Residual Fuel in the United States, on First of Month In Millions of Barrels

Year	Jan.	Feb.	Mar.	Apr.	May	June	July	Aug.	Sept.	Oct.	Nov.	Dec.	Residual Fuel --- Oil Stocks --- Jan. 1	July 1
2002	136.9	130.0	123.1	122.4	127.0	133.1	133.8	130.6	126.9	121.4	124.4	134.1	41.0	41.7
2003	112.6	97.7	98.6	97.2	106.7	112.2	118.0	126.5	131.3	132.1	136.1	136.5	31.3	32.7
2004	122.8	112.2	104.4	101.5	107.5	114.3	121.9	130.8	127.7	124.7	133.7	126.3	37.8	35.3
2005	121.9	117.3	105.4	105.4	112.4	119.7	133.3	139.1	149.3	142.8	140.6	143.7	37.4	37.5
2006	139.4	135.6	120.5	116.5	124.0	129.9	137.5	145.1	134.6	134.4	134.8	133.9	42.4	37.7
2007	139.6	123.7	120.0	121.3	125.1	123.8	130.3	134.6	134.2	134.4	134.8	133.9	42.4	42.7
2008	131.0	117.6	107.8	107.1	113.9	121.7	130.9	133.0	127.7	127.6	135.9	146.0	39.3	36.1
2009	143.7	148.1	145.3	150.1	156.7	162.7	165.9	168.6	172.7	171.2	171.1	166.0	36.1	41.2
2010	163.5	155.3	146.8	144.8	150.0	157.9	166.6	170.3	166.7	161.5	162.0	164.3	37.2	36.9
2011[1]	162.2	153.8	148.5	142.9	144.7	143.7	158.1	156.9	153.7	142.9	144.0	149.7	41.3	42.3

[1] Preliminary.   *Source: Energy Information Administration; U.S. Department of Energy (EIA-DOE)*

Production of Distillate Fuel Oil in the United States In Thousand Barrels per Day

Year	Jan.	Feb.	Mar.	Apr.	May	June	July	Aug.	Sept.	Oct.	Nov.	Dec.	Average
2002	3,508	3,498	3,360	3,647	3,709	3,679	3,561	3,538	3,536	3,380	3,768	3,922	3,592
2003	3,403	3,459	3,732	3,796	3,833	3,728	3,673	3,730	3,721	3,750	3,800	3,845	3,707
2004	3,592	3,446	3,550	3,874	3,857	3,956	3,902	3,981	3,625	3,808	4,004	4,159	3,813
2005	3,777	3,797	3,874	4,028	4,179	4,274	4,236	4,108	3,570	3,585	3,966	4,044	3,953
2006	3,840	3,941	3,736	3,833	4,105	4,107	4,065	4,234	4,300	4,090	4,070	4,159	4,040
2007	4,256	4,582	4,334	4,214	4,068	4,114	4,026	4,146	4,161	4,213	4,074	4,193	4,198
2008	4,130	3,980	3,953	4,287	4,459	4,587	4,523	4,466	3,681	4,435	4,489	4,511	4,292
2009	4,284	4,231	3,939	4,132	4,093	4,047	3,929	3,965	4,099	3,984	4,018	3,877	4,050
2010	3,551	3,658	3,835	4,156	4,375	4,408	4,425	4,404	4,341	4,315	4,503	4,670	4,220
2011[1]	4,305	4,032	4,284	4,187	4,277	4,469	4,655	4,667	4,574	4,534	4,786	4,917	4,474

[1] Preliminary.   *Source: Energy Information Administration; U.S. Department of Energy (EIA-DOE)*

HEATING OIL

Imports of Distillate Fuel Oil in the United States   In Thousand of Barrels per Day

Year	Jan.	Feb.	Mar.	Apr.	May	June	July	Aug.	Sept.	Oct.	Nov.	Dec.	Average
2004	370	507	449	267	275	324	283	313	272	243	319	292	326
2005	353	344	257	264	281	236	243	263	275	507	486	435	329
2006	552	388	292	297	437	297	361	363	438	307	288	355	365
2007	352	334	360	322	272	273	318	346	261	288	245	241	301
2008	309	249	249	266	188	180	181	109	195	166	203	262	213
2009	368	327	269	166	206	245	191	166	205	177	164	224	226
2010	462	293	179	220	189	237	170	246	189	163	178	219	229
2011[1]	326	206	190	186	167	126	153	148	177	127	135	162	175

[1] Preliminary.   *Source: Energy Information Administration, U.S. Department of Energy (EIA-DOE)*

Exports of Distillate Fuel Oil from the United States   In Thousand of Barrels per Day

Year	Jan.	Feb.	Mar.	Apr.	May	June	July	Aug.	Sept.	Oct.	Nov.	Dec.	Average
2004	72	86	99	92	100	163	113	120	88	101	102	176	109
2005	49	102	165	192	199	227	189	163	108	109	92	65	138
2006	123	156	120	200	229	187	231	191	456	291	252	149	215
2007	253	202	155	167	227	240	243	311	274	173	188	NA	221
2008	NA	NA	NA	NA	NA	NA	NA	NA	NA	NA	NA	NA	NA
2009	NA	NA	NA	NA	NA	NA	NA	NA	NA	NA	NA	NA	NA
2010	NA	NA	NA	NA	NA	NA	NA	NA	NA	NA	NA	NA	NA
2011[1]	NA	NA	NA	NA	NA	NA	NA	NA	NA	NA	NA	NA	NA

[1] Preliminary.   *Source: Energy Information Administration, U.S. Department of Energy (EIA-DOE)*

Disposition of Distillate Fuel Oil, Total Product Supplied in the United States   In Thousand of Barrels per Day

Year	Jan.	Feb.	Mar.	Apr.	May	June	July	Aug.	Sept.	Oct.	Nov.	Dec.	Average
2004	4,334	4,232	4,152	4,145	3,840	3,888	3,827	3,887	4,065	4,104	4,058	4,176	4,059
2005	4,223	4,202	4,349	4,101	4,037	4,038	3,854	4,020	4,116	4,079	4,061	4,339	4,118
2006	4,159	4,308	4,395	4,065	4,072	4,019	3,950	4,162	4,141	4,315	4,180	4,268	4,170
2007	4,256	4,582	4,334	4,214	4,068	4,114	4,026	4,146	4,161	4,213	4,074	4,193	4,198
2008	4,192	4,281	4,161	4,106	3,931	3,763	3,688	3,659	3,740	4,182	3,872	3,783	3,947
2009	4,079	3,864	3,744	3,455	3,436	3,513	3,395	3,426	3,560	3,654	3,596	3,861	3,632
2010	3,701	3,854	3,835	3,759	3,639	3,743	3,544	3,830	3,886	3,773	3,873	4,176	3,801
2011[1]	3,968	3,871	3,993	3,689	3,657	3,903	3,452	3,959	3,929	3,944	3,903	3,880	3,846

[1] Preliminary.   *Source: Energy Information Administration, U.S. Department of Energy (EIA-DOE)*

Production of Residual Fuel Oil in the United States   In Thousands of Barrels per Day

Year	Jan.	Feb.	Mar.	Apr.	May	June	July	Aug.	Sept.	Oct.	Nov.	Dec.	Average
2004	656	659	635	701	668	648	618	631	617	610	703	723	656
2005	701	691	619	598	645	673	614	594	555	530	642	674	628
2006	670	635	644	643	580	645	658	652	619	597	624	656	635
2007	667	650	656	658	647	628	708	698	698	689	694	676	672
2008	588	643	662	710	734	695	584	579	485	575	588	597	620
2009	585	571	583	475	605	613	586	631	604	672	624	624	598
2010	633	632	581	598	615	559	576	554	588	528	564	595	585
2011[1]	552	529	519	535	557	553	562	604	516	529	493	477	536

[1] Preliminary.   *Source: Energy Information Administration, U.S. Department of Energy (EIA-DOE)*

Supply and Disposition of Residual Fuel Oil in the United States

| | -------- Supply -------- | | ------------ Disposition ------------ | | | Ending | Average |
Year	Total Production	Imports	Stock Change	Exports	Product Supplied	Stocks (Million Barrels)	Sales to End Users[3] (Cents per Gallon)
	------------------------------- In Tousands of Barrels Per Day -------------------------------						
2004	655	426	12	205	865	42	73.9
2005	628	530	-14	251	920	37	104.8
2006	635	350	14	283	689	42	121.8
2007	673	372	-13	309	723	39	137.4
2008	620	349	NA	NA	622	36	196.4
2009	598	331	NA	NA	511	37	134.1
2010	585	366	NA	NA	534	41	171.3
2011[1]	541	359	NA	NA		38	

[1] Preliminary.   [2] Less than +500 barrels per day and greater than -500 barrels per day.   [3] Refiner price excluding taxes.
Source: Energy Information Administration, U.S. Department of Energy (EIA-DOE)

Hides and Leather

Hides and leather have been used since ancient times for boots, clothing, shields, armor, tents, bottles, buckets, and cups. Leather is produced through the tanning of hides, pelts, and skins of animals. The remains of leather have been found in the Middle East dating back at least 7,000 years.

Today, most leather is made of cowhide but it is also made from the hides of lamb, deer, ostrich, snakes, crocodiles, and even stingray. Cattle hides are the most valuable byproduct of the meat packing industry. U.S. exports of cowhides bring more than $1 billion in foreign trade, and U.S. finished leather production is worth about $4 billion.

Prices – The average monthly price of wholesale cattle hides (packer heavy native steers FOB Chicago) in 2011 fell -7.5% yr/yr to 82.15 cents per pound, below 2007's record high of 90.53 cents per pound.

Supply – World production of cattle and buffalo hides in 2010 fell by -1.0% yr/yr to 9.040, down from 2009's record high of 9.135 million metric tons. The world's largest producers of cattle and buffalo hides in 2010 were the U.S. with 12.2% of world production, Brazil with 10.1%, and Argentina with 3.9%. U.S. new supply of cattle hides from domestic slaughter in 2009 fell 3.0% yr/yr to 33.338 million hides, which is far below the record high of 43.582 million

hides posted in 1976. U.S. production of leather footwear has been dropping off sharply in recent years due to the movement of production offshore to lower cost producers. U.S. production of leather footwear in 2003 (latest data available) fell -46% yr/yr to 22.3 million pairs and was a mere 4% of the 562.3 million pairs produced in 1970.

Demand – World consumption of cowhides and skins in 2000, the last reporting year for the series, rose +1.4% to 4,774 metric tons, which was a record high for the data series, which goes back to 1984. The world's largest consumers of cowhides and skins in 2000 were the U.S. with 13.0% of world consumption, Italy (10.6%), Brazil (8.9%), Mexico, (6.0%), Argentina (6.0%), and South Korea (5.9%).

Trade – U.S. net exports of cattle hides in 2004 (latest data) fell –4.3% yr/yr to 17.388 million hides from the 15-year high of 21.750 million hides posted in 2001. The total value of U.S. leather exports in 2004 rose +16.8% yr/yr to $1.344 billion. The largest destinations for U.S. exports in 2011 were South Korea (which took 16.0% of U.S. exports), Italy (9.1%), Taiwan (6.4%), Mexico (5.6%), and Thailand (2.0%). World imports of cowhides and skins in 2000 (latest data) rose +2.8% yr/yr to a record high of 2,058 metric tons. The world's largest importers of cowhides and skins in 2000 were South Korea (with 13% of world imports in 2000), Italy (11%) and Taiwan (7%).

World Production of Cattle and Buffalo Hides   In Thousands of Metric Tons

Year	Argentina	Australia	Brazil	Canada	Colombia	France	Germany	Italy	Mexico	Russia	United Kingdom	United States	World Total
2001	348	254	725	95	76	156	153	130	178	220	61	1,086	8,066
2002	345	243	750	96	72	162	151	132	178	224	65	1,128	8,242
2003	375	256	770	88	72	160	141	130	180	229	63	1,093	8,355
2004	429	243	792	111	80	150	145	128	191	223	66	1,009	8,477
2005	428	245	850	112	86	148	132	126	192	203	68	1,016	8,602
2006	403	233	886	104	85	143	135	124	197	183	74	1,076	8,811
2007	449	252	914	96	88	142	132	122	199	180	75	1,086	8,953
2008	440	239	914	96	94	143	132	121	199	182	75	1,104	9,028
2009[1]	482	236	914	93	96	144	132	122	199	179	75	1,104	9,135
2010[2]	356	230	914	94	95	144	132	122	199	181	75	1,104	9,040

[1] Preliminary.   [2] Forecast.   *Source: Food and Agricultural Organization of the United Nations (FAO-UN)*

Salient Statistics of Hides and Leather in the United States   In Thousands of Equivalent Hides

Year	Federally Inspected	Uninspected[4]	Total Production	Net Exports	Heavy Native Cows[2]	Heavy Native[3] Steers	All U.S. Tanning	Cattle-hide	Value of Leather Exports ($1,000)	Men	Women	Production[5]	Exports
	----- Thousands of Equivalent Hides -----				Cents Per Pound		In 1,000 Equiv. Hides			(1982 = 100)		Million Pairs	
2000	35,631	615	36,246	19,670	83.41	80.2	17,332	16,746	1,125,957	157.2	133.6	58,870	20,157
2001	34,771	599	35,370	21,750	85.52	85.8	14,212	13,779	1,221,131	158.4	133.8	55,600	19,472
2002	35,120	614	35,735	19,484	85.73	82.3		16,403	1,161,944	158.8	133.5	41,100	21,582
2003	34,907	587	35,493	18,177	88.34	83.8		17,470	1,150,212	161.4	132.1	22,300	21,319
2004	32,156	573	32,728	17,388	57.07	67.1		15,492	1,344,017	161.7	129.2		21,464
2005	31,832	556	32,388		57.89	65.6				163.5	132.1		
2006	33,145	553	33,698		60.30	68.9				164.6	134.2		
2007	33,721	543	34,264		65.70	72.0				167.0	137.0		
2008	33,805	560	34,365		58.35	63.9				173.7	139.7		
2009[1]	32,765	573	33,338		29.22	44.8				177.6	139.9		

[1] Preliminary.   [2] Central U.S., heifers.   [3] F.O.B. Chicago.   [4] Includes farm slaughter; diseased & condemned animals & hides taken off fallen animals.
[5] Other than rubber.   *Sources: Leather Industries of America (LIA); Bureau of Labor Statistics, U.S. Department of Commerce (BLS)*

HIDES AND LEATHER

Production of All Footwear (Shoes, Sandals, Slippers, Athletic, Etc.) in the United States   In Millions of Pairs

Year	First Quarter	Second Quarter	Third Quarter	Fourth Quarter	Total	Year	First Quarter	Second Quarter	Third Quarter	Fourth Quarter	Total
1994	42.5	40.8	40.1	39.5	163.0	1999	26.7	26.1	24.5	21.7	78.5
1995	37.2	38.3	34.8	36.7	147.0	2000	----	----	----	----	58.8
1996	33.2	31.8	29.7	33.2	128.0	2001	----	----	----	----	55.6
1997	31.4	33.1	28.6	30.6	124.4	2002	----	----	----	----	41.1
1998	32.8	31.8	29.3	28.6	108.5	2003[1]	----	----	----	----	22.3

[1] Preliminary.   *Source: Bureau of the Census, U.S. Department of Commerce*

Average Factory Price[2] of Footwear in the United States   In Dollars Per Pair

Year	First Quarter	Second Quarter	Third Quarter	Fourth Quarter	Total	Year	First Quarter	Second Quarter	Third Quarter	Fourth Quarter	Total
1994	25.77	23.60	21.49	22.44	23.22	1999	23.33	22.70	19.90	19.50	21.19
1995	19.61	21.46	25.37	21.26	21.79	2000	----	----	----	----	24.14
1996	23.65	22.78	22.14	20.38	22.07	2001	----	----	----	----	25.66
1997	22.42	21.56	22.21	22.24	22.11	2002	----	----	----	----	24.12
1998	24.39	24.21	20.27	19.78	21.84	2003[1]	----	----	----	----	45.95

[1] Preliminary.   [2] Average value of factory shipments per pair.   *Source: Bureau of the Census, U.S. Department of Commerce*

Imports and Exports of All Cattle Hides in the United States   In Thousands of Hides

Year	Imports Total	From Canada	U.S. Exports Total	Canada	Italy	Japan	Rep of Korea	Mexico	Portugal	Romania	Spain	Taiwan	Thailand
2002	1,298	1,227	20,784	837	1,099	584	5,812	1,470	14	0	189	2,145	914
2003	4,051	1,921	19,139	530	779	483	4,784	1,257	6	0	63	1,982	788
2004	9,000	6,171	18,795	346	417	468	4,218	1,419	4	0	16	1,842	684
2005	4,517	2,897	19,231	141	568	334	4,048	1,288	2	0	8	1,730	652
2006	2,491	1,786	20,059	57	523	277	3,455	1,225	5	0	41	1,902	441
2007	1,986	1,243	17,687	91	191	234	2,867	1,243	3	0	44	1,260	724
2008	1,863	1,182	16,015	113	265	175	2,346	1,135	0	0	99	795	453
2009	1,475	975	16,661	345	407	189	2,379	1,510	11	0	62	1,249	574
2010	1,388	1,064	15,436	193	1,010	148	2,042	1,423	1	0	90	1,446	460
2011[1]			18,807	179	1,703	347	2,999	1,063	5	1	51	1,194	382

[1] Preliminary.   *Source: Leather Industries of America*

Imports of Bovine Hides and Skins by Selected Countries   In Metric Tons

Year	Brazil	Canada	Hong Kong	Italy	Japan	Mexico	Portugal	Rep. of Korea	Spain	Taiwan	Turkey	United States	World Total
1992	11	17	80	131	188	71	32	385	26	91	28	65	1,266
1993	21	26	81	141	188	71	39	372	35	94	37	57	1,426
1994	16	28	95	243	139	60	56	356	29	112	17	49	1,556
1995	33	35	100	250	152	30	43	342	42	112	43	57	1,715
1996	20	34	79	263	123	71	42	341	33	124	50	60	1,692
1997	13	39	64	254	114	96	37	323	44	140	68	60	1,985
1998	10	42	71	249	96	110	39	229	44	142	45	59	1,876
1999[1]	8	34	91	215	95	115	42	254	29	142	55	57	2,002
2000[2]	8	36	93	220	95	115	43	260	30	142	60	57	2,058

[1] Preliminary.   [2] Forecast.   *Source: Foreign Agricultural Service, U.S. Department of Agriculture (FAS-USDA)*

Exports of Bovine Hides and Skins by Selected Countries   In Metric Tons

Year	Australia	Brazil	Canada	Germany	Hong Kong	Italy	Nether-lands	New Zealand	Poland	Russia	United Kingdom	United States	World Total
1992	144	71	74	38	75	9	66	31	17	28	19	610	1,261
1993	142	76	87	40	76	7	35	21	5	150	25	581	1,374
1994	96	84	79	24	93	10	37	22	2	216	22	455	1,271
1995	85	148	90	34	100	10	47	22	2	195	22	510	1,351
1996	93	174	97	33	72	20	47	28	3	212	24	506	1,423
1997	115	216	97	35	60	16	48	27	3	210	25	473	1,475
1998	111	220	86	31	69	24	32	28	6	202	17	443	1,400
1999[1]	115	230	83	28	90	7	30	30	7	190	15	436	1,389
2000[2]	108	250	85	31	92	8	25	30	7	170	15	427	1,399

[1] Preliminary.   [2] Forecast.   *Source: Foreign Agricultural Service, U.S. Department of Agriculture (FAS-USDA)*

Hides (monthly average) through December 2011   Cents per pound

Utilization of Bovine Hides and Skins by Selected Countries   In Metric Tons

Year	Argentina	Brazil	Colombia	Germany	Italy	Japan	Mexico	Rep. of Korea	Spain	Taiwan	Turkey	United States	World Total
1992	298	382	97	129	435	229	231	400	98	91	90	528	3,977
1993	302	510	94	100	435	226	232	385	98	94	95	554	4,322
1994	304	505	96	83	550	200	226	374	94	112	85	536	4,282
1995	300	493	89	79	570	191	200	355	98	112	100	523	4,365
1996	308	461	91	80	615	165	230	353	95	124	110	548	4,332
1997	332	387	89	101	570	150	251	347	106	140	120	572	4,609
1998	285	412	91	100	540	135	275	265	108	142	100	603	4,584
1999[1]	300	415	89	102	500	130	280	280	104	142	110	623	4,707
2000[2]	285	425	89	103	505	130	285	283	108	142	120	623	4,774

[1] Preliminary.   [2] Forecast.   *Source: Foreign Agricultural Service, U.S. Department of Agriculture (FAS-USDA)*

Wholesale Price of Hides (Packer Heavy Native Steers) F.O.B. Chicago   In Cents Per Pound

Year	Jan.	Feb.	Mar.	Apr.	May	June	July	Aug.	Sept.	Oct.	Nov.	Dec.	Average
2002	68.23	72.39	80.41	83.21	84.32	86.72	84.43	85.77	85.84	85.75	83.35	85.18	82.13
2003	83.77	85.81	86.04	85.81	79.42	77.64	80.53	84.09	86.78	86.13	85.89	86.05	84.00
2004	85.17	81.79	82.89	79.15	80.16	82.43	85.11	84.54	85.05	82.23	81.42	78.02	82.33
2005	78.14	80.90	79.04	80.45	79.49	83.07	82.70	81.78	80.58	80.44	80.07	79.03	80.47
2006	79.28	81.01	83.86	84.95	87.76	88.07	87.93	87.15	88.29	88.08	88.81	90.50	86.31
2007	93.75	95.85	95.66	98.13	97.68	93.19	87.36	86.95	86.14	83.08	84.72	83.83	90.53
2008	79.55	79.43	82.79	85.58	85.82	87.01	87.55	87.49	85.10	85.31	78.38	44.98	80.75
2009	43.75	43.09	34.55	36.22	38.33	46.84	53.76	73.02	68.86	65.35	74.23	77.51	54.63
2010	79.31	78.31	83.78	91.83	93.38	93.69	92.86	91.36	88.90	90.68	90.44	90.90	88.79
2011	78.24	81.78	85.20	88.18	84.12	86.26	85.60	85.66	82.40	79.54	76.76	72.10	82.15

Source: National Agricultural Statistics Service, U.S. Department of Agriculture (NASS-USDA)

Hogs

Hogs are generally bred twice a year in a continuous cycle designed to provide a steady flow of production. The gestation period for hogs is 3-1/2 months and the average litter size is 9 pigs. The pigs are weaned at 3-4 weeks of age. The pigs are then fed so as to maximize weight gain. The feed consists primarily of grains such as corn, barley, milo, oats, and wheat. Protein is added from oilseed meals. Hogs typically gain 3.1 pounds per pound of feed. The time from birth to slaughter is typically 6 months. Hogs are ready for slaughter at about 254 pounds, producing a dressed carcass weight of around 190 pounds and an average 88.6 pounds of lean meat. The lean meat consists of 21% ham, 20% loin, 14% belly, 3% spareribs, 7% Boston butt roast and blade steaks, and 10% picnic, with the remaining 25% going into jowl, lean trim, fat, miscellaneous cuts, and trimmings. Futures on lean hogs are traded at the Chicago Mercantile Exchange. The futures contract is settled in cash based on the CME Lean Hog Index price, meaning that no physical delivery of hogs occurs. The CME Lean Hog Index is based on the 2-day average net price of slaughtered hogs at the average lean percentage level.

Prices – Lean hog futures prices began 2011 on firm footing and ratcheted higher into August 2011 when they posted a record high of 107.475 cents a pound, the highest since hog futures trading began in 1966. The main bullish factors were the prospects of increased U.S. pork exports to Japan from the March 2011 earthquake crisis and increased exports to South Korea after it culled 25% of its hog herd from foot-and-mouth disease. Lean hog prices then moved lower the rest of 2011 and dropped to a 1-year low in December 2011, finishing the year +5.7% at 84.300 cents a pound. Bearish factors for hog prices the second half of 2011 included (1) increased output with 2011 U.S. pork production up +1.4% y/y to 22.8 billion pounds, and (2) the December 2011 Quarterly Hog & Pigs report that showed a +1.5% y/y increase in the U.S. hog inventory to 65.9 million hogs and a rise in pig litters to a record 10.02 pigs in the 3 months ended November 2011. Foreign demand strengthened in 2011 with U.S. pork exports up 21% y/y, although the USDA projects that 2012 U.S. pork production will to increase by +1.9% y/y to 23.2 billion pounds.

Supply – World pork production in 2011 fell 1.6% yr/yr to 101.127 million metric tons. The USDA is forecasting a rise of +2.2% to 103.433 million metric tons in 2012. The world's largest pork producers are China with 49% of world production in 2011, the European Union with 22%, and the U.S. with 10%.

U.S. pork production in 2011 rose +0.9% to 10.278 million metric tons. The USDA is forecasting that U.S. pork production in 2012 will rise by 1.8% to 10.466 million metric tons. The number of hogs and pigs on U.S. farms in 2011 (Dec 1) rose by +0.1% to 65.850 million, down from the more than 6-decade high of 68.117 in 2007. The federally-inspected hog slaughter in the U.S. in 2011 rose +0.6% to 109.956, down from the 2008 record high of 115.421 million head.

Demand – World consumption of pork in 2011 fell by -1.7% yr/yr to 100.849 million metric tons. The USDA is forecasting an increase of +2.0% in 2012 to 102.898 million metric tons. U.S. consumption of pork in 2011 fell by -3.1% to 8.384 million metric tons. The USDA is forecasting a +1.7% yr/yr increase in U.S. pork consumption to 8.526 million metric tons in 2012. The U.S. accounted for 8.3% of world consumption in 2011.

Trade – World pork exports in 2011 rose +8.9% yr/yr to 6.574 million metric tons but the USDA is forecasting a decline of -0.4% for 2012 to 6.545 million metric tons. The world's largest pork exporters are the U.S. with 34% of world exports in 2011, the European Union with 30%, Canada with 18%, and Brazil with 9%. U.S. pork exports in 2011 rose +17.2% yr/yr to 2.246 million metric tons and the USDA is forecasting a rise of +2.8% in 2012 to 2.309 million metric tons.

World pork imports in 2011 rose +7.2% to 6.266 million metric tons, but the USDA is forecasting a decline of -4.0% to 6.018 million metric tons in 2012. The world's largest pork importers are Japan, which accounted for 19% of world imports in 2011, Russia (15%), Mexico (10%), South Korea (10%), and China (9%).

Salient Statistics of Pigs and Hogs in the United States

	Pig Crop Spring[3]			Pig Crop Fall[4]			Value of Hogs on Farms, Dec. 1-		Hog Mar-ketings	Quantity Pro-duced	Value of Pro-duction	Hogs Slaughtered, Thousand Head Commercial				
Year	Sows Farrowed	Pig Crop	Pigs Per Litter	Sows Farrowed	Pig Crop	Pigs Per Litter	$ Per Head	Total Million $	(1,000 Head)	(Live Wt.) (Mil. Lbs.)	(Million $)	Federally Inspected	Other	Total	Farm	Total
	--- 1,000 Head ---			--- 1,000 Head ---												
2002	5,776	50,858	8.81	5,716	50,820	8.89	71.0	4,231	124,013	26,274	8,691	98,915	1,348	100,263	115	100,378
2003	5,655	50,029	8.85	5,773	51,462	8.91	67.0	4,025	124,383	26,260	9,663	99,685	1,233	100,931	116	101,047
2004	5,706	50,737	8.89	5,793	52,043	8.98	103.0	6,306	127,563	26,689	13,072	102,361	1,103	103,463	114	103,577
2005	5,716	51,330	8.98	5,818	52,635	9.05	95.0	5,834	129,056	27,416	13,607	102,519	1,063	103,582	109	103,690
2006	5,768	52,242	9.06	5,862	53,376	9.11	90.0	5,599	132,262	28,149	12,702	103,689	1,048	104,737	105	104,842
2007	5,935	54,266	9.14	6,312	58,608	9.28	73.0	4,986	137,519	29,606	13,468	108,138	1,034	109,172	106	109,278
2008	6,123	57,019	9.31	6,103	58,011	9.51	89.0	5,958	148,986	31,411	14,457	115,421	1,026	116,446	106	116,553
2009	6,029	57,564	9.55	5,874	56,978	9.70	83.0	5,465	150,107	31,359	12,590	112,612	1,001	113,614	114	113,727
2010[1]	5,801	56,326	9.71	5,824	57,359	9.85			144,259	30,391	16,073	109,315	948	110,263	107	110,370
2011[2]	5,760	57,118	9.92	5,795	58,098	10.03						109,956	908	110,864		110,864

[1] Preliminary. [2] Estimate. [3] December-May. [4] June-November. *Source: Economic Research Service, U.S. Department of Agriculture (ERS-USDA)*

World Hog Numbers in Specified Countries as of January 1   In Thousands of Head

Year	Brazil	Canada	China	European Union	Japan	Rep. of Korea	Mexico	Philip-pines	Russia	Taiwan	Ukraine	United States	World Total
2003	32,655	14,745	417,762	160,486	9,725	8,110	9,284	12,218	17,601	6,794	9,204	59,554	789,879
2004	32,081	14,725	413,818	158,970	9,724	8,367	9,389	12,518	16,278	6,779	7,321	60,453	783,419
2005	32,323	14,810	421,234	156,973	9,600	8,044	9,068	12,139	13,717	6,819	6,466	60,982	786,588
2006	32,938	15,110	433,191	159,115	9,620	8,098	8,911	13,041	13,812	7,172	7,052	61,463	805,406
2007	33,147	14,907	418,504	161,526	9,759	8,518	9,021	13,693	16,185	7,092	8,055	62,516	800,035
2008	32,947	13,810	439,895	159,732	9,745	8,742	9,401	----	16,340	----	7,020	68,177	774,410
2009	33,892	12,180	462,913	153,067	9,899	8,223	9,310	----	16,165	----	6,526	67,148	785,439
2010	35,122	11,835	469,960	152,198	10,000	8,721	8,979	----	17,236	----	7,577	64,887	792,606
2011[1]	36,652	11,895	477,115	151,084	9,768	8,449	9,007	----	17,200	----	7,960	64,925	800,270
2012[2]	38,282	11,905	459,146	149,100	9,800	6,806	9,240	----	17,545	----	7,570	65,850	781,524

[1] Preliminary.   [2] Forecast.   Source: Foreign Agricultural Service, U.S. Department of Agriculture (FAS-USDA)

Hogs and Pigs on Farms in the United States on December 1   In Thousands of Head

Year	Georgia	Illinois	Indiana	Iowa	Kansas	Minne-sota	Missouri	Nebraska	North Carolina	Ohio	South Dakota	Wisconsin	Total
2002	345	4,150	3,250	15,500	1,530	6,100	2,950	3,000	9,700	1,440	1,330	520	59,554
2003	295	4,000	3,100	15,900	1,650	6,500	2,950	2,900	10,000	1,520	1,280	480	60,444
2004	275	4,100	3,200	16,300	1,710	6,500	2,900	2,850	9,900	1,450	1,340	430	60,975
2005	270	4,000	3,250	16,600	1,790	6,600	2,700	2,850	9,800	1,560	1,490	430	61,449
2006	245	4,200	3,350	17,300	1,840	6,900	2,800	3,050	9,500	1,690	1,270	450	62,490
2007	265	4,350	3,700	19,400	1,880	7,700	3,150	3,350	10,200	1,830	1,460	440	68,177
2008	235	4,350	3,550	19,900	1,740	7,500	3,150	3,350	9,700	1,940	1,280	360	67,148
2009	195	4,250	3,600	19,000	1,810	7,200	3,100	3,100	9,600	2,010	1,190	350	64,887
2010	160	4,400	3,650	19,100	1,820	7,700	2,900	3,150	9,000	2,040	1,290	340	64,925
2011[1]	155	4,600	3,850	19,800	1,890	7,800	2,750	3,150	8,800	2,290	1,390	340	65,931

[1] Preliminary.   Source: National Agricultural Statistics Service, U.S. Department of Agriculture (NASS-USDA)

Hog-Corn Price Ratio[2] in the United States

Year	Jan.	Feb.	Mar.	Apr.	May	June	July	Aug.	Sept.	Oct.	Nov.	Dec.	Average
2002	19.1	19.9	18.6	16.6	17.2	18.2	18.4	13.4	10.7	13.2	12.2	13.1	15.9
2003	14.2	14.7	14.9	14.9	17.4	19.2	19.7	18.4	18.0	17.3	15.8	14.8	16.6
2004	15.4	16.3	17.2	16.4	19.7	20.3	22.7	23.6	24.9	24.4	27.1	25.7	21.1
2005	25.1	26.0	25.3	25.6	27.7	24.4	23.6	26.2	26.0	25.8	24.6	23.1	25.3
2006	20.4	21.1	20.8	19.6	22.2	25.1	23.5	24.7	22.2	18.2	15.6	14.5	20.7
2007	14.0	13.8	13.1	14.0	15.2	15.4	15.7	15.7	14.3	12.9	11.0	10.5	13.8
2008	9.3	9.3	8.6	8.6	10.5	9.8	10.3	11.5	10.5	11.1	9.6	10.2	9.9
2009	9.8	11.3	11.4	11.4	11.3	10.8	12.0	11.2	11.6	10.5	11.0	12.5	11.2
2010	13.2	13.8	14.7	16.6	17.9	17.1	16.8	16.8	15.0	12.3	10.5	10.9	14.6
2011[1]	11.3	10.9	11.4	10.7	10.9	10.9	11.3	11.0	10.5	12.0	11.0	10.8	11.1

[1] Preliminary.   [2] Bushels of corn equal in value to 100 pounds of hog, live weight.   Source: Economic Research Service, U.S. Department of Agriculture (ERS-USDA)

Cold Storage Holdings of Frozen Pork[2] in the United States, on First of Month   In Millions of Pounds

Year	Jan.	Feb.	Mar.	Apr.	May	June	July	Aug.	Sept.	Oct.	Nov.	Dec.
2002	465.0	503.9	510.9	531.5	567.7	548.0	497.8	472.2	464.4	480.2	489.8	463.9
2003	468.5	512.7	519.7	530.5	520.0	499.7	460.0	440.7	430.2	435.2	446.8	438.9
2004	470.7	504.1	477.1	447.3	448.6	412.8	373.0	366.8	382.1	413.8	423.1	436.3
2005	482.9	496.8	538.2	540.2	562.8	511.2	488.6	442.9	408.5	425.6	440.7	431.3
2006	421.3	527.7	528.0	505.0	520.0	477.0	412.6	417.8	415.6	458.4	488.4	468.5
2007	442.5	484.3	483.2	494.8	528.5	492.0	467.9	455.9	458.3	484.9	494.8	474.6
2008	458.7	574.9	611.8	657.3	663.4	579.4	530.1	505.3	502.7	526.2	528.0	526.7
2009	555.6	606.9	624.5	594.1	612.3	584.5	577.9	539.7	530.1	528.7	516.3	482.8
2010	471.1	492.3	515.9	513.1	483.7	446.0	413.0	391.2	388.3	424.3	481.7	468.0
2011[1]	475.8	538.8	574.2	577.2	549.3	548.3	495.1	454.3	442.9	491.9	488.7	495.1

[1] Preliminary.   [2] Excludes lard.   Source: Economic Research Service, U.S. Department of Agriculture (ERS-USDA)

Hogs (monthly average) through December 2011 — Cents per pound

Average Price of Hogs, National Base 51-52% lean — In Dollars Per Hundred Pounds (Cwt.)

Year	Jan.	Feb.	Mar.	Apr.	May	June	July	Aug.	Sept.	Oct.	Nov.	Dec.	Average
2002	40.16	40.65	37.47	32.97	34.64	37.32	40.53	34.00	26.98	31.69	29.99	32.35	34.90
2003	34.39	35.64	36.11	36.42	43.62	47.88	44.98	41.90	41.82	38.63	36.02	36.02	39.45
2004	39.02	45.21	48.30	48.34	58.45	57.95	58.21	56.19	55.34	53.68	56.23	53.15	52.51
2005	53.36	51.11	51.30	51.00	55.40	49.86	49.96	51.60	49.98	47.49	37.70	44.81	49.46
2006	41.37	43.17	43.34	41.45	49.00	54.90	51.89	53.32	50.28	47.57	45.97	44.84	47.26
2007	44.04	48.60	45.47	48.43	54.40	54.82	52.39	52.01	46.61	41.96	36.95	39.40	47.09
2008	36.77	42.74	39.40	45.06	57.75	54.71	56.48	62.56	52.76	47.06	38.90	39.80	47.83
2009	41.43	42.43	42.47	42.83	43.18	42.21	42.74	36.56	37.41	37.65	40.12	45.82	41.24
2010	49.81	48.98	52.43	57.43	63.13	58.23	58.25	61.49	60.64	52.41	47.00	50.92	55.06
2011[1]	55.56	61.62	62.63	68.10	68.41	69.88	71.65	76.09	65.45	68.44	63.40	62.14	66.11

[1] Preliminary.　*Source: Economic Research Service, U.S. Department of Agriculture (ERS-USDA)*

Average Price Received by Farmers for Hogs in the United States — In Cents Per Pound

Year	Jan.	Feb.	Mar.	Apr.	May	June	July	Aug.	Sept.	Oct.	Nov.	Dec.	Average
2002	37.7	38.5	36.0	31.7	33.2	35.8	39.2	31.9	26.5	30.8	27.8	30.3	33.3
2003	33.0	34.3	34.7	34.8	41.3	45.0	42.7	39.6	39.7	36.7	34.7	34.2	37.6
2004	36.8	42.6	47.2	47.4	56.6	56.7	57.1	55.3	54.8	52.2	55.6	52.4	51.2
2005	53.2	50.7	51.2	51.1	54.9	49.5	49.8	51.0	49.4	47.0	43.5	44.3	49.6
2006	40.7	42.6	42.8	41.3	48.2	53.8	50.2	51.6	48.9	46.5	44.9	43.5	46.3
2007	42.7	47.5	44.9	47.3	53.1	54.3	52.2	51.3	46.8	42.4	37.9	39.6	46.7
2008	37.2	42.2	40.3	44.4	55.3	53.4	54.3	60.7	52.6	48.5	40.7	41.9	47.6
2009	42.8	43.8	43.9	44.0	44.6	43.3	43.3	37.3	37.7	37.8	40.3	45.0	42.0
2010	48.4	48.9	52.1	56.5	62.2	58.2	58.5	58.2	61.0	53.3	47.8	52.3	54.8
2011[1]	55.8	61.4	63.1	67.7	68.6	69.7	68.6	75.8	67.1	68.7	64.4	63.5	66.2

[1] Preliminary.　*Source: Economic Research Service, U.S. Department of Agriculture (ERS-USDA)*

Quarterly Hogs and Pigs Report in the United States, 10 States   In Thousands of Head

Year[2]	Inventory[3]	Breeding[3]	Market[3]	Farrowings	Pig Crop
2002	59,804	6,209	53,594	11,492	101,677
I	59,804	6,209	53,594	2,835	24,857
II	59,256	6,230	53,026	2,941	26,001
III	60,391	6,208	54,183	2,883	25,725
IV	60,753	6,051	54,702	2,833	25,094
2003	59,554	6,058	53,496	11,429	101,491
I	59,554	6,058	53,496	2,769	24,400
II	58,183	6,027	52,156	2,886	25,629
III	59,602	6,026	53,576	2,918	25,974
IV	61,009	5,938	55,071	2,856	25,488
2004	60,444	6,009	54,434	11,499	102,781
I	60,444	6,009	54,434	2,836	25,105
II	59,520	5,961	53,558	2,870	25,633
III	60,698	5,937	54,760	2,905	26,162
IV	61,519	5,962	55,556	2,888	25,881
2005	60,975	5,969	55,005	11,535	103,965
I	60,975	5,969	55,005	2,835	25,343
II	59,699	5,941	53,757	2,882	25,986
III	60,732	5,977	54,754	2,918	26,449
IV	61,846	5,972	55,873	2,900	26,187
2006	61,449	6,011	55,438	11,629	105,618
I	61,449	6,011	55,438	2,841	25,662
II	60,326	6,025	54,301	2,927	26,580
III	61,687	6,060	55,627	2,912	26,519
IV	62,914	6,079	56,835	2,949	26,857
2007	62,490	6,087	56,402	12,248	112,873
I	62,490	6,087	56,402	2,905	26,395
II	61,896	6,149	55,746	3,030	27,870
III	63,947	6,169	57,777	3,133	29,095
IV	67,275	6,208	66,708	3,180	29,513
2008	68,177	6,233	61,944	12,226	115,030
I	68,177	6,233	61,944	3,071	28,388
II	67,218	6,200	61,018	3,052	28,631
III	67,400	6,131	61,269	3,075	29,240
IV	68,196	6,061	62,135	3,028	28,771
2009	67,148	6,062	61,087	11,903	114,542
I	67,148	6,062	61,087	3,011	28,552
II	65,819	5,992	59,828	3,018	29,012
III	66,809	5,968	60,842	2,959	28,718
IV	66,716	5,875	60,842	2,915	28,260
2010	64,887	5,850	59,037	11,626	113,687
I	64,887	5,850	59,037	2,872	27,597
II	63,568	5,760	57,808	2,929	28,730
III	64,650	5,788	58,862	2,944	28,871
IV	65,971	5,770	60,201	2,881	28,489
2011[1]	64,625	5,778	59,147	11,496	114,405
I	64,625	5,778	59,147	2,844	27,869
II	63,684	5,788	57,896	2,877	28,851
III	64,700	5,803	58,897	2,901	29,084
IV	66,599	5,806	60,793	2,874	

[1] Preliminary.   [2] Quarters are Dec. preceding year-Feb.(I), Mar.-May(II), June-Aug.(III) and Sept.-Nov.(IV).
[3] Beginning of period.   *Source: National Agricultural Statistics Service, U.S. Department of Agriculture (NASS-USDA)*

Federally Inspected Hog Slaughter in the United States   In Thousands of Head

Year	Jan.	Feb.	Mar.	Apr.	May	June	July	Aug.	Sept.	Oct.	Nov.	Dec.	Total
2002	8,552	7,400	7,879	8,321	8,215	7,425	7,957	8,425	8,384	9,276	8,548	8,534	98,915
2003	8,680	7,587	8,069	8,238	7,715	7,665	8,008	7,951	8,466	9,547	8,506	9,254	99,685
2004	8,704	7,805	8,942	8,567	7,494	8,415	8,008	8,616	8,897	8,883	8,881	9,150	102,361
2005	8,402	8,031	8,858	8,369	7,939	8,470	7,582	8,888	8,778	9,027	9,038	9,138	102,519
2006	8,834	7,978	9,148	7,884	8,450	8,256	7,805	8,991	8,738	9,541	9,276	8,788	103,689
2007	9,281	8,040	9,119	8,389	8,680	8,218	8,312	9,296	8,683	10,555	9,964	9,601	108,138
2008	10,474	9,297	9,579	9,911	8,981	8,801	9,373	9,170	9,878	10,654	9,250	10,053	115,421
2009	9,846	8,840	9,574	9,353	8,379	9,101	9,062	9,250	9,848	10,230	9,385	9,742	112,612
2010	8,838	8,619	9,947	8,980	7,897	8,968	8,396	9,030	9,257	9,651	9,895	9,838	109,315
2011[1]	9,036	8,440	9,795	8,559	8,470	8,866	8,089	9,440	9,604	9,822	9,968	9,868	109,956

[1] Preliminary. *Source: National Agricultural Statistics Service, U.S. Department of Agriculture (NASS-USDA)*

Average Live Weight of all Hogs Slaughtered Under Federal Inspection   In Pounds Per Head

Year	Jan.	Feb.	Mar.	Apr.	May	June	July	Aug.	Sept.	Oct.	Nov.	Dec.	Average
2002	268	267	267	268	267	266	261	259	261	264	268	268	265
2003	268	267	268	268	268	265	263	261	263	268	270	269	267
2004	269	268	268	268	266	265	263	263	266	267	270	270	267
2005	270	270	271	271	270	269	265	263	265	269	272	272	269
2006	273	272	272	272	271	267	264	262	267	269	272	271	269
2007	271	270	271	270	269	266	265	264	267	270	273	272	269
2008	273	271	271	270	268	266	263	261	266	270	271	271	268
2009	272	272	272	272	272	270	268	268	270	272	272	270	271
2010	272	272	272	272	272	271	269	267	271	276	278	278	273
2011[1]	278	278	278	277	276	273	268	266	271	276	279	278	275

[1] Preliminary. *Source: National Agricultural Statistics Service, U.S. Department of Agriculture (NASS-USDA)*

Average Open Interest of Lean Hog Futures in Chicago   In Contracts

Year	Jan.	Feb.	Mar.	Apr.	May	June	July	Aug.	Sept.	Oct.	Nov.	Dec.
2002	28,720	31,662	33,056	33,472	33,161	28,719	29,338	32,030	36,136	35,245	42,852	43,974
2003	40,660	39,862	40,446	37,883	43,672	47,338	39,706	37,700	49,469	46,295	43,552	43,352
2004	46,380	55,058	63,889	77,756	80,271	81,370	79,860	84,840	86,092	86,423	94,336	98,328
2005	102,580	97,550	95,841	94,008	96,662	91,871	97,160	95,841	107,617	113,754	116,005	124,492
2006	133,258	144,506	145,020	144,250	157,259	158,276	157,899	165,781	176,336	174,971	188,965	179,057
2007	174,424	182,146	178,296	174,233	176,897	177,274	174,144	176,425	175,093	179,402	204,475	206,458
2008	212,644	227,377	219,938	232,309	252,497	242,588	238,162	231,283	206,602	171,506	168,129	159,600
2009	137,693	122,594	126,377	134,363	143,493	135,606	131,683	130,844	143,952	152,820	164,819	174,739
2010	194,351	179,300	197,407	217,304	217,779	190,933	197,940	214,535	230,240	209,159	198,160	200,932
2011	218,818	243,878	226,344	233,168	222,193	221,633	242,921	253,224	247,476	273,568	257,632	246,758

Contract size = 40,000 lbs.   *Source: Chicago Mercantile Exchange (CME)*

Volume of Trading of Lean Hog Futures in Chicago   In Contracts

Year	Jan.	Feb.	Mar.	Apr.	May	June	July	Aug.	Sept.	Oct.	Nov.	Dec.	Total
2002	145,266	120,994	168,929	196,956	163,816	158,074	166,064	140,154	174,797	167,065	165,039	164,106	1,931,260
2003	186,436	137,479	186,511	156,370	209,740	210,901	199,782	124,677	232,705	207,247	164,190	148,117	2,164,155
2004	212,420	170,270	249,205	211,501	295,271	304,279	315,197	215,233	356,295	242,204	376,823	255,488	3,204,186
2005	347,467	237,079	380,658	287,828	412,655	398,201	354,819	315,949	391,121	295,817	421,714	310,235	4,153,543
2006	561,152	319,827	597,852	356,950	658,973	826,312	578,656	478,837	577,375	533,532	649,293	342,242	6,481,001
2007	687,585	449,649	721,014	423,223	620,985	744,799	865,371	559,139	591,564	485,066	730,036	386,401	7,264,832
2008	800,566	527,093	809,724	736,404	796,703	938,662	968,358	617,855	781,563	506,765	576,326	445,119	8,505,138
2009	614,928	390,054	593,621	503,180	620,260	727,565	644,070	510,721	657,827	540,591	590,062	426,182	6,819,061
2010	672,191	464,868	706,267	567,410	740,462	803,035	763,584	627,870	808,561	683,542	753,457	485,288	8,076,535
2011	879,859	660,332	925,083	660,983	881,184	991,400	900,953	770,608	1,047,769	785,722	857,709	608,359	9,969,961

Contract size = 40,000 lbs.   *Source: Chicago Mercantile Exchange (CME)*

Honey

Honey is the thick, supersaturated sugar solution produced by bees to feed their larvae. It is composed of fructose, glucose and water in varying proportions and also contains several enzymes and oils. The color of honey varies due to the source of nectar and age of the honey. Light colored honeys are usually of higher quality than darker honeys. The average honeybee colony can produce more than 700 pounds of honey per year but only 10 percent is usually harvested by the beekeeper. The rest of the honey is consumed by the colony during the year. American per capita honey consumption is 1 pound per person per year. Honey is said to be humanity's oldest sweet, and beeswax the first plastic.

Honey is used in many ways, including direct human consumption, baking, and medicine. Honey has several healing properties. Its high sugar content nourishes injured tissues, thus enhancing faster healing time. Honey's phytochemicals create a form of hydrogen peroxide that cleans out the wound, and the thick consistency protects the wound from contact with air. Honey has also proven superior to antibiotic ointments for reducing rates of infection in people with burns.

Prices – U.S. average domestic honey prices in 2010 rose by +8.8% to a record high of 160.3 cents per pound.

The value of U.S. honey production in 2010 rose +30.7% to $281.97 million, a new record high.

Supply – World production of honey in 2010 rose +0.4% to 1.541 million metric tons, not far below the 2008 record high of 1.554 million metric tons. The major producer of honey by far is China with 398,000 metric tons in 2010 which is 25.8% of total world production. Other major producers in 2010 were the U.S. with 79,789 metric tons, Argentina with 59,000 metric tons, Mexico with 55,684 metric tons, and Russia with 54,000 metric tons.

U.S. production of honey in 2010 rose +20.1% to 175.904 million pounds, remaining well below the 14-year high of 220.339 million pounds posted in 2000. Stocks rose by +20.8% to 45.307 million pounds in 2010 (Jan 1), which is a down from 2000's decade high of 220.339 million pounds. Yield per colony in 2010 rose +11.8% to 65.5 pounds per colony. The number of colonies in 2010 rose +7.5% to 2.684, a decade record high.

Trade – U.S. imports of honey in 2010 rose by +19.3% to 251.2 million pounds, below the 2006 record high of 277.7 million pounds. U.S. exports of honey are generally small and in 2010 they totaled only 9.6 million pounds, which was only 5.4% of U.S. production.

World Production of Honey   In Metric Tons

Year	Argentina	Australia	Brazil	Canada	China	Germany	Japan	Mexico	Russia	United States	Total
2004	80,000	14,632	32,290	34,241	297,987	25,575	3,585	56,917	52,666	83,272	1,350,286
2005	110,000	15,335	33,750	36,109	299,527	21,232	3,290	50,631	52,123	72,927	1,404,838
2006	105,000	17,500	36,194	48,353	337,578	25,199	3,133	55,970	55,678	70,238	1,507,508
2007	81,000	18,000	34,747	31,489	357,220	18,266	3,373	55,459	53,655	67,286	1,471,191
2008	72,000	17,059	37,792	29,440	407,219	15,727	3,384	55,271	57,440	74,293	1,554,240
2009	62,000	16,595	38,764	31,920	407,367	16,460	2,940	56,071	53,598	66,413	1,534,998
2010[1]	59,000	16,200	44,600	33,710	398,000	23,137	2,300	55,684	54,000	79,789	1,541,282

[1] Preliminary.   NA = Not available.   *Source: Food and Agricultural Organization of the United Nations (FAO)*

Salient Statistics of Honey in the United States   In Millions of Pounds

Year	Number of Colonies (1,000)	Yield Per Colony (Pounds)	Stocks Jan. 1	Total U.S. Production	Imports for Consumption	Domestic Disappearance	Exports	Total Supply	Placed Under Loan	CCC Take Over	Net Gov't. Expenditure[3] (Million $)	Domestic Avg. Price All Honey - Cents Per Pound -	National Avg. Price Support	Per Capita Consumption (Pounds)
2005	2,413	72.4	62.5	174.8	233.0	----	7.6	470.3	----	----	----	91.8	----	----
2006	2,393	64.7	60.5	154.9	277.7	----	7.0	493.1	----	----	----	103.6	----	----
2007	2,443	60.7	52.6	148.3	233.0	----	8.3	434.0	----	----	----	107.7	----	----
2008	2,342	69.9	51.2	163.8	231.4	----	10.1	446.4	----	----	----	142.1	----	----
2009[1]	2,498	58.6	37.5	146.4	210.5	----	9.7	394.4	----	----	----	147.3	----	----
2010[2]	2,684	65.5	45.3	175.9	251.2	----	9.6	472.4	----	----	----	160.3	----	----

[1] Preliminary.   [2] Forecast.   [3] Fiscal year.   *Source: Economic Research Service, U.S. Department of Agriculture (ERS-USDA)*

Production and Yield of Honey in the United States

	--------------- Production in Thousands of Pounds ---------------						Value of Production ($1,000)	-------------------- Yield Per Colony in Pounds --------------------					
Year	California	Florida	Minnesota	North Dakota	South Dakota	Total		California	Florida	Minnesota	North Dakota	South Dakota	Average
2005	30,000	13,760	8,880	33,670	17,380	174,818	160,428	75	86	74	91	79	72.4
2006	19,760	13,770	10,000	25,900	10,575	154,907	160,484	52	81	80	74	47	64.7
2007	13,600	11,360	8,840	31,080	13,260	148,341	159,763	40	71	68	74	52	60.8
2008	18,360	11,850	9,516	36,000	21,375	163,789	232,744	51	79	78	90	95	69.9
2009	11,715	11,560	7,930	34,650	17,820	146,416	215,671	33	68	65	77	66	58.6
2010[1]	27,470	13,800	8,316	46,410	15,635	175,904	281,974	67	69	66	91	59	65.5

[1] Preliminary.   *Source: National Agricultural Statistics Service, U.S. Department of Agriculture (NASS-USDA)*

Interest Rates - U.S.

U.S. interest rates can be characterized in two main ways, by credit quality and by maturity. Credit quality refers to the level of risk associated with a particular borrower. U.S. Treasury securities, for example, carry the lowest risk. Maturity refers to the time at which the security matures and must be repaid. Treasury securities carry the full spectrum of maturities, from short-term cash management bills, to T-bills (4-weeks, 3-months, and 6-months), T-notes (2-year, 3-year, 5-year and 10-year), and 30-year T-bonds. The most active futures markets are the Treasury note and bond futures and the Eurodollar futures, which are all traded at the CME Group.

Prices – 10-year T-note futures prices showed some weakness in early 2011 due to the strengthening U.S. economy and talk that the Fed might soon be forced to start retracting some of its extraordinary liquidity. However, T-note prices then started a sharp rally in April 2011 that eventually took T-note prices to new record highs. The T-note rally during spring was caused by several factors including the weak U.S. economy seen during the first half of 2011 and safe-haven demand caused by the worsening European debt crisis.

T-note prices in early 2011 also continued to benefit from the Federal Reserve's second quantitative easing program, which was known as QE2. During the QE2 program, the Federal Reserve purchased a total of $600 billion of Treasury securities from November 2010 through July 2011. That added to the Fed's existing program announced in August 2010 of reinvesting the proceeds from maturing securities in the purchase of new Treasury securities. The Fed's QE2 program brought the Fed's balance sheet asset level to about $2.9 billion by June 2011, representing an extra $2 trillion of liquidity above the Fed's normal asset level of $900 billion.

T-note prices were also boosted in early summer 2011 by the U.S. debt ceiling debacle, which hurt the U.S. economy by causing fears among investors that the U.S. Treasury might default on its debt for the first time in history. Budget hawks initially refused to go along with a routine U.S. debt ceiling hike and only backed down after some alarming brinkmanship. Standard & Poors subsequently downgraded the U.S. credit rating to AA+ from AAA, which was the first time in history that the U.S. lost its triple A credit rating. S&P took away the AAA rating because of the lack of progress by the federal government in curbing is massive budget deficit and its growing national debt. There were some fears at the time that T-note prices might plunge on the perception of higher risk on U.S. Treasury securities. However, T-note prices actually rallied because of the damage to the U.S. economy and because the U.S. credit rating downgrade made clear that Europe would be next in line for downgrades.

The Fed in mid 2011 once again became alarmed about the weak U.S. economy. In an attempt to bring long-term Treasury yields down even further, the Fed in September 2011 began its $400 billion Operation Twist program. The Fed with that program sold shorter-term Treasury securities from its portfolio and used the cash to buy longer-term T-note securities. The program, which is due to last until June 2012, was a significant factor in boosting longer-term T-note prices in late 2011. T-note prices were also boosted in the second half of 2011 by safe-haven demand tied to the European banking crisis, which nearly caused an all-out European systemic banking crisis before the European Central Bank cut rates and announced unlimited 36-month loan operations in November and December 2011.

U.S. Producer Price Index[2] for All Commodities   1982 = 100

Year	Jan.	Feb.	Mar.	Apr.	May	June	July	Aug.	Sept.	Oct.	Nov.	Dec.	Average
2002	128.5	128.4	129.8	130.8	130.8	130.9	131.2	131.5	132.3	133.2	133.1	132.9	131.1
2003	135.3	137.6	141.2	136.8	136.7	138.0	137.7	138.0	138.5	139.3	138.9	139.5	138.1
2004	141.4	142.1	143.1	144.8	146.8	147.2	147.4	148.0	147.7	150.0	151.4	150.2	146.7
2005	150.9	151.6	153.7	155.0	154.3	154.3	156.3	157.6	162.2	166.2	163.7	163.0	157.4
2006	164.3	161.8	162.2	164.3	165.8	166.1	166.8	167.9	165.4	162.2	164.6	165.6	164.8
2007	164.0	166.8	169.3	171.4	173.3	173.8	175.1	172.4	173.5	174.7	179.0	178.6	172.7
2008	181.0	182.7	187.9	190.9	196.6	200.5	205.5	199.0	196.9	186.4	176.8	170.9	189.6
2009	171.2	169.3	168.1	169.1	170.8	174.1	172.5	175.0	174.1	175.2	177.4	178.1	172.9
2010	181.9	181.0	183.3	184.4	184.8	183.5	184.1	184.9	184.9	186.6	187.7	189.7	184.7
2011[1]	192.7	195.8	199.2	203.1	204.1	203.9	204.6	203.2	203.7	201.3	202.0	200.2	201.2

[1] Preliminary.   [2] Not seasonally adjusted.   *Source: Bureau of Labor Statistics, U.S. Department of Commerce (BLS)*

U.S. Consumer Price Index[2] for All Urban Consumers   1982-84 = 100

Year	Jan.	Feb.	Mar.	Apr.	May	June	July	Aug.	Sept.	Oct.	Nov.	Dec.	Average
2002	177.1	177.8	178.8	179.8	179.8	179.9	180.1	180.7	181.0	181.3	181.3	180.9	179.9
2003	181.7	183.1	184.2	183.8	183.5	183.7	183.9	184.6	185.2	185.0	184.5	184.3	184.0
2004	185.2	186.2	187.4	188.0	189.1	189.7	189.4	189.5	189.9	190.9	191.0	190.3	188.9
2005	190.7	191.8	193.3	194.6	194.4	194.5	195.4	196.4	198.8	199.2	197.6	196.8	195.3
2006	198.3	198.7	199.8	201.5	202.5	202.9	203.5	203.9	202.9	201.8	201.5	201.8	201.6
2007	202.4	203.5	205.4	206.7	207.9	208.4	208.3	207.9	208.5	208.9	210.2	210.0	207.3
2008	211.1	211.7	213.5	214.8	216.6	218.8	220.0	219.1	218.8	216.6	212.4	210.2	215.3
2009	211.1	212.2	212.7	213.2	213.9	215.7	215.4	215.8	216.0	216.2	216.3	215.9	214.5
2010	216.7	216.7	217.6	218.0	218.2	218.0	218.0	218.3	218.4	218.7	218.8	219.2	218.1
2011[1]	220.2	221.3	223.5	224.9	226.0	225.7	225.9	226.5	226.9	226.4	226.2	225.7	224.9

[1] Preliminary.   [2] Not seasonally adjusted.   *Source: Bureau of Labor Statistics, U.S. Department of Commerce (BLS)*

3-Month Eurodollar Futures - CME Group
(weekly close) as of December 30, 2011
Points of 100%

Volume of Trading of 3-month Eurodollar Futures in Chicago   In Thousands of Contracts

Year	Jan.	Feb.	Mar.	Apr.	May	June	July	Aug.	Sept.	Oct.	Nov.	Dec.	Total
2002	19,487.1	14,491.2	17,986.7	17,946.9	18,717.5	17,931.8	20,366.9	17,757.9	15,309.9	18,495.9	13,348.6	10,240.5	202,081
2003	13,534.2	12,314.9	18,275.3	15,392.9	19,403.0	21,162.6	18,732.5	18,724.3	18,817.0	20,004.3	15,431.9	16,978.2	208,771
2004	20,808.8	16,042.4	22,583.6	26,673.6	25,548.9	28,067.1	25,114.4	24,859.3	32,283.0	25,737.3	27,945.3	21,920.2	297,584
2005	27,793.8	28,549.2	34,472.4	42,437.2	36,599.9	37,997.0	26,794.7	32,920.8	45,483.5	35,148.8	34,775.7	27,382.0	410,355
2006	35,602.4	34,218.0	47,463.8	37,752.2	44,154.6	45,443.4	36,794.1	45,126.7	45,180.3	46,453.5	42,700.7	41,187.7	502,077
2007	43,204.2	46,365.8	63,154.7	39,567.7	50,305.2	58,372.0	53,290.3	77,539.0	49,528.8	45,862.8	53,795.1	40,484.5	621,470
2008	70,787.1	59,378.2	60,956.1	56,371.5	48,683.4	60,086.5	54,178.8	36,521.6	58,497.7	40,508.5	24,515.5	26,489.2	596,974
2009	31,370.9	29,422.6	35,280.3	29,706.3	34,665.5	51,021.4	40,062.0	36,483.1	39,604.4	40,397.6	32,914.4	36,656.6	437,585
2010	36,569.3	37,746.7	47,459.2	52,132.3	57,806.8	36,986.7	32,120.3	34,582.2	38,196.5	34,205.0	55,512.9	47,637.1	510,955
2011	42,213.1	51,117.3	62,877.0	49,748.5	46,199.0	62,516.2	46,462.8	61,739.9	38,864.4	34,186.8	39,340.0	28,821.7	564,087

Contract size = $1,000,000.   *Source: CME Group; International Monetary Market (IOM), division of the Chicago Mercantile Exchange (CME)*

Average Open Interest of 3-month Eurodollar Futures in Chicago   In Thousands of Contracts

Year	Jan.	Feb.	Mar.	Apr.	May	June	July	Aug.	Sept.	Oct.	Nov.	Dec.
2002	4,592.0	4,937.0	4,727.9	4,411.6	4,421.0	4,295.5	4,123.7	4,482.4	4,243.4	4,237.9	4,553.7	4,072.5
2003	4,007.1	4,500.1	4,517.3	4,448.6	5,098.7	5,514.2	5,218.4	5,277.9	5,034.1	4,935.4	5,024.2	4,936.1
2004	5,128.0	5,624.1	5,640.5	5,602.2	6,060.0	6,117.3	6,026.7	6,236.3	5,992.8	5,968.9	6,527.8	6,706.7
2005	7,163.3	7,858.5	8,124.1	8,244.1	8,604.5	8,045.7	7,416.0	8,044.7	8,054.2	8,471.9	9,264.8	9,145.1
2006	8,833.5	9,574.0	9,586.0	9,679.6	10,126.2	9,995.4	9,572.4	10,153.9	9,949.4	9,809.8	10,345.5	10,201.1
2007	9,682.3	10,400.5	10,847.9	10,827.1	11,895.5	11,285.2	11,166.9	11,416.3	10,782.6	10,019.4	10,631.2	10,515.5
2008	11,033.0	11,206.7	10,356.6	9,225.3	9,282.5	9,266.0	9,589.0	9,882.1	8,953.0	8,141.7	8,286.9	7,389.1
2009	6,772.8	6,857.6	6,371.3	6,055.5	6,480.5	6,383.2	6,540.1	6,748.5	6,659.5	6,937.8	7,382.3	6,876.4
2010	6,957.6	7,607.2	7,643.6	7,850.9	7,728.4	7,297.3	7,652.9	7,876.1	7,528.6	7,953.2	8,245.8	7,433.0
2011	7,675.5	8,820.5	9,086.9	9,494.8	10,101.6	10,117.4	10,018.2	9,997.3	9,011.2	8,239.0	8,624.3	8,123.4

Contract size = $1,000,000.   *Source: CME Group; International Monetary Market (IOM), division of the Chicago Mercantile Exchange (CME)*

2-Year Treasury Note Futures - CME Group (CBT)
(weekly close) as of December 31, 2011

Nominal Value

Volume of Trading of 2-Year U.S. Treasury Note Futures in Chicago   In Thousands of Contracts

Year	Jan.	Feb.	Mar.	Apr.	May	June	July	Aug.	Sept.	Oct.	Nov.	Dec.	Total
2002	195.0	332.9	290.4	159.2	377.0	242.9	177.0	377.0	253.0	174.8	387.2	232.3	3,199
2003	146.8	392.9	292.5	153.3	513.9	339.2	274.1	514.0	522.8	281.1	496.7	488.5	4,416
2004	310.4	829.8	630.0	462.4	872.2	788.8	406.7	1,009.9	1,014.5	678.0	1,393.3	1,058.5	9,455
2005	953.7	1,997.5	1,706.1	1,548.3	2,306.3	1,811.4	1,153.0	2,144.2	2,118.0	1,344.1	2,451.5	1,671.3	21,205
2006	2,053.3	3,223.3	3,206.5	2,090.0	4,690.9	2,837.1	2,525.1	4,461.0	2,768.3	2,422.9	4,826.4	2,862.0	37,967
2007	2,892.6	5,666.6	5,321.4	3,128.3	7,197.4	5,495.7	4,793.7	10,567.2	4,788.1	4,771.2	8,849.7	5,138.5	68,610
2008	7,526.1	10,092.8	7,515.4	5,102.6	8,195.6	7,207.2	6,366.1	7,529.6	8,126.5	5,355.3	4,067.9	2,225.8	79,311
2009	2,117.4	3,797.2	2,486.1	2,219.7	4,409.0	3,818.7	3,094.7	5,931.9	3,915.7	5,012.4	7,205.5	4,150.6	48,159
2010	4,487.2	8,143.4	6,164.3	6,164.1	9,494.2	4,398.8	4,083.6	6,491.7	3,719.2	3,189.8	6,849.9	3,791.0	66,977
2011	4,172.3	9,276.8	7,161.9	5,363.7	8,520.4	6,814.1	5,166.5	9,198.7	3,990.7	3,743.3	6,105.9	2,664.6	72,179

Contract size = $200,000.   *Source: CME Group; Chicago Board of Trade (CBT)*

Average Open Interest of 2-Year U.S. Treasury Note Futures in Chicago   In Thousands of Contracts

Year	Jan.	Feb.	Mar.	Apr.	May	June	July	Aug.	Sept.	Oct.	Nov.	Dec.
2002	86.5	103.3	103.6	87.9	102.0	105.9	99.4	108.0	110.4	108.1	115.5	113.6
2003	107.1	114.2	123.9	109.0	120.3	118.8	112.1	149.1	151.9	144.6	149.0	156.5
2004	161.9	195.2	186.8	172.4	198.9	210.7	191.7	207.1	216.4	205.5	221.6	248.5
2005	287.3	345.7	329.6	307.0	341.5	372.9	362.3	371.1	364.4	351.3	357.3	363.2
2006	437.8	489.3	469.0	489.5	607.6	541.1	595.1	701.4	683.6	680.7	698.4	716.0
2007	764.5	826.7	896.3	1,003.3	1,125.5	965.1	1,016.8	985.4	902.3	993.1	1,043.6	997.3
2008	1,101.2	1,313.0	1,187.3	1,110.0	1,166.8	972.5	895.4	922.6	783.7	735.0	648.0	503.4
2009	505.7	495.1	473.4	487.5	514.2	535.3	627.8	741.6	772.4	935.2	1,052.2	911.8
2010	885.7	982.1	891.3	1,001.7	1,022.3	900.3	847.1	805.6	708.2	734.8	710.8	664.9
2011	711.7	900.2	892.0	1,031.0	1,066.2	1,030.5	1,012.9	976.2	772.3	714.5	748.0	698.8

Contract size = $200,000.   *Source: CME Group; Chicago Board of Trade (CBT)*

5-Year Treasury Note Futures - CME Group (CBT)
(weekly close) as of December 30, 2011

Volume of Trading of 5-Year U.S. Treasury Note Futures in Chicago   In Thousands of Contracts

Year	Jan.	Feb.	Mar.	Apr.	May	June	July	Aug.	Sept.	Oct.	Nov.	Dec.	Total
2002	2,867.9	3,826.0	3,848.2	3,092.4	4,637.6	4,095.7	4,437.4	5,354.4	4,859.3	5,026.7	5,013.2	3,453.2	50,512
2003	4,435.6	5,178.5	5,533.7	4,623.6	7,267.6	6,165.7	6,462.6	7,090.2	7,453.9	6,364.3	6,885.3	6,285.6	73,746
2004	5,856.9	7,388.8	7,775.6	7,793.1	10,979.4	9,458.2	7,109.8	10,656.0	10,311.6	7,686.2	11,036.9	9,416.8	105,469
2005	7,797.7	11,168.4	11,848.9	10,720.3	12,320.4	9,164.3	7,698.0	12,662.9	10,999.9	8,510.5	11,996.4	7,021.1	121,909
2006	9,388.4	12,141.7	11,865.2	7,869.8	12,971.9	9,368.7	8,102.0	13,347.5	9,369.3	8,730.9	13,423.5	8,291.5	124,870
2007	9,208.6	14,410.2	14,156.0	8,372.3	15,673.4	13,243.1	13,001.7	22,354.8	11,376.0	12,495.6	21,271.6	10,644.1	166,207
2008	15,479.7	20,790.4	17,424.0	12,474.7	17,616.2	14,904.3	14,514.1	15,085.6	16,979.1	10,079.8	8,057.9	4,721.7	168,127
2009	4,821.3	8,349.9	7,388.4	5,837.7	9,658.3	8,314.8	8,034.1	10,588.0	8,259.3	9,242.9	10,231.8	7,664.7	98,391
2010	7,434.9	11,815.6	10,096.3	9,631.3	16,093.0	10,212.4	9,662.0	13,062.2	9,627.7	9,404.1	14,828.5	10,282.0	132,150
2011	10,654.1	16,398.4	16,604.1	11,371.9	17,958.8	16,524.9	13,314.4	21,004.3	12,074.6	11,607.0	15,320.7	7,729.7	170,563

Contract size = $100,000.   *Source: CME Group; Chicago Board of Trade (CBT)*

Average Open Interest of 5-Year U.S. Treasury Note Futures in Chicago   In Thousands of Contracts

Year	Jan.	Feb.	Mar.	Apr.	May	June	July	Aug.	Sept.	Oct.	Nov.	Dec.
2002	507.2	576.2	585.6	632.2	656.4	594.9	554.9	652.8	655.0	662.5	720.7	692.8
2003	685.1	743.2	777.8	835.5	856.3	827.5	781.7	840.4	737.0	819.4	925.6	880.1
2004	874.2	1,008.1	987.2	1,043.0	1,145.4	1,118.5	1,217.3	1,322.5	1,168.1	1,099.4	1,290.7	1,318.7
2005	1,160.2	1,237.0	1,325.0	1,257.2	1,326.0	1,264.7	1,258.3	1,409.8	1,341.3	1,413.8	1,484.4	1,423.8
2006	1,105.1	1,404.8	1,238.0	1,614.9	1,763.5	1,601.5	1,586.9	1,648.0	1,564.9	1,666.1	1,932.4	1,841.2
2007	1,468.1	1,499.6	1,481.0	1,850.9	1,851.0	1,669.6	1,574.5	1,600.7	1,483.4	1,378.1	1,267.1	1,057.8
2008	1,940.6	2,101.2	1,923.8	812.7	860.8	774.2	761.1	831.9	800.3	770.9	854.0	831.6
2009	965.5	964.7	897.8	937.2	1,045.8	932.2	940.4	1,095.6	925.0	1,012.8	1,136.6	1,010.9
2010	805.1	939.1	942.4	937.2	1,524.6	1,576.9	940.4	1,095.6	1,326.7	1,200.4	1,136.6	1,010.9
2011	1,075.8	1,293.9	1,223.4	1,364.8	1,524.6	1,576.9	1,513.4	1,435.6	1,326.7	1,200.4	1,277.5	1,261.2

Contract size = $100,000.   *Source: CME Group; Chicago Board of Trade (CBT)*

10-Year Treasury Note Futures - CME Group (CBT)
(weekly close) as of December 30, 2011

Nominal Value

Volume of Trading of 10-year U.S. Treasury Note Futures in Chicago   In Thousands of Contracts

Year	Jan.	Feb.	Mar.	Apr.	May	June	July	Aug.	Sept.	Oct.	Nov.	Dec.	Total
2002	5,539.7	6,407.2	6,520.6	5,463.3	8,309.1	7,547.7	8,980.8	10,590.5	8,529.1	11,198.8	9,679.2	7,020.2	95,786
2003	9,120.6	10,746.5	11,320.5	9,377.2	13,817.0	12,149.5	15,285.0	14,248.7	13,706.7	13,586.9	12,474.5	10,912.2	146,745
2004	13,608.5	14,569.4	16,984.0	16,478.4	17,785.8	15,184.2	12,954.3	17,419.5	18,467.8	16,622.0	21,006.4	15,038.9	196,119
2005	13,901.3	19,565.4	21,132.8	19,487.3	22,688.8	16,778.7	13,894.5	20,120.1	18,348.2	15,357.3	20,705.4	13,144.2	215,124
2006	17,188.6	21,262.7	22,739.9	17,241.5	26,174.6	20,311.2	16,645.2	24,796.6	22,125.2	20,602.6	28,413.8	18,070.1	255,572
2007	21,492.5	30,367.2	30,210.2	18,529.8	34,343.9	37,171.0	32,361.3	38,785.6	24,375.6	25,280.4	36,890.7	19,421.3	349,229
2008	28,924.8	33,426.2	23,331.5	19,043.9	27,414.0	22,591.8	22,903.0	21,069.7	23,265.1	15,101.1	11,826.6	7,873.1	256,771
2009	9,778.0	14,548.1	15,116.1	11,893.7	17,309.8	16,994.6	16,420.7	19,292.8	16,099.0	19,268.8	19,037.2	14,093.3	189,852
2010	16,865.3	23,588.6	19,582.2	22,070.6	35,156.5	24,198.2	22,294.5	30,744.0	26,070.6	22,947.9	29,360.3	20,840.2	293,719
2011	22,260.8	27,531.8	29,500.1	20,162.8	31,149.4	31,897.7	25,851.1	39,911.1	24,612.4	23,559.8	26,614.2	14,351.4	317,403

Contract size = $100,000.   *Source: CME Group; Chicago Board of Trade (CBT)*

Average Open Interest of 10-year U.S. Treasury Note Futures in Chicago   In Thousands of Contracts

Year	Jan.	Feb.	Mar.	Apr.	May	June	July	Aug.	Sept.	Oct.	Nov.	Dec.
2002	572.9	643.9	679.6	699.1	806.5	793.0	877.6	958.3	888.7	970.2	938.0	751.6
2003	772.9	896.9	914.9	897.1	968.1	993.6	1,009.5	1,032.5	856.2	985.7	1,140.7	965.0
2004	1,145.9	1,320.6	1,312.9	1,347.7	1,392.4	1,300.3	1,348.2	1,456.6	1,503.6	1,626.9	1,767.4	1,642.0
2005	1,671.3	1,888.6	1,980.2	2,003.5	2,140.8	1,869.0	1,859.3	1,992.8	1,749.4	1,677.7	1,778.6	1,635.6
2006	1,700.0	1,990.4	2,048.7	2,259.7	2,321.0	2,054.2	2,087.1	2,265.3	2,271.5	2,408.2	2,398.2	2,236.0
2007	2,343.6	2,367.3	2,294.0	2,586.9	2,878.3	2,853.9	2,871.5	2,820.5	2,269.5	2,497.2	2,661.6	2,313.2
2008	2,431.2	2,517.6	2,179.8	2,073.7	2,144.6	1,978.8	1,802.6	1,835.2	1,658.2	1,385.2	1,226.4	1,074.2
2009	1,034.9	1,027.6	1,007.0	1,010.0	1,132.3	1,070.9	1,056.2	1,139.7	1,120.2	1,239.1	1,327.5	1,203.9
2010	1,292.9	1,420.4	1,423.8	1,632.0	1,838.8	1,756.8	1,802.2	1,973.0	1,686.3	1,617.2	1,527.4	1,335.3
2011	1,360.1	1,521.3	1,563.5	1,643.4	1,854.0	1,834.0	1,843.5	1,937.7	1,627.4	1,504.3	1,505.7	1,460.6

Contract size = $100,000.   *Source: CME Group; Chicago Board of Trade (CBT)*

30-Year Treasury Bond Futures - CME Group (CBT)
(weekly close) as of December 30, 2011

Nominal Value

Volume of Trading of 30-year U.S. Treasury Bond Futures in Chicago — In Thousands of Contracts

Year	Jan.	Feb.	Mar.	Apr.	May	June	July	Aug.	Sept.	Oct.	Nov.	Dec.	Total
2002	4,132.7	4,721.1	4,504.8	3,932.8	5,191.4	4,722.2	5,157.9	5,666.5	4,534.5	5,190.1	4,722.8	3,605.6	56,082
2003	3,625.3	4,840.9	5,106.9	3,795.0	7,188.4	5,896.2	6,352.1	6,198.0	5,738.4	5,121.8	4,823.4	4,835.2	63,522
2004	5,025.4	5,762.8	6,687.9	5,983.2	6,463.8	5,556.9	4,540.1	6,343.5	7,638.7	5,658.6	7,374.2	5,914.0	72,949
2005	6,134.8	8,973.5	8,573.7	7,293.5	8,558.9	7,407.2	5,367.0	7,771.3	7,193.6	6,450.4	7,928.8	5,274.0	86,927
2006	7,044.8	8,511.6	8,980.6	6,969.2	10,354.4	7,564.5	5,854.2	8,736.7	7,553.9	6,375.1	9,461.6	6,348.2	93,755
2007	7,108.8	10,060.2	10,338.3	6,108.4	10,578.5	11,338.4	9,452.1	11,439.3	6,864.4	7,232.1	11,146.2	5,963.6	107,630
2008	9,667.3	11,646.2	8,739.1	5,835.3	9,173.4	7,176.8	7,429.4	7,521.6	7,830.0	5,559.1	5,267.6	3,618.7	89,465
2009	3,805.9	6,062.7	4,525.5	3,224.8	6,465.1	5,192.0	4,995.2	7,238.3	4,297.6	5,133.4	6,978.4	4,313.9	62,233
2010	4,617.8	7,345.1	5,748.7	6,033.7	10,457.5	5,899.4	5,711.8	9,165.6	6,774.8	6,806.7	9,379.5	5,569.2	83,510
2011	6,272.2	8,551.9	7,823.2	5,528.4	9,231.3	8,358.3	6,471.5	11,892.5	7,487.1	6,694.3	9,057.7	4,969.9	92,339

Contract size = $100,000.   *Source: CME Group; Chicago Board of Trade (CBT)*

Average Open Interest of 30-year U.S. Treasury Bond Futures in Chicago — In Contracts

Year	Jan.	Feb.	Mar.	Apr.	May	June	July	Aug.	Sept.	Oct.	Nov.	Dec.
2002	468,455	520,573	479,939	463,100	472,778	458,020	427,896	465,971	496,815	467,440	459,877	440,225
2003	420,797	506,910	487,277	449,286	566,887	596,186	554,632	521,928	423,995	443,177	489,185	471,848
2004	488,484	571,445	557,595	488,921	735,910	665,235	579,724	600,565	595,736	586,653	618,647	574,121
2005	674,170	792,247	749,403	710,061	858,812	760,240	760,749	813,905	763,092	737,070	810,426	803,020
2006	601,094	662,314	622,927	739,601	949,173	980,004	988,995	991,513	915,693	948,940	1,022,623	947,588
2007	816,747	903,121	852,305	875,810	941,317	879,149	891,111	880,157	877,623	756,790	731,186	754,687
2008	1,033,106	1,041,505	979,695	893,308	724,577	706,818	696,641	727,674	749,290	739,723	777,241	704,259
2009	726,062	733,323	712,813	708,243	740,180	663,330	682,310	738,206	669,950	683,476	654,901	563,632
2010	656,438	676,778	648,845	663,991	702,197	668,848	628,174	661,826	647,168	618,884	634,941	597,183
2011	552,937	613,356	609,003	573,206	702,197	668,848	628,174	661,826	647,168	618,884	634,941	597,183

Contract size = $100,000.   *Source: CME Group; Chicago Board of Trade (CBT)*

Municipal Note Futures - Chicago Board of Trade
(weekly close) as of March 22, 2006

Nominal Value

U.S. Federal Funds Rate   In Percent

Year	Jan.	Feb.	Mar.	Apr.	May	June	July	Aug.	Sept.	Oct.	Nov.	Dec.	Average
2002	1.73	1.74	1.73	1.75	1.75	1.75	1.73	1.74	1.75	1.75	1.34	1.24	1.67
2003	1.24	1.26	1.25	1.26	1.26	1.22	1.01	1.03	1.01	1.01	1.00	0.98	1.13
2004	1.00	1.01	1.00	1.00	1.00	1.03	1.26	1.43	1.61	1.76	1.93	2.16	1.35
2005	2.28	2.50	2.63	2.79	3.00	3.04	3.26	3.50	3.62	3.78	4.00	4.16	3.21
2006	4.29	4.49	4.59	4.79	4.94	4.99	5.24	5.25	5.25	5.25	5.25	5.24	4.96
2007	5.25	5.26	5.26	5.25	5.25	5.25	5.26	5.02	4.94	4.76	4.49	4.24	5.02
2008	3.94	2.98	2.61	2.28	1.98	2.00	2.01	2.00	1.81	0.97	0.39	0.16	1.93
2009	0.15	0.22	0.18	0.15	0.18	0.21	0.16	0.16	0.15	0.12	0.12	0.12	0.16
2010	0.11	0.13	0.16	0.20	0.20	0.18	0.18	0.19	0.19	0.19	0.19	0.18	0.18
2011	0.17	0.16	0.14	0.10	0.09	0.09	0.07	0.10	0.08	0.07	0.08	0.07	0.10

Source: Bureau of Economic Analysis, U.S. Department of Commerce (BEA)

U.S. Municipal Bond Yield[1]   In Percent

Year	Jan.	Feb.	Mar.	Apr.	May	June	July	Aug.	Sept.	Oct.	Nov.	Dec.	Average
2002	5.16	5.11	5.29	5.22	5.19	5.09	5.02	4.95	4.74	4.88	4.95	4.85	5.04
2003	4.90	4.81	4.76	4.74	4.41	4.33	4.74	5.10	4.92	4.89	4.73	4.65	4.75
2004	4.61	4.55	4.41	4.82	5.07	5.05	4.87	4.70	4.56	4.49	4.52	4.48	4.68
2005	4.41	4.35	4.57	4.46	4.31	4.23	4.31	4.32	4.29	4.48	4.57	4.46	4.40
2006	4.37	4.41	4.44	4.58	4.59	4.60	4.61	4.39	4.27	4.30	4.14	4.11	4.40
2007	4.23	4.22	4.15	4.26	4.31	4.60	4.56	4.64	4.51	4.39	4.46	4.42	4.40
2008	4.27	4.64	4.93	4.70	4.58	4.69	4.68	4.69	4.86	5.50	5.23	5.56	4.86
2009	5.07	4.90	4.99	4.78	4.56	4.81	4.72	4.60	4.24	4.20	4.37	4.21	4.62
2010	4.33	4.36	4.36	4.41	4.29	4.36	4.32	4.03	3.87	3.87	4.40	4.92	4.29
2011	5.28	5.15	4.92	4.99	4.59	4.51	4.52	4.02	4.01	4.13	4.05	3.95	4.51

[1] 20-bond average.   *Source: Bureau of Economic Analysis, U.S. Department of Commerce (BEA)*

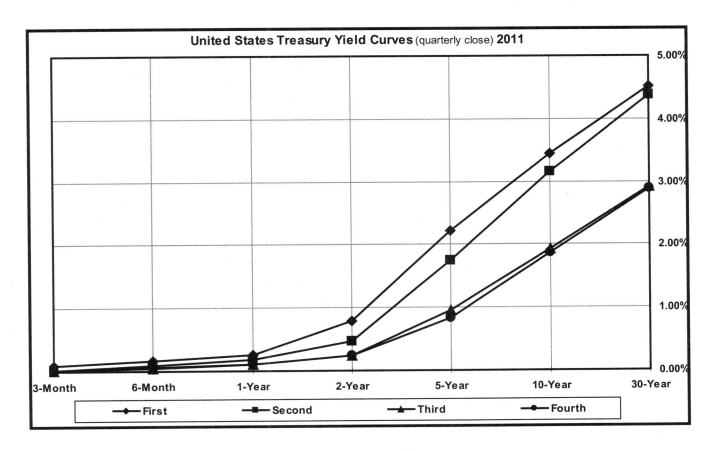

United States Treasury Yield Curves (quarterly close) 2011

Legend: First — Second — Third — Fourth

X-axis: 3-Month, 6-Month, 1-Year, 2-Year, 5-Year, 10-Year, 30-Year

Y-axis: 0.00%, 1.00%, 2.00%, 3.00%, 4.00%, 5.00%

U.S. Industrial Production Index[1]   1997 = 100

Year	Jan.	Feb.	Mar.	Apr.	May	June	July	Aug.	Sept.	Oct.	Nov.	Dec.	Average
2002	87.6	87.5	88.2	88.6	89.1	89.9	89.6	89.8	89.9	89.5	90.0	89.5	89.1
2003	90.2	90.5	90.4	89.6	89.6	89.7	89.9	89.9	90.4	90.4	91.1	91.1	90.2
2004	91.3	91.8	91.3	91.7	92.4	91.5	92.2	92.4	92.4	93.3	93.5	94.1	92.3
2005	94.6	95.3	95.2	95.2	95.4	95.7	95.6	95.7	93.8	95.0	95.9	96.4	95.3
2006	96.6	96.7	96.9	97.3	97.1	97.5	97.6	97.8	97.7	97.7	97.6	98.6	97.4
2007	98.3	99.4	99.4	100.2	100.1	100.1	100.2	100.2	100.7	100.1	100.5	100.7	100.0
2008	100.4	100.2	99.8	98.9	98.3	98.1	97.7	96.1	92.1	92.9	91.7	89.3	96.3
2009	87.5	87.0	85.5	84.8	83.9	83.5	84.4	85.2	85.8	86.0	86.2	86.7	85.5
2010	87.7	87.9	88.4	88.7	89.9	90.0	90.8	91.0	91.2	91.1	91.4	92.6	90.1
2011[1]	92.8	92.5	93.1	92.7	93.0	93.1	94.1	94.4	94.6	95.1	94.9	95.3	93.8

[1] Total Index of the Federal Reserve Index of Quantity Output, seasonally adjusted.   [2] Preliminary.   *Source: Bureau of Economic Analysis, U.S. Department of Commerce (BEA)*

U.S. Gross National Product, National Income, and Personal Income   In Billions of Constant Dollars[1]

	Gross Domestic Product					National Income					Personal Income				
Year	First Quarter	Second Quarter	Third Quarter	Fourth Quarter	Total	First Quarter	Second Quarter	Third Quarter	Fourth Quarter	Total	First Quarter	Second Quarter	Third Quarter	Fourth Quarter	Total
2002	10,499	10,602	10,702	10,767	10,642	9,305	9,381	9,418	9,531	9,409	8,978	9,061	9,075	9,127	9,060
2003	10,887	11,012	11,255	11,415	11,142	9,614	9,757	9,899	10,090	9,840	9,195	9,321	9,419	9,578	9,378
2004	11,590	11,763	11,936	12,124	11,853	10,281	10,445	10,642	10,769	10,534	9,680	9,847	9,999	10,223	9,937
2005	12,362	12,500	12,729	12,901	12,623	11,020	11,157	11,360	11,559	11,274	10,239	10,387	10,578	10,741	10,486
2006	13,161	13,330	13,433	13,584	13,377	11,838	11,966	12,093	12,228	12,031	11,027	11,204	11,337	11,505	11,268
2007	13,759	13,977	14,126	14,253	14,029	12,261	12,361	12,407	12,556	12,396	11,714	11,839	11,954	12,141	11,912
2008	14,274	14,416	14,395	14,082	14,292	12,694	12,725	12,733	12,284	12,609	12,416	12,572	12,513	12,340	12,460
2009	13,894	13,854	13,921	14,087	13,939	12,099	12,036	12,126	12,330	12,148	11,964	11,944	11,874	11,938	11,930
2010	14,278	14,468	14,606	14,755	14,527	12,596	12,804	12,942	13,019	12,840	12,138	12,326	12,453	12,578	12,374
2011[2]	14,868	15,013	15,176	15,294	15,088	13,233	13,344	13,431		13,336	12,847	12,955	12,980	13,062	12,961

[1] Seasonally adjusted at annual rates.   [2] Preliminary.   *Source: Bureau of Economic Analysis, U.S. Department of Commerce (BEA)*

INTEREST RATES - U.S.

U.S. Money Supply M1[2]   In Billions of Dollars

Year	Jan.	Feb.	Mar.	Apr.	May	June	July	Aug.	Sept.	Oct.	Nov.	Dec.	Average
2002	1,191.1	1,191.1	1,193.8	1,185.9	1,189.6	1,193.5	1,200.3	1,186.1	1,195.1	1,204.5	1,209.6	1,220.6	1,196.8
2003	1,226.9	1,238.7	1,239.9	1,248.8	1,268.3	1,281.0	1,288.7	1,294.7	1,296.6	1,297.3	1,298.8	1,307.0	1,273.9
2004	1,305.4	1,322.0	1,330.0	1,331.1	1,332.5	1,343.0	1,340.5	1,353.4	1,362.0	1,361.2	1,374.9	1,376.7	1,344.4
2005	1,366.5	1,372.4	1,372.4	1,356.7	1,365.1	1,379.7	1,367.7	1,377.2	1,377.2	1,375.7	1,376.6	1,375.0	1,371.9
2006	1,380.2	1,380.0	1,383.5	1,380.7	1,386.0	1,373.1	1,370.8	1,371.5	1,362.5	1,369.8	1,370.9	1,367.2	1,374.7
2007	1,373.9	1,365.0	1,366.1	1,378.1	1,380.0	1,364.4	1,370.2	1,374.4	1,373.3	1,378.7	1,371.1	1,375.4	1,372.6
2008	1,381.9	1,382.6	1,387.8	1,392.7	1,392.1	1,399.6	1,420.4	1,404.3	1,459.7	1,472.0	1,513.5	1,606.9	1,434.5
2009	1,589.6	1,570.7	1,578.1	1,613.0	1,614.0	1,651.6	1,661.7	1,655.7	1,660.9	1,674.6	1,680.0	1,697.8	1,637.3
2010	1,684.3	1,705.0	1,712.5	1,701.7	1,706.0	1,722.4	1,724.6	1,743.7	1,762.1	1,777.0	1,822.6	1,840.3	1,741.9
2011[1]	1,868.4	1,878.9	1,891.2	1,903.8	1,931.6	1,945.2	2,004.7	2,106.3	2,122.7	2,138.9	2,158.3	2,173.9	2,010.3

[1] Preliminary.   [2] M1 -- The sum of currency held outside the vaults of depository institutions, Federal Reserve Banks, and the U.S. Treasury; travelers checks; and demand and other checkable deposits issued by financial institutions (except demand deposits due to the Treasury and depository institutions), minus cash items in process of collection and Federal Reserve float. Seasonally adjusted.   *Source: Board of Governors of the Federal Reserve System*

U.S. Money Supply M2[2]   In Billions of Dollars

Year	Jan.	Feb.	Mar.	Apr.	May	June	July	Aug.	Sept.	Oct.	Nov.	Dec.	Average
2002	5,453.5	5,480.6	5,490.7	5,493.6	5,516.6	5,540.3	5,586.6	5,623.9	5,648.1	5,699.4	5,743.6	5,768.7	5,587.1
2003	5,798.0	5,833.0	5,850.8	5,894.2	5,947.8	5,985.4	6,040.1	6,087.1	6,063.2	6,052.4	6,055.7	6,058.6	5,972.2
2004	6,063.4	6,103.6	6,141.8	6,182.9	6,254.6	6,263.3	6,271.5	6,295.2	6,332.9	6,355.3	6,387.3	6,404.4	6,254.7
2005	6,407.2	6,419.2	6,435.1	6,442.3	6,460.6	6,497.3	6,524.8	6,555.8	6,589.1	6,621.5	6,644.4	6,667.9	6,522.1
2006	6,711.3	6,736.8	6,751.8	6,786.9	6,798.9	6,835.7	6,875.0	6,904.3	6,927.8	6,983.0	7,018.6	7,059.7	6,865.8
2007	7,103.6	7,118.6	7,151.8	7,223.8	7,248.5	7,274.3	7,308.8	7,372.9	7,403.1	7,426.9	7,451.3	7,484.5	7,297.3
2008	7,529.1	7,610.0	7,678.7	7,732.3	7,740.2	7,753.7	7,807.1	7,794.4	7,879.8	7,993.9	8,043.0	8,231.7	7,816.2
2009	8,313.8	8,342.9	8,405.3	8,407.8	8,452.5	8,463.1	8,458.6	8,426.7	8,434.9	8,464.8	8,497.9	8,514.2	8,431.9
2010	8,479.9	8,531.0	8,524.4	8,549.5	8,596.3	8,616.4	8,613.1	8,639.2	8,673.7	8,726.2	8,756.0	8,796.4	8,625.2
2011[1]	8,860.4	8,903.5	8,949.9	8,996.9	9,046.1	9,120.8	9,293.2	9,483.0	9,502.5	9,549.7	9,596.0	9,640.1	9,245.2

[1] Preliminary.   [2] M2 -- M1 plus savings deposits (including money market deposit accounts) and small-denomination (less than $100,000) time deposits issued by financial institutions; and shares in retail money market mutual funds (funds with initial investments of less than $50,000), net of retirement accounts. Seasonally adjusted.   *Source: Board of Governors of the Federal Reserve System*

U.S. Money Supply M3[2]   In Billions of Dollars

Year	Jan.	Feb.	Mar.	Apr.	May	June	July	Aug.	Sept.	Oct.	Nov.	Dec.	Average
1997	5,013.2	5,041.7	5,080.2	5,119.8	5,147.1	5,177.4	5,235.8	5,291.4	5,332.3	5,376.3	5,417.1	5,460.5	5,224.4
1998	5,508.8	5,541.3	5,611.5	5,647.3	5,686.9	5,728.4	5,750.0	5,815.0	5,882.0	5,953.7	6,010.1	6,051.9	5,765.6
1999	6,080.7	6,129.5	6,133.6	6,172.3	6,201.0	6,237.7	6,269.0	6,299.1	6,323.0	6,378.4	6,464.1	6,551.8	6,270.0
2000	6,605.5	6,642.2	6,704.0	6,767.3	6,776.9	6,823.6	6,875.2	6,945.0	7,003.5	7,027.0	7,038.3	7,117.6	6,860.5
2001	7,237.2	7,308.5	7,372.0	7,507.8	7,564.1	7,644.7	7,691.9	7,696.3	7,853.2	7,897.8	7,973.0	8,035.4	7,648.5
2002	8,063.9	8,109.3	8,117.3	8,142.6	8,175.1	8,190.8	8,244.2	8,298.1	8,331.5	8,368.9	8,498.8	8,568.0	8,259.0
2003	8,588.1	8,628.7	8,648.8	8,686.0	8,741.9	8,791.6	8,888.7	8,918.2	8,906.5	8,896.8	8,880.3	8,872.3	8,787.3
2004	8,930.2	9,000.3	9,080.7	9,149.6	9,243.8	9,275.7	9,282.7	9,314.4	9,351.8	9,359.4	9,395.1	9,433.0	9,234.7
2005	9,487.2	9,531.6	9,565.3	9,620.9	9,665.0	9,725.3	9,762.4	9,864.6	9,950.8	10,032.0	10,078.5	10,154.0	9,786.5
2006[1]	10,242.8	10,298.7	Discontinued										10,270.8

[1] Preliminary.   [2] M3 -- M2 plus large-denomination ($100,000 or more) time deposits; repurchase agreements issued by depository institutions; Eurodollar deposits, specifically, dollar-denominated deposits due to nonbank U.S. addresses held at foreign offices of U.S. banks worldwide and all banking offices in Canada and the United Kingdom; and institutional money market mutual funds (funds with initial investments of $50,000 or more). Seasonally adjusted.
Source: Board of Governors of the Federal Reserve System

U.S. Money Supply MZM[2]   In Billions of Dollars

Year	Jan.	Feb.	Mar.	Apr.	May	June	July	Aug.	Sept.	Oct.	Nov.	Dec.	Average
2002	5,716.5	5,762.1	5,784.0	5,802.3	5,835.1	5,858.3	5,907.2	5,936.2	5,947.6	5,983.3	6,106.2	6,161.6	5,900.0
2003	6,172.4	6,204.7	6,210.8	6,237.7	6,277.8	6,326.7	6,432.5	6,455.1	6,433.8	6,415.6	6,407.6	6,383.8	6,329.9
2004	6,392.8	6,431.1	6,477.4	6,523.2	6,601.6	6,607.9	6,605.6	6,617.6	6,639.1	6,639.1	6,663.3	6,668.6	6,572.3
2005	6,653.7	6,646.0	6,642.2	6,641.5	6,640.5	6,674.3	6,702.4	6,725.9	6,763.5	6,796.2	6,809.0	6,836.0	6,710.9
2006	6,875.7	6,884.5	6,889.5	6,919.3	6,926.9	6,965.3	7,000.1	7,023.8	7,048.2	7,109.5	7,153.9	7,225.4	7,001.8
2007	7,250.3	7,268.0	7,322.9	7,416.4	7,473.6	7,529.1	7,603.8	7,739.5	7,862.7	7,970.3	8,060.5	8,131.4	7,635.7
2008	8,190.0	8,396.7	8,554.2	8,649.6	8,687.5	8,733.6	8,789.4	8,770.5	8,788.6	8,829.0	8,946.0	9,178.7	8,709.5
2009	9,334.7	9,404.7	9,501.4	9,535.0	9,618.2	9,634.7	9,639.9	9,587.0	9,582.8	9,570.1	9,569.3	9,549.6	9,544.0
2010	9,504.1	9,511.8	9,454.2	9,414.4	9,434.1	9,446.3	9,467.0	9,522.7	9,587.3	9,651.7	9,701.9	9,737.3	9,536.1
2011[1]	9,771.6	9,803.2	9,885.6	9,971.6	10,054.7	10,119.0	10,273.8	10,391.4	10,450.4	10,506.4	10,557.9	10,618.9	10,200.4

[1] Preliminary.   [2] MZM (money, zero maturity): M2 minus small-denomination time deposits, plus institutional money market mutual funds (that is, those included in M3 but excluded from M2). The label MZM was coined by William Poole (1991); the aggregate itself was proposed earlier by Motley (1988). Seasonally adjusted.   *Source: Board of Governors of the Federal Reserve System*

Prime Rate and Discount Rate
(monthly close) through December 2011

Percent

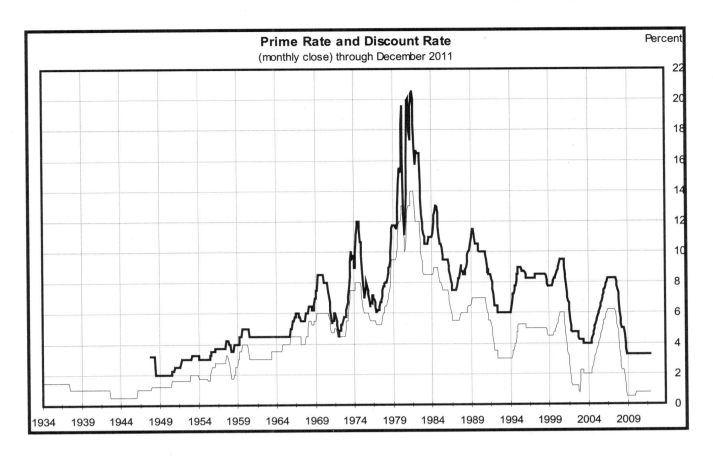

Municipal Bonds and Corporate AAA Bond Yields
(monthly average) through December 2011

Percent

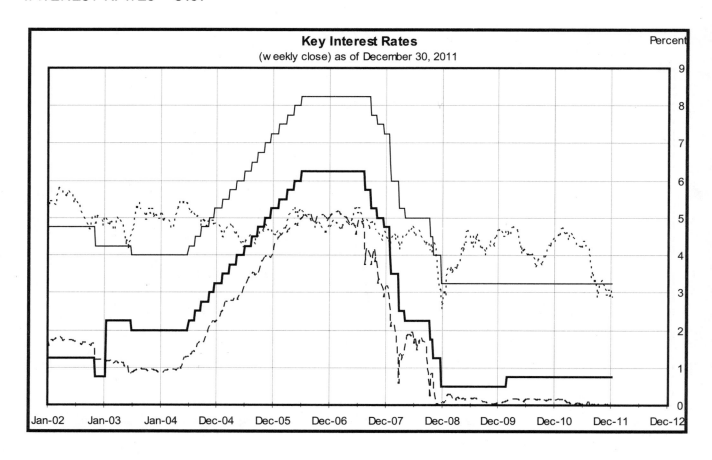

Key Interest Rates
(weekly close) as of December 30, 2011

5-Year Treasury Note Yield
(monthly average) through December 2011

Interest Rates - Worldwide

Interest rate futures contracts are widely traded throughout the world. The most popular futures contracts are generally the 10-year government bond and the 3-month interest rate contracts. In Europe, futures on German interest rates are traded at the all-electronic Eurex Exchange in Frankfurt. Futures on UK interest rates are traded at the Liffe Exchange in London. Futures on Canadian interest rates are traded at the Montreal Exchange. Futures on Japanese interest rates are traded at the Singapore Exchange (Simex) and at the Tokyo Stock Exchange. A variety of other interest rate futures contracts are traded throughout the rest of the world (please see the front of this Yearbook for a complete list).

Euro-Zone – The Eurex 10-year Euro Bund futures contract in early 2011 continued the sell-off that started in September 2010 and posted a 2-year low in April. That sell-off was due to some temporary optimism on the European debt crisis and an improvement in the European economy. However, Bund futures then rallied sharply through the remainder of 2011 and closed sharply higher on the year. The 10-year German bund yield dropped from its peak of 3.5% in April 2011 to a record low of 1.67% in September 2011, consolidating most of the rest of the year below 2%.

The strength in Bund prices during 2011 was due to the severe worsening on the European debt crisis which began a year earlier in 2010. Portugal required a bailout by April 2011, joining Ireland, which received a bailout in November 2010, and Greece, which received its first bailout in May 2010. Even worse, Spain and Italy were on the ropes in 2011. The markets knew that the Eurozone countries did not have enough firepower or political will to bail out Italy with its massive debt load of 1.9 trillion euros. Greece failed to enact its promised reforms and its debt load was set to soar to nearly 200% of GDP, a debt that Greece could not possibly repay. There was the constant threat during the year of an outright Greek default, which it was feared would spread even more contagion to the other troubled Eurozone countries. By early 2012, Greece finally met the conditions for a voluntary write-down of its debt and a second 130 billion euro bailout package.

The Greek 10-year bond yield rose above 30% and Irish and Portuguese 10-year bond yields rose as high as 12% in July 2011. Even French bond yields rose during late 2011 on fears that the troubled Eurozone nations would sink French banks and French government finances. German bond yields, on the other hand, remained low near 2% in late 2011, benefiting from safe-haven demand.

Eurozone officials finally started getting a handle on the European debt crisis in late 2011. Eurozone officials accelerated the operation of the permanent 500 billion euro European Stability Mechanism to July 2012. Eurozone officials addressed the structural defects in the Eurozone by agreeing upon a fiscal compact that required Eurozone nations to enshrine debt limits in their national constitutions and mandated automatic sanctions on nations that broke the fiscal rules. Most importantly, the European Central Bank in late 2011 cut its refinancing rate by a total of 50 bp to 1.00% and also announced two unlimited 36-month lending operations that flooded the European banking system with liquidity. These measures finally started to contain the European debt crisis. Yet as 2011 ended, the Eurozone economy was in at least a mild recession and Germany Bund yields remained low into early 2012.

UK – The Liffe 10-year Gilt futures contract rallied sharply during most of 2011. The 10-year UK gilt yield fell from the high 3% area in early 2011 to 2% by the end of the year. Gilt prices were supported during 2011 by the European debt crisis, the poor UK economy, and the government's tight fiscal policy. The Bank of England (BOE) during 2011 maintained its extremely easy monetary policy with the base rate at 0.50% and its quantitative easing program remaining in place. The BOE was unable to ease monetary policy during the year because the UK CPI rose from the low 3% area in late 2010 to a peak of +5.2% in September 2011. The CPI eased going into early 2012, however, which allowed the BOE in February 2012 to at least extend its quantitative easing program. UK GDP was dismal during 2011, falling from +1.7% y/y in Q4-2010 to as low as +0.5% y/y in Q3-2011. On the brighter side, the UK government's action to tighten fiscal policy and bring down the government's budget deficit gave investors more confidence in the UK's finances and allowed the UK to avoid spill-over contagion from the European debt crisis.

Canada – The Montreal Exchange's Canadian 10-year government note futures contract showed some weakness in early 2011 as the Canadian and U.S. economies showed some temporary signs of progress. However, 10-year Canadian note futures then rallied through most of the rest of 2011 due to the weaker Canadian and U.S. economies and increased concern about the European debt crisis. Canada's GDP was strong at +4% in December 2010, but then headed lower to +2.1% by May and June 2011. Canada's GDP temporarily improved to +3% by September 2011 but then headed lower again and hit a 2-year low of +2.0% in November 2011. The Bank of Canada during 2011 left its policy rate unchanged at 1.00% all year. Canada's CPI rose as high as +3.7% in May 2011, which prevented the Bank of Canada from considering a new easing move. However, the CPI eased to +2.1% by December 2011.

Japan – The SGX 10-year JGB futures rallied mildly during most of 2011. The 10-year JGB yield during 2011 drifted lower from a high of 1.30% in early 2011 to the 1.00% area late in the year. Japan was hit by the massive Tohoku earthquake in March 2011, which caused an enormous tsunami and a nuclear disaster. The earthquake caused Japanese GDP to fall by -6.8% (quarter-on-quarter annualized) in Q1-2011 and by -1.5% in Q2-2011. Japan's GDP showed a temporary +7.0% rise in Q3 on earthquake rebuilding, but then turned negative again to -2.3% by Q4-2011. Japan's economy was also hurt during the year by a slow-down in exports caused by weaker economic growth in China and Europe. The Bank of Japan kept its overnight rate near zero all year and continued to engage in a large quantitative easing program in an attempt to revive the Japanese economy.

Long Gilt Futures - Euronext-LIFFE
(weekly close) as of December 30, 2011

Nominal Value

3-Month Sterling Futures - Euronext-LIFFE
(weekly close) as of December 30, 2011

Points of 100%

10-Year Japanese Government Bond Futures - Tokyo Stock Exch.
(weekly close) as December 30, 2011

Nominal Value

3-Month Euroyen Futures - TIFFE
(weekly close) as of December 30, 2011

Points of 100%

10-Year Canadian Government Bond Futures - Montreal Exch.
(weekly close) as of December 30, 2011

Nominal Value

3-Month Canadian Bankers' Acceptance Futures - Montreal Exch.
(weekly close) as of December 30, 2011

Points of 100%

Australia -- Economic Statistics Percentage Change from Previous Period

Year	Real GDP	Nominal GDP	Real Private Consump-tion	Real Public Consump-tion	Grossed Fixed Invest-ment	Real Total Domestic Demand	Real Exports of Goods & Services	Real Imports of Goods & Services	Consumer Prices[3]	Unem-ployment Rate
2004	3.2	7.5	5.3	3.9	6.2	4.9	4.0	15.1	2.3	5.4
2005	3.5	8.1	3.7	2.2	9.6	5.0	2.4	8.6	2.7	5.0
2006	2.4	7.8	3.0	3.6	4.1	2.8	3.4	7.2	3.5	4.8
2007	5.0	9.2	5.2	3.3	9.8	7.0	3.3	12.2	2.3	4.4
2008	2.1	8.6	1.9	3.3	9.0	3.7	3.1	11.1	4.4	4.2
2009	1.2	1.6	1.7	2.8	-1.1	.5	1.0	-8.3	1.8	5.6
2010	3.3	9.3	3.3	5.2	7.0	5.1	4.7	13.3	2.9	5.2
2011[1]	3.6	7.2	3.2	2.1	6.6	4.0	6.1	8.1	2.8	4.9
2012[2]	4.0	6.7	3.2	1.7	8.5	4.5	6.5	8.4	2.9	4.7

[1] Estimate. [2] Projection. [3] National accounts implicit private consumption deflator. *Source: Organization for Economic Co-operation and Development (OECD)*

Canada -- Economic Statistics Percentage Change from Previous Period

Year	Real GDP	Nominal GDP	Real Private Consump-tion	Real Public Consump-tion	Grossed Fixed Invest-ment	Real Total Domestic Demand	Real Exports of Goods & Services	Real Imports of Goods & Services	Consumer Prices[3]	Unem-ployment Rate
2004	3.1	6.4	3.3	2.0	7.8	4.1	5.0	8.0	1.8	7.2
2005	3.0	6.4	3.7	1.4	9.3	4.9	1.9	7.1	2.2	6.8
2006	2.8	5.6	4.2	3.0	7.1	4.4	.6	4.9	2.0	6.3
2007	2.2	5.5	4.6	2.7	3.5	3.9	1.2	5.9	2.1	6.0
2008	.5	4.6	2.9	3.9	1.4	2.5	-4.6	1.2	2.4	6.2
2009	-2.5	-4.5	.4	3.5	-11.7	-2.6	-14.2	-13.9	.3	8.3
2010	3.0	5.8	3.2	3.3	6.6	4.8	6.8	12.7	1.6	8.1
2011[1]	2.3	3.9	2.1	.8	4.8	2.5	5.3	5.7	1.7	7.8
2012[2]	3.0	4.6	3.0	-.3	2.6	2.2	9.4	6.6	1.5	7.4

[1] Estimate. [2] Projection. [3] National accounts implicit private consumption deflator. *Source: Organization for Economic Co-operation and Development (OECD)*

France -- Economic Statistics Percentage Change from Previous Period

Year	Real GDP	Nominal GDP	Real Private Consump-tion	Real Public Consump-tion	Grossed Fixed Invest-ment	Real Total Domestic Demand	Real Exports of Goods & Services	Real Imports of Goods & Services	Consumer Prices[3]	Unem-ployment Rate
2004	2.3	3.9	2.4	2.2	3.3	3.0	3.5	6.4	2.3	8.8
2005	2.0	4.0	2.5	1.3	4.5	2.7	3.5	6.3	1.9	8.9
2006	2.4	4.9	2.6	1.3	4.5	2.7	5.0	5.9	1.9	8.8
2007	2.3	4.9	2.5	1.5	5.9	3.2	2.5	5.7	1.6	8.0
2008	.1	2.7	.5	1.6	.3	.4	-.8	.3	3.2	7.4
2009	-2.5	-2.0	.6	2.8	-7.0	-2.3	-12.2	-10.6	.1	9.1
2010	1.6	2.0	1.5	1.6	-1.8	1.5	9.9	8.8	1.6	9.3
2011[1]	1.6	2.6	1.6	.6	2.8	2.0	6.4	7.5	1.1	9.1
2012[2]	2.0	3.1	2.2	.0	4.3	2.1	6.3	6.2	1.1	8.8

[1] Estimate. [2] Projection. [3] National accounts implicit private consumption deflator. *Source: Organization for Economic Co-operation and Development (OECD)*

Germany -- Economic Statistics Percentage Change from Previous Period

Year	Real GDP	Nominal GDP	Real Private Consump-tion	Real Public Consump-tion	Grossed Fixed Invest-ment	Real Total Domestic Demand	Real Exports of Goods & Services	Real Imports of Goods & Services	Consumer Prices[3]	Unem-ployment Rate
2004	.7	1.7	-.2	-.7	-1.3	-.5	9.2	6.5	1.8	9.7
2005	.9	1.6	.4	.4	1.1	.1	8.0	6.9	1.9	10.5
2006	3.6	4.0	1.5	1.0	8.7	2.5	13.5	12.3	1.8	9.8
2007	2.8	4.7	-.2	1.6	4.9	1.3	7.9	5.2	2.3	8.3
2008	.7	1.7	.6	2.3	1.8	1.0	2.0	2.9	2.8	7.3
2009	-4.7	-3.3	-.1	2.9	-10.0	-1.9	-14.3	-9.4	.2	7.4
2010	3.5	4.3	-.1	2.6	4.9	2.3	15.2	13.6	1.0	6.9
2011[1]	2.5	3.6	1.3	.7	2.7	1.5	9.0	7.4	1.2	6.3
2012[2]	2.2	3.4	1.6	.6	1.2	1.3	5.6	4.1	1.4	6.2

[1] Estimate. [2] Projection. [3] National accounts implicit private consumption deflator. *Source: Organization for Economic Co-operation and Development (OECD)*

Italy -- Economic Statistics   Percentage Change from Previous Period

Year	Real GDP	Nominal GDP	Real Private Consumption	Real Public Consumption	Grossed Fixed Investment	Real Total Domestic Demand	Real Exports of Goods & Services	Real Imports of Goods & Services	Consumer Prices[3]	Unemployment Rate
2004	1.4	4.0	.8	2.2	1.5	1.3	3.6	3.3	2.3	8.0
2005	.8	2.9	1.2	1.9	1.4	1.0	2.0	2.7	2.2	7.7
2006	2.1	4.0	1.3	.5	3.1	2.0	6.5	6.2	2.2	6.8
2007	1.4	4.0	1.1	.9	1.3	1.2	3.9	3.3	2.0	6.2
2008	-1.3	1.4	-.8	.8	-4.0	-1.4	-3.9	-4.3	3.5	6.7
2009	-5.1	-3.0	-1.7	.6	-12.2	-3.8	-19.1	-14.6	.8	7.8
2010	1.0	1.7	.4	-.3	2.0	.7	7.9	6.6	1.5	8.6
2011[1]	1.3	2.5	.6	.1	1.5	.6	6.7	3.7	1.4	8.5
2012[2]	1.6	2.7	1.0	.0	3.1	1.2	5.3	3.9	1.4	8.3

[1] Estimate.   [2] Projection.   [3] National accounts implicit private consumption deflator.   *Source: Organization for Economic Co-operation and Development (OECD)*

Japan -- Economic Statistics   Percentage Change from Previous Period

Year	Real GDP	Nominal GDP	Real Private Consumption	Real Public Consumption	Grossed Fixed Investment	Real Total Domestic Demand	Real Exports of Goods & Services	Real Imports of Goods & Services	Consumer Prices[3]	Unemployment Rate
2004	2.7	1.6	1.6	1.9	1.4	1.9	13.9	8.1	.0	4.7
2005	1.9	.7	1.3	1.6	3.1	1.7	7.0	5.8	-.6	4.4
2006	2.0	1.1	1.5	.4	.5	1.2	9.7	4.2	.2	4.1
2007	2.4	1.6	1.6	1.5	-1.2	1.3	8.4	1.6	.1	3.8
2008	-1.2	-2.0	-.7	.3	-2.6	-1.3	1.6	1.2	1.4	4.0
2009	-5.2	-6.1	-1.0	1.5	-14.0	-4.0	-23.9	-16.7	-1.4	5.1
2010	3.7	1.8	2.4	1.6	-.1	1.7	25.4	10.5	-.9	5.1
2011[1]	1.7	.9	1.0	1.7	3.2	1.6	6.7	6.6	-.8	4.9
2012[2]	1.3	.5	1.4	.3	2.3	1.4	5.8	6.5	-.5	4.5

[1] Estimate.   [2] Projection.   [3] National accounts implicit private consumption deflator.   *Source: Organization for Economic Co-operation and Development (OECD)*

Switzerland -- Economic Statistics   Percentage Change from Previous Period

Year	Real GDP	Nominal GDP	Real Private Consumption	Real Public Consumption	Grossed Fixed Investment	Real Total Domestic Demand	Real Exports of Goods & Services	Real Imports of Goods & Services	Consumer Prices[3]	Unemployment Rate
2004	2.5	3.1	1.6	.8	4.5	1.9	7.9	7.3	.8	4.4
2005	2.6	2.8	1.7	1.2	3.8	1.8	7.8	6.6	1.2	4.4
2006	3.6	5.8	1.6	.3	4.7	1.4	10.3	6.5	1.1	4.0
2007	3.6	6.2	2.3	.3	5.1	1.4	9.6	6.1	.7	3.6
2008	1.9	4.4	1.3	1.7	.5	.2	3.3	.3	2.4	3.5
2009	-1.9	-1.6	1.0	1.6	-4.9	.6	-8.7	-5.4	-.5	4.4
2010	2.7	2.8	1.7	.2	3.7	.7	10.6	8.3	.5	4.4
2011[1]	2.2	2.9	2.0	.4	4.2	2.6	4.8	6.4	.1	4.3
2012[2]	2.5	3.2	2.4	.9	2.8	2.3	5.5	6.2	1.1	4.1

[1] Estimate.   [2] Projection.   [3] National accounts implicit private consumption deflator.   *Source: Organization for Economic Co-operation and Development (OECD)*

United Kingdom -- Economic Statistics   Percentage Change from Previous Period

Year	Real GDP	Nominal GDP	Real Private Consumption	Real Public Consumption	Grossed Fixed Investment	Real Total Domestic Demand	Real Exports of Goods & Services	Real Imports of Goods & Services	Consumer Prices[3]	Unemployment Rate
2004	3.0	5.5	3.1	3.0	5.1	3.5	5.0	6.9	1.3	4.8
2005	2.2	4.2	2.2	2.0	2.4	2.1	7.9	7.1	2.0	4.8
2006	2.8	5.9	1.7	1.4	6.4	2.4	11.1	9.1	2.3	5.4
2007	2.7	5.8	2.2	1.3	7.8	3.1	-2.6	-.8	2.3	5.4
2008	-.1	2.9	.4	1.6	-5.0	-.7	1.0	-1.2	3.6	5.7
2009	-5.0	-3.7	-3.3	1.0	-15.1	-5.5	-11.1	-12.3	2.2	7.6
2010	1.8	5.1	1.2	1.9	2.0	2.7	4.4	7.5	3.1	7.9
2011[1]	1.7	3.7	1.7	-1.1	2.3	1.3	5.0	3.1	2.6	7.8
2012[2]	2.0	3.2	1.8	-1.7	4.3	1.4	6.4	4.0	1.6	7.6

[1] Estimate.   [2] Projection.   [3] National accounts implicit private consumption deflator.   *Source: Organization for Economic Co-operation and Development (OECD)*

Iron and Steel

Iron (symbol Fe) is a soft, malleable, and ductile metallic element. Next to aluminum, iron is the most abundant of all metals. Pure iron melts at about 1,535 degrees Celsius and boils at 2,750 degrees Celsius. Archaeologists in Egypt discovered the earliest iron implements dating back to about 3,000 BC, and iron ornaments were used even earlier.

Steel is an alloy of iron and carbon, often with an admixture of other elements. The physical properties of various types of steel and steel alloys depend primarily on the amount of carbon present and how it is distributed in the iron. Steel is marketed in a variety of sizes and shapes, such as rods, pipes, railroad rails, tees, channels, and I-beams. Steel mills roll and form heated ingots into the required shapes. The working of steel improves the quality of the steel by refining its crystalline structure and making the metal tougher. There are five classifications of steel: carbon steels, alloy steels, high-strength low-alloy steels, stainless steel, and tool steels.

Prices – In 2011 the average wholesale price for No. 1 heavy-melting steel scrap in Chicago rose +24.8% to $416.87 per metric ton. That was a new record high for the average price but in January of 2011 the price hit $429.00 per metric ton but then moved lower the rest of the year.

Supply – World production of iron ore in 2011 rose by +8.1% to 2.800 billion metric tons, which was a new record high. The world's largest producers of iron ore are China with 43% of world production, Australia with 17%, and Brazil with 14%. The U.S. accounted for only 2.0% of world iron ore production in 2011. World production of raw steel (ingots and castings) in 2011 rose +6.4 % yr/yr to 1,500 million metric tons, with the largest producers being China with 47% of world production, Japan with 7%, and the U.S. with 6%.

U.S. production of steel ingots in 2011 rose by 5.7% to 86.000 million short tons, up from the 2009 record low of 59.400 million short tons. U.S. production of pig iron (excluding ferro-alloys) in 2011 (annualized through October) rose +6.7% to 31.920 million short tons.

Demand – U.S. consumption of ferrous scrap and pig iron fell −17.6% yr/yr in 2009 (latest data available) to 84.660 million metric tons which is a record low. The largest consumers of ferrous scrap and pig iron were the manufacturers of pig iron and steel ingots and castings with 91% of consumption at 77.240 million metric tons in 2009. Iron foundries and miscellaneous users accounted for 1.0% of consumption and manufacturers of steel castings (scrap) accounted for 1% of consumption.

Trade – The U.S. imported 4.360 million metric tons of iron ore in 2010, up +12.7% yr/yr from 3.870 million metric tons in 2009. The bulk of U.S. iron ore imports came from Canada (81% with 3.520 million metric tons), Brazil (3.6% with 158,000 metric tons), and Chili (2.8% with 121,000 metric tons).

World Production of Raw Steel (Ingots and Castings)   In Thousands of Metric Tons

Year	Brazil	Canada	China	France	Germany	Italy	Japan	Rep. of Korea	Russia	Ukraine	United Kindom	United States	World Total
2002	29,605	16,300	182,370	20,524	44,999	25,930	107,745	45,390	59,777	34,538	11,718	91,600	907,000
2003	31,150	15,928	222,340	19,803	44,809	26,832	110,511	46,310	62,710	36,900	13,128	93,700	974,000
2004	32,918	16,305	272,450	20,770	46,374	28,317	112,718	47,521	65,646	38,740	13,766	99,700	1,060,000
2005	31,631	15,327	353,240	19,481	44,524	29,061	112,471	47,820	66,186	38,636	13,210	94,900	1,140,000
2006	30,901	15,493	419,150	19,857	47,224	31,550	116,266	48,455	70,816	40,899	13,931	98,200	1,250,000
2007	33,782	15,569	489,290	19,252	48,550	31,990	120,203	51,517	72,389	42,830	14,300	98,100	1,350,000
2008	33,716	15,100	500,490	17,874	45,833	30,477	118,739	53,322	68,700	37,107	13,538	91,900	1,330,000
2009	33,750	9,000	567,840	12,836	32,671	19,737	87,500	53,300	59,166	29,757	10,080	59,400	1,240,000
2010[1]	33,000		627,000	15,000	44,000		110,000	49,000	67,000	34,000	10,000	81,000	1,410,000
2011[2]	36,000		700,000	16,000	46,000		110,000	68,000	69,000	35,000	10,000	86,000	1,500,000

[1] Preliminary.   [2] Estimate.   *Source: U.S. Geological Survey (USGS)*

Average Wholesale Prices of Iron and Steel in the United States

	No. 1 Heavy Melting Steel Scrap		---- Sheet Bars ----			Pittsburg Prices					
	Pittsburg	Chicago	Hot Rolled	Hot Rolled	Cold Finished	Hot Rolled Strip	Carbon Steel Plates	Cold Rolled Strip	Galvan-ized Sheets	Rail Road Steel Scrap[2]	Used Steel Cans[3]
Year	----- $ Per Gross Ton -----		-------------------------------------- Cents Per Pound --------------------------------------							---- $ Per Gross Ton ----	
2002	101.06	89.92	16.46	----	23.26	----	----	----	22.00	NA	66.71
2003	128.32	113.82	14.80	----	25.15	----	----	----	20.08	----	116.21
2004	221.05	220.13	30.84	----	38.67	----	----	----	36.69	----	192.80
2005	199.10	196.75	27.83	----	44.96	----	----	----	33.77	----	172.00
2006	222.39	225.21	29.78	----	44.02	----	----	----	38.09	----	212.63
2007	250.98	262.80	26.89	----	45.26	----	----	----	38.25	----	244.65
2008	365.62	357.88	44.56	----	61.67	----	----	----	54.91	----	314.63
2009	204.21	206.14	24.60	----	42.10	----	----	----	34.23	----	121.84
2010	339.54	334.48	31.65	----	50.82	----	----	----	41.72	----	296.91
2011[1]	408.64	417.00	38.02	----	63.63	----	----	----	48.45	----	391.50

[1] Preliminary.   [2] Specialties scrap.   [3] Consumer buying prices.   NA = Not available.   *Source: American Metal Market (AMM)*

IRON AND STEEL

Salient Statistics of Steel in the United States   In Thousands of Short Tons

Year	Pig Iron Production	Producer Price Index for Steel Mill Products (1982=100)	Basic Oxygen	Open Hearth	Electric[2]	Stainless	Carbon	Alloy	Total	Net Shipments Steel Mill Products	Exports	Imports
2001	46,424	101.3	52,204	----	47,118	1,836	92,946	4,666	99,322	99,448	6,144	30,080
2002	44,341	104.8	50,114	----	51,564	1,894	92,518	4,779	101,679	99,191	6,009	32,686
2003	43,122	109.5	50,942	----	48,751	1,952	98,772	4,901	99,693	105,625	8,220	23,125
2004	44,731	147.2	50,613	----	58,456	2,073	105,161	4,851	109,069	112,085	7,933	35,808
2005	40,036	159.7	45,231	----	57,599	1,903	96,636	4,935	102,830	103,474	9,393	32,108
2006	37,900	174.1	39,298	----	50,346	1,775	78,846	9,025	89,645	99,300	8,830	41,100
2007	36,300	182.9	36,147	----	53,161	1,713	86,958	8,026	96,697	96,500	10,100	30,200
2008	33,700	220.6	W	W	W	1,511	73,899	9,051	84,461	89,300	12,200	29,000
2009	19,000	165.2	W	W	W	880	33,230	3,726	37,836	56,400	8,400	14,700
2010[1]	29,000	192.1								76,000	11,000	22,000

[1] Preliminary.   [2] Includes crucible steels.   *Sources: American Iron & Steel Institute (AISI); U.S. Geological Survey (USGS)*

Production of Steel Ingots, Rate of Capability Utilization[1] in the United States   In Percent

Year	Jan.	Feb.	Mar.	Apr.	May	June	July	Aug.	Sept.	Oct.	Nov.	Dec.	Average
2002	84.5	88.4	86.7	90.3	89.4	92.5	86.8	91.0	94.0	90.8	86.8	83.9	88.8
2003	83.1	87.3	85.0	87.8	81.1	86.2	78.9	78.3	80.7	82.8	82.8	81.9	83.0
2004	88.0	90.9	93.8	93.3	92.9	94.4	93.5	95.0	97.3	97.5	94.8	91.5	93.6
2005	90.9	92.9	88.4	89.2	84.2	79.8	77.1	81.3	86.4	89.3	88.1	85.0	86.1
2006	85.6	89.5	92.8	91.4	92.5	92.1	88.7	88.7	91.2	86.2	81.5	75.0	87.9
2007	78.2	87.8	86.3	85.0	88.4	88.6	87.0	87.7	86.5	88.5	88.5	88.1	86.7
2008	90.3	91.6	89.7	90.3	91.1	90.3	88.8	90.4	84.5	70.5	50.7	40.9	80.8
2009	42.6	45.5	42.9	40.8	42.8	46.9	52.4	57.7	62.1	62.3	61.4	60.9	51.5
2010	64.2	71.1	73.2	74.0	74.8	75.4	69.6	68.1	70.2	67.3	68.3	68.4	70.4
2011[2]	73.2	75.4	75.0	74.2	72.7	76.2	75.0	75.7	76.1	71.9			74.5

[1] Based on tonnage capability to produce raw steel for a full order book.   [2] Preliminary.   *Sources: American Iron and Steel Institute (AISI); U.S. Geological Survey (USGS)*

Production of Steel Ingots in the United States   In Thousands of Short Tons

Year	Jan.	Feb.	Mar.	Apr.	May	June	July	Aug.	Sept.	Oct.	Nov.	Dec.	Total
1997	8,735	8,266	9,175	8,882	9,048	8,662	8,692	8,818	9,006	9,128	9,116	9,071	107,488
1998	9,510	9,087	9,839	9,524	9,483	8,863	8,832	9,194	8,548	8,681	7,710	8,013	107,643
1999	8,422	7,837	8,854	8,643	8,914	8,413	8,619	8,993	8,650	9,574	9,357	9,604	105,882
2000	9,838	9,170	10,009	9,843	10,097	9,592	9,411	9,213	8,830	8,978	8,054	7,982	111,015
2001	8,475	8,122	8,932	8,685	8,832	8,550	8,459	8,525	8,263	8,125	7,226	6,695	98,889
2002	8,050	7,609	8,261	8,214	8,401	8,414	8,510	8,918	8,916	9,015	8,340	8,329	100,976
2003	8,617	8,175	8,817	8,692	8,047	8,534	8,163	8,096	8,026	8,514	8,347	8,414	100,442
2004	8,656	8,400	9,268	8,901	9,163	9,006	9,164	9,314	9,234	9,551	8,989	8,660	108,305
2005	9,123	8,419	9,028	8,757	8,543	7,837	7,896	8,330	8,562	9,032	8,629	8,599	102,754
2006[1]	8,918	8,506	9,770	9,382	9,811	9,458	9,324	9,320	9,282	8,922	8,169	7,760	108,621

[1] Preliminary.   *Source: American Iron and Steel Institute (AISI)*

Shipments of Steel Products[1] by Market Classifications in the United States   In Thousands of Short Tons

Year	Appliances Utensils & Cutlery	Automotive	Containers, Packaging & Shipping Materials	Construction Including Maint.	Contactors Products	Electrical Equipment	Export	Machinery, Industrial Equip. & Tools	Oil and Gas	Rail Transportation	Steel for Converting & Processing[2]	Steel Service Center & Distributors	All Other[3]	Total Shipments
1997	1,635	15,251	4,163	15,885	[5]	2,434	2,610	2,355	3,811	1,410	11,263	27,800	17,241	105,858
1998	1,729	15,842	3,829	15,289	[5]	2,255	2,556	2,147	2,649	1,657	9,975	27,751	16,741	102,420
1999	1,712	15,639	3,768	14,685	[5]	2,260	2,292	1,547	1,544	876	7,599	21,439	32,840	106,201
2000	1,530	14,697	3,684	14,763	[5]	2,039	2,752	1,513	2,268	994	7,753	22,537	35,093	109,624
2001	1,675	12,767	3,193	16,339	[5]	1,694	2,281	1,210	2,134	720	7,462	23,887	26,086	99,448
2002	1,734	12,562	3,251	15,729	[5]	1,336	1,844	1,137	1,658	751	7,201	22,828	29,160	99,191
2003	1,891	11,937	2,949	14,403	[5]	1,200	2,572	1,108	1,800	799	6,798	24,266	35,905	105,628
2004	1,919	12,527	2,978	15,114	[5]	1,139	2,426	1,332	2,043	957	7,295	25,385	38,969	112,085
2005	1,895	13,031	2,504	15,858	[5]	1,088	2,592	1,300	2,056	1,019	7,559	23,213	31,359	103,474
2006[4]	1,781	14,003	2,535	17,544	[5]	1,228	3,068	1,360	2,459	1,242	8,531	23,706	31,153	108,609

[1] All grades including carbon, alloy and stainless steel.   [2] Net total after deducting shipments to reporting companies for conversion or resale.
[3] Includes agricultural; bolts, nuts rivets & screws; forgings (other than automotive); shipbuilding & marine equipment; aircraft; mining, quarrying & lumbering; other domestic & commercial equipment machinery; ordnance & other direct military; and shipments of non-reporting companies.
[4] Preliminary.   [5] Included in Construction.   *Source: American Iron and Steel Institute (AISI)*

Net Shipments of Steel Products[2] in the United States   In Thousands of Short Tons

Year	Cold Finished Bars	Rails & Accessories	Wire Drawn	Tin Mill Products	Plates Cut & Coils	Sheet & Strip[3] Galv, Hot Dipped	Hot Rolled Bars	Pipe & Tubing	Structural Shapes & Steel Piling	Reinforcing Bars	Hot Rolled Sheets	Cold Rolled Sheets	Carbon	Alloy	Stainless
1997	1,809	875	619	4,057	8,855	12,439	8,153	6,548	6,029	6,188	18,221	13,322	97,509	6,282	2,067
1998	1,780	938	725	3,714	8,864	13,481	8,189	5,409	5,595	5,909	15,715	13,185	94,536	5,847	2,037
1999	1,775	646	611	3,771	8,200	14,870	8,078	4,772	5,995	6,183	17,740	13,874	98,694	5,421	2,086
2000	1,756	783	579	3,742	8,898	14,917	7,901	5,385	7,402	6,893	19,236	14,802	102,141	5,379	2,104
2001	1,369	630	481	3,202	8,349	14,310	7,032	5,377	6,789	6,976	18,866	12,352	92,314	4,789	1,837
2002	1,404	789	733	3,419	8,769	14,944	6,581	4,809	6,729	6,359	19,243	12,673	92,518	4,779	1,894
2003	1,426	739	684	3,513	9,230	15,221	6,486	4,597	7,437	7,970	22,218	13,485	98,772	4,901	1,952
2004	1,520	843	428	3,247	10,740	16,306	7,181	5,328	7,812	8,274	23,106	14,762	105,161	4,851	2,073
2005	1,495	920	560	2,874	10,274	15,249	6,674	5,096	8,070	7,464	20,569	12,793	97,884	5,183	1,903
2006[1]	1,487	1,016	603	2,880	10,827	16,358	7,595	5,426	8,652	7,419	20,862	13,281	101,572	4,956	2,081

[1] Preliminary.   [2] All grades, including carbon, alloy and stainless steel.   *Source: American Iron and Steel Institute (AISI)*

World Production of Pig Iron (Excludes Ferro-Alloys)   In Thousands of Metric Tons

Year	Belgium	Brazil	China	France	Germany	India	Italy	Japan	Russia	Ukraine	United Kingdom	United States	World Total
2001	7,732	27,623	155,540	12,004	29,184	21,900	10,650	78,836	44,980	26,400	9,861	42,125	624,086
2002	8,053	29,667	170,850	13,217	29,427	24,315	9,736	80,979	46,060	27,560	8,561	40,200	653,000
2003	7,813	32,036	213,660	12,756	29,481	26,550	10,604	82,092	48,368	29,570	10,228	40,600	719,000
2004	8,224	34,558	251,850	13,198	30,018	25,117	10,664	82,974	50,427	31,000	10,180	42,300	773,000
2005	7,254	33,884	343,750	12,705	28,854	27,125	11,423	83,058	49,175	30,747	10,236	37,200	858,000
2006	7,516	32,452	412,450	13,013	30,360	28,300	11,497	84,270	51,683	32,926	10,736	37,900	939,000
2007	6,576	35,571	476,520	12,426	31,149	28,800	11,100	86,771	51,523	35,647	10,960	36,300	1,020,000
2008	7,125	35,286	470,670	11,372	29,111	29,000	10,373	86,171	48,300	30,982	10,137	33,700	997,000
2009[1]	3,087	35,300	543,750	8,105	20,127	29,500	5,719	86,000	43,930	25,676	7,674	19,000	1,000,000
2010[2]		23,000	600,000	10,000	29,000	39,000		82,000	47,000	26,000	7,000	29,000	1,000,000

[1] Preliminary.   [2] Estimate.   *Source: U.S. Geological Survey (USGS)*

Production of Pig Iron (Excludes Ferro-Alloys) in the United States   In Thousands of Short Tons

Year	Jan.	Feb.	Mar.	Apr.	May	June	July	Aug.	Sept.	Oct.	Nov.	Dec.	Total
2002	3,493	3,308	3,616	3,480	3,584	3,612	3,854	3,983	4,006	4,018	3,710	3,677	44,341
2003	3,832	3,631	3,906	3,810	3,381	3,569	3,395	3,253	3,289	3,527	3,530	3,733	42,856
2004	3,682	3,524	4,018	3,749	3,670	3,633	3,590	3,839	3,818	3,940	3,668	3,389	44,520
2005	3,773	3,592	4,030	3,397	3,395	2,962	2,895	3,183	3,127	3,237	3,310	3,135	40,036
2006	3,519	3,421	3,765	3,612	3,816	3,667	3,540	3,525	3,544	3,403	3,059	2,909	41,780
2007	2,850	2,610	3,040	3,010	3,130	3,120	3,080	3,010	3,010	3,200	2,940	3,160	36,160
2008	2,900	3,110	3,280	3,240	3,210	3,020	3,090	3,290	2,900	2,770	2,040	1,690	34,540
2009	1,450	1,510	1,630	1,410	1,370	1,380	1,840	2,090	1,930	2,510	2,240	2,410	21,770
2010	2,350	2,530	2,870	2,030	2,830	2,800	2,450	2,490	2,600	2,150	2,470	2,340	29,910
2011[1]	2,400	2,490	2,790	2,550	2,870	2,820	2,520	2,610	2,540	3,010			31,920

[1] Preliminary.   *Source: American Iron and Steel Institute*

Salient Statistics of Ferrous Scrap and Pig Iron in the United States   In Thousands of Metric Tons

	Consumption: Ferrous Scrap & Pig Iron Charged To											Stocks, Dec. 31		
	Mfg. of Pig Iron & Steel Ingots & Castings			Iron Foundries & Misc. Users			Mfg. of Steel	All Uses			Imports	Exports	Ferrous Scrap & Pig Iron at Consumers	
Year	Scrap	Pig Iron	Total	Scrap	Pig Iron	Total	Castings (Scrap)	Ferrous Scrap	Pig Iron	Grand Total	of Scrap[2]	of Scrap[3]		Total
2000	59,000	49,000	110,300	13,000	1,200	14,216	2,200	74,000	50,000	126,300	3,040	5,230	5,320	930	6,250
2001	56,700	46,900	105,400	12,000	1,100	13,113	2,200	71,000	48,000	120,800	2,630	7,440	4,880	787	5,667
2002	56,400	42,500	101,100	11,000	1,500	12,513	1,800	69,000	44,000	115,200	3,130	8,950	4,930	754	5,684
2003	55,200	39,700	96,670	4,460	655	5,119	2,680	61,900	41,000	104,670	3,480	10,800	4,410	381	4,791
2004	57,100	38,000	96,590	8,490	1,020	9,514	1,330	66,500	39,100	107,100	4,660	11,800	5,400	721	6,121
2005	54,600	36,900	93,240	9,010	1,090	10,103	1,810	65,400	38,000	105,150	3,840	13,000	4,970	664	5,897
2006	54,500	36,700	92,730	9,370	857	10,232	1,640	65,600	37,600	104,740	4,820	14,900	4,370	700	5,389
2007	54,600	36,500	93,140	9,080	1,290	10,374	1,380	65,000	37,800	104,850	3,700	16,500	4,420	771	5,555
2008	56,600	33,500	92,050	7,760	844	8,608	2,070	66,400	34,400	102,760	3,600	21,500	4,620	885	5,940
2009[1]	47,600	28,300	77,240	838	17	859	838	53,100	30,200	84,660	2,990	22,400	3,410	507	4,151

[1] Preliminary.   [2] Includes tinplate and terneplate.   [3] Excludes used rails for rerolling and other uses and ships, boats, and other vessels for scrapping.
Source: U.S. Geological Survey (USGS)

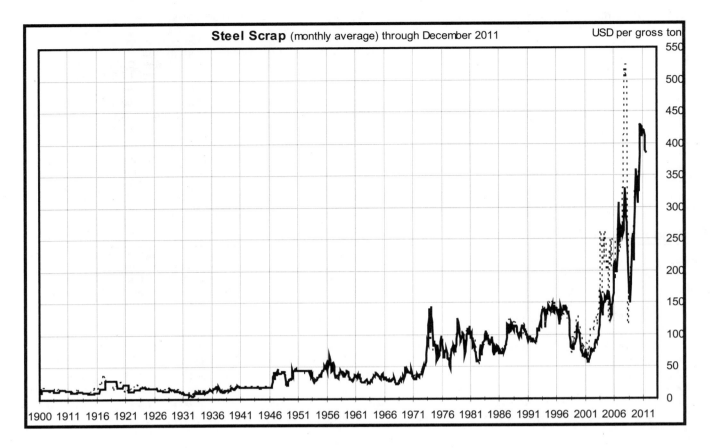

Steel Scrap (monthly average) through December 2011 — USD per gross ton

Consumption of Pig Iron in the United States, by Type of Furance or Equipment — In Thousands of Metric Tons

Year	Open Hearth	Electric	Cupola	Basic Oxygen Process	Air & Other Furnace	Direct Casting	Total
2000	----	2,900	530	47,000	W	35	50,000
2001	----	2,700	500	45,000	W	36	48,000
2002	----	3,200	520	40,000	W	36	44,000
2003	----	2,310	792	37,900	W	36	41,000
2004	----	3,030	354	35,700	W	36	39,100
2005	----	3,040	528	34,400	W	36	38,000
2006	----	3,380	435	33,800	W	36	37,600
2007	----	3,980	401	33,400	8	36	37,800
2008[1]	----	3,350	401	30,600	5	36	33,600
2009[2]	----	4,140	148	25,900	----	36	30,200

[1] Preliminary. [2] Estimate. W = Withheld. *Source: U.S. Geological Survey (USGS)*

Wholesale Price of No. 1 Heavy Melting Steel Scrap in Chicago — In Dollars Per Metric Ton

Year	Jan.	Feb.	Mar.	Apr.	May	June	July	Aug.	Sept.	Oct.	Nov.	Dec.	Average
2002	70.21	75.03	75.50	85.05	93.09	97.10	97.50	97.50	100.50	98.85	93.50	93.50	89.78
2003	96.93	101.97	105.07	105.50	101.69	96.88	101.05	116.79	122.02	122.50	138.22	159.74	114.03
2004	187.75	219.92	250.85	224.55	181.90	180.00	222.50	249.32	217.38	237.62	248.00	223.57	220.28
2005	203.00	190.00	190.00	217.14	180.95	124.32	135.50	189.78	241.19	204.29	246.25	242.43	197.07
2006	222.70	237.76	237.07	245.00	249.23	249.23	245.25	204.41	207.25	202.55	197.90	203.55	225.16
2007	225.24	252.37	305.00	291.90	255.36	254.71	250.71	257.04	268.74	265.65	252.10	273.42	262.69
2008	334.00	338.70	352.57	482.73	513.10	498.10	510.45	466.43	313.62	188.00	91.67	169.29	354.89
2009	183.00	176.68	157.73	150.00	179.25	185.00	230.00	244.29	257.86	244.76	216.32	251.05	206.33
2010	297.63	305.00	352.83	360.00	338.75	335.00	305.00	325.91	347.14	324.29	338.00	380.00	334.13
2011	429.00	427.37	425.00	425.00	407.86	419.32	420.00	420.00	420.00	411.43	388.75	408.68	416.87

Source: American Metal Market (AMM)

World Production of Iron Ore[3]   In Thousands of Metric Tons (Gross Weight)

Year	Australia	Brazil	Canada	China	India	Maur-itania	Russia	South Africa	Sweden	Ukraine	United States	Venezula	World Total
2002	187,198	214,560	30,902	231,000	86,400	9,553	84,236	36,484	20,300	58,900	51,600	16,684	1,100,000
2003	212,981	230,707	33,322	261,000	99,100	10,377	91,760	38,086	21,500	62,498	48,600	17,954	1,210,000
2004	234,000	261,696	28,596	320,000	120,600	10,505	96,980	39,322	22,300	65,550	54,700	19,196	1,360,000
2005	262,000	281,462	30,387	420,000	152,000	11,133	96,764	39,542	23,300	68,570	54,329	21,200	1,550,000
2006	275,000	317,800	33,543	601,000	181,000	10,658	102,000	41,326	23,300	74,000	52,749	22,100	1,840,000
2007	299,000	354,674	32,744	707,000	202,000	11,817	105,000	42,082	24,700	77,900	52,489	20,700	2,040,000
2008	342,000	351,246	31,273	824,000	220,000	11,200	99,900	48,983	23,800	72,700	53,560	20,650	2,210,000
2009	394,000	300,000	31,700	880,000	245,000	10,400	92,000	55,313	17,700	66,476	26,696	14,900	2,240,000
2010[1]	433,000	370,000	37,000	1,070,000	230,000	11,000	101,000	59,000	25,000	78,000	50,000	14,000	2,590,000
2011[2]	480,000	390,000	37,000	1,200,000	240,000	11,000	100,000	55,000	25,000	80,000	54,000	16,000	2,800,000

[1] Preliminary.   [2] Estimate.   [3] Iron ore, iron ore concentrates and iron ore agglomerates.   *Source: U.S. Geological Survey (USGS)*

Salient Statistics of Iron Ore[3] in the United States   In Thousands of Metric Tons

Year	Net Import Reliance As a % of Apparent Consumption	Production Total	Production Lake Superior	Production Other Regions	Ship-ments	Value Million $ (at Mine)	Average Value $ at Mine Per Ton	Stock, Dec. 31 Mines	Stock, Dec. 31 Con-suming Plants	Stock, Dec. 31 Lake Erie Docks	Imports	Exports	Con-sumption	Total
2002	11	51,600	51,500	NA	51,500	1,340.0	26.04	4,090	12,400	1,820	12,500	6,750	59,700	313.0
2003	11	48,600	NA	NA	46,100	1,490.0	32.30	4,910	10,900	1,630	12,600	6,770	61,600	328.0
2004	6	54,700	NA	NA	54,900	2,080.0	37.92	3,930	NA	NA	11,800	8,400	64,500	371.0
2005	4	54,300	NA	NA	53,200	2,370.0	44.50	2,040	NA	NA	13,000	11,800	60,100	532.0
2006	8	52,700	NA	NA	52,700	2,840.0	53.88	1,650	NA	NA	11,500	8,270	58,200	611.0
2007	E	52,500	NA	NA	50,900	3,040.0	59.64	2,090	NA	NA	9,400	9,310	54,700	543.0
2008	E	53,600	NA	NA	53,600	3,770.0	70.43	4,070	NA	NA	9,250	11,100	51,900	918.0
2009	E	26,700	NA	NA	27,600	2,560.0	92.80	5,060	NA	NA	3,900	3,900	31,000	376.0
2010[1]	E	49,900	NA	NA	50,600		98.80				7,000	11,000	42,300	
2011[2]	E	54,000	NA	NA	52,000		120.00						49,000	

[1] Preliminary.   [2] Estimate.   [3] Usable iron ore exclusive of ore containing 5% or more manganese and includes byproduct ore.
NA = Not available.   *Source: U.S. Geological Survey (USGS)*

U.S. Imports (for Consumption) of Iron Ore[2]   In Thousands of Metric Tons

Year	Australia	Brazil	Canada	Chile	Mauritania	Peru	Sweden	Venezuela	Total
2001	576	4,260	4,530	711	----	71	70	87	10,700
2002	567	5,750	5,540	319	----	86	44	49	12,500
2003	128	4,980	6,970	296	----	77	88	21	12,600
2004	3	5,020	5,830	244	----	56	111	262	11,800
2005	1	4,180	7,510	270	----	33	133	148	13,000
2006	8	4,530	6,240	283	----	52	3	23	11,500
2007	----	3,210	5,520	279	----	140	141	58	9,400
2008	----	2,620	5,900	215	----	59	88	68	9,250
2009	----	188	3,140	203	----	34	31	21	3,870
2010[1]	----	158	3,520	121	----	14	42	239	4,360

[1] Preliminary.   [2] Including agglomerates.   [3] Less than 1/2 unit.   *Source: U.S. Geological Survey (USGS)*

Iron Ore Stocks in the United States, at End of Month   In Thousands of Metric Tons

Year	Jan.	Feb.	Mar.	Apr.	May	June	July	Aug.	Sept.	Oct.	Nov.	Dec.
2002	4,980	6,810	8,270	7,740	7,270	6,330	5,020	4,080	3,420	3,290	3,540	3,210
2003	4,640	7,790	10,100	9,500	8,180	7,080	6,550	6,160	5,820	5,640	5,240	3,860
2004	4,220	7,260	8,780	8,360	7,660	7,080	5,670	4,500	3,470	3,850	3,700	2,990
2005	4,060	6,770	8,410	7,690	7,730	7,370	7,420	7,240	6,550	5,840	6,250	5,750
2006	6,750	9,620	11,900	11,100	10,800	10,100	9,353	8,760	8,090	8,120	7,590	5,880
2007	7,330	10,100	11,800	11,000	10,300	9,870	9,340	8,700	7,950	7,660	7,110	6,490
2008	6,930	9,820	12,400	11,300	9,950	9,370	8,170	6,910	6,110	5,800	5,830	6,630
2009	8,680	10,900	12,500	12,300	10,600	9,010	7,410	5,990	5,430	5,130	3,900	3,120
2010	3,760	6,080	7,040	6,070	5,400	4,160	3,730	3,240	3,150	3,410	3,320	3,390
2011[1]	4,250	7,470	9,750	9,250	8,970	8,200	7,060	6,380	5,150	4,660	4,250	

[1] Preliminary.   *Source: U.S. Geological Survey (USGS)*

Lard

Lard is the layer of fat found along the back and underneath the skin of a hog. The hog's fat is purified by washing it with water, melting it under constant heat, and straining it several times. Lard is an important byproduct of the meatpacking industry. It is valued highly as cooking oil because there is very little smoke when it is heated. However, demand for lard in cooking is declining because of the trend toward healthier eating. Lard is also used for medicinal purposes such as ointments, plasters, liniments, and occasionally as a laxative for children. Lard production is directly proportional to commercial hog production, meaning the largest producers of hogs are the largest producers of lard.

Prices – The average monthly wholesale price of lard in 2011 rose by +355.3% to 54.55 per pound, a new record high.

Supply – World production of lard in the 2010-11 marketing year rose by +3.0% yr/yr to 8.187 million metric tons, which was a new record high. The world's largest lard producers were China (with 43.1% of world production), the U.S (7.2%), Germany (6.7%), the former USSR (5.5%), Brazil (5.2%), Spain (3.7%), and Poland (2.9%). U.S. production of lard in 2010-11 rose +2.8% yr/yr to 1.396 billion pounds.

Demand – U.S. consumption of lard in 2010 rose +19.1% to 360.017 million pounds, down from 2008 record high of 490.602 million pounds. The current level of consumption is less than 20% of the consumption of 1.574 billion pounds in 1971.

Exports – U.S. exports of lard in 2009-10 (latest data) fell by -12.21% to 71.4 million pounds, and accounted for only 6% of U.S. production.

World Production of Lard   In Thousands of Metric Tons

Year	Brazil	Canada	China	France	Germany	Italy	Japan	Poland	Romania	Spain	United States	Ex-USSR	World Total
2002-03	350.2	124.2	3,040.4	156.2	433.7	204.8	59.3	272.5	60.1	280.9	510.0	346.0	7,166.8
2003-04	337.2	127.0	3,154.3	155.5	439.5	208.3	59.3	257.7	69.4	273.4	531.7	334.1	7,308.2
2004-05	344.2	127.4	3,317.8	153.4	456.9	199.2	59.4	243.8	58.9	278.1	532.4	314.4	7,475.3
2005-06	368.9	126.5	3,371.0	151.3	471.3	200.9	55.9	266.4	66.7	282.1	541.3	330.5	7,653.5
2006-07	382.5	126.1	3,181.3	152.2	501.2	207.7	54.2	270.9	76.2	300.5	552.7	369.5	7,636.6
2007-08	386.0	123.7	3,192.7	153.0	520.1	208.7	54.7	249.9	75.0	308.5	605.3	387.0	7,734.1
2008-09[1]	405.2	120.4	3,280.9	140.6	532.9	207.9	52.9	208.9	72.1	297.8	597.3	385.5	7,743.8
2009-10[2]	411.9	122.7	3,402.7	136.5	552.7	210.4	52.5	220.4	71.9	289.9	576.7	430.0	7,946.2
2010-11[3]	425.9	125.0	3,531.2	138.8	547.8	211.3	52.5	238.2	76.2	304.8	592.6	451.3	8,187.2

[1] Preliminary.   [2] Estimate.   [3] Forecast.   *Source: The Oil World*

Supply and Distribution of Lard in the United States   In Millions of Pounds

	Supply			Disappearance						
Year	Production	Stocks Oct. 1	Total Supply	Domestic	Baking or Frying Fats	Margarine[3]	Exports	Total Disappearance	Direct Use	Per Capita (Lbs.)
2002-03	1,083.0	13.6	1,105.0	670.9	W	7.0	84.2	755.2	370.3	1.3
2003-04	1,090.0	10.5	1,108.0	639.6	W	16.0	117.3	756.9	368.5	1.3
2004-05	1,117.0	13.3	1,136.0	487.8	W	6.0	289.2	777.0	220.2	0.7
2005-06	1,193.3	13.8	1,207.1	694.8	W	3.0	93.8	788.6	459.7	1.5
2006-07	1,218.5	9.4	1,227.9	718.5	W	W	71.9	790.4	498.6	1.7
2007-08	1,334.4	14.2	1,348.6	756.8	W	W	72.9	829.7	486.7	1.6
2008-09	1,316.8	13.9	1,330.7	800.9	W	W	81.4	882.3	310.3	1.0
2009-10[1]	1,271.4	17.5	1,288.9	775.8	W	W	71.6	847.4	479.8	1.5
2010-11[2]	1,306.4	25.6	1,332.1		W	W	78.8			

[1] Preliminary.   [2] Forecast.   [3] Includes edible tallow.   W = Withheld.
Source: Economic Research Service, U.S. Department of Agriculture (ERS-USDA)

Consumption of Lard (Edible and Inedible) in the United States   In Millions of Pounds

Year	Jan.	Feb.	Mar.	Apr.	May	June	July	Aug.	Sept.	Oct.	Nov.	Dec.	Total
2002	26.4	26.1	21.8	26.7	24.8	21.2	22.9	26.4	23.6	26.4	28.1	28.7	303.2
2003	22.6	22.3	23.4	21.4	23.3	24.0	23.0	21.4	22.5	24.3	20.2	21.0	269.5
2004	22.9	25.8	25.9	23.9	23.5	22.0	19.1	19.7	21.3	22.4	21.9	19.9	268.1
2005	19.0	15.4	21.4	18.7	19.9	20.4	18.9	19.5	20.1	19.7	22.2	17.9	233.1
2006	15.7	16.4	20.6	21.4	20.2	16.7	14.9	17.7	17.8	18.9	22.3	20.9	223.4
2007	21.6	16.2	22.2	19.7	20.5	20.8	22.8	23.9	22.8	31.1	29.7	31.4	282.8
2008	34.8	32.2	44.6	50.7	50.8	44.4	47.8	39.7	44.0	37.5	31.7	32.2	490.6
2009	23.4	17.3	26.8	26.0	26.3	25.8	21.3	20.5	25.4	32.4	29.9	27.0	302.3
2010	22.2	W	38.8	W	30.4	30.8	30.4	32.4	30.1	31.1	30.4	28.8	366.6
2011[1]	22.2	26.3	36.0	W	28.8	29.6	31.4	W	W	W	W	W	348.7

[1] Preliminary.   *Source: Bureau of the Census, U.S. Department of Commerce*

Lard (monthly average) through December 2011 — Cents per pound

Average Wholesale Price of Lard--Loose, Tank Cars, in Chicago In Cents Per Pound

Year	Jan.	Feb.	Mar.	Apr.	May	June	July	Aug.	Sept.	Oct.	Nov.	Dec.	Average
2002	12.69	12.50	13.07	12.42	11.38	14.64	14.60	15.00	15.21	14.39	16.28	18.42	14.22
2003	18.61	17.11	16.85	16.72	17.29	18.90	18.93	20.08	23.98	27.50	26.40	25.18	20.63
2004	26.50	25.83	23.77	22.58	21.31	22.50	27.53	32.06	32.38	27.95	27.26	26.50	26.35
2005	22.10	18.30	17.71	20.72	22.95	21.30	18.08	17.75	20.97	27.38	27.76	18.60	21.14
2006	17.16	16.44	16.82	18.00	17.13	17.63	22.21	29.91	31.86	23.55	20.78	22.58	21.17
2007	23.00	23.82	30.75	27.71	28.60	32.64	36.00	35.77	36.00	35.09	33.78	32.66	31.32
2008	33.01	38.33	46.00	43.04	42.27	44.93	52.82	46.50	41.73	37.07	26.40	20.00	39.34
2009	25.36	20.31	19.49	23.36	29.00	30.06	27.63	32.20	29.73	25.75	30.07	28.75	26.81
2010	28.60	28.25	32.95	33.95	34.24	32.98	31.42	33.33	43.59	46.64	37.32	38.30	35.13
2011	48.50	49.60	52.00	51.50	54.31	56.75	63.00	58.96	61.33	61.10	48.86	48.71	54.55

Source: Economic Research Service, U.S. Department of Agriculture (ERS-USDA)

Cold Storage Holdings of all Lard[1] in the United States, on First of Month In Millions of Pounds

Year	Jan.	Feb.	Mar.	Apr.	May	June	July	Aug.	Sept.	Oct.	Nov.	Dec.
2002	13.2	18.0	16.4	16.5	20.3	22.4	18.9	18.3	12.0	10.5	14.6	11.3
2003	10.5	14.0	19.6	18.7	16.5	13.5	11.9	9.7	8.4	9.3	10.1	12.4
2004	13.3	19.8	18.6	20.3	20.5	15.0	12.9	10.8	10.3	11.8	11.4	13.2
2005	13.7	14.6	20.6	19.0	17.8	12.3	12.0	12.3	12.5	13.0	12.2	14.7
2006	9.6	11.5	13.7	13.6	9.3	9.9	13.0	12.4	13.0	11.5	16.1	16.0
2007	16.4	14.9	13.3	18.5	10.9	14.6	11.3	12.8	11.0	9.2	14.6	18.8
2008	14.0	22.4	20.4	22.9	23.0	19.5	22.7	13.6	18.0	17.8	16.1	20.4
2009	12.1	13.6	15.4	16.2	14.5	18.8	17.3	21.6	20.5	26.7	18.5	15.4
2010	13.9	14.5	21.0	22.9	26.1	15.7	19.4	17.9	14.1	13.8	15.6	15.5
2011[2]	17.5	20.5	25.3	20.9	26.2	19.9	23.4	23.9				

[1] Stocks in factories and warehouses (except that in hands of retailers).   [2] Preliminary.   *Source: Bureau of the Census, U.S. Department of Commerce*

Lead

Lead (symbol Pb) is a dense, toxic, bluish-gray metallic element, and is the heaviest stable element. Lead was one of the first known metals. The ancients used lead in face powders, rouges, mascaras, paints, condiments, wine preservatives, and water supply plumbing. The Romans were slowly poisoned from lead because of its diverse daily usage.

Lead is usually found in ore with zinc, silver, and most often copper. The most common lead ore is galena, containing 86.6% lead. Cerussite and angleside are other common varieties of lead. More than half of the lead currently used comes from recycling.

Lead is used in building construction, bullets and shot, tank and pipe lining, storage batteries, and electric cable sheathing. Lead is used extensively as a protective shielding for radioactive material (e.g., X-ray apparatus) because of its high density and nuclear properties. Lead is also part of solder, pewter, and fusible alloys.

Lead futures and options trade at the London Metal Exchange (LME). The LME lead futures contract calls for the delivery of 25 metric tons of at least 99.970% purity lead ingots (pigs). The contract is priced in U.S. dollars per metric ton. Lead first started trading on the LME in 1903.

Prices – The price of lead at the beginning of 2011 was about $2,600 per metric ton. The price then rallied to about $2,900 in March, and then moved lower to about $2,300 in May. From there the price moved higher to about $2,700 in August but then fell to close the year at about $2,000. By February of 2012 the price had moved higher to about $2,300 per metric ton.

Supply – World smelter production of lead (both primary and secondary) in 2010 (the latest data available)

rose +6.7% yr/yr to 9.490 million metric tons to post a new record high production level. The world's largest smelter producers of lead (both primary and secondary) are China with 44% of world production in 2010, followed by the U.S. with 13%, Germany with 4%, and with the UK, Canada, and Japan, each with about 3%.

U.S. mine production of recoverable lead fell -9.9% yr/yr to an 18-year low of 356,000 metric tons in 2010 (latest data available). Missouri was responsible for 94% of U.S. production, with the remainder produced mainly by Idaho and Montana. Lead recovered from scrap in the U.S. (secondary production) rose +4.9% yr/yr in 2011 (annualized through November) to 1.193 million metric tons, down from the 2008 record high of 1.220 metric tons. The amount of lead recovered from scrap is almost three times the amount of lead produced in the U.S. from mines (primary production). The value of U.S. secondary lead production in 2010 (latest data available) rose by +28.2% to $2.730 billion, but still below the 2007 record high of $3.220 billion.

Demand – U.S. lead consumption in 2011 (annualized through November) rose +9.9% to 1.544 million metric tons. The record high level of U.S. lead consumption was 1.680 million metric tons posted in 1999.

Trade – The U.S. relied on imports for 8% of its lead consumption in 2001 but has been a net exporter ever since. U.S. imports of lead pigs and bars in 2010 (latest data available) rose +8.0% yr/yr to 271,000 metric tons. U.S. lead exports in 2010 were comprised of ore concentrate (299,000 metric tons), unwrought lead (77,700 metric tons), scrap (43,500 metric tons), and wrought lead (5,590 metric tons).

World Smelter (Primary and Secondary) Production of Lead   In Thousands of Metric Tons

Year	Australia[3]	Belgium[4]	Canada[3]	China[2]	France	Germany	Italy	Japan	Mexico[3]	Spain	United Kingdom[3]	United States	World Total
2002	304.0	88.0	251.6	1,330.0	204.0	379.9	205.0	285.8	237.2	116.0	374.6	1,360	6,800
2003	295.0	65.0	223.4	1,580.0	96.7	356.9	246.0	295.3	247.5	102.0	364.6	1,380	6,990
2004	268.0	63.0	241.2	1,940.0	105.6	359.2	202.0	282.9	217.4	105.6	245.9	1,280	7,040
2005	263.0	83.4	230.2	2,390.0	105.0	417.7	211.5	274.6	226.5	110.0	304.4	1,300	7,660
2006	233.0	101.4	250.5	2,720.0	100.2	379.0	190.5	280.0	212.5	129.0	318.7	1,310	8,100
2007	229.0	117.2	236.7	2,790.0	100.2	405.1	210.0	276.3	212.0	128.0	263.0	1,300	8,300
2008	248.0	109.0	259.1	3,200.0	88.0	415.1	211.8	279.5	199.8	125.0	283.0	1,280	8,770
2009[1]	229.0	109.0	258.9	3,710.0	88.0	390.6	149.0	247.8	210.4	125.0	279.0	1,210	8,890
2010[2]	204.0	121.0	272.9	4,200.0	88.0	405.0	149.0	258.0	210.0	125.0	294.0	1,250	9,490

[1] Preliminary.   [2] Estimate.   [3] Refinded & bullion.   [4] Includes scrap.   *Source: U.S. Geological Survey (USGS)*

Consumption of Lead in the United States, by Products   In Metric Tons

Year	Ammunition	Bearing Metals	Pipes, Traps & Bends[2]	Cable Covering	Calking Lead	Casting Metals	Other Metal Products[3]	Total Other Oxides[4]	Sheet Lead	Solder	Storage Battery — Grids, Post, etc.	Oxides	Brass and Bronze	Total Consumption
2002	57,600	406	2,250	W	1,060	34,800	24,200	51,900	25,600	6,450	554,000	641,000	2,730	1,440,000
2003	48,800	13,500	1,550	W	822	31,700	9,730	35,600	24,400	6,310	523,000	642,000	2,810	1,390,000
2004	61,500	1,300	W	W	W	17,900	W	25,700	31,600	7,440	657,000	630,000	2,390	1,480,000
2005	61,300	1,180	1,220	W	W	30,400	22,200	14,100	29,100	8,370	579,000	705,000	2,100	1,490,000
2006	65,700	1,240	1,440	W	W	29,900	23,400	16,000	28,400	7,280	586,000	710,000	3,130	1,490,000
2007	69,400	1,410	1,230	W	W	31,500	23,600	15,800	28,600	7,220	640,000	738,000	2,870	1,570,000
2008	67,400	1,250	1,190	W	W	20,100	7,670	10,700	26,400	6,610	575,000	715,000	2,460	1,440,000
2009	67,900	1,100	1,130	W	W	15,900	5,790	10,100	25,400	6,450	389,000	750,000	1,370	1,290,000
2010[1]	65,700	1,230	990	W	W	16,400	8,800	9,760	23,400	6,420	478,000	806,000	1,410	1,430,000

[1] Preliminary.   [2] Including building.   [3] Including terne metal, type metal, and lead consumed in foil, collapsible tubes, annealing, plating, galvanizing and fishing weights.   [4] Includes paints, glass and ceramic products, and other pigments and chemicals.   W = Withheld.
Source: U.S. Geological Survey (USGS)

Salient Statistics of Lead in the United States   In Thousands of Metric Tons

Year	Net Import Reliance as a % of Apparent Consumption	Production of Refined Lead From Domestic Ores[3]	Foreighn Ores[3]	Total Primary	Total Value of Refined Million $	Secondary Lead Recovered — As Soft Lead	In Antimonial Lead	In Other Alloys	Total	Total Value of Secondary Million USD	Stocks, Dec. 31 — Primary	Con-sumer[4]	Average Price Cents Per Pound — New York	London
2002	E	262.0	W	262.0	252.0	754.0	289.0	72.8	1,120.0	1,070.0	W	111.0	43.56	20.52
2003	E	245.0	W	245.0	236.0	829.0	303.0	4.2	1,140.0	1,110.0	W	84.6	43.76	23.34
2004	E	148.0	W	148.0	143.0	841.0	283.0	3.0	1,130.0	1,370.0	W	59.0	55.14	40.19
2005	E	143.0	W	143.0	----	869.0	271.0	4.5	1,150.0	1,550.0	W	46.8	61.03	44.23
2006	E	153.0	W	153.0	----	948.0	200.0	12.4	1,160.0	1,980.0	W	54.8	77.40	58.00
2007	E	123.0	W	123.0	----	1,020.0	160.0	2.4	1,180.0	3,220.0	W	39.0	123.84	117.00
2008	E	135.0	W	135.0	----	1,000.0	140.0	2.4	1,140.0	3,040.0	W	72.5	120.33	94.79
2009	E	103.0	W	103.0	----	960.0	151.0	NA	1,110.0	2,130.0	W	63.0	86.87	77.95
2010[1]	E	115.0	W	115.0	----	962.0	175.0	NA	1,140.0	2,730.0	W	65.0	109.00	97.40
2011[2]	E	117.0	W	117.0	----				1,200.0		W	60.0	124.00	113.00

[1] Preliminary.   [2] Estimate.   [3] And base bullion.   [4] Also at secondary smelters.   W = Withheld.   E = Net exporter.
Source: U.S. Geological Survey (USGS)

U.S. Foreign Trade of Lead   In Thousands of Metric Tons

Year	Exports — Ore Con-centrate	Un-wrought Lead[3]	Wrought Lead[4]	Scrap	Ash & Re-sidues[5]	Imports for Consumption — Ores, Flue Dust or Fume & Mattes	Base Bullion	Pigs & Bars	Re-claimed Scrap, Etc.	Value Million $	General Import From: Ore, Flue, Dust & Matte — Aus-tralia	Can-ada	Peru	Pigs & Bars — Can-ada	Mexico	Peru
2001	181.0	17.0	17.7	108.0	14.2	2.2	----	271.0	10.2	166.8	----	.....	----	167.0	12.4	2.3
2002	241.0	31.4	11.7	106.0	----	0.0	----	210.0	2.6	124.9	----	----	----	172.0	7.5	----
2003	253.0	92.1	30.5	92.8	----	----	----	175.0	4.2	111.9	----	----	----	167.0	8.3	----
2004	292.0	58.6	23.8	56.3	----	----	----	197.0	4.8	235.3	----	----	----	166.0	8.8	7.3
2005	390.2	45.5	19.0	67.3	----	----	----	298.0	3.3	334.8	----	----	----	190.0	15.2	23.9
2006	297.6	52.7	15.8	120.9	----	----	0.5	331.0	1.6	450.8	----	----	----	222.0	15.8	34.6
2007	300.0	51.8	4.6	129.0	----	----	2.0	263.0	2.4	591.4	----	----	----	208.0	35.6	16.5
2008	277.0	68.1	6.2	175.0	----	----	2.7	309.0	1.3	681.6	----	----	----	219.0	58.1	10.6
2009[1]	287.0	77.6	4.3	140.0	----	----	0.8	251.0	1.3	418.8	----	----	----	205.0	41.1	1.0
2010[2]	299.0	77.7	5.6	43.5	----	----	0.6	271.0	3.7	575.9	----	----	----	237.0	29.4	----

[1] Preliminary.   [2] Estimate.   [3] And lead alloys.   [4] Blocks, pigs, etc.   [5] Less than 1/2 unit.   Source: U.S. Geological Survey (USGS)

Annual Mine Production of Recoverable Lead in the United States   In Metric Tons

Year	Total	Idaho	Missouri	Montana	Other States	Missouri's % of Total
2001	454,000	W	423,000	W	30,900	93%
2002	440,000	W	428,000	W	12,300	97%
2003	449,000	W	432,000	W	17,200	96%
2004	430,000	W	407,000	W	23,400	95%
2005	426,000	W	397,000	W	29,500	93%
2006	419,000	W	393,000	W	26,100	94%
2007	434,000	W	400,000	W	34,200	92%
2008	399,000	W	360,000	W	38,600	90%
2009[1]	395,000	W	370,000	W	24,900	94%
2010[2]	356,000	W	W	W	W	W

[1] Preliminary.   [2] Estimate.   W = Withheld, included in Other States.   Source: U.S. Geological Survey (USGS)

Mine Production of Recoverable Lead in the United States   In Thousands of Metric Tons

Year	Jan.	Feb.	Mar.	Apr.	May	June	July	Aug.	Sept.	Oct.	Nov.	Dec.	Total
2002	39.5	35.5	41.2	36.1	39.3	36.1	35.0	39.6	33.2	34.8	34.1	34.2	438.6
2003	33.7	34.9	38.5	36.2	38.8	39.2	41.3	38.0	38.3	37.2	34.0	33.9	444.0
2004	33.4	32.8	33.5	35.1	31.2	33.1	33.8	36.9	36.9	36.2	35.0	31.8	409.7
2005	31.1	31.1	34.6	35.2	33.4	41.4	39.5	37.4	38.2	37.9	34.6	37.9	432.3
2006	36.7	33.3	38.1	33.6	33.4	33.9	36.6	36.3	37.0	38.0	35.0	29.6	421.5
2007	38.1	33.9	36.7	31.6	36.9	34.5	38.7	41.3	34.6	39.4	31.5	37.1	434.3
2008	38.0	36.9	36.1	33.0	31.0	34.4	37.8	34.2	33.8	29.1	27.8	33.7	405.8
2009	33.8	30.5	32.8	34.7	33.6	33.7	29.9	35.7	35.6	36.9	28.5	32.8	398.5
2010	31.8	28.6	32.7	31.5	29.7	26.5	29.5	26.9	30.1	31.3	27.8	30.0	356.4
2011[1]	30.4	25.1	29.5	32.5	27.4	27.2	29.3	24.4	29.2	25.2	27.0		335.1

[1] Preliminary.   Source: U.S. Geological Survey (USGS)

LEAD

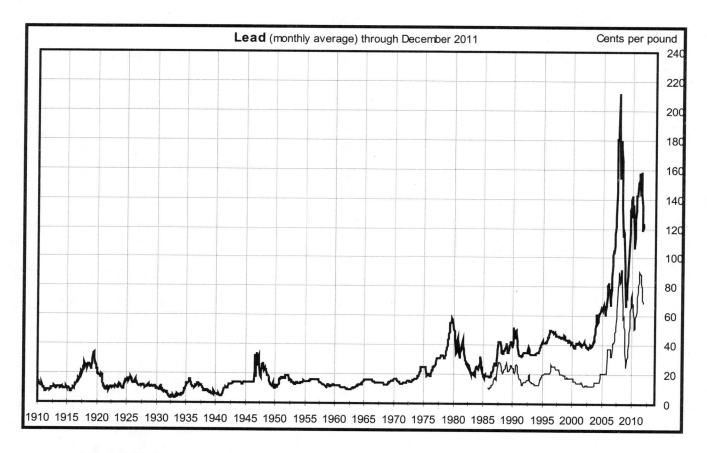

Lead (monthly average) through December 2011 — Cents per pound

Average Price of Pig Lead, U.S. Primary Producers (Common Corroding)[1]   In Cents Per Pound

Year	Jan.	Feb.	Mar.	Apr.	May	June	July	Aug.	Sept.	Oct.	Nov.	Dec.	Average
2002	45.00	45.00	45.00	45.00	45.00	45.00	45.00	45.00	45.00	45.00	45.00	45.00	45.00
2003	23.14	24.65	23.81	23.13	24.56	24.77	26.93	26.05	27.23	30.16	32.09	35.46	26.83
2004	38.48	44.79	45.30	39.93	42.44	45.16	48.20	47.46	48.08	48.01	49.54	49.75	45.60
2005	50.46	52.20	54.00	53.25	53.41	53.26	47.22	47.53	49.76	54.01	54.68	59.63	52.45
2006	66.16	67.16	63.28	61.58	61.16	51.92	56.07	61.48	69.24	77.64	82.09	86.22	67.00
2007	83.62	88.42	94.72	98.73	103.14	117.95	148.17	148.47	153.50	175.59	159.80	124.81	124.74
2008	125.37	146.72	141.77	134.92	106.42	88.93	93.68	92.49	90.49	73.02	65.52	49.58	100.74
2009	57.27	55.74	61.81	67.86	70.02	80.87	81.05	91.57	104.06	105.75	109.61	110.96	83.05
2010	113.15	102.18	104.73	108.78	92.43	83.23	89.48	99.29	104.31	113.11	113.59	114.22	103.21
2011	123.37	122.83	124.67	130.68	117.43	121.38	129.14	116.63	111.36	95.84	97.61	100.19	115.93

[1] New York Delivery.   Source: American Metal Market

Refiners Production[1] of Lead in the United States   In Metric Tons

Year	Jan.	Feb.	Mar.	Apr.	May	June	July	Aug.	Sept.	Oct.	Nov.	Dec.	Total
2001	NA	NA	NA	NA	NA	NA	NA	NA	NA	NA	NA	NA	290,000
2002	NA	NA	NA	NA	NA	NA	NA	NA	NA	NA	NA	NA	262,000
2003	NA	NA	NA	NA	NA	NA	NA	NA	NA	NA	NA	NA	245,000
2004	NA	NA	NA	NA	NA	NA	NA	NA	NA	NA	NA	NA	NA
2005	NA	NA	NA	NA	NA	NA	NA	NA	NA	NA	NA	NA	143,000
2006	NA	NA	NA	NA	NA	NA	NA	NA	NA	NA	NA	NA	143,000
2007	NA	NA	NA	NA	NA	NA	NA	NA	NA	NA	NA	NA	NA
2008	NA	NA	NA	NA	NA	NA	NA	NA	NA	NA	NA	NA	NA
2009	NA	NA	NA	NA	NA	NA	NA	NA	NA	NA	NA	NA	NA
2010[2]	NA	NA	NA	NA	NA	NA	NA	NA	NA	NA	NA	NA	NA

[1] Represents refined lead produced from domestic ores by primary smelters plus small amounts of secondary material passing through these smelters. Includes GSA metal purchased for remelt.   [2] Preliminary.   NA = Not available.   Source: U.S. Geological Survey (USGS)

Total Stocks of Lead[1] in the United States at Refiners, at End of Month   In Metric Tons

Year	Jan.	Feb.	Mar.	Apr.	May	June	July	Aug.	Sept.	Oct.	Nov.	Dec.
2001	NA	NA	NA	NA	NA	NA	NA	NA	NA	NA	NA	NA
2002	NA	NA	NA	NA	NA	NA	NA	NA	NA	NA	NA	NA
2003	NA	NA	NA	NA	NA	NA	NA	NA	NA	NA	NA	NA
2004	NA	NA	NA	NA	NA	NA	NA	NA	NA	NA	NA	NA
2005	NA	NA	NA	NA	NA	NA	NA	NA	NA	NA	NA	NA
2006	NA	NA	NA	NA	NA	NA	NA	NA	NA	NA	NA	NA
2007	NA	NA	NA	NA	NA	NA	NA	NA	NA	NA	NA	NA
2008	NA	NA	NA	NA	NA	NA	NA	NA	NA	NA	NA	NA
2009	NA	NA	NA	NA	NA	NA	NA	NA	NA	NA	NA	NA
2010[2]	NA	NA	NA	NA	NA	NA	NA	NA	NA	NA	NA	NA

[1] Primary refineries.   [2] Preliminary.   NA = Not available.   *Source: U.S. Geological Survey (USGS)*

Total[1] Lead Consumption in the United States   In Thousands of Metric Tons

Year	Jan.	Feb.	Mar.	Apr.	May	June	July	Aug.	Sept.	Oct.	Nov.	Dec.	Total
2002	132.0	131.0	133.0	142.0	142.0	144.0	143.0	145.0	141.0	145.0	142.0	133.0	1,673
2003	134.0	129.0	126.0	120.0	121.0	121.0	121.0	122.0	123.0	127.0	122.0	125.0	1,491
2004	119.0	118.0	119.0	119.0	117.0	119.0	118.0	118.0	117.0	117.0	117.0	119.0	1,417
2005	125.0	117.0	109.0	108.0	134.0	130.0	124.0	129.0	126.0	126.0	126.0	126.0	1,480
2006	124.0	130.0	129.0	128.0	128.0	128.0	125.0	126.0	127.0	128.0	126.0	126.0	1,525
2007	130.0	128.0	129.0	128.0	131.0	139.0	131.0	134.0	132.0	137.0	132.0	127.0	1,578
2008	140.0	136.0	130.0	135.0	135.0	141.0	134.0	129.0	134.0	136.0	127.0	126.0	1,603
2009	123.0	119.0	116.0	124.0	116.0	117.0	116.0	115.0	118.0	122.0	121.0	117.0	1,424
2010	120.0	118.0	114.0	115.0	117.0	118.0	116.0	117.0	118.0	117.0	118.0	117.0	1,405
2011[2]	120.0	118.0	118.0	133.0	132.0	133.0	132.0	133.0	132.0	132.0	132.0		1,544

[1] Represents total consumption of primary & secondary lead as metal, in chemicals, or in alloys.   [2] Preliminary.   *Source: U.S. Geological Survey (USGS)*

Lead Recovered from Scrap in the United States   In Thousands of Metric Tons (Lead Content)

Year	Jan.	Feb.	Mar.	Apr.	May	June	July	Aug.	Sept.	Oct.	Nov.	Dec.	Total
2002	89.3	82.3	88.2	93.1	93.9	93.6	88.0	96.1	93.3	97.5	95.0	95.7	1,106.0
2003	95.7	83.6	86.2	85.1	94.0	94.8	95.7	93.9	93.3	102.0	93.7	95.2	1,113.2
2004	94.0	94.2	96.3	97.9	94.4	96.6	97.4	96.3	94.8	96.8	94.9	95.4	1,149.0
2005	94.4	95.1	86.8	86.8	87.1	94.6	94.7	94.8	93.0	95.9	96.4	92.4	1,112.0
2006	90.2	96.7	97.4	98.2	99.5	95.7	94.9	97.0	95.6	98.4	98.4	95.9	1,157.9
2007	99.0	96.5	98.6	93.5	94.5	100.0	103.0	103.0	101.0	104.0	104.0	94.6	1,191.7
2008	104.0	98.2	102.0	100.0	105.0	102.0	92.0	102.0	91.7	100.0	122.0	101.0	1,219.9
2009	97.3	99.0	101.0	90.2	91.6	93.8	97.0	97.2	90.9	96.3	98.0	98.0	1,150.3
2010	96.2	95.2	92.1	86.3	89.8	92.9	94.2	98.0	95.6	101.0	100.0	96.3	1,137.6
2011[1]	102.0	96.2	95.5	104.0	101.0	100.0	102.0	103.0	95.4	95.9	98.8		1,193.2

[1] Preliminary.   *Source: U.S. Geological Survey (USGS)*

Domestic Shipments[1] of Lead in the United States, by Refiners   In Thousands of Short Tons

Year	Jan.	Feb.	Mar.	Apr.	May	June	July	Aug.	Sept.	Oct.	Nov.	Dec.	Total
1989	29.3	28.5	32.2	35.7	45.1	36.4	32.8	41.5	40.0	44.2	40.2	31.1	437.1
1990	39.3	33.9	39.1	33.5	38.4	32.9	32.6	38.9	36.6	38.9	37.9	31.7	433.7
1991	35.4	33.8	34.3	39.8	33.9	26.0	31.8	37.9	35.1	35.7	28.7	26.7	399.2
1992	31.3	23.9	30.4	26.3	25.6	27.2	27.3	28.7	26.3	28.5	26.3	21.7	323.5
1993	24.6	23.6	32.5	30.0	31.3	35.1	28.9	34.0	35.5	35.5	31.7	33.5	376.2
1994	35.9	32.8	35.2	32.7	34.7	36.7	31.6	33.4	34.8	34.3	34.0	33.3	409.3
1995	36.5	30.3	35.1	31.1	33.7	31.9	28.6	40.3	34.9	40.9	33.2	29.8	406.4
1996	37.2	32.4	29.5	30.2	29.4	26.7	27.7	33.5	30.1	33.5	28.1	27.6	366.0
1997[2]	31.5	27.8	24.7	35.2	39.2	36.1	33.4	29.4	26.4	31.5	30.4	28.1	377.8
1998[2]	Data no longer available.												

[1] Includes GSA metal.   [2] Preliminary.   *Source: American Metal Market (AMM)*

Lumber and Plywood

Humans have utilized lumber for construction for thousands of years, but due to the heaviness of timber and the manual methods of harvesting, large-scale lumbering didn't occur until the mechanical advances of the Industrial Revolution. Lumber is produced from both hardwood and softwood. Hardwood lumber comes from deciduous trees that have broad leaves. Most hardwood lumber is used for miscellaneous industrial applications, primarily wood pallets, and includes oak, gum, maple, and ash. Hardwood species with beautiful colors and patterns are used for such high-grade products as furniture, flooring, paneling, and cabinets and include black walnut, black cherry, and red oak. Wood from cone-bearing trees is called softwood, regardless of its actual hardness. Most lumber from the U.S. is softwood. Softwoods, such as southern yellow pine, Douglas fir, ponderosa pine, and true firs, are primarily used as structural lumber such as 2x4s and 2x6s, poles, paper and cardboard.

Plywood consists of several thin layers of veneer bonded together with adhesives. The veneer sheets are layered so that the grain of one sheet is perpendicular to that of the next, which makes plywood exceptionally strong for its weight. Most plywood has from three to nine layers of wood. Plywood manufacturers use both hard and soft woods, although hardwoods serve primarily for appearance and are not as strong as those made from softwoods. Plywood is primarily used in construction, particularly for floors, roofs, walls, and doors. Homebuilding and remodeling account for two-thirds of U.S. lumber consumption. The price of lumber and plywood is highly correlated with the strength of the U.S. home-building market.

The forest and wood products industry is dominated by Weyerhaeuser Company (ticker symbol WY), which has about $20 billion in annual sales. Weyerhaeuser is a forest products conglomerate that engages not only in growing and harvesting timber, but also in the production and distribution of forest products, real estate development, and construction of single-family homes. Forest products include wood products, pulp and paper, and containerboard. The timberland segment of the business manages 7.2 million acres of company-owned land and 800,000 acres of leased commercial forestlands in North America. The company's Canadian division has renewable, long-term licenses on about 35 million acres of forestland in five Canadian provinces. In order to maximize its long-term yield from its acreage, Weyerhaeuser engages in a number of forest management activities such as extensive planting, suppression of non-merchantable species, thinning, fertilization, and operational pruning.

Lumber futures and options are traded on the Chicago Mercantile Exchange (CME). The CME's lumber futures contract calls for the delivery of 111,000 board feet (one 73 foot rail car) of random length 8 to 12 foot 2 x 4s, the type used in construction. The contract is priced in terms of dollars per thousand board feet.

Prices – CME lumber futures prices in early 2011 extended the rally that started in the second half of 2010 but were unable to exceed the 5-year high of $327 posted in April 2010. Lumber prices then fell sharply in April along with most other commodity prices on the weak economy and consolidated the remainder the year, closing 2011 down 18% at $247.10 per thousand board feet.

Supply – The U.S. led the world in the production of industrial round wood and in 2010 production rose +2.8% yr/yr to 300.218 million cubic meters, followed by Russia with 132.800 million cubic meters (+17.6% yr/yr) and Canada with 129.558 million cubic meters (+12.3% yr/yr). The U.S. also led the world in the production of plywood with 9.397 million cubic meters of production in 2010 (+5.2% yr/yr), followed by Russia with 2.679 million cubic meters (+27.2% yr/yr), and then Japan with 2.645 million cubic meters (+15.7% yr/yr). U.S. softwood lumber production in latest data from the series of 2006 (latest data annualized through November) fell 4.4% yr/yr to 38.503 billion board feet.

Demand – U.S. consumption of softwood lumber in 2006 (latest data), the last reporting year, fell by 1.9% yr/yr to 63.080 billion board feet.

Trade – U.S. total lumber imports in 2006 (latest data), the last reporting year, fell 1.8% to 25.285 billion board feet, down from last year's record high. U.S. imports of hardwood in 2006 fell by 3.1% to 1,042 million board feet. U.S. imports of softwood in 2006 fell by 1.7% to 24.214 billion board feet. The leading softwood import was spruce with 1.730 billion board feet of imports in 20065, followed by cedar at 721 million board feet.

Total U.S. exports of lumber in 2006 (latest data) rose +3.6% yr/yr to 2.779 billion board feet, which is a 6-year high. The record high was 4.528 billion board feet in 1988. U.S. exports of hardwood in 2006 rose by +21.7% yr/yr to 1.797 billion board feet. U.S. exports of softwood in 2006 rose by 9.5% yr/yr to 982 million board feet. The largest types of U.S. softwood exports in 2006 were southern pine with 232 million board feet of exports, Ponderosa white pine (114 million board feet), and Douglas Fir (76 million board feet). The world's largest exporter of plywood in 2009 was Russia with 1.334 million cubic meters of exports, followed by Finland with 683 million cubic meters, and Belgium with 379 thousand cubic meters.

LUMBER AND PLYWOOD

World Production of Industrial Roundwood by Selected Countries   In Thousands of Cubic Meters

Year	Austria	Canada	Czech Republic	Finland	France	Germany	Poland	Romania	Russia	Spain	Sweden	Turkey	United States
2001	10,562	182,945	13,364	47,727	33,792	36,502	23,375	9,806	117,800	13,276	57,300	9,976	403,212
2002	11,810	195,211	13,534	48,529	29,384	37,755	24,995	12,092	118,600	13,850	60,700	11,191	404,958
2003	13,719	176,799	13,960	49,246	27,459	45,415	27,204	12,537	126,600	14,075	61,200	10,729	405,613
2004	12,943	205,273	14,411	49,281	28,187	48,657	29,337	12,794	130,600	14,235	61,400	11,225	418,131
2005	12,786	200,247	14,285	47,116	27,944	50,905	28,531	11,542	138,000	13,351	92,300	11,202	423,456
2006	14,430	181,010	16,333	45,521	28,592	54,000	28,767	9,454	144,600	14,109	58,700	12,253	412,134
2007	16,521	157,609	16,738	51,406	29,817	68,029	32,461	11,572	162,000	12,546	72,300	13,674	378,771
2008	16,772	132,232	14,307	45,965	27,724	46,806	30,470	9,517	136,700	14,427	64,900	14,462	336,895
2009[1]	12,144	115,353	13,769	36,701	29,081	38,987	30,475	8,587	112,900	11,900	59,200	14,252	292,091
2010[2]	13,281	129,558	14,907	45,977	29,304	45,388	31,343	10,548	132,800	13,168	64,300	15,695	300,218

[1] Preliminary.   [2] Estimate.   NA = Not available.   *Source: Food and Agriculture Organization of the United Nations (FAO)*

U.S. Housing Starts: Seasonally Adjusted Annual Rate   In Thousands

Year	Jan.	Feb.	Mar.	Apr.	May	June	July	Aug.	Sept.	Oct.	Nov.	Dec.	Average
2002	1,698	1,829	1,642	1,592	1,764	1,717	1,655	1,633	1,804	1,648	1,753	1,788	1,710
2003	1,853	1,629	1,726	1,643	1,751	1,867	1,897	1,833	1,939	1,967	2,083	2,057	1,854
2004	1,911	1,846	1,998	2,003	1,981	1,828	2,002	2,024	1,905	2,072	1,782	2,042	1,950
2005	2,144	2,207	1,864	2,061	2,025	2,068	2,054	2,095	2,151	2,065	2,147	1,994	2,073
2006	2,273	2,119	1,969	1,821	1,942	1,802	1,737	1,650	1,720	1,491	1,570	1,649	1,812
2007	1,409	1,480	1,495	1,490	1,415	1,448	1,354	1,330	1,183	1,264	1,197	1,037	1,342
2008	1,084	1,103	1,005	1,013	973	1,046	923	844	820	777	652	560	900
2009	490	582	505	478	540	585	594	586	585	534	588	581	554
2010	615	603	626	687	580	539	550	606	597	539	551	526	585
2011[1]	636	518	593	549	553	615	615	585	646	628	685	657	607

[1] Preliminary.   Total Privately owned.   *Source: Bureau of the Census, U.S. Department of Commerce*

Stocks (Gross) of Softwood Lumber in the United States, on First of Month   In Millions of Board Feet

Year	Jan.	Feb.	Mar.	Apr.	May	June	July	Aug.	Sept.	Oct.	Nov.	Dec.
1997	3,973	4,019	4,113	4,067	3,963	4,017	3,915	3,871	3,875	3,927	3,925	3,865
1998	3,884	3,970	4,048	4,062	4,158	4,084	NA	NA	NA	NA	NA	NA
1999	3,519	3,595	3,688	3,726	3,698	3,581	3,512	3,485	3,533	3,491	3,562	3,536
2000	3,639	3,704	3,811	3,887	3,960	2,738	3,902	3,936	3,878	3,848	3,957	3,875
2001	3,919	3,864	4,013	3,951	4,095	3,955	NA	3,961	3,938	4,076	4,100	4,248
2002	4,784	3,735	3,826	3,756	3,273	3,316	3,242	3,230	3,136	3,098	3,173	3,127
2003	3,175	3,177	3,202	3,249	3,308	3,211	3,075	3,085	3,081	3,158	3,076	3,055
2004	2,904	2,904	2,904	2,873	2,966	2,966	2,966	2,966	3,030	3,030	3,031	2,450
2005	2,912	2,994	3,076	3,056	2,866	2,687	2,554	2,641	2,497	2,986	3,059	2,913
2006[1]	3,004	3,100	3,111	2,978	2,952	2,925	2,918	2,917	2,956	2,960	2,954	

[1] Preliminary.   NA = Not available.   *Source: American Forest & Paper Association (AFPA)*

Lumber (Softwood) Production in the United States   In Millions of Board Feet

Year	Jan.	Feb.	Mar.	Apr.	May	June	July	Aug.	Sept.	Oct.	Nov.	Dec.	Total
1997	3,012	2,791	2,866	3,149	2,890	3,027	3,097	2,889	2,905	3,094	2,536	2,487	34,743
1998	2,767	2,760	2,928	3,084	2,647	3,051	3,079	2,930	2,953	3,167	2,667	2,754	34,787
1999	2,783	2,921	3,190	3,227	3,071	3,318	3,115	3,054	2,992	3,096	2,954	2,795	36,516
2000	3,020	3,128	3,474	3,058	3,276	3,249	2,730	2,971	2,839	3,041	2,761	2,342	35,889
2001	2,832	2,457	2,918	2,928	NA	3,032	2,812	3,240	2,743	3,188	2,740	2,372	34,104
2002	3,019	2,761	3,074	3,284	3,126	3,200	3,104	3,128	2,862	3,386	2,599	2,482	36,025
2003	2,971	2,801	2,937	2,994	2,931	3,109	3,088	2,981	3,052	3,335	2,793	2,740	35,732
2004	3,037	2,978	3,380	3,434	3,021	3,329	3,227	3,271	3,147	3,321	3,082	2,931	38,158
2005	3,233	3,169	3,596	3,486	3,339	3,535	3,248	3,490	3,385	3,574	3,180	3,052	40,287
2006[1]	3,511	3,216	3,550	3,294	3,360	3,420	3,195	3,349	2,877	3,154	2,368		38,503

[1] Preliminary.   *Source: American Forest & Paper Association (AFPA)*

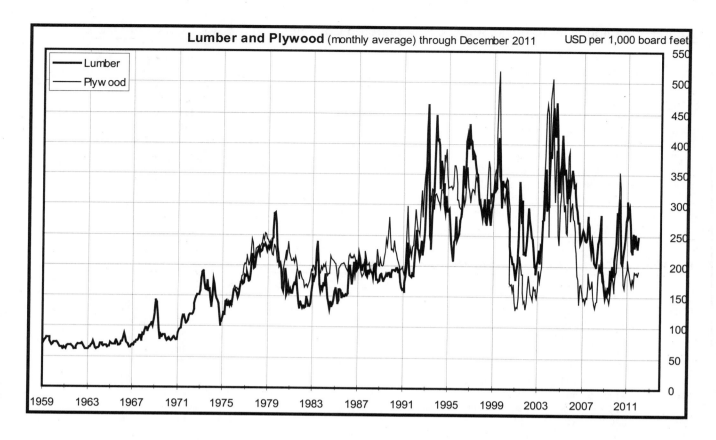

Lumber and Plywood (monthly average) through December 2011 — USD per 1,000 board feet

Lumber (Softwood) Shipments in the United States   In Millions of Board Feet

Year	Jan.	Feb.	Mar.	Apr.	May	June	July	Aug.	Sept.	Oct.	Nov.	Dec.	Total
1997	2,966	2,697	2,890	3,253	2,834	3,126	3,139	2,885	2,852	3,096	2,598	2,461	34,797
1998	2,685	2,685	2,863	3,019	2,684	3,175	3,132	2,963	2,948	3,205	2,703	2,865	34,927
1999	2,689	2,829	3,177	3,227	3,071	3,383	3,141	3,004	3,037	3,021	2,944	2,691	36,214
2000	2,953	3,039	3,394	2,974	3,292	3,309	2,686	3,027	2,871	2,931	2,752	2,444	35,672
2001	2,859	2,372	2,981	2,974	NA	2,961	2,936	3,279	2,644	3,166	2,732	2,396	34,145
2002	3,032	2,815	3,049	3,212	3,064	3,260	3,234	3,111	2,858	3,299	2,675	2,501	36,110
2003	3,018	2,742	2,843	3,134	2,969	3,173	3,209	3,137	3,030	3,413	2,787	2,722	36,177
2004	3,067	2,840	3,262	3,582	3,061	3,385	3,485	3,372	3,086	3,345	3,135	2,964	38,584
2005	3,264	3,087	3,506	3,506	3,542	3,696	3,389	3,512	3,413	3,542	3,145	3,196	40,798
2006[1]	3,423	3,122	3,536	3,280	3,386	3,447	3,202	3,349	2,838	3,151	2,374		38,300

[1] Preliminary.   *Source: American Forest & Paper Association (AFPA)*

Imports and Exports of Lumber in the United States, by Type   In Millions of Board Feet

	Imports[2] Softwood					Total Hard-wood	Total Lumber	Exports[2] Softwood		Pond-erosa/	South-		Total Hard-wood	Total Lumber
Year	Cedar	Douglas Fir	Hem-lock	Pine	Spruce	Total		Douglas Fir	Hem-lock	White Pine	ern Pine	Total		
1997	586	264	250	314	1,040	18,014	465	18,506	436	105	122	299	1,820	1,281	3,189
1998	514	417	268	363	849	18,686	589	19,306	252	39	113	279	1,265	1,119	2,601
1999	591	426	259	449	803	19,178	708	19,903	249	54	140	326	1,431	1,242	2,867
2000	694	455	184	450	812	19,449	795	20,268	232	46	116	298	1,355	1,319	2,822
2001	667	471	199	365	838	20,075	645	20,737	168	26	86	232	968	1,222	2,351
2002	648	385	69	445	1,046	20,986	739	21,774	111	19	83	205	848	1,219	2,313
2003	536	356	53	472	854	21,188	794	22,023	96	18	100	132	948	1,236	2,368
2004	630	570	67	580	1,183	23,483	995	24,499	88	19	93	156	821	1,496	2,533
2005	637	494	76	439	1,769	24,626	1,075	25,738	93	19	112	235	897	1,477	2,682
2006[1] I	180	88	31	100	432	6,054	261	6,321	19	3	29	58	246	449	695
II															
III															

Lumber Futures - CME Group
(weekly close) as of December 30, 2011

USD per 1,000 board feet

Average Open Interest of Random Lumber Futures in Chicago   In Contracts

Year	Jan.	Feb.	Mar.	Apr.	May	June	July	Aug.	Sept.	Oct.	Nov.	Dec.
2002	2,106	2,382	2,441	2,011	1,502	2,136	1,879	2,265	2,654	2,974	3,315	3,249
2003	3,238	3,222	2,521	2,804	2,937	3,188	2,370	2,827	3,492	3,033	1,824	1,887
2004	2,884	3,996	3,790	5,414	5,436	5,042	5,123	6,216	4,667	3,826	3,489	3,540
2005	3,759	5,169	5,040	4,705	3,463	3,576	3,401	4,227	3,913	3,883	4,713	5,202
2006	5,893	5,144	4,084	4,959	4,586	5,449	5,317	6,429	5,912	6,351	6,121	7,018
2007	6,466	7,807	7,684	8,680	7,726	8,206	7,130	7,666	6,493	9,356	8,960	9,731
2008	9,827	13,134	13,385	14,637	14,801	14,275	14,417	14,016	12,110	9,466	7,744	8,084
2009	7,912	7,937	6,852	7,732	7,815	9,039	7,910	8,873	9,248	9,593	10,174	9,557
2010	9,674	10,231	9,538	10,571	8,358	9,402	8,675	9,498	8,812	9,707	9,620	10,018
2011	11,235	10,223	9,471	9,813	10,090	10,408	9,233	10,170	9,465	10,314	9,663	10,768

Contract size = 110,000 board feet.   *Source: CME Group; Chicago Mercantile Exchange (CME)*

Volume of Trading of Random Lumber Futures in Chicago   In Contracts

Year	Jan.	Feb.	Mar.	Apr.	May	June	July	Aug.	Sept.	Oct.	Nov.	Dec.	Total
2002	15,328	13,239	16,401	13,910	12,427	11,950	12,046	10,154	13,518	13,442	15,828	16,180	164,423
2003	24,241	17,533	17,027	11,573	20,132	21,840	21,097	22,418	22,891	19,387	12,480	13,272	223,891
2004	17,921	17,713	22,544	25,743	19,951	17,190	22,672	20,902	24,238	17,111	17,271	19,617	242,873
2005	20,838	20,257	24,595	20,360	17,338	17,115	16,244	19,590	22,895	15,896	23,404	17,709	236,241
2006	26,803	19,152	18,504	21,358	21,619	23,959	21,568	23,800	22,618	24,804	22,385	24,454	271,024
2007	26,214	28,328	24,741	26,433	31,540	28,545	23,462	28,610	24,841	33,876	29,738	28,361	334,689
2008	31,401	43,338	37,899	50,586	37,909	38,362	41,612	40,693	32,155	36,226	20,277	27,155	437,613
2009	18,478	29,930	22,193	25,349	24,351	34,027	24,340	29,548	22,271	33,768	21,817	31,155	317,227
2010	25,483	26,365	20,928	32,393	24,763	29,446	18,360	24,660	26,107	31,689	23,662	28,046	311,902
2011	22,691	25,642	25,141	32,161	20,134	30,740	18,440	32,615	28,562	26,650	22,589	33,968	319,333

Contract size = 110,000 board feet.   *Source: CME Group; Chicago Mercantile Exchange (CME)*

LUMBER AND PLYWOOD

Production of Plywood by Selected Countries   In Thousands of Cubic Meters

Year	Austria	Canada	Finland	France	Germany	Italy	Japan	Poland	Romania	Russia	Spain	Sweden	United States
2003	186	2,206	1,300	415	245	511	3,024	289	94	1,978	370	75	14,870
2004	186	2,344	1,350	435	283	485	3,149	342	117	2,246	375	71	14,833
2005	195	2,322	1,305	415	236	390	3,212	361	126	2,556	557	92	14,449
2006	178	2,252	1,415	431	235	334	3,314	385	188	2,614	468	92	13,651
2007	258	2,639	1,410	378	229	420	3,073	440	107	2,777	450	72	12,402
2008	268	2,225	1,273	360	174	421	2,586	391	152	2,592	250	56	10,376
2009[1]	163	1,810	800	265	193	337	2,287	312	212	2,107	233	65	8,934
2010[2]	286	1,973	980	271	191	310	2,645	407	266	2,679	409	69	9,397

[1] Preliminary.   [2] Estimate.   NA = Not available.   Source: Food and Agricultural Organization of the United Nations (FAO)

Imports of Plywood by Selected Countries   In Thousands of Cubic Meters

Year	Austria	Belgium	Canada	Denmark	France	Germany	Italy	Japan	Nether-lands	Sweden	Switzer-land	United Kingdom	United States
2003	180	572	509	394	363	1,103	558	4,221	527	161	130	1,253	4,249
2004	144	624	350	413	383	1,214	581	5,122	542	164	140	1,474	5,900
2005	140	521	690	371	411	1,142	532	4,732	526	189	145	1,456	6,181
2006	140	610	685	1,821	445	1,314	575	5,046	603	197	128	1,497	6,393
2007	172	672	1,827	1,047	459	1,516	588	4,064	608	240	126	1,624	4,397
2008	133	633	2,149	429	581	1,459	530	3,583	635	192	131	1,486	3,059
2009[1]	116	527	861	585	397	1,066	417	2,948	457	144	53	1,164	2,647
2010[2]	155	548	1,909	716	453	1,264	485	3,255	547	152	68	1,264	2,937

[1] Preliminary.   [2] Estimate.   NA = Not available.   Source: Food and Agricultural Organization of the United Nations (FAO)

Exports of Plywood by Selected Countries   In Thousands of Cubic Meters

Year	Austria	Baltic States	Belgium	Canada	Finland	France	Germany	Italy	Nether-lands	Poland	Russia	Spain	United States
2003	262	245	436	1,017	1,172	187	200	208	32	149	1,201	88	512
2004	265	255	474	1,027	1,234	192	265	201	46	171	1,438	114	525
2005	287	253	423	1,118	1,173	196	287	146	40	177	1,527	117	503
2006	311	282	470	950	1,250	225	321	239	60	137	1,577	124	492
2007	285	318	386	964	1,229	227	368	295	55	148	1,503	162	443
2008	278	197	470	583	1,083	275	342	184	51	133	1,326	213	506
2009[1]	278	211	374	306	683	162	277	148	49	117	1,334	122	448
2010[2]	304	286	459	294	833	157	327	218	121	133	1,512	141	772

[1] Preliminary.   [2] Estimate.   NA = Not available.   Source: Food and Agricultural Organization of the United Nations (FAO)

Imports of Industrial Roundwood by Selected Countries   In Thousands of Cubic Meters

Year	Austria	Belgium	Canada	Finland	France	Germany	Italy	Norway	Poland	Portugal	Spain	Sweden	United States
2003	7,498	2,667	6,615	12,869	2,250	2,519	4,323	2,722	663	468	3,191	9,021	2,551
2004	8,812	2,879	5,961	12,961	2,175	2,227	4,614	2,866	943	364	2,973	9,398	2,437
2005	8,629	3,188	6,274	16,031	2,344	3,005	4,755	3,145	2,009	362	3,640	8,686	3,569
2006	9,102	3,284	5,787	14,655	2,601	3,669	4,486	2,333	1,814	335	3,841	6,664	2,922
2007	8,722	4,094	5,100	12,942	3,181	4,692	4,299	2,539	2,088	746	3,965	7,364	2,242
2008	7,550	3,669	4,608	13,371	2,358	5,758	3,478	1,808	1,868	521	2,860	6,781	1,430
2009[1]	8,036	3,031	4,636	3,761	1,503	4,534	2,703	933	1,874	473	1,777	4,676	2,065
2010[2]	8,041	4,277	4,745	6,256	1,689	6,829	3,198	1,288	2,289	878	1,956	6,276	1,318

[1] Preliminary.   [2] Estimate.   NA = Not available.   Source: Food and Agricultural Organization of the United Nations (FAO)

Exports of Industrial Roundwood by Selected Countries   In Thousands of Cubic Meters

Year	Canada	Czech Republic	Estonia	France	Germany	Hungary	Latvia	Lithuania	Russia	Slovakia	Sweden	Switzer-land	United States
2003	5,004	2,955	3,029	4,111	4,592	1,366	3,922	1,378	37,518	1,034	1,520	1,748	10,288
2004	3,899	2,858	2,297	3,851	5,589	1,137	4,136	1,178	41,553	1,142	1,522	1,741	10,402
2005	5,592	2,942	1,806	3,862	6,819	871	3,919	1,131	48,020	1,691	3,095	1,416	9,815
2006	4,640	2,679	1,606	3,695	7,557	1,095	3,419	1,061	50,900	1,218	3,004	1,667	9,638
2007	3,560	2,456	1,502	3,966	7,674	1,054	3,690	1,671	49,100	1,457	3,808	1,310	9,949
2008	2,839	3,449	1,469	3,547	7,037	661	3,193	1,171	36,784	2,192	2,349	1,087	10,200
2009[1]	2,723	4,267	1,080	5,047	3,857	684	2,503	673	21,700	2,538	1,177	825	9,619
2010[2]	4,019	4,200	2,250	6,656	3,310	873	4,158	1,329	21,243	2,434	1,217	748	11,586

[1] Preliminary.   [2] Estimate.   NA = Not available.   Source: Food and Agricultural Organization of the United Nations (FAO)

Magnesium

Magnesium (symbol Mg) is a silvery-white, light, and fairly tough, metallic element and is relatively stable. Magnesium is one of the alkaline earth metals. Magnesium is the eighth most abundant element in the earth's crust and the third most plentiful element found in seawater. Magnesium is ductile and malleable when heated, and with the exception of beryllium, is the lightest metal that remains stable under ordinary conditions. First isolated by the British chemist Sir Humphrey Davy in 1808, magnesium today is obtained mainly by electrolysis of fused magnesium chloride.

Magnesium compounds, primarily magnesium oxide, are used in the refractory material that line the furnaces used to produce iron and steel, nonferrous metals, glass, and cement. Magnesium oxide and other compounds are also used in the chemical, agricultural, and construction industries. Magnesium's principal use is as an alloying addition for aluminum. These aluminum-magnesium alloys are used primarily in beverage cans. Due to their lightness and considerable tensile strength, the alloys are also used in structural components in airplanes and automobiles.

Prices – The average price of magnesium in 2011 fell -7.3% to $2.42 per pound, well below the 2008 record high of $3.38 per pound.

Supply – World primary production of magnesium in 2011 rose +3.0% yr/yr to 780,000 metric tons, which was a new record high. The current level of magnesium production has more than tripled since the mid-1970s when 1976's production was 249,367 metric tons.

The world's largest primary producers of magnesium in 2011 were China with 670,000 metric tons, Russia with 37,000 metric tons, and Israel with 28,000 metric tons. The U.S. production amount is not available because it is considered proprietary data but is probably less than about 50,000 metric tons. China's production has increased over the past 10 years from 70,500 metric tons in 1998 to a record high of 670,000 metric tons in 2011. By 2006 Canada's production had grown by more than seven-fold from the mid-1980s, but that fell sharply in 2007 to 16,300 metric tons and down to 2,000 in 2008.

Demand – Total U.S. consumption of primary magnesium in 2010 (latest data available) rose +9.4% to 55,707 from 50,907metric tons. U.S. consumption of magnesium for structural products in 2010 rose +7.7% yr/yr to 22,307 metric tons. Of the structural product consumption category, 90% was for castings and the remaining 10% was for wrought products. U.S. consumption of magnesium for aluminum alloys rose +3.5% yr/yr in 2010 to 23,800 metric tons. The consumption of magnesium for other uses fell by -30.1% yr/yr in 2010 to 9,600 metric tons.

Trade – U.S. exports of magnesium in 2011 fell -20.0% yr/yr to 12,000 metric tons, but still above the 2005 record low of 9,650 metric tons. U.S. imports of magnesium in 2011 fell -5.7% yr/yr to 50,000 metric tons.

World Production of Magnesium (Primary)   In Metric Tons

Year	Brazil	Canada	China	Israel	Kazakhstan	Russia	Serbia	Ukraine	United States	Total
2006	6,000	65,000	520,000	24,581	21,000	35,000	1,500	2,200	W	675,000
2007	18,000	16,300	625,000	29,618	21,000	37,000	2,000	2,500	W	751,000
2008	15,000	2,000	559,000	32,051	21,000	37,000	1,500	2,000	W	670,000
2009	16,000	----	501,000	19,405	21,000	37,000	1,500	2,000	W	608,000
2010[1]	16,000	----	654,000	25,000	21,000	37,000	2,000	2,000	W	757,000
2011[2]	16,000	----	670,000	28,000	20,000	37,000	2,000	2,000	W	780,000

[1] Preliminary.   [2] Estimate.   W = Withheld.   *Source: U.S. Geological Survey (USGS)*

Salient Statistics of Magnesium in the United States   In Metric Tons

Year	Primary (Ingot)	New Scrap	Old Scrap	Total	Total Exports[3]	Imports for Consumption	Stocks Dec. 31[4]	Price $ Per Pound[5]	Castings	Wrought	Total	Aluminum Alloys	Other Uses	Total
		---- Secondary ----							**----- Structural Products -----**					
2006	W	60,500	21,700	81,900	12,300	75,300	W	1.40	26,007	2,410	28,417	33,700	15,400	49,100
2007	W	59,900	23,500	84,100	14,800	71,800	W	2.25	23,727	2,820	26,547	32,000	13,600	45,600
2008	W	61,100	22,600	83,700	14,400	83,300	W	3.15	16,647	2,480	19,127	35,000	10,300	45,300
2009	W	48,100	20,500	66,600	19,600	47,300	W	2.30	19,617	1,090	20,707	23,000	7,200	30,200
2010[1]	W	51,500	20,500	72,000	15,000	53,000	W	2.43	20,187	2,120	22,307	23,800	9,600	33,400
2011[2]				75,000	12,000	50,000	W	2.35						

[1] Preliminary.   [2] Estimate.   [3] Metal & alloys in crude form & scrap.   [4] Estimate of Industry Stocks, metal.   [5] Magnesium ingots (99.8%), f.o.b. Valasco, Texas.   [6] Distributive or sacrificial purposes.   W = Withheld proprietary data.   *Source: U.S. Geological Survey (USGS)*

Average Price of Magnesium   In Dollars Per Pound

Year	Jan.	Feb.	Mar.	Apr.	May	June	July	Aug.	Sept.	Oct.	Nov.	Dec.	Average
2007	1.42	1.56	1.58	1.62	1.65	1.65	1.65	1.65	1.65	1.98	2.09	2.20	1.73
2008	2.89	3.08	3.27	3.39	3.55	3.55	3.55	3.55	3.55	3.50	3.43	3.22	3.38
2009	3.13	2.99	2.83	2.73	2.73	2.73	2.52	2.35	2.30	2.25	2.23	2.23	2.59
2010	2.43	2.65	2.65	2.68	2.65	2.65	2.67	2.66	2.63	2.60	2.55	2.55	2.61
2011	2.55	2.53	2.53	2.53	2.53	2.58	2.42	2.40	2.40	2.22	2.19	2.20	2.42

Source: American Metal Market (AMM)

Manganese

Manganese (symbol Mn) is a silvery-white, very brittle, metallic element used primarily in making alloys. Manganese was first distinguished as an element and isolated in 1774 by Johan Gottlieb Gahn. Manganese dissolves in acid and corrodes in moist air.

Manganese is found in the earth's crust in the form of ores such as rhodochrosite, franklinite, psilomelane, and manganite. Pyrolusite is the principal ore of manganese. Pure manganese is produced by igniting pyrolusite with aluminum powder or by electrolyzing manganese sulfate.

Manganese is used primarily in the steel industry for creating alloys, the most important ones being ferromanganese and spiegeleisen. In steel, manganese improves forging and rolling qualities, strength, toughness, stiffness, wear resistance, and hardness. Manganese is also used in plant fertilizers, animal feed, pigments, and dry cell batteries.

Prices – The average monthly price of ferromanganese (high carbon, FOB plant) fell by -4.9% yr/yr in 2011 to $1,323.05 per gross ton and still below the 2008 record high of $2,953.84 per gross ton. The 2011 price, however, is still almost three times the 25-year low price of $447.44 per gross ton posted as recently as 2001.

Supply – World production of manganese ore in 2009 (latest data available) fell by -11.8% to 33.6 million metric tons, down from the 2008 record high of 38,100 metric tons. The 2009 level was still well above the record low of 17.8 million metric tons posted in 1999. The world's largest producers of manganese ore are China with 36% of world production in 2009, South Africa with 14%, Australia with 13%, Brazil with 7%, and the Ukraine with 3%. China's production in 2009 rose by +9.0% yr/yr to 12.000 million metric tons.

Demand – U.S. consumption of manganese ore in 2011 rose +0.4% to 470,000 metric tons, up further from the 2007 record low of 351,000 metric tons. U.S. consumption of ferromanganese in 2011 rose +2.7% yr/yr to 300,000 metric tons, but still below the 12-year high of 315,000 metric tons posted in 2004. The 2011 figure is about 25% of the U.S. consumption in the early 1970s.

Trade – The U.S. still relies on imports for 100% of its manganese consumption, as it has since 1985. U.S. imports of manganese ore for consumption in 2011 rose +16.6% yr/yr to 470,000 metric tons, up from 2009's 18-year low of 269 metric tons. U.S. imports of ferromanganese for consumption in 2011 rose +19.6% yr/yr to 390,000 metric tons. U.S. imports of silico-manganese in 2011 rose +34.7% yr/yr to 400,000 metric tons, up from 2009's 27-year low of 130,000 metric tons. The primary sources of U.S. imports of manganese ore in 2009 were Gabon with 63% imports and Australia with 10%.

World Production of Manganese Ore   In Thousands of Metric Tons (Gross Weight)

Year	Australia[2] 37-53[4]	Brazil 37[4]	China 20-30[4]	Gabon 45-53[4]	Georgia[5] 29-30[4]	Ghana 32-34[4]	India 10-54[4]	Kazakhstan[5] 29-30[4]	Mexico 27-50[4]	South Africa 30-48+[4]	Ukraine[5] 30-35[4]	Other	World Total
2000	1,614	1,925	3,500	1,743	----	896	1,550	1,136	435	3,635	2,741	433	19,600
2001	2,069	1,970	4,300	1,791	----	1,077	1,600	1,387	277	3,266	2,700	490	20,900
2002	2,189	2,529	4,500	1,856	----	1,136	1,553	1,792	245	3,322	2,470	526	22,100
2003	2,564	2,544	4,600	2,000	----	1,509	1,650	2,361	320	3,501	2,591	547	24,200
2004	3,431	3,143	5,500	2,460	----	1,597	1,776	2,318	377	4,282	2,362	656	27,900
2005	3,136	3,200	7,500	2,859	----	1,715	2,386	2,208	369	4,612	2,260	745	31,000
2006	4,556	3,390	8,000	3,000	----	1,659	2,084	2,531	346	5,213	1,606	772	33,200
2007	5,289	1,570	10,000	3,300	----	1,173	2,300	2,482	423	5,996	1,720	843	35,100
2008	4,812	3,160	11,000	3,250	----	1,261	2,400	2,485	472	6,807	1,447	1,000	38,100
2009[1]	4,451	2,200	12,000	2,000	----	1,007	2,500	2,467	470	4,576	932	965	33,600

[1] Preliminary.   [2] Metallurgical Ore.   [3] Concentrate.   [4] Ranges of percentage of manganese.   *Source: U.S. Geological Survey (USGS)*

Salient Statistics of Manganese in the United States   In Thousands of Metric Tons (Gross Weight)

Year	Net Import Reliance As a % of Apparent Consumption	Manganese Ore (35% or More Manganese) Imports for Consumption	Exports	Consumption	Stocks Dec. 31[3]	Ferromanganese Imports for Consumption	Exports	Consumption	Avg Price Mn. Metallurgical Ore $/Lg. Ton Unit[4]	Silicomanganese Exports	Imports
2002	100	427	15	360	151	275	9	253	2.30	0.5	247.0
2003	100	347	18	398	156	238	11	248	2.41	0.6	267.0
2004	100	451	123	441	159	429	9	315	2.89	0.5	422.0
2005	100	656	13	368	337	255	14	286	4.39	0.9	327.0
2006	100	572	2	365	153	358	22	297	3.22	0.9	400.0
2007	100	602	29	351	190	315	29	272	3.10	3.3	414.0
2008	100	571	48	464	255	448	23	304	12.15	7.1	365.0
2009	100	269	15	422	115	153	24	242	7.95	19.0	130.0
2010[1]	100	489	14	468	89	326	19	292	9.18	9.0	297.0
2011[2]	100	570	1	470	90	390	8	300	9.10	10.0	400.0

[1] Preliminary.   [2] Estimate.   [3] Including bonded warehouses; excludes Gov't stocks; also excludes small tonnages of dealers' stocks.
[4] 46-48% Mn, C.I.F. U.S. Ports.   *Source: U.S. Geological Survey (USGS)*

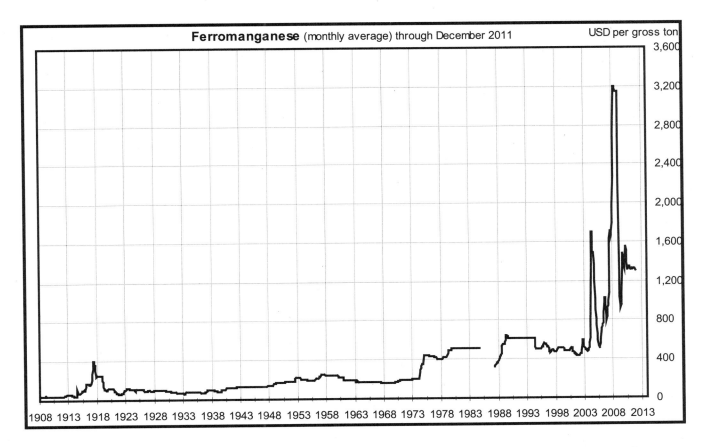

Ferromanganese (monthly average) through December 2011 — USD per gross ton

Imports[3] of Manganese Ore (20% or More Mn) in the United States — In Metric Tons (Mn Content)

Year	Australia	Brazil	Gabon	Mexico	Morocco	South Africa	Total	Customs Value ($1,000)
2000	18,100	3,250	188,000	3,250	----	----	219,000	32,100
2001	18,000	3,480	158,000	1,720	----	17,400	199,000	28,000
2002	18,400	12,900	140,000	1,100	----	41,800	214,000	29,200
2003	12,900	7	123,000	1,520	----	36,900	175,000	27,000
2004	27,700	----	188,000	1,640	----	13,200	234,000	37,700
2005	21,300	7,020	252,000	4,320	----	33,100	334,000	58,200
2006	12,800	5,800	120,000	1,320	----	91,200	270,000	53,900
2007	34,900	20,000	170,000	3,670	----	53,600	298,000	57,600
2008[1]	51,900	34,400	181,000	----	----	14,600	289,000	154,000
2009[2]	15,400	1,540	96,500	671	9	----	154,000	82,600

[1] Preliminary.   [2] Estimate.   [3] Imports for consumption.   *Source: U.S. Geological Survey (USGS)*

Average Price of Ferromanganese[1] — In Dollars Per Gross Ton -- Carloads

Year	Jan.	Feb.	Mar.	Apr.	May	June	July	Aug.	Sept.	Oct.	Nov.	Dec.	Average
2002	430.00	430.00	437.14	447.73	449.55	456.75	481.82	556.14	597.00	589.67	552.89	518.93	495.64
2003	509.52	510.00	502.38	497.61	492.50	481.79	477.27	470.00	478.57	497.83	516.67	559.76	499.49
2004	610.00	790.00	1,382.61	1,700.00	1,700.00	1,674.43	1,490.34	1,488.64	1,500.00	1,371.43	1,207.50	1,019.52	1,327.87
2005	904.50	818.68	739.46	651.67	586.19	547.39	528.13	512.07	522.14	550.24	597.75	694.05	637.69
2006	707.25	712.50	737.50	759.00	764.55	870.23	987.50	1,025.00	1,021.25	946.25	836.25	790.00	846.44
2007	834.29	930.00	949.55	1,000.00	1,074.43	1,633.33	1,705.00	1,620.00	1,620.00	1,656.96	1,700.00	1,785.53	1,375.76
2008	1,978.57	2,262.75	2,734.29	3,145.45	3,200.00	3,200.00	3,175.00	3,150.00	3,150.00	3,150.00	3,150.00	3,150.00	2,953.84
2009	2,225.00	1,300.00	1,300.00	1,038.10	950.00	928.18	955.45	1,071.43	1,344.52	1,481.67	1,431.84	1,365.26	1,282.62
2010	1,326.58	1,387.50	1,530.43	1,559.09	1,507.00	1,389.09	1,310.00	1,320.45	1,327.38	1,345.00	1,345.00	1,345.00	1,391.04
2011	1,336.25	1,320.00	1,320.00	1,327.62	1,321.43	1,315.00	1,315.00	1,327.39	1,330.00	1,330.00	1,330.00	1,303.95	1,323.05

[1] Domestic standard, high carbon, FOB plant, carloads.   *Source: American Metal Market (AMM)*

Meats

U.S. commercial red meat includes beef, veal, lamb, and pork. Red meat is a good source of iron, vitamin B12, and protein, and eliminating it from the diet can lead to iron and zinc deficiencies. Today, red meat is far leaner than it was 30 years ago due to newer breeds of livestock that carry less fat. The leanest cuts of beef include tenderloin, sirloin, and flank. The leanest cuts of pork include pork tenderloin, loin chops, and rib chops.

The USDA (United States Department of Agriculture) grades various cuts of meat. "Prime" is the highest USDA grade for beef, veal, and lamb. "Choice" is the grade designation below Prime for beef, veal, and lamb. "Commercial" and "Cutter" grades are two of the lower designations for beef, usually sold as ground meat, sausage, and canned meat. "Canner" is the lowest USDA grade designation for beef and is used primarily in canned meats not sold at retail.

Supply – World meat production in 2012 is expected to rise +1.4% to a new record high of 160.231 million metric tons. China is projected to be the world's largest meat producer in 2012 with 56.800 million metric tons of production (up +3.2% yr/yr), accounting for 35.5% of world production.

U.S. production of meat in 2010 fell -0.5% yr/yr to 48.189 billion pounds, below the 2008 record high of 50.362 billion pounds. U.S. production of beef in 2010 rose +1.4% yr/yr to 26.419 billion pounds, which will be just moderately below the record of 27.192 billion pounds in 2002. Beef accounted for 53.7% of all U.S. meat production. U.S. production of pork in 2010 fell -17.7% yr/yr to 18.952, below the 2008 record high of 23.367 billion pounds. Pork accounts for 38.5% of U.S. meat production. Veal accounts for only 0.3% of U.S. meat production, and lamb and mutton account for only 0.4% of U.S. meat production.

Demand – U.S. per capita meat consumption in 2010 fell by -3.6% yr/yr to 108.6 pounds per person per year, but that is only slightly below the 2006-07 record low of 117.5 pounds per person reflecting the trend towards eating more chicken and fish and the availability of meat substitutes. Per capita beef consumption in 2010 fell -2.5% yr/yr to 59.6 pounds per person per year, which was about half the record high of 127.5 pounds seen in 1976. Per capita pork consumption in 2010 fell by -4.8% yr/yr to 47.7 pounds per person per year, a new record low. Per capita consumption of veal is negligible at 0.4 pounds per person and lamb/mutton consumption is also negligible at 1.0 pound per person.

Trade – World red meat exports in 2012 are expected to rise +2.3% to 14.776 million metric tons, a new record high. The world's largest red meat exporters will be the U.S. with 24.1% of world exports in 2012, European Union with 16.0%, Brazil with 13.2%, Canada with 10.9%, and Australia with 9.6%.

World Total Meat Production[4]   In Thousands of Metric Tons

Year	Argentina	Australia	Brazil	Canada	China[4]	European Union	India	Mexico	New Zealand	Russia	South Africa	United States	World Total
2003	2,950	2,492	9,945	2,934	47,811	30,016	----	2,985	729	3,161	756	21,095	144,155
2004	3,308	2,475	10,575	3,280	49,014	29,998	----	2,964	749	3,073	800	20,574	146,651
2005	3,388	2,487	11,302	3,235	51,234	29,766	----	2,828	711	2,854	826	20,710	149,656
2006	3,310	2,572	11,855	3,077	52,272	29,941	----	2,659	699	2,894	876	21,539	152,897
2007	3,515	2,558	12,293	3,024	49,012	31,046	----	2,752	658	3,070	830	22,059	152,390
2008	3,370	2,507	12,039	3,075	52,337	30,686	----	2,828	695	3,226	826	22,762	156,044
2009	3,605	2,456	12,065	3,041	54,669	30,347	----	2,862	671	3,304	829	22,333	157,553
2010	2,838	2,427	12,310	3,044	56,670	30,574	----	2,916	693	3,355	835	22,233	159,788
2011[1]	2,715	2,485	12,257	2,908	55,050	30,580	----	3,000	660	3,370	825	22,326	157,975
2012[2]	2,815	2,530	12,505	2,965	56,800	30,480	----	3,025	664	3,405	815	21,929	160,231

[1] Preliminary.   [2] Forecast.   [3] Data through 2000, includes beef, veal, pork, sheep and goat meat. Beginning 2001, excludes sheep and goat.
[4] Predominately pork production.   *Source: Foreign Agricultural Service, U.S. Department of Agriculture (FAS-USDA)*

Production and Consumption of Red Meats in The United States

	Beef			Veal			Lamb & Mutton			Pork (Excluding Lard)			All Meats		
	Commercial Production	Consumption		Commercial Production	Consumption		Commercial Production	Consumption		Commercial Production	Consumption		Commercial Production	Consumption	
Year	- Million Pounds -	Total	Per Capita Lbs.	- Million Pounds -	Total	Per Capita Lbs.	- Million Pounds -	Total	Per Capita Lbs.	- Million Pounds -	Total	Per Capita Lbs.	- Million Pounds -	Total	Per Capita Lbs.
2002	27,192	27,877	68.0	205	204	1.0	223	381	1.0	19,685	19,146	52.0	47,305	47,608	121.0
2003	26,339	27,000	65.0	202	204	0.6	203	367	1.0	19,966	19,436	52.0	46,710	47,006	118.0
2004	24,650	27,750	66.0	176	177	0.6	200	373	1.0	20,529	19,437	51.0	45,555	47,737	119.0
2005	24,787	27,754	66.0	165	164	0.6	191	355	1.0	20,705	19,112	50.0	45,848	47,385	117.0
2006	26,256	28,137	65.9	156	155	0.4	190	356	1.1	21,074	19,055	49.4	47,675	47,703	116.8
2007	26,523	28,141	65.2	146	145	0.4	189	385	1.1	21,962	19,763	50.8	48,820	48,434	117.5
2008	26,664	27,194	62.4	152	150	0.4	180	343	1.0	23,367	19,431	49.5	50,362	47,118	113.3
2009	26,068	26,836	61.1	147	147	0.4	177	338	1.0	23,020	19,870	50.1	49,412	47,191	112.6
2010[1]	26,414	26,392	59.6	145	150	0.4	168	318	0.9	22,456	19,075	47.8	49,183	45,935	108.7
2011[2]	26,309	25,562	57.3							22,779	18,388	45.7	49,382	44,387	104.3

[1] Preliminary.   [2] Estimate.   [3] Forecast.   *Source: Economic Research Service, U.S. Department of Agriculture (ERS-USDA)*

Total Red Meat Imports[3] (Carcass Weight Equivalent) of Principal Countries   In Thousands of Metric Tons

Year	Brazil	Canada	European Union	Egypt	Hong Kong	Japan	Rep of Korea	Mexico	Philip-pines	Russia	Taiwan	United States	World Total
2003	62	395	593	128	339	1,924	620	752	149	1,452	144	1,901	10,335
2004	52	228	694	174	364	1,903	457	754	185	1,385	134	2,168	10,762
2005	48	290	810	222	351	2,000	595	755	160	1,790	129	2,096	11,565
2006	28	326	842	292	366	1,832	708	829	160	1,853	128	1,848	11,780
2007	30	413	676	293	392	1,896	755	854	179	1,981	120	1,823	12,288
2008	29	424	522	166	464	1,926	725	943	205	2,253	141	1,528	13,158
2009	35	427	535	180	523	1,835	705	1,000	182	1,850	182	1,569	12,344
2010	36	426	462	260	501	1,919	748	983	242	1,900	188	1,432	12,748
2011[1]	46	470	385	230	480	1,935	1,035	910	235	1,980	195	1,290	13,128
2012[2]	51	460	390	250	510	1,935	920	920	240	1,760	197	1,322	13,118

[1] Preliminary.   [2] Forecast.   [3] Data through 2000, includes beef, veal, pork, sheep and goat meat. Beginning 2001, excludes sheep and goat.
Source: Foreign Agricultural Service, U.S. Department of Agriculture (FAS-USDA)

Total Red Meat Exports[3] (Carcass Weight Equivalent) of Principal Countries   In Thousands of Metric Tons

Year	Argentina	Australia	Brazil	Canada	China	Denmark	France	India	Ireland	Nether-lands	New Zealand	United States	World Total
2003	382	1,318	1,765	1,388	433	1,578	432	548	10	227	1,921	282	10,722
2004	616	1,431	2,231	1,575	589	1,665	492	594	9	127	1,198	354	11,439
2005	755	1,444	2,606	1,680	578	1,396	617	577	11	91	1,525	418	12,401
2006	553	1,490	2,723	1,558	629	1,503	681	530	8	24	1,878	461	12,842
2007	535	1,454	2,919	1,490	431	1,426	678	496	8	52	2,075	386	12,803
2008	425	1,455	2,426	1,623	281	1,931	672	533	11	24	3,015	361	13,775
2009	657	1,404	2,303	1,603	270	1,563	609	514	9	27	2,735	376	13,091
2010	299	1,409	2,177	1,682	329	2,091	917	530	6	20	2,959	347	13,795
2011[1]	261	1,392	1,907	1,575	320	2,475	1,100	501	5	31	3,487	310	14,444
2012[2]	301	1,422	1,945	1,610	345	2,365	1,275	504	5	23	3,559	320	14,776

[1] Preliminary.   [2] Forecast.   [3] Data through 2000, includes beef, veal, pork, sheep and goat meat. Beginning 2001, excludes sheep and goat.
Source: Foreign Agricultural Service, U.S. Department of Agriculture (FAS-USDA)

United States Meat Imports by Type of Product   In Metric Tons

Year	Beef and Veal Fresh	Beef and Veal Frozen	Beef and Veal Other Prepared or Preserved	Lamb, Mutton and Goat, Except Canned	Pork Fresh and Chilled	Pork Frozen	Pork Other Prepared or Preserved	Variety Meats, Fresh or Frozen	Other Livestock Meats NSE	Total
1996	227,874	412,805	66,719	33,009	125,220	58,336	72,650	32,579	13,744	1,042,934
1997	262,985	469,949	63,181	37,848	126,061	65,000	72,903	44,317	14,215	1,156,457
1998	295,820	527,063	68,884	51,630	146,965	70,227	76,230	47,031	13,058	1,296,907
1999	337,899	542,524	82,669	50,209	188,556	77,638	84,207	51,640	13,625	1,428,966
2000	336,117	608,737	73,750	59,968	229,395	91,446	92,672	57,388	14,281	1,563,753
2001	368,529	618,897	73,713	66,785	240,275	84,687	83,724	62,541	16,723	1,615,873
2002	400,484	586,500	84,640	73,863	276,639	90,423	91,379	55,384	19,401	1,678,713
2003	285,772	612,569	85,439	77,546	293,169	107,749	107,964	47,688	21,367	1,639,263
2004	387,758	717,942	92,123	82,930	266,583	109,915	96,840	33,776	55,737	1,843,604
2005[1]	406,431	669,935	96,181	83,957	266,544	93,063	78,594	41,067	25,426	1,761,198

[1] Preliminary.   NSE = Not specified elsewhere.   *Source: Foreign Agricultural Service, U.S. Department of Agriculture (FAS-USDA)*

United States Meat Exports by Type of Product   In Metric Tons

Year	Beef and Veal Fresh	Beef and Veal Frozen	Beef and Veal Other Prepared or Preserved	Lamb and Mutton, Fresh or Frozen	Pork Fresh and Chilled	Pork Frozen	Pork Other Prepared or Preserved	Variety Meats, Fresh, Chilled or Frozen	Other Meats	Total
1996	273,276	324,329	14,577	2,478	101,975	166,057	32,190	495,343	434,759	1,844,984
1997	316,534	359,460	15,227	2,545	134,706	151,121	31,215	469,789	435,258	1,915,854
1998	346,403	352,050	17,966	2,528	147,006	209,135	37,907	495,643	423,980	2,032,618
1999	370,184	414,458	19,323	2,219	160,910	225,492	40,463	524,325	455,561	2,212,935
2000	395,588	417,538	21,791	2,184	208,055	185,240	36,915	604,738	503,942	2,372,990
2001	393,105	362,972	23,932	2,770	227,807	247,461	44,494	685,063	513,969	2,501,573
2002	407,599	393,836	27,232	3,042	235,547	231,274	69,030	592,185	619,491	2,579,236
2003	430,071	390,543	37,572	2,909	237,129	257,360	69,693	598,726	567,565	2,591,568
2004	114,966	20,458	9,068	3,671	352,173	298,786	74,963	456,480	189,127	1,519,691
2005[1]	173,337	31,714	19,027	4,885	404,601	401,115	75,096	497,346	274,990	1,882,111

[1] Preliminary.   *Source: Foreign Agricultural Service, U.S. Department of Agriculture (FAS-USDA)*

MEATS

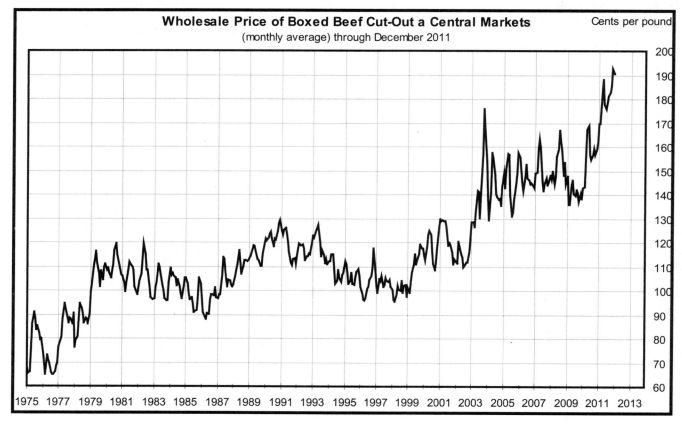

Wholesale Price of Boxed Beef Cut-Out a Central Markets
(monthly average) through December 2011
Cents per pound

Exports and Imports of Meats in the United States (Carcass Weight Equivalent)[3]

	Exports				Imports			
Year	Beef and Veal	Lamb and Mutton	Pork[3]	All Meat	Beef and Veal	Lamb and Mutton	Pork[3]	All Meat
2002	2,448	7	1,612	4,067	3,218	160	1,071	4,448
2003	2,518	7	1,717	4,242	3,006	168	1,185	4,359
2004	460	8	2,181	2,649	3,679	181	1,099	4,960
2005	697	9	2,666	3,373	3,599	180	1,024	4,803
2006	1,145	18	2,995	4,158	3,085	190	990	4,265
2007	1,434	9	3,141	4,585	3,052	203	968	4,223
2008	1,996	12	4,667	6,660	2,538	183	832	3,553
2009	1,935	16	4,126	6,045	2,626	171	834	3,631
2010[1]	2,299	16	4,224	6,539	2,297	166	859	3,322
2011[2]	2,779		5,112	7,891	2,052	172	800	3,024

[1] Preliminary.　　[2] Estimate.　　[3] Includes meat content of minor meats and of mixed products.
Source: Economic Research Service, U.S. Department of Agriculture (FAS-USDA)

Average Wholesale Prices of Meats in the United States · In Cent Per Pound

	Composite Retail Price		Wholesale Value[4]		Net Farm Value[5] of Pork	Cow Beef Canner & Cutter, Central US	Boxed Beef Cut-out, Choice1-3, Central US 550-700 Lb.	Pork Carcass Cut-out, U.S., No. 2	Lamb Carcass, Choice-Prime, E. Coast, 55-65 lbs.	Pork[6] Loins, Central US 14-18 lbs.	Skinned Ham, Central US 17-20 lbs.	Pork Bellies, Central US 12-14 lbs.
Year	of Beef, Choice, Grade 3	of Pork[3]	Beef	Pork								
2002	331.53	265.75	180.02	100.70	61.90	NA	114.42	53.49	151.28	97.98	47.52	69.91
2003	374.62	265.82	222.90	107.40	69.60	NA	143.58	58.87	185.21	100.96	45.48	86.42
2004	406.53	279.16	218.90	127.40	92.10	NA	142.15	73.53	189.08	117.14	64.98	99.35
2005	409.22	282.69	226.10	124.90	88.00	NA	145.78	69.84	209.88	113.22	64.07	81.46
2006	397.02	280.72	228.17	121.38	83.27	NA	146.82	67.62	199.10	104.46	64.04	82.81
2007	415.85	287.03	231.08	121.44	81.98	NA	149.80	67.54	215.96	104.17	57.96	88.97
2008	432.45	293.65	235.04	124.73	82.48	NA	153.17	69.24	226.63	106.63	63.52	69.86
2009	425.98	291.97	217.18	111.19	71.56	NA	140.77	58.13	225.45	92.81	51.34	60.91
2010[1]	439.44	311.36	241.08	141.16	95.68	NA	156.91	81.25	263.02	115.96	76.41	93.63
2011[2]	482.72	343.35	275.82	158.89	113.93	NA	181.29	93.69	364.95	129.51	82.19	123.60

[1] Preliminary.　　[2] Estimate.　　[3] Sold as retail cuts (ham, bacon, loin, etc.).　　[4] Quantity equivalent to 1 pound of retail cuts.
[5] Portion of gross farm value minus farm by-product allowance.　　Source: Economic Research Service, U.S. Department of Agriculture (ERS-USDA)

Average Wholesale Price of Boxed Beef Cut-Out[1], Choice 1-3, at Central US   In Cents Per Pound

Year	Jan.	Feb.	Mar.	Apr.	May	June	July	Aug.	Sept.	Oct.	Nov.	Dec.	Average
2002	111.99	111.53	120.54	116.61	115.14	114.06	109.88	110.93	111.83	111.64	116.41	122.45	114.42
2003	128.59	128.77	126.35	133.03	141.44	141.16	130.13	139.91	156.64	176.06	167.15	153.71	143.58
2004	138.60	129.29	141.34	157.53	155.70	148.54	140.27	139.33	137.82	138.45	135.64	143.31	142.15
2005	148.93	143.02	150.66	157.34	156.82	140.02	131.19	132.85	137.97	144.30	148.81	157.49	145.78
2006	155.60	149.71	144.94	141.83	147.45	153.09	147.01	146.22	144.69	144.79	143.64	142.92	146.82
2007	149.15	149.54	159.23	163.23	160.20	145.59	141.47	144.51	146.99	144.09	145.39	148.25	149.80
2008	146.41	149.63	144.42	147.47	156.07	159.10	167.33	162.31	159.56	148.03	153.29	144.42	153.17
2009	147.68	136.03	135.91	144.42	146.22	140.22	139.59	142.13	140.94	137.15	140.60	138.35	140.77
2010	142.87	143.22	155.73	167.37	168.80	156.54	154.53	156.67	159.20	156.58	159.25	162.20	156.91
2011[2]	169.96	169.82	182.52	188.05	177.96	176.02	178.44	181.12	183.05	185.34	192.51	190.72	181.29

[1] Data through 2004: 550-750 pounds; beginning 2005: 600-900 pounds.   [2] Preliminary.   *Source: Economic Research Service, U.S. Department of Agriculture (ERS-USDA)*

Production (Commercial) of All Red Meats in the United States   In Millions of Pounds (Carcass Weight)

Year	Jan.	Feb.	Mar.	Apr.	May	June	July	Aug.	Sept.	Oct.	Nov.	Dec.	Total
2002	4,081	3,501	3,677	3,902	4,018	3,813	4,016	4,141	3,873	4,382	3,908	3,859	47,171
2003	4,075	3,496	3,705	3,845	3,944	3,948	4,046	3,913	4,007	4,155	3,524	3,876	46,534
2004	3,713	3,404	3,944	3,713	3,597	3,928	3,708	3,878	3,905	3,921	3,770	3,931	45,412
2005	3,648	3,423	3,879	3,622	3,714	3,963	3,616	4,100	3,933	3,926	3,942	3,954	45,719
2006	3,890	3,485	4,111	3,614	4,048	4,120	3,782	4,245	3,933	4,182	4,136	3,862	47,408
2007	4,091	3,615	4,013	3,753	4,075	4,028	3,940	4,026	3,864	4,614	4,300	4,059	48,378
2008	4,416	3,968	4,090	4,297	4,223	4,050	4,252	4,097	4,273	4,530	3,872	4,162	50,230
2009	4,169	3,825	4,142	4,084	3,919	4,162	4,124	4,077	4,262	4,391	3,963	4,148	49,264
2010	3,918	3,736	4,282	4,013	3,732	4,177	3,956	4,127	4,161	4,265	4,329	4,355	49,050
2011[1]	4,042	3,811	4,347	3,869	3,914	4,219	3,793	4,303	4,192	4,271	4,260	4,216	49,236

[1] Preliminary.   *Source: Economic Research Service, U.S. Department of Agriculture (ERS-USDA)*

Cold Storage Holdings of All[2] Meats in the United States, on First of Month   In Millions of Pounds

Year	Jan.	Feb.	Mar.	Apr.	May	June	July	Aug.	Sept.	Oct.	Nov.	Dec.
2002	946.8	982.6	970.7	961.9	996.6	973.0	918.0	912.6	950.7	997.8	1,038.9	997.7
2003	1,011.5	1,015.2	978.2	951.9	926.8	901.5	847.5	825.0	817.3	832.1	836.9	828.1
2004	879.0	953.7	926.9	879.4	883.6	829.3	797.9	807.7	841.9	886.1	889.2	912.6
2005	979.0	965.0	953.2	928.0	908.5	847.0	847.8	850.8	842.9	884.9	900.1	882.1
2006	877.2	1,012.4	987.3	959.8	979.1	940.8	880.9	915.5	918.2	969.4	994.0	1,009.9
2007	946.6	977.3	963.4	943.5	970.3	925.7	919.7	943.5	958.7	991.8	1,003.2	968.4
2008	961.6	1,047.5	1,072.6	1,106.9	1,103.9	1,024.5	983.8	960.5	970.9	1,009.4	1,027.8	1,037.8
2009	1,078.5	1,096.2	1,084.9	1,045.3	1,050.6	1,030.1	1,043.1	1,014.7	980.2	984.0	968.4	936.8
2010	924.9	938.4	941.9	921.8	876.3	837.8	816.1	808.6	803.4	844.7	918.6	925.3
2011[1]	939.9	1,017.4	1,050.6	1,042.7	1,009.5	1,014.9	949.4	894.2	896.7	944.9	927.0	958.9

[1] Preliminary.   [2] Includes beef and veal, mutton and lamb, pork and products, rendered pork fat, and miscellaneous meats. Excludes lard.
Source: Economic Research Service, U.S. Department of Agriculture (ERS-USDA)

Cold Storage Holdings of Frozen Beef in the United States, on First of Month   In Millions of Pounds

Year	Jan.	Feb.	Mar.	Apr.	May	June	July	Aug.	Sept.	Oct.	Nov.	Dec.
2002	460.7	455.5	439.0	410.5	405.7	401.8	396.9	416.5	461.8	494.9	525.2	512.6
2003	524.6	482.4	441.9	403.1	389.7	385.1	371.5	368.2	371.0	379.8	375.2	373.8
2004	395.1	434.4	435.0	416.8	421.2	402.8	411.8	427.0	446.0	457.2	452.6	463.3
2005	484.3	453.3	400.2	372.3	329.4	318.2	342.1	385.2	410.6	438.8	439.2	429.9
2006	434.4	465.9	440.6	436.2	441.3	446.3	449.1	479.2	484.5	491.9	485.7	520.3
2007	482.1	470.6	458.9	427.2	417.3	411.5	430.3	467.7	480.9	486.7	488.0	475.3
2008	482.5	450.8	436.5	426.7	416.4	420.4	428.1	430.8	441.2	454.5	471.0	481.6
2009	492.6	462.5	435.5	425.9	410.7	417.9	434.8	444.8	420.1	428.9	427.7	430.9
2010	430.3	426.3	404.5	384.6	369.5	362.8	374.2	388.8	387.4	396.8	414.6	435.2
2011[1]	445.0	461.7	459.8	448.8	443.2	447.6	432.8	415.2	428.6	427.6	414.6	441.5

[1] Preliminary.   *Source: Economic Research Service, U.S. Department of Agriculture (ERS-USDA)*

Mercury

Mercury (symbol Hg) was known to the ancient Hindus and Chinese, and was also found in Egyptian tombs dating back to 1500 BC. The ancient Greeks used mercury in ointments, and the Romans used it in cosmetics. Alchemists thought mercury turned into gold when it hardened.

Mercury, also called quicksilver, is a heavy, silvery, toxic, transitional metal. Mercury is the only common metal that is liquid at room temperatures. When subjected to a pressure of 7,640 atmospheres (7.7 million millibars), mercury becomes a solid. Mercury dissolves in nitric or concentrated sulfuric acid, but is resistant to alkalis. It is a poor conductor of heat. Mercury has superconductivity when cooled to sufficiently low temperatures. It has a freezing point of about −39 degrees Celsius and a boiling point of about 357 degrees Celsius.

Mercury is found in its pure form or combined in small amounts with silvers, but is found most often in the ore cinnabar, a mineral consisting of mercuric sulfide. By heating the cinnabar ore in air until the mercuric sulfide breaks down, pure mercury metal is produced. Mercury forms alloys called amalgams with all common metals except iron and platinum. Most mercury is used for the manufacture of industrial chemicals and for electrical and electronic applications. Other uses for mercury include its use in gold recovery from ores, barometers, diffusion pumps, laboratory instruments, mercury-vapor lamps, pesticides, batteries, and catalysts. A decline in mercury production and usage since the 1970s reflects a trend for using mercury substitutes due to its toxicity.

Prices – The average monthly price of mercury in 2011 rose by +65.4% yr/yr to $1,649.51 per flask (34.5 kilograms), which is a new record average high. In September of 2011 the monthly price had risen to $2,100.00 per flask and remained there the rest of the year.

Supply – World mine production of mercury in 2011 fell by -14.2% yr/yr to 1,930, down from the 15-year high of 2,250 metric tons in 2010. The record low of 1,150 metric tons was posted in 2006. The world's largest miners of mercury are China with 73% of world production and Kyrgyzstan with 13%. China's production in 2010 was a record high of 1,600 metric tons. China's record low of 190 metric tons was posted only 11 years ago in 2001.

Demand – The breakdown of domestic consumption of mercury by particular categories is no longer available. However, as of 1997 records showed that chlorine and caustic soda accounted for 46% of U.S. mercury consumption, followed by wiring devices and switches (17%), dental equipment (12%), electrical lighting (8%), and measuring control instruments (7%). Substitutes for mercury include lithium and composite ceramic materials.

Trade – U.S. foreign trade in mercury has been relatively small but U.S. imports of mercury in 2011 fell -45.6% yr/yr to 160 metric tons but still above 2007's 7-year low of 67 metric tons. By contrast the U.S.'s record high imports were in 1974 at 1,799 metric tons. U.S. imports were mostly from Chile and Peru. U.S. exports of mercury in 2011 fell by -56.4% to 200 metric tons, but still well above 2007's 13-year low of 84 metric tons.

World Mine Production of Mercury — In Metric Tons (1 tonne = 29.008216 flasks)

Year	Chile (byproduct)	China	Finland	Kyrgyzstan	Mexico	Morocco	Peru (exports)	Russia	Tajikistan	United States	World Total
2002	----	495	51	300	15	10	----	50	20	NA	1,980
2003	----	610	25	300	15	10	----	50	30	NA	1,730
2004	----	1,140	24	300	15	10	----	50	30	NA	1,900
2005	----	1,100	20	200	6	10	102	50	30	NA	1,520
2006	----	760	20	250	8	10	22	50	30	NA	1,150
2007	----	800	20	250	8	10	34	50	30	NA	1,200
2008	----	1,300	20	250	21	10	136	50	30	NA	1,820
2009	88	1,400	15	250	21	10	92	50	30	NA	1,960
2010[1]	176	1,600	15	250	21	10	102	50	30	NA	2,250
2011[2]	100	1,400		250	15		35				1,930

[1] Preliminary. [2] Estimate. NA = Not available. W = Withheld. Source: U.S. Geological Survey (USGS)

Salient Statistics of Mercury in the United States — In Metric Tons

Year	Producing Mines	Secondary Production — Industrial	Secondary Production — Government[3]	NDS[4] Shipments	Consumer & Dealer Stocks, Dec. 31	Industrial Demand	Exports	Imports
2003	NA	NA	----	----	94	72	287	46
2004	NA	NA	----	----	62	91	278	92
2005	NA	NA	----	----	38	40	319	212
2006	NA	NA	----	----	19	38	390	94
2007	NA	NA	----	----	18	31	84	67
2008	NA	NA	----	----	24	NA	732	155
2009	NA	NA	----	----	30	NA	753	206
2010[1]	NA	NA	----	----	30	NA	459	294
2011[2]	NA	NA	----	----			200	160

[1] Preliminary. [2] Estimate. [3] Secondary mercury shipped from the Department of Energy. [4] National Defense Stockpile. NA = Not available.
E = Net exporter. Source: U.S. Geological Survey (USGS)

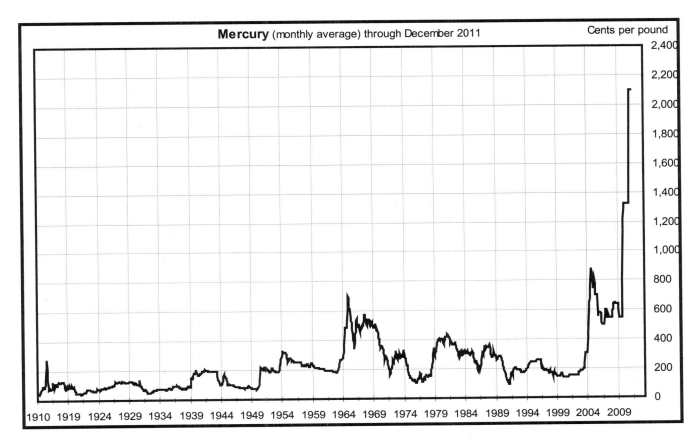

Mercury (monthly average) through December 2011 — Cents per pound

Average Price of Mercury in New York   In Dollars Per Flask of 76 Pounds (34.5 Kilograms)

Year	Jan.	Feb.	Mar.	Apr.	May	June	July	Aug.	Sept.	Oct.	Nov.	Dec.	Average
2002	154.00	154.00	154.00	154.00	154.00	154.00	154.00	154.00	154.00	154.00	154.00	154.00	154.00
2003	165.43	175.00	175.00	175.00	185.23	187.50	187.50	187.50	187.50	187.50	195.63	200.00	184.07
2004	200.00	256.25	297.61	305.00	305.00	305.00	305.00	305.00	417.05	485.12	649.24	650.00	373.36
2005	678.57	747.50	867.39	873.81	850.00	817.05	759.52	750.00	813.64	730.95	700.00	700.00	774.04
2006	700.00	700.00	691.30	552.50	574.02	582.50	582.50	582.50	582.50	576.59	513.64	500.00	594.84
2007	500.00	500.00	500.00	500.00	500.00	573.81	600.00	600.00	572.50	550.00	550.00	550.00	541.36
2008	550.00	550.00	550.00	550.00	550.00	550.00	550.00	550.00	590.91	600.00	645.00	650.00	573.83
2009	650.00	647.00	640.00	640.00	642.86	640.00	640.00	640.00	603.18	550.00	550.00	550.00	616.09
2010	550.00	550.00	550.00	550.00	828.57	1,129.55	1,213.64	1,293.18	1,325.00	1,325.00	1,325.00	1,325.00	997.08
2011	1,325.00	1,325.00	1,325.00	1,325.00	1,325.00	1,325.00	1,370.24	2,073.91	2,100.00	2,100.00	2,100.00	2,100.00	1,649.51

Source: American Metal Market (AMM)

Mercury Consumed in the United States   In Metric Tons

Year	Batteries[3]	Chlorine & Caustic Soda	Catalysts, Misc.	Dental Equip.	Electrical Lighting[3]	General Lab Use	Measuring Control Instrument	Paints	Wiring Devices & Switches[3]	Other Uses	Grand Total
1989	250	379	40	39	31	18	87	192	141	32	1,212
1990	106	247	29	44	33	32	108	14	70	38	720
1991	18	184	26	41	39	30	90	6	71	49	554
1992	13	209	20	42	55	28	80	----	82	92	621
1993	10	180	18	35	38	26	65	----	83	103	558
1994	6	135	25	24	27	24	53	----	79	110	483
1995	----	154	----	32	30	----	43	----	84	93	436
1996[1]	----	136	----	31	29	----	41	----	49	86	372
1997[2]	----	160	----	40	29	----	24	----	57	36	346
	Data No Longer Available										

[1] Preliminary.   [2] Estimate.   W = Withheld proprietary data.   *Source: U.S. Geological Survey (USGS)*

Milk

Evidence of man's use of animal milk as food was discovered in a temple in the Euphrates Valley near Babylon, dating back to 3,000 BC. Humans drink the milk produced from a variety of domesticated mammals, including cows, goats, sheep, camels, reindeer, buffaloes, and llama. In India, half of all milk consumed is from water buffalo. Camels' milk spoils slower than other types of milk in the hot desert, but the vast majority of milk used for commercial production and consumption comes from cows.

Milk directly from a cow in its natural form is called raw milk. Raw milk is processed by spinning it in a centrifuge, homogenizing it to create a consistent texture (i.e., by forcing hot milk under high pressure through small nozzles), and then sterilizing it through pasteurization (i.e., heating to a high temperature for a specified length of time to destroy pathogenic bacteria). Condensed, powdered, and evaporated milk are produced by evaporating some or all of the water content. Whole milk contains 3.5% milk fat. Lower-fat milks include 2% low-fat milk, 1% low- fat milk, and skim milk, which has only 1/2 gram of milk fat per serving.

The Chicago Mercantile Exchange has three different milk futures contracts: Milk Class III which is milk used in the manufacturing of cheese, Milk Class IV which is milk used in the production of butter and all dried milk products, and Nonfat Dry Milk which is used in commercial or consumer cooking or to reconstitute nonfat milk by the consumer. The Milk Class III contract has the largest volume and open interest.

Prices – The average monthly price received by farmers for all milk sold to plants in 2011 rose by +24% yr/yr to a new record annual high of $20.14 per hundred pounds.

Supply – World milk production in 2012 is expected to rise +1.8% to 460.425 million metric tons. The biggest producers will be the European Union with 30.2% of world production, the U.S. with 19.6%, and India with 12.0%. U.S. 2012 milk production in pounds is expected to rise +3.6% yr/yr to 203.340 billion pounds, setting a new record high. The number of dairy cows on U.S. farms has fallen sharply in the past 3 decades from the 12 million seen in 1970. In 2012, there is expected to be 9.236 million dairy cows on U.S. farms, up +0.5% yr/yr. Dairy farmers have been able to increase milk production even with fewer cows because of a dramatic increase in milk yield per cow. In 2012, the average cow is expected to produce a record 22,020 pounds of milk per year, more than double the 9,751 pounds seen in 1970.

Demand – Per capita consumption of milk in the U.S. fell to a new record low of 204 pounds per year in 2008 (latest data), down sharply by 26% from 277 pounds in 1977. The utilization breakdown for 2002 (latest data) shows the largest manufacturing usage categories are cheese (64.504 billion pounds of milk) and creamery butter (30.250 billion pounds).

Trade – U.S. imports of milk in 2011 fell -4.9% yr/yr to 3.900 billion pounds, still well below the record high of 7.500 billion pounds posted in 2005-06.

World Fluid Milk Production (Cow's Milk)   In Thousands of Metric Tons

Year	Argentina	Australia	Brazil	China	European Union	India	Japan	Mexico	New Zealand	Russia	Ukraine	United States	World Total
2005	9,500	10,429	24,250	27,534	134,672	37,520	8,285	9,855	14,724	32,000	13,423	80,255	421,622
2006	10,200	10,395	25,230	31,934	132,206	41,000	8,137	10,051	15,337	31,100	12,890	82,455	427,850
2007	9,550	9,500	26,750	35,252	132,604	42,890	8,007	10,657	15,918	32,200	11,997	84,211	436,691
2008	10,010	9,500	27,820	34,300	133,848	44,500	7,982	10,907	15,580	32,500	11,524	86,174	435,393
2009	10,350	9,326	28,795	28,445	133,700	48,160	7,910	10,866	16,983	32,600	11,370	85,881	435,113
2010	10,600	9,327	29,948	29,300	135,435	50,300	7,721	11,033	17,173	31,900	10,977	87,461	441,960
2011[1]	11,990	9,550	30,610	30,700	137,800	52,500	7,450	10,878	18,681	31,800	10,800	88,950	452,344
2012[2]	12,450	9,750	31,300	32,150	138,950	55,000	7,500	10,975	19,130	31,900	10,550	90,038	460,425

[1] Preliminary.   [2] Forecast.   *Source: Foreign Agricultural Service, U.S. Department of Agriculture (FAS-USDA)*

Salient Statistics of Milk in the United States   In Millions of Pounds

Year	Number of Milk Cows on Farms[3] (Thousands)	Production Per Cow[4] (Pounds)	Production Total[4]	Beginning Stocks[5]	Imports	Total Supply	Exports[5]	Domestic Fed to Calves	Domestic Humans	Total Use	All Milk, Wholesale	Milk, Eligible for Fluid Market	Milk, Manufacturing Grade	Per Capita Consumption[6] (Fluid Milk in Lbs)
2004	9,010	18,958	170,805	8,333	5,278	184,416	3,400	956	169,699	174,055	16.04	16.04	15.41	207
2005	9,040	19,577	176,989	7,154	7,500	191,643	3,300	987	175,788	180,075	15.14	15.14	14.45	206
2006	9,112	19,951	181,798	8,007	7,500	197,305	3,400	943	180,700	185,043	12.91	12.92	12.28	208
2007	9,158	20,266	185,602	9,500	7,200	202,302	5,700	952	184,565	191,217	19.13	19.13	18.18	206
2008	9,315	20,396	189,992	10,356	5,300	205,648	8,700	942	188,917	198,559	18.30	18.28	17.98	204
2009	9,200	20,576	189,320	10,045	5,600	204,965	4,500	899	188,322	193,721	12.84	12.84	12.18	
2010[1]	9,117	21,149	192,819	11,334	4,100	208,253	8,100	883	191,827	200,810	16.27	16.29	14.79	
2011[2]	9,194	21,346	196,245	10,800	3,900	210,945	6,400				20.14	NA	NA	

[1] Preliminary.   [2] Estimate.   [3] Average number on farms during year including dry cows, excluding heifers not yet fresh.   [4] Excludes milk sucked by calves.   [5] Government and commercial.   [6] Product pounds of commercial sales and on farm consumption.
Source: Economic Research Service, U.S. Department of Agriculture (ERS-USDA)

Milk-Feed Price Ratio[1] in the United States   In Pounds

Year	Jan.	Feb.	Mar.	Apr.	May	June	July	Aug.	Sept.	Oct.	Nov.	Dec.	Average
2003	2.40	2.35	2.27	2.25	2.19	2.21	2.60	2.89	3.16	3.23	3.05	2.89	2.62
2004	2.70	2.60	2.80	3.11	3.15	3.12	2.96	2.93	3.22	3.27	3.57	3.67	3.09
2005	3.45	3.50	3.35	3.18	2.93	2.87	2.93	3.08	3.27	3.42	3.45	3.28	3.23
2006	3.17	2.93	2.70	2.48	2.32	2.35	2.33	2.48	2.61	2.53	2.44	2.43	2.56
2007	2.45	2.33	2.39	2.51	2.54	2.88	3.16	3.19	3.19	3.10	3.05	2.85	2.80
2008	2.65	2.24	2.07	1.88	1.81	1.88	1.90	1.81	1.90	2.02	2.01	1.92	2.01
2009	1.60	1.51	1.56	1.59	1.48	1.45	1.57	1.80	2.00	2.11	2.26	2.42	1.78
2010	2.33	2.36	2.18	2.19	2.17	2.26	2.31	2.36	2.36	2.40	2.23	1.98	2.26
2011[1]	1.96	2.01	2.14	1.83	1.73	1.88	1.92	1.84	1.84	1.82	1.87	1.81	1.89

[1] Pounds of 16% protein mixed dairy feed equal in value to one pound of whole milk.   [2] Preliminary.   *Source: Economic Research Service, U.S. Department of Agriculture (ERS-USDA)*

Milk Production[2] in the United States   In Millions of Pounds

Year	Jan.	Feb.	Mar.	Apr.	May	June	July	Aug.	Sept.	Oct.	Nov.	Dec.	Total
2003	14,584	13,441	15,044	14,634	15,003	14,328	14,263	14,015	13,468	13,898	13,470	14,164	170,394
2004	14,402	13,595	14,762	14,519	15,012	14,293	14,405	14,215	13,619	14,070	13,610	14,303	170,805
2005	14,614	13,530	15,206	15,047	15,697	15,324	15,168	15,061	14,481	14,857	14,523	15,231	181,798
2006	15,343	14,238	15,966	15,538	16,068	15,476	15,714	15,525	14,871	15,370	15,013	15,632	185,602
2007	15,605	14,321	16,132	15,763	16,180	15,942	15,995	15,757	15,129	15,615	15,212	15,900	189,992
2008	15,976	15,176	16,458	16,125	16,707	15,935	16,018	15,737	15,038	15,420	15,070	15,775	189,320
2009	16,135	14,754	16,485	16,148	16,805	16,353	16,436	16,094	15,540	15,900	15,498	16,150	192,819
2010	16,020	14,758	16,614	16,416	17,040	16,518	16,479	16,422	15,783	16,278	15,820	16,556	196,245
2011[1]	16,393	15,077	16,989	16,652	17,278	16,518	16,479	16,422	15,783	16,278	15,820	16,556	196,245

[1] Preliminary.   [2] Excludes milk sucked by calves.   *Source: Economic Research Service, U.S. Department of Agriculture (ERS-USDA)*

Milk Cows[2] in the United States   In Thousands of Head

Year	Jan.	Feb.	Mar.	Apr.	May	June	July	Aug.	Sept.	Oct.	Nov.	Dec.	Total
2003	9,147	9,145	9,141	9,125	9,104	9,097	9,087	9,072	9,061	9,034	9,005	8,994	9,083
2004	8,985	8,993	9,002	8,999	8,991	9,014	9,028	9,029	9,025	9,023	9,021	9,013	9,010
2005	9,000	8,996	9,009	9,030	9,042	9,050	9,053	9,060	9,066	9,060	9,056	9,063	9,040
2006	9,081	9,088	9,106	9,116	9,129	9,139	9,119	9,114	9,107	9,107	9,111	9,126	9,112
2007	9,135	9,136	9,142	9,132	9,138	9,144	9,153	9,159	9,166	9,181	9,196	9,217	9,158
2008	9,276	9,287	9,295	9,307	9,318	9,321	9,335	9,331	9,323	9,324	9,333	9,334	9,315
2009	9,312	9,289	9,283	9,282	9,270	9,228	9,191	9,162	9,123	9,094	9,085	9,082	9,200
2010	9,089	9,092	9,099	9,108	9,119	9,129	9,135	9,123	9,121	9,123	9,125	9,141	9,117
2011[1]	9,160	9,163	9,180	9,182	9,194	9,196	9,198	9,200	9,201	9,212	9,213	9,223	9,194

[1] Preliminary.   [2] Includes dry cows, excludes heifers not yet fresh.   *Source: Economic Research Service, U.S. Department of Agriculture (ERS-USDA)*

Milk Per Cow[2] in the United States   In Pounds

Year	Jan.	Feb.	Mar.	Apr.	May	June	July	Aug.	Sept.	Oct.	Nov.	Dec.	Total
2003	1,594	1,470	1,646	1,604	1,648	1,575	1,570	1,545	1,486	1,538	1,496	1,575	18,761
2004	1,603	1,512	1,640	1,613	1,670	1,586	1,596	1,574	1,509	1,559	1,509	1,587	18,958
2005	1,624	1,504	1,688	1,666	1,735	1,668	1,656	1,643	1,572	1,613	1,569	1,639	19,577
2006	1,690	1,567	1,753	1,705	1,760	1,676	1,663	1,653	1,590	1,631	1,594	1,669	19,951
2007	1,708	1,567	1,765	1,726	1,771	1,692	1,717	1,695	1,622	1,674	1,633	1,696	20,266
2008	1,722	1,634	1,771	1,733	1,793	1,710	1,713	1,689	1,623	1,675	1,630	1,703	20,396
2009	1,733	1,588	1,776	1,740	1,812	1,726	1,744	1,718	1,649	1,695	1,658	1,737	20,576
2010	1,763	1,623	1,826	1,802	1,869	1,791	1,799	1,764	1,704	1,743	1,698	1,767	21,149
2011[1]	1,790	1,645	1,851	1,814	1,879	1,796	1,792	1,785	1,715	1,767	1,717	1,795	21,346

[1] Preliminary.   [2] Excludes milk sucked by calves.   *Source: Economic Research Service, U.S. Department of Agriculture (ERS-USDA)*

Average Price Received by Farmers for All Milk (Sold to Plants)   In Dollars Per Hundred Pounds (Cwt.)

Year	Jan.	Feb.	Mar.	Apr.	May	June	July	Aug.	Sept.	Oct.	Nov.	Dec.	Average
2003	11.70	11.40	11.00	11.00	11.00	11.00	12.10	13.30	14.50	15.00	14.40	13.80	12.52
2004	13.20	13.60	15.40	18.10	19.30	18.20	16.10	14.90	15.50	15.60	16.20	16.40	16.04
2005	15.90	15.50	15.60	15.20	14.70	14.40	14.80	14.80	15.30	15.60	15.10	14.80	15.14
2006	14.50	13.50	12.60	12.10	11.90	11.90	11.70	12.00	13.00	13.60	13.90	14.20	12.91
2007	14.50	14.90	15.60	16.60	18.00	20.20	21.60	21.60	21.80	21.40	21.90	21.50	19.13
2008	20.50	19.10	18.10	18.00	18.30	19.30	19.30	18.40	18.20	17.80	17.10	15.50	18.30
2009	13.30	11.60	11.80	11.90	11.60	11.30	11.30	12.10	13.00	14.30	15.40	16.50	12.84
2010	16.10	15.90	14.80	14.60	15.00	15.40	15.90	16.70	17.70	18.50	17.90	16.70	16.27
2011[1]	16.70	19.10	20.40	19.60	19.60	21.20	21.90	22.00	21.10	19.90	20.40	19.80	20.14

[1] Preliminary.   *Source: Economic Research Service, U.S. Department of Agriculture (ERS-USDA)*

Molybdenum

Molybdenum (symbol Mo) is a silvery-white, hard, malleable, metallic element. Molybdenum melts at about 2,610 degrees Celsius and boils at about 4,640 degrees Celsius. Swedish chemist Carl Wilhelm Scheele discovered molybdenum in 1778.

Molybdenum occurs in nature in the form of molybdenite and wulfenite. Contributing to the growth of plants, it is an important trace element in soils. Approximately 70% of the world supply of molybdenum is obtained as a by-product of copper mining. -Molybdenum is chiefly used as an alloy to strengthen steel and resist corrosion. It is used for structural work, aircraft parts, and forged automobile parts because it withstands high temperatures and pressures and adds strength. Other uses include lubricants, a refractory metal in chemical applications, electron tubing, and as a catalyst.

Prices – The average monthly U.S. merchant price of molybdic oxide in 2011 fell by -0.9% yr/yr to $15.71 per pound. That was still far below the 2005 record high of $32.70 per pound but more than six times higher than the 2001 record low of $2.37.

Supply – World production of molybdenum in 2011 rose by +6.8% yr/yr to a record high of 250,000 metric tons.

The 18-year low of 122,000 metric tons was seen in 2002. The world's largest producers of molybdenum are China with 38% of world production in 2011, the U.S. with 26%, and Chili with 15%.

U.S. production of molybdenum concentrate in 2011 rose +7.7% yr/yr to 64,000 metric tons, well above the 29-year low of 32,300 metric tons posted in 2002. U.S. net production of molybdic oxide in 2009 (latest data available) rose +1.9% to 32,100 metric tons. U.S. net production of molybdenum metal powder is now being withheld as proprietary data but in 2008 the figure was 1,640 metric tons.

Demand – U.S. consumption of molybdenum concentrate in 2010 (latest data) rose by +57.4% yr/yr to 48,000 metric tons, remaining well above the 14-year low of 21,200 metric tons posted in 2002. U.S. consumption of molybdenum concentrate has more than doubled over the last 13 years. U.S. consumption of molybdenum primary products in 2011 fell by -1.0% yr/yr to 19,000 metric tons.

Trade – U.S. imports of molybdenum concentrate for consumption in 2009 (latest data) fell by 26.3% yr/yr to 7,520 metric tons, but still well above the 16-year low of 4,710 metric tons posted in 2002.

World Mine Production of Molybdenum   In Metric Tons (Contained Molybdenum)

Year	Armenia	Canada[3]	Chile	China	Iran	Kazak-hstan	Mexico	Mongolia	Peru	Russia	United States	Uzbek-isten	World Total
2005	3,000	7,667	48,041	40,000	2,476	230	4,246	1,188	17,325	3,000	58,000	575	186,000
2006	3,900	7,117	43,278	43,900	2,500	250	2,516	1,404	17,209	3,100	59,800	600	186,000
2007	4,080	6,819	44,912	66,700	3,600	400	6,159	1,978	16,737	3,300	57,000	600	213,000
2008	4,250	7,724	33,687	81,000	3,800	400	7,812	1,899	16,721	3,600	55,900	500	218,000
2009	4,150	8,836	34,925	93,500	3,700	380	7,800	3,000	12,295	3,800	47,800	550	221,000
2010[1]	4,200	9,100	39,000	94,000	3,700	400	8,000	3,000	12,000	3,800	56,000	550	234,000
2011[2]	4,200	8,300	38,000	94,000	3,700	360	12,000	2,000	18,000	3,800	64,000	550	250,000

[1] Preliminary.   [2] Estimate.   [3] Shipments.   *Source: U.S. Geological Survey (USGS)*

Salient Statistics of Molybdenum in the United States   In Metric Tons (Contained Molybdenum)

| | Concentrate | | | | | | | | Primary Products[4] Net Production | | Shipments | | | |
| | Shipments | | | | | | | | | | | | | |
Year	Pro-duction	Total (Including Exports)	Value Million $	For Exports	Con-sumption	Imports For Con-sumption	Stocks Dec. 31[3]	Grand Total	Molybolic Oxide[5]	Molyb-denum Metal Powder	Avg Price Value $ / Kg.[6]	To Oxide for Domestic Dest-inations	Exports, Gross Weight	Con-sumption	Producer Stocks, Dec. 31
2004	41,500	42,000	1,420.0	----	38,700	8,780	2,610	24,300	23,400	868	36.73	39,300	5,280	17,400	2,840
2005	58,000	57,900	NA	----	46,600	11,900	3,620	29,800	28,700	1,050	70.11	46,700	14,600	18,900	3,770
2006	59,800	60,100	NA	----	44,400	10,900	2,120	30,600	29,000	1,620	54.62	51,000	11,600	19,000	3,210
2007	57,000	57,100	NA	----	43,900	12,400	2,630	31,100	29,500	1,620	66.79	48,700	14,900	21,000	3,140
2008	55,900	57,800	NA	----	44,500	10,200	1,690	33,200	31,500	1,640	62.99	51,300	16,700	21,100	3,680
2009[1]	47,800	63,700	NA	----	W	7,520	2,420	W	32,100	W	25.84	43,300	10,600	17,700	3,660
2010[2]	59,400				48,000				34.83					19,200	

[1] Preliminary.   [2] Estimate.   [3] At mines & at plants making molybdenum products.   [4] Comprises ferromolybdenum, molybdic oxide, & molybdenum salts & metal.   [5] Includes molybdic oxide briquets, molybdic acid, molybdenum trioxide, all other.   [6] U.S. producer price per kilogram of molybdenum oxide contained in technical-grade molybdic oxide.   W = Withheld proprietary data.   E = Net exporter.   *Source: U.S. Geological Survey (USGS)*

US Merchant Price of Molybdic Oxide   In Dollars Per Pound

Year	Jan.	Feb.	Mar.	Apr.	May	June	July	Aug.	Sept.	Oct.	Nov.	Dec.	Average
2005	33.00	30.15	33.59	34.79	36.41	38.32	32.79	30.00	31.93	32.33	30.33	28.72	32.70
2006	23.70	24.54	23.12	22.93	24.82	26.31	26.01	25.60	26.96	26.02	25.41	25.50	25.08
2007	25.22	25.53	27.77	28.52	30.05	33.71	32.23	31.39	23.00	32.00	32.80	32.63	29.57
2008	32.74	32.88	32.88	32.88	32.88	32.88	32.88	33.17	33.75	33.75	15.58	10.62	29.74
2009	9.78	9.61	9.03	8.55	9.08	10.34	11.56	17.35	15.24	13.22	10.86	11.15	11.31
2010	14.04	15.91	17.68	17.89	17.34	14.60	14.13	15.57	16.20	15.20	15.65	16.03	15.85
2011	16.73	17.63	17.70	17.36	17.25	16.87	14.95	14.83	14.70	13.80	13.24	13.47	15.71

Source: American Metal Market (AMM)

Nickel

Nickel (symbol Ni) is a hard, malleable, ductile metal that has a silvery tinge that can take on a high polish. Nickel is somewhat ferromagnetic and is a fair conductor of heat and electricity. Nickel is primarily used in the production of stainless steel and other corrosion-resistant alloys. Nickel is used in coins to replace silver, in rechargeable batteries, and in electronic circuitry. Nickel plating techniques, like electro-less coating or single-slurry coating, are employed in such applications as turbine blades, helicopter rotors, extrusion dies, and rolled steel strip.

Nickel futures and options trade at the London Metal Exchange (LME). The nickel futures contract calls for the delivery of 6 metric tons of primary nickel with at least 99.80% purity in the form of full plate, cut cathodes, pellets or briquettes. The contract is priced in terms of U.S. dollars per metric ton.

Prices – Nickel started the year 2011 at about $24,700 per metric ton and rose rapidly to a high of $29,000 per metric ton in February. From there the price fell sharply to a low of $18,700 per metric ton by the end of 2011. The price then began to rally and hit about $20,800 per metric ton in January of 2012.

Supply – World mine production of nickel in 2011 rose +13.2% yr/yr to 1.800 million metric tons, which was a new record high. The current levels are almost triple the production seen in 1970. The world's largest mine producers of nickel in 2011 were Russia (with 16% of world production), Indonesia (13%), Canada (11%), Australia (10%), and New Caledonia (8%). In 2008 (latest data available) U.S. secondary nickel production fell -6.5% to 79,720 metric tons which was a 10 year low.

Demand – U.S. consumption of nickel in 2009 (latest data available) fell -21.1% to 101,000 metric tons, which was a 27-year low. The primary U.S. nickel consumption use is for stainless and heat-resisting steels, which accounted for 88% of U.S. consumption in 2008 (latest data). Other consumption uses in 2008 were super alloys (18%), nickel alloys (17%), electro-plating anodes (7%), alloy steels (6%), copper base alloys (4%), and chemicals (1%).

Trade – The U.S. relied on imports for 47% of its nickel consumption in 2011, down from 64% in 1998. U.S. imports of primary and secondary nickel in 2011 rose +5.7% to 161,500 metric tons, up from the 2009 record low of 117,600 metric tons. U.S. exports of primary and secondary nickel in 2011 fell -16.0% to 78,000 metric tons.

World Mine Production of Nickel   In Metric Tons (Contained Nickel)

Year	Australia[3]	Botswana	Brazil	Canada	China	Republic	Greece	Indonesia	New Caledonia	Philippines	Russia	South Africa	Total
2005	188,900	39,305	74,198	199,932	72,700	53,124	23,210	135,000	111,939	26,636	277,177	42,392	1,470,000
2006	185,000	38,000	82,492	232,948	82,100	47,516	21,670	157,000	102,986	64,705	276,985	41,599	1,570,000
2007	184,900	27,600	58,317	254,915	67,000	47,125	21,190	229,000	125,364	91,367	279,773	37,917	1,680,000
2008	199,200	28,940	67,116	259,651	72,000	31,300	18,646	192,600	102,583	80,644	266,807	31,675	1,600,000
2009	165,000	28,595	67,000	136,594	79,355	----	10,203	202,800	92,846	137,351	261,852	34,606	1,400,000
2010[1]	139,000	32,400	66,200	155,000	77,000	3,100	----	232,000	138,000	156,000	265,000	41,800	1,590,000
2011[2]	180,000	32,000	83,000	200,000	80,000	14,000	----	230,000	140,000	230,000	280,000	42,000	1,800,000

[1] Preliminary.   [2] Estimate.   [3] Content of nickel sulfate and concentrates.   *Source: U.S. Geological Survey (USGS)*

Salient Statistics of Nickel in the United States   In Metric Tons (Contained Nickel)

Year	Net Import Reliance As a % of Apparent Consumption	Production - Plant[4]	Secondary[5]	Alloy Sheets	Cast Iron	Copper Base Alloys	Electro-plating Anodes	Nickel Alloys	Stainless & Heat Resisting Steels	Super Alloys	Chemicals	Apparent Consumption	Stocks, Dec. 31 At Consumer Plants	Stocks, Dec. 31 At Producer Plants	Primary & Secondary Exports	Primary & Secondary Imports	Avg. Price LME $/Lb.
2004	49	----	99,700	3,770	306	5,990	11,900	15,400	115,000	15,700	6,270	183,000	11,380	6,580	56,300	154,800	6.27
2005	48	----	98,520	4,020	179	6,090	11,300	18,800	131,000	18,000	2,030	196,000	13,180	5,940	63,230	158,500	6.69
2006	50	----	103,360	4,170	201	7,010	10,700	19,600	136,000	20,000	1,930	208,000	14,090	6,450	67,350	173,300	11.00
2007	17	----	98,920	7,130	212	5,720	10,300	17,900	127,000	22,000	2,880	119,000	19,150	5,690	116,100	141,200	16.88
2008	33	----	85,240	8,680	232	4,930	9,560	22,200	110,400	22,900	844	128,000	19,170	5,860	106,200	149,100	9.57
2009[1]	21	----	79,720	6,300	205	2,600	11,500	19,900	104,000	12,000	1,740	101,000	17,760	6,150	97,030	117,600	6.65
2010[2]	34												22,200	6,620	92,900	152,800	9.89

[1] Exclusive of scrap.   [2] Preliminary.   [3] Estimate.   [4] Smelter & refinery.   [5] From purchased scrap (ferrous & nonferrous).
W = Withheld proprietary data.   NA = Not available.   *Source: U.S. Geological Survey (USGS)*

Average Price of Nickel[1] in the United States   In Cents Per Pound

Year	Jan.	Feb.	Mar.	Apr.	May	June	July	Aug.	Sept.	Oct.	Nov.	Dec.	Average
2007	1,734.23	1,930.47	2,172.62	2,378.64	2,476.96	2,002.41	1,618.56	1,342.03	1,425.77	1,489.95	1,477.33	1,254.00	1,775.25
2008	1,328.12	1,341.80	1,475.21	1,376.29	1,243.11	1,094.23	986.01	929.79	870.45	612.68	551.36	501.41	1,025.87
2009	575.83	535.25	501.88	567.31	610.15	720.34	766.47	950.67	860.98	912.94	862.14	850.66	726.22
2010	929.69	958.30	1,124.71	1,290.79	1,130.91	1,006.54	1,041.32	1,109.42	1,153.47	1,186.36	1,133.19	1,174.23	1,103.24
2011	1,242.88	1,361.67	1,298.06	1,275.63	1,180.33	1,090.85	1,154.75	1,077.02	1,000.59	933.70	891.56	899.85	1,117.24

[1] Plating material, briquettes.   *Source: American Metal Market (AMM)*

Oats

Oats are seeds or grains of a genus of plants that thrive in cool, moist climates. There are about 25 species of oats that grow worldwide in the cooler temperate regions. The oldest known cultivated oats were found inside caves in Switzerland and are believed to be from the Bronze Age. Oats are usually sown in early spring and harvested in mid to late summer, but in southern regions of the northern hemisphere, they may be sown in the fall. Oats are used in many processed foods such as flour, livestock feed, and furfural, a chemical used as a solvent in various refining industries. The oat crop year begins in June and ends in May. Oat futures and options are traded on the Chicago Board of Trade (CBOT).

Prices – Oat prices on the CBOT weekly nearest futures chart in early 2011 extended the rally that started in mid-2010 and posted a new 3-year high of $4.25 per bushel in March 2011. However, oat prices then slowly sank during the remainder of the year to close 2011 down -21% at $3.09 per bushel.

Regarding cash prices, the average monthly price received by farmers for oats in the U.S. in the first eight months of the 2011-12 marketing year (June/May) rose +10.3% yr/yr to $2.31 per bushel.

Supply – World oat production in 2011-12 rose +18% yr/yr to 23.204 million metric tons, moderately above the record low of 19.625 million metric tons posted in 2010/11. World annual oat production in the past three decades has dropped very sharply from levels above 50 million metric

tons in the early 1970s. The world's largest oat producers are the European Union with 34.5% of world production in 2011-12, Russia 23.0%, Canada with 12.9%, and Australia with 7.1%.

U.S. oat production in the 2011-12 marketing year fell -33.9% yr/yr to 53.649 million bushels, which is a new record low. U.S. oat production has fallen sharply from levels mostly above 1 billion bushels seen from the early 1900s into the early 1960s. U.S. farmers harvested only 939 million acres of oats in 2011-12, which was down −25.6% from the previous year and posted a new record low. That is down from the almost 40 million acres harvested back in the 1950s. The oat yield in 2011-12 fell -11.2% to 57.1 bushels per acre. Oat stocks in the U.S. as of September 2011 were down −33.0% yr/yr to a 79.391 million bushels. The largest U.S. oat-producing states in 2011 were the states of Wisconsin (with 13.3% of U.S. production), Minnesota (11.1%), North Dakota (8.2%), South Dakota (7.7%), Iowa (6.1%), and Pennsylvania (5.1%).

Demand – U.S. usage of oats in 2011-12 fell -4.5% yr/yr to 169.000 million bushels, a new record low. Regarding U.S. usage of oats in 2011-12, 53.2% was for feed and residual, 39.8% for food, alcohol and industrial, 5.2% for seed, and 1.8% for exports.

Trade – U.S. exports of oats remained unchanged at 3.0 million bushels in 2011-12. U.S. imports of oats in 2011-12 rose +8.4% yr/yr to 90.0 million bushels, below the 2007 record high of 123.29 million bushels.

World Production of Oats   In Thousands of Metric Tons

Crop Year	Argentina	Australia	Belarus	Brazil	Canada	China	European Union	Norway	Turkey	Ukraine	United States	Russia	World Total
2002-03	488	957	575	299	2,911	493	9,680	279	290	943	1,684	5,683	25,455
2003-04	332	2,018	500	435	3,377	654	9,019	333	270	941	2,096	5,169	26,359
2004-05	536	1,283	770	460	3,467	600	9,146	367	270	1,007	1,679	4,937	25,722
2005-06	350	1,690	609	522	3,283	700	7,968	279	270	791	1,667	4,545	23,927
2006-07	400	748	555	406	3,852	400	7,768	248	210	690	1,357	4,860	22,772
2007-08	472	1,502	580	238	4,696	350	8,634	276	189	544	1,313	5,384	25,454
2008-09	291	1,160	605	239	4,273	300	8,935	328	196	944	1,294	5,835	25,567
2009-10/1	182	1,162	552	253	2,906	410	8,579	245	218	731	1,351	5,401	23,320
2010-11/2	660	1,141	442	379	2,480	420	7,370	245	210	458	1,178	3,218	19,625
2011-12/3	345	1,650	800	370	3,000	420	8,013	245	210	550	779	5,334	23,204

¹ Preliminary.   ² Estimate.   ³ Forecast.   *Source: Foreign Agricultural Service, U.S. Department of Agriculture (FAS-USDA)*

Official Oats Crop Production Reports in the United States   In Thousands of Bushels

Year	July 1	Aug. 1	Sept. 1	Oct. 1	Dec. 1	Final	Year	July 1	Aug. 1	Sept. 1	Oct. 1	Dec. 1	Final
2000	151,380	152,745	----	----	----	149,165	2006	110,322	107,423	----	----	----	93,522
2001	132,150	135,445	----	----	----	117,024	2007	100,921	98,341	----	----	----	90,430
2002	147,584	142,580	----	----	----	116,002	2008	92,872	89,897	----	----	----	89,135
2003	147,895	151,345	----	----	----	144,383	2009	91,277	91,960	----	----	----	93,081
2004	121,860	127,950	----	----	----	115,695	2010	87,726	87,239	----	----	----	81,190
2005	131,314	127,819	----	----	----	114,878	2011¹	56,551	57,489	----	----	----	53,649

¹ Preliminary.   *Source: National Agricultural Statistics Service, U.S. Department of Agriculture (NASS-USDA)*

Oat Stocks in the United States   In Thousands of Bushels

	On Farms				Off Farms				Total Stocks			
Year	Mar. 1	June 1	Sept. 1	Dec. 1	Mar. 1	June 1	Sept. 1	Dec. 1	Mar. 1	June 1	Sept. 1	Dec. 1
2002	40,200	28,650	70,500	52,500	53,158	34,552	41,212	51,284	93,358	63,202	111,712	103,784
2003	35,000	20,600	82,100	64,400	47,879	29,233	49,637	54,900	82,879	49,833	131,737	119,300
2004	45,600	27,500	74,300	60,400	49,414	37,348	41,458	44,513	95,014	64,848	115,758	104,913
2005	43,500	25,350	71,700	60,100	38,946	32,592	41,803	35,617	82,446	57,942	113,503	95,717
2006	42,200	25,190	60,800	53,000	32,673	27,376	39,284	45,889	74,873	52,566	100,084	98,889
2007	33,900	18,400	53,650	43,100	37,158	32,198	34,710	51,331	71,058	50,598	88,360	94,431
2008	31,000	16,100	52,800	42,600	47,988	50,674	66,296	72,322	78,988	66,774	119,096	114,922
2009	30,200	17,480	54,500	43,000	65,250	66,619	73,875	67,629	95,450	84,099	128,375	110,629
2010	30,900	17,600	46,250	34,100	67,091	62,716	70,722	66,911	97,991	80,316	116,972	101,011
2011[1]	26,950	14,580	31,000	24,400	59,361	53,049	47,391	54,233	86,311	67,629	78,391	78,633

[1] Preliminary.   Source: National Agricultural Statistics Service, U.S. Department of Agriculture (NASS-USDA)

Supply and Utilization of Oats in the United States   In Millions of Bushels

Crop Year Beginning June 1	Acreage Planted	Harvested	Yield Per Acre	Pro-duction	Imports	Total Supply	Feed & Residual	Food, Alcohol & Industrial	Seed	Exports	Total Use	Ending Stocks	Farm Price	Findley Loan Rate	Target Price
	--- 1,000 Acres ---		(Bushels)					In Millions of Bushels					Dollars Per Bushel		
2002-03	4,995	2,058	56.4	116.0	95.1	274.3	149.9	60.2	11.8	2.6	224.5	49.8	1.81	1.35	1.40
2003-04	4,597	2,220	65.0	144.4	89.7	284.0	143.7	62.4	10.5	2.5	219.1	64.9	1.48	1.35	1.40
2004-05	4,085	1,787	64.7	115.7	90.3	270.9	136.3	63.0	11.0	2.7	212.9	57.9	1.48	1.33	1.44
2005-06	4,246	1,823	63.0	114.9	91.2	264.0	135.7	62.9	10.8	2.1	211.4	52.6	1.63	1.33	1.44
2006-07	4,168	1,566	59.8	93.5	106.2	252.3	124.9	64.5	9.7	2.6	201.7	50.6	1.87	1.33	1.44
2007-08	3,763	1,504	60.1	90.4	123.3	264.3	120.2	66.0	8.5	2.9	197.5	66.8	2.63	1.33	1.44
2008-09	3,247	1,400	63.7	89.1	114.6	270.5	108.1	66.1	8.9	3.3	186.4	84.1	3.15	1.33	1.44
2009-10	3,404	1,379	67.5	93.1	94.9	272.1	115.1	66.2	8.3	2.2	191.8	80.3	2.02	1.33	1.44
2010-11[1]	3,138	1,263	64.3	81.2	83.0	244.5	97.9	67.2	8.8	3.0	176.9	67.6	2.40-2.50	1.33	1.44
2011-12[2]	2,496	939	57.1	53.6	90.0	214.2	90.0	67.2	8.8	3.0	169.0	45.2			

[1] Preliminary.   [2] Forecast.   [3] Less than 500,000 bushels.   NA = Not available.
Source: Economic Research Service, U.S. Department of Agiculture (ERS-USDA)

Production of Oats in the United States, by States   In Thousands of Bushels

Year	Illinois	Iowa	Michigan	Minne-sota	Nebraska	New York	North Dakota	Ohio	Penn-sylvania	South Dakota	Texas	Wisconsin	Total
2002	3,285	13,300	4,160	14,840	2,365	4,160	12,600	3,355	7,015	5,400	6,160	15,000	116,002
2003	4,450	10,790	5,250	18,815	6,570	4,410	21,240	3,960	6,490	15,640	6,300	15,410	144,383
2004	2,450	10,080	4,420	13,300	3,400	3,250	14,080	3,150	6,050	13,940	6,400	13,650	115,695
2005	3,160	9,875	4,575	12,710	4,380	4,050	14,160	3,600	6,050	12,960	4,730	13,760	114,878
2006	3,080	8,360	4,030	11,200	2,025	4,958	4,920	4,125	7,040	5,415	3,700	14,490	93,522
2007	1,488	4,757	3,080	10,800	2,135	3,480	15,340	3,100	4,480	9,360	4,000	10,720	90,430
2008	2,100	4,875	3,960	11,900	2,450	4,224	6,630	3,500	4,640	8,760	5,000	11,780	89,135
2009	1,625	6,175	3,465	12,070	2,070	4,620	11,220	3,375	4,880	6,570	2,820	13,260	93,081
2010	1,950	4,340	4,080	11,385	1,700	3,886	6,405	3,500	4,720	7,560	4,160	9,860	81,190
2011[1]	1,360	3,250	1,920	5,940	1,300	1,700	4,420	2,052	2,760	4,130	2,100	7,130	53,649

[1] Preliminary.   Source: National Agricultural Statistics Service, U.S. Department of Agriculture (NASS-USDA)

Average Cash Price of No. 2 Heavy White Oats in Toledo   In Dollars Per Bushel

Year	Jan.	Feb.	Mar.	Apr.	May	June	July	Aug.	Sept.	Oct.	Nov.	Dec.	Average
1996-97	NQ	2.45	2.34	2.19	2.02	1.96	1.96	1.99	2.16	2.26	2.12	2.08	2.14
1997-98	2.12	1.79	1.84	1.80	1.77	NQ	NQ	NQ	NQ	NQ	NQ	NQ	1.86
1998-99	NQ	NQ	NQ	NQ	NQ	NQ	NQ	NQ	NQ	NQ	NQ	NQ	NQ
1999-00	NQ	NQ	NQ	NQ	NQ	NQ	NQ	NQ	NQ	NQ	NQ	NQ	NQ
2000-01	NQ	NQ	NQ	NQ	NQ	NQ	NQ	NQ	NQ	NQ	NQ	NQ	NQ
2001-02	NQ	NQ	NQ	NQ	NQ	NQ	NQ	NQ	NQ	NQ	NQ	NQ	NQ
2002-03	NQ	NQ	NQ	NQ	NQ	NQ	NQ	NQ	NQ	NQ	NQ	NQ	NQ
2003-04	NQ	NQ	NQ	NQ	NQ	NQ	NQ	NQ	NQ	NQ	NQ	NQ	NQ
2004-05	NQ	NQ	NQ	NQ	NQ	NQ	NQ	NQ	NQ	NQ	NQ	NQ	NQ
2005-06[1]	NQ	NQ	NQ										

[1] Preliminary.   NQ = No quotes.   Source: Economic Research Service, U.S. Department of Agriculture (ERS-USDA)

OATS

Volume of Trading in Oats Futures in Chicago   In Contracts

Year	Jan.	Feb.	Mar.	Apr.	May	June	July	Aug.	Sept.	Oct.	Nov.	Dec.	Total
2002	41,516	46,435	30,662	51,889	32,386	39,229	35,217	29,647	23,968	32,847	35,412	15,932	415,140
2003	26,149	31,892	27,766	26,022	20,442	24,113	23,230	21,562	26,658	33,621	30,273	27,170	318,898
2004	33,743	34,605	55,216	49,746	38,951	35,356	25,451	31,023	32,322	25,443	33,942	20,650	416,448
2005	26,439	35,921	36,808	35,199	24,696	33,748	28,353	26,134	17,708	27,080	32,687	26,766	351,539
2006	25,667	40,534	30,437	35,799	39,362	42,812	35,751	30,790	25,700	43,724	51,304	25,435	427,315
2007	42,231	41,327	41,259	46,054	31,288	43,157	32,977	30,240	24,565	29,484	48,488	21,671	432,741
2008	44,184	61,469	44,478	47,918	37,813	52,116	27,923	32,074	19,009	31,829	23,978	18,797	441,588
2009	17,494	34,259	19,035	34,277	25,365	41,961	19,370	24,801	20,076	29,720	29,328	18,619	314,305
2010	31,060	32,283	23,890	37,409	21,363	54,174	26,097	23,735	22,430	25,743	30,649	15,754	344,587
2011	28,513	41,210	32,798	35,451	25,962	42,810	17,687	26,037	24,613	23,352	41,624	9,259	349,316

Contract size = 5,000 bu.   *Source: CME Group; Chicago Board of Trade (CBT)*

Average Open Interest of Oats in Chicago   In Contracts

Year	Jan.	Feb.	Mar.	Apr.	May	June	July	Aug.	Sept.	Oct.	Nov.	Dec.
2002	12,640	13,137	11,833	10,976	9,047	10,381	10,230	10,970	9,881	9,550	9,134	6,008
2003	6,929	6,715	5,945	6,135	5,833	5,640	5,811	5,958	6,261	6,194	6,268	5,122
2004	6,284	6,314	10,018	12,988	11,903	11,339	10,293	9,153	6,669	7,010	7,753	6,724
2005	7,691	8,482	7,346	8,110	7,746	7,686	7,779	6,721	5,847	6,914	7,565	9,385
2006	10,200	11,697	10,960	10,961	13,529	14,128	13,965	11,620	11,178	13,483	14,714	13,818
2007	16,176	18,406	19,178	19,255	18,061	17,909	14,824	13,387	14,158	14,251	13,223	10,914
2008	13,696	14,812	14,764	15,097	15,957	16,802	16,667	15,027	14,740	15,495	15,108	16,848
2009	16,519	16,927	14,367	15,142	13,304	14,380	13,805	13,649	13,684	13,526	13,593	11,976
2010	12,601	13,869	15,662	17,612	17,244	16,838	10,329	10,956	11,664	13,477	13,452	11,707
2011	13,104	14,297	13,191	13,677	12,577	12,457	12,287	13,127	14,082	15,902	16,557	12,802

Contract size = 5,000 bu.   *Source: CME Group; Chicago Board of Trade (CBT)*

Oats (monthly average) through December 2011 — Cents per bushel

Average Cash Price of No. 2 Heavy White Oats in Minneapolis   In Dollars Per Bushel

Year	June	July	Aug.	Sept.	Oct.	Nov.	Dec.	Jan.	Feb.	Mar.	Apr.	May	Average
2002-03	1.40	1.24	1.23	1.36	1.36	1.33	1.36	1.44	1.28	1.28	1.22	1.08	1.30
2003-04	1.05	NQ	.98	1.01	1.00	.99	1.04	.99	1.14	1.08	1.22	1.08	1.05
2004-05	1.04	.96	.99	1.11	1.01	1.04	1.13	1.18	1.15	1.16	1.13	.99	1.07
2005-06	.99	1.20	1.12	1.09	1.16	1.16	1.37	1.33	1.29	1.23	1.25	1.33	1.21
2006-07	1.38	1.41	1.29	1.36	1.52	1.69	1.76	1.74	1.66	1.78	1.76	1.73	1.59
2007-08	1.81	1.68	1.63	1.67	NQ	1.74	2.43	2.02	2.28	3.18	2.35	2.47	2.12
2008-09	2.54	2.60	NQ	NQ	NQ	1.33	1.33	1.36	1.18	1.23	1.26	1.45	1.59
2009-10	1.46	1.35	1.33	1.27	1.46	1.60	1.60	1.53	1.43	1.37	1.31	1.19	1.41
2010-11	1.49	1.49	1.68	1.96	2.23	2.21	2.43	2.45	2.54	2.22	2.22	2.22	2.10
2011-12[1]	2.31	2.30	2.30	2.33	2.19	2.10	2.06	1.97	2.16				2.19

[1] Preliminary.   NQ = No qoute.   *Source: Economic Research Service, U.S. Department of Agriculture (ERS-USDA)*

Average Price Received by Farmers for Oats in the United States   In Dollars Per Bushel

Year	June	July	Aug.	Sept.	Oct.	Nov.	Dec.	Jan.	Feb.	Mar.	Apr.	May	Average
2002-03	1.95	1.69	1.67	1.80	1.80	1.91	1.95	2.04	2.11	2.08	1.98	1.95	1.91
2003-04	1.83	1.46	1.39	1.39	1.44	1.29	1.58	1.48	1.58	1.60	1.63	1.70	1.53
2004-05	1.61	1.36	1.32	1.42	1.45	1.51	1.60	1.64	1.67	1.73	1.65	1.64	1.55
2005-06	1.75	1.59	1.49	1.54	1.59	1.64	1.73	1.73	1.82	1.82	1.75	1.85	1.69
2006-07	1.90	1.78	1.67	1.70	1.77	2.05	2.01	2.20	2.35	2.40	2.46	2.49	2.07
2007-08	2.54	2.32	2.24	2.47	2.45	2.63	2.69	2.88	3.19	3.43	3.47	3.63	2.83
2008-09	3.56	3.44	3.16	3.29	3.26	3.00	3.12	2.77	2.69	2.77	2.37	2.64	3.01
2009-10	2.37	2.03	1.86	1.82	2.03	2.02	2.22	2.19	2.10	2.29	2.25	2.19	2.11
2010-11	2.11	2.11	2.09	2.30	2.55	3.07	2.94	3.13	3.27	3.28	3.53	3.55	2.83
2011-12[1]	3.41	3.35	3.19	3.67	3.70	3.36	3.57	3.56	3.66				3.50

[1] Preliminary.   *Source: National Agricultural Statistics Service, U.S. Department of Agriculture (NASS-USDA)*

Olive Oil

Olive oil is derived from the fruit of the olive tree and originated in the Mediterranean area. Olives designated for oil are picked before ripening in the fall. Olive picking is usually done by hand. The olives are then weighed and washed in cold water. The olives, along with their oil-rich pits, are then crushed and kneaded until a homogeneous paste is formed. The paste is spread by hand onto metal plates, which are then stacked and pressed hydraulically to yield a liquid. The liquid is then centrifuged to separate the oil. It takes 1,300 to 2,000 olives to produce 1 quart of olive oil. The best olive oil is still produced from the first pressing, which is usually performed within 24 to 72 hours after harvest and is called extra virgin olive oil.

Supply – World production of olive oil (pressed oil) in the marketing year 2010-11 rose +2.7% to 3.390 million metric tons, which was a new record high. The world's largest producers of olive oil in 2010-11 were Spain (with 44.6% of world production), Italy (15.9%), Greece (10.7%), Syria (6.1%), Turkey (5.0%), and Morocco (4.8%). Production levels in the various countries vary considerable from year-to-year depending on various weather and crop conditions.

Demand – World consumption of olive oil in the 2010-11 marketing year rose +2.1% yr/yr to a new record high of 3.250 million metric tons. The U.S. is the world's largest consumer of olive oil with 8.6% of world consumption in 2010-11. The U.S. consumption of olive oil set a new record high of 278,000 metric tons.

Trade – World olive oil imports in 2010-11 rose +8.3% to 800,000 metric tons. The U.S. was the world's largest importer in 2010-11 with 280,000 metric tons, representing 35.0% of world imports. World olive oil exports in 2010-11 rose +6.4% to 790,000 metric tons. The world's largest exporters were Spain (with 26.6% of world exports), Italy (22.8%), Tunisia (14.4%), and Turkey (5.1%).

World Production of Olive Oil (Pressed Oil) In Thousands of Metric Tons

Crop Year	Algeria	Argentina	Greece	Italy	Jordan	Libya	Morocco	Portugal	Spain	Syria	Tunisia	Turkey	World Total
2002-03	15.0	11.0	449.0	620.0	30.0	6.5	48.5	31.9	949.4	184.5	76.0	187.0	2,698.0
2003-04	69.5	13.5	332.0	470.0	21.0	6.5	110.0	38.2	1,566.0	121.5	296.0	80.0	3,178.1
2004-05	33.5	18.0	470.0	785.0	49.0	12.5	54.0	46.7	1,034.0	195.0	139.5	157.0	3,077.6
2005-06	32.0	23.0	455.5	635.0	23.0	9.0	81.0	35.5	887.0	110.0	236.5	119.0	2,711.6
2006-07	21.5	15.0	398.0	532.0	39.0	11.0	81.0	51.3	1,139.0	171.5	172.5	174.5	2,916.7
2007-08	24.0	27.0	353.2	553.0	22.5	13.0	92.0	39.3	1,280.0	111.0	183.0	79.0	2,880.0
2008-09[1]	61.5	23.0	329.0	586.0	20.0	15.0	92.0	57.0	1,125.3	142.0	179.0	140.0	2,888.0
2009-10[2]	26.5	16.0	346.0	565.0	29.5	15.0	173.0	63.7	1,475.0	163.0	170.0	157.0	3,300.0
2010-11[3]	48.0	17.5	363.0	515.0	22.0	15.0	163.5	72.5	1,512.0	206.5	140.0	171.0	3,390.0

[1] Preliminary. [2] Estimate. [3] Forecast. *Source: The Oil World*

World Imports and Exports of Olive Oil (Pressed Oil) In Thousands of Metric Tons

Crop Year	Australia	Brazil	Italy	Japan	Spain	United States	World Total	Greece	Italy	Spain	Tunisia	Turkey	World Total
	---- Imports ----							---- Exports ----					
2002-03	32.0	21.1	70.1	31.4	16.6	220.1	536.5	10.4	197.3	118.4	42.9	60.8	532.9
2003-04	30.5	23.2	178.2	33.1	49.1	244.8	721.6	9.3	199.9	123.0	197.0	55.9	725.9
2004-05	28.9	25.7	154.6	32.8	40.7	248.7	719.1	8.9	217.0	125.1	128.3	88.4	734.2
2005-06	32.7	26.0	136.6	30.2	51.1	242.0	700.9	9.8	203.6	114.6	123.3	56.0	686.1
2006-07	42.1	36.6	154.1	32.0	71.3	262.5	801.6	17.8	208.6	148.5	220.7	47.2	804.2
2007-08	27.8	42.9	119.4	30.4	41.8	264.5	738.0	12.0	197.9	158.8	187.4	18.3	740.0
2008-09[1]	29.0	41.4	82.6	33.3	12.1	276.5	714.7	13.7	196.6	179.5	152.2	27.9	720.1
2009-10[2]	35.6	51.3	56.7	42.6	17.9	272.0	738.7	14.2	214.6	208.7	108.6	27.2	742.4
2010-11[3]	34.0	53.0	106.0	44.0	18.0	280.0	800.0	18.0	180.0	210.0	114.0	40.0	790.0

[1] Preliminary. [2] Estimate. [3] Forecast. *Source: The Oil World*

World Consumption and Ending Stocks of Olive Oil (Pressed Oil) In Thousands of Metric Tons

Crop Year	Brazil	Morocco	Syria	Tunisia	Turkey	United States	World Total	European Union	Morocco	Syria	Tunisia	Turkey	World Total
	---- Consumption ----							---- Ending Stocks ----					
2002-03	21.1	64.2	117.7	31.7	91.6	218.7	2,797.3	535.0	19.0	130.9	4.6	47.0	799.6
2003-04	23.2	69.8	133.4	59.2	61.8	225.3	2,924.9	791.0	35.0	95.0	45.0	10.0	1,048.6
2004-05	25.7	62.4	142.8	40.9	65.7	235.9	2,918.6	964.7	11.0	105.0	42.0	13.0	1,219.1
2005-06	26.0	60.4	117.8	46.2	68.1	232.7	2,865.6	863.4	3.0	55.0	110.0	8.0	1,079.9
2006-07	36.6	71.8	128.3	26.8	90.3	244.2	3,003.8	782.3	14.0	43.0	38.0	45.0	990.2
2007-08	42.9	77.9	105.2	28.1	97.8	258.7	3,039.0	728.3	25.0	5.0	8.0	8.0	829.2
2008-09[1]	41.4	92.8	111.0	30.8	105.2	266.3	3,079.4	477.0	34.0	8.0	8.0	15.0	632.4
2009-10[2]	51.3	103.9	120.5	35.9	116.8	272.0	3,184.5	495.1	93.0	20.0	35.0	28.0	744.2
2010-11[3]	53.0	109.5	130.0	36.0	125.0	278.0	3,250.0	599.7	115.0	37.5	27.0	34.0	894.2

[1] Preliminary. [2] Estimate. [3] Forecast. *Source: The Oil World*

Onions

Onions are the bulbs of plants in the lily family. Onions can be eaten raw, cooked, pickled, used as a flavoring or seasoning, or dehydrated. Onions rank in the top 10 vegetables produced in the U.S. in terms of dollar value. Since 1629, onions have been cultivated in the U.S., but are believed to be indigenous to Asia.

The two main types of onions produced in the U.S. are yellow and white onions. Yellow varieties comprise approximately 75% of all onions grown for bulb production in the U.S. Onions that are planted as a winter crop in warm areas are milder in taste and odor than onions planted during the summer in cooler regions.

Prices – Onion prices in 2011 averaged $12.20 per hundred pounds, down -43.5% from $21.60 in 2010. Monthly onion prices were weak in early 2011 at a low of $6.79 per hundred pounds in March, moved up to a high of $20.00 in June, but then faded to end the year at $9.48 per hundred pounds.

Supply – U.S. production in 2011 rose +2.1% to 7.517 billion pounds, still below the 2004 record high of 8.307 billion pounds. The farm value of the U.S. production crop in 2010 rose +9.6% to $1.154 million, down from the 2006 record high of $1.084 billion. U.S. farmers harvested a 17-year low of 149.160 acres in 2011, down –0.7% yr/yr. The yield per acre in 2011 was 504 pounds per acre.

Demand – U.S. per capita consumption of onions in 2011 remained unchanged at 21.3 pounds.

Trade – U.S. exports of fresh onions in 2009 (latest data) totaled 561 million pounds, and imports totaled 681 million pounds.

Salient Statistics of Onions in the United States

Crop Year	Harvested Acres	Yield Per Acre	Pro- duction 1,000 Cwt.	Price Per Cwt.	Farm Value $1,000	Jan. 1 Pack Frozen	Anual Pack Frozen	Imports Canned	Exports (Fresh)	Imports (Fresh)	Per Capita[3] Utilization -- Lbs., Farm Weight -- All	Fresh
							In Millions of Pounds					
2005	165,220	445	73,504	12.40	848,798	39.9	----	22.9	667.2	659.2	22.0	20.9
2006	163,780	444	73,066	16.10	1,084,099	48.1	----	19.7	658.8	643.2	21.7	19.9
2007	160,080	497	79,638	11.10	816,061	44.9	----	14.0	550.8	902.5	22.6	21.6
2008	153,490	489	75,120	11.90	834,386	39.4	----	19.7	612.2	714.2	21.7	20.2
2009	151,060	500	75,599	15.00	1,054,227	36.2	----	18.9	561.2	681.6	21.5	19.6
2010[1]	149,270	493	73,599	15.60	1,049,704	39.0	----	17.7	713.8	862.7	21.4	19.9
2011[2]	149,160	504	75,173	11.20	762,143	37.5					21.4	19.9

[1] Preliminary. [2] Forecast. [3] Includes fresh and processing. *Source: Economic Research Service, U.S. Department of Agiculture (ERS-USDA)*

Production of Onions in the United States   In Thousands of Hundredweight (Cwt.)

| | | ----- Spring ----- | | | ----- Summer ----- | | | | | | | | | | |
Crop Year	Arizona	Cali- fornia	Texas	Total (All)	Cali- fornia	Colo- rado	Idaho	Mich- igan	Minne- sota	Mexico	New York	Oregon, Malheur	Texas	Total (All)	Grand Total
2005	920	3,800	4,650	11,575	12,240	4,180	6,080	754	----	----	3,808	7,360	----	61,929	73,504
2006	490	3,279	4,104	11,128	13,515	3,800	5,076	650	----	----	4,224	6,084	----	62,049	73,177
2007	495	3,015	3,120	9,870	12,325	3,157	6,825	988	----	----	3,780	9,828	----	69,768	79,638
2008	660	2,860	2,403	9,498	13,303	2,850	6,192	1,008	----	----	4,141	8,662	----	65,622	75,120
2009	576	2,460	3,003	8,523	14,287	2,739	6,512	1,330	----	----	4,275	7,840	----	67,076	75,599
2010	----	2,542	2,666	7,484	13,050	2,880	6,840	880	----	----	3,087	8,588	----	66,115	73,599
2011[1]	----	2,520	4,144	9,629	12,980	2,988	6,900	925	----	----	2,952	8,475	----	65,544	75,173

[1] Preliminary. *Source: Agricultural Statistics Board, U.S. Department of Agiculture (ASB-USDA)*

Cold Storage Stocks of Frozen[2] Onions in the United States, on First of Month   In Thousands of Pounds

Year	Jan.	Feb.	Mar.	Apr.	May	June	July	Aug.	Sept.	Oct.	Nov.	Dec.
2006	48,106	52,207	55,141	54,638	54,276	53,331	45,724	43,707	47,176	47,636	50,175	48,731
2007	44,919	42,027	45,810	46,244	40,350	32,240	34,663	30,966	36,734	39,096	37,653	37,929
2008	39,438	40,120	43,487	44,181	39,503	42,726	45,115	41,242	42,324	42,786	41,006	40,102
2009	36,192	35,247	34,714	32,696	32,860	33,258	31,005	31,252	34,647	36,935	40,862	42,488
2010	38,967	38,348	35,231	29,333	26,484	25,109	25,119	23,805	30,594	32,146	29,197	30,444
2011[1]	37,504	33,942	34,401	38,114	49,076	58,596	53,773	56,913	68,638	74,735	58,109	68,618

[1] Preliminary. *Source: National Agricultural Statistics Service, U.S. Department of Agiculture (NASS-USDA)*

Average Price Received by Growers for Onions in the United States   In Dollars Per Hundred Pounds (Cwt.)

Year	Jan.	Feb.	Mar.	Apr.	May	June	July	Aug.	Sept.	Oct.	Nov.	Dec.	Season Average
2006	11.70	8.04	7.45	15.10	15.60	17.00	16.80	13.70	12.30	10.90	11.10	16.60	16.10
2007	22.10	26.20	35.00	55.20	24.20	24.60	15.40	10.80	5.57	4.47	4.70	4.39	11.10
2008	4.13	3.15	2.53	10.60	23.90	17.60	13.10	8.52	10.50	10.70	10.50	13.40	11.90
2009	9.47	8.44	6.99	18.40	13.40	18.00	10.80	8.56	9.27	8.19	7.93	7.83	15.00
2010	11.20	15.00	34.20	29.90	19.30	16.10	16.30	13.10	11.70	9.61	12.10	11.60	15.60
2011[1]	12.40	9.97	6.79	8.43	17.90	20.00	18.90	13.20	10.40	9.50	9.47	9.48	11.20

[1] Preliminary. *Source: Economic Research Service, U.S. Department of Agiculture (ERS-USDA)*

Oranges and Orange Juice

The orange tree is a semi-tropical, non-deciduous tree, and the fruit is technically a hesperidium, a kind of berry. The three major varieties of oranges include the sweet orange, the sour orange, and the mandarin orange (or tangerine). In the U.S., only sweet oranges are grown commercially. Those include Hamlin, Jaffa, navel, Pineapple, blood orange, and Valencia. Sour oranges are mainly used in marmalade and in liqueurs such as triple sec and curacao.

Frozen Concentrated Orange Juice (FCOJ) was developed in 1945, which led to oranges becoming the main fruit crop in the U.S.. The world's largest producer of orange juice is Brazil, followed by Florida. Two to four medium-sized oranges will produce about 1 cup of juice, and modern mechanical extractors can remove the juice from 400 to 700 oranges per minute. Before juice extraction, orange oil is recovered from the peel. Approximately 50% of the orange weight is juice, the remainder is peel, pulp, and seeds, which are dried to produce nutritious cattle feed.

The U.S. marketing year for oranges begins December 1 of the first year shown (e.g., the 2005-06 marketing year extends from December 1, 2005 to November 30, 2006). Orange juice futures prices are subject to upward spikes during the U.S. hurricane season (officially June 1 to November 30), and the Florida freeze season (late-November through March).

Frozen concentrated orange juice future and options are traded on the ICE Futures U.S. (ICE) exchange. The ICE orange juice futures contract calls for the delivery of 15,000 pounds of orange solids and is priced in terms of cents per pound.

Prices – ICE orange juice futures prices in 2011 traded sideways to higher into April when they pushed up to a 4-year high of 205.50 cents on the worst drought in Florida in a decade. The USDA also said Florida's orange-crop acreage fell to a 25-year low of 473,086 acres in 2010 as the number of orange trees declined 2% y/y to 62.5 million because of citrus canker. FCOJ prices fell back to a 1-year low of 148.50 cents in September 2011 after Brazil, the world's leading orange grower, said its orange output would increase 17% y/y to 377.1 million boxes. Orange juice prices finished 2011 down -2% at 169.00 cents. FCOJ prices then exploded higher in January 2012 to a record 226.95 cents after the USDA stopped juice imports into the US to check for the banned fungicide carbendazim.

Supply – World production of oranges in the 2011-12 marketing year fell -4.0% y/y to 51.352 million metric tons, down from the 2008-09 record high of 51.751 million metric tons. The world's largest producers of oranges in 2011-12 were Brazil with 35.4% of world production, followed by the U.S. (15.8%), and Mexico (6.2%).

U.S. production of oranges in 2010-11 (latest data) rose +5.7% y/y to 203.749 million boxes (1 box equals 90 lbs.) Florida's production in 2010-11 rose +5.0% y/y to 140.300 million boxes and California's production rose +7.0% to 61.500 million boxes.

World Production of Oranges   In Thousands of Metric Tons

Year	Argentina	Australia	Brazil	Egypt	Greece	Italy	Mexico	Morocco	South Africa	Spain	Turkey	United States	World Total
2002-03	700	407	15,382	1,767	1,145	1,723	3,734	800	1,148	2,950	1,250	10,527	45,862
2003-04	750	453	19,054	1,850	550	1,835	3,901	705	1,113	3,052	1,250	11,734	50,915
2004-05	770	547	16,565	1,940	764	2,105	4,000	813	1,038	2,691	1,300	8,419	45,658
2005-06	840	470	17,993	2,120	1,017	2,261	4,157	784	1,167	2,376	1,445	8,212	47,773
2006-07	990	419	18,482	2,054	----	----	4,248	721	1,412	----	1,536	6,917	49,554
2007-08	940	403	16,850	2,138	----	----	4,297	732	1,526	----	1,427	9,141	50,720
2008-09	900	430	17,014	2,372	----	----	4,193	790	1,445	----	1,430	8,281	50,568
2009-10[1]	770	380	15,422	2,401	----	----	4,051	823	1,428	----	1,690	7,479	48,478
2010-11[2]	580	440	20,645	2,430	----	----	4,100	904	1,350	----	1,710	8,035	53,481
2011-12[3]	750	440	18,155	2,350	----	----	3,200	949	1,400	----	1,730	8,150	51,352

[1] Preliminary.   [2] Estimate.   [3] Forecast.   NA = Not available.   *Source: Foreign Agricultural Service, U.S. Department of Agriculture (FAS-USDA)*

Salient Statistics of Oranges & Orange Juice in the United States

	Production[4]				Florida Crop Processed					Frozen Concentrated Orange Juice - Florida			
Year	California	Florida	Total U.S.	Farm Price $ Per Box	Farm Value Million $	Frozen Concentrates	Chilled Products	Total Pro-cessed	Yield Per Box Gallons[5]	Carry-in	Pack	Total Supply	Total Season Movement
	Million Boxes				Million $	Million Boxes				In Millions of Gallons (42 Deg. Brix)			
2001-02	51.5	230.0	283.8	6.37	1,846.2	136.0	85.9	223.2	1.6	128.3	253.2	381.5	249.9
2002-03	62.0	203.0	267.0	5.80	1,564.7	102.1	92.5	196.0	1.5	120.2	203.3	323.5	200.1
2003-04	50.5	242.0	294.6	5.88	1,774.5	139.7	93.4	233.6	1.6	124.0	249.7	373.7	213.8
2004-05	64.5	149.8	216.5	6.68	1,475.4	54.3	88.5	143.9	1.6	151.8	86.3	238.1	175.2
2005-06	61.0	147.7	210.8	8.60	1,829.9	51.9	88.7	141.7	1.6	107.8	85.2	193.0	160.8
2006-07	46.0	129.0	177.3	12.56	2,216.5	48.0	74.5	123.4	1.6	67.2	79.6	146.8	149.2
2007-08	62.0	170.2	234.4	9.36	2,198.8	80.8	84.7	165.5	1.7	52.1	135.6	187.7	137.7
2008-09[1]	46.5	162.5	210.7	9.22	1,970.1	72.5	82.6	156.2	1.7	108.1	121.5	229.6	143.9
2009-10[2]	57.5	133.7	192.8	10.25	1,999.2	52.7	74.9	128.2	1.6	118.0	82.3	200.3	130.2
2010-11[3]	61.5	140.3	203.7	9.68	197.4	51.8	82.6	135.1	1.6	95.0	105.1	200.1	148.5

[1] Preliminary.   [2] Estimate.   [3] Forecast.   4/ Fruit ripened on trees, but destroyed prior to picking not included.   [5] 42 deg. Brix equivalent.
Source: Economic Research Service, U.S. Department of Agriculture (ERS-USDA); Florida Department of Citrus

Frozen Concentrate Orange Juice - ICE Futures U.S.
(weekly close) as December 30, 2011

Cents per pound

Average Open Interest of Frozen Concentrated Orange Juice Futures in New York   In Contracts

Year	Jan.	Feb.	Mar.	Apr.	May	June	July	Aug.	Sept.	Oct.	Nov.	Dec.
2002	15,716	16,593	18,515	22,328	23,498	26,581	28,137	33,206	27,323	23,758	22,651	23,461
2003	25,080	26,588	22,707	21,466	20,634	23,794	25,467	26,518	27,788	30,767	31,575	36,336
2004	36,079	35,325	32,806	36,112	34,704	42,299	39,970	38,259	39,877	38,990	33,342	36,072
2005	33,821	33,619	30,008	32,523	26,171	28,730	32,221	29,034	23,603	28,602	34,966	35,795
2006	30,485	35,479	36,603	36,617	34,418	29,180	27,169	29,872	29,515	30,852	29,873	28,342
2007	29,484	28,370	32,312	29,430	28,830	31,917	30,457	29,540	28,335	29,599	26,608	27,412
2008	24,919	26,603	29,806	32,831	32,102	33,136	28,353	31,133	29,112	31,060	28,254	28,802
2009	27,889	28,234	26,905	27,982	29,370	31,608	30,602	31,281	28,806	30,805	29,677	34,210
2010	35,442	34,435	35,991	31,854	29,524	29,143	26,424	27,037	27,400	29,340	28,707	29,996
2011	31,885	31,086	27,618	27,153	31,594	36,039	35,046	28,253	23,967	25,308	27,118	27,105

Contract size = 15,000 lbs.   *Source: ICE Futures U.S. (ICE)*

Volume of Trading of Frozen Concentrated Orange Juice Futures in New York   In Contracts

Year	Jan.	Feb.	Mar.	Apr.	May	June	July	Aug.	Sept.	Oct.	Nov.	Dec.	Total
2002	31,709	50,898	30,316	58,644	37,283	52,238	45,316	78,111	36,053	71,635	24,111	61,443	577,757
2003	45,945	63,224	23,926	70,846	35,791	64,209	27,056	73,792	40,782	87,055	42,084	78,005	652,715
2004	52,908	86,600	41,941	99,532	45,741	123,815	105,220	118,021	65,655	89,064	56,502	85,438	970,437
2005	54,140	85,349	57,557	87,595	40,785	94,913	61,610	92,195	46,868	117,355	50,098	113,574	902,039
2006	65,978	98,034	82,293	92,312	73,517	87,429	63,429	84,160	50,871	95,955	54,975	74,743	923,696
2007	70,773	84,076	63,417	87,759	59,937	84,150	50,721	78,502	48,392	103,218	45,539	69,308	845,792
2008	57,421	78,860	52,166	80,331	43,942	70,780	51,859	67,402	41,353	78,327	29,013	59,058	710,512
2009	28,514	63,757	31,766	67,156	30,396	81,964	56,197	65,286	40,276	86,071	28,426	77,186	656,995
2010	55,002	62,671	42,726	73,654	36,599	63,734	37,098	64,224	50,953	72,996	34,959	96,967	691,583
2011	39,184	63,134	43,077	63,680	41,142	89,150	28,260	80,733	32,920	59,502	24,493	62,335	627,610

Contract size = 15,000 lbs.   *Source: ICE Futures U.S. (ICE)*

ORANGES AND ORANGE JUICE

Cold Storage Stocks of Orange Juice Concentrate[2] in the U.S., on First of Month — In Millions of Pounds

Year	Jan.	Feb.	Mar.	Apr.	May	June	July	Aug.	Sept.	Oct.	Nov.	Dec.
2002	1,571.7	1,721.3	1,770.9	1,794.4	1,886.0	1,982.8	1,934.0	1,870.9	1,680.9	1,543.6	1,409.6	1,471.2
2003	1,673.6	1,851.9	1,833.4	1,856.6	1,936.8	2,102.6	2,021.2	1,848.9	1,672.2	1,529.9	1,335.6	1,428.5
2004	1,585.8	1,613.0	1,646.1	1,790.5	1,987.6	2,128.7	2,075.7	1,953.4	1,823.3	1,644.2	1,516.8	1,458.0
2005	1,468.8	1,553.8	1,578.9	1,578.2	1,652.4	1,668.1	1,548.8	1,501.6	1,397.3	1,243.3	1,139.9	1,027.5
2006	1,044.7	1,065.9	1,076.8	1,005.7	1,087.5	1,157.7	1,104.1	1,002.6	888.8	776.0	714.3	650.3
2007	678.2	726.0	751.1	825.1	901.5	960.7	909.7	849.1	761.2	620.4	582.2	563.7
2008	682.5	837.8	942.4	1,031.9	1,210.6	1,442.7	1,514.9	1,424.9	1,319.4	1,199.7	1,086.0	1,034.6
2009	1,088.0	1,193.2	1,261.2	1,291.4	1,415.4	1,497.2	1,519.7	1,404.3	1,316.7	1,252.2	1,150.3	1,127.2
2010	1,185.2	1,289.7	1,300.4	1,305.1	1,377.6	1,434.2	1,353.1	1,235.7	1,133.9	1,036.8	903.6	795.3
2011[1]	809.7	834.7	869.2	842.0	835.2	864.5	797.3	732.0	641.5	588.9	522.3	479.6

[1] Preliminary.　[2] Adjusted to 42.0 degrees Brix equivalent (9.896 pounds per gallon).　Source: Agricultural Statistics Board, U.S. Department of Agriculture (ASB-USDA)

Producer Price Index of Frozen Orange Juice Concentrate — 1982 = 100

Year	Jan.	Feb.	Mar.	Apr.	May	June	July	Aug.	Sept.	Oct.	Nov.	Dec.	Average
2002	103.0	102.9	103.1	102.9	102.8	103.2	103.2	103.5	107.4	107.4	109.7	110.2	104.9
2003	110.2	110.2	110.7	110.4	108.5	109.4	109.1	108.9	107.1	106.6	105.1	103.0	108.3
2004	103.4	103.2	102.7	101.6	101.6	101.6	98.9	98.9	98.9	98.9	103.3	103.3	101.4
2005	103.3	103.3	105.0	109.0	109.0	109.0	109.3	109.3	108.1	107.9	108.4	126.4	109.0
2006	138.3	142.1	150.1	160.9	161.0	164.1	172.3	174.8	185.4	197.6	208.9	208.7	172.0
2007	198.1	191.7	198.5	179.6	187.7	184.1	173.6	171.5	152.9	159.3	162.6	168.2	177.3
2008	168.0	166.6	160.0	159.2	159.3	159.6	126.0	121.8	121.4	116.8	115.2	124.3	141.5
2009	124.6	124.4	124.4	117.6	125.0	118.0	118.0	119.8	119.1	119.0	119.0	128.8	121.5
2010	141.3	141.1	141.5	144.5	144.5	144.5	144.7	145.0	150.0	150.4	150.4	150.6	145.7
2011[1]	164.1	163.9	163.9	169.6	169.8	170.4	170.8	188.8	187.6	181.7	190.5	175.7	174.7

[1] Preliminary.　NA = Not avaliable.　Source: Bureau of Labor Statistics, U.S. Department of Labor (BLS)

Average Price Received by Farmers for Oranges (Equivalent On-Tree) in the U.S. — In Dollars Per Box

Year	Jan.	Feb.	Mar.	Apr.	May	June	July	Aug.	Sept.	Oct.	Nov.	Dec.	Average
2002	3.75	4.05	4.64	4.65	4.47	4.00	4.06	6.61	5.33	5.18	3.11	3.23	4.42
2003	3.00	3.14	4.17	4.43	4.43	4.41	3.91	4.27	2.80	2.78	2.32	2.55	3.52
2004	2.45	3.02	3.68	3.68	3.60	4.13	8.85	8.49	15.85	20.87	5.34	3.27	6.94
2005	3.39	3.69	4.84	4.80	5.11	5.43	6.55	4.90	4.29	4.04	5.90	4.46	4.78
2006	5.16	5.27	5.78	6.44	7.13	7.05	6.56	12.03	17.96	13.89	6.95	7.28	8.46
2007	8.25	8.11	10.58	10.62	11.12	11.07	8.95	8.81	7.84	9.60	8.14	5.80	9.07
2008	5.77	5.83	6.20	6.40	7.01	6.75	5.79	4.78	5.92	5.57	7.53	5.39	6.08
2009	5.74	6.04	7.08	6.54	6.61	7.04	7.38	8.58	W	W	11.61	6.13	7.28
2010	6.41	6.78	7.97	7.49	8.00	8.85	7.10	7.49	6.88	6.96	11.47	6.66	7.67
2011[1]	6.58	6.50	6.69	7.01	7.45	8.12	7.74	9.58	8.44	8.26	9.95	7.02	7.78

[1] Preliminary.　Source: Economic Research Service, U.S. Department of Agriculture (ERS-USDA)

Oranges (monthly average) through December 2011 — USD per box

Palm Oil

Palm oil is an edible vegetable oil produced from the flesh of the fruit of the oil palm tree. The oil palm tree is a tropical palm tree that is a native of the west coast of Africa and is different from the coconut palm tree. The fruit of the oil palm tree is reddish, about the size of a large plum, and grows in large bunches. A single seed, the palm kernel, is contained in each fruit. Oil is extracted from both the pulp of the fruit (becoming palm oil) and the kernel (palm kernel oil). About 1 metric ton of palm kernel oil is obtained for every 10 metric tons of palm oil.

Palm oil is commercially used in soap, ointments, cosmetics, detergents, and machinery lubricants. It is also used worldwide as cooking oil, shortening, and margarine. Palm kernel oil is a lighter oil and is used exclusively for food use. Crude palm oil and crude palm kernel oil are traded on the Kuala Lumpur Commodity Exchange.

Prices – The monthly average wholesale price of palm oil (CIF, bulk, U.S. ports) in 2010 rose by +29.7% yr/yr to 43.93 cents per pound, below the 2008 record high of 48.09 cents per pound.

Supply – World production of palm oil in the 2011-12 marketing year rose by +5.5% to 50.566 million metric tons. World palm oil production has grown by over twenty times the production level of 1.922 million metric tons seen back in 1970. Indonesia and Malaysia are the world's two major global producers of palm oil. Indonesian production rose +7.6% to a record high of 25.400 million metric tons in 2011-12 and Indonesian production accounted for 50.3% of world production. Malaysian production in 2011-12 rose +2.7% to a record high of 18.700 million metric tons and Malaysian production accounted for 37.0% of world production. Other smaller global producers include Thailand with 2.9% of world production, Columbia with 1.8% and Nigeria with 1.7%.

Demand – U.S. total disappearance of palm oil in 2011-12 rose +40.0% yr/yr to 1.190 million metric tons which was a new record high.

Trade – World palm oil exports in 2010-11 rose by +2.2% to 37.480 million metric tons, which was a new record high. The world's largest exporters are Indonesia with a 47.0% share of world exports and Malaysia with a share of 43.8%. World palm oil imports in 2010-11 rose +2.2% to 37.440 million metric tons. The world's largest importers are India with a 17.2% share of world imports and China with a 16.4% share.

World Production of Palm Oil   In Thousands of Metric Tons

Crop Year	Brazil	Came-roon	Colombia	Costa Rica	Ecuador	Ghana	Indonesia	Ivory Coast	Malaysia	Nigeria	Papua New Guinea	Thailand	World Total
2002-03	129	144	540	155	234	265	120	10,300	13,180	770	316	640	27,683
2003-04	142	147	614	180	308	270	120	11,970	13,420	780	326	840	30,049
2004-05	160	150	655	173	298	315	120	13,560	15,194	790	345	820	33,498
2005-06	170	150	700	181	236	320	120	15,560	15,485	800	350	784	35,784
2006-07	190	165	755	189	281	410	120	16,600	15,290	810	361	1,170	37,329
2007-08	205	165	780	202	289	405	120	18,000	17,567	820	448	1,050	41,084
2008-09	230	182	795	210	290	440	120	20,500	17,259	850	451	1,540	43,992
2009-10[1]	240	190	770	225	300	430	120	22,000	17,763	850	487	1,345	45,862
2010-11[2]	265	190	775	225	300	460	120	23,600	18,215	850	500	1,288	47,930
2011-12[3]	275	190	885	225	300	500	120	25,400	18,700	850	530	1,450	50,566

[1] Preliminary.   [2] Estimate.   [3] Forecast.   *Source: The Oil World*

World Trade of Palm Oil   In Thousands of Metric Tons

Crop Year	China	Germany	India	Nether-lands	Pakistan	United Kingdom	Total	Hong Kong	Indonesia	Malaysia	Guinea	Sing-apore	Total
	--- Imports ---							--- Exports ---					
2001-02	2,600	592	3,233	1,101	1,333	721	18,590	302	6,094	10,758	332	217	18,917
2002-03	3,167	562	4,110	1,132	1,442	776	21,467	209	7,167	12,133	329	253	21,531
2003-04	3,570	646	3,574	1,174	1,405	819	23,459	154	8,706	12,186	336	227	23,474
2004-05	4,319	766	3,342	1,438	1,683	869	26,328	59	9,862	13,585	322	223	26,152
2005-06	5,182	662	2,820	1,589	1,728	885	27,885	14	11,590	13,718	317	206	28,088
2006-07	5,543	711	3,664	1,710	1,743	734	29,157	27	12,465	13,768	406	185	29,601
2007-08	5,559	654	5,019	2,011	1,860	595	32,697	11	14,100	15,041	385	199	32,857
2008-09	6,297	983	6,875	2,048	1,870	516	36,090	19	16,209	15,990	494	198	35,639
2009-10[1]	5,853	928	6,606	1,946	1,970	546	36,626	2	16,596	16,610	500	201	36,680
2010-11[2]	6,130	810	6,450	1,550	2,020	525	37,440	4	17,620	16,430	505	170	37,480

[1] Preliminary.   [2] Estimate.   [3] Forecast.   *Source: The Oil World*

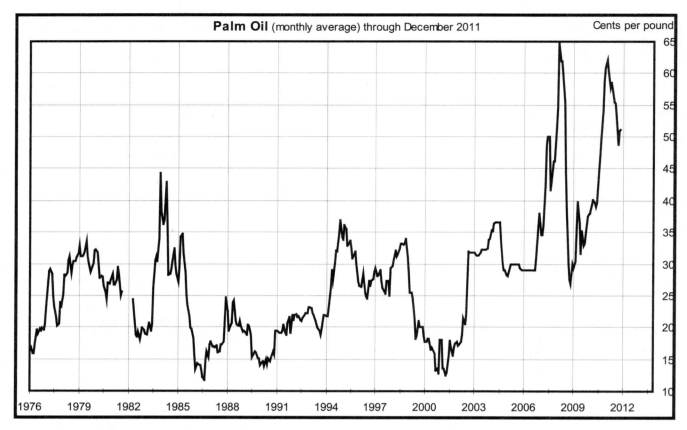

Palm Oil (monthly average) through December 2011 — Cents per pound

Supply and Distribution of Palm Oil in the United States   In Thousands of Metric Tons

Crop Year Beginning Oct. 1	Stocks Oct. 1	Imports	Total Supply	Edible Products	Inedible Products	Total End Products	Total Disappearance	Exports	U.S. Import Value[4]	Malaysia, F.O.B., RBD	Palm Kernel Oil, Malaysia, C.I.F Rotterdam
				-------- In Millions of Pounds ---------					---------- U.S. $ Per Metric Ton ----------		
2002-03	24.1	174.4	198.5	W	W	76.7	168.5	8.1	----	428	439
2003-04	22.1	281.5	303.6	51.9	37.5	67.9	226.4	13.1	----	489	619
2004-05	64.0	349.0	413.0	62.3	W	62.3	319.4	17.2	----	420	638
2005-06	76.4	603.8	680.2	436.4	W	436.4	555.6	30.6	----	452	583
2006-07	94.0	692.0	786.0	568.5	W	568.5	635.8	58.7	----	685	768
2007-08	91.5	954.7	1,046.2	789.3	W	789.3	934.7	38.3	----	1053	1248
2008-09	73.2	1,035.5	1,108.7	973.6	W	973.6	917.0	62.1	----	628	662
2009-10[1]	129.6	996.6	1,126.2	1,140.8	W	1,140.8	892.7	83.3	----	807	972
2010-11[2]	150.3	900.0	1,050.3	1,049.7	W	1,049.7	850.0	90.3	----	1175	1879
2011-12[3]	110.0	1,190.0	1,300.0	NA	W	NA	1,190.0	29.0	----		

[1] Preliminary.   [2] Estimate.   [3] Forecast.   [4] Market value in the foreign country, excluding import duties, ocean freight and marine insurance.
W = Withheld.   *Sources: The Oil World; Economic Research Service, U.S. Department of Agriculture (ERS-USDA)*

Average Wholesale Palm Oil Prices, CIF, Bulk, U.S. Ports   In Cents Per Pound

Year	Jan.	Feb.	Mar.	Apr.	May	June	July	Aug.	Sept.	Oct.	Nov.	Dec.	Average
2002	17.75	17.06	17.30	17.75	18.85	21.44	20.50	21.85	32.00	31.75	31.75	31.75	23.31
2003	31.75	31.75	31.35	31.25	31.25	31.75	32.25	32.25	32.25	32.25	32.44	33.75	32.02
2004	34.00	35.38	35.25	36.40	36.50	36.50	36.50	36.50	34.00	30.00	29.00	29.00	34.09
2005	28.20	28.00	28.67	30.00	30.00	30.00	30.00	30.00	30.00	30.00	29.25	29.00	29.43
2006	29.00	29.00	29.00	29.00	29.00	29.00	29.00	29.00	29.00	29.00	31.00	35.75	29.73
2007	38.00	34.50	34.50	36.00	42.38	48.63	50.00	NA	41.67	43.19	46.20	46.20	41.93
2008	51.48	54.66	64.63	61.96	61.90	59.70	55.41	44.43	38.52	30.11	27.41	26.91	48.09
2009	29.98	29.32	30.32	35.46	39.86	36.45	31.40	35.39	32.90	33.24	34.66	37.53	33.88
2010	37.83	37.91	39.35	40.11	39.60	38.97	39.64	44.57	47.00	49.55	54.00	58.60	43.93
2011	60.88	62.06	60.44	57.80	58.44	57.56	55.40	55.25	53.25	48.63	51.00	51.05	55.98

Source: Economic Research Service, U.S. Department of Agriculture (ERS-USDA)

Paper

The earliest known paper that is still in existence was made from cotton rags around 150 AD. Around 800 AD, paper made its appearance in Egypt but was not manufactured there until 900 AD. The Moors introduced the use of paper to Europe, and around 1150, the first papermaking mill was established in Spain, followed by England in 1495, and the U.S. in 1690.

During the 17th and 18th centuries, the increased usage of paper created a shortage of cotton rags, which were the only source for papermaking. The solution to this problem lead to the introduction of the ground-wood process of pulp-making in 1840 and the first chemical pulp process 10 years later.

Today, the paper and paperboard industries, including newsprint, are sensitive to the economic cycle. As the economy strengthens, paper use increases, and vice versa.

Prices – The average monthly index price (1982 = 100) for paperboard in 2011 rose +2.8% yr/yr to 230.1, down from last year's record high 231.1. The average monthly producer price index of standard newsprint paper in 2011 rose by +9.3% to 138.8, down from the 12-year high of 151.8 posted in 2006.

Supply – U.S. production of paper and paperboard in 2010 rose +6.2% yr/yr to 75.768 million metric tons. The U.S. is the world's largest producer of paper and paperboard by far, followed by Germany with 23.202 million metric tons and Canada with 12.733 million metric tons.

U.S. production of newsprint fell by −2.4% yr/yr to a record low of 414.6 metric tons per month in 2005 which is the latest data available. U.S. production of newsprint is second in the world, after Canada, which had production of 657.167 metric tons per month in 2005.

Production of Paper and Paperboard by Selected Countries   In Thousands of Metric Tons

Year	Austria	Canada	Finland	France	Germany	Italy	Nether-lands	Norway	Russia/3	Spain	Sweden	United Kingdom	United States
2005	4,950	19,498	12,391	10,332	21,679	9,999	3,471	2,223	7,126	5,697	11,775	6,241	83,697
2006	5,213	18,189	14,189	10,006	22,656	10,008	3,367	2,109	7,434	6,898	12,066	5,454	84,317
2007	5,199	17,367	14,334	9,871	23,317	10,112	3,224	2,010	7,581	6,713	11,511	5,228	83,916
2008	5,153	15,789	13,126	9,404	22,828	9,467	2,977	1,900	7,700	6,414	11,663	4,983	80,178
2009	4,606	12,823	10,602	8,332	20,870	8,404	2,609	1,577	7,373	5,700	10,932	4,293	71,355
2010[1]	5,009	12,733	11,759	8,830	23,202	8,988	3,105	1,695	7,282	6,193	11,410	4,300	75,786

[1] Preliminary.   Source: Food and Agriculture Organization of the United Nations (FAO)

Production of Newsprint by Selected Countires (Monthly Average)   In Thousands of Metric Tons

Year	Australia	Brazil	Canada	China	Finland	France	Germany	India	Japan	Rep. of Korea	Russia/3	Sweden	United States
2006	NA	11.3	NA	334.0	NA	91.6	225.9	85.1	314.3	137.9	166.1	211.4	NA
2007	NA	11.6	NA	382.4	NA	90.6	218.6	85.8	317.0	138.8	159.8	214.1	NA
2008	NA	11.8	NA	387.1	NA	90.3	227.9	95.5	306.7	133.3	165.6	210.3	NA
2009	NA	NA	NA	403.6	NA	NA	207.3	80.7	287.9	124.8	167.3	200.6	NA
2010[1]	NA	NA	NA	358.9	NA	NA	213.4	80.9	280.1	132.6	162.8	201.2	NA
2011[2]	NA	NA	NA	305.5	NA	NA	NA	74.4	265.4	131.3	159.6	189.6	NA

[1] Preliminary.   [2] Estimate.   NA = Not available.   Source: Food and Agriculture Organization of the United Nations (FAO)

Index Price of Paperboard   (1982 = 100)

Year	Jan.	Feb.	Mar.	Apr.	May	June	July	Aug.	Sept.	Oct.	Nov.	Dec.	Average
2005	179.7	180.0	180.1	180.7	180.9	176.6	174.6	168.5	168.5	168.6	174.1	173.9	175.5
2006	175.3	184.0	184.3	184.3	193.7	196.7	196.8	197.2	197.5	197.7	198.4	197.5	192.0
2007	198.0	198.1	198.2	199.0	198.8	198.7	199.0	199.1	203.1	209.5	209.2	209.4	201.7
2008	209.7	209.8	209.7	209.7	209.7	210.3	211.5	226.0	229.5	230.0	229.6	229.1	217.9
2009	224.6	221.3	216.7	211.8	205.3	203.0	202.8	202.0	202.4	199.1	198.8	197.9	207.1
2010	198.0	210.3	212.6	214.5	229.2	231.4	232.2	232.3	236.3	234.2	233.7	233.8	224.9
2011[1]	233.6	230.6	230.7	230.6	230.0	232.0	232.6	231.6	231.6	230.1	230.1	230.1	231.1

[1] Preliminary.   Source: Bureau of Labor Statistics, U.S. Department of Commerce (BLS) (0914)

Producer Price Index of Standard Newsprint   (1982 = 100)

Year	Jan.	Feb.	Mar.	Apr.	May	June	July	Aug.	Sept.	Oct.	Nov.	Dec.	Average
2005	130.3	131.9	131.6	132.8	133.2	135.9	138.8	141.4	152.2	143.5	144.9	145.6	138.5
2006	148.8	148.0	150.5	149.8	152.0	153.7	154.3	153.3	153.9	153.7	151.9	151.3	151.8
2007	150.3	146.1	145.0	143.1	127.9	127.5	125.8	124.1	122.5	121.8	121.1	124.4	131.6
2008	125.8	129.6	133.4	136.2	142.7	146.5	151.0	156.1	158.6	162.4	167.6	166.1	148.0
2009	162.3	158.9	153.0	141.1	129.6	120.3	107.5	105.3	105.5	107.7	111.0	114.6	126.4
2010	116.5	116.9	118.3	114.8	122.3	124.8	128.6	129.5	132.5	133.5	135.3	134.7	125.6
2011[1]	137.3	137.8	136.2	136.1	136.0	137.5	135.2	137.1	138.2	138.2	138.8	138.8	137.3

[1] Preliminary.   Source: Bureau of Labor Statistics, U.S. Department of Commerce (BLS) (0913-02)

Peanuts and Peanut Oil

Peanuts are the edible seeds of a plant from the pea family. Although called a nut, the peanut is actually a legume. Ancient South American Inca Indians were the first to grind peanuts to make peanut butter. Peanuts originated in Brazil and were later brought to the U.S. via Africa. The first major use of peanuts was as feed for pigs. It wasn't until the Civil War that peanuts were used as human food when both Northern and Southern troops used the peanut as a food source during hard times. In 1903, Dr. George Washington Carver, a talented botanist who is considered the "father of commercial peanuts," introduced peanuts as a rotation crop in cotton-growing areas. Carver discovered over 300 uses for the peanut including shaving cream, leather dye, coffee, ink, cheese, and shampoo.

Peanuts come in many varieties, but there are four basic types grown in the U.S.: Runner, Spanish, Valencia, and Virginia. Over half of Runner peanuts are used to make peanut butter. Spanish peanuts are primarily used to make candies and peanut oil. Valencia peanuts are the sweetest of the four types. Virginia peanuts are mainly roasted and sold in and out of the shell.

Peanut oil is extracted from shelled and crushed peanuts through hydraulic pressing, expelled pressing, or solvent extraction. Crude peanut oil is used as a flavoring agent, salad oil, and cooking oil. Refined, bleached and deodorized peanut oil is used for cooking and in margarines and shortenings. The by-product called press cake is used for cattle feed along with the tops of the plants after the pods are removed. The dry shells can be burned as fuel.

Prices – The average monthly price received by farmers for peanuts (in the shell) in the first six months of the 2011-12 marketing year (Aug/July) rose +27.7% to 28.8 cents per pound. The record high is 34.7 cents posted in 1990-91. The average monthly price of peanut oil in the 2011-12 marketing year (through December 2011) rose +18.3% yr/yr to 96.92 cents per pound, below the 2007-08 record high of 100.91 per pound.

Supply – World peanut production in 2011-12 rose +0.4% to 35.531 million metric tons, a new record high. The world's largest peanut producers are China with 45.6% of world production, India with 15.1%, U.S. with 4.6%, and Nigeria with 4.4%. U.S. peanut production in the 2011-12 marketing year fell by -12.5% to 3.636 billion pounds, down from the 2008-09 record high of 5.1462 billion pounds.

U.S. farmers harvested 1.098 million acres of peanuts in 2011-12, down -12.5% yr/yr. That was down from the 16-year high harvest of 1.629 million acres in 2005-06. U.S. peanut yield in 2011-12 rose +0.1% yr/yr to 3,313 pounds per acre, down from 2008-09 record high of 3,426 pounds per acre. The largest peanut producing states in the U.S. in 2011 are Georgia (with 45.0% of U.S. production), Florida (15.1%), Alabama (13.7%), North Carolina (8.0%), and South Carolina (6.4%). U.S. crude peanut oil production in 2011 rose +31.8% to 202.476 million pounds, which was only about 40% of the record high level of 358,195 million pounds posted in 1996.

Demand – U.S. disposition of peanuts in 2010-11 rose by +2.5% yr/yr to 4.376 billion pounds. Of that disposition, 65.0% of the peanuts went for food, 13.7% for exports, 11.4% for crushing into peanut oil, and 9.9% for seed, loss and residual. The most popular type of peanut grown in the U.S. is the Runner peanut with 87.8% of U.S. production in 2010-11. This was followed by the Virginia peanut with 10.5% of production and the Spanish peanut far behind with only 1.7% of production. Peanut butter is a primary use for Runner and Virginia peanuts. It accounts for 57.7% of Runner peanut usage and 60.7% of Virginia peanut usage. In a poor third place, only about 5% of Spanish peanuts are used for peanut butter. Snack peanuts is also a key usage category and accounts for 36.7% of Spanish peanut usage, 18.0% of Virginia peanut usage, and 26.7% of Runner peanut usage. Candy accounts for 40.1% of Spanish peanut usage, 20.6% of Runner peanut usage, and 7.6% of Virginia peanut usage.

Trade – U.S. exports of peanuts in 2010-11 rose +13.7% yr/yr to 600 million pounds. U.S. imports of peanuts fell by −16.7% yr/yr in 2010-11 to 60 million pounds.

World Production of Peanuts (in the Shell)   In Thousands of Metric Tons

Crop Year	Argentina	Burma	China	India	Indonesia	Nigeria	Senegal	South Africa	Sudan	Thailand	United States	Zaire	World Total
2002-03	316	756	14,818	355	5,400	1,086	1,510	260	60	370	112	1,506	30,862
2003-04	420	878	13,420	360	7,700	1,130	1,510	445	115	370	113	1,880	32,834
2004-05	585	916	14,340	364	7,000	1,150	1,520	573	85	370	114	1,945	33,606
2005-06	510	931	14,340	365	6,300	1,170	1,520	703	93	370	114	2,209	33,239
2006-07	775	1,023	12,887	370	5,385	1,200	1,520	460	77	850	117	1,571	31,032
2007-08	800	1,000	13,027	370	6,800	1,150	1,550	331	118	850	114	1,666	32,592
2008-09	860	1,000	14,286	370	6,250	1,250	1,550	731	128	850	115	2,342	34,752
2009-10	836	1,000	14,708	370	4,900	1,250	1,550	1,033	117	850	115	1,675	33,358
2010-11[1]	736	1,000	15,640	370	5,850	1,250	1,550	1,100	115	850	115	1,885	35,394
2011-12[2]	1,100	1,000	16,200	370	5,350	1,250	1,550	1,000	120	850	115	1,649	35,531

[1] Preliminary.   [2] Estimate.   *Source: Foreign Agricultural Service, U.S. Department of Agriculture (FAS-USDA)*

Salient Statistics of Peanuts in the United States

Crop Year Beginning Aug. 1	Acreage Planted	Acreage Harvested for Nuts	Average Yield Per Acre In Lbs.	Production (1,000 Lbs)	Season Farm Price (Cents Lb.)	Farm Value (Million Dollars)	In Thousands of Pounds			
							Exports		Imports	
	1,000 Acres						Unshelled	Shelled	Unshelled	Shelled
2002-03	1,353.0	1,291.7	2,571	3,321,040	18.2	599.7	489,900	----	75,372	----
2003-04	1,344.0	1,312.0	3,159	4,144,150	19.3	799.4	515,900	----	38,088	----
2004-05	1,430.0	1,394.0	3,076	4,288,200	18.9	813.6	491,000	----	36,863	----
2005-06	1,657.0	1,629.0	2,989	4,869,860	17.3	843.4	491,000	----	32,100	----
2006-07	1,243.0	1,210.0	2,863	3,464,250	17.7	612.8	603,000	----	61,000	----
2007-08	1,230.0	1,195.0	3,130	3,740,650	20.5	758.6	750,000	----	73,000	----
2008-09	1,534.0	1,507.0	3,426	5,162,400	23.0	1,193.6	727,000	----	86,000	----
2009-10	1,116.0	1,079.0	3,421	3,691,650	21.7	793.1	592,000	----	72,000	----
2010-11[1]	1,288.0	1,255.0	3,312	4,156,840	22.5	938.6	600,000	----	60,000	----
2011-12[2]	1,140.6	1,097.6	3,313	3,636,320	29.0-31.0	1,024.9				

[1] Preliminary. [2] Estimate. Source: Economic Research Service, U.S. Department of Agriculture (ERS-USDA)

Supply and Disposition of Peanuts (Farmer's Stock Basis) & Support Program in the United States

Crop Year Beginning Aug. 1	Supply				Disposition					Government Support Program		Amount Put Under Support	
	Production	Imports	Stocks Aug. 1	Total	Exports	Crushed for Oil	Seed, Loss & Residual	Food	Total Disappearance	Support Price	Additional	Quantity (Mil. Lbs.)	% of Production
	In Millions of Pounds									Cents Per Lb.			
2003-04	4,144	38	875	5,057	516	536	429	2,456	3,936	36.00	----	1,657	80.0
2004-05	4,288	37	1,121	5,446	491	393	547	2,600	4,031	36.00	----	1,948	91.4
2005-06	4,870	32	1,415	6,317	491	542	501	2,616	4,150	36.00	----	2,300	96.1
2006-07	3,464	61	2,167	5,692	603	513	471	2,585	4,172	36.00	----	1,694	97.9
2007-08	3,741	73	1,520	5,265	750	496	471	2,517	4,234	36.00	----	1,363	74.2
2008-09	5,162	86	1,031	6,280	727	445	407	2,571	4,150	36.00	----	2,073	80.5
2009-10	3,692	72	2,130	5,894	592	435	569	2,675	4,271	36.00	----	1,674	90.7
2010-11[1]	4,157	65	1,829	6,050	606	587	350	2,840	4,382				
2011-12[2]	3,636	100	1,516	5,252	525	445	372	2,890	4,232				

[1] Preliminary. [2] Estimate. Source: Economic Research Service, U.S. Department of Agriculture (ERS-USDA)

Production of Peanuts (Harvested for Nuts) in the United States, by States   In Thousands of Pounds

Crop Year	Alabama	Florida	Georgia	New Mexico	North Carolina	Oklahoma	South Carolina	Texas	Virginia	Total
2002	379,800	197,800	1,313,000	54,000	210,000	159,600	19,140	868,000	119,700	3,321,040
2003	508,750	345,000	1,863,000	45,900	320,000	98,000	57,800	810,000	95,700	4,144,150
2004	557,200	364,000	1,817,800	59,500	367,500	102,300	112,800	803,700	104,000	4,288,200
2005	613,250	410,400	2,130,000	66,500	288,000	107,910	168,000	975,000	66,000	4,869,860
2006	407,500	300,000	1,598,500	43,200	268,800	62,700	168,000	514,750	54,400	3,464,250
2007	400,350	321,300	1,622,400	32,000	261,000	57,800	173,600	691,900	52,500	3,740,650
2008	675,500	448,000	2,329,000	25,600	358,900	63,000	265,200	834,900	80,400	5,162,400
2009	495,000	336,000	1,797,800	21,700	244,200	42,900	148,800	506,850	44,400	3,691,650
2010	481,000	472,500	1,959,150	34,000	232,200	70,350	224,000	586,800	33,840	4,156,840
2011[1]	498,000	549,500	1,636,800	17,820	291,600	59,400	233,600	232,800	33,840	3,636,320

[1] Preliminary. Source: Agricultural Statistics Board, U.S. Department of Agriculture (ASB-USDA)

Supply and Reported Uses of Shelled Peanuts and Products in the United States   In Thousands of Pounds

Crop Year Beginning Aug. 1	Shelled Peanuts Stocks, Aug. 1		Shelled Peanuts Production		Reported Used (Shelled Peanuts - Raw Basis)						Shelled Peanuts Crushed[6]	Crude Oil Production	Cake & Meal Production
					Edible Grades Used In								
	Edible	Oil Stock[2]	Edible	Oil Stock[2]	Candy[3]	Snack[4]	Sandwich Spread	Butter[5]	Other Products	Total			
2002-03	504,186	24,231	1,983,016	611,627	354,232	344,913	----	828,529	24,379	1,552,053	644,194	285,685	356,888
2003-04	603,529	17,686	2,439,231	390,893	365,983	414,588	----	901,637	15,930	1,698,138	402,958	172,977	226,995
2004-05	621,190	17,686	2,357,314	246,663	389,696	450,781	----	938,514	22,547	1,801,538	295,769	126,249	172,668
2005-06	501,868	15,305	2,411,471	357,600	376,777	454,324	----	974,223	12,092	1,817,416	407,817	181,085	232,868
2006-07	510,097	21,499	2,415,495	347,243	373,684	415,131	----	993,445	9,397	1,791,657	385,375	166,450	223,537
2007-08	528,918	33,401	2,291,603	319,186	320,467	425,166	----	1,012,263	10,676	1,768,572	372,980	158,144	211,733
2008-09	431,593	39,508	2,442,345	253,778	316,275	367,478	----	1,102,698	9,840	1,796,291	334,296	142,666	190,748
2009-10	554,295	35,498	2,457,434	280,888	315,595	352,963	----	1,191,821	15,840	1,876,219	326,779	139,903	185,452
2010-11[1]	473,878	43,380	2,450,639	357,130	395,452	395,177	----	1,213,229	16,890	2,020,748	441,017	190,110	250,043

[1] Preliminary. [2] Includes straight run oil stock peanuts. [3] Includes peanut butter made by manufacturers for own use in candy. [4] Formerly titled "Salted Peanuts." [5] Includes peanut butter made by manufacturers for own use in cookies and sandwiches, but excludes peanut butter used in candy. [6] All crushings regardless of grade. Source: National Agricultural Statistics Service, U.S. Department of Agriculture (NASS-USDA)

PEANUTS AND PEANUT OIL

Shelled Peanuts (Raw Basis) Used in Primary Products, by Type   In Thousands of Pounds

Crop Year Beginning Aug. 1	Virginia Candy[2]	Peanuts	Butter[3]	Total	Runner Candy[2]	Peanuts	Butter[3]	Total	Spanish Candy[2]	Peanuts	Butter[3]	Total
2001-02	26,640	97,046	106,573	233,356	303,668	250,079	702,454	1,269,776	19,421	13,791	9,900	43,724
2002-03	26,930	75,100	77,018	183,226	312,192	257,259	734,844	1,323,846	15,110	12,555	16,667	44,981
2003-04	23,580	68,257	88,053	181,559	328,560	333,198	805,852	1,481,457	13,843	13,133	7,732	35,122
2004-05	25,466	70,216	112,027	209,411	349,437	367,671	824,876	1,562,692	14,793	12,894	1,611	29,435
2005-06	25,738	81,617	123,402	231,893	335,748	361,176	849,176	1,557,025	15,291	11,531	W	28,498
2006-07	29,542	75,858	113,689	220,196	329,806	328,167	869,014	1,535,250	14,335	11,104	W	36,211
2007-08	27,909	71,059	125,497	225,445	279,564	344,551	878,026	1,511,807	12,994	9,556	W	31,321
2008-09	26,342	52,925	110,737	191,770	276,212	303,730	981,546	1,569,531	13,721	10,823	W	34,990
2009-10	17,361	50,812	W	198,497	286,277	290,358	1,056,699	1,646,454	11,957	11,793	W	31,269
2010-11[1]	16,070	62,708	W	211,194	365,260	319,529	1,076,521	1,774,346	14,122	12,940	W	35,207

[1] Preliminary.   [2] Includes peanut butter made by manufacturers for own use in candy.   [3] Includes peanut butter made by manufacturers for own use in cookies and sandwiches, but excludes peanut butter used in candy.
Source: National Agricultural Statistics Service, U.S. Department of Agriculture (NASS-USDA)

Production, Consumption, Stocks and Foreign Trade of Peanut Oil in the United States   In Millions of Pounds

Crop Year Beginning Aug. 1	Production Crude	Refined	Consumption In Refining	In End Products	Stocks, Dec. 31 Crude	Refined	Imports for Consumption	Exports
2001-02	278.5	179.1	291.9	282.5	8.2	1.7	----	----
2002-03	267.7	166.3	W	277.6	52.9	3.5	----	----
2003-04	180.7	115.8	W	203.8	23.0	1.8	----	----
2004-05	135.7	91.0	W	181.9	40.3	2.4	----	----
2005-06	188.0	119.9	W	152.1	15.4	3.7	----	----
2006-07	173.8	115.1	W	W	35.5	5.6	----	----
2007-08	168.7	111.2	W	W	14.1	1.8	----	----
2008-09	150.8	99.9	W	W	17.6	3.0	----	----
2009-10[1]	146.3	96.6	W	W	18.1	2.1	----	----
2010-11[2]	196.9	132.0	W	W	----	----	----	----

[1] Preliminary.   [2] Forecast.   W = Withheld.   *Source: Bureau of the Census, U.S. Department of Commerce*

Production of Crude Peanut Oil in the United States   In Millions of Pounds

Year	Jan.	Feb.	Mar.	Apr.	May	June	July	Aug.	Sept.	Oct.	Nov.	Dec.	Total
2002	24.8	25.5	32.8	28.5	33.8	24.3	22.6	27.7	27.2	26.5	24.9	20.2	319.0
2003	21.7	16.6	19.4	20.5	20.0	23.2	19.8	17.3	18.3	24.1	15.6	13.2	229.6
2004	12.6	15.7	13.0	14.7	11.8	13.7	10.7	9.8	5.8	10.0	11.9	12.6	142.4
2005	14.4	13.1	9.9	11.3	13.3	14.6	8.9	14.5	11.3	15.3	16.4	17.7	160.8
2006	W	16.5	W	15.6	18.1	15.6	15.7	19.7	16.2	18.0	14.4	10.1	159.8
2007	14.3	12.8	14.3	14.9	9.7	15.2	14.1	17.7	19.0	17.3	12.0	14.0	175.3
2008	14.9	6.0	14.3	14.2	13.8	12.6	13.0	11.8	14.6	17.8	12.4	13.9	159.2
2009	13.8	6.8	14.1	12.2	11.9	12.2	9.4	10.9	12.5	15.1	13.6	11.5	143.8
2010	16.0	10.7	12.1	10.0	13.8	7.8	12.3	12.8	13.9	W	15.7	15.7	153.6
2011[1]	16.9	15.3	20.0	17.9	17.3	18.0	17.1						209.8

[1] Preliminary.   W = Withheld.   *Source: Bureau of the Census, U.S. Department of Commerce*

Average Price of Peanut Meal 50% Southeast Mills   In Dollars Per Short Ton

Year	Jan.	Feb.	Mar.	Apr.	May	June	July	Aug.	Sept.	Oct.	Nov.	Dec.	Average
2002-03	NA	130.00	122.50	118.50	114.25	124.00	125.00	135.00	135.00	135.75	130.00	130.00	127.27
2003-04	147.10	161.00	163.25	163.35	168.75	200.40	226.00	237.50	204.00	199.33	143.33	133.00	178.92
2004-05	100.38	99.25	93.50	93.25	99.25	112.00	122.75	137.25	145.25	140.83	132.50	109.00	115.43
2005-06	105.50	102.50	100.88	NA	114.50	113.50	113.17	113.33	107.13	107.50	100.00	98.75	106.98
2006-07	98.50	98.50	98.00	98.50	98.50	NA	NA	NA	NA	NA	NA	NA	98.40
2007-08	NA	NA	NA	NA	NA	NA	NA	NA	NA	NA	NA	NA	NA
2008-09	NA	NA	NA	NA	NA	NA	NA	NA	NA	NA	NA	NA	NA
2009-10	NA	NA	NA	NA	NA	NA	NA	NA	NA	NA	NA	NA	NA
2010-11	NA	NA	NA	NA	NA	NA	NA	NA	NA	NA	NA	NA	NA
2011-12[1]	NA	NA	NA	NA									

[1] Preliminary.   NA = Not available.   *Source: Agricultural Marketing Service, U.S. Department of Agriculture (AMS-USDA)*

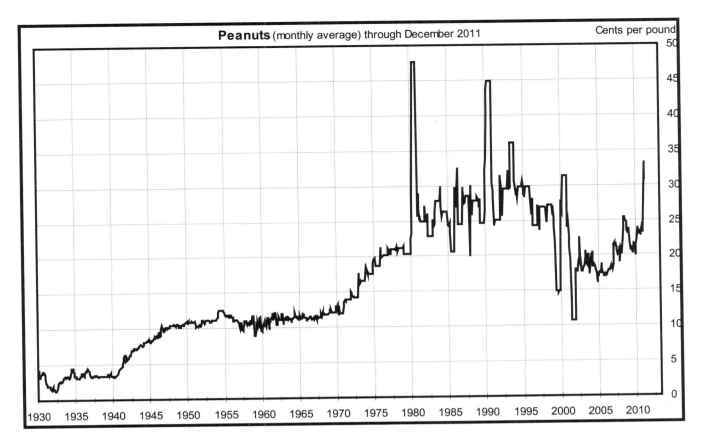

Peanuts (monthly average) through December 2011   Cents per pound

Average Price Received by Farmers for Peanuts (in the Shell) in the United States   In Cents Per Pound

Year	Jan.	Feb.	Mar.	Apr.	May	June	July	Aug.	Sept.	Oct.	Nov.	Dec.	Average[1]
2002-03	NQ	17.9	17.9	18.0	17.5	19.1	19.6	22.6	18.4	19.6	17.7	NQ	18.8
2003-04	NQ	18.3	18.5	18.4	19.6	20.6	18.9	18.6	19.8	20.6	20.3	17.4	19.2
2004-05	19.0	19.2	20.1	20.3	18.3	18.9	18.6	18.5	18.0	17.8	17.6	16.0	18.5
2005-06	17.0	17.0	17.4	17.5	17.4	17.3	18.6	16.9	17.4	17.3	17.0	17.0	17.3
2006-07	17.0	17.3	17.2	17.2	17.6	17.8	17.8	17.8	18.3	17.9	18.1	18.7	17.7
2007-08	18.0	18.6	21.4	21.7	21.3	21.6	21.0	20.7	20.0	20.4	20.1	21.1	20.5
2008-09	18.9	21.0	20.6	20.1	21.7	23.9	25.3	25.4	25.2	24.8	24.7	23.4	22.9
2009-10	23.1	23.3	23.7	21.7	21.7	20.7	21.0	20.6	20.4	20.5	21.6	21.5	21.7
2010-11	20.7	19.9	21.4	22.3	24.0	23.0	23.5	23.4	23.2	22.9	23.2	23.9	22.6
2011-12[2]	23.2	23.2	28.3	33.1	30.8	33.6	32.1						29.2

[1] Weighted average by sales.   [2] Preliminarily.   NQ = No quote.   *Source: National Agricultural Statistics Service, U.S. Department of Agriculture (NASS-USDA)*

Average Price of Domestic Crude Peanut Oil (in Tanks) F.O.B. Southeast Mills   In Cents Per Pound

Year	Jan.	Feb.	Mar.	Apr.	May	June	July	Aug.	Sept.	Oct.	Nov.	Dec.	Average
2002-03	NA	42.00	43.67	45.75	46.00	47.00	50.25	52.75	56.60	58.25	60.00	60.67	51.18
2003-04	61.60	63.25	64.50	65.00	61.67	60.00	60.00	56.50	NA	56.00	53.75	55.00	59.75
2004-05	55.00	55.00	55.67	56.00	55.00	50.00	50.00	53.25	52.50	52.38	52.25	50.06	53.09
2005-06	45.50	45.50	45.00	42.50	42.50	42.50	42.50	42.50	43.75	45.00	47.30	49.25	44.48
2006-07	52.67	52.50	50.00	49.25	46.25	48.20	52.63	55.63	62.56	69.63	70.00	73.00	56.86
2007-08	76.75	93.20	98.50	97.33	99.00	100.00	104.38	104.80	107.00	110.00	110.00	110.00	100.91
2008-09	97.00	90.00	85.25	79.10	75.00	62.50	58.75	56.60	57.00	60.70	62.00	54.00	69.83
2009-10	51.20	52.00	52.20	59.00	59.50	58.75	63.60	67.63	67.75	67.80	68.38	68.81	61.39
2010-11	71.40	75.13	77.90	80.06	79.63	77.50	78.70	82.81	78.50	88.05	95.56	97.50	81.90
2011-12[1]	97.00	98.75	96.10	95.81									96.92

[1] Preliminary.   NA = Not available.   *Source: Agricultural Marketing Service, U.S. Department of Agriculture (AMS-USDA)*

Pepper

The pepper plant is a perennial climbing shrub that originated in India and Sri Lanka. Pepper is considered the world's most important spice and has been used to flavor foods for over 3,000 years. Pepper was once considered so valuable that it was used to ransom Rome from Attila the Hun. Black pepper alone accounts for nearly 35% of the world's spice trade. Unlike many other popular herbs and spices, pepper can only be cultivated in tropical climates. The pepper plant produces a berry called a peppercorn. Both black and white pepper are obtained from the same plant. The colors of pepper are determined by the maturity of the berry at harvest and by different processing methods.

Black pepper is picked when the berries are still green and immature. The peppercorns are then dried in the sun until they turn black. White pepper is picked when the berries are fully ripe and bright red. The red peppercorns are then soaked, washed to remove the skin of the berry, and dried to produce a white to yellowish-white peppercorn. Black pepper has a slightly hotter flavor and stronger aroma than white pepper. Piperine, an alkaloid of pyridine, is the active ingredient in pepper that makes it hot.

Black pepper oil is obtained from crushed berries using solvent extraction. Black pepper oil is used in the treatment of pain, chills, flu, muscular aches, and in some perfumes. It is also helpful in promoting digestion in the colon.

The world's key pepper varieties are known by their place of origin. Popular types of pepper include Lampong Black and Muntok White from Indonesia, Brazilian Black, and Malabar Black and Tellicherry from India.

Trade – The world's largest exporters of pepper in 2008 (latest data available) were Vietnam (with 134,300 metric tons of exports), Indonesia (50,642), India (26,281), Brazil (35,770), and Malaysia (13,153). U.S. imports of black pepper in 2008 (latest data) fell -2.6% yr/yr to 49,625 metric tons. The primary source of U.S. imports of black pepper in 2008 was Indonesia which accounted for 41% of U.S. imports, followed by India with 20%, and Brazil with 17%. Imports from Malaysia have dropped by over 95% since 2003. U.S. imports of white pepper in 2008 rose by +25.1% yr/yr to 6,960 metric tons. The primary source of U.S. imports of white pepper was Indonesia, which accounted for 69% of U.S. imports, followed by Malaysia with 5%, Brazil with 1%, and China with 1%.

World Exports of Pepper (Black and White) and Prices in the United States   In Metric Tons

| | Exports (In Metric Tons) | | | | | | | | New York Spot Prices (Cents Per Pound) | | | | |
| | | | | | | | | | Indonesian | | Indian | | |
Year	Brazil	India	Indo-nesia	Mada-gascar	Malaysia	Mexico	Sri Lanka	Vietnam	Lampong Black	Muntok White	Brazilian Black	Malabar Black	Telli-cherry[2]
2000	20,469	19,125	47,502	588	23,684	4,534	4,855	36,400	228.1	227.1	228.1	228.1	282.6
2001	36,975	19,641	53,432	811	25,537	4,658	2,161	57,000	116.2	132.6	116.2	116.2	179.3
2002	38,230	21,066	63,214	880	22,840	4,344	7,915	78,400	92.9	120.6	92.9	92.9	127.8
2003	38,972	15,319	51,546	863	18,346	3,861	7,740	73,900	85.8	139.3	85.8	85.8	128.8
2004	43,003	15,429	32,364	1,243	19,788	5,785	4,852	111,000	75.6	120.9	75.6	75.6	118.8
2005	38,424	21,470	34,531	1,229	18,097	4,485	8,131	109,900	76.0	116.0	76.0	76.0	109.9
2006	42,200	35,499	36,953	1,776	16,610	6,593	7,596	115,000	103.9	153.5	103.9	103.9	136.4
2007	38,679	47,464	38,447	1,892	15,165	4,081	6,940	83,000	161.8	216.4	161.8	161.8	
2008	36,728	39,645	52,407	1,209	13,592	5,376	6,237	90,300					
2009[1]	35,770	26,281	50,642	1,606	13,153	6,175	6,576	134,300					

[1] Preliminary.   [2] Extra bold.   NA = not avaliable.   *Source: Foreign Agricultural Service, U.S. Department of Agriculture (FAS-USDA)*

United States Imports of Unground Pepper from Specified Countries   In Metric Tons

| | Black Pepper | | | | | | | White Pepper | | | | | |
Year	Brazil	India	Indonesia	Malaysia	Sing-apore	Sri Lanka	Total	Brazil	China	Indonesia	Malaysia	Sing-apore	Total
1999	7,093	24,931	8,429	2,392	525	441	47,591	32	451	5,202	420	342	6,789
2000	7,853	10,981	15,713	4,148	306	516	43,539	15	210	6,345	185	215	7,311
2001	11,699	7,998	19,606	2,957	508	279	48,749	48	7	5,807	120	161	6,365
2002	11,300	7,407	13,638	3,213	110	564	50,155	18	73	6,559	103	219	7,207
2003	13,792	4,950	16,370	1,416	163	504	51,124	198	180	4,567	224	904	6,758
2004	15,606	2,039	13,210	97	25	187	50,925	472	98	4,034	192	422	7,290
2005	13,935	3,828	13,502	144	50	269	52,152	460	73	4,134	192	300	7,248
2006	15,622	7,272	12,941	249	90	342	55,523	615	106	3,809	419	344	7,805
2007	14,148	14,763	14,201	162	75	281	50,934	122	121	3,991	520	140	5,564
2008[1]	8,224	9,699	20,180	35	126	665	49,626	88	82	4,783	381	36	6,960

[1] Preliminary.   *Source: Foreign Agricultural Service, U.S. Department of Agriculture (FAS-USDA)*

Pepper (monthly average) through June 2007 — Cents per pound

Average Black Pepper in New York (Brazilian)   In Cents Per Pound

Year	Jan.	Feb.	Mar.	Apr.	May	June	July	Aug.	Sept.	Oct.	Nov.	Dec.	Average
1998	199.4	205.5	243.8	262.8	262.8	247.5	253.0	253.8	246.3	243.0	231.3	225.0	239.5
1999	222.5	225.8	252.5	248.0	252.5	250.0	229.0	249.3	263.8	282.0	297.5	281.0	254.5
2000	260.0	256.3	246.0	260.0	265.0	265.0	263.8	252.5	205.0	167.5	147.5	149.0	228.1
2001	157.5	146.3	144.0	150.0	143.8	123.0	97.3	87.0	90.0	89.3	81.6	85.3	116.2
2002	85.0	80.0	81.4	100.5	101.0	92.0	84.8	86.8	93.5	103.5	106.0	100.8	92.9
2003	93.8	89.0	88.5	85.5	83.8	89.0	90.0	86.6	83.5	81.6	80.0	78.0	85.8
2004	78.0	75.5	75.5	75.4	77.3	78.0	76.8	75.0	75.0	74.2	73.3	73.0	75.6
2005	73.0	73.0	73.8	75.2	75.5	77.0	77.0	77.0	77.6	78.0	77.0	77.4	76.0
2006	78.0	78.0	77.8	78.5	80.0	80.4	89.0	112.7	146.0	152.0	139.5	134.3	103.9
2007	132.5	136.0	137.2	177.5	194.5	193.0							161.8

NA = Not available.   *Source: Foreign Agricultural Service, U.S. Department of Agriculture (FAS-USDA)*

Average White Pepper in New York (Indonesian)[1]   In Cents Per Pound

Year	Jan.	Feb.	Mar.	Apr.	May	June	July	Aug.	Sept.	Oct.	Nov.	Dec.	Average
1998	348.0	346.3	362.5	390.0	393.0	358.8	354.0	356.3	348.8	340.0	340.0	340.0	356.5
1999	361.3	355.0	365.0	355.0	352.5	335.0	310.0	313.8	325.0	327.0	316.3	303.0	334.9
2000	295.0	293.8	264.0	253.8	246.3	242.0	226.3	227.5	205.0	171.3	150.0	150.0	227.1
2001	159.0	151.3	144.0	133.8	130.0	127.0	122.5	129.6	128.0	125.5	120.0	120.0	132.6
2002	111.3	100.3	95.6	108.8	108.0	105.0	104.5	118.8	130.0	154.0	157.5	153.0	120.6
2003	152.4	148.8	150.0	150.0	142.6	133.0	133.0	138.2	137.5	133.6	127.5	125.0	139.3
2004	118.0	118.0	125.8	130.0	130.0	125.0	127.0	120.5	119.0	113.8	109.5	114.6	120.9
2005	119.0	118.0	118.0	116.4	115.0	115.0	115.0	115.0	115.2	115.0	115.0	115.0	116.0
2006	115.0	117.5	125.0	125.0	125.0	126.2	145.0	160.0	210.0	212.5	192.5	188.8	153.5
2007	191.3	195.0	197.0	225.0	245.0	245.0							216.4

[1] Muntok White.   *Source: Foreign Agricultural Service, U.S. Department of Agriculture (FAS-USDA)*

Petroleum

Crude oil is petroleum that is acquired directly from the ground. Crude oil was formed millions of years ago from the remains of tiny aquatic plants and animals that lived in ancient seas. Ancient societies such as the Persians, 10th century Sumatrans, and pre-Columbian Indians believed that crude oil had medicinal benefits. Around 4,000 BC in Mesopotamia, bitumen, a tarry crude, was used as caulking for ships, as a setting for jewels and mosaics, and as an adhesive to secure weapon handles. The walls of Babylon and the famed pyramids were held together with bitumen, and Egyptians used it for embalming. During the 19th century in America, an oil find was often met with dismay. Pioneers who dug wells to find water or brine, were disappointed when they struck oil. It wasn't until 1854, with the invention of the kerosene lamp, that the first large-scale demand for petroleum emerged. Crude oil is a relatively abundant commodity. The world has produced approximately 650 billion barrels of oil, but another trillion barrels of proved reserves have yet to be extracted. Crude oil was the world's first trillion-dollar industry and accounts for the single largest product in world trade.

Futures and options on crude oil trade at the New York Mercantile Exchange (Nymex) and at the International Petroleum Exchange in London (IPE). The Nymex trades two main types of crude oil: light sweet crude oil and Brent crude oil. The light sweet futures contract calls for the delivery of 1,000 barrels of crude oil in Cushing, Oklahoma. Light sweet crude is preferred by refiners because of its low sulfur content and relatively high yield of high-value products such as gasoline, diesel fuel, heating oil, and jet fuel. The Brent blend crude is based on a light, sweet North Sea crude oil. Brent blend crude production is approximately 500,000 barrels per day, and is shipped from Sullom Voe in the Shetland Islands.

Prices – NYMEX West-Texas Intermediate crude oil prices extended the 2009/2010 rally into early 2011 and reached a 3-year high of $113.89 per barrel in May 2011. That rally was driven by general strength in commodity prices caused by the Fed's second quantitative easing move from November 2010 to June 2011 totaling $600 billion. Crude oil prices were also boosted in early 2011 by the virtual shut-down of Libyan crude oil production due to

the revolution that eventually ousted former Libyan leader Colonel Gaddafi. Libya's oil production plunged from normal levels of 1.58 million barrels per day in January 2011 to only 390,000 bpd in March 2011 and to virtually zero by August 2011. After the revolution was over, Libya production rose in late 2011 but still only reached 925,000 bpd in January 2012, about 60% of its normal level. After peaking in May 2011, oil prices then fell through October 2011 due to (1) increased production by Saudi Arabia and its Persian Gulf partners to offset the loss of Libyan crude oil production, (2) the European debt crisis and the mild European recession seen by Q4-2011, (3) reduced demand from China as its economy slowed during 2011, and (4) weak demand from the U.S. due to a weaker economy, record ethanol production, and energy conservation efforts. Crude oil prices then rallied sharply in the late 2011 and early 2012 as the U.S. economy strengthened and as tensions increased with Iran over its nuclear program.

Supply – World crude oil production in 2010 (latest data) rose +2.4% yr/yr to 74.098 million barrels per day, which was a new record high. The world's largest oil producers in 2010 were Russia (with 13.1%), Saudi Arabia (12.0%), the United States (7.4%), Iran (5.5%), China (5.5%), and Canada (3.7%). U.S. crude oil production in 2011 rose +3.5% yr/yr to 5.664 million barrels per day. Alaskan production in 2011 fell −6.8% yr/yr to 558,000 barrels per day, the lowest level since 1977 and only 34% of the peak level of 2.017 million barrels per day seen in 1988.

Demand – U.S. demand for crude oil in 2011 rose +0.6% yr/yr to 14.814 million barrels per day, below the 2004 record high of 15.475. Most of that demand went for U.S. refinery production of products such as gasoline fuel, diesel fuel, aviation fuel, heating oil, kerosene, asphalt, and lubricants.

Trade – The U.S. is highly dependent on imports of crude oil to meet its energy needs. U.S. imports in 2011 fell -3.2% yr/yr to 8.917 million barrels per day, down from the 2005 record high of 10.126. U.S. imports of petroleum products in 2011 fell −3.7% to 1.913 million barrels per day, imports of distillate fuel oil fell -22.8% yr/yr to 176,000 barrels per day, and imports of residual fuel oil fell -1.9% yr/yr to 359,000 barrels per day.

World Production of Crude Petroleum In Thousands of Barrels Per Day

Year	Canada	China	Indo-nesia	Iran	Kuwait	Mexico	Nigeria	Russia/3	Saudi Arabia	United Kingdom	United States	Vene-zuela	World Total
2002	2,171	3,390	1,249	3,444	1,894	3,263	2,118	7,408	7,634	2,292	5,746	2,604	67,262
2003	2,306	3,409	1,155	3,743	2,136	3,459	2,275	8,132	8,775	2,093	5,681	2,335	69,400
2004	2,398	3,485	1,096	4,001	2,376	3,476	2,329	8,805	9,101	1,845	5,419	2,557	72,446
2005	2,369	3,609	1,067	4,139	2,529	3,423	2,627	9,043	9,550	1,649	5,178	2,565	73,671
2006	2,525	3,673	1,019	4,028	2,535	3,345	2,440	9,247	9,152	1,490	5,102	2,511	73,378
2007	2,628	3,729	963	3,912	2,464	3,143	2,350	9,437	8,722	1,498	5,064	2,433	72,906
2008	2,579	3,790	986	4,050	2,586	2,839	2,165	9,357	9,261	1,391	4,950	2,394	73,590
2009	2,579	3,799	969	4,037	2,350	2,646	2,208	9,495	8,250	1,328	5,361	2,239	72,182
2010[1]	2,734	4,076	953	4,080	2,300	2,621	2,455	9,694	8,900	1,233	5,474	2,146	73,889
2011[2]	2,906	4,073	896	4,054	2,530	2,596	2,525	9,774	9,475		5,673	2,240	73,964

Includes lease condensate. [1] Preliminary. [2] Estimate. *Source: Energy Information Administration, U.S. Department of Energy (EIA-DOE)*

Refiner Sales Prices of Residual Fuel Oil   In Cents Per Gallon

Year	Jan.	Feb.	Mar.	Apr.	May	June	July	Aug.	Sept.	Oct.	Nov.	Dec.	Average
2006	134.6	137.8	136.0	139.7	143.5	148.1	145.1	145.1	132.4	120.1	117.6	119.9	135.0
2007	117.2	121.4	122.1	125.8	135.9	142.1	153.9	158.4	161.0	166.1	183.2	194.8	148.5
2008	203.9	200.4	204.8	222.1	234.9	265.8	294.5	300.5	266.6	216.6	165.4	121.1	224.7
2009	116.4	120.0	118.3	117.4	121.3	144.0	148.8	164.1	168.9	171.7	173.9	181.3	145.5
2010	185.2	186.2	186.2	188.7	189.8	187.4	185.8	189.5	188.3	191.3	202.5	221.5	191.9
2011[1]	230.2	245.1	265.4	274.1	278.6	290.5	287.7	289.6	288.2	289.1			273.9

Sulfur 1% or less, excluding taxes.   [1] Preliminary.   *Source: Energy Information Administration, U.S. Department of Energy (EIA-DOE)*

Refiner Sales Prices of No. 2 Fuel Oil   In Cents Per Gallon

Year	Jan.	Feb.	Mar.	Apr.	May	June	July	Aug.	Sept.	Oct.	Nov.	Dec.	Average
2006	175.6	171.1	179.1	197.2	201.3	198.4	200.6	206.1	179.7	172.2	169.9	175.3	185.5
2007	161.2	172.9	178.1	191.0	194.9	201.4	207.1	202.1	213.3	226.0	256.9	257.0	205.2
2008	256.4	260.7	297.7	319.5	353.6	376.2	380.2	328.7	300.3	240.0	194.7	157.9	288.8
2009	154.8	142.7	135.8	139.7	146.8	174.4	165.8	180.4	177.4	191.8	200.4	198.9	167.4
2010	207.5	198.6	210.0	221.4	212.9	203.7	200.1	204.1	209.3	222.1	230.8	243.5	213.7
2011[1]	258.5	273.7	299.6	316.7	303.9	295.6	302.4	292.7	292.7	291.5			292.7

Excluding taxes.   [1] Preliminary.   *Source: Energy Information Administration, U.S. Department of Energy (EIA-DOE)*

Refiner Sales Prices of No. 2 Diesel Fuel   In Cents Per Gallon

Year	Jan.	Feb.	Mar.	Apr.	May	June	July	Aug.	Sept.	Oct.	Nov.	Dec.	Average
2006	181.0	180.6	190.1	212.2	218.7	218.7	225.0	234.3	191.3	182.7	186.8	188.6	200.8
2007	169.5	182.4	197.9	211.6	210.1	214.7	222.0	219.3	232.2	242.6	269.8	259.9	219.3
2008	258.0	273.8	315.8	335.6	371.2	385.9	387.6	333.8	316.0	251.4	195.5	146.9	297.6
2009	148.0	132.6	131.5	145.6	153.1	182.8	174.5	193.7	184.8	197.8	203.7	199.7	170.7
2010	207.8	202.5	216.3	231.2	217.7	212.0	209.8	216.1	219.0	232.5	239.2	248.6	221.1
2011[1]	262.1	282.0	313.4	329.6	311.6	307.9	313.5	303.2	303.5	303.5			303.0

Excluding taxes.   [1] Preliminary.   *Source: Energy Information Administration, U.S. Department of Energy (EIA-DOE)*

Refiner Sales Prices of Kerosine-Type Jet Fuel   In Cents Per Gallon

Year	Jan.	Feb.	Mar.	Apr.	May	June	July	Aug.	Sept.	Oct.	Nov.	Dec.	Average
2006	182.4	182.5	186.2	203.2	213.2	213.3	217.4	221.4	194.7	181.5	177.8	190.6	197.0
2007	172.7	176.6	184.6	202.1	207.9	211.4	216.7	215.1	225.6	235.3	265.6	265.5	214.9
2008	266.5	267.4	310.6	331.5	364.2	391.2	397.8	339.3	327.8	256.9	197.4	147.0	299.8
2009	147.2	135.2	126.6	142.5	146.0	178.0	175.9	189.4	182.2	191.7	206.0	201.2	168.5
2010	212.1	199.9	212.9	224.7	218.6	209.4	210.0	213.8	213.1	226.3	234.2	245.9	218.4
2011[1]	258.5	278.3	309.5	325.9	318.8	310.1	309.0	304.0	302.5	296.1			301.3

Excluding taxes.   [1] Preliminary.   *Source: Energy Information Administration, U.S. Department of Energy (EIA-DOE)*

Refiner Sales Prices of Propane[2]   In Cents Per Gallon

Year	Jan.	Feb.	Mar.	Apr.	May	June	July	Aug.	Sept.	Oct.	Nov.	Dec.	Average
2006	104.4	97.5	96.7	102.3	102.9	106.7	110.8	111.3	103.2	100.3	101.3	103.3	103.4
2007	99.5	103.3	104.9	106.7	111.2	109.4	115.9	116.7	124.8	135.1	147.1	146.1	118.4
2008	151.9	146.9	149.5	157.1	167.5	176.1	183.3	166.7	156.5	124.2	100.5	91.6	147.7
2009	97.4	89.0	80.5	71.9	72.8	83.8	76.0	83.7	92.3	100.4	108.8	117.8	89.5
2010	133.2	132.4	117.9	114.4	109.8	104.9	101.2	108.4	115.1	125.3	127.7	132.2	118.5
2011[1]	138.0	140.1	140.3	143.3	151.5	150.3	151.3	152.2	155.7	151.1			147.4

[1] Preliminary.   [2] Consumer Grade, Excluding taxes.   *Source: Energy Information Administration, U.S. Department of Energy (EIA-DOE)*

Supply and Disposition of Crude Oil in the United States   In Thousands of Barrels Per Day

	Supply					Unaccounted for Crude Oil	Stock Withdrawal[3]		Disposition		Ending Stocks		
	-- Field Production --		------ Imports ------				---- Withdrawal[3] ----		Refinery				Other
	Total Domestic	Alskan	Total	SPR[2]	Other		SPR[2]	Other	Inputs	Exports	Total	SPR[2]	Primary
Year	---------- In Thousands of Barrels Per Day ----------								----- In Millions of Barrels -----				
2004	5,419	908	10,088	77	10,010	143	102	46	15,475	27	961	676	286
2005	5,178	864	10,126	52	10,074	76	25	104	15,220	32	1,008	685	324
2006	5,102	741	10,118	8	10,089	8	11	-37	15,242	25	1,001	689	312
2007	5,064	722	10,031	7					15,156	27	983	697	286
2008	4,950	683	9,783	19					14,648	29	1,028	702	326
2009	5,361	645	9,013	56					14,336	44	1,052	727	325
2010	5,474	599	9,213	----					14,724	42	1,060	727	333
2011[1]	5,664	558	8,917	----					14,814	43	1,032	696	336

[1] Preliminary.   [2] Strategic Petroleum Reserve.   [3] A negative number indicates a decrease in stocks and a positive number indicates an increase.
Source: Energy Information Administration, U.S. Department of Energy (EIA-DOE)

PETROLEUM

Crude Petroleum Refinery Operations Ratio[2] in the United States   In Percent of Capacity

Year	Jan.	Feb.	Mar.	Apr.	May	June	July	Aug.	Sept.	Oct.	Nov.	Dec.	Average
2002	87.7	86.6	87.9	93.0	91.5	93.1	93.5	92.9	90.4	87.5	92.6	91.1	90.7
2003	87.2	87.4	90.5	94.1	95.8	94.7	94.0	95.0	93.1	92.4	93.6	93.0	92.6
2004	89.1	88.8	88.5	92.5	95.6	97.5	96.8	97.1	90.1	90.2	94.4	95.0	93.0
2005	91.3	90.6	90.8	92.8	94.2	97.1	94.2	92.7	83.6	81.3	89.3	89.4	90.6
2006	87.0	86.5	85.8	88.0	91.2	93.0	92.5	93.2	93.0	87.9	88.0	90.6	89.7
2007	88.2	84.7	87.1	88.1	89.7	88.5	91.2	90.8	88.9	87.4	88.9	88.7	88.5
2008	85.8	85.0	83.2	86.2	88.8	89.5	88.8	87.1	74.6	85.3	85.8	83.9	85.3
2009	82.3	81.5	81.5	82.7	84.0	86.0	84.2	84.1	84.9	81.5	81.1	81.3	82.9
2010	79.9	81.1	83.2	88.7	88.2	90.7	91.2	89.1	86.5	82.5	86.5	88.4	86.3
2011[1]	84.9	79.8	84.0	83.1	85.3	89.1	90.3	90.4	88.8	84.8	87.0	86.6	86.2

[1] Preliminary.   [2] Based on the ration of the daily average crude runs to stills to the rated capacity of refineries per day.   *Source: Energy Information Administration, U.S. Department of Energy (EIA-DOE)*

Crude Oil Refinery Inputs in the United States   In Thousands of Barrels Per Day

Year	Jan.	Feb.	Mar.	Apr.	May	June	July	Aug.	Sept.	Oct.	Nov.	Dec.	Average
2002	14,487	14,306	14,526	15,325	15,301	15,397	15,430	15,338	14,861	14,303	15,155	14,900	14,947
2003	14,338	14,381	14,933	15,575	15,910	15,620	15,546	15,693	15,446	15,342	15,455	15,345	15,304
2004	14,782	14,706	14,787	15,541	15,992	16,240	16,142	16,142	14,980	14,941	15,664	15,750	15,472
2005	15,254	15,142	15,214	15,494	15,905	16,401	15,850	15,664	13,986	13,646	15,032	15,046	15,220
2006	14,805	14,581	14,582	14,928	15,516	15,843	15,702	15,792	15,739	15,008	15,009	15,354	15,238
2007	14,992	14,435	14,840	15,045	15,380	15,248	15,671	15,685	15,226	14,933	15,151	15,202	15,151
2008	14,804	14,625	14,364	14,799	15,263	15,417	15,255	14,947	12,759	14,552	14,606	14,352	14,645
2009	14,146	14,134	14,118	14,382	14,483	14,850	14,636	14,593	14,710	14,095	13,898	13,983	14,336
2010	13,666	13,950	14,314	15,131	15,215	15,382	15,519	15,110	14,740	14,000	14,637	14,976	14,720
2011[1]	14,446	13,745	14,453	14,302	14,776	15,365	15,617	15,592	15,269	14,543	14,759	14,688	14,796

[1] Preliminary.   *Source: Energy Information Administration, U.S. Department of Energy (EIA-DOE)*

Production of Major Refined Petroleum Products in Continental United States   In Millions of Barrels

Year	Asphalt	Aviation Gasoline	Fuel Oil Distillate	Fuel Oil Residual	Gasoline	Jet Fuel	Kero-sene	Natural Gas Plant Liquids	Lubri-cants	Liquified Gasses Total	Liquified Gasses at L.P.G.[2]	Liquified Gasses AT L.P.G.[3]
2001	177.3	6.5	1,348.4	262.8	2,913	558.2	26.7	680.3	64.1	810.1	569.1	241.0
2002	179.9	6.4	1,309.8	218.8	2,983	552.3	20.8	686.5	63.3	822.5	576.8	245.7
2003	181.0	5.8	1,355.5	241.8	2,992	543.1	20.4	626.7	60.6	766.1	526.4	239.6
2004	185.6	6.2	1,397.6	238.0	3,013	566.3	23.2	662.7	62.0	797.2	561.3	235.9
2005	186.0	6.1	1,441.4	227.9	3,014	561.5	23.6	623.9	60.8	736.9	527.2	209.8
2006	184.8	6.6	1,478.1	231.5	3,036	540.4	17.3	633.4	66.8	757.6	537.8	219.9
2007	166.1	6.0	1,507.7	244.4	3,045	528.6	12.7	648.3	65.1	789.0	552.8	236.2
2008	150.9	5.5	1,569.5	227.1	3,072	539.5	12.0	651.9	63.2	786.1	556.2	229.9
2009	131.0	5.0	1,476.7	218.6	3,199	510.2	6.9	688.5	55.4	821.1	591.3	229.8
2010[1]	132.1	5.4	1,384.7	200.8	3,298	519.7	7.2	730.4	47.6	869.3	631.7	237.6

[1] Preliminary.   [2] Gas processing plants.   [3] Refineries.   *Source: Energy Information Administration, U.S. Department of Energy (EIA-DOE)*

Stocks of Petroleum and Products in the United States on January 1   In Millions of Barrels

Year	Crude Petroleum	Strategic Reserve	Total	Asphalt	Aviation Gasoline	Fuel Oil Distillate	Fuel Oil Residual	Finished Gasoline	Jet Fuel	Kero-sene	Gases[2]	Lubri-cants	Motor Gasoline Total	Motor Gasoline Finished[3]
2002	862.2	550.2	445.6	20.6	1.5	144.5	41.0	161.5	42.0	5.4	120.9	13.8	214	161
2003	876.7	599.1	425.1	21.3	1.4	134.1	31.3	161.9	39.2	5.5	105.7	12.0	199	162
2004	906.3	638.4	413.1	19.3	1.2	136.8	37.8	146.8	38.7	5.6	94.4	10.0	----	147
2005	961.9	675.6	405.6	22.1	1.3	126.0	42.4	143.1	40.2	4.9	111.0	10.4	----	143
2006	1,007.8	684.5	403.6	21.0	1.2	136.0	37.3	134.8	41.8	5.1	117.6	9.7	----	135
2007	998.4	688.6	405.9	28.8	1.4	143.7	42.4	118.3	39.1	3.4	125.2	12.4	----	118
2008	982.8	696.9	374.3	22.2	1.2	133.5	38.6	110.0	39.5	2.8	105.5	10.6	----	110
2009	1,026.1	701.8	367.8	20.3	1.2	145.9	36.2	98.2	38.2	2.2	126.9	10.7	----	98
2010	1,051.8	726.6	375.1	17.9	1.0	164.7	37.8	85.9	43.4	2.5	113.2	8.9	----	86
2011[1]	1,058.5	726.5	357.4	19.9	1.1	164.5	41.3	63.4	43.2	2.4	121.3	8.2	----	63

[1] Preliminary.   [2] Includes ethane & ethylene at plants and refineries.   [3] Includes oxygenated.
Source: Energy Information Administration, U.S. Department of Energy (EIA-DOE)

Stocks of Crude Petroleum in the United States, on First of Month   In Millions of Barrels

Year	Jan.	Feb.	Mar.	Apr.	May	June	July	Aug.	Sept.	Oct.	Nov.	Dec.
2002	874.9	887.3	895.0	891.4	898.3	894.0	882.8	878.5	857.9	881.1	884.0	876.7
2003	873.3	870.3	880.8	891.0	888.6	893.1	897.3	897.8	911.0	925.5	914.8	907.3
2004	912.8	931.2	949.5	961.5	965.8	967.2	960.1	947.6	943.2	957.0	961.0	961.3
2005	965.7	984.2	1,008.0	1,029.5	1,030.1	1,024.3	1,017.2	1,010.3	1,000.0	1,007.4	1,008.1	1,008.2
2006	1,006.8	1,027.4	1,028.8	1,035.5	1,029.2	1,024.6	1,019.4	1,020.7	1,020.6	1,027.9	1,023.1	1,000.9
2007	1,013.2	1,006.2	1,019.5	1,031.4	1,043.6	1,044.3	1,027.0	1,011.0	1,003.9	1,001.4	995.0	983.0
2008	994.6	1,001.1	1,015.0	1,021.2	1,007.9	1,001.7	1,002.4	1,009.7	1,006.4	1,014.5	1,023.4	1,027.7
2009	1,055.1	1,063.1	1,079.7	1,089.7	1,081.2	1,071.2	1,069.5	1,059.7	1,060.1	1,057.6	1,063.0	1,051.8
2010	1,063.4	1,069.8	1,085.8	1,089.9	1,088.5	1,092.1	1,084.2	1,085.9	1,089.3	1,094.1	1,079.0	1,060.0
2011[1]	1,074.0	1,076.8	1,089.1	1,095.9	1,096.3	1,085.0	1,066.4	1,045.8	1,027.7	1,034.6	1,033.6	1,026.8

[1] Preliminary.   Source: Energy Information Administration; U.S. Department of Energy

Production of Crude Petroleum in the United States   In Thousands of Barrels Per Day

Year	Jan.	Feb.	Mar.	Apr.	May	June	July	Aug.	Sept.	Oct.	Nov.	Dec.	Average
2002	5,848	5,871	5,883	5,859	5,924	5,915	5,770	5,811	5,411	5,363	5,597	5,699	5,746
2003	5,785	5,791	5,817	5,774	5,733	5,701	5,526	5,595	5,683	5,635	5,560	5,579	5,681
2004	5,570	5,556	5,607	5,527	5,548	5,398	5,458	5,333	5,062	5,156	5,396	5,413	5,419
2005	5,441	5,494	5,601	5,556	5,581	5,460	5,240	5,218	4,204	4,534	4,837	4,984	5,179
2006	5,106	5,045	5,045	5,128	5,161	5,160	5,102	5,059	5,037	5,106	5,105	5,166	5,102
2007	5,123	5,125	5,106	5,189	5,197	5,096	5,024	4,914	4,884	5,043	5,017	5,056	5,065
2008	5,100	5,122	5,151	5,117	5,102	5,098	5,133	4,894	3,930	4,669	5,024	5,056	4,950
2009	5,154	5,260	5,227	5,273	5,379	5,281	5,402	5,418	5,547	5,501	5,427	5,451	5,360
2010	5,406	5,578	5,505	5,390	5,390	5,425	5,288	5,440	5,652	5,571	5,553	5,507	5,475
2011[1]	5,483	5,612	5,633	5,594	5,612	5,624	5,610	5,754	5,641	5,784	5,874	5,855	5,673

[1] Preliminary.   Source: Energy Information Administration, U.S. Department of Energy (EIA-DOE)

U.S. Foreign Trade of Petroleum and Products   In Thousands of Barrels Per Day

	---------------- Exports ----------------		-------------------------------------- Imports --------------------------------------				
Year	Total[2]	Petroleum Products	Crude	Petroleum Products	Distillate Fuel Oil	Residual Fuel Oil	Net Imports[3]
2002	984	975	9,140	2,390	267	249	10,546
2003	1,027	1,014	9,665	2,599	333	327	11,237
2004	1,048	1,021	10,088	3,057	325	426	12,097
2005	1,165	1,133	10,126	3,588	329	530	12,549
2006	1,317	1,292	10,118	3,517	365	350	12,390
2007	1,433	1,405	10,031	2,761	304	372	12,035
2008	1,802	1,773	9,783	2,570	213	349	11,113
2009	2,024	1,980	9,013	2,122	225	331	9,667
2010	2,353	2,311	9,213	1,986	228	366	9,440
2011[1]	2,802	2,759	8,917	1,913	176	359	8,563

[1] Preliminary.   [2] Includes crude oil.   [3] Equals imports minus exports.
Source: Energy Information Administration, U.S. Department of Energy (EIA-DOE)

Domestic First Purchase Price of Crude Petroleum at Wells[1]   In Dollars Per Barrel

Year	Jan.	Feb.	Mar.	Apr.	May	June	July	Aug.	Sept.	Oct.	Nov.	Dec.	Average
2002	15.89	16.92	20.04	22.14	23.51	22.59	23.51	24.76	26.08	25.29	23.38	25.29	22.51
2003	28.35	31.85	30.09	25.46	24.96	26.83	27.53	27.94	25.23	26.52	27.21	28.54	27.54
2004	30.35	31.21	32.86	33.23	36.07	34.53	36.54	40.10	40.62	46.28	42.81	38.22	36.90
2005	40.18	42.19	47.56	47.26	44.03	49.83	53.35	58.90	59.64	56.99	53.20	53.24	50.53
2006	57.85	55.69	55.59	62.51	64.31	64.36	67.72	67.21	59.36	53.26	52.42	55.03	59.61
2007	49.32	52.94	54.95	58.20	58.90	62.35	69.23	67.78	73.16	79.32	87.16	85.29	66.55
2008	87.06	89.41	98.44	106.64	118.55	127.47	128.08	112.83	98.50	73.22	53.67	36.80	94.22
2009	35.00	34.14	42.46	45.22	52.69	63.08	60.43	65.28	65.27	69.82	71.99	70.42	56.32
2010	72.89	72.74	75.77	78.80	70.90	70.77	71.37	72.07	71.23	76.02	79.20	83.98	74.65
2011[2]	85.66	86.69	99.19	108.80	102.46	97.30	97.82	89.00	90.22	92.28			94.94

[1] Buyers posted prices.   [2] Preliminary.   Source: Energy Information Administration, U.S. Department of Energy (EIA-DOE)

Light Crude Oil Futures - CME Group (NYMEX)
(weekly close) as of December 30, 2011

USD per barrel

Volume of Trading of Crude Oil Futures in New York   In Thousands of Contracts

Year	Jan.	Feb.	Mar.	Apr.	May	June	July	Aug.	Sept.	Oct.	Nov.	Dec.	Total
2002	3,481	3,150	3,790	4,315	4,317	3,429	3,466	3,883	3,939	4,397	3,478	4,034	45,679
2003	4,553	4,039	4,151	3,355	3,329	3,534	3,401	3,732	3,826	4,248	3,624	3,646	45,437
2004	4,118	3,887	4,495	4,326	4,250	4,633	4,063	4,987	4,711	4,794	4,510	4,108	52,883
2005	4,352	4,032	5,721	5,404	5,045	5,326	4,629	6,091	5,252	5,022	4,488	4,288	59,650
2006	5,482	5,594	5,937	5,285	5,861	5,134	4,500	5,409	6,067	7,492	7,555	6,739	71,053
2007	10,367	9,092	10,069	9,287	9,487	9,862	9,656	10,647	10,670	12,390	11,307	8,692	121,526
2008	10,815	10,100	12,577	11,066	13,497	12,453	11,321	10,589	11,554	11,638	8,662	9,910	134,183
2009	11,369	11,411	11,340	10,106	9,939	11,367	11,924	11,823	11,462	13,179	11,600	11,906	137,428
2010	10,894	12,772	13,298	17,433	17,591	14,458	11,427	14,494	16,018	14,423	13,429	12,416	168,652
2011	17,948	17,757	15,675	12,089	15,126	15,815	11,571	17,178	13,488	14,785	13,609	9,994	175,036

Contract size = 1,000 bbl.   *Source: CME Group; New York Mercantile Exchange (NYMEX)*

Average Open Interest of Crude Oil Futures in New York   In Thousands of Contracts

Year	Jan.	Feb.	Mar.	Apr.	May	June	July	Aug.	Sept.	Oct.	Nov.	Dec.
2002	448.1	454.2	497.4	488.1	512.4	474.1	457.0	454.2	505.5	528.5	482.2	531.1
2003	608.3	641.0	568.5	495.5	478.9	494.1	517.5	542.6	507.2	532.0	550.4	580.6
2004	647.7	656.9	673.5	690.0	722.5	705.1	692.9	705.6	684.8	717.0	705.2	676.3
2005	707.9	745.2	829.2	833.8	799.0	785.4	820.1	901.6	870.6	848.7	832.3	841.3
2006	903.5	927.5	954.2	1,000.4	1,055.7	1,016.2	1,068.7	1,164.0	1,181.8	1,168.7	1,176.6	1,200.0
2007	1,284.9	1,281.7	1,314.3	1,328.0	1,390.4	1,431.6	1,523.6	1,477.4	1,483.3	1,447.1	1,451.8	1,362.3
2008	1,393.5	1,384.6	1,428.5	1,393.8	1,396.5	1,351.8	1,277.9	1,224.1	1,171.2	1,076.8	1,139.7	1,160.9
2009	1,232.4	1,223.3	1,190.2	1,163.0	1,159.6	1,180.5	1,170.7	1,176.0	1,174.2	1,231.2	1,207.8	1,200.4
2010	1,303.5	1,304.8	1,324.1	1,375.8	1,416.3	1,307.3	1,252.7	1,262.3	1,338.2	1,419.1	1,414.1	1,380.0
2011	1,494.0	1,540.7	1,551.4	1,565.5	1,591.3	1,531.0	1,517.1	1,521.8	1,433.7	1,406.6	1,332.6	1,321.5

Contract size = 1,000 bbl.   *Source: CME Group; New York Mercantile Exchange (NYMEX)*

Plastics

Plastics are moldable, chemically fabricated materials produced mostly from fossil fuels, such as oil, coal, or natural gas. The word plastic is derived from the Greek *plastikos*, meaning "to mold," and the Latin *plasticus*, meaning "capable of molding." Leo Baekeland created the first commercially successful thermosetting synthetic resin in 1909. More than 50 families of plastics have since been produced.

All plastics can be divided into either thermoplastics or thermosetting plastics. The difference is the way in which they respond to heat. Thermoplastics can be repeatedly softened by heat and hardened by cooling. Thermosetting plastics harden permanently after being heated once.

Prices – The average monthly producer price index (1982=100) of plastic resins and materials in the U.S. in 2011 rose +10.0% yr/yr to 231.1, a new record high. The average monthly producer price index of thermoplastic resins in the U.S. in 2011 rose +10.8% yr/yr to 234.0, a new record high. The average monthly producer price index of thermosetting resins in the U.S. in 2011 rose +5.5% to 228.3, a new record high.

Supply – Total U.S. plastics production in 2010 rose +4.2% yr/yr to 102.806 billion pounds, down from the 2007 record high of 115.793 billion pounds. U.S. plastics production has more than doubled in the past two decades. By sector, the thermoplastics sector is by far the largest, with 2010 production rising +4.2% yr/yr to 89.592 billion pounds and accounting for 87.2% of total U.S. plastic production. Production in the thermosetting plastic sector (polyester unsaturated, phenolic, and epoxy) rose +3.9% yr/yr in 2010 to 13.214 billion pounds and accounted for 12.9% of total U.S. plastics production. The category of "other plastics" fell -14.7% to 11.952 billion pounds and accounted for 12% of total U.S. plastics production.

Demand – Total usage of plastic resins by important markets in 2010 in the U.S. rose by +3.5% to 74.624 billion pounds. The breakdown by market shows that the largest single consumption category is "Packaging" with 2.502 billion pounds of usage in 2010, accounting for 32% of total U.S. consumption. After packaging, the largest categories are "Consumer and Industrial" (19.8% of U.S. consumption), and "Building and Construction" (14.7% of U.S. consumption).

Trade – U.S. exports of plastics in 2010 fell -0.1% yr/yr to 14.723 billion pounds, just under last year's record of 14.738 billion pounds. U.S. exports accounted for 19.7% of U.S. supply disappearance in 2010.

Plastics Production by Resin in the United States — In Millions of Pounds

	Thermosets				Thermoplastics										
Year	Polyester Unsat-urated	Phenolic	Epoxy	Total Thermo-sets	Thermo-plastic Polyester	Polyvinyl Chloride	Poly-styrene	Poly-propy-lene	Nylon	Low Density Polye-thylene[1]	High Density Polye-thylene	Total Thermo-plastics	Total Selected Plastics	Other Plastics	Total Plastics
2001	3,021	3,894	597	7,512	6,972	14,626	6,223	16,135	1,159	18,389	15,195	81,726	89,238	12,720	101,958
2002	3,197	4,076	620	7,893	7,480	15,250	6,768	17,084	1,284	19,515	16,190	86,762	94,655	13,607	108,262
2003	3,152	4,015	587	7,754	7,950	14,938	6,478	17,497	1,306	18,915	15,906	86,071	93,825	12,641	106,466
2004	3,294	4,200	658	8,152	8,632	15,883	6,765	18,523	1,357	20,390	17,519	92,317	100,469	13,471	113,940
2005	3,359	4,689	609	8,657	7,749	15,259	6,293	17,965	1,252	19,736	16,155	87,524	96,181	13,595	109,776
2006	3,430	4,809	624	8,863	8,290	14,919	6,269	18,775	1,270	20,926	17,645	91,204	100,067	13,970	114,037
2007	3,471	4,838	642	8,951	8,745	14,606	6,015	19,445	1,295	21,511	18,222	92,835	101,786	14,007	115,793
2008	2,798	4,233	583	15,091	8,159	12,789	5,220	16,768	1,148	19,061	16,247	86,455	89,594	11,952	101,546
2009	NA	NA	535	12,713	NA	12,754	4,865	16,623	943	19,793	16,956	85,983	98,696	NA	98,696
2010	NA	NA	610	13,214	NA	14,017	5,055	17,254	1,027	20,530	16,887	89,592	102,806	NA	102,806

[1] Includes LDPE and LLDPE. *Source: American Plastics Council (APC)*

Total Resin Sales and Captive Use by Important Markets — In Millions of Pounds (Dry Weight Basis)

Year	Adhesive, Inks & Coatings	Building & Con-struction	Consumer & Indust-rial	Electrical & Elect-ronics	Exports	Furniture & Fur-nishings	Industrial & Mach-inary	Pack-aging	Trans-portation	Other	Total
2001	1,143	13,988	16,510	2,501	9,295	3,226	968	22,847	4,207	2,705	77,390
2002	1,165	14,729	17,649	3,037	10,048	3,507	998	24,170	4,738	2,283	82,324
2003	1,170	14,495	17,571	2,862	9,009	3,361	962	24,087	4,732	2,021	80,270
2004	1,196	15,676	18,714	3,096	9,900	3,458	1,042	25,952	4,899	2,168	86,101
2005	1,160	15,483	17,400	2,917	9,790	3,406	1,087	25,144	4,711	2,133	83,231
2006	1,078	15,486	17,823	2,641	10,244	3,332	1,004	26,280	4,559	2,031	84,478
2007	1,069	14,289	17,193	1,980	12,346	3,091	943	26,527	3,312	1,604	82,354
2008	937	12,313	15,461	1,755	11,962	2,671	834	24,097	2,751	1,375	74,156
2009	835	11,139	14,862	1,495	14,738	2,008	657	23,391	1,941	1,004	72,071
2010	846	10,975	14,793	1,629	14,723	1,892	854	25,020	2,611	1,281	74,624

[1] Included in other. *Source: American Plastics Council (APC)*

PLASTICS

Average Producer Price Index of Plastic Resins and Materials (066) in the United States   (1982 = 100)

Year	Jan.	Feb.	Mar.	Apr.	May	June	July	Aug.	Sept.	Oct.	Nov.	Dec.	Average
2002	122.0	121.3	123.1	125.4	128.0	130.1	135.3	136.4	136.7	138.2	137.0	135.3	130.7
2003	137.2	141.8	149.6	153.2	152.4	149.2	144.9	143.6	144.9	146.2	145.8	144.0	146.1
2004	146.2	150.4	151.4	154.8	156.5	159.6	161.1	164.9	170.6	175.6	181.4	185.2	163.1
2005	190.3	190.8	192.1	192.3	190.3	186.3	185.0	183.4	188.2	203.9	208.6	205.2	193.0
2006	203.9	200.0	198.9	194.3	195.9	198.5	199.2	202.3	202.4	200.0	196.2	189.1	198.4
2007	187.6	185.5	187.0	192.1	193.8	196.9	198.6	198.7	198.0	199.3	205.9	207.5	195.9
2008	209.7	209.6	210.8	212.1	216.4	219.1	229.2	233.3	227.1	222.3	200.3	190.3	215.0
2009	184.6	190.1	188.6	183.5	185.9	185.9	194.4	194.5	196.4	194.5	194.5	196.8	190.8
2010	195.0	206.4	208.2	222.4	213.1	208.1	212.7	211.1	210.7	215.0	210.3	208.4	210.1
2011[1]	213.2	218.8	223.2	229.1	239.5	238.4	236.7	233.8	235.3	235.4	240.0	229.3	231.1

[1] Preliminary.   Source: Bureau of Labor Statistics, U.S. Department of Commerce (BLS)

Average Producer Price Index of Thermoplastic Resins (0662) in the United States   (1982 = 100)

Year	Jan.	Feb.	Mar.	Apr.	May	June	July	Aug.	Sept.	Oct.	Nov.	Dec.	Average
2002	118.4	117.8	120.3	123.8	126.2	128.6	135.0	135.9	136.2	137.6	136.1	133.8	129.1
2003	136.3	142.2	151.4	155.8	153.6	149.5	144.3	142.8	144.7	146.3	146.2	143.9	146.4
2004	146.7	151.9	152.6	156.4	157.5	160.9	162.3	165.5	171.3	176.6	182.3	186.9	164.2
2005	193.2	193.8	195.3	194.9	192.0	187.0	185.4	183.7	189.3	208.4	213.7	209.4	195.5
2006	207.9	202.8	201.5	195.6	197.6	201.1	201.6	205.1	205.0	201.6	196.8	188.1	200.4
2007	186.0	183.4	185.3	190.7	193.0	196.2	198.2	198.4	197.6	199.3	206.6	208.2	195.2
2008	209.9	209.9	211.5	213.2	218.4	221.2	232.4	236.5	229.0	223.5	197.6	187.1	215.9
2009	179.3	187.1	185.9	180.3	183.1	183.2	193.2	192.9	194.5	192.2	192.8	194.9	188.3
2010	193.2	206.8	208.8	225.7	214.9	208.8	214.3	212.6	212.1	217.2	211.7	209.3	211.3
2011[1]	214.7	221.1	226.0	232.6	244.6	242.1	239.9	236.3	238.1	238.1	243.6	231.1	234.0

[1] Preliminary.   Source: Bureau of Labor Statistics, U.S. Department of Commerce (BLS)

Average Producer Price Index of Thermosetting Resins (0663) in the United States   (1982 = 100)

Year	Jan.	Feb.	Mar.	Apr.	May	June	July	Aug.	Sept.	Oct.	Nov.	Dec.	Average
2002	146.2	144.6	143.8	141.2	144.1	145.5	145.8	147.6	148.4	150.3	150.3	150.6	146.5
2003	150.4	149.7	151.7	152.0	156.8	157.9	157.1	156.4	155.7	155.6	153.8	153.8	154.2
2004	154.0	154.2	155.9	158.3	162.2	164.3	166.4	173.2	179.0	183.0	189.3	189.8	169.1
2005	189.9	190.3	190.5	193.5	195.8	195.8	195.5	194.6	196.1	197.5	199.9	200.2	195.0
2006	200.0	200.8	200.8	201.7	201.6	200.5	202.1	203.6	204.2	206.3	206.6	206.3	202.9
2007	207.8	208.3	207.8	211.7	210.0	212.6	212.3	212.4	211.9	211.6	214.7	216.8	211.5
2008	221.4	220.7	220.0	219.0	218.5	220.3	224.8	229.3	229.8	229.6	228.3	220.7	223.5
2009	226.7	219.3	216.2	213.5	213.9	213.7	213.5	215.5	219.7	220.0	216.2	220.0	217.4
2010	218.0	216.8	217.1	216.7	216.1	217.2	216.3	215.2	215.3	215.4	215.3	216.1	216.3
2011[1]	218.0	219.4	220.6	223.0	224.8	231.9	233.0	233.7	234.0	233.9	233.8	233.1	228.3

[1] Preliminary.   Source: Bureau of Labor Statistics, U.S. Department of Commerce (BLS)

Average Producer Price Index of Styrene Plastics Materials (0662-06) in the United States   (1982 = 100)

Year	Jan.	Feb.	Mar.	Apr.	May	June	July	Aug.	Sept.	Oct.	Nov.	Dec.	Average
1995	129.0	127.0	132.5	134.7	135.9	137.5	135.1	133.2	132.1	130.1	127.9	126.1	131.8
1996	125.7	123.5	125.0	118.3	120.1	122.7	123.4	123.3	123.6	122.8	122.0	120.9	122.6
1997	120.6	123.1	123.0	121.6	121.6	121.6	122.7	117.7	118.0	116.5	113.5	113.7	119.5
1998	113.3	113.9	115.5	114.9	114.1	112.8	111.3	111.2	107.6	107.9	107.1	106.3	111.3
1999	103.5	102.4	103.5	104.7	103.0	102.3	103.1	101.5	101.4	99.8	99.4	100.5	102.1
2000	103.0	104.3	110.5	113.0	116.2	116.9	118.5	116.5	115.0	114.1	112.1	110.4	112.5
2001	110.5	109.2	107.9	108.0	101.8	99.9	97.6	95.7	87.3	89.4	90.0	85.4	98.6
2002	85.7	85.8	87.9	88.5	90.4	91.7	93.7	100.6	100.5	108.9	108.1	103.9	95.5
2003[1]	102.9	110.2	119.5	127.2	126.7	119.1	118.0	113.3	112.8	113.6	113.7	111.6	115.7
2004[1]	Data no longer available												

[1] Preliminary.   Source: Bureau of Labor Statistics, U.S. Department of Commerce (BLS)

Platinum-Group Metals

Platinum is a relatively rare, chemically inert metallic element that is more valuable than gold. Platinum is a grayish-white metal that has a high fusing point, is malleable and ductile, and has a high electrical resistance. Chemically, platinum is relatively inert and resists attack by air, water, single acids, and ordinary reagents. Platinum is the most important of the six-metal group, which also includes ruthenium, rhodium, palladium, osmium, and iridium. The word "platinum" is derived from the Spanish word platina meaning silver.

Platinum is one of the world's rarest metals with new mine production totaling only about 5 million troy ounces a year. All the platinum mined to date would fit in the average-size living room. Platinum is mined all over the world with supplies concentrated in South Africa. South Africa accounts for nearly 80% of world supply, followed by Russia, and North America.

Because platinum will never tarnish, lose its rich white luster, or even wear down after many years, it is prized by the jewelry industry. The international jewelry industry is the largest consumer sector for platinum, accounting for 51% of total platinum demand. In Europe and the U.S., the normal purity of platinum is 95%. Ten tons of ore must be mined and a five-month process is needed to produce one ounce of pure platinum.

The second major consumer sector for platinum is for auto catalysts, with 21% of total platinum demand. Catalysts in autos are used to convert most of vehicle emissions into less harmful carbon dioxide, nitrogen, and water vapor. Platinum is also used in the production of hard disk drive coatings, fiber optic cables, infra-red detectors, fertilizers, explosives, petrol additives, platinum-tipped spark plugs, glassmaking equipment, biodegradable elements for household detergents, dental restorations, and in anti-cancer drugs.

Palladium is very similar to platinum and is part of the same general metals group. Palladium is mined with platinum, but it is somewhat more common because it is also a by-product of nickel mining. The primary use for palladium is in the use of automotive catalysts, with that sector accounting for about 63% of total palladium demand. Other uses for palladium include electronic equipment (21%), dental alloys (12%), and jewelry (4%).

Rhodium, another member of the platinum group, is also used in the automotive industry in pollution control devices. To some extent palladium has replaced rhodium. Iridium is used to process catalysts and it has also found use in some auto catalysts. Iridium and ruthenium are used in the production of polyvinyl chloride. As the prices of these metals change, there is some substitution. Therefore, strength of platinum prices relative to palladium should lead to the substitution of palladium for platinum in catalytic converters.

Platinum futures and options and palladium futures are traded on the New York Mercantile Exchange (NYMEX). Platinum and palladium futures are traded on the Tokyo Commodity Exchange (TOCOM). The NYMEX platinum futures contract calls for the delivery of 50 troy ounces of platinum (0.9995 fineness) and the contract trades in terms of dollars and cents per troy ounce. The NYMEX palladium futures contract calls for the delivery of 50 troy ounces of palladium (0.9995 fineness) and the contract is priced in terms of dollars and cents per troy ounce.

Prices – NYMEX platinum futures prices started the year 2011 at about $1,735 per troy ounce and, except for dips in March and June, moved higher to reach $1,885 in August. The price then turned lower and except for a brief rally in October ended the year at about $1,400 per troy ounce. The price began to rise again and hit about $1,650 per troy ounce in February 2012.

NYMEX palladium futures prices started the year 2011 at about $756 per troy ounce and moved steadily lower all year to finally end the year at about $614 per troy ounce. The price then began to rise and hit about $703 in February of 2012.

Supply – World mine production of platinum in 2011 was unchanged yr/yr at 192,000 kilograms, and remained below the record high of 217,000 kilograms in 2006. South Africa is the world's largest producer of platinum by far with 72% of world production in 2011, followed by Russia (14%), Canada (5%) and the U.S. (2%). World mine production of palladium in 2011 rose +2.5% to 207,000 kilograms, which was still below the record high production level of 222,000 in 2006. The world's largest palladium producers are Russia with 41% of world production in 2011, South Africa with 38%, Canada with 9%, and the U.S. with 6%. World production of platinum group metals other than platinum and palladium in 2010 (latest data available) rose by +3.4% yr/yr to 73,200 kilograms, but still below the 2007 record high of 79,600 kilograms.

U.S. mine production of platinum in 2011 rose by +7.2% yr/yr to 3,700 kilograms, but still below the record high of 4,390 kilograms posted in 2002. U.S. mine production of palladium in 2011 rose by +7.8% yr/yr to 12,500 kilograms, but still below the record high of 14,800 kilograms posted in 2002. U.S. refinery production of scrap platinum and palladium in 2010, latest data available, fell 4.1% to 14,420 kilograms, but still above the 2005 record low of 11,580 kilograms but still well below the 13-year high of 24,790 kilograms in 2001.

Demand – The total of platinum-group metals sold to consuming industries in the U.S. in 2004 (the latest data available) rose +7.1% to 91,434 kilograms. The two main U.S. industries that use platinum are the auto industry, which accounted for about 74% of U.S. platinum usage in 2004, and the jewelry industry, which accounted for about 26% of U.S. platinum usage.

Trade – U.S. imports of refined platinum and palladium in 2011 for consumption fell -5.3% yr/yr to 239,880 kilograms. U.S. exports of refined platinum and palladium in 2011 fell by -24.8% to 45,900 kilograms, and still well below the record high of 103,590 kilograms in 2006. The U.S. relied on imports for 88% of its platinum and palladium consumption in 2011.

PLATINUM-GROUP METALS

World Mine Production of Platinum   In Kilograms

Year	Australia	Canada	Colombia[3]	Finland	Japan	Russia	Serbia/Montenegro	Africa	United States	Zimbabwe	World Total
2002	200	9,202	661	508	762	27,000	5	132,897	4,390	2,306	178,000
2003	225	6,990	828	461	770	28,000	1	148,348	4,170	4,270	195,000
2004	200	1,000	1,209	705	750	28,000	----	153,239	4,040	4,438	194,000
2005	111	6,075	1,082	800	760	29,000	3	163,711	3,920	4,834	211,000
2006	209	8,510	1,438	800	760	29,000	2	168,125	4,290	4,998	218,000
2007	142	8,000	1,526	800	770	27,000	2	160,940	3,860	5,306	209,000
2008	120	8,500	1,369	800	770	25,000	2	146,140	3,580	5,642	193,000
2009	130	4,600	929	800	780	24,500	2	140,819	3,830	7,230	184,000
2010[1]	130	3,900	998	800	780	25,100	2	147,790	3,450	8,800	192,000
2011[2]		10,000	1,000			26,000		139,000	3,700	9,400	192,000

[1] Preliminary.   [2] Estimate.   [3] Placer platinum.   W = Withheld.   *Source: U.S. Geological Survey (USGS)*

World Mine Production of Palladium and Other Group Metals   In Kilograms

	Palladium										Other Group Metals		
Year	Australia	Canada	Finland	Japan	Russia	Serbia/Montenegro	Africa	United States	Zimbabwe	Total	Russia	South Africa	World Total
2002	810	12,210	----	5,618	96,000	25	63,758	14,800	1,943	196,000	14,500	39,986	57,900
2003	820	12,808	----	5,500	97,000	8	70,946	14,000	3,449	207,000	15,000	46,856	64,400
2004	800	12,000	----	5,300	97,000	19	76,403	13,700	3,564	211,000	15,000	46,759	66,600
2005	550	10,415	----	5,400	97,400	19	82,961	13,300	3,879	216,000	15,500	56,309	77,700
2006	750	10,493	----	5,400	98,400	15	86,265	14,400	4,022	222,000	15,600	53,138	74,600
2007	600	14,100	----	5,500	96,800	15	83,643	12,800	4,180	223,000	14,500	59,449	79,600
2008	580	14,700	----	5,500	87,700	15	75,537	11,900	4,386	203,000	12,500	53,999	72,300
2009	590	8,100	----	5,600	83,200	15	75,118	12,700	5,680	194,000	11,900	55,456	70,800
2010[1]	580	6,700	----	5,600	84,700	15	82,222	11,600	7,000	202,000	12,000	57,292	73,200
2011[2]		18,000			85,000		78,000	12,500	7,400	207,000			

[1] Preliminary.   [2] Estimate.   *Source: U.S. Geological Survey (USGS)*

Platinum Group Metals Sold to Consuming Industries in the United States   In Kilograms

	Automotive		Chemical		Electrical		Dental & Medical		Jewelry & Decorative		Petroleum		All Platinum Group Metals			
Year	Platinum	Other[3]	Platinum	Other[3]	Platinum	Other[3]	Platinum	Other[3]	Platinum	Other[3]	Platinum	Other[3]	Platinum	Palladium	Other[3]	Total
1996	28,550	19,282	2,115	2,457	4,541	17,665	778	6,285	1,493	1,493	3,514	902	44,489	45,157	----	89,646
1997	28,923	20,402	2,239	2,426	4,945	19,997	840	6,376	2,115	1,617	3,390	871	46,184	50,227	----	96,411
1998	29,483	26,528	2,301	2,488	5,194	20,215	902	6,376	2,333	1,617	3,390	809	47,396	61,827	----	109,223
1999	31,100	29,390	2,364	2,519	5,443	21,148	933	6,065	3,110	1,679	3,514	778	50,310	65,248	----	115,558
2000	32,344	31,100	2,457	2,139	5,691	19,282	964	3,732	3,670	1,400	3,639	660	52,808	61,889	----	114,697
2001	33,411	34,832	2,644	715	5,909	17,354	995	3,670	4,043	1,431	4,199	715	55,399	62,293	----	117,692
2002	17,727	19,904	3,110	2,333	2,955	6,531	1,244	6,687	9,641		1,400		33,433	28,768	----	62,200
2003[1]	27,524	37,476	2,955	2,177	2,644	6,687	778	6,998	9,641		1,244		37,476	47,894	----	85,370
2004[2]	24,880	44,940	2,799	2,644	2,799	6,376	622	7,309	9,019		1,089		33,588	57,846	----	91,434

[1] Preliminary.   [2] Estimate.   [3] Includes Palladium, iridium, osmium, rhodium, and ruthenium.
Sources: U.S. Geological Survey (USGS); American Metal Market (AMM)

Salient Statistics of Platinum and Allied Metals[3] in the United States   In Kilograms

	Net Import Reliance as a % of Apparent Consumption	Mine Production		Refinery Production (Secondary)	Total Refined	Refiner, Importer & Dealer Stocks as of Dec. 31				Imports		Exports		Apparent Consumption
Year		Platinum	Palladium		Refined	Platinum	Palladium	Other[4]	Total	Refined	Total	Refined	Total	
2002	93	4,390	14,800	20,900	20,900	649	5,870	784	7,303	222,356	----	70,943	----	----
2003	91	4,170	14,000	24,250	24,250	649	1,170	562	2,381	223,653	----	45,124	----	----
2004	92	4,040	13,700	22,180	22,180	649	568	501	1,718	248,705	----	52,897	----	----
2005	93	3,920	13,300	11,580	11,580	261	----	189	450	284,849	----	49,395	----	----
2006	90	4,290	14,400	12,530	12,530	261	----	111	372	287,756	----	103,590	----	----
2007	91	3,860	12,800	16,340	16,340	261	----	18	279	362,733	----	81,100	----	----
2008	89	3,580	11,900	15,050	15,050	261	----	18	279	334,961	----	50,430	----	----
2009	95	3,830	12,700	15,030	15,030	261	----	18	279	286,688	----	51,140	----	----
2010[1]	91	3,450	11,600	14,420	14,420	261	----	18	279	253,206	----	61,040	----	----
2011[2]	88	3,700	12,500							239,880	----	45,900	----	----

[1] Preliminary.   [2] Estimate.   [3] Includes platinum, palladium, iridium, osmium, rhodium, and ruthenium.   [4] Includes iridium, osmium, rhodium, and ruthenium.   W = Withheld.   *Source: U.S. Geological Survey (USGS)*

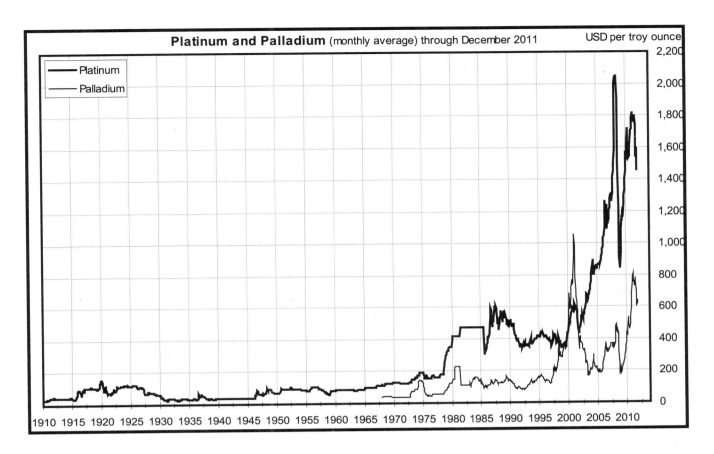

Platinum and Palladium (monthly average) through December 2011 — USD per troy ounce

Average Merchant's Price of Platinum in the United States — In Dollars Per Troy Ounce

Year	Jan.	Feb.	Mar.	Apr.	May	June	July	Aug.	Sept.	Oct.	Nov.	Dec.	Average
2002	471.52	470.68	511.95	539.20	533.66	554.70	526.32	545.48	556.05	580.11	588.15	594.89	539.39
2003	633.09	684.47	677.05	627.19	651.43	664.19	684.68	695.12	707.90	734.91	762.78	810.48	691.78
2004	855.95	849.53	902.78	884.76	814.05	810.59	813.48	851.91	851.05	843.76	856.15	854.55	849.05
2005	861.80	867.40	870.23	867.71	869.00	883.23	876.60	901.04	918.10	933.76	964.00	9,890.48	1,641.95
2006	1,032.48	1,045.16	1,044.39	1,105.00	1,264.05	1,192.73	1,233.03	1,236.74	1,183.30	1,085.32	1,183.73	1,124.79	1,144.23
2007	1,151.90	1,206.47	1,222.77	1,280.90	1,306.50	1,289.14	1,307.38	1,267.30	1,313.00	1,413.87	1,449.45	1,492.47	1,308.43
2008	1,585.09	2,002.55	2,043.65	1,991.32	2,053.57	2,042.24	1,904.68	1,492.52	1,221.71	917.13	841.22	842.40	1,578.17
2009	949.76	1,037.26	1,084.59	1,169.57	1,134.45	1,220.41	1,163.82	1,248.24	1,294.71	1,335.86	1,401.26	1,447.20	1,207.26
2010	1,567.15	1,525.63	1,602.65	1,718.33	1,633.45	1,556.77	1,530.57	1,543.82	1,598.57	1,692.29	1,702.35	1,715.05	1,615.55
2011	1,790.62	1,828.68	1,773.26	1,804.00	1,792.24	1,771.45	1,766.65	1,810.52	1,745.43	1,539.81	1,607.65	1,461.81	1,724.34

Source: American Metal Market (AMM)

Average Dealer Price[1] of Palladium in the United States — In Dollars Per Troy Ounce

Year	Jan.	Feb.	Mar.	Apr.	May	June	July	Aug.	Sept.	Oct.	Nov.	Dec.	Average
2002	412.62	377.79	377.15	372.50	360.00	339.20	325.41	327.55	330.50	319.09	289.20	243.57	339.55
2003	258.41	255.68	226.38	164.76	169.00	181.76	175.27	185.76	214.29	203.74	200.17	200.86	203.01
2004	220.70	237.95	272.43	299.57	249.57	231.32	222.95	217.55	213.95	220.43	215.85	193.00	232.94
2005	188.45	184.15	200.09	200.76	191.38	188.50	186.95	188.13	191.19	209.71	246.35	266.24	203.49
2006	275.95	291.58	312.70	355.74	372.82	319.36	320.21	332.57	324.40	315.18	326.91	328.00	322.95
2007	339.81	344.26	352.27	370.35	369.50	370.76	368.67	344.61	337.63	368.70	366.75	355.42	357.39
2008	376.95	473.65	490.35	449.05	438.29	453.57	428.27	318.29	250.19	193.30	212.61	178.00	355.21
2009	189.81	207.63	203.73	228.29	230.45	247.18	250.64	278.38	295.86	324.45	354.84	376.60	265.66
2010	437.15	429.16	464.48	535.33	495.05	465.18	459.86	493.45	543.24	596.33	687.75	760.05	530.59
2011	797.48	823.47	766.48	777.30	743.38	774.55	794.80	766.57	710.14	620.45	637.70	650.57	738.57

[1] Based on wholesale quantities, prompt delivery.   *Source: American Metal Market (AMM)*

Volume of Trading of Platinum Futures in New York   In Contracts

Year	Jan.	Feb.	Mar.	Apr.	May	June	July	Aug.	Sept.	Oct.	Nov.	Dec.	Total
2002	12,848	13,807	24,434	11,066	12,294	27,176	14,198	18,583	29,762	11,834	9,878	33,891	219,771
2003	15,545	15,157	38,170	13,472	18,968	30,961	10,852	11,878	37,686	19,275	14,040	42,301	268,305
2004	16,337	15,574	42,249	29,228	13,125	28,495	15,598	18,180	34,076	24,393	18,606	39,834	295,695
2005	15,410	20,253	41,297	16,267	20,135	55,588	25,132	26,604	52,535	21,827	30,447	50,684	376,179
2006	20,604	27,572	42,804	17,215	34,684	45,985	16,220	21,428	44,000	21,182	46,754	34,671	373,119
2007	20,534	26,975	59,099	26,457	35,525	66,968	35,371	35,975	58,091	34,100	36,126	66,324	501,545
2008	54,479	71,978	84,901	41,283	54,476	66,398	43,127	47,539	74,165	38,107	30,011	69,079	675,543
2009	31,090	35,199	82,949	30,849	34,962	104,413	46,045	48,650	134,462	55,865	63,896	134,504	802,884
2010	85,446	83,630	176,594	91,365	133,781	144,344	71,314	74,099	188,874	99,204	151,998	185,858	1,486,507
2011	123,012	97,150	235,375	105,524	113,655	216,647	95,589	188,066	293,142	156,172	136,109	232,822	1,993,263

Contract size = 50 oz.   *Source: CME Group; New York Mercantile Exchange (NYMEX)*

Average Open Interest of Platinum Futures in New York   In Contracts

Year	Jan.	Feb.	Mar.	Apr.	May	June	July	Aug.	Sept.	Oct.	Nov.	Dec.
2002	6,587	6,213	7,121	6,823	6,031	6,901	5,516	6,405	6,930	7,211	7,406	8,388
2003	8,694	8,132	8,034	6,322	6,599	6,847	7,450	8,556	8,794	8,489	9,421	9,373
2004	8,210	7,379	8,879	7,698	5,555	5,590	5,376	6,282	6,091	6,092	7,208	7,184
2005	6,800	7,486	8,047	8,132	8,496	10,109	8,497	11,729	12,478	13,024	12,377	11,327
2006	10,625	9,995	8,407	9,486	9,681	8,265	8,575	9,889	9,076	7,276	8,332	8,186
2007	8,810	10,752	11,154	13,413	15,173	15,033	16,641	12,347	12,341	15,199	14,427	15,404
2008	17,912	15,770	12,966	12,977	15,869	15,821	14,198	12,325	13,904	15,111	16,530	17,267
2009	18,300	20,041	20,388	20,506	21,045	23,755	21,952	25,303	28,571	31,236	33,730	33,542
2010	34,160	34,637	36,720	37,368	33,840	30,242	28,369	31,026	35,528	38,402	36,959	37,115
2011	40,572	41,823	35,986	35,925	36,214	35,150	32,278	37,063	39,229	37,910	38,779	42,652

Contract size = 50 oz.   *Source: CME Group; New York Mercantile Exchange (NYMEX)*

Palladium Futures - CME Group (NYMEX)
(weekly close) as of December 30, 2011
USD Per Troy Ounce

Volume of Trading of Palladium Futures in New York   In Contracts

Year	Jan.	Feb.	Mar.	Apr.	May	June	July	Aug.	Sept.	Oct.	Nov.	Dec.	Total
2002	1,275	3,372	1,538	1,527	6,126	2,166	2,154	8,971	1,452	1,710	8,118	2,644	41,053
2003	4,200	7,266	3,256	3,971	8,420	3,430	4,221	15,645	8,152	7,587	18,323	11,142	95,613
2004	17,093	41,036	20,508	30,214	27,343	11,433	7,606	28,895	10,690	15,036	41,269	16,429	267,552
2005	7,728	43,268	16,979	13,316	46,112	13,594	17,185	49,268	17,747	21,680	50,643	24,403	321,923
2006	28,447	59,279	32,573	23,135	64,863	25,857	13,464	41,123	16,222	14,351	47,797	11,005	378,116
2007	23,636	62,815	14,987	25,166	69,089	16,322	15,072	65,106	16,975	26,385	52,411	13,029	400,993
2008	26,954	105,845	49,411	24,750	66,939	18,934	26,245	53,692	25,253	28,627	43,879	13,299	483,828
2009	14,284	41,726	14,509	17,332	51,635	23,403	25,689	57,502	25,393	29,401	71,228	28,719	400,821
2010	48,438	90,368	48,314	58,104	134,435	45,840	45,847	87,366	55,399	69,623	156,495	61,355	901,584
2011	72,121	121,271	94,402	85,897	132,608	80,665	66,290	139,208	80,932	72,895	119,732	73,508	1,139,529

Contract size = 100 oz.   *Source: CME Group; New York Mercantile Exchange (NYMEX)*

Average Open Interest of Palladium Futures in New York   In Contracts

Year	Jan.	Feb.	Mar.	Apr.	May	June	July	Aug.	Sept.	Oct.	Nov.	Dec.
2002	1,217	1,208	1,042	1,199	1,554	1,806	2,103	2,298	1,878	1,976	1,977	2,025
2003	2,000	2,039	1,948	1,997	2,315	2,609	2,680	3,605	5,184	5,533	6,096	6,737
2004	9,119	11,878	11,465	11,039	8,828	7,861	8,055	8,688	8,933	9,965	11,192	12,188
2005	12,824	13,821	12,946	13,116	13,345	13,527	13,794	14,465	13,340	13,488	14,676	14,477
2006	14,353	16,632	15,426	17,783	18,002	14,251	14,087	13,166	11,247	11,836	12,511	11,210
2007	13,794	16,132	15,587	18,126	19,682	18,288	18,152	18,035	16,062	16,286	17,194	14,820
2008	18,184	20,999	20,227	19,571	19,197	17,106	15,223	13,821	14,294	14,656	13,435	12,688
2009	12,442	12,596	12,230	14,237	15,594	16,288	17,150	20,669	21,877	21,881	22,650	22,692
2010	23,356	22,566	22,944	23,905	23,152	21,271	19,732	19,808	23,036	24,706	24,747	23,089
2011	22,340	22,939	21,584	21,325	20,376	20,615	21,809	21,576	19,590	19,074	19,368	18,558

Contract size = 100 oz.   *Source: CME Group; New York Mercantile Exchange (NYMEX)*

Pork Bellies

Pork bellies are the cut of meat from a hog from which bacon is produced. A hog has two belly slabs, generally weighing 8-18 pounds each, depending on the hog's commercial slaughter weight. Total hog slaughter weights average around 255 pounds, equal to a dressed carcass weight of about 190 pounds. Bellies account for about 12% of a hog's live weight, but represent a larger 14% of the total cutout value of the realized pork products. Pork bellies can be frozen and stored for up to a year before processing. The pork belly futures contract at the Chicago Mercantile Exchange calls for the physical delivery of 40,000 pounds of frozen pork bellies, which have been slaughtered at USDA federally inspected slaughtering plants. Each deliverable belly typically weighs 12-14 pounds each.

There are definite seasonal patterns in pork belly prices. Bellies are storable and the movement into cold storage builds early in the calendar year, peaking about mid-year. Net withdrawals from storage then carry stocks to a low around October. The cycle then starts again. Retail bacon demand also follows a time worn trend, peaking in the summer and tapering off to a low during the winter months. While demand patterns would suggest the highest prices in the summer and the lowest in the winter, just the opposite is not unusual. Such contra-seasonal price moves can be partially attributed to supply logistics, notably the availability of frozen storage stocks deliverable against futures at CME exchange-approved warehouses. When stocks prove either too large or small, the underlying demand variables for bacon can be relegated to the backburner as a market-moving factor. The fact that no contract months are traded between August and the following February adds to the late fall futures price distortion.

Belly prices are sensitive to the inventory in cold storage and to the weekly net movement in and out of storage, which affords some insight to demand, although a better measure is the weekly quantity of bellies being sliced into bacon. Higher retail prices tend to encourage placing more supply into storage because of lower retail bacon demand. Bacon is not a necessary foodstuff so demand can be buoyed by favorable consumer disposable income. However, dietary standards have changed dramatically in recent years and do not favor the consumption of high fat and salt content food, such as bacon. In addition, alternatives to pork bacon have emerged in recent years such as turkey bacon, which has lower fat and calorie content.

Supply – The average monthly level of frozen pork belly storage stocks in 2011 rose by +1.2% to 37.806 million pounds, down from the 2008 10-year high of 60.932 million pounds. As of December 2011, there were 26.599 million pounds of pork bellies in storage.

Average Retail Price of Bacon, Sliced   In Dollars Per Pound

Year	Jan.	Feb.	Mar.	Apr.	May	June	July	Aug.	Sept.	Oct.	Nov.	Dec.	Average
2002	3.27	3.32	3.27	3.26	3.18	3.19	3.23	3.27	3.16	3.24	3.21	3.24	3.24
2003	3.20	3.28	3.22	3.29	3.09	3.14	3.16	3.23	3.22	3.16	3.23	3.18	3.20
2004	3.16	3.19	3.13	3.20	3.33	3.42	3.47	3.62	3.59	3.61	3.44	3.37	3.38
2005	3.37	3.40	3.36	3.33	3.56	3.46	3.48	3.44	3.40	3.33	3.26	3.33	3.39
2006	3.36	3.39	3.40	3.34	3.31	3.40	3.51	3.56	3.55	3.61	3.44	3.46	3.44
2007	3.51	3.57	3.46	3.50	3.65	3.66	3.72	3.80	3.78	3.88	3.66	3.69	3.66
2008	3.65	3.62	3.62	3.55	3.64	3.66	3.61	3.84	3.73	3.75	3.60	3.67	3.66
2009	3.73	3.62	3.59	3.58	3.66	3.62	3.64	3.59	3.59	3.60	3.50	3.57	3.61
2010	3.63	3.64	3.67	3.64	3.86	4.05	4.21	4.35	4.57	4.77	4.70	4.16	4.11
2011[1]	4.25	4.37	4.54	4.66	4.77	4.84	4.76	4.77	4.82	4.59	4.64	4.55	4.63

[1] Preliminary.   Source: Economic Research Service, U.S. Department of Agriculture (ERS-USDA)

Frozen Pork Belly Storage Stocks in the United States, on First of Month   In Thousands of Pounds

Year	Jan.	Feb.	Mar.	Apr.	May	June	July	Aug.	Sept.	Oct.	Nov.	Dec.
2002	44,301	50,849	57,569	60,721	63,293	62,269	51,019	29,925	14,250	9,452	10,354	18,059
2003	28,254	35,354	38,278	42,971	48,542	45,870	43,504	32,075	17,900	10,180	21,135	33,073
2004	49,017	63,095	57,123	50,126	48,363	41,366	37,185	23,383	15,230	11,344	15,970	33,955
2005	56,026	61,528	72,324	77,718	88,367	80,033	66,775	45,254	16,175	8,094	9,421	22,490
2006	40,707	54,902	58,861	61,628	62,665	58,803	46,056	30,506	11,962	10,199	15,597	30,553
2007	41,917	46,227	46,643	55,160	61,796	57,294	47,214	31,619	21,410	17,050	20,356	34,328
2008	54,746	70,647	79,282	98,896	100,189	87,428	74,372	57,964	31,878	21,270	21,696	33,490
2009	51,593	69,166	75,668	72,940	79,543	78,801	76,333	60,238	48,958	38,481	37,127	44,638
2010	56,764	53,584	55,552	58,762	49,656	44,201	35,369	21,380	7,202	4,817	23,248	37,696
2011[1]	50,677	51,326	50,900	52,521	53,185	57,123	48,645	29,503	15,162	9,297	8,734	26,599

[1] Preliminary.   Source: National Agricultural Statistics Service, U.S. Department of Agriculture (NASS-USDA)

Weekly Pork Belly Storage Movement

------------- Stocks[1] in Thousands of Pounds ----------------					------------- Stocks[1] in Thousands of Pounds ----------------			
Week Ending	In	Out	On Hand	Net Move-ment	Week Ending	In	Out	On Hand	Net Move-ment
Jan 02, 2010	2,057	-84	37,083	1,973	Jan 01, 2011	2,176	-642	58,660	1,534
Jan 09, 2010	953	-647	37,389	306	Jan 08, 2011	1,327	-787	59,200	540
Jan 16, 2010	930	-1,542	36,777	-612	Jan 15, 2011	743	-288	59,655	455
Jan 23, 2010	1,384	-3,558	34,603	-2,174	Jan 22, 2011	382	-280	59,756	102
Jan 30, 2010	1,102	-2,200	33,505	-1,089	Jan 29, 2011	0	-163	59,593	-163
Feb 06, 2010	335	-820	33,020	-485	Feb 05, 2011	83	-164	59,000	-81
Feb 13, 2010	622	-923	32,719	-301	Feb 12, 2011	83	-38	57,941	55
Feb 20, 2010	624	-324	33,019	300	Feb 19, 2011	198	-233	59,009	-35
Feb 27, 2010	1,047	-83	33,983	964	Feb 26, 2011	0	-124	58,885	-124
Mar 06, 2010	1,170	-1,739	34,705	-569	Mar 05, 2011	231	-100	59,016	131
Mar 13, 2010	736	-571	35,112	165	Mar 12, 2011	250	-450	58,816	-200
Mar 20, 2010	563	-246	35,429	317	Mar 19, 2011	166	-329	58,453	-163
Mar 27, 2010	736	-551	35,614	185	Mar 26, 2011	123	-407	58,169	-284
Apr 03, 2010	1,389	-364	36,639	1,025	Apr 02, 2011			58,329	160
Apr 10, 2010	964	-444	37,159	520	Apr 09, 2011	109	-83	58,355	26
Apr 17, 2010	856	-1,901	36,114	-1,045	Apr 16, 2011	0	398	57,564	-398
Apr 24, 2010	940	-2,796	34,258	-1,856	Apr 23, 2011	0	80	57,484	-80
May 01, 2010	756	-3,451	31,563	-2,695	Apr 30, 2011	792	-712	31,964	80
May 08, 2010	0	-1,581	29,982	-1,581	May 07, 2011	1,152	0	33,199	1,152
May 15, 2010	212	-887	29,307	-675	May 14, 2011	1,471	-167	38,512	1,304
May 22, 2010	82	-775	28,614	-693	May 21, 2011	1,087	0	40,672	1,087
May 29, 2010	359	-414	28,559	-55	May 28, 2011	2,010	-209	42,473	1,801
Jun 05, 2010	337	-1,304	27,592	-967	Jun 04, 2011	779	-372	41,960	407
Jun 12, 2010	209	-1,407	26,394	-1,198	Jun 11, 2011	186	-533	42,532	347
Jun 19, 2010	446	-1,527	25,313	-1,081	Jun 18, 2011	530	-2,746	40,317	-2,216
Jun 26, 2010	0	-1,639	23,674	-1,639	Jun 25, 2011	921	-3,357	37,881	-2,436
Jul 03, 2010	0	-1,177	22,497	-1,177	Jul 02, 2011	204	-3,255	34,830	-3,051
Jul 10, 2010	127	-1,470	21,154	-1,343	Jul 09, 2011		Discontinued		
Jul 17, 2010	41	-3,375	17,820	-3,334	Jul 16, 2011	----	----	----	----
Jul 24, 2010	122	-3,833	14,109	-3,711	Jul 23, 2011	----	----	----	----
Jul 31, 2010	195	-2,841	11,463	-2,646	Jul 30, 2011	----	----	----	----
Aug 07, 2010	243	-3,496	8,210	-3,253	Aug 06, 2011	----	----	----	----
Aug 14, 2010	42	-2,943	5,309	-2,901	Aug 13, 2011	----	----	----	----
Aug 21, 2010	77	-2,445	2,941	-2,368	Aug 20, 2011	----	----	----	----
Aug 28, 2010	0	-1,471	1,470	-1,471	Aug 27, 2011	----	----	----	----
Sep 04, 2010	0	-1,046	424	-1,046	Sep 03, 2011	----	----	----	----
Sep 11, 2010	0	-415	9	-415	Sep 10, 2011	----	----	----	----
Sep 18, 2010	0	-5	4	-5	Sep 17, 2011	----	----	----	----
Sep 25, 2010	0	-2	2	-2	Sep 24, 2011	----	----	----	----
Oct 02, 2010	0	0	2	0	Oct 01, 2011	----	----	----	----
Oct 09, 2010	1,189	0	1,191	1,189	Oct 08, 2011	----	----	----	----
Oct 16, 2010	3,448	0	4,639	3,448	Oct 15, 2011	----	----	----	----
Oct 23, 2010	3,695	0	8,334	3,695	Oct 22, 2011	----	----	----	----
Oct 30, 2010	4,985	0	13,319	4,985	Oct 29, 2011	----	----	----	----
Nov 06, 2010	4,698	0	18,017	4,698	Nov 05, 2011	----	----	----	----
Nov 13, 2010	6,032	-4	24,045	6,028	Nov 12, 2011	----	----	----	----
Nov 20, 2010	5,185	0	29,230	5,185	Nov 19, 2011	----	----	----	----
Nov 27, 2010	5,748	0	34,978	5,748	Nov 26, 2011	----	----	----	----
Dec 04, 2010	5,592	-75	40,495	5,517	Dec 03, 2011	----	----	----	----
Dec 11, 2010	5,669	-783	45,381	4,886	Dec 10, 2011	----	----	----	----
Dec 18, 2010	6,586	-958	51,009	5,628	Dec 17, 2011	----	----	----	----
Dec 25, 2010	6,661	-544	57,126	6,117	Dec 24, 2011	----	----	----	----

[1] 59 Chicago and Outside Combined Chicago Mercantile Exchange approved warehouses.   *Source: Chicago Mercantile Exchange (CME)*

PORK BELLIES

Pork Belly Futures - CME Group
(weekly close) as of July 15, 2011

Cents Per Pound

Average Open Interest of Pork Belly Futures in Chicago   In Contracts

Year	Jan.	Feb.	Mar.	Apr.	May	June	July	Aug.	Sept.	Oct.	Nov.	Dec.
2002	2,574	2,768	2,879	3,271	3,224	2,821	1,885	986	1,116	1,329	2,020	2,548
2003	2,842	2,805	2,915	3,082	3,383	3,410	2,858	1,632	1,899	1,885	2,075	2,484
2004	2,431	3,213	3,491	3,998	3,880	3,158	2,675	1,473	1,399	1,200	1,491	1,900
2005	2,013	3,010	2,858	2,891	3,743	3,725	2,507	1,599	1,143	1,451	1,323	1,868
2006	2,273	2,407	1,949	2,146	2,049	1,938	1,812	1,006	782	907	1,039	1,069
2007	1,257	1,520	1,391	1,259	1,256	1,369	1,146	851	941	1,532	1,911	1,850
2008	2,047	1,718	1,763	2,051	1,976	2,219	1,816	702	704	805	1,140	1,164
2009	1,192	1,291	1,090	894	860	865	667	573	657	642	595	565
2010	475	404	317	268	198	124	48	18	11	10	6	4
2011	3	2	0	0	0	0	Delisted	----	----	----	----	----

Contract size = 40,000 lbs.   *Source: Chicago Mercantile Exchange (CME)*

Volume of Trading of Pork Belly Futures in Chicago   In Contracts

Year	Jan.	Feb.	Mar.	Apr.	May	June	July	Aug.	Sept.	Oct.	Nov.	Dec.	Total
2002	16,495	16,650	14,279	17,758	13,648	15,764	16,773	7,490	6,857	8,107	8,659	9,574	152,054
2003	13,635	13,956	13,137	18,279	18,112	16,993	19,540	9,967	7,909	10,235	8,542	11,024	161,329
2004	11,519	14,738	17,699	18,412	17,366	15,136	16,012	10,518	9,410	5,713	7,643	7,783	151,949
2005	7,736	13,995	10,767	13,713	11,020	15,226	12,869	11,275	5,099	9,370	6,438	6,910	124,418
2006	10,806	12,890	11,682	13,183	10,342	12,616	9,842	9,634	4,885	4,375	4,568	2,741	107,564
2007	7,767	7,117	6,102	6,200	6,072	6,369	6,965	5,873	3,296	4,006	5,140	3,502	68,409
2008	6,159	5,741	5,396	6,289	4,695	5,608	7,993	4,163	2,377	2,463	2,060	3,761	56,705
2009	3,559	3,340	3,400	2,716	2,538	3,610	2,369	1,614	1,211	1,431	776	1,288	27,852
2010	1,170	1,174	892	659	352	292	115	53	5	2	6	2	4,722
2011	2	----	----	----	----	----	Delisted	----	----	----	----	----	2

Contract size = 40,000 lbs.   *Source: Chicago Mercantile Exchange (CME)*

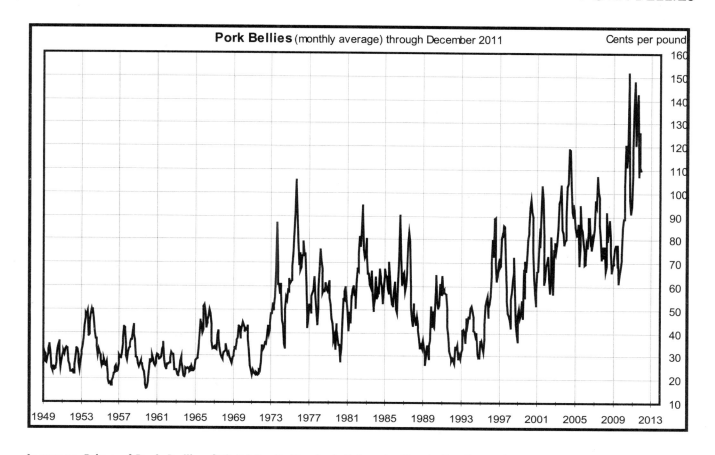

Pork Bellies (monthly average) through December 2011 — Cents per pound

Average Price of Pork Bellies (12-14 lbs.), Central, U.S.   In Cents Per Pound

Year	Jan.	Feb.	Mar.	Apr.	May	June	July	Aug.	Sept.	Oct.	Nov.	Dec.	Average
2002	70.87	70.75	72.55	63.48	58.65	65.90	81.06	67.98	57.05	76.24	75.50	78.92	69.91
2003	78.02	79.54	85.80	84.94	96.58	97.05	102.37	85.65	83.15	84.46	78.53	81.00	86.42
2004	79.78	90.76	103.67	109.15	117.53	113.00	118.22	99.92	92.00	88.90	91.50	87.81	99.35
2005	78.00	82.13	84.20	78.13	87.31	68.73	77.48	94.00	89.67	84.07	78.82	75.00	81.46
2006	75.00	71.83	78.67	78.83	87.00	101.25	94.29	90.67	82.56	75.44	78.64	79.50	82.81
2007	86.25	96.08	93.25	93.47	106.30	101.06	99.83	86.58	80.42	71.58	75.69	77.08	88.97
2008	75.56	78.94	67.26	61.08	79.00	64.54	78.75	74.17	63.50	77.00	57.25	61.25	69.86
2009	69.88	71.00	65.25	77.50	57.00	50.00	80.36	42.25	45.83	47.33	60.50	64.00	60.91
2010	82.00	73.50	89.00	NA	NA	NA	73.50	122.50	88.00	76.67	143.00	94.50	93.63
2011[1]	110.00	NA	143.00	147.00	143.00	119.00	121.00	135.09	133.00	111.00	91.33	NA	125.34

[1] Preliminary.   *Source: Economic Research Service, U.S. Department of Agriculture (ERS-USDA)*

Average Price of Pork Loins (12-14 lbs.)[2], Central, U.S.   In Cents Per Pound

Year	Jan.	Feb.	Mar.	Apr.	May	June	July	Aug.	Sept.	Oct.	Nov.	Dec.	Average
2002	106.95	105.73	100.08	94.13	101.71	104.80	108.64	97.85	87.17	93.04	82.60	93.03	97.98
2003	91.83	95.75	92.43	96.90	108.93	126.51	102.50	104.85	111.38	97.71	89.06	93.72	100.96
2004	111.98	117.30	110.00	115.48	140.65	130.30	121.36	116.93	119.22	110.00	102.92	109.50	117.14
2005	116.08	114.83	115.88	115.03	133.45	115.62	115.03	119.82	111.31	103.78	96.72	101.12	113.22
2006	95.00	96.21	101.31	107.25	112.77	124.61	114.95	109.35	99.58	99.27	92.02	101.15	104.46
2007	100.96	112.08	101.04	108.99	121.61	113.58	111.78	111.66	100.18	93.41	88.25	86.46	104.17
2008	87.70	90.22	90.33	108.10	130.43	115.19	117.11	128.86	114.54	111.10	92.88	93.10	106.63
2009	94.96	94.83	90.46	92.10	97.73	91.58	101.03	90.33	89.08	85.98	82.63	103.03	92.81
2010	110.94	104.08	108.14	122.64	137.62	114.17	118.47	132.73	120.09	110.36	104.06	108.22	115.96
2011[1]	119.02	119.98	123.08	131.20	138.84	136.21	139.57	149.33	131.78	131.07	116.40	117.61	129.51

[1] Preliminary.   *Source: Economic Research Service, U.S. Department of Agriculture (ERS-USDA)*

Potatoes

The potato is a member of the nightshade family. The leaves of the potato plant are poisonous and a potato will begin to turn green if left too long in the light. This green skin contains solanine, a substance that can cause the potato to taste bitter and even cause illness in humans.

In Peru, the Inca Indians were the first to cultivate potatoes around 200 BC. The Indians developed potato crops because their staple diet of corn would not grow above an altitude of 3,350 meters. In 1536, after conquering the Incas, the Spanish Conquistadors brought potatoes back to Europe. At first, Europeans did not accept the potato because it was not mentioned in the Bible and was therefore considered an "evil" food. But after Marie Antoinette wore a crown of potato flowers, it finally became a popular food. In 1897, during the Alaskan Klondike gold rush, potatoes were so valued for their vitamin C content that miners traded gold for potatoes. The potato became the first vegetable to be grown in outer space in October 1995.

The potato is a highly nutritious, fat-free, cholesterol-free and sodium-free food, and is an important dietary staple in over 130 countries. A medium-sized potato contains only 100 calories. Potatoes are an excellent source of vitamin C and provide B vitamins as well as potassium, copper, magnesium, and iron. According to the U.S. Department of Agriculture, "a diet of whole milk and potatoes would supply almost all of the food elements necessary for the maintenance of the human body."

Potatoes are one of the largest vegetable crops grown in the U.S., and are grown in all fifty states. The U.S. ranks about 4th in world potato production. The top three types of potatoes grown extensively in the U.S. are white, red, and Russets (Russets account for about two-thirds the U.S. crop). Potatoes in the U.S. are harvested in all four seasons, but the vast majority of the crop is harvested in fall. Potatoes harvested in the winter, spring and summer are used mainly to supplement fresh supplies of fall-harvested potatoes and are also important to the processing industries. The four principal categories for U.S. potato exports are frozen, potato chips, fresh, and dehydrated. Fries account for approximately 95% of U.S. frozen potato exports.

Prices – The average monthly price received for potatoes by U.S. farmers in 2011 rose +14.6% to $10.08 per hundred pounds, a new record high.

Supply – The total potato crop in 2010 fell by -7.1% to 39.923 billion pounds, well below the record high of 50.936 billion pounds posted in 2000. The fall crop in 2011 rose by +6.1% to 38.887 billion pounds and it accounted for 92% of the total crop. Stocks of the fall crop (as of Dec 1, 2011) were 25.000 billion pounds. In 2011, the spring crop rose +3.1% to 2.557 billion pounds, the summer crop fell -0.1% to 1.296 billion pounds, and the winter crop fell -15.7% to 213.20 million billion pounds.

The largest producing states for the fall 2011 crop were Idaho (with 32.7% of the crop), Washington (25.3%), Wisconsin (6.4%), Colorado (5.5%), and North Dakota (4.6%). For the spring crop, the largest producing states were California with 42.7% of the crop and Florida with 35.6% of the crop. Farmers harvested 1.077 million acres in 2011, up +6.8% from last year's record low The yield per harvested acre in 2011 fell -1.0% to 39,700 pounds per acre.

Demand – Total utilization of potatoes in 2010 fell -6.6% yr/yr to 40.427 billion pounds, a new record low. The breakdown shows that the largest consumption category for potatoes is frozen French fries with 36.1% of total consumption, followed closely by table stock (28.6%), dehydration (10.3%), and chips and shoestrings (9.1%). U.S. per capita consumption of potatoes in 2012 is expected to rise +0.2% to 112.4 pounds, well below the record high of 145.0 pounds per capita seen in 1996.

Trade – U.S. exports of potatoes in 2010 rose +18.5% to 808,354 thousand pounds, a new record high. U.S. imports in 2010 fell -4.0% to 762,925 thousand pounds, down from the 2008 record high of 1.071 million pounds.

Salient Statistics of Potatoes in the United States

Crop Year	Acreage Planted (1,000 Acres)	Acreage Harvested (1,000 Acres)	Yield Per Harvested Acre Cwt.	Total Pro-duction	Farm Disposition — Used Where Grown — Seed & Feed	Shrinkage & Loss	Sold[2]	Farm Price ($ Cwt.)	Value of Pro-duction[3] (Million $)	sales	Stocks Jan. 1 (1,000 Cwt)	Foreign Trade[4] Exports (Fresh)	Imports (Millions of Lbs.)	Consumption[4] Per Capita — In Pounds — Fresh	Total
				In Thousands of Cwt.					Million $			Millions of Lbs.			
2002	1,300	1,266	362	458,171	5,622	30,905	421,644	6.67	3,045	2,812	231,490	647,120	621,461	44.3	131.9
2003	1,273	1,249	367	457,814	5,541	35,296	416,977	5.89	2,686	2,458	233,590	541,775	635,007	46.8	137.9
2004	1,193	1,167	391	456,041	4,796	37,408	413,837	5.67	2,575	2,344	236,700	433,712	575,374	45.8	134.6
2005	1,109	1,087	390	423,926	4,791	28,519	390,616	7.04	2,982	2,750	220,500	586,226	631,252	41.3	125.4
2006	1,139	1,120	393	440,698	4,750	29,639	406,309	7.31	3,209	2,970	225,800	600,715	611,229	38.6	123.7
2007	1,142	1,122	396	444,873	4,105	29,561	411,209	7.51	3,340	3,089	232,300	615,784	923,574	38.7	124.4
2008	1,060	1,047	396	415,055	4,138	26,438	384,478	9.09	3,770	3,494	213,200	616,290	1,071,973	37.8	118.3
2009	1,071	1,044	414	432,601	4,535	29,135	398,931	8.19	3,558	3,292	234,300	682,190	794,611	36.4	113.1
2010	1,026	1,008	401	404,273	4,220	24,990	375,063	8.79	3,722	3,449	204,500	808,354	762,925	35.6	112.8
2011[1]	1,099	1,077	397	427,406					4,006					33.6	109.9

[1] Preliminary.   [2] For all purposes, including food, seed processing & livestock feed.   [3] Farm weight basis, excluding canned and frozen potatoes.
[4] Calendar year.   *Source: Economic Research Service, U.S. Department of Agriculture (ERS-USDA)*

Cold Storage Stocks of All Frozen Potatoes in the United States, on First of Month   In Millions of Pounds

Year	Jan.	Feb.	Mar.	Apr.	May	June	July	Aug.	Sept.	Oct.	Nov.	Dec.
2002	1,239.8	1,274.2	1,271.5	1,271.4	1,222.7	1,182.3	1,223.5	1,106.6	1,040.6	1,141.4	1,252.2	1,214.4
2003	1,131.2	1,173.1	1,211.0	1,217.4	1,150.5	1,106.6	1,181.8	1,130.4	1,070.4	1,151.7	1,248.0	1,232.8
2004	1,120.4	1,167.3	1,207.4	1,192.5	1,158.7	1,185.9	1,128.7	1,117.1	1,127.0	1,178.6	1,274.9	1,219.3
2005	1,074.8	1,168.8	1,152.8	1,093.7	1,174.3	1,178.1	1,190.5	1,154.9	1,121.3	1,180.4	1,200.0	1,122.5
2006	1,051.1	1,076.2	1,147.0	1,158.9	1,176.6	1,104.9	1,108.1	996.4	964.1	1,009.6	1,066.6	1,052.1
2007	954.8	1,041.3	1,063.6	1,116.2	1,102.2	1,070.7	1,078.2	991.8	1,000.4	1,080.0	1,133.8	1,078.4
2008	1,012.4	1,089.1	1,117.5	1,087.7	1,134.4	1,074.9	1,190.0	1,107.5	1,126.7	1,180.8	1,200.5	1,212.1
2009	1,098.6	1,171.0	1,192.1	1,226.8	1,221.4	1,203.2	1,245.1	1,187.5	1,094.8	1,130.2	1,162.9	1,108.1
2010	1,043.8	1,091.3	1,113.6	1,100.5	1,093.7	1,077.3	1,141.9	1,063.9	1,036.3	1,070.1	1,122.9	1,127.5
2011[1]	1,018.9	1,095.0	1,102.9	1,090.8	1,070.3	1,073.8	1,073.8	1,073.8	1,073.8	1,073.8	1,073.8	1,073.8

[1] Preliminary.   Source: Agricultural Statistics Board, U.S. Department of Agriculture (ASB-USDA)

Potato Crop Production Estimates, Stocks and Disappearance in the United States   In Millions of Cwt.

											Fall Crop			
	------ Crop Production Estimates ------			------------ Total Storage Stocks[2] ------------						----------- 1,000 Cwt. -----------				
	------ Total Crop ------			------ Fall Crop ------			----------- Following Year -----------						Disap-	Stocks	Average Price	Value of Sales
Year	Oct. 1	Nov. 1	Dec. 1	Oct. 1	Nov. 1	Dec. 1	Jan. 1	Feb. 1	Mar. 1	Apr. 1	May 1	Pro- duction	pearance (Sold)	Dec. 1	($/Cwt.)	($1,000)
2002	----	459.7	----	----	415.0	264.5	231.5	199.0	165.2	125.8	83.0	413,581	378,796	264,485	5.89	2,232,627
2003	----	459.2	----	----	413.5	267.9	233.6	200.2	166.3	126.1	85.0	410,588	371,755	267,900	5.22	1,943,986
2004	----	450.2	----	----	407.8	271.1	236.7	203.5	168.0	128.9	88.6	410,253	369,781	271,100	5.12	1,877,912
2005	----	421.3	----	----	382.2	253.8	220.5	189.1	155.5	115.7	75.9	382,743	351,083	253,800	6.53	2,290,850
2006	----	434.8	----	----	390.9	258.9	225.8	192.2	159.5	120.9	79.1	398,921	365,863	258,900	6.67	2,442,474
2007	----	448.0	----	----	408.3	265.5	232.3	199.3	163.4	125.5	84.0	406,800	374,617	265,500	7.04	2,636,885
2008	----	415.1	----	----	373.5	243.7	213.2	183.9	152.7	115.8	78.1	378,588	349,580	243,700	8.49	2,967,871
2009	----	429.7	----	----	391.5	265.8	234.3	203.5	169.7	128.7	89.6	393,544	361,316	265,800	7.62	2,751,550
2010	----	399.2	----	----	361.4	240.2	209.4	180.3	148.5	111.0	72.0	366,505	339,051	240,200	8.79	2,981,528
2011[1]	----	----	----	----	----	250.0	NA	186.9				388,873		250,000		

[1] Preliminary.   [2] Held by growers and local dealers in the fall producing areas.
Source: Agricultural Statistics Board, U.S. Department of Agriculture (ASB-USDA)

Production of Potatoes by Seasonal Groups in the United States   In Thousands of Cwt.

	- Winter -	---------- Spring ----------			-------- Summer --------			------------------------------------- Fall -------------------------------------							
Year	Total	Cali- fornia	Florida	Total	Mexico	Virgina	Total	Colo- rado	Idaho	Maine	Minne- sota	North Dakota	Oregan	Washing- ton	Wis- consin	Total
2002	4,206	7,695	7,381	22,452	736	1,386	17,932	27,885	133,385	16,960	18,810	23,460	24,936	92,340	30,750	413,581
2003	4,027	8,360	8,008	24,433	532	1,550	18,766	23,652	123,180	17,030	22,330	27,440	20,991	93,150	32,800	410,588
2004	4,818	8,313	7,678	22,663	340	1,200	18,307	23,791	131,970	19,065	18,920	26,765	19,775	93,810	30,450	410,253
2005	4,892	6,116	6,527	18,724	----	1,029	17,567	22,910	118,288	15,455	17,630	20,500	22,023	95,480	27,880	382,743
2006	4,495	6,044	6,441	19,766	----	1,512	18,166	22,686	128,915	17,980	20,400	25,480	18,533	89,900	29,370	398,921
2007	2,258	6,123	7,807	19,817	----	1,134	15,997	20,981	130,010	16,668	21,560	23,660	20,294	100,800	28,160	406,800
2008	2,530	6,930	7,952	20,132	----	1,254	13,805	21,907	116,475	14,769	20,400	22,680	18,674	93,000	25,730	378,588
2009	2,132	7,175	7,700	21,321	----	1,416	14,321	22,080	132,500	15,263	20,700	19,125	21,460	87,230	28,980	393,544
2010	NA	10,935	7,950	24,797	----	952	12,971	21,528	112,970	15,892	17,010	22,000	20,058	88,440	24,293	366,505
2011[1]	NA	10,920	9,112	25,573	----	1,180	12,960	21,291	127,070	14,310	16,685	18,865	23,342	98,400	25,000	388,873

[1] Preliminary.   Source: Agricultural Statistics Board, U.S. Department of Agriculture (ASB-USDA)

Utilization of Potatoes in the United States   In Thousands of Cwt.

	--- Sales ---											------------- Non-Sales -------------			
				-------------------------- For Processing --------------------------					-------- Other Sales --------		Used on			
Crop Year	Table Stock	Chips, Shoe- strings	Dehyd- ration	Frozen French Fries	Other Frozen Products	Canned Potatoes	Other Canned Products[2]	Starch & Flour	Live- stock Feed	Seed	Total Sales	Farms Where Grown	Shrink- age & Loss	Total Non- Sales	Total
2001	122,552	54,080	40,759	126,711	23,598	2,590	1,722	1,015	3,496	24,537	401,060	4,088	31,227	36,613	437,673
2002	131,889	51,640	51,357	124,875	28,951	2,744	2,089	1,050	3,044	24,005	421,644	4,144	30,905	36,527	458,171
2003	133,143	52,790	48,418	126,515	23,870	3,086	1,168	1,379	2,005	24,603	416,977	4,000	35,294	40,837	457,814
2004	130,418	50,068	48,541	131,592	23,003	2,843	984	1,531	1,942	22,915	413,837	3,601	37,408	42,204	456,041
2005	114,123	52,294	43,387	126,429	25,376	2,174	958	1,622	1,999	22,254	390,616	3,595	28,519	33,310	423,926
2006	113,335	64,377	48,809	126,083	24,229	1,957	930	1,369	1,610	23,610	406,309	3,520	29,639	34,389	440,698
2007	110,860	54,343	49,021	139,624	26,571	2,504	800	4,029	1,160	22,297	411,209	2,986	29,561	33,666	444,875
2008	109,351	50,988	40,646	134,123	19,519	2,070	790	5,288	803	20,900	384,478	3,315	26,438	30,576	415,055
2009	116,326	42,548	44,477	138,589	21,004	1,983	748	6,504	6,533	20,219	398,931	3,346	29,135	33,670	432,601
2010[1]	107,407	54,692	34,130	135,557	13,360	1,658	689	6,356	593	20,621	375,063	3,002	24,990	29,210	404,273

[1] Preliminary.   [2] Hash, stews and soups.   Source: Agricultural Statistics Board, U.S. Department of Agriculture (ASB-USDA)

POTATOES

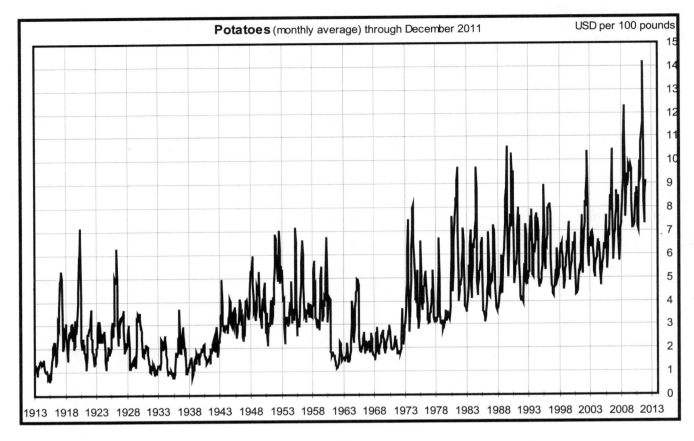

Potatoes (monthly average) through December 2011 — USD per 100 pounds

Per Capita Utilization of Potatoes in the United States — In Pounds (Farm Weight)

Year	Total	Fresh	Freezing	Chips & Shoe-string	Dehy-drating	Canning	Total Processing
2003	137.9	46.8	57.1	17.2	15.5	1.4	91.2
2004	134.6	45.8	57.4	16.4	13.8	1.2	88.8
2005	125.4	41.3	54.4	16.1	12.8	0.9	84.1
2006	123.7	38.6	53.3	18.6	12.4	0.8	85.1
2007	124.4	38.7	53.2	18.6	13.0	0.9	85.7
2008	118.3	37.8	51.5	15.7	12.4	0.9	80.5
2009	113.5	36.7	50.5	13.7	11.8	0.8	76.8
2010	113.9	36.8	50.1	15.0	11.2	0.7	77.1
2011[1]	112.2	35.0	49.5	16.0	11.0	0.7	77.2
2012[2]	112.4	35.2	49.7	14.9	11.9	0.8	77.2

[1] Preliminary.   [2] Forecast.   Source: Agricultural Statistics Board, U.S. Department of Agriculture (ASB-USDA)

Average Price Received by Farmers for Potatoes in the U.S. — In Dollars Per Hundred Pounds (Cwt.)

Year	Jan.	Feb.	Mar.	Apr.	May	June	July	Aug.	Sept.	Oct.	Nov.	Dec.	Season Average
2002	6.90	7.34	8.26	8.00	8.62	9.39	10.40	8.00	6.14	5.44	6.38	6.67	6.67
2003	6.67	6.33	6.87	6.94	6.96	6.68	6.30	5.75	5.24	5.03	5.46	5.77	5.88
2004	5.75	5.87	6.09	6.62	6.47	6.16	6.46	5.77	5.32	4.70	5.02	5.36	5.65
2005	5.59	5.79	6.44	6.20	6.23	6.29	7.63	7.02	5.69	5.37	6.26	6.83	7.04
2006	7.07	6.76	8.50	8.35	7.83	8.41	10.46	8.23	6.12	5.76	6.59	6.79	7.31
2007	7.06	7.42	7.93	8.71	7.95	7.75	8.48	6.85	5.81	5.68	6.47	7.02	7.51
2008	7.33	7.51	8.37	8.45	9.16	10.78	12.33	11.33	8.65	7.60	8.77	9.30	9.09
2009	9.40	8.87	9.27	9.81	9.62	9.48	9.81	9.61	8.27	7.11	7.22	7.47	8.19
2010	7.17	7.34	7.42	8.42	8.57	8.25	8.83	7.78	7.22	7.03	8.01	9.94	8.79
2011[1]	9.08	9.26	10.74	11.17	11.17	11.59	14.19	10.47	8.30	7.33	8.54	9.08	

[1] Preliminary.   Source: Agricultural Statistics Board, U.S. Department of Agriculture (ASB-USDA)

Potatoes Processed[1] in the United States, Eight States   In Thousands of Cwt.

States	Storage Season	to Dec. 1	to Jan. 1	to Feb. 1	to Mar. 1	to Apr. 1	to May 1	to June 1	Entire Season
Idaho and Oregon-Malheur Co.	2003-04	24,310	30,730	36,260	43,640	49,570	56,380	63,770	77,530
	2004-05	24,360	30,840	36,820	44,610	51,000	58,090	65,800	84,600
	2005-06	22,840	29,300	35,970	43,300	50,820	57,830	65,030	77,360
	2006-07	27,090	34,070	41,350	49,840	56,650	63,680	71,220	85,630
	2007-08	26,230	33,250	40,310	48,660	55,460	63,000	70,700	88,030
	2008-09	22,380	28,980	35,430	42,150	49,030	55,570	62,940	77,340
	2009-10	23,110	29,180	35,170	42,050	49,200	56,100	62,930	79,400
	2010-11	21,040	26,840	32,700	39,240	46,180	52,830	59,440	70,050
	2011-12	28,060	34,800	41,800					
Maine[2]	2003-04	1,590	2,085	2,720	3,420	4,095	4,740	5,400	7,270
	2004-05	1,540	1,970	2,600	3,135	3,700	4,340	4,910	6,590
	2005-06	1,365	1,880	2,485	3,090	3,800	4,450	5,130	6,825
	2006-07	1,755	2,360	2,910	3,465	4,185	4,810	5,470	7,560
	2007-08	1,700	2,170	2,815	3,440	3,990	4,670	5,240	7,550
	2008-09	1,635	2,240	2,895	3,515	4,005	4,795	5,540	7,545
	2009-10	1,575	2,060	2,680	3,265	3,915	4,550	5,260	7,160
	2010-11	1,860	2,390	3,000	3,620	4,320	4,980	5,645	7,490
	2011-12	1,860	2,365	3,070					
Washington & Oregon-Other	2003-04	32,670	38,520	43,610	51,210	58,500	64,160	72,350	79,800
	2004-05	32,305	38,130	43,570	50,730	57,140	63,855	71,355	78,680
	2005-06	30,310	35,895	40,545	48,290	55,320	61,855	69,360	78,550
	2006-07	30,980	37,060	41,290	49,930	56,690	63,170	70,410	77,355
	2007-08	30,595	36,940	42,350	50,165	57,160	67,690	72,380	82,770
	2008-09	32,560	38,050	42,795	49,865	56,350	62,635	70,625	81,260
	2009-10	25,395	31,245	36,530	43,780	50,130	56,700	64,805	75,690
	2010-11	27,670	33,570	38,815	46,700	53,660	60,145	67,655	77,940
	2011-12	31,745	38,160	44,465					
Other States[3]	2003-04	13,835	16,505	19,590	22,685	25,920	29,480	32,845	42,160
	2004-05	12,490	15,000	17,965	20,910	24,150	27,480	30,945	41,175
	2005-06	11,055	14,070	17,005	19,895	22,520	25,270	27,740	35,535
	2006-07	14,355	17,800	21,415	24,690	28,205	31,560	35,040	43,565
	2007-08	15,040	17,535	20,755	23,900	26,650	29,710	32,600	39,430
	2008-09	12,480	15,120	18,165	21,030	24,025	26,515	29,590	37,285
	2009-10	10,865	13,565	16,305	18,995	21,600	24,355	27,375	34,240
	2010-11	11,820	14,785	17,435	20,370	23,215	25,775	28,690	35,430
	2011-12	11,215	13,650	16,330					
Total	2003-04	72,405	87,840	102,180	120,955	138,085	154,760	174,365	206,760
	2004-05	70,695	85,940	100,955	119,385	135,990	153,765	173,010	211,045
	2005-06	65,570	81,145	96,005	114,575	132,460	149,405	167,260	198,270
	2006-07	74,210	91,320	107,895	127,050	145,760	163,250	182,170	214,225
	2007-08	73,565	89,895	106,230	126,165	143,260	165,070	180,920	217,780
	2008-09	68,975	84,280	99,155	116,400	133,220	149,285	168,420	203,005
	2009-10	60,945	76,050	90,685	108,090	124,845	141,705	160,370	196,490
	2010-11	62,390	77,585	91,950	109,930	127,375	143,730	161,430	190,910
	2011-12	72,880	88,975	105,665					
Dehy-drated[4]	2003-04	14,250	18,440	22,050	26,090	30,290	34,630	39,070	47,750
	2004-05	14,525	18,540	21,875	25,970	30,020	33,685	38,505	47,805
	2005-06	11,920	15,655	19,225	22,765	26,605	30,065	34,130	41,625
	2006-07	14,590	19,250	23,635	27,885	32,210	36,480	40,915	49,375
	2007-08	12,815	16,785	21,040	25,350	29,500	33,650	37,975	46,660
	2008-09	10,675	14,490	18,335	21,465	24,875	28,195	31,870	39,345
	2009-10	10,985	14,035	17,150	19,895	23,155	26,630	30,045	38,915
	2010-11	7,960	10,795	13,645	16,485	19,415	22,740	25,855	32,700
	2011-12	13,375	16,845	20,860					

[1] Total quantity received and used for processing regardless of the State in which the potatoes were produced. Amount excludes quantities used for potato chips in Maine, Michigan and Wisconsin.   [2] Includes Maine grown potatoes only.   [3] Colorado, Minnesota, , Nevada, North Dakota and Wisconsin.
[4] Dehydrated products except starch and flour. Included in above totals. Includes CO, ID, NV, ND, OR, WA, and WI.
Source: National Agricultural Statistics Service, U.S. Department of Agriculture (NASS-USDA)

Rayon and Other Synthetic Fibers

World Cellulosic Fiber Production   In Thousands of Metric Tons

Year	Brazil	Bulgaria	China	CIS	Czech Republic	India	Indonesia	Japan	Mexico	Taiwan	Thailand	United States	World Total
2002	34.2	5.6	682.1	72.9	7.3	285.7	214.0	68.1	16.8	114.2	71.1	80.7	2,125
2003	47.2	5.2	800.2	78.8	9.1	283.0	223.0	68.3	8.4	121.5	73.8	75.3	2,249
2004	46.8	5.0	966.1	77.2	9.2	311.5	234.0	67.1	8.4	134.9	79.4	66.8	2,465
2005	40.1	5.0	1,056.0	46.6	9.5	295.4	245.0	66.6	3.8	114.5	78.2	49.1	2,483
2006	34.3	5.0	1,179.0	29.2	9.4	309.5	280.0	65.1	----	132.3	80.2	27.2	2,635
2007	39.7	5.0	1,360.2	27.9	9.3	345.4	325.0	71.5	----	136.3	95.4	25.3	2,914
2008	15.9	5.0	1,206.8	9.2	5.9	301.0	282.0	69.1	----	105.5	80.2	22.8	2,545
2009	30.3	4.6	1,401.1	4.5	9.0	327.1	295.0	54.5	----	115.4	104.0	17.1	2,763
2010[1]	42.0	6.0	2,010.0	16.3	13.0	340.6	407.0	96.0	----	150.0	142.0	25.0	3,765
2011[2]	42.0	6.0	2,260.0	16.3	13.0	340.6	407.0	96.0	----	150.0	142.0	25.0	4,015

[1] Preliminary. [2] Producing capacity. *Source: Fiber Economics Bureau, Inc. (FEB)*

World Noncellulosic Fiber Production (Except Olefin)   In Thousands of Metric Tons

Year	Brazil	China	India	Indonesia	Japan	Rep. of Korea	Mexico	Pakistan	Taiwan	Thailand	Turkey	United States	World Total
2002	293.1	8,849.4	1,695.3	1,132.8	1,129.1	2,455.7	509.6	581.5	3,091.3	852.6	728.1	2,805.0	28,052
2003	314.2	10,456.0	1,792.0	1,144.2	1,030.3	2,418.0	474.9	646.8	3,060.9	872.5	766.9	2,719.5	29,450
2004	330.9	12,474.1	1,904.2	1,064.5	989.2	2,194.3	474.9	659.3	2,965.0	905.9	792.0	2,858.2	31,429
2005	255.6	16,097.9	1,849.2	1,072.0	955.4	1,697.4	390.6	565.2	2,587.8	920.7	788.8	2,479.3	35,261
2006	274.2	18,383.1	2,263.9	1,100.7	923.9	1,484.6	271.0	550.7	2,292.4	869.9	788.8	2,479.3	35,261
2007	275.8	21,356.5	2,652.6	1,148.2	901.1	1,540.2	252.6	558.1	2,345.1	831.0	740.1	2,311.8	38,403
2008	282.4	21,681.1	2,669.4	1,116.3	771.1	1,354.9	195.5	528.8	1,947.3	842.3	580.0	1,908.4	37,023
2009	265.4	23,129.8	2,977.8	1,110.8	569.6	1,300.5	177.4	526.0	1,899.4	842.3	551.0	1,614.8	37,771
2010[1]	331.4	31,151.0	4,221.0	1,399.0	981.2	1,673.0	268.0	746.0	2,162.1	1,051.0	805.0	2,182.6	50,861
2011[2]	385.5	32,776.0	4,551.0	1,409.0	946.2	1,618.0	268.0	746.0	1,961.1	1,145.0	805.0	2,247.7	52,763

[1] Preliminary. [2] Producing capacity. *Source: Fiber Economics Bureau, Inc. (FEB)*

World Production of Synthetic Fibers   In Thousands of Metric Tons

	Noncellulosic Fiber Production (Except Olefin)							Glass Fiber Production							Cigarette Tow Production
	By Fibers				World Total										
Year	Acrylic & Mod-acrylic	Nylon & Aramid	Polyester	Other	Yarn & Monofilaments	Staple & Tow & Fiberfill	Total	Europe	Japan	Other Americas	United States	Total	China	USSR	
2002	2,713	3,941	21,048	350	15,993	12,059	28,052	718	251	96	1,222	90	34	2,661	612
2003	2,707	3,951	22,365	427	16,853	12,597	29,450	724	250	100	1,307	120	37	2,790	633
2004	2,824	3,976	24,136	492	17,957	13,472	31,429	740	250	104	1,363	150	40	2,903	651
2005	2,698	3,893	26,410	510	19,293	14,218	33,511								665
2006	2,525	3,953	28,200	583	20,712	14,549	35,261								680
2007	2,407	3,954	31,406	636	23,027	15,375	38,403								679
2008	1,837	3,596	30,991	600	22,620	14,402	37,023								699
2009	1,938	3,305	31,937	592	23,104	14,667	37,771								740
2010[1]	2,641	4,800	42,568	852	31,046	19,815	50,861								
2011[2]	2,646	4,729	44,503	885	32,687	20,076	52,763								

[1] Preliminary. [2] Producing capacity. [3] Alginate, azion, spandex, saran, etc. *Source: Fiber Economics Bureau, Inc. (FEB)*

Artificial (Cellulosic) Fiber Distribution in the United States   In Millions of Pounds

	Yarn & Monofilament					Staple & Tow					Glass Fiber Shipments
	Producers' Shipments			Imports	Domestic Consumption	Producers' Shipments			Imports	Domestic Consumption	
Year	Domestic	Exports	Total			Domestic	Exports	Total			
2001	54.3	33.7	88.0	14.5	68.8	117.2	35.5	152.7	33.9	151.2	----
2002	41.2	33.2	74.4	12.7	53.9	91.1	12.6	103.7	56.2	147.4	----
2003	32.5	35.5	68.0	11.7	44.2	86.7	13.1	99.8	44.5	131.2	----
2004	26.7	38.7	65.4	12.2	38.9	77.4	9.9	87.2	63.9	141.3	----
2005	22.6	41.4	64.0	9.3	31.9	40.2	8.1	48.2	91.0	131.2	----
2006	22.4	37.6	60.0	7.7	30.1	----	8.9	8.9	141.4	141.4	----
2007	18.7	41.1	59.8	17.0	35.7	----	5.4	5.4	200.7	200.7	----
2008	15.4	44.5	59.9	11.8	27.2	----	6.8	6.8	179.8	179.8	----
2009	12.7	43.2	55.9	7.4	20.1	----	3.5	3.5	168.3	168.3	----
2010[1]	13.9	46.1	60.0	10.8	24.7	----	3.1	3.1	164.6	164.6	----

[1] Preliminary. *Source: Fiber Economice Bureau, Inc.*

Man-Made Fiber Production in the United States   In Millions of Pounds

	- Artificial (Cellulosic) Fibers - - Rayon & Acetate -			------- Synthetic (Noncellulosic) Fibers -----------										
	Filament Yarn & Monofil-	Staple	Total Cellu-	----- Yarn & Monofilament -----				Staple & Tow				Total Noncel-	Total Manu-	Total Glass
Year	ament	& Tow	lostic	Nylon	Polyester	Olefin	Total Yarn	Nylon	Polyester	Acrylic & Mod-acrylic	Olefin	Total Staple	lulosic Fibers	factured Fibers	Fiber
2002	----	104	104	1,772	1,218	2,331	5,321	681	2,050	340	749	3,820	9,141	----	2,759
2003	----	100	100	1,762	1,145	2,349	5,255	697	1,886	270	680	3,533	8,788	----	2,789
2004	----	----	----	1,837	1,242	2,383	5,462	680	2,064	240	676	3,660	9,123	----	----
2005	----	----	----	1,788	1,111	2,395	5,295	598	2,019	140	699	3,455	8,750	----	----
2006	----	----	----	1,739	1,072	2,223	5,034	515	1,864	----	622	3,001	8,035	----	----
2007	----	----	----	1,636	1,017	2,266	4,918	429	1,719	----	588	2,736	7,654	----	----
2008	----	----	----	1,348	915	1,915	4,178	266	1,423	----	487	2,177	6,355	----	----
2009[1]	----	----	----	1,127	837	1,622	3,586	178	1,163	----	410	1,752	5,338	----	----
2010[2]	----	----	----	1,268	1,088	1,855	4,211	90	1,310	----	431	1,831	6,042	----	----

[1] Preliminary.   [2] Estimate.   Source: Fiber Economics Bureau, Inc. (FEB)

Domestic Distribution of Synthetic (Noncellulosic) Fibers in the United States   In Millions of Pounds

	---------- Yarn & Monofilament ----------							--------------- Staple & Tow ---------------							
	----- Producers' Shipments ----- ----- Domestic -----						Domestic Consumption	----- Producers' Shipments ----- ----- Domestic -----							Domestic Consumption
Year	Nylon	Poly-ester	Olefin	Total	Exports	Total	Imports		Nylon	Poly-ester	Acrylic & Mod-acrylic	Olefin	Total	Exports	Total Imports	
2002	1,668	1,139	2,289	5,092	189	5,281	765	5,856	637	1,823	255	723	3,438	353	3,791	875	4,312
2003	1,666	1,088	2,318	5,061	179	5,240	766	5,827	673	1,688	211	635	3,206	246	3,452	829	4,035
2004	1,722	1,119	2,347	5,167	249	5,416	785	5,952	658	1,788	200	641	3,287	296	3,583	766	4,053
2005	1,688	1,014	2,369	5,053	197	5,250	849	5,903	582	1,765	122	650	3,120	292	3,411	914	4,034
2006	1,589	914	2,198	4,664	211	4,875	819	5,482	492	1,624	----	596	2,713	268	2,981	1,007	3,719
2007	1,526	928	2,219	4,672	199	4,871	739	5,411	407	1,506	----	549	2,461	256	2,717	1,029	3,490
2008	1,336	841	1,921	4,098	144	4,242	692	4,790	252	1,279	----	448	1,979	184	2,163	1,038	3,017
2009	1,120	781	1,621	3,522	82	3,603	568	4,090	150	1,080	----	363	1,594	135	1,728	841	2,435
2010[1]	1,232	1,002	1,852	4,086	104	4,190	670	4,755	57	1,157	----	390	1,604	169	1,773	969	2,573

[1] Preliminary.   Source: Fiber Economics Bureau, Inc. (FEB)

Mill Consumption of Fiber & Products and Per Capita Consumption in the United States   In Millions of Pounds

	------- Cellulosic Fibers -------				-- Noncellulosic Fibers --			Total Manu-factured Fibers[2]					- Per Capita[4] Mill Consumption (Lbs.) -				
Year	Yarn & Monofil-ament	Staple & Tow	Net Waste	Total Cell-ulosic	Non-cellu-losic	Net Waste	Total Non-cellulosic		Cotton	Wool	Other Fibers[3]	Grand Total	Man-made Finers	Cotton	Wool	Other Fibers[3]	Total
2001	69	151	2.4	222	9,556	193	9,749	9,971	3,983	87	168.1	1,210	43.5	33.1	1.4	2.1	80.0
2002	54	147	1.8	203	10,173	190	10,363	10,566	3,576	56	110.3	14,308	47.7	34.3	1.3	2.2	85.5
2003	44	131	1.3	177	9,873	177	10,050	10,226	3,210	43	106.3	13,586	48.5	34.8	1.4	2.7	87.4
2004	39	141	1.5	182	10,025	144	10,169	10,351	3,126	44	123.4	13,644	48.7	35.1	1.4	3.4	88.7
2005	32	131	2.0	165	9,954	136	10,090	10,255	3,005	36	141.3	13,437	49.8	37.7	1.4	3.1	92.0
2006	30	141	2.9	174	9,240	73	9,312	9,487	2,729	34	106.7	12,357	48.5	38.3	1.4	2.9	91.1
2007	36	201	2.8	239	8,901	77	8,978	9,218	2,624	26	101.1	11,969	47.6	38.5	1.4	2.6	90.1
2008	27	180	2.9	210	7,807	59	7,866	8,076	2,093	30	96.6	10,296	43.4	32.8	1.3	2.4	79.8
2009[1]	20	168	0.6	189	6,583	23	6,606	6,795	1,580	25	84.2	8,484	38.5	29.0	1.1	1.8	70.4

[1] Preliminary.   [2] Excludes Glass Fiber.   [3] Includes silk, linen, jute and sisal & others.   [4] Mill consumption plus inports less exports of semimanufactured and unmanufactured products.   Source: Fiber Economics Bureau, Inc. (FEB)

Producer Price Index of Grey Synthetic Broadwovens   (1982 = 100)

Year	Jan.	Feb.	Mar.	Apr.	May	June	July	Aug.	Sept.	Oct.	Nov.	Dec.	Average
2002	106.7	106.4	108.0	108.5	107.7	108.2	107.3	108.1	108.0	107.2	107.3	108.4	107.7
2003	108.2	108.2	107.6	107.7	110.1	106.0	105.7	107.1	106.7	106.0	106.6	107.7	107.3
2004	107.3	106.9	106.2	107.4	108.9	109.0	107.5	106.2	106.3	106.3	106.2	106.2	107.0
2005	108.5	108.8	109.1	110.5	110.2	110.0	110.7	110.9	110.8	112.4	113.3	116.2	111.0
2006	118.2	119.5	119.8	119.2	119.4	119.4	119.5	120.4	119.1	119.5	119.0	118.1	119.3
2007	117.8	118.8	118.9	119.1	119.6	119.8	120.3	121.5	122.9	122.7	123.0	122.9	120.6
2008	122.9	123.0	122.8	123.0	123.3	123.3	123.6	121.8	122.0	121.2	122.0	120.1	122.4
2009	121.7	122.6	122.6	125.9	125.8	127.5	127.2	124.3	124.2	124.3	124.7	125.0	124.7
2010	124.9	125.1	125.2	125.9	125.2	127.3	127.8	127.5	127.5	123.4	126.8	129.4	126.3
2011[1]	131.1	133.0	133.9	135.5	138.2	140.0	140.9	139.4	139.3	138.9	138.5	138.7	137.3

[1] Preliminary.   Source: Bureau of Labor Statistics, U.S. Department of Commerce (BLS) (0337-03)

Rice

Rice is a grain that is cultivated on every continent except Antarctica and is the primary food for half the people in the world. Rice cultivation probably originated as early as 10,000 BC in Asia. Rice is grown at varying altitudes (sea level to about 3,000 meters), in varying climates (tropical to temperate), and on dry to flooded land. The growth duration of rice plants is 3-6 months, depending on variety and growing conditions. Rice is harvested by hand in developing countries or by combines in industrialized countries. Asian countries produce about 90% of rice grown worldwide. Rough rice futures and options are traded on the Chicago Board of Trade (CBOT).

Prices – Rough rice prices on the CBOT nearest-futures chart rallied in mid-2011 and posted a new 3-year high of $18.255 per hundred pounds in September 2011. However, rough rice prices then sank during the remainder of the year and closed 2011 up +4.3% at $14.605 per hundred pounds.

Regarding cash prices, the average monthly price of rice received by farmers in the U.S. in the first six months of the 2011-12 marketing year (i.e., August 2011 through July 2012) rose by +13.8% yr/yr to $14.28 per hundred pounds (cwt.).

Supply – World rice production in the 2011-12 marketing year rose +2.5% to 693.247 million metric tons, which is a new record high. The world's largest rice producers were China with 29.0% of world production in 2011-12, India with 22.1%, Indonesia with 8.5%, Bangladesh with 7.4%, Vietnam with 6.0%, and Thailand with 4.4%. U.S. production of rice in 2011-12 fell -24.0% yr/yr to 108.009 million cwt (hundred pounds), below last year's record high of 243.104 million cwt (hundred pounds).

Demand – World utilization of rice in 2011-12 rose +2.3% to a record high of 456.788 million metric tons. U.S. rice consumption in 2011-12 fell -7.8% yr/yr to 127.0 million cwt (hundred pounds), below last year's record high of 137.8 million cwt (hundred pounds).

Trade – World exports of rice in 2011-12 fell -2.8% yr/yr to 33.186 million metric tons, below last year's record high of 34.129 million metric tons. The world's largest rice exporters are Thailand, India, and the U.S. with 19.6% each of world exports, Pakistan with 11.3%, Uruguay with 8.5%, Vietnam 2.7%, and Burma with 2.3%. U.S. rice imports in 2011-12 rose +3.8% yr/yr to 19.0 million cwt (hundred pounds), but still below the 2007-08 record high of 23.9 million cwt. U.S. rice exports in 2011-12 fell by -18.5% yr/yr to 91.0 million cwt.

World Rice Supply and Distribution   In Thousands of Metric Tons

| | | | -------- Imports -------- | | | | | | ---------- Utilization ---------- | | -------- Ending Stocks ---------- | | |
Crop Year	Brazil	Indo-nesia	European Union	Iran	Nigeria	Saudi Arabia	Total	China	India	Total	China	India	Total
2005-06	750	539	1,124	1,500	1,650	1,357	26,475	128,000	85,088	412,337	36,783	10,520	76,614
2006-07	732	2,000	1,340	1,460	1,500	958	28,339	127,200	86,700	418,407	35,915	11,430	75,098
2007-08	422	350	1,568	1,150	1,800	1,166	29,893	127,450	90,466	425,625	37,762	13,000	79,966
2008-09	675	250	1,339	1,670	1,750	1,072	27,177	133,000	91,090	434,182	38,546	19,000	91,533
2009-10[1]	688	1,150	1,317	1,100	1,750	1,069	28,075	134,320	85,508	434,592	40,534	20,500	94,163
2010-11[2]	600	2,775	1,150	1,300	2,400	1,100	32,557	135,000	90,680	446,463	42,572	23,000	97,227
2011-12[3]	600	1,000	1,170	1,500	2,300	1,150	30,115	138,500	94,000	456,788	44,447	24,500	100,120

[1] Preliminary.   [2] Estimate.   [3] Forecast.   *Source: Foreign Agricultural Service, U.S. Department of Agriculture (FAS-USDA)*

World Production of Rough Rice   In Thousands of Metric Tons

Year	Bang-ladesh	Brazil	Burma	China	India	Indo-nesia	Japan	Korea	Pakistan	Philip-pines	Thailand	Vietnam	World Total
2005-06	43,141	11,579	18,000	180,591	137,699	54,200	11,342	6,435	8,321	15,109	27,576	34,503	622,897
2006-07	43,504	11,316	18,276	181,714	140,039	54,729	10,695	6,306	8,176	15,516	27,652	34,730	626,220
2007-08	43,204	12,057	18,500	186,034	145,050	57,364	10,893	5,962	8,551	16,633	30,000	36,932	644,750
2008-09	46,505	12,603	17,500	191,900	148,785	59,395	11,029	6,468	10,351	17,071	30,076	38,904	669,135
2009-10[1]	46,505	11,660	18,190	195,100	133,648	57,276	10,592	6,502	10,201	15,511	30,697	39,989	659,422
2010-11[2]	49,805	13,676	18,534	195,714	143,984	56,349	10,604	5,810	7,501	16,729	30,700	42,080	676,419
2011-12[3]	51,005	11,500	18,103	200,714	153,015	58,740	10,503	5,616	9,826	16,889	30,758	41,840	693,247

[1] Preliminary.   [2] Estimate.   [3] Forecast.   *Source: Foreign Agricultural Service, U.S. Department of Agriculture (FAS-USDA)*

World Exports of Rice (Milled Basis)   In Thousands of Metric Tons

Year	Argentina	Australia	Burma	China	European Union	Guyana	India	Pakistan	Thailand	Uruguay	Vietnam	United States	World Total
2005-06	485	326	47	1,216	161	170	4,688	3,664	7,376	3,660	834	4,705	29,724
2006-07	452	166	31	1,340	148	190	5,740	2,839	9,557	2,923	734	4,522	31,432
2007-08	443	36	541	1,372	152	254	4,654	2,982	10,011	3,336	778	4,649	31,667
2008-09	554	15	1,052	747	140	185	2,090	2,910	8,570	3,032	987	5,950	28,925
2009-10[1]	488	59	445	650	244	244	2,082	4,000	9,047	3,514	711	6,734	31,374
2010-11[2]	645	350	750	502	250	275	2,800	3,200	10,500	3,487	995	7,000	34,129
2011-12[3]	630	450	750	600	350	260	6,500	3,750	6,500	2,826	900	6,500	33,186

[1] Preliminary.   [2] Estimate.   [3] Forecast.   *Source: Foreign Agricultural Service, U.S. Department of Agriculture (FAS-USDA)*

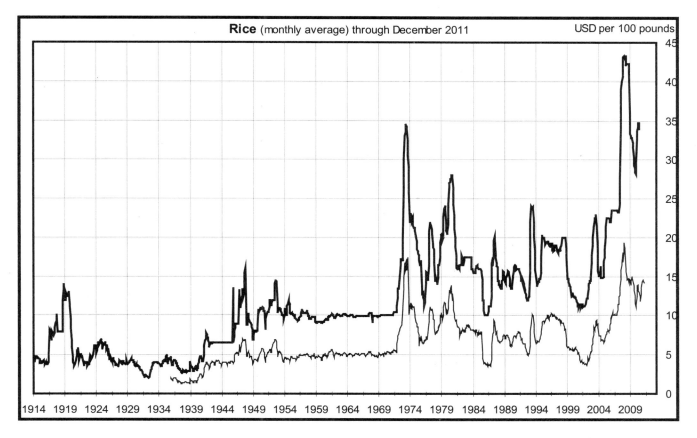

Rice (monthly average) through December 2011 — USD per 100 pounds

Average Wholesale Price of Rice No. 2 (Medium)[1] Southwest Louisiana   In Dollars Per Cwt. Bagged

Year	Jan.	Feb.	Mar.	Apr.	May	June	July	Aug.	Sept.	Oct.	Nov.	Dec.	Average
2001-02	11.06	11.50	11.50	11.50	11.08	11.50	11.50	11.43	10.94	11.13	11.13	11.13	11.28
2002-03	11.13	11.50	12.25	12.25	12.25	12.63	13.50	14.05	14.25	14.44	14.50	14.88	13.13
2003-04	16.75	17.70	19.00	19.95	21.25	21.38	22.30	22.46	22.50	23.00	21.50	21.50	20.77
2004-05	18.60	15.69	15.23	15.13	15.13	16.31	14.88	14.88	14.88	14.88	14.88	14.94	15.45
2005-06	17.00	17.50	18.45	20.13	21.38	22.50	22.50	22.50	22.50	22.50	22.50	22.35	20.98
2006-07	21.94	22.00	22.00	23.50	23.50	23.50	23.50	23.50	23.50	23.50	23.50	23.50	23.12
2007-08	23.50	23.50	23.30	23.25	23.25	23.25	24.31	27.45	34.00	39.00	40.00	40.00	28.73
2008-09	40.63	43.10	43.25	43.06	42.88	43.25	43.25	42.15	42.25	42.25	42.25	42.25	42.55
2009-10	41.05	35.75	33.25	33.05	32.75	32.75	32.63	32.15	31.56	30.35	29.25	28.88	32.79
2010-11[2]	28.35	28.16	29.69	32.70	33.75	34.15	34.75	34.75	34.00				32.26

[1] U.S. No. 2 -- broken not to exceed 4%.   [2] Preliminary.   *Source: Economic Research Service, U.S. Department of Agriculture (ERS-USDA)*

Average Price Received by Farmers for Rice (Rough) in the United States   In Dollars Per Hundred Pounds (Cwt.)

Year	Jan.	Feb.	Mar.	Apr.	May	June	July	Aug.	Sept.	Oct.	Nov.	Dec.	Average[2]
2002-03	3.71	3.94	3.69	3.70	4.13	4.66	4.24	4.31	4.61	4.84	5.43	5.31	4.38
2003-04	5.47	6.18	6.44	6.99	7.57	8.57	8.23	8.45	8.65	9.30	9.37	8.79	7.83
2004-05	8.96	8.47	7.60	7.36	7.37	7.39	6.90	6.97	6.98	6.98	6.96	6.82	7.40
2005-06	6.58	6.76	6.99	7.46	7.49	7.80	8.02	8.05	8.16	8.03	8.41	8.18	7.66
2006-07	8.81	9.03	9.65	10.10	9.91	10.40	10.10	10.00	10.20	10.00	10.00	10.10	9.86
2007-08	10.10	10.30	10.70	11.40	11.50	12.40	12.60	13.60	14.60	15.90	16.50	16.80	13.03
2008-09	18.10	16.90	18.10	19.40	18.60	18.20	16.00	15.60	15.00	14.60	14.70	14.20	16.62
2009-10	14.70	14.60	14.30	14.00	14.40	15.00	14.80	14.30	14.30	13.80	13.20	12.60	14.17
2010-11	11.60	11.10	11.50	12.50	13.80	14.00	13.40	13.00	13.00	12.40	11.80	12.70	12.57
2011-12[1]	13.60	14.30	14.60	14.50	14.20	14.20	13.90						14.19

[1] Preliminary.   [2] Weighted average by sales.   *Source: Economic Research Service, U.S. Department of Agriculture (ERS-USDA)*

RICE

Salient Statistics of Rice, Rough & Milled (Rough Equivalent) in the United States   In Millions of Cwt.

Crop Year Beginning Aug. 1	Stocks Aug. 1	Pro-duction	Imports	Total Supply	Food	Brewers	Seed	Total	Resi-dual	Exports	Total Disap-pearance	CCC Stocks July 31	Put Under Price Support	Long	Med-ium	All Classes	Milled Long
2006-07	43.0	193.7	20.6	258.2	124.7	4	3.4	128.1	4	90.8	218.8	0	----	6.64	6.07	6.50	10.52
2007-08	39.3	198.4	23.9	261.6	123.2	4	3.7	126.8	4	105.3	232.1	0	----	6.57	6.37	6.50	10.12
2008-09	29.5	203.7	19.2	252.4	123.8	4	3.9	127.6	4	94.4	222.0	0	----	6.54	6.52	6.50	10.00
2009-10	30.4	219.9	19.0	269.3	120.0	4	4.5	124.5	4	108.3	232.8	0	----	6.64	6.63	6.50	9.94
2010-11[1]	36.5	243.1	18.3	297.9	129.7	4	3.3	137.8	4	111.6	249.5	0	----	6.23	6.50	6.50	9.93
2011-12[2]	48.5	185.0	19.0	255.5	123.3	4	3.7	127.0	4	91.0	218.0						

Government Support Program / Loan Rate ($ Per Cwt.) / Rough[3]

[1] Preliminary.   [2] Forecast.   [3] Loan rate for each class of rice is the sum of the whole kernels' loan rate weighted by its milling yield (average 56%) and the broken kernels' loan rate weighted by its milling yield (average 12%).   [4] Included in Food.
Source: Economic Research Service, U.S. Department of Agriculture (ERS-USDA)

Acreage, Yield, Production and Prices of Rice in the United States

Crop Year Beginning Aug. 1	Southern States	Cali-fornia	United States	Cali-fornia	United States	Southern States	Cali-fornia	United States	Value of Pro-duction ($1,000)	Arkan-sas[2]	Hous-ton[2]	U.S. No. 2[4]	Thai "A"[5]	Thai "B"[5]
2006-07	2,298	523	2,821	7,660	6,868	153,696	40,040	193,736	1,990,783	22.18	21.10			
2007-08	2,215	533	2,748	8,220	7,185	154,704	43,684	198,388	2,600,871	29.92	29.58			
2008-09	2,459	517	2,976	8,320	6,846	160,703	43,030	203,733	3,603,460	45.05	33.01			
2009-10	2,547	556	3,103	8,600	7,085	172,046	47,804	219,850	3,209,236	31.47	26.52			
2010-11	3,062	553	3,615	8,020	6,725	198,778	44,326	243,104	3,183,213	32.36	27.67			
2011-12[1]	2,038	580	2,618	8,350	7,067	136,607	48,402	185,009	2,631,681					

Acreage Harvested — 1,000 Acres; Yield Per Harvested Acre (In Lbs.); Production — 1,000 Cwt.; Wholesale Prices — $ Per Cwt.; Milled Rice, Average C.I.F. Rotterdam — $ Per Metric Ton

[1] Preliminary.   [2] F.O.B. mills, Arkansas, medium.   [3] Houston, Texas (long grain).   [4] Milled, 4%, container, FAS.
[5] SWR, 100%, bulk.   NA = Not available.   *Source: Economic Research Service, U.S. Department of Agriculture (ERS-USDA)*

U.S. Exports of Milled Rice, by Country of Destination   In Thousands of Metric Tons

Trade Year Beginning October	Canada	Haiti	Iran	Ivory Coast	Jamaica	Mexico	Nether-lands	Peru	Saudi Arabia	South Africa	Switzer-land	United Kingdom	Total
2005-06	236.9	340.3	0	25.0	53.5	822.3	38.2	1.7	93.4	.0	12.4	118.0	4,014
2006-07	243.9	279.3	0	0	42.6	810.2	4.0	.1	96.8	.7	.2	37.6	3,306
2007-08	251.5	314.1	0	15.0	56.4	783.0	6.2	2.9	150.0	20.2	1.0	63.5	3,899
2008-09	207.8	15.3	239.7	31.7	26.4	790.9	6.9	.3	129.8	.7	1.3	57.1	3,388
2009-10	220.0	.4	327.5	.0	28.3	827.0	4.4	3.2	116.1	1.2	.3	65.5	4,258
2010-11[1]	229.1	1.9	334.6		26.6	943.2	5.1	1.6	120.9	1.7	.6	47.4	3,901

[1] Preliminary.   *Source: Economic Research Service, U.S. Department of Agriculture (ERS-USDA)*

U.S. Rice Exports by Export Program   In Thousands of Metric Tons

Year	PL 480	Section 416	CCC Credit Pro-grams[2]	CCC African Relief Exports	EEP[3]	Export Pro-grams[4]	Exports Outside Specified Export Programs	Total U.S. Rice Exports	% Export Programs as a Share of Total Exports
2004	124	0	----	0	0	239	3,460	3,699	6
2005	128	0	----	0	0	159	4,099	4,258	4
2006	59	0	----	0	0	107	3,917	4,024	3
2007	103	0	----	0	0	142	3,174	3,316	4
2008	65	0	----	0	0	91	3,818	3,909	2
2009[1]	44	0	----	0	0	54	3,358	3,411	2

[1] Preliminary.   [2] May not completely reflect exports made under these programs.   [3] Sales not shipments.   [4] Adjusted for estimated overlap between CCC export credit and EEP shipments.   *Source: Economice Research Service, U.S. Department of Agriculture (ERS-USDA)*

Production of Rice (Rough) in the United States, by Type and Variety   In Thousands of Cwt.

Year	Long Grain	Medium Grain	Short Grain	Total	Year	Long Grain	Medium Grain	Short Grain	Total
2002	157,243	52,201	1,516	210,960	2007	143,235	51,063	4,090	198,388
2003	149,011	48,180	2,706	199,897	2008	153,257	47,166	3,310	203,733
2004	170,445	58,689	3,228	230,818	2009	152,725	63,291	3,834	219,850
2005	177,527	42,408	3,300	223,235	2010	183,296	57,144	2,664	243,104
2006	146,214	43,802	3,720	193,736	2011[1]	116,420	65,562	3,027	185,009

[1] Preliminary.   *Source: National Agricultural Statistics Service, U.S. Department of Agriculture (NASS-USDA)*

Rubber

Rubber is a natural or synthetic substance characterized by elasticity, water repellence, and electrical resistance. Pre-Columbian Native South Americans discovered many uses for rubber such as containers, balls, shoes, and waterproofing for fabrics such as coats and capes. The first commercial application of rubber began in 1791 when Samuel Peal patented a method of waterproofing cloth by treating it with a solution of rubber and turpentine. In 1839, Charles Goodyear revolutionized the rubber industry with his discovery of a process called vulcanization, which involves combining rubber and sulfur and heating the mixture.

Natural rubber is obtained from latex, a milky white fluid, from the Hevea Brasiliensis tree. The latex is gathered by cutting a chevron shape through the bark of the rubber tree. The latex is collected in a small cup, with approximately 1 fluid ounce per cutting. The cuttings are usually done every other day until the cuttings reach the ground. The tree is then allowed to renew itself before a new tapping is started. The collected latex is strained, diluted with water, and treated with acid to bind the rubber particles together. The rubber is then pressed between rollers to consolidate the rubber into slabs or thin sheets and is air-dried or smoke-dried for shipment.

During World War II, natural rubber supplies from the Far East were cut off, and the rubber shortage accelerated the development of synthetic rubber in the U.S. Synthetic rubber is produced by chemical reactions, condensation or polymerization, of certain unsaturated hydrocarbons.

Synthetic rubber is made of raw material derived from petroleum, coal, oil, natural gas, and acetylene and is almost identical to natural rubber in chemical and physical properties.

Rubber futures are traded on the Central Japan Commodity Exchange (CJCE). The CJCE's natural rubber contract is based on the RSS3 ribbed smoked sheet No. 3. The CJCE's Rubber Index Futures Contract is based on a composite of 8 component grades from 6 rubber markets in the world. Rubber futures are also traded on the Shanghai Futures Exchange (SHFE) and the Tokyo Commodity Exchange (TOCOM).

Supply – World production of natural rubber in 2010 rose +1.2% to 10.537 million metric tons, which was below the record high of 10.721 million metric tons posted in 2008. The world's largest producers of natural rubber in 2010 were Thailand with 29.0% of world production, Indonesia (26.5%), Malaysia (8.2%), India (8.1%), Vietnam (7.2%), and China (6.6%).

Trade – World exports of natural rubber in 2009 rose +11.2% to a record 1.148 million metric tons. The world's largest exporter of natural rubber in 2009 by far was Thailand with 87.8% of world exports. World imports of natural rubber in 2009 fell by -1.6% to 1.117 million metric tons. The world's largest importers of natural rubber are China with 27.6% of world imports, Malaysia with 32.0%, and the European Union with 11.6%.

World Production of Natural Rubber   In Thousands of Metric Tons

Year	Brazil	China	Côte d'Ivoire	India	Indonesia	Liberia	Malaysia	Nigeria	Philippines	Sri Lanka	Thailand	Vietnam	Total
2001	88.1	477.4	127.9	631.0	1,607.5	107.0	882.0	108.0	85.6	86.2	2,522.5	312.6	7,291.6
2002	95.9	527.4	135.5	649.4	1,630.4	109.0	890.0	112.0	86.9	90.5	2,633.1	298.2	7,517.0
2003	93.8	565.0	124.5	711.7	1,792.4	107.0	985.6	142.0	88.0	92.0	2,860.1	363.5	8,182.7
2004	98.8	574.7	136.8	749.7	2,065.8	114.5	1,168.7	142.0	311.3	94.7	3,006.7	419.0	9,160.0
2005	103.7	513.6	170.1	802.6	2,270.9	111.0	1,126.0	158.6	315.6	104.4	2,979.7	481.6	9,418.0
2006	105.4	538.0	178.3	852.9	2,637.2	93.5	1,283.6	142.5	351.6	109.1	3,070.5	555.4	10,201.3
2007	113.3	588.4	188.5	825.3	2,755.2	120.8	1,199.6	143.0	404.1	117.6	3,022.3	605.8	10,380.8
2008	201.5	547.9	203.0	864.0	2,921.9	84.8	1,072.4	110.4	411.0	129.2	3,166.9	660.0	10,721.3
2009	211.6	618.9	209.5	830.6	2,789.9	59.5	857.0	145.0	391.0	136.0	3,090.3	711.3	10,410.3
2010[1]	221.8	690.8	215.0	851.0	2,788.3	62.1	858.9	143.2	395.2	139.3	3,051.8	754.5	10,537.2

[1] Preliminary.   [2] Estimate.   *Source: Food and Agricultural Organization of the United Nations (FAO-UN)*

World Imports of Natural Rubber   In Metric Tons

Year	Brazil	Canada	China	European Union	Germany	Italy	Malaysia	Mexico	Pakistan	Rep of Korea	United Kingdom	United States	Total
2000	12,096	4,607	58,826	91,070	24,310	12,730	546,757	14,763	17,533	26,359	21,353	121,380	1,042,949
2001	12,880	4,419	110,688	116,120	22,501	27,828	431,206	24,032	18,589	25,680	20,944	115,428	998,326
2002	13,088	3,739	109,299	132,809	34,468	35,623	261,628	27,380	22,291	24,833	19,067	205,635	940,408
2003	11,735	8,489	141,379	136,659	33,683	38,137	293,924	25,457	23,152	25,467	16,904	113,882	923,783
2004	12,345	18,959	200,094	167,011	60,530	34,402	303,345	23,483	26,860	24,189	20,042	112,514	1,066,745
2005	12,358	17,657	190,600	162,664	56,039	34,518	303,852	22,469	24,235	23,636	24,348	97,156	1,011,026
2006	12,100	19,771	266,444	158,632	81,842	35,949	330,408	22,937	29,645	22,964	22,818	68,215	1,124,447
2007	13,024	20,366	246,855	191,235	114,432	38,012	361,713	22,527	22,497	23,399	22,635	89,160	1,196,246
2008[1]	13,649	20,552	251,613	185,746	75,878	34,597	341,173	22,928	22,293	21,342	22,772	93,714	1,134,574
2009[2]	14,003	14,233	307,906	129,105	67,388	24,955	357,254	18,918	16,634	21,036	15,620	69,930	1,116,923

[1] Preliminary.   [2] Estimate.   *Source: Food and Agricultural Organization of the United Nations (FAO-UN)*

RUBBER

World Exports of Natural Rubber In Metric Tons

Year	Belgium	Came-roon	Hong Kong	Germany	Guate-mala	India	Indonesia	Malaysia	Myanmar	Nether-lands	Thailand	United States	Total
2000	3,387	6,451	17,224	5,022	14,260	554	9,095	91,803	20,100	1,330	323,024	11,538	517,111
2001	4,159	6,033	10,334	4,019	12,856	585	10,375	80,424	25,000	1,148	410,458	9,072	589,260
2002	5,002	7,816	9,536	8,553	13,861	3,299	8,637	77,974	22,600	1,106	438,889	8,136	621,554
2003	6,386	8,502	8,403	10,253	12,136	8,627	12,526	76,866	30,000	927	491,926	21,795	703,057
2004	8,193	9,115	10,230	13,560	12,870	5,403	11,755	73,331	31,500	600	853,403	8,624	1,052,181
2005	11,138	9,482	9,627	9,255	20,096	11,125	4,014	55,602	34,000	1,449	814,613	4,094	1,001,942
2006	22,047	9,553	10,262	7,178	17,234	6,763	8,334	58,211	407	16,952	947,755	1,987	1,130,383
2007	42,653	9,173	8,487	10,563	22,800	13,069	7,610	56,704	947	16,650	887,544	5,365	1,118,348
2008[1]	31,402	6,396	5,723	6,732	20,355	13,141	8,547	44,599	1,388	22,650	836,404	5,888	1,032,795
2009[2]	13,266	6,614	3,813	5,076	19,821	7,690	9,147	38,752	1,170	5,857	1,007,960	3,386	1,148,578

[1] Preliminary. [2] Estimate. *Source: Food and Agricultural Organization of the United Nations (FAO-UN)*

World Imports of Natural Dry Rubber In Metric Tons

Year	Brazil	Canada	China	European Union	France	Germany	Italy	Japan	Malaysia	Rep of Korea	Spain	United States	Total
2000	128,009	146,240	858,662	1,215,563	294,868	252,232	136,876	794,728	235,125	305,403	166,404	1,094,960	5,472,935
2001	114,999	129,089	966,399	1,187,979	296,309	243,130	131,306	705,619	227,590	305,337	178,737	877,230	5,093,166
2002	131,646	156,069	957,233	1,117,621	248,610	244,889	124,583	770,473	195,172	298,965	178,377	1,007,540	5,235,206
2003	150,077	140,140	1,181,192	1,248,305	314,400	262,320	126,255	793,889	142,204	315,808	183,802	1,005,900	5,674,075
2004	171,015	133,676	1,209,413	1,172,116	239,751	210,307	137,872	795,542	148,800	328,117	187,364	1,045,540	5,751,971
2005	183,329	142,460	1,334,140	1,185,635	240,984	248,544	137,884	842,766	173,950	346,866	185,521	1,071,860	6,107,832
2006	166,448	129,971	1,451,064	1,194,464	230,784	246,444	139,991	879,987	190,200	341,772	175,035	943,348	6,198,163
2007	208,453	123,287	1,481,813	1,233,869	233,711	261,495	136,895	842,246	245,317	354,553	199,911	939,367	6,382,040
2008[1]	220,959	121,907	1,498,355	1,103,069	208,921	234,608	123,850	839,170	219,637	337,790	181,472	958,558	6,218,358
2009[2]	138,010	91,646	1,495,789	744,649	131,546	189,322	80,071	731,498	381,483	311,067	126,787	634,888	5,461,209

[1] Preliminary. [2] Estimate. *Source: Food and Agricultural Organization of the United Nations (FAO-UN)*

World Exports of Natural Dry Rubber In Metric Tons

Year	Côte d'Ivoire	Germany	Guate-mala	India	Indonesia	Liberia	Malaysia	Nigeria	Philip-pines	Sri Lanka	Thailand	Vietnam	Total
2000	119,531	21,374	17,794	3,451	1,370,520	105,000	886,155	36,000	30,684	32,302	2,003,700	273,400	5,054,379
2001	125,929	16,007	18,225	4,936	1,443,010	107,000	740,427	30,000	39,067	31,453	1,865,000	308,073	4,904,381
2002	123,527	17,814	22,481	36,781	1,487,350	109,000	808,900	24,000	44,559	34,676	2,053,820	351,000	5,316,645
2003	129,080	16,049	24,258	42,045	1,648,390	107,000	868,018	22,000	55,241	34,648	2,307,740	345,000	5,829,930
2004	137,539	18,995	32,106	31,999	1,862,510	114,500	1,360,980	29,000	43,305	38,460	2,167,960	513,300	6,545,322
2005	155,981	13,634	36,304	48,197	2,019,770	111,000	1,091,510	25,000	41,088	30,595	2,137,540	249,423	6,125,620
2006	172,437	22,006	33,059	41,014	2,277,660	100,500	1,073,190	24,000	33,833	46,022	2,109,080	246,081	6,349,022
2007	182,397	40,572	45,474	39,294	2,399,150	120,800	960,241	33,792	30,417	46,083	2,077,770	247,331	6,426,742
2008[1]	199,721	28,113	53,008	26,031	2,286,910	84,800	870,997	25,900	36,323	42,476	1,995,520	247,331	6,059,046
2009[2]	218,555	56,089	57,770	12,787	1,982,120	59,500	664,306	31,700	24,899	50,246	1,731,790	213,544	5,350,377

[1] Preliminary. [2] Estimate. *Source: Food and Agricultural Organization of the United Nations (FAO-UN)*

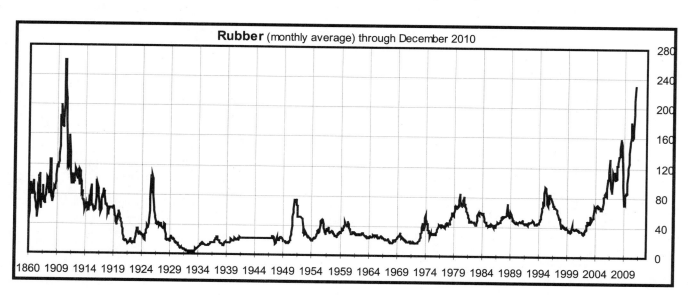

Rubber (monthly average) through December 2010

Rye

Rye is a cereal grain and a member of the grass family. Hardy varieties of rye have been developed for winter planting. Rye is most widely grown in northern Europe and Asia. In the U.S., rye is used as an animal feed and as an ingredient in bread and some whiskeys. Bread using rye was developed in northern Europe in the Middle Ages where bakers developed dark, hearty bread consisting of rye, oat and barley flours. Those were crops that grew more readily in the wet and damp climate of northern Europe, as opposed to wheat which fares better in the warmer and drier climates in central Europe. Modern rye bread is made with a mixture of white and rye flours. Coarsely ground rye flour is also used in pumpernickel bread and helps provide the dark color and course texture, along with molasses. The major producing states are North and South Dakota, Oklahoma, and Georgia. The crop year runs from June to May.

Supply – World rye production in 2011-12 marketing year rose by +10.4% yr/yr to 12.733 million metric tons, just above from the 2006-07 record low of 12.402 million metric tons. The world's largest producers of rye are the European Union with 54.1% of world production in 2011-12, followed by Russia with 23.3%, Belarus with 11.8%, and the Ukraine with 4.3%. U.S. production of rye accounted for only 1.3% of world production.

U.S. production of rye in 2011 fell -14.9% to 6.326 million bushels, far below the production levels of over 20 million bushels seen from the late 1800s through the 1960s. U.S. production of rye fell off in the 1970s, and fell to a record low of 6.311 million bushels in 2007.

U.S. acreage harvested with rye in 2011-12 fell -8.7 to 242,000 acres. U.S. farmers in the late 1800s through the 1960s typically harvested more than 1 million acres of rye, showing how domestic planting of rye has dropped off sharply in the past several decades. Rye yield in 2011-12 fell -6.8% to 26.1 bushels per acre, and that is still well below the record high of 33.1 bushels per acre posted in 1984-85. Modern rye production yields are, however, more than double the levels in the teens seen prior to the 1960s when yields started to rise.

Demand – Total U.S. domestic usage of rye in 2010-11 rose +9.0% yr/yr to 11.713 million bushels. The breakdown of domestic usage shows that 28.2% of rye in 2010-11 was used for food, industry, and seed, and 20.6% as feed and residual.

Trade – World exports of rye in the 2011-12 marketing year fell -26.8% yr/yr to 360,000 metric tons, still above the record low of 270,000 metric tons in 2008-09. The largest exporters were Canada with 125,000 metric tons and the European Union with 100,000 metric tons of exports. World imports of rye fell -37.0% to 288,000 metric tons. U.S. imports of rye in 2011-12 fell -10.0% yr/yr to 127,000 metric tons.

World Production of Rye   In Thousands of Metric Tons

Crop Year	Argentina	Australia	Belarus	Canada	European Union	Kazakhstan	Romania	Russia	Switzerland	Turkey	Ukraine	United States	World Total
2002-03	80	20	1,600	134	9,255	106	----	7,122	20	255	1,511	165	20,338
2003-04	37	20	1,200	327	6,972	42	----	4,147	20	240	624	219	13,922
2004-05	89	20	1,400	398	10,031	20	----	2,864	20	270	1,592	210	17,013
2005-06	55	20	1,155	330	7,688	24	----	3,622	20	270	1,054	191	14,524
2006-07	55	20	1,072	383	6,541	30	----	2,959	20	271	584	183	12,195
2007-08	77	20	1,305	252	7,679	68	----	3,909	20	241	562	160	14,394
2008-09	55	20	1,492	316	9,262	40	----	4,505	20	247	1,051	203	17,321
2009-10[1]	55	20	1,227	280	9,952	75	----	4,333	20	343	954	178	17,524
2010-11[2]	40	20	735	232	7,796	42	----	1,642	20	270	464	189	11,536
2011-12[3]	50	20	1,500	195	6,884	28	----	2,969	20	270	550	161	12,733

[1] Preliminary.   [2] Estimate.   [3] Forecast.   Source: Foreign Agricultural Service, U.S. Department of Agriculture (FAS-USDA)

World Imports and Exports of Rye   In Thousands of Metric Tons

	Imports							Exports					
Year	European Union	Japan	Rep, of Korea	Turkey	Russia	United States	World Total	Belarus	Canada	European Union	Russia	United States	World Total
2002-03	436	414	31	14	----	156	1,356	110	53	669	291	3	1,414
2003-04	99	341	114	43	6	83	845	60	173	506	156	1	907
2004-05	----	261	8	59	172	143	783	50	122	574	----	4	854
2005-06	9	279	7	2	49	139	620	50	132	359	----	----	610
2006-07	25	258	8	18	32	150	583	50	208	424	26	2	712
2007-08	98	83	6	13	----	179	415	75	191	76	119	6	470
2008-09	9	57	7	8	----	100	212	50	76	114	16	8	270
2009-10[1]	----	103	7	----	----	108	248	25	124	99	12	2	318
2010-11[2]	19	101	11	----	150	141	457	150	191	106	----	4	492
2011-12[3]	50	75	5	5	----	127	288	75	125	100	50	5	360

[1] Preliminary.   [2] Estimate.   [3] Forecast.   Source: Foreign Agricultural Service, U.S. Department of Agriculture (FAS-USDA)

RYE

Rye (monthly average) through 2010/11 — Cents per bushel

Production of Rye in the United States — In Thousands of Bushels

Year	Georgia	Kansas	Mich-igan	Minne-sota	Neb-raska	Dakota	Okla-homa	Penn-ylvania	Carolina	Dakota	Texas	Wis-consin	Total
2002	560	[2]	[2]	[2]	[2]	210	1,300	[2]	[2]	270	[2]	[2]	6,488
2003	800	[2]	[2]	[2]	[2]	750	1,540	[2]	[2]	672	[2]	[2]	8,634
2004	600	[2]	[2]	[2]	[2]	780	1,620	[2]	[2]	649	[2]	[2]	8,255
2005	810	[2]	[2]	[2]	[2]	[2]	1,400	[2]	[2]	[2]	[2]	[2]	7,537
2006	650	[2]	[2]	[2]	[2]	[2]	1,040	[2]	[2]	[2]	[2]	[2]	7,193
2007	800	[2]	[2]	[2]	[2]	[2]	1,080	[2]	[2]	[2]	[2]	[2]	6,311
2008	1,200	[2]	[2]	[2]	[2]	[2]	1,045	[2]	[2]	[2]	[2]	[2]	7,979
2009	525	[2]	[2]	[2]	[2]	[2]	560	[2]	[2]	[2]	[2]	[2]	6,993
2010	960	[2]	[2]	[2]	[2]	[2]	1,500	[2]	[2]	[2]	[2]	[2]	7,431
2011[1]	945	[2]	[2]	[2]	[2]	[2]	825	[2]	[2]	[2]	[2]	[2]	6,326

[1] Preliminary.   [2] Estimates not published beginning in 2000.   Source: Agricultural Statistics Board, U.S. Department of Agriculture (ASB-USDA)

Salient Statistics of Rye in the United States — In Thousands of Bushels

Crop Year Beginning June 1	Supply				Disappearance — Domestic Use						Total Disap-pearance	Acreage		Yield Per Harvested Acre (Bushels)
	Stocks June 1	Pro-duction	Imports	Total Supply	Food	Industry	Seed	Feed & Residual	Total	Exports		Planted	Harvested for Grain	
												1,000 Acres		
2002-03	568	6,488	6,140	13,196	3,300	3,000	3,000	3,329	12,629	122	12,751	1,355	263	24.8
2003-04	445	8,634	3,286	12,365	3,300	3,000	3,000	2,425	11,725	60	11,771	1,348	319	27.1
2004-05	594	8,255	5,626	14,475	3,300	3,000	3,000	4,237	13,537	145	13,682	1,380	300	27.5
2005-06	793	7,537	5,481	13,811	3,300	3,000	3,000	3,791	13,091	14	13,105	1,433	279	27.0
2006-07	706	7,193	5,899	13,798	3,300	3,000	3,000	3,947	13,247	70	13,317	1,396	274	26.3
2007-08	481	6,311	7,064	13,856	3,300	3,000	3,000	3,909	13,209	251	13,460	1,334	252	25.0
2008-09	396	7,979	3,953	12,328	3,300	3,000	3,000	2,203	11,503	316	11,819	1,260	269	29.7
2009-10[1]	509	6,993	4,251	11,753	3,300	3,000	3,000	1,448	10,748	73	10,821	1,241	252	27.8
2010-11[2]	932	7,431	5,551	13,914	3,300	3,000	3,000	3,664	12,964	149	13,113	1,211	265	28.0
2011-12[3]	801	6,326	6,000	13,127	3,310	3,000	3,010	2,707	12,027	200	12,227	1,266	242	26.1

[1] Preliminary.   [2] Estimate.   [3] Forecast   Source: Economic Research Service, U.S. Department of Agriculture (ERS-USDA)

Salt

Salt, also known as sodium chloride, is a chemical compound that is an essential element in the diet of humans, animals, and even many plants. Since prehistoric times, salt has been used to preserve foods and was commonly used in the religious rites of the Greeks, Romans, Hebrews, and Christians. Salt, in the form of salt cakes, served as money in ancient Ethiopia and Tibet. As long ago as 1450 BC, Egyptian art shows records of salt production.

The simplest method of obtaining salt is through the evaporation of salt water from areas near oceans or seas. In most regions, rock salt is obtained from underground mining or by wells sunk into deposits. Salt is soluble in water, is slightly soluble in alcohol, but is insoluble in concentrated hydrochloric acid. In its crystalline form, salt is transparent and colorless, shining with an ice-like luster.

Prices – Salt prices in 2011 (FOB mine, vacuum and open pan) fell slightly -0.1% yr/yr to $180.00 per ton, below the record high of $180.08 posted in 2010.

Supply – World production of salt in 2011 rose +3.6% yr/yr to 290.000 million metric tons. The world's largest salt producers were China with 22.4% and the U.S. with 15.2% of world production in 2011. U.S. salt production in 2011 rose +1.6% yr/yr to 44.000 million metric tons.

Demand – U.S. consumption of salt in 2011 rose +2.2% to 57.000 million metric tons, below the 2008 record high of 60.200 million metric tons.

Trade – The U.S. relied on imports for 22% of its salt consumption in 2011, down from the record high of 24% in 2009. U.S. imports of salt for consumption in 2011 rose +0.8% yr/yr to 13.000 million metric tons, below the 2009 record high of 14.700 million metric tons. U.S. exports of salt in 2011 fell by -32.8% to 400,000 metric tons, with the bulk of those exports going to Canada.

World Production of All Salt   In Thousands of Metric Tons

Year	Australia	Canada	China	France	Germany	India	Italy	Mexico	Poland	Spain	United Kingdom	United States	World Total
2004	11,088	14,096	37,101	6,910	18,838	15,000	2,876	8,566	5,142	3,993	5,800	46,500	235,000
2005	12,444	13,643	46,610	6,730	19,333	15,500	3,476	9,508	4,023	4,550	5,800	45,200	249,000
2006	11,424	14,389	56,630	8,718	19,846	15,500	3,438	8,371	4,029	4,303	5,800	44,500	261,000
2007	10,855	11,862	59,760	6,140	15,951	16,000	2,214	8,400	3,522	4,350	5,800	44,600	266,000
2008	11,160	14,386	59,520	6,100	15,833	16,000	2,200	8,809	3,401	4,350	5,800	48,100	276,000
2009	10,316	14,615	58,450	6,100	18,939	16,500	2,200	7,445	3,523	4,350	5,800	46,100	279,000
2010[1]	11,968	10,537	60,000	6,100	19,100	17,000	2,200	8,431	3,520	4,350	5,800	43,300	280,000
2011[2]	13,000	11,000	65,000	6,000	20,000	18,000		8,800	4,000	4,400	5,800	44,000	290,000

[1] Preliminary.   [2] Estimate.   *Source: U.S. Geological Survey (USGS)*

Salient Statistics of the Salt Industry in the United States   In Thousands of Metric Tons

Year	Net Import Reliance As a % of Apparent Consumption	Average Value FOB Mine Vacuum & Open Pan ($ Per Ton)	Production — Total	Production — Open & Vacuum Pan	Production — Solar	Production — Rock	Production — Brine	Sold or Used, Producers — Open & Vacuum Pan	Sold or Used, Producers — Rock	Sold or Used, Producers — Brine	Sold or Used, Producers — Total Salt	Sold or Used, Producers — Value[3] Million $	Imports for Consumption	Exports — Total	Exports — To Canada	Apparent Consumption
2004	23	128.39	46,500	4,100	3,520	18,300	20,500	4,040	17,400	20,500	45,000	1,270.0	11,900	1,110	971	55,800
2005	20	130.75	45,100	4,170	3,430	17,700	19,900	3,970	18,100	19,800	45,000	1,310.0	12,100	879	686	56,200
2006	17	145.90	44,400	4,450	3,640	16,500	19,800	4,300	13,500	19,800	40,600	1,310.0	9,490	973	775	49,100
2007	15	154.95	44,500	4,420	3,650	16,800	19,700	4,310	18,400	19,600	45,500	1,520.0	8,640	833	588	53,300
2008	21	158.59	48,000	4,200	4,070	20,900	18,900	4,120	21,100	18,800	47,400	1,690.0	13,800	1,030	896	60,200
2009	24	178.67	46,000	4,030	3,880	20,300	17,800	3,960	18,200	17,800	43,100	1,750.0	14,700	1,450	1,360	56,400
2010[1]	22	180.08	43,300	4,100	4,830	15,800	18,500	4,020	16,300	18,500	43,500	1,690.0	12,900	595	451	55,800
2011[2]	22	180.00	44,000								44,000		13,000	400		57,000

[1] Preliminary.   [2] Estimate.   [3] Values are f.o.b. mine or refinery & do not include cost of cooperage or containers.   *Source: U.S. Geological Survey (USGS)*

Salt Sold or Used by Producers in the U.S. by Classes & Consumers or Uses   In Thousands of Metric Tons

Year	Chemical[2]	Tanning Leather	Textile & Dyeing	Meat Packers[3]	Canning	Baking	Agricultural Distribution	Feed Dealers	Feed Manufacturers	Rubber	Oil	Paper & Pulp	Metal Processing	Water Treatment	Grocery Stores	Water Conditioning Distrib.	Ice Control and/or Stabilization
2003	20,100	71	151	374	231	210	215	1,090	460	67	2,210	88	126	777	802	537	18,500
2004	20,400	56	145	385	225	209	242	1,090	451	69	2,350	86	112	858	794	514	18,000
2005	19,700	55	149	398	211	204	227	1,140	477	65	2,210	81	107	1,140	803	511	21,000
2006	18,400	50	121	380	208	203	211	1,090	502	66	2,150	72	49	952	770	489	12,400
2007	21,500	41	98	305	198	149	385	1,160	457	6	211	61	36	1,030	943	522	20,800
2008	18,600	37	78	283	190	144	436	1,260	405	6	286	77	42	1,330	992	464	22,600
2009	17,900	32	48	271	215	324	357	1,310	377	5	314	58	24	1,010	812	469	16,900
2010[1]	20,200	39	59	275	258	364	359	1,330	425	5	325	59	26	913	761	461	18,700

[1] Preliminary.   [2] Chloralkali producers and other chemical.   *Source: U.S. Geological Survey (USGS)*

Sheep and Lambs

Sheep and lambs are raised for both their wool and meat. In countries that have high wool production, there is also demand for sheep and lamb meat due to the easy availability. Production levels have declined in New Zealand and Australia, but that has been counteracted by a substantial increase in China.

Prices – The average monthly price received by farmers for lambs in the U.S. in 2011 rose by +42.7% to 177.33 cents per pound, a new record high. The average monthly price received by U.S. farmers for sheep in 2011 rose by +27.7% to a 64.33 cents per pound, a new record high. The average monthly wholesale price of slaughter lambs (choice) at San Angelo, Texas in 2011 rose by +37.7% to 146.00 cents per pound, down from the record high of 160.87cents per pound posted in 2010.

Supply – World sheep and goat numbers in 2009 (latest data) fell by -0.6% to 1.939 billion head, just below the 2008 record high of 1.940 billion head. The world's largest producers of sheep and goats are China with 14.5% of world production in 2009, India (9.9%), Australia (3.8%), and New Zealand (1.7%). The number of sheep and lambs on U.S. farms in 2010 (Jan 1) fell –1.6% to 5.530 million head. The U.S. states with the most sheep and lambs were Texas (with 15.9% of the U.S. total), California (11.0%), Wyoming (6.6%), Colorado (6.7%), and South Dakota (5.0%).

World Sheep and Goat Numbers in Specified Countries on January 1   In Thousands of Head

Year	Argen-tina	Australia	China	India	Kazak-hstan	New Zealand	Romania	Russia	South Africa	Spain	Turkey	United Kingdom	World Total
2001	16,887	113,040	279,767	183,918	9,981	40,173	8,195	14,773	35,350	27,276	35,693	36,792	1,801,563
2002	16,400	108,916	276,501	184,864	10,479	39,725	7,776	15,327	32,452	26,860	33,994	35,909	1,803,561
2003	16,650	101,782	282,651	185,827	11,273	39,707	7,945	16,051	32,178	26,650	31,954	35,939	1,829,496
2004	17,700	104,127	293,324	192,061	12,247	39,424	8,125	17,030	31,732	25,743	32,203	35,937	1,885,041
2005	18,700	104,525	304,254	198,507	13,409	40,035	8,086	17,771	31,690	25,654	31,811	35,345	1,941,689
2006	19,676	94,778	298,195	205,171	14,335	40,253	8,298	18,213	31,383	25,408	31,822	34,820	1,953,969
2007	19,750	88,711	283,948	212,100	15,350	38,572	8,405	19,675	31,347	25,086	32,260	34,041	1,970,616
2008	19,950	83,138	280,031	217,360	16,080	34,184	9,334	21,503	31,623	22,912	31,749	33,223	1,984,122
2009[1]	20,050	77,240	281,056	222,172	16,770	32,466	9,780	21,770	31,347	21,983	29,568	32,126	1,991,985
2010[2]	20,050	72,586	284,728	227,991	17,370	32,658	10,059	21,988	30,776	21,485	26,923	31,085	2,000,380

[1] Preliminary.   [2] Forecast.   Source: Food and Agricultural Organization of the United Nations (FAO-UN)

Salient Statistics of Sheep & Lambs in the United States (Average Live Weight)   In Thousands of Head

Year	Inventory, Jan. 1 - Without New Crop Lambs	Inventory, Jan. 1 - With New Crop Lambs	Lamb Crop	Total Supply	Marketings[3] Sheep	Marketings[3] Lambs	Slaughter Farm	Slaughter Commercial	Slaughter Total[4]	Net Exports	Total Disappearance	Production (Live Weight) (Mil. Lbs.)	Farm Value Jan. 1	Farm Value Total
2002	6,685	6,685	4,357	11,042	855	4,794	66	3,286	3,352	266	4,380	485.1	614.5	92.0
2003	6,300	6,321	4,140	10,461	828	4,387	67	2,979	3,046	105	3,804	470.1	656.6	104.0
2004	6,105	6,105	4,096	10,201	695	4,184	65	2,839	2,904			464.0	720.4	119.0
2005	6,135	6,135	4,117	10,252	669	4,200	64	2,698	2,762			473.3	798.2	13.0
2006	6,230	6,230	3,950	10,180	692	4,196	69	2,699	2,768			463.1	872.4	141.0
2007	6,165	6,273	3,895	10,168	780	3,927	85	2,694	2,778			473.1	818.5	134.0
2008	5,950	6,055	3,710	9,765	737	3,652	92	2,556	2,647			417.0	823.4	138.0
2009	5,747	5,855	3,690	9,545	625	3,532	95	2,516	2,611			421.6	765.2	133.0
2010[1]	5,620	5,727	3,570	9,297	645	3,429	95	2,458	2,553			405.3	762.3	135.0
2011[2]	5,530	5,639	3,510	9,149			93							

[1] Preliminary.   [2] Estimate.   [3] Excludes interfarm sales.   [4] Includes all commercial and farm.
Source: Economic Research Service, U.S. Department of Agriculture (ERS-USDA)

Sheep and Lambs[3] on Farms in the United States on January 1   In Thousands of Head

Year	California	Colorado	Idaho	Iowa	Minnesota	Montana	Mexico	Ohio	Dakota	Texas	Utah	Wyoming	Total
2004	680	360	260	250	140	300	160	140	370	1,100	265	430	6,105
2005	670	365	270	245	145	305	145	142	375	1,070	270	450	6,135
2006	650	390	260	235	155	295	155	141	385	1,090	280	450	6,230
2007	610	400	260	235	150	290	130	141	380	1,050	295	460	6,165
2008	620	420	235	225	145	270	130	125	340	960	280	425	5,950
2009	660	410	210	200	140	255	120	130	305	870	290	420	5,747
2010	610	370	220	210	130	245	120	128	325	830	290	375	5,620
2011[1]	600	370	235	200	130	230	110	129	265	850	280	365	5,480
2012[2]	570	460	240	195	150	225	100	126	285	650	305	370	5,345

[1] Preliminary.   [2] Estimate.   [3] Includes sheep & lambs on feed for market and stock sheep & lambs.   Source: Economic Research Service, U.S. Department of Agriculture (ERS-USDA)

Average Wholesale Price of Slaughter Lambs (Choice[2]) at San Angelo Texas   In Dollars Per Hundred Pounds (Cwt.)

Year	Jan.	Feb.	Mar.	Apr.	May	June	July	Aug.	Sept.	Oct.	Nov.	Dec.	Average
2003	89.25	90.25	96.25	88.13	95.75	97.25	87.88	85.81	91.44	91.31	91.00	96.17	91.71
2004	99.44	99.94	102.50	92.31	97.50	101.37	97.50	91.12	92.25	91.75	95.58	99.12	96.70
2005	107.25	109.69	101.37	99.37	96.94	99.50	95.00	92.14	91.56	93.00	93.33	94.00	97.76
2006	86.75	76.87	67.47	60.60	68.16	70.94	74.00	84.00	85.30	85.18	85.40	83.00	77.31
2007	81.00	82.27	84.50	85.25	84.20	77.40	86.38	86.19	89.44	84.90	84.83	92.92	84.94
2008	86.63	88.82	83.25	74.70	77.75	86.75	88.81	88.13	89.54	85.55	85.46	95.83	85.94
2009	88.74	89.25	92.75	89.38	95.23	93.91	88.00	88.88	88.17	89.50	89.66	92.25	90.48
2010	95.04	106.63	109.95	112.00	104.47	102.05	109.17	112.15	125.38	129.69	138.50	156.67	116.81
2011[1]	164.19	182.63	177.15	152.88	160.20	160.88	169.47	162.13	152.80	154.00	158.25	135.83	160.87

[1] Preliminary.   *Source: Economic Research Service, U.S. Department of Agriculture (ERS-USDA)*

Federally Inspected Slaughter of Sheep & Lambs in the United States   In Thousands of Head

Year	Jan.	Feb.	Mar.	Apr.	May	June	July	Aug.	Sept.	Oct.	Nov.	Dec.	Total
2003	227	211	252	280	209	216	225	226	241	251	223	246	2,805
2004	207	199	295	238	175	220	207	219	231	228	228	229	2,676
2005	195	204	268	208	198	210	188	216	219	217	213	219	2,555
2006	210	193	240	234	215	200	191	213	205	223	212	212	2,547
2007	204	194	267	203	205	188	191	212	197	232	223	212	2,529
2008	202	202	219	207	195	181	193	186	207	209	180	213	2,393
2009	179	169	210	213	167	185	189	187	207	201	200	217	2,323
2010	173	167	249	175	167	194	178	185	186	185	201	200	2,261
2011[1]	151	146	184	192	166	168	150	183	163	161	172	167	2,000

[1] Preliminary.   *Source: Economic Research Service, U.S. Department of Agriculture (ERS-USDA)*

Cold Storage Holdings of Lamb and Mutton in the United States, on First of Month   In Thousands of Pounds

Year	Jan.	Feb.	Mar.	Apr.	May	June	July	Aug.	Sept.	Oct.	Nov.	Dec.
2003	7,124	6,232	4,063	3,900	5,016	5,838	5,427	5,929	5,855	6,210	4,485	4,883
2004	3,795	3,671	3,355	3,164	3,251	3,504	3,872	3,376	3,878	4,179	4,166	3,715
2005	3,497	7,549	7,585	7,650	8,739	9,719	9,362	11,756	11,790	10,942	10,137	9,332
2006	9,967	15,730	15,777	15,454	15,247	15,215	15,126	15,254	15,353	15,228	15,452	15,862
2007	15,769	15,640	15,570	15,996	18,206	16,644	15,410	13,811	15,692	14,734	13,944	13,096
2008	12,918	15,177	18,157	17,118	17,783	18,411	19,598	19,723	21,147	20,796	21,331	21,659
2009	21,001	19,469	18,279	19,274	19,801	19,694	21,568	20,062	19,045	17,426	15,301	15,052
2010	14,519	11,759	12,922	16,313	16,453	20,448	22,972	22,059	19,859	18,046	16,189	16,500
2011[1]	15,206	13,278	12,582	12,861	13,279	15,062	18,097	21,034	21,209	22,218	20,021	19,014

[1] Preliminary.   *Source: Economic Research Service, U.S. Department of Agriculture (ERS-USDA)*

Average Price Received by Farmers for Sheep in the United States   In Dollars Per Hundred Pounds (Cwt.)

Year	Jan.	Feb.	Mar.	Apr.	May	June	July	Aug.	Sept.	Oct.	Nov.	Dec.	Average
2003	41.30	44.00	40.90	31.10	31.30	29.40	28.60	29.20	32.50	35.00	40.50	45.10	35.74
2004	43.80	40.80	36.70	36.70	36.00	31.30	37.10	37.30	41.20	40.40	41.40	44.60	38.94
2005	53.50	52.40	49.00	45.10	43.70	41.20	41.00	43.00	43.70	43.60	46.20	49.30	45.98
2006	47.70	45.90	40.10	35.20	32.50	28.20	27.60	27.90	32.20	31.40	30.30	34.80	34.48
2007	37.10	37.30	36.60	34.20	30.80	28.20	29.20	28.30	26.70	25.50	27.10	30.20	30.93
2008	31.90	29.90	28.70	28.40	25.40	24.50	26.10	26.60	24.50	21.70	27.30	32.90	27.33
2009	31.40	31.90	32.10	34.70	31.70	28.90	29.60	31.30	29.70	29.80	36.30	44.40	32.65
2010	52.40	54.80	51.30	49.40	46.20	42.10	43.80	47.60	48.70	48.40	54.20	65.70	50.38
2011[1]	81.90	76.00	NA	68.80	55.40	50.80	56.50	66.80	58.40	NA	NA	NA	64.33

[1] Preliminary.   *Source: Economic Research Service, U.S. Department of Agriculture (ERS-USDA)*

Average Price Received by Farmers for Lambs in the United States   In Dollars Per Hundred Pounds (Cwt.)

Year	Jan.	Feb.	Mar.	Apr.	May	June	July	Aug.	Sept.	Oct.	Nov.	Dec.	Average
2003	92.00	92.40	97.10	93.70	97.60	89.30	89.40	88.60	95.10	96.80	99.70	97.70	94.12
2004	104.00	106.00	103.00	100.00	103.00	105.00	101.00	97.90	100.00	97.70	99.90	101.00	101.54
2005	114.00	114.00	114.00	114.00	114.00	114.00	110.00	109.00	110.00	108.00	107.00	100.00	110.67
2006	96.10	97.80	92.10	87.20	88.90	92.10	93.40	95.40	98.30	98.50	95.60	94.00	94.12
2007	96.50	94.80	95.50	97.10	97.10	96.80	98.70	97.90	99.00	97.00	97.10	98.40	97.16
2008	97.50	96.50	97.40	99.40	101.00	102.00	103.00	99.90	99.40	97.40	100.00	101.00	99.54
2009	100.00	100.00	100.00	101.00	102.00	104.00	102.00	97.10	98.10	96.80	97.70	98.70	99.78
2010	102.00	106.00	115.00	118.00	122.00	119.00	122.00	127.00	135.00	137.00	142.00	146.00	124.25
2011[1]	149.00	155.00	169.00	181.00	181.00	189.00	194.00	189.00	189.00	NA	NA	NA	177.33

[1] Preliminary.   *Source: Economic Research Service, U.S. Department of Agriculture (ERS-USDA)*

Silk

Silk is a fine, tough, elastic fiber produced by caterpillars, commonly called silkworms. Silk is one of the oldest known textile fibers. Chinese tradition credits Lady Hsi-Ling-Shih, wife of the Emperor Huang Ti, with the discovery of the silkworm and the invention of the first silk reel. Dating to around 3000 BC, a group of ribbons, threads, and woven fragments was found in China. Also found, along the lower Yangzi River, were 7,000 year-old spinning tools, silk thread, and fabric fragments.

Silk filament was first woven into cloth in Ancient China. The Chinese successfully guarded this secret until 300AD, when Japan, and later India, learned the secret. In 550 AD, two Nestorian monks were sent to China to steal mulberry seeds and silkworm eggs, which they hid in their walking staffs, and then brought them back to Rome. By the 17th century, France was the silk center of the West. Unfortunately, the silkworm did not flourish in the English climate, nor has it ever flourished in the U.S.

Sericulture is the term for the raising of silkworms. The blind, flightless moth, Bombyx mori, lays more than 500 tiny eggs. After hatching, the tiny worms eat chopped mulberry leaves continuously until they are ready to spin their cocoons. After gathering the complete cocoons, the first step in silk manufacturing is to kill the insects inside the cocoons with heat. The cocoons are then placed in boiling water to loosen the gummy substance, sericin, holding the filament together. The filament is unwound, and then rewound in a process called reeling. Each cocoon's silk filament is between 600 and 900 meters long. Four different types of silk thread may be produced: organzine, crepe, tram, and thrown singles. During the last 30 years, in spite of the use of man-made fibers, world silk production has doubled.

Raw silk is traded on the Kansai Agricultural Commodities Exchange (KANEX) in Japan. Dried cocoons are traded on the Chuba Commodity Exchange (CCE). Raw silk and dried cocoons are traded on the Yokohama Commodity Exchange.

Supply – World production of silk in 2010, was unchanged at164,971 metric tons, below the 2007 record high of 166,139. China is the world's largest producer of silk by far with a 76.4% share of world production in 2010. Other key producers include India with 11.5% of world production, Vietnam (4.5%), and Turkmenistan (2.7%).

Trade – In 2009, the world's largest exporters of silk were China with 84.7% of world exports, North Korea with 1.3%, and Japan with 0.3%. In 2009, the world's largest importers of silk were India (with 57.9% of world imports), Japan (5.8%), South Korea (5.2%), and Italy (4.0%).

World Production of Raw Silk   In Metric Tons

Year	Brazil	China	India	Iran	Japan	North Korea	Rep. of Korea	Kyrgy-zstan	Thailand	Turkmen-istan	Uzbek-istan	Viet Nam	World Total
2001	1,554	94,201	15,857	900	559	150	6	76	1,510	5,000	1,260	10,866	132,496
2002	1,620	100,101	17,347	900	391	200	4	96	1,550	4,500	1,200	12,124	140,551
2003	1,700	95,761	16,319	900	287	320	3	50	1,550	4,500	1,200	11,582	134,816
2004	1,750	104,801	15,742	900	263	350	3	17	1,600	4,500	1,200	12,323	145,943
2005	1,200	111,951	16,500	900	150	350	3	50	1,600	4,500	1,200	11,475	152,448
2006	1,250	123,491	17,305	900	117	350	3	50	1,600	4,500	1,200	10,413	163,774
2007	1,250	125,001	18,475	900	105	350	3	50	1,600	4,500	1,200	10,110	166,139
2008	1,300	126,001	18,500	900	105	350	3	50	1,600	4,500	1,200	7,746	164,850
2009[1]	1,300	126,001	19,000	900	105	350	3	50	1,600	4,500	1,200	7,367	164,971
2010[2]	1,300	126,001	19,000	900	105	350	3	50	1,600	4,500	1,200	7,367	164,971

[1] Preliminary.   [2] Estimate.   NA = Not avaliable.   *Source: Food and Agricultural Organization of the United Nations (FAO-UN)*

World Trade of Silk by Selected Countries   In Metric Tons

	Imports							Exports					
Year	France	Hong Kong	India	Italy	Japan	Rep. of Korea	World Total	Brazil	China	Hong Kong	Japan	Rep. of Korea	World Total
2000	323	561	4,713	3,177	2,581	1,769	17,267	3	12,531	676	9	120	15,183
2001	327	175	6,809	2,760	1,893	1,582	16,410	23	11,266	186	2	90	13,003
2002	262	38	9,054	2,363	2,025	1,845	18,548	4	14,702	102	2	170	16,117
2003	147	67	9,258	2,219	1,949	1,648	18,439	2	13,931	31	96	296	15,866
2004	181	3	7,948	1,983	1,581	1,338	16,607	7	11,288	20	688	227	14,321
2005	262	14	8,383	1,974	1,406	1,359	18,114	36	10,972	11	202	219	13,699
2006	212	3	5,565	2,146	1,295	1,095	14,944	4	6,712	4	11	223	10,008
2007	150	2	7,922	1,463	791	989	15,343	18	13,756	2	10	277	15,696
2008	191		8,392	1,040	932	724	15,945	13	13,431		16	137	14,903
2009[1]	111	17	7,338	501	737	656	12,675	8	9,227	16	36	137	10,896

[1] Preliminary.   *Source: Food and Agricultural Organization of the United Nations (FAO-UN)*

Silver

Silver is a white, lustrous metallic element that conducts heat and electricity better than any other metal. In ancient times, many silver deposits were on or near the earth's surface. Before 2,500 BC, silver mines were worked in Asia Minor. Around 700 BC, ancient Greeks stamped a turtle on their first silver coins. Silver assumed a key role in the U.S. monetary system in 1792 when Congress based the currency on the silver dollar. However, the U.S. discontinued the use of silver in coinage in 1965. Today Mexico is the only country that uses silver in its circulating coinage.

Silver is the most malleable and ductile of all metals, with the exception of gold. Silver melts at about 962 degrees Celsius and boils at about 2212 degrees Celsius. Silver is not very chemically active, although tarnishing occurs when sulfur and sulfides attack silver, forming silver sulfide on the surface of the metal. Because silver is too soft in its pure form, a hardening agent, usually copper, is mixed into the silver. Copper is usually used as the hardening agent because it does not discolor the silver. The term "sterling silver" refers to silver that contains at least 925 parts of silver per thousand (92.5%) to 75 parts of copper (7.5%).

Silver is usually found combined with other elements in minerals and ores. In the U.S., silver is mined in conjunction with lead, copper, and zinc. In the U.S., Nevada, Idaho, Alaska, and Arizona are the leading silver-producing states. For industrial purposes, silver is used for photography, electrical appliances, glass, and as an antibacterial agent for the health industry.

Silver futures and options are traded on the New York Mercantile Exchange (NYMEX), the NYSE-LIFEE exchange, and the London Metal Exchange (LME). Silver futures are traded on the Tokyo Commodity Exchange (TOCOM). The Nymex silver futures contract calls for the delivery of 5,000 troy ounces of silver (0.999 fineness) and is priced in terms of dollars and cents per troy ounce.

Prices – Nymex silver futures prices in Q1 2011 rallied sharply and in April 2011 posted a 32-year high of $49.82 an ounce, just below the all-time high from 1980 at $50.35 an ounce. Silver prices then embarked on a zigzag downward correction the rest of the year and fell to a 1-year low of $26.385 an ounce in December 2011. Silver prices ended 2011 down -9.8% at $27.875 per troy ounce. Major bullish factors in 2011 included (1) increased demand for precious metals as an inflation hedge with the central banks of the U.S., England, and Japan all engaging in quantitative easing, and (2) a surge in demand for precious metals as an alternative asset after the credit ratings of the U.S., Japan, Italy and other countries were all downgraded. Bearish factors included (1) dollar strength which prompted liquidation of most commodities, and (2) a slowdown in the global economy due to the European debt crisis.

Supply – World mine production of silver in 2011 rose +3.1% yr/yr to a new record high of 23,800 metric tons, continuing to show some improvement after flat production figures in 2000-03. The world's largest silver producers in 2011 were Mexico with 18.9% of world production, Peru and China (16.8%), Australia (7.8%), Chile and Russia (5.9%), and the Bolivia (5.7%). U.S. production of refined silver in 2011 (through August, annualized) fell by -4.9% to 5,311 metric tons, down from last year's record high of 5,583 metric tons.

Demand – U.S. consumption of silver in 2009 (latest data available) fell –11.8% yr/yr to 164.4 million troy ounces. The largest consumption of silver is for electrical contacts and conductors with 31.9% of total usage, followed by coinage (20.6%), photographic materials (13.4%), jewelry (7.1%), and brazing alloys and solders (3.2%). The world's largest consuming nation of silver for industrial purposes is the U.S. with 20% of world consumption in 2004 (latest data), followed by Japan (16%), India (10%), and Italy (7%).

Trade – U.S. exports of refined silver in 2010 (latest data available) rose +69.2% yr/yr to 22.794 million troy ounces, which about half of the record high of 99.022 million troy ounces seen in 1997. The major destinations for U.S. silver exports are Canada (14.8%), Germany (9.9%), and South Korea (8.7%). U.S. imports of silver ore and concentrates in 2010 rose from 3,000 troy ounces to 104,000 troy ounces. U.S. imports of refined silver bullion in 2010 rose +91.8% yr/yr to 172.646 million troy ounces. The bulk of those imports came from Mexico (82.947 million troy ounces), Canada (51.119 million troy ounces), and Peru (9.999 million troy ounces).

World Mine Production of Silver   In Thousands of Kilograms (Metric Ton)

Year	Australia	Bolivia	Canada[3]	Chile	China	Kazak-hstan	Mexico	Peru	Poland	Russia	Sweden	United States	World Total[2]
2002	2,077	450	1,408	1,210	2,200	893	2,727	2,870	1,229	400	294	1,350	18,800
2003	1,868	465	1,310	1,313	2,400	827	2,569	2,921	1,237	700	307	1,240	18,800
2004	2,224	407	1,337	1,360	2,450	733	2,569	3,060	1,419	1,277	293	1,250	20,000
2005	2,417	420	1,124	1,400	2,500	832	2,894	3,206	1,263	1,350	310	1,230	20,800
2006	1,727	472	995	1,607	2,600	806	2,970	3,471	1,266	974	268	1,160	20,100
2007	1,879	525	860	1,936	2,700	723	3,135	3,494	1,199	911	270	1,280	20,800
2008	1,926	1,114	728	1,405	2,800	646	3,236	3,686	1,161	1,132	265	1,250	21,400
2009	1,635	1,326	631	1,301	2,900	618	3,554	3,854	1,207	1,313	265	1,250	22,000
2010[1]	1,864	1,259	596	1,276	3,500	551	4,411	3,640	1,181	1,145	270	1,280	23,100
2011[2]	1,900	1,350	700	1,400	4,000		4,500	4,000	1,200	1,400		1,160	23,800

[1] Preliminary.   [2] Estimate.   [3] Shipments.   *Source: U.S. Geological Survey (USGS)*

SILVER

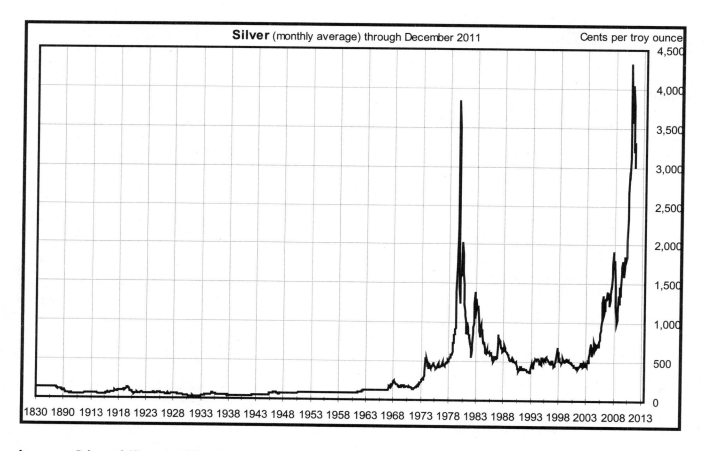

Silver (monthly average) through December 2011 — Cents per troy ounce

Average Price of Silver in New York (Handy & Harman)   In Cents Per Troy Ounce (.999 Fine)

Year	Jan.	Feb.	Mar.	Apr.	May	June	July	Aug.	Sept.	Oct.	Nov.	Dec.	Average
2002	450.17	444.79	457.00	460.50	473.55	492.13	494.57	456.16	458.93	442.28	453.87	465.78	462.39
2003	485.62	468.11	454.74	453.40	475.29	455.62	486.48	502.90	520.62	503.91	520.64	565.33	491.06
2004	637.13	647.71	729.48	708.57	589.19	588.38	637.55	670.98	641.93	717.55	751.43	712.43	669.36
2005	665.45	709.18	728.50	715.74	705.29	733.64	704.40	702.72	719.33	769.90	786.35	865.88	733.87
2006	918.48	952.13	1,037.52	1,263.71	1,337.84	1,077.41	1,121.24	1,225.39	1,159.93	1,161.55	1,298.45	1,329.83	1,156.96
2007	1,286.63	1,394.58	1,316.27	1,373.23	1,319.27	1,315.48	1,295.21	1,233.22	1,292.92	1,372.17	1,467.15	1,431.24	1,341.45
2008	1,605.90	1,766.63	1,921.60	1,751.57	1,704.90	1,703.95	1,806.41	1,457.81	1,219.33	1,042.72	986.78	1,031.66	1,499.94
2009	1,139.90	1,343.68	1,311.50	1,252.02	1,411.30	1,465.93	1,338.64	1,443.05	1,648.74	1,726.34	1,787.68	1,765.68	1,469.54
2010	1,775.05	1,587.21	1,717.11	1,816.83	1,841.90	1,853.43	1,793.98	1,849.25	2,061.12	2,346.86	2,657.20	2,933.00	2,019.41
2011	2,855.15	3,085.61	3,594.61	4,264.45	3,702.67	3,584.09	3,832.95	4,035.17	3,802.10	3,206.33	3,336.08	3,028.07	3,527.27

Source: American Metal Market (AMM)

Average Price of Silver in London (Spot Fix)   In Pence Per Troy Ounce (.999 Fine)

Year	Jan.	Feb.	Mar.	Apr.	May	June	July	Aug.	Sept.	Oct.	Nov.	Dec.	Average
2002	315.08	310.55	318.27	316.61	322.58	329.32	316.07	295.93	292.38	282.49	286.93	291.52	306.48
2003	297.21	289.23	287.39	285.06	292.05	272.79	295.53	313.01	320.30	298.01	306.53	320.48	298.13
2004	347.36	339.49	395.67	391.14	327.03	320.36	342.32	368.78	356.35	392.94	402.52	368.43	362.70
2005	354.28	375.57	382.74	377.48	380.46	403.56	402.10	391.55	397.90	436.23	453.10	496.09	404.26
2006	519.94	544.76	594.70	714.36	715.69	584.44	607.69	647.19	615.09	618.97	678.96	677.31	626.59
2007	656.95	712.03	675.74	690.95	665.15	662.06	636.65	613.19	639.99	670.90	708.45	709.65	670.14
2008	815.50	899.50	960.24	883.98	867.12	866.05	907.89	772.57	677.51	617.03	645.37	693.86	800.55
2009	787.02	931.98	923.81	850.16	912.88	894.99	816.90	872.89	1,010.76	1,065.91	1,076.27	1,087.91	935.96
2010	1,098.45	1,016.07	1,140.22	1,184.58	1,256.63	1,255.90	1,172.41	1,181.47	1,323.37	1,479.95	1,665.70	1,880.21	1,304.58
2011	1,808.34	1,912.09	2,224.65	2,602.69	2,266.24	2,209.81	2,373.37	2,466.59	2,410.10	2,032.85	2,111.63	1,942.66	2,196.75

Source: American Metal Market (AMM)

Silver Futures - CME Group (NYMEX)
(weekly close) as of December 30, 2011

Cents per troy ounce

Average Open Interest of Silver Futures in New York (COMEX)   In Contracts

Year	Jan.	Feb.	Mar.	Apr.	May	June	July	Aug.	Sept.	Oct.	Nov.	Dec.
2002	67,442	65,355	67,405	76,158	82,525	100,837	94,731	82,349	80,511	89,094	85,434	78,174
2003	98,561	94,472	84,485	87,445	85,232	80,001	91,544	108,118	110,423	92,216	101,303	103,007
2004	109,860	113,764	117,848	113,172	90,493	87,201	89,062	97,844	85,245	108,762	121,221	107,136
2005	97,744	98,644	101,200	103,562	104,680	124,317	124,521	121,133	117,121	135,335	146,409	136,502
2006	131,767	129,928	132,140	137,121	110,400	110,631	98,733	110,635	102,159	105,167	114,132	105,741
2007	105,692	122,515	113,749	118,275	109,070	120,179	117,817	118,292	110,958	123,781	144,897	146,891
2008	174,969	182,076	157,971	143,333	123,649	128,645	136,866	131,931	110,333	97,927	91,983	84,986
2009	87,525	96,902	92,756	93,855	95,420	106,283	99,018	103,076	122,052	133,409	137,261	124,797
2010	126,921	118,619	112,234	123,849	122,547	129,561	118,619	126,117	145,022	153,013	148,547	133,596
2011	133,030	138,901	135,793	143,245	124,278	118,740	115,246	117,217	109,908	103,939	107,600	100,220

Contract size = 5,000 oz.   *Source: CME Group; New York Mercantile Exchange (NYMEX), COMEX Division*

Volume of Trading of Silver Futures in New York (COMEX)   In Thousands of Contracts

Year	Jan.	Feb.	Mar.	Apr.	May	June	July	Aug.	Sept.	Oct.	Nov.	Dec.	Total
2002	265.8	271.3	163.9	325.9	243.5	389.8	281.2	296.6	164.5	209.2	292.9	231.0	3,135.6
2003	291.1	409.7	216.7	315.2	251.1	352.7	407.9	442.8	335.5	373.5	464.2	250.8	4,111.4
2004	385.1	544.9	408.4	671.2	278.7	425.5	316.3	428.0	281.7	364.2	541.4	360.8	5,006.1
2005	285.4	513.6	370.3	485.8	392.2	621.6	334.9	601.0	455.0	425.0	652.9	398.5	5,536.4
2006	495.6	624.5	562.3	807.3	513.8	508.7	255.8	452.6	268.4	244.2	424.8	275.1	5,433.1
2007	364.6	589.3	479.9	635.0	417.3	680.6	404.1	784.0	469.5	581.1	1,018.5	393.2	6,817.1
2008	719.3	989.6	881.8	913.0	581.0	860.0	722.7	953.1	792.1	594.3	578.0	332.4	8,917.2
2009	415.6	652.2	433.8	575.7	418.4	869.1	476.6	842.9	657.0	809.6	1,159.3	680.3	7,990.5
2010	755.9	1,065.2	750.2	994.8	936.9	1,079.3	642.8	978.6	757.1	1,314.2	2,282.2	1,269.6	12,826.7
2011	1,429.7	1,674.7	1,685.7	3,014.6	2,461.1	1,768.9	1,325.0	1,982.8	1,220.4	952.6	1,327.4	765.6	19,608.6

Contract size = 5,000 oz.   *Source: CME Group; New York Mercantile Exchange (NYMEX), COMEX Division*

SILVER

Mine Production of Recoverable Silver in the United States   In Metric Tons

Year	Arizona	Cali-fornia	Colo-rado	Idaho	Missouri	Montana	Nevada	New Mexico	South Dakota	Wash-ington	Other States	Total
2002	W	3	W	W	W	W	424	W	W	W	927	1,350
2003	W	1	W	W	W	W	322	W	W	W	916	1,240
2004	W	1	W	W	W	W	302	W	W	W	943	1,250
2005	W	W	W	W	W	W	276	W	W	W	949	1,230
2006	W	W	W	W	W	W	260	W	W	W	895	1,160
2007	W	W	W	W	W	W	243	W	W	W	1,040	1,280
2008	W	W	W	W	W	W	235	W	W	W	1,020	1,250
2009	W	W	W	W	W	W	203	W	W	W	1,040	1,250
2010	W	W	W	W	W	W	217	W	W	W	1,050	1,250
2011[1]	W	W	W	W	W	W	193	W	W	W	824	1,020

[1] Preliminary.   W = Withheld proprietary data; included in "Other States".   *Source: U.S. Geological Survey (USGS)*

Consumption of Silver in the United States, by End Use   In Millions of Troy Ounces

Year	Brazing Alloys & Solders	Catalysts	Batteries	Mirrors	Electrical Contacts & Con-ductors	Photo-graphic Materials	Silver-plate	Jewerly	Sterling Ware	Total Net Industrial Con-sumption	Coinage	Total Con-sumption
2000	8.7	6.3	5.2	2.6	51.5	70.2	4.5	6.1	5.6	178.8	13.4	192.2
2001	8.3	6.1	5.3	2.5	34.1	65.5	4.0	4.9	4.6	157.3	12.3	169.6
2002	8.4	NA	NA	NA	37.6	64.8	[3]	13.7	[3]	161.7	15.3	177.0
2003	7.9	NA	NA	NA	39.5	58.9	[3]	15.1	[3]	160.8	14.5	175.3
2004	7.3	NA	NA	NA	47.4	55.2	[3]	15.4	[3]	164.8	15.5	180.3
2005	7.7	NA	NA	NA	52.1	56.4	[3]	15.7	[3]	172.8	16.6	189.4
2006	7.2	NA	NA	NA	55.0	46.4	[3]	15.0	[3]	168.2	17.6	185.8
2007	7.7	NA	NA	NA	57.7	35.9	[3]	14.2	[3]	164.2	16.0	180.2
2008	7.2	NA	NA	NA	61.4	29.3	[3]	13.0	[3]	161.0	25.4	186.4
2009[1]	5.2	NA	NA	NA	52.4	22.0	[3]	11.6	[3]	130.5	33.9	164.4

[1] Preliminary.   [3] Included in Jewelry beginning 2002.   NA = Not available.   *Source: American Metal Market*

Commodity Exchange, Inc. (COMEX) Warehouse of Stocks of Silver   In Thousands of Troy Ounces

Year	Jan.	Feb.	Mar.	Apr.	May	June	July	Aug.	Sept.	Oct.	Nov.	Dec.
2002	104,547	102,395	100,983	102,540	104,526	107,766	105,938	105,563	108,090	107,495	107,440	107,090
2003	107,394	107,610	109,153	108,521	108,168	105,092	107,222	105,406	104,862	106,283	118,238	124,498
2004	124,271	124,181	123,195	122,087	122,687	118,442	118,369	116,253	109,311	107,789	104,624	102,831
2005	103,590	102,390	101,494	103,627	103,995	104,257	104,719	109,467	115,588	116,687	116,257	117,608
2006	119,974	124,793	127,898	125,763	123,627	108,443	102,268	102,086	103,634	105,451	105,313	107,770
2007	111,071	113,970	117,637	126,433	131,343	130,497	139,935	132,106	133,057	133,474	133,891	134,533
2008	130,072	135,414	135,037	135,881	133,512	134,896	135,959	138,061	137,821	135,719	130,204	127,170
2009	NA	123,902	124,121	123,615	119,910	120,879	118,519	117,818	117,796	116,159	116,159	112,494
2010	110,588	110,588	110,588	115,786	116,178	119,452	114,015	110,244	110,765	111,075	107,785	107,393
2011	104,548	103,594	102,549	105,495	102,014	100,968	101,720	104,176	104,085	106,012	107,096	110,415

Source: CME Group; New York Mercantile Exchange (NYMEX), COMEX Division

Production[2] of Refined Silver in the United States, from All Sources   In Metric Tons

Year	Jan.	Feb.	Mar.	Apr.	May	June	July	Aug.	Sept.	Oct.	Nov.	Dec.	Total
2002	544	387	465	532	509	398	398	419	473	437	394	485	5,441
2003	483	426	320	412	357	431	430	373	361	809	363	471	5,235
2004	407	418	460	337	361	177	175	351	433	255	390	678	4,442
2005	402	505	515	568	450	558	556	440	356	376	485	439	5,650
2006	506	434	500	445	381	554	489	431	349	387	209	305	4,990
2007	401	405	445	436	476	452	335	438	290	388	267	339	4,671
2008	325	360	394	460	401	417	420	428	460	445	422	393	4,925
2009	456	182	270	326	337	394	363	495	535	676	530	778	5,342
2010	553	504	794	503	510	356	383	534	439	460	547	441	6,024
2011[1]	626	512	748	477	486	462	491	491	499	520			6,374

[1] Preliminary.   [2] Includes U.S. mine production of recoverable silver plus imports of refined silver.   *Source: U.S. Geological Survey (USGS)*

U.S. Exports of Refined Silver to Selected Countries   In Thousands of Troy Ounces

Year	Canada	France	Germany	Hong Kong	Japan	Rep of Korea	Singapore	Switzerland	United Arab Emirates	United Kingdom	Uruguay	Other Countries	Total
2001	1,598	----	----	11	1,202	----	2	354	----	20,029	105	7,659	30,960
2002	466	----	1	4	466	----	10	727	----	14,532	----	11,990	28,196
2003	524	3	----	3	17	16	2	630	----	3,086	----	2,534	6,816
2004	7,009	1	3	24	585	1	166	2,321	----	3	108	2,125	12,346
2005	3,729	----	25	3	1	18	95	2,829	----	1,145	563	1,302	9,709
2006	5,433	----	874	----	547	----	120	2,154	2	37,937	----	3,730	50,797
2007	3,762	3	1,537	1,804	801	25	103	990	----	1,061	498	12,790	23,373
2008	4,051	13	1,283	5	2,115	1,424	131	527	----	1,929	437	8,597	20,512
2009	395	1	1,399	159	2	1,816	113	823	----	1,765	----	6,997	13,471
2010[1]	3,376	----	2,247	139	1,241	1,974	1,010	733	----	1,331	----	10,744	22,794

[1] Preliminary.   [2] Included in "Other Countries", if any.   NA = Not available.   *Source: American Bureau of Metal Statistics, Inc. (ABMS)*

U.S. Imports of Silver From Selected Countries   In Thousands of Troy Ounces

Year	Canada	Mexico	Other Countries	Total	Canada	Chile	Mexico	Peru	Uruguay	Other Countries	Total
2001	243	----	----	243	44,046	2,054	41,152	5,498	----	1,771	94,521
2002	149	1,813	----	1,961	48,868	2,331	67,837	6,430	----	6,350	131,815
2003	82	----	----	82	41,795	1,987	62,050	18,261	----	12,223	136,316
2004	71	----	----	71	37,616	2,042	59,156	17,297	----	4,774	120,884
2005	14	----	----	14	41,474	2,514	65,908	20,319	----	4,173	134,387
2006	----	----	----	----	47,261	1,106	73,945	13,214	----	2,077	137,602
2007	----	----	12	12	34,722	1,206	78,125	18,358	----	2,942	135,352
2008	----	----	1	1	25,109	2,234	76,196	16,075	----	4,485	124,099
2009	----	----	----	3	24,016	4,019	52,405	6,559	----	3,022	90,020
2010[1]	104	----	----	104	51,119	2,578	82,947	9,999	----	26,003	172,646

[1] Preliminary.   [2] Included in "Other Countries", if any.   NA = Not available.   Source: American Bureau of Metal Statistics, Inc. (ABMS)

World Silver Consumption   In Millions of Troy Ounces

Year	Industrial Uses										Coinage							
	Canada	France	Germany	India	Italy	Japan	Mexico	United Kingdom	United States	World Total	Austria	Canada	France	Germany	Mexico	United States	Total Coinage	World Total
1995	2.0	30.0	43.6	101.3	49.5	112.7	16.9	31.6	148.7	752.7	.5	.7	1.2	2.4	.6	9.0	24.7	777.4
1996	2.0	26.9	41.0	122.2	51.7	112.1	20.3	33.8	155.0	785.8	.5	.7	.3	4.6	.5	7.1	23.3	809.1
1997	2.2	28.3	42.3	122.9	56.1	119.9	23.3	34.9	166.3	828.2	.4	.6	.3	3.7	.4	6.5	28.5	856.7
1998	2.3	28.4	38.4	114.7	55.9	112.8	21.7	38.6	162.6	801.2	.3	1.1	.3	10.0	.2	7.0	27.8	829.0
1999	2.1	26.6	35.1	121.5	61.8	122.5	21.3	39.3	175.2	838.7	.3	1.4	.3	7.0	.4	10.7	29.2	867.8
2000	2.0	28.8	31.8	131.0	65.1	135.0	16.6	42.7	179.1	871.8	.3	1.0	.4	8.8	.6	13.4	32.1	904.0
2001	2.0	28.7	32.4	154.0	58.2	119.3	15.9	45.9	157.3	836.5	.3	.9	.4	8.1	1.1	12.3	30.5	867.0
2002	2.1	27.1	29.4	122.5	56.0	118.7	17.0	43.1	161.6	807.0	.4	1.0	.5	6.0	1.1	15.3	31.6	838.6
2003	2.2	25.6	29.4	122.5	55.0	115.9	18.7	44.1	160.8	817.5	.4	.3	.5	10.3	1.1	14.5	35.8	853.4
2004[2]	2.1	12.0	30.7	79.2	54.8	125.1	18.6	52.2	164.8	807.0	.5	1.3	.5	10.3	.9	15.5	41.1	836.6

[2] Preliminary.   NA = Not available.   *Source: The Silver Institute*

Soybean Meal

Soybean meal is produced through processing and separating soybeans into oil and meal components. By weight, soybean meal accounts for about 35% of the weight of raw soybeans (at 13% moisture). If the soybeans are of particularly good quality, then the processor can get more meal weight by including more hulls in the meal while still meeting the 48% protein minimum. Soybean meal can be further processed into soy flour and isolated soy protein, but the bulk of soybean meal is used as animal feed for poultry, hogs and cattle. Soybean meal accounts for about two-thirds of the world's high-protein animal feed, followed by cottonseed and rapeseed meal, which together account for less than 20%. Soybean meal consumption has been moving to record highs in recent years. The soybean meal marketing year begins in October and ends in September. Soybean meal futures and options are traded on the Chicago Board of Trade (CBOT). The CBOT soybean meal futures contract calls for the delivery of 100 tons of soybean meal produced by conditioning ground soybeans and reducing the oil content of the conditioned product and having a minimum of 48.0% protein, minimum of 0.5% fat, maximum of 3.5% fiber, and maximum of 12.0% moisture.

Soybean crush – The term soybean "crush" refers to both the physical processing of soybeans and also to the dollar-value premium received for processing soybeans into their component products of meal and oil. The conventional model says that processing 60 pounds (one bushel) of soybeans produces 11 pounds of soybean oil, 44 pounds of 48% protein soybean meal, 3 pounds of hulls, and 1 pound of waste. The Gross Processing Margin (GPM) or crush equals (0.22 times Soybean Meal Prices in dollars per ton) + (11 times Soybean Oil prices in cents/pound) – Soybean prices in $/bushel. A higher crush value will occur when the price of the meal and oil products are strong relative to soybeans, e.g., because of supply disruptions or because of an increase in demand for the products. When the crush value is high, companies will have a strong incentive to buy raw soybeans and boost the output of the products. That supply increase should eventually bring the crush value back into line with the long-term equilibrium.

Prices – Soybean meal futures prices at the Chicago Board of Trade traded sideways in early 2011 and then sold off fairly sharply late in the year to post a 1-1/2 year low in November and close 2011 down -16% at $309.4 per ton.

Regarding cash prices, the average price of soybean meal (48% solvent) in Decatur, Illinois in the 2011-12 marketing year (i.e., October 2011 to September 2012) through December of 2011, averaged $296.03 per short ton, down by -14.3% yr/yr.

Supply – World soybean meal production in 2011-12 rose +3.5% yr/yr to a new record high of 183.289 million metric tons. The world's largest soybean meal producers are China with 26.6% of world production in 2011-12, the US with 19.5%, Brazil with 15.6%, and the European Union with 6.7%. U.S. production of soybean meal in 2011-12 fell -1.4% yr/yr to 38.685 million short tons, below the 2006-07 record high of 43.054. U.S. soybean meal stocks in 2011-12 (Oct 1) rose +15.9% yr/yr to 350,000 short tons, below the decade high of 383,000 short tons in 2001-02.

Demand – World consumption of soybean meal in 2011-12 rose +3.7% yr/yr to 181.427 million metric tons, a new record high. The U.S. accounted for 15.4% of that consumption and the European Union accounted for 18.2%. U.S. consumption of soybean meal in 2011-12 rose +0.7% yr/yr to 27.941 million metric tons.

Trade – World exports of soybean meal in 2011-12 rose +1.6% to 60.607 million metric tons. Brazil accounted for 24.1% of world exports and the U.S. accounted for 13.0%. World imports of soybean meal in 2011-12 rose +1.5% yr/yr to 58.894 million metric tons. U.S. exports of soybean meal in 2011-12 fell -3.3% yr/yr to 8.800 million short tons. U.S. imports of soybean meal in 2011-12 fell -7.8% yr/yr to 165,000 short tons, remaining well below the record high of 285,000 short tons seen in 2003-04.

World Supply and Distribution of Soybean Meal   In Thousands of Metric Tons

Crop Year Beginning Oct. 1	Production Brazil	China	European Union	United States	Total	Exports Brazil	United States	Total	Imports European Union	Total	Consumption European Union	United States	Total	Ending Stocks Brazil	United States	Total
2002-03	21,449	21,000	12,950	34,649	130,265	13,657	5,728	43,070	20,545	42,481	33,335	29,096	130,085	1,647	200	5,421
2003-04	22,360	20,190	11,084	32,953	129,032	14,792	4,690	46,085	22,012	44,901	32,729	28,531	127,654	1,801	191	5,615
2004-05	22,740	24,026	11,300	36,936	138,568	14,256	6,659	47,701	21,910	46,080	32,680	30,446	136,722	1,577	156	5,840
2005-06	21,920	27,296	10,760	37,416	146,556	12,895	7,301	52,519	22,829	51,437	32,875	30,114	145,390	1,469	285	5,924
2006-07	24,110	28,465	11,550	39,037	154,248	12,715	7,987	55,321	22,213	52,933	33,228	31,166	151,508	1,913	311	6,276
2007-08	24,890	31,280	11,715	38,359	159,218	12,138	8,384	56,601	24,074	54,600	35,169	30,148	157,044	2,588	266	6,449
2008-09	24,700	32,475	10,131	35,473	151,870	13,109	7,708	52,801	20,980	51,342	31,579	27,898	152,367	1,844	213	4,493
2009-10	26,150	38,644	9,880	37,830	165,304	12,985	10,137	55,718	20,730	53,151	30,138	27,777	161,213	2,260	274	6,017
2010-11[1]	27,510	44,431	10,714	35,910	176,965	14,100	8,301	59,642	23,250	58,050	33,256	27,760	174,894	2,340	272	6,496
2011-12[2]	28,520	48,708	10,400	35,639	183,189	14,585	7,847	60,607	23,000	58,894	33,057	27,941	181,427	2,430	272	6,545

[1] Preliminary.   [2] Forecast.   *Source: Foreign Agricultural Service, U.S. Department of Agriculture (FAS-USDA)*

Soybean Meal Futures - CME Group (CBT)
(weekly close) as of December 30, 2011

USD per ton

Volume of Trading of Soybean Meal Futures in Chicago   In Thousands of Contracts

Year	Jan.	Feb.	Mar.	Apr.	May	June	July	Aug.	Sept.	Oct.	Nov.	Dec.	Total
2002	610.3	398.3	424.7	618.9	567.2	664.7	806.4	673.7	581.2	613.7	657.8	557.7	7,174.5
2003	639.6	551.4	527.7	676.7	599.6	749.8	772.1	692.8	677.2	896.4	700.7	674.3	8,158.4
2004	648.7	767.1	740.7	819.6	795.8	821.6	873.2	638.9	547.3	559.7	703.5	653.2	8,569.2
2005	658.7	857.6	713.4	661.8	571.3	1,025.0	632.8	693.4	602.9	497.9	694.0	715.8	8,324.6
2006	506.9	605.0	575.3	785.6	716.8	976.1	801.5	819.1	807.7	906.1	1,064.2	785.7	9,350.0
2007	768.9	1,018.8	822.1	985.7	798.9	1,217.3	1,107.9	1,025.1	1,028.6	1,016.4	1,218.8	1,204.7	12,213.3
2008	1,260.6	1,235.1	1,240.4	1,257.7	922.5	1,359.0	1,258.6	1,074.5	1,069.3	1,020.3	837.1	818.9	13,354.2
2009	909.2	988.7	841.7	1,195.1	1,071.4	1,390.1	1,146.6	1,071.8	974.6	1,012.1	1,222.7	1,056.6	12,880.8
2010	994.1	1,134.5	1,330.1	1,264.3	850.7	1,349.0	1,134.2	1,057.8	1,136.4	1,054.7	1,590.7	1,156.3	14,052.8
2011	1,115.7	1,437.9	1,475.1	1,546.9	1,141.0	1,642.3	1,211.5	1,485.3	1,726.2	1,329.8	1,511.7	1,296.8	16,920.2

Contract size = 100 tons.   *Source: CME Group; Chicago Board of Trade (CBT)*

Average Open Interest of Soybean Meal Futures in Chicago   In Contracts

Year	Jan.	Feb.	Mar.	Apr.	May	June	July	Aug.	Sept.	Oct.	Nov.	Dec.
2002	146,674	137,425	134,880	130,138	132,376	143,956	142,728	132,996	137,799	131,249	137,836	140,902
2003	154,821	168,036	157,670	163,532	163,096	154,985	152,121	146,582	153,505	169,709	170,707	176,191
2004	183,462	186,137	185,647	175,069	162,284	149,584	135,675	134,987	133,045	137,447	152,846	147,307
2005	154,984	165,403	146,326	133,578	129,372	149,882	122,088	109,976	121,833	135,970	140,102	140,959
2006	127,922	132,833	147,837	172,905	181,823	182,940	196,236	230,082	236,351	206,002	216,854	206,762
2007	201,214	227,905	213,708	216,258	212,398	217,576	210,612	201,339	219,046	225,683	248,277	251,133
2008	234,286	234,695	225,607	218,126	199,422	216,039	208,444	178,191	163,511	152,968	138,111	124,898
2009	118,930	121,722	110,580	123,445	160,515	190,481	174,733	167,301	155,388	150,639	159,393	165,141
2010	170,924	198,651	200,438	196,464	177,726	187,838	197,981	200,131	208,773	195,256	201,589	194,033
2011	203,340	215,886	213,717	226,365	228,210	223,375	180,790	176,598	187,326	186,973	204,468	206,053

Contract size = 100 tons.   *Source: CME Group; Chicago Board of Trade (CBT)*

SOYBEAN MEAL

Supply and Distribution of Soybean Meal in the United States   In Thousands of Short Tons

Crop Year Beginning Oct. 1	For Stocks Oct. 1	Pro- duction	Total Supply	Domestic	Exports	Total	Decatur 48% Protein Solvent	Decatur 44% Protein Solvent	Brazil FOB 45-46% Protein	Rotter- dam CIF
2002-03	240	38,194	38,600	32,361	6,019	38,380	181.57	200	163	197
2003-04	220	36,324	36,830	31,449	5,170	36,619	256.05	282	211	273
2004-05	211	40,715	41,073	33,559	7,343	40,902	182.90	202	172	231
2005-06	172	41,244	41,557	33,195	8,048	41,243	174.17	192	176	215
2006-07	314	43,054	43,524	34,374	8,804	43,178	205.44	226	199	276
2007-08	343	42,284	42,768	33,232	9,242	42,474	335.94	370	337	469
2008-09	294	39,102	39,484	30,752	8,497	39,249	331.17	365	333	401
2009-10[1]	235	41,707	42,101	30,640	11,159	41,800	311.27	343	327	391
2010-11[2]	302	39,251	39,731	30,278	9,104	39,381	340-380			
2011-12[3]	350	38,685	39,200	30,100	8,800	38,900				

[1] Preliminary.   [2] Estimate.   [3] Forecast.   *Source: Economic Research Service, U.S. Department of Agriculture (ERS-USDA)*

U.S. Exports of Soybean Cake & Meal by Country of Destination   In Thousands of Metric Tons

Year	Algeria	Australia	Canada	Dominican Republic	Italy	Japan	Mexico	Nether- lands	Philip- pines	Russia	Spain	Vene- zuela	Total
2002	266.5	294.1	1,100.2	358.7	34.1	157.2	435.1	78.4	756.6	121.3	----	59.8	6,703
2003	184.7	383.9	1,056.4	317.5	0.0	329.0	693.7	10.2	238.5	60.7	0.0	190.5	5,582
2004	176.2	209.2	1,140.6	156.9	0.5	220.3	824.1	2.0	299.0	18.2	0.1	193.4	4,937
2005	63.0	74.9	1,155.9	264.2	0.2	523.4	1,356.3	10.1	442.0	16.8	5.0	112.5	6,352
2006	18.4	54.3	1,390.4	423.6	1.3	481.1	1,705.7	6.5	519.4	31.1	----	27.9	7,479
2007	39.5	1.2	1,467.4	448.7	0.1	451.3	1,638.4	8.2	626.9	31.8	0.6	49.3	7,922
2008	50.1	45.3	1,365.0	368.5	58.5	385.8	1,447.3	36.8	551.2	27.3	0.0	545.0	7,996
2009	----	121.9	1,154.3	362.4	48.5	366.3	1,323.0	0.2	803.4	20.0	90.0	487.1	8,791
2010	----	208.0	1,068.9	384.4	28.1	389.2	1,382.0	0.8	860.1	22.0	50.6	571.0	9,317
2011[1]	17.4	0.5	1,047.9	358.4	27.3	356.9	1,426.0	0.4	869.1	22.6	0.2	636.4	7,835

[1] Preliminary.   *Source: Foreign Agricultural Service, U.S. Department of Agriculture (FAS-USDA)*

Production of Soybean Cake & Meal[2] in the United States   In Thousands of Short Tons

Year	Oct.	Nov.	Dec.	Jan.	Feb.	Mar.	Apr.	May	June	July	Aug.	Sept.	Total	Yield in lbs.
2001-02	3,534.4	3,538.7	3,655.3	3,703.1	3,313.2	3,589.7	3,315.7	3,344.2	3,194.1	3,085.4	3,106.7	2,911.3	40,292	44.27
2002-03	3,499.3	3,424.7	3,526.8	3,358.4	3,048.4	3,360.1	2,994.7	3,072.4	2,873.4	3,064.4	2,966.6	3,023.5	38,213	43.90
2003-04	3,462.1	3,465.9	3,483.7	3,479.3	3,144.9	3,092.4	2,682.4	2,792.4	2,616.2	2,752.2	2,480.2	2,872.6	36,324	44.32
2004-05	3,685.2	3,584.2	3,567.9	3,553.6	3,293.3	3,547.6	3,328.0	3,396.8	3,160.9	3,320.4	3,122.1	3,157.0	40,717	44.26
2005-06	3,700.9	3,562.3	3,518.0	3,589.5	3,215.3	3,504.0	3,212.6	3,474.6	3,250.9	3,507.8	3,351.7	3,354.5	41,242	43.83
2006-07	3,823.2	3,671.9	3,733.0	3,697.5	3,257.2	3,721.5	3,444.5	3,627.3	3,532.6	3,572.4	3,474.6	3,498.2	43,054	44.03
2007-08	3,869.5	3,709.4	3,887.5	3,791.2	3,473.7	3,701.1	3,500.6	3,633.8	3,352.3	3,316.3	3,052.4	2,996.3	42,284	43.95
2008-09	3,519.4	3,413.5	3,346.0	3,439.8	3,203.7	3,425.4	3,335.2	3,502.8	3,323.2	3,066.7	2,844.9	2,683.5	39,104	43.93
2009-10	3,845.7	3,976.5	4,076.1	3,932.5	3,635.5	3,680.0	3,214.0	3,144.5	3,049.2	3,056.1	3,030.6	3,059.7	41,700	43.81
2010-11[1]	3,738.1	3,720.0	3,675.5	3,569.5	3,126.2	3,371.6	3,112.9	3,100.5	2,988.4				40,537	

[1] Preliminary.   [2] At oil mills; including millfeed and lecithin.   *Sources: Economic Research Service, U.S. Department of Agriculture (ERS-USDA)*

Stocks (at Oil Mills)[2] of Soybean Cake & Meal in the United States, on First of Month   In Thousands of Short Tons

Year	Jan.	Feb.	Mar.	Apr.	May	June	July	Aug.	Sept.	Oct.	Nov.	Dec.
2001-02	383.3	305.5	302.9	393.7	289.7	272.0	336.5	253.8	212.7	343.3	202.4	256.5
2002-03	240.0	285.2	371.7	337.0	299.1	259.5	335.7	263.5	311.8	271.6	228.4	266.9
2003-04	219.9	317.8	432.4	280.7	328.9	415.8	375.0	338.6	465.5	314.9	344.6	196.3
2004-05	210.7	357.7	286.8	271.3	340.9	310.4	248.0	307.5	349.0	244.8	362.3	238.3
2005-06	171.8	316.1	304.9	338.0	326.6	301.6	286.5	415.4	303.5	266.2	372.6	225.8
2006-07	313.8	388.4	373.6	468.9	372.4	289.4	329.9	328.6	279.0	316.8	314.9	231.9
2007-08	343.0	305.1	295.5	421.6	287.4	331.3	395.4	339.9	433.0	424.3	297.4	415.2
2008-09	293.8	372.0	599.1	413.9	448.0	437.2	360.9	421.8	577.6	426.3	328.4	316.3
2009-10	234.7	446.2	627.4	568.8	630.5	702.4	361.7	296.2	467.7	341.1	425.0	272.5
2010-11[1]	301.6	516.5	484.4	510.7	449.1	466.6	325.1	442.9	375.0			

[1] Preliminary.   [2] Including millfeed and lecithin.   *Sources: Economic Research Service, U.S. Department of Agriculture (ERS-USDA)*

Average Price of Soybean Meal (48% Solvent) in Decatur Illinois   In Dollars Per Short Ton -- Bulk

Year	Jan.	Feb.	Mar.	Apr.	May	June	July	Aug.	Sept.	Oct.	Nov.	Dec.	Average
2002-03	168.20	163.20	163.60	167.40	176.80	175.40	182.10	195.40	191.90	187.30	189.70	217.95	181.58
2003-04	225.20	242.00	231.54	252.15	257.39	301.14	311.83	300.69	285.81	284.05	205.34	175.51	256.05
2004-05	155.37	153.90	161.60	167.34	167.95	187.96	193.19	198.68	219.28	215.75	198.43	175.40	182.90
2005-06	166.22	170.32	193.17	183.64	176.73	175.07	174.64	175.77	176.83	168.97	159.76	168.87	174.17
2006-07	177.71	190.67	180.63	190.36	208.81	205.26	189.37	198.66	229.70	222.05	217.63	254.41	205.44
2007-08	260.55	280.76	314.78	331.28	345.87	331.57	329.94	325.48	390.72	412.25	355.35	352.70	335.94
2008-09	260.66	267.37	268.24	306.85	297.42	292.22	324.27	380.37	418.47	373.18	405.27	379.68	331.17
2009-10	325.69	328.18	333.93	314.23	295.79	277.61	291.21	287.85	305.78	325.56	331.76	317.65	311.27
2010-11	321.92	341.78	351.93	368.54	358.59	345.43	335.87	342.30	347.45	346.52	349.60	336.32	345.52
2011-12	301.45	290.37	281.65	310.65									296.03

Source: Economic Research Service, U.S. Department of Agriculture (ERS-USDA)

Average Price of Soybean Meal (44% Solvent) in Decatur Illinois   In Dollars Per Short Ton -- Bulk

Year	Jan.	Feb.	Mar.	Apr.	May	June	July	Aug.	Sept.	Oct.	Nov.	Dec.	Average
1992-93	168.6	170.9	176.4	175.6	167.5	172.4	175.6	181.7	181.3	217.6	206.9	186.5	181.8
1993-94	180.6	195.7	192.5	185.9	184.4	182.0	176.4	191.1	183.0	168.1	165.6	162.5	180.7
1994-95	156.4	150.9	145.4	145.1	149.4	145.7	151.0	148.1	149.1	160.1	157.5	171.8	152.5
1995-96	183.4	194.1	213.6	220.5	216.7	215.7	237.9	232.3	227.9	242.3	251.1	265.5	225.1
1996-97	238.0	242.7	240.9	240.7	253.6	270.4	277.7	296.0	275.9	261.5	261.6	265.7	260.4
1997-98	216.0	231.6	214.9	193.1	182.1	165.3	152.8	150.3	157.8	173.3	135.7	126.9	175.0
1998-99	129.4	139.3	139.6	131.0	124.4	127.2	128.6	127.0	131.7	125.7	135.9	144.1	132.0
1999-00	147.2	148.1	145.4	155.0	163.6	166.6	168.1	180.1	170.2	156.8	151.4	166.9	160.0
2000-01	166.0	173.7	187.9	175.6	158.3	149.1	149.7	155.6	163.1	183.9	170.6	163.5	166.4
2001-02	157.7	157.2	146.6	Disc.	Disc.	Disc.	Disc.	Disc.	Disc.	Disc.	Disc.	Disc.	153.8

Source: Economic Research Service, U.S. Department of Agriculture (ERS-USDA)

Soybean Oil

Soybean oil is the natural oil extracted from whole soybeans. Typically, about 19% of a soybean's weight can be extracted as crude soybean oil. The oil content of U.S. soybeans correlates directly with the temperatures and amount of sunshine during the soybean pod-filling stages. Edible products produced with soybean oil include cooking and salad oils, shortening, and margarine. Soybean oil is the most widely used cooking oil in the U.S. It accounts for 80% of margarine production and for more than 75% of total U.S. consumer vegetable fat and oil consumption. Soy oil is cholesterol-free and high in polyunsaturated fat. Soy oil is also used to produce inedible products such as paints, varnish, resins, and plastics. Of the edible vegetable oils, soy oil is the world's largest at about 32%, followed by palm oil and rapeseed oil. Soybean oil futures and options are traded on the Chicago Board of Trade (CBOT).

Prices – Soybean oil futures prices at the Chicago Board of Trade in 2011 traded sideways early in the year. Soybean oil futures prices then sold off moderately in September and closed 2011 down -10% at 52.09 cents per pound.

Regarding cash prices, for the year 2011-12 (through December 2011), the average monthly price of crude domestic soybean oil (in tank cars) in Decatur (F.O.B.) fell by -4.0% yr/yr to 51.08 cents per pound.

Supply – World production of soybean oil in 2011-12 rose +3.4% yr/yr to a new record high of 43,266 million metric tons. The U.S. accounts for 19.8% of world soybean oil production, while Brazil accounts for 16.3%, and the European Union accounts for 5.6%. U.S. production of soybean oil in 2011-12 fell -0.7% yr/yr to 18.605 billion pounds.

Demand – World consumption of soybean oil in 2011-12 rose +4.0% yr/yr to a new record high of 43.396 million metric tons. The U.S. accounted for 18.7% of world consumption, while Brazil accounted for 12.8%, the European Union for 6.6%, and India for 5.6%. U.S. consumption of soybean oil in 2011-12 rose +5.4% yr/yr to 17.700 billion pounds.

Trade – World exports of soybean oil in 2011-12 fell -8.0% yr/yr to 9.197 million metric tons. U.S. exports of soybean oil in 2011-12 fell -63.9% yr/yr to 1.200 billion pounds, well below 2009-10 record high of 3.359 billion pounds.

World Supply and Demand of Soybean Oil   In Thousands of Metric Tons

Crop Year Beginning Oct. 1	Production Brazil	Production European Union	Production United States	Production Total	Exports Brazil	Exports United States	Exports Total	Imports India	Imports Total	Consumption Brazil	Consumption European Union	Consumption India	Consumption United States	Consumption Total	End Stocks[3] United States	End Stocks[3] Total
2002-03	5,205	2,950	8,360	30,511	2,394	1,027	8,803	1,197	8,186	2,925	2,304	1,910	7,748	30,187	676	2,913
2003-04	5,588	2,531	7,748	30,299	2,718	425	8,698	906	8,391	2,959	2,112	1,942	7,650	30,261	488	2,644
2004-05	5,630	2,575	8,782	32,550	2,414	600	9,098	2,026	8,883	3,060	2,200	2,737	7,911	31,807	771	3,172
2005-06	5,430	2,480	9,248	34,852	2,466	523	9,833	1,727	9,111	3,113	2,905	3,000	8,147	33,756	1,365	3,546
2006-07	5,970	2,670	9,294	36,532	2,462	851	10,643	1,447	9,928	3,395	3,408	2,500	8,426	35,473	1,399	3,890
2007-08	6,160	2,710	9,335	37,826	2,388	1,320	10,991	733	10,416	3,955	3,422	2,330	8,317	37,722	1,127	3,419
2008-09	6,120	2,350	8,503	35,893	1,909	995	9,177	1,060	9,076	4,295	2,749	2,300	7,378	36,011	1,298	3,200
2009-10	6,470	2,280	8,897	38,893	1,449	1,523	9,265	1,598	8,704	5,020	2,397	2,760	7,195	38,260	1,523	3,272
2010-11[1]	6,810	2,480	8,636	41,838	1,600	1,496	9,999	1,000	9,422	5,290	3,053	2,750	7,620	41,841	1,122	2,692
2011-12[2]	7,060	2,412	8,573	43,266	1,610	726	9,197	800	8,914	5,550	2,870	2,450	8,142	43,496	911	2,179

[1] Preliminary.   [2] Forecast.   [3] End of season.   Source: Foreign Agricultural Service, U.S. Department of Agriculture (FAS-USDA)

Supply and Distribution of Soybean Oil in the United States   In Millions of Pounds

Crop Year Beginning Oct. 1	Pro-duction	Imports	Stocks Oct. 1	Exports	Total Domestic	Food Short-ening	Food Mar-garine	Food Cooking & Salad Oils	Food Other Edible	Total Food	Non-Food Paint & Varnish	Non-Food Resins & Plastics	Total Non-Food	Total Disap-pearance
2002-03	18,430	46	2,359	2,261	17,085	8,566	1,212	7,886	119	17,783	64	88	520	19,346
2003-04	17,080	306	1,489	936	16,864	8,304	1,138	7,933	NA	17,375	71	100	623	17,800
2004-05	19,360	26	1,076	1,324	17,439	7,938	1,227	7,790	NA	16,955	81	81	747	18,763
2005-06	20,387	35	1,699	1,153	17,959	7,799	848	8,657	NA	17,304	117	85	1,866	19,112
2006-07	20,489	37	3,010	1,877	18,574	6,225	961	8,708	NA	15,894	63	98	3,445	20,451
2007-08	20,580	65	3,085	2,911	18,335	5,271	902	9,612	NA	15,785	33	108	3,466	21,246
2008-09	18,745	90	2,485	2,193	16,265	4,445	W	10,321	NA	14,766	W	106	2,182	18,459
2009-10	19,615	103	2,861	3,359	15,814	3,883	W	9,339	NA	13,222	W	W	3,166	19,173
2010-11[1]	18,888	159	3,406	3,233	16,794									20,027
2011-12[2]	18,605	185	2,425	1,200	17,700									18,900

[1] Preliminary .   [2] Forecast.   Source: Economic Research Service, U.S. Department of Agriculture (ERS-USDA)

Stocks of Crude Soybean Oil in the United States, at End of Month

Year	Oct	Nov	Dec	Jan	Feb	Mar	Apr	May	June	July	Aug	Sept
2004-05	1,019.5	1,013.1	1,111.1	1,348.2	1,425.3	1,588.7	1,560.0	1,658.1	1,622.4	1,715.6	1,525.2	1,505.9
2005-06	1,641.0	1,706.5	2,029.6	2,247.4	2,392.2	2,433.1	2,454.7	2,576.8	2,605.3	2,762.9	2,740.2	2,703.5
2006-07	2,680.0	2,719.5	2,700.0	2,739.4	2,853.0	2,974.9	2,897.9	2,928.5	2,962.3	2,816.3	2,666.4	2,558.1
2007-08	2,701.1	2,736.4	2,713.9	2,860.0	2,713.1	2,714.6	2,573.4	2,633.8	2,554.7	2,482.8	2,265.2	2,200.4
2008-09	2,084.0	2,197.8	2,346.7	2,625.6	2,739.6	2,816.2	2,868.5	2,931.6	3,125.9	3,031.2	2,741.3	2,495.8
2009-10	2,452.0	2,611.1	2,836.9	2,933.3	2,992.2	2,995.7	3,094.6	3,186.0	3,249.6	3,266.2	3,029.6	3,080.0
2010-11[1]	2,957.7	2,994.3	3,165.7	3,078.7	3,075.1	3,109.8	3,010.4	2,917.4	2,868.2	2,824.3	NA	NA

Crop year beginning October 1.   [1] Preliminary.   *Source: Bureau of the Census, U.S. Department of Commerce*

Stocks of Refined Soybean Oil in the United States, at End of Month   In Millions of Pounds

Year	Oct	Nov	Dec	Jan	Feb	Mar	Apr	May	June	July	Aug	Sept
2004-05	235.8	178.4	200.3	212.6	222.0	222.7	243.4	236.6	216.2	273.8	200.7	193.6
2005-06	254.1	178.9	199.4	251.3	281.2	285.0	300.8	308.2	313.9	343.2	320.9	315.3
2006-07	334.7	355.6	381.7	442.4	427.7	386.5	403.5	382.4	397.9	408.2	380.0	346.1
2007-08	352.1	319.3	364.8	374.5	362.5	360.7	344.1	344.7	338.8	300.8	286.3	282.3
2008-09	307.3	337.6	298.5	282.7	283.1	284.8	294.3	302.8	291.4	298.9	268.8	246.5
2009-10	260.7	275.1	273.5	283.7	294.7	265.9	258.9	279.1	303.3	278.5	253.1	278.4
2010-11[1]	272.2	301.4	309.0	336.7	300.4	299.9	331.7	260.0	284.9	304.5	NA	NA

Crop year beginning October 1.   [1] Preliminary.   *Source: Bureau of the Census, U.S. Department of Commerce*

U.S. Exports of Soybean Oil[1], by Country of Destination   In Metric Tons

Crop Year Beginning Oct. 1	Canada	Ecuador	Ethiopia	Haiti	India	Mexico	Morocco	Pakistan	Panama	Peru	Turkey	Vene-zuela	Total
2001-02	87,047	0	2,225	9,452	88,529	161,760	39,439	59,999	12,616	37,677	85,199	635	1,142,755
2002-03	124,667	0	11,997	1,997	42,727	188,993	26,517	38,215	2,241	20,349	26,500	311	1,026,638
2003-04	96,450	10	3,665	1,298	14,561	97,099	15,518	17	2,834	25,097	0	169	424,554
2004-05	68,162	0	1,529	4,375	29,385	162,913	6,579	15,506	7,247	15,459	21	6,063	600,399
2005-06	76,342	2	3,270	3,972	23,031	108,515	21,951	12,000	1,546	19,588	4,032	38	523,153
2006-07	80,068	3	550	1,962	14,301	151,641	60,347	2	3,409	5,940	16	26,806	851,221
2007-08	90,361	3,009	2,141	14,138	11	269,249	107,323	0	6,817	183	73	82,035	1,320,430
2008-09	41,500	0	840	19,127	146,086	173,041	110,249	0	1,715	37,061	2,598	54,438	994,927
2009-10	41,369	0	720	24,616	162,342	211,456	231,996	6,795	5,151	92,004	54	52,702	1,523,466
2010-11[2]	34,996	8,722	700	13,314	45	167,664	291,890	20,900	6,123	44,999	1,120	57,707	1,466,327

[1] Crude & Refined oil combined as such.   [2] Preliminary.   *Source: Foreign Agricultural Service, U.S. Department of Agriculture (FAS-USDA)*

Production of Crude Soybean Oil in the United States   In Millions of Pounds

Year	Oct.	Nov.	Dec.	Jan.	Feb.	Mar.	Apr.	May	June	July	Aug.	Sept.	Total
2002-03	1,692.6	1,631.5	1,696.0	1,612.8	1,473.6	1,633.3	1,447.5	1,491.7	1,391.0	1,482.4	1,440.4	1,445.2	18,438
2003-04	1,630.8	1,610.6	1,604.6	1,618.3	1,462.4	1,461.4	1,260.3	1,314.6	1,236.0	1,304.0	1,185.9	1,391.7	17,081
2004-05	1,759.6	1,688.0	1,682.3	1,680.2	1,564.1	1,686.4	1,579.6	1,620.1	1,497.3	1,586.7	1,484.4	1,531.1	19,360
2005-06	1,828.6	1,756.7	1,717.3	1,765.2	1,594.8	1,746.5	1,586.3	1,709.3	1,608.7	1,737.6	1,657.7	1,684.1	20,393
2006-07	1,829.5	1,725.0	1,771.0	1,747.2	1,548.3	1,766.9	1,626.3	1,729.9	1,693.5	1,710.7	1,662.8	1,678.0	20,489
2007-08	1,868.6	1,805.4	1,879.4	1,845.2	1,687.7	1,827.8	1,707.0	1,756.4	1,632.8	1,616.4	1,507.5	1,445.5	20,580
2008-09	1,715.9	1,622.9	1,597.0	1,615.1	1,536.1	1,636.0	1,596.0	1,683.2	1,604.3	1,469.2	1,369.4	1,299.9	18,745
2009-10	1,825.2	1,854.0	1,898.3	1,845.0	1,690.1	1,728.8	1,519.2	1,481.6	1,438.8	1,440.5	1,418.4	1,474.4	19,614
2010-11[1]	1,790.5	1,771.2	1,739.4	1,722.9	1,500.0	1,623.8	1,504.6	1,491.2	1,445.8				19,453

Crop year beginning October 1.   [1] Preliminary.   *Source: Bureau of the Census, U.S. Department of Commerce*

Production of Refined Soybean Oil in the United States   In Millions of Pounds

Year	Oct.	Nov.	Dec.	Jan.	Feb.	Mar.	Apr.	May	June	July	Aug.	Sept.	Total
2002-03	1,451.2	1,367.2	1,262.2	1,224.5	1,181.0	1,308.2	1,238.6	1,378.8	1,316.1	1,293.8	1,290.5	1,334.8	15,647
2003-04	1,393.0	1,350.9	1,226.6	1,205.6	1,196.0	1,330.6	1,210.3	1,267.4	1,195.9	1,246.8	1,268.8	1,306.3	15,198
2004-05	1,377.6	1,331.1	1,243.2	1,243.4	1,188.1	1,321.6	1,324.5	1,287.4	1,253.6	1,329.1	1,324.1	1,324.7	15,515
2005-06	1,389.3	1,307.4	1,245.2	1,273.9	1,132.9	1,409.3	1,326.6	1,361.5	1,352.9	1,329.1	1,399.7	1,400.0	15,928
2006-07	1,477.9	1,309.3	1,303.9	1,269.3	1,165.2	1,361.0	1,361.8	1,409.8	1,340.8	1,457.5	1,404.0	1,421.0	16,281
2007-08	1,468.6	1,372.3	1,359.7	1,350.5	1,259.6	1,400.0	1,346.2	1,277.0	1,257.6	1,354.7	1,371.8	1,314.7	16,133
2008-09	1,388.0	1,248.3	1,102.6	1,121.7	1,088.2	1,200.0	1,185.0	1,210.7	1,139.9	1,239.8	1,200.8	1,227.8	14,353
2009-10	1,377.3	1,294.4	1,193.2	1,148.4	1,122.9	1,245.1	1,121.4	1,133.4	1,104.9	1,135.9	1,141.4	1,154.9	14,173
2010-11[1]	1,269.0	1,211.7	1,103.5	1,157.9	1,085.5	1,281.4	1,235.1	1,229.7	1,239.5	1,238.7	NA	NA	14,463

Crop year beginning October 1.   [1] Preliminary.   *Source: Bureau of the Census, U.S. Department of Commerce*

Coconut Oil and Corn Oil (monthly average) through December 2011

Consumption of Soybean Oil in End Products in the United States   In Millions of Pounds

Year	Jan.	Feb.	Mar.	Apr.	May	June	July	Aug.	Sept.	Oct.	Nov.	Dec.	Total
2002	1,461.5	1,395.3	1,568.0	1,505.1	1,549.7	1,492.4	1,490.5	1,545.5	1,543.7	1,710.2	1,587.2	1,458.8	18,308
2003	1,418.1	1,347.4	1,490.0	1,494.9	1,552.6	1,493.1	1,509.5	1,483.5	1,577.7	1,660.7	1,544.2	1,451.4	18,023
2004	1,388.1	1,417.6	1,555.2	1,468.0	1,506.7	1,421.1	1,429.2	1,473.6	1,483.2	1,558.3	1,533.7	1,368.9	17,604
2005	1,365.4	1,609.2	1,609.6	1,587.2	1,589.5	1,496.2	1,523.3	1,570.4	1,527.2	1,589.6	1,546.9	1,416.2	18,430
2006	1,505.2	1,368.8	1,661.4	1,561.1	1,634.9	1,653.2	1,575.5	1,746.2	1,727.9	1,775.6	1,638.6	1,571.5	19,420
2007	1,547.3	1,357.8	1,624.8	1,586.7	1,728.6	1,640.3	1,812.9	1,793.1	1,699.5	1,757.8	1,618.9	1,548.4	19,716
2008	1,623.6	1,476.9	1,625.3	1,580.9	1,510.8	1,528.4	1,589.8	1,624.2	1,559.2	1,662.7	1,500.3	1,348.5	18,630
2009	1,251.8	1,245.9	1,346.9	1,282.5	1,275.3	1,283.6	1,357.4	1,374.8	1,397.9	1,606.5	1,468.2	1,377.4	16,268
2010	1,231.8	1,227.6	1,350.0	1,215.6	1,183.4	1,232.8	1,229.6	1,274.4	1,262.6	1,342.1	1,293.8	1,192.1	15,036
2011[1]	1,222.6	1,190.1	1,458.3	1,413.2	1,421.6	1,500.8	1,508.7	NA	NA	NA	NA	NA	16,655

[1] Preliminary.   *Source: Bureau of the Census, U.S. Department of Commerce*

U.S. Exports of Soybean Oil (Crude and Refined)   In Millions of Pounds

Year	Jan.	Feb.	Mar.	Apr.	May	June	July	Aug.	Sept.	Oct.	Nov.	Dec.	Total
2002	249.9	446.7	233.3	233.3	87.3	345.4	180.8	95.3	109.8	113.5	194.9	210.2	2,501
2003	277.5	319.1	273.9	211.6	109.5	96.6	234.5	116.0	105.9	152.5	111.3	133.2	2,142
2004	71.2	62.8	73.5	38.8	44.0	39.3	53.9	68.8	86.8	59.9	184.5	239.5	1,023
2005	77.0	217.2	74.6	74.8	71.9	68.5	52.4	137.3	65.9	76.3	154.1	107.8	1,178
2006	71.3	67.0	178.2	96.8	53.8	82.0	89.4	64.7	111.8	167.1	120.3	276.7	1,379
2007	176.4	118.2	75.2	102.7	121.3	123.5	202.0	202.3	190.8	132.9	198.0	391.3	2,035
2008	157.7	509.9	385.5	427.1	163.4	171.7	125.5	183.8	64.2	138.1	102.3	119.9	2,549
2009	96.4	145.9	161.3	350.3	277.9	86.5	247.6	302.9	164.2	332.1	241.1	390.3	2,797
2010	513.9	399.5	408.0	148.0	77.2	129.1	179.3	365.6	174.5	440.3	432.5	394.5	3,662
2011[1]	466.1	301.4	330.1	188.6	91.7	129.6	119.7	114.6	223.5	78.1	107.8	59.5	2,211

[1] Preliminary.   *Source: Bureau of the Census, U.S. Department of Commerce*

Soybean Oil (monthly average) through December 2011   Cents per pound

Stocks of Soybean Oil (Crude and Refined) at Factories and Warehouses in the U.S.   In Millions of Pounds

Year	Oct.	Nov.	Dec.	Jan.	Feb.	Mar.	Apr.	May	June	July	Aug.	Sept.
2001-02	2,877.2	2,724.9	2,787.4	2,868.1	3,038.5	2,896.4	2,952.7	2,856.8	2,943.2	2,735.9	2,529.7	2,521.7
2002-03	2,358.6	2,280.1	2,326.1	2,398.0	2,395.7	2,271.9	2,244.6	2,120.2	2,053.9	1,928.5	1,794.2	1,654.4
2003-04	1,490.6	1,411.8	1,530.4	1,579.9	1,945.6	1,988.0	1,855.9	1,644.1	1,651.6	1,514.0	1,412.0	1,180.6
2004-05	1,075.6	1,269.4	1,191.2	1,311.1	1,560.1	1,646.8	1,812.7	1,797.1	1,888.7	1,838.0	1,988.8	1,727.0
2005-06	1,699.0	1,883.5	1,851.8	2,190.5	2,498.7	2,673.4	2,718.1	2,755.4	2,885.0	2,919.2	3,106.1	3,061.2
2006-07	3,009.8	3,012.3	3,081.9	3,090.6	3,356.7	3,477.7	3,558.4	3,500.0	3,468.7	3,549.8	3,399.6	3,200.4
2007-08	3,085.2	3,224.9	3,235.2	3,277.0	3,408.0	3,278.3	3,083.5	2,925.8	2,989.0	2,906.0	2,793.2	2,567.4
2008-09	2,484.6	2,388.5	2,519.0	2,629.6	2,992.3	3,124.1	3,191.6	3,279.4	3,338.8	3,530.3	3,448.9	3,134.0
2009-10	2,860.5	2,809.4	2,990.5	3,150.5	3,221.7	3,295.7	3,317.6	3,152.1	3,521.9	3,597.5	3,594.1	3,337.8
2010-11[1]	3,405.8	3,285.0	3,349.5	3,474.6	3,415.4	3,375.5	3,409.8	3,342.1	3,177.3	3,153.1	3,128.9	

On First of Month.   [1] Preliminary.   *Source: Economic Research Service, U.S. Department of Agriculture (ERS-USDA)*

Average Price of Crude Domestic Soybean Oil (in Tank Cars) F.O.B. Decatur   In Cents Per Pound

Year	Oct.	Nov.	Dec.	Jan.	Feb.	Mar.	Apr.	May	June	July	Aug.	Sept.	Average
2002-03	20.75	23.00	22.60	21.50	21.20	21.56	22.40	23.17	22.90	21.80	20.40	23.20	22.04
2003-04	27.40	27.76	29.54	30.34	33.05	34.66	34.19	32.68	30.07	28.05	25.98	25.87	29.97
2004-05	23.23	22.95	21.79	20.46	20.70	23.60	23.09	23.38	24.70	25.46	23.59	23.19	23.01
2005-06	24.26	22.52	21.00	21.63	22.21	23.21	22.98	24.76	24.20	25.86	24.80	23.54	23.41
2006-07	24.80	27.64	27.63	28.00	28.94	29.74	31.06	32.90	34.01	35.74	34.87	36.89	31.02
2007-08	38.10	42.68	45.16	49.77	56.68	57.27	56.58	58.27	62.43	60.54	50.78	46.09	52.03
2008-09	35.50	31.55	29.30	32.16	28.93	28.23	32.76	36.06	35.66	31.08	33.69	30.96	32.16
2009-10	33.15	36.59	36.81	34.88	34.69	36.39	37.11	35.41	34.47	35.07	37.57	39.21	35.95
2010-11	44.02	47.62	51.51	53.84	54.21	54.07	56.65	56.09	55.68	55.16	54.39	55.13	53.20
2011-12[1]	51.73	51.44	50.17	50.99									51.08

[1] Preliminary.   *Source: Economic Research Service, U.S. Department of Agriculture (ERS-USDA)*

SOYBEAN OIL

Soybean Oil Futures - CME Group (CBT)
(weekly close) as of December 30, 2011

Cents per pound

Volume of Trading of Soybean Oil Futures in Chicago   In Thousands of Contracts

Year	Jan.	Feb.	Mar.	Apr.	May	June	July	Aug.	Sept.	Oct.	Nov.	Dec.	Total
2002	474.8	497.4	468.9	497.0	526.9	588.4	701.5	648.9	529.4	549.9	705.4	628.0	6,816.5
2003	522.9	540.6	473.7	618.5	520.0	740.5	761.5	594.7	636.5	733.4	656.5	618.5	7,417.3
2004	521.3	722.6	736.2	760.2	631.2	642.9	657.5	549.5	565.4	552.9	654.3	599.3	7,593.3
2005	475.1	799.9	579.6	636.3	565.5	852.3	548.3	637.1	594.8	607.1	672.8	707.4	7,676.1
2006	531.9	611.2	597.6	866.4	688.6	1,024.5	801.2	816.7	729.0	939.3	1,003.3	878.8	9,488.5
2007	784.1	1,091.9	765.0	1,218.3	805.3	1,476.9	1,113.7	1,092.0	947.7	1,213.6	1,324.4	1,337.9	13,170.9
2008	1,294.7	1,541.4	1,291.0	1,551.1	1,107.0	1,467.6	1,624.2	1,386.9	1,441.7	1,414.4	1,252.4	1,455.9	16,828.4
2009	1,211.9	1,518.5	1,189.8	1,429.7	1,202.9	1,993.4	1,543.9	1,400.4	1,217.9	1,342.1	1,527.1	1,554.4	17,132.1
2010	1,184.3	1,787.0	1,414.2	1,924.2	1,224.4	2,198.2	1,721.4	1,646.8	1,561.7	1,588.9	2,297.3	2,242.9	20,791.2
2011	1,660.1	2,427.9	2,153.7	2,276.7	1,613.1	2,427.4	1,616.1	1,924.0	2,027.5	1,866.4	2,296.1	1,867.6	24,156.5

Contract size = 60,000 lbs.   *Source: CME Group; Chicago Board of Trade (CBT)*

Average Open Interest of Soybean Oil Futures in Chicago   In Contracts

Year	Jan.	Feb.	Mar.	Apr.	May	June	July	Aug.	Sept.	Oct.	Nov.	Dec.
2002	149,103	158,157	149,913	136,198	128,707	129,480	135,762	143,144	146,759	139,626	169,978	155,871
2003	143,607	140,272	131,323	142,123	147,584	143,218	147,610	157,066	141,596	161,556	183,747	191,176
2004	198,361	212,204	186,745	159,478	141,772	136,887	135,649	142,574	132,936	147,046	154,316	151,800
2005	159,229	174,091	161,971	145,808	135,515	155,962	147,542	132,351	139,489	165,634	175,229	186,760
2006	171,317	183,717	192,643	204,132	244,580	241,962	276,251	269,208	259,464	256,153	279,091	273,375
2007	256,800	283,761	285,436	312,454	301,566	309,109	294,005	285,255	277,219	276,874	306,390	298,906
2008	289,892	292,918	287,995	275,016	253,974	259,416	258,412	254,496	256,621	257,226	252,077	220,725
2009	204,502	211,632	206,299	208,101	217,198	246,451	245,978	239,386	217,068	229,387	248,176	229,970
2010	219,042	283,115	282,973	290,577	299,379	319,098	284,484	292,426	290,685	325,697	358,850	347,185
2011	375,563	391,930	358,625	357,657	313,673	322,642	287,408	278,784	287,250	297,663	305,955	305,279

Contract size = 60,000 lbs.   *Source: CME Group; Chicago Board of Trade (CBT)*

Soybeans

Soybean is the common name for the annual leguminous plant and its seed. The soybean is a member of the oilseed family and is not considered a grain. The soybean seeds are contained in pods and are nearly spherical in shape. The seeds are usually light yellow in color. The seeds contain 20% oil and 40% protein. Soybeans were an ancient food crop in China, Japan, and Korea and were only introduced to the U.S. in the early 1800s. Today, soybeans are the second largest crop produced in the U.S. behind corn. Soybean production in the U.S. is concentrated in the Midwest and the lower Mississippi Valley. Soybean crops in the U.S. are planted in May or June and are harvested in autumn. Soybean plants usually reach maturity 100-150 days after planting depending on growing conditions.

Soybeans are used to produce a wide variety of food products. The key value of soybeans lies in the relatively high protein content, which makes it an excellent source of protein without many of the negative factors of animal meat. Popular soy-based food products include whole soybeans (roasted for snacks or used in sauces, stews and soups), soy oil for cooking and baking, soy flour, protein concentrates, isolated soy protein (which contains up to 92% protein), soy milk and baby formula (as an alternative to dairy products), soy yogurt, soy cheese, soy nut butter, soy sprouts, tofu and tofu products (soybean curd), soy sauce (which is produced by a fermentation process), and meat alternatives (hamburgers, breakfast sausage, etc).

The primary market for soybean futures is at the Chicago Board of Trade. The CBOT's soybean contract calls for the delivery of 5,000 bushels of No. 2 yellow soybeans (at contract par), No. 1 yellow soybeans (at 6 cents per bushel above the contract price), or No. 3 yellow soybeans (at a 6 cents under the contract price). Soybean futures are also traded at exchanges in Brazil, Argentina, China, and Tokyo.

Prices – Soybean futures prices in 2011 posted a 2-1/2 year high of $14.5575 a bushel in February due to strong foreign demand after 2010 China soybean imports surged 29% y/y to a record 54.8 MMT and the USDA hiked is 2010/11 U.S. soybean export estimate to a record 1.59 billion bushels. Prices then consolidated moderately below that high into summer and remained well supported by the fact that the USDA in June 2011 cut its U.S. soybean acreage estimate to a 4-year low of 75.208 million acres due to a cold wet spring. Prices then eked out a 3-1/4 year high in August 2011 at $14.56 a bushel after the USDA cut its 2011 U.S. soybean production estimate to a 2-year low of 3.056 billion bushels as it cut its yield estimate to an 8-year low of 41.5 bushels per acre. Soybean prices then turned lower into the fall after the USDA in October 2011 cut its 2011 U.S. soybean export forecast and hiked its 2011/12 global ending stocks estimate to 63.01 MMT from 62.55 MMT projected in September. Soybean prices continued lower into year-end and posted a 1-1/4 year low of $10.94 a bushel in December and finished 2011 down -14% at $11.9850 a bushel. Another bearish factor for soybean prices was reduced Chinese demand for U.S. soybeans in favor of South American supplies after Oil World said Brazil and Argentina shipped a record 6.45

MMT of soybeans to China in the 3 months thru November 2011. Overall 2011 China soybean imports fell -3.9% to 52.64 MMT, the first annual decline in seven years. Going into 2012, a drought in South America has the potential to keep soybean prices well supported, along with a tight U.S. 2011/12 stocks/use ratio of 9.1%. However, global supplies are near normal with the 2011/12 world stocks/use ratio at 23.4%.

Supply – World soybean production during the 2011-12 marketing year (Sep-Aug) fell by -4.8% yr/yr to 251.465 million metric tons. World soybean production has more than quadrupled from the 62 million metric ton level seen in 1980. The world's largest soybean producers were the U.S. with 33.1% of world production in 2011-12, Brazil (28.6%), Argentina (19.1%), China (5.4%), and India (4.4%). China's soybean production has roughly doubled since 1980. Brazil's production has risen just over four times since 1980.

U.S. soybean production in 2011-12 fell by -8.2% yr/yr to 3.056 billion bushels, below the record high of 3.359 in 2009-10. U.S. farmers harvested 73.636 million acres of soybeans in 2011-12, which fell -3.9% yr/yr from last year's record high of 76.616 million acres. The average yield in 2011-12 is down -4.6% yr/yr to 41.5 bushels per acre, under the record high of 44.0 bushels per acre. U.S. ending stocks for the 2011-12 marketing year (September 1), rose by +42.5% to 215.0 million bushels, still above the 3-decade low of 112.4 million bushels seen in 2004-05.

Demand – Total U.S. distribution in 2011-12 fell -8.2% to 3.011 billion bushels. The distribution tables for U.S. soybeans for the 2011-12 marketing year show that 53.6% of U.S. soybean usage went for crushing into soybean oil and meal, 42.4% for exports, and 4.0% for seed and residual. The quantity of U.S. soybeans that went for crushing fell -2.0% yr/yr in 2011-12 to 1.615 billion bushels. The world soybean crush rose +2.9% yr/yr in 2011-12 to a new record high of 227.423 million metric tons, which was about double the level seen in 1993-94.

Trade – World exports of soybeans in 2011-12 rose +0.9% yr/yr to a new record high of 92.792 million metric tons. The world's largest soybean exporters in 2011-12 were the U.S. with 37.4% of world exports, Brazil with 40.7% of world exports, and Argentina with 9.6% of world exports. U.S. soybean exports in 2011-12 fell -15.1% yr/yr to a 34.700 million metric tons, down from last year's record high of 40.859. Brazil's soybean exports have more than doubled in the past decade and Canada's exports have almost tripled.

World imports in 2011-12 rose +2.2% yr/yr to a new record high of 90.762 million metric tons. The world's largest importers of soybeans in 2011-12 were China with 61.2% of world imports, the European Union with 12.7%, Mexico with 3.9%, and Japan with 3.1%. China's imports in 2011-12 rose +6.0% yr/yr to a record level of 55.500 million metric tons, which is far from negligible levels prior to 1994.

SOYBEANS

World Production of Soybeans   In Thousands of Metric Tons

Crop Year[4]	Argen-tina	Bolivia	Brazil	Canada	China	India	Indo-nesia	Mexico	Para-guay	Thailand	United States	Russia	World Total
2002-03	35,500	1,650	52,000	2,336	16,510	4,000	780	89	4,500	423	250	75,010	196,869
2003-04	33,000	1,850	51,000	2,263	15,394	6,800	820	125	3,911	393	220	66,783	186,638
2004-05	39,000	2,027	53,000	3,042	17,400	5,850	825	132	4,040	555	217	85,019	215,777
2005-06	40,500	2,060	57,000	3,156	16,350	7,000	832	187	3,640	689	226	83,507	220,670
2006-07	48,800	1,650	59,000	3,466	15,074	7,690	815	80	5,856	807	210	87,001	236,233
2007-08	46,200	1,050	61,000	2,696	13,400	9,470	780	88	6,900	652	210	72,859	220,469
2008-09	32,000	1,600	57,800	3,336	15,540	9,100	800	153	4,000	744	180	80,749	211,960
2009-10[1]	54,500	1,665	69,000	3,507	14,980	9,700	700	121	7,200	942	170	91,417	260,854
2010-11[2]	49,000	1,580	75,500	4,345	15,100	9,800	650	168	8,300	1,222	180	90,606	264,180
2011-12[3]	48,000	1,580	72,000	4,246	13,500	11,000	640	200	6,400	1,749	180	83,172	251,465

[1] Preliminary.   [2] Estimate.   [3] Forecast.   [4] Spilt year includes Northern Hemisphere crops harvested in the late months of the first year shown combined with Southern Hemisphere crops harvested in the early months of the following year.   *Sources: Oil World; Foreign Agricultural Service, U.S. Department of Agriculture (FAS-USDA)*

World Crushings and Ending Stocks of Soybeans   In Thousands of Metric Tons

Crop Year	Argen-tina	Brazil	China	European Union	India	Japan	Mexico	Taiwan	United States	World Total	Brazil	United States	World Total
2002-03	23,533	27,168	26,540	16,480	3,375	4,217	4,335	2,135	43,948	165,189	16,636	4,853	43,193
2003-04	25,040	29,323	25,439	14,084	5,580	3,536	3,889	2,046	41,632	164,227	15,507	3,059	38,086
2004-05	27,313	29,344	30,362	14,350	4,530	3,149	3,729	2,013	46,160	175,272	16,658	6,960	48,380
2005-06	31,888	28,285	34,500	13,670	6,940	2,820	3,823	2,190	47,324	186,154	16,641	12,229	53,417
2006-07	33,586	31,110	35,970	14,670	6,485	2,925	3,900	2,161	49,198	196,090	18,189	15,617	62,093
2007-08	34,607	32,117	39,518	14,870	8,400	2,890	3,650	1,965	49,081	202,851	18,898	5,580	51,607
2008-09	31,243	31,868	41,035	12,860	7,200	2,497	3,465	1,917	45,230	193,325	12,037	3,761	42,719
2009-10[1]	34,127	33,700	48,830	12,510	7,500	2,370	3,600	2,150	47,673	209,500	15,836	4,106	59,598
2010-11[2]	37,613	35,933	55,000	12,265	9,600	2,070	3,625	2,150	44,851	221,094	22,189	5,852	68,902
2011-12[3]	38,900	37,000	59,600	11,700	9,800	1,920	3,650	2,160	43,953	227,423	16,029	7,490	60,284

[1] Preliminary.   [2] Estimate.   [3] Forecast.   *Sources: Oil World; Foreign Agricultural Service, U.S. Department of Agriculture (FAS-USDA)*

World Imports and Exports of Soybeans   In Thousands of Metric Tons

Crop Year	China	European Union	Japan	Rep. of Korea	Mexico	Taiwan	World Total	Argen-tina	Brazil	Canada	Para-guay	United States	World Total
2002-03	21,417	16,943	5,087	1,516	4,230	2,351	62,884	8,624	19,629	726	3,070	28,423	61,242
2003-04	16,933	14,675	4,688	1,368	3,797	2,218	53,996	6,741	20,417	914	2,667	24,128	56,042
2004-05	25,802	14,539	4,295	1,240	3,640	2,256	63,726	9,568	20,137	1,124	2,950	29,860	64,820
2005-06	28,317	13,937	3,962	1,190	3,667	2,498	63,940	7,249	25,911	1,326	2,011	25,579	63,432
2006-07	28,726	15,180	4,094	1,231	3,844	2,436	68,901	9,560	23,485	1,683	3,907	30,386	70,862
2007-08	37,816	15,129	4,014	1,232	3,614	2,148	78,322	13,839	25,364	1,753	4,585	31,538	78,774
2008-09	41,098	13,213	3,396	1,167	3,327	2,216	77,395	5,590	29,987	2,017	2,234	34,817	76,845
2009-10[1]	50,338	12,675	3,401	1,197	3,523	2,469	86,825	13,088	28,578	2,247	5,350	40,798	92,550
2010-11[2]	52,339	12,465	2,917	1,239	3,498	2,454	88,828	9,205	29,951	2,946	6,000	40,859	91,969
2011-12[3]	55,500	11,500	2,850	1,160	3,500	2,400	90,762	8,900	37,800	2,880	5,000	34,700	92,792

[1] Preliminary.   [2] Estimate.   [3] Forecast.   *Sources: Oil World; Foreign Agricultural Service, U.S. Department of Agriculture (FAS-USDA)*

Supply and Distribution of Soybeans in the United States   In Millions of Bushels

Crop Year Beginning Sept. 1	Farms	Mills, Elevators[3]	Total	Production	Total Supply	Crushings	Exports	Seed, Feed & Residual Use	Total Distribution
2002-03	62.7	145.3	208.0	2,756.1	2,969.0	1,615.0	1,044.0	131.0	2,791.0
2003-04	58.0	120.3	178.3	2,453.7	2,638.0	1,530.0	887.0	109.0	2,525.0
2004-05	29.4	83.0	112.4	3,123.7	3,242.0	1,696.0	1,097.0	193.0	2,986.0
2005-06	99.7	156.0	255.7	3,063.2	3,322.0	1,739.0	940.0	194.0	2,873.0
2006-07	176.3	273.0	449.3	3,188.2	3,655.0	1,808.0	1,116.0	157.0	3,081.0
2007-08	143.0	430.8	573.8	2,675.8	3,261.0	1,803.0	1,159.0	94.0	3,056.0
2008-09	47.0	158.0	205.0	2,967.0	3,185.0	1,662.0	1,279.0	106.0	3,047.0
2009-10	35.1	103.1	138.2	3,359.0	3,512.0	1,752.0	1,499.0	110.0	3,361.0
2010-11[1]	35.4	115.5	150.9	3,329.2	3,495.0	1,648.0	1,501.0	130.0	3,280.0
2011-12[2]	48.5	166.5	215.0	3,056.0	3,286.0	1,615.0	1,275.0	121.0	3,011.0

[1] Preliminary.   [2] Estimate.   [3] Also warehouses.   *Source: Economic Research Service, U.S. Department of Agriculture (ERS-USDA)*

Salient Statistics & Official Crop Production Reports of Soybeans in the United States   In Millions of Bushels

Year	Planted ---- 1,000 Acres ----	Acreage Harvested	Yield Per Acre (Bu.)	Farm Price ($/Bu.)	Farm Value (Million Dollars)	Yield of Oil (Lbs. Per Bushel Crushed)	Yield of Meal (Lbs. Per Bushel Crushed)	Aug. 1	Sept. 1	Oct. 1	Nov. 1	Dec. 1	Final
									Crop Production Reports -- In Thousands of Bushels --				
2002-03	73,963	72,497	38.0	5.64	15,253	11.39	43.90	2,628,387	2,655,819	2,653,798	2,689,691	----	2,756,147
2003-04	73,404	72,476	33.9	7.95	18,014	11.20	44.32	2,862,039	2,642,644	2,468,390	2,451,759	----	2,453,665
2004-05	75,208	73,958	42.2	5.90	17,895	11.33	44.26	2,876,627	2,835,989	3,106,861	3,150,441	----	3,123,686
2005-06	72,032	71,251	43.0	5.63	17,269	11.64	43.83	2,791,133	2,856,449	2,967,075	3,043,116	----	3,063,237
2006-07	75,522	74,602	42.9	6.67	20,468	11.34	44.03	2,927,634	3,092,970	3,188,576	3,203,908	----	3,188,247
2007-08	64,741	64,146	41.7	11.02	26,974	11.54	43.95	2,625,274	2,618,796	2,598,046	2,594,275	----	2,675,822
2008-09	75,718	74,681	39.7	10.13	29,458	11.36	43.93	2,972,577	2,933,888	2,983,023	2,920,589	----	2,967,007
2009-10	77,451	76,372	44.0	9.61	32,145	11.10	43.82	3,199,172	3,245,292	3,250,113	3,319,270	----	3,359,011
2010-11[1]	77,404	76,610	43.5	12.17	37,547	11.54	44.39	3,433,370	3,482,899	3,408,211	3,375,067	----	3,329,181
2011-12[2]	74,976	73,636	41.5	11.88	35,784			3,055,882	3,085,340	3,059,987	3,045,558	----	3,056,032

[1] Preliminary.   [2] Forecast.   NA = Not available.   Source: National Agricultural Statistics Service, U.S. Department of Agriculture (NASS-USDA)

Stocks of Soybeans in the United States   In Thousands of Bushels

Year	On Farms Mar. 1	June 1	Sept. 1	Dec. 1	Off Farms Mar. 1	June 1	Sept. 1	Dec. 1	Total Stocks Mar. 1	June 1	Sept. 1	Dec. 1
2002	687,000	301,200	62,700	1,170,000	648,987	383,721	145,320	943,641	1,335,987	684,921	208,020	2,113,641
2003	636,500	272,500	58,000	820,000	565,528	329,862	120,329	868,653	1,201,028	602,362	178,329	1,688,653
2004	355,900	110,000	29,400	1,300,000	549,947	300,604	83,014	1,004,640	905,847	410,604	112,414	2,304,640
2005	795,000	356,100	99,700	1,345,000	586,364	343,174	156,038	1,157,098	1,381,364	699,274	255,738	2,502,098
2006	872,000	495,500	176,300	1,461,000	797,206	495,199	273,026	1,240,366	1,669,206	990,699	449,326	2,701,366
2007	910,000	500,000	143,000	1,100,000	876,887	592,185	430,810	1,231,860	1,786,887	1,092,185	573,810	2,331,860
2008	593,000	226,600	47,000	1,189,000	840,982	449,543	158,034	1,086,432	1,433,982	676,143	205,034	2,275,432
2009	656,500	226,300	35,100	1,229,500	645,289	369,859	103,098	1,109,050	1,301,789	596,159	138,198	2,338,550
2010	609,200	232,600	35,400	1,091,000	660,868	338,523	115,485	1,187,084	1,270,068	571,123	150,885	2,278,084
2011[1]	505,000	217,700	48,500	1,138,500	743,800	401,583	166,513	1,227,284	1,248,800	619,283	215,013	2,365,784

[1] Preliminary.   Source: National Agricultural Statistics Service, U.S. Department of Agriculture (NASS-USDA)

Commercial Stocks of Soybeans in the United States, on First of Month   In Millions of Bushels

Year	Jan.	Feb.	Mar.	Apr.	May	June	July	Aug.	Sept.	Oct.	Nov.	Dec.
2002	29.6	27.0	22.2	21.0	18.4	15.4	14.4	10.2	4.6	8.4	26.9	28.4
2003	25.9	13.2	13.9	12.8	9.7	9.4	11.7	7.6	4.5	7.0	33.0	36.7
2004	35.5	26.2	26.0	19.4	15.7	13.5	8.0	5.9	4.4	10.8	31.1	32.9
2005	26.5	21.5	19.5	16.0	14.8	12.1	11.5	8.8	5.4	17.0	36.7	36.1
2006	36.8	30.2	26.1	25.7	17.6	20.5	14.6	14.5	14.5	19.0	40.1	43.7
2007	42.0	36.5	37.3	34.3	29.7	27.4	26.6	24.6	25.5	32.0	54.0	61.3
2008	51.1	45.5	41.8	36.3	28.2	25.6	19.2	14.8	11.4	19.6	40.5	46.1
2009	44.6	36.8	27.0	15.6	13.9	11.8	10.0	5.8	5.9	24.7	40.5	44.3
2010	30.0	28.5	20.1	22.3	10.8	8.0	8.2	4.5	3.3	19.2	45.0	32.0
2011	32.6	23.2	16.0	11.3	10.2	5.9	6.2	5.7	4.6	9.8	49.4	50.7

Source: Livestock Division, U.S. Department of Agriculture (LD-USDA)

Stocks of Soybeans at Mills in the United States, on First of Month   In Millions of Bushels

Year	Sept.	Oct.	Nov.	Dec.	Jan.	Feb.	Mar.	Apr.	May	June	July	Aug.
2000-01	52.1	56.8	179.4	166.8	137.8	143.3	127.0	120.6	94.9	86.1	79.3	69.0
2001-02	69.0	41.3	152.8	137.1	121.4	129.6	128.2	112.9	104.2	88.2	67.9	65.4
2002-03	46.4	36.3	114.5	113.5	106.0	109.2	102.9	91.5	91.6	76.0	64.9	55.6
2003-04	35.3	31.9	129.9	121.0	121.7	125.6	124.5	134.3	114.8	91.2	76.0	61.4
2004-05	37.0	74.8	114.1	113.1	100.3	85.6	88.1	88.8	70.9	59.2	66.1	51.7
2005-06	43.7	66.2	158.3	129.7	114.1	117.4	108.0	90.0	69.5	64.0	63.1	51.5
2006-07	52.7	48.7	124.7	132.4	127.0	133.0	121.8	123.8	113.8	102.0	103.5	99.1
2007-08	92.6	101.6	157.2	139.5	117.9	135.5	122.0	104.4	100.8	78.9	74.8	73.7
2008-09	53.3	50.1	130.4	121.7	116.4	103.4	99.8	100.5	98.8	82.5	89.6	75.0
2009-10[1]	45.2	31.5	99.2	129.6	108.0	101.6	95.3	96.8	80.5	62.7	66.6	63.5

[1] Preliminary.   Source: Economic Research Service, U.S. Department of Agriculture (ERS-USDA)

SOYBEANS

Production of Soybeans for Beans in the United States, by State In Millions of Bushels

Year	Arkansas	Illinois	Indiana	Iowa	Ken-tucky	Mich-igan	Minn-esota	Miss-issippi	Missouri	Neb-raska	Ohio	Tenn-essee	Total
2002-03	96.5	453.7	239.5	499.2	42.6	78.5	308.9	43.8	170.0	176.3	151.0	34.7	2,756.1
2003-04	111.3	379.6	204.1	342.9	53.9	54.7	238.4	55.8	146.0	182.3	164.8	47.0	2,453.7
2004-05	122.9	495.0	284.3	497.4	57.2	75.2	232.7	61.5	223.2	218.5	207.7	48.4	3,123.7
2005-06	102.0	439.4	263.6	525.0	53.3	76.6	306.0	58.0	181.7	235.3	201.6	41.8	3,063.2
2006-07	107.5	482.4	284.0	510.1	60.3	89.6	319.0	42.9	191.2	250.5	217.1	44.1	3,188.2
2007-08	101.5	360.2	220.3	448.8	30.3	70.7	267.3	58.3	175.1	196.4	199.3	19.2	2,675.8
2008-09	123.5	428.6	244.4	449.7	47.6	69.9	264.9	78.4	191.1	226.0	161.3	49.6	2,967.0
2009-10	122.6	430.1	266.6	486.0	68.2	79.6	284.8	77.1	230.6	259.4	222.0	68.9	3,359.0
2010-11	110.3	466.1	258.5	496.2	47.3	88.7	329.0	76.2	210.4	267.8	220.3	43.7	3,329.2
2011-12[1]	124.3	416.4	238.1	466.1	57.7	85.4	270.3	70.2	189.8	258.4	215.7	40.0	3,056.0

[1] Preliminary.   *Source: Agricultural Statistics Board, U.S. Department of Agriculture (ASB-USDA)*

U. S. Exports of Soybeans In Millions of Bushels

Year	Sept.	Oct.	Nov.	Dec.	Jan.	Feb.	Mar.	Apr.	May	June	July	Aug.	Total
2001-02	31.7	158.9	158.0	133.2	157.2	132.0	63.8	46.0	45.6	43.2	56.0	38.0	1,063.7
2002-03	30.9	136.7	152.8	114.7	159.3	151.5	92.1	66.4	35.9	31.9	37.9	34.3	1,044.4
2003-04	34.0	165.3	186.4	143.2	109.3	82.6	69.9	28.7	19.1	20.2	14.8	10.8	884.2
2004-05	47.2	177.7	181.0	155.0	121.9	123.2	96.4	65.2	49.6	35.2	20.0	30.3	1,102.7
2005-06	32.3	143.1	140.1	83.1	111.8	111.3	95.6	43.4	46.5	39.0	47.6	51.0	944.8
2006-07	64.9	182.6	126.4	122.7	147.2	126.5	96.9	71.1	41.9	48.9	37.9	49.6	1,116.5
2007-08	62.0	138.6	127.4	146.0	146.1	139.2	114.8	72.7	56.2	58.7	51.2	45.9	1,158.8
2008-09	34.3	179.3	173.3	170.9	152.9	159.1	101.6	82.0	60.0	60.5	49.9	55.4	1,279.3
2009-10	39.1	198.0	298.8	225.9	226.4	170.0	131.5	55.4	32.0	28.2	37.4	56.3	1,499.0
2010-11[1]	68.1	293.9	255.9	195.8	185.3	171.8	123.7	66.5	34.3	31.5	30.4	44.0	1,501.3

[1] Preliminary.   *Source: Economic Research Service, U.S. Department of Agriculture (ERS-USDA)*

Spread Between Value of Products and Soybean Price in the United States In Cents Per Bushel

Year	Sept.	Oct.	Nov.	Dec.	Jan.	Feb.	Mar.	Apr.	May	June	July	Aug.	Average
2001-02	102	108	106	83	86	65	65	65	57	63	64	89	79
2002-03	77	73	52	60	53	52	61	53	62	59	72	74	62
2003-04	117	88	94	81	84	81	96	96	85	97	150	127	99
2004-05	132	95	70	66	75	76	67	78	69	75	73	82	79
2005-06	100	102	70	91	90	83	94	102	107	104	106	110	97
2006-07	126	105	81	74	73	72	80	64	78	113	110	88	89
2007-08	90	83	100	109	105	103	114	114	84	105	122	114	104
2008-09	195	95	68	72	59	61	61	77	109	106	92	156	96
2009-10	192	123	127	115	104	103	77	88	85	113	89	93	109
2010-11[1]	89	89	80	88	87	72	71	86	82	70	56	70	78

[1] Preliminary.   *Source: Economic Research Service, U.S. Department of Agriculture (ERS-USDA)*

Soybean Crushed (Factory Consumption) in the United States In Millions of Bushels

Year	Jan.	Feb.	Mar.	Apr.	May	June	July	Aug.	Sept.	Oct.	Nov.	Dec.	Total
2001-02	128.2	150.2	149.1	153.4	155.1	139.0	149.8	139.2	140.6	134.6	129.8	130.6	1,700
2002-03	122.3	149.5	145.7	150.2	142.7	129.2	142.8	127.0	129.8	121.4	129.3	125.1	1,615
2003-04	127.6	146.2	145.6	145.8	146.0	131.4	129.6	112.5	117.5	109.4	115.3	103.0	1,530
2004-05	121.0	155.3	151.1	150.0	148.6	137.6	148.5	139.4	142.8	132.0	139.5	130.3	1,696
2005-06	133.2	157.7	151.5	148.4	152.4	136.3	149.5	135.5	146.2	137.4	148.5	142.1	1,739
2006-07	142.4	161.7	155.1	157.4	155.5	136.9	156.1	145.0	152.1	148.9	150.4	146.2	1,808
2007-08	147.3	163.7	156.3	164.1	160.5	146.5	156.0	147.5	152.6	141.0	139.3	128.6	1,803
2008-09	125.7	150.0	144.7	141.3	145.2	135.4	144.4	140.3	146.2	140.1	128.8	119.8	1,662
2009-10	113.3	163.5	168.7	173.1	167.2	153.9	156.1	136.5	133.0	129.2	129.4	128.1	1,752
2010-11[1]	130.4	157.2	155.1	153.0	149.2	129.4	140.3	128.0	128.0	123.6	129.6	125.0	1,649

[1] Preliminary.   *Source: Economic Research Service, U.S. Department of Agriculture (ERS-USDA)*

Soybean Futures - CME Group (CBT)
(weekly close) as of December 30, 2011

Cents per bushel

Volume of Trading of Soybean Futures in Chicago · In Thousands of Contracts

Year	Jan.	Feb.	Mar.	Apr.	May	June	July	Aug.	Sept.	Oct.	Nov.	Dec.	Total
2002	156,898	169,242	169,882	164,388	156,548	188,692	220,758	201,494	201,808	210,033	208,099	213,868	12,150
2003	201,536	217,680	226,421	251,314	230,325	222,185	190,206	190,533	232,030	265,088	241,320	252,874	14,475
2004	258,708	267,482	263,737	262,919	222,310	199,108	172,194	171,791	190,006	242,654	228,700	241,972	17,546
2005	244,197	266,745	295,324	268,081	252,582	313,724	278,738	256,853	249,030	285,070	275,308	290,370	18,846
2006	315,640	359,379	354,211	374,507	375,124	371,155	336,000	348,321	361,643	384,069	394,259	414,374	20,216
2007	416,459	478,579	474,466	470,517	465,303	549,655	536,595	495,302	526,913	580,446	586,635	582,502	22,648
2008	563,927	598,278	543,451	506,423	458,047	489,069	446,006	388,939	364,679	348,438	312,905	304,252	31,726
2009	297,316	313,704	292,160	358,857	415,599	454,846	410,718	401,752	428,320	461,463	438,531	464,281	36,373
2010	446,212	465,666	434,272	477,138	459,342	462,796	470,087	514,703	553,196	633,086	624,213	643,091	35,759
2011	643,422	673,796	618,157	624,350	559,493	582,529	529,949	524,547	590,297	567,081	521,277	525,510	36,934

Contract size = 5,000 bu.   *Source: CME Group; Chicago Board of Trade (CBT)*

Average Open Interest of Soybean Futures in Chicago · In Contracts

Year	Jan.	Feb.	Mar.	Apr.	May	June	July	Aug.	Sept.	Oct.	Nov.	Dec.	
2002	1,078.8	899.9	1,065.7	1,238.6	1,048.3	1,311.8	1,762.2	1,346.4	1,002.9	1,486.1	1,070.9	1,163.5	14,475
2003	1,267.3	1,222.9	997.1	1,588.9	1,368.2	1,723.4	1,385.7	1,193.5	1,308.5	2,416.3	1,535.4	1,538.5	17,546
2004	1,509.7	1,879.6	1,957.2	2,036.2	1,593.2	1,601.7	1,551.3	1,107.6	1,052.8	1,635.3	1,395.3	1,526.1	18,846
2005	1,398.6	2,085.8	1,959.9	1,656.5	1,454.6	2,577.3	1,675.4	1,487.2	1,069.1	1,765.0	1,241.5	1,845.1	20,216
2006	1,503.4	1,889.1	1,501.2	1,916.6	1,682.6	2,443.2	1,798.2	1,638.5	1,420.2	2,884.7	2,017.4	1,952.6	22,648
2007	1,976.3	2,620.6	2,251.0	2,641.2	2,107.2	3,461.3	2,734.6	2,323.7	2,315.2	3,680.4	2,521.3	3,093.5	31,726
2008	3,528.7	3,746.2	2,895.0	3,786.1	2,272.2	3,731.2	3,134.9	2,454.4	2,615.1	3,719.0	1,910.5	2,579.7	36,373
2009	2,773.7	2,892.5	2,576.2	3,638.9	2,635.5	3,439.7	2,845.7	2,417.6	2,348.2	3,996.4	2,820.8	3,373.7	35,759
2010	2,659.0	3,392.5	2,932.8	3,414.4	2,078.2	2,946.5	2,546.1	2,266.1	2,553.0	4,660.2	3,455.9	4,029.3	36,934
2011	3,572.5	4,577.6	3,906.0	4,143.1	2,790.6	3,822.9	2,708.7	3,332.7	4,053.1	5,309.5	3,004.7	3,922.4	45,144

Contract size = 5,000 bu.   *Source: CME Group; Chicago Board of Trade (CBT)*

SOYBEANS

Soybeans (monthly average) through December 2011 — Cents per bushel

Average Cash Price of No. 1 Yellow Soybeans at Illinois Processor   In Cents Per Bushel

Year	Jan.	Feb.	Mar.	Apr.	May	June	July	Aug.	Sept.	Oct.	Nov.	Dec.	Average
2001-02	469	430	441	438	437	440	464	471	492	519	575	567	479
2002-03	579	541	575	566	570	590	580	611	640	635	601	589	590
2003-04	639	729	763	772	823	872	975	992	958	890	809	641	822
2004-05	562	519	534	545	539	544	628	622	644	701	703	639	598
2005-06	565	553	574	592	576	575	569	562	581	576	577	542	570
2006-07	535	580	661	657	683	735	730	718	749	792	801	804	704
2007-08	907	944	1,032	1,123	1,216	1,335	1,312	1,292	1,324	1,499	1,516	1,288	1,232
2008-09	1,140	903	893	868	991	938	917	1,025	1,166	1,237	1,096	1,136	1,026
2009-10	1,012	978	1,009	1,033	984	944	949	975	955	955	1,030	1,066	991
2010-11[1]	1,065	1,148	1,252	1,311	1,378	1,386	1,350	1,364	1,368	1,382	1,384	1,381	1,314

[1] Preliminary.   *Source: Economic Research Service, U.S. Department of Agriculture (ERS-USDA)*

Average Price Received by Farmers for Soybeans in the United States   In Dollars Per Bushel

Year	Jan.	Feb.	Mar.	Apr.	May	June	July	Aug.	Sept.	Oct.	Nov.	Dec.	Average
2002-03	5.39	5.20	5.46	5.46	5.51	5.55	5.59	5.82	6.07	6.09	5.82	5.68	5.64
2003-04	6.06	6.60	7.05	7.17	7.35	8.28	9.28	9.62	9.56	9.08	8.46	6.83	7.95
2004-05	5.83	5.56	5.36	5.45	5.57	5.42	5.95	6.03	6.21	6.58	6.65	6.15	5.90
2005-06	5.77	5.67	5.62	5.78	5.87	5.67	5.57	5.52	5.68	5.62	5.61	5.23	5.63
2006-07	5.23	5.52	6.08	6.18	6.37	6.87	6.95	6.88	7.12	7.51	7.56	7.72	6.67
2007-08	8.15	8.36	9.42	10.00	9.95	11.70	11.40	12.00	12.10	13.10	13.30	12.80	11.02
2008-09	10.80	9.95	9.39	9.24	9.97	9.54	9.12	9.79	10.70	11.40	10.80	10.80	10.13
2009-10	9.75	9.43	9.53	9.80	9.79	9.41	9.39	9.47	9.41	9.45	9.79	10.10	9.61
2010-11	9.98	10.20	11.10	11.60	11.60	12.70	12.70	13.10	13.20	13.20	13.20	13.40	12.17
2011-12[1]	12.20	11.70	11.70	11.50	11.90	12.30							11.88

[1] Preliminary.   *Source: Economic Research Service, U.S. Department of Agriculture (ERS-USDA)*

Stock Index Futures - U.S.

A stock index simply represents a basket of underlying stocks. Indices can be either price-weighted or capitalization-weighted. In a price-weighted index, such as the Dow Jones Industrials Average, the individual stock prices are simply added up and then divided by a divisor, meaning that stocks with higher prices have a higher weighting in the index value. In a capitalization-weighted index, such as the Standard and Poor's 500 index, the weighting of each stock corresponds to the size of the company as determined by its capitalization (i.e., the total dollar value of its stock). Stock indices cover a variety of different sectors. For example, the Dow Jones Industrials Average contains 30 blue-chip stocks that represent the industrial sector. The S&P 500 index includes 500 of the largest blue-chip U.S. companies. The NYSE index includes all the stocks that are traded at the New York Stock Exchange. The Nasdaq 100 includes the largest 100 companies that are traded on the Nasdaq Exchange. The most popular U.S. stock index futures contract is the S&P 500 at the Chicago Mercantile Exchange (CME).

Prices – The S&P 500 index showed weakness early in early 2011 on a confluence of negative events that included high gasoline prices, the European debt crisis, the massive Japanese earthquake in March, and the U.S. debt ceiling debacle that resulted in a downgrade of America's AAA rating from Standard & Poors.

However, the S&P 500 bottomed out in October 2011 and then rallied through the remainder of the year and into early 2012. The S&P 500 ended 2011 virtually unchanged. By early 2012, the S&P 500 was trading just below the 3-3/4 year high posted in May 2011 and was back down at the levels seen in June 2008 before the worst of the 2008/09 financial crisis came with the bankruptcy of Lehman Brothers in September 2008. The stock market was able to rally in late 2011 and early 2012 on a substantial improvement in the U.S. economy along with optimism that progress was being made on containing the European debt crisis.

The stock market in 2011 was also helped by Federal Reserve policy. The Fed's second quantitative easing program totaling $600 billion ended in June 2011. However, the Fed remained dissatisfied with the high unemployment and the slow pace of the economic recovery. The Fed in September 2011 therefore began its $400 billion "Operation Twist" program, which involved selling short-term securities in its portfolio and buying longer-term securities with the goal of keeping long-term Treasury yields low. The Fed was very successful in keeping Treasury yields near record lows through 2011 and early 2012, which was a highly bullish factor for the stock market.

The stock market in late 2011 was also able to recover because of the continued impressive pace of U.S. corporate earnings growth. U.S. corporations were very successful in the aftermath of the 2008/09 financial crisis in cutting their expenses and managing to find ways to force a recovery in earnings growth. In fact, earnings growth for the S&P 500 companies was strong at about +10% in 2011, adding to the increase of +30% seen in 2010. The consensus is for earnings growth in 2012 to remain firm at about +8%.

The strength in earnings in turn allowed stock market valuations to remain at very reasonable levels even as stock prices rallied. As of early 2012, the S&P 500 was trading at a very reasonable price-to-earnings ratio based on forward-looking earnings of 13.1, which was below the 5-year average of 14.9 and the 10-year average of 16.7. The reasonable valuation level leaves room on the upside for further gains in stock prices as earnings and the economy gain traction.

Average Value of Dow Jones Industrials Index (30 Stocks)

Year	Jan.	Feb.	Mar.	Apr.	May	June	July	Aug.	Sept.	Oct.	Nov.	Dec.	Average
2002	9,923.8	9,891.1	10,501.0	10,165.2	10,080.5	9,492.4	8,616.5	8,685.5	8,160.2	8,048.1	8,625.7	8,526.7	9,226.4
2003	8,474.4	7,916.2	7,977.7	8,332.1	8,623.4	9,098.1	9,154.5	9,284.8	9,492.5	9,683.6	9,762.2	10,124.7	8,993.7
2004	10,540.1	10,601.5	10,323.7	10,419.9	10,083.8	10,364.9	10,152.1	10,032.8	10,204.6	10,001.6	10,411.8	10,673.4	10,317.5
2005	10,539.5	10,723.8	10,682.1	10,283.2	10,377.2	10,486.6	10,545.4	10,554.3	10,532.5	10,324.3	10,695.3	10,827.8	10,547.7
2006	10,872.5	10,971.2	11,144.5	11,234.7	11,333.9	10,998.0	11,032.5	11,257.4	11,533.6	11,963.1	12,185.2	12,377.6	11,408.7
2007	12,512.9	12,631.5	12,268.5	12,754.8	13,407.8	13,480.2	13,677.9	13,239.7	13,557.7	13,901.3	13,200.5	13,406.9	13,170.0
2008	12,537.4	12,419.6	12,193.9	12,656.6	12,812.5	12,056.7	11,322.4	11,530.8	11,114.1	9,176.7	8,614.6	8,595.6	11,252.6
2009	8,396.2	7,690.5	7,235.5	7,992.1	8,398.4	8,593.0	8,679.8	9,375.1	9,635.0	9,857.3	10,227.6	10,433.4	8,876.1
2010	10,471.2	1,021.5	10,677.5	11,052.2	10,500.2	10,159.3	10,222.6	10,350.4	10,598.1	11,044.5	11,198.6	11,465.3	9,896.7
2011	11,802.4	12,190.0	12,081.5	12,434.9	12,580.0	12,097.3	12,512.3	11,326.6	11,175.5	11,515.9	11,804.2	12,075.7	11,966.4

Source: New York Stock Exchange (NYSE)

Average Value of Dow Jones Transportation Index (20 Stocks)

Year	Jan.	Feb.	Mar.	Apr.	May	June	July	Aug.	Sept.	Oct.	Nov.	Dec.	Average
2002	2,735.3	2,719.1	2,942.9	2,776.0	2,734.8	2,702.2	2,432.1	2,318.5	2,216.0	2,216.6	2,321.6	2,331.7	2,537.2
2003	2,297.3	2,102.5	2,094.6	2,278.7	2,429.9	2,459.6	2,554.5	2,617.3	2,744.7	2,841.3	2,920.0	2,969.3	2,525.8
2004	3,021.0	2,889.4	2,838.3	2,941.1	2,877.1	3,069.0	3,099.8	3,065.8	3,205.1	3,372.6	3,589.4	3,750.0	3,143.2
2005	3,587.0	3,614.5	3,779.4	3,527.8	3,548.8	3,542.1	3,663.1	3,726.1	3,637.0	3,673.1	4,051.7	4,152.1	3,708.6
2006	4,224.5	4,362.5	4,519.5	4,679.6	4,761.4	4,663.1	4,636.1	4,291.1	4,363.3	4,654.7	4,761.6	4,660.0	4,548.1
2007	4,752.2	5,024.6	4,817.3	5,059.2	5,174.8	5,137.2	5,258.8	4,889.0	4,812.7	4,891.2	4,605.9	4,686.4	4,925.8
2008	4,348.7	4,720.0	4,641.9	4,996.9	5,304.5	5,166.7	4,899.2	5,057.0	4,889.3	3,815.4	3,518.5	3,369.2	4,560.6
2009	3,238.3	2,857.3	2,499.9	2,986.8	3,163.7	3,266.6	3,321.5	3,697.2	3,863.1	3,844.4	3,915.2	4,117.2	3,397.6
2010	4,119.6	3,971.7	4,308.5	4,597.7	4,427.6	4,259.5	4,217.9	4,280.6	4,439.9	4,670.6	4,846.8	5,067.4	4,434.0
2011	5,135.4	5,130.2	5,110.7	5,319.1	5,431.5	5,212.9	5,395.0	4,569.8	4,420.8	4,628.8	4,820.8	4,943.3	5,009.8

Source: New York Stock Exchange (NYSE)

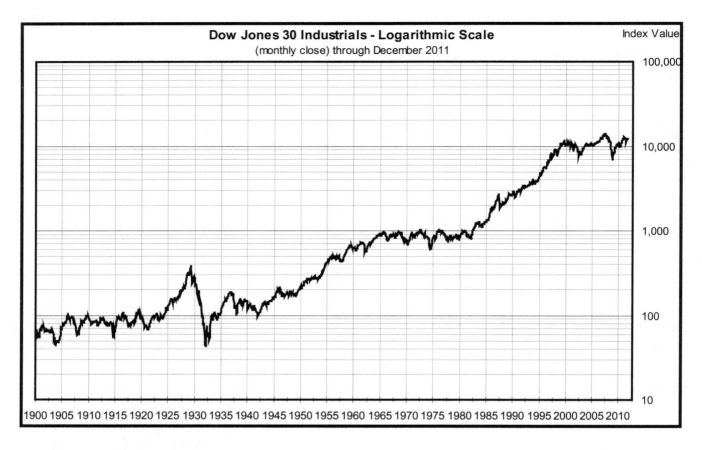

Dow Jones 30 Industrials - Logarithmic Scale
(monthly close) through December 2011

Average Value of Dow Jones Utilities Index (15 Stocks)

Year	Jan.	Feb.	Mar.	Apr.	May	June	July	Aug.	Sept.	Oct.	Nov.	Dec.	Average
2002	290.7	279.6	298.4	305.1	297.3	276.1	235.5	241.0	221.7	189.2	200.4	208.5	253.6
2003	217.7	199.5	203.3	215.9	232.3	250.4	240.3	236.8	246.5	253.1	249.2	258.4	233.6
2004	268.8	272.2	278.2	275.6	268.4	275.4	278.8	285.3	293.3	303.3	324.9	327.8	287.7
2005	331.9	351.5	356.3	364.5	364.4	376.3	392.5	397.4	422.7	401.3	395.3	409.0	380.2
2006	416.7	408.2	401.7	392.1	401.0	409.2	424.1	436.9	430.1	439.8	449.1	458.5	422.3
2007	449.9	474.1	486.1	516.9	526.2	498.2	502.3	489.0	499.5	514.0	523.5	540.9	501.7
2008	518.8	499.0	480.3	506.2	516.7	519.1	500.8	472.4	446.3	370.1	368.1	362.7	463.4
2009	371.3	356.3	315.8	331.6	339.3	350.6	361.4	373.3	376.0	375.6	373.4	398.9	360.3
2010	393.8	371.9	378.1	384.3	372.7	366.9	379.8	389.8	396.6	404.8	400.5	400.8	386.7
2011	410.1	411.9	409.9	416.5	434.8	427.0	435.3	419.9	431.7	439.9	443.0	451.5	427.6

Source: New York Stock Exchange (NYSE)

Average Value of Standard & Poor's 500 Index

Year	Jan.	Feb.	Mar.	Apr.	May	June	July	Aug.	Sept.	Oct.	Nov.	Dec.	Average
2002	1,140.2	1,100.7	1,153.8	1,112.0	1,079.3	1,014.1	903.6	912.6	867.8	854.6	909.9	899.2	995.6
2003	895.8	837.6	846.6	890.0	936.0	988.0	992.5	989.5	1,019.4	1,038.7	1,049.9	1,080.6	963.7
2004	1,132.5	1,143.4	1,124.0	1,133.1	1,102.8	1,132.8	1,105.9	1,088.9	1,117.7	1,118.1	1,168.9	1,199.2	1,130.6
2005	1,181.4	1,199.6	1,194.9	1,164.4	1,178.3	1,202.3	1,222.2	1,224.3	1,225.9	1,192.0	1,237.3	1,262.1	1,207.1
2006	1,278.7	1,276.7	1,293.7	1,302.2	1,290.0	1,253.1	1,260.2	1,287.2	1,317.8	1,363.3	1,388.6	1,416.4	1,310.7
2007	1,424.2	1,444.8	1,407.0	1,463.7	1,511.1	1,514.5	1,520.7	1,454.6	1,497.1	1,539.7	1,463.4	1,479.2	1,476.7
2008	1,378.8	1,354.9	1,316.9	1,370.5	1,403.2	1,341.3	1,257.3	1,281.5	1,217.0	968.8	883.0	877.4	1,220.9
2009	865.6	805.2	757.1	848.2	902.4	926.1	935.8	1,009.7	1,044.6	1,067.7	1,088.1	1,110.4	946.7
2010	1,123.6	1,089.2	1,152.1	1,197.3	1,125.1	1,083.4	1,079.8	1,087.3	1,122.1	1,171.6	1,198.9	1,241.5	1,139.3
2011	1,282.6	1,321.1	1,304.5	1,331.5	1,338.3	1,287.3	1,325.2	1,185.3	1,173.9	1,207.2	1,226.4	1,243.3	1,268.9

Source: Index and Option Market (IOM), division of the Chicago Mercantile Exchange (CME)

Composite Index of Leading Indicators   (1992 = 100)

Year	Jan.	Feb.	Mar.	Apr.	May	June	July	Aug.	Sept.	Oct.	Nov.	Dec.	Average
2002	87.1	87.7	88.0	88.1	89.0	89.0	89.1	89.3	89.3	89.4	90.2	90.5	88.9
2003	90.6	90.5	90.6	91.1	92.5	93.1	93.8	94.3	95.0	95.8	96.4	96.9	93.4
2004	97.5	97.8	99.1	99.3	100.0	100.2	100.6	100.6	100.8	100.7	101.4	102.0	100.0
2005	101.8	102.2	101.7	101.8	102.1	103.1	102.9	103.1	102.4	103.3	104.2	104.2	102.7
2006	104.7	104.4	104.6	104.4	103.7	103.9	103.7	103.3	103.7	103.9	103.8	104.4	104.0
2007	104.0	103.7	104.1	103.9	104.0	103.9	104.6	103.6	103.7	103.2	102.6	102.6	103.7
2008	102.1	101.9	101.9	102.0	101.9	101.9	101.2	100.3	100.3	99.4	99.0	98.8	100.9
2009	98.8	98.3	98.1	99.2	100.6	101.3	102.5	103.1	104.2	104.7	105.8	106.2	101.9
2010	106.7	107.2	108.6	108.6	109.0	108.8	109.0	109.1	109.9	110.1	111.4	112.3	109.2
2011[1]	91.8	92.7	93.7	93.7	94.2	94.2	94.4	93.7	93.1	93.7	93.9	94.3	93.6

[1] Preliminary.   *Source: The Conference Board*

Consumer Confidence, The Conference Board   (2004 = 100)

Year	Jan.	Feb.	Mar.	Apr.	May	June	July	Aug.	Sept.	Oct.	Nov.	Dec.	Average
2002	97.8	95.0	110.7	108.5	110.3	106.3	97.4	94.5	93.7	79.6	84.9	80.7	96.6
2003	78.8	64.8	61.4	81.0	83.6	83.5	77.0	81.7	77.0	81.7	92.5	94.8	79.8
2004	97.7	88.5	88.5	93.0	93.1	102.8	105.7	98.7	96.7	92.9	92.6	102.7	96.1
2005	105.1	104.4	103.0	97.5	103.1	106.2	103.6	105.5	87.5	85.2	98.3	103.8	100.3
2006	106.8	102.7	107.5	109.8	104.7	105.4	107.0	100.2	105.9	105.1	105.3	110.0	105.9
2007	110.2	111.2	108.2	106.3	108.5	105.3	111.9	105.6	99.5	95.2	87.8	90.6	103.4
2008	87.3	76.4	65.9	62.8	58.1	51.0	51.9	58.5	61.4	38.8	44.7	38.6	58.0
2009	37.4	25.3	26.9	40.8	54.8	49.3	47.4	54.5	53.4	48.7	50.6	53.6	45.2
2010	56.5	46.4	52.3	57.7	62.7	54.3	51.0	53.2	48.6	49.9	57.8	63.4	54.5
2011[1]	64.8	72.0	63.8	66.0	61.7	57.6	59.2	45.2	46.4	40.9	55.2	64.5	58.1

[1] Preliminary.   *Source: The Conference Board (TCB) Copyrighted.*

Capacity Utilization Rates (Total Industry)   In Percent

Year	Jan.	Feb.	Mar.	Apr.	May	June	July	Aug.	Sept.	Oct.	Nov.	Dec.	Average
2002	73.8	73.7	74.2	74.4	74.8	75.4	75.2	75.3	75.4	75.1	75.5	75.1	74.8
2003	75.7	76.0	75.9	75.4	75.4	75.5	75.7	75.7	76.2	76.2	76.8	76.8	75.9
2004	77.0	77.4	77.0	77.3	77.9	77.2	77.8	78.0	77.9	78.7	78.8	79.4	77.9
2005	79.8	80.3	80.1	80.1	80.2	80.4	80.2	80.2	78.5	79.4	80.0	80.4	80.0
2006	80.4	80.3	80.4	80.6	80.3	80.5	80.5	80.5	80.3	80.1	79.9	80.5	80.4
2007	80.2	80.9	80.8	81.2	81.1	81.0	81.0	81.0	81.3	80.8	81.1	81.3	81.0
2008	81.1	81.0	80.6	80.0	79.5	79.3	79.0	77.6	74.3	74.9	73.9	71.9	77.8
2009	70.4	70.0	68.8	68.2	67.5	67.3	68.2	68.9	69.5	69.9	70.2	70.8	69.1
2010	71.9	72.2	72.8	73.2	74.3	74.5	75.3	75.5	75.7	75.7	75.8	76.8	74.5
2011[1]	76.9	76.5	77.0	76.6	76.7	76.7	77.5	77.6	77.7	78.1	77.8	78.1	77.3

[1] Preliminary.   *Source: Bureau of Economic Analysis, U.S. Department of Commerce (BEA)*

Manufacturers New Orders, Durable Goods   In Billions of Constant Dollars

Year	Jan.	Feb.	Mar.	Apr.	May	June	July	Aug.	Sept.	Oct.	Nov.	Dec.	Average
2002	161.90	171.00	167.88	171.36	172.11	165.25	174.66	177.23	167.40	168.12	169.58	163.44	169.16
2003	168.22	173.13	173.81	169.08	171.03	172.81	173.80	173.44	177.60	183.07	181.63	181.07	174.89
2004	175.91	179.56	191.69	183.62	183.67	183.99	187.38	184.80	187.59	184.98	193.13	193.21	185.79
2005	192.38	194.42	187.78	194.90	205.89	209.49	196.08	203.65	203.08	209.65	220.63	220.26	203.18
2006	205.94	215.50	226.01	213.98	214.52	221.40	211.77	209.99	234.09	214.99	224.95	231.08	218.68
2007	215.84	220.66	228.74	234.19	227.71	230.28	237.90	230.94	226.32	228.40	231.02	245.13	229.76
2008	232.62	232.27	229.26	228.97	227.81	228.44	225.43	213.56	211.83	191.97	183.97	175.97	215.17
2009	152.70	153.13	148.71	148.67	154.54	149.79	162.90	157.96	161.32	163.56	160.57	163.78	156.47
2010	174.36	174.89	172.74	180.32	179.45	178.36	184.50	179.64	190.96	183.95	184.70	183.36	180.60
2011[1]	190.71	188.69	197.33	192.35	196.21	193.95	202.08	202.22	199.46	199.63	208.01	214.31	198.75

[1] Preliminary.   *Source: Bureau of Economic Analysis, U.S. Department of Commerce (BEA)*

Corporate Profits After Tax -- Quarterly   In Billions of Dollars

Year	First Quarter	Second Quarter	Third Quarter	Fourth Quarter	Total	Year	First Quarter	Second Quarter	Third Quarter	Fourth Quarter	Total
2000	566.2	558.6	560.0	531.8	554.2	2006	1,130.2	1,122.6	1,158.5	1,128.8	1,135.0
2001	558.3	595.6	569.9	599.6	580.9	2007	1,041.4	1,097.4	1,070.0	1,052.0	1,065.2
2002	651.1	666.0	676.0	726.3	679.9	2008	1,004.8	989.7	1,016.1	746.9	939.4
2003	685.9	723.1	745.5	781.6	734.0	2009	966.4	1,017.5	1,137.3	1,237.2	1,089.6
2004	909.6	928.7	971.8	953.3	940.9	2010	1,314.5	1,386.3	1,402.8	1,452.7	1,389.1
2005	1,003.1	1,033.3	1,051.6	1,086.8	1,043.7	2011[1]	1,454.1	1,517.1	1,558.7		1,510.0

[1] Preliminary.   *Source: Bureau of Economic Analysis, U.S. Department of Commerce (BEA)*

STOCK INDEX FUTURES - U.S.

Change in Manufacturing and Trade Inventories   In Billions of Dollars

Year	Jan.	Feb.	Mar.	Apr.	May	June	July	Aug.	Sept.	Oct.	Nov.	Dec.	Average
2002	-0.9	-31.5	-47.8	-20.1	33.6	27.8	78.5	3.5	-106.8	18.5	33.0	-86.0	17.6
2003	-118.4	-60.3	-18.3	0.1	111.8	89.5	24.1	-39.4	78.7	54.4	57.5	45.7	17.6
2004	16.6	108.5	107.0	101.2	88.6	153.5	139.9	373.6	-12.2	54.3	166.0	29.5	72.8
2005	130.5	84.6	60.3	40.0	218.4	-5.7	-66.0	57.9	272.9	81.3	78.8	305.6	54.5
2006	85.9	-49.7	129.5	82.7	169.3	169.3	92.2	93.2	65.9	22.9	28.3	4.2	85.2
2007	37.8	43.6	-17.0	59.5	68.1	55.0	75.6	62.7	87.7	23.8	53.3	96.3	53.4
2008	169.4	78.5	35.6	81.4	66.2	133.3	202.6	34.8	-64.9	-99.6		-250.0	35.2
2009	-170.2	-188.5	-232.1	-197.4	-196.7	-218.1	-159.1	-232.5	-46.8	59.8	75.6	-14.9	-126.7
2010	27.9	104.4	95.5	95.3	54.9	136.3	173.2	139.3	179.6	190.5	63.3	173.4	119.5
2011[1]	167.1	129.1	220.2	169.5	167.8	74.0	93.7	66.1	4.0	139.4			123.1

[1] Preliminary.   *Source: Bureau of Economic Analysis, U.S. Department of Commerce (BEA)*

Productivity: Index of Output per Hour, All Persons, Nonfarm Business -- Quarterly   (1992 = 100)

Year	First Quarter	Second Quarter	Third Quarter	Fourth Quarter	Total	Year	First Quarter	Second Quarter	Third Quarter	Fourth Quarter	Total
2000	84.2	86.1	86.1	87.0	85.8	2006	100.9	101.0	100.5	101.1	100.9
2001	86.7	88.2	88.8	90.0	88.4	2007	101.1	101.9	103.1	103.6	102.4
2002	91.9	92.1	92.9	92.9	92.4	2008	103.0	103.6	103.4	102.5	103.1
2003	93.7	95.0	97.2	97.5	95.8	2009	102.8	104.8	106.5	107.9	105.5
2004	97.7	98.5	98.6	98.8	98.4	2010	109.2	109.5	110.1	110.7	109.8
2005	99.8	99.6	100.3	100.3	100.0	2011[1]	110.5	110.5	111.0	111.2	110.8

[1] Preliminary.   *Source: Bureau of Economic Analysis, U.S. Department of Commerce (BEA)*

Civilian Unemployment Rate

Year	Jan.	Feb.	Mar.	Apr.	May	June	July	Aug.	Sept.	Oct.	Nov.	Dec.	Average
2002	5.6	5.5	5.7	6.0	5.8	5.9	5.9	5.7	5.6	5.7	6.0	6.0	5.8
2003	5.7	5.8	5.8	6.0	6.1	6.4	6.2	6.1	6.1	6.0	5.9	5.7	6.0
2004	5.6	5.6	5.7	5.6	5.6	5.6	5.5	5.4	5.4	5.5	5.4	5.4	5.5
2005	5.2	5.4	5.1	5.1	5.1	5.0	5.0	4.9	5.1	4.9	5.0	4.9	5.1
2006	4.7	4.8	4.7	4.7	4.6	4.6	4.8	4.7	4.6	4.4	4.5	4.5	4.6
2007	4.6	4.5	4.4	4.5	4.5	4.6	4.7	4.7	4.7	4.8	4.7	5.0	4.6
2008	5.0	4.8	5.1	5.0	5.4	5.5	5.8	6.1	6.2	6.6	6.9	7.4	5.8
2009	7.7	8.2	8.6	8.9	9.4	9.5	9.4	9.7	9.8	10.1	10.0	10.0	9.3
2010	9.7	9.8	9.8	9.9	9.6	9.4	9.5	9.6	9.5	9.5	9.8	9.4	9.6
2011[1]	9.1	9.0	8.9	9.0	9.0	9.1	9.1	9.1	9.0	8.9	8.7	8.5	9.0

[1] Preliminary.   *Source: Bureau of Economic Analysis, U.S. Department of Commerce (BEA)*

S&P 500 Index - Logarithmic Scale
(monthly close) through December 2011

Dow Jones 30 Industrials Index (weekly close) as of December 30, 2011

S&P 500 Index (weekly close) as of December 30, 2011

NASDAQ 100 Index (weekly close) as of December 30, 2011

Value Line 'A' Index (weekly close) as of December 30, 2011

STOCK INDEX FUTURES - U.S.

Volume of Trading of S&P 500 Stock Index Futures in Chicago   In Thousands of Contracts

Year	Jan.	Feb.	Mar.	Apr.	May	June	July	Aug.	Sept.	Oct.	Nov.	Dec.	Total
2002	1,459.2	1,677.0	2,251.4	1,472.8	1,584.6	2,720.9	2,205.7	1,615.1	2,943.1	1,930.5	1,374.3	2,465.0	23,700
2003	1,442.8	1,343.0	2,900.2	1,256.8	1,415.6	2,782.4	1,222.9	1,079.4	2,411.7	1,118.1	921.3	2,281.5	20,175
2004	944.8	838.6	2,487.0	880.3	937.7	2,135.8	837.4	964.6	2,076.5	866.3	1,105.3	2,101.3	16,176
2005	764.5	873.6	2,330.2	916.2	891.6	2,090.1	618.4	979.1	2,090.2	902.1	880.2	2,041.4	15,377
2006	711.3	772.9	2,198.8	607.5	1,122.0	2,321.6	726.3	890.8	1,883.1	686.3	935.6	1,988.6	14,845
2007	696.3	765.0	2,341.9	614.6	937.9	2,237.8	803.4	1,546.1	1,941.4	854.5	1,130.8	1,967.9	15,838
2008	1,187.3	907.8	2,374.7	761.0	768.2	1,978.9	921.9	729.7	2,491.2	1,588.1	942.0	2,112.2	16,763
2009	674.4	744.3	2,026.3	555.3	534.7	1,637.5	453.5	427.3	1,338.3	473.3	384.6	1,186.4	10,436
2010	403.6	432.0	1,084.5	363.5	650.7	1,195.3	412.7	433.1	1,027.9	296.8	415.8	974.1	7,690
2011	321.2	330.8	1,162.0	306.6	309.8	1,027.3	283.4	713.6	1,124.3	389.1	394.8	857.8	7,221

Contract value = $250.   *Source: Index and Option Market (IOM), division of the Chicago Mercantile Exchange (CME)*

Average Open Interest of S&P 500 Stock Index Futures in Chicago   In Contracts

Year	Jan.	Feb.	Mar.	Apr.	May	June	July	Aug.	Sept.	Oct.	Nov.	Dec.
2002	495,352	519,023	542,358	513,048	542,839	592,888	594,727	621,558	644,806	607,848	631,224	647,022
2003	596,064	619,738	658,749	622,917	643,030	691,003	611,564	611,578	631,509	582,111	589,392	633,997
2004	612,911	614,843	624,209	595,593	587,717	604,154	586,760	597,581	632,050	636,566	686,531	714,420
2005	678,739	686,413	719,141	681,149	697,818	700,618	656,266	653,430	669,849	642,704	657,097	681,868
2006	655,483	668,113	682,218	653,044	664,790	670,449	625,142	634,579	634,817	609,410	640,481	679,221
2007	634,075	639,584	654,891	634,576	662,438	652,951	602,222	643,716	663,165	595,908	623,469	623,631
2008	566,839	602,738	607,396	560,088	559,320	558,810	551,609	565,810	578,027	627,531	633,531	603,664
2009	518,589	583,132	566,284	439,705	467,060	456,209	391,596	393,499	400,489	386,593	398,242	379,761
2010	334,063	379,277	384,532	320,130	323,367	354,304	308,220	320,409	327,551	314,245	352,215	341,358
2011	295,221	328,406	351,308	312,007	326,135	314,542	277,586	351,944	367,322	292,018	295,609	285,435

Contract value = $250.   *Source: Index and Option Market (IOM), division of the Chicago Mercantile Exchange (CME)*

Volume of Trading of E-mini S&P 500 Index Futures in Chicago   In Thousands of Contracts

Year	Jan.	Feb.	Mar.	Apr.	May	June	July	Aug.	Sept.	Oct.	Nov.	Dec.	Total
2002	4,933	5,337	5,609	7,165	7,564	9,772	14,277	11,200	11,765	17,175	11,054	9,892	115,742
2003	13,584	12,631	15,820	13,520	12,846	15,040	14,854	10,860	15,354	14,558	11,002	11,108	161,177
2004	13,087	11,355	18,033	14,993	15,889	12,428	14,361	12,921	12,755	14,636	13,705	13,039	167,203
2005	15,447	12,561	18,478	20,182	16,591	17,371	14,400	17,759	18,786	22,929	16,088	16,503	207,096
2006	18,716	16,095	21,357	18,174	24,750	30,359	21,629	19,107	21,986	22,377	23,616	19,760	257,927
2007	21,632	22,507	37,944	20,399	26,266	39,351	35,295	55,547	37,578	38,649	46,727	33,454	415,348
2008	55,257	40,368	56,108	38,472	36,217	49,724	53,375	36,400	76,696	84,259	56,426	50,587	633,889
2009	45,814	49,498	69,321	49,293	46,060	48,779	42,273	38,448	46,864	46,352	36,951	36,662	556,314
2010	40,765	42,986	46,644	43,563	64,388	61,258	44,454	42,196	46,366	41,921	45,468	35,320	555,329
2011	38,684	36,326	60,446	32,705	43,114	59,186	43,083	82,693	71,646	55,044	51,593	45,850	620,369

Contract value = $50.   *Source: Index and Option Market (IOM), division of the Chicago Mercantile Exchange (CME)*

Average Open Interest of E-mini S&P 500 Index Futures in Chicago   In Thousands of Contracts

Year	Jan.	Feb.	Mar.	Apr.	May	June	July	Aug.	Sept.	Oct.	Nov.	Dec.
2002	86.3	120.1	140.0	156.4	225.6	246.3	291.7	349.0	319.3	312.9	419.0	385.2
2003	265.2	356.6	490.0	567.6	741.8	718.5	399.5	492.5	513.4	460.9	467.7	525.3
2004	510.5	576.4	643.1	545.4	579.9	645.8	603.8	698.0	693.5	708.4	979.9	969.3
2005	827.3	901.7	1,013.6	943.3	1,014.9	986.8	932.6	1,060.8	1,110.1	1,042.2	1,166.4	1,211.3
2006	1,149.2	1,194.6	1,334.1	1,211.3	1,402.5	1,525.3	1,371.2	1,512.3	1,582.4	1,549.5	1,754.4	1,810.9
2007	1,625.6	1,825.1	2,037.4	1,943.7	2,088.7	2,060.5	1,735.6	2,105.4	2,151.5	1,972.4	2,095.4	2,172.5
2008	2,208.2	2,418.8	2,442.6	2,076.5	2,180.8	2,311.5	2,405.0	2,467.2	2,566.1	2,987.6	3,114.1	2,942.0
2009	2,512.9	2,896.4	3,123.3	2,489.2	2,680.4	2,690.2	2,429.6	2,622.9	2,582.3	2,397.1	2,593.6	2,688.5
2010	2,510.1	2,808.4	2,866.0	2,468.7	2,680.5	2,937.2	2,797.2	2,839.5	2,872.0	2,668.2	2,810.5	2,826.7
2011	2,581.7	2,829.5	2,960.3	2,704.1	2,762.3	2,887.0	2,578.6	3,318.6	3,424.6	3,008.7	2,955.1	2,903.6

Contract value = $50.   *Source: Index and Option Market (IOM), division of the Chicago Mercantile Exchange (CME)*

Volume of Trading of NASDAQ 100 Index Futures in Chicago   In Contracts

Year	Jan.	Feb.	Mar.	Apr.	May	June	July	Aug.	Sept.	Oct.	Nov.	Dec.	Total
2002	380,076	367,561	436,495	378,294	443,579	529,496	454,630	334,242	466,898	367,750	315,925	428,341	4,903,287
2003	360,307	301,454	487,916	301,395	330,640	519,597	350,514	251,058	488,363	322,898	259,960	447,119	4,421,221
2004	271,404	268,590	591,556	321,242	297,320	427,805	286,693	245,050	433,251	286,048	226,853	356,171	4,011,983
2005	254,437	198,956	375,435	217,304	170,882	281,483	125,500	159,789	289,113	200,952	155,141	253,066	2,682,058
2006	186,649	162,841	295,163	113,885	169,399	305,557	132,661	149,906	256,605	136,433	140,407	220,364	2,269,870
2007	122,055	111,962	255,491	73,881	97,857	226,877	94,964	124,717	178,645	112,930	121,891	162,108	1,683,378
2008	137,810	90,886	188,815	72,775	80,472	192,723	103,965	83,158	171,532	125,975	58,023	101,279	1,407,413
2009	61,110	61,943	119,432	47,289	53,465	76,479	46,606	55,012	84,170	45,122	48,519	57,772	756,919
2010	50,060	37,696	55,326	34,026	44,200	47,702	28,137	32,035	46,609	24,746	57,965	49,322	507,824
2011	36,142	21,771	58,401	35,746	27,603	43,952	38,356	50,565	57,793	39,421	31,149	31,693	472,592

Contract value = $100.   *Source: Index and Option Market (IOM), division of the Chicago Mercantile Exchange (CME)*

Average Open Interest of NASDAQ 100 Index Futures in Chicago   In Contracts

Year	Jan.	Feb.	Mar.	Apr.	May	June	July	Aug.	Sept.	Oct.	Nov.	Dec.
2002	49,992	52,883	52,617	51,157	65,219	73,151	60,625	67,760	84,317	72,229	77,451	76,660
2003	71,219	79,905	87,252	71,636	77,717	88,914	80,002	83,940	91,685	75,191	85,651	86,480
2004	73,805	74,892	89,874	81,220	80,905	83,282	69,818	71,711	84,355	74,161	83,675	87,172
2005	72,299	81,327	78,387	56,668	57,116	56,836	49,357	53,270	61,369	60,918	59,754	63,712
2006	61,254	62,994	69,322	60,603	65,224	65,908	54,289	57,585	54,235	53,832	68,347	61,397
2007	47,832	51,655	55,782	50,905	59,586	63,132	63,492	67,870	64,324	50,761	53,292	50,372
2008	42,272	52,260	51,385	31,738	37,017	34,864	28,456	30,588	27,761	27,770	31,473	29,459
2009	23,558	29,607	29,090	21,525	24,228	21,913	17,299	21,266	22,113	19,389	21,267	18,502
2010	15,446	28,890	20,717	17,115	23,509	19,880	12,821	18,414	18,068	22,008	29,505	19,916
2011	14,571	18,006	17,336	17,887	21,448	14,400	16,130	21,731	20,622	20,112	30,793	19,188

Contract value = $100.   *Source: Index and Option Market (IOM), division of the Chicago Mercantile Exchange (CME)*

Volume of Trading of E-mini NASDAQ 100 Index Futures in Chicago   In Thousands of Contracts

Year	Jan.	Feb.	Mar.	Apr.	May	June	July	Aug.	Sept.	Oct.	Nov.	Dec.	Total
2002	3,719	3,649	3,652	4,227	4,625	4,713	5,789	4,225	4,337	6,252	4,812	4,490	54,491
2003	5,200	4,620	5,749	5,132	5,075	6,323	6,369	4,816	7,095	6,601	5,254	5,655	67,889
2004	6,157	5,640	8,011	6,387	6,749	5,646	7,139	6,123	6,476	7,322	5,844	5,675	77,169
2005	7,174	6,149	7,336	7,256	5,735	6,233	4,895	5,171	5,624	6,583	5,288	5,008	72,453
2006	6,628	5,803	7,479	5,459	7,386	8,258	6,741	6,315	7,074	6,769	6,333	5,696	79,940
2007	7,122	6,685	8,700	4,976	7,069	8,426	8,122	10,558	6,856	8,916	11,147	6,733	95,309
2008	11,604	8,072	9,677	6,988	7,042	9,912	10,151	7,607	11,523	12,287	7,300	6,571	108,734
2009	5,713	6,789	8,800	6,383	6,241	6,722	6,243	5,959	6,808	7,048	5,686	5,579	77,972
2010	6,712	6,180	6,448	5,938	8,666	8,055	6,905	6,619	7,366	6,249	5,997	4,505	79,638
2011	4,986	4,764	8,138	4,913	5,944	6,778	5,276	8,884	8,035	6,814	5,808	4,826	75,166

Contract value = $20.   *Source: Index and Option Market (IOM), division of the Chicago Mercantile Exchange (CME)*

Average Open Interest of E-mini NASDAQ 100 Index Futures in Chicago   In Contracts

Year	Jan.	Feb.	Mar.	Apr.	May	June	July	Aug.	Sept.	Oct.	Nov.	Dec.
2002	78,070	94,150	98,159	100,849	153,348	176,394	130,337	171,043	162,133	110,952	154,104	155,987
2003	169,160	227,905	258,023	196,739	240,759	257,390	262,564	316,032	287,936	214,659	279,379	244,333
2004	205,078	251,011	251,486	257,573	304,034	261,067	213,080	256,749	299,794	279,170	374,750	384,492
2005	339,077	419,715	382,805	310,664	331,447	290,759	270,134	325,508	307,007	365,277	382,667	371,388
2006	351,240	361,807	345,533	396,080	381,178	427,387	386,930	421,179	437,975	457,275	498,584	433,456
2007	360,663	354,765	423,270	320,046	463,422	454,010	418,512	429,654	451,180	415,073	439,054	408,021
2008	347,374	410,404	424,513	256,064	377,029	358,774	316,037	333,976	336,525	379,643	359,028	302,534
2009	245,830	281,273	302,750	329,709	286,754	284,962	272,424	332,576	341,802	321,653	329,991	338,692
2010	338,217	402,622	362,520	351,601	353,999	353,720	316,651	349,380	397,910	441,782	442,146	401,214
2011	367,204	361,772	350,534	351,601	370,994	321,623	346,518	350,282	369,902	321,427	325,938	308,063

Contract value = $20.   *Source: Index and Option Market (IOM), division of the Chicago Mercantile Exchange (CME)*

STOCK INDEX FUTURES - U.S.

Volume of Trading of S&P 400 Midcap Stock Index Futures in Chicago   In Contracts

Year	Jan.	Feb.	Mar.	Apr.	May	June	July	Aug.	Sept.	Oct.	Nov.	Dec.	Total
2002	22,322	22,814	43,819	23,019	22,484	51,775	30,607	23,075	52,375	25,593	21,262	48,105	387,250
2003	18,827	18,392	44,454	15,841	15,194	40,603	15,153	12,082	43,112	15,253	13,109	50,797	302,817
2004	13,647	10,361	46,214	13,921	13,078	45,940	12,602	13,582	36,701	7,923	9,824	36,971	260,764
2005	6,486	5,736	36,685	5,130	7,235	39,025	4,603	7,699	42,503	5,736	4,988	39,232	205,058
2006	5,668	3,739	34,668	3,671	4,619	31,924	2,656	3,311	23,289	3,718	6,409	29,596	153,268
2007	2,854	3,205	26,948	3,716	3,937	22,210	3,906	4,271	17,518	3,610	10,570	15,395	118,140
2008	5,581	3,286	14,864	2,796	3,124	15,896	4,670	3,369	19,246	6,432	4,397	13,563	97,224
2009	2,330	4,802	11,017	4,668	1,707	10,037	1,642	1,822	8,854	3,229	2,285	6,967	59,360
2010	1,852	3,043	5,412	1,019	3,956	6,944	1,580	2,582	4,072	2,330	1,117	4,560	38,467
2011	2,827	879	4,887	2,098	824	2,839	2,792	6,161	4,604	6,310	5,453	3,050	42,724

Contract value = $500.   *Source: Index and Option Market (IOM), division of the Chicago Mercantile Exchange (CME)*

Average Open Interest of S&P 400 Midcap Stock Index Futures in Chicago   In Contracts

Year	Jan.	Feb.	Mar.	Apr.	May	June	July	Aug.	Sept.	Oct.	Nov.	Dec.
2002	13,691	14,109	14,954	14,340	16,402	16,611	15,121	16,213	17,006	14,695	15,394	16,432
2003	13,793	13,498	14,530	13,120	13,353	13,986	13,123	13,029	13,726	14,014	15,465	17,446
2004	15,911	15,988	16,554	15,870	15,819	17,148	13,939	13,600	14,213	13,339	14,046	14,755
2005	13,078	13,313	14,861	11,812	11,832	13,811	12,380	12,420	14,477	12,890	12,955	13,822
2006	12,168	11,940	12,409	10,999	10,892	10,447	9,307	9,687	9,194	8,442	9,884	9,794
2007	7,793	8,143	8,267	7,972	9,187	8,425	6,729	6,671	6,951	6,166	8,580	8,839
2008	6,501	7,622	7,512	4,254	5,358	5,700	4,578	5,756	6,847	6,601	6,766	5,761
2009	3,785	4,755	5,227	4,433	4,580	3,781	2,481	2,887	2,847	2,586	2,273	2,437
2010	1,552	2,791	2,274	1,549	2,580	3,250	2,268	2,799	2,334	2,418	3,389	2,539
2011	2,112	2,802	2,290	1,682	1,727	1,558	2,090	4,372	3,291	4,399	5,756	3,581

Contract value = $500.   *Source: Index and Option Market (IOM), division of the Chicago Mercantile Exchange (CME)*

Volume of Trading of Dow Jones Industrials Index Futures in Chicago   In Contracts

Year	Jan.	Feb.	Mar.	Apr.	May	June	July	Aug.	Sept.	Oct.	Nov.	Dec.	Total
2002	409,009	472,893	538,804	467,571	456,210	616,754	811,518	539,507	639,154	699,005	427,235	407,665	6,485,325
2003	452,579	426,198	559,372	428,972	410,967	473,432	368,277	286,508	367,845	218,394	157,726	266,032	4,416,302
2004	224,713	207,423	362,668	203,745	208,229	246,564	183,469	149,931	230,829	169,627	152,412	237,528	2,577,138
2005	149,353	107,824	226,113	157,010	124,999	192,165	96,885	121,793	188,541	133,636	108,737	180,349	1,787,405
2006	119,593	111,738	220,880	106,325	152,340	272,494	108,053	97,964	237,988	121,736	111,993	258,743	1,919,847
2007	97,032	97,537	231,466	76,661	127,981	197,380	101,710	119,985	135,432	95,101	91,014	112,518	1,483,817
2008	105,901	82,432	135,860	71,571	51,097	121,220	122,305	76,031	170,465	99,607	53,397	57,771	1,147,657
2009	32,235	36,568	54,497	35,502	32,590	50,874	27,114	17,541	47,003	18,659	13,769	29,232	395,584
2010	13,279	11,251	23,512	14,352	14,189	28,257	9,843	10,761	18,012	9,749	10,888	24,016	188,109
2011	14,006	12,520	30,645	22,807	16,017	38,755	19,825	27,233	40,956	11,931	14,659	37,343	286,697

Contract value = $10.   *Source: Chicago Board of Trade (CBT)*

Average Open Interest of Dow Jones Industrials Index Futures in Chicago   In Contracts

Year	Jan.	Feb.	Mar.	Apr.	May	June	July	Aug.	Sept.	Oct.	Nov.	Dec.
2002	23,862	35,588	37,582	28,714	32,810	34,482	32,412	32,272	34,665	31,923	34,045	31,892
2003	27,032	30,429	34,371	31,160	34,936	36,352	36,773	43,974	41,747	34,066	37,835	39,727
2004	34,656	44,306	50,172	44,494	45,304	46,641	42,790	42,042	45,940	41,250	43,662	53,469
2005	47,754	48,665	48,423	40,068	41,367	36,909	29,042	30,921	37,232	36,378	37,588	43,819
2006	39,641	39,943	43,595	43,351	45,756	53,833	56,451	58,799	60,497	61,996	63,061	69,927
2007	67,567	72,788	54,933	41,615	48,211	42,631	33,406	37,757	35,894	30,936	35,735	34,375
2008	27,564	32,212	33,736	29,240	31,425	32,987	31,175	34,663	36,423	26,685	27,638	23,708
2009	14,401	22,146	19,045	10,306	15,681	18,781	10,880	11,614	12,693	13,764	16,046	12,915
2010	12,142	13,855	10,785	7,616	11,884	10,945	7,250	8,945	7,325	5,155	7,631	7,591
2011	8,937	11,647	11,005	15,685	23,810	16,465	14,001	15,038	13,834	13,114	17,338	17,038

Contract value = $10.   *Source: Chicago Board of Trade (CBT)*

Stock Index Futures - WorldWide

World Stocks – World stock markets in 2011 closed generally lower. The MSCI World Index, a benchmark for large companies based in 23 developed countries, closed down -7.6% in 2011, giving back most of the +9.6% gain seen in 2011. The index had rallied sharply by +27.0% in 2009.

The MSCI World Index fell in 2011 mainly because of the European debt crisis, which hurt global business confidence and pushed Europe into a mild recession by late 2011. The Eurozone GDP in Q4-2011 fell by an annualized -1.2% and likely showed another decline in Q1-2012. Other bearish factors in 2011 included the generally weak U.S. economy, which was weighed down by high gasoline prices, political battles, and the continued depression in the housing market.

In addition, China's economy weakened during the year to a growth rate of only +8.9% by Q4-2011, down from pace of over 10% seen in early 2010. China's central bank from late 2010 through early 2011 was forced to raise its 1-year lending rate by a total of one percentage point to 6.56% in order to battle a surge in inflation. The weaker Chinese economy had a negative economic impact on Asia and indeed the whole world. The market consensus as of early 2012 was that Chinese officials would be able to engineer a soft landing for the Chinese economy and avoid any disasters.

Small-Capitalization Stocks – The MSCI World Small-Cap Index, which tracks companies with market caps between $200 million and $1.5 billion, fell by -10.5% in 2011, giving back some ground after the sharp rallies of +24.3% in 2010 and +41.7% in 2009. The -10.5% decline in the MSCI World Small-Cap Index in 2011 was 2.9 percentage points weaker than the -7.6% decline seen in the large-cap MSCI World Index. The underperformance by small-caps could have been expected in 2011 after the sharp outperformance by small-caps in the two previous years. The small-caps outperformed the large-caps by an impressive 14.7 points in both 2010 and 2009.

World Industry Groups – The MSCI industry sectors in 2011 produced the following ranked annual returns: Health Care +7.2%, Consumer Staples +6.0%, Energy -1.9%, Information Technology -3.4%, Telecom -4.1%, Consumer Discretionary -6.3%, Utilities -6.8%, Industrials -10.0%, Financials -20.7%, and Materials -21.2%. The defensive Health Care (+7.2%) and Consumer Staples (+6.0%) sectors were the only two sectors that showed gains for the year as investors remained cautious with the weak economy seen in 2011. The Energy sector came in third with a decline of -1.9%. The three sectors that did the best in 2010 put in a poor performances in 2011 with a -6.3% decline in Consumer Discretionary, a -10.0% decline in Industrials, and a -21.2% decline in Materials. Financials saw a sharp drop of -20.7% in 2011 due to the ongoing European debt crisis and concerns about reduced profitability with tougher post-crisis regulations.

Emerging markets – Emerging stock markets fell sharply by -20% in 2011 due to the weak growth in the industrialized world, which hurt the emerging markets despite generally strong economic growth in their domestic economies. Specifically, the MSCI Emerging Markets Free Index, which tracks companies based in 26 emerging countries, fell by -20.4% in 2011 following the rallies seen in the two previous years of +16.4% in 2010 and +74.5% in 2009.

G7 – In 2011, all of the G7 stock markets saw sell-offs, except for the S&P 500 index, which closed essentially unchanged on the year. Europe had a dismal year due to the European debt crisis. Japan's stock market fell sharply due to the March earthquake disaster. The ranked returns for the G7 stock markets for 2011 are as follows: U.S. S&P 500 unchanged, UK FTSE 100 -5.6%, Canadian Toronto Composite -11.1%, German DAX index -14.7%, French CAC40 -17.0%, Japanese Nikkei 225 -17.3%, and Italian MIB -25.2%.

North America – In North America, Mexico's Bolsa Index ended 2011 down -3.8%, falling behind the unchanged close in the U.S. S&P 500 index and ending its streak of outperforming the U.S. and Canadian stock markets for ten straight years. The Mexican Bolsa index has posted double-digit gains in seven of the last nine years (2011 -3.8%, 2010 +20.0%, 2009 +43.5%, 2008 −24.2%, 2007 +11.7%, 2006 +48.6%, 2005 +37.8%, 2004 +46.9%, 2003 +43.5%). The Toronto Composite index in 2011 fell by -11.1%, underperforming the unchanged close in the S&P 500 and ending its 7-year streak of outperforming the S&P 500.

Latin America – Most of the large Latin America stock markets showed declines in 2011 along with the rest of the global emerging markets: Venezuela's Stock Market Index +79.1%, Jamaica's Stock Exchange Index +11.8%, Costa Rica's Stock Market Index +2.4% Ecuador's Guayaqui Bolsa Index +1.9%, Chile's Stock Market Select Index -15.2%, Peru's Lima General Index -16.7%, Brazil's Bovespa Index -18.1%, Columbia's General Index -18.3%, and Argentina's Merval Index -30.1%.

Europe – European stocks in 2011 closed lower as the European debt crisis hurt the economy and caused concern about a systemic European banking crisis. The Dow Jones Stoxx 50 index fell -8.4% after being unchanged in 2010 and rising +24.1% in 2009. The big European countries all saw declines in 2011: UK FTSE 100 index -5.6%, Spanish IBEX 35 index -13.1%, German DAX index -14.7%, French CAC 40 index -17.0%, and Italian MIB index −25.2%.

Asia – The Asian stock markets in 2011 closed mostly lower along with the rest of the world's stock markets. The MSCI Far East Index in 2011 fell by -14.6%, reversing most of the +16.6% gain seen in 2010. Asia was hurt by the European debt crisis and by interest rate hikes that were made necessary by higher inflation. China's Shanghai Composite Index in 2011 fell by -21.7%, adding to the -14.3% decline seen in 2010. Japan closed down -17.3% due to the major economic dislocations from the March 2011 earthquake disaster. The ranked closes for the Asian stock markets in 2011 were as follows: Philippines' Composite index +4.1%, Indonesia's Jakarta Composite Index +3.2%, Malaysia's Kuala Lumpur Composite index +0.8%, Thailand's Stock Exchange index -0.7%, New Zealand's Exchange 50 Index -1.0%, Pakistan's 100 Index -5.6%, South Korea's Composite Index -11.0%, Australia's All-Ordinaries Index -15.2%, Singapore's Straights Times Index -17.0%, Japan's Nikkei 225 Index -17.3%, Hong Kong's Hang Seng -20.0%, Taiwan's TAIEX Index of -21.2%, China's Shanghai Composite Index -21.7%, and India's Mumbai Sensex 30 index -24.6%, Vietnam's Stock Index -27.5%.

STOCK INDEX FUTURES - WORLDWIDE

Year	Jan.	Feb.	Mar.	Apr.	May	June	July	Aug.	Sept.	Oct.	Nov.	Dec.	Average
United States													
2005	355.1	361.8	354.9	347.7	358.2	358.1	371.0	366.8	369.4	362.8	375.6	375.2	363.1
2006	384.8	385.0	389.2	394.0	381.8	381.8	383.8	391.9	401.5	414.2	421.0	426.3	396.3
2007	432.3	422.9	427.1	445.6	460.1	451.9	437.4	443.1	458.9	465.7	445.2	441.4	444.3
2008	414.4	400.0	397.6	416.5	420.9	384.8	381.0	385.6	350.6	291.2	269.4	271.5	365.3
2009	248.3	221.0	239.8	262.4	276.3	276.3	296.8	306.8	317.7	311.5	329.3	335.2	285.1
2010	322.8	332.0	351.5	356.7	327.5	309.8	331.1	315.4	343.0	355.7	354.9	378.0	339.9
2011	386.6	398.9	398.5	409.9	404.4	397.0	388.4	366.4	340.1	376.7	374.8	378.0	385.0
Canada													
2005	269.0	282.6	281.0	273.9	280.8	289.5	304.7	311.9	321.9	303.5	316.4	329.5	297.1
2006	349.2	341.7	354.0	356.7	343.3	339.4	345.8	352.9	343.8	360.8	372.8	377.3	353.1
2007	381.0	381.3	384.8	392.2	410.9	406.5	405.4	399.3	412.1	427.5	400.1	404.3	400.5
2008	384.5	397.0	390.2	407.4	430.1	422.9	397.3	402.5	343.5	285.4	271.0	262.7	366.2
2009	254.2	237.4	254.9	272.6	303.1	303.3	315.3	317.7	333.1	318.9	334.6	343.3	299.0
2010	324.3	339.9	351.9	356.9	343.8	330.1	342.4	348.2	361.5	370.5	378.6	392.9	353.4
2011	396.1	413.2	412.6	407.6	403.5	388.8	378.4	373.2	339.8	358.1	356.7	349.5	381.5
France													
2005	215.3	221.6	223.8	215.2	226.7	232.7	244.9	242.1	253.1	244.1	251.3	259.4	235.9
2006	272.2	275.1	287.3	285.5	271.3	273.2	275.6	284.2	288.9	294.3	293.1	304.9	283.8
2007	308.6	303.5	310.0	327.9	335.9	333.2	316.4	311.6	314.5	321.8	312.0	308.9	317.0
2008	267.9	263.6	259.0	274.9	275.9	244.0	241.7	246.6	221.9	191.9	179.5	177.1	237.0
2009	163.6	148.7	154.5	173.9	180.3	172.8	188.5	201.0	208.8	198.5	202.5	216.6	184.1
2010	205.8	204.1	218.7	210.0	193.0	189.4	200.5	192.1	204.4	210.9	198.7	209.3	203.1
2011	220.4	226.2	219.5	226.0	220.5	219.1	202.0	179.2	164.1	178.4	173.6	173.9	200.2
Germany													
2005	251.6	257.2	257.1	247.4	263.7	271.2	288.9	285.6	298.2	291.4	307.1	319.8	278.3
2006	335.5	342.7	353.0	355.3	336.6	336.0	335.9	346.4	355.0	370.6	373.0	390.0	352.5
2007	401.4	397.0	409.0	438.0	466.1	473.4	448.4	451.6	464.8	474.1	465.3	477.0	447.2
2008	405.1	399.0	386.4	410.8	419.6	379.5	383.1	379.7	344.8	294.9	276.1	284.4	363.6
2009	256.5	227.3	241.5	282.0	292.1	284.3	315.3	323.1	335.5	320.2	332.6	352.2	296.9
2010	331.6	331.0	363.8	362.8	352.6	352.7	363.5	350.3	368.3	390.3	395.5	408.8	364.3
2011	418.5	430.0	416.3	444.3	431.2	436.1	423.3	342.0	325.3	363.1	360.0	348.7	394.9
Italy													
2005	234.9	237.8	241.0	230.5	237.0	241.1	251.9	249.5	261.7	242.9	252.5	261.4	245.2
2006	271.8	282.9	286.3	285.5	269.9	271.5	274.1	283.7	287.2	296.4	304.2	310.9	285.4
2007	317.4	310.9	317.2	331.5	329.5	319.9	307.4	304.6	302.4	307.0	291.2	286.7	310.5
2008	252.1	251.6	236.2	251.1	249.8	221.0	213.6	217.1	190.3	158.0	151.0	146.8	211.6
2009	139.5	121.7	123.5	148.7	154.9	149.1	158.5	169.1	178.2	171.6	168.3	177.1	155.0
2010	168.9	163.2	177.2	169.7	153.6	151.4	162.2	153.3	160.8	168.0	153.6	163.2	162.1
2011	173.3	176.7	174.3	179.1	169.9	161.8	150.3	129.3	123.8	134.8	125.4	125.5	152.0
Japan													
2005	39.5	40.7	40.5	38.2	39.1	40.2	41.3	43.1	47.1	47.2	51.6	55.9	43.7
2006	57.8	56.2	59.2	58.6	53.7	53.8	53.6	56.0	55.9	56.9	56.5	59.8	56.5
2007	60.3	61.1	60.0	60.4	62.0	62.9	59.8	57.5	58.2	58.1	54.4	53.1	59.0
2008	47.2	47.2	43.5	48.0	49.7	46.8	46.4	45.4	39.1	29.8	29.5	30.7	41.9
2009	27.7	26.3	28.1	30.6	33.0	34.5	35.9	36.4	35.2	34.8	32.4	36.6	32.6
2010	35.4	35.1	38.5	38.4	33.9	32.5	33.1	30.6	32.5	31.9	34.5	35.5	34.3
2011	35.5	36.9	33.8	34.2	33.6	34.1	34.1	31.1	30.2	31.2	29.3	29.3	32.8
United Kingdom													
2005	225.5	230.5	227.0	221.4	229.4	236.5	244.3	245.6	253.6	246.1	253.2	263.0	239.7
2006	270.5	273.1	281.6	284.0	269.4	274.1	277.5	277.8	281.8	290.1	288.2	297.6	280.5
2007	296.7	295.4	303.3	310.0	317.7	314.5	303.8	301.2	306.4	319.1	303.1	303.6	306.2
2008	277.1	278.3	270.4	286.4	284.7	263.8	254.0	265.0	229.4	201.7	197.1	204.1	251.0
2009	192.0	178.3	183.3	200.7	208.1	200.6	217.4	232.8	243.4	238.8	244.7	255.0	216.3
2010	245.8	252.8	268.8	264.5	246.9	235.0	250.8	249.1	264.9	271.2	264.3	282.9	258.1
2011	281.2	287.0	283.4	291.4	288.3	286.1	279.5	258.7	245.2	264.3	262.0	264.0	274.3

Not Seasonally Adjusted. *Source: Economic and Statistics Administration, U.S. Department of Commerce (ESA)*

FT-SE 100 Stock Index (weekly close) as of December 30, 2011

Deutscher Aktienindex (DAX) (weekly close) as of December 30, 2011

STOCK INDEX FUTURES - WORLDWIDE

Toronto 300 Stock Index (weekly close) as of December 30, 2011

CAC-40 Stock Index (weekly close) as of December 30, 2011

Hang Seng Stock Index (weekly close) as of December 30, 2011

Nikkei 225 Stock Index (weekly close) as of December 30, 2011

Sugar

The white crystalline substance called "sugar" is the organic chemical compound sucrose, one of several related compounds all known as sugars. These include glucose, dextrose, fructose, and lactose. All sugars are members of the larger group of compounds called carbohydrates and are characterized by a sweet taste. Sucrose is considered a double sugar because it is composed of one molecule of glucose and one molecule of fructose. While sucrose is common in many plants, it occurs in the highest concentration in sugarcane (Saccharum officinarum) and sugar beets (Beta vulgaris). Sugarcane is about 7 to 18 percent sugar by weight while sugar beets are 8 to 22 percent.

Sugarcane is a member of the grass family and is a perennial. Sugarcane is cultivated in tropical and subtropical regions around the world roughly between the Tropics of Cancer and Capricorn. It grows best in hot, wet climates where there is heavy rainfall followed by a dry season. The largest cane producers are Florida, Louisiana, Texas, and Hawaii. On a commercial basis, sugarcane is not grown from seeds but from cuttings or pieces of the stalk.

Sugar beets, which are produced in temperate or colder climates, are annuals grown from seeds. Sugar beets do best with moderate temperatures and evenly distributed rainfall. The beets are planted in the spring and harvested in the fall. The sugar is contained in the root of the beet, but the sugars from beets and cane are identical. Sugar beet production takes place mostly in Europe, the U.S., China, and Japan. The largest sugar beet producing states are Minnesota, Idaho, North Dakota, and Michigan. Sugar beets are refined to yield white sugar and very little raw sugar is produced.

Sugar beets and sugarcane are produced in over 100 countries around the world. Of all the sugar produced, about 25% is processed from sugar beets and the remaining 75% is from sugar cane. The trend has been that production of sugar from cane is increasing relative to that produced from beets. The significance of this in that sugarcane is a perennial plant while the sugar beet is an annual, and due to the longer production cycle, sugarcane production and the sugar processed from that cane, may not be quite as responsive to changes in price.

Sugar futures are traded on the Bolsa de Mercadorias & Futuros (BM&F), Kansai Commodities Exchange (KANEX), the Tokyo Grain Exchange (TGE), the NYSE-LIFFE exchange in London, and the ICE Futures U.S. (ICE) exchange. Options are traded on the BM&F, the TGE, the NYSE-LIFFE and the ICE.

Raw sugar is traded on the ICE Futures U.S. (ICE) exchange while white sugar is traded on the NYSE-LIFFE exchange in London. The most actively traded contract is the No. 11 (World) sugar contract at the ICE. The No. 11 contract calls for the delivery of 112,000 pounds (50 long tons) of raw cane centrifugal sugar from any of 28 foreign countries of origin and the United States. The ICE also trades the No. 16 sugar contract (Domestic), which calls for the delivery of raw centrifugal cane sugar in the United States. Futures on white sugar are traded on the NYSE-LIFFE and call for the delivery of 50 metric tons of white beet sugar, cane crystal sugar, or refined sugar of any origin from the crop current at the time of delivery.

Prices – World sugar prices on the ICE No.11 sugar nearest-futures chart rallied early in 2011 and posted a 31-year high of 36.08 cents per pound in February after the ISO forecast a 1.7% increase in 2011 global sugar demand that cut the inventory–to-consumption ratio to a 20-year low of 32%. Reduced sugar output in Australia, the world's third-largest sugar exporter, also underpinned prices after floods and cyclones cut its 2011 output to a 9-year low of 3.58 MMT. Sugar prices then collapsed into late-spring and posted a 1-1/4 year low of 20.40 cents a pound in May 2011 after the ISO hiked its 2010/11 global sugar surplus estimate to 1 MMT on higher output from Thailand and forecast a 4 MMT global sugar surplus in 2011/12 on increased sugar production in Brazil and India. Sugar prices rebounded sharply to a 1-year high of 31.85 cents a pound in August 2011 after the USDA forecast record global sugar consumption in 2011/12 of 162 MMT along with export delays in Brazil where as many as 75 vessels were waiting to load sugar, the longest wait in 2 years. Prices faded into year-end after India allowed another 1 MMT of sugar exports and the ISO raised its 2011/12 global sugar production estimate to a record 172.4 MMT. Sugar prices finished 2011 down -27% at 23.30 cents per pound.

Supply – World production of centrifugal (raw) sugar in the 2011-12 marketing year (Oct 1 to Sep 30) rose +4.2% to 168.247 million metric tons, a new record high. The world's largest sugar producers in 2011-12 were Brazil with 21.3% of world production, India with 16.8%, and the European Union with 10.0%. U.S. centrifugal sugar production in 2011-12 rose +36.5% to 2.300 million metric tons. World ending stocks in 2011-12 rose +1.8% to 30.018 million metric tons. The stocks/consumption ratio fell -0.3% in 2011-12 to 18,800 metric tons. U.S. production of cane sugar in 2011-12 rose +5.5% to 3.345 million short tons and beet sugar production fell -2.9% yr/yr to 4.525 million short tons.

Demand – World domestic consumption of centrifugal (raw) sugar in 2011-12 rose by +2.8% yr/yr to 159.320 million metric tons, below last year's record high of 156.080 million metric tons. U.S. domestic disappearance (consumption) of sugar in 2011-12 rose by +0.5% yr/yr to 11.615 million short tons. U.S. per capita sugar consumption in 2010-11 (latest data) rose +3.9% to 65.98 pounds per year, which is only about two-thirds of the levels seen in the early 1970s.

Trade – World exports of centrifugal sugar in 2011-12 rose +1.0% yr/yr to 56.694 million metric tons, a new record high. The world's largest sugar exporter was Brazil, where exports in 2011-12 fell -7.8% yr/yr to 23.800 million metric tons, which accounted for 42.0% of total world exports. The next largest exporters are Thailand with 15.4% of world exports and Australia with 5.2%. U.S. sugar exports in 2011-12 fell -19.4% yr/yr to 200,000 short tons, which is down from the 15-year high of 422,000 seen in 2006-07. U.S. sugar imports in 2011-12 fell -6.6% yr/yr to 3.135 million short tons, down from the decade high of 3.355 in 2010-11.

SUGAR

World Production, Supply & Stocks/Consumption Ratio of Sugar   In 1000's of Metric Tons (Raw Value)

Marketing Year	Beginning Stocks	Production	Imports	Total Supply	Exports	Domestic Consumption	Ending Stocks	Stocks As a % of Consumption
2002-03	36,629	148,552	41,699	226,880	47,205	138,033	40,593	29.4
2003-04	40,593	142,487	41,256	224,336	46,535	138,923	38,055	27.4
2004-05	38,055	140,734	45,478	224,267	46,950	141,646	34,739	24.5
2005-06	34,739	144,303	44,720	223,762	49,533	142,942	30,572	21.4
2006-07	30,572	164,458	44,306	239,336	51,107	149,307	36,890	24.7
2007-08	36,890	163,536	45,721	246,147	50,721	152,037	42,656	28.1
2008-09	42,656	144,144	46,714	233,514	47,786	153,717	31,169	20.3
2009-10[1]	31,169	153,687	51,396	236,252	51,617	154,653	29,258	18.9
2010-11[2]	29,258	161,437	51,728	242,423	56,136	156,080	29,499	18.9
2011-12[3]	29,499	168,247	49,014	246,760	56,694	159,320	30,018	18.8

[1] Preliminary.   [2] Estimate.   [3] Forecast.   *Source: Foreign Agricultural Service, U.S. Department of Agriculture (FAS-USDA)*

World Production of Sugar (Centrifugal Sugar-Raw Value)   In Thousands of Metric Tons

Year	Australia	Brazil	China	Cuba	European Union	India	Indonesia	Mexico	Pakistan	Thailand	United States	Ukraine	World Total
2002-03	5,461	23,810	11,380	2,250	18,675	22,140	1,755	5,229	3,944	7,286	1,550	7,644	148,552
2003-04	5,178	26,400	10,734	2,550	17,132	15,150	1,730	5,330	4,047	7,010	1,580	7,847	142,487
2004-05	5,388	28,175	9,826	1,350	21,648	14,170	2,050	6,149	2,937	5,187	2,054	7,146	140,734
2005-06	5,297	26,850	9,446	1,240	21,373	21,140	2,100	5,604	2,597	4,835	2,054	6,713	144,303
2006-07	5,212	31,450	12,855	1,200	17,757	30,780	1,900	5,633	3,615	6,720	2,850	7,662	164,458
2007-08	4,939	31,600	15,898	1,420	15,614	28,630	2,000	5,852	4,163	7,820	2,020	7,396	163,536
2008-09	4,814	31,850	13,317	1,340	14,014	15,950	2,053	5,260	3,512	7,200	1,710	6,833	144,144
2009-10[1]	4,700	36,400	11,429	1,250	16,687	20,637	1,910	5,115	3,420	6,930	1,382	7,224	153,687
2010-11[2]	3,700	38,350	11,199	1,100	15,090	26,650	1,770	5,495	3,920	9,663	1,685	7,110	161,437
2011-12[3]	4,150	35,750	11,840	1,250	16,740	28,300	2,088	5,650	4,220	10,170	2,300	7,153	168,247

[1] Preliminary.   [2] Estimate.   [3] Forecast.   *Source: Foreign Agricultural Service, U.S. Department of Agriculture (FAS-USDA)*

World Stocks of Centrifugal Sugar at Beginning of Marketing Year   In Thousands of Metric Tons (Raw Value)

Year	Australia	Brazil	China	Cuba	European Union	India	Indonesia	Iran	Mexico	Philippines	Russia	United States	World Total
2002-03	507	210	869	360	2,717	11,670	1,385	167	1,172	239	2,130	1,386	36,629
2003-04	662	270	2,021	267	3,581	12,150	1,340	267	1,194	277	1,050	1,515	40,593
2004-05	543	1,030	2,323	275	4,699	8,485	1,170	402	1,237	405	440	1,721	38,055
2005-06	343	585	1,757	215	5,339	5,160	1,120	542	2,045	239	580	1,208	34,739
2006-07	291	-285	703	225	5,088	4,000	1,170	932	1,294	253	470	1,540	30,572
2007-08	402	-485	1,401	155	2,720	11,701	570	1,292	1,718	262	440	1,632	36,890
2008-09	400	215	3,965	135	3,130	11,301	590	1,362	1,975	547	550	1,510	42,656
2009-10[1]	487	-1,135	3,784	45	2,232	5,361	340	842	624	322	481	1,392	31,169
2010-11[2]	413	-835	2,355	75	1,433	5,204	750	757	973	394	399	1,359	29,258
2011-12[3]	193	-285	1,607	75	1,814	6,059	515	422	806	492	400	1,349	29,499

[1] Preliminary.   [2] Estimate.   [3] Forecast.   *Source: Foreign Agricultural Service, U.S. Department of Agriculture (FAS-USDA)*

Centrifugal Sugar (Raw Value) Imported into Selected Countries   In Thousands of Metric Tons

Year	Algeria	Canada	China	European Union	Indonesia	Iran	Japan	Rep. of Korea	Malaysia	Nigeria	Russia	United States	World Total
2002-03	1,094	1,329	842	2,150	1,600	955	1,483	1,590	1,406	1,000	4,000	1,569	41,699
2003-04	1,185	1,323	1,235	1,900	1,500	760	1,442	1,682	1,484	1,150	3,670	1,591	41,256
2004-05	1,153	1,274	1,360	2,549	1,450	865	1,328	1,652	1,459	1,150	4,300	1,905	45,478
2005-06	1,130	1,445	1,234	2,630	1,800	1,450	1,385	1,669	1,414	1,200	2,900	3,124	44,720
2006-07	1,110	1,161	1,465	3,530	1,800	1,600	1,432	1,475	1,670	1,240	2,950	1,887	44,306
2007-08	1,105	1,445	972	2,948	2,420	1,200	1,477	1,805	1,425	1,485	3,100	2,377	45,721
2008-09	1,180	1,264	1,077	3,180	2,197	1,200	1,287	1,685	1,520	1,250	2,150	2,796	46,714
2009-10[1]	1,501	1,336	1,535	2,561	3,200	1,400	1,322	1,595	1,595	1,400	2,223	3,010	51,396
2010-11[2]	1,465	1,391	2,130	3,800	2,995	1,550	1,582	1,605	1,630	1,500	2,950	3,355	51,728
2011-12[3]	1,320	1,400	2,200	3,150	3,010	1,500	1,600	1,620	1,650	1,525	1,675	3,135	49,014

[1] Preliminary.   [2] Estimate.   [3] Forecast.   *Source: Foreign Agricultural Service, U.S. Department of Agriculture (FAS-USDA)*

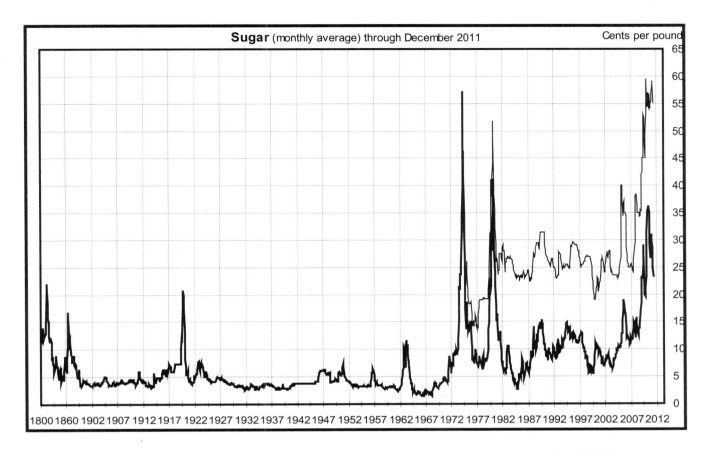

Sugar (monthly average) through December 2011 — Cents per pound

Years axis: 1800 1860 1902 1907 1912 1917 1922 1927 1932 1937 1942 1947 1952 1957 1962 1967 1972 1977 1982 1987 1992 1997 2002 2007 2012

Centrifugal Sugar (Raw Value) Exported From Selected Countries   In Thousands of Metric Tons

Year	Australia	Brazil	Colombia	Cuba	Dominican Republic	European Union	Guate-mala	India	Mauritius	South Africa	Swazi-land	Thailand	World Total
2002-03	4,114	14,000	1,306	1,798	185	5,600	1,335	1,410	542	1,296	278	5,280	47,205
2003-04	4,157	15,240	1,200	1,942	185	4,900	1,335	250	587	1,025	285	4,860	46,535
2004-05	4,447	18,020	1,231	770	185	6,028	1,386	40	581	1,010	298	3,115	46,950
2005-06	4,208	17,090	988	730	251	8,345	1,391	1,510	548	1,230	320	2,242	49,533
2006-07	3,860	20,850	942	795	225	2,439	1,500	2,680	510	1,267	358	4,705	51,107
2007-08	3,700	19,500	661	960	217	1,656	1,333	5,830	465	1,154	350	4,914	50,721
2008-09	3,522	21,550	585	785	217	1,332	1,654	176	480	1,185	350	5,295	47,786
2009-10[1]	3,600	24,300	870	565	250	2,647	1,815	225	500	830	350	4,930	51,617
2010-11[2]	2,750	25,800	790	500	209	1,009	1,808	3,200	481	430	365	7,400	56,136
2011-12[3]	2,950	23,800	800	615	191	2,210	1,808	2,500	480	480	370	8,700	56,694

[1] Preliminary.   [2] Estimate.   [3] Forecast.   *Source: Foreign Agricultural Service, U.S. Department of Agriculture (FAS-USDA)*

Average Wholesale Price of Refined Beet Sugar[2]--Midwest Market   In Cents Per Pound

Year	Jan.	Feb.	Mar.	Apr.	May	June	July	Aug.	Sept.	Oct.	Nov.	Dec.	Average
2002	26.75	26.00	25.95	24.63	24.50	24.00	24.00	25.40	26.25	26.75	27.40	27.88	25.79
2003	27.80	26.50	27.13	27.63	28.00	28.00	27.63	25.50	24.00	24.70	23.94	23.63	26.21
2004	23.70	23.50	23.50	23.50	23.50	23.50	23.50	23.50	23.50	23.50	23.38	23.20	23.48
2005	23.50	23.50	23.25	23.80	24.75	25.88	26.00	26.75	40.10	40.00	40.00	36.90	29.54
2006	34.50	36.50	37.10	36.38	35.00	35.00	35.00	34.50	31.20	28.75	27.19	26.10	33.10
2007	25.50	25.00	24.90	25.00	25.00	25.00	25.38	25.60	25.38	25.00	24.50	24.50	25.06
2008	24.13	26.40	28.00	28.00	29.60	33.25	38.00	38.40	38.50	36.20	35.00	35.00	32.54
2009	35.00	35.00	35.00	34.25	34.40	35.50	35.40	38.00	42.00	42.60	45.00	45.00	38.10
2010	50.50	53.00	52.25	48.20	45.00	50.00	53.40	59.50	59.00	54.40	56.50	57.00	53.23
2011[1]	54.50	54.00	56.50	56.80	54.00	55.00	55.40	57.00	58.60	59.00	58.75	55.10	56.22

[1] Preliminary.   [2] These are f.o.b. basis prices in bulk, not delivered prices.   *Source: Economic Research Service, U.S. Department of Agriculture (ERS-)*

SUGAR

Average Price of World Raw Sugar[1]   In Cents Per Pound

Year	Jan.	Feb.	Mar.	Apr.	May	June	July	Aug.	Sept.	Oct.	Nov.	Dec.	Average
2002	7.96	6.81	7.27	7.12	7.33	7.07	8.02	7.86	8.54	8.84	8.87	8.81	7.88
2003	8.56	9.14	8.50	7.92	7.41	6.85	7.18	7.30	6.70	6.74	6.83	6.95	7.51
2004	6.42	7.01	8.23	8.21	8.08	8.41	9.19	8.99	9.10	9.84	9.65	10.19	8.61
2005	10.33	10.51	10.57	10.19	10.23	10.45	10.89	11.09	11.59	12.40	12.86	15.09	11.35
2006	17.27	18.93	18.01	18.21	17.83	16.19	16.61	13.58	12.42	12.09	12.38	12.47	15.50
2007	11.85	11.63	11.44	10.85	10.78	11.05	12.18	11.66	11.61	11.86	11.83	12.47	11.60
2008	13.75	15.16	14.60	13.68	12.23	13.29	14.90	15.58	14.74	12.99	12.87	12.31	13.84
2009	13.09	13.90	13.83	14.43	16.89	16.94	18.57	22.37	23.11	23.22	22.96	25.28	18.72
2010	28.94	27.29	21.36	19.87	19.59	21.24	23.42	25.09	31.19	34.80	35.44	36.10	27.03
2011[1]	36.11	35.01	33.22	29.35	26.64	29.75	30.51	28.87	27.71	26.30	24.52	23.42	29.28

[1] Contract No. 11, f.o.b. stowed Caribbean port, including Brazil, bulk spot price.   [2] Preliminary.   Source: Economic Research Service, U.S. Department of Agriculture (ERS-USDA)

Average Price of Raw Sugar in New York (C.I.F., Duty/Free Paid, Contract #12 & #14)   In Cents Per Pound

Year	Jan.	Feb.	Mar.	Apr.	May	June	July	Aug.	Sept.	Oct.	Nov.	Dec.	Average
2002	21.03	20.69	19.92	19.73	19.52	19.93	20.86	20.91	21.65	21.94	22.22	22.03	20.87
2003	21.62	21.91	22.14	21.87	21.80	21.62	21.32	21.26	21.34	20.92	20.91	20.37	21.42
2004	20.54	20.57	20.86	20.88	20.69	20.03	20.14	20.10	20.47	20.31	20.40	20.55	20.46
2005	20.57	20.36	20.54	21.21	21.96	21.89	21.94	20.49	21.10	21.71	21.83	21.74	21.28
2006	23.61	24.05	23.10	23.56	23.48	23.32	22.44	21.38	21.27	20.22	19.66	19.59	22.14
2007	20.03	20.59	20.85	20.91	21.27	21.33	22.72	21.80	21.42	20.56	20.25	20.12	20.99
2008	20.24	20.21	20.65	20.54	20.83	21.80	23.76	23.15	23.10	21.46	19.83	20.00	21.30
2009	20.15	19.83	19.75	21.58	21.64	22.47	23.02	26.18	28.91	30.48	31.86	33.30	24.93
2010	39.36	40.13	35.11	30.86	30.89	32.73	33.66	34.24	38.17	39.30	38.84	38.35	35.97
2011[1]	38.46	39.69	39.65	38.32	35.04	35.65	37.93	40.16	40.15	38.19	37.92	36.32	38.12

[1] Preliminary.   Source: Economic Research Service, U.S. Department of Agriculture (ERS-USDA)

Supply and Utilization of Sugar (Cane and Beet) in the United States   In Thousands of Short Tons (Raw Value)

	Supply								Utilization					
	Production			Offshore Receipts							Net		Domestic Disappearance		
Year	Cane	Beet	Total	Foreign	Terri-tories	Total	Beginning Stocks	Total Supply	Total Use	Exports	Changes in Invisible Stocks	Refining Loss Adjustment	In Poly-hydric Alcohol[4]	Total	Per Capita Pounds
2002-03	3,964	4,462	8,426	1,730	0	1,730	1,528	11,684	10,014	142	161	0	24	9,504	63.3
2003-04	3,957	4,692	8,649	1,750	0	1,750	1,670	12,070	10,172	288	23	0	41	9,678	61.0
2004-05	3,265	4,611	7,876	2,100	0	2,100	1,897	11,873	10,542	259	94	0	48	10,019	61.6
2005-06	2,955	4,444	7,399	3,443	0	3,443	1,332	12,174	10,476	203	-67	0	51	10,184	63.1
2006-07	3,438	5,008	8,445	2,080	0	2,080	1,698	12,223	10,424	422	-132	0	53	9,913	62.2
2007-08	3,431	4,721	8,152	2,620	0	2,620	1,799	12,571	10,907	203	0	0	61	10,501	61.2
2008-09	3,317	4,214	7,531	3,082	0	3,082	1,664	12,277	10,743	136	0	0	46	10,441	65.2
2009-10[1]	3,387	4,575	7,963	3,320	0	3,320	1,534	12,817	11,319	211	-45	0	35	10,917	63.5
2010-11[2]	3,172	4,659	7,831	3,698	0	3,698	1,498	13,027	11,555	248	-30	0	31	11,109	66.0
2011-12[3]	3,345	4,525	7,870	2,893	0	2,893	1,472	12,235	11,615	200	0	0	40	11,225	

[1] Preliminary.   [2] Estimate.   [3] Forecast.   [4] Includes feed use.   Source: Economic Research Service, U.S. Department of Agriculture (ERS-USDA)

Sugar Cane for Sugar & Seed and Production of Cane Sugar and Molasses in the United States

			Production					Farm Value		Sugar Production				
	Acreage Harvested (1,000 Acres)	Yield of Cane Per Havested Acre Net Tons	for Sugar	for Seed	Total	Sugar Yield Per Acre (Short Tons)	Farm Price ($ Per Ton)	of Cane Used for Sugar	of Cane Used for Sugar & Seed	Raw Value Total (1,000 Tons)	Per Ton of Cane (In Lbs.)	Refined Basis (1,000 Tons)	Molasses Made Edible	Total[3]
Year			1,000 Tons					1,000 Dollars					1,000 Gallons	
2002	1,023.2	34.7	33,903	1,650	35,553	4.07	28.4	961,896	1,007,142	----	----	----	----	----
2003	992.3	34.1	31,942	1,916	33,858	4.26	29.5	943,646	998,269	----	----	----	----	----
2004	938.2	30.9	27,243	1,770	29,013	3.71	28.3	771,734	821,118	----	----	----	----	----
2005	921.9	28.9	24,728	1,878	26,606	3.49	28.4	701,920	754,529	----	----	----	----	----
2006	897.7	32.9	27,962	1,602	29,564	4.05	30.4	849,157	897,601	----	----	----	----	----
2007	879.6	34.1	28,273	1,696	29,969	4.17	29.4	831,218	880,616	----	----	----	----	----
2008	868.0	31.8	26,131	1,472	27,603	4.03	29.5	771,134	814,479	----	----	----	----	----
2009	873.9	34.8	28,494	1,938	30,432	4.17	34.8	NA	1,056,613	----	----	----	----	----
2010[1]	877.5	31.2	25,663	1,697	27,360	3.87	41.7	NA	1,140,636	----	----	----	----	----
2011[2]	873.0	32.4	26,705	1,574	28,279									

[1] Preliminary.   [2] Estimate.   [3] Excludes edible molasses.   Source: Economic Research Service, U.S. Department of Agriculture (ERS-USDA)

U.S. Sugar Beets, Beet Sugar, Pulp & Molasses Produced from Sugar Beets and Raw Sugar Spot Prices

								- Sugar Production -		------- Raw Sugar Prices --------				Wholesale
	------ Acreage ------		Yield Per Harvested Acre	Pro- duction	Sugar Yield Per Acre		Farm Value	Equiv- alent Raw Value[4]	Refined Basis	World[5] Refined #5	------- CSCE --------			List Price HFCS (42%)
											#11 World	N.Y. Duty Paid		
Year of Harvest	Planted	Harvested	Acre (Sh. Tons)	(1,000 Tons)	(Sh. Tons)	Price[3] (Dollars)	Value (1,000 $)	- 1,000 Short Tons -		------ In Cents Per Pound ------				Midwest
	---- 1,000 Acres ----													
2002	1,427	1,361	20.4	27,707	3.28	39.60	1,097,329	4,462	----	10.35	7.88	20.87		13.05
2003	1,365	1,348	22.8	30,710	3.48	41.40	1,270,026	4,692	----	9.74	7.51	21.42		13.24
2004	1,346	1,307	23.0	30,021	3.53	36.90	1,109,272	4,611	----	10.87	8.61	20.46		13.20
2005	1,300	1,243	22.1	27,433	3.58	43.50	1,193,151	4,444	----	13.19	11.35	21.28		13.58
2006	1,366	1,304	26.1	34,064	3.84	44.20	1,506,985	5,008	----	19.01	15.50	22.14		17.03
2007	1,269	1,247	25.5	31,834	3.79	42.00	1,337,173	4,721	----	14.00	11.60	20.99		21.22
2008	1,091	1,005	26.8	26,881	4.15	48.10	1,294,144	4,166	----	15.96	13.84	21.30		24.50
2009	1,186	1,149	25.9	29,783	3.98	51.50	1,532,634	4,575	----	22.13	18.72	24.93		25.88
2010[1]	1,172	1,156	27.7	32,034	4.15	66.70	2,135,530	4,800	----	27.78	27.03	35.97		21.82
2011[2]	1,233	1,213	23.7	28,789						31.68	29.28	38.12		21.65

[1] Preliminary. [2] Estimate. [3] Includes support payments, but excludes Gov't. sugar beet payments. [4] Refined sugar multiplied by factor of 1.07.
[5] F.O.B. Europe. *Source: Economic Research Service, U.S. Department of Agriculture (ERS-USDA)*

Sugar Deliveries and Stocks in the United States   In Thousands of Short Tons (Raw Value)

			------- Deliveries by Primary Distributors ---------					Total ----------------------		---------------------- Stocks, Jan. 1 ----------------------					
			Cane Sugar Refineries Deliveries	Beet Sugar Factories Deliveries	Importers of Direct Con- sumption Sugar	Mainland Cane Sugar Mills[3]	Total Deliveries	Domestic Con- sumption	Cane Sugar Re- fineries	Beet Sugar Factories	CCC	Refiners' Raw	Mainland Cane Mills	Total
Year	Quota Allocation	Actual Imports												
2002	----	----	5,407	4,291	109	----	9,808	9,994	288	1,472	634	351	1,781	4,525
2003	----	----	5,232	4,219	60	----	9,511	9,713	298	1,300	246	299	1,289	3,432
2004	----	----	4,989	4,668	64	----	9,722	9,901	326	1,817	0	286	1,659	4,088
2005	----	----	5,136	4,710	197	----	10,043	10,212	368	1,753	28	245	1,635	4,029
2006	----	----	5,230	4,195	577	----	10,002	10,162	328	1,429	0	217	1,382	3,357
2007	----	----	5,123	4,707	116	----	9,946	10,173	452	1,792	0	358	1,437	4,039
2008	----	----	5,075	4,867	773	----	10,715	10,900	400	1,806	0	304	1,500	4,009
2009	----	----	5,493	4,324	667	----	10,485	10,657	440	1,464	0	468	1,612	3,984
2010[1]	----	----	5,619	4,514	843	----	10,975	11,215	484	1,456	0	346	1,274	3,559
2011[2]	----	----	5,553	4,552	968	----	11,074	11,326	487	1,691	0	257	1,455	3,890

[1] Preliminary. [2] Estimate. [3] Sugar for direct consumption only. [4] Refined. *Source: Economic Research Service,*
U.S. Department of Agriculture (ERS-USDA)

Sugar, Refined--Deliveries to End User in the United States   In Thousands of Short Tons

Year	Bakery & Cereal Products	Bev- erages	Confec- tionery[2]	Hotels, Restar. & Insti- tutions	Ice Cream & Dairy Products	Canned, Bottled & Frozen Foods	All Other Food Uses	Retail Grocers[3]	Wholesale Grocers[4]	Non-food Uses	Non- Industrial Uses	Industrial Uses	Total Deliveries
2002	2,075	189	1,223	53	529	297	725	1,322	2,406	99	4,076	5,128	9,203
2003	2,108	214	1,130	52	548	303	632	1,279	2,387	99	4,214	4,886	9,100
2004	2,180	242	1,125	76	603	315	697	1,267	2,398	91	4,071	5,252	9,323
2005	2,297	237	1,131	115	587	336	606	1,262	2,401	92	4,026	5,286	9,312
2006	2,231	228	1,069	88	553	335	535	1,204	2,389	107	3,856	5,056	8,912
2007	2,399	312	1,110	74	609	360	569	1,211	2,411	102	3,888	5,460	9,348
2008	2,312	341	1,108	115	612	427	676	1,212	2,317	97	3,835	5,572	9,407
2009	2,286	351	1,085	127	587	427	573	1,241	2,360	84	3,907	5,393	9,300
2010	2,400	422	1,070	124	583	391	609	1,270	2,471	111	4,079	5,587	9,666
2011[1]	2,318	405	1,048	119	619	411	625	1,239	2,503	128	4,075	5,554	9,630

[1] Preliminary. [2] And related products. [3] Chain stores, supermarkets. [4] Jobbers, sugar dealers.
Source: Economic Research Service, U.S. Department of Agriculture (ERS-USDA)

Deliveries[1] of All Sugar by Primary Distributors in the United States, by Quarters   In Thousands of Short Tons

Year	First Quarter	Second Quarter	Third Quarter	Fourth Quarter	Total	Year	First Quarter	Second Quarter	Third Quarter	Fourth Quarter	Total
2000	2,318	2,484	2,611	2,564	9,977	2006	2,436	2,487	2,690	2,389	10,002
2001	2,370	2,486	2,580	2,474	9,911	2007	2,307	2,535	2,682	2,422	9,946
2002	2,227	2,439	2,645	2,497	9,808	2008	2,489	2,676	2,807	2,743	10,715
2003	2,183	2,360	2,464	2,504	9,511	2009	2,387	2,602	2,780	2,715	10,485
2004	2,286	2,368	2,520	2,547	9,722	2010	2,504	2,692	3,005	2,774	10,975
2005	2,335	2,471	2,666	2,571	10,043	2011[2]	2,602	2,739	2,994	2,739	11,074

[1] Includes for domestic consumption and for export. [2] Preliminary. *Source: Economic Research Service, U.S. Department of Agriculture (ERS-USDA)*

SUGAR

Volume of Trading of World Sugar #11 Futures in New York In Contracts

Year	Jan.	Feb.	Mar.	Apr.	May	June	July	Aug.	Sept.	Oct.	Nov.	Dec.	Total
2002	568.8	629.5	417.3	693.6	412.2	610.3	529.5	381.0	756.0	402.8	432.1	340.6	6,174
2003	566.0	797.6	443.8	729.5	489.2	719.8	535.9	545.9	760.2	475.3	403.1	674.4	7,141
2004	513.6	1,018.7	1,181.1	993.7	617.3	1,100.6	614.6	679.5	1,248.7	626.5	539.5	632.7	9,767
2005	981.5	1,279.3	957.1	1,258.6	657.6	1,366.8	779.2	1,198.3	1,803.5	915.8	816.6	992.8	13,007
2006	1,444.2	1,601.2	1,092.2	1,467.4	1,147.7	1,459.1	825.0	1,278.6	1,746.7	1,095.7	918.7	1,024.0	15,101
2007	1,322.9	2,189.7	1,659.6	2,023.2	1,819.5	2,679.8	1,559.7	1,326.6	2,175.7	1,565.3	1,452.1	1,489.7	21,264
2008	3,566.7	3,280.8	2,237.7	2,889.5	1,941.8	3,067.4	1,820.2	1,721.4	2,540.9	1,629.9	1,085.5	1,238.1	27,020
2009	1,624.6	2,040.3	1,867.0	2,995.5	2,229.3	3,359.1	1,741.5	2,833.2	3,219.5	1,824.3	1,576.4	1,989.5	27,300
2010	2,348.9	2,986.5	2,772.9	2,754.5	1,730.0	2,936.0	1,840.3	2,184.6	3,366.7	1,978.1	2,629.3	1,524.7	29,053
2011	2,180.8	3,341.9	1,774.8	2,338.8	1,832.4	3,266.1	1,702.0	1,986.6	2,555.9	1,258.7	1,286.7	1,104.7	24,629

Contract size = 112,000 lbs.   *Source: ICE Futures U.S. (ICE)*

Average Open Interest of World Sugar #11 Futures in New York   In Contracts

Year	Jan.	Feb.	Mar.	Apr.	May	June	July	Aug.	Sept.	Oct.	Nov.	Dec.
2002	184,096	205,138	194,541	187,415	157,738	158,276	149,202	170,667	202,144	207,456	207,598	217,904
2003	244,036	265,758	220,971	192,497	170,867	184,257	180,898	196,857	195,200	185,917	200,605	207,995
2004	246,347	269,863	268,250	275,423	267,362	282,842	300,961	309,436	292,917	322,079	304,462	332,803
2005	375,713	391,006	357,056	352,521	355,922	366,568	404,141	473,757	468,737	464,829	478,097	523,820
2006	526,575	501,074	462,871	474,241	490,201	453,021	457,301	479,420	493,931	447,817	503,364	563,844
2007	632,783	695,426	652,346	686,648	738,708	695,249	674,318	667,523	656,128	681,403	763,910	835,526
2008	1,035,301	1,013,324	973,541	939,615	915,325	885,082	809,433	804,956	774,839	664,164	636,078	644,852
2009	664,303	656,033	644,829	681,177	703,355	764,799	735,556	838,638	821,646	770,085	772,808	813,238
2010	842,463	830,888	745,170	667,291	656,182	635,744	587,509	627,022	651,093	585,353	584,909	592,044
2011	619,904	648,027	597,384	613,301	583,047	627,566	630,027	598,737	651,093	489,135	495,699	533,588

Contract size = 112,000 lbs.   *Source: ICE Futures U.S. (ICE)*

Sulfur

Sulfur (symbol S) is an odorless, tasteless, light yellow, nonmetallic element. As early as 2000 BC, Egyptians used sulfur compounds to bleach fabric. The Chinese used sulfur as an essential component when they developed gunpowder in the 13th century.

Sulfur is widely found in both its free and combined states. Free sulfur is found mixed with gypsum and pumice stone in volcanic regions. Sulfur dioxide is an air pollutant released from the combustion of fossil fuels. The most important use of sulfur is the production of sulfur compounds. Sulfur is used in skin ointments, matches, dyes, gunpowder, and phosphoric acid.

Supply – World production of all forms of sulfur in 2011 rose +1.3% yr/yr to a new record high production of 69.000 million metric tons. The world's largest producers of sulfur are China with 14% of world production, the U.S.

with 13%, Canada with 10%, and Russia with 10%. U.S. production of sulfur in 2011 fell by -3.0% yr/yr to a record low of 8.800 million metric tons.

Demand – U.S. consumption of all forms of sulfur rose by +2.7% in 2011 to 12.600 million metric tons, and that was well above the 4-decade low of 9.520 million metric tons seen in 2009. U.S. consumption of elemental sulfur in 2010 (latest data) rose +14.3% to 10.600 million metric tons. U.S. consumption of sulfuric acid in 2009 (latest data) rose by +0.8% yr/yr to 7.740 million metric tons.

Trade – U.S. exports of recovered sulfur in 2010 (latest data available) fell -15.5% yr/yr to 1.200 million metric tons, but still above the 16-year low of 635,000 metric tons in 2006. U.S. imports of recovered sulfur in 2010 rose by +65.7% yr/yr to 2.800 million metric tons, but still below the 2008 record high of 3.000 million metric tons.

World Production of Sulfur (All Forms)   In Thousands of Metric Tons

Year	Canada	China	France	Germany	Iraq	Japan	Mexico	Poland	Russia	Saudi Arabia	Spain	United States	World Total
2004	9,101	7,150	1,405	2,094	----	3,158	1,825	1,290	6,920	2,249	651	10,100	66,400
2005	8,973	7,710	616	3,877	----	3,256	1,767	1,280	6,950	2,717	613	9,500	67,200
2006	9,082	7,760	650	4,123	----	3,293	1,724	1,310	6,950	2,907	618	9,060	67,000
2007	8,789	8,460	650	4,091	----	3,216	1,576	1,350	7,050	3,089	637	9,100	67,500
2008	8,156	8,610	650	4,167	----	3,334	1,741	1,280	7,170	3,163	637	9,300	68,800
2009	7,467	9,370	650	3,760	----	3,214	1,700	727	7,070	3,214	637	8,940	67,900
2010[1]	7,255	9,600	1,305	3,905	----	3,292	1,810	732	7,070	3,300	637	9,070	68,100
2011[2]	7,100	9,600	1,300	3,700	----	3,100	1,800	1,000	7,100	3,300	640	8,800	69,000

[1] Preliminary.   [2] Estimate.   *Source: U.S. Geological Survey (USGS)*

Salient Statistics of Sulfur in the United States   In Thousands of Metric Tons (Sulfur Content)

	Production of										Sales Value of Shipments		
	Elemental Sulfur					By-product Sulfuric Acid[4]	Other Sulf. Acid Com-pounds	Imports Sulfuric Acid[4]	Exports Sulfuric Acid[4]	Producer Stocks, Dec. 31[5]	Apparent Con-sumption (All Forms)	F.O.B. Mine/Plant		
	Native - Sulfur[3]	Recovered			Total Elemental Sulfur							Frasch	Recovered	Average
Year	Frasch	Petroleum & Cole	Natural Gas	Total										Total
2004	----	7,390	1,990	9,380	739	----	10,100	2,400	204	185	12,800	----	----	32.62
2005	----	6,940	1,850	8,790	711	----	9,500	2,680	338	160	12,400	----	----	30.88
2006	----	6,960	1,440	8,390	674	----	9,060	2,430	248	221	12,000	----	----	32.85
2007	----	7,000	1,280	8,280	817	----	9,100	2,600	336	187	11,900	----	----	36.49
2008	----	7,380	1,320	8,550	753	----	9,300	3,440	261	211	12,900	----	----	264.04
2009	----	7,840	1,220	8,190	749	----	8,940	1,270	254	232	9,520	----	----	1.73
2010[1]	----			8,280	791	----	9,070	1,500	188	164	11,300		----	70.48
2011[2]	----			8,100	710	----	8,800			165	11,600			200.00

Sulfur Consumption & Foreign Trade of the United States   In Thousands of Metric Tons (Sulfur Content)

	Consumption			Sulfuric Acid Sold or Used, by End Use[2]						Foreign Trade				
										Exports			Imports	
	Native Sulfur	Rec-overed	Total Elemental	Pulpmills & Paper	Inorganic Chem-icals[3]	Synthetic Rubber & Plastic	Phosph-atic Fertilizers	Petro-leum Refining[4]			Re-covered	Value $1,000	Re-covered	Value $1,000
Year	(Frasch)	Sulfur	Form	Products					Frasch	Frasch			Frasch	
2003	W	10,900	10,900	10,100	225	71	82	6,660	140	----	840	54,400	----	2,870	70,600
2004	W	11,300	11,300	9,290	272	154	70	6,870	248	----	949	63,300	----	2,850	76,800
2005	W	10,900	10,900	9,680	267	312	64	7,000	188	----	684	55,200	----	2,820	70,500
2006	W	10,600	10,600	8,750	246	426	250	6,220	262	----	635	43,800	----	2,950	70,400
2007	W	10,300	10,300	8,330	245	245	117	6,280	264	----	922	84,800	----	2,930	79,400
2008	W	10,700	10,700	7,680	187	293	69	5,690	244	----	952	272,000	----	3,000	753,000
2009	W	9,270	9,270							----	1,420		----	1,690	
2010[1]	W	10,600	10,600							----	1,200		----	2,800	

[1] Preliminary.   [2] Sulfur equivalent.   [3] Including inorganic pigments, paints & allied products, and other inorganic chemicals & products.
[4] Including other petroleum and coal products.   W = Withheld proprietary data.   NA = Not available.   *Source: U.S. Geological Survey (USGS)*

Sunflowerseed, Meal and Oil

Sunflowers are native to South and North America, but are now grown almost worldwide. Sunflower-seed oil accounts for approximately 14% of the world production of seed oils. Sunflower varieties that are commercially grown contain from 39% to 49% oil in the seed. Sunflower crops produce about 50 bushels of seed per acre on average, which yields approximately 50 gallons of oil.

Sunflower-seed oil accounts for around 80% of the value of the sunflower crop. Refined sunflower-seed oil is edible and used primarily as a salad and cooking oil and in margarine. Crude sunflower-seed oil is used industrially for making soaps, candles, varnishes, and detergents. Sunflower-seed oil contains 93% of the energy of U.S. No. 2 diesel fuel and is being explored as a potential alternate fuel source in diesel engines. Sunflower meal is used in livestock feed and when fed to poultry, increases the yield of eggs. Sunflower seeds are also used for birdfeed and as a snack for humans.

Prices – The average monthly price received by U.S. farmers for sunflower seeds in the first five months of the 2011-12 marketing year (Sep/Aug) rose +18.4% to $30.14 per hundred pounds, a new record high.

Supply – World sunflower-seed production in the 2010-11 rose +0.6% yr/yr to 33.011 million metric tons. The world's largest sunflower-seed producers are Russia with 43.7% of world production, Argentina with 10.3%, China with 5.2%, France with 5.0%, and Romania with 4.0%, and Bulgaria and the U.S. with about 3.9%.

U.S. production of sunflower seeds in 2011-12 fell by -25.5% yr/yr to 925,000 metric tons, far below the record production level of 3.309 million metric tons posted in 1979-80. U.S. farmers harvested 1.458 million acres of sunflowers in 2011-12, down -22.2% yr/yr, well below the 9-year high of 2.610 million acres posted in 2005-06. U.S sunflower yield in 2011-12 was 13.98 hundred pounds per acre, below 2009-10 record high of 15.54 hundred pounds per acre.

Demand – Total U.S. disappearance of sunflower seeds in 2011-12 fell -25.2% yr/yr to 1.004 million metric tons, of which 36.2% went to crushing for oil and meal, 49.1% went to non-oil and seed use, and 14.7% went to exports.

Trade – World sunflower-seed exports in 2010-11 rose +8.8% yr/yr to 1.725 million metric tons. The world's largest exporters are Russia which accounted for 33.8% of world exports in 2010-11 and the U.S. which accounted for 8.1% of world exports. World sunflower-seed imports in 2010-11 rose +2.6% yr/yr to 1.700 million metric tons. The world's largest importers are Turkey which accounted for 38.8% of world exports and France with 4.7% of world imports.

World Production of Sunflowerseed   In Thousands of Metric Tons

Crop Year	Argentina	Bulgaria	China	France	Hungary	India	Romania	Africa	Spain	Turkey	States	USSR	Total
2001-02	3,730	405	1,478	1,584	632	726	824	929	871	530	1,551	5,468	21,302
2002-03	3,350	645	1,946	1,497	777	1,060	1,003	643	757	830	1,112	7,836	23,985
2003-04	2,990	789	1,743	1,530	992	1,160	1,506	648	763	560	1,209	10,179	26,984
2004-05	3,730	1,030	1,700	1,462	1,186	1,350	1,220	620	785	640	930	8,830	26,461
2005-06	3,840	830	1,928	1,510	1,108	1,490	1,180	520	381	780	1,720	12,132	30,572
2006-07	3,190	1,060	1,803	1,440	1,100	1,450	1,390	300	607	820	997	12,697	30,389
2007-08	4,620	635	1,670	1,311	950	1,460	700	872	733	670	1,309	10,889	29,322
2008-09	3,200	1,036	1,750	1,598	1,550	1,150	1,170	801	873	850	1,553	15,087	34,713
2009-10[1]	2,650	1,257	1,650	1,720	1,370	1,000	1,102	490	861	790	1,377	14,717	32,824
2010-11[2]	3,400	1,341	1,710	1,633	1,100	650	1,300	809	889	990	1,241	14,416	33,011

[1] Preliminary.   [2] Forecast.   Source: Economic Research Service, U.S. Department of Agriculture (ERS-USDA)

World Imports and Exports of Sunflowerseed   In Thousands of Metric Tons

Crop Year	France	Germany	Nether-lands	Spain	Turkey	World Total	Argen-tina	France	Hungary	Former USSR	United States	Uraquay	World Total
	------- Imports -------						------- Exports -------						
2001-02	43	58	180	172	164	1,202	342	24	14	186	176	130	1,184
2002-03	62	65	148	151	287	1,462	232	3	19	577	123	223	1,586
2003-04	202	60	167	218	630	2,287	45	25	14	1,374	138	127	2,307
2004-05	5	71	24	188	518	1,302	99	20	52	131	117	134	1,187
2005-06	28	63	90	235	391	1,517	45	9	31	664	156	59	1,548
2006-07	49	73	64	233	495	1,954	63	5	42	606	156	13	1,922
2007-08	9	74	55	64	529	1,336	41	5	51	130	168	38	1,333
2008-09	180	82	77	107	477	2,178	64	5	32	1,071	159	----	2,250
2009-10[1]	13	43	44	45	704	1,657	67	6	21	490	160	14	1,585
2010-11[2]	80	43	40	53	660	1,700	100	9	14	584	140	4	1,725

[1] Preliminary.   [2] Forecast.   Source: Economic Research Service, U.S. Department of Agriculture (ERS-USDA)

Sunflowerseed Statistics in the United States   In Thousands of Metric Tons

Crop Year Beginning Sept. 1	Acres Harvested (1,000)	Harvested Yield Per CWT	Farm Price ($/Metric Ton)	Value of Pro- duction (Million $)	Stocks, Sept. 1	Production	Imports	Total Supply	Crush	Exports	Non-Oil Use & Seed	Total Disap- pearance
2004-05	1,711	11.98	302	272.7	163	930	44	1,137	276	141	630	1,047
2005-06	2,610	15.40	267	487.7	90	1,822	39	1,951	566	178	851	1,595
2006-07	1,770	12.11	320	308.8	356	972	112	1,440	659	182	462	1,303
2007-08	2,012	14.26	478	614.7	137	1,301	87	1,525	683	200	522	1,405
2008-09	2,396	14.29	481	704.1	120	1,553	70	1,743	661	184	675	1,520
2009-10	1,954	15.54	333	459.0	223	1,377	46	1,646	776	179	514	1,469
2010-11[1]	1,874	14.60	514	633.8	177	1,241	41	1,459	588	162	592	1,342
2011-12[2]	1,458	13.98	648	603.6	117	925	50	1,092	363	148	493	1,004

[1] Preliminary.   [2] Forecast.   *Source: Economic Research Service, U.S. Department of Agriculture (ERS-USDA)*

World Production of Sunflowerseed Oil and Meal   In Thousands of Metric Tons

Year	Sunflowerseed Oil Argentina	France	Spain	Turkey	Ex- USSR	World Total	Sunflowerseed Meal Argentina	France	Spain	Turkey	United States	Ex- USSR	World Total
2003-04	1,204	565	459	486	3,394	9,551	1,184	734	534	616	305	3,385	10,982
2004-05	1,507	416	457	451	3,292	9,441	1,509	508	531	572	138	3,432	10,850
2005-06	1,631	400	421	464	4,634	11,050	1,653	494	490	589	288	4,536	12,318
2006-07	1,315	453	411	496	5,004	11,309	1,407	556	478	629	311	4,993	12,767
2007-08	1,575	443	357	459	4,108	10,165	1,609	484	415	604	329	4,242	11,558
2008-09	1,484	573	444	490	5,795	12,830	1,531	651	516	621	355	5,740	14,280
2009-10[1]	1,156	572	438	595	5,997	12,501	1,209	668	509	757	398	5,985	13,947
2010-11[2]	1,312	594	444	626	5,573	12,107	1,356	734	516	802	344	5,614	13,599

[1] Preliminary.   [2] Forecast.   *Source: Economic Research Service, U.S. Department of Agriculture (ERS-USDA)*

Sunflower Oil Statistics in the United States   In Thousands of Metric Tons

Crop Year Beginning Sept. 1	Stocks, Oct. 1	Production	Imports	Total Supply	Exports	Domestic Use	Total Disap- pearance	Price $ Per Metric Ton (Crude Mpls.)
2004-05	18	116	34	168	57	101	158	938
2005-06	10	238	26	274	95	154	249	893
2006-07	25	277	71	373	77	269	346	1,242
2007-08	27	287	47	361	77	272	349	1,978
2008-09	12	296	30	338	91	197	288	1,170
2009-10	50	331	22	403	98	267	365	1,163
2010-11[1]	38	224	47	309	38	243	281	
2011-12[2]	28	152	45	225	23	179	202	

[1] Preliminary.   [2] Forecast.   *Source: Economic Research Service, U.S. Department of Agriculture (ERS-USDA)*

Sunflower Meal Statistics in the United States   In Thousands of Metric Tons

Crop Year Beginning Sept. 1	Stocks, Oct. 1	Production	Imports	Total Supply	Exports	Domestic Use	Total Disap- pearance	Price USD Per Metric Ton 28% Protein
2004-05	5	133		138	3	130	138	91
2005-06	5	272	5	282	6	271	282	88
2006-07	5	316	20	341	13	323	341	114
2007-08	5	328		333	17	311	333	183
2008-09	5	335		340	7	328	340	172
2009-10	5	374		379	6	368	379	164
2010-11[1]	5	253		258	3	250	258	233
2011-12[2]	5	172		177	5	167	177	258

[1] Preliminary.   [2] Forecast.   *Source: Economic Research Service, U.S. Department of Agriculture (ERS-USDA)*

Average Price Received by Farmers for Sunflower[2] in the United States   In Dollars Per Hundred Pounds (Cwt.)

Year	Jan.	Feb.	Mar.	Apr.	May	June	July	Aug.	Sept.	Oct.	Nov.	Dec.	Average
2006-07	11.70	12.10	12.50	13.60	13.80	14.90	15.60	15.90	16.60	17.00	18.20	18.40	15.03
2007-08	17.70	17.80	18.30	19.20	19.10	24.20	25.90	24.50	27.40	28.10	28.40	26.40	23.08
2008-09	28.20	25.30	23.10	22.80	22.10	22.60	22.10	20.20	21.50	18.40	17.70	20.60	22.05
2009-10	13.90	16.20	14.20	14.80	15.50	16.70	15.80	15.80	14.90	15.10	15.40	14.50	15.23
2010-11	17.30	20.80	18.70	20.60	21.90	27.40	28.60	28.90	29.70	29.10	30.30	32.20	25.46
2011-12[1]	32.90	29.60	29.00	29.60	28.70	27.80							29.60

[1] Preliminary.   [2] KS, MN, ND and SD average.   *Source: Economic Research Service, U.S. Department of Agriculture (ERS-USDA)*

Tall Oil

Tall oil is a product of the paper and pulping industry. Crude tall oil is the major byproduct of the kraft or sulfate processing of pinewood. Crude tall oil starts as tall oil soap which is separated from recovered black liquor in the kraft pulping process. The tall oil soap is acidified to yield crude tall oil. The resulting tall oil is then fractionated to produce fatty acids, rosin, and pitch. Crude tall oil contains 40-50 percent fatty acids such as oleic and linoleic acids; 5-10 percent sterols, alcohols, and other neutral components. The demand is for the tall oil rosin and fatty acids which are used to produce adhesives, coatings, and ink resins. The products find use in lubricants, soaps, linoleum, flotation and waterproofing agents, paints, varnishes, and drying oils.

Since tall oil and its production are derived from the paper and pulping industry, the amount of tall oil produced is related in part to the pulp industry and in part to the U.S. economy.

Consumption of Tall Oil in Inedible Products in the United States   In Millions of Pounds

Year	Jan.	Feb.	Mar.	Apr.	May	June	July	Aug.	Sept.	Oct.	Nov.	Dec.	Total
2003	136.1	119.9	136.9	126.3	121.7	121.9	119.3	111.6	131.4	124.1	104.9	120.1	1,474
2004	126.8	109.4	136.1	123.7	135.7	160.5	166.9	140.8	125.3	124.6	129.4	110.7	1,590
2005	134.9	115.4	124.5	97.3	144.4	128.3	125.0	127.5	115.6	137.0	120.3	118.2	1,488
2006	120.4	112.1	135.8	120.2	153.2	131.0	140.6	144.3	134.3	129.6	134.8	133.2	1,590
2007	130.9	126.6	117.7	127.0	130.7	128.7	131.2	129.9	128.5	131.1	128.6	123.8	1,535
2008	135.8	131.8	127.4	130.8	144.0	145.9	144.5	151.0	141.2	148.5	127.6	103.7	1,632
2009	117.1	102.4	103.6	96.2	110.3	110.0	115.0	129.3	115.9	125.8	123.5	107.0	1,356
2010	110.1	127.9	135.3	135.6	146.1	121.2	147.0	142.0	136.4	135.9	131.0	119.2	1,588
2011[1]	139.3	92.1	129.0	136.4	132.3	130.8	137.8	NA	NA	NA	NA	NA	1,539

[1] Preliminary.   *Source: Bureau of the Census, U.S. Department of Commerce*

Production of Crude Tall Oil in the United States   In Millions of Pounds

Year	Oct.	Nov.	Dec.	Jan.	Feb.	Mar.	Apr.	May	June	July	Aug.	Sept.	Total
2002-03	102.5	87.3	101.8	108.7	89.8	111.5	108.3	99.6	91.8	109.2	100.8	97.1	1,208.6
2003-04	102.1	87.9	109.0	113.7	96.1	112.1	102.8	106.8	99.2	94.4	108.9	104.1	1,236.9
2004-05	88.1	93.7	99.6	110.0	97.9	109.4	107.3	109.8	101.5	101.0	101.0	98.9	1,218.1
2005-06	95.5	92.1	100.3	103.9	103.4	108.1	110.4	117.6	101.4	104.6	109.7	99.7	1,246.8
2006-07	104.8	103.7	108.5	107.5	105.0	104.5	121.5	125.5	98.1	108.5	122.2	107.9	1,317.7
2007-08	100.0	99.7	107.2	113.6	112.1	115.9	117.2	112.9	103.2	102.8	107.4	105.0	1,297.0
2008-09	107.6	100.7	87.0	90.3	93.0	107.2	105.9	104.7	103.1	94.0	106.6	102.2	1,202.2
2009-10	105.8	102.0	102.8	106.0	104.2	115.8	117.2	119.7	120.2	113.2	106.2	111.5	1,324.6
2010-11[1]	113.3	109.8	104.5	113.8	105.9	110.2	108.6	119.5	107.8	114.6	NA	NA	1,329.5

[1] Preliminary.   *Source: Bureau of the Census, U.S. Department of Commerce*

Stocks of Crude Tall Oil in the United States, on First of Month   In Millions of Pounds

Year	Oct.	Nov.	Dec.	Jan.	Feb.	Mar.	Apr.	May	June	July	Aug.	Sept.
2002-03	160.2	154.1	155.7	160.5	176.0	167.4	156.3	173.4	163.7	180.3	199.3	209.5
2003-04	210.7	207.3	203.0	210.2	209.6	216.3	205.3	207.1	194.1	190.5	196.1	162.2
2004-05	174.1	140.3	124.4	95.0	109.9	108.8	134.0	132.1	130.5	126.3	122.0	121.8
2005-06	107.5	97.3	83.4	81.5	102.8	118.7	82.6	88.3	94.7	93.9	82.0	92.7
2006-07	73.9	61.7	72.1	75.7	97.8	83.4	115.7	132.5	156.1	162.5	164.3	198.4
2007-08	186.8	185.6	168.5	177.0	176.3	162.9	156.3	187.7	182.2	145.1	137.8	138.6
2008-09	135.7	110.8	95.7	110.8	102.2	112.5	116.2	135.3	134.3	138.3	126.2	108.8
2009-10	98.3	85.9	104.2	87.2	108.9	84.9	126.8	103.0	113.6	111.6	112.0	101.6
2010-11[1]	113.0	111.3	89.0	86.5	87.7	93.4	101.9	107.6	105.2	109.8	103.5	NA

[1] Preliminary.   *Source: Bureau of the Census, U.S. Department of Commerce*

Stocks of Refined Tall Oil in the United States, on First of Month   In Millions of Pounds

Year	Oct.	Nov.	Dec.	Jan.	Feb.	Mar.	Apr.	May	June	July	Aug.	Sept.
2002-03	13.3	16.5	18.7	20.1	20.1	18.6	20.4	19.7	15.8	14.5	13.5	13.9
2003-04	13.1	20.1	19.6	19.9	19.2	13.7	14.3	12.7	16.3	14.2	16.6	17.7
2004-05	14.8	16.6	16.9	17.0	15.2	20.4	16.0	18.2	16.9	17.2	14.5	17.5
2005-06	18.7	28.1	26.9	32.9	28.5	W	6.1	5.3	6.6	4.5	5.9	6.9
2006-07	7.7	7.5	5.3	5.3	5.8	7.3	7.5	7.3	7.9	9.2	6.6	4.2
2007-08	5.9	6.7	5.2	6.4	6.0	7.5	6.8	7.3	6.5	5.4	5.3	8.2
2008-09	6.6	5.0	6.6	5.2	5.3	4.1	5.0	4.3	3.8	6.0	4.1	5.6
2009-10	5.2	7.4	7.4	6.9	5.2	6.0	5.3	5.5	5.9	4.7	4.4	6.1
2010-11[1]	6.4	5.5	3.5	5.3	5.5	5.0	3.4	5.3	5.5	16.5	7.3	NA

[1] Preliminary.   W = Withheld proprietary data.   *Source: Bureau of the Census, U.S. Department of Commerce*

Tallow and Greases

Tallow and grease are derived from processing (rendering) the fat of cattle. Tallow is used to produce both edible and inedible products. Edible tallow products include margarine, cooking oil, and baking products. Inedible tallow products include soap, candles, and lubricants. Production of tallow and greases is directly related to the number of cattle produced. Those countries that are the leading cattle producers are also the largest producers of tallow. The American Fats and Oils Association provides specifications for a variety of different types of tallow and grease, including edible tallow, lard (edible), top white tallow, all beef packer tallow, extra fancy tallow, fancy tallow, bleachable fancy tallow, prime tallow, choice white grease, and yellow grease. The specifications include such characteristics as the melting point, color, density, moisture content, insoluble impurities, and others.

Prices – The monthly average price of tallow (inedible, No. 1 Packers-Prime, delivered Chicago) in 2011 rose +48.8% yr/yr to 49.61 cents per pound, a new record high. The wholesale price of inedible tallow in 2011 rose +27.3% yr/yr to 35.05 cents per pound, below the 2008 record high of 38.02 cents per pound.

Supply – World production of tallow and greases (edible and inedible) in 2010 (latest data), rose by +1.2% yr/yr to 8.464 million metric tons, below the 2007 record high of 8.530 million metric tons. The world's largest producer of tallow and greases by far is the U.S. with 43.6% of world production, followed by Brazil with 7.0%, Australia with 5.8%, and Canada with 3.1%.

U.S. production of edible tallow in 2010 fell –0.8% yr/yr to 1.823 billion pounds, down from the 2002 record high of 1.974. U.S. production of inedible tallow and greases in 2010 rose +0.2% yr/yr to 5.887 billion pounds, well below the record high of 7.156 billion pounds posted in 2002.

Demand – U.S. consumption of inedible tallow and greases in 2010 fell 11.1% yr/yr to 1.573 billion pounds, of which virtually all went for animal feed. U.S. consumption of edible tallow in 2010 fell -2.9% yr/yr to 1.661 billion pounds, down from last year's record high of 1.710 billion pounds. U.S. per capita consumption of edible tallow in 2010 rose from 0.7 pounds per person to 3.3 pounds per person yr/yr, down from the 2000 and 2004 record high of 4.0 pounds.

Trade – U.S. exports of inedible tallow and grease in 2010 rose +7.0 yr/yr to 352.735 million pounds, and accounted for 5.7% of total U.S. supply. U.S. exports of edible tallow in 2010 rose +18.7% yr/yr to 192 million pounds, and accounted for 10.3% of U.S. supply.

World Production of Tallow and Greases (Edible and Inedible)   In Thousands of Metric Tons

Year	Argentina	Australia	Brazil	Canada	France	Germany	Korea	Nether-lands	New Zealand	Russia	United Kingdom	United States	World Total
2001	142	507	446	296	140	126	15	151	173	171	115	3,503	7,689
2002	147	469	474	305	154	124	14	125	162	178	123	3,826	8,062
2003	154	456	493	289	164	121	15	121	174	183	120	3,707	8,015
2004	178	486	528	343	166	124	15	113	192	181	124	3,714	8,247
2005	184	493	554	339	171	121	15	106	168	175	128	3,797	8,389
2006	181	503	574	285	195	124	16	107	187	179	135	3,808	8,474
2007	195	501	589	276	192	128	16	116	184	184	140	3,818	8,530
2008	189	499	573	261	193	131	16	122	189	187	138	3,695	8,403
2009[1]	204	483	587	252	187	131	16	123	182	189	134	3,655	8,364
2010[2]	160	488	592	262	196	134	16	131	182	191	141	3,688	8,465

[1] Preliminary.   [2] Forecast.   *Source: Foreign Agricultural Service, U.S. Department of Agriculture (FAS-USDA)*

Salient Statistics of Tallow and Greases (Inedible) in the United States   In Millions of Pounds

	Supply				Consumption			Wholesale Prices, Cents Per Lb.	
Year	Production	Stocks, Jan. 1	Total	Exports	Soap	Feed	Total	Edible, (Loose) Chicago	Inedible, Chicago No. 1
2002	7,156	327	7,482	384	W	2,886	2,886	14.8	13.5
2003	6,246	240	6,486	307	W	2,434	2,434	20.3	18.3
2004	6,173	282	6,455	336	W	2,536	2,536	19.8	18.0
2005	6,204	281	6,485	276	W	2,456	2,456	19.0	17.5
2006	6,460	309	6,769	331	W	2,585	2,585	18.6	16.9
2007	6,369	291	6,661	361	W	2,385	2,385	30.7	27.8
2008	6,224	350	6,573	319	W	2,095	2,095	38.0	34.2
2009	5,878	315	6,193	330	W	1,770	1,770	27.5	25.2
2010[1]	5,887	286	6,174	353	W	1,574	1,574	35.1	33.3
2011[2]	3,654	281	3,934	342	W	1,560	1,560	53.2	49.6

[1] Preliminary.   [2] Forecast.   *Source: Foreign Agricultural Service, U.S. Department of Agriculture (FAS-USDA)*

TALLOW AND GREASES

Tallow (monthly average) through December 2011 — Cents per pound

Supply and Disappearance of Edible Tallow in the United States — In Millions of Pounds, Rendered Basis

	-------------------- Supply --------------------			-- Disappearance --					
Year	Stocks, Jan. 1	Production	Total Supply	Domestic Disap- pearance	Exports	Total Disap- pearance	Direct Use	Baking or Frying Fats	Per Capita (Lbs.)
2001	37	1,792	1,859	1,455	364	1,819	869	W	3.0
2002	40	1,974	2,023	1,486	511	1,998	974	W	3.4
2003	25	1,966	1,996	1,552	420	1,972	1,108	W	3.8
2004	24	1,818	1,842	1,565	255	1,820	1,163	W	4.0
2005	22	1,813	1,836	1,518	293	1,811	1,116	W	3.8
2006	25	1,861	1,893	1,583	275	1,858	1,160	W	3.9
2007	35	1,789	1,831	1,404	388	1,792	889	W	2.9
2008	39	1,794	1,863	1,648	185	1,833	896	W	2.9
2009[1]	30	1,837	1,903	1,710	162	1,872	212	W	0.7
2010[2]	31	1,823	1,877	1,661	192	1,853	1,023	W	3.3

[1] Preliminary.   [2] Forecast.   W = Withheld.   *Sources: Economic Research Service, U.S. Department of Agriculture (ERS-USDA); Bureau of the Census, U.S. Department of Commerce*

Average Wholesale Price of Tallow, Inedible, No. 1 Packers (Prime), Delivered, Chicago — In Cents Per Pound

Year	Jan.	Feb.	Mar.	Apr.	May	June	July	Aug.	Sept.	Oct.	Nov.	Dec.	Average
2002	10.00	10.54	12.64	11.06	11.59	15.47	14.80	14.00	14.23	13.98	15.91	18.08	13.53
2003	17.13	15.65	16.60	16.54	16.48	17.30	16.08	15.85	18.70	22.78	23.37	23.08	18.30
2004	23.23	16.72	17.80	21.05	18.01	18.08	19.55	16.92	17.20	14.33	15.61	16.97	17.96
2005	16.20	16.03	18.73	20.95	19.38	18.23	15.11	15.31	17.54	17.40	17.96	16.67	17.46
2006	17.52	17.05	14.98	13.47	14.77	15.27	17.05	17.35	15.59	17.71	20.42	21.46	16.89
2007	22.02	20.78	21.74	25.04	29.16	33.08	32.58	27.67	30.14	31.29	32.87	27.64	27.83
2008	32.19	36.08	40.03	39.66	40.02	45.36	47.55	40.14	36.17	24.39	14.29	14.23	34.18
2009	22.86	19.57	16.72	21.83	25.80	29.53	26.17	31.75	30.44	22.27	25.89	29.09	25.16
2010	28.37	27.42	31.57	32.74	33.08	32.73	32.15	32.28	32.93	33.88	40.52	42.50	33.35
2011[1]	47.83	47.61	49.49	51.59	52.33	54.52	53.69	49.36	50.02	47.36	44.35	47.21	49.61

[1] Preliminary.   *Sources: Economic Research Service, U.S. Department of Agriculture (ERS-USDA)*

Tea

Tea is the common name for a family of mostly woody flowering plants. The tea family contains about 600 species placed in 28 genera and they are distributed throughout the tropical and subtropical areas, with most species occurring in eastern Asia and South America. The tea plant is native to Southeast Asia. There are more than 3,000 varieties of tea, each with its own distinct character, and each is generally named for the area in which it is grown. Tea may have been consumed in China as long ago as 2700 BC and certainly since 1000 BC. In 2737 BC, the Chinese Emperor Shen Nung, according to Chinese mythology, was a scholar and herbalist. While his servant boiled drinking water, a leaf from the wild tea tree he was sitting under dropped into the water and Shen Nung decided to try the brew. Today, half the world's population drinks tea. Tea is the world's most popular beverage next to water.

Tea is a healthful drink and contains antioxidants, fluoride, niacin, folic acid, and as much vitamin C as a lemon. The average 5 oz. cup of brewed tea contains approximately 40 to 60 milligrams of caffeine (compared to 80 to 115 mg in brewed coffee). Decaffeinated tea has been available since the 1980s. Herbal tea contains no true tea leaves but is actually brewed from a collection of herbs and spices.

Tea grows mainly between the tropic of Cancer and the tropic of Capricorn, requiring 40 to 50 inches of rain per year and a temperature ideally between 50 to 86 degrees Fahrenheit. In order to rejuvenate the bush and keep it at a convenient height for the pickers to access, the bushes must be pruned every four to five years. A tea bush can produce tea for 50 to 70 years, but after 50 years, the yield is reduced.

The two key factors in determining different varieties of tea are the production process (sorting, withering, rolling, fermentation, and drying methods) and the growing conditions (geographical region, growing altitude, and soil type). Black tea, often referred to as fully fermented tea, is produced by allowing picked tea leaves to wither and ferment for up to 24 hours. After fermenting, the leaves are fired, which stops oxidation. Green tea, or unfermented tea, is produced by immediately and completely drying the leaves and omitting the oxidization process, thus allowing the tea to remain green in color.

Supply – World production of tea in 2010 rose +6.5% to 4.518 million metric tons, a new record high. The world's largest producers of tea in 2010 were China (with 32.5% of world production), India (21.9%), Kenya (8.8%), Sri Lanka (6.3%), Turkey (5.2%), and Iran (3.7%).

Trade – U.S. tea imports in 2011 (annualized through May) fell -0.4% to 211,560 metric tons, down from last year's record high of 212,328 metric tons. World tea imports in 2009 (latest data) fell -7.0% to 1.568 million metric tons. The world's largest tea importers were Russia (with 11.6% of total world imports), the United Kingdom (9.3%), Pakistan (6.2%), and the U.S. (7.1%). World exports of tea in 2009 (latest data) fell -6.4% to 1.774 million metric tons. The world's largest exporters were Kenya (with 18.7% of world exports), China (17.2%), Sri Lanka (16.3%), India (11.5%), Indonesia (5.2%), Vietnam (4.6%), and Argentina (4.0%).

World Tea Production, in Major Producing Countries In Metric Tons

Year	Argentina	Bang-ladesh	China	India	Indo-nesia	Iran	Japan	Kenya	Malawi	Sri Lanka	Turkey	Ex-USSR[2]	World Total
2004	70,389	57,580	855,422	879,000	171,200	40,250	100,700	324,600	50,090	308,090	201,663	22,288	3,450,569
2005	67,871	57,580	953,660	907,000	177,700	59,180	100,000	328,500	38,000	317,200	217,540	24,752	3,660,637
2006	72,129	58,000	1,047,345	949,000	146,858	46,500	91,800	310,580	45,009	310,800	201,866	8,405	3,703,751
2007	76,000	58,500	1,183,002	973,000	150,224	49,680	94,100	369,600	48,140	305,220	206,160	8,614	3,974,514
2008	80,142	59,000	1,274,984	987,000	150,851	165,717	96,500	345,800	41,639	318,700	198,046	6,543	4,211,397
2009	71,715	59,500	1,375,780	972,700	146,440	165,717	86,000	314,100	52,559	290,000	198,601	6,877	4,242,280
2010[1]	88,574	60,000	1,467,467	991,180	150,000	165,717	85,000	399,000	66,600	282,300	235,000	4,415	4,518,060

[1] Preliminary.   [2] Mostly Georgia and Azerbaijan.   Sources: Foreign Agricultural Service, U.S. Department of Agriculture (FAS-USDA); Food and Agriculture Organization of the United Nations (FAO-UN)

World Exports of Tea from Producing Countries   In Metric Tons

Year	Argentina	Bang-ladesh	Brazil	China	India	Indonesia	Kenya	Malawi	Papua New Guinea	Sri Lanka	Vietnam	Zim-babwe	Total
2003	59,062	7,348	4,209	262,663	174,246	88,176	293,751	36,924	6,600	297,003	58,600	13,355	1,529,666
2004	67,819	10,635	3,593	282,643	174,728	98,572	284,309	46,200	8,100	298,909	104,000	14,968	1,634,553
2005	68,270	12,560	3,407	288,814	159,121	102,294	347,971	44,600	6,900	307,793	88,000	4,825	1,718,526
2006	72,056	7,842	3,238	288,625	181,326	95,339	325,066	27,503	6,600	204,240	105,000	11,532	1,629,242
2007	75,767	5,269	3,298	292,199	193,459	83,659	374,329	54,397	6,400	190,203	114,000	6,840	1,711,388
2008[1]	77,498	8,259	3,034	299,789	203,207	96,210	396,641	30,435	5,937	318,329	104,700	5,979	1,895,979
2009[2]	69,816	5,339	2,326	305,352	203,863	92,304	331,594	47,356	6,250	288,528	82,416	7,874	1,774,815

[1] Preliminary.   [2] Estimate.   Source: Food and Agriculture Organization of the United Nations (FAO-UN)

Imports of Tea in the United States   In Metric Tons

Year	Jan.	Feb.	Mar.	Apr.	May	June	July	Aug.	Sept.	Oct.	Nov.	Dec.	Total
2006	15,278	14,469	17,148	18,533	21,840	20,057	15,683	16,378	14,650	11,836	15,432	12,547	193,851
2007	14,094	12,830	17,312	19,165	18,957	20,707	16,623	15,829	16,136	14,475	14,636	13,969	194,734
2008	15,685	17,751	19,648	21,127	19,540	18,409	17,657	16,418	17,221	16,783	14,357	13,363	207,957
2009	15,525	14,737	19,304	18,124	19,177	18,666	17,092	18,666	17,551	13,217	13,429	12,201	197,689
2010	14,752	15,682	18,907	20,421	20,967	19,845	19,856	19,150	18,747	15,722	14,464	13,815	212,329
2011[1]	13,933	15,361	18,571	18,087	21,777	19,848	19,085	19,260	21,599	13,868	15,152	15,021	211,560

[1] Preliminary.   Source: Foreign Agricultural Service, U.S. Department of Agriculture (FAS-USDA)

Tin

Tin (symbol Sn) is a silvery-white, lustrous gray metallic element. Tin is soft, pliable and has a highly crystalline structure. When a tin bar is bent or broken, a crackling sound called a "tin cry" is produced due to the breaking of the tin crystals. People have been using tin for at least 5,500 years. Tin has been found in the tombs of ancient Egyptians. In ancient times, tin and lead were considered different forms of the same metal. Tin was exported to Europe in large quantities from Cornwall, England, during the Roman period, from approximately 2100 BC to 1500 BC. Cornwall was one of the world's leading sources of tin for much of its known history and into the late 1800s.

The principal ore of tin is the mineral cassiterite, which is found in Malaya, Bolivia, Indonesia, Thailand, and Nigeria. About 80% of the world's tin deposits occur in unconsolidated placer deposits in riverbeds and valleys, or on the sea floor, with only about 20% occurring as primary hard-rock lodes. Tin deposits are generally small and are almost always found closely allied to the granite from which it originates. Tin is also recovered as a by-product of mining tungsten, tantalum, and lead. After extraction, tin ore is ground and washed to remove impurities, roasted to oxidize the sulfides of iron and copper, washed a second time, and then reduced by carbon in a reverberatory furnace. Electrolysis may also be used to purify tin.

Pure tin, rarely used by itself, was used as currency in the form of tin blocks and was considered legal tender for taxes in Phuket, Thailand, until 1932. Tin is used in the manufacture of coatings for steel containers used to preserve food and beverages. Tin is also used in solder alloys, electroplating, ceramics, and in plastic. The world's major tin research and development laboratory, ITRI Ltd, is funded by companies that produce and consume tin. The focus of the research efforts have been on possible new uses for tin that would take advantage of tin's relative non-toxicity to replace other metals in various products. Some of the replacements could be lead-free solders, antimony-free flame-retardant chemicals, and lead-free shotgun pellets. No tin is currently mined in the U.S.

Tin futures and options trade on the London Metal Exchange (LME). Tin has traded on the LME since 1877 and the standard tin contract began in 1912. The futures contract calls for the delivery of 5 metric tons of tin ingots of at least 99.85% purity. The contract trades in terms of U.S. dollars per metric ton.

Prices – The average monthly price of tin (straights) in New York in 2011 rose by +26.9% yr/yr to $15.87 per pound, which is a new record high. The 2011 price is more than five times the 3-decade low of $2.83 per pound seen as recently as 2002. The average monthly price of ex-dock tin in New York in 2011 rose +27.8% yr/yr to $12.15 per pound.

Supply – World mine production of tin in 2011 fell by -2.5% yr/yr to 270,000 metric tons, remaining below the 2007 record high of 301,000 metric tons. The world's largest mine producers of tin are China with 41% of world production in 2011, Indonesia with 19%, and Peru with 13%. World smelter production of tin in 2009 (latest data available) rose +6.6% yr/yr to 325,000 metric tons, down from the 2007 record high of 327,000 metric tons. The world's largest producers of smelted tin are China with 42% of world production in 2009, Indonesia with 17%, and Malaysia with 11%.

The U.S. does not mine tin, and therefore its supply consists only of scrap and imports. U.S. tin recovery in 2010 (latest data) rose +6.5% to 6,600, up from the 2009 record low of 6,200 metric tons.

Demand – U.S. consumption of tin (pig) in 2011 rose +6.9% to 34,763 metric tons (annualized through October), up from the 2009 record low of 31,110 metric tons. The breakdown of U.S. consumption of tin by finished products in 2010 (latest data) shows that the largest consuming industry of tin is tinplate (with 30% of consumption), followed by solder (17%, chemicals (12%), and bronze and brass (9%).

Trade – The U.S. relied on imports for 69% of its tin consumption in 2010. U.S. imports of unwrought tin metal in 2010 (latest data) rose +7.0% to 35,300 metric tons, up from the 14-year low in 2009. The largest sources of U.S. imports in 2010 were Bolivia (17%), Indonesia (11%), and China (2%). U.S. exports of tin in 2010 rose +77.6% yr/yr to 5,630 metric tons.

World Mine Production of Tin   In Metric Tons (Contained Tin)

Year	Australia	Bolivia	Brazil	China	Indonesia	Malaysia	Nigeria	Peru	Portugal	Russia	Thailand	United Kingdom	World Total
2002	7,017	15,242	12,063	62,000	88,142	4,215	790	38,815	574	1,300	1,130	1,700	235,000
2003	3,864	16,755	12,217	102,000	71,694	3,359	1,800	40,202	218	2,000	793	2,100	261,000
2004	1,196	17,569	12,202	118,000	65,772	2,745	1,000	67,675	220	2,500	586	3,500	302,000
2005	2,819	18,433	11,739	126,000	78,404	2,857	1,300	42,145	243	3,000	158	3,500	296,000
2006	1,478	18,444	9,528	126,000	80,933	2,398	1,400	38,470	25	3,000	190	3,500	291,000
2007	2,071	15,972	11,835	146,000	66,137	2,263	180	39,019	41	2,500	120	3,500	301,000
2008	1,783	17,320	13,000	110,000	53,228	2,605	185	39,037	29	1,500	120	3,500	257,000
2009	1,400	19,273	13,000	115,000	55,000	2,380	180	37,503	30	1,200	120	3,500	260,000
2010[1]	2,000	20,200	11,000	120,000	56,000	1,770		33,800	30	1,100	150	5,500	277,000
2011[2]		20,700	12,000	110,000	51,000	2,000		34,600	100	1,000	100	6,000	270,000

[1] Preliminary.   [2] Estimate.   *Source: U.S. Geological Survey (USGS)*

World Smelter Production of Primary Tin   In Metric Tons

Year	Australia	Bolivia	Brazil	China	Indo-nesia	Japan	Malaysia	Mexico	Russia	South Africa	Spain	Thailand	World Total
2000	775	9,353	13,825	112,000	46,432	593	26,228	1,204	4,800	----	----	17,076	272,000
2001	1,171	11,292	12,168	105,000	53,470	668	30,417	1,789	4,569	----	----	22,387	272,000
2002	791	10,976	11,675	82,000	67,455	659	30,887	1,748	4,615	----	----	17,548	266,000
2003	597	12,836	10,761	98,000	66,284	662	18,250	1,769	4,100	----	----	15,400	270,000
2004	467	13,627	11,512	115,000	49,872	707	33,914	25	4,570	----	----	20,800	295,000
2005	594	13,941	8,986	122,000	65,300	754	36,924	17	5,000	----	----	31,600	324,000
2006	572	14,089	8,780	132,000	65,357	854	22,850	25	4,980	----	----	27,540	320,000
2007	118	12,251	9,384	149,000	64,127	879	25,263	25	3,800	----	----	23,104	327,000
2008	170	12,666	10,308	129,000	53,417	986	31,630	15	2,000	----	----	21,860	305,000
2009[1]	7,637	14,715	10,550	135,000	54,000	980	36,407	15	1,700	----	----	21,000	325,000

[1] Preliminary.   Source: U.S. Geological Survey (USGS)

United States Foreign Trade of Tin   In Metric Tons

| | ----- Concentrates[2] (Ore) ----- | | | -------- Imports for Consumption -------- Unwrought Tin Metal -------- | | | | | | | | |
Year	Exports (Metal)	Total All Ore	Bolivia	Peru	Total All Metal	Bolivia	Brazil	China	Indo-nesia	Malaysia	Singa-pore	Thailand	Kingdom
2001	4,350	----	----	----	37,500	6,040	5,510	6,360	3,880	674	145	----	118
2002	2,940	----	----	----	42,200	6,150	4,840	7,600	3,340	122	----	----	2
2003	3,690	----	----	----	37,100	5,720	3,000	4,340	3,070	490	----	----	143
2004	3,650	----	----	----	47,600	5,060	4,330	5,310	4,660	6,600	----	500	97
2005	4,330	----	----	----	37,500	5,400	2,150	4,510	5,220	1,530	194	45	67
2006	5,490	----	----	----	43,300	8,160	1,300	4,440	4,600	245	1,090	210	1,370
2007	6,410	----	----	----	34,600	4,340	2,600	4,230	1,680	14	1,730	15	881
2008	9,800	----	----	----	36,300	4,980	1,570	2,380	2,000	1,740	706	1,670	225
2009	3,170	----	----	----	33,000	6,300	1,050	1,210	3,220	169	451	15	----
2010[1]	5,630	----	----	----	35,300	6,060	75	641	3,970	4,500	996	1,310	----

[1] Preliminary.   [2] Tin content.   Source: U.S. Geological Survey (USGS)

Consumption (Total) of Tin (Pig) in the United States   In Metric Tons

Year	Jan.	Feb.	Mar.	Apr.	May	June	July	Aug.	Sept.	Oct.	Nov.	Dec.	Total
2002	3,965	3,866	3,868	3,819	4,087	3,887	3,887	3,842	3,835	3,966	3,822	3,811	46,655
2003	3,814	3,808	3,851	3,891	3,701	3,814	3,841	3,850	3,803	3,816	3,764	3,887	45,840
2004	3,851	3,632	3,887	3,837	3,874	4,001	3,844	3,871	3,850	3,870	3,947	3,772	46,236
2005	4,097	3,990	4,027	3,874	3,825	3,918	3,806	3,900	3,824	3,833	3,849	3,699	46,642
2006	3,877	3,694	3,508	3,439	3,447	3,580	3,475	3,420	3,456	3,442	3,407	3,356	42,101
2007	3,381	3,342	3,601	3,365	3,716	3,811	3,585	4,070	3,910	3,734	3,586	3,628	43,729
2008	2,653	2,626	2,630	2,693	2,639	2,641	2,665	2,697	2,687	2,607	2,662	2,653	31,853
2009	2,642	2,546	2,610	2,573	2,525	2,521	2,630	2,552	2,626	2,646	2,675	2,564	31,110
2010	2,678	2,673	2,689	2,698	2,666	2,655	2,706	2,740	2,724	2,730	2,599	2,951	32,509
2011[1]	2,782	2,769	2,833	2,831	2,862	2,983	2,961	2,823	3,064	3,061			34,763

[1] Preliminary.   Source: U.S. Geological Survey (USGS)

Tin Stocks (Pig-Industrial) in the United States, on First of Month   In Metric Tons

Year	Jan.	Feb.	Mar.	Apr.	May	June	July	Aug.	Sept.	Oct.	Nov.	Dec.
2002	7,700	7,320	7,020	6,990	6,870	6,600	6,540	6,590	6,670	7,130	6,880	6,950
2003	7,280	6,980	6,690	6,640	6,390	6,400	6,380	6,420	6,250	6,180	6,190	6,340
2004	6,520	6,010	6,130	6,280	5,850	6,000	5,900	6,290	6,110	6,030	5,900	6,410
2005	6,140	5,260	5,570	5,420	5,770	5,400	5,670	5,830	5,540	5,350	5,330	5,410
2006	5,400	5,380	5,330	5,350	5,400	5,380	5,420	5,400	5,740	5,650	5,650	5,830
2007	5,700	5,970	6,030	6,030	5,860	5,570	5,270	5,270	5,260	5,310	5,920	6,000
2008	6,140	8,070	8,280	8,020	8,000	7,970	7,930	7,960	7,980	7,960	7,990	7,940
2009	7,970	7,890	7,660	7,640	7,620	7,640	7,570	7,630	7,590	7,540	7,520	7,470
2010	7,450	7,030	7,080	7,060	7,080	7,180	7,270	7,220	7,130	7,060	7,090	7,090
2011[1]	6,920	6,660	6,710	6,740	6,750	6,820	6,860	6,880	6,860	6,860	6,800	

[1] Preliminary.   Source: U.S. Geological Survey (USGS)

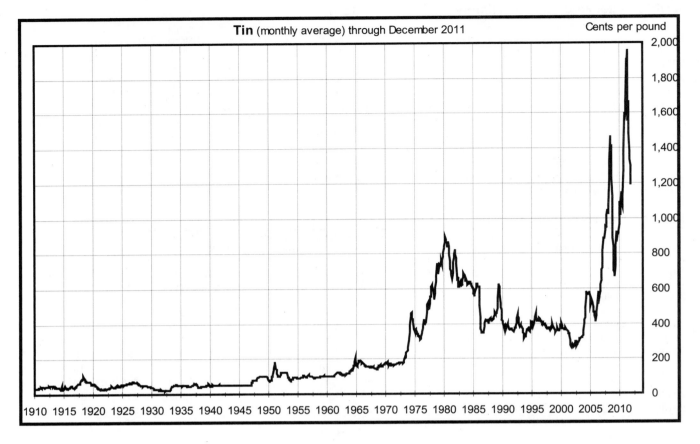

Tin (monthly average) through December 2011   Cents per pound

Average Price of Ex-Dock Tin in New York[1]   In Cents Per Pound

Year	Jan.	Feb.	Mar.	Apr.	May	June	July	Aug.	Sept.	Oct.	Nov.	Dec.	Average
2002	189.23	183.23	187.65	195.36	201.95	208.01	211.51	188.36	193.79	206.67	205.94	206.63	199.15
2003	212.68	217.98	219.58	217.90	225.40	223.69	225.81	229.58	233.59	248.22	252.93	285.40	232.73
2004	305.34	313.55	357.66	418.57	449.29	438.72	439.24	437.68	438.91	436.80	439.24	414.16	407.43
2005	376.37	393.05	408.41	395.40	394.68	367.81	347.78	347.96	331.01	313.73	300.96	323.43	358.38
2006	338.27	373.87	378.76	420.35	420.53	376.76	400.64	404.26	428.83	461.66	475.57	524.69	417.02
2007	535.46	604.14	648.82	656.53	661.04	659.63	689.99	705.01	700.45	748.39	777.74	756.89	678.67
2008	760.82	800.60	917.15	1,001.99	1,108.30	1,027.62	1,070.50	930.65	850.83	672.97	646.77	532.54	860.06
2009	539.32	523.68	508.12	554.44	646.09	702.56	657.47	694.15	695.88	701.13	698.44	721.79	636.92
2010	823.31	764.25	818.62	870.50	821.34	809.88	851.80	967.17	1,057.81	1,223.59	1,191.80	1,211.71	950.98
2011	1,274.29	1,456.60	1,422.69	1,501.64	1,339.50	1,188.91	1,271.42	1,137.37	1,055.80	1,019.31	998.78	913.27	1,214.96

Source: American Metal Market (AMM)

Average Price of Tin (Straights) in New York   In Cents Per Pound

Year	Jan.	Feb.	Mar.	Apr.	May	June	July	Aug.	Sept.	Oct.	Nov.	Dec.	Average
2002	271.59	263.91	270.54	280.98	288.74	296.02	299.39	269.30	277.60	293.79	292.40	292.95	283.10
2003	304.44	312.32	314.52	312.26	321.92	319.67	322.10	327.16	332.21	350.90	356.46	396.46	330.87
2004	422.33	433.50	485.99	557.29	575.39	570.99	565.68	568.14	572.72	573.79	577.07	550.97	537.82
2005	500.93	519.61	539.30	522.71	522.18	492.64	467.71	466.67	444.80	426.36	411.23	440.30	479.54
2006	464.54	509.45	519.31	574.53	575.57	517.52	548.29	552.06	583.57	623.07	644.19	705.62	568.14
2007	719.05	811.07	873.03	883.74	886.54	884.67	931.50	954.26	949.21	1,012.46	1,049.78	1,025.36	915.06
2008	1,025.05	1,071.97	1,224.20	1,325.79	1,461.85	1,357.22	1,410.60	1,229.27	1,124.02	887.70	841.86	694.41	1,137.83
2009	711.20	686.02	664.21	724.55	841.83	920.39	862.04	902.14	899.35	911.42	922.75	964.64	834.21
2010	1,090.89	1,011.26	1,082.71	1,149.23	1,084.11	1,067.12	1,117.84	1,268.74	1,386.44	1,597.89	1,552.75	1,588.29	1,249.77
2011	1,661.33	1,906.31	1,857.97	1,958.08	1,750.23	1,555.57	1,663.54	1,486.24	1,378.26	1,330.78	1,298.42	1,191.48	1,586.52

Source: U.S. Geological Survey (USGS)

Tin Plate Production & Tin Recovered in the United States   In Metric Tons

	------ Tin Content of Tinplate Produced ------				---------------------------- Tin Recovered from Scrap by Form of Recovery ----------------------------								
	------- Tinplate (All Forms) -------													
Year	Tinplate Waste ----- Gross Weight -----		Tin Content (Met. Ton)	Tin per Tonne of Plate (Kilograms)	Tin Metal	Bronze & Brass	Solder	Type Metal	Babbitt	Anti-monial Lead	Chemical Com-pounds	Misc.[2]	Grand Total
2001	97,800	2,000,000	7,800	3.9	----	----	----	----	----	----	----	----	----
2002	45,900	2,450,000	7,750	3.2	----	----	----	----	----	----	----	----	----
2003	W	2,500,000	7,750	3.1	----	----	----	----	----	----	----	----	----
2004	W	2,550,000	7,700	3.0	----	----	----	----	----	----	----	----	----
2005	W	2,270,000	7,670	3.4	----	----	----	----	----	----	----	----	----
2006	56,400	2,130,000	6,810	3.2	----	----	----	----	----	----	----	----	----
2007	58,900	1,780,000	7,010	3.9	----	----	----	----	----	----	----	----	----
2008	30,900	2,280,000	6,690	2.9	----	----	----	----	----	----	----	----	----
2009	14,500	1,150,000	6,200	5.4	----	----	----	----	----	----	----	----	----
2010[1]	18,200	1,150,000	6,600	5.8	----	----	----	----	----	----	----	----	----

[1] Preliminary.   [2] Includes foil, terne metal, cable lead, and items indicated by symbol "W".   W = Withheld.   NA = Not available.
Source: U.S. Geological Survey (USGS)

Consumption of Primary and Secondary Tin in the United States   In Metric Tons

Year	Net Import Reliance as a % of Apparent Consumption	Stocks, Jan. 1[2]	---------------------- Net Receipts ----------------------				Available Supply	Stocks, Dec. 31 (Total Available Less Total Processed)	Total Pro-cessed	Consumed in Manu-facturing Products
			Primary	Secondary	Scrap	Total				
2000	86	8,910	41,400	2,990	6,050	50,400	59,300	12,200	47,100	47,000
2001	88	8,830	34,500	2,180	4,770	41,400	50,200	8,220	42,000	41,900
2002	79	8,500	34,200	1,610	4,230	40,100	48,600	8,550	40,000	39,800
2003	89	8,220	32,400	1,380	3,440	37,300	45,500	7,770	37,700	37,400
2004	92	7,680	40,800	4,160	4,350	49,300	57,000	11,800	45,200	44,700
2005	78	8,060	32,500	5,790	3,840	42,200	50,200	9,120	41,000	40,600
2006	80	7,640	29,900	5,040	4,100	39,000	46,600	8,520	38,100	37,700
2007	72	7,230	25,600	4,950	3,030	33,600	40,800	8,980	31,700	31,100
2008	70	8,760	22,700	4,300	2,410	29,400	38,200	8,460	29,800	29,400
2009[1]	74	8,940	26,200	5,890	2,170	34,300	43,200	10,300	32,900	32,600

[1] Preliminary.   [2] Includes tin in transit in the U.S.   NA = Not available.   *Source: U.S. Geological Survey (USGS)*

Consumption of Tin in the United States, by Finished Products   In Metric Tons (Contained Tin)

Year	Tin-plate[2]	Solder	Babbitt	Bronze & Brass	Tinning	Chem-icals[3]	Tin Powder	Bar Tin & Anodes	White Metal	Other	Total	Total Primary	Total Secondary
2001	7,800	17,000	770	3,430	1,070	7,590	W	570	1,390	2,230	41,900	34,200	7,630
2002	7,750	13,800	1,310	3,040	679	8,400	W	617	1,320	2,920	39,800	34,000	5,830
2003	7,790	10,600	2,570	2,600	833	8,720	W	852	1,220	2,180	37,400	32,900	4,510
2004	7,700	19,000	728	3,070	798	9,120	W	680	937	2,630	44,700	36,700	7,990
2005	7,250	16,700	554	3,200	790	8,360	W	709	W	3,030	40,600	31,400	9,170
2006	7,110	12,800	484	3,300	696	9,290	W	698	W	1,040	37,700	29,200	8,480
2007	7,010	10,400	604	2,800	451	6,070	W	788	W	1,120	31,100	23,700	7,490
2008	6,840	5,110	604	2,460	395	5,440	227	767	W	5,370	29,200	23,100	6,250
2009	6,200	6,210	427	2,110	318	3,080	193	270	W	379	21,100	24,900	10,800
2010[1]	6,600	3,710	220	2,000	331	2,590	192	239	W	416	22,400	26,900	6,220

[1] Preliminary.   [2] Includes small quantity of secondary pig tin and tin acquired in chemicals.   [3] Including tin oxide.
W = Withheld proprietary data.   *Source: U.S. Geological Survey (USGS)*

Titanium

Titanium (symbol Ti) is a silver-white, metallic element used primarily to make light, strong alloys. It ranks ninth in abundance among the elements in the crust of the earth but is never found in the pure state. It occurs as an oxide in various minerals. It was first discovered in 1791 by Rev. William Gregor and was first isolated as a basic element in 1910. Titanium was named after the mythological Greek god Titan for its strength.

Titanium is extremely brittle when cold, but is malleable and ductile at a low red heat, and thus easily fabricated. Due to its strength, low weight, and resistance to corrosion, titanium is used in metallic alloys and as a substitute for aluminum. It is used extensively in the aerospace industry, in desalinization plants, construction, medical implants, paints, pigments, and lacquers.

Prices – The price of the mineral ilmenite, a primary source of titanium, in 2009 fell an average of about -34% to $72 per metric ton. The price of titanium metal sponge in 2009 (latest data) traded in the range of $4.50 to $7.07 per pound versus $6.16 to $8.02 in 2008. The price of titanium dioxide pigments (Anatase) in 2005 (latest data available) traded in the range of $.95-$1.00 per pound versus 90-95 cents per pound in 2004.

Supply – World production of titanium ilmenite concentrates in 2011 rose +3.4% yr/yr to 6.000 million metric tons, down from the 2007 record high of 7.120 million metric tons. The world's largest producers of titanium ilmenite concentrates are Australia with 15% of world production in 2011, India (9%), China (8%), Vietnam (8%), and Norway (5%). World production of titanium rutile concentrates in 2011 rose +4.5% yr/yr to 700,000 metric tons, which is a new record high. The world's largest producers are Australia with 57% of world production in 2011 followed by South Africa with 19% and Sierra Leone with 9%.

Demand – U.S. consumption of titanium dioxide pigment in 2011 rose +2.3% yr/yr to 785,000 metric tons, but still down from 2004's record high of 1.170 million metric tons. U.S. consumption of ilmenite in 2005 (latest data available) fell −12.8% to 1.290 million metric tons, down from 2004's 8-year high of 1.480 million metric tons. U.S. consumption of rutile in 2005 (latest data available) fell 4.7% yr/yr to a 7-year low of 424,000 metric tons.

Trade – U.S. imports of titanium dioxide pigment in 2011 fell by -11.8% yr/yr to 180,000 metric tons, well below the 2005 record high of 341,000 metric tons. U.S. imports of ilmenite in 2008 (latest data) rose +76.0% yr/yr to 433,000 metric tons.

World Produciton of Titanium Illmenite Concentrates   In Thousands of Metric Tons

Year	Australia[2]	Brazil	China	Egypt	India	Malaysia	Norway	Ukraine	United States	Vietnam	World Total	-- Titaniferous Slag[4] --- Canada	Africa
2002	1,956	177	750	125	460	106	750	512	400	170	5,400	900	973
2003	2,063	218	800	125	562	95	840	421	500	314	5,950	873	1,010
2004	1,965	75	840	----	621	61	860	370	500	550	5,850	863	1,020
2005	2,080	82	900	----	686	38	810	375	500	523	6,050	860	1,020
2006	2,508	95	1,000	----	690	46	850	470	500	605	6,850	930	1,230
2007	2,503	100	1,100	----	700	60	882	500	400	643	7,120	960	1,270
2008	2,199	175	1,000	----	610	37	915	520	300	693	6,870	1,000	1,230
2009	1,700	71	900	----	700	16	671	500	300	687	6,180	765	1,230
2010	991	45	550	----	540			300	300	200	485	5,800	
2011[1]	900	45	500		550			300	300	300	490	6,000	

[1] Preliminary.   [2] Includes leucoxene.   [3] Approximately 10% of total production is ilmenite. Beginning in 1988, 25% of Norway's ilmenite production was used to produce slag containing 75% TiO2.   NA = Not available.   *Source: U.S. Geological Survey (USGS)*

Salient Statistics of Titanium in the United States   In Metric Tons

Year	Titanium Dioxide Pigment Pro-duction	Imports[3]	Apparent Con-sumption	Ilmenite Imports[3]	Con-sumption	Titanium Slag Imports[3]	Con-sumption	Rutile[4] Imports[3]	Con-sumption	Exports of Titanium Products Ores & Concen-trates	Scrap	Dioxide & Pigments	Ingots, Billets, Etc.
2002	1,410,000	231,000	1,110,000	840,000	1,300,000	445,000	----	390,000	487,000	3,810	6,000	485,000	3,460
2003	1,420,000	240,000	1,070,000	804,000	1,300,000	409,000	----	427,000	489,000	10,300	5,320	518,000	3,960
2004	1,540,000	264,000	1,170,000	701,000	1,480,000	457,000	----	360,000	445,000	8,690	9,760	576,000	4,990
2005	1,310,000	341,000	1,130,000	822,000	1,290,000	667,000	----	366,000	424,000	20,900	20,600	486,000	6,350
2006	1,370,000	288,000	1,080,000	187,000		693,000		355,000		32,800	10,800	513,000	7,900
2007	1,440,000	221,000	979,000	246,000		749,000		463,800		9,730	9,510	564,000	8,670
2008	1,350,000	183,000	800,000	433,000		461,000		487,000		14,900	8,180	668,000	10,500
2009	1,230,000	175,000	757,000										
2010[1]	1,320,000	204,000	767,000										
2011[2]	1,420,000	180,000	785,000										

[1] Preliminary.   [2] Estimate.   [3] For consumption.   [4] Natural and synthetic.   W = Withheld.   *Source: U.S. Geological Survey (USGS)*

World Production of Titanium Rutile Concentrates   In Metric Tons

Year	Australia	Brazil	India	Sierra Leone	South Africa	Sri Lanka	Thailand	Ukraine	World Total
2003	173,000	2,450	18,000	----	108,000	----	----	60,000	384,000
2004	162,000	2,500	19,600	----	110,000	----	----	60,000	354,000
2005	177,000	2,500	20,100	----	115,000	----	----	60,000	374,000
2006	232,000	2,500	21,000	73,802	123,000	----	----	60,000	512,000
2007	312,000	2,500	21,000	82,527	114,000	----	----	60,000	594,000
2008	325,000	2,500	21,000	78,908	121,000	----	----	57,000	608,000
2009	266,000	3,000	20,000	61,000	127,000	11,000	----	57,000	550,000
2010[1]	280,000	3,000	20,000	67,000	130,000	12,000	----	57,000	580,000

[1] Preliminary.   NA = Not available.   *Source: U.S. Geological Survey (USGS)*

World Production of Titanium Sponge Metal & U.S. Consumption of Titanium Concentrates

	Production of Titanium (In Metric Tons) Sponge Metal[2]					U.S. Consumption of Titanium Concentrates, by Products (In Metric Tons) Ilmenite (TiO$_2$ Content)				Rutile (TiO$_2$ Content)			
Year	China	Japan	Russia	United Kingdom	United States	Total	Pigments	Misc.	Total	Welding Rod Coatings	Pigments	Misc.	Total
2004	4,800	23,100	23,000	----	W	75,000	1,460,000	19,300	1,480,000	----	418,000	26,700	445,000
2005	9,510	30,800	29,000	----	W	96,000	1,260,000	34,000	1,390,000	----	394,000	30,000	424,000
2006	18,000	37,800	32,000	----	W	121,000	NA	NA	1,510,000	----	----	----	----
2007	45,200	38,900	34,200	----	W	153,000	NA	NA	1,600,000	----	----	----	----
2008	49,600	40,900	29,500	----	W	155,000	NA	NA	1,440,000	----	----	----	----
2009	61,500	25,000	26,600	----	W	136,000	NA	NA	1,360,000	----	----	----	----
2010	57,800	31,600	25,800	----	W	137,000							
2011/1	60,000	56,000	40,000	----	W	186,000							

[1] Preliminary.   [2] Unconsolidated metal in various forms.   [4] Included in Pigments.   NA = Not available.   W = Withheld.
Source: U.S. Geological Survey (USGS)

Average Prices of Titanium in the United States

Year	Ilmenite FOB Australian Ports[2]	Slag, 85% TiO2 FOB Richards Bay, South Africa	Rutile Large Lots Bulk, FOB U.S. East Coast[3]	Rutile Bagged FOB Australian Ports	Avg. Price of Grade A Titanium Sponge, FOB Shipping Point	Titanium Metal Sponge	Titanium Dioxide Pigments FOB US Plants Anatase	Titanium Dioxide Pigments FOB US Plants Rutile
	-------- Dollars Per Metric Ton --------					-------- Dollars Per Pound --------		
2002	$85 - $100	$445.00	$430 - $470	$400 - $540	----	$3.64	$0.85 - $0.95	$0.85 - $0.95
2003	$80 - $100	$401.00	$415 - $445	$430 - $540	----	$2.72 - $3.95	$0.85 - $0.95	$0.85 - $0.90
2004	$81.00	$347 - $466	$430 - $480	$550 - $650	----	$3.55 - $6.44	$0.90 - $0.95	$0.90 - $0.95
2005	$80.00	$390 - $555	$460 - $480	$550 - $650	----	$3.46 - $12.22	$0.95 - $1.00	$0.95 - $1.00
2006	$75 - $85	$402 - $454	$450 - $500	$570 - $700	----	$5.87 - $12.84	----	----
2007	$75 - $85	$418 - $457	$475 - $500	$650 - $700	----	$6.33 - $7.06	----	----
2008	$84 - $137	$393 - $407	$500 - $550	$675 - $725	----	$6.16 - $8.02	----	----
2009[1]	$60 - $85	$401 - $439	$525 - $540	$700 - $800	----	$4.50 - $7.07	----	----

[1] Preliminary.   NA = Not available.   *Source: U.S. Geological Survey (USGS)*

Average Price of Titanium[1] in United States   In Dollars Per Pound

Year	Jan.	Feb.	Mar.	Apr.	May	June	July	Aug.	Sept.	Oct.	Nov.	Dec. Average
2006	24.75	24.75	25.53	26.10	27.50	27.58	27.75	27.75	27.75	27.75	27.75	27.75	26.89
2007	27.21	26.50	26.50	25.69	25.32	24.50	24.50	22.15	21.50	20.63	18.90	17.79	23.43
2008	16.62	16.00	15.60	15.50	15.50	15.14	14.95	14.50	14.50	14.50	13.56	13.17	14.96
2009	12.93	12.50	10.50	9.93	9.20	9.00	9.00	9.00	8.92	8.75	8.75	8.75	9.77
2010	8.75	8.75	8.92	9.13	10.10	10.70	11.00	11.00	11.00	11.00	11.43	11.50	10.27
2011	11.50	11.76	12.00	12.00	12.00	12.00	12.00	12.00	12.23	12.25	12.25	12.25	12.02

[1] Ingot, 6Al - 4V.   NA = Not available.   *Source: American Metal Market (AMM)*

Average Price of Titanium[1] in United States   In Dollars Per Pound

Year	Jan.	Feb.	Mar.	Apr.	May	June	July	Aug.	Sept.	Oct.	Nov.	Dec. Average
2006	33.50	33.50	40.54	42.50	42.50	43.14	44.50	44.50	44.50	44.50	44.50	44.50	41.89
2007	44.50	44.50	44.50	40.45	39.50	39.50	39.50	39.50	39.50	37.76	37.50	37.50	40.35
2008	36.74	35.50	35.50	35.50	35.50	35.50	35.50	35.50	34.55	33.00	33.00	33.00	34.90
2009	31.20	31.00	31.00	29.76	29.00	29.00	29.00	29.00	29.00	27.10	26.50	26.50	29.01
2010	26.50	25.55	24.50	25.50	26.50	26.50	28.50	28.50	28.50	28.50	30.20	30.50	27.48
2011	30.50	30.50	30.50	30.50	30.50	30.50	30.50	30.50	30.50	30.50	30.50	30.50	30.50

[1] Plate, Alloy.   NA = Not available.   *Source: American Metal Market (AMM)*

Tobacco

Tobacco is a member of the nightshade family. It is commercially grown for its leaves and stems, which are rolled into cigars, shredded for use in cigarettes and pipes, processed for chewing, or ground into snuff. Christopher Columbus introduced tobacco cultivation and use to Spain after observing natives from the Americas smoking loosely rolled tobacco-stuffed tobacco leaves.

Tobacco is cured, or dried, after harvesting and then aged to improve its flavor. The four common methods of curing are: air cured, fire cured, sun cured, and flue cured. Flue curing is the fastest method of curing and requires only about a week compared with up to 10 weeks for other methods. Cured tobacco is tied into small bundles of about 20 leaves and aged one to three years.

Virginia tobacco is by far the most popular type used in pipe tobacco since it is the mildest of all blending tobaccos. Approximately 60% of the U.S. tobacco crop is Virginia-type tobacco. Burley tobacco is the next most popular tobacco. It is air-cured, burns slowly and provides a relatively cool smoke. Other tobacco varieties include Perique, Kentucky, Oriental, and Latakia.

Prices – U.S. tobacco farm prices in 2011 rose +4.8% to 186.7 cents per pound, below the record high of 198.4 cents per pound posted in 2004.

Supply – World production of tobacco in 2010 fell by -0.2% yr/yr to 7.113 million metric tons, below last year's decade high of 7.127 million metric tons. The world's largest producers of tobacco are China with 42.3% of world production, followed at a distance by Brazil (with 11.0% of world production), India (10.6%), and the U.S. (4.6%). U.S. production in 2010 fell by -12.6% yr/yr to 326,080 metric tons, where it was down by more than half from the 2-decade high of 810,750 metric tons posted in 1997. Tobacco in the U.S. is grown primarily in the Mid-Atlantic States and they account for the vast majority of U.S. production. Specifically, the largest tobacco producing states in the U.S. are North Carolina (with 41.9% of U.S. production in 2011), Kentucky (28.6%), Virginia (8.6%), Tennessee (7.6%), South Carolina and Georgia with (4.4%).

U.S. production of flue-cured tobacco (type 11-14), the most popular tobacco type grown in the U.S., fell by -23.0% yr/yr to 347.475 million pounds in 2011. The second most popular type is burley tobacco (type 31), which saw U.S. production in 2011 fall -8.2% to 172.265 million pounds.

Total U.S. production of tobacco in 2011 fell -16.5% yr/yr to 601.029 million pounds, which is less than half of the 2-decade high of 1.787 billion pounds posted in 1997. U.S. farmers have sharply reduced the planting acreage for tobacco. In 2011, harvested tobacco acreage fell by 3.7% yr/yr to 324,830 acres, which is up from the 2005 record low of 297,080 but still far below the 25-year high of 836,230 posted in 1997. Yield in 2011 fell -13.1% to 1,850 down from a 15-year high of 2,325 pounds per acre in 2009. The farm value of the U.S. tobacco crop in 2011 fell by -12.3% yr/yr to $1.121 billion.

U.S. marketings of flue-cured tobacco (Types 11-14) in the 2006-07 (latest data) marketing year rose by +18.5% yr/yr to 454.7 million pounds. U.S. marketings of burley tobacco (Type 31) in the 2006-07 marketing year rose by +6.9% yr/yr to 224.6 million pounds.

U.S. production of cigarettes in 2009 (latest data) fell -14.6% to 338.1 billion cigarettes, which was still down sharply from the record high of 754.5 million posted in 1996. U.S. production of cigars rose by +65.2% yr/yr to 8.231 billion in 2009. U.S. production of chewing tobacco in 2009 fell by 9.8% to 29.3 million pounds, which was a record low.

Demand – U.S. per capita consumption of tobacco products in 2006 (latest data) was unchanged at 3.69 pounds per person but there appears to be a shifting from cigarettes to cigars. The 3.69 pounds per capita consumption of tobacco in 2006 is less than half the record high of 9.68 pounds per person that occurred at the beginning of the series in 1970. Per capita cigarette consumption in 2006 fell 1.5% yr/yr to 1,691 cigarettes per person, which was a record low. Per capita consumption of cigars in 2006 rose +1.9% yr/yr to a record high of 47.80 cigars per person. Per capita consumption of loose smoking tobacco in 2006 fell −6.3% yr/yr to 0.15 pounds.

Trade – U.S. tobacco exports in 2004 (latest data) rose +3.5% yr/yr to 354.0 million pounds, rebounding further from the record low of 325.8 million pounds seen in 2002. Meanwhile, U.S. tobacco imports in 2004 fell −10.9% yr/yr to 561.7 million pounds from the 11-year high of 630.1 million pounds see in 2003. The U.S. exported 111.3 billion cigarettes and 180 million cigars in 2006.

World Production of Leaf Tobacco   In Metric Tons

Year	Brazil	Canada	China	Greece	India	Indo-nesia	Italy	Japan	Pakistan	Turkey	United States	Zim-babwe	World Total
2001	568,505	58,606	2,358,845	142,000	340,000	201,900	130,487	60,600	85,100	144,786	449,643	195,905	6,157,481
2002	670,309	54,550	2,454,108	133,000	550,000	194,500	122,231	58,200	94,500	152,856	395,134	178,408	6,519,512
2003	656,200	46,338	2,262,663	136,000	490,000	200,875	124,985	50,662	88,200	112,158	364,035	102,683	6,029,034
2004	921,281	42,430	2,411,490	133,937	549,900	165,108	117,882	52,659	86,200	133,913	400,012	78,312	6,590,541
2005	889,426	43,000	2,685,743	124,351	549,100	153,470	115,983	46,800	100,500	135,247	292,574	83,230	6,760,958
2006	900,381	48,525	2,746,193	37,405	552,200	146,265	96,600	37,700	112,592	98,137	330,169	44,451	6,601,867
2007	908,679	44,000	2,397,152	29,370	520,000	164,851	110,000	37,800	103,240	74,584	357,273	79,000	6,194,918
2008	851,058	44,718	2,839,945	20,500	490,000	169,668	121,281	38,500	107,765	93,403	363,103	81,952	6,641,100
2009[1]	863,079	45,991	3,067,928	22,600	620,000	181,319	119,119	36,600	104,996	85,000	373,117	96,367	7,127,501
2010[2]	780,942	40,200	3,005,753	22,000	755,500	195,000	97,200	29,300	119,323	55,000	326,080	109,737	7,113,965

[1] Preliminary.   [2] Estimate.   *Source: Food and Agriculture Organization of the United Nations (FAO-UN)*

Production and Consumption of Tobacco Products in the United States

Year	Cigar-ettes - Billions -	Cigars[3] - Millions -	Plug	Twist	Loose-leaf	Smoking Total Tobacco	Snuff[4]	Cigar-ettes Number	Cigars[3]	Cigar-ettes	Cigars[3]	Smoking Tobacco In Pounds	Chewing Tobacco	Total Products
					In Millions of Pounds			*Number*						
2000	593.2	2,825	2.6	0.8	46.0	49.4	13.6	69.5	2,049	38.0	3.40	.62	.13	.48	4.10
2001	562.8	3,741	2.4	0.8	43.9	47.1	12.8	70.9	2,051	41.2	3.50	.68	.15	.47	4.30
2002	484.3	3,816	2.2	0.8	41.5	44.5	15.5	72.7	1,982	41.8	3.40	.68	.16	.43	4.16
2003	499.4	4,017	1.7	0.7	39.2	41.6	17.8	73.8	1,890	44.5	3.20	.73	.16	.40	3.97
2004	492.7	4,342	1.7	0.7	37.0	39.3	16.1	79.3	1,814	47.9	3.10	.79	.15	.37	3.87
2005	498.7	3,674	1.4	0.6	37.2	39.2	17.4	86.7	1,716	46.9	2.90	.77	.16	.36	3.69
2006	483.7	4,256	1.3	0.6	36.4	38.3	16.5	81.8	1,691	47.8	2.90	.78	.15	.37	3.69
2007	449.7	4,797	1.2	0.5	35.1	36.8	NA	NA	NA	NA	NA	NA	NA	NA	NA
2008[1]	396.1	4,984	1.1	0.5	30.9	32.5	----	----	----	----	----	----	----	----	----
2009[2]	338.1	8,232	0.9	0.5	28.0	29.3	----	----	----	----	----	----	----	----	----

[1] Preliminary. [2] Estimate. [3] Large cigars and cigarillos. [4] Includes loose-leaf. [5] Consumption of tax-paid tobacco products. Unstemmed rocessing weight. [6] 18 years and older. NA = Not available. *Source: Economic Research Service, U.S. Department of Agriculture (ERS-USDA)*

Production of Tobacco in the United States, by States In Thousands of Pounds

Year	Florida	Georgia	Indiana	Kentucky	Maryland	North Carolina	Ohio	Pennsyl-vania	South Carolina	Tenn-essee	Virginia	Wisconsin	Total
2002	11,960	53,000	7,800	222,991	1,800	347,920	9,625	6,815	59,475	71,331	64,407	3,817	871,122
2003	11,000	59,400	8,190	225,042	1,595	299,995	8,745	7,880	63,000	65,632	67,285	4,255	802,560
2004	9,800	46,690	8,610	235,003	1,870	350,560	10,976	8,100	63,450	65,381	67,285	3,541	881,875
2005	5,500	27,760	----	174,260	----	278,900	6,732	10,700	39,900	51,670	40,351	----	645,015
2006	2,860	30,090	----	186,780	----	330,580	7,000	16,790	48,300	49,135	47,322	----	727,897
2007	----	39,775	----	197,040	----	383,420	7,175	18,310	46,125	38,636	46,142	----	787,653
2008	----	33,600	----	205,850	----	390,360	6,970	17,630	39,900	52,380	45,970	----	800,504
2009	----	28,014	----	206,900	----	423,856	6,800	18,660	38,850	49,960	46,530	----	822,581
2010	----	26,790	----	181,760	----	352,625	5,125	19,965	36,000	45,740	44,299	----	718,190
2011[1]	----	26,325	----	172,140	----	251,565	3,360	20,655	26,350	45,363	51,360	----	601,029

[1] Preliminary. *Source: Agricultural Statistics Board, U.S. Department of Agriculture (ASB-USDA)*

Salient Statistics of Tobacco in the United States

Year	Acres Harvested 1,000 Acres	Yield Per Acre Pounds	Pro-duction Million Pounds	Farm Price cents Lb.	Farm Value Million $	Tobacco (June - July) Exports[2] Million Pounds	Imports[3]	Cigar-ettes In Millions	Cigars & Cheroots	All Tobacco	Smoking Tobacco[4]	All Tobacco In Millions of Pounds	Fire Cured[6]	Cigar Filler[7]	Mary-land
2002	427.3	2,039	871	193.6	1,687	325.8	549.7	127,400	123	338	144.0	1,738	99.5	12.3	9.7
2003	411.2	1,952	803	196.7	1,576	342.1	630.1	121,500	130	343	121.2	1,584	100.5	10.7	8.2
2004	408.1	2,161	882	198.4	1,750	354.0	561.7	118,700	171	361	45.4	1,529	101.5	9.7	7.2
2005	297.1	2,171	645	164.2	1,059	----	----	113,300	301	----	----	1,455	----	9.9	5.0
2006	339.0	2,144	728	166.5	1,211	----	----	111,317	180	----	----	1,167	----	10.8	0.8
2007	356.0	2,213	788	169.3	1,329	----	----	----	----	----	----	----	----	----	----
2008	354.5	2,258	801	185.9	1,488	----	----	----	----	----	----	----	----	----	----
2009	354.0	2,323	823	183.7	1,511	----	----	----	----	----	----	----	----	----	----
2010	337.5	2,128	718	178.2	1,280	----	----	----	----	----	----	----	----	----	----
2011[1]	324.8	1,850	601	186.7	1,122	----	----	----	----	----	----	----	----	----	----

[1] Preliminary. [2] Domestic. [3] For consumption. [4] In bulk. [5] Flue-cured and cigar wrapper, year beginning July 1; for all other types, October 1. [6] Kentucky-Tennessee types 22-23. [7] Types 41-46. *Source: Economic Research Service, U.S. Department of Agriculture (ERS-USDA)*

Tobacco Production in the United States, by Types In Thousands of Pounds (Farm-Sale Weight)

Year	11-14	21	22	23	31	32	35-36	37	41	41-61	51	54	55	61
2002	514,385	1,471	23,292	10,145	293,537	4,205	10,570	116	4,410	13,401	4,021	3,151	666	1,153
2003	456,690	839	23,504	10,165	281,698	4,195	11,230	84	5,280	14,155	3,386	3,472	783	1,234
2004	521,535	1,345	24,800	11,006	292,172	5,830	11,798	124	4,140	13,265	3,767	2,744	797	1,915
2005	380,850	----	----	----	203,383	3,000	----	----	2,860	8,621	4,117	----	----	----
2006	447,190	----	----	----	217,255	2,090	----	----	2,600	8,265	4,434	----	----	----
2007	503,760	----	----	----	216,087	2,420	----	----	4,140	11,442	5,473	----	----	1,829
2008	499,220	----	----	----	201,530	3,780	----	----	3,960	8,444	3,076	----	----	1,408
2009	525,414	----	----	----	214,896	4,830	----	----	4,400	7,411	1,872	----	----	1,139
2010	451,290	----	----	----	187,570	4,950	----	----	4,935	10,821	4,776	----	----	1,110
2011[1]	347,475	----	----	----	172,265	6,000	----	----	3,655	7,566	2,891	----	----	1,020

[1] Preliminary. *Source: Agricultural Statistics Board, U.S. Department of Agriculture (ASB-USDA)*

TOBACCO

U.S. Exports of Unmanufactured Tobacco   In Millions of Pounds (Declared Weight)

Year	Australia	Belgium-Luxem.	Denmark	France	Germany	Italy	Japan	Nether-lands	Sweden	Switzer-land	Thailand	United Kingdom	Total U.S. Exports
2002	4.5	29.4	13.6	10.3	59.5	8.6	49.6	10.3	1.2	27.3	12.6	6.0	338.2
2003	6.3	61.7	13.5	8.8	55.8	7.6	42.4	9.8	1.6	34.8	3.6	4.8	343.3
2004	3.6	27.4	10.2	16.3	53.5	6.6	34.6	15.8	.6	9.4	8.5	4.0	360.9
2005	2.9	12.7	8.4	10.7	55.3	5.8	21.7	25.4	.7	15.6	4.1	3.2	339.0
2006	4.9	16.8	8.4	7.5	81.2	3.2	3.9	37.0	.7	38.5	3.0	1.1	397.6
2007	3.5	18.0	9.7	13.2	63.1	.7	4.0	24.0	.3	41.7	1.8	.0	411.5
2008	1.3	3.9	6.5	7.0	39.2	.0	.0	46.3	.3	69.3	3.0	.1	372.3
2009	6.4	3.6	6.4	7.7	23.9	.4	.0	37.7	.3	59.1	2.8	.1	380.3
2010	5.2	44.6	4.5	8.3	20.8	.6	.0	44.7	.4	34.7	3.0	1.1	393.9
2011[1]	.8	10.0	.7	8.9	25.9	.8	.0	27.2	.5	65.6	3.7	6.0	406.3

[1] Preliminary.   *Source: Economic Research Service, U.S. Department of Agriculture (ERS-USDA)*

U.S. Salient Statistics for Flue-Cured Tobacco (Types 11-14) in the United States   In Millions of Pounds

Year	Acres Harvested 1,000	Yield Per Acre Pounds	Mar-ketings	Stocks Oct. 1	Total Supply	Exports	Domestic Disap-pearance	Total Disap-pearance	Farm Price cents/Lb.	Placed Under Gov't Loan (Mil. Lb.)	Price Support Level (cents/) Lb.	Loan Stocks Nov. 30	Loan Stocks Uncom-mitted
2002-03	245.6	2,094	565	916	1,481	220	423	643	182.0	24.8	165.6	17.8	12.8
2003-04	233.4	1,957	508	838	1,345	216	307	522	185.1	59.8	166.3	70.6	68.7
2004-05	228.4	2,283	499	823	1,322	189	338	526	184.5	94.9	169.0	108.2	128.5
2005-06	174.5	2,182	383	796	1,179	258	317	575	147.4	----	----	79.0	----
2006-07	213.1	2,095	455	604	1,058	270	248	518	149.6	----	----	----	----
2007-08	223.0	2,259	----	----	----	----	----	----	152.7	----	----	----	----
2008-09	223.0	2,239	----	----	----	----	----	----	175.7	----	----	----	----
2009-10	223.8	2,348	----	----	----	----	----	----	175.4	----	----	----	----
2010-11[1]	210.9	2,140	----	----	----	----	----	----	----	----	----	----	----
2011-12[2]	206.7	1,681	----	----	----	----	----	----	----	----	----	----	----

[1] Preliminary.   [2] Estimate.   NA = Not available.   *Source: Economic Research Service, U.S. Department of Agriculture (ERS-USDA)*

Salient Statistics for Burley Tobacco (Type 31) in the United States   In Millions of Pounds

Year	Acres Harvested 1,000	Yield Per Acre Pounds	Mar-ketings	Stocks Oct. 1	Total Supply	Exports	Domestic Disap-pearance	Total Disap-pearance	Farm Price cents/Lb.	Gross Sales[3]	Price Support Level cents/Lb.	Loan Stocks Nov. 30	Loan Stocks Uncom-mitted
2002-03	157.7	1,861	300	648	948	149	221	370	197.4	217.7	183.5	124.2	46.1
2003-04	152.3	1,850	272	578	1,850	174	136	310	197.7	197.3	184.9	91.7	26.5
2004-05	153.2	1,908	280	540	820	228	100	328	199.4	202.3	187.3	115.1	8.5
2005-06	100.2	2,031	203	493	696	208	84	293	156.4	----	----	78.7	----
2006-07	103.6	2,095	225	403	628	190	56	246	163.8	----	----	----	----
2007-08	106.3	2,033	----	----	----	----	----	----	160.1	----	----	----	----
2008-09	97.5	2,067	----	----	----	----	----	----	166.9	----	----	----	----
2009-10	101.9	2,109	----	----	----	----	----	----	170.9	----	----	----	----
2010-11[1]	97.6	1,922	----	----	----	----	----	----	----	----	----	----	----
2011-12[2]	88.9	1,938	----	----	----	----	----	----	----	----	----	----	----

[1] Preliminary.   [2] Estimate.   [3] Before Christmas holidays.   NA = Not available.
Source: Economic Research Service, U.S. Department of Agriculture (ERS-USDA)

Exports of Tobacco from the United States (Quantity and Value)   In Metric Tons

Year	Unmanufactured Flue-Cured	Value 1,000 USD	Burley	Value 1,000 USD	Total	Value 1,000 USD	Manu-factured	Value 1,000 USD
2002	73,125	532,713	40,170	334,621	153,427	1,049,709	110,092	1,950,188
2003	70,669	519,732	41,876	346,504	155,722	1,038,073	102,351	1,843,922
2004	67,183	490,547	58,764	373,001	163,693	1,044,440	60,770	1,566,223
2005	62,779	420,532	61,606	412,588	153,762	989,588	19,364	1,301,834
2006	88,020	569,431	63,214	409,272	180,368	1,141,374	22,261	1,320,283
2007	82,093	541,816	75,905	498,168	186,643	1,207,945	17,552	1,122,176
2008	100,848	730,677	44,506	342,732	168,885	1,238,047	25,474	824,638
2009	86,429	659,772	37,395	300,744	172,504	1,158,970	4,654	489,480
2010[1]	85,727	662,346	32,687	265,927	178,664	1,167,342	5,008	454,346
2011[2]	88,933	644,101	33,385	256,006	184,300	1,149,031	7,457	488,636

[1] Preliminary.   [2] Forecast.   *Source: Foreign Agricultural Service, U.S. Department of Agriculture (FAS-USDA)*

Tung Oil

Tung oil is a yellow drying oil produced from the seed of the tung tree. The seeds or nuts of the tung tree are harvested and pressed to yield tung oil. Tung oil is used mostly as an industrial lubricant and drying agent, and is the most powerful drying agent known. It is also used in paints and varnishes, soaps, inks, and electrical insulators. Tung oil is poisonous, containing glycerol esters of unsaturated fats. The oil is also used as a substitute for linseed oil in paints, varnishes, and linoleum, and as a waterproofing agent.

Prices – The price of tung oil in 2010 fell by -4.3% yr/yr to 130.0 cents per pound, below 2008's record high of 143.03 cents per pound.

Demand – U.S. consumption of tung oil has fallen sharply over the past decade. In 2008 (latest data annualized) U.S. consumption rose by +1.8% yr/yr to 1.314 million pounds but that 2008 consumption level was only about 7% of 1996's 18-year high of 21.645 million pounds.

Trade – World imports of tung oil in 2010 rose +8.4% yr/yr to 16,312 metric tons. U.S. imports of tung oil in 2010 fell by -16.2% to 1,400 metric tons. The world's largest importers of tung oil are South Korea with 11.0% of world imports, Netherlands with 10.2%, Japan with 8.8%, the U.S. with 8.6%, Germany with 8.3%, and the Taiwan with 7.2%. The world's largest exporter of tung oil by far is China with 7,173 metric tons of exports in 2010, accounting for 49.1% of total world exports.

World Tung Oil Trade — In Metric Tons

| | Imports | | | | | | | | Exports | | | | |
Year	Germany	Hong Kong	Japan	Nether-lands	Rep. of Korea	Taiwan	United States	World Total	Argen-tina	China	Hong Kong	Para-guay	World Total
2004	100	207	1,900	1,778	5,486	3,529	2,975	24,961	1,299	18,850	240	3,626	25,501
2005	43	154	2,067	2,376	3,769	2,938	1,866	22,476	1,035	16,563	171	4,306	23,459
2006	478	104	1,984	2,342	1,828	2,891	2,076	20,183	733	14,668	104	2,876	19,539
2007	1,307	120	1,858	2,119	2,685	2,021	1,630	18,899	956	13,313	100	2,085	18,542
2008	1,251	120	1,937	1,693	1,894	1,884	1,750	16,762	364	12,245	100	2,148	16,351
2009[1]	1,288	90	1,178	1,394	2,036	1,621	1,670	15,051	262	8,913	70	3,024	14,924
2010[2]	1,349	30	1,429	1,660	1,799	1,173	1,400	16,312	790	7,173	80	5,541	17,042

[1] Preliminary.   [2] Estimate.   *Source: The Oil World*

Consumption of Tung Oil in Inedible Products in the United States — In Thousands of Pounds

Year	Jan.	Feb.	Mar.	Apr.	May	June	July	Aug.	Sept.	Oct.	Nov.	Dec.	Total
2005	128	110	144	151	371	127	161	189	92	171	146	110	1,900
2006	174	175	138	103	128	193	198	114	198	134	136	75	1,766
2007	170	81	108	104	176	117	153	83	68	92	75	64	1,291
2008	W	W	141	91	98	W	108	W	W	W	W	W	1,314
2009	W	W	W	W	W	W	W	W	W	W	W	W	W
2010	W	W	W	W	W	W	W	W	W	W	W	W	W
2011[1]	W	W	W	W	W	W	W	W	W	W	W	W	W

[1] Preliminary.   W = Withheld.   *Source: Bureau of the Census, U.S. Department of Commerce*

Stocks of Tung Oil at Factories & Warehouses in the United States, on First of Month — In Thousands of Pounds

Year	Jan.	Feb.	Mar.	Apr.	May	June	July	Aug.	Sept.	Oct.	Nov.	Dec.
2005	90	128	107	182	130	141	134	122	114	93	116	70
2006	109	99	98	124	81	116	128	85	128	125	76	98
2007	109	135	109	92	66	110	117	153	101	100	36	59
2008	82	87	94	63	29	79	50	78	86	73	W	W
2009	W	W	W	W	W	W	W	W	W	W	W	W
2010	W	W	W	W	W	W	W	W	W	W	W	W
2011[1]	W	W	W	W	W	W	W	W	W	W	W	W

[1] Preliminary.   W = Withheld.   *Source: Bureau of the Census, U.S. Department of Commerce*

Average Price of Tung Oil (Imported, Drums) F.O.B. in New York — In Cents Per Pound

Year	Jan.	Feb.	Mar.	Apr.	May	June	July	Aug.	Sept.	Oct.	Nov.	Dec.	Average
2005	92.50	95.00	97.50	97.50	97.50	97.50	97.50	102.50	105.00	105.00	97.50	95.00	98.33
2006	95.00	95.00	95.00	95.00	95.00	93.75	90.00	90.00	89.00	89.00	89.00	89.00	92.06
2007	85.40	84.33	87.00	85.00	85.00	85.00	85.00	NA	90.00	99.50	100.00	100.71	89.72
2008	107.62	110.79	126.00	130.00	130.00	135.14	139.86	147.62	164.29	175.00	175.00	175.00	143.03
2009	170.00	151.32	135.00	133.33	130.00	130.00	130.00	130.00	130.00	130.00	130.00	130.00	135.80
2010	130.00	130.00	130.00	130.00	130.00	130.00	130.00	130.00	NA	NA	NA	NA	130.00
2011[1]	NA	NA	NA	NA	NA	NA	NA	NA	NA	NA	NA	NA	NA

[1] Preliminary.   *Source: Economic Research Service, U.S. Department of Agriculture (ERS-USDA)*

Tungsten

Tungsten (symbol W) is a grayish-white, lustrous, metallic element. The atomic symbol for tungsten is W because of its former name of Wolfram. Tungsten has the highest melting point of any metal at about 3410 degrees Celsius and boils at about 5660 degrees Celsius. In 1781, the Swedish chemist Carl Wilhelm Scheele discovered tungsten.

Tungsten is never found in nature but is instead found in the minerals wolframite, scheelite, huebnertite, and ferberite. Tungsten has excellent corrosion resistance qualities and is resistant to most mineral acids. Tungsten is used as filaments in incandescent lamps, electron and television tubes, alloys of steel, spark plugs, electrical contact points, cutting tools, and in the chemical and tanning industries.

Prices – The average monthly price of tungsten at U.S. ports in 2011 rose by +69.2% yr/yr to $329.59 per short ton, which is a new record high.

Supply – World concentrate production of tungsten in 2011 rose by +4.7% yr/yr to 72,000 metric tons, which is a new record high. The world's largest producer of tungsten by far is China with 60,000 metric tons of production in 2011, which was 83% of total world production. Russia is the next largest producer at 4% with only a miniscule production of only 3,100 metric tons.

Trade – The U.S. in 2011 relied on imports for 36% of its tungsten consumption. U.S. imports for consumption in 2011 rose by +38.7% yr/yr to 3,800 metric tons. U.S. exports in 2011 were negligible at 50 metric tons.

World Concentrate Production of Tungsten   In Metric Tons (Contained Tungsten[3])

Year	Austria	Bolivia	Brazil	Burma	Canada	China	Mongolia	Korea	Portugal	Russia	Rwanda	Thailand	Total
2004	1,335	403	262	107	----	59,900	77	280	746	2,800	90	187	66,600
2005	1,280	531	577	168	384	51,200	78	650	816	2,800	318	345	59,500
2006	1,153	868	525	197	1,983	45,000	182	930	780	2,800	820	303	56,400
2007	1,117	1,107	537	183	2,305	41,000	245	230	846	3,300	1,534	477	54,100
2008	1,122	1,148	408	136	2,277	43,500	142	270	850	3,000	975	617	62,200
2009	900	1,000	500	87	2,000	51,000	39	100	900	2,500	499	600	61,300
2010[1]	1,000	1,200			420	59,000			1,200	2,800			68,800
2011[2]	1,100	1,200			2,000	60,000			1,300	3,100			72,000

[1] Preliminary.   [2] Estimate.   [3] Conversion Factors: WO_3 to W, multiply by 0.7931; 60% WO_3 to W, multiply by 0.4758.
Source: U.S. Geological Survey (USGS)

Salient Statistics of Tungsten in the United States   In Metric Tons (Contained Tungsten)

Year	Net Import Reliance as a % Apparent Consumption	Total Con- sumption	Tool	Stainless & Heat Assisting	Alloy Steel[3]	Super- alloys	Cutting & Wear Resistant Materials	Products Made From Metal Powder	Miscel- laneous	Chemical and Ceramic	Exports	Imports for Con- sumption	Con- sumers	Pro- ducers
2003	63	W	W	312	W	W	5,210	W	----	129	20	4,690	W	W
2004	73	W	W	259	W	W	6,020	W	----	130	43	2,310	W	W
2005	68	W	W	280	W	W	6,020	W	----	130	52	2,080	W	W
2006	67	W	W	292	W	W	6,710	W	----	118	130	2,290	W	W
2007	67	W	W	282	W	W	6,090	W	----	89	109	3,880	W	W
2008	60	W	W	283	W	W	6,650	W	----	80	496	3,990	W	W
2009[1]	68	W									38	3,590	W	W
2010[2]	68	W									400	3,000	W	W

Consumption of Tungsten Products by End Uses — Steel; Stocks, Dec. 31 — Concentrates —

[1] Preliminary.   [2] Estimate.   [3] Other than tool.   [4] Included with stainless & heat assisting.   W = Withheld.
Source: U.S. Geological Survey (USGS)

Average Price of Tungsten at U.S. Ports (Including Duty)   In Dollars Per Short Ton

Year	Jan.	Feb.	Mar.	Apr.	May	June	July	Aug.	Sept.	Oct.	Nov.	Dec.	Average
2004	63.00	63.00	66.83	89.77	92.50	92.50	88.95	86.09	87.00	89.86	92.00	93.83	83.78
2005	97.08	109.32	134.13	178.21	272.26	277.61	275.25	237.28	232.50	244.05	255.00	255.00	213.97
2006	255.00	265.66	282.50	275.00	266.36	265.00	265.00	265.00	266.13	267.50	262.00	253.00	265.68
2007	252.50	256.71	261.36	262.50	262.50	262.50	262.50	261.63	252.50	252.50	252.50	252.50	257.68
2008	252.50	252.50	252.50	252.50	252.50	252.50	252.50	252.50	252.50	252.50	252.50	252.50	252.50
2009	252.50	215.00	205.00	205.00	165.00	165.00	165.00	165.00	165.00	165.00	166.58	180.00	184.51
2010	173.95	175.00	175.65	177.50	177.50	177.50	175.12	169.46	217.50	238.21	240.00	240.00	194.78
2011	263.45	307.00	307.00	307.00	307.00	307.00	307.00	307.00	307.00	385.67	425.00	425.00	329.59

U.S. Spot Quotations, 65% WO_3, Basis C.I.F.   *Source: U.S. Geological Survey (USGS)*

Turkeys

During the past three decades, the turkey industry has experienced tremendous growth in the U.S. Turkey production has more than tripled since 1970, with a current value of over $7 billion. Turkey was not a popular dish in Europe until a roast turkey was eaten on June 27, 1570, at the wedding feast of Charles XI of France and Elizabeth of Austria. The King was so impressed with the birds that the turkey subsequently became a popular dish at banquets held by French nobility.

The most popular turkey product continues to be the whole bird, with heavy demand at Thanksgiving and Christmas. The primary breeders maintain and develop the quality stock, concentrating on growth and conformation in males and fecundity in females, as well as characteristics important to general health and welfare. Turkey producers include large companies that produce turkeys all year round, and relatively small companies and farmers who produce turkeys primarily for the seasonal Thanksgiving market.

Prices – The average monthly price received by farmers for turkeys in the U.S. in 2011 rose by +11.0% yr/yr to 66.0 cents per pound, below the record high of 67.9 cents per pound posted in 2010. The monthly average retail price of turkeys (whole frozen) in the U.S. in 2011 rose by +7.3% yr/yr to a record high of 167.1 cents per pound. Turkey prices have more than tripled from the low 40-cent area seen in the early 1970s.

Supply – World production of turkeys in 2012 fell -0.2% yr/yr to 5.304 million metric tons. World production of turkeys has grown by more than two and one-half times since 1980 when production was 2.090 million metric tons. The U.S. is the largest producer of turkeys in the world by far with 2.567 million metric tons of production in 2012, which is 48.4% of world production. The value of U.S. turkey production in the U.S. in 2010 was $4.371 billion.

Demand – World consumption of turkeys in 2012 rose by +0.5% to 5.084 million metric tons. U.S. turkey consumption was 2.298 million metric tons in 2012, which accounted for 45.2% of world consumption. U.S. per capita consumption of turkeys in 2012 is forecasted to rise +0.6% yr/yr to 16.3 pounds per person per year. U.S. per capital consumption of turkeys has been in the range of 16-18 pounds since 1990, but the USDA is projecting that per capita consumption will drop somewhat.

Production and Consumption of Turkey Meat, by Selected Countries — In Thousands of Metric Tons (RTC)

	Production							Consumption						
Year	Brazil	Canada	European Union	Mexico	Russia	United States	World Total	Brazil	Canada	European Union	Mexico	Russia	United States	World Total
2003	272	148	2,028	14	8	2,529	5,011	160	137	1,939	167	122	2,301	4,952
2004	315	145	2,032	13	9	2,441	4,968	179	139	1,966	152	106	2,272	4,876
2005	360	155	1,919	14	11	2,464	4,936	199	143	1,888	194	118	2,247	4,857
2006	353	163	1,858	14	16	2,543	4,960	197	144	1,841	197	107	2,297	4,866
2007	458	170	1,790	15	30	2,664	5,143	281	150	1,769	211	105	2,404	5,025
2008	465	180	1,830	15	39	2,796	5,337	261	163	1,835	212	107	2,434	5,100
2009	466	167	1,795	11	31	2,535	5,018	302	151	1,801	155	72	2,363	4,910
2010	485	159	1,946	11	70	2,526	5,211	327	143	1,911	163	105	2,305	5,020
2011[1]	505	160	1,940	10	90	2,593	5,312	365	145	1,880	169	123	2,297	5,057
2012[2]	531	162	1,910	10	110	2,567	5,304	389	145	1,850	173	140	2,298	5,084

[1] Preliminary. [2] Forecast. *Source: Foreign Agricultural Service, U.S. Department of Agriculture (FAS-USDA)*

Salient Statistics of Turkeys in the United States

			Liveweight		Value of Production		Ready-to-Cook Basis		Consumption		Production Costs		Wholesale Ready-to-Cook	
	Poults Placed[3]	Number Raised[4]	Produced	Price cents	Value of Production	Production	Beginning Stocks	Exports	Total	Per Capita	Feed	Total	Production	3-Region Weighted
Year	In Thousands		Mil Lbs	Per Lb.	Million $	In Millions of Pounds				Lbs.	Liveweight Basis		Costs	Avg Price[5]
2001	301,721	272,059	7,154.8	39.0	2,796.8	5,489	241	487	5,004	17.5	20.55	34.25	59.11	63.63
2002	296,877	275,477	7,494.9	36.5	2,732.5	5,638	241	439	5,108	17.7	20.85	34.55	59.48	61.09
2003	289,542	274,048	7,487.3	36.1	2,699.7	5,576	333	484	5,074	17.4	22.59	36.29	61.66	60.41
2004	277,717	263,207	7,278.4	42.0	3,054.3	5,383	354	442	5,003	17.0	----	----	----	----
2005	293,683	252,053	7,096.0	44.9	3,182.8	5,432	288	570	4,952	16.7	----	----	----	----
2006	293,137	262,460	7,463.9	47.9	3,573.7	5,607	206	547	5,060	16.9	----	----	----	----
2007	308,402	266,828	7,566.3	52.3	3,954.5	5,873	218	547	5,294	17.5	----	----	----	----
2008	297,590	273,088	7,922.1	56.5	4,477.1	6,165	261	676	5,361	17.6	----	----	----	----
2009[1]	273,904	247,359	7,149.5	50.0	3,573.4	5,588	396	535	5,201	16.9	----	----	----	----
2010[2]	276,931	244,188	7,107.3		4,371.4	5,643	262	582		16.4	----	----	----	----

[1] Preliminary. [2] Estimate. [3] Poults placed for slaughter by hatcheries. [4] Turkeys place August 1-July 31. [5] Regions include central, eastern and western. Central region receives twice the weight of the other regions in calculating the average.
Source: Economic Research Service, U.S. Department of Agriculture (ERS-USDA)

TURKEYS

Turkey-Feed Price Ratio in the United States   In Pounds[2]

Year	Jan.	Feb.	Mar.	Apr.	May	June	July	Aug.	Sept.	Oct.	Nov.	Dec.	Average
2002	7.2	7.2	6.8	6.8	7.3	7.3	6.9	6.3	6.0	6.1	6.5	6.4	6.7
2003	5.7	5.7	5.9	5.9	5.7	5.8	5.9	5.7	6.0	6.3	6.3	5.7	5.9
2004	5.1	4.6	4.5	4.5	4.8	5.2	5.8	7.0	7.9	8.4	8.7	8.2	6.2
2005	6.9	6.9	6.6	6.7	6.9	7.0	7.3	8.0	9.0	9.5	10.0	9.5	7.9
2006	7.0	6.9	6.9	7.3	7.1	7.6	7.7	8.5	9.1	9.6	9.4	5.9	7.8
2007	5.6	5.3	5.5	5.8	5.9	6.1	6.6	6.7	6.6	6.4	6.1	4.9	6.0
2008	4.1	3.6	4.0	4.0	4.3	4.3	4.5	4.7	5.4	5.9	5.6	4.4	4.6
2009	4.1	4.6	4.8	4.7	4.7	4.8	5.1	5.2	5.3	5.6	5.7	5.6	5.0
2010	4.8	5.3	5.6	5.9	6.2	6.9	6.9	6.7	6.6	6.8	6.4	5.6	6.1
2011[1]	4.6	4.2	4.4	4.4	4.6	4.8	4.7	4.7	5.2	5.9	5.9	5.4	4.9

[1] Preliminary.   [2] Pounds of feed equal in value to one pound of turkey, liveweight.   Source: Economic Research Service, U.S. Department of Agriculture (ERS-USDA)

Average Price Received by Farmers for Turkeys in the United States (Liveweight)   In Cents Per Pound

Year	Jan.	Feb.	Mar.	Apr.	May	June	July	Aug.	Sept.	Oct.	Nov.	Dec.	Average
2002	34.1	34.1	32.9	32.9	35.8	37.2	38.6	38.2	37.2	37.2	39.8	38.7	36.4
2003	34.6	34.5	35.1	35.6	34.9	34.9	33.6	32.7	36.2	39.1	41.2	38.2	35.9
2004	34.9	35.0	36.6	38.4	40.1	41.7	43.3	45.1	46.2	48.1	48.7	45.9	42.0
2005	39.3	38.0	38.1	38.8	40.7	42.1	44.6	46.5	50.3	52.5	54.5	53.9	44.9
2006	40.8	39.6	40.3	42.5	43.3	45.4	45.9	48.6	53.3	62.7	66.3	42.7	47.6
2007	40.8	42.4	44.3	46.8	48.3	52.0	55.5	57.2	60.4	61.5	61.6	52.6	52.0
2008	44.8	47.5	52.9	55.1	58.1	59.8	60.9	63.2	66.4	64.6	58.6	44.5	56.4
2009	43.8	46.5	47.1	47.6	50.1	52.5	52.0	51.1	48.5	52.1	54.1	53.7	49.9
2010	46.5	49.1	52.2	53.7	56.1	61.7	64.7	66.8	69.0	73.4	73.6	67.7	61.2
2011[1]	56.4	57.8	59.9	65.4	67.9	69.5	67.5	70.7	73.1	77.3	78.0	71.4	67.9

[1] Preliminary.   Source: Economic Research Service, U.S. Department of Agriculture (ERS-USDA)

Average Wholesale Price of Turkeys[1] (Hens, 8-16 Lbs.) in New York   In Cents Per Pound

Year	Jan.	Feb.	Mar.	Apr.	May	June	July	Aug.	Sept.	Oct.	Nov.	Dec.	Average
2002	60.86	60.03	59.00	59.52	63.52	65.68	66.52	66.56	67.15	67.75	69.79	66.96	64.45
2003	61.04	61.13	61.24	61.43	60.36	60.12	58.18	57.74	61.52	66.08	69.33	66.85	62.09
2004	62.13	61.61	62.62	64.52	66.41	68.95	71.21	73.32	74.69	76.89	78.29	76.05	69.72
2005	67.63	65.34	64.68	65.86	67.69	69.50	72.56	75.98	80.90	82.40	85.75	82.60	73.41
2006	68.29	65.84	67.67	69.75	71.27	72.95	74.95	78.70	84.40	95.83	99.51	74.20	76.95
2007	67.63	69.84	71.66	74.45	76.98	82.12	86.89	89.70	93.12	95.20	94.71	82.47	82.06
2008	73.74	76.40	82.20	85.99	89.19	91.45	92.91	96.85	99.62	97.27	87.44	74.88	87.33
2009	71.20	74.32	75.22	76.59	78.71	82.00	82.68	81.33	80.26	82.52	84.96	83.95	79.48
2010	76.50	78.72	82.64	83.90	86.45	93.38	98.68	102.45	105.81	111.03	109.29	101.16	94.17
2011[2]	88.14	89.97	92.38	96.68	99.75	103.14	104.00	105.39	109.79	114.83	113.57	106.54	102.02

[1] Ready-to-cook.   [2] Preliminary.   Source: Economic Research Service, U.S. Department of Agriculture (ERS-USDA)

Certified Federally Inspected Turkey Slaughter in the U.S. (Ready-to-Cook Weights)   In Millions of Pounds

Year	Jan.	Feb.	Mar.	Apr.	May	June	July	Aug.	Sept.	Oct.	Nov.	Dec.	Total
2002	477.2	442.1	447.8	487.2	496.7	448.0	474.7	475.9	439.4	519.0	488.2	457.9	5,654
2003	473.6	427.1	464.6	471.1	475.8	478.0	483.9	449.3	453.6	522.8	450.3	436.1	5,586
2004	435.5	389.0	466.6	445.2	445.1	462.8	455.4	462.2	451.2	461.5	479.6	434.4	5,389
2005	439.0	396.3	459.4	439.7	456.3	485.8	427.5	483.7	450.6	479.1	478.2	434.4	5,430
2006	443.0	412.4	487.9	430.3	492.8	504.4	453.5	493.6	456.5	535.8	499.7	423.5	5,633
2007	479.0	442.7	478.8	459.6	507.5	495.7	502.0	517.3	456.4	577.8	520.3	457.3	5,894
2008	544.6	504.0	484.5	515.9	517.9	519.7	544.1	503.8	511.5	570.1	507.9	488.2	6,212
2009	465.5	441.6	467.7	472.2	448.8	490.7	482.3	460.7	463.8	504.4	475.3	453.2	5,626
2010	421.1	423.3	488.0	452.8	437.5	487.0	463.9	478.2	464.1	521.7	518.0	458.6	5,614
2011[1]	460.9	432.8	500.4	453.8	494.6	516.3	445.7	499.1	470.8	521.5	509.3	456.9	5,762

[1] Preliminary.   Source: Economic Research Service, U.S. Department of Agriculture (ERS-USDA)

Per Capita Consumption of Turkeys in the United States   In Pounds

Year	First Quarter	Second Quarter	Third Quarter	Fourth Quarter	Total	Year	First Quarter	Second Quarter	Third Quarter	Fourth Quarter	Total
2001	3.9	3.8	4.3	5.6	17.5	2007	3.8	4.1	4.2	5.5	17.5
2002	3.5	3.9	4.4	5.9	17.7	2008	4.0	4.1	4.3	5.3	17.6
2003	3.6	3.9	4.6	5.3	17.4	2009	3.7	3.9	4.0	5.3	16.9
2004	3.6	4.0	4.5	5.0	17.0	2010	3.5	3.6	4.1	5.1	16.4
2005	3.6	3.9	4.2	5.1	16.7	2011[1]	3.5	3.5	3.9	5.2	16.2
2006	3.5	3.9	4.3	5.2	16.9	2012[2]	3.5	3.6	4.0	5.2	16.3

[1] Preliminary.   [2] Estimate.   Source: Economic Research Service, U.S. Department of Agriculture (ERS-USDA)

Storage Stocks of Turkeys (Frozen) in the United States on First of Month   In Millions of Pounds

Year	Jan.	Feb.	Mar.	Apr.	May	June	July	Aug.	Sept.	Oct.	Nov.	Dec.
2002	240.5	327.1	413.2	457.6	515.2	578.2	644.1	706.2	685.6	672.4	624.9	334.3
2003	333.0	451.9	492.7	549.3	573.5	658.8	718.2	722.5	706.5	647.5	582.7	350.7
2004	354.0	420.5	471.7	504.6	548.8	571.1	597.6	599.6	600.2	527.4	472.3	294.9
2005	288.4	332.9	379.4	414.2	440.1	465.9	506.3	518.9	523.1	477.8	417.6	194.7
2006	206.2	260.5	315.7	377.7	423.7	466.5	507.5	512.2	500.3	464.2	404.2	214.5
2007	218.4	293.4	312.9	346.8	360.2	398.0	448.4	503.5	524.4	504.9	417.0	206.9
2008	260.6	327.6	416.7	428.1	491.3	522.4	562.7	620.7	629.2	621.5	578.0	360.4
2009	396.1	446.2	462.4	513.4	571.7	585.7	594.7	641.1	653.5	613.9	517.5	244.5
2010	261.8	302.1	342.4	379.7	422.1	461.8	507.2	501.5	502.2	473.7	410.2	174.1
2011[1]	191.6	253.5	289.0	331.1	364.5	447.9	508.7	524.8	528.4	509.7	406.9	194.2

[1] Preliminary.   Source: Economic Research Service, U.S. Department of Agriculture (ERS-USDA)

Average Retail Price of Turkeys (Whole frozen) in the United States   In Cents Per Pound

Year	Jan.	Feb.	Mar.	Apr.	May	June	July	Aug.	Sept.	Oct.	Nov.	Dec.	Average
2002	102.2	105.1	106.6	104.0	102.5	107.3	108.0	106.8	106.6	111.7	103.8	98.8	105.3
2003	106.6	105.8	105.5	100.1	106.0	110.6	113.4	116.2	116.7	111.2	100.6	105.4	108.2
2004	108.4	109.4	113.4	108.4	109.0	111.7	112.9	114.2	108.8	112.3	99.6	100.3	109.0
2005	105.8	106.3	106.1	105.8	106.9	108.0	106.8	106.3	112.1	113.7	102.3	106.6	107.2
2006	106.9	119.7	120.9	111.1	108.4	112.8	113.0	110.6	115.1	114.9	97.3	99.1	110.8
2007	110.3	113.6	107.9	108.1	114.6	122.3	122.2	122.9	121.6	124.1	111.3	101.0	115.0
2008	120.7	123.0	115.1	117.0	125.8	123.8	127.0	128.8	132.0	122.2	130.9	133.2	125.0
2009	136.5	136.9	134.7	135.4	136.6	141.0	144.5	146.1	145.4	148.0	133.6	136.5	139.6
2010	139.8	137.5	142.5	147.9	146.4	147.4	155.4	152.1	156.6	167.7	140.7	138.0	147.7
2011[1]	145.9	152.6	157.2	156.2	159.6	158.1	160.3	164.1	167.6	167.3	154.1	157.4	158.4

[1] Preliminary.   Source: Economic Research Service, U.S. Department of Agriculture (ERS-USDA)

Average Retail-to-Consumer Price Spread of Turkeys (Whole) in the United States   In Cents Per Pound

Year	Jan.	Feb.	Mar.	Apr.	May	June	July	Aug.	Sept.	Oct.	Nov.	Dec.	Average
2002	34.2	37.9	40.7	38.3	32.9	35.9	35.9	34.9	35.4	40.2	29.8	24.6	35.1
2003	38.4	37.6	36.8	31.2	38.1	42.9	47.1	50.0	47.2	37.8	25.1	33.2	38.8
2004	39.4	40.4	42.5	35.0	33.5	33.9	33.3	32.5	25.7	26.9	14.0	18.0	31.3
2005	31.3	33.4	33.3	31.5	30.9	29.4	25.6	22.4	24.1	22.9	8.7	16.8	25.9
2006	29.4	44.5	44.8	32.8	28.6	30.8	29.6	22.9	21.5	9.3	-11.3	15.9	24.9
2007	33.7	34.3	27.2	25.2	28.7	30.9	26.5	24.6	19.7	20.0	7.4	9.8	24.0
2008	38.0	37.5	23.7	21.6	27.3	23.4	25.1	23.0	23.4	18.0	33.9	48.8	28.6
2009						51.0	53.9	56.0	56.2	56.3	39.4	43.7	50.9
2010	55.6	50.6	51.9	55.5	52.2			42.8	42.9	49.3	22.7	28.8	45.2
2011[1]	48.8							49.7	48.8	43.5	31.5	41.9	44.0

[1] Preliminary.   Source: Economic Research Service, U.S. Department of Agriculture (ERS-USDA)

Uranium

Uranium (symbol U) is a chemically reactive, radioactive, steel-gray, metallic element and is the main fuel used in nuclear reactors. Uranium is the heaviest of all the natural elements. Traces of uranium have been found in archeological artifacts dating back to 79 AD. Uranium was discovered in pitchblende by German chemist Martin Heinrich Klaproth in 1789. Klaproth named it uranium after the recently discovered planet Uranus. French physicist Antoine Henri Becquerel discovered the radioactive properties of uranium in 1896 when he produced an image on a photographic plate covered with a light-absorbing substance. Following Becquerel's experiments, investigations of radioactivity led to the discovery of radium and to new concepts of atomic organization.

The principal use for uranium is fuel in nuclear power plants. Demand for uranium concentrates is directly linked to the level of electricity generated by nuclear power plants. Uranium ores are widely distributed throughout the world and are primarily found in Canada, DRC (formerly Zaire), and the U.S... Uranium is obtained from primary mine production and secondary sources. Two Canadian companies are the primary producers of uranium from deposits in the Athabasca Basin of northern Saskatchewan. Specifically, the companies Cameco accounted for 19% of global mine production in 2000 and Cogema Resources accounted for 15% of world production. Secondary sources of uranium include excess inventories from utilities and other fuel cycle participants, used reactor fuel, and dismantled Russian nuclear weapons.

Prices – The average price of delivered uranium in 2010 (latest data available) rose by +7.5% yr/yr to $49.29 per pound, which is a record high. The 2001 price of $10.15 was the record low for the data series that goes back to 1981.

Supply – World production of uranium oxide (U308) concentrate in 2003 (latest data available) rose +7.3% yr/yr to a 13-year high of 56,552 short tons; up from 2002's production of 52,709 short tons. The world's largest uranium producers in 2003 were Canada with 17,050 short tons of production in 2003 (30% of world production), the U.S. with 10,200 short tons of production (18% of world production), and Australia with 9,326 short tons of production (16% of world production).

U.S. uranium production in 2003 (latest data available) rose +64.4% yr/yr to a 20-year high of 10,200 short tons, up sharply from the record low of 1,315 short tons in 2001. U.S. production had reached a peak of 21,850 short tons in 1980 and production had fallen steadily to the record low in 2001, which was only 6% of the record level of production. In the last two years production has increased significantly.

Trade – U.S. imports of uranium in 2010 (latest data available) fell -6.1% yr/yr to 55.300 million pounds. The record high of 66.100 million pounds was posted in 2004. The U.S. has generally been forced to import more uranium as domestic production steadily declined. U.S. exports of uranium in 2010 fell -1.7% yr/yr to 23.100 million pounds, which is slightly below the record high of 23.100 million pounds posted in 2009.

World Production of Uranium Oxide (U_3O_8) Concentrate — In Short Tons (Uranium Content)

Year	Australia	Canada	China	Czech Rep. & Slovakia	France	Gabon	Germany	Namibia	Niger	South Africa	United States	Ex-USSR	World Total
1994	3,050	11,950	----	----	1,700	750	----	2,500	3,800	2,250	1,950	----	41,750
1995	4,900	13,600	----	----	1,250	800	----	2,600	3,750	1,850	3,050	----	43,050
1996	6,450	15,250	----	----	1,200	750	----	3,150	4,300	2,200	3,150	----	46,650
1997	7,150	15,650	----	----	940	600	----	3,770	4,500	1,065	2,900	----	46,550
1998	6,350	14,200	----	----	660	950	----	3,590	4,850	1,250	2,435	----	44,110
1999	7,875	10,680	----	----	450	380	----	3,495	3,790	1,195	2,325	----	39,640
2000	9,830	13,875	655	795	525	----	45	2,430	3,270	1,305	1,890	655	43,475
2001	10,035	16,270	650	595	195	----	----	2,910	3,795	1,135	1,315	1,050	47,395
2002[1]	10,857	17,153	W	0	----	W	W	1,082	W	764	6,206	W	52,709
2003[2]	9,326	17,050	W	W	----	0	0	1,034	0	1,438	10,200	W	56,552

[1] Preliminary. [2] Estimate. W = Withheld. *Source: American Bureau of Metal Statistics, Inc. (ABMS)*

Commercial and U.S. Government Stocks of Uranium, End of Year — In Millions of Pounds U_3O_8 Equivalent

| | Utility | | Domestic Supplier | | Total | DOE Owned & USEC Held | |
Year	Natural Uranium	Enriched Uranium[1]	Natural Uranium	Enriched Uranium[1]	Commercial Stocks	Natural Uranium	Enriched Uranium[1]
2001	34.4	21.2	9.2	39.0	103.8	53.1	----
2002	31.0	22.4	15.0	32.9	102.1	51.8	----
2003	22.7	23.0	[2]	39.9	85.5	W	W
2004	27.9	29.8	[2]	37.5	95.2	W	W
2005	45.3	19.4	[2]	29.1	93.8	W	W
2006	54.3	23.2	[2]	29.1	106.6	W	W
2007	55.9	25.3	[2]	31.2	112.4	W	W
2008	58.8	24.2	[2]	27.0	110.0	W	W
2009	53.6	31.2	[2]	26.8	111.5	W	W
2010	48.8	37.7	[2]	25.7	112.3	W	W

[1] Includes amount reported as UF_6 at enrichment suppliers. [2] Included in Enriched beginning 2003. DOE = Department of Energy
USEC = U.S. Energy Commission *Source: Energy Information Administration, U.S. Department of Energy (EIA-DOE)*

Uranium Futures - CME Group (NYMEX)
(weekly close) as of December 30, 2011

Reported Average Price Settlements for Purchases by U.S. Utilities and Domestic Suppliers   In Dollars Per Pound

Year of Delivery	Contract Price	Market Price[1]	Price & Cost Floor	Total	Contract & Market	Year of Delivery	Contract Price	Market Price[1]	Price & Cost Floor	Total	Contract & Market
	----- Averages of Reported Prices -----						----- Averages of Reported Prices -----				
2001	11.72	8.04	----	10.15	----	2006	----	----	----	18.61	----
2002	10.73	9.79	----	10.36	----	2007	----	----	----	32.78	----
2003	----	----	----	10.81	----	2008	----	----	----	45.88	----
2004	----	----	----	12.61	----	2009	----	----	----	45.86	----
2005	----	----	----	14.36	----	2010	----	----	----	49.29	----

[1] No floor.   Note: Price excludes uranium delivered under litigation settlements. Price is given in year-of-delivery dollars.   *Source: Energy Information Administration, U.S. Department of Energy (EIA-DOE)*

Uranium Industry Statistics in the United States   In Millions of Pounds U_3O_8

Year	Production Mine	Production Concentrate	Concentrate Shipments	Exploration	Employment - Person Years Mining	Milling	Processing	Total[1]	Deliveries to U.S. Utilities[2]	Avg Price Delivered Uranium $/lb U_3O_8	Imports	Avg Price Delivered Uranium Imports $/lb U_3O_8	Exports
2006	4.7	4.106	3.838	188	121	W	W	755	66.5	18.61	64.8	19.31	18.7
2007	4.5	4.534	4.050	375	378	107	216	1,231	51.0	32.78	54.1	34.18	14.8
2008	3.9	3.902	4.130	457	558	W	W	1,563	53.4	45.88	57.1	41.30	17.2
2009	4.1	3.708	3.620	175	441	W	W	1,096	49.8	45.86	58.9	41.23	23.5
2010	4.2	4.228	5.137	211	400	W	W	1,073	46.6	49.29	55.3	47.01	23.1

[1] From suppliers under domestic purchases.   *Source: Energy Information Administration, U.S. Department of Energy (EIA-DOE)*

Volume of Trading of Uranium Futures in New York   In Contracts

Year	Jan.	Feb.	Mar.	Apr.	May	June	July	Aug.	Sept.	Oct.	Nov.	Dec.	Total
2007	----	----	----	----	220	50	38	372	164	116	250	58	1,268
2008	157	22	719	617	511	14	1,617	10	7,553	2,000	30	41	13,291
2009	408	40	1,400	16	1	600	1,300	400	403	0	1,581	0	6,149
2010	152	2	101	2,031	4,024	1,743	4,728	330	750	2,933	7,619	1,684	26,097
2011	537	2,483	2,996	845	2,049	10,438	436	1,026	466	906	211	205	22,598

Contract size = 250 pounds of U308.   *Source: CME Group; New York Mercantile Exchange (NYMEX)*

Average Open Interest of Uranium Futures in New York   In Contracts

Year	Jan.	Feb.	Mar.	Apr.	May	June	July	Aug.	Sept.	Oct.	Nov.	Dec.
2007	----	----	----	----	68	81	95	362	463	460	675	696
2008	552	508	1,158	1,479	1,949	1,912	2,200	2,206	2,644	2,604	2,544	2,343
2009	1,951	1,951	2,651	2,666	2,665	2,865	3,465	3,865	3,568	3,568	3,395	3,395
2010	3,277	3,279	2,980	4,710	8,013	9,753	11,742	11,649	12,274	13,534	15,154	15,622
2011	14,734	15,406	15,761	15,033	15,417	8,951	7,861	6,595	6,799	6,736	6,326	5,866

Contract size = 250 pounds of U308.   *Source: CME Group; New York Mercantile Exchange (NYMEX)*

Vanadium

Vanadium (symbol V) is a silvery-white, soft, ductile, metallic element. Discovered in 1801, but mistaken for chromium, vanadium was rediscovered in 1830 by Swedish chemist Nils Sefstrom, who named the element in honor of the Scandinavian goddess Vanadis.

Never found in the pure state, vanadium is found in about 65 different minerals such as carnotite, roscoelite, vanadinite, and patronite, as well as in phosphate rock, certain iron ores, some crude oils, and meteorites. Vanadium is one of the hardest of all metals. It melts at about 1890 degrees Celsius and boils at about 3380 degrees Celsius.

Vanadium has good structural strength and is used as an alloying agent with iron, steel, and titanium. It is used in aerospace applications, transmission gears, photography, as a reducing agent, and as a drying agent in various paints.

Prices – The price of vanadium in 2011 rose by +4.6% to $6.60 per pound but still well below the record high of $16.28 per pound in 2005.

Supply – Virtually all (99%) of vanadium is produced from ores, concentrates, and slag, with the remainder coming from petroleum residues, ash, and spent catalysts.

World production in 2011 from ore, concentrates and slag rose +4.2% to 60,000 metric tons. World production of all vanadium in 2010 (latest data available) rose +12.1% yr/yr to 57,600 metric tons.

The world's largest producer of vanadium from ores, concentrates and slag is China with 23,000 metric tons of production in 2011 which was 38% of total world production. The two other major producers are South Africa with 20,000 metric tons of production in 2011, which was 33% of world production, and Russia with 15,000 metric tons of production which was 25% of world production. Production in Russia and South Africa has been relatively stable in recent years, while China's production grew sharply in the late 1990s. China's production level of 23,000 metric tons in 2011 is a new record high and more than four times the levels seen in the early 1990s.

Trade – U.S. exports of vanadium in 2011 were in the forms of oxides & hydroxides (700 metric tons, -36.4% yr/yr), ferro-vanadium (300 metric tons, -50.9%), and vanadium pent-oxide, anhydride (100 metric tons, -28.6%). U.S. imports of vanadium in 2011 were in the forms of vanadium pent-oxide, anhydride (2,400 metric tons, -40.0% yr/yr); ferro-vanadium (1,000 metric tons, -25.4% yr/yr); ore, slag and residues (900 metric tons), +72.7% yr/yr; and oxides & hydroxides (650 metric tons), +289.2% yr/yr).

World Production of Vanadium — In Metric Tons (Contained Vanadium)

	------- From Ores, Concentrates and Slag -------						From Petroleum Residues Ash, Spent Catalysts			
Year	Australia	China[3]	Kazak-hstan	Russia	South Africa	Total[4]	Japan[5]	United States[6]	Total	World Total
2006	----	17,500	1,000	15,100	23,780	57,400	560	----	560	57,900
2007	----	19,000	1,000	14,500	23,486	58,000	560	----	560	58,500
2008	----	20,000	1,000	14,500	20,295	55,800	560	----	560	56,400
2009	----	21,000	1,000	14,500	14,353	50,900	560	----	560	51,400
2010[1]	----	22,000	1,000	14,500	19,000	57,600	560	----	560	57,600
2011[2]	----	23,000		15,000	20,000	60,000				

[1] Preliminary. [2] Estimate. [3] In vanadiferous slag product. [4] Excludes U.S. production. [5] In vanadium pentoxide product.
[6] In vanadium pentoxide and ferrovanadium products. Source: U.S. Geological Survey (USGS)

Salient Statistics of Vanadium in the United States — In Metric Tons (Contained Vanadium)

Year	Con-sumer & Producer Stocks, Dec. 31	Tool Steel	Cast Irons	High Strength, Low Alloy	Stainless & Heat Resisting	Super-alloys	Carbon	Full Alloy	Total	Average $ Per Lb. V₂O₅	Vanadium Pent-oxide Anhydride	Oxides & Hydr-oxides	Ferro-Vana-dium	Ores, Slag, Residues	Vanadium Pent-oxide Anhydride	Oxides & Hydr-oxides	Ferro-Vana-dium
2006	330	323	W	1,020	61	40	1,210	1,030	4,030	7.86	341	832	515	637	1,920	129	2,140
2007	324	379	W	1,560	61	44	1,190	1,380	4,970	7.40	327	626	206	1,000	2,390	42	2,220
2008	335	152	W	W	116	39	1,010	2,030	5,170	12.92	249	1,040	452	1,040	3,700	144	2,800
2009	295	W	W	1,540	119	12	832	1,920	4,690	5.43	401	506	672	791	1,120	25	353
2010[1]	248	W	W	W	120	9	843	2,030	5,030	6.50	140	1,100	611	521	4,000	167	1,340
2011[2]	190									6.80	100	700	300	900	2,400	650	1,000

Column group headers: Vanadium Consumption by Uses in the U.S. (Tool Steel, Cast Irons, High Strength Low Alloy, Stainless & Heat Resisting, Super-alloys, Carbon, Full Alloy, Total); Exports (Vanadium Pent-oxide Anhydride, Oxides & Hydroxides, Ferro-Vanadium); Imports (Ores Slag Residues, Vanadium Pent-oxide Anhydride, Oxides & Hydroxides, Ferro-Vanadium)

[1] Preliminary. [2] Estimate. W = Withheld. Source: U.S. Geological Survey (USGS)

Average Price of Vanadium Pentoxide — In Dollars Per Pound

Year	Jan.	Feb.	Mar.	Apr.	May	June	July	Aug.	Sept.	Oct.	Nov.	Dec.	Average
2005	9.65	10.24	13.75	15.00	20.36	26.16	19.96	11.63	11.10	13.74	13.75	11.00	14.70
2006	8.73	9.11	8.78	7.92	8.15	8.08	7.40	7.07	7.85	7.70	7.27	6.70	7.90
2007	6.21	6.34	7.22	8.10	7.98	7.67	7.48	7.36	7.64	7.74	7.67	7.40	7.40
2008	8.03	13.11	15.80	14.60	15.85	17.61	15.65	16.39	15.23	12.83	9.85	8.66	13.63
2009	6.50	6.05	5.66	4.75	3.73	4.78	5.25	6.11	6.93	6.69	6.13	6.13	5.73
2010	6.97	7.25	7.72	8.00	7.85	6.96	6.23	6.41	6.75	6.63	6.63	6.63	7.00

Source: American Metal Market (AMM)

Vegetables

Vegetables are the edible products of herbaceous plants, which are plants with soft stems. Vegetables are grouped according to the edible part of each plant including leaves (e.g., lettuce), stalks (celery), roots (carrot), tubers (potato), bulbs (onion), fruits (tomato), seeds (pea), and flowers (broccoli). Each of these groups contributes to the human diet in its own way. Fleshy roots are high in energy value and good sources of the vitamin B group, seeds are relatively high in carbohydrates and proteins, while leaves, stalks, and fruits are excellent sources of minerals, vitamins, water, and roughage. Vegetables are an important food for the maintenance of health and prevention of disease. Higher intakes of vegetables have been shown to lower the risks of cancer and coronary heart disease.

Vegetables are best consumed fresh in their raw state in order to derive the maximum benefits from their nutrients. While canned and frozen vegetables are often thought to be inferior to fresh vegetables, they are sometimes nutritionally superior to fresh produce because they are usually processed immediately after harvest when nutrient content is at its peak. When cooking vegetables, aluminum utensils should not be used, because aluminum is a soft metal that is affected by food acids and alkalis. Scientific evidence shows that tiny particles of aluminum from foods cooked in aluminum utensils enter the stomach and can injure the sensitive lining of the stomach.

Prices – The monthly average index of fresh vegetable prices received by growers in the U.S. in 2011 rose by +0.7% to 195.4, a new record high.

Demand – The leading vegetable in terms of U.S. per capita consumption in 2011 was the potato with 109.9 pounds of consumption. Runner-up vegetables were tomatoes (93.6 pounds), sweet corn (24.6 pounds), lettuce (27.1 pounds), and onions (21.3 pounds). Total U.S. per capita vegetable consumption in 2011 rose +6.3% to 417.5 pounds.

Index of Prices Received by Growers for Commercial Vegetables[2] in the United States   (1990-92=100)

Year	Jan.	Feb.	Mar.	Apr.	May	June	July	Aug.	Sept.	Oct.	Nov.	Dec.	Average
2006	128	115	133	151	156	131	119	152	160	123	119	150	136
2007	177	165	192	181	144	133	126	146	155	196	139	138	158
2008	138	118	134	162	154	153	143	143	174	178	154	155	151
2009	173	139	151	176	141	155	135	140	135	167	216	208	161
2010	148	147	210	190	172	152	150	151	149	142	183	155	162
2011[1]	193	274	218	164	173	159	158	148	139	129	129		171

[1] Preliminary.   [2] Includes fresh and processing vegetables.   Not seasonally adjusted.   Source: National Agricultural Statistics Service, U.S. Department of Agriculture (NASS-USDA)

Index of Prices Received by Growers for Fresh Vegetables in the United States   (1990-92=100)

Year	Jan.	Feb.	Mar.	Apr.	May	June	July	Aug.	Sept.	Oct.	Nov.	Dec.	Average
2006	207.6	138.8	137.6	174.4	147.9	128.7	134.1	179.5	193.1	167.7	138.3	178.4	160.5
2007	175.3	190.3	222.4	222.5	142.1	145.4	146.0	137.8	162.7	218.3	177.4	204.5	178.7
2008	200.2	158.3	194.1	179.3	170.7	191.7	168.3	146.1	158.7	185.1	200.3	155.9	175.7
2009	179.8	163.6	167.4	182.3	134.1	182.5	149.8	144.3	140.4	180.6	197.8	210.4	169.4
2010	178.6	190.6	310.4	274.1	215.4	158.6	177.1	157.3	171.2	153.7	156.0	186.7	194.1
2011[1]	211.2	341.1	267.7	184.7	156.9	174.2	148.7	146.6	174.1	171.4	199.1	169.2	195.4

[1] Preliminary.   Not seasonally adjusted.   Source: National Agricultural Statistics Service, U.S. Department of Agriculture (NASS-USDA)

Producer Price Index of Canned[2] Processed Vegetables in the United States   (1982 = 100)

Year	Jan.	Feb.	Mar.	Apr.	May	June	July	Aug.	Sept.	Oct.	Nov.	Dec.	Average
2006	138.0	136.8	137.1	137.3	138.8	140.2	140.0	140.5	141.4	141.5	142.2	142.2	139.7
2007	142.8	142.9	143.1	143.3	143.5	143.6	143.1	143.1	144.0	143.9	144.2	144.6	143.5
2008	147.8	148.4	149.6	151.2	150.2	151.3	153.3	158.6	162.5	163.0	164.2	167.8	155.7
2009	168.9	169.0	170.5	170.7	171.0	171.1	171.3	170.9	170.6	170.7	169.9	169.2	170.3
2010	169.8	167.3	167.2	167.0	166.7	166.0	164.1	164.6	161.6	161.1	162.0	161.7	164.9
2011[1]	162.2	162.0	162.7	164.4	164.4	164.9	166.9	168.1	169.8	170.2	170.6	171.3	166.5

[1] Preliminary.   [2] Includes canned vegetables and juices, including hominy and mushrooms.   Not seasonally adjusted.   Source: Bureau of Labor Statistics, U.S. Department of Labor (BLS)

Producer Price Index of Frozen Processed Vegetables in the United States   (1982 = 100)

Year	Jan.	Feb.	Mar.	Apr.	May	June	July	Aug.	Sept.	Oct.	Nov.	Dec.	Average
2006	137.3	137.7	138.7	138.6	138.8	139.5	139.4	139.3	139.9	142.0	142.7	142.6	139.7
2007	144.0	144.0	144.0	145.2	145.9	146.7	148.2	149.3	149.9	151.5	152.5	153.2	147.9
2008	153.3	153.8	155.6	156.5	156.7	157.1	158.8	161.1	163.9	170.6	172.7	177.9	161.5
2009	176.5	178.1	178.5	178.1	178.1	178.5	178.1	177.4	179.3	180.3	180.4	180.1	178.6
2010	179.9	180.3	180.8	180.2	180.5	180.3	179.6	179.8	179.0	174.9	175.5	175.9	178.9
2011[1]	174.8	175.2	175.3	176.0	176.1	177.7	183.9	185.1	186.0	186.7	191.6	193.3	181.8

[1] Preliminary.   Not seasonally adjusted.   Source: Bureau of Labor Statistics, U.S. Department of Labor (BLS)

Per Capita Use of Selected Commercially Produced Fresh and Processing Vegetables and Melons in the United States
In Pounds, farm weight basis

Crop	2003	2004	2005	2006	2007	2008	2009	2010	2011[10]	2012[11]
Asparagus, All	1.3	1.4	1.4	1.4	1.4	1.5	1.5	1.6	1.6	1.6
Fresh	1.0	1.1	1.1	1.1	1.2	1.2	1.3	1.4	1.4	1.4
Canning	0.2	0.2	0.2	0.2	0.1	0.2	0.2	0.1	0.1	0.1
Freezing	0.1	0.1	0.1	0.1	0.1	0.1	0.1	0.1	0.1	0.1
Snap beans, All	7.5	7.6	7.6	7.9	7.8	7.4	7.2	7.5	7.2	6.7
Fresh	2.0	1.9	1.8	2.1	2.2	2.0	1.8	1.9	1.9	1.9
Canning	3.7	3.7	4.0	3.9	3.5	3.3	3.6	3.7	3.4	3.1
Freezing	1.9	1.9	1.8	1.9	2.1	2.1	1.9	2.0	1.9	1.8
Broccoli, All [1]	7.9	8.0	8.1	8.0	8.3	8.7	8.7	8.0	8.5	8.3
Fresh	5.4	5.3	5.3	5.8	5.6	6.0	6.2	5.6	5.9	5.8
Freezing	2.6	2.7	2.7	2.3	2.7	2.7	2.5	2.5	2.5	2.5
Cabbage, All	8.5	9.1	9.0	9.0	9.0	9.0	8.1	8.3	8.4	8.1
Fresh	7.4	8.0	7.8	7.8	8.0	8.1	7.3	7.5	7.5	7.3
Canning (kraut)	1.1	1.1	1.2	1.2	1.0	0.9	0.9	0.8	0.8	0.8
Carrots, All [2]	11.9	11.8	11.8	11.2	10.5	10.6	9.7	9.8	10.0	10.0
Fresh	8.8	8.7	8.7	8.1	8.1	8.1	7.4	7.6	7.6	7.5
Canning	1.1	1.1	1.1	1.0	0.9	1.0	0.9	0.7	0.9	0.9
Freezing	2.0	2.0	2.0	2.1	1.5	1.5	1.5	1.5	1.5	1.7
Cauliflower, All [1]	1.9	1.9	2.1	2.1	2.0	2.0	2.1	1.7	1.8	1.8
Fresh	1.6	1.6	1.8	1.7	1.7	1.6	1.7	1.3	1.4	1.4
Freezing	0.4	0.4	0.4	0.4	0.4	0.4	0.4	0.4	0.4	0.4
Celery	6.3	6.2	5.9	6.1	6.3	6.2	6.2	6.2	6.2	6.2
Sweet Corn, All [3]	26.5	26.2	26.7	26.1	26.1	25.1	25.8	24.6	24.3	24.2
Fresh	9.2	9.0	8.7	8.3	9.2	9.1	9.2	9.2	9.2	9.1
Canning	8.3	8.2	8.6	8.4	6.9	6.7	7.6	6.8	6.5	6.2
Freezing	9.0	9.1	9.5	9.4	10.0	9.3	9.1	8.5	8.6	9.0
Cucumbers, All	10.6	11.3	10.0	9.1	10.2	9.9	11.9	10.5	10.0	10.5
Fresh	6.2	6.4	6.2	6.2	6.4	6.4	6.8	6.8	6.6	6.6
Pickling	4.5	4.9	3.8	3.0	3.7	3.5	5.1	3.7	3.3	3.9
Melons	27.1	25.4	25.6	26.9	26.4	26.7	26.2	26.1	25.9	25.6
Watermelon	13.5	13.0	13.6	15.1	14.4	15.6	14.9	15.5	15.1	15.0
Cantaloupe	10.8	9.8	9.6	9.3	9.6	8.9	9.1	8.5	8.5	8.4
Honeydew	2.2	2.1	1.9	1.9	1.8	1.7	1.6	1.5	1.5	1.5
Other	0.6	0.5	0.6	0.6	0.6	0.5	0.5	0.6	0.8	0.7
Lettuce, All	33.1	33.2	30.6	32.0	29.9	27.3	26.1	26.9	26.7	26.8
Head lettuce	22.2	21.3	20.9	20.1	18.4	16.9	16.1	16.1	16.2	16.0
Romaine & Leaf	10.8	12.0	9.7	12.0	11.5	10.4	10.0	10.7	10.6	10.8
Onions, All	21.4	23.4	22.0	21.7	22.6	21.7	21.5	21.4	21.2	21.1
Fresh	19.5	21.9	20.9	19.9	21.6	20.2	19.6	19.9	19.7	19.5
Dehydrating	1.8	1.5	1.1	1.8	1.0	1.5	1.9	1.5	1.5	1.5
Green Peas, All [4]	3.1	2.8	2.7	2.8	3.0	2.9	3.0	2.7	2.7	2.6
Canning	1.3	1.2	1.1	1.2	1.2	1.1	1.3	1.2	1.1	1.1
Freezing	1.8	1.6	1.6	1.6	1.8	1.8	1.7	1.6	1.6	1.5
Peppers, All	14.0	14.8	15.3	15.8	15.2	15.8	16.4	16.4	16.4	16.4
Bell Peppers, All	8.4	8.6	9.2	9.5	9.4	9.6	9.8	9.9	9.8	9.7
Chile Peppers, All	5.6	6.1	6.1	6.4	5.9	6.2	6.6	6.5	6.6	6.7
Tomatoes, All	89.3	90.5	93.9	84.3	87.9	85.6	89.9	91.8	93.5	91.3
Fresh	19.4	20.0	20.2	19.8	19.2	18.5	19.6	20.8	20.6	20.8
Canning	69.9	70.5	73.7	64.5	68.7	67.1	70.3	71.0	72.9	70.6
Other, Fresh [5]	18.6	19.4	20.1	20.1	19.4	19.1	18.6	18.6	18.1	18.3
Other, Canning [6]	2.3	2.7	2.9	2.6	2.6	2.5	2.3	2.6	2.4	2.4
Other, Freezing [7]	3.9	3.8	4.1	4.1	4.1	4.0	4.3	4.4	4.1	4.1
Subtotal, All [8]	295.2	299.5	299.5	291.1	292.7	286.0	289.5	289.2	288.8	286.0
Fresh	173.7	176.8	173.7	175.2	174.5	170.0	167.6	169.6	168.6	167.9
Canning	98.0	99.7	102.7	92.3	94.5	92.6	98.7	97.1	98.0	95.6
Freezing	21.6	21.5	22.1	21.8	22.6	21.9	21.4	20.9	20.7	21.0
Potatoes, All	137.9	134.6	125.4	123.7	124.4	118.3	113.5	113.9	112.2	112.4
Fresh	46.8	45.8	41.3	38.6	38.7	37.8	36.7	36.8	35.0	35.2
Processing	91.2	88.8	84.1	85.1	85.7	80.5	76.8	77.1	77.2	77.2
Sweet Potatoes	4.7	4.6	4.5	4.6	5.1	5.0	5.2	6.3	6.9	6.9
Mushrooms	4.1	4.2	3.9	4.0	3.9	3.6	3.6	3.8	3.9	3.9
Dry Peas & Lentils [9]	0.6	0.7	0.8	1.2	0.7	0.4	1.0	1.2	0.9	0.8
Dry Edible Beans	6.7	5.9	6.1	6.5	6.4	6.4	6.0	7.1	6.2	6.4
Total, All Items	449.3	449.5	440.2	431.0	433.1	419.7	418.8	421.4	418.9	416.3

[1] All production for processing broccoli and cauliflower is for freezing. [2] Industry allocation suggests that 27 percent of processing carrot production is for canning and 73 percent is for freezing. [3] On-cob basis. [4] In-shell basis. [5] Includes artichokes, brussels sprouts, eggplant, endive/escarole, garlic, radishes, green limas, squash, and spinach. In 2000, okra, pumpkins, kale, collards, turnip greens and mustard greens added. [6] Includes beets, green limas (1992-2003), spinach, and miscellaneous imports (1990-2001). [7] Includes green limas, spinach, and miscellaneous freezing vegetables. [8] Fresh, canning, and freezing data do not sum to the total because onions for dehydrating are included in the total. [9] Production from new areas in upper midwest added in 1998. A portion of this is likely for feed use. [10] Preliminary. [11] Forecast. NA = Not available. *Source: Economic Research Service, U.S. Department of Agriculture (ERS-USDA)*

Average Price Received by Growers for Broccoli in the United States In Dollars Per Cwt

Year	Jan.	Feb.	Mar.	Apr.	May	June	July	Aug.	Sept.	Oct.	Nov.	Dec.	Season Average
2004	33.60	28.50	21.60	24.00	27.20	28.70	24.20	29.70	57.00	43.90	44.20	45.40	33.20
2005	22.60	33.30	42.60	39.80	22.40	39.70	22.40	30.50	27.70	22.40	20.90	34.10	28.50
2006	32.50	23.80	27.60	32.40	29.00	51.10	26.20	56.90	39.40	24.60	27.50	53.10	33.70
2007	69.80	25.40	27.60	36.90	26.70	24.80	28.80	38.20	41.80	61.00	38.10	40.70	36.70
2008	47.90	24.40	30.80	52.10	25.20	29.60	26.70	26.60	41.10	57.50	41.20	33.70	36.20
2009	44.60	29.50	46.90	41.90	32.80	31.00	26.50	29.70	31.60	64.60	57.10	53.50	37.80
2010	26.50	26.70	48.30	35.40	43.50	34.50	29.30	25.70	33.30	30.40	55.30	66.60	35.40
2011[1]	57.10	45.40	41.10	33.90	40.20	55.70	28.70	35.60	33.60	33.10	43.00	51.60	

[1]Preliminary.   Source: National Agricultural Statistics Service, U.S. Department of Agriculture (NASS-USDA)

Average Price Received by Growers for Carrots in the United States In Dollars Per Cwt

Year	Jan.	Feb.	Mar.	Apr.	May	June	July	Aug.	Sept.	Oct.	Nov.	Dec.	Season Average
2004	24.50	24.90	24.60	24.20	24.90	22.50	20.20	18.00	16.70	16.40	17.20	18.00	20.20
2005	20.30	21.00	21.00	21.10	21.20	21.30	21.80	21.40	20.00	21.40	23.10	22.00	20.90
2006	21.40	21.50	21.50	21.50	20.80	21.40	21.50	22.40	19.30	19.80	20.20	19.10	20.60
2007	21.00	28.10	28.30	29.60	32.00	25.90	19.70	17.10	16.10	15.80	15.80	16.20	22.10
2008	16.20	25.90	25.90	25.50	32.00	25.60	25.60	25.60	25.30	25.20	24.70	25.20	24.50
2009	25.20	25.20	25.20	25.20	25.50	25.80	25.60	24.00	25.20	25.30	27.20	27.80	25.20
2010	28.50	23.90	27.50	27.40	27.40	26.20	27.10	27.10	26.80	26.90	27.60	33.00	26.20
2011[1]	38.00	40.70	44.60	46.20	44.80	35.10	28.40	28.00	27.60	27.50	26.80	25.50	

[1]Preliminary.   Source: National Agricultural Statistics Service, U.S. Department of Agriculture (NASS-USDA)

Average Price Received by Growers for Cauliflower in the United States In Dollars Per Cwt

Year	Jan.	Feb.	Mar.	Apr.	May	June	July	Aug.	Sept.	Oct.	Nov.	Dec.	Season Average
2004	27.30	42.20	24.20	23.50	28.80	46.20	27.60	26.30	31.10	32.20	43.80	54.40	30.80
2005	27.70	38.20	50.60	36.70	29.70	38.10	25.60	31.50	28.50	19.70	25.50	43.90	30.30
2006	33.10	26.40	31.40	32.80	29.00	51.10	26.20	56.90	39.40	24.60	34.80	41.60	32.30
2007	45.70	29.40	51.40	51.60	24.90	30.00	22.30	27.90	27.20	46.20	26.60	52.40	34.40
2008	51.80	30.00	41.70	63.80	24.90	53.90	38.20	43.20	29.50	48.50	29.50	43.90	40.70
2009	68.20	30.00	51.30	41.40	46.60	43.50	41.70	31.90	26.90	58.10	54.40	47.10	44.40
2010	33.20	36.70	50.40	58.00	68.60	32.90	31.20	26.30	27.70	31.50	52.60	66.40	39.60
2011[1]	41.10	55.90	51.50	42.90	56.80	52.80	38.40	30.90	29.70	30.30	66.90	66.20	

[1]Preliminary.   Source: National Agricultural Statistics Service, U.S. Department of Agriculture (NASS-USDA)

Average Price Received by Growers for Celery in the United States In Dollars Per Cwt

Year	Jan.	Feb.	Mar.	Apr.	May	June	July	Aug.	Sept.	Oct.	Nov.	Dec.	Season Average
2004	20.80	24.40	13.90	15.60	15.00	13.80	12.00	10.00	11.90	15.10	18.10	13.40	14.80
2005	12.90	22.90	28.40	20.80	15.50	9.62	10.00	10.80	12.80	12.20	13.10	10.70	13.90
2006	9.64	10.80	14.90	16.60	12.70	17.80	21.00	23.30	27.70	27.10	22.00	20.20	18.20
2007	33.90	58.90	31.90	18.80	18.30	11.60	11.60	9.64	13.80	13.30	18.60	13.50	20.40
2008	16.20	13.20	13.40	14.00	37.40	30.10	22.10	12.40	11.90	17.10	16.90	20.30	18.50
2009	35.10	29.70	15.00	17.40	17.40	11.70	11.30	11.40	12.00	20.90	21.10	38.80	18.50
2010	37.40	21.60	25.70	17.10	20.00	15.80	16.00	13.90	15.10	15.00	14.30	20.20	19.70
2011[1]	25.10	46.50	29.50	19.30	33.10	17.10	17.50	14.30	12.50	12.00	15.00	14.90	

[1]Preliminary.   Source: National Agricultural Statistics Service, U.S. Department of Agriculture (NASS-USDA)

Average Price Received by Growers for Sweet Corn in the United States In Dollars Per Cwt

Year	Jan.	Feb.	Mar.	Apr.	May	June	July	Aug.	Sept.	Oct.	Nov.	Dec.	Season Average
2004	30.80	20.70	20.20	17.60	18.10	22.80	21.80	22.90	24.10	33.50	46.70	36.80	20.80
2005	21.30	28.60	26.10	21.50	18.10	22.60	22.20	20.30	24.70	25.50	37.30	21.20	22.10
2006	36.50	35.00	34.00	27.20	15.40	21.60	21.10	22.70	25.90	21.20	20.00	14.40	23.00
2007	27.40	23.60	30.20	25.60	21.40	17.30	22.20	22.80	23.20	21.40	20.60	34.10	22.70
2008	30.80	23.00	28.60	20.50	21.90	19.90	28.50	27.20	27.10	23.70	30.80	22.20	25.90
2009	24.90	46.40	59.30	32.50	20.80	25.40	34.60	26.40	23.70	23.30	19.80	19.40	29.40
2010	37.80	58.50	62.70	40.10	25.10	16.00	20.20	23.10	24.00	28.00	20.60	31.60	25.70
2011[1]	62.20	51.80	42.40	23.80	22.20	24.00	33.00	28.30	24.60	28.40	25.00	14.90	

[1]Preliminary.   Source: National Agricultural Statistics Service, U.S. Department of Agriculture (NASS-USDA)

VEGETABLES

Average Price Received by Growers for Head Lettuce in the United States   In Dollars Per Cwt

Year	Jan.	Feb.	Mar.	Apr.	May	June	July	Aug.	Sept.	Oct.	Nov.	Dec.	Season Average
2002	26.20	44.10	86.40	14.10	10.20	10.60	11.30	14.60	14.30	13.50	11.90	30.00	21.10
2003	12.10	11.80	9.64	12.50	21.20	32.20	11.90	21.50	23.90	26.30	31.70	21.30	18.10
2004	15.40	19.80	10.40	14.80	10.50	13.30	10.70	17.10	15.20	24.10	14.90	15.70	16.90
2005	11.50	11.70	27.90	30.10	13.90	17.30	11.00	13.50	12.70	12.40	9.81	16.60	15.50
2006	10.50	12.00	19.10	22.40	33.70	11.80	12.20	20.70	16.30	11.80	12.50	22.40	16.90
2007	20.80	15.50	29.70	17.80	13.60	17.80	17.30	23.10	29.20	44.40	17.40	16.00	21.70
2008	17.60	13.40	14.70	21.60	15.50	17.70	17.30	17.20	31.90	32.90	18.80	23.50	20.10
2009	28.50	17.80	19.40	27.70	18.20	18.90	16.90	16.70	16.60	27.20	49.60	38.70	21.70
2010	17.30	14.10	20.80	19.00	24.30	25.70	26.00	23.30	17.20	20.20	35.40	17.50	23.80
2011[1]	27.20	54.40	35.20	17.80	26.40	17.10	19.40	14.70	14.80	17.00	30.50	17.40	

[1]Preliminary.   Source: National Agricultural Statistics Service, U.S. Department of Agriculture (NASS-USDA)

Average Price Received by Growers for Tomatoes in the United States   In Dollars Per Cwt

Year	Jan.	Feb.	Mar.	Apr.	May	June	July	Aug.	Sept.	Oct.	Nov.	Dec.	Season Average
2002	40.50	26.60	38.50	34.30	29.60	33.00	28.50	25.80	23.70	27.60	40.10	38.00	31.60
2003	47.20	31.70	53.30	30.00	23.70	45.70	37.60	41.00	35.70	30.10	30.50	29.10	37.40
2004	34.50	36.30	42.20	44.20	32.20	21.70	23.40	37.80	38.20	67.90	89.00	47.10	37.60
2005	15.40	40.90	40.70	65.10	49.40	40.00	28.00	26.10	46.10	37.30	36.50	96.80	41.80
2006	79.20	46.50	24.80	34.40	23.30	30.90	25.10	27.80	79.80	53.20	28.10	24.80	43.70
2007	35.60	31.20	26.30	52.60	35.60	29.60	26.70	28.60	33.10	41.60	58.70	81.20	34.80
2008	58.20	45.50	66.10	47.40	48.20	56.80	40.90	29.40	25.60	33.80	64.90	37.90	45.50
2009	29.30	32.70	41.50	45.40	33.20	67.20	31.70	35.90	34.40	40.20	73.70	65.00	40.60
2010	58.90	84.60	109.00	103.00	65.20	37.30	33.60	35.50	38.40	32.00	38.10	37.30	48.10
2011[1]	51.90	108.00	98.70	67.60	49.10	43.50	33.70	30.40	35.30	26.60	44.70	26.50	

[1]Preliminary.   Source: National Agricultural Statistics Service, U.S. Department of Agriculture (NASS-USDA)

Frozen Vegetables: January 1 and July 1 Cold Storage Holdings in the United States   In Thousands of Pounds

	2007	2008		2009		2010		2011		2012[1]
Crop	July 1	Jan. 1	July 1	Jan. 1	July 1	Jan. 1	July 1	Jan. 1	July 1	Jan. 1
Asparagus	9,952	5,409	9,964	7,368	12,279	9,057	11,127	7,630	10,018	6,615
Limas, Fordhook	2,619	7,442	2,209	3,676	960	2,973	2,622	7,255	----	----
Limas, Baby	18,367	40,364	16,213	41,020	20,264	58,390	31,238	49,100	34,313	54,711
Green Beans, Reg. Cut	72,177	183,696	70,854	211,997	95,706	176,371	70,842	166,011	61,436	192,235
Green Beans, Fr. Style	9,303	32,284	12,675	29,298	13,140	25,325	13,169	19,028	8,220	22,509
Broccoli, Spears	23,878	24,078	33,587	36,649	37,560	29,456	35,163	20,851	32,338	25,164
Broccoli, Chopped & Cut	40,715	36,422	49,873	45,513	24,864	41,547	48,760	34,885	37,149	44,822
Brussels sprouts	11,535	21,491	10,392	21,049	12,898	20,789	13,813	17,845	10,510	11,135
Carrots, Diced	53,574	128,121	68,556	156,398	95,309	165,191	94,385	159,405	91,040	158,524
Carrots, Other	51,911	142,063	85,955	150,459	99,242	155,247	86,154	150,944	79,677	145,066
Cauliflower	17,768	36,694	20,334	27,564	16,266	27,066	19,977	23,524	16,707	23,433
Corn, Cut	161,547	461,503	172,494	463,724	202,653	584,048	305,686	571,012	216,687	458,788
Corn, Cob	69,152	256,464	78,251	264,562	98,389	252,108	102,824	249,387	101,891	249,459
Mixed vegetables	43,342	43,868	46,341	47,729	54,394	50,129	46,561	38,245	45,834	49,143
Okra	16,638	23,720	21,505	24,115	21,470	29,030	14,933	21,457	24,921	34,611
Onion Rings	8,136	7,428	5,925	6,628	4,306	3,456	5,382	4,955	5,611	4,435
Onions, Other	26,527	32,010	39,190	29,564	26,699	35,511	19,737	32,549	48,162	69,243
Blackeye Peas	3,136	4,394	2,815	2,737	1,519	3,653	2,757	2,764	2,447	1,756
Green Peas	241,116	232,647	198,133	255,471	252,937	275,625	298,995	276,587	234,439	238,909
Peas and Carrots Mixed	4,654	5,090	4,756	5,109	5,258	6,075	7,096	5,992	6,294	5,082
Spinach	70,443	47,467	80,320	42,505	87,057	47,993	96,542	52,103	84,296	49,062
Squash, Summer/Zucchini	49,275	62,534	46,531	56,537	40,733	52,275	39,685	64,783	39,010	73,109
Southern greens	10,741	12,833	14,231	12,632	16,551	11,621	16,742	13,507	20,022	15,084
Other Vegetables	220,569	373,370	275,882	423,684	293,501	408,829	280,686	360,009	264,367	372,890
Total	1,237,075	2,221,392	1,366,986	2,365,988	1,563,955	2,471,765	1,664,876	2,354,112	1,475,389	2,305,785
Potatoes, French Fries	871,947	820,461	947,666	874,095	1,011,186	847,238	899,847	820,872	866,965	802,278
Potatoes, Other Frozen	206,261	191,894	242,365	224,485	233,941	196,607	242,099	198,033	220,707	197,635
Potatoes, Total	1,078,208	1,012,355	1,190,031	1,098,580	1,245,127	1,043,845	1,141,946	1,018,905	1,087,672	999,913
Grand Total	2,315,283	3,233,747	2,557,017	3,464,568	2,809,082	3,515,610	2,806,822	3,373,017	2,563,061	3,305,698

Cold Storage Stocks of Frozen Green Beans[2] in the United States, on First of Month In Thousands of Pounds

Year	Jan.	Feb.	Mar.	Apr.	May	June	July	Aug.	Sept.	Oct.	Nov.	Dec.
2006	171,319	143,654	121,644	101,480	81,681	66,245	54,377	122,147	199,238	249,492	232,397	219,053
2007	183,610	159,544	141,661	117,447	98,894	83,761	72,177	123,094	201,269	234,744	220,553	205,671
2008	183,696	163,431	138,508	121,767	100,988	86,190	70,854	122,470	203,585	246,495	238,098	231,706
2009	211,997	188,915	169,346	147,596	126,359	116,493	95,706	139,967	197,238	240,107	211,003	194,184
2010	176,371	159,532	142,137	123,047	92,954	80,754	70,842	109,413	164,357	223,928	198,883	182,202
2011[1]	166,011	139,152	124,368	104,929	86,575	76,704	61,436	94,272	168,094	233,617	207,954	195,509

[1] Preliminary.   [2] Regular cut.   *Source: Economic Research Service, U.S. Department of Agriculture (ERS-USDA)*

Cold Storage Stocks of Frozen Corn[2] in the United States, on First of Month In Thousands of Pounds

Year	Jan.	Feb.	Mar.	Apr.	May	June	July	Aug.	Sept.	Oct.	Nov.	Dec.
2006	464,177	419,971	363,830	320,651	275,131	221,912	188,557	180,971	392,687	567,303	602,333	541,422
2007	475,671	416,423	372,526	307,655	252,007	208,089	161,547	165,472	337,746	519,243	539,506	500,697
2008	461,503	421,154	352,171	318,052	246,808	208,127	172,494	157,387	342,614	518,630	559,266	511,933
2009	463,724	406,206	368,520	326,868	290,734	238,292	202,653	193,401	396,474	601,205	658,972	630,159
2010	584,048	547,232	497,712	448,133	401,942	343,136	305,686	291,404	472,963	629,274	676,527	617,660
2011[1]	571,012	521,993	467,481	405,201	340,257	283,392	216,687	181,404	302,134	506,672	541,408	504,957

[1] Preliminary.   [2] Cut.   *Source: Economic Research Service, U.S. Department of Agriculture (ERS-USDA)*

Cold Storage Stocks of Frozen Corn[2] in the United States, on First of Month In Thousands of Pounds

Year	Jan.	Feb.	Mar.	Apr.	May	June	July	Aug.	Sept.	Oct.	Nov.	Dec.
2006	263,818	234,464	199,446	163,904	130,581	87,100	71,738	71,608	189,243	316,029	324,324	305,843
2007	281,694	239,973	205,823	172,282	142,308	103,175	69,152	79,662	190,260	295,144	291,044	274,619
2008	256,464	225,602	185,562	163,020	123,090	105,895	78,251	80,325	182,022	295,216	321,617	297,614
2009	264,562	247,402	218,649	192,534	169,269	131,665	98,389	107,043	181,263	292,652	293,967	265,665
2010	252,108	236,435	214,708	188,317	164,144	132,229	102,824	100,184	203,300	259,187	260,414	254,363
2011[1]	249,387	230,771	210,381	180,610	156,146	132,393	101,891	89,845	181,470	270,417	261,722	254,865

[1] Preliminary .   [2] Cob.   *Source: Economic Research Service, U.S. Department of Agriculture (ERS-USDA)*

Cold Storage Stocks of Frozen Green Peas in the United States, on First of Month In Thousands of Pounds

Year	Jan.	Feb.	Mar.	Apr.	May	June	July	Aug.	Sept.	Oct.	Nov.	Dec.
2006	214,851	186,693	149,406	124,143	104,255	84,184	222,513	389,734	390,822	360,778	322,057	271,839
2007	230,351	192,339	164,492	124,968	90,684	67,839	241,116	400,957	374,470	330,052	294,144	260,036
2008	232,647	200,278	173,323	132,601	105,832	78,501	198,133	387,597	372,967	342,420	312,439	288,190
2009	255,471	232,757	199,313	167,606	143,908	121,027	252,937	437,572	403,023	376,205	335,817	303,632
2010	275,625	255,309	236,609	203,325	172,781	149,428	298,995	456,725	437,177	384,187	348,511	311,507
2011[1]	276,587	234,314	209,119	175,895	147,077	126,467	234,439	440,127	392,908	345,682	321,423	275,522

[1] Preliminary.   *Source: Economic Research Service, U.S. Department of Agriculture (ERS-USDA)*

Cold Storage Stocks of Other Frozen Vegetables in the United States, on First of Month In Thousands of lbs

Year	Jan.	Feb.	Mar.	Apr.	May	June	July	Aug.	Sept.	Oct.	Nov.	Dec.
2006	421,491	399,423	353,776	301,890	274,713	249,472	224,001	212,044	160,851	172,959	424,987	495,447
2007	458,222	396,189	371,397	319,167	276,074	254,816	232,344	215,691	196,806	209,121	451,052	498,790
2008	464,609	425,313	402,895	350,167	312,823	269,330	251,309	234,242	206,201	219,247	537,319	527,876
2009	509,807	467,363	414,907	360,587	343,101	311,835	286,675	246,058	215,985	198,200	551,910	530,591
2010	486,760	449,112	399,408	355,773	318,497	289,097	246,690	209,745	174,476	225,587	502,560	473,224
2011[1]	439,996	404,540	367,245	345,891	294,806	254,167	217,588	189,747	150,499	160,415	452,305	452,560

[1] Preliminary.   *Source: Economic Research Service, U.S. Department of Agriculture (ERS-USDA)*

Cold Storage Stocks of Total Frozen Vegetables in the United States, on First of Month In Millions of Pounds

Year	Jan.	Feb.	Mar.	Apr.	May	June	July	Aug.	Sept.	Oct.	Nov.	Dec.
2006	2,250.9	2,048.1	1,869.7	1,711.2	1,551.8	1,369.6	1,412.9	1,654.4	2,084.8	2,476.6	2,592.2	2,483.7
2007	2,225.4	1,963.9	1,766.6	1,533.9	1,316.8	1,183.8	1,237.1	1,516.5	1,952.2	2,340.1	2,403.6	2,366.5
2008	2,221.4	2,011.5	1,769.6	1,626.4	1,438.1	1,334.2	1,367.0	1,632.2	2,059.1	2,461.3	2,621.5	2,558.7
2009	2,366.0	2,172.1	1,984.1	1,830.5	1,716.8	1,572.1	1,564.0	1,832.2	2,186.4	2,624.7	2,724.6	2,603.6
2010	2,471.8	2,315.0	2,151.8	1,959.8	1,808.8	1,621.6	1,664.9	1,859.8	2,263.4	2,529.3	2,619.7	2,517.1
2011[1]	2,354.1	2,117.0	1,934.9	1,741.7	1,602.4	1,503.7	1,475.4	1,654.6	1,984.8	2,372.8	2,480.2	2,398.5

[1] Preliminary.   *Source: Economic Research Service, U.S. Department of Agriculture (ERS-USDA)*

Wheat

Wheat is a cereal grass, but before cultivation it was a wild grass. It has been grown in temperate regions and cultivated for food since prehistoric times. Wheat is believed to have originated in southwestern Asia. Archeological research indicates that wheat was grown as a crop in the Nile Valley about 5,000 BC. Wheat is not native to the U.S. and was first grown here in 1602 near the Massachusetts coast. The common types of wheat grown in the U.S. are spring and winter wheat. Wheat planted in the spring for summer or autumn harvest is mostly red wheat. Wheat planted in the fall or winter for spring harvest is mostly white wheat. Winter wheat accounts for nearly three-fourths of total U.S. production. Wheat is used mainly as a human food and supplies about 20% of the food calories for the world's population. The primary use for wheat is flour, but it is also used for brewing and distilling, and for making oil, gluten, straw for livestock bedding, livestock feed, hay or silage, newsprint, and other products.

Wheat futures and options are traded on the Mercado a Termino de Buenos Aires (MATBA), Sydney Futures Exchange (SFE), JSE Securities Exchange of South Africa, National Commodity & Derivatives Exchange of India, NYSE-LIFFE exchange in London and Paris, Budapest Stock Exchange (BSE), the Chicago Board of Trade (CBOT), the Kansas City Board of Trade (KCBT), and the Minneapolis Grain Exchange (MGE). The Chicago Board of Trade's wheat futures contract calls for the delivery of soft red wheat (No. 1 and 2), hard red winter wheat (No. 1 and 2), dark northern spring wheat (No. 1 and 2), No.1 northern spring at 3 cents/bushel premium, or No. 2 northern spring at par.

Prices – CBOT wheat prices started out 2011 on a strong note as they posted a 3-1/2 year high of $8.93 a bushel in February 2011 due to strong demand for U.S. wheat on scant European supplies, Russia's ban on wheat exports, and on quality issues for Australian supplies because of flooding. Another bullish factor was reduced wheat plantings in Canada, the world's second-largest exporter, after 2011 Canada wheat acres planted estimate dropped to 20.35 million acres, the second-smallest acreage since 1971. Wheat prices then ratcheted lower into summer and in July 2011 posted a 1-1/2 year low of $5.65 a bushel after Russia announced it would lift its wheat export ban starting July 1 and after the USDA hiked its U.S. winter-wheat production estimate for the second straight month to 1.492 billion bushels from a May estimate of 1.424 billion bushels. Wheat prices moved sideways the remainder of the year and finished 2011 down -17.8% at $6.53 a bushel. Keeping pressure on wheat prices in late 2011 was (1) the action by Australia, the world's third-largest wheat exporter, to raise its 2011/12 wheat crop estimate to a record 28.3 MMT and to raise its wheat export estimate to a record 21.6 MMT, (2) Argentina's action to boost its 2011 wheat exports to a record 11.1 MMT and (3) the USDA's hike in its 2012 global wheat ending stocks estimate to a 12-year high of 208.52 MMT. The 2011/12 wheat supply situation is ample with the stocks-to-use ratio at 39.5% for the U.S. and 31.2% globally.

Supply – World wheat production in the 2011-12 marketing year rose +6.3% to 692.875 million metric tons, a new record high. The world's largest wheat producers were the European Union with 19.8% of world production in 2011-12, China (17.0%), India (12.5%), Russia (8.1%), the U.S. (7.8%), and Australia (4.1%). China's wheat production in 2011-12 rose +2.4% yr/yr to 117.920 million metric tons, but is still below its record high of 123.289 million metric tons seen in 1997-98. Australia's wheat production rose +1.5% yr/yr to 28.300 million metric tons in 2011-12, a new record high. The world land area harvested with wheat in 2011-12 fell -0.2% yr/yr to 222.3 million hectares (1 hectare equals 10,000 square meters or 2.471 acres), remaining above the 209.6 million hectares in 2003-04, which was the smallest wheat harvest area since 1970-71. World wheat yield in 2011-12 rose +5.5% to 3.07 metric tons per acre, a new record high.

U.S. wheat production in 2011-12 fell -9.4% yr/yr to 1.999 billion bushels, well below the record crop of 2.785 billion bushels seen in 1981-82. The U.S. winter wheat crop in 2011 rose +0.6% yr/yr to 1.493 billion bushels, which was well below the record winter wheat crop of 2.097 billion bushels seen in 1981. U.S. production of durum wheat in 2011 fell -52.4% yr/yr to 50.482 million bushels. U.S. production of other spring wheat in 2011 fell -26.1% yr/yr to 455.188 million bushels. The largest U.S. producing states of winter wheat in 2011 were Kansas with 5.2% of U.S. production, Washington with 8.7%, Montana with 6.0%, and Colorado with 7.9%. U.S. farmers planted 54.409 million acres of wheat in 2011, which was up +1.5% yr/yr. U.S. wheat yield in 2011-12 was 43.7 bushels per acre, under last year's record high of 46.3 bushels per acre. Ending stocks for U.S. wheat for 2010-11 (latest data) were at 818.0 million bushels, down 16.2% yr/yr.

Demand – World wheat utilization in 2011-12 rose +3.3% yr/yr to a record high of 673.3 million metric tons. U.S. consumption of wheat in 2011-12 rose +2.9% yr/yr to 1.161 billion bushels, which was below the record high of 1.381 billion bushels seen in 1998-99. The consumption breakdown shows that 80.5% of U.S. wheat consumption in 2011-12 went for food, 12.5% for feed and residuals, and 7.0% for seed.

Trade – World trade in wheat in 2011-12 rose +3.2% yr/yr to 136.6 million metric tons, down from 2008-09 record high of 143.0 million metric tons. U.S. exports of wheat in 2011-12 fell -26.3% yr/yr to 950.000 million bushes, and remained below the record of 1.771 billion bushels of exports seen in 1981-82. U.S. imports of wheat in 2011-12 rose +23.8% to 120.0 million bushels, down from the 2006-07 record high of 127.0 million bushels.

WHEAT

World Production of Wheat — In Thousands of Metric Tons

Crop Year	Argentina	Australia	Canada	China	European Union	India	Iran	Kazakhstan	Pakistan	Russia	Turkey	United States	World Total
2002-03	12,700	10,132	16,198	90,290	132,579	72,770	12,450	12,700	18,227	50,609	16,800	43,705	569,597
2003-04	15,100	26,132	23,049	86,490	110,578	65,760	13,440	11,537	19,183	34,070	16,800	63,805	555,435
2004-05	16,900	21,905	24,796	91,952	146,886	72,150	14,568	9,937	19,500	45,434	18,500	58,698	626,734
2005-06	13,800	25,173	25,748	97,445	132,356	68,640	14,308	11,197	21,612	47,615	18,500	57,243	618,810
2006-07	16,300	10,822	25,265	108,466	124,870	69,350	14,664	13,460	21,277	44,927	17,500	49,217	596,078
2007-08	18,600	13,569	20,054	109,298	120,133	75,810	15,887	16,466	23,295	49,368	15,500	55,821	611,991
2008-09	11,000	21,420	28,611	112,464	151,122	78,570	7,957	12,538	20,959	63,765	16,800	68,016	682,785
2009-10[1]	12,000	21,834	26,848	115,120	138,816	80,680	13,485	17,051	24,000	61,770	18,450	60,366	685,426
2010-11[2]	16,100	27,891	23,167	115,180	135,674	80,800	15,500	9,638	23,900	41,508	17,000	60,062	651,607
2011-12[3]	14,500	28,300	25,260	117,920	137,486	86,870	13,750	22,732	24,000	56,231	18,800	54,413	692,875

[1] Preliminary. [2] Estimate. [3] Forecast. *Source: Foreign Agricultural Service, U.S. Department of Agriculture (FAS-USDA)*

World Supply and Demand of Wheat — In Millions of Metric Tons/Hectares

Year	Area Harvested	Yield	Production	World Trade	Utilization Total	Ending Stocks	Stocks as a % of Utilization
2002-03	215.0	2.65	569.6	106.8	602.6	170.0	28.2
2003-04	210.0	2.65	555.4	103.6	581.4	135.9	23.4
2004-05	217.2	2.89	626.7	113.9	605.3	155.5	25.7
2005-06	219.7	2.82	619.1	114.1	616.8	152.5	24.7
2006-07	213.0	2.80	596.3	115.6	618.2	132.6	21.4
2007-08	218.2	2.81	612.1	116.4	613.8	127.0	20.7
2008-09	225.3	3.03	682.8	143.0	636.2	167.1	26.3
2009-10[1]	227.2	3.01	684.3	134.4	648.3	200.9	31.0
2010-11[2]	222.6	2.91	648.7	132.3	652.0	196.1	30.1
2011-12[3]	222.3	3.07	683.3	136.6	673.3	202.6	30.1

[1] Preliminary. [2] Estimate. [3] Forecast. *Source: Foreign Agricultural Service, U.S. Department of Agriculture (FAS-USDA)*

Salient Statistics of Wheat in the United States

Year	Planting Intentions	Winter	Spring	All	Average All Yield Per Acre in Bushels	Value of Production $1,000	Domestic Exports[2]	Imports[3]	Flour	Cereal
2002-03	60,318	29,742	16,166	45,824	35.0	5,637,416	850.2	77.4	136.8	3.7
2003-04	62,141	36,753	16,310	53,063	44.2	7,929,039	1,158.3	63.0	136.7	3.7
2004-05	59,674	34,462	15,537	49,999	43.2	7,283,324	1,065.9	70.6	134.5	3.6
2005-06	57,229	33,794	16,325	50,119	42.0	7,171,441	1,002.8	81.4	134.3	3.6
2006-07	57,344	31,117	16,769	46,810	38.7	7,694,734	908.5	121.9	135.7	----
2007-08	60,460	35,938	15,061	50,999	40.5	13,289,326	1,262.6	112.6	138.1	----
2008-09	63,193	39,608	16,091	55,699	44.9	16,625,759	1,015.4	127.0	136.5	----
2009-10	59,168	34,510	15,383	49,893	44.5	10,654,115	879.3	118.6	134.7	----
2010-11	53,593	31,741	15,878	47,619	46.3	12,827,254	1,288.8	96.9		
2011-12[1]	54,409	32,314	13,401	45,705	43.7	14,367,556	950.0	120.0		

[1] Preliminary. [2] Includes flour milled from imported wheat. [3] Total wheat, flour & other products. [4] Civilian only. [5] Year beginning June.
Source: Economic Research Service, U.S. Department of Agriculture (ERS-USDA)

Supply and Distribution of Wheat in the United States — In Millions of Bushels

Crop Year Beginning June 1	On Farms	Mills, Elevators[3]	Total Stocks	Production	Imports[4]	Total Supply	Food	Seed	Feed & Residual[5]	Total	Exports[4]	Total Disappearance
2002-03	216.8	560.3	777.1	1,605.9	77.4	2,460.4	918.6	84.4	115.7	1,118.7	850.2	1,968.9
2003-04	132.1	359.3	491.4	2,344.8	63.0	2,898.9	911.9	79.7	202.5	1,194.1	1,158.3	2,352.4
2004-05	131.9	414.6	546.4	2,158.2	70.6	2,773.8	909.6	77.6	180.6	1,167.8	1,065.9	2,233.7
2005-06	161.3	378.8	540.1	2,104.7	81.4	2,724.8	917.1	77.1	156.6	1,150.8	1,002.8	2,153.6
2006-07	111.0	460.2	571.2	1,812.0	121.9	2,501.5	937.9	81.9	117.1	1,136.8	1,262.6	2,314.1
2007-08	73.2	383.0	456.2	2,051.1	112.6	2,619.9	947.9	87.6	16.0	1,051.4	1,015.4	2,275.4
2008-09	25.6	280.2	305.8	2,499.2	127.0	2,932.0	926.8	78.0	255.2	1,260.0	879.3	2,017.5
2009-10	140.7	515.8	656.5	2,218.1	118.6	2,993.2	918.9	69.5	149.9	1,138.2	1,288.8	2,417.2
2010-11[1]	209.9	765.7	975.6	2,206.9	96.9	3,279.5	925.6	70.9	131.9	1,128.4	950.0	2,111.6
2011-12[2]	130.9	731.3	862.2	1,999.3	120.0	2,981.6	935.0	81.6	145.0	1,161.6		

[1] Preliminary. [2] Estimate. [3] Also warehouses and all off-farm storage not otherwise designated, including flour mills. [4] Imports & exports are for wheat, including flour & other products in terms of wheat. [5] Mostly feed use.
Source: Economic Research Service, U.S. Department of Agriculture (ERS-USDA)

WHEAT

Year	Hard Spring Stocks June 1	Hard Spring Production	Hard Spring Exports[3]	Durum[2] Stocks June 1	Durum[2] Production	Durum[2] Exports[3]	Hard Winter Stocks June 1	Hard Winter Production	Hard Winter Exports[3]	Soft Red Winter Stocks June 1	Soft Red Winter Production	Soft Red Winter Exports[3]	White Stocks June 1	White Production	White Exports[3]
2002-03	230	351	259	33	80	32	363	620	309	78	321	105	73	233	148
2003-04	145	500	272	28	97	44	188	1,071	512	55	380	140	75	297	192
2004-05	157	525	314	26	90	31	227	856	388	64	380	122	72	306	207
2005-06	159	467	282	38	101	47	193	930	430	88	309	76	63	298	175
2006-07	132	432	250	40	53	35	215	682	281	106	390	146	78	254	197
2007-08	117	450	305	21	72	42	165	956	538	109	352	209	44	221	170
2008-09	68	512	210	8	84	24	138	1,035	447	55	614	199	37	255	136
2009-10	142	548	214	25	109	44	254	920	370	171	404	109	64	237	143
2010-11	234	570	339	35	106	43	385	1,018	616	242	237	109	80	275	182
2011-12[1]	185	398	240	35	50	20	386	780	390	171	458	115	85	314	185

[1] Preliminary.   [2] Includes "Red Durum."   [3] Includes four made from U.S. wheat & shipments to territories.
Source: Economic Research Service, U.S. Department of Agriculture (ERS-USDA)

Seeded Acreage, Yield and Production of all Wheat in the United States

Year	Seed Acreage - 1,000 Acres Winter	Other Spring	Durum	All	Yield Per Harvested Acre (Bushels) Winter	Other Spring	Durum	All	Production (Million Bushels) Winter	Other Spring	Durum	All
2002	41,766	15,639	2,913	60,318	38.2	29.1	29.5	35.0	1,137.0	388.9	80.0	1,605.9
2003	45,384	13,842	2,915	62,141	46.7	39.5	33.7	44.2	1,716.7	531.4	96.6	2,344.8
2004	43,350	13,763	2,561	59,674	43.5	43.2	38.0	43.2	1,499.4	568.9	89.9	2,158.2
2005	40,433	14,036	2,760	57,229	44.4	37.1	37.2	42.0	1,499.1	504.5	101.1	2,104.7
2006	40,575	14,899	1,870	57,344	41.7	33.2	29.5	38.7	1,298.1	460.5	53.5	1,812.0
2007	45,012	13,292	2,156	60,460	41.7	37.1	34.1	40.2	1,499.2	479.6	72.2	2,051.1
2008	46,307	14,165	2,721	63,193	47.1	40.5	32.6	44.9	1,867.3	548.0	83.8	2,499.2
2009	43,346	13,268	2,554	59,168	44.2	45.1	44.9	44.5	1,524.6	584.4	109.0	2,218.1
2010	37,335	13,698	2,560	53,593	46.8	46.1	42.1	46.3	1,484.9	616.0	106.1	2,206.9
2011[1]	40,646	12,394	1,369	54,409	46.2	37.7	38.5	43.7	1,493.7	455.2	50.5	1,999.3

[1] Preliminary.   *Source: Economic Research Service, U.S. Department of Agriculture (ERS-USDA)*

Production of Winter Wheat in the United States, by State   In Thousands of Bushels

Year	Colorado	Idaho	Illinois	Kansas	Missouri	Montana	Nebraska	Ohio	Oklahoma	Oregon	Texas	Washington	Total
2002	36,300	48,510	30,870	270,600	33,440	21,840	50,160	50,220	103,600	29,820	78,300	104,400	1,137,001
2003	77,000	57,600	52,650	480,000	53,070	67,340	83,720	68,000	179,400	47,940	96,600	117,000	1,716,721
2004	45,900	63,000	53,100	314,500	48,360	66,830	61,050	55,180	164,500	47,580	108,500	117,250	1,499,434
2005	52,800	66,430	36,600	380,000	29,160	94,500	68,640	58,930	128,000	47,580	96,000	120,600	1,499,129
2006	39,900	54,670	60,970	291,200	49,140	82,560	61,200	65,280	81,600	38,690	33,600	118,800	1,298,081
2007	91,650	51,830	48,950	283,800	37,840	83,220	84,280	44,530	98,000	38,160	140,600	104,780	1,499,241
2008	57,000	60,000	73,600	356,000	55,680	94,380	73,480	74,120	166,500	44,950	99,000	96,320	1,867,333
2009	98,000	56,700	45,920	369,600	34,310	89,540	76,800	70,560	77,000	42,000	61,250	96,760	1,524,608
2010	105,750	58,220	16,520	360,000	12,600	93,600	64,070	45,750	120,900	54,270	127,500	117,990	1,484,861
2011[1]	78,000	63,140	46,665	276,500	34,000	89,790	65,250	49,300	70,400	63,525	49,400	129,750	1,493,677

[1] Preliminary.   *Source: Crop Reporting Board, U.S. Department of Agriculture (CRB-USDA)*

Official Winter Wheat Crop Production Reports in the United States   In Thousands of Bushels

Crop Year	May 1	June 1	July 1	August 1	September 1	Current December	Final
2002-03	1,300,726	1,237,671	1,178,320	1,158,710	----	----	1,137,001
2003-04	1,563,314	1,626,376	1,715,912	1,712,150	----	----	1,716,721
2004-05	1,550,395	1,530,742	1,469,735	1,489,408	----	----	1,499,434
2005-06	1,590,862	1,545,971	1,525,302	1,520,848	----	----	1,499,129
2006-07	1,322,831	1,263,766	1,280,005	1,283,134	----	----	1,298,081
2007-08	1,615,613	1,609,679	1,561,907	1,537,262	----	----	1,499,241
2008-09	1,777,532	1,817,364	1,864,245	1,874,857	----	----	1,867,333
2009-10	1,502,074	1,491,769	1,524,771	1,537,348	----	----	1,524,608
2010-11	1,458,350	1,482,364	1,505,493	1,522,902	----	----	1,484,861
2011-12[1]	1,424,357	1,450,115	1,491,739	1,497,429	----	----	1,493,677

[1] Preliminary.   *Source: Crop Reporting Board, U.S. Department of Agriculture (CRB-USDA)*

Production of All Spring Wheat in the United States, by State In Thousands of Bushels

| | Durum Wheat | | | | | | Other Spring Wheat | | | | | | | |
Year	Arizona	Cali-fornia	Montana	North Dakota	South Dakota	Total	Idaho	Minne-sota	Montana	North Dakota	Oregon	South Dakota	Wash-ington	Total
2002	8,928	9,000	12,995	48,750	147	79,960	29,900	61,200	75,900	165,200	4,680	24,000	25,370	388,917
2003	11,500	11,500	14,490	58,410	621	96,637	27,060	104,400	60,500	252,800	5,600	56,280	22,345	531,402
2004	9,603	9,000	17,985	52,800	450	89,893	38,710	88,550	88,350	243,950	8,400	71,910	26,250	568,918
2005	7,900	6,555	16,380	68,250	260	101,105	32,400	70,930	81,600	224,400	5,980	67,600	18,700	504,456
2006	7,400	6,435	6,715	31,500	90	53,475	34,310	77,550	63,800	212,350	5,750	42,600	21,250	460,480
2007	8,364	8,000	11,400	43,070	175	72,224	30,600	79,200	55,200	234,000	5,520	52,260	20,562	479,623
2008	14,602	15,225	10,830	42,250	190	83,827	37,440	100,800	59,520	246,400	7,650	68,400	22,470	548,004
2009	12,400	17,000	16,585	61,230	207	109,042	40,810	82,150	70,500	289,800	6,858	64,680	26,325	584,411
2010	9,085	10,450	18,020	66,750	555	106,080	47,970	85,250	103,740	277,200	9,316	59,220	29,900	615,975
2011[1]	7,979	12,535	10,780	18,233	196	50,482	52,080	69,000	74,400	167,750	10,990	37,820	38,130	455,188

[1] Preliminary. *Source: Crop Reporting Board, U.S. Department of Agriculture (CRB-USDA)*

Grindings of Wheat by Mills in the United States   In Millions of Bushels -- of 60 Pounds Each

Year	Jan.	Feb.	Mar.	Apr.	May	June	July	Aug.	Sept.	Oct.	Nov.	Dec.	Total
2002-03	-----	230.3	-----	-----	224.4	-----	-----	215.8	-----	-----	217.4	-----	888.0
2003-04	-----	231.8	-----	-----	224.2	-----	-----	214.7	-----	-----	214.5	-----	885.2
2004-05	-----	224.8	-----	-----	222.1	-----	-----	214.9	-----	-----	216.5	-----	878.3
2005-06	-----	229.3	-----	-----	223.4	-----	-----	216.1	-----	-----	217.1	-----	885.9
2006-07	-----	233.3	-----	-----	228.0	-----	-----	222.0	-----	-----	226.1	-----	909.5
2007-08	-----	239.3	-----	-----	236.3	-----	-----	223.2	-----	-----	224.3	-----	923.1
2008-09	-----	235.2	-----	-----	225.3	-----	-----	217.6	-----	-----	221.2	-----	899.3
2009-10	-----	232.7	-----	-----	224.6	-----	-----	221.2	-----	-----	219.2	-----	897.6
2010-11	-----	234.6	-----	-----	226.9	-----	-----	218.2	-----	-----	216.4	-----	896.1
2011-12[1]	-----	NA	-----	-----	NA	-----	-----		-----	-----		-----	

[1] Preliminary. *Source: Bureau of the Census, U.S. Department of Commerce*

Stocks of Wheat in the United States   In Millions of Bushels

| | On Farms | | | | Off Farms | | | | Total Stocks | | | |
Year	Mar. 1	June 1	Sept. 1	Dec. 1	Mar. 1	June 1	Sept. 1	Dec. 1	Mar. 1	June 1	Sept. 1	Dec. 1
2002	338.5	216.8	580.2	384.8	871.3	560.3	1,170.8	935.1	1,209.8	777.1	1,751.0	1,319.9
2003	236.3	132.1	687.3	491.9	670.3	359.3	1,351.7	1,028.4	906.6	491.4	2,039.0	1,520.3
2004	257.9	131.9	790.6	531.0	762.7	414.6	1,147.8	899.3	1,020.6	546.4	1,938.4	1,430.3
2005	304.7	161.3	721.4	513.0	679.7	378.8	1,201.9	916.4	984.4	540.1	1,923.3	1,429.4
2006	256.0	111.0	572.0	403.3	716.2	460.2	1,178.5	911.4	972.2	571.2	1,750.5	1,314.7
2007	192.5	73.2	495.0	289.5	664.3	383.0	1,221.9	842.4	856.7	456.2	1,716.9	1,131.9
2008	92.0	25.6	635.7	454.0	617.3	280.2	1,222.2	968.1	709.3	305.8	1,857.9	1,422.1
2009	280.4	140.7	836.0	558.8	759.7	515.8	1,373.3	1,222.9	1,040.1	656.5	2,209.3	1,781.7
2010	348.3	209.9	812.1	550.0	1,008.1	765.7	1,637.5	1,382.9	1,356.4	975.6	2,449.6	1,932.9
2011[1]	288.0	130.9	633.0	405.0	1,137.3	731.3	1,513.7	1,251.4	1,425.3	862.2	2,146.7	1,656.4

[1] Preliminary. *Source: National Agricultural Statistics Service, U.S. Department of Agriculture (NASS-USDA)*

Wheat Supply and Distribution in Canada, Australia and Argentina   In Millions of Metric Tons

| | Canada (Year Beginning Aug. 1) | | | | | Australia (Year Beginning Oct. 1) | | | | | Argentina (Year Beginning Dec. 1) | | | | |
| | Supply | | | Disappearance | | Supply | | | Disappearance | | Supply | | | Disappearance | |
Crop Year	Stocks Aug. 1	New Crop	Total Supply	Domestic	Exports[3]	Stocks Oct. 1	New Crop	Total Supply	Domestic	Exports[3]	Stocks Dec. 1	New Crop	Total Supply	Domestic	Exports[3]
2002-03	6.5	16.2	22.7	8.0	9.4	8.0	10.1	18.1	6.1	9.1	1.1	12.7	13.8	5.3	6.8
2003-04	5.7	23.0	28.7	7.2	15.8	3.2	26.1	29.3	6.0	18.0	1.3	15.1	16.4	5.4	9.5
2004-05	6.0	24.8	30.8	8.2	14.9	5.4	21.9	27.3	6.0	14.7	1.6	16.9	18.5	5.4	11.9
2005-06	7.9	25.7	33.6	8.2	16.0	6.7	25.2	31.9	6.6	16.0	1.3	13.8	15.1	5.1	9.6
2006-07	9.7	25.3	35.0	9.0	19.4	9.4	10.8	20.2	7.4	8.7	.4	16.3	16.7	5.4	10.7
2007-08	6.9	20.1	27.0	6.8	16.1	4.2	13.6	17.8	6.5	7.5	.6	18.6	19.2	5.3	11.2
2008-09	4.4	28.6	33.0	8.0	18.9	3.9	21.4	25.3	7.3	14.7	2.4	11.0	13.4	5.8	6.8
2009-10	6.5	26.8	33.3	6.9	19.0	3.4	21.8	25.2	4.9	14.8	1.3	12.0	13.3	5.9	5.1
2010-11[1]	7.8	23.2	31.0	7.7	16.6	5.6	27.9	33.5	6.1	18.7	2.4	16.1	18.5	5.9	9.5
2011-12[2]	7.2	25.3	32.5	8.8	18.0	8.8	28.3	37.1	7.1	21.5	3.1	14.5	17.6	5.9	8.5

[1] Preliminary.   [2] Forecast.   [3] Including flour.   *Source: Foreign Agricultural Service, U.S. Department of Agriculture (FAS-USDA)*

WHEAT

Quarterly Supply and Disappearance of Wheat in the United States   In Millions of Bushels

		Supply			Disappearance — Domestic Use					Total Disap-pearance	Ending Stocks		
Crop Year Beginning June 1	Beginning Stocks	Pro-duction	Imports³	Total Supply	Food	Seed	Feed & Residual	Total	Exports³		Gov't Owned⁴	Privately Owned⁵	Total Stocks
2001-02	876.2	1,947.5	107.6	2,931.2	926.4	83.4	182.0	1,191.8	962.3	2,154.1	99.0	678.1	777.1
June-Aug.	876.2	1,947.5	25.7	2,849.3	233.8	3.5	237.9	475.2	218.3	693.5	97.7	2,058.1	2,155.8
Sept.-Nov.	2,155.8	----	29.0	2,184.9	245.1	51.6	-23.1	273.6	287.8	561.4	96.9	1,526.6	1,623.5
Dec.-Feb.	1,623.5	----	27.6	1,651.0	221.1	2.0	-6.6	216.5	224.7	441.2	96.9	1,112.9	1,209.8
Mar.-May	1,209.8	----	25.2	1,235.0	226.4	26.3	-26.2	226.4	231.5	457.9	99.0	678.1	777.1
2002-03	777.1	1,605.9	77.4	2,460.4	918.6	84.4	115.7	1,118.7	850.2	1,968.9	66.4	425.0	491.4
June-Aug.	777.1	1,605.9	26.7	2,409.6	233.2	2.7	184.5	420.4	240.2	660.7	91.4	1,657.6	1,749.0
Sept.-Nov.	1,749.0	----	23.1	1,772.1	237.8	54.6	-74.7	217.7	234.5	454.2	80.9	1,239.0	1,319.9
Dec.-Feb.	1,319.9	----	12.7	1,332.6	218.9	3.1	14.1	236.1	189.8	425.9	74.1	832.5	906.6
Mar.-May	906.6	----	14.9	921.6	228.4	23.9	-8.2	244.5	185.7	430.2	66.4	425.0	491.4
2003-04	491.4	2,344.8	63.1	2,899.3	911.9	79.6	202.9	1,194.4	1,158.1	2,352.5	60.9	485.5	546.4
June-Aug.	491.4	2,344.8	15.7	2,851.9	230.5	2.1	315.3	547.9	264.9	812.8	60.3	1,978.7	2,039.0
Sept.-Nov.	2,039.0	----	17.8	2,056.7	239.6	53.3	-61.9	231.0	305.4	536.4	60.4	1,459.6	1,520.3
Dec.-Feb.	1,520.3	----	12.9	1,533.2	215.9	2.2	3.1	221.2	291.4	512.6	60.0	960.6	1,020.6
Mar.-May	1,020.6	----	16.7	1,037.3	225.9	22.0	-53.6	194.3	296.4	490.7	60.9	485.5	546.4
2004-05	546.4	2,158.2	70.6	2,775.2	904.6	78.9	188.9	1,172.4	1,062.9	2,235.3	54.0	486.1	540.1
June-Aug.	546.4	2,158.2	17.4	2,722.1	227.5	4.1	265.2	496.8	286.8	783.6	61.9	1,876.5	1,938.4
Sept.-Nov.	1,938.4	----	18.7	1,957.1	235.6	48.2	-57.0	226.8	300.0	526.8	61.7	1,369.0	1,430.3
Dec.-Feb.	1,430.3	----	17.8	1,448.1	216.3	2.4	7.7	226.4	237.4	463.8	55.9	928.5	984.4
Mar.-May	984.4	----	16.7	1,001.1	225.2	24.2	-27.0	222.4	238.7	461.1	54.5	485.6	540.1
2005-06	2,105.0	2,104.7	81.0	4,290.7	914.0	78.0	154.0	1,146.0	1,009.0	2,155.0			571.0
June-Aug.	540.1	2,104.7	19.0	2,663.0	231.0	2.0	263.0	496.0	244.0	740.0	48.3	1,875.0	1,923.0
Sept.-Nov.	1,923.0	----	20.0	1,944.0	238.0	51.0	-61.0	228.0	286.0	514.0	44.1	1,385.4	1,429.0
Dec.-Feb.	1,429.0	----	20.0	1,450.0	219.0	1.0	1.0	221.0	257.0	478.0			972.0
Mar.-May	972.0	----	22.0	995.0	226.0	24.0	-49.0	201.0	222.0	423.0			571.0
2006-07	571.0	1,808.0	121.0	2,500.0	937.0	81.0	117.0	1,135.0	908.0	2,043.0			456.0
June-Aug.	571.0	1,808.0	26.0	2,406.0	235.0	2.0	205.0	442.0	214.0	656.0			1,751.0
Sept.-Nov.	1,751.0	----	29.0	1,780.0	243.0	56.0	-47.0	252.0	212.0	464.0			1,315.0
Dec.-Feb.	1,315.0	----	32.0	1,346.0	225.0	1.0	28.0	254.0	235.0	489.0			857.0
Mar.-May	857.0	----	34.0	891.0	234.0	22.0	-69.0	187.0	247.0	434.0			456.0
2007-08	456.0	2,051.0	112.0	2,619.0	947.0	88.0	16.0	1,051.0	1,262.0	2,313.0			306.0
June-Aug.	456.0	2,051.0	30.0	2,538.0	240.0	1.0	257.0	498.0	323.0	821.0			1,717.0
Sept.-Nov.	1,717.0	----	21.0	1,738.0	245.0	60.0	-120.0	185.0	421.0	606.0			1,132.0
Dec.-Feb.	1,132.0	----	24.0	1,156.0	227.0	2.0	-42.0	187.0	261.0	448.0			709.0
Mar.-May	709.0	----	37.0	746.0	235.0	25.0	-79.0	181.0	257.0	438.0			306.0
2008-09	306.0	2,499.0	127.0	2,932.0	924.0	75.0	256.0	1,255.0	1,016.0	2,271.0			657.0
June-Aug.	306.0	2,499.0	28.0	2,833.0	236.0	2.0	393.0	631.0	345.0	976.0			1,858.0
Sept.-Nov.	1,858.0	----	28.0	1,886.0	238.0	54.0	-124.0	168.0	295.0	463.0			1,422.0
Dec.-Feb.	1,422.0	----	36.0	1,459.0	219.0	1.0	28.0	248.0	170.0	418.0			1,040.0
Mar.-May	1,040.0	----	35.0	1,075.0	231.0	18.0	-41.0	208.0	206.0	414.0			657.0
2009-10	657.0	2,218.0	119.0	2,994.0	917.0	69.0	150.0	1,136.0	881.0	2,017.0			976.0
June-Aug.	657.0	2,218.0	28.0	2,902.0	231.0	1.0	261.0	493.0	200.0	693.0			2,209.0
Sept.-Nov.	2,209.0	----	24.0	2,234.0	237.0	46.0	-83.0	200.0	252.0	452.0			1,782.0
Dec.-Feb.	1,782.0	----	30.0	1,812.0	221.0	1.0	31.0	253.0	202.0	455.0			1,356.0
Mar.-May	1,356.0	----	37.0	1,393.0	228.0	21.0	-59.0	190.0	227.0	417.0			976.0
2010-11¹	976.0	2,207.0	96.0	3,279.0	930.0	80.0	170.0	1,180.0	1,288.0	2,468.0			862.0
June-Aug.	976.0	2,207.0	27.0	3,212.0	235.0	2.0	262.0	499.0	266.0	765.0			2,450.0
Sept.-Nov.	2,450.0	----	24.0	2,473.0	242.0	52.0	-63.0	231.0	310.0	541.0			1,933.0
Dec.-Feb.	1,933.0	----	23.0	1,956.0	221.0	1.0	-2.0	220.0	311.0	531.0			1,425.0
Mar.-May	1,425.0	----	22.0	1,448.0	233.0	73.0	-65.0	241.0	401.0	642.0			862.0
2011-12²	862.0	1,999.0	120.0	2,982.0	935.0	82.0	145.0	1,162.0	950.0	2,112.0			870.0
June-Aug.	862.0	1,999.0	21.0	2,882.0	230.0	6.0	203.0	439.0	296.0	735.0			2,147.0
Sept.-Nov.	2,147.0	----	32.0	2,179.0	246.0	52.0	-27.0	271.0	250.0	521.0			1,656.0

¹ Preliminary.   ² Forecast.   ³ Imports & exports include flour and other products expressed in wheat equivalent.   ⁴ Uncommitted, Government only.
⁵ Includes total loans.   ⁶ Includes alcoholic beverages.   *Source: Economic Research Service, U.S. Department of Agriculture (ERS-USDA)*

Wheat Government Loan Program Data in the United States   Loan Rates--Cents Per Bushel

Crop Year Beginning June 1	National Average[3]	Target Rate[4]	Corn Belt (Soft Red Winter)	Central & Southern Plains (Hard Winter)	Northern Plains (Spring & Durum)	Pacific Northwest (White)	Placed Under Loan	% of Production Under Program	Acquired by CCC Under Program	Total Stocks May 31	Total CCC Stocks May 31	Outstanding CCC Loans	Outstanding Farmer-Owned Reserve	"Free"
										In Millions of Bushels				
2000-01	258	NA	253	257	258	271	181	8.1	27	876	97	42	0	779
2001-02	258	NA	NA	NA	NA	NA	197	10.1	17	777	99	78	0	678
2002-03	280	386	NA	NA	NA	NA	120	7.5	2	491	66	55	0	425
2003-04	280	386	NA	NA	NA	NA	186	7.9	3	546	61	37	0	485
2004-05	275	392	NA	NA	NA	NA	178	8.3	10	540	55	58	0	486
2005-06	275	392	NA	NA	NA	NA	170	8.1	1	571	43	NA	0	528
2006-07	275	392	NA	NA	NA	NA	94	5.2	0	456	41	NA	0	437
2007-08	275	392	NA	NA	NA	NA	36	1.8	0	306	0	NA	NA	NA
2008-09[1]	275	392	NA	NA	NA	NA	84	3.4	0	657	0	NA	NA	NA
2009-10[2]	275	392	NA	NA	NA	NA				976	NA	NA	NA	NA

[1] Preliminary.   [2] Estimate.   [3] The national average loan rate at the farm as a percentage of the parity-priced wheat at the beginning of the marketing year.   [4] 1996-97 through 2001-02 marketing year, target prices not applicable.   NA = Not avaliable.
Source: Agricultural Marketing Service, U.S. Department of Agriculture (AMS-USDA)

Exports of Wheat (Only)[2] from the United States   In Thousands of Bushels

Year	June	July	Aug.	Sept.	Oct.	Nov.	Dec.	Jan.	Feb.	Mar.	Apr.	May	Total
2002-03	63,219	78,013	92,345	73,606	78,866	75,678	69,485	62,769	48,618	65,990	55,764	59,438	823,791
2003-04	54,665	88,042	115,869	125,312	101,168	76,222	79,811	109,607	94,480	96,685	102,588	91,917	1,136,366
2004-05	80,599	97,962	103,222	119,965	92,634	83,947	81,718	77,349	73,131	76,612	81,885	75,575	1,044,599
2005-06	64,553	90,760	83,173	102,761	103,423	77,164	91,531	84,659	71,175	74,420	69,050	72,209	984,878
2006-07	63,115	67,846	78,225	76,431	70,752	60,595	72,226	84,629	75,412	76,512	75,130	85,565	886,438
2007-08	73,088	80,285	153,223	149,168	158,064	116,504	82,343	87,539	84,414	92,251	82,781	79,725	1,239,385
2008-09	77,176	119,492	141,173	117,332	93,462	75,311	54,389	56,634	55,825	75,580	61,048	65,884	993,306
2009-10	63,851	58,627	68,321	100,213	77,627	68,117	54,438	65,060	76,522	73,780	76,958	68,473	851,987
2010-11	74,400	80,546	104,145	130,529	86,525	92,159	85,582	108,741	105,409	120,873	146,979	126,991	1,262,879
2011-12[1]	107,349	83,260	100,294	99,523	71,073								1,107,598

[1] Preliminary.   [2] Grains.   *Source: Economic Research Service, U.S. Department of Agriculture (ERS-USDA)*

United States Wheat and Wheat Flour Imports and Exports   In Thousands of Bushels

Crop Year Beginning June 1	Wheat Suitable for Milling Consump.	Wheat Unfit for Human Consump.	Grain	Flour & Products[2]	Total	Foreign Donations P.L. 480	Foreign Donations Sec. 416	Aid[3]	Total concessional	CCC Export Credit	Export Enhancement Program	Total U.S. Wheat
	-- Wheat Equivalent --						In Thousands of Metric Tons					
2004-05	44,499	----	44,499	26,071	70,570	1,867	12	----	2,139	2,554	0	26,505
2005-06	54,073	----	54,073	27,281	81,354	969	17	----	1,191	1,052	0	25,005
2006-07	92,928	----	92,928	21,752	121,870	767	0	----	961	1,008	0	29,636
2007-08	85,806	----	85,806	26,702	112,631	734	12	----	841	1,360	0	32,847
2008-09	101,964	----	101,964	22,356	126,970	722	12	----	965	2,691	0	22,545
2009-10	93,003	----	93,003	29,217	118,591	793	16	----	901	2,078	0	25,762
2010-11[1]	69,053	----	69,053	23,434	96,919							

[1] Preliminary.   [2] Includes macaroni, semolina & similar products.   [3] Shipment mostly under the Commodity Import Program, financed with foreign aid funds.   NA = Not available.   *Source: Economic Research Service, U.S. Department of Agriculture (ERS-USDA)*

Comparative Average Cash Wheat Prices   In Dollars Per Bushel

Crop Year June to May	Received by U.S. Farmers	No. 2 Soft Red Winter, Chicago	No 1 Hard Red Ordinary Protein, Kansas City	No 2 Soft Red Winter, St. Louis	No 1 Dark Northern Spring 14%	No 1 Hard Amber Durum	No 1 Soft White, Portland, Oregon	No 2 Western White Pacific Northwest	No 2 Soft White, Standard Toledo	Australian No 1	Canada Vancouver No 1 CWRS 13 1/2%	Argentina F.O.B. B.A.	U.S. Gulf No. 2 Hard Winter	Rotterdam C.I.F. U.S. No 2 Hard Winter
				-- Minneapolis --						------- Export Prices[2] (U.S. $ Per Metric Ton) -------				
2004-05	3.40	3.01	3.99	3.40	4.66	----	3.93	4.04	3.08	177	202	127	151	213
2005-06	3.42	3.13	4.45	3.20	4.98	----	3.57	4.35	3.15	191	204	140	168	224
2006-07	4.26	3.98	5.38	4.11	5.41	----	4.87	5.48	3.85	230	230	192	204	257
2007-08	6.48	7.71	9.11	7.43	10.81	13.08	9.97	8.68	8.06	294	447	298	340	321
2008-09	6.78	5.04	7.03	4.86	8.53	----	6.25	6.62	4.98	217	350	244	292	----
2009-10	4.87	4.39	5.24	3.88	6.96	----	4.91	5.00	4.31	209	280	227	205	----
2010-11	5.70	6.60	7.55	6.88	9.93		6.77	4.63	6.62	273	394	302		
2011-12[1]	7.05-7.75	6.38	8.08	6.78	10.61		6.59		6.51	245	431	282		

[1] Preliminary.   [2] Calendar year.   NA = Not available.   *Source: Economic Research Service, U.S. Department of Agriculture (ERS-USDA)*

WHEAT

Wheat (monthly average) through December 2011   Cents per bushel

1860 1902 1907 1912 1917 1922 1927 1932 1937 1942 1947 1952 1957 1962 1967 1972 1977 1982 1987 1992 1997 2002 2007 2012

Average Price of No. 2 Soft Red Winter (30 Days) Wheat in Chicago   In Dollars Per Bushel

Year	June	July	Aug.	Sept.	Oct.	Nov.	Dec.	Jan.	Feb.	Mar.	Apr.	May	Average
2002-03	2.81	3.19	3.42	3.92	3.89	3.85	3.53	3.32	3.44	3.14	3.08	3.25	3.40
2003-04	3.11	3.23	3.63	3.46	3.42	3.87	3.92	3.90	3.84	3.85	3.92	3.73	3.66
2004-05	3.46	3.26	2.92	2.97	2.82	2.79	2.88	2.93	2.95	3.28	2.92	2.96	3.01
2005-06	3.09	3.22	3.04	2.93	2.99	2.83	2.98	3.11	3.34	3.29	3.21	3.54	3.13
2006-07	3.26	3.43	3.20	3.39	4.40	4.35	4.49	4.19	4.20	4.07	4.25	4.50	3.98
2007-08	5.25	5.52	6.24	7.98	7.89	7.57	8.69	8.55	10.12	10.40	7.72	6.59	7.71
2008-09	7.20	6.87	6.77	5.45	3.76	3.68	4.01	4.62	4.28	4.40	4.43	4.96	5.04
2009-10	4.96	4.45	4.18	3.70	4.01	4.53	4.67	4.55	4.37	4.38	4.43	4.49	4.39
2010-11	4.26	5.38	6.29	6.43	5.97	6.20	7.20	7.55	7.99	6.95	7.56	7.44	6.60
2011-12[1]	6.71	6.54	7.03	6.40	5.96	6.09	5.94						6.38

[1] Preliminary.   *Source: Economic Research Service, U.S. Department of Agriculture (ERS-USDA)*

Average Price Received by Farmers for Wheat in the United States   In Dollars Per Bushel

Year	June	July	Aug.	Sept.	Oct.	Nov.	Dec.	Jan.	Feb.	Mar.	Apr.	May	Average
2002-03	2.92	3.21	3.63	4.21	4.38	4.25	4.06	3.89	3.70	3.55	3.37	3.33	3.71
2003-04	3.08	2.95	3.35	3.39	3.44	3.61	3.68	3.68	3.77	3.83	3.88	3.82	3.54
2004-05	3.55	3.37	3.27	3.36	3.43	3.46	3.40	3.43	3.36	3.42	3.35	3.31	3.39
2005-06	3.23	3.20	3.24	3.36	3.43	3.45	3.53	3.52	3.66	3.79	3.81	4.09	3.53
2006-07	3.98	3.88	3.91	4.06	4.59	4.59	4.52	4.53	4.71	4.75	4.89	4.88	4.44
2007-08	5.03	5.17	5.64	6.76	7.65	7.39	7.71	7.96	10.10	10.50	10.10	8.87	7.74
2008-09	7.62	7.15	7.61	7.43	6.65	6.29	5.95	6.20	5.79	5.71	5.75	5.84	6.50
2009-10	5.72	5.17	4.85	4.48	4.47	4.79	4.87	4.90	4.73	4.70	4.41	4.33	4.79
2010-11	4.16	4.49	5.44	5.79	5.88	6.10	6.44	6.69	7.42	7.54	8.04	8.16	6.35
2011-12[1]	7.40	7.10	7.61	7.55	7.29	7.26	7.19	7.04	7.09				7.28

[1] Preliminary.   *Source: Economic Research Service, U.S. Department of Agriculture (ERS-USDA)*

Average Price of No. 1 Hard Red Winter (Ordinary Protein) Wheat in Kansas City   In Dollars Per Bushel

Year	June	July	Aug.	Sept.	Oct.	Nov.	Dec.	Jan.	Feb.	Mar.	Apr.	May	Average
2002-03	3.55	3.92	4.29	5.04	5.10	4.76	4.40	4.06	4.08	3.80	3.79	3.87	4.22
2003-04	3.63	3.34	3.87	3.74	3.79	4.21	4.31	4.32	4.25	4.30	4.35	4.28	4.03
2004-05	4.13	3.97	3.73	4.01	3.95	4.22	4.22	4.14	4.00	4.00	3.76	3.80	3.99
2005-06	3.87	3.83	3.96	4.30	4.57	4.53	4.52	4.46	4.72	4.62	4.86	5.21	4.45
2006-07	5.25	5.27	5.00	5.16	5.62	5.61	5.49	5.29	5.39	5.40	5.52	5.54	5.38
2007-08	6.22	6.28	6.84	8.52	8.89	8.62	9.80	9.97	12.28	12.29	10.29	9.33	9.11
2008-09	9.19	8.68	8.64	7.52	6.17	6.21	6.06	6.59	6.21	6.23	6.10	6.70	7.03
2009-10	6.63	5.58	5.15	4.56	5.06	5.58	5.37	5.24	5.10	4.99	4.86	4.78	5.24
2010-11	4.50	5.26	6.76	7.01	7.04	7.13	8.04	8.54	9.23	8.44	9.28	9.38	7.55
2011-12[1]	8.61	8.03	8.63	8.30	7.77	7.74	7.46						8.08

[1] Preliminary.   *Source: Economic Research Service, U.S. Department of Agriculture (ERS-USDA)*

Average Price of No. 1 Dark Northern Spring (14% Protein) Wheat in Minneapolis   In Dollars Per Bushel

Year	June	July	Aug.	Sept.	Oct.	Nov.	Dec.	Jan.	Feb.	Mar.	Apr.	May	Average
2002-03	3.64	4.03	4.37	5.24	5.20	4.99	4.47	4.34	4.52	4.36	4.22	4.20	4.47
2003-04	4.12	4.00	4.15	4.03	4.31	4.59	4.43	4.44	4.64	4.63	4.69	4.69	4.39
2004-05	4.56	4.31	4.12	4.68	4.87	5.14	4.93	5.01	4.13	4.79	4.69	4.69	4.66
2005-06	5.03	4.71	4.83	4.80	5.11	5.11	5.28	4.87	4.90	4.83	4.94	5.31	4.98
2006-07	5.59	5.65	4.94	4.86	5.36	5.55	5.44	5.27	5.40	5.55	5.65	5.64	5.41
2007-08	6.19	6.60	6.88	8.20	9.27	9.39	11.06	12.59	19.00	15.60	12.93	12.06	10.81
2008-09	11.46	11.46	9.87	8.51	7.37	6.80	7.78	8.02	7.64	7.57	7.72	8.13	8.53
2009-10	7.96	6.82	6.17	6.30	6.36	7.29	6.79	7.39	7.57	7.48	6.88	6.55	6.96
2010-11	6.90	6.89	7.92	8.35	8.61	8.67	10.14	11.24	12.22	12.36	12.76	13.04	9.93
2011-12[1]	12.97	11.16	10.21	9.80	9.80	10.61	9.69						10.61

[1] Preliminary.   *Source: Economic Research Service, U.S. Department of Agriculture (ERS-USDA)*

Average Farm Prices of Winter Wheat in the United States   In Dollars Per Bushel

Year	June	July	Aug.	Sept.	Oct.	Nov.	Dec.	Jan.	Feb.	Mar.	Apr.	May	Average
2004-05	3.46	3.31	3.19	3.26	3.34	3.39	3.34	3.28	3.27	3.32	3.27	3.23	3.31
2005-06	3.15	3.15	3.16	3.28	3.34	3.27	3.45	3.45	3.59	3.82	3.74	4.06	3.46
2006-07	3.95	3.82	3.77	4.03	4.63	4.67	4.53	4.53	4.67	4.67	4.87	4.77	4.41
2007-08	5.00	5.13	5.66	6.89	7.55	7.31	7.70	7.75	9.17	9.96	9.62	8.17	7.49
2008-09	7.51	7.10	7.30	6.99	6.03	5.65	5.40	5.70	5.26	5.27	5.26	5.52	6.08
2009-10	5.47	5.02	4.67	4.20	4.27	4.60	4.68	4.57	4.53	4.45	4.19	4.21	4.57
2010-11	4.05	4.47	5.47	5.76	5.83	6.02	6.40	6.35	7.03	7.02	7.39	7.80	6.13
2011-12[1]	7.13	6.77	7.26	7.01	6.54	6.42	6.41	6.57	6.49				6.73

[1] Preliminary.   *Source: Economic Research Service, U.S. Department of Agriculture (ERS-USDA)*

Average Farm Prices of Durum Wheat in the United States   In Dollars Per Bushel

Year	June	July	Aug.	Sept.	Oct.	Nov.	Dec.	Jan.	Feb.	Mar.	Apr.	May	Average
2004-05	4.35	4.09	3.86	3.89	3.87	3.79	3.67	3.64	3.72	3.70	3.63	3.67	3.82
2005-06	3.67	3.72	3.35	3.38	3.39	3.28	3.37	3.29	3.34	3.39	3.41	3.94	3.46
2006-07	3.81	3.83	4.09	4.07	4.55	4.62	4.53	4.71	5.16	5.32	5.46	5.39	4.63
2007-08	5.49	6.69	7.00	8.98	11.70	11.70	11.50	13.10	14.10	15.40	14.30	13.50	11.12
2008-09	8.48	11.70	12.60	11.90	11.50	8.93	8.40	8.26	7.53	7.40	7.18	7.05	9.24
2009-10	6.83	7.57	4.95	4.86	4.59	4.91	4.94	4.94	4.61	4.57	4.17	4.28	5.10
2010-11	4.58	4.44	4.45	4.89	5.07	5.55	5.71	7.09	8.45	8.15	8.60	7.86	6.24
2011-12[1]	8.97	10.20	10.20	10.70	9.58	10.40	10.00	8.80	8.88				9.75

[1] Preliminary.   *Source: Economic Research Service, U.S. Department of Agriculture (ERS-USDA)*

Average Farm Prices of Other Spring Wheat in the United States   In Dollars Per Bushel

Year	June	July	Aug.	Sept.	Oct.	Nov.	Dec.	Jan.	Feb.	Mar.	Apr.	May	Average
2004-05	3.83	3.55	3.38	3.48	3.50	3.57	3.48	3.61	3.49	3.51	3.39	3.37	3.51
2005-06	3.51	3.45	3.43	3.51	3.61	3.71	3.68	3.70	3.83	3.85	3.95	4.18	3.70
2006-07	4.18	4.41	4.11	4.11	4.48	4.48	4.74	4.51	4.73	4.73	4.87	4.98	4.53
2007-08	5.17	5.43	5.53	6.26	6.99	7.00	7.39	8.01	11.20	10.90	10.50	10.70	7.92
2008-09	10.10	9.52	8.18	7.76	7.20	7.10	6.89	7.02	6.61	6.50	6.49	6.76	7.51
2009-10	6.66	5.96	5.54	4.85	5.00	5.19	5.18	5.30	5.04	5.04	4.89	4.61	5.27
2010-11	4.58	4.71	5.47	5.97	6.14	6.35	6.60	7.14	7.68	8.02	8.67	8.85	6.68
2011-12[1]	9.26	8.41	8.30	8.05	8.20	8.46	8.26	8.12	7.97				8.34

[1] Preliminary.   *Source: Economic Research Service, U.S. Department of Agriculture (ERS-USDA)*

WHEAT

Wheat Futures - CME Group (CBT) — Cents per bushel
(weekly close) as December 30, 2011

Volume of Trading of Wheat Futures in Chicago   In Thousands of Contracts

Year	Jan.	Feb.	Mar.	Apr.	May	June	July	Aug.	Sept.	Oct.	Nov.	Dec.	Total
2002	603.0	593.1	501.1	563.1	419.3	689.8	586.4	651.6	682.9	609.4	594.4	378.8	6,872.9
2003	438.0	526.0	411.0	496.8	638.6	661.8	585.1	689.6	536.5	778.9	739.8	465.4	6,967.4
2004	656.9	771.7	783.1	786.2	606.1	786.5	501.7	747.4	520.9	478.7	913.7	402.3	7,955.2
2005	613.0	1,053.6	827.8	937.5	694.7	1,088.0	690.3	1,024.8	660.0	717.4	1,164.5	642.4	10,114.1
2006	889.2	1,421.3	1,059.6	1,300.0	1,511.6	1,617.1	1,067.4	1,659.9	1,365.9	1,938.1	1,613.7	781.2	16,224.9
2007	1,346.2	1,506.0	1,148.0	2,082.5	1,170.5	2,343.7	1,514.4	2,111.3	1,320.3	1,648.4	2,109.7	1,281.8	19,582.7
2008	1,861.3	2,527.7	1,398.7	1,558.6	1,121.6	2,185.7	1,314.2	2,093.6	1,228.1	1,139.0	1,644.5	939.0	19,011.9
2009	986.9	1,505.7	1,213.8	1,747.8	1,300.1	2,350.9	1,298.1	1,926.4	1,040.0	1,451.2	1,952.5	904.2	17,677.5
2010	1,297.9	1,936.2	1,289.8	2,029.8	1,392.3	2,547.3	2,394.8	3,386.6	1,501.6	1,527.8	2,383.2	1,402.9	23,090.3
2011	1,651.7	2,601.4	2,131.8	2,475.9	2,095.9	2,857.2	1,699.9	2,301.0	1,470.5	1,594.4	2,217.0	1,186.8	24,283.3

Contract size = 5,000 bu.   *Source: CME Group; Chicago Board of Trade (CBT)*

Average Open Interest of Wheat Futures in Chicago   In Contracts

Year	Jan.	Feb.	Mar.	Apr.	May	June	July	Aug.	Sept.	Oct.	Nov.	Dec.
2002	118,192	118,484	112,469	112,870	96,050	98,047	118,041	131,303	129,913	114,544	101,354	82,934
2003	92,679	99,882	95,464	99,500	97,750	96,230	92,484	119,817	110,703	109,449	125,335	120,376
2004	130,101	137,459	141,239	155,383	127,086	135,322	154,623	166,422	154,431	156,290	172,064	182,402
2005	201,297	223,108	218,153	208,149	207,407	223,014	239,219	256,533	276,741	297,319	301,838	298,523
2006	320,974	380,405	389,284	385,698	466,013	491,343	473,749	459,650	455,755	476,906	435,059	426,976
2007	453,140	441,924	405,383	377,162	363,297	401,509	411,971	404,940	379,871	407,669	414,509	423,198
2008	443,193	440,137	400,426	375,845	362,835	359,429	332,360	331,301	294,696	279,041	283,832	250,914
2009	268,513	297,116	291,831	309,503	302,088	335,407	317,024	327,977	320,607	331,678	355,414	353,774
2010	388,660	431,434	427,821	457,548	469,103	490,351	477,461	504,547	487,184	516,982	507,512	480,059
2011	515,137	538,874	482,060	482,702	457,289	451,965	428,043	427,516	411,468	426,188	411,485	376,671

Contract size = 5,000 bu.   *Source: CME Group; Chicago Board of Trade (CBT)*

Commercial Stocks of Domestic Wheat[1] in the United States, on First of Month   In Millions of Bushels

Year	July	Aug.	Sept.	Oct.	Nov.	Dec.	Jan.	Feb.	Mar.	Apr.	May	June
2002-03	193.9	207.7	237.2	241.0	237.7	218.8	195.1	179.7	158.3	133.1	107.2	93.8
2003-04	133.3	171.9	212.0	226.3	220.7	198.1	145.0	126.3	113.1	94.0	89.6	85.4
2004-05	118.3	147.6	174.3	173.5	161.6	137.8	129.8	122.5	113.4	103.8	92.2	88.8
2005-06	127.5	138.6	159.9	163.5	158.5	147.8	137.9	130.9	128.8	122.9	116.7	126.2
2006-07	154.3	172.5	190.3	170.9	166.8	159.5	154.7	146.7	136.3	129.3	116.6	99.2
2007-08	108.6	155.9	173.1	185.7	164.8	151.2	148.3	138.9	123.5	112.3	87.1	78.7
2008-09	98.2	150.4	176.4	214.5	212.9	179.7	167.8	135.9	126.1	124.9	119.5	115.0
2009-10	152.4	198.2	221.3	224.5	219.8	208.8	199.8	192.9	184.1	177.1	181.2	174.8
2010-11	229.8	237.4	247.3	242.3	235.4	229.5	222.6	234.4	223.0	201.9	190.8	178.1
2011-12	202.9	220.3	232.6	236.2	219.9	203.8	193.4					

[1] Domestic wheat in storage in public and private elevators in 39 markets and wheat afloat in vessels or barges at lake and seaboard ports, the first Saturday of the month.   *Source: Livestock Division, U.S. Department of Agriculture (LD-USDA)*

Stocks of Wheat Flour Held by Mills in the United States   In Thousands of Sacks--100 Pounds

Year	Jan. 1	April 1	July 1	Oct. 1	Year	Jan. 1	April 1	July 1	Oct. 1
2000	5,099	5,217	5,062	5,244	2006	5,211	5,775	5,576	5,587
2001	5,241	5,506	5,178	5,393	2007	5,919	5,884	5,587	6,188
2002	5,377	5,164	4,632	4,184	2008	6,374	6,219	6,157	6,719
2003	4,265	4,707	4,622	4,554	2009	5,831	5,561	5,607	5,430
2004	4,764	4,666	4,700	4,868	2010	5,407	5,637	5,596	5,517
2005	5,085	4,268	4,637	4,781	2011[1]	5,660	5,680	NA	NA

[1] Preliminary.   *Source: Bureau of the Census, U.S. Department of Commerce*

Average Producer Price Index of Wheat Flour (Spring[2])   June 1983 = 100

Year	Jan.	Feb.	Mar.	Apr.	May	June	July	Aug.	Sept.	Oct.	Nov.	Dec.	Average
2002	109.6	109.6	110.6	106.5	108.2	108.8	112.6	115.5	120.9	123.0	119.3	116.6	113.4
2003	119.4	121.6	120.2	120.3	122.6	121.6	119.2	122.2	120.4	117.2	121.1	122.4	120.7
2004	123.5	125.1	123.9	124.0	127.6	126.4	125.2	121.0	128.5	127.2	130.2	128.5	125.9
2005	128.5	130.4	130.8	127.6	129.6	130.8	130.3	129.7	130.6	131.4	133.6	131.8	130.4
2006	130.2	134.2	132.8	139.4	142.2	144.2	148.5	141.6	144.2	151.9	151.8	147.5	142.4
2007	144.8	144.6	148.2	153.2	154.3	161.9	167.4	174.0	196.2	209.4	207.1	229.5	174.2
2008	239.6	278.9	293.6	262.8	248.1	246.5	228.5	229.5	214.6	194.8	190.8	181.5	234.1
2009	187.4	185.3	186.5	183.4	185.0	196.2	176.4	171.1	165.2	168.0	169.2	168.5	178.5
2010	167.2	168.1	163.7	162.5	167.1	161.7	169.7	190.5	190.6	190.1	200.5	204.9	178.1
2011[1]	212.0	228.4	211.8	226.5	225.2	219.5	217.0	224.1	224.8	201.5	209.3	207.1	217.3

[1] Preliminary.   [2] Standard patent.   *Source: Bureau of Labor Statistics, U.S. Department of Commerce (BLS) (0212-0301)*

World Wheat Flour Production (Monthly Average)   In Thousands of Metric Tons

Year	Australia	France	Germany	Hungary	India	Japan	Kazakhstan	Rep. of Korea	Mexico	Poland	Russia	Turkey	United Kingdom
2002	NA	473.9	415.3	67.6	211.6	389.4	143.4	151.2	218.3	135.2	797.3	139.6	369.0
2003	NA	467.3	424.4	70.7	234.1	391.0	144.2	149.3	220.6	143.1	821.4	159.8	365.0
2004	NA	465.8	441.8	67.6	238.5	390.1	145.2	157.6	217.4	135.2	799.5	176.8	370.0
2005	NA	464.5	437.9	67.3	205.4	384.6	197.6	153.1	239.1	207.3	765.8	299.0	368.0
2006	NA	472.3	444.2	62.2	180.3	384.6	207.9	154.2	243.8	211.9	776.1	290.4	366.0
2007	NA	478.2	437.7	59.7	181.1	387.8	224.6	146.7	243.8	124.3	547.7	309.8	NA
2008	NA	477.8	453.0	57.6	178.6	387.3	242.0	140.1	244.1	109.8	762.4	327.8	NA
2009	NA	449.5	429.1	59.2	195.1	379.9	255.0	150.7	249.3	143.2	774.1	349.7	NA
2010[1]	NA	461.9	458.0	NA	212.5	401.0	NA	160.5	257.5	122.6	746.7	371.4	NA
2011[2]	NA	443.8	438.5	NA	215.0	404.1	NA	158.9	263.5	116.7	740.1	409.3	NA

[1] Preliminary.   [2] Estimate.   NA = Not available.   *Source: United Nations (UN)*

WHEAT

Production of Wheat Flour in the United States   In Millions of Sacks--100 Pounds Each

Year	July	Aug.	Sept.	Oct.	Nov.	Dec.	Jan.	Feb.	Mar.	Apr.	May	June	Total
2002-03	-----	102.1	-----	-----	100.3	-----	-----	95.9	-----	-----	96.8	-----	395.0
2003-04	-----	103.1	-----	-----	100.5	-----	-----	96.6	-----	-----	96.8	-----	396.9
2004-05	-----	100.9	-----	-----	99.7	-----	-----	95.9	-----	-----	96.2	-----	392.7
2005-06	-----	102.5	-----	-----	100.3	-----	-----	98.1	-----	-----	98.0	-----	398.9
2006-07	-----	104.9	-----	-----	102.5	-----	-----	100.3	-----	-----	102.5	-----	410.1
2007-08	-----	109.0	-----	-----	107.1	-----	-----	101.4	-----	-----	102.5	-----	420.0
2008-09	-----	108.2	-----	-----	104.2	-----	-----	100.7	-----	-----	102.9	-----	416.0
2009-10	-----	107.4	-----	-----	103.7	-----	-----	102.5	-----	-----	101.5	-----	415.1
2010-11	-----	108.6	-----	-----	104.8	-----	-----	100.0	-----	-----	100.3	-----	413.7
2011-12[1]	-----	NA	-----	-----	NA	-----	-----		-----	-----		-----	

[1] Preliminary.   Source: Bureau of the Census, U.S. Department of Commerce

United States Wheat Flour Exports (Grain Equivalent[2])   In Thousands of Bushels

Year	June	July	Aug.	Sept.	Oct.	Nov.	Dec.	Jan.	Feb.	Mar.	Apr.	May	Total
2002-03	1,474	1,547	753	1,373	2,437	2,854	4,645	1,049	884	1,146	1,083	541	19,786
2003-04	824	1,074	3,444	1,087	765	1,295	1,673	1,789	1,342	1,020	732	1,386	16,431
2004-05	742	1,220	885	770	834	1,005	1,347	955	617	756	722	781	10,634
2005-06	859	686	839	720	840	871	734	572	620	937	1,188	966	9,832
2006-07	720	488	780	610	532	754	756	786	999	941	1,425	2,711	11,502
2007-08	1,467	1,220	1,277	1,135	1,758	2,515	1,960	1,224	1,544	1,328	1,114	1,126	17,668
2008-09	1,417	1,052	1,093	1,053	856	1,055	958	969	858	750	687	793	11,541
2009-10	865	1,515	1,704	1,473	2,255	1,609	1,194	1,231	1,722	2,525	1,652	1,993	19,738
2010-11	1,158	915	898	1,005	1,727	988	1,130	1,638	1,641	1,239	1,982	1,116	15,437
2011-12[1]	1,078	874	1,774	1,101	1,002								13,990

[1] Preliminary.   [2] Includes meal, groats and durum.   Source: Economic Research Service, U.S. Department of Agriculture (ERS-USDA)

Supply and Distribution of Wheat Flour in the United States

Year	Wheat Ground -- 1,000 Bu. --	Milfeed Production - 1,000 Tons -	Flour Production[3]	Flour & Product Imports[2]	Total Supply	Exports Flour	Exports Products	Domestic Disap-pearance	Total Population July 1 -- Millions --	Per Capita Disap-pearance -- Pounds --
					In 1,000 Cwt.					
2002	889,412	6,893	394,700	11,291	405,991	9,226	2,683	394,082	288.1	136.8
2003	889,188	7,029	396,215	11,145	407,360	5,768	3,953	397,639	290.8	136.7
2004	876,047	6,764	393,925	10,726	404,651	5,152	4,662	394,837	293.5	134.5
2005	884,101	6,826	394,973	11,262	406,235	3,747	4,741	397,748	296.2	134.3
2006	894,527	6,916	403,391	11,740	415,131	3,412	5,867	405,852	299.1	135.7
2007	923,756	7,103	418,836	11,511	430,347	6,707	6,486	417,155	302.0	138.1
2008	907,979	6,753	416,283	10,822	427,105	4,925	6,179	416,001	304.8	136.5
2009	896,060	6,460	414,658	10,313	424,971	5,911	5,338	413,722	307.5	134.6
2010	899,523	6,458	417,396	11,206	428,602	7,004	3,931	417,667	310.1	134.7
2011[1]			305,747	11,696	316,406	6,299	3,604	307,034		

[1] Preliminary.   [2] Commercial production of wheat flour, whole wheat, industrial and durum flour and farina reported by Bureau of Census.
Source: Economic Research Service, U.S. Department of Agriculture (ERS-USDA)

Wheat and Flour Price Relationships at Milling Centers in the United States   In Dollars

	At Kansas City					At Minneapolis				
	Cost of Wheat to Produce 100 lb. Flour[1]	Wholesale Price of Bakery Flour 100 lb. Flour[2]	By-Products Obtained 100 lb. Flour[3]	Total Products Actual	Total Products Over Cost of Wheat	Cost of Wheat to Produce 100 lb. Flour[1]	Wholesale Price of Bakery Flour 100 lb. Flour[2]	By-Products Obtained 100 lb. Flour[3]	Total Products Actual	Total Products Over Cost of Wheat
2004-05	9.33	10.88	.95	11.83	2.50	10.62	11.31	.94	12.25	1.62
2005-06	10.38	11.73	1.03	12.76	2.38	11.35	12.25	.93	13.19	1.84
2006-07	12.41	13.27	1.57	14.85	2.44	12.33	12.92	1.50	14.41	2.08
2007-08	22.67	22.83	2.00	24.83	2.16	24.66	24.94	2.03	26.98	2.32
2008-09	17.14	17.60	2.18	19.77	2.63	19.44	19.18	2.15	21.33	1.89
2009-10	13.29	14.13	1.51	15.64	2.35	16.16	15.90	1.55	17.45	1.29
2010-11	18.97	18.78	2.35	21.13	2.16	22.97	21.56	2.40	23.96	.99
2011-12	20.07	19.36	3.34	22.69	2.63	24.53	23.18	3.37	26.55	2.02
June-Aug.	20.61	20.40	3.27	23.67	3.06	26.10	25.28	3.21	28.49	2.39
Sept.-Nov.	19.52	18.32	3.40	21.71	2.19	22.96	21.07	3.53	24.60	1.64

[1] Based on 73% extraction rate, cost of 2.28 bushels: At Kansas City, No. 1 hard winter 13% protein; and at Minneapolis, No. 1 dark northern spring, 14% protein.   [2] quoted as mid-month bakers' standard patent at Kansas City and spring standard patent at Minneapolis, bulk basis.   [3] Assumed 50-50 millfeed distribution between bran and shorts or middlings, bulk basis.   Source: Agricultural Marketing Service, U.S. Department of Agriculture

Wool

Wool is light, warm, absorbs moisture, and is resistant to fire. Wool is also used for insulation in houses, for carpets and furnishing, and for bedding. Sheep are sheared once a year and produce about 4.3 kg of "greasy" wool per year.

Greasy wool is wool that has not been washed or cleaned. Wool fineness is determined by fiber diameter, which is measured in microns (one millionth of a meter). Fine wool is softer, lightweight, and produces fine clothing. Merino sheep produce the finest wool.

Wool futures and options are traded on the Sydney Futures Exchange (SFE), where there are futures and options contracts on greasy wool, and futures on fine wool and broad wool. All three futures contracts call for the delivery of merino combing wool. Wool yarn futures are traded on the Chubu Commodity Exchange (CCE), the Osaka Mercantile Exchange (OME) and the Tokyo Commodity Exchange (TOCOM).

Prices – Average monthly wool prices at U.S. mills in 2011 (through November) rose by +60.0% yr/yr to $5.16 per pound, a new record high. The value of U.S. wool production in 2011 rose +39.7% to $48.925 million, a new record high.

Supply – World production of wool has been falling in the past decade due to the increased use of polyester fabrics. Greasy wool world production in 2010 (latest data), the latest reporting year for the data series, fell -2.9% yr/yr to 2.058 million metric tons. The world's largest producers of greasy wool in 2010 were China with 18.8% of world production, followed by Australia (18.6%), and New Zealand (8.1%).

U.S. wool production of 13,770 metric tons in 2010 accounted for only 0.7% of world production. U.S. production of wool goods rose +16.5% yr/yr in 2010 (9 months annualized) to 6.4 million yards, up from the 2009 record low of 4.8 million yards. That was less than 4% of the record high of 222.5 million yards of wool goods production seen in 1969. The U.S. sheep herd in 2011 fell -3.6% to 4.030 million sheep, a new record low.

Trade – U.S. exports of domestic wool in 2011 fell -10.0% yr/yr to 9.000 million pounds. U.S. imports in 2010 fell -6.0% to 3.108 million pounds.

World Production of Wool, Greasy   In Metric Tons

Year	Argen-tina	Australia	China	Kazak-hstan	New Zealand	Pakistan	Rom-ania	Russia	South Africa	United Kingdom	United States	Uruguay	World Total
2001	56,000	657,000	298,254	23,612	236,661	39,200	16,880	39,210	48,649	55,000	19,122	56,744	2,243,271
2002	65,000	587,274	307,588	24,818	228,300	39,400	16,659	41,428	47,502	60,000	18,633	39,376	2,163,278
2003	72,000	551,107	338,058	26,782	229,600	39,700	16,879	44,586	44,156	60,000	17,326	34,922	2,179,069
2004	60,000	509,473	373,902	28,499	217,700	39,900	17,505	47,111	46,539	60,000	17,046	37,271	2,201,996
2005	63,696	519,660	393,172	30,444	215,500	40,000	17,600	48,033	45,000	60,000	16,865	42,009	2,260,715
2006	67,794	519,900	388,777	32,389	224,700	40,100	19,378	50,276	38,414	57,552	16,284	46,709	2,248,272
2007	68,743	502,300	363,470	34,200	217,900	40,600	21,025	52,022	29,700	62,000	15,750	46,709	2,226,769
2008	65,000	458,700	367,687	35,200	197,273	41,000	17,700	53,491	41,583	63,290	14,952	45,085	2,178,469
2009[1]	65,000	420,300	364,002	36,400	179,242	41,540	18,038	54,658	43,320	65,393	13,770	41,057	2,121,071
2010[2]	54,000	382,300	386,768	37,600	165,800	42,000	17,600	53,280	41,091	67,000	13,770	34,700	2,058,978

[1] Preliminary.   [2] Estimate.   NA = Not avaliable.   *Source: Food and Agriculture Organization of the United Nations (FAO-UN)*

Production of Wool Goods[2] in the United States   In Millions of Yards

Year	First Quarter	Second Quarter	Third Quarter	Fourth Quarter	Total	Year	First Quarter	Second Quarter	Third Quarter	Fourth Quarter	Total
2002	7.4	8.6	6.2	5.5	27.7	2007	2.6	2.5	2.2	2.1	9.5
2003	6.5	6.4	5.2	4.9	23.0	2008	2.3	2.1	1.7	1.5	7.5
2004	5.5	5.9	4.2	4.2	19.8	2009	1.4	1.2	1.0	1.1	4.8
2005	4.9	6.9	4.2	4.3	20.3	2010	1.5	1.5	1.2	1.3	5.5
2006	4.1	3.9	2.8	2.8	13.7	2011[1]	1.7	1.6	X	X	6.4

[1] Preliminary.   [2] Woolen and worsted woven goods, except woven felts.   *Source: Bureau of the Census, U.S. Department of Commerce*

Consumption of Apparel Wool[2] in the United States   In Millions of Pounds--Clean Basis

Year	First Quarter	Second Quarter	Third Quarter	Fourth Quarter	Total	Year	First Quarter	Second Quarter	Third Quarter	Fourth Quarter	Total
1997	33.1	33.8	30.6	32.8	130.4	2002	11.0	10.5	6.5	W	36.0
1998	29.3	29.6	21.9	17.5	98.4	2003	W	W	W	W	W
1999	17.3	16.8	15.8	13.6	63.5	2004	W	W	W	W	W
2000	17.4	16.1	14.6	13.9	63.0	2005	2.3	5.2	3.9	4.0	15.4
2001	17.0	13.5	11.6	10.9	53.0	2006[1]	3.7	3.8	2.8	3.0	13.3

[1] Preliminary.   [2] Woolen and worsted woven goods, except woven felts.   W = Withheld.   *Source: Bureau of the Census, U.S. Department of Commerce*

WOOL

Salient Statistics of Wool in the United States

Year	Sheep & Lambs Shorn[4] -1,000's-	Weight per Fleece -In Lbs.-	Shorn Wool Production 1,000 Lbs.	Price per Lb.	Value of Production -$1,000-	Shorn Wool Payment Support -- Cents Per Lb. --	Shorn Wool Payment Rate -- Cents Per Lb. --	Total Wool Production	Domestic Production	Domestic Wool Exports	Dutiable Imports for Consumption[3] (48's & Finer)	Total New Supply[2]	Duty Free Raw Imports (Not Finer than 46's)	Mill Consumption Apparel	Mill Consumption Carpet
2003	5,074	7.50	38,229	73.0	28,126	100	40.0	38,197	20,168	11,067	4,986	29,836	15,749	43,869	6,017
2004	5,073	7.40	37,622	80.0	29,921	100	40.0	37,581	19,843	11,168	6,204	31,334	16,455	NA	NA
2005	5,072	7.30	37,232	71.0	26,272	100	40.0	37,182	19,632	12,573	6,220	25,434	12,156	NA	NA
2006	4,852	7.40	36,019	68.0	24,510	100	40.0	35,899	18,955	17,998	7,324	18,210	9,929	NA	NA
2007	4,657	7.50	34,723	87.0	30,242	100	40.0	34,723	18,334	17,077	5,245	15,527	9,025	NA	NA
2008	4,434	7.43	32,963	99.0	32,486	100	40.0	32,963	17,404	10,307	4,551	20,279	8,631	NA	NA
2009	4,195	7.40	38,060	79.0	24,337	100	40.0	30,900	16,400	10,200	3,306		6,046		
2010	4,180	7.30	30,370	115.0	35,018			30,600	16,200	10,000	3,108		4,928		
2011[1]	4,030	7.30	29,290	167.0	48,925			30,000	16,000	9,000					

[1] Preliminary.   [2] Production minus exports plus imports; stocks not taken into consideration.   [3] Apparel wool includes all dutiable wool; carpet wool includes all duty-free wool.   [4] Includes sheep shorn at commercial feeding yards.
Source: Economic Research Service, U.S. Department of Agriculture (ERS-USDA)

Shorn Wool Prices   In Dollars Per Pound

Year	US Farm Price Shorn Wool Greasy Basis[1] -- cents/Lb --	Grade 70's type 61	Grade 64's type 63	Grade 62's type 64	Grade 60/62's type 64A	Grade 58's-56's 433-34	Market Indicator[3] Cents/Kg.	62's Staple 3"& up	60's Staple 3"& up	58's Staple 3 1/4"& up	56's Staple 3 1/4"& up	54's Staple 3 1/2"& up
2002	53.0	2.87	2.68	2.70	2.63	2.55	1,051	1.90	1.41	1.40	1.19	1.02
2003	73.0	3.23	3.14	3.16	3.02	2.81	821	2.41	1.73	1.79	1.48	1.24
2004	80.0	3.21	2.75	2.89	2.49	2.33	NA	2.35	1.59	1.74	1.50	1.25
2005	71.0	2.99	2.57	2.65	2.42	2.23	NA	1.86	1.46	1.39	1.41	1.03
2006	68.0	3.17	2.65	2.75	2.47	2.26	NA	1.79	1.45	1.30	1.00	.94
2007	87.0	4.41	3.73	3.90	3.31	2.77	NA	2.65	2.24	1.82	1.32	1.04
2008	99.0	4.35	3.47	3.59	3.19	2.71	NA	3.09	2.45	2.25	1.82	1.20
2009	79.0	3.48	3.02	3.08	2.86	2.46	NA	2.27	1.89	1.73	1.36	1.34
2010	115.0	5.34	3.10	4.24	3.78	2.78	NA	3.27	2.54	2.15	1.89	1.48

Columns 2–6 are the Australian Offering Price, Clean[2]; columns 8–12 are Graded Territory Shorn Wool, Clean Basis[4].

[1] Annual weighted average.   [2] F.O.B. Australian Wool Corporation South Carolina warehouse in bond.   [3] Index of prices of all wool sold in Australia for the crop year July-June.   [4] Wool principally produced in Texas and the Rocky Mountain States.
Source: Economic Research Service, U.S. Department of Agriculture (ERS-USDA)

Average Wool Prices[1] --Australian-- 64's, Type 62, Duty Paid--U.S. Mills   In Cents Per Pound

Year	Jan.	Feb.	Mar.	Apr.	May	June	July	Aug.	Sept.	Oct.	Nov.	Dec.	Average
2002	218	243	250	251	249	259	255	254	268	312	322	328	267
2003	344	346	326	333	296	326	316	308	306	292	285	290	314
2004	304	294	288	281	261	275	277	263	255	255	270	271	275
2005	273	271	268	242	265	266	270	259	252	244	233	236	257
2006	243	256	259	251	258	254	260	260	258	260	308	315	265
2007	352	344	355	367	381	380	378	359	364	393	405	400	373
2008	416	411	407	404	378	376	386	346	317	257	226	239	347
2009	229	223	230	250	287	295	295	318	339	379	386	392	302
2010	423	404	412	404	381	379	381	381	390	419	450	479	409
2011	517	544	586	638	670	742	713	649	610	562	450		607

[1] Raw, clean basis.   *Source: Economic Research Service, U.S. Department of Agriculture (ERS-USDA)*

Average Wool Prices --Domestic[1]-- Graded Territory, 64's, Staple 2 3/4 & Up--U.S. Mills   In Cents Per Pound

Year	Jan.	Feb.	Mar.	Apr.	May	June	July	Aug.	Sept.	Oct.	Nov.	Dec.	Average
2002	134	150	170	181	189	200	200	200	198	204	223	233	190
2003	236	260	258	250	223	234	239	243	243	243	232	233	241
2004	233	239	240	240	235	229	233	236	240	236	230	230	235
2005	215	207	200	185	185	185	179	186	195	181	168	140	186
2006	NQ	NQ	162	183	173	171	165	165	165	NQ	212	220	180
2007	186	242	245	279	311	295	285	270	276	NQ	NQ	NQ	265
2008	290	318	319	325	285	295	305	NQ	NQ	NQ	NQ	NQ	305
2009	NQ	NQ	NQ	157	215	226	228	223	NQ	270	NQ	NQ	220
2010	NQ	NQ	310	337	341	313	300	NQ	NQ	NQ	NQ	334	323
2011	NQ	NQ	NQ	NQ	516	NQ	NQ	NQ	NQ	NQ	NQ		516

[1] Raw, shorn, clean basis.   NQ = No quote.   *Source: Economic Research Service, U.S. Department of Agriculture (ERS-USDA)*

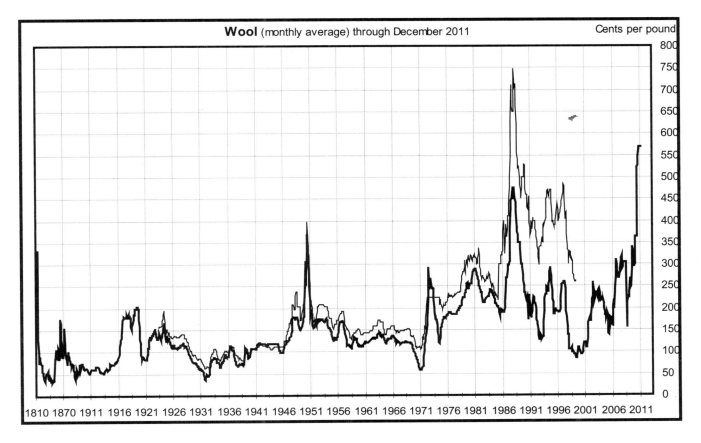

Wool (monthly average) through December 2011   Cents per pound

Wool: Mill Consumption, by Grades in the U.S., Scoured Basis   In Millions of Pounds

| | Apparel Class[1] | | | | | | | | |
| | Woolen System | | | Worsted System | | | | |
Year	60's & Finer	Coarser Than 60's	Total	60's & Finer	Coarser Than 60's	Total	All Total	Carpet Wool[2]
1998	31,258	15,079	46,337	42,243	9,793	52,036	98,373	16,331
1999	18,379	10,772	29,151	27,429	6,955	34,384	63,535	13,950
2000	18,503	13,432	31,935	21,732	8,374	30,106	62,041	15,205
2001	16,062	9,849	25,911	NA	NA	27,058	52,969	13,310
2002	9,627	8,482	18,109	NA	NA	17,906	36,015	6,891
2003	6,681	5,309	11,990	NA	NA	31,879	43,869	6,017
2004	NA	NA	NA	NA	NA	NA	NA	NA
2005	NA	NA	NA	NA	NA	NA	NA	NA
2006[3]	NA	NA	NA	NA	NA	NA	NA	NA
2007[4]	NA	NA	NA	NA	NA	NA	NA	NA

[1] Domestic & duty-paid foreign.   [2] Duty-free foreign.   [3] Preliminary.   [4] Estimate.   NA = Not available.   *Source: Economic Research Service, U.S. Department of Agriculture (ERS-USDA)*

United States Imports[2] of Unmanufactured Wool (Clean Yield)   In Thousands of Pounds

Year	Jan.	Feb.	Mar.	Apr.	May	June	July	Aug.	Sept.	Oct.	Nov.	Dec.	Total
2002	1,860.5	1,781.0	2,560.3	2,357.0	2,291.0	1,451.5	1,640.3	1,183.7	1,854.5	2,358.5	2,146.6	3,106.7	24,591.6
2003	2,541.1	2,817.2	2,337.2	2,165.2	2,134.8	1,793.4	1,237.2	1,065.4	793.3	1,618.4	1,113.5	1,210.7	20,827.4
2004	1,315.8	1,523.3	2,080.3	1,847.4	1,364.1	2,795.0	1,637.9	1,935.1	2,697.5	2,400.3	1,856.4	1,205.5	22,658.6
2005	2,286.3	1,060.3	1,979.4	1,466.0	1,482.0	2,024.5	1,502.9	1,372.5	989.5	1,712.4	1,460.1	1,017.4	18,353.3
2006	1,886.2	975.3	1,755.7	1,451.4	1,254.9	1,592.2	880.8	1,536.9	1,178.3	1,524.9	1,612.6	1,604.2	17,253.4
2007	1,250.1	1,097.3	1,429.4	1,417.0	1,356.5	1,302.7	1,141.2	892.5	846.7	1,252.0	1,328.0	956.3	14,269.7
2008	1,753.3	888.8	1,405.6	1,090.1	1,269.2	1,100.0	1,259.0	825.6	1,231.3	980.6	706.8	671.5	13,181.8
2009	1,061.7	982.9	1,043.0	803.5	536.2	745.1	833.8	847.4	447.4	798.8	626.0	627.0	9,352.8
2010	705.5	340.8	663.7	757.1	424.3	576.4	1,183.0	702.2	652.4	607.1	594.8	385.4	7,592.7
2011[1]	857.1	451.2	564.5	681.2	698.5	503.3	1,046.5	1,306.0	1,590.9				10,265.6

[1] Preliminary.   [2] Data are imports for consumption.   *Source: Economic Research Service, U.S. Department of Agriculture (ERS-USDA)*

Zinc

Zinc (symbol Zn) is a bluish-while metallic element that is the 24th most abundant element in the earth's crust. Zinc is never found in its pure state but rather in zinc oxide, zinc silicate, zinc carbonate, zinc sulfide, and in minerals such as zincite, hemimorphite, smithsonite, franklinite, and sphalerite. Zinc is utilized as a protective coating for other metals, such as iron and steel, in a process known as galvanizing. Zinc is used as an alloy with copper to make brass and also as an alloy with aluminum and magnesium. There are, however, a number of substitutes for zinc in chemicals, electronics, and pigments. For example, with aluminum, steel and plastics can substitute for galvanized sheets. Aluminum alloys can also replace brass. Zinc is used as the negative electrode in dry cell (flashlight) batteries and also in the zinc-mercuric-oxide battery cell, which is the round, flat battery typically used in watches, cameras, and other electronic devices. Zinc is also used in medicine as an antiseptic ointment.

Zinc futures and options are traded on the London Metals Exchange (LME). The LME zinc futures contract calls for the delivery of 25 metric tons of at least 99.995% purity zinc ingots (slabs and plates). The contract trades in terms of U.S. dollars per metric ton. Zinc first started trading on the LME in 1915.

Prices – Zinc prices in 2011 rose 3.7% to a monthly average of 105.88 cents per pound, but still below the 2006 record high of 158.44 cents per pound.

Supply – World smelter production of zinc in 2011 fell slightly by 2.4% to 12.400 million metric tons from the record high of 12.700 million metric tons posted in 2010. The world's largest producer of zinc in 2010 (latest data available) was China with 41% of world smelter production, followed by Canada with 5.4%, Japan with 4.5%, and Australia with 4.0%. China's production of 5.2 million metric tons in 2010 has more quintupled 1.0 million metric tons in 1994.

U.S. smelter production in 2010 rose by +23% to 249,000 metric tons. U.S. mine production of recoverable zinc in 2011 rose +2.2% yr/yr to 741,491 metric tons. U.S. production in 2011 of slab zinc on a primary basis fell -2.5% yr/yr to 117,000 metric tons, while secondary production rose +3.9% yr/yr to 134,000 metric tons.

Demand – U.S. consumption of slab zinc in 2011 rose by +1.9% yr/yr to 924,000 metric tons, up from the 29-year low of 893,000 metric tons seen in 2009. U.S. consumption of slab zinc by fabricators in 2011 rose by +31.3% yr/yr to 279,491 metric tons, up from the 2010 record low of 212,900 metric tons.

The breakdown of consumption by industries for 2010 showed that 78% of slab zinc consumption was for galvanizers, 10% for brass products, and the rest for other miscellaneous industries. The consumption breakdown by grades for 2010 showed that 43% was for special high grade, 26% for re-melt and other, 19% for high grade, and 12% for prime western.

Trade – The U.S. in 2011 relied on imports for 73% of its consumption of zinc, up sharply from the 35% average seen in the 1990s. U.S. imports for consumption of slab zinc rose by +2.8% yr/yr to 690,000 metric tons in 2011, while imports of zinc ore fell -6.3% yr/yr to 30,000 metric tons. The dollar value of U.S. zinc imports in 201 rose by 1.0% yr/yr to $1.864, below the 2007 record high $3.091 billion. The breakdown of imports in 2011 shows that most zinc is imported as blocks, pigs and slabs (690,000 metric tons); followed by dust, powder and flakes (84,800 metric tons); ores (30,000 metric tons); waste and scrap (16,600 metric tons); dross, ashes and fume (12,400 metric tons); and sheets, plates and other (3,450 metric tons).

Salient Statistics of Zinc in the United States   In Metric Tons

Year	Slab Zinc Production Primary	Slab Zinc Production Secondary	Mine Production Recovered	Imports for Consumption Slab Zinc	Imports for Consumption Ore (Zinc Content)	Exports Slab Zinc	Exports Ore (Zinc Content)	Consumption Slab Zinc	Consumption Consumed as Ore	Consumption All Classes[3]	Net Import Reliance As a % of Apparent Consumption	High-Grade, Price -Cents/Lb.-
2002	182,000	113,000	754,000	874,000	122,000	1,160	822,000	1,170,000	----	1,420,000	60	38.64
2003	187,000	150,000	768,000	792,000	164,000	1,680	841,000	1,120,000	----	1,390,000	58	40.63
2004	194,000	156,000	739,000	868,000	231,000	3,300	745,000	1,190,000	----	1,430,000	72	52.47
2005	195,000	156,000	748,000	700,000	156,000	784	786,000	1,080,000	----	1,290,000	67	67.11
2006	113,000	156,000	727,000	895,000	383,000	2,530	825,000	1,190,000	----	1,400,000	78	158.89
2007	121,000	157,000	803,000	758,000	271,000	8,070	816,000	1,040,000	----	1,170,000	73	154.40
2008	125,000	161,000	778,000	725,000	63,200	3,250	725,000	1,010,000	----	----	72	88.93
2009	94,000	109,000	736,000	686,000	74,200	2,960	785,000	893,000	----	----	77	77.91
2010[1]	120,000	129,000	748,000	671,000	32,000	4,000	752,000	907,000	----	----	73	102.00
2011[2]	117,000	134,000	760,000	690,000	30,000	20,000	630,000	924,000	----	----	73	106.00

[1] Preliminary.   [2] Estimate.   [3] Based on apparent consumption of slab zinc plus zinc content of ores and concentrates and secondary materials used to make zinc dust and chemicals.   *Source: U.S. Geological Survey (USGS)*

World Smelter Production of Zinc[3]   In Thousands of Metric Tons

Year	Australia	Belgium	Canada	China	France	Germany	Italy	Japan	Kazak-hstan	Mexico	Spain	United States	World Total
2001	558.5	259.3	661.2	2,040.0	347.0	358.3	177.8	684.1	277.1	303.8	418.0	311.0	9,320
2002	573.0	260.0	793.4	2,100.0	350.0	378.6	176.0	673.9	286.3	302.1	488.0	362.0	9,840
2003	613.0	244.0	761.2	2,320.0	268.0	388.1	123.0	686.1	316.7	320.4	519.0	351.0	10,100
2004	538.0	263.0	805.4	2,720.0	268.4	382.0	118.0	667.2	357.1	316.9	524.8	350.0	10,600
2005	463.3	257.0	724.0	2,780.0	267.5	344.9	121.0	675.2	364.8	327.2	506.2	351.0	10,300
2006	469.0	251.0	824.5	3,170.0	127.8	342.6	109.0	654.2	364.8	279.7	507.4	269.0	10,800
2007	508.0	241.0	802.1	3,740.0	129.1	294.7	109.0	638.7	358.2	321.9	494.1	278.0	11,400
2008	505.0	251.0	764.3	4,000.0	117.9	292.3	100.0	650.9	365.6	305.4	456.1	286.0	11,700
2009[1]	531.0	26.0	685.5	4,280.0	161.0	153.0	100.0	540.6	327.9	300.0	500.8	203.0	11,300
2010[2]	505.0	260.0	691.2	5,160.0	163.0	165.0	100.0	574.0	318.8	300.0	501.0	249.0	12,700

[1] Preliminary.   [2] Estimate.   [3] Secondary metal included.   *Source: U.S. Geological Survey (USGS)*

Consumption (Reported) of Slab Zinc in the United States, by Industries and Grades   In Metric Tons

Year	Total	Galvanizers	Brass Products	Zinc-Base Alloy[3]	Zinc Oxide	Other	Special High Grade	High Grade	Remelt and Other	Prime Western
2001	543,000	281,000	74,400	91,200	[4]	NA	294,000	54,000	30,300	165,000
2002	496,000	265,000	86,800	103,000	[4]	NA	294,000	61,400	28,000	113,000
2003	506,000	264,000	87,400	113,000	[4]	NA	310,000	60,000	27,600	109,000
2004	510,000	248,000	96,700	W	[4]	NA	321,000	58,800	33,600	96,200
2005	486,000	238,000	83,900	W	[4]	NA	316,000	62,100	40,300	68,000
2006	504,000	259,000	42,300	W	[4]	203,000	315,000	69,100	73,900	75,400
2007	484,000	304,000	39,700	W	[4]	141,000	242,000	80,700	92,700	69,000
2008	433,000	262,000	107,000	23,200	[4]	40,600	195,000	60,400	75,800	102,000
2009/1	306,000	226,000	45,500	17,900	[4]	17,200	170,000	46,600	55,000	34,600
2010/2	475,000	369,000	45,800	35,000	[4]	25,100	205,000	91,900	121,684	56,500

[1] Preliminary.   [2] Estimated.   [3] Die casters.   [4] Included in other.   W = Withheld.   NA = Not applicable.   *Source: U.S. Geological Survey (USGS)*

United States Foreign Trade of Zinc   In Metric Tons

| | | | | | | | | Zinc Ore & Manufactures Exported | | | | | | |
| | | Imports for Consumption | | | | | | Blocks, Pigs, Anodes, etc. | | Wrought & Alloys | | | | Zinc Ore & Concentrates |
Year	Ores[3]	Blocks, Pigs, Slabs	Sheets, Plates, Other & Scrap	Waste & Scrap	Dross, Ashes, Fume	Dust, Powder & Flakes	Total Value $1,000	Un-wrought	Un-wrought Alloys	Sheets, Plates & Strips	Angles, Bars, Rods, etc.	Waste & Scrap	Dust (Blue Powder)	Zinc Ore & Concentrates
2002	122,000	874,000	1,640	31,200	15,500	30,900	887,785	----	----	----	----	47,700	5,660	822,000
2003	164,000	792,000	1,790	10,300	14,100	27,400	839,705	----	----	----	----	50,200	6,550	841,000
2004	231,000	868,000	2,500	10,800	16,100	24,800	1,142,733	----	----	----	----	53,900	7,640	745,000
2005	156,000	700,000	3,630	9,580	15,800	23,400	1,198,040	----	----	----	----	56,000	9,310	786,000
2006	383,000	895,000	2,050	14,200	31,100	30,100	2,771,580	2,530	19,900	3,780	11,200	83,800	16,400	825,000
2007	271,000	758,000	2,160	21,800	18,600	31,300	3,090,910	8,070	22,500	4,310	26,700	102,000	19,400	816,000
2008	63,200	725,000	3,330	17,000	13,200	28,500	1,919,030	3,250	8,550	4,970	28,100	91,000	13,000	725,000
2009	74,200	686,000	3,010	9,100	8,610	20,400	1,336,134	2,960	6,280	6,160	16,600	47,100	12,100	785,000
2010[1]	32,200	671,000	3,440	15,600	17,900	31,600	1,846,320	4,200	11,400	7,380	27,800	77,900	14,900	752,000
2011[2]	30,000	690,000	3,450	16,600	12,400	84,800	1,864,260	17,700	12,500	7,740	24,300	78,200	14,400	630,000

[1] Preliminary.   [2] Estimate.   [3] Zinc content.   *Source: U.S. Geological Survey (USGS)*

Mine Production of Recoverable Zinc in the United States   In Thousands of Metric Tons

Year	Jan.	Feb.	Mar.	Apr.	May	June	July	Aug.	Sept.	Oct.	Nov.	Dec.	Total
2002	61.3	60.4	67.8	55.2	63.4	63.8	66.0	67.2	54.4	68.3	61.3	65.5	754.6
2003	65.2	60.2	62.7	54.0	65.2	64.0	64.5	59.6	63.3	58.6	61.0	60.5	738.8
2004	60.4	55.3	57.9	58.5	56.1	59.0	60.8	62.0	61.6	61.6	56.8	56.5	706.5
2005	53.6	56.0	64.1	56.7	53.3	64.6	64.5	68.9	61.8	64.4	51.2	62.3	721.4
2006	58.1	51.4	61.5	54.2	54.3	59.8	64.7	62.3	65.8	66.3	51.5	47.4	697.3
2007	60.3	55.8	63.5	56.6	61.2	64.1	63.1	69.5	61.3	64.6	53.9	69.6	743.5
2008	72.4	67.3	72.1	65.6	67.8	72.5	72.4	61.6	58.7	52.2	52.8	64.7	780.1
2009	69.3	54.0	55.2	58.4	56.1	58.6	57.0	62.1	60.5	65.2	49.9	62.1	708.4
2010	59.4	56.5	63.5	61.6	62.6	57.4	64.8	60.3	60.0	66.0	50.0	63.2	725.3
2011[1]	69.5	54.9	62.1	59.3	66.2	57.9	70.0	63.6	60.0	55.4	60.8		741.5

[1] Preliminary.   *Source: U.S. Geological Survey (USGS)*

ZINC

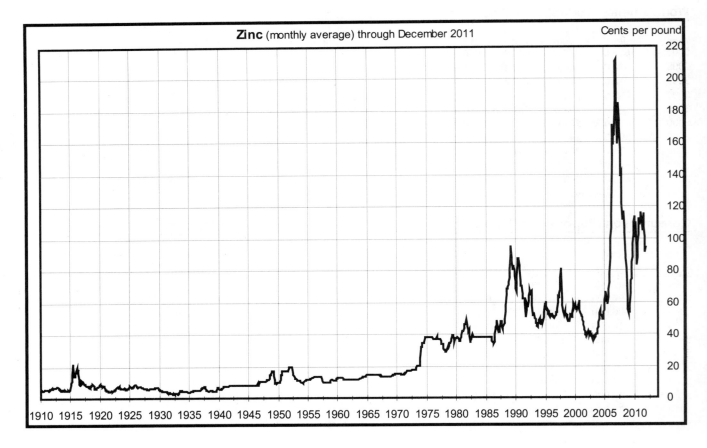

Zinc (monthly average) through December 2011 — Cents per pound

Consumption of Slab Zinc by Fabricators in the United States   In Thousands of Metric Tons

Year	Jan.	Feb.	Mar.	Apr.	May	June	July	Aug.	Sept.	Oct.	Nov.	Dec.	Total
2002	31.2	31.3	30.4	33.1	34.9	34.4	34.3	35.8	36.1	36.1	32.7	33.3	403.6
2003	33.1	33.1	34.4	35.2	34.7	38.2	34.2	35.5	36.8	36.8	35.3	36.4	423.7
2004	35.1	36.2	36.6	36.7	35.9	37.0	33.7	33.6	33.8	34.6	34.3	33.4	420.9
2005	33.6	33.9	34.1	33.5	33.8	34.1	31.3	33.7	34.8	34.7	33.8	34.1	405.4
2006	34.8	34.5	34.8	34.0	33.1	34.2	32.4	33.4	31.4	32.8	32.0	32.4	399.8
2007	33.0	23.1	22.3	23.1	22.7	23.5	22.3	22.7	23.2	23.4	23.4	17.4	280.1
2008	19.7	19.8	21.0	18.6	24.8	23.3	21.5	21.5	22.1	20.2	19.5	19.4	251.4
2009	18.8	20.5	17.4	16.5	17.3	17.3	17.8	20.2	21.0	20.3	18.6	20.4	226.1
2010	19.7	19.1	20.4	20.8	18.3	18.8	19.1	18.3	16.4	14.9	14.0	13.1	212.9
2011[1]	20.5	20.0	22.0	20.9	22.7	21.3	25.3	26.3	25.8	25.8	25.6		279.5

[1] Preliminary.   *Source: U.S. Geological Survey (USGS)*

Average Price of Zinc, Prime Western Slab (Delivered U.S. Basis)   In Cents Per Pound

Year	Jan.	Feb.	Mar.	Apr.	May	June	July	Aug.	Sept.	Oct.	Nov.	Dec.	Average
2002	40.98	39.97	42.15	41.66	39.97	39.70	41.01	38.91	39.26	39.08	36.99	38.52	39.64
2003	38.88	38.46	38.48	36.99	37.86	38.57	40.30	39.77	39.84	43.44	44.11	47.60	40.36
2004	49.61	53.31	54.63	51.89	51.88	51.53	49.85	49.31	49.37	53.36	54.61	58.32	52.31
2005	61.10	64.57	66.59	63.55	60.70	61.97	58.26	62.76	67.73	72.10	77.60	87.45	67.03
2006	100.02	106.57	116.10	147.28	170.57	158.11	163.89	164.23	166.56	185.80	210.32	211.82	158.44
2007	183.91	161.21	158.81	171.08	184.68	173.23	169.81	155.93	139.28	140.84	122.63	112.65	156.17
2008	111.49	115.37	117.27	107.07	102.59	89.16	87.44	81.53	81.83	62.25	55.26	53.22	88.71
2009	57.28	53.96	57.96	65.19	69.91	73.34	74.38	85.30	88.25	97.11	102.32	109.97	77.91
2010	113.30	100.72	106.15	110.33	93.02	83.34	88.25	97.11	102.16	112.55	109.67	108.04	102.05
2011	112.47	116.61	111.76	112.83	104.86	108.12	115.41	107.26	101.03	91.28	94.18	94.73	105.88

Source: American Metal Market (AMM)